I0225474

Hill: The Ferry Keeper's Family

Other Books by George J. Hill

Leprosy in Five Young Men

Outpatient Surgery

Cancer Chemotherapy:
Therapy of Solid Tumors in Adults

Clinical Oncology

Edison's Environment:
Invention and Pollution in the Career of Thomas Edison

Intimate Relationships:
Church and State in the U.S. and Liberia, 1917-1947

High and Dry:
Adventures of a U.S. Navy Officer on the Indian-Afghan Border
in November-December 1943

Ranch Hand:
Two Dot, Montana, in the Summer of 1954

From Fox to Purity, 1955:
In the Southern Selkirks, British Columbia, Canada

John Saxe, Loyalist (1732-1808) and His Descendants for Five Generations

Edited Work

A Lesson in Reality:
Poems and Essays, 1991-2000
By David Hedgcock Hill

HILL: The Ferry Keeper's Family

Luke Hill and Mary Hout, Who Were Married
in Windsor, Connecticut, in 1651
and
Fourteen Generations of Their Known
and Possible Descendants

By

George J. Hill, M.D., D.Litt.

Additional Contributions By

William Edwin Hill, deceased
Diane Snyder Ptak, C.A.L.S.
Avis Boyington Hill
Jeanine Humbert Johnson
Thom Carlson, Ph.D.
Dennis O'Connell
Mark Norris
James D. Hill

HERITAGE BOOKS
2011

HERITAGE BOOKS

AN IMPRINT OF HERITAGE BOOKS, INC.

Books, CDs, and more—Worldwide

For our listing of thousands of titles see our website
at
www.HeritageBooks.com

Published 2011 by
HERITAGE BOOKS, INC.
Publishing Division
100 Railroad Ave. #104
Westminster, Maryland 21157

Copyright © 2011 George J. Hill, M.D., D.Litt.

Other Heritage Books by the author:
John Saxe, Loyalist (1732–1808) and His Descendants for Five Generations

Cover photograph of Hill's Ferry site, Farmington River, Windsor, Connecticut, by George J. Hill, 2011. Image of marriage record of Luke Hill and Mary Hout in Windsor Old Church Records, reprinted with permission from The Connecticut Historical Society, Hartford, Connecticut. Image of birth of Ebenezer Hill from Farmington, Conn., Land Records 2:328, on microfilm at Connecticut State Library, courtesy of Connecticut Historical Society. Cover designed by Debbie Riley.

All rights reserved. No part of this book may be reproduced or transmitted in any form or by any means, electronic or mechanical, including photocopying, recording or by any information storage and retrieval system without written permission from the author, except for the inclusion of brief quotations in a review.

International Standard Book Numbers
Paperbound: 978-0-7884-5367-0
Clothbound: 978-0-7884-8968-6

"Luke Hill married Mary Hout, May 5, 1651"

"Ebenezer Hill Son of Luik Hill was born
March a bought the 20th one thousand Six hundred
fifty and Six"

Abbreviations

abt or abt. = about
aka or a k a = also known as
B. or b or b. = birth
b.d. = birth date
bp or bp. = baptism
b.p. = birth place
br or b.r. = birth record
ch = child or children, or church
cv or *cf* = which see
D. or d or d. = death
dau or dau. = daughter
d.d. = death date
dsp or d.s.p. = died without progeny
d.p. = death place
f = father
h = husband
Ibid. = the same
infra = below
m or m. or md = married
m.r. = marriage record
MS = manuscript
O.C.R. or OCR = Old Church Records of Windsor, Conn.
op. cit. = the same work cited
s or s. = son
supra = above
unm = unmarried
v.r. or VR or V.R. = vital records
w = wife
wid = widow

Contents

List of Illustrations

Foreword

Fortunate readers who find themselves consulting the pages of this book will become fascinated by this recreation of the lives of Luke Hill and Mary Hout and fourteen generations of their known and possible descendants. Solidly based on previously published family histories augmented by a multitude of facts gathered from the historical public records of the communities in which they lived, this book takes us through the lives and accomplishments of this early Colonial family and of their descendants in a way which really succeeds in depicting their lives in this spacious new country.

As is often the case, this book starts with a mystery: where did Luke Hill originate? He first appears in the historical record about 38 years old on 6 May 1651 when he married Mary Hout in Windsor, Conn. We know three further things about him: first, he was not a devout Puritan; second, he is recorded as having put his mark, not his signature, on an early Connecticut document and was therefore illiterate; third, both in Windsor and in Simsbury he took over the running of the local ferries which could indicate he was apprenticed to a waterman as a boy; and fourth, he did not distinguish himself in any way in the course of his service in the local trainband, and so was probably never in the organized military. Also, no earlier trace of his arrival in the Colonies can be found. These facts lead me to think that he had been apprenticed to a country waterman (not London, or other major seaport, because Queen Elizabeth's law, "that all apprentices be educated" [i.e., taught to read and write so that they could read their Bibles] was carefully enforced in London and in other major cities) probably in the West Country or the South of England where the more rigorous Protestant sects were not located. He was probably dislodged from a quiet rural life by the Civil War, and forced to flee abroad, but not as a soldier. He could very likely have joined the crew of a sailing ship and then decided to desert his ship during a visit to New York City, which would explain the informality of his arrival and the absence of his name on any passenger lists as well as his unusual decision to leave the community from which his wife came in order to settle in a different Colony where neither of them appear to have had any friends or connections. This theory could be tested by tracing the ancestry of the male Hill descendant who believes that his ancestry came from Sheffield, England in the 19th century. Sheffield was an industrial city which specialized in high quality iron and steel because of the coal and limestone which are found in abundance nearby. It really grew during the 18th century and attracted workers from all over the Kingdom to work in its mines and forges, so that most of its inhabitants in later years were descended from immigrants from other places in England. If this Mr. Hill's English ancestors could be shown to have originated from a different – coastal? – area during the previous century, this could well be the place of common origin. As for his name, spelling was phonetic and erratic in his time, especially for people who were illiterate and therefore had no firm notions on how their names should be spelled, but it would have been extremely unusual for a man to have ever changed his name.

This book is also typical of modern comprehensive family histories in that the author freely admits the problems involved in compiling accurate information off the internet today. How does an author differentiate between information which is right, information which is largely correct but inaccurate in some of its details, and information which is only the product of a vivid imagination? It is easy enough to say that you need to go with the preponderance of the logically probable information, but this sometimes produces some strange and potentially misleading conclusions. It is very hard to convincingly forge a very old document itself, so if old documents appear "right" when they are physically examined, it is normally acceptable to rely on them. But the internet is different – all you have is an electronic transcription of the words, and this can be misleading. Old Uncle Henry's version of his family's history often differs from that of old Aunt Sally, and how is a poor genealogist to tell which version is closer to the truth?

    Hill: the Ferry Keeper's Family is an excellent example of both the old and the new genealogical research systems. *The First Generation: Luke Hill and Mary Hout* is solidly based on the "old" system of family history compilation, where the few facts which are known are taken from solidly documented sources, and where the principal problems arise from a lack of any kind of evidence. *The Fifth Generation: Descendants of the Great-Grandchildren*, in contrast, is clearly based on the "new" system of family history compilation, where there are many, many facts on offer on the internet, and the principal problems result from attempts to reconcile conflicting facts and theories and differentiate between internet information based on verifiable facts and internet information based primarily on vivid imaginations masquerading as family traditions. The transition between the two types of family histories is handled seamlessly and carefully, with all attributions to questionable sources fully noted in the text. How we wish that more family traditions had been preserved on the earlier family members, and how we wish that more vital record documentation was available on the later family members! But the author of this book has made excellent use of all the material available at this time, and readers will know far more about the Ferry Keeper's Family, its members and their histories, after consulting this book than they ever did before.

Dennis Woodfield, D.Phil. (Oxon.)
Princeton, New Jersey

Introduction

This book has been long in the making, and even now, it is incomplete and imperfect. This is probably always the case for a work of genealogy and family history, for such books are of necessity always works in progress. Each compiler had therefore best think modestly of his product. His task is to assemble and then pass along the scraps and notes he has gathered so another compiler can carry the project forward in another generation.

The successful study of genealogy is a cooperative venture, like a team sport, or the production of an opera, or a symphony orchestra. I am greatly indebted to many others who have studied the Hill family and gathered information about them, which they were willing to share with others. Some of this information came directly to me, and other information came indirectly, through relatives and other genealogists.

This genealogy of the Hill Family was started more than ninety years ago, when William Edwin Hill prepared a 14-page typescript that he called *Genealogy of the Hill Family in America*. William Edwin Hill prepared this typescript anonymously in 1921 in his role as Secretary of the Hill Family Reunion in Caton, Steuben County, New York. William Edwin Hill's *Genealogy* was an account of the then-known descendants of a Revolutionary War soldier named Isaac Hill, who was born in 1740, in the line of one of his sons, Ephraim Hill, who came to Caton, N.Y., in about 1824.

William Edwin Hill's *Genealogy* was printed on what we now refer to as legal-sized paper, 8½ by 14 inches. Many copies of this *Genealogy* were prepared using a technique called mimeographing, and they were distributed to the adult members of the descendants of Ephraim Hill who were then living in New York State and in Iowa. The paper on which the *Genealogy* was printed was coarse and the typed lines ran to the very edges of the pages, which conspired to make the document difficult to preserve and reproduce. There is an enormous amount of useful information about this branch of the Hill family in America in this *Genealogy*, but even a cursory reading shows that it was burdened with many small inconsistencies and typographical errors.

When I was a boy, twelve years old or thereabouts, I began to exhibit some interest in family history, and my mother then showed me a copy of William Edwin Hill's *Genealogy*. I eventually was given two copies of the document to keep, both of which had been marked up a bit with additions and corrections. I have since referred to this *Genealogy* on many occasions and I have used it as a guide in searching for photographs and other documents related to the descendants and ancestors of Isaac Hill. In 1994, after I bought a computer and acquired my first genealogy software, I began to enter the information from the *Genealogy* into a computerized family tree. After six years, with the help of several others in my family who were also searching for our ancestors and relatives, I felt that it was time to prepare an updated version of William Edwin Hill's *Genealogy*. I therefore compiled in the year 2000 what I called a Second Edition of the *Genealogy of the Hill Family in America*. The Second Edition included a photocopy of the First Edition, reduced to 80% of its original size, its pages facing pages on which I had made corrections and additions. I brought the Second Edition down to the end of the 7th generation of descent from Isaac Hill, which was only partially entered in the First Edition in 1921. I added to the Second Edition a brief statement of what I then knew of the ancestors of Isaac Hill, beginning with his great-grandfather Luke Hill, Sr.

The most important documents that helped me in my research were the D.A.R. applications[1] of three of my relatives who were descendants of Isaac Hill, who was born in Connecticut in 1740; the Revolutionary War Pension Record of Isaac Hill[2]; and a letter from Donald Lines Jacobus, in which he showed the evidence and his conclusion for the descent of this Isaac Hill from Luke and Mary Hill, who were married in Windsor, Connecticut, in 1651.[3] These documents were kindly provided to me by relatives who hoped they would help me in my study of the genealogy of the Hill family. They certainly did.

In the past fifteen years, I have received much information from distant cousins who are descendants of other children of Luke Hill Sr.; from cousins who are descendants of his grandson Isaac Hill Sr.; and from cousins who are descendants of the children of Isaac Hill Jr. Some of this information is very thoroughly referenced, and some of it is probably best regarded as interesting hearsay. I have added it all to the genealogy, showing the sources, except when I believed it was inaccurate, based on other information that I have discovered. I also considered whether to include unverified information from family trees on Ancestry.com and from the synthesis of information from these family trees that appears on OneWorldTree. I decided that I must either include this as "possibly" or "probably" true, depending on whether or not there is any corroborative evidence for it, or I must leave it out of this book and make no reference to it. On balance, I finally decided to include this unverified information for the convenience of the reader, because at my age – now 78 – it is unlikely that I will have the time to study it completely, and some of it – perhaps much of it – may eventually prove to be true. Whenever I have included information from Ancestry.com or OneWorldTree, I have indicated this in my End Notes.

I should add that I have not attempted to trace the lines of any person named Hill (or Hills) except those who are believed to descend from Luke Hill of Windsor, Connecticut. It is now reasonably certain from Y-DNA analysis that his descendants are not connected in any way with others of this name who came to America in the first part of the seventeenth century, or thereafter. Two other men whose surname is Hill have the same Y-DNA chromosome, with only one variation. All three of us have the same Hill ancestor – Luke Hill – and none of the forty or so other Hill lines in the Genographic Project have the same ancestor. I therefore conclude at this time that Luke Hill is not related to any of the other Hills. It would be interesting to examine all of those with this surname, but if that happens, it will be the task of some other person.

---

[1] Five women have joined the Daughters of the American Revolution by right of descent from Private Isaac Hill, b. 1740 in Connecticut. He is Ancestor #A055756 in the D.A.R. Patriot Index.

[2] Isaac Hill's Revolutionary War Pension Application is S31747. A copy was obtained from the War Department in 1926 by Camp Stanley, M.D., and it has been passed along to Isaac Hill's descendants.

[3] Donald Lines Jacobus, letter regarding the ancestry of Isaac Hill (b. 1740) to Mrs. H. A. Thomas (1952), 10 pp., forwarded from Allen R. Yale of Connecticut Historical Society to Jeanine Humbert Johnson, 17 July 1992. See also: H. A. Thomas, "Notes: Luke Hill of Windsor, Conn., and John Hill of Guilford, Conn., and Their Descendants: Additions and Corrections" *NEHGR* 107 (Jan. 1953): 71. "These additions and corrections are to the article which appeared in *The Register*, vol. 57, p. 87 et seq., and are taken from the notes of Donald Lines Jacobus."

Acknowledgments

To those cited on the Title Page, I am especially grateful, especially to the late William Edwin Hill, who was the Secretary of the Hill Family Association, and who compiled the original version of the *Genealogy of the Hill Family in America*. To the others, thank you for your assistance: Avis Boyington Hill, wife of my first cousin Dale Hill, was always helpful; she was the genealogist in that generation of the family. Jeanine Hubert Johnson, a granddaughter of my uncle Ben, I owe much; she is the genealogist in the next generation of our family. To Dennis O'Connell, thanks for the enormous line of Abraham Hill, younger brother of my great-grandfather Isaac Hill. James D. Hill, who I don't know personally, thanks for the research you did on the youngest son of the founder, Luke Hill Sr. To Thom Carlson, Ph.D., many thanks for the research that you did, which is so well-documented on your line. And to Mark Norris, thank you very much for your contributions; you opened up an entirely new line, unknown to me. And most of all, to Diane Snyder Ptak, C.A.L.S., many thanks for your help in identifying new sources and for showing me how a genealogist looks at the evidence.

To those who are not cited on the title page, I am grateful for the encouragement that I received from my mother and father, both of whom are now deceased – Essie Mae (Thompson) Hill and Gerald Leslie Hill. And in no particular order, the following cousins, aunts, and uncles: The late Ruby (neé Hill) Woodin, and her daughter Jessie (neé Woodin) Kent; Charles Eugene Hill; Dean Edwin Hill; the late Paul Frank Hill of Corning, N.Y.; the late Paul Francis Hill, son of William Benjamin Hill; Donald Hill; Alton and Kathleen Eileen (neé Ferranti) Herrick; Dolly Jean (neé Goldsberry) Koon; Mrs. Kenneth (Natalie) Rose; Leslie Franklin Schroader; Foster Paul Stockwell and his father, the late Rev. Francis Olin Stockwell.

To the genealogists and officers of many societies that I have joined, I am grateful for the support (and the constructive criticism) of Timothy Field Beard; James Raywalt (aka Alex Bannerman); the late Paul Wentworth Cook; Robert Pond Vivian; Francis M. Clarke, Jr., M.D., F.A.C.S.; William Beckett Brown III; Harry P. Folger III; Tim Jacobs; Phyllis Hansen; Gerald G. DeGroat; John Mauk Hilliard; David Carline Smith; and Richard Burr. I am forever grateful to Leslie Wolfinger, Publications Division Director, and Debbie Riley, Editor, of Heritage Books, Inc., for creating this book out of the manuscript that they received, and for their many useful suggestions.

I am also pleased to acknowledge the help I received from the Connecticut Historical Society, which provided the marriage record and record of births of seven children of Luke Hill and Mary Hout (crediting The Connecticut Historical Society, Hartford, Connecticut). They require that the entire page be published, and I have done this in the frontispiece. The Society also located the record of birth of one child in the Farmington, Conn., Land Records (v.2, p.238). This record is reproduced in the frontispiece from microfilm at the Connecticut State Library.

I am very grateful for the research done by the late Donald Lines Jacobus; and my distant cousin (unbeknownst to me until I began this work), Brigadier General Lucius Barnes Barbour, creator of the Barbour Collection. And for writing the Foreword, for his suggestions, and for his constant support, I am forever indebted to Denis Buchanan Woodfield, D.Phil (Oxon.).

1

First Generation – The Ferry Keeper and His Family
Luke Hill and Mary Hout

----

1. Luke HILL Sr. was probably born in England in about 1613, and he died in Connecticut sometime between 9 May 1695 and the end of the year 1696. He probably died in Simsbury, Hartford County, Connecticut, where he lived at the time of his death.[1]

Luke Hill was an early settler in Windsor, Conn., where he first appears in the historical record on 6 May 1651 at the time of his marriage. After his marriage, he became a freeman of the town of Windsor, where he was a yeoman farmer and the official keeper of the ferry on the Farmington River. When his children were young, he began to acquire land in the wooded wilderness north of Windsor, and he moved there after his last child was born. He thus became one of the original settlers of Simsbury, Conn., where he also was a freeman, the ferry keeper, and patriarch of a large family. He was survived by his wife, five of his children, and many grandchildren and great-grandchildren. He was about 38 years old when he was married in May 1651. His relatively advanced age at that time and his secondary occupation in Connecticut as a ferry keeper – a sort of waterman – suggest that he may have been a sailor who had earned enough prize money to come ashore, buy a farm, and start raising a family.[2]

The exact date and place of Luke Hill's birth is unknown, and his parents' names are also unknown. The surname Hill is known throughout England and Scotland, and his ancestry surely must be English or Scottish, for he settled in an English colonial town in Connecticut and became a freeman there. He was probably born in England, although it is possible that he was born to English parents who had left the British Isles and were living in one of the places where Englishmen had gone by 1613, such as India, the Netherlands, West Indies, New Netherland, and Jamestowne, Virginia. We wonder how he spent his first 38 years, which we now know was the first half of his life, because the answer to that question could be a guide to locating information about his birthplace, his ancestry, and his original occupation.

England was in turmoil during the two decades before Luke Hill appeared in Windsor, Connecticut, in May 1651. England had been at war with France from 1626 until 1630, and during this time, Parliament challenged the King, Charles I, by passing the Petition of Right, which prohibited taxation without consent of Parliament. In 1637, the city of Edinburgh rioted to protest the order to read the English liturgy in Scotland, and Scots Presbyterians organized to resist the episcopacy. In 1641, some 30,000 Irish Protestants were massacred in Ulster, and the Great Rebellion against the King – the First Civil War – began in July 1642. In May 1645, Royalist forces under Prince Rupert, a nephew of Charles I, destroyed Leicester, but one year later, on 5 May 1646, the king himself was forced to surrender at Newark-on-Trent in Nottinghamshire. In 1648, the Second Civil War broke out between the Royalists and Roundheads. Charles was again seized by the army on 1 December 1648 and he was beheaded a little less than two months later, on 30 January 1648/9. The period of the Commonwealth then began, and it was during this interregnum in English history that Luke Hill appeared in Windsor, Connecticut. Oliver Cromwell, as Lord Protector, ruled England, Scotland, and Ireland from 20 April 1653 until he died on 3 September 1658.

Hill: The Ferry Keeper and His Family for 14 Generations

Luke Hill may have lived in England until 1650 or so, and then came directly to America, where he settled in Connecticut. But no trace of his passage on any ship to New England has been discovered. He was not a notably religious person in America – he was not a devout Puritan – nor was he a professional soldier. He was therefore more likely a farmer and a trader, who simply did his duty by bearing arms in the local militia, which was called the trainband, and attending church. Or perhaps he had gone to sea as a young man; in those days, a boy might be put to work on ships at the age of 12, or even younger than that. He probably did not leave England for reasons of conscience. Although he might have come directly to American in 1650 or so, when he was in his late 30s, I think it is more likely that he left England as a young man, perhaps to work as a sailor, and, if so, he might have come ashore in New Netherland. He would not have been the first, or the last, to jump ship. Under such circumstances, his departure from England would not have been a matter of public record, although his name might someday be found on the manifest of a ship's crew or of its passengers. After a long absence from England, Luke Hill may have seen the opportunity to become a settler in the new English colony of Connecticut.[3]

In the years after his marriage in 1651, Luke Hill's name appears many times in the early records of Connecticut, but only once is he recorded as having put his mark on a document – and never his signature. We may therefore presume that he was not much of a scholar, and probably couldn't even write his own name. His given name was, nevertheless, rather consistently recorded as either Luke or "luke" or "luk" Hill. And his surname was almost always spelled "Hill" except when it appeared as "Hills," when its meaning was either plural or possessive, and once in which it was spelled "Hil." For example, in Bassette's summary of references to Luke Hill in the records of Connecticut from 1651-1696, his given name was spelled Luke sixteen times, Luk (or luk) seven times, and once as Luck.[4]

DNA studies of two of Luke Hill's male descendants show that his Y-chromosome is in so-called "Haplogroup *I* (M170)," a marker that appeared about 20,000 years ago in the Middle East. The descendants of M170 (Haplogroup *I*) migrated from Africa to southeastern Europe. They probably spread throughout Europe in the mid-first millennium B.C. during the rise of Celtic culture. M170 is derived from M89, a male who appeared 45,000 years ago in Northern Africa or the Middle East; M89 is therefore a male-line ancestor of M170. M89 was descended from the so-called "Eurasian Adam" (M168), who lived about 60,000 years ago in Africa. M168 is the common ancestor of every non-African male living today.

The DNA of Luke Hill's descendants and of his ancestors has been studied in the Genographic Project of the National Geographic Society. By 2010, two men with identical haplotypes had been found who claim descent from Luke Hill Sr., and more than two dozen other men had been identified who have haplotypes that are very similar to the two who believe that Luke Hill Sr. is their male-line ancestor in America. All of these men believe that their male-line ancestor came to America from England. Most of them do not have the surname of Hill, so their ancestral lines probably diverged from that of Luke Hill's before surnames came into use in England. One of the men with nearly identical haplotypes, whose surname happens to be Hill, believes that his male-line ancestor came to America from Sheffield, England, in the 19th century. This man has a haplotype that is very similar to the two who claim descent from Luke Hill Sr. This information may be a clue to where Luke Hill and his ancestors lived in England, from where Luke Hill came to America in the seventeenth century.[5]

It is not known when and where Luke Hill arrived in America, and it is also unknown if he was related to any of the other men named Hill who came to America in the mid-seventeenth century. Family relationships were often recorded in wills and deeds and other legal documents in those days, by such references as, "my cousin" (which sometimes meant only that they had an ancestor-in-common) or "my brother" (which could mean brother, or brother-in-law, or even the husband of a sister-in-law). However, no contemporaneous documents have come to light that suggest a relationship of Luke Hill with any other family named Hill. I therefore conclude that Luke Hill of Windsor, Conn., is not related to any of the many other men named Hill or Hills who emigrated from England in the mid-seventeenth century.[6]

Luke Hill first appears in the historical record on 6 May 1651 in Windsor, Connecticut, when he married a woman named Mary Hout. The record of the marriage has been preserved, along with the births of seven of their children. It is seen on the frontispiece of this book, but because his wife's name has been spelled various ways by different authors, I have enlarged and reproduced it here.

Her ancestry and the dates of her birth and death are unknown, but it is known that she was alive several years after he made his will, providing for her, when he was over 80 years of age. Given the record of her childbearing, from February 1651/2 to November 1668, she must have been younger than her husband, probably by at least a decade or more. If she had her first child when she was as young as, say, 18, and her last child when she was as old as, say, 45, she would have been born between 1623-1634.

Mary Hout might be the woman named "Mary Hout," who is said to have been born in 1630, somewhere in Connecticut, about whom nothing more is known. She may, indeed, be the Mary Hout of this genealogy, and her name has been entered gratuitously without giving her ancestry. Another possibility is that she was "an unrecorded daughter of Reverend Ephraim Huit [who was] one of the earliest settlers of Windsor," whose eldest daughter, like the eldest daughter of Luke Hill, was named Lydia. Both of these possibilities are not likely; the first because there is nothing known about her, and the second because the Rev. Huit was so prominent that an "unrecorded daughter" is not likely. A third possibility is that her name is a variant of Hoyt. For example, Thomas Hyatt, who appeared in Stamford in 1641, and who died there, 16 July 1662, spelled his name in the records as Hyote, hiout, Hiout, hout, hyout, hiat, hyat, Hyat, and Hyatt. The word "hout" is one of these ways, and he was twice recorded as having this spelling of his surname. His daughters would have been the right age. However, his will names six children, and all six are shown (Caleb, Ruth, Deborah, John, Rebecca, and Thomas). The only way he could have a daughter named Mary Hout would be if she eloped and was not recognized by him. This possibility exists, and it is also possible that one of many others named Hoyt or Hyatt in Connecticut has a daughter whose surname was spelled Hout.[7]

Yet another possibility is that Mary was Dutch, for the surname Hout was well-known at that time; it means "wood" or "woods" in Dutch. The Dutch considered that the Connecticut River (which they called "Fresh River") was the northern border of New Netherland, and a small Dutch settlement existed until 1654 near what is now Hartford, three years after Luke Hill and Mary Hout were married in the adjacent town of Windsor. Perhaps he and Mary Hout simply slipped across the border from the Dutch outpost near Hartford in May 1651, got married in Windsor, and started raising a family there.[8]

Windsor had only been in existence for eighteen years when Luke Hill and Mary Hout were married there in 1651. Windsor and the nearby towns of Hartford (to the south),

Farmington (to the west), and Wethersfield (south of Hartford) on the Connecticut River were first settled in 1633-40 by Puritans from Massachusetts, under the leadership of Pastor Thomas Hooker. The union of these towns in 1637 was the origin of the Colony of Connecticut, of which Hartford was the capital. In the same year, 1637, about 500 Puritans from England came to America under the leadership of the Rev. James Davenport and spent the winter in Massachusetts. In the next year, 1638, they came to the mouth of the Quinnipiac River in Connecticut, where they founded a settlement which they named, in 1640, New Haven. In 1643 New Haven and four adjacent towns in Connecticut and Southold, Long Island, joined to form the New Haven Colony, which later merged with the Connecticut Colony, the capital of which continued to be Hartford.[9]

Luke and Mary's first child, Lydia, was born in February 1651/2, about nine months after they were married. Their second child, Mary, was born in September 1654. In June 1655 Luke Hill purchased a home lot of six acres in Windsor from John Strong, between "high ways" on the east and west, and between the property of Walter Gaylord on the north and "John brook" on the south. This lot was probably at the south-east corner of the Palisado, facing the Rivulet (now known as the Farmington River).[10] He apparently was living in Farmington in March 1656/7 when his first son and third child, Eleazer (originally known as Ebenezer), was born.[11] The record of the births of the other seven children are shown in the frontispiece, along with the marriage of Luke Hill and Mary Hout. The birth of Ebenezer (later known as Eleazer) is shown here, from Farmington records. The name of the father is enlarged to show its spelling. I believe it is spelled Luik Hill, which is an acceptable variant of Luke Hill:

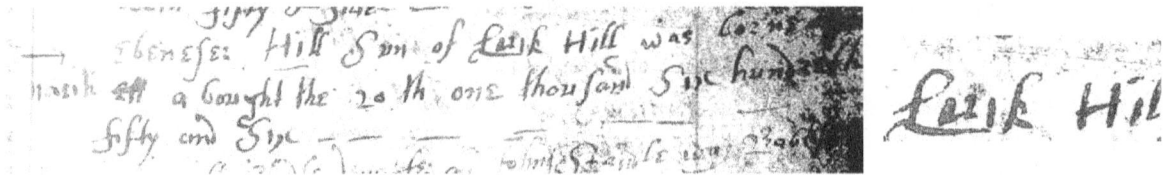

Luke Hill must have stayed in Farmington for a year or so at most, because in 1658 he purchased from Tahan Grant in Windsor a dwelling house, a house lot, and common privileges to seven and a half acres of land. Grant's land was at the north-east corner of the Palisado, adjacent to the Great Meadow that stretched down to the Connecticut River. Luke may also have lived for a while at about this time in Middletown.[12] In any event, Luke and Mary's next child, a son Tahan, was born in Windsor in November 1659. And also at about this time, Luke was granted fifteen acres of land at Massaco (later called Simsbury), about 12 miles north of Windsor, "on the west side of the river bounded out by Mr. Grant Apl. 19, 1660." This was the Farmington River, which flows north on a great loop from Simsbury and then turns south to pass through Windsor, where it enters the Connecticut River. Luke Hill also bought twenty acres of meadow and seventy-seven acres of upland from Aron Cooke at that time, probably somewhere between the center of Windsor and the new settlement at Massaco. Luke continued to live in Windsor, however, and his next child, another boy, was born there in March 1661/2; he was named Luke, and as an adult, he was known as Luke Jr. while his father was still alive.[13]

In December 1663 Captain Aran Cooke sued Luke Hill for moneys due, but the captain lost his suit; the jury found for the defendant. Cooke was thereupon ordered to pay court costs of twelve shillings, and to pay thirty-one shillings and four pence to Luke Hill. Soon after the trial was over, Luke and Mary had their next child, Abigail (in April 1664); she was followed by Elizabeth (in October 1666).[14]

As recently as January 1659/60, a canoe had been used as the ferry across the Rivulet, operated by a Thomas Parsons, but on 1 April 1667, the Town Acts note that Luke Hill took charge of the Rivulet ferry, "for £12 per annum besides what he gets from travellers and persons by night." By the end of that month, however, Luke Hill "made a sad complaint" about the inadequate amount that the town allowed him, and he threatened to "leave the ferry." His wife, too, "came in and sadly bemoaned their condition." It appears that the town must have reduced the stipend by £3 when the Hills took over the job, because after hearing from Luke and his wife, "it was voted that they would add the other £3 as it was before." Little more than a year later, in September 1668, the Town Acts show that it was "Voted that the town should be at the cost to procure a new rope for the ferry because Luke Hill is not able to be at the cost himself." It appears that the canoe had been retired, for a boat was now being used as the ferry, which was kept on a steady course across the Rivulet by a rope. The "old ferry Boat" was also retired in November 1668, sold to Samuel Marshall "to make the best of her" for 10*s*. Marshall was a clever fellow, because in July 1671, he leased the ferry back to the town for 13 weeks, for 50*s*.[15]

On 11 May 1669, the town of Windsor made an agreement with John Willington to keep the Rivulet ferry and to "have the use of the cellar" which the town had bought from Luke Hill, as well as "the little House by it" to dwell in. Willington was granted £16 for his wages in addition to "the use of a corner of land … for his improvement," thus profiting by the complaint that Luke Hill and his wife had made about their poor compensation a year earlier. We thus see that by May 1669, Luke had moved to Massaco. His youngest child, John, was born in Windsor in November 1668, and the family now consisted of two adults and eight children – if we count Ebenezer, now called Eleazer.[16]

On 11 October 1669, the census of Massaco was turned in to the General Court of Connecticut, showing 13 freemen there, "who had first been freemen at Windsor." Luke Hill was on that list, so we see that he had been a freeman at Windsor, and now had that privilege in Massaco.[17] On 12 May 1670 Massaco was officially renamed "Simmsbury," and in November of that year, Luke Hill's eldest daughter was married, although she and her husband continued to live in Simsbury. Luke soon became responsible for the Simsbury ferry, which went back and forth across what was called locally "the river" (actually, the same Rivulet that flows through Windsor, now called the Farmington River). "Hill's Ferry" in was on Pent Road. The location of Hill's Ferry can still be seen; Pent Road is a short dead end street on the west side of the river, opposite the end of Ferry Lane on the east side of the river in Simsbury. The ferry site was sold to Timothy Woodbridge in 1742. The old "Hill House" was later torn down by the Rev. Benejah Roots but it was replaced in 1762, and Roots' house stood for many years at that location.[18]

On 5 May 1671, it was voted to erect a meeting house at Simsbury near "Luke Hills in Hope Meadow," which was near the location of a Dr. Barber's place in 1897. "Hope Meadow" can still be identified; it is undoubtedly smaller than it was in 1671, but its name has been given to the main street through Simsbury as Hopmeadow Street (U.S. Route 202 and State Route 10). Pent Road joins it from the east in Simsbury Center, and the Hopmeadow Country Club is across Hopmeadow Street to the west.

In 1676, the residents of Simsbury fled to Windsor when the town was invaded and burned by Indians in King Philip's War. Simsbury was the most heavily damaged town in Connecticut during that brief but violent conflict between Native American warriors and the English settlers, which lasted from June 1675-August 1676. The town was not rebuilt until 1679.

In August 1677, it was noted in Windsor church records that Luke Hill had seven children born at Windsor. This is reasonably consistent with information in other records about the births of his eight children, six of whom are said to have been born in Windsor, one in Farmington, and one in East Hartford (I believe the latter statement is incorrect; seven were born in Windsor). In May 1678, Luke and Mary lost the first of their children, with the death of Mary (Hill) Saxton; she left four children, the youngest only four years of age. In October 1679, Simsbury was rebuilt after it had been laid waste during the war, and Luke Hill was one of the men who were ordered to perform the rebuilding. In 1681, Luke Hill was granted three shillings and six pence per week for keeping the wife of the late John Brookes for ten weeks.[19]

There were many disputes as to the location of the meeting house in Simsbury until a decision was finally made in 1683 that it should be near Thomas Rowel's, and that it would be 24 x 28 x 14 ft high.[20] In June 1687, Luke Hill's son-in-law, Arthur Henbury (also spelled Henbery), provided that his daughter Lydia would be cared for by his "Honored father Hill" until she reached the age of eighteen. Henbury's wife, Lydia (Hill) Henbury, was Luke's oldest child. She is believed to have died in 1689, probably related to the birth of her last child. She had six children by Henbury, the youngest of whom was born in 1689. Some accounts of this bequest imply that Arthur Henbury's provision for his daughter Lydia was made on his death bed, but it appears that he recovered after making his will. After Henbury's wife Lydia (née Hill) died, he married a widow, Mrs. Martha Bement, by whom he had two more children.[21]

In May 1688, Luke Hill was granted fifty rods (825 feet) in breadth in Simsbury, "over the Mountain towards Stony Brook to go from our east lyn towards or to the mountain." The next March, a highway was laid out to run between Luke Hill's house and Jonathan Gillett's house, and thence to the cove. Jonathan and his brother Nathan Gillett (a k a Gillet and Gillette) had lived across the Rivulet from Luke Hill in Windsor, and they now lived near him in Simsbury. Several descendants of Jonathan and Nathan Gillett married descendants of Luke Hill, and these families were intermarried for several generations. In February 1692, "luk Hil Senior" received his allotment, formerly laid out at the East Corner, and a year later Nathaniel Holcomb was noted to desire two acres, northerly of "Goodman Hils hom lot." Luke and Mary's fourth child, Tahan, was the next to die; he left one descendant at his death in December 1692. In September 1693, "Luke Hill, senr of Simsbury, aged 80 years or there aboutts" testified regarding a grant of land by the town of Simsbury five years previously, in May 1688.[22]

On 26 February 1693/4 Luke Hill, Sr., "being agged above seventy years and through this my agg utterly disenabled & In capacitated to labr," made his will and Covenant. He appointed his youngest son John Hill as executor and directed him to care for his aged mother and to pay his sister, Abigail Pamerly, fourteen pounds. Abigail was to receive several items from the house, including the "grat Iron Pot," but she not to have this "till after her parants death." On 9 May 1695, the General Court freed "Luk Hill" and two others "from the list of estates by which rates are made," presumably for age as well as a good past record. Following this relief from taxes, there are no further references to Luke Hill, Sr., in the records of Simsbury or Windsor, so he probably died soon thereafter. In 1696, a Luke Hill paid taxes of 11*s*-03*d* in Simsbury, presumably Luke Hill, Jr. Mary (Hout) Hill survived her husband, and in October 1697, she was recorded as having observed the conditions of a marriage that was performed in 1688.[23]

Luke Hill married, on 6 May 1651 in Windsor, Connecticut, Mary Hout, whose ancestry is unknown; probably born between 1623 and1634, say 1630, in England or New England; died after October 1697, probably at Simsbury, Conn. Luke and Mary (Hout) Hill had eight children: Lydia (1651/52-abt. 1688-9); Mary (1654-1678); Eleazer, probably known as Ebenezer at birth (b. 1656/57-1724/5); Tahan (1659-1692); Luke, Jr. (1661/2-1740); Abigail (1664-1737); Elizabeth (1666-1725); and John (1668-1740). All but one of the children were born in

Windsor, Connecticut, between 18 February 1651 and 28 November 1668. The first child, Lydia, was born a little more than nine months after her parents were married. The third child, Eleazer (various spellings), was born in Farmington. The children married members of the Henbury/Henbery, Saxton/Sexton, Gillett/Gilet/Gilette, Parmelee/Pamerly, Butler, Adams, Phelps, and Terry families. Two of the children married Parmelees, and Luke Jr. and John were married twice. Luke Hill Sr. had at least 37 grandchildren: Lydia had six children; Mary had three, Eleazer had four, Tahan had two, Luke Jr., had seven, Abigail had six, Elizabeth had two, and John had seven. Two of Luke Hill's sons (Eleazer and John) were chosen as hayward ("hedge ward," guardian of fences) of Simsbury, and Eleazer was also a perambulator of Simsbury.[24]

Mary HOUT was probably born between 1623 and 1634, say 1630, in England or New England, and died in Connecticut, probably Simsbury, soon after October 1697. Her surname was spelled Hout in the record of her marriage, as we saw above. Hout is an ancient Dutch family name, meaning "wood" or "woods," and the surname Ten Hout ("near the woods") can be found in the records of New Netherland as early as 1681.[25] Hout is also an alternate spelling of the German surname Haut ("high"). Mary's name has been spelled many other ways by different authors, such as Hoyt, Hart, Haught, Haight, Holt, and Huit. One unreferenced account says that she was the daughter of Simon and Susannah (Smith) Haight, born at Upway, Dorsetshire, England, 20 September 1635, and died at Simsbury, Hartford County, Connecticut, in 1692. And in July 2001, the FamilySearch.org genealogy, also without a reference, showed her parents as Simon and Susannah (Smith) Haight. Others have said that she was a child of Simon Hoyt who lived at Windsor, Connecticut, from 1639 to about 1648. However, the Lyon genealogy shows that Simon Hoyt's daughter Mary married Thomas Lyon Sr. This Mary Lyon was the heir of Simon Hoyt, so the wife of Luke Hill could not be the daughter of Simon Hoyt.[26] With such confusion, and no facts to support any supposition, we must conclude that Mary Hout's origin is unknown as of February 2010.

There is little in the historical record about Mary Hout. She appears but four times in Windsor records. She first appears at the time of her marriage to Luke Hill on 6 May 1651, the only time that her maiden name appears in a contemporaneous document. In April 1667, she and her husband complained to the town about what they believed was inadequate compensation for keeping the Rivulet Ferry. In February 1693/4 her husband made a covenant with their son John, providing that he take care of "me and his agged mother." And in October 1697, she was recorded as having observed the conditions of a marriage that was performed in 1688.[27]

Luke and Mary (Hout) Hill had the following children:

2	i.	Lydia (1651/2-~1689)
3	ii.	Mary (1654-1678)
4	iii.	Eleazer (known as Ebenezer at birth) (1656/7-1724/5)
5	iv.	Tahan "Tahay" (1659-1692)
6	v.	Luke (1661/2-1740)
7	vi.	Abigail (1664-1737)
8	vii.	Elizabeth (1666-1725)
9	vii.	John (1668-1740)

Descendants of Luke and Mary (Hout) Hill married descendants of other early setters of Windsor and Simsbury, Connecticut, such as the Parmelee and Case families. And in later generations, descendants of Luke and Mary Hill married each other, unaware that they were distant cousins.[28]

Fig. 1-1: Farmington River, Windsor, Conn., looking downstream from Palisado Avenue
Bridge. Hill's Ferry site is shown by the arrow, midway in the picture

Fig. 1-2: Congregational Church, Windsor, Conn.
The first settlers of Windsor are buried in the Palisado Cemetery behind the church

From Google Images

Fig. 1-3: Lt. Walter Fyler House, 96 Palisado Ave, Windsor, Conn. (built 1640).
Perhaps the oldest wooden house in Connecticut, contemporaneous with Luke Hill's. It
is on the SW side of the Palisado. Hill's Ferry is near the south corner, off to the right.

SOME EARLY
RECORDS AND DOCUMENTS
OF AND RELATING TO
THE TOWN OF
WINDSOR CONNECTICUT
1639-1703

*

HARTFORD
CONNECTICUT HISTORICAL SOCIETY

[53] Luke Hill married mary Hout . may . 6 . 1651 .
his Daughter liddya was Borne . febury . 18 . 1651 .
his Daughter mary² was Borne . feptemᵣ . 20 . 1654 .
his fonn Tahan Hill was Borne . noumbr . 23 . 1659 .
his fonn Luke Hill was Borne . march . 6 . 1661 .
his Daughte Abigayl was Borne . Aprell . 16 . 1664 .
his Daughter elifabeth was Born . octobr . 8 . 1666 .
his fonn John Hill was borne . noumber . 28 . 1668 .

Fig. 1-4: *Some Early Records and Documents of ...Windsor*, p. 47
Hill marriage and births, transcribed from the Old Church Records (OCR)

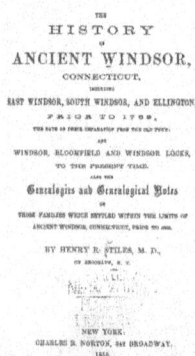

THE
HISTORY
OF
ANCIENT WINDSOR,
CONNECTICUT,
INCLUDING
EAST WINDSOR, SOUTH WINDSOR, AND ELLINGTON,
PRIOR TO 1768,
THE DATE OF THEIR SEPARATION FROM THE OLD TOWN;
AND
WINDSOR, BLOOMFIELD AND WINDSOR LOCKS,
TO THE PRESENT TIME.
ALSO THE
Genealogies and Genealogical Notes
OF
THOSE FAMILIES WHICH SETTLED WITHIN THE LIMITS OF
ANCIENT WINDSOR, CONNECTICUT, PRIOR TO 1640.

BY HENRY R. STILES, M. D.,
OF BROOKLYN, N. Y.

NEW YORK:
CHARLES B. NORTON, 841 BROADWAY,
1859.

HILL, WILLIAM, early at Dorchester, where he had land granted Nov.
1635; removed to W., probably rot with the first company; possibly
brother of John, mentioned on page 59 of the *Hist. of Dorchester;* was a
pointed in 1639 to view arms and ammunition in the towns; deputy
'39-41 and 44; auditor of public accounts in '39; after which he was an a
sistant, and in 1659 was collector of customs at Fairfield.

LUKE, m. Mary Hout, May 6, 1651. *Children*—Lydia, b. Feb. 18, 1651-
Mary, b. Sept. 20, 1654; Tahan, b. Nov. 23, 1659; Luke, b. March 6, 1661
Abigail, b. April 16, 1664; Elizabeth, Oct. 8, 1666; John, b. Nov. 28, 166

Sgt. ELEAZER, m. Elizabeth Gillet, July 8, 1731; he d. March 3, 1724-
Children—Eleazer, b. May 15, 1732; Benjamin, b. July 17, 1735; Stephe
b. Oct. 2, 1737.

Wid. SARAH, d. Sept. 30, 1737.

Fig. 1-5: Stiles, *Ancient Windsor*, (1859), 664 – Luke Hill m. Mary Hout, May 6, 1651.
The earliest records, Figs. 1-4 and 1-5, show Mary's name spelled as Hout.

PLAN
OF
PALISADO.

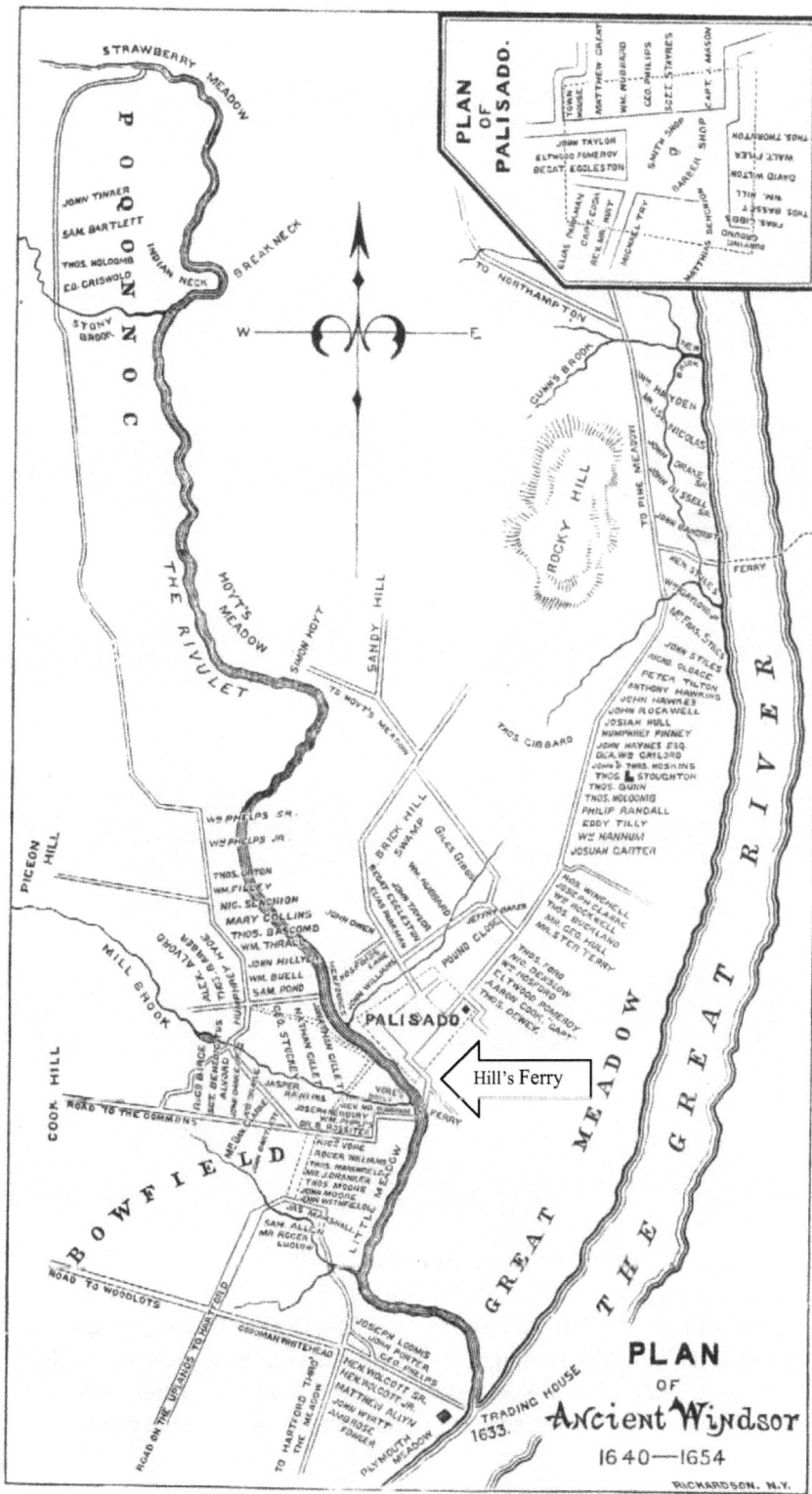

Fig. 1-6:
Stiles,
*History of
Ancient
Windsor*
(1859)
"Plan of
Ancient
Windsor
1650-54"
facing p.123

Hill's Ferry
site is
marked with
arrow

STRAWBERRY MEADOW

POQUONOC

JOHN TINKER
SAM. BARTLETT
THOS. HOLCOMB
ED. CRISWOLD

INDIAN NECK
BREAK NECK
STONY BROOK

THE RIVULET

HOYT'S MEADOW
SIMON HOYT

SANDY HILL

TO HOYT'S MEADOW

TO NORTHAMPTON

CUNN'S BROOK

TO PINE MEADOW

ROCKY HILL

THOS. GIBBARD

WM HAYDEN
NICOLAS
DRAKE
JOHN BISSELL SR.
ALEX. ALVORD
CAPT THOS. STILES
JOHN STILES
RICHD. OLDAGE
PETER TILTON
ANTHONY HAWKINS
JOHN ROCKWELL
JOSIAK HULL
HUMPHREY PINNEY
JOHN HAYNES ESQ.
DEA. WE GAYLORD
JOHN & THOS. HOSKINS
THOS. QUIN
THOS. L STOUGHTON
THOS. HOLCOMB
PHILIP RANDALL
EDDY TILLY
WM HANNUM
JOSUAH CARTER

TO NORTHAMPTON FERRY

WS PHELPS SR.
WM PHELPS JR.

THOS. ORTON
WM. FILLEY
NIC. SENCHION
MARY COLLINS
THOS. BASCOMB
WM. THRALL
JOHN HILLYER
WM. BUELL
SAM. POND

PIGEON HILL

MILL BROOK

ALEX. ALVORD
JNO. BARBER
JOHN OWEN

BRICK HILL SWAMP
GILES GIBBS
JOHN TAYLOR
EDCT. EGGLESTON
ELIAS PARKMAN
WM. HANNUM

POUND CLOSE
BETHIA BAKER

THOS. FORD
TWO. DEASLOW
ELTWOOD POMEROY
AARON COOK
THOS. DEWEY

THOS. WINCHELL
JOSEPH CLARK
WM ROCKWELL
THOS. BUCKLAND
MR. GEO. HULL
MR STETH FERRY

PALISADO

Hill's Ferry

BIGG BRICK
WM ALVORD
THOS. BUCKLAND
NATHAN GILLET
JASPER RAWINS
JOSEPH NEWBERY
WM. PERRY
DR. B. ROSSTER

COOK HILL
ROAD TO THE COMMONS

BOWFIELD

ALICE KORK
ROGER WILLIAMS
THOS. MARSHFIELD
MR J. DRANLIER
THOS. MOORE
JOHN MOORE
JOHN WHITFIELD

ROAD ON THE WAYSIDES TO HARTFORD

ROAD TO WOODLOTS

TO HARTFORD THIRD
THE MEADOW

GOODMAN WHITEHEAD

JOSEPH LOOMIS
JOHN PORTER
C.F.O. PHELPS
NICH. WOLCOTT SR.
NICH. WOLCOTT JR.
MATTHEW ALLYN
JOHN WYATT
AMBROSE FINGER

TRADING HOUSE
1633

PLYMOUTH MEADOW

PLAN
OF
Ancient Windsor
1640—1654

THE GREAT RIVER

GREAT MEADOW

LITTLE MEADOW

RICHARDSON, N.Y.

NO. 1 MAP.

PLAN OF PALISADO:
TOWN HOUSE
MATTHEW GRANT
WM. HUBBARD
GEO PHILIPS
ROGET STAYRES
CAPT J. MASON
JOHN TAYLOR
ELTWOOD POMEROY
DEACT. EGGLESTON
SMITH SHOP
BARBER SHOP
MICHAEL TRY
MATTHIAS SENCHION
THOS. THORNTON
WALT. FYLER
DAVID WILTON
WM. HILL
THAS. GIBBS
THOS. BASSET
BURYING GROUND

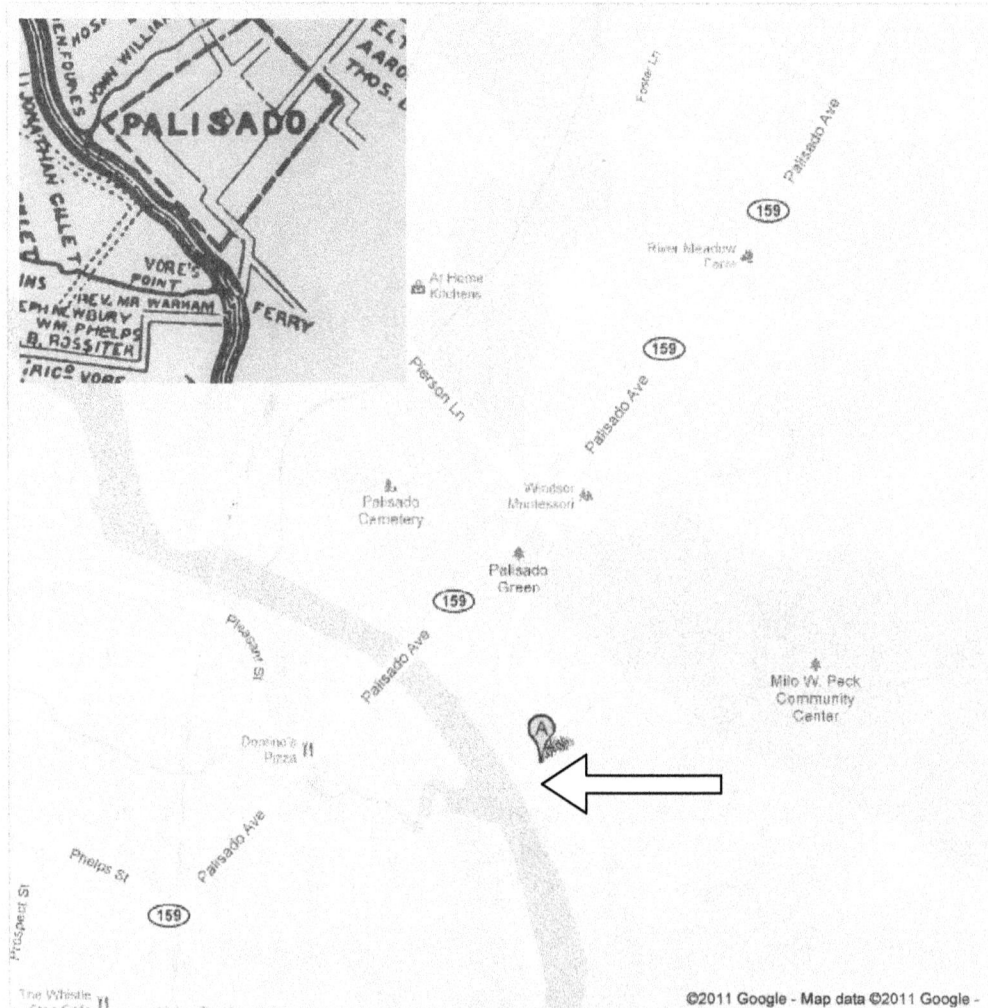

Fig. 1-7: Ferry Crossing in Windsor, Conn.
Modern map of Palisado District, Windsor, showing Hill's Ferry location (A), now at 80 North Meadow Rd. Inset shows the ferry site on Stiles' map (1859). Both maps show the road at south corner of the Palisado, leading to the ferry and continuing down into the Great Meadow. Palisado Avenue now crosses the Farmington River on a bridge which did not then exist. The cover shows the river, viewed from the point of the arrow

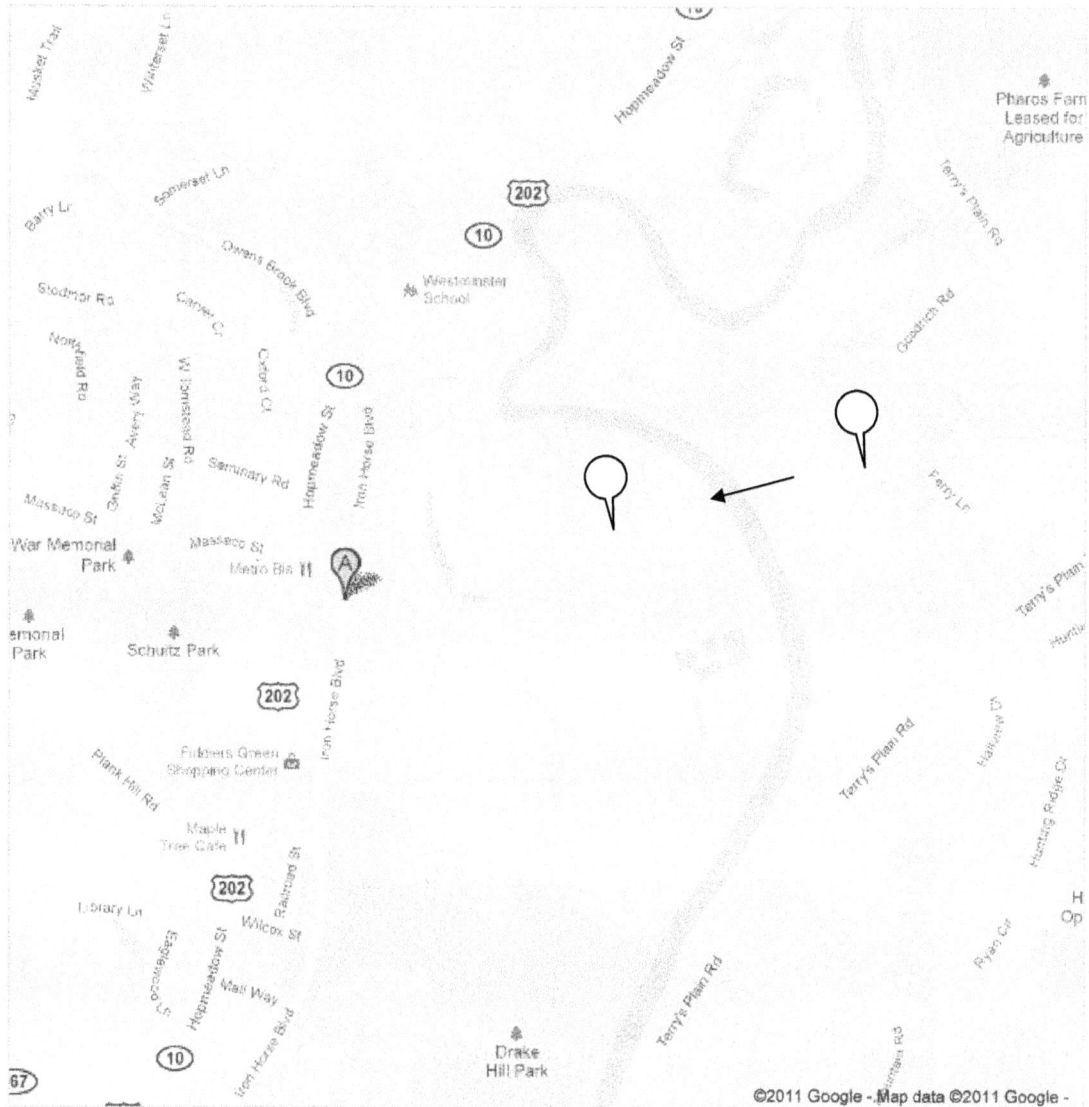

Fig. 1-8: Ferry crossing in Simsbury, Conn.
The Luke Hill home was near Hopmeadow Street, on Pent Road (unmarked, 1 block
long), marked (A) on the teardrop at what is now Iron Horse Blvd. The river was wider
in colonial days, and the ferry crossed between the the unmarked teardrops   The arrow
shows the direction of the photo of the ferry site in Fig. 1-9, taken from the east.

Fig. 1-9: Hill's Ferry Site, Simsbury, Conn. View to the west from the east bank of the
Farmington River, shown in Fig. 1-8 with arrow.

© 2004 Steve Schar, Google Images

Fig. 1-10: Simsbury Cemetery, Simsbury, Conn.

2

Second Generation – The Eight Children of the Ferry Keeper

Line 1 - Lydia

2. Lydia HILL, **eldest child** of Luke and Mary (Hout) Hill, was born at Windsor, Hartford County, Connecticut, 18 February 1651/2; died at Simsbury, Hartford Co., Conn., before 25 June 1687. She married, on 5 November 1670, in Simsbury, Conn., as his first wife, **Arthur HENBURY** (aka Henbery); born about 1646; died in Hartford, Conn., 1 August 1697.[29]

There is no written record that describes Lydia Hill's childhood, but it is not difficult to imagine something of her life. She was born about nine months after her parents were married, and as the eldest child and first daughter, she would have been her mother's main helper throughout her early years. Her father was older than most men then were at the time of his marriage, and her mother was probably much younger than her husband. At first, they lived on the north side of a stream called The Rivulet, now known as the Farmington River, near its point of entry into the Connecticut River. Her father was a farmer and also keeper of the ferry across The Rivulet. They lived in a newly settled village called Windsor, north of the other new English settlements of Hartford and Wethersfield, and east of the new town of Farmington. By the time Lydia was old enough to be able to remember her surroundings, they had moved into the wooden-walled center of Windsor, known as the Palisado, while her father continued to operate the ferry. Between 1651 and 1668, her parents had three more girls and four boys, all of whom survived. It was a large family to take care of and Lydia was surely busy, although she was only thirteen years old when her youngest brother was born. By that time, her father was looking for a way to enlarge his property, and in the next year, 1669, he relocated his family to a new settlement in the wilderness known as Masacco, about fifteen miles north of Windsor. The next year, Masacco was given the name Simsbury, by which it is known to this day. Lydia's father continued to operate a ferry across the Farmington River, at the point where it flowed through Simsbury on its way to join the Connecticut River to the south. The Hill family lived in the center of Simsbury, just east of the main street that ran north and south through town.

In 1670, at the age of eighteen, Lydia married **Arthur Henbury**, a Simsbury man who was about six years older than she was. Her husband, like her father and one of her brothers, was one of the registered voters of Simsbury, a man of substance in that little community. Her first child was born in 1672 and her second child in 1674. Her third child, a daughter like the others, was born in about 1676. In that year, New England erupted in a war between the English colonists and the Native Americans, led by Massasoit's son, known as King Philip. Simsbury was invaded and burned to the ground by the Indians in 1676. The residents fled for their lives to Windsor, and the town was not rebuilt until 1679. In 1682, after returning to Simsbury, Lydia's fourth child was born, another daughter. She then had a son who was born in 1686, and another daughter who was born about a year later. Lydia probably died about that time, when she was, say, 35 years of age. Her husband also became very ill, and thinking he might die, he wrote his will in June 1687. His will shows that Lydia had died, because he refers to what remained of his wife's "portion." He divided his assets equally between his five surviving daughters, except that for what remained of his wife's "portion," he gave to Lydia's father and mother to care for his youngest daughter, just a baby, with a "wekly body." Sad to say, his baby daughter probably died soon after that, for she is not mentioned again in historical records.

Lydia's husband remarried in about 1689, to a widow with no children of her own, and two years later, in 1691, he left Simsbury with his new wife and his children and relocated to Hartford. He died there six years later, in August 1697, at about 51 years of age. His estate was valued at £108-06-04, which was rather substantial for that time and place, and it was still being adjudicated two years later. Two of Lydia's daughters had married before their father died. The oldest daughter was married by 1694, and the next surviving daughter was married about six weeks before her father died. His widow, now alone and responsible for two young stepdaughters, married a widower. Lydia's last two surviving daughters were cared for until they married in April and December 1703; their husbands happened to be each other's first cousins.

Arthur Henbury married (2) in 1688 or 1689, a widow, Mrs. Martha Bement, by whom he had no children. After Henbury died, his widow, Martha (Bement) Henbury, married (3), as his third wife, Thomas Shepard.[30]

Arthur and Lydia (Hill) Henbury had the following children[31]:

10	i.	Mary (1672-1759)
11	ii.	Hannah (~1674-1759)
12	iii.	Susanna (1682/3-1767)
13	iv.	Elizabeth (~1684-1767)
14	v.	Samuel (1686-<1687)
15	vi.	Lydia (<1687-1689)

Line 2 - Mary

3. Mary HILL,[32] second daughter and **second** of the eight children of Luke and Mary (Hout) Hill, was born at Windsor, Hartford Co., Conn., 20 September 1654; died, probably at Simsbury, Hartford Co., Conn., sometime after the birth of her last child in, say, 1682; probably later than that, say about 1714. She married, on 30 July 1677, at Simsbury, **John SAXTON** (a k a Sexton), son of Richard and Sarah (Cook) Sexton; born at Windsor, 4 March 1649/50; died at Simsbury, 4 December 1718. The marriage is recorded in the Old Church Records of Windsor, but it was probably performed in the adjacent town of Simsbury, where her father was then living.

Little is known about Mary (Hill) Saxton/Sexton, except that the birth of her daughter Mary was recorded on 4 May 1678. Richard Sexton/Saxton had two other children, both sons, and inasmuch as another marriage for Richard has not been recorded, we can assume that they are Mary's children. A record of the sons' births has not been preserved, although they were baptized on the same day as adults more than two decades later. Mary was truly a *femme covert*, and her name does not appear again in the historical records. She probably lived to an old age, but she was not mentioned when Richard made his will in 1716, so we may presume that she died at, say, age 60, perhaps around 1714. There were no feminine items in the inventory of his estate when it was taken after his death in 1718, so her personal effects had probably already been distributed to her daughter, her two daughters-in-law, and perhaps to their daughters.

John SAXTON (a k a **SEXTON**),[33] eldest of the two sons and second of the six children of Richard and Sarah (Cook) Sexton, was born at Windsor, Hartford Co., Conn., 4 March 1649/50; died at Simsbury, Hartford Co., Conn., 4 December 1718.

Richard Sexton and a contemporary immigrant, George Sexton, arrived in New England within about the same decade, George having arrived after Richard. It has been speculated that the two men were brothers, and that both are descendants of the first earl of Limerick, who was originally of Yorkshire, England. The name of George Sexton appears in records of Windsor,

Conn., in 1663, a year after Richard died there. George and his family appear to have removed from Windsor, Conn., to Westfield, Mass., in about 1671.

Richard Sexton came to America on the *Blessing*, Master John Lester, which sailed from London to America in July 1635. "Richard Sexton, age 14" was one of 30 passengers on this small ship; his age at that time indicates that he was born in about 1621. Five and a half years later, in January 1640/1, a "Richard Saxton" purchased a half-acre house lot in Windsor, Conn., on the west side of the street in the Palisado, north of the burying ground, adjacent to the land of William Hill. "Richard Saxton" was recorded as being of Windsor in 1643. In September 1644, the Rev. Ephraim Huit died in Windsor; his estate showed a debt of £16 that was owed by Richard Sexton, which Sexton had apparently borrowed to buy this house lot.

Three years later, in April 1647, Richard Sexton married Sarah Cook, sister of Nathaniel Cook, a leading citizen of Windsor. The Sextons initially lived on the green near the Palisado, and they later moved to several other locations in Windsor. Richard Sexton was listed as an owner of land in Windsor in 1653, and his last home was on the west side of the Tunxis River, close to his first house lot in Windsor. Sixteen residents of Windsor died in 1662, including Richard Sexton, on 3 May; and three days later, his youngest daughter died, only four months old. He was survived by his wife and five other children, ranging from a little over four to 14 and one-half years of age. Richard Sexton was about 41 when he died, and his wife was probably under 40. She never remarried, and like his father had been on arrival in America, their son John Sexton, though only 12, was suddenly thrust into the role of an adult.

John Sexton had first appeared in the historical record in the Windsor town records as follows: "John Saxton, Son of Richard Saxton was born on March: 4th: 1649." He next appears as being paid £0-8-0 for killing a wolf in March 1674, the first of several for which he would be paid by the town. His mother died in June of that year, and then, at age 24, he was appointed administrator of his mother's estate. His only brother, Richard Jr., died in December 1675 in King Philip's War, and in June 1676, John contributed 1*s* 3*d* to the Connecticut Relief fund for the poor of other Colonies who had been distressed by that war.

"John Saxton" was fined 30*s* "for retailing of cyder Contrary to Law" in September 1676. In the next summer, on 30 July 1677, he married Mary Hill, daughter of Luke Hill, who had operated the ferry across the Farmington River at Windsor and was then living a few miles upstream as the ferry operator in Simsbury. John may already have been living in Simsbury, and some accounts even suggest that the first child of John Saxton and Mary Hill was born a year before they were married. They would eventually have three children, although the birth of only one of the three was recorded, a year after they were married. The other two children, who were sons, were baptized as adults.

John Saxton/Sexton appears in many other records of Simsbury. He was one of 14 citizens of Simsbury who were "propounded for freemen" of the Connecticut Colony in 1686, and he was accepted as a freeman in October of that year. His property lines were shown in town meetings in February 1685/6 and again in May 1688. He paid a tax of 10*s* in 1693/4 and he was chosen as a Fence Viewer in March 1694/5. He was granted a small sum for helping to frame a barn in 1698 and he was granted 30 acres of land in January 1698/9. He purchased another 33 acres of land for £20 and ten barrels of tar in 1699. "John Sextone" was sued for payment of a debt in 1699/1700, and although the suit was withdrawn, it was reinstituted the next year and he lost on the second round. He killed a wolf and was paid for it in 1700, and he repeated the task in 1706/7 and in 1716, and, so he claimed, again in 1717. In 1701, his property was valued at £46, while his son, John Jr., had property valued at £93 at a time when the highest on the roll was only £129. In 1708 he was chosen as a fence viewer for the town.

On 8 June 1714, "John Sexton of Symbsury was presented by the Grandjury for neglecting to attend the publick Worship of God." He pleaded not guilty but was fined 5s. It is not clear whether this was John Sr. or John Jr., but it may have been the son, who was then 33 years old. "John Sexton Snr of Symsbury" made his will on 9 March 1716/7. He gave most of his land and goods to his son John Jr., except for specific grants to his "daughter" Hannah, who was the widow of his late son Richard, on condition that she keep her children with her, including her three daughters, who were referred to as "orphans." He also gave six acres of land in Bissell's Marsh to his son-in-law William Gillett. His remaining outlands were to be divided into three equal parts and given to his "son" William Gillett, Richard's three daughters, and his "Loving son John," who was named as his sole executor. His wife was not mentioned, so she was surely deceased by that time. He had not remarried, so she probably lived long after her last child was born, and she perhaps died shortly before he died.

John Saxton/Sexton died on 4 December 1718. On 5 January 1718/19, his estate was inventoried. It included more than 143 acres of land and was valued at £295-17-08. There were no feminine items included in the inventory, which suggests that his wife had died at least a few years earlier and that her effects had already been given to her daughter and daughter-in-law. The distribution of his property by John Sexton Jr. was contested in Court in April 1727 by Ariziah Wilcoxson, who was married to one John Sr.'s three granddaughters by his son Richard, and by David Enno, who was married to the daughter of his son-in-law William Gillett. Enno (aka Eno) appears to have settled for £10, although he claimed (probably correctly) that his wife should have inherited a full third of her grandfather's property, rather than one-fourth, which was the amount that was allotted to her by her uncle John.

John Saxton/Sexton married, at Simsbury, Hartford Co., Conn., 30 July 1677, Mary Hill, daughter of Luke and Mary (Hout) Hill, born at Windsor, Hartford Co., Conn., 20 September 1654; died, probably at Simsbury, sometime before 1716. A record of her death has not been found, but she probably lived long after her last child was born in, say, 1682, so she may have lived until, say, age 60, which would be about 1714.

John and Mary (Hill) Saxton/Sexton had three children: Mary (1678-aft 1721)[34]; Richard (perhaps b. 1673/4, but more likely about 1680; d. 1714); and John (b. say 1682-d. 1766). Mary married William Gillett and was the grandmother of General Roger Enos, head of Vermont forces in the Revolutionary War. His daughter Jerusha Hayden Enos married General Ira Allen, who is sometimes referred to as a (or the) Founder of Vermont, and who was a brother of the famed Ethan Allen. Richard and John Saxton were both baptized as adults on 14 April 1706. Richard, as noted above, was survived by his wife and three daughters, two of whom survived to adulthood and had many descendants; a son is also described in some accounts, but he is not known to have descendants. John apparently never married and died without known progeny at the age of about 84.

They had the following children:

16	i.	Richard (perhaps b. 1673, more likely 1680-d.1714)
17	ii.	Mary (1678-)
18	iii.	John (~1682-1766)

Mary married William Gillett, and her daughter, Mary Gillett, married David Eno. Their son, whose surname was spelled with a terminal "s," was Roger Enos, a hero of the Revolutionary War and later Major General and head of the Vermont militia. His daughter, Jerusha Hayden Enos, married Ira Allen, who is said to have given her the town of Irasburg as a wedding present.

Ira Allen was a brother of the famed Ethan Allen of the Green Mountain Boys. Roger Enos is the most important historical figure in the descendants of Luke and Mary (Hout) Hill. He is buried in the Greenwood Cemetery, Burlington, Vermont.

Line 3 - Eleazer

4. Eleazer (? aka Ebenezer) HILL,[35] probably the eldest son and **third** child of Luke and Mary (Hout) Hill, was born at Farmington, Hartford County, Connecticut, about 20 March 1656/7; died at Windsor, Hartford County, Connecticut, 3 March 1724/5. He married, in Simsbury, Hartford County, Connecticut, on 29 December 1679, **Sarah GILLETT**, daughter of Nathan and Elizabeth Gillett; born at Simsbury, 13 July 1651; died at Simsbury or Windsor, 30 September 1737. Nathan Gillett was the brother of Jonathan Gillett, both of whom emigrated from England and were early settlers in Windsor, Conn.[36] Several descendants of Jonathan and Nathan Gillett married descendants of Luke Hill.[37]

The name of Eleazer Hill first appears in the records of Simsbury, Mass., when he married Sarah Gillett on 29 December 1679.[38] He was said to have been born in Connecticut in 1656, and his wife was said to have been born in Connecticut in 1651.[39] Their first child, a daughter, was born one and a half years later, on 29 July 1681. On 7 May 1683, he was one of the signers of a resolution to allow the location of the meeting-house to be chosen by lot, inasmuch as the town had been unable to agree whether to build it at Hop Meadow or on Terry's Plain. Luke Hill was one of the other signers of this resolution. Eleazer's second child, another daughter, was born on 6 December 1685, and a third daughter was born in about 1687.

In April 1688 Eleazer Hill, as a son-in-law of Nathan Gillett, was granted land in the Nathan Gillett Weatogue Meadow tract in Simsbury. His lot abutted that of his brother-in-law Nicholas Gozzard. He was a constable in January 1692/3, and his only son, Eleazer, Jr., was born a year and a half later, on 20 July 1694. In the same year, 1694, Eleazer Hill was listed as one of those who were taxed for the town, and in 1695 he was chosen perambulator, fence viewer and hayward of Simsbury. In 1696, he was taxed for support of the minister. In 1697, when a new minister arrived, "Eliezer Hill" was one of those who signed the covenant of the church at Simsbury; his daughter Mary died in that year. This covenant was also signed by his wife, Sarah Hill.[40]

Some time prior to August 1717, and probably prior to 1708, he relocated to Windsor, which adjoined Simsbury to the south. In 1708 Eleazer Hill and Daniel and Timothy Loomis performed the inventory of the estate of Thomas Rowley of Windsor, which was distributed in 1710. In 1715 he and Daniel Loomis inventoried the estate of Daniel Clark of Windsor, and on 3 January 1715/16, he and Elias Slater inventoried the estate of William Goring of Windsor. On 5 July 1715, the court ruled that Eleazer Hill would be the guardian of two of the four children of Jeremiah Alverd, recently deceased. Johanna Alverd, age 14, chose Eleazer to be her guardian, and the court recognized this for £50. The court assigned Eleazer to be the guardian of her younger sister, Elizabeth, age 9, also for £50. Three years later, in 1718, the family of four minor children was temporarily reunited by court action, but conflicts between adult members of the Alverd family apparently persisted, and the final outcome was neither pleasant nor clear-cut. Eleazer was, however, no longer involved in this sad situation.[41]

Eleazer Hill's will was dated 17 August 1717, naming his son Eleazer (Jr.) as his principal heir and executor, providing that he care for his mother, if she was still alive, and that he pay £7 to each of his two sisters – Elizabeth and Sarah – who were alive when he wrote his will. Eleazer Hill's will was witnessed by Daniel Loomis, James Enno, and Timothy Loomis.

Eleazer died on 3 March 1724/5 and the will was recorded on 12 April 1725.[42]

Sarah (Gillett) Hill was probably still alive when Eleazer died in March 1724/5. She is probably the Widow Sarah Hill who died at Windsor, Conn., on 30 September 1737.[43] Eleazer and Sarah (Gillett) Hill had four children,[44] of whom only the youngest, his son and namesake, is known to have had descendants His son, Sgt. Eleazer Hill, married Elizabeth Gillett, who was probably an unrecorded descendant of either Jonathan or Nathan Gillett and thus very likely was a relative of his mother, Sarah (Gillett) Hill. Sgt. Eleazer and Elizabeth Hill had three sons, one of whom, also named Eleazer (or Eliezer) [III], married a Gillett; the mother of Eleazer [III]'s wife Hannah Hayes was Ann (Gillett) Hayes, who was a daughter of Nathan and Hannah (Buckland) Gillett.

The children of Eleazer and Sarah (Gillett) Hill were:

19	i.	Elizabeth (1681-1725)
20	ii.	Mary (1685-1697)
21	iii.	Sarah (~1687-1725)
22	iv.	Eleazer (1694-1741)

Line 4 - Tahan

5. Tahan "Tahay" HILL,[45] probably the second son and **fourth** child of Luke and Mary (Hout) Hill, was born at Windsor, Hartford County, Conn., 23 November 1659; died, probably at Guilford, Conn., 16 December 1692. He married, probably at Hartford, Conn., 29 November 1688, **Hannah PARMELEE**, elder daughter and fifth of the nine children of John and Hannah Parmelee; born at Hartford, Conn., 5 November 1667.[46]

Tahan Hill was the third child of Luke Hill whose birth was recorded at Windsor, Conn. It appears that Luke Hill probably had another son, known originally as Ebenezer and later as Eleazer, who was born at Farmington in March 1656/7. If this is a correct assumption, Luke's wife Mary was surely in Farmington at that time, and very likely the entire Luke Hill family lived in Farmington for a year or two before returning to Windsor. All of the rest of Luke Hill's children were born in Windsor.

When Tahan was born, his father was operating the ferry across the Farmington River, which was then called "The Rivulet," in Windsor, just upstream from the wide mouth of the Farmington River, where it emptied into the Connecticut River. Luke Hill owned a house lot within the Palisado on the left (north) bank of the Farmington River, and, like all of the early colonists, he undoubtedly had a small farm there. Four more children were born to Luke and Mary Hill in Windsor. Soon after his last child was born in 1668, Luke Hill moved to what was then a wooded wilderness a few miles north of Windsor. He and several others created a village there which they initially called Massaco, and which was later renamed Simsbury. Soon after Massaco/Simsbury was settled, war with the Indians broke out in a conflict that became known as King Philip's War. Indians destroyed the village of Simsbury in 1676 and the colonists fled to Windsor until the war was over. By 1679, Luke Hill was back in Simsbury and he and his sons were involved in the rebuilding of the village. Tahan was then a sturdy young man, 20 years of age. As he had previously done in Windsor, Luke Hill had a small farm on the bank of the Farmington River and operated the ferry across the river.

Eleazer Hill, who was presumably Tahan's older brother, and Tahan's youngest brother John were both active in the affairs of Simsbury for many years. Eleazer prospered in Simsbury. He became a constable and had several positions in the town government. Eleazer then returned with his family to Windsor, where he continued to be active in community affairs. Eleazer left a comfortable estate when he died. Tahan's youngest brother, John, inherited his father's farm and became a man of substance in Simsbury. The two middle brothers, Tahan and Luke Jr. – who was about two years younger than Tahan – left Simsbury and relocated to Guilford, Conn., when they were in their twenties. Both men soon married, Luke Jr. in 1685 and Tahan in 1688. Luke's wife had her first child in 1687 and her next child was born in 1692. Tahan stayed on in Guilford after Luke Jr. returned to Simsbury in about 1693.

When he was 29, Tahan married a 21-year old woman from a prominent family in the nearby town of Hartford, Conn. Her first child was born in 1689, followed by another in 1691. Tahan was a resident of Guilford in 1690. He died the following year, in December 1692, when he was but 33 years old, leaving his widow to care for a one-year old baby and a three-year-old child. She soon married again, however, and may have had additional children with her second husband. Nothing is known of her son by Tahan Hill, who was but a baby when his father died, but her daughter by Tahan later married into a prominent family and had many descendants.

Tahan Hill married Hannah Parmelee,[47] daughter of John Jr. and Hannah Parmelee and granddaughter of John Parmelee, founder of a large Parmelee family of early Connecticut. Hannah Parmelee's brother Caleb Parmelee married Tahan Hill's sister Abigail (See below).

Tahan and Hannah (Parmelee) Hill had two children: Hannah (1689-), who married Samuel Bushnell and had descendants; and Tahan [Jr.] (1691-), of whom nothing more is known. Following the untimely death of Tahan Hill, his widow married (2), in Saybrook, Conn., 25 May 1693, Thomas Merrill[48]; b. at Hartford, 1646; d. 7 November 1711. It is unknown if Hannah (Parmelee) (Hill) Merrill had progeny by her second marriage.[49]

Tahan and Hannah (Parmelee) Hill had the following children:

    23   i.   Hannah (1689-1775)
    24   ii.   Tahan (1691-)

Line 5 – Luke, Jr.

6. Luke HILL Jr.,[50] third son and **fifth** child of Luke and Mary (Hout) Hill, was born at Windsor, Hartford County, Connecticut, 6 March 1661; died at Wallingford, New Haven County, Connecticut, 26 May 1740. He married (1), at Branford, New Haven County, Connecticut, 14 October 1685, **Hannah BUTLER**, daughter of John and Benedicta Butler, born at Simsbury, Hartford County, Connecticut, in 1664; died sometime after her sixth child was born in 1703. He then married (2) **Deliverance _____**, probably **Mrs. Deliverance COOKE FALCONER**, widow of Patrick Falconer Jr., by whom he had one child.[51]

Luke Hill moved from Windsor to Simsbury with his parents and his brothers and sisters in about 1669, when Simsbury – originally called Massaco – was first being settled. They were forced to flee back to Windsor in 1676, when their village was overrun by Indians in King Philip's War and the town was burned to the ground. By about 1676, the settlers had returned and were rebuilding the village. In 1679, Luke Hill's father was declared a freeman of Massaco (Simsbury), which was, nevertheless, still under the jurisdiction of Windsor. Luke Jr. was 18 years old at that time. As one of the middle sons of man without great wealth, he would soon have had to find his own way in the world. He would have no experience with a craft or trade except that of farming, and of the operation of a ferry across a small river. So it is not surprising that he and his brother Tahan, two years his senior in age, left home when they were in their twenties and relocated to the coastal community of Guilford, about 50 miles south of Simsbury.

Luke Jr. soon married a girl from Guilford, Hannah Butler; he was then twenty-four and his bride was twenty-one. Their first child, a son, named Ebenezer for Luke's oldest brother, was born two years later, in 1687, at Guilford, and a daughter, Anna, who was named for her mother, was born there five years later, in 1692. In about 1693, Luke and Hannah moved a few miles north into the Connecticut River valley, and Hannah's third child, Keziah, was born at Wethersfield in 1695, in the tenth year of their marriage. They then moved back to Simsbury, where Luke's father and mother and several of his siblings, cousins, and in-laws were still living. Luke was one of 68 citizens of Simsbury who were taxed in 1696, and he paid £00-11-03. Luke and Hannah's fourth child – another son and namesake of his father and paternal grandfather – was born at Simsbury in 1698, followed two years later by another daughter, who they named Lydia for Luke's eldest sister. They then moved back to the coast again to settle in Branford, about eight miles west of Guilford, mid-way between Guilford and New Haven. Luke and Hannah's youngest child, Isaac – the first of several to bear that name in successive generations – was born at Branford in 1703. By this time, Luke and Hannah's family consisted of at least five children, ranging in age from the newborn baby to their oldest son, now sixteen. Nothing more has been found about their third child, so she may have died young. Hannah died some time after Isaac was born, perhaps about 1735, for Luke married again and had a seventh child in Guilford in 1738.[52]

Luke Hill's second wife was named Deliverance, perhaps Deliverance Cooke Falconer. If that was her full name, she would have been a widow named Mrs. Deliverance Falconer, daughter of Thomas Cooke Jr. and Sarah Mason, and widow of Patrick Falconer Jr. However, no record has been found about the name of Luke's second wife except her given name, Deliverance. Her daughter, Deliverance Hill, was married in 1764 in Woodbury, Litchfield Co., Connecticut, and has many descendants.[53]

Within the next decade, Luke and Hannah's children began to leave home. His eldest daughter, Anna, was married in 1715, but she continued to live in Branford until 1718 when she was living a few miles inland, in Wallingford. His eldest son, Ebenezer, was married in 1717, and he, too, lived in Branford until 1719, when he, too, was in Wallingford. Ebenezer and his wife had seven children in Wallingford between 1717 and 1734. Ebenezer was a freeman of the part of Wallingford now known as Cheshire in 1730, but he soon moved about 40 miles north to Goshen, in Litchfield County, in the north-west corner of the state. Luke [III] was married in Wallingford in 1723 but he, too, moved to Goshen. Lydia was married in Wallingford in 1725, and her children were all born there except for the second, who was born in Goshen. Luke and Hannah's youngest child, Isaac, was married in Wallingford in 1733 and he was a freeman there in 1730. He then joined his older brothers in Litchfield County. By 1735, all three brothers – Ebenezer, Luke [III], by now called Luke Jr., and Isaac – were living in Goshen, where they formed an informal partnership in land operations. Isaac's son Bilious Hill was the first white child born in Goshen, and he was probably born at the home of his uncle Ebenezer Hill.

Sometime after the birth of his last child by Hannah Butler, and probably by 1718 or 1719, Luke moved to the part of Wallingford that is now Cheshire, and he died there in 1740. In the meantime, however, he married a second wife, by whom he had a child in Guilford in 1738. Some say that he was a freeman in Wallingford (Cheshire) in 1730, but I believe the names of Luke, Isaac, and Ebenezer Hill that appear on the list of freemen of Cheshire in 1730 more likely refer to the three sons of Luke and Hannah Hill. I suppose that in 1730, Luke Hill Jr., perhaps because he was elderly – 69 at that time – or perhaps because he was impecunious, was no longer was regarded as a freeman of the town.[54]

Luke and Hannah and their daughters continued to live in the older towns of Connecticut, near the coast. But their three sons – Ebenezer, Luke [III], and Isaac – moved to Litchfield

County, in the wild, unsettled north-west corner of Connecticut. One of their daughters was also there for at least a year or so with her husband. Luke [III]'s wife had a daughter who was born in Goshen in 1733, and Isaac's second child was born there in 1738. In 1736 Ebenezer's son Ebenezer, Jr., and his uncles Luke [III] and Isaac were involved in a land transaction on the border of the towns of Torrington and Litchfield, a few miles from Goshen. This was not country for the faint-hearted: the Deerfield Massacre of 1704 took place about 80 miles north of Goshen in the north-west corner of Massachusetts. Luke's sons' half-sister Deliverance (Hill) Blackmun also moved with her husband to Litchfield County, and she had a son who was born there, in the town of Woodbury, in 1775.[55]

R. D. Smyth said in 1903 that Luke Hill "seems to have been of roving disposition." Smyth presumably meant that Luke chose to travel rather than settle in one place. It is of course a matter of record that he lived in various towns in Connecticut including Windsor, Simsbury, Guilford, Wethersfield, then Simsbury again, Branford, and finally Wallingford. All of these towns were within a radius of 20 miles, from Simsbury in the north to Guilford and Branford on the coast. Windsor, Simsbury, and Wethersfield were on or near the Connecticut River in Hartford County, and Guilford, Branford, and Wallingford were near the Quinnipiac River in New Haven County. Whether Luke Hill had "a roving disposition," or whether he simply moved from time to time to make the best of his opportunities would be a matter of conjecture. However, the record clearly shows that Luke and Hannah Hill succeeded in raising at least five of their six children, and that these children in turn married and raised their own families. What more should be expected of a man?

Luke Hill Jr. and his wife Hannah (Butler) Hill had the following children[56]:

25	i.	Ebenezer (1687-?1758)[57]
26	ii.	Anna (1692-)[58]
27	iii.	Keziah (1695-)
28	iv.	Luke (1698-?1772)[59]
29	v.	Lydia (1700-)[60]
30	vi.	Isaac (1703-1741)[61]

Luke Hill Jr. and his wife Deliverance (probably Mrs. Deliverance Cooke Falconer) had one daughter,

31	i.	Deliverance (1738-)[62]

Luke Jr.'s daughter Lydia married John Dibble; their daughter Lydia Dibble married Elijah Birge; and their son David Birge married Abigail Howland, who was a descendant of the *Mayflower* Pilgrim, John Howland. Their son, Elijah Birge, had a son Martin, whose son George Kingsley Birge (1849-1918) was a notable figure in the history of Buffalo and of American industry. George K. Birge made a fortune in the wallpaper business and another fortune as president and principal owner (from 1908-1916) of the Pierce-Arrow automobile company, which he sold for $7,000,000 two years before he died (present value about $140 million). George K. Birge married Caroline "Carrie" Humphrey, daughter of a U.S. Congressman, the Hon. James H. Humphrey. Their daughter Allithea married George Cary, a Harvard graduate who designed what is now known as the Birge mansion on Symphony Circle, and who became the leading architect of Buffalo.

Luke Jr.'s daughter Anna married Isaac Cook; their son Waitstill Cook married Elizabeth White; and their son John married Lucy Cruttenden (probably an alternate spelling of Crittenden). John and Lucy's daughter Amanda Cook married Benjamin Leete (1804-1883), who was born on Leetes Island in Guilford, Conn. Leetes Island had been in this family since early in the seventeenth century. Benjamin's grandfather was a first cousin of Pelatiah Leete III, whose home was built on the island in 1765 and is still standing there.

Luke Jr.'s youngest child, Isaac, who died in 1741, was the father of five children. His fourth child, Isaac Jr., was born the year before he died, and his fifth, Abraham, was born posthumously, in 1741. Isaac Jr. was a soldier in the last French and Indian War and he was again a soldier in the Revolutionary War. No less than three of Isaac Jr.'s eight sons went west, and they became pioneer settlers in the southern tier of counties in New York State, and in Ohio, Indiana, Illinois, and Iowa. Isaac Jr.'s son Ephraim founded a branch of the family in Caton, Steuben County, N.Y., that has held reunions annually in that village for more than eighty years. Abraham's son Richard went to Caton with his first cousin Ephraim, and the two branches of the Hill family have lived in Steuben County since about 1824. Abraham was buried in Carmel, Putnam County, N.Y., in 1817, and his gravestone in the Baptist cemetery in Carmel is the oldest known gravestone of a male-line descendant of the patriarch Luke Hill, Sr.

Line 6 - Abigail

7. Abigail HILL,[63] third daughter and **sixth** child of Luke and Mary (Hout) Hill, was born at Windsor, Hartford County, Connecticut, 16 April 1664; died at Branford, New Haven County, Connecticut, 6 October 1737. She married, at Guilford, New Haven County, Connecticut, on 23 April 1693, as his second wife, **Caleb PARMELEE,**[64] fourth son and seventh of the nine children of John [Jr.] and Hannah Parmelee, and grandson of John [Sr.] and Hannah Parmelee; born at Guilford in about 1675; died at Branford in 1714. Caleb Parmelee had married (1) on 11 April 1690, Abigail Johnson,[65] who died 8 May 1692, 12 days after giving birth to their son Samuel, who died at the age of seven months. Caleb Parmelee's sister Hannah married Abigail Hill's brother Tahan (see above). Parmelees and Hills also intermarried in later generations of both families.

Caleb Parmelee was a member of a large and prominent family in Guilford, and it is therefore not surprising that he and Abigail Hill were married in Guilford, rather than in Simsbury, where her parents lived. She was then 29 years old, almost a spinster. Abigail probably came to Guilford with her older brother Tahan, who married Caleb's older sister Hannah Parmelee in 1688. Tahan died in 1692, leaving a daughter and a son, born in 1689 and 1691, respectively, and a widow who remarried in May 1693, just a month after Abigail and Caleb were married.

Caleb Parmelee was a husbandman – a farmer. He was therefore accustomed to hard work, although his family was prosperous, one of the leading families in Guilford. His grandfather John Parmelee Sr. had been one of the founders of Guilford and he was one of the twenty-five signers of the Guilford Covenant in 1689. When John Parmelee Sr. died in New Haven in 1659, he left property valued at more than £78. His two-and-a-half acre home lot in Guilford later became the site of the First Congregational Church.

Caleb's father, John Parmelee Jr., obtained the Plaine house lot and four-and-a-half acres of marsh land in Guilford through his second wife, the widow of William Plaine.[66] Caleb's older brother Nathaniel, the only child of John Jr. and his first wife Rebecca Parmelee, was killed at the age of 31 in King Philip's War, leaving a widow and three children who would have been a concern for the rest of the family until she remarried the following year. One of Nathaniel's children, Nathaniel Jr., had a son, Ezra, who married Tahan and Hannah (Parmelee)'s granddaughter, Jemima Bushnell. Nathaniel's younger brother and the eldest child of John Jr. and his third wife Hannah Parmelee, Sergeant John Parmelee, also a farmer, was also prosperous; he had property valued at £154 in 1716.

The next son of John Parmelee Jr., Joshua Parmelee, married twice; his second wife, Hannah (DeWolf) Stone, was the widow of Benjamin Stone Jr. Their daughter, Esther Stone, would, in 1733, marry Isaac Hill Sr., son of Abigail Hill's brother Luke Hill Jr. Hannah (De Wolf) (Stone) Parmelee would later marry a third and then a fourth husband, and her daughter Esther (Stone) Hill would later marry a second husband. No widow or widower stayed unmarried very long in those days if they had small children to take care of, and inter-family marriages kept the families close together. Caleb Parmelee's younger brother Isaac married Elizabeth Hyland, daughter of George Hyland, whose house, built in 1660, still stands as one of the oldest houses in Guilford.

Although the Parmelee family was well-connected in Guilford, Caleb and his bride moved to Branford, a few miles down the coast, where they spent the rest of their lives.[67] Sometime in the first months of 1693/4, Abigail received £14 in the settlement of her father's will.[68] Soon after that, her first child, Hannah, was born in March 1694 in Guilford, eleven months after Abigail and Caleb were married. Hannah joined the Branford church in 1714 when she was 20. The next child, Caleb Jr., was born in 1696. Caleb Jr. married three times and had six children, all of whom were born in and around Branford, although it is not recorded that he became a member of the church. Abigail's third child, Lydia, was born in 1699; she joined the Branford church in 1716 at the age of 17 and was married ten years later. The fourth child, Josiah, was born in 1701 and he joined the Branford church when he was 14. Abigail and Caleb Parmelee had two more children, Abigail (1703) and Benjamin (1705). Abigail died at the age of 73, having outlived her husband and at least two and probably four of her six children. She had seven grandchildren and one great-grandchild, all by her son Caleb Jr.

Caleb and Abigail (Hill) Parmelee had the following children:

32	i.	Hannah (1694-1761)
33	ii.	Caleb (1696-1750)
34	iii.	Lydia (1699/70-1726)
35	iv.	Josiah (1701-1720)
36	v.	Abigail (1702/3-)
37	vi.	Benjamin (1705-)

Caleb Parmelee Jr. married Jemima Harrison (1692-1766), daughter of Lieutenant Thomas Harrison. Her gravestone in Branford Center Cemetery is the earliest marked grave that I have found in the family of Luke Hill Sr.[69]

Line 7 - Elizabeth

8. Elizabeth HILL,[70] fourth daughter and **seventh** child of Luke and Mary (Hout) Hill, was born at Windsor, Hartford County, Connecticut, on 8 or 18 Oct 1666; died, probably at Simsbury, Hartford County, Connecticut, sometime after 1689. She married, at Simsbury, in about 1685, **Samuel ADAMS**, possibly a son of George and Frances (Taylor) Adams; born about 1664 in Watertown, Massachusetts; died at Simsbury after 1689, probably after 1701.

There is little in the historical record about Luke Hill's daughter Elizabeth. There are some 730 references to "Elizabeth Hill(s)" in the on-line data base of the New England Historic Genealogical Society, dozens of references to "Elizabeth Hill(s)" in Family Tree Maker's CD179 and CD515 of Connecticut Family Histories, and countless citations elsewhere on the internet. These references are to women with this name at birth or as their married name, over a span of about three centuries, ranging in location from New England to Virginia. In a search of these citations, I found only two that relate specifically to Luke Hill's daughter Elizabeth. These are the transcriptions of the record of the marriage of Luke Hill Sr. and of the birth of his children, from the Old Church Records in Windsor, Conn., published by Parsons, "Record of Marriages and Births, in Windsor, Ct." *NEHGR* 5 (April 1851): 225-8ff; and Smith and Steiner, "Luke Hill of Windsor, Conn., and John Hill of Guilford, Conn., and Their Descendants," *NEHGR* 57 (Jan. 1903): 87-93. Also, James Savage wrote in *A Genealogical Dictionary of the First Settlers of New England* (1861) that an Elizabeth Hill who was born in Connecticut in 1666.[71]

Elizabeth Hill, daughter of Luke, was long said to have married, in about 1700, William Buckland, son of William [Sr.] and Elizabeth (Williams) Buckland, born in East Hartford, Conn., in, say, 1667; died there, 12 December 1724. This was first stated by Henry Stiles (1892) and this information was restated and amplified by Bassette in 1926.[72] However, in 1957 Donald Lines Jacobus wrote in *The American Genealogist* that William Buckland married Elizabeth Hills, daughter of John Hills of East Hartford. (Their family name is spelled Hills, with an "s.") And then in 1977, the posthumous publication of Lucius Barbour's *Families of Early Hartford, Conn.* provided additional details regarding the children of John Hills, naming his daughter Elizabeth; of the marriage of Elizabeth Hills to William Buckland; and of their children.[73] It is now clear that William Buckland married Elizabeth Hills, daughter of John Hills of East Hartford, not Elizabeth Hill, daughter of Luke Hill of Simsbury. All of the children of William Buckland are thus descendants of John Hills, with an "s," not Luke Hill.

Another candidate to be considered as the husband of Luke Hill's daughter Elizabeth is James Lord of Guilford, Conn. A woman named Elizabeth Hill appears in the *Barbour Collection* in which it is said that "LORD, James, b. Apr. 2, 1668; m. Elizabeth HILL, of Guilford, Dec. 13, 1693; d. Feb. 10, 1730/1."[74] I had no particular reason to accept or reject this as the marriage of Luke Hill's daughter, inasmuch as two of Elizabeth's siblings went to Guilford and married Parmelee siblings, and another of Elizabeth's brothers lived for a while in Guilford before moving to Wallingford. However, a better candidate for the husband of Luke Hill's daughter Elizabeth appeared in 1962, when George McCracken wrote in *The American Genealogist* that Ephraim Griffin (born at Windsor 1 March 1668/9 and died at Simsbury 21 February 1687/7) married Elizabeth Adams (born Simsbury 21 February 1686/7), daughter of Samuel and Elizabeth (Hill) Adams.[75] With this statement by McCracken, Samuel Adams of Simsbury became the most promising candidate to be the husband of Luke Hill's daughter Elizabeth. But this begs the question: Who is this Samuel Adams of Simsbury?

The Hill family and the Adams family were early settlers in the town of Simsbury, Connecticut, and these families had much to do with each other. The history of Luke Hill Sr. in Simsbury was given above, in Chapter 1. The Adams family was larger and somewhat more prominent politically than the Hill family, and references to Adamses persist longer in Simsbury history than references to Hills. These two families were neighbors and of the same social class. There are references to Adamses on a dozen or more pages in Noah Phelps, *History of Simsbury*, and many citations to Adamses on some of these pages. The first reference is to "Adamses" on p. 13, as a family that in 1667 received one of the original grants of land in Simsbury. Their grant was in the meadows later known as Westover Plains. Other initial grantees of meadow land in Simsbury included John Gillett, whose grandnephew William Gillett married Luke's granddaughter Mary Saxton; Nathan Gillett, whose daughter married Luke's son Eleazer; and Joseph Phelps, whose daughter married Luke's son John. The first Adams who appears by name in the historical record of Simsbury was Daniel Adams Sr., whose name continued in a second generation as Sgt. Daniel Adams and also as Daniel Adams in a third generation. Daniel Adams

– presumably Daniel Sr. – and Luke Hill Sr. were adjacent signatories on the petition for determining the site of the church in Simsbury on 7 May 1683 (p. 47). The names of Daniel Adams and Sgt. Daniel Adams appear on many additional pages. Daniel Adams was representative to the General Assembly in 1699, 1702, and 1703 (p. 156). The name of Samuel Adams appears on the Town Rate in 1694 and on the Minister's Rates in 1696 and 1701 (pp. 152-3). "Samuel Adams Sen." was on the list of freeman before 1717 (p. 153). I speculate that this latter Samuel Adams is husband of Luke Hill's daughter Elizabeth and the father of her two children. In Simsbury Vital Records, he is called Samuel Adams "Senior," apparently to distinguish him from another man known as Samuel Adams "the Elder," of whom more below.[76]

There are also references in Phelps' *History of Simsbury* to Lieut. David Adams (p. 138), who had four sons and four daughters, and references elsewhere to Hannah, John, Benjamin, Edward, Joseph, James, Ambrose, Abel, and Ezra Adams, Jr. Samuel Adams, Sr. appears on p. 153 on the list of freemen of Simsbury, probably before 1717. Samuel Adams "the Elder" married Elizabeth Reade and had several children including Elizabeth (b. 1715) and Samuel [Jr.] (b. 1720). The man known as Samuel Adams "the Elder" could not have been the Samuel Adams who married Elizabeth Hill and was the father of her children Elizabeth (b. 1686/7) and Samuel (b. 1689), for both of them were still alive when Samuel and Elizabeth (Reade) Adams' children were born. Furthermore, the husband of Elizabeth Hill and father of her daughter Elizabeth was called Samuel Adams "Senior" in the vital records, whereas the husband of Elizabeth Reade and the father of her children was referred to in Simsbury vital records as Samuel Adams "the Elder."

The complicated and confusing genealogy of the Adams family in Simsbury can best be interpreted by studying the family of George Adams of Watertown and Cambridge, Massachusetts. This George Adams, who married Frances – probably Frances Taylor – is said to be the ancestor of such notable Adamses as Presidents John and John Quincy Adams. Many books and papers have been written about this Adams family. It is generally agreed that they had at least five children, namely John, George, Daniel, Joseph, and Mary. Some of the genealogies of George and Frances Adams say they had six children, or "possibly others," without naming the others. George Adams's sons Daniel and John married, respectively, Mary and Abigail Pinney, who were daughters of Humphrey and Mary (Hull) Pinney. Daniel Adams and Mary Pinney were married in Simsbury in 1677 and John Adams and Abigail Pinney were married in the same year in Windsor, Connecticut. Daniel and John Adams thus lived in the adjacent towns of Simsbury and Windsor and raised large families. Many of their descendants bore the same names – Daniel and Samuel appear many times – which of course has led to much confusion. I speculate that they had another brother, Samuel, who came to Simsbury. I believe it is this Samuel Adams who appears in the Town Rate in 1694 (*supra*) and is known in the vital records as "Samuel Addams Senior." It would be unlikely that Daniel's son Samuel Adams, known as "the Elder," would have been subject to town taxes in 1694, for Samuel Adams "the Elder" was not even married until 1713.[77]

Samuel and Elizabeth (Hill) Adams "Senior" had two children, and perhaps more that are unknown to me, who were born at Simsbury. A daughter, Elizabeth, was born on 21 February 1686/7. She married (1) in 1707, Ephraim Griffin, by whom she had five children, at least two of whom had descendants; and (2) in 1725, Caleb Holcomb. A son, Samuel, was born on 26 October 1689. Nothing more is known about this son, who would be Samuel Jr. The historical record is silent after 1689 about Elizabeth (Hill) Adams, and there is no further mention of her husband Samuel after 1701, when he last appears in the tax rates for Simsbury.

Children of Samuel and Elizabeth (Hill) Adams:

38. i. Elizabeth (1686/7-aft 1726)

39. ii. Samuel (1689-)

Line 8 – John Hill

9. John HILL,[78] fourth son and **eighth** and youngest child of Luke and Mary (Hout) Hill, was born at Windsor, Hartford County, Connecticut, 28 November 1668; died at Simsbury, Hartford County, Connecticut, 1 November 1740. He married (1), at Simsbury, in about 1696, **Sarah PHELPS**, daughter of Joseph and Hannah (Newton) Phelps, Sr.; born at Simsbury in May 1672; died there in about 1707. They had five children. He then married (2) **Sarah TERRY**, daughter of Lieutenant John Terry, by whom he had another child.[79]

John was only a year old when his father became one of the first permanent settlers on the banks of the Tunxis River – later called the Farmington River – in the wooded wilderness north of Windsor that was then occupied by the Massaco Indians. The earliest settler, a man named John Griffin, came to this area in 1648 and obtained a conveyance of land from the Massacos on which he harvested pitch. Additional grants were made by the Indians in this area and were recognized by the General Court of Connecticut in 1653 and some land was cultivated as early as 1663. The first formal grants of land were made in 1666 and 1667, the earliest names including John Gillett, Nathan Gillett, Joseph Phelps, whose children later married children of Luke Hill, and – although he was not on the initial list – apparently Luke Hill was also there by 1668. His name appears on the list of 13 freemen of Massaco, as it was then called, in 1669. The inhabitants petitioned the General Court for town privileges in 1670, and the Court accepted this request, giving the town the name of Simsbury. Thus Simsbury became the twenty-first town in Connecticut, although it continued to be known locally as Massaco or Massaco Plantation until 1742. In 1674 the town ordered a ferry to be established at the mouth of the Hop Brook, where it entered the Farmington River.[80]

The outbreak of war with the Indians in 1675 – a ferocious conflict known as King Philip's War – forced the settlers to flee from Simsbury in March 1676. Some, including the Hill family, returned to Windsor until the war was over, while others went to Hartford. The Indians burned the entire village to the ground on 26 March 1676, and it has been said that no other town in Connecticut ever suffered such devastation in the Indian Wars as did Simsbury in 1676. The settlers returned in March 1677, and Luke Hill was soon living once again on the Hop Meadow, near the west bank of the river. In 1671, it was agreed by the town that the new meeting house would be built at "at the Hope meadow by Luke Hills." The location was, however, somewhat "miry" and subject to occasional flooding, even though it was set back from the river. New buildings later avoided these low lands, but Luke stayed on and operated one of the unofficial ferries across the river.

In February 1693/4, Luke Hill made a covenant, which was in effect his last will and testament. He addressed his youngest son, John, then 25 years old, who was present at that moment in time, professing his good will and affection to the young man. He agreed to give John virtually all of his property, including his real estate and a long list of household items, farm implements, and livestock, provided that John would care for his father and mother for the rest of their lives. Luke excepted from this list of possessions that passed to John only a portion that was due to his daughter Abigail, now Abigail Parmelee, consisting of £14, a great iron pot, and a feather bed, bolster, and pillow, which would go to her after her parents' deaths. John and his heirs and executors would oversee the distribution of Luke's estate. Luke died within a year or so after making this covenant with John, and his widow, Mary, died about a year after her husband died. It was not unusual in those days for the youngest son to receive the family home and most if not all of the father's farm in exchange for agreeing to take care of his widowed mother. This covenant is thus typical of such an arrangement. It is, however, unusual to have only one other child named in the covenant or will, when there were others alive at that time. Often others would be named, if only to say that they had already received their share. Why Luke chose to name only Abigail, who had apparently married well and was not living in Simsbury, and why he did not name any of the others such as Luke Jr., who was still living in Simsbury, will probably never be known.[81]

In other words, John agreed to take care of his parents for the rest of their lives, to provide for his sister Abigail's small share in the estate, and the rest would be his alone. Within a month, John was named a hayward – a fence watcher – of Simsbury. It is not known if the making of the covenant with his father and his appointment by the town were in any way related matters, but it is clear that when the covenant went into effect, he became a man of substance in the town. Luke Hill Sr. died in 1695 or 1696, and his property on Pent Road then became John Hill's without any residual encumbrance. Luke's widow, Mary, died at about the same time, probably soon after her husband. In 1696, John Hill appears for the first time in the Simsbury records, as one of those who were to be taxed for the Minister's Rate. And at about the same time in, say, 1696, John married Sarah Phelps, daughter of Joseph Phelps Sr., one of the founders of Simsbury and one of its most prominent and prosperous citizens. Their first child, a daughter who was named for her mother, was born in July 1697. John and Sarah's second child was dead at birth in January 1700/01, and another child died as an infant in April 1702. John's namesake, called "John Jur." in Simsbury records was probably born at about this time. In the meantime, in 1701, John, now 32, had been made a freeman of Simsbury. Two more daughters were then born, Mary and Hannah, probably two years apart. They were probably Sarah's children, and Sarah appears to have died at the time the second of these daughters was born, or shortly thereafter. John then had four young children to take care of, including one who was perhaps just a newborn – Sarah, John Jr., Mary, and Hannah.[82]

John married again in April 1708. His second wife, Sarah Terry, daughter of Lieutenant John Terry, also came from one of the old and successful families of Simsbury. They had a daughter, Elizabeth, born in 1710. John's four daughters later married men from Simsbury and had descendants, although his eldest daughter predeceased him. His son, John Jr., also known as John 2nd, also had descendants.

In 1723 John Hill owned a "long lot" (660 ft. wide and 2 miles deep) near the Hill Ferry in Simsbury. This is a substantial piece of property, amounting to exactly three-fourths of a square mile, or 480 acres, located along a well-watered, fertile riverbank. The following year, when he was fifty-five years old, John Hill spent about four months on active military service; he was on duty from 4 June until October 1724. He was not an officer, and there is no indication that this was arduous duty. In fact, such service often was an opportunity for men to get away and "rough it" with the other men. Who would have taken care of his crops during that summer is unknown, but his son John Jr. was 22 and old enough to take over the farm. John Jr. was married the following February and soon began to raise his own family.[83]

The ferry business in Simsbury was hurt by the building of a bridge across the river in 1734, although local operators such as the Hills continued to use canoes as ferries for many more years. Eventually broad-bottomed boats were used as ferries, but by that time the Hills were out of the ferry business. Simsbury's first legal ferry was established in 1756 when Thomas Marvin obtained a grant from the General Assembly. This was long after Luke Sr. had died in 1693, and it was sixteen years after his son John – who had continued to operate the family's ferry business – died in November 1740. Marvin had bought the Hill farm at Pent Road from Timothy Woodbridge, who had bought it from John Hill's heirs after his rather substantial estate, valued at more than £1339, was distributed on 6 July 1742.[84] Thomas Marvin was permitted to charge the following rates, which seem quite modest to us, although this was probably the going rate at that time for private ferry operators, too:[85]

 For man, horse, and load, one penny.

 Single man, or single horse, one halfpenny.

 Neat cattle, per head, one halfpenny.

 Sheep and swine, per head, one farthing.

In 1757, Thomas Marvin sold his "house and home lot and meadow land" and his "right in Said Simsbury and privilege of a ferry across the River between Hopmeadow and Terry's Plain" to the Rev. Benejah Roots. Mr. Roots tore down the old Hill house and built one in 1762 that stood for many years. Pent Road is presently a dead end street about one hundred yards long, extending east from the main thoroughfare in Simsbury to its end at what is now called Iron Horse Boulevard, adjacent to a hiking trail along the course of the former Farmington Canal. The early canals in America were often replaced by railroads that ran along their routes, and this apparently was the history of this piece of land in Simsbury, although both the railroad and the canal are now gone, memorialized only by their names. Open land slopes gently down to the Farmington River to the east of the Farmington Canal Heritage Trail. This land was once subject to flooding and was not considered suitable for permanent buildings in the colonial era. Industrial buildings are now located along the north side of Pent Road, facing a shopping center on the south side of the street. The John Hill family resided in the Connecticut River Valley for over 150 years before moving to the Sixtown area of Jefferson County, New York.[86]

The Google Map and Satellite view shows that Pent Road is about 100 yards long, extending from Hopmeadow Road (US 202) on the west to Iron Horse Blvd. on the east, with the Farmington Canal Heritage Trail running N and S adjacent to and just to the E of Iron Horse Blvd. There is a shopping center on the S side of Pent Road (Simsburytown Shops) and industrial buildings on the N side of Pent Road. The Farmington River is about 200 yards E of the E end of Pent Road at Iron Horse Blvd.

John Hill married (1) Sarah Phelps, and (2) Sarah Terry. My analysis regarding the births of John Hill's children, and the conclusion that all were the children of Sarah Phelps except the last, who was born of Sarah Terry, goes as follows: The marriage of Sarah Phelps to John Hill appears in Phelps, *History of Simsbury*, although a date/year is not given. She is said there to be the daughter of Joseph Phelps and granddaughter of William Phelps, a founder of Simsbury. Her first child, Sarah (who m. Samuel Strickland) was born 28 July 1697, by which we can conclude that Sarah Phelps probably married John Hill in about 1696, when he was 30 and she was 26. We can presume that she was also the mother of John 2d (aka John, Jr.), because he was born 2 April 1702. Sarah (Phelps) Hill may have had additional children after that and then she died, at a date unknown.

Sarah (Hill) Strickland was 23 when she married Samuel Strickland, age 22, in 1720. She died before her father, John Hill, died, and her unnamed heirs, presumably children, were provided for in his will. Three other daughters of John Hill were named in the will. Each is shown in the will by her married name: Mary Read, Hannah Wilcock, and Elizabeth Hoskins. They are presumably listed in the order in which they were born. Vital Records show that Mary was married in 1724 to Dr. Jacob Reed, age 24. If Mary's birth year was, say, 1704, she would have been 20. Vital Records show that Hannah was married in 1726 to Ephriam Wilcox, age 19. If Hannah's birth year was in, say, 1706, she would have been 20. The youngest child of John Hill, Elizabeth, is shown in the Barbour Collection to have been a daughter of John Hill and Sarah Terry, born 14 December 1710. She married in 1698, at age 18, Joseph Hoskins, age 30.

We can presume that Mary and Hannah were born before Elizabeth, because they appear before her in the order of the estate of their older sister, Sarah Strickland, and children were traditionally listed in the order of their births, with all the males listed together and all of the females together. One or both of these daughters – Mary and Hannah – are probably children of Sarah Phelps, because John Hill married Sarah Terry on 22 April 1708. However, it is just barely possible that Sarah Terry could have had two children before she had Elizabeth (and if so, it would have been Mary in about January 1708/9 and then Hannah in, say, December 1709), followed by Elizabeth in December 1710. (James D. Hill gives Sarah Phelps another child who died at birth; I have not been able to verify the birth of this child, but I will accept it.)

James D. Hill believes that both Mary and Hannah were children of Sarah Terry, assigning them estimated birth years after Elizabeth. I believe, however, that the order in which these children are listed in John Hill's estate shows that Mary and Hannah were born after Sarah but before Elizabeth, so I reject the order that James D. Hill proposed, viz.: Elizabeth, Hannah, and Mary. (If they were born after Elizabeth, Hannah and Mary would have been too young to marry when they did.) On Ancestry.com family trees and on OneWorldTree, Hannah is shown as a child of Sarah Phelps. I believe that is correct. If Mary and Hannah were children of Sarah Terry, she would have had her children very quickly – not in the usual "every two years" that was typical of New England's colonial women. Also, it would have been unusual for John Hill to wait very long before marrying after Sarah Phelps died. He had young children and he needed a new wife and stepmother for them. So he probably married Sarah Terry within a year after Sarah Phelps died. If my reasoning is correct, Sarah Terry had but one child, Elizabeth, born about two and a half years after she married John Hill. In the meantime, the new wife, Sarah (Terry) Hill, was raising Sarah (who was ten when Sarah Terry married John), John Jr. (who was then six), and Mary and Hannah (who were no older than four and two, respectively).

In about 1696 when John was 27, he first married **Sarah PHELPS**, daughter of Joseph Phelps Sr. and Hannah Newton, in Simsbury, Conn; born in May 1672 in Simsbury, Conn.; died in Simsbury, Conn., in about 1707; she was 34.

John Hill and Sarah Phelps had the following children:

40	i.	Sarah (1697-1736)
41	ii.	Infant (~1700-1701)
42	iii.	Dead child (~1700/01-1700/01)
43	iv.	John, Jur. (~1702-1771)
44	v.	Mary (~1704-1773)
45	vi.	Hannah (~1706-1766)

He is said by some to have next married **Sarah BUSHNELL** and lived for a time in Saybrook, Conn., although there is no evidence for this assertion.

On 22 April 1708 when John was 39, he second married **Sarah TERRY**, daughter of Lieut. John Terry, in Simsbury, Conn.; born on 16 Nov 1668 in Simsbury, Conn.; died about 1740, she was 71.

John Hill and Sarah Terry had the following child, and perhaps also Mary and Hannah, who are listed above as probably being children of Sarah Phelps:

46	i.	Elizabeth (1710-)

Findagrave   Google Images   Google Images

Fig. 2-1: From left to right: Gravestone of Roger Enos (1729-1808), Burlington,
Vermont (L), Ira Allen (center), and Ethan Allen (R) (From Google Images). Gen. Roger
Enos was a grandson of Luke Hill, Sr. His gravestone is the oldest known of the
descendants of Luke and Mary (Hout) Hill. His daughter Jerusha married Ira Allen,
brother of Ethan Allen.

Fig. 2-2: Whitfield House, 1639, Guilford, Conn.
The Whitfield House, built by Henry Whitfield in 1639, the year that Guilford was first
settled. It is the oldest house in Connecticut and the oldest stone house in New England.
This house was standing when two children of Luke Hill Jr. were born in Guilford in
1687 and 1692. The house is not related to Hill family. (From Google Images)

From Barbour, in Google Images

Fig. 2-3: Goshen, Conn.

The township of Goshen was sold to new owners in New Haven in December 1737 and settlement of the new township commenced a year or two later. This image shows the center of town with a Congregational church and a smaller building with a spire on the right, called the Academy. The main school house is the brick building beside the church. Luke Hill Jr.'s sons Ebenezer, Luke III, and Isaac were early settlers here.

Fig. 2-4
Congregational Church
Cheshire, Connecticut
From Google Images

Luke Hill Jr. moved to Cheshire at the end of his life, and was one of the first settlers here.

From Google Images
Fig. 2-5: Pelatiah Leete III House (1765) – Leetes Island, Guilford, Conn.
A great-granddaughter of Luke Hill Jr. married a grandson of Pelatiah Leete I.

Fig. 2-6: First Congregational Church, on the Green, Guilford, Conn.
Site of the home of John Parmelee Sr. Tahan Hill, son of Luke Sr, married Hannah
Parmelee, granddaughter of John Parmelee Sr.

Fig. 2-7: Hyland House, Guilford, Conn. (1660). Owned by Isaac Parmelee (1665-1749) "The Hyland House" (1660), 84 Boston St., Guilford, Conn. This 17th-Century frame house with an added-on lean-to is one of the oldest in Guilford. Built by George Hyland, it was owned by three generations of the Parmelee family. The Parmelees were related by marriage to the Hills.

Fig. 2-8: Congregational Church, Branford, Conn.
Hannah, Lydia, and Josiah Parmelee, children of Caleb and Abigail (Hill) Parmelee, were members of this church

Fig. 2-9: Jemima (Harrison) Parmelee (1692-1766)
Branford, Connecticut, Center Cemetery
From findagrave.com

Fig. 2-10: John Hill's farm at Pent Road and Farmington River, Simsbury, Conn.
(enlargement of the view in Fig. 1-8)

Luke Hill Sr. and his youngest son John Hill lived on Pent Road, near Hopmeadow Street on the west side of the Farmington River. Their house location is shown with a teardrop, marked "A." The house would have been set back from the river in order to be out of danger from flooding, but the Hills' property must have extended down to the river bank.

3

Third Generation
Grandchildren of Luke and Mary (Hout) Hill

Line 1. Children of Lydia Hill and Arthur Henbury

10. Mary HENBURY,[87] eldest child of Arthur and Lydia (Hill) Henbury and first grandchild of Luke and Mary (Hout) Hill, was born in Simsbury, Hartford Co., Conn., 31 Aug 1672; died in Coventry, Tolland Co., Conn., in Feb 1759, at age 86.

Mary's mother, Lydia Henbury, was married in 1870, when she was eighteen, to a man who was six years her senior in age and who, although only 24, was already a man of some substance in the frontier town of Simsbury. When Mary was born in 1672, she was only four years younger that her mother's youngest brother, John. The second and third generations in Luke Hill's family thus began to overlap in age and they continued to do so forever after. In 1676, when she was four years old, Mary and the rest of her family, and indeed all of Simsbury's English inhabitants, fled from the Indians in King Philip's War, and Simsbury was burned to the ground. The town was rebuilt in 1679, and in 1682, the Henburys were back in Simsbury, where the last of Lydia's six children were born. Lydia died at about that time, leaving her husband, Arthur Henbury, to care for the children alone. He became ill and thought he would die, but he recovered and married a widow without any children of her own. His two youngest children soon died, but Mary and three of her sisters survived, and in 1691, Henbury moved to the nearby town of Hartford. He was successful there and when he died six years later, he left a comfortable estate. By then, his two elder daughters had married and left home, while their two younger sisters remained with their stepmother.

Mary Henbury was admitted to 1st Church Hartford on 1 March 1695/6, so she was probably married by then. It would therefore have been in, say, about 1694, when she married William Long of Hartford. Mary and William Long had five children, four of whose baptisms are recorded in church records in Barbour, *Families of Early Hartford*, and a fifth child whose birth date is in Simsbury Vital Records. Her children were William (bp 25 Jun 1699), Mary (bp 30 May 1703), Ebenezer (bp 29 June 1707), all baptized at 1st Church Hartford; Sarah (bp 1 June 1701, at 2d Church); Lydia, d. 2 Aug 1689 (Simsbury Vital Records)

In about 1694 when Mary was 21, she married **William LONG**, son of Thomas LONG and Sarah WILCOX, in Hartford, Hartford Co., Conn.; he was born on 4 Feb 1689 in Hartford, Hartford Co., Conn.; died in Coventry, Tolland Co., Conn. in Jul 1740, at age 51. They had five children, of whom two are known to have married; one married a Grover, and the other married a Babcock. Their daughter Mary Babcock had six children, two of whom had further descendants. They had the following children:

47	i.	Lydia (1697-)
48	ii.	William (~1699)
49	iii.	Sarah (~1701-)
50	iv.	Mary (~1703-)
51	v.	Ebenezer (~1707-)

11. Hannah HENBURY,[88] second daughter and second of the six children of Arthur and Lydia (Hill) Henbury, was born in Simsbury, Hartford Co., Conn., in about 1674; died in February 1759 in Coventry, Tolland Co., Conn.; she was about 85 years old.

Hannah was but two years old when her parents and the rest of the Simsbury community fled to Windsor during King Philip's War and the town was burned to the ground. Her parents returned sometime after 1679 and her mother had four more children before she died about 1688, at about age 35. Her father soon married again, to a childless widow, and in 1691 he left Simsbury and moved to Hartford. Hannah lived with her father and stepmother and her three surviving sisters until her older sister, Mary, was married in about 1694. In June 1697, six weeks before her father died, Hannah married Samuel Richards in Simsbury. They had at least five and perhaps as many as eight children.[89]

On 14 Jun 1697 when Hannah was 23, she married, in Hartford, Conn., as his second wife, **Samuel RICHARDS**, son of John RICHARDS and Lydia STOCKING(S). Samuel married (1), in say 1695, Mary Graves, by whom he had a daughter, Lydia, born in Hartford, Conn., 14 March 1695/6. Lydia Richards later married John Merrill, but has no known descendants. Mary (Graves) Richards died sometime in the next year, perhaps even as early as March 1695/6, and in June 1697, Samuel Richards married (2) Hannah Henbury; he died in about 1732 in Hartford. Hannah (Henbury) Richards lived on for another twenty-seven or so years and died in Coventry, Conn., which is north of Hartford, near the Massachusetts border. How and why Hannah went to Coventry is a mystery, for the migratory patterns of her children and her brothers and sisters were mainly to the south and northwest – to Guilford and Branford on the ocean and to Litchfield County in the northwestern corner of Connecticut.

Five of the children of Samuel and Hannah (Henbury) Richards are known to have married. Their daughter Hannah married Ebenezer Judd and had two daughters, both of whom died young. Josiah (aka Jonah) and Mary Palmer had one daughter; she has had many descendants, some of whom are living today. James and Anna Ensign had two children but neither of them have descendants who are recorded. Daniel and Jane Buckland had five children and at least 14 grandchildren. Esther and Araron Merrill have no known descendants. They had the following children:

52	i.	Hannah (1700-)
53	ii.	Josiah (aka Jonah) (1702/3-~1746)
54	iii.	Mary (1705-)
55	iv.	James (1705/6-1754)
56	v.	Daniel (1708-1750)
57	vi.	Esther (1713-1798)
58	vii.	Samuel
59	viii.	Hezekiah (~1715-)

12. Susanna HENBURY,[90] third daughter and third of the six children of Arthur and Lydia (Hill) Henbury, was born at Simsbury, Hartford Co., Conn., 20 February 1682/3, and was baptized at First Church, Hartford, Conn., 26 March 1693; died at North Branford, New Haven Co., Conn., 17 May 1767.

Susannah's parents had returned to Simsbury after this village was rebuilt following its destruction during King Philip's War, and it was there that they had their last four children were born. Susanna's birth date is known, and I believe she was their next child. However, her sister Elizabeth may have been born next, but Elizabeth's birth date is unknown. Susannah and Elizabeth were both baptized on the same day, as recorded at First Church, Hartford; Susannah was then ten years old. Susannah and Elizabeth both married men who were first cousins, and following the custom of the time, the first to marry one of these sisters was the older cousin, and he probably married the older of the two sisters. I have therefore assigned a probable birth year for Elizabeth that follows the known birth year of Susannah.

We do not know how Susannah met her husband, but it was not a long journey from Simsbury, near the Connecticut River in central Connecticut, to the coast and then a few miles west to Branford. This journey had been made already by others in Susannah's family and she had relatives in Branford and the adjacent town of Guilford. At the age of twenty, she was married in Branford to John Frisbie, a man from a family that was prominent in that town. Eight months later, her sister Elizabeth married John's cousin Benjamin Frisbie. Ten months after she was married, Susannah had the first of what would become a family of ten children, who were born between April 1703 and November 1724.

Susannah and John Frisbie's eldest child was married in 1731 and their fourth child was also married later that year. Two of their children died young, but when John died in 1736, Susannah was left to care for six children, who ranged in age from twelve to twenty-one. Her oldest son at home did not marry immediately. Presumably he stayed to be the man of the house until his mother remarried in 1741, after which he was free to marry, and he did so in 1743, when he was 37 years old. Susannah was 58 when she married for the second time. Seven of her children are known to have married and she had at least 30 grandchildren, many of whose descendants have been traced to the twentieth century.

On 7 April 1703 when Susanna was 21, she married (1) **John FRISBIE**,[91] son of Sgt. John FRISBIE and Ruth BOWERS, in Branford, Conn. He was born on 23 May 1676 in Branford, Conn., and died there, 14 Jan 1736/7; he was 59. Two of their children died young, and nothing more is known of the youngest, Jonah. He must therefore be regarded as a possible but unproved child. The other seven children married members of the Barker, Munson, Grannis, Frost, Matthews, Culver, and Gaylord families.
They had the following children:

60	i.	John (1703-1786)
61	ii.	Jedediah (1705-1736)
62	iii.	Samuel (~1707-1708)
63	iv.	Israel (1709-1787)
64	v.	Nathaniel (1711-1711)
65	vi.	Susannah (1713-)
66	vii.	Huldah (1715-1797)
67	viii.	Elijah (1717-1800)
68	ix.	Hannah (1720-1803)
69	x.	Jonah (1724-)

On 8 Sep 1741 when Susanna was 59, she married (2) **Joseph FOOTE**[92] in Wallingford, Conn.

12. Elizabeth HENBURY,[93] a daughter, probably the fourth daughter and fourth child, of Arthur and Lydia (Hill) Henbury, was born in Simsbury, Conn., in, say, 1684, and was christened on the same day as her sister Susannah, 26 Mar 1693. Their baptisms are recorded at First Church, Hartford. Susannah was then ten years old, and Elizabeth was perhaps nine.

Nothing more is known of Elizabeth until she married Benjamin Frisbie of Branford, a bit younger than his first cousin John Frisbie, who eight months earlier had married Elizabeth's sister Susannah. Elizabeth and Benjamin Frisbie had seven children between 1705 and March 1723. Benjamin died in September 1724 and Elizabeth, then perhaps 40 years old, was left to care for her children. Two of the children may already have died but Elizabeth had at least five at home, ranging in age from a one-year old baby to a twenty-year old man. Her oldest son married the next year and moved to Goshen, far away in Litchfield County. It is unlikely that

Elizabeth could have lived alone for long with her young children, and indeed it is recorded that she married again, to a man named Caleb Matthews, of whom nothing more is known. Her four other surviving children were eventually married and had children of their own. Her two daughters married within the next five years at age 21 and 22, respectively, although her other two sons took longer to find wives, one marrying at the age of 23 and the other at the rather advanced age of 33. Her children married members of the Pardee, Ives, Gaylord, and Lewis families. She is known to have had at least nineteen grandchildren; the first was born in 1726 when her own youngest child was only three years old. No record has been found of her death.

She married (1), at Branford, New Haven, Co., Conn., 8 December 1703, **Benjamin FRISBIE**,[94] son of Benoni and Hannah (Rose) Frisbie; born in Branford, 24 January 1679; died there, 10 September 1724, age 45. Benjamin Frisbie's father Benoni was the son of Edward and Hannah (?Culpepper) Frisbie, who were also the parents of Sgt. John Frisbie, husband of Benjamin's sister-in-law, Susannah Henbury.

Benjamin and Elizabeth (Henbury) Frisbie had the following children:

70	i.	Benjamin (1705-?1758)
71	ii.	Abigail (1709-1778)
72	iii.	Jerusha (1712-)
73	iv.	Mary (1714-)
74	v.	Zebulon (1717-1800)
75	vi.	Levi (1719-)
76	vii.	Theodore (1723-1764)

Elizabeth married (2) **Caleb MATTHEWS**, who died without recorded descendants.

14. Samuel HENBURY,[95] only son and fifth child of Arthur and Lydia (Hill) Henbury, was born in Simsbury, Conn., 2 Apr 1686, and died before 25 June 1687, at the age of one or less.

15. Lydia HENBURY,[96] fifth daughter and youngest of the six children of Arthur and Lydia (Hill) Henbury, was born sometime between, say, February 1686/7 and 25 June 1687, surely in Simsbury, Conn., and died there, 2 Aug 1689, at age 2.

Line 2. Children of Mary Hill and John Saxton

Two of the children of Mary and John Saxton were probably the youngest grandchildren of Luke and Mary Hill who would remember their grandparents, and could tell about them to their own children. Richard, born in 1673, and Mary, born in 1678, were in their early twenties when their grandfather and grandmother Hill died. No other grandchildren of Luke and Mary Hill who were born after Richard and Mary Saxton, and had children, were alive when Luke and Mary died.

16. Richard SAXTON,[97] eldest child of John and Mary (Hill) Saxton, was born at Simsbury, Hartford Co., Conn, 24 February 1673; died there, 27 March 1714, age 41. Richard Saxton was one of the oldest grandchildren of Luke and Mary (Hout) Hill to be living in Simsbury while they were still alive. He would surely have remembered his grandparents, for he was twenty when Luke died, and Mary died after Luke. Other children and grandchildren of Luke and Mary (Hout) Hill had moved away from Simsbury by the time their grandson Richard Saxton was born there, and he continued to live in Simsbury for the rest of his life.

When Richard was 33 he married a 22-year old woman from Simsbury. They had four children, born over a span of five years. When Richard died, his youngest child was only two years old. How his widow and children coped with the loss of her husband and their father is unknown, for she apparently did not remarry, and she, too, died before her children were married. Richard's will provides some information about the disposition of his estate. However, it is likely that his fatherless and then orphaned children were dependent on their relatives until they could support themselves. One daughter died at age 18 in the same year that her mother died, but the other three children lived long lives. The two surviving daughters married members of the Wilcox and Adams families, and they had a total of at least 17 children.

On 20 June 1706 when Richard Saxton was 33, he married **Hannah BUELL**,[98] daughter of Peter Buell, in Simsbury, Hartford Co., Conn.; born there in 1684 and d. 23 July 1725, age 41. Richard and Hannah (Buell) Saxton had the following children:

77	i.	Hannah (1707-1725)
78	ii.	Mary (1709-1776)
79	iii.	Adam (1710-1774)
80	iv.	Lucy (1712-1784)

17. Mary SAXTON (a k a SEXTON),[99] daughter and second of the three children of John and Mary (Hill) Saxton, was born in Simsbury, Hartford Co., Conn., 4 May 1678; died sometime after 1721. When she was twenty-one years old, she married William Gillett, son and grandson of men named Jonathan Gillett (Sr. and Jr.) who were instrumental in the founding of Windsor and Simsbury. William and Mary Gillett had five children over the next seven years. William died in 1718/19, leaving Mary to care for this young family, which then ranged from about eleven to eighteen years of age. Mary married again three years later, and the children all survived for a time. Two of the boys died young, however, one at age twelve and the other when he was eighteen, but the other three children survived; the two daughters married and had children. One daughter married David Eno, who died in service at Cape Breton in 1745, but their son Roger Enos became famous as a colonel in the Revolutionary War and his daughter Jerusha married the famous – some say notorious – Ira Allen, a founder of Vermont. William and Mary Gillett's other daughter married David Gaines and had one child. Mary (Saxton) Gillett had no children by her second husband.

On 14 Sep 1699 when Mary was 21, she married (1) **William GILLETT**,[100] son of Jonathan GILLETT Jr. and Anna KELSEY, in Simsbury, Conn.; born on 4 Dec 1673 in Windsor, Conn., and died in Simsbury, Conn. on 27 Jan 1718/9, age 44.

William and Mary (Saxton) Gillett had the following children:

81	i.	William (1700-1736)
82	ii.	Jonathan (1701-1719)
83	iii.	Mary (1703-1760)
84	iv.	Richard (1705-1719)
85	v.	Eunice (1707-1740)

On 22 June 1721 at age 43, Mary (Saxton) Gillett married (2) Jonathan **HOLCOMB** in Simsbury, Conn.[101]

18. John SAXTON,[102] second son and third and youngest child of John and Mary (Hill) Saxton, was probably born about 1682 in Simsbury, Hartford Co., Conn.; he died there on 13 Oct 1766, at about age 84. He was named in 1716 as the sole executor of the will of his father, John Sexton, but nothing else is known about him except the date of his death. He presumably did have descendants and probably did not marry.

Line 3. Children of Eleazer Hill and Sarah Gillett

The clearest exposition of the children of Eleazer and Sarah Hill is by Leon S. Pitman, "Some Descendants of Nathan Gillett of Windsor and Simsbury, Connecticut" (Modesto, California, [1999] 2002), which is available on-line by a search under that author and title. Pitman wrote:

Children of Nathan Gillett:

... vi. SARAH, b. 13 July 1651, m. 29 Dec. 1679 in Simsbury 29 Dec. 1659 to ELEAZER HILL, who was b. 7 March 1656/7 in Farmington, Conn.[28] He d. at Windsor 3 Mar. 1724/5. In April 1688 Eleazer Hill, as a son-in-law of Nathan Gillett, was granted land in the Nathan Gillett Weatogue Meadow tract in Simsbury.[29] His lot abutted that of brother-in-law Nicholas Gozzard. Children born in Simsbury, surname **Hill**, include: (1) *Elizabeth*, b. 29 July 1681; (2) *Mary*, b. 6 Dec. 1685, d. 5 Dec. 1697 in Simsbury; (3) *Eleazer*, b. 20 Jul. 1694, (4) *Sarah*.[30].[103]

I have advanced Sarah to be shown as the third child of Eleazer and Sarah (Gillett), because of the long interval between the recorded births of Mary (1685) and Eleazer (1694), and I have given Sarah a possible birth year of about 1687. Three of the children died without known issue, but the son, Eleazer, who would be Eleazer III, married and had descendants.

19. Elizabeth HILL,[104] eldest child of Eleazer and Sarah (Gillett) Hill, was born in Simsbury, Conn., 29 July 1681.

20. Mary HILL,[105] second daughter and second child of Eleazer and Sarah (Gillett) Hill, was born at Simsbury, Conn., 5 December 1685; she died there on 5 December 1697, at age 11. She was buried on 26 December 1697.

21. Sarah HILL,[106] third daughter of Eleazer and Sarah (Gillett) Hill, was born at Simsbury, Conn., in, say, about 1687.

22. Sergeant Eleazer HILL,[107] son and probably the youngest child of Eleazer and Sarah (Gillett) Hill, was born at Simsbury, Hartford Co., Conn., 20 July 1694, and died on 3 Mar 1741, age 46. He was called "Sgt." in the records of Simsbury although the nature of his military service is unknown. On 8 July 1731 when Eleazer was 36, he married **Elizabeth GILLET**.[108] Her ancestry is unknown but she is doubtless a descendant of either Jonathan or Nathan Gillett of Simsbury, or a widow of one of their male descendants. Sgt. Eleazer and Elizabeth Hill had three children, all of whom were sons. One son, his namesake, is said to have had a child by a wife whose name is unknown.

Eleazer and Elizabeth (Gillett) Hill had the following children:

86	i.	Eleazer (1732-)
87	ii.	Benjamin (1735-)
88	iii.	Stephen (1737-)

Line 4. Children of Tahan and Hannah (Parmelee) Hill

Tahan Hill was born in Windsor and grew up in Simsbury, Connecticut. He and his younger brother, Luke, Jr., and their younger sister Abigail moved to Guilford, on the coast. Luke Jr. moved on to nearby Branford, while Tahan and Abigail stayed in Guilford and married into the prominent Parmelee family. Tahan and his sister married a sister and brother who were children of the patriarch, John Parmelee Jr. Tahan died soon after his second child was born and his widow remarried to provide a secure home for herself and her children. Her second husband was from Saybrook, Conn., and she probably died there. It is hardly a surprise that her daughter married a man from Saybrook, which was then in New London County. Branford is eight miles west of Guilford, and Saybrook – now known as Old Saybrook, Middlesex County – is eighteen miles east of Guilford, at the mouth of the Connecticut River.

23. Hannah HILL,[109] daughter and elder child of Tahan and Hannah (Parmelee) Hill, was born in Guilford, New Haven Co., 17 November 1689; may have died in Saybrook, New London Co., Conn., 16 October 1775, age 85. On 3 March 1709/10 when Hannah was 20, she married in Saybrook, **Samuel BUSHNELL** Jr., son of Samuel and Patience (Rudd) Bushnell; he was born at Saybrook, 21 August 1692.

Samuel Bushnell Jr. and Hannah Hill had the following children[110]:

89	i.	Jeremiah (1710-1790)
90	ii.	Jemima (1712-1783)
91	iii.	Hannah (1718-1782)
92	iv.	Samuel (1724-1793) [unconfirmed]
93	v.	Patience (1725-1764) [unconfirmed]

24. Tahan HILL,[111] son of Tahan and Hannah (Parmelee) Hill, was born in 1691 in Guilford, Conn. Nothing more is known of him, and he probably died young.

Line 5. Children of Luke Hill Jr.
Children of Luke Jr. and Hannah (Butler) Hill

The six children of Luke Hill Jr. and his first wife Hannah Butler grew up experiencing travel and relocation more than any of their cousins in the Hill family, for their father was by far the most peripatetic of the children of Luke Hill Sr. Luke Jr. was born in Windsor and grew up in Simsbury, but as a young adult, he moved to Guilford with his older brother Tahan and their younger sister Abigail. Tahan and Abigail soon married a brother and sister in Guilford and they stayed on in Guilford, while Luke Jr. married a young woman from Branford, eight miles away. He must have soon moved back to Guilford, though, because his first two children were born there. His third child is said to have been born in Wethersfield, and the next two were born in his home town of Simsbury. His youngest child was born in Branford. Luke Jr. then moved to Wallingford, accompanied by some of his children. His first wife died in about 1736 and he married a younger woman and had one more child. He died in the part of Wallingford now known as Cheshire in 1740. Windsor, Simsbury, and Wethersfield were in Hartford County, in the center of Connecticut; and Guilford, Branford, and Wallingford/Cheshire were in adjacent New Haven County, on the coast.[112]

In spite of these perigrinations, the family must have been close, for Luke Jr.'s oldest son's children were born in Wallingford and he died there. Luke Jr's second child stayed in Branford and her children were born there. We know nothing more of the daughter who was born in Wethersfield, but Luke Jr.'s fourth child was married in Wallingford and his children were born there. This child moved to Litchfield late in life, where he was joined by several cousins who were among the earliest settlers in the remote north-west corner of Connecticut. Luke Jr.'s fifth child was married in Wallingford and her first children were born there, but she and her husband moved to Litchfield county, where her last children were born and where her husband died. The youngest child of Luke Hill, Jr., named Isaac, was born in Branford and was married and died in Wallingford. Isaac's youngest child may have been born posthumously in Goshen, but his wife later returned to Guilford and died there.

The records of these births, marriages, and deaths appear in various sources and the actual locations of the events are not necessarily the same as the source would suggest. Furthermore, records are not always consistent or in agreement. Many of the locations are close to each other, and it is probably impossible to be absolutely certain where a specific event took place, except that births were at home (no matter where they were recorded), baptisms were ordinarily done in church, and burials were usually in churchyards, even if unmarked.

25. Ebenezer HILL,[113] eldest child of Luke Jr. and Hannah (Butler) Hill, was born at Guilford, New Haven Co., Conn., 23 November 1687; died in Wallingford (now Cheshire), New Haven Co., Conn., sometime after January 1740, at which time he was 52.

The history of Cheshire, Connecticut shows that on 30 April 1730, the names of Luke,

Isaac, and Ebenezer Hill were recorded as freemen and present at the "freemans meeting" in Wallingford and Cheshire. By 1735, Ebenezer Hill was in Litchfield County, living in an area north of the town of Litchfield then known as New Bantam which became Goshen in 1738. Luke Jr. (who we would think of as Luke III) and his brothers Ebenezer and Isaac Hill bought 100 acres of land there in February 1735 and in February 1737 they divided it into three equal parts. In June 1737, Luke sold his part to Benjamin Frisbie of Wallingford. In December 1739, Isaac sold all but one acre of his part to Ebenezer, which somehow had already come into Ebenezer's possession. Thus by the first month of 1740, Ebenezer Hill owned 66 and 2/3 acres in Goshen, adjacent to a piece of land half that size that was owned by a Benjamin Frisbie, to whom he was closely related. A Benjamin Frisbie (b. 1679) was married to Ebenezer's cousin Elizabeth, daughter of his older sister Lydia, but there is no indication that he came to Goshen. However, their son, Benjamin [Jr.] (b. 1705), who was Ebenezer's first cousin, once removed, came to Goshen and lived there until he died in the French and Indian War in 1758. Sometime after 1740 Ebenezer may have returned to Wallingford, where his father was living with his second wife and a baby who was his half sister, for his death is said to be recorded in Wallingford records.

On 3 Jan 1717 when Ebenezer was 29, he married **Martha DIBBLE**,[114] daughter of Josiah and Hannah DIBBLE; born on 14 Nov 1697 in Saybrook, Conn.; died in Litchfield, Conn., 20 May 1764, at age 67.
They may have had some or all of the following children:

94	i.	Ebenezer (1717-)
95	ii.	Asa (1719-1809)
96	iii.	Martha (1724-1764)
97	iv.	Titus (Linas) (1726-)
98	v.	Zenas (1730-)
99	vi.	Luke (1732-1740)
100	vii.	Dan (1734-)
101	viii.	Huldah (1736-7)
102	ix.	Hulda (1742-)

26. Anna HILL,[115] eldest daughter and second child of Luke Jr. and Hannah (Butler) Hill, was born in Guilford, Conn., 30 December 1692. In 1715 when Anna was 22, she married, in Branford, Conn., **Isaac COOK**, son of Henry and Mary (Hall) COOK; born in 1692 in Salem, Essex Co., Mass.; died in Branford, New Haven Co., Conn., in 1762, age 70. Isaac Cook was born in the year of the witchcraft delusion in Salem. Many residents of Salem slipped away to other places in the years after that tragic episode, and apparently Isaac Cook's family was part of that migration. They moved to Branford and were living there when Isaac married Anna Hill.

Isaac and Anna Cook must have soon moved to Wallingford, Conn., for seven children were born to them in Wallingford between 1716 and 1729. An eighth child is said to have been born in Canton, which is about thirty-five miles north of Wallingford. Canton is midway between her parents' home in Simsbury and the town of Goshen, where she also had many relatives, so it is possible the she was en route to Goshen or some where else in northern Connecticut when this child was born. I will therefore include Jerusha Cook as a possible child of Isaac and Anna Cook. A record of Anna's death has not been found, but Isaac apparently returned to Branford in later life and he died there in 1762.
They had seven children, born in Wallingford, and possibly one more:

103	i.	Isaac (1716-1760)
104	ii.	Demetrius (1718-)
105	iii.	Uzziel (1722-)
106	iv.	Anna (1724-1759)
107	v.	Waitstill (1727-1780)
108	vi.	Desire (1729-)
109	vii.	Lydia (1732-)
110	viii.	Jerusha (1736-) [perhaps]

27. Keziah HILL,[116] second daughter and third child of Luke Jr. and Hannah (Butler) Hill, was born on 24 February 1695 in Wethersfield, Hartford Co., Conn. She was named for Job's second daughter, born after he prospered. Nothing else is known about her, or how it was that she was the only child of Luke and Hannah who was born in Wethersfield.

28. Luke HILL [III],[117] second son and fourth child of Luke Jr. and Hannah (Butler) Hill, was born on 16 Sep 1698 in Simsbury, Hartford Co., Conn.; died in Litchfield, Litchfield Co., Conn., in 1772, at about 73. A Luke Hill was a Freeman of Wallingford (now Cheshire), in April 1730. It is unknown if it was Luke Hill (b. 1698) or his father Luke Hill Jr. (1661-1740), but it was probably his father, who was living in Wallingford/Cheshire at that time. However, his father may have been impecunious (his peregrinations being unusual even for those times), so the burden of participation in government may have fallen on the son. Luke1698, who became known as Luke Jr., soon moved on to Litchfield County, where he was involved in land transactions with his brothers Ebenezer and Isaac. Their joint purchase of 100 acres in what is now Goshen, and Luke Jr.'s sale of his portion of this property, is described above in the notes for Ebenezer. How Luke [III] survived and where he lived in Litchfield County after he sold his property to his brother Ebenezer is unknown, but he had several other close relatives in that part of Connecticut and he was probably given a home with one or more of them. His son Uri, who died sometime before 1769, had married twice, and had two children before he died. This was three years before Luke [III] died. Uri's second wife remarried and continued to live in Goshen until she died in 1826, having nine children by her second husband, Ephraim Starr. She could well have been the one who provided a home for her former father-in-law in his last years.

On 19 December 1723 when Luke was 25, he married **Sarah FREDERICK**,[118] daughter of William and Abigail (Doolittle) FREDERICK, in Wallingford, New Haven Co., Conn.; born on 18 October 1704 in Wallingford, New Haven Co., Conn.
They had the following children:

111	i.	Kezia (1724-1726)
112	ii.	Uri (1729-<1769)
113	iii.	Kezia (1733-1801)
114	iv.	Sarah (1737-)
115	v.	Abigail (1741-)

29. Lydia HILL,[119] third daughter and fifth child of Luke Hill Jr. and Hannah Butler, was born at Simsbury, Hartford Co., Connecticut, 25 February 1700; died at Goshen, Litchfield Co., Conn.

Lydia was named for her father's oldest sister, Lydia (Hill) Henbury, and she was her parents' youngest daughter. She married, on 14 April 1725, at Wallingford, New Haven Co., Connecticut, John Dibble; born at Saybrook, New London Co. (now Middlesex Co.), Conn., 13 December 1702; died at Goshen, Litchfield Co., Conn., 7 April 1756.

John and Lydia (Hill) Dibble probably had eight children. Their first six children were born at Wallingford between 1725 and 1737, and the last two were born at Goshen in 1740 and

35

1746.[120] Their first daughter was named Lydia, thus continuing this name for a third generation. Sometime between 1737 and 1740 they relocated to Goshen, in the northwest corner of Connecticut, where many of her close relatives had moved, and they were recorded as living there in 1753. Both of them died in Goshen. John died in the spring of 1756. The record of Lydia's death and burial has not been preserved.

On 14 April 1725 when Lydia was 25, she married **John DIBBLE**,[121] son of John and Mary (Severance) DIBBLE, in Wallingford, New Haven Co., Conn.; born 13 December 1702 in Saybrook, Conn; died in Goshen, Litchfield Co., Conn., 7 April 1756, age 53.
They had the following children:

116	i.	John (1725-1790)
117	ii.	Reuben (1727-1779)
118	iii.	Israel (1729-)
119	iv.	Lydia (1731-1805)
120	v.	Susannah (1735-)
121	vi.	Josiah (1737-)
122	vii.	Rachel (1740-)
123	viii.	Mary (1747-1825)

30. Isaac HILL, Sr.,[122] third son and youngest child of Luke, Jr., and Hannah (Butler) Hill, was born at Branford, New Haven Co., Conn., probably on 27 May 1703; died at Wallingford, Connecticut, very likely on 25 October 1741, at age 38. Other dates have been given for his birth and death. There is, however, no doubt that Isaac Hill Sr. was dead by the time his widow Esther (Stone) Hill was named Executrix of his estate on 29 January 1741/2; that Isaac Hill Sr. had five children who were named when she was made their guardian on 26 October 1743; and that those children were Chloe, Billious, Phineas, Isaac, and Abraham.[123]

Isaac, Luke, and Ebenezer Hill, appear on the list of Freemen of Wallingford (now Cheshire), Conn., on the last day of April 1730. We cannot be certain who these three men were, but they were probably sons of Luke Hill, Jr. They were thus were the brothers Luke [III], Ebenezer, and Isaac Hill, who was later known as Isaac Hill, Sr., and who died at Wallingford eleven years later. This document places Isaac Hill Sr. in Wallingford in the spring of 1730 and he was probably still there in 1733, when his first child was born. The three brothers soon moved to Litchfield County, where they were among the earliest settlers in the wilderness of northwestern Connecticut. In 1735 they bought property in the part of that county that became Goshen before Goshen was established. Luke sold his portion to Benjamin Frisbie in 1737 and Isaac sold his portion to Ebenezer in 1738.

Isaac's second child was born in Goshen in 1738 and his third child was probably born there, too, in 1739, although Isaac and his wife are also said to have been early settlers in Woodbury, 23 miles south of Goshen, in 1738.[124] Luke apparently continued to live in Litchfield County until he died, but Isaac returned to Wallingford – probably the part now known as Cheshire, where his father was living – and he was probably living there by 1740 when his fourth child, Isaac Jr., was born. Isaac Sr. died in Wallingford in 1741. In 1741 his wife had another son, her fifth child, who was born either shortly before or after Isaac Sr. died. His widow was still living in Wallingford when she was made Executrix of Isaac Sr.'s estate in January 1741/2 and when she was granted guardianship of her children in 1743. In 1745 she remarried and moved to Guilford, where she had another son by her second husband. Not surprisingly, her sons by Isaac Hill Sr. later remembered Guilford as their home. Isaac Jr. said that he was born in Guilford, when he gave his deposition as a soldier in the Revolutionary War many years later.

Isaac Hill Sr. married, at Wallingford, New Haven County, Connecticut, 16 January 1733, **Esther** (aka Ester, Hester) **STONE**, daughter of Benajah Jr. and Hannah (De Wolf) Stone; born in 1711; died, probably in Guilford, Conn., 11 March 1797. Nothing else is known of her father. After her father died, her mother married (2) Joshua Parmelee (who was of the prominent Parmelee family that appears many times in the present genealogy), and then (3) Dr. Benjamin Hull, and lastly (4) Benjamin Hart. Following the death of Isaac Hill, Esther married (2), 8 May 1745, Ebenezer Shelley of Guilford, Connecticut, who had previously married (1), Comfort Everest, who died in 1743. By this marriage Esther had a son, Ebenezer Shelley, Jr., born 18 April 1746. Following Esther's death, Ebenezer, Sr., married (3), 20 May 1766, Sarah Pierson of Guilford. The number of step-siblings, step-parents, and half-siblings that these marriages produced is probably incalculable.[125]

Isaac Sr. and Esther (Stone) Hill had five children: Chloe [aka Cloe] (1733-1749); Billious [aka Billie, Bellas] (1738-1807); Phineas (abt. 1739-1826); Isaac Jr. (1740-1833); and Abraham (abt 1740/41-1817). Following the death of Isaac Hill Sr., Esther moved from Wallingford to Guilford and married (2), 9 May 1745, as his second wife, Ebenezer Shelley, Sr., by whom she had a son, Ebenezer Shelley, Jr. (b. 1746).[126]

Isaac and Esther's five children continued the migratory patterns that has been seen in the previous generations of this family. The first child, Chloe, died in Woodbury, Fairfield Co., Conn., at age 15. Woodbury, about 23 miles south of Goshen, appears later in the history of the descendants of Isaac Sr., and Chloe was apparently the first to go there. The next two children, Billious and Phineas, moved to northwestern Vermont. Having been the first English child to be born in Goshen,[127] Billious took his wife and five children to Addison County, Vermont, near Lake Champlain, after the Revolutionary War. Billious and his wife died there in 1807 and 1805, respectively. Phineas moved further north, to Chittenden County, Vermont, with his wife and four children, and his fifth child was born there in 1800. Isaac Jr. married a woman from Stratford, on the coast in Fairfield County, and he stayed in Connecticut. After his first child was born in Stratford in 1763, he moved back to Litchfield County, where his next two children were born. The rest of his eleven children were born in towns in Litchfield and Fairfield Counties, the last in 1788 in Shelton, Fairfield County. Isaac Jr. then settled in Southbury, near the border between Litchfield and Fairfield Counties, and he remained there until he died in 1833. Sometime before or during the Revolutionary War, Abraham and his wife moved across the border into the adjoining area of Dutchess County in eastern New York State. The last of Abraham's five children were born there in 1779 in Carmel, which is now in Putnam County. Isaac Sr. and Esther (Stone) Hill had the following children:

124	i.	Cloe (1733-1749)
125	ii.	Billious (aka Billie, aka Bellas) (1738-1807)
126	iii.	Phineas (~1739-1826)
127	iv.	Isaac [1] (1740-1833)
128	v.	Abraham (~1740-1817)

Child of Luke Sr. and Deliverance Hill

31. Deliverance HILL,[128] only child of Luke Hill Sr. and his second wife, Deliverance, who was perhaps Deliverance (Cooke) Falconer, was born on 20 July 1738 in Guilford, New Haven County, Conn. Her origin and her life is a bit of a mystery. There is much information in historical records about Deliverance Cooke, who may be her mother, and of this Deliverance

Cooke's marriage to Patrick Falconer and of the birth of their five children. Deliverance Cooke was the youngest of ten children of Thomas Cooke Jr., a carpenter of Guilford, and his wife Sarah Mason. His father, Thomas Cooke Sr., was one of the original signers of the plantation covenant of Guilford and he served for a time as Representative to the General Assembly. One of Deliverance Cooke's older brothers, the Rev. Samuel Cooke, A.B. (Yale 1705), was the head of a prominent family of Yale graduates and clergymen. Deliverance Cooke's husband Patrick Falconer died in 1735 in Guilford, Conn., leaving her with five children that ranged in age from one to 12 years in age. Deliverance Cooke is said to have died 12 February 1781, at age 85. No record of her marriage to Luke Hill Jr. has been located, but there is nothing inconsistent in these records with the assertion that she married (2) Luke Hill Jr., as his second wife, for she was widowed in 1735 and resided at that time in Guilford, where Luke Hill had previously lived for some time and still had close relatives. She had borne five children to Falconer between 1723 and 1734, so she would likely have sought a second husband to help rear her young children. And it would not have been impossible for her to conceive and have a child in 1738 by Luke Hill, in Guilford (where Luke's daughter Deliverance was born), at which time she would have been 42 years old.

All in all, it is reasonable to believe that Luke Hill married Deliverance (Cooke) Falconer, accepted responsibility for her five children, and then had another child, who was born about two years before he died. This child, Deliverance Hill, was a half-sister of Luke's six children by his first marriage, some of whom were old enough to be her aunts and uncles, and she may also have been a half-sister of the five children of Patrick Falconer. Deliverance's only child, who was named for her father, was born in Woodbury in 1775. Nothing is known about her later life. Her husband moved to upstate New York, on the western side of Lake Champlain and died there many years later.

On 11 January 1764 when Deliverance was 25, she married **Andrew BLACKMAN**, in Woodbury, Conn.; born on 3 January 1740; he died in Clinton, Mooers Co., N.Y., 2 October 1821, age 81.

They had one child:

   129   i.   Luke Sherman (1775-1855)

Line 6. Children of Abigail Hill and Caleb Parmelee

Abigail married Caleb Parmelee as his second wife, eleven months after the death of his first wife, who died twelve days after giving birth to a son, who in turn died eight months later. Caleb's younger sister Hannah had married Abigail's older brother Tahan. Hannah was soon widowed and her young son died, too, but her daughter Hannah Hill lived to have many descendants who were "double cousins" of the children of Caleb and Abigail Parmelee. The Parmelee family was prominent in Guilford at that time, and for many decades thereafter. Soon after they were married, however, Caleb and Hannah Parmelee moved to Branford, a few miles away in New Haven County, and it is there that their six children were born. Nothing is known about the descendants, if any, of five of these children, but Caleb Jr., who married twice, is believed to have descendants who are alive today.

32. Hannah PARMELEE,[129] eldest child of Caleb and Abigail (Hill) Parmelee, was born on 28 March 1694 in Branford, New Haven Co., Conn.; died there 24 January 1761, at age 66. There is little in the historical record about Hannah Parmelee. *Families of Early Guilford* and the Parmelee Family section of *Early Connecticut Families* agree that she was the first child of Caleb and Abigail (Hill) Parmelee. *Early Connecticut Families* adds that she joined the

Branford Church on 5 November 1714.

Ordinarily, by the traditions of the writers of those publications, if she had been married, this would have been noted and her death would have been a matter of record under her married name. I would ordinarily assume, therefore, that she lived into her 66th year, unmarried, and died a spinster. However, there are countless websites that appear on Google and in family trees in Ancestry.com when her name is entered as a search term, in which she is said to have married John Parish (aka Parrish) in Branford, Conn., on 18 April 1709, when she was 15 years old. This John Parish/Parrish is said in these websites and family trees to have been born in 1671 and died in 1748. Many of the websites and family trees say that he was born in Mendon, Mass., and that he died on 23 March 1748 in Branford, Conn. Some websites and family trees show no descendants of this marriage, some show one or two children, and a few show as many as eight children of John and Hannah (Parmelee) Parish/Parrish. None of the websites or family trees on Ancestry.com provide a source for the marriage of John and Hannah, or for the births of any children from this marriage.

After a long search of records in the NEHGS website and in *The American Genealogist*, I cannot confirm the marriage of John Parish/Parrish and Hannah Parmelee at any time, much less on 18 April 1709, the date usually given. This date is stated on many Ancestry.com family trees and other family trees published on-line that can be found on Google. I also cannot confirm that the John Parish who died on 23 March 1748 was the same John Parish who was the third son and fourth child of John and Hannah (Jewell) Parish of Mendon, Mass. I therefore will list John Parish/Parrish as a possible husband of Hannah Parmelee, and I will list the children whose names appear on various websites, but I will not assign them numbers in the genealogy of the family of Luke and Mary (Hout) Hill.

On 18 April 1709 when Hannah was 15, she may have married **John PARRISH** in Branford, New Haven Co., Conn.; born in say 1671 in Mendon, Mass.; died in Branford, Conn. on 23 March 1748, at about age 77.[130]

They may have had the following children[131]:

Mary Parish 1713-1737
Hannah Parish 1720-1758
Lucy Parish 1722-
Josiah Parish 1724-1806
Abigail Parish 1727-
Gideon Parish 1730-
Joel Parish 1733-

33. Caleb PARMELEE Jr.,[132] elder son and second child of Caleb and Abigail (Hill) Parmelee, was born 23 August 1696 in Branford, New Haven Co., Conn.; died there 14 July 1750, age 53. In 1720 when Caleb was 23, he married (1) **Elizabeth FOOTE,**[133] daughter of John FOOTE, in Guilford, New Haven Co., Conn.; born in 1697 in Branford, Conn.; died in Branford, Conn. in 1725, age 28.

They had the following children:

130	i.	Abigail (1721-)
131	ii.	Mary (1722-)
132	iii.	Sarah (1724-1767)

On 25 March 1725 when Caleb was 28, he married (2) **Jemima HARRISON,**[134] daughter of Lt. Thomas HARRISON and his wife, Margaret STENT; born in 1692; died in Branford, Conn., 9 June 1766, and was buried there at about age 76. Jemima (Harrison) Parmelee's father, Thomas

Harrison, served in King Philip's War, was an ensign in 1697 and a lieutenant in 1709 in Queen Anne's War, and he was also in the expedition to Canada. He was the father of nine children by Margaret Stent, daughter of his step-mother.
They had one child:

> **133**   i.   Jerusha (1729-)

On 11 January 1737 when Caleb was 40, he m. (3) **Mary DURHAM**,[135] who d. in October 1770.
They had the following children:

> **134**   i.   Chloe (1739-)
> **135**   ii.   Rebecca (1741-)

34. Lydia PARMELEE,[136] second daughter and third child of Caleb and Abigail (Hill) Parmelee, was born 8 March 1699 in Branford, Conn.; died 8 October 1726, age 27. She joined the Branford church on 2 September 1716, and on 3 February 1725/6 at the age of 25, she married **John YOUNG**.

35. Josiah PARMELEE,[137] second son and fourth child of Caleb and Abigail (Hill) Parmelee, was born 28 December 1701 in Branford, Conn.; died there 9 September 1720, age 18. He joined the Branford church on 2 September 1716.

36. Abigail PARMELEE,[138] third daughter and fifth child of Caleb and Abigail (Hill) Parmelee, was born 12 March 1703 in Branford, Conn.; died there 8 February 1733, age 29. On 3 May 1727 when she was 24, she married **John READ** in Branford, Conn.

37. Benjamin PARMELEE,[139] third son and sixth child of Caleb and Abigail (Hill) Parmelee, was born 26 June 1705 in Branford, Conn., and he died there.

Line 7. Children of Elizabeth Hill and Samuel Adams

Samuel Adams and Elizabeth Hill had two children, who were born in Simsbury and lived there for the rest of their lives. Their elder child was a daughter who married twice and is believed to have descendants who are alive today. Nothing more is known about their younger child, a son.

38. Elizabeth ADAMS,[140] eldest child of Samuel and Elizabeth (Hill) Adams, was b. 21 Feb 1686/7 in Simsbury, Hartford Co., Conn.; d. there 6 Dec 1726, age 40. She had five children by her first marriage, two of whom had descendants, and no children by her second marriage.

On 9 December 1707 when Elizabeth was 21, she married (1) **Ephraim GRIFFIN**, son of John GRIFFIN and Ann BANCROFT, in Simsbury, Hartford Co., Conn.; born 1 March 1668/9 in Windsor, Hartford Co., Conn.; died in Simsbury, 26 Sep 1725, at age 57.
They had the following children:

> **136**   i.   Elizabeth (~1709-1800)
> **137**   ii.   Anna (Hannah) (1713-)
> **138**   iii.   Silence (~1716->1726)
> **139**   iv.   Ephraim (~1718-)
> **140**   v.   Sheba (Phoebe, Pheba) (~1722-)

In September 1725 when Elizabeth was 39, she married (2) **Caleb HOLCOMB** in Simsbury; born 1 May 1695 in Simsbury; died there, 27 Aug 1758, age 63; apparently without progeny.

39. Samuel ADAMS,[141] son and second child of Caleb and Abigail (Hill) Parmelee, was born 26 October 1689 in Simsbury, Hartford Co., Conn. Nothing more is known about him. He could be, but is probably not, the man known in Simsbury V.R. as Samuel Adams 3rd.

Line 8. Children of John Hill

John Hill, youngest of the eight children of Luke and Sarah (Hout) Hill, married twice and had seven children. His oldest children were the product of his first marriage, to Sarah Phelps, whereas the mother of his youngest child, and perhaps more, was his second wife, Sarah Terry. It is not possible to be sure who was the mother of some of the middle children, although as I have indicated above, I believe the preponderance of evidence favors the conclusion that Sarah Phelps was the mother of the first six children and Sarah Terry was the mother only of his youngest child. John Hill and some of his children lived for their entire lives in Simsbury, and they were probably the last of the descendants of Luke Hill Sr., to live there. One of the last of the Hill family to live in Simsbury were John Hill's daughter Mary, who died there in 1773, and her husband, Dr. Jacob Reed, who died in Simsbury in 1775.

The children inherited a substantial amount of money and property when their father died on 1 November 1740. The total inventory amounted to £1339-09-07. The older children's step-mother applied to receive back her dower, but after the dower was set out and the property was distributed in April 1741, there was still over £213 in cash to be divided. The widow Sarah (Terry) Hill received one-third (£71-06-02), and the children or their heirs received two-thirds. John Jr. received his "double part" of £47-10-08 and the rest was divided equally, with allocations of £23-15-05 going to the heirs of the oldest child, Sarah Strickland, and to Mary Read, Hannah Wilcox, and Elizabeth Hoskins – who appear in the distribution by their married names. This was enough money and property to keep the family together for at least one more generation in Simsbury.

40. Sarah HILL,[142] eldest child of John and Sarah (Phelps) Hill, was born on 28 July 1697 in Simsbury, Hartford Co., Conn.; christened there 28 November1697; and died there 25 Dec 1736, at age 39. She was the mother of three children, or perhaps six, and probably died when her youngest child was two years old. Her daughter Sarah is said to have had descendants, some of whom are probably alive today.

On 28 Jul 1720 when Sarah was 23, she married **Samuel STRICKLAND,**[143] son of Joseph Strickland, in Simsbury, Hartford Co., Conn.; born there on 11 Nov 1697; christened there on 14 Nov 1697; and probably died there.

They had the following children:

141	i.	Joseph (1721-)
142	ii.	Mary (1722-)
143	iii.	Sarah (1724-1769)
144	iv.	Hannah (1729-)
145	v.	Elizabeth (1731-)
146	vi.	Orpha (1733-)

41. Infant HILL,[144] probably the second child of Samuel and Sarah (Hill) Strickland, was born about 1700 in Simsbury, Hartford Co., Conn.; died there on 2 Apr 1702, at about age 2.

42. Dead child HILL,[145] probably the third child of Samuel and Sarah (Hill) Strickland, was born dead on 29 Jan 1700/01 in Simsbury, Conn.

43. John HILL, Jr.,[146] only surviving son and probably the fourth child of Samuel and Sarah (Phelps) Hill, was born about 1702 in Simsbury, Hartford Co., Conn.; died in Canton, Hartford Co., Conn., 1 Aug 1771, about 69 years of age. He was buried on 8 Aug 1771 in Collinsville, Conn. He received a "double part" of the two-thirds of his father's estate that was divided between him and four of his sisters, as if two-thirds of the estate was divided into six parts. He probably continued for some time to farm on the historic Hill family property in the center of Simsbury. He may also have operated the ferry that his father and grandfather had run across the

Farmington River, until the ferry service in Simsbury was commercialized by the town and state. He was, however, probably living in the western part of Simsbury that had become the town of Canton, for that is where he died.

John Hill Jr. married three times and had ten children. How and where he met his first wife is unknown, but she was the first person with a French surname to marry into the family of Luke and Mary (Hout) Hill, and she was probably the first to marry one of these Hills who was born in the colony of New York. She died eight months after giving birth to her fourth child. John married again within a year or so and had two more children by his second wife, who died ten months after giving birth to her second child. He married again five months later, and had four more children by his third wife.

On 17 February 1724/5 when John was 22, he married (1) **Jane LaDIEU**,[147] daughter of Pierre LADIEU and Martha ANNERAUD, in Simsbury, Conn.; born about 1708 in New Rochelle, N.Y.; died in Simsbury, 8 November 1732, at about 24. Her parents were Huguenots. They had the following children[148]:

147	i.	John 3rd (1725-1795)
148	ii.	Eleazer B. (1727->1790)
149	iii.	Martha (1730-)
150	iv.	Mary (1732-1733)

John married (2) **Elizabeth _____**,[149] who was born about 1700 and died in Simsbury, Conn., 21 September 1738, at about 38.
They had the following children:

151	i.	Seth (1734-1736)
152	ii.	Benoni (1736-1737)

On 21 February 1738/9 when John was 36, he married (3) **Abigail WILCOXSON**,[150] in Simsbury, Conn.; born about 1708, she was "of Simsbury." She may have moved to the adjacent town of Canton, which is where her husband died in 1771, but no record has been found that mentions her after 1753, when her last child was born.
They had the following children:

153	i.	Sarah (1740-)
154	ii.	Phebe (1746-)
155	iii.	Darius (1749-)
156	iv.	Mary (1753-)

44. Mary HILL,[151] sixth child of John Hill Jr., was probably a daughter of his first wife, Sarah Phelps, or perhaps a daughter of his second wife, Sarah Terry. She was born about 1704 in Simsbury, Conn.; died there in May 1773, about 69. She was mother of 11 children, 10 of whom are documented in Simsbury Vital Records and one more who is found in the distribution of her husband's estate. Her husband, Dr. Jacob Reed, was notable in that he was a third generation physician, which was rare in colonial America.

On 9 April 1724 when Mary was 20, she married **Dr. Jacob REED** (aka READ, READE),[152] son of Dr. Jacob READE and Elizabeth LAW, in Simsbury, Conn.; born on 15 May 1700 in Simsbury; died there 8 Jan 1775, age 74. His father, Dr. Jacob Reade [Sr.], son of Dr. Philip Reade, was mentioned twice in Noah Phelps' *History of Simsbury*, in the list for Minister's Rate in 1701, and as being taxed in 1701.[153]
They had the following children:

157	i.	Mary (1724-)
158	ii.	Lydia (1726-1806)

159	iii.	John (1728-<1775)
160	iv.	Elizabeth (1729-<1775)
161	v.	Jacob (1731-)
162	vi.	Sarah (1733-1736)
163	vii.	Titus (1735-1788)
164	viii.	Silas (1738-)
165	ix.	Sarah (1740-)
166	x.	Abijah (1743->1775)
167	xi.	Amy (->1775)

45. Hannah HILL,[154] sixth child and third surviving daughter of John Hill Jr., was probably the last child of his first wife, Sarah Phelps, or possibly a daughter of his second wife, Sarah Terry. She was born about 1706 in Simsbury, Conn.; died in New Haven Co., Conn., 8 June 1766, about 60. She married Ephraim Wilcox and was the mother of many children, perhaps as many as eight.

There are 14 pages of citations to the birth, death, and marriage of members of the Wilcox family (spelled variously) in Simsbury Vital Records, but very few that can be identified as specifically relating to Ephraim Wilcox and Hannah Hill. Most of the entries in their branch of the family are derived from Ancestry.com. I have used the synthesis in OneWorldTree for Hannah Hill and Ephraim Wilcox to organize this list, although it is almost completely unverified.

She received a portion of her father's estate: "To Mary Read, to Hannah Wilcock, and to Elizabeth Hoskins, to each of them the sum of 23-15-05." Her birth was not recorded in the *Barbour Collection*, so it is not clear if she was the daughter of Sarah (Phelps) Hill or Sarah (Terry) Hill. In OneWorldTree, her birth is said to be in 1707, which would make her a child of Sarah Phelps, although James D. Hill lists her as a child of Sarah Terry. I have discussed this question above, in the entry for John Hill Sr., in which I conclude that she probably was a daughter of Sarah Phelps. Various Family Trees in Ancestry.com list different children for Hannah Hill and Ephraim Wilcox (aka Wilcoxson). These lists have been consolidated in OneWorldTree, and that list of eight children will be quoted here. All are said to have been b. in Simsbury except Elnathan (in Killgsworth) and Dijah (of whom it is said: "b. Connecticut").

On 5 April 1726 when Hannah was 20, she married **Ephraim WILCOX,**[155] son of Samuel WILLCOXSON, in Simsbury, Hartford Co., Conn.; he was born in Simsbury, 24 February 1707; died there in 1770, about age 62. He was taxed at Salmon Brook, Simsbury, Conn., in 1734.[156]

They had the following children[157]:

168	i.	Ephraim (1727-)
169	ii.	Susannah (1731-1803)
170	iii.	Sylvanus (1733-1821)
171	iv.	Elnathan (1734-1826)
172	v.	Zachariah (1735-1821)
173	vi.	Willard (1737-1825)
174	vii.	Dijah (1739-1805)
175	viii.	Rosannah (1741-)

46. Elizabeth HILL,[158] daughter of John and Sarah (Terry) Hill, was born at Simsbury, Hartford Co., Conn., 14 December 1710; died sometime after 1742. Her grandfather, Lieutenant John Terry, was an important figure in the early history of Simsbury. Elizabeth and her mother were both named as heirs in the estate of her father, who died in 1740. Elizabeth received one-sixth of the two-thirds of the estate that went to the children when it was distributed in 1742. Her mother received the "widow's third," and also the return of her dowry, and this may have benefited Elizabeth if she survived her mother.

On 26 December 1728 when Elizabeth was 18, she married **Joseph HOSKINS**, son of Robert HOSKINS and Mary GILLETT, in Simsbury, Hartford Co., Conn.; born 8 October 1698 in Simsbury, Hartford Co.; died there 29 Sep 1782, he was 83. Mary Gillett was presumably a descendant of either Jonathan Gillett or his brother Nathan, of Windsor, Conn., and thus was related to other Gilletts who married descendants of Luke Hill and Mary Hout, but her specific ancestry is unknown. Joseph and Elizabeth (Hill) Hoskins had one child, a son, who is said to have married Eunice Coe, a descendant of John Parmelee of Guilford, and may have descendants who are alive today.

They had one child:

   176   i.   Joseph (1731-1818)[159]

4

Fourth Generation
The Great-Grandchildren of Luke and Mary (Hout) Hill

Line 1 (continued). Grandchildren of Arthur and Lydia (Hill) Henbury

The following five children were christened, and were probably born, in Hartford, Conn.[160]

47. Lydia LONG was born 23 February 1697. On 19 August 1725, at age 28, she married **Matthew GROVER**, in Coventry, Tolland Co., Conn.[161]

48. William LONG was christened on 25 June 1699 in Hartford, Conn.

49. Sarah LONG was christened on 1 June 1701 in Hartford, Conn.

50. Mary LONG was born on 26 April 1703; christened on 30 May 1703 in Hartford, Conn. On 10 February 1730, at age 26, she married **Benjamin BABCOCK**, in Coventry, Tolland Co., Conn.; born in 1697 in Coventry, Tolland Co., Conn.; died there on 28 February 1751, about 54. They had the following children:

177	i.	Ebenezer (1730-)
178	ii.	William (1732-)
179	iii.	Sarah (1734-)
180	iv.	Hannah (1736-)
181	v.	Mary (1737-)
182	vi.	Benjamin (1757-)

51. Ebenezer LONG was christened on 29 June 1707 in Hartford, Conn.

The next eight children were probably born in Hartford, Conn.; they were christened there.[162]

52. Hannah RICHARDS was born on 17 June 1700. On 5 November 1729 when Hannah was 29, she married **Ebenezer JUDD**, son of Thomas JUDD & Sarah GAYLORD, in Hartford, Conn.; born on 3 March 1703 in Hartford, Conn.; died there on 20 May 1734, age 31. They had the following children:

183	i.	Ruth (1733-1736)
184	ii.	Hannah (1731-1736)

53. Josiah (Jonah) RICHARDS, christened "Jonah" Richards on 7 February 1702/3 in Hartford, Conn., although he was known as Josiah as an adult; died in New Hartford, Litchfield Co., Conn., in 1746, about age 43. On 27 July 1726 at about age 24, he married **Mary PALMER** in Branford, Conn.; born on 4 June 1708.[163] They had one child:

185	i.	Hannah (1739-)

54. Mary RICHARDS was born on 1 July 1705.

55. James RICHARDS was born 2 February 1705/6; christened 3 Feb 1705/6 in Hartford, Conn.; died in 1754, age 48. He married **Anna ENSIGN**, born in 1706; died in 1786, about 80. They had the following children:

186	i.	Aaron (1743-1795)
187	ii.	Anna (1748-1780)

56. Daniel RICHARDS was born on 25 December 1708; christened on 26 December 1708 in Hartford, Conn.; died in Goshen, Litchfield Co., Conn. in 1750, about age 41. On 26 December

1734 when he was 26, he married **Jane BUCKLAND**, daughter of Charles BUCKLAND and Hannah SHEPARD, in Hartford, Hartford Co., Conn.; born in New Hartford, Litchfield Co., Conn.; died in Goshen, Litchfield Co., Conn. She was the mother of five, three of whom had descendants.

They had the following children:

188	i.	Samuel (1735-)
189	ii.	Daniel (1738-1819)
190	iii.	Charles (1742-1817)
191	iv.	Hanah (Twin) (1746-)
192	v.	Abijah (Twin) (1746-1750)

57. Esther RICHARDS was born on 18 June 1713 and was christened on 21 June 1713 in Hartford, Conn.; died in West Hartford, Hartford Co., Conn. on 28 November 1798, age 85. On 9 April 1740 when she was 26, she married **Aaron MERRILL**.[164]

58. Samuel? RICHARDS. No further information about this person in Ancestry.com.

59. Hezekiah RICHARDS was born about 1715. No further information in Ancestry.com.

Children of John and Susannah (Henbury) Frisbie[165]

60. John FRISBIE[166] was born on 11 March 1703/4; died in Branford, Conn., 17 September 1786, age 83. On 8 February 1731, at age 27, he married **Anna BARKER**,[167] daughter of William BARKER and Elizabeth HARRISON, in Branford, Conn.; born in September 1706 in Branford, Conn.; died there 7 Sep 1762, age 56.

They had the following children:

193	i.	John (1731-1817)
194	ii.	Jonathan (1734-1818)
195	iii.	William (1737-1813)
196	iv.	Jacob (1740-1823)
197	v.	Elizabeth (1744-)
198	vi.	Joel (1747-)

61. Jedediah FRISBIE was born 2 October 1705; died in Branford, Conn. on 14 January 1736, age 30. On 10 May 1743 when he was 37, he married **Elizabeth MUNSON**, daughter of Caleb MUNSON and Elizabeth HARMON, in Wallingford, Conn.; born on 31 March 1717 in Wallingford, Conn.; died in Branford, Conn. on 11 November 1777, age 60. She was the mother of 6, five of whom married and three had descendants.[168]

They had the following children:

199	i.	Simon (1743-1777)
200	ii.	Miriam (1746-1824)
201	iii.	Keziah (1748-1821)
202	iv.	Susannah (1750-)
203	v.	Moses (1754-)
204	vi.	Elizabeth (1757-1827)

62. Samuel FRISBIE[169] was born in about 1707/8 and was christened in February 1707/8 in Branford, Conn.; died there in 1708, about age 1.

63. Israel FRISBIE[170] was born on 22 June 1709; died in Branford, New Haven Co., Conn., on 12 January 1787, age 77. On 1 July 1731, at age 22, he married (1) **Elizabeth GRANNIS**, daughter of John GRANNIS and Elizabeth BROCKETT, in Branford, Conn.; born 1 September 1708 in New Haven, New Haven Co., Conn.; died in North Branford, New Haven Co., Conn., 9 Jun 1760, age 51.

They had the following children:

205	i.	James (1732-)
206	ii.	Jonah (1734-)
207	iii.	Chloe (1737-1749)
208	iv.	Tamer (1739-)
209	v.	Chloe (1750-)
210	vi.	Israel (1754-)

Israel married (2) **Hannah** _____, widow of Timothy Johnson.

64. Nathaniel FRISBIE[171] was born on 3 September 1711; died in 1711 in Branford, Conn.

65. Susannah FRISBIE[172] was born on 11 May 1713. On 17 January 1738 when she was 24, she married **Joseph FROST** in Branford, New Haven Co., Conn.; born in 1711 in Branford. They had one child:

211	i.	Solomon (1742-1838)

66. Huldah FRISBIE[173] was born on 15 November 1715; died in Plymouth, Conn., on 27 April 1797, age 81. On 14 January 1742, when she was 26, she married **Aaron MATTHEWS** in Wallingford, Conn.; born on 19 November 1721 in New Haven, New Haven Co., Conn.; died in Plymouth, Conn., 24 April 1806, age 84.
They had the following children:

212	i.	Reuben (1743-1777)
213	ii.	Aaron (1744-1802)
214	iii.	Samuel (1761-1812)

67. Elijah FRISBIE[174] was born on 1 November 1717; died in Waterbury, Conn., 15 February 1800, age 82. He married (1) **Abigail CULVER**, daughter of Samuel CULVER and Ruth TYLER; born 17 December 1718 in Wallingford, Conn.; died in Waterbury, Conn., 19 April 1771, age 52.
They had the following children:

215	i.	Esther (1743-1795)
216	ii.	Judah (1744-1817)
217	iii.	Reuben (1746-1824)
218	iv.	Abigail (1746-)
219	v.	Charles (1752-)
220	vi.	Hannah Amelia (1738-1810)
221	vii.	Sarah (1756-1842)
222	viii.	John (1762-1846)

He married (2) **Elizabeth IVES**, who died on 11 October 1776.
He married (3) **Lydia REDFIELD**.

68. Hannah FRISBIE was born on 24 January 1720; died in Hamden, Conn., 25 February 1803, age 83. On 12 February 1747, at age 27, she married **Benjamin GAYLORD**, son of John GAYLORD and Elizabeth HICKOX, in Wallingford, Conn.; born in 1722 in Durham, New Haven, Conn.; died in Hamden, New Haven, Conn., 18 May 1801, age 79.[175]
They had the following children:

223	i.	Susannah (1749-1749)
224	ii.	Hannah (1749-1791)
225	iii.	John (1750-1750)
226	iv.	Benjamin (1755-1825)
227	v.	Elizabeth (1756-1756)

69. Jonah FRISBIE was born on 22 November 1724. He married **Anna BARKER**, born on 11

September 1706 in Branford, New Haven Co., Conn.; died on 7 September 1762, age 55.[176]

The seven children of Benjamin and Elizabeth (Henbury) Frisbie were born in Branford, Conn.

70. Benjamin FRISBIE was born on 16 July 1705; he or his son Benjamin died in the French and Indian War on 30 August 1758. He resided in Goshen and Litchfield, Conn. He married **Elizabeth PARDEE**, daughter of George PARDEE and Mercy DENISON.[177]

They had the following children:

228	i.	Hephzibah (1726-)
229	ii.	James (1793-)
230	iii.	Jabez (1730-)
231	iv.	Elizabeth (1732-)
232	v.	Jerusha (1735-)
233	vi.	Mary (~1737-)
234	vii.	Benjamin (1739-?1758)
235	viii.	Joseph (1741-)

71. Abigail FRISBIE was born on 23 January 1709; died in Bristol, Hartford Co., Conn., in 1778, she was about 68. On 7 May 1730 when she was 21, she married **Elnathan IVES**, son of Gideon IVES and Mary ROYCE, in Wallingford, Conn.[178]

They had one child:

236	i.	Jerusha

72. Jerusha FRISBIE was born on 10 March 1712/3. On 8 January 1729, at age 16, she married **Benjamin GAYLORD**, son of Joseph GAYLORD and Sarah STANLEY, in Wallingford, Conn.[179]

They had the following children:

237	i.	Levi (1730-)
238	ii.	Jersusha (1731-)
239	iii.	Enos (1733-1834)

73. Mary FRISBIE was born on 10 October 1714 in Branford, Conn.[180]

74. Zebulon FRISBIE was born on 10 May 1717; died in Bristol, Hartford Co., Conn., 12 August 1800, age 83. On 2 April 1740, at age 22, he married **Lucy LEWIS**, daughter of Barnabas LEWIS and Elizabeth _____ in Wallingford, Conn.; born 23 March 1724 in Wallingford; died in Bristol, Hartford Co., Conn.; 18 September 1789, age 65.[181]

They had the following children:

240	i.	Lucy (1741-1823)
241	ii.	Mary (1745-1757)
242	iii.	Elizabeth (1747-)
243	iv.	Lola "Lowly" (1749-)
244	v.	Zebulon (1752-1836)
245	vi.	Levi (1753-1755)
246	vii.	Abel (1755-)
247	viii.	Levi (1759-1842)
248	ix.	Daniel (1761-)
249	x.	Samuel (1763-1831)

75. Levi FRISBIE was born on 3 Dec 1719.[182]

76. Theodore FRISBIE was born on 27 Mar 1723; died in Wallingford, Conn., 31 January 1764, age 40. He married (1) **Phillis _____**, who died in June 1757 in Cheshire, Conn. She was the "wife of Theodore," and thus apparently a widow when she married Theodore Frisbie.[183]

They had one child:

| 250 | i. | Levi (1757-) |

On 11 June 1758 when he was 35, he married (2) **Mehitabel WHEELER**, daughter of William WHEELER and Jemima PLUMB, in Wallingford, Conn.

They had the following children:

251	i.	Theodore (1759-1830)
252	ii.	Luman (1760-)
253	iii.	Mary (1763-1774)

Line 2 (continued). Grandchildren of John and Mary (Hill) Saxton

The four children of Richard and Hannah (Buell) Saxton were born at Simsbury., Conn.[184]

77. Hannah SAXTON was born in 1707; died in Simsbury, Conn., 23 July 1725, about 18.

78. Mary SAXTON was born in 1709; died in West Simsbury, Hartford Co., Conn., 9 April 1776, about age 67. On 15 December 1726, when she was 17, she married **Azariah WILCOX**, in Simsbury, Conn.; born on 27 July 1706 in Simsbury; died there on 31 March 1776, age 69.

They had the following children:

254	i.	Desiah (1739-1750)
255	ii.	Elisha (1728-1812)
256	iii.	Hannah (1732-1802)
257	iv.	Mary (1734-1816)
258	v.	Lydia (1737-1750)
259	vi.	Rachel (1743-1817)
260	vii.	Aaron (1745-1750)
261	viii.	Ziba (1749-1808)

79. Adam SAXTON was born in 1710; died in Simsbury, Conn., 12 October 1774, about 64.

80. Lucy SAXTON was born in 1712; died in Simsbury, Conn., 18 September 1784, at about age 72. On 11 January 1732 when she was about 20, she married **Daniel ADAMS** in Simsbury; born in 1706 in Simsbury; died there 21 May 1779, at about age 73.

They had the following children:

262	i.	Richard Saxton (1734-1726)
263	ii.	Lucy (1736-1801)
264	iii.	Daniel (1738-1758)
265	iv.	Child (1740-1741)
266	v.	Thanks (1742-1816)
267	vi.	Elizabeth (1745-1833)
268	vii.	Parmenio (aka Permena, Pernene) (1747-1809)
269	viii.	Oliver (1750-1804)
270	ix.	John (1752-1778)

These five children were all born in Simsbury, Hartford Co., Conn.

81. William GILLETT[185] was born on 1 September 1700; died in Simsbury, 16 Jul 1736 or 1737, age 35 or 36.

82. Jonathan GILLETT[186] was born 1 October 1701; died in Simsbury, 7 January 1719, age 17.

83. Mary GILLETT[187] was born 28 February 1703; died in Simsbury, Conn., 23 November 1760, at age 57. A mother of five, she was widowed at the age of 43 when her husband died in the Siege of Louisbourg, in King George's War. Four of her children had descendants.

On 20 October 1723, when was 20, she married **David ENO**, in Simsbury, Conn.; born 12 August 1702 in Simsbury; died at Cape Breton (i.e., Louisbourg) in Jun 1745, at age 42. His children ranged from 5 to 18 years of age at the time he died. The Siege of Fort Louisbourg on the Ile-Royale (now called Cape Breton Island) took place from 1 May – 16 June 1745. Louisbourg surrendered to a combined assault in which a British fleet commanded by Peter Warren was supported by soldiers from New England commanded by William Pepperell. The fort had good seaward defenses but it was vulnerable to land-based siege batteries, and it surrendered in the face of the attack that was about to occur. Capture of the fort was a major success for Britain. However, in spite of strenuous objections from the colonists, it was used as a bargaining chip in the negotiations that ended the war, which was known in Europe as the War of Austrian Succession. Louisbourg was returned to France in 1748 by the Treaty of Aix-la-Chapelle.

They had the following children:

271	i.	Mary (1727-1804)
272	ii.	Roger (1729-1808)
273	iii.	Mercy (1734-1860)
274	iv.	Jonathan (1739-1813)
275	v.	Abigail (1740-1782)

84. Richard GILLETT was born in 1705; died in Simsbury, 3 January 1719, about age 14.[188]

85. Eunice GILLETT was born in 1707; died 24 May 1740, at about age 33. On 3 December 1728 when she was about 21, she married **Daniel (aka David) GAINES**, in Simsbury. He was born in Simsbury in 1700.[189]

They had one child:

276	i.	Daniel (1732-)

Line 3 (continued). Grandchildren of Eleazer and Sarah (Gillett) Hill

86. Eleazer HILL [III],[190] eldest of the three children, all of whom were sons, of Eleazer [Jr.] and Elizabeth (Gillett) Hill, was born on 15 May 1732 in Simsbury or Windsor, Conn.

Child of Eleazer Hill [III] by a wife whose name is unknown:

277	i.	Benjamin (1767-)

87. Benjamin HILL was born on 17 July 1735 in Simsbury or Windsor, Conn.[191]

88. Stephen HILL was born on 2 October 1737 in Simsbury or Windsor, Conn.[192]

Line 4. (cont'd). Grandchildren of Tahan and Hannah (Parmelee) Hill

The children were born in Saybrook, which was originally in New London County, and later in Middlesex County, Connecticut.

89. Jeremiah BUSHNELL[193] was born on 27 September 1710; died in Saybrook, Middlesex Co., Conn., 14 February 1790, at age 79.

90. Jemima BUSHNELL[194] was born on 19 February 1712; died 27 December 1783, age 71. On 22 February 1737/8, when she was 25, she married **Ezra (aka Ezrah) PARMELEE**, son of Deacon Nathaniel PARMELEE and Mrs. Esther (KELSEY) WARD, in Killingworth, Middlesex Co., Conn.; born 28 April 1714; died in 1800, about 85. He lived in Killingworth, Conn., and later in Claremont, N.H., and he probably died there.

They had the following children:

278	i.	Daniel (1739-1800)
279	ii.	Jerusha (1741-1819)

280	iii.	Samuel (1743-1808)
281	iv.	Ezra (1745-1838)
282	v.	Oliver (1748-1821)
283	vi.	Jemima (1750-)
284	vii.	Justin (1750-)
285	viii.	Elias (1752-1829)
286	ix.	Hiel (1756-1836)

91. Hannah BUSHNELL was born in 1718 and died in 1782, at about age 64.[195]

92. Samuel BUSHNELL was born in 1724; died in Sheffield, Berkshire Co., Mass., 21 January 1793, about age 69.[196]

93. Patience BUSHNELL was born 28 October1725; died in Saybrook, Middlesex Co., Conn. on 28 June 1764, age 38.[197]

Line 5 (continued). Grandchildren of Luke Hill Jr. and Hannah Butler

Seven of the next eight children were born in Wallingford, New Haven Co., Conn.; the second child was born in Branford, New Haven Co., Conn. One of the children married a first cousin who was also born in Wallingford.

94. Ens. Ebenezer HILL Jr. was born on 24 October 1717 in Wallingford, Conn.; died in Stephen Town, N.Y. He married **Elizabeth BALDWIN**.[198]

They had the following children:

287	i.	Ambrose (1743-1816)
288	ii.	Ebenezer (1746-1753)
289	iii.	Samuel (1748-1766)
290	iv.	Reuben (1751-1765)
291	v.	Chloe (Cloe) (1754-)
292	vi.	Ebenezer (1756-)
293	vii.	Lucina (1761-)

95. Asa HILL,[199] second son and second child of Ebenezer and Martha Wealthy (Dibble) Hill, was born at Goshen, Litchfield Co., Conn., 22 November 1719; died 14 September 1809, probably at Norwalk, Conn. He is buried in the Mill Hill Burying Ground in Norwalk. He was a gravestone carver and at least two of his sons - Ithuel and Phineas - also became gravestone carvers and stone masons. At the age of 22, on 2 December 1741, he sold 20 acres of land to John Willoughby in the southeast part of Goshen. This was part of the "Squire's Farms" that had been in his father's hands. He married, in Goshen, 13 March 1745, **Elizabeth RICHARDS**,[200] who was born in about 1725. They lived in the south part of Goshen near his older brother, Ebenezer Jr. and Elisha Buel, and on 9 March 1759 he sold land in that part of Goshen to Isaac Pratt. Asa and Elizabeth (Richards) Hill had five children, born between 1745 and 1760.

They had the following children:

294	i.	Jonah (1745-)
295	ii.	David (1748-1749)
296	iii.	Elizabeth (1751-1825)
297	iv.	Martha (1759-)
298	v.	Sarah (1760-)

Elizabeth died sometime thereafter and he married (2), in about 1769, **Gloriana WHEELER**, daughter of William WHEELER and Jemima PLUMB, who was born about 1749. Asa and Gloriana (Wheeler) Hill had four children, born between 1769 and 1778.[201]

They had the following children:

299	i.	Ithuel (1769-1821)
300	ii.	Uri (Uriah) (1771-)
301	iii.	Asa (1776-1776)
302	iv.	Phineas (1778-1844)

96. Martha HILL was born on 17 February 1724 in Wallingford, Conn.; died in Litchfield, Litchfield Co., Conn., 20 May 1764, at age 40. On 18 November 1747 when she was 23, she married **Ebenezer GRANT**, son of Josiah GRANT and Sarah COOK, in Litchfield, Conn.; born 2 March 1723 in Windsor, Hartford Co., Conn.; died in Litchfield, Conn., 9 July 1765, age 42.[202] A story about his son, Dr. Isaac Grant, in the *[Albion, Mich.] Morning Star* (21 January 2001) says he is a descendant of Matthew Grant, from whom President Grant is also descended. They had the following children:

303	i.	Sarah (1748-1769)
304	ii.	Martha (1751-1769)
305	iii.	Lydia (1753-1767)
306	iv.	Elihu (1756-)
307	v.	Isaac (1760-1841)
308	vi.	Huldah (1763-1764)

97. Titus (Linas) HILL.[203] Born on 22 Mar 1725/6 in Wallingford, New Haven Co., Conn.; died in probably Richmond, Berkshire Co., Mass., aft 1790. He was a soldier in the French & Indian War. He served at Lake George, N.Y., in August 1757, in the alarm for the defense of Fort William Henry. He purchased a farm in the S.E. corner of the town of Richmond, Mass., in 1766, and he resided there at age 64, when the U.S. census was taken in 1790. On 13 Dec 1750 when Titus (Linas) was 25, he married **Mindwell HALL** in Goshen, Conn. Born in 1730.[204] They had the following children:

309	i.	Titus (aka Silas) (1752-1820)
310	ii.	Arunah (1754-)
311	iii.	Nancy (1757-)
312	iv.	Elisha (1759-1827)
313	v.	Mary (1763-)
314	vi.	Lois (1766-1766)

98. Zenas HILL[205] was born 4 January 1730 in Wallingford, Conn. On 21 December 1752 when he was 22, he married his first cousin **Kezia HILL** (113), daughter of Luke HILL [III] (28) and Sarah FREDERICK, in Goshen, Litchfield Co., Conn.; born on 1 Dec 1733 in Wallingford, Conn.; died in Tinmouth, Rutland Co., Vt., in 1801, at about age 67.[206] They had the following children:

315	i.	Frederick (aka Jaldiacek) (1753-)
316	ii.	Ira (1755-1841)
317	iii.	Uri (1759-)
318	iv.	Amelia (1761-)
319	v.	Sarah (1762-)
320	vi.	Zenas (1764-)
321	vii.	Jesse (1766-)
322	viii.	Abigail (1769-)
323	ix.	Urania (1773-1774)

99. Luke HILL was born 2 April 1732 in Wallingford, Conn., and died 26 May 1740, age 8.[207]

100. Daniel HILL was born 14 June 1734 in Wallingford, New Haven Co., Conn.; died aft 1810. On 20 Dec 1757, he married **Hannah MATTHEWS** in Goshen, Conn.[208]
They had one child:

    324   i.   Miles (1766-1815)

101. Huldah HILL was born 15 Nov 1736 in Goshen, Conn.; died there, 6 September 1737.[209]

102. Hulda HILL [II] was born 4 June 1742 in Goshen, Conn. Hulda [II] married **Benjamin REEVES**. She apparently d.s.p.

103. Isaac COOK[210] was born in July 1716 in Wallingford, New Haven Co., Conn.; died in Branford, New Haven Co., Conn. in 1760, about age 43.

104. Demetrius COOK[211] was born 2 April 1718 in Wallingford, New Haven Co., Conn. On 26 April 1739 when he was 21, he married **Elizabeth ROGERS**, in Branford, New Haven Co., Conn.; born 24 Sep 1720 in Branford; died in Conn. in Sep 1807, about age 86.

105. Uzziel COOK[212] was born 9 May 1722 in Wallingford, New Haven Co., Conn.

106. Anna COOK was born on 24 Jun 1724 in Wallingford, New Haven Co., Conn.; died in Branford, New Haven Co., Conn., in 1759, about age 34. She was the mother of three, one of whom had descendants. On 3 December 1749 when she was 25, she married **Jonathan WHEADON** in Branford, New Haven Co., Conn.; born 15 July 1721 in Branford, Conn.; died in Conn. in 1783, about age 61.[213]
They had the following children:

    325   i.   Chille (1751-)
    326   ii.   Lucene (1753-)
    327   iii.   Jonathan (1755-)

107. Waitstill COOK was born 8 January 1727 in Wallingford, New Haven Co., Conn.; died in Branford, New Haven Co., Conn., 26 January 1780, age 53. In about 1750 when he was about 22, he married **Elizabeth WHITE** in Canoe Brook Swamp, N.J.; she was born in 1727; died in North Underhill, Vt., 11 July 1812, about age 85. Two of their nine children are said to have had descendants.[214]
They had the following children:

    328   i.   Jane (1751-)
    329   ii.   Hannah (1753-)
    330   iii.   Jacob (1755-)
    331   iv.   Ebenezer Hubbard (1759-1847)
    332   v.   William (1762-)
    333   vi.   Elizabeth "Betsy" (1764-)
    334   vii.   John (1768-)
    335   viii.   Hulda (1768-)
    336   ix.   Benjamin (1771-)

108. Desire COOK was born 21 July 1729 in Wallingford, New Haven Co., Conn.[215]

109. Lydia COOK was born 4 February 1732 in Wallingford, New Haven Co., Conn.[216]

110. Jerusha COOK was born 19 Nov 1736 in Canton, Hartford Co., Conn.[217]

111. Kezla HILL[218] was born 28 September 1724 in Wallingford, New Haven Co., Conn.; died there 14 October 1726, at age 2.

112. Uri HILL[219] was born 19 June 1729 in Wallingford, Conn., and died before 1769. On 15 March 1756 when he was 26, he married (1) **Mary ROOT** in Goshen, Litchfield Co., Conn.
They had one child:

    337   i.   Uri (1760-)

On 20 October 1764 when he was 35, he married (2), as her second husband, Hannah **BEACH (BEECH)**, in Goshen, Conn.; born 28 February 1745 in Goshen; died there 28 Feb 1826, age 81. She was the mother of 1 by Uri Hill and mother of 9 by her first husband, Ephraim Starr. They had one child:

 338   i.   Mary Ann (1766-)

113. Kezia HILL[220] was born 1 December 1733 in Wallingford, New Haven Co., Conn.; died in Tinmouth, Rutland Co., Vt. in 1801, about age 67. On 21 December 1752 when she was 19, she married **Zenas HILL** (98),[221] son of Ebenezer HILL (25) and Martha DIBBLE, in Goshen, Litchfield Co., Conn.; born 4 January 1730 in Wallingford.

They had the following children, whose numbers were assigned above under Zenas Hill (98):

 315   i.   Frederick (aka Jaldiacek) (1753-)
 316   ii.   Ira (1755-1841)
 317   iii.   Uri (1759-)
 318   iv.   Amelia (1761-)
 319   v.   Sarah (1762-)
 320   vi.   Zenas (1764-)
 321   vii.   Jesse (1766-)
 322   viii.   Abigail (1769-)
 323   ix.   Urania (1773-1774)

114. Sarah HILL[222] was born 2 October 1737 in Wallingford, New Haven Co., Conn.

115. Abigail HILL[223] was born 12 June 1741 in Wallingford, New Haven Co., Conn.

116. John DIBBLE Jr.[224] was born 26 July 1725 in Wallingford, New Haven Co., Conn.; died in Stratford, Conn., in 1790, about age 64. On 6 October 1746 when he was 21, he married (1) **Elizabeth HOLLAND** in Goshen, Litchfield Co., Conn.; born in 1729 in Wallingford.

They had one child:

 339   i.   David (1749-)

On 26 June 1751 when he was 25, he married (2) **Sybil KILBOURN** in Goshen, Conn.; born there, 31 Jan 1732, and died in 1789, about age 56.

They had the following children:

 340   i.   Reuben (1755-)
 341   ii.   Harris (1756-)
 342   iii.   ?

117. Reuben DIBBLE[225] was born on 6 March 1727 in Wallingford, New Haven Co., Conn.; died in Conn. in 1779, about age 51. On 16 March 1758 when he was 31, he married **Ann SHERWOOD** in Stamford, Fairfield Co., Conn.; born there, 15 April 1731; died in Darien, Fairfield Co., Conn., in 1829, about age 97.

They had the following children:

 343   i.   John (1758-1852)
 344   ii.   Abigail (1762-1789)
 345   iii.   Anna (1765-1802)
 346   iv.   Sarah (1771-)

118. Israel DIBBLE was born in 1729 in Wallingford, New Haven Co., Conn. He married **Hannah _____**.[226]

They had one child:

 347   i.   Alexander (1760-1819)

119. Lydia DIBBLE[227] was born 19 May 1731, probably in Wallingford, New Haven Co.,

Conn.; died in New Haven, Addison Co., Vt., 12 May 1805, at age 73. On 12 September 1751 when she was 20, she married (1) **Elijah BIRGE** in Litchfield, Litchfield Co., Conn.; born there on 22 June 1731; died in 1756, age 24.

They had the following children:

348	i.	Rhoda (1751-)
349	ii.	David (1753-1836)
350	iii.	Elijah (1756-1829)

On 9 August 1758, when she was 27, she married (2) **Billious (aka Billie, aka Bellas) HILL** (125), son of Isaac HILL Sr. (30) and Esther (Ester, Hester) STONE, in Goshen, Litchfield Co., Conn.; born there in 1738; died in New Haven, Vt., 17 October 1807, at age 69. He was the first white child born in Goshen and he was later a skilled cabinetmaker. He enlisted for three years service in the Continental Army in April 1781 and was on muster rolls as late as July 1783. He was Captain of Artificers at West Point, N.Y., where he planned and laid out the works. (See his entry in the kindred of Isaac Hill Sr. for further details.)

They had the following children:

351	i.	Mabel Leanna (~1758-)
352	ii.	Chloe (1759-1814)
353	iii.	William (1761-1761)
354	iv.	Reuben (1766-1833)
355	v.	Lydia (1769-)

120. Susannah DIBBLE[228] was born 30 March 1735 in Wallingford, Conn.

121. Josiah DIBBLE was born 3 March 1737 in Wallingford, Conn. On 18 March 1756, when he was 19, he married **Sibble PLUMB** in Goshen, Litchfield Co., Conn.[229]

122. Rachel DIBBLE[230] was born 30 January 1740 in Goshen, Conn.

123. Mary DIBBLE was born 30 May 1747 in Goshen, Conn.; probably died in Hull, Lower Canada, 24 August 1825, at age 78. On 14 February 1771, when she was 23, she probably married **Samuel BENEDICT** in Sharon, Vt.; born 23 April 1744 in Ridgefield, Fairfield Co., Conn.; died in Aylmer, Quebec, Canada, 30 August 1820, at age 76.[231]

They are said to have had the following children:

356	i.	Lucy (1772-)
357	ii.	David (1773-1807)
358	iii.	Miriam (1775-1834)
359	iv.	Samuel (1778-1869)
360	v.	Ezra (1780-1854)
361	vi.	Mary (1785-1796)
362	vii.	Rachel (1789-1870)
363	viii.	Hannah (1791-1812)

124. Cloe HILL[232] was born on 20 November 1733 in Wallingford, Conn.; died in Woodbury, Conn. on 30 September 1749, age 15.

125. Billious (aka Billie, aka Bellas) HILL,[233] second child and eldest of the four sons of Isaac and Ester (Stone) Hill, was born at Goshen, Litchfield Co., Conn., in 1738; died 17 October 1807, at New Haven, Addison Co., Vt., and was buried at the River Cemetery there. He was the first white child born in Goshen. He was probably born at the house of his uncle, Ebenezer Hill, in the south part of the town. He removed to Woodbury in about 1762 although his name appears in a survey of Goshen taken in 1770. He was a skilled woodworker, and he was a soldier in the Revolutionary War. He was also a Captain of Artificers and was responsible for the works at West Point.

On 9 August 1758 when he was about 20, he married, as her second husband, his first cousin **Lydia DIBBLE** (119), daughter of John DIBBLE and Lydia HILL (29), in Goshen, Litchfield Co., Conn.; born on 19 May 1731, probably in Wallingford, New Haven Co., Conn.; died in New Haven, Addison Co., Vt., 12 May 1805, she was 73. She was probably buried there in the River Cemetery, where her husband was buried two years later. She was the mother of three children by her first husband, Elijah Birge, and of four by her second husband, Billious Hill. (See her record *supra* in the descendants of John and Lydia [Hill] Dibble for her children by Elijah Birge).

Billious and Lydia (Dibble) Hill had the following children, numbered *supra* for Lydia (119):

351	i.	Mabel Leanna (~1758-)
352	ii.	Chloe (1759-1814)
353	iii.	William (1761-1761)
354	iv.	Reuben (1766-1833)
355	v.	Lydia (1769-)

126. Phineas HILL,[234] second son and third child of Isaac and Ester (Stone) Hill, was born about 1739, probably at Goshen, Litchfield Co., Conn.; died 2 November 1826, probably at Shelburne, Chittenden Co., Vermont. On 31 March 1784, when he was 45, he married in Litchfield, Litchfield Co., Conn., **Rhoda KILBOURNE** (aka Kilborn, aka Kilbourn), daughter of Giles and Chloe (Monger) Kilbourne; born at Litchfield, 9 March 1759; died, probably at Shelburne, Vt., after 1849, when she was 89 or older. They had five children.

Between 1786 and 1789, when his family was still young, he relocated to Shelburne, Vermont, when that town was still a wilderness. He built a cabin there during one season and his wife joined him in the following season, riding through the woods for five miles on a horse with a babe in arms and a bed strapped to the horse behind her. In 1791, he was a member of a committee that sought to find a place for a house of worship and meetinghouse, and in 1800 he was one of the founding members of the Methodist Church in Shelburne. He last appeared in the census records in Shelburne in 1810.

Phineas and Rhoda (Kilbourne) Hill had the following children:

364	i.	Kilbourn (Kilborn) (1786->1849)
365	ii.	Seymour (1788-1796)
366	iii.	Clarissa (1789-1821)
367	iv.	Rose (1792-)
368	v.	Olive Amanda (1800-1836)

127. Isaac HILL [Jr.],[235] third son and fourth child of Isaac and Esther (Stone) Hill, was probably born at Wallingford, New Haven County, Connecticut, 16 April 1740; died 1 April 1833, probably in Southbury, Conn. His death is recorded in the South Britain Congregational Church Records; South Britain was then part of Southbury.

Isaac Hill owned property in various towns in Connecticut during his nearly 93 years of life. In 1757, during the French and Indian War, he was a resident of Stratford and served for three years in the Stratford, Connecticut, militia. In the Revolutionary War he served in the fall of 1776 as a private in the Connecticut forces under Captain John Yates and Colonel Enos. Colonel (later General) Roger Enos was his cousin, although he may not have known this. Isaac Hill also served for three weeks in April 1781 under Captain Robert Lewis, and from June or July until 11 December 1781 he served under Colonel Zebulon Butler. At some time when he was "out of service," he developed measles and "lost one of his eyes."

In 1790 he was living in Fairfield County with a son and daughter. On 13 August 1832 he was a resident of Southbury, New Haven County, when he applied in Woodbury District Probate Court for a pension for service in the Connecticut militia in the Revolutionary War. His service number was S31747; the pension was granted. By 1832 he must have been one of the oldest surviving veterans of the French and Indian War and the Revolutionary War. He was a member of the South Britain Congregational Church in Southbury.

On 10 January 1834 the Clerk of the Court of Probate for the District of Woodbury certified that the original proceedings in the matter of the application of Isaac Hill for a pension were contained in the documents that were submitted and appeared above his signature and seal. The pension was to be paid at the rate of $15.66 per annum, commencing (retroactively) on 4 March 1831. The initial payment of $89.81 apparently included the arrears, and a semi-annual allowance for the period ending 4 September.

Isaac Hill married, at Stratford, Fairfield County, Connecticut, 29 September 1762, when he was 22, **Eunice MALLORY**,[236] daughter of Benajah and Elizabeth (Wakelee) Mallory; born 7 January 1747 at Stratford; died 8 January 1805, probably at Southbury, New Haven Co., or Shelton, Fairfield County, Conn. Isaac and Eunice (Mallory) Hill had nine, ten, or 11 children, according to various sources, the correct number apparently being 11. The births of six of the children are recorded at Shelton, Conn. Six of the children reached maturity.

They had the following children:

369	i.	Abraham Enoch (1763-1778)
370	ii.	Luke [3] (~1764-1838)
371	iii.	Esther (~1765-)
372	iv.	Isaac [5] (1772-1860)
373	v.	Benajah (1774-1862)
374	vi.	Seth [6] Slone (1776-1853)
375	vii.	Ephraim [2] (1778-1832)
376	viii.	Sally Betsey (1781-1828)
377	ix.	Dolly (1784-1784)
378	x.	VanAger [4] (~1785-)
379	xi.	Roswell (1788-1844)

128. **Abraham HILL**,[237] fourth son and fifth child of Isaac Hill Sr. and his wife Esther (Stone) Hill, was born between February 1740/41 and 6 November 1741, perhaps posthumously, in Goshen, Litchfield Co., Conn.; died in Carmel, Putnam Co., N.Y., 11 May 1817, at about age 76. He was buried in May 1817 in the Baptist Church Cemetery, Carmel, N.Y., his gravestone showing his age as "~ 70." His grave is in the midst of several Revolutionary War soldiers, all of which are festooned with flags on Memorial Day. Inasmuch as he lived for many years during and after the Revolutionary War in this part of Putnam County, and is buried with these Patriots, I would assume that he was considered a Patriot by them. However, proof of his participation in or support for the Revolutionary cause has not yet been found. He married **Hannah FERRIS**,[238] daughter of John FERRIS and Hannah MEAD, born about 1748; died in Carmel, N.Y., 5 June 1818, about 70.

They had the following children:

380	i.	Amy (1769-1818)
381	ii.	Elizabeth (1771-)
382	iii.	Ferris (1774-1863)
383	iv.	Annie (1779-)

384   v.   Samuel (1781-)

Line 5 (cont'd). Grandchild of Luke Hill Jr. and Deliverance Cooke

129. Luke Sherman BLACKMUN,[239] son of Andrew and Deliverance (Hill) Blackman, and only grandson of Luke Hill Jr. and his second wife Deliverance (Cooke) Falconer, was born on 12 January 1775 in Woodbury, Litchfield Co., Conn.; died in Mooers, Clinton Co., N.Y., 4 Oct 1855, age 80. He is said to have married **Sally FOSTER,** who was born in 1780 and died in 1827. They reportedly had one child:

385   i.   William Sherman (1816-1874)

Line 6 (continued). Grandchildren of Caleb and Abigail (Hill) Parmelee

130. Abigail PARMELEE,[240] eldest child of Caleb Parmelee Jr. and Elizabeth Foote, was born on 16 April 1721 in Branford, New Haven Co., Conn. In 1742, she married (1) **Cornelius JOHNSON,**[241] born 18 August 1705 in Branford, Conn.; died there, 31 December 1768, age 63. They had the following children:

386   i.   Cornelius (1744-)
387   ii.   Lemuel (1745-)
388   iii.   Caleb (1746-1771)
389   iv.   Ruphus (1747-)
390   v.   Orphana (1748-)

Abigail married (2) **Demetrius CRAMPTON.**[242]

131. Mary PARMELEE,[243] second child and second daughter of Caleb Parmelee Jr. and Elizabeth Foote, was born on 25 December 1722. On 2 August 1739 when she was 16, she married **Samuel BARNES** in Branford, New Haven Co., Conn.; born about 1714/15; christened on 13 February 1714/15. He was of East Haven, Conn. They had no progeny.

132. Sarah PARMELEE, third child and youngest daughter of Caleb Parmelee Jr. and Elizabeth Foote, was born on 16 October 1724 in Branford, Conn.; died in 1767, about age 42. She joined the Branford church on 30 August 1741. On 23 Nov 1744 when she was 20, she married **Timothy ALLEN** in Branford, Conn.; born 31 August 1715 in Norwich, New London Co., Conn.; died in Chesterfield, Mass., 12 January 1806, age 90.[244]

They had the following children:

391   i.   Parmelee [aka Parmlee, Parmalee] (1746-1806)
392   ii.   Caleb (1759-1804)

133. Jerusha PARMELEE, only child of Caleb Parmelee Jr. and Jemima Harrison, was born on 16 February 1729. In September 1747 when she was 18, she married **Stephen SMITH.**[245]

134. Chloe PARMELEE,[246] elder child of Caleb Parmelee Jr. and Mary Durham, was born on 2 April 1739.

135. Rebecca PARMELEE,[247] younger child of Caleb Parmelee Jr. and Mary Durham, was born on 12 April 1741.

Line 7 (cont'd). Grandchildren of Samuel and Elizabeth (Hill) Adams

136. Elizabeth GRIFFIN was born about 1709 in Simsbury, Conn.; died there in 1800, about age 91. She married **Nathaniel GRIFFIN,** son of Thomas GRIFFIN; born in 1706; died in 1786, about age 80.[248]

They had the following children:

393   i.   Elizabeth (1728-1801)

394	ii.	Chloe (1731-1805)
395	iii.	Nathaniel (1732-1790)
396	iv.	Stephen (1735-1803)
397	v.	Micah (1738-1815)
398	vi.	Elisha (1740-<1747)
399	vii.	Elisha (1747-)
400	viii.	Seth (1747-1817)
401	ix.	Martin (1754-1830)

137. Anna (Hannah) GRIFFIN was born on 26 July 1713 in Simsbury, Conn.; christened 26 September 1713. On 17 May 1736, she married **Ebenezer LOOMIS** in Simsbury.[249]

138. Silence GRIFFIN was born abt 1716 in Windsor, Hartford Co., Conn.; died after 1726.[250]

139. Ephraim GRIFFIN was born about 1718 in Windsor, Hartford Co., Conn. He chose Michael Humphrey as guardian on 6 March 1731/2. He married **Elizabeth TERRY**, daughter of John TERRY and Mary ROBE; born on 3 February 1724/5 in Simsbury, Hartford Co., Conn. Elizabeth was the sister of Solomon Terry, who married Ephraim's sister Sheba (140).[251]

140. Sheba (Phoebe, Pheba) GRIFFIN was born about 1722. She was the mother of 6, born at Simsbury between 1749-1759. She married **Solomon TERRY**, son of John TERRY and Mary ROBE; born on 5 March 1720 in Simsbury, Hartford Co., Conn. Solomon was the older brother of Elizabeth, who married Ephraim Griffin (139).[252]
They had the following children:

402	i.	Elizabeth (1749-)
403	ii.	Stephen (1751-1835)
404	iii.	4 unnamed children of Solomon and Sheba (Griffin)

Line 8 (continued). Grandchildren of John Hill

141. Joseph STRICKLAND[253] was born 10 May 1721 in Simsbury, Hartford Co., Conn.

142. Mary STRICKLAND[254] was born 23 October 1722 in Simsbury, Conn.

143. Sarah STRICKLAND was born 10 December 1724 in Simsbury, Conn.; died in East Windsor, Hartford Co., Conn., 13 May 1769, age 44. On 26 December 1753 when she was 29, she married **Timothy STRONG**, son of Jacob STRONG and Abigail BISSELL, in East Windsor, Hartford Co., Conn.; born in 1719 in Litchfield, Woodbury, Conn.; died in East Windsor, Conn. 19 August 1803, about age 84.[255]
They had the following children:

405	i.	Alexander (1754-1755)
406	ii.	Eli (1755-1825)
407	iii.	Sarah (1758-1806)
408	iv.	Samuel (1761-1821)
409	v.	David (1764-)

144. Hannah STRICKLAND[256] was born in September 1729 in Simsbury, Conn.

145. Elizabeth STRICKLAND[257] was born on 25 Jun 1731 in Simsbury, Conn.

146. Orpha STRICKLAND[258] was born 4 January 1733/4 in Simsbury, Conn.

147. John HILL [III],[259] eldest child and elder son of John Hill Jr. and his wife Jane Ladieu (aka Ladou, LaDou), was born 3 February 1725/6 in Simsbury, Conn.; died in Conn., 9 October 1795, age 71. He was buried in Oct 1795 in Canton, Conn. In about 1748 when he was about 22, he married (1) **Isabell ALFORD**, born in 1733 in Simsbury, Conn.
They had the following children:

| **410** | i. | John 4th (~1749-) |
| **411** | ii. | Mary (1753-) |

In about 1754 when he was about 28, he married (2) **Isabel EGGLESTON**, daughter of Jedediah EGGLESTON Sr. and Sarah MOORE; born 11 April 1732 in Windsor, Conn.; died in Canton, Conn., in 1818, about 85 years old.
They had the following children:

412	i.	Elijah (~1754-)
413	ii.	Chloe (~1755-)
414	iii.	Keziah (~1759-)
415	iv.	Anna (~1761-)
416	v.	Jedediah (1761-1841)
417	vi.	Wealthy (1767-1852)

148. Eleazer B. HILL,[260] second child and second son of John Hill Jr. and his wife Jane Ladieu, was born 21 October 1727 in Simsbury, Conn.; died after 1790. He married (1) **Aphia _____**; born about 1731 in New Hartford, Conn.
They had one child:

| **418** | i. | Jenny (1756-) |

He married (2) **Zervia B. _____** in about 1731. She was "of Simsbury," Conn.
They had the following children:

419	i.	Zeruiah (1763-)
420	ii.	Aphia (1764-)
421	iii.	Asenath (1766-)
422	iv.	Cynthia (1776-)
423	v.	Eleazer (~1778-)

149. Martha HILL,[261] third child and elder daughter of John Hill Jr. and his wife Jane Ladieu, was born 21 June 1730 in Simsbury, Conn.

150. Mary HILL,[262] fourth child and second daughter of John Hill Jr. and his wife Jane Ladieu, was born 28 February 1732 in Simsbury, Conn.; died there 12 November 1733, age 1.

151. Seth HILL,[263] elder son of John Hill Jr. and his wife Elizabeth _____, was born 20 October 1734 in Simsbury, Conn.; died there 18 Mar 1736, age 1.

152. Benoni HILL,[264] second child and second son of John Hill Jr. and his wife Elizabeth _____, was born 9 June 1736 in Simsbury, Conn.; died there 21 November 1737, age 1.

153. Sarah HILL, elder daughter and first child of John Hill Jr. and Abigail Wilcoxson, was born 6 January 1739/40 in Simsbury, Conn. She married _____ **DAILEY**, born about 1737.[265]

154. Phebe HILL, second daughter and second child of John Hill Jr. and his wife Abigail Wilcoxson, was born 17 July 1746 in Simsbury, Conn. She married **Hezekiah HARRINGDEN**, who was born about 1744.[266]

155. Darius HILL, third child and son of John Hill Jr. and his wife Abigail Wilcoxson, was born 4 December 1749 in Simsbury, Conn. He married **Lois MOSES**, born 5 December 1749.[267]
They had the following children:

424	i.	Lois (1770-)
425	ii.	Darius (1772-)
426	iii.	Arden (1775-)
427	iv.	Sarah (1778-)
428	v.	Elias (1780-)
429	vi.	Rachel (1784-)

> **430** vii. Asa (1787-)

156. Mary HILL, third daughter and fourth child of John Hill Jr. and his wife Abigail Wilcoxson, was born 18 August 1753. She married **Ozias CASE**.[268]

157. Mary REED (aka READ, READE),[269] eldest daughter and eldest child of Jacob and Mary (Hill) Reed, was born 10 January 1724/5 in Simsbury, Hartford Co., Conn. She was probably the mother of one child, who was brought up as a step-child in the family of her second husband. On 9 November 1752 when she was 28, she married (1) **Phinehas BUNCE**, son of James BUNCE and Elizabeth _____, in Simsbury, Hartford Co., Conn.; born about 1727/8 in Hartford, Hartford Co., Conn.; christened there 25 February 1727; probably died there before 1 February 1763, before he was 36. Phinehas Bunce was mentioned in the will of his father, made 19 December 1757 and proved 9 March 1762. Phinehas had died at Simsbury before 1 February 1763, when his widow Mary and her brother Titus Reade were appointed administrators. The widow Mary Edgerton was named in the will of her mother, Mary (Hill) Reade, who died May 1773 and had a probate distribution on 3 June 1775. The distribution included "Mary Edgerton wife of Jonathan Edgerton." Titus Read of Simsbury conveyed on 1 Nov 1780 land of her own patrimony, "she being now the wife of Jonathan Edgerton of Simsbury."
They had one child:

> **431** i. Mary (1753-1849)

In 1773 when Mary was 48, she married (2) **Jonathan EDGERTON**.

158. Lydia REED (aka READ, READE),[270] second child and second daughter of Jacob and Mary (Hill) Reed, was born 18 November 1726 in Simsbury, Hartford Co., Conn.; died there 1 October 1806, age 79. On 22 January 1746/7 when she was 19, she married **John BARBER**,[271] son of Samuel BARBER and Sarah HOLCOMB, in Simsbury. Born 4 December 1719 in Simsbury; died there 27 December 1797, age 78. He was the son of Samuel[3], Thomas[2], Thomas[1] in the "Barber Genealogy."
They had the following children:

> **432** i. Lydia (1747-1783)
> **433** ii. John (1749-1825)
> **434** iii. Sarah (1754-1761)
> **435** iv. Reuben (1755-)
> **436** v. Rhoda (1757-1761)
> **437** vi. Benjamin (1759-1836)
> **438** vii. Jonathan (1763-1817)
> **439** viii. Abel (1765-1817)

159. John READ,[272] eldest son and third child of Jacob and Mary (Hill) Reed, was born 20 June 1728 in Simsbury, Conn.; died before 1775.

160. Elizabeth REED (aka READ, READE),[273] third daughter and fourth child of Jacob and Mary (Hill) Reed, was b 27 April 1729 in Simsbury; died before 1775; married **John SEGAR**.
They probably had more than one child, whose names are unknown:

> **440** i. Children of John and Mary (Reade)

161. Jacob READE (aka REED, READ) Jr.,[274] second son and fifth child of Jacob and Mary (Hill) Reed, was born 20 August 1731 in Simsbury, Conn. On 7 December 1766 when he was 35, he married **Rebecca WOOD** of New Haven, Conn.
They had the following children, and perhaps more:

> **441** i. Jacob (1767-)
> **442** ii. Elizabeth (1769-)

443   iii.   Rhoda (1772-)

162. Sarah READE,[275] fourth daughter and sixth child of Jacob and Mary (Hill) Reed, was born in say Oct 1733 in Simsbury, Hartford Co., Conn.; died there, 11 Dec 1736, age 3.

163. Titus READE,[276] third son and seventh child of Jacob and Mary (Hill) Reed was born 9 January 1735/6 in Simsbury, Conn.; died there, 22 September 1788, age 52. In 1763 when he was about 27, he married **Amy CASE**, daughter of Noah CASE and Miriam HOLCOMBE, in Granby, Hartford Co., Conn.; born 1 November 1744 in Simsbury, Conn.; died 30 October 1782, age 37. She was probably the daughter of Richard Case, and surely a descendant of his father, John Case of Simsbury.

They had the following children:

444   i.   Titus (1765-)
445   ii.   David (1767-)
446   iii.   George (1769-)
447   iv.   Amy (1772-)
448   v.   Daniel (1774-)
449   vi.   Roswell (1776-1852)
450   vii.   Phinehas (1781-)
451   viii.   Ruth (1782-)

164. Silas READE (aka READ),[277] fourth son and eighth child of Jacob and Mary (Hill) Reed, was born 22 June 1738 in Simsbury, Conn. On 5 May 1763 when he was 24, he married **Thanks ADAMS** in Simsbury, Conn.

They had the following children:

452   i.   Orpha (1764-)
453   ii.   Ruth (1766-1775)
454   iii.   Hannah (1771-)
455   iv.   Alvin (1774-)

165. Sarah READE,[278] fifth daughter and ninth child of Jacob and Mary (Hill) Reed, was born 8 July 1740 in Simsbury, Conn. On 5 May 1763 when she was 22, she married **Joseph CASE** in Simsbury, Conn.; born 30 November 1722; died there, 13 February 1801, age 78.

166. Abijah READE,[279] fifth son and tenth child of Jacob and Mary (Hill) Reed, was born 13 July 1743 in Simsbury, Conn.; died after 1775.

167. Amy REED (aka READ, READE),[280] sixth daughter and eleventh child of Jacob and Mary (Hill) Reed, was born in Simsbury, Hartford Co., Conn.; died after 1775.

168. Ephraim WILCOX,[281] eldest son and eldest of the eight children of Ephraim and Hannah (Hill) Wilcox, was born 24 May 1727 in Simsbury, Hartford Co., Conn. He married **Ruhamah PINNEY**, who died in 1776.

They had the following children:

456   i.   Asa (1747-)
457   ii.   Chloe (1747-)
458   iii.   Jehiel (1751-1848)
459   iv.   Philander (1752-1813)
460   v.   Martin (1759-1813)

169. Susannah WILCOX,[282] elder daughter and second child of Ephraim and Hannah (Hill) Wilcox, was born 17 April 1731 in Simsbury, Conn.; died in Pownal, Vt., 15 March 1803, age 71. Three of her seven children had descendants. On 4 June 1755, when she was 24, she married **Michael JACKSON**, son of Joseph JACKSON and Esther NORMAN, in Simsbury,

Conn.; born 28 March 1735 in Canterbury, Conn.; died in Pownal, Vt., 24 October 1802, age 67. They had the following children:

461	i.	Lyman (1756-1835)
462	ii.	Esther (1758->1837)
463	iii.	Jesse (1760-1783)
464	iv.	Abigail (1762-1784)
465	v.	Ebenezer (1765-1839)
466	vi.	Keziah (1767-1811)
467	vii.	Mindwell (1769-1800)

Esther Jackson (462) married Isaiah J. Hendryx, who was a sergeant in the Continental Army in the Revolutionary War. Isaiah and Esther (Jackson) Hendryx were the parents of Susannah Hendryx (aka Hendrix), who married Josiah Riley; their son Simeon Riley m. Katherine Gillett, a descendant of Jonathan Gillett of Windsor, Conn.; their daughter Adelia Riley married Charles W. Hill, who was a descendant of Luke Hill Jr. The marriage of Adelia Riley and Charles Hill thus united descendants of Luke Hill Jr. and his younger brother John Hill.

170. Sylvanus WILCOX,[283] second son and third child of Ephraim and Hannah (Hill) Wilcox, was born 14 November 1733 in Simsbury, Conn.; died in Alford, Mass., 5 July 1821, age 87. In 1759 when he was about 25, he married **Chestina (Justina) CURTIS**, in Simsbury, Conn.; born in 1742 in Southington, Hartford Co., Conn.; died in Alford, Berkshire Co., Mass., 27 May 1816, about age 74. Seven of their ten children are said to have descendants.
They are reported to have had the following children:

468	i.	Israel (1776-1817)
469	ii.	Asenath (1760-1790)
470	iii.	Sylvanus (1762-1846)
471	iv.	Rufus (1764-1813)
472	v.	Reuben (1767-1849)
473	vi.	Ralph (1769-)
474	vii.	Oliver (1772-1831)
475	viii.	Chestina (1774-)
476	ix.	Lavina (1782-)
477	x.	Pluma (1783-)

171. Elnathan WILCOX, third son and fourth child of Ephraim and Hannah (Hill) Wilcox, was born 10 February 1734 in Killingworth, Middlesex Co., Conn.; died in East Bloomfield, Ontario Co., N.Y., 25 May 1826, at age 92. On 17 June 1761, when he was 27, he married **Hannah ADAMS** in Alford, Berkshire Co., Mass.; born in 1742 in East Bloomfield, N.Y.; died there, 14 September 1825, about age 83. Six of their eight children are said to have descendants.
They are reported to have had the following children:

478	i.	William (1761-1828)
479	ii.	Abigail (1762-1830)
480	iii.	Nathan (1763-1844)
481	iv.	Enoch (1765-1835)
482	v.	Ezra P. (1769-1832)
483	vi.	Smith (1774-1831)
484	vii.	Benjamin (1776-1859)
485	viii.	Polly (1779-1833)

172. Zachariah WILCOX, fourth son and fifth child of Ephraim and Hannah (Hill) Wilcox, was born in 1735 in Simsbury, Conn.; died in Conquest, Cayuga Co., N.Y. in 1821, about age 86. He married **Martha HILL**, whose ancestry is unknown.

173. Willard WILCOX, fifth son and sixth child of Ephraim and Hannah (Hill) Wilcox, was born in 1737 in Simsbury, Hartford Co., Conn.; died on 25 May 1825, about age 88.

174. Dijah WILCOX, sixth son and seventh child of Ephraim and Hannah (Hill) Wilcox, was born in 1739 in Conn.; died in Cayuga, Cayuga Co., N.Y. in 1805, about age 66. He is said to have married **Silence HAYS**, who was born in 1737.

They reportedly had the following children:

486	i.	Jedediah (1770-1823)
487	ii.	Jesse (1774-1841)
488	iii.	Stephen (1776-)
489	iv.	Jeremiah (1780-)
490	v.	Joseph (1791-1865)

175. Rosannah WILCOX, younger daughter and eighth child of Ephraim and Hannah (Hill) Wilcox, was born in 1741 in Simsbury, Hartford Co., Conn. Nothing more is known about her.

176. Joseph HOSKINS [Jr.][284] was born 21 January 1731 in Simsbury, Conn.; died in Winsted, Litchfield Co., Conn., in December 1818, about age 87. On 30 August 1761, when he was 30, he married **Eunice COE**, daughter of Ebenezer COE and Jane ELMER, in Torrington, Litchfield Co., Conn.; born 29 April 1742 in Torrington; died there, 23 February 1810, age 67. It is said that Eunice Coe's paternal grandmother was Barbara Parmelee, who was a descendant of John Parmelee Jr. of Guilford, Conn.

They had one child:

491	i.	Theodore (1766-1839)

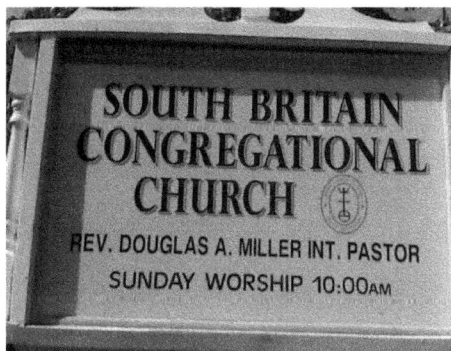

Fig. 4-1: South Britain Congregational Church, Southbury, Ct.
Isaac Hill Jr.'s death is recorded here (1833); his burial site is unknown
(photos by George J. Hill)

Fig. 4-2: Abraham Hill's grave,
Carmel, N.Y. (1817)

From Dennis O'Connell 2-2-04

5

Fifth Generation
Luke and Mary (Hout) Hill's Great-Great-Grandchildren

Line 1. Great-Grandchildren of Lydia Hill

177. Ebenezer BABCOCK[285] was born 17 January 1730 in Coventry, Tolland Co., Conn. On 26 August 1754, he m. **Hannah PRESTON** in Coventry; born 21 January 1734 in Windham, Windham Co., Conn. They had the following children:

492	i.	Benjamin (1755-1796)
493	ii.	Daniel (1756-1805)
494	iii.	Joseph (1758-1759)
495	iv.	Redolphus (1761-1762)
496	v.	Hannah (1763-1852)
497	vi.	Nathaniel (1765-1839)
498	vii.	Mary (1767-1768)
499	viii.	Ebenezer (1767-1808)
500	ix.	Tabitha (1770-1786)
501	x.	Elisabeth (1773-1789)
502	xi.	Lydia (1774-1803)
503	xii.	Esther (1776-1827)
504	xiii.	Olive (1779-1793)

178. William BABCOCK was born 1 May 1732 in Coventry, Conn.

179. Sarah BABCOCK was born 7 May 1734 in Coventry, Conn. On 1 March 1753, she married **Samuel PARKER** in Coventry; b. there about 1730; died in Peru, Berkshire Co., Mass., 1 May 1814. They had the following children:

505	i.	Marah (1754-1844)
506	ii.	William (1755-1791)
507	iii.	Sarah (1757-)
508	iv.	Samuel (1759-1844)
509	v.	Hannah (1761-)
510	vi.	Bettie (1763-)
511	vii.	Elias (1765-1813)
512	viii.	Daniel (1767-)
513	ix.	Triphene (1769-1842)
514	x.	Phebe (1771-1830)
515	xi.	Eli (1774-)

180. Hannah BABCOCK was born 8 October 1736 in Coventry, Conn.

181. Mary BABCOCK was born 19 October 1737 in Coventry, Conn.

182. Benjamin BABCOCK was born 28 January 1757 in Coventry, Conn.

183. Ruth JUDD[286] was born 10 March 1733 in Hartford, Conn.; died there, 9 Nov 1736, age 3.

184. Hannah JUDD was born 4 April 1731 in Hartford, Conn.; died there, 10 Nov 1736, age 5.

The eight children of Josiah and Mary (Palmer) Richards [287]

185. Hannah RICHARDS was born in 1739 in New Hartford, Litchfield Co., Conn. On 9 May 1759, she married **Solomon Damon BARKER** in Waterbury, New Haven Co., Conn.; born about 1737. They had one child:

516	i.	Theodore Theodorus (~1780-~1850)

186. Aaron RICHARDS was born 11 March 1743; died 28 November 1795. He married **Jerusha ALVORD**; born 10 March 1743; died 27 November 1793. It is remarkable, if true, that they were born within a day of each other and that their death dates, two years apart, were on successive days in the year.

187. Anna RICHARDS was born in 1748 in Hartford, Conn.; died there, 27 May 1780, about age 32.

188. Samuel RICHARDS was born 17 September 1735 in Goshen, Litchfield Co., Conn., and died in Connecticut. On 14 February 1754, he married **Mary BROWN** in Goshen, Conn. She was born in 1732. They had the following children:

517	i.	Clorinda (1755-1755)
518	ii.	Charity (1757-)
519	iii.	Abijah (1759-)

189. Daniel RICHARDS was born 20 June 1738 in Goshen, Conn.; died in Richfield, Otsego Co., N.Y., 19 May 1819, age 80. On 2 June 1763, when he was 24, he married **Ann RICHARDS** in Norfolk, Litchfield Co., Conn. She was born in 1743 and died in 1809, about age 66. They had the following children:

520	i.	Ann
521	ii.	Joseph
522	iii.	Lydia
523	iv.	Polly
524	v.	Sarah
525	vi.	Samuel (1765-1813)

190. Charles RICHARDS was born in 1742 in Goshen, Conn.; died there, 1 July 1817, about age 75. In 1770, when he was about 28, he married **Comfort CURTIS** in Connecticut. She was born in 1744 in Connecticut and died in 1825, about age 81. They had the following children:

526	i.	Chester (1770-)
527	ii.	Russell (1773-1853)
528	iii.	Mary (1774-1774)
529	iv.	Esther
530	v.	Enos (-1815)

191. Hanah RICHARDS was born 7 July 1746 in Goshen, Conn., apparently a twin of Abijah.

192. Abijah RICHARDS was born 7 July 1746 in Goshen, Conn.; died there in 1750, about age 3. He was apparently a twin of his sister Hanah.

The grandchildren of John and Susannah (Henbury) Frisbie are from Ancestry.com.[288]

193. John FRISBIE was born 1 December 1731 in Northford, Conn., and died in Harwinton, Conn., 1 Mar 1817, age 85. On 31 July 1760, when he was 28, he married **Freelove ROGERS**, who was born in 1737, and died in Harwinton, 25 May 1806, about age 69. They had the following children:

531	i.	Anna (1761-1825)
532	ii.	John (1762-1837)
533	iii.	Isaac (1764-1826)
534	iv.	Enos (1766-1829)
535	v.	Tryphena (1768-1799)
536	vi.	Adah (1769-1730)
537	vii.	Ezra (1771-1818)
538	viii.	Bede Beda (1774-1809)
539	ix.	Clarissa (1778-1837)

194. Jonathan FRISBIE was born 27 May 1734 in Northford, New Haven Co., Conn., and died in Middletown, Windsor Co., Vt., in September 1818, age 84. He also resided in Fort Edward, N.Y. He married **Anna MOSS**, who was born on 13 February 1750. They had the following children:

540	i.	Relief (1769-1822)

541	ii.	Anna (1777-)
542	iii.	Simeon (1781-1807)
543	iv.	Salome (1785-1811)
544	v.	Elizabeth (1788-)

195. William FRISBIE was born 14 February 1737 in Northford, Conn.; died in Middletown, Windsor Co., Vt., 1 Mar 1813, age 76. He resided in Woodbury, Conn., Stillwater, N.Y., and Middlebury, Vt. On 22 May 1769, when he was 32, he married **Sarah CAMPBELL**, in Stillwater, Saratoga Co., N.Y.; born 15 October 1745 in Voluntown, New London Co., Conn.; died in Stillwater, N.Y., 22 June 1772, age 26. They had one child:

545	i.	William (1769-1837)

196. Jacob FRISBIE was born in 1740; died in No. Branford, Conn.., 30 November 1823, about age 83. He married **Kezia BARKER**, born about 1743; died in No. Branford, Conn., on 9 Jul 1788, about age 45. They had the following children:

546	i.	Jacob (1767-1842)
547	ii.	Augustus (1768-)
548	iii.	Philemon (1772-)
549	iv.	Bede (1774-)
550	v.	Eli (1776-)
551	vi.	Eunice (1779-)
552	vii.	Salmon (1782-)

197. Elizabeth FRISBIE was born in 1744. She married ____**ROOT** of Stillwater, N.Y.

198. Joel FRISBIE was born in 1747. He resided in Rutland, Vt.

199. Simon FRISBIE was born 24 March 1743 in Branford, Conn., and died on 11 November 1777, age 34. On 11 February 1768, when he was 24, he married **Hannah MALTBY** in Wallingford, Conn.; born 25 September 1746 in Branford, Conn., and died on 7 Jan 1778, age 31. They had one child:

553	i.	Sarah (1795-)

200. Miriam FRISBIE was born 2 April 1746 in Branford, Conn.; died in Wolcott, Conn., 10 September 1824, age 78. She had eight children, all of whom married, and five of whom had descendants. On 11 March 1772 when she was 25, she married **Ozias NORTON** in Southington, Hartford Co., Conn.; born 10 February 1753 in Wolcott, Conn.; died there, 6 February 1840, age 86. They had the following children:

554	i.	Elizabeth (Twin) (1774-)
555	ii.	Susannah (Twin) (1774-1806)
556	iii.	Keziah (1776-1863)
557	iv.	Jonathan Fowler (1778-1849)
558	v.	Moses Frisbie (1780-)
559	vi.	Ziba (1782-)
560	vii.	Jedediah Harmon (1788-1874)
561	viii.	Simeon Newton (1791-1847)

201. Keziah FRISBIE was born 28 March 1748 in Branford, Conn.; died 31 January 1821, age 72. On 7 October 1772, when she was 24, she married **Samuel MUNSON** in Wallingford, New Haven Co., Conn.; born 8 December 1741 in Branford, Conn.; died in Wallingford, 18 August 1791, age 49.

202. Susannah FRISBIE was born 21 December 1750 in Branford, Conn.

203. Moses FRISBIE was born 30 September 1754 in Branford, Conn.

204. Elizabeth FRISBIE was born 6 June 1757 in Branford, Conn.; died there, 20 February 1827, age 69. On 15 January 1783, when she was 25, she married **Waitstill MUNSON** in Wallingford, New Haven Co., Conn.; born in 1755 in Branford, Conn. They had the following children:

562	i.	Russell (1784-)
563	ii.	Lucretia (1786-)

564	iii.	Sophia (1789-)
565	iv.	Unetia (1789-)
566	v.	Orpha (1792-)
567	vi.	Aaron (1796-)
568	vii.	Eli (1797-)
569	viii.	Chauncey (1806-)

205. James FRISBIE was born 22 April 1732.

206. Jonah FRISBIE was born 14 December 1734 in Branford, Conn.; died in Charleston, So. Car. On 27 September 1758, when he was 23, he married **Elizabeth HICKOK** in Durham, Conn.; born 17 September 1738 in Branford, Conn. Five of their ten children had descendants.
They had the following children:

570	i.	Timothy (1769-1842)
571	ii.	Thaddeus Granice (1760-)
572	iii.	Elizabeth (1761-)
573	iv.	Rachel (1763-)
574	v.	Jonah (1765-)
575	vi.	Dorcas (1767-1848)
576	vii.	James (1771-)
577	viii.	Asa (1776-1857)
578	ix.	Archibald (1777-)
579	x.	Satira

207. Chloe FRISBIE was born 1 January 1737; died 27 January 1749, at age 12.

208. Tamer FRISBIE was born 22 August 1739. On 5 May 1763, she married **Abraham PLANT.**

209. Chloe FRISBIE was born 31 May 1750. On 3 February 1773, she married **Isaac HALL**.

210. Israel FRISBIE was born 22 June 1754.

211. Solomon FROST, born 14 May 1742 in Woodbury, Conn.; died in Windsor, Broome Co., N.Y., 8 September 1838, age 96. He married **Thankful EDWARDS**, born 23 April 1742 in Middletown, Conn. They had one child:

580	i.	Sarah (1789-1845)

212. Reuben MATTHEWS was born 29 March 1743 in Wallingford, New Haven Co., Conn.; died in Cheshire, New Haven Co., Conn. 22 February 1777, age 33. On 31 October 1765, when he was 22, he married **Elizabeth McKEAN**.
They had the following children:

581	i.	Sarah (1767-)
582	ii.	William (1772-)
583	iii.	Reuben (1774-)
584	iv.	Ruth Elizabeth (1776-)

213. Aaron MATTHEWS was born in 1744 in Camden, N.Y.; died in Camden, Oneida Co., N.Y., in 1802, about age 58. He married **Hannah TUTTLE**, born 4 January 1747 in Wallingford, New Haven Co., Conn.; died in New York in 1813, about age 65. Hannah (Tuttle) Matthews is said in OWT to be the mother of 3, but the children named (Lucy, Darius, and Lyman) do not look likely for this family.

214. Samuel MATTHEWS was born on 23 February 1761 in Wallingford, New Haven Co., Conn., and died in 1812, about age 50. He is said to have married **Marne CATLIN**, who was born in 1744. OneWorldTree says she was the mother of Randal, Caroline, and Samuel.

The children of Elijah and Abigail (Culver) Frisbie are from Jacobus, *Ancient New Haven*[289]

215. Esther FRISBIE was born in 1743 and died in 1795, about age 52.

216. Judah FRISBIE was born 13 September 1744 in Branford, Conn.; died in Wolcott, Conn. on 27 January 1817, age 72. On 12 August 1779, when he was 34, he married **Hannah BALDWIN,** daughter of Israel BALDWIN; born in 1746 in Waterbury, Conn.; died in Wolcott, Conn., 27 Aug 1829, age 83.
They had the following children:

585	i.	Mary (1780-1852)

586	ii.	David (1782-1829)
587	iii.	Hannah (1783-1816)

217. Reuben FRISBIE was born 8 August 1746 in Branford, Conn.; died in Wolcott, Conn., 10 September 1824, age 78. On 25 May 1769, when he was 22, he married (1) **Hannah WAKELEE** in Waterbury, Conn.; born 16 February 1751 in Waterbury, Conn.; died there 22 November 1778, age 27. They had the following children:

588	i.	Elizabeth (1769-1857)
589	ii.	Daniel (1771-1850)
590	iii.	Ebenezer (1773-1835)
591	iv.	Abigail (1775-)

On 3 Jun 1779 when Reuben was 32, he married (2) **Ruth SEWARD**, who was born in 1755 and died in Waterbury, Conn., in 1833, about age 78. They had the following children:

592	i.	Ruth
593	ii.	Sally
594	iii.	Samuel
595	iv.	Polly (1784-)

218. Abigail FRISBIE was born in 1746 in Branford, Conn. On 26 January 1769, when she was about 23, she married **Dan TUTTLE** in Waterbury, Conn.; born 27 November 1746 in Wallingford, Conn.; died in Camden, N.Y. in 1816, about age 69. They had the following children:

596	i.	Abigail
597	ii.	Benoni
598	iii.	Hannah
599	iv.	Levi
600	v.	Nancy
601	vi.	Lyman (1769-1813)
602	vii.	Solomon (1773-)
603	viii.	Zophar (1776-)
604	ix.	Lucinda (1780-)
605	x.	Lucy (1796-1847)

219. Charles FRISBIE was born in 1752.

220. Hannah Amelia FRISBIE was born in 1738 in Branford, Conn.; died in Stafford, Tolland Co., Conn. in 1810, about age 72. On 26 March 1778, when she was about 40, she married **Elnathan THRASHER** in Waterbury, Conn.; born in 1750 in Taunton, Bristol Co., Mass.; died in Oneida, N.Y., in 1810, about age 60. They had the following children:

606	i.	John (1779-1856)
607	ii.	Abigail Lucy (1781-1855)

221. Sarah FRISBIE was born 13 March 1756 in Wolcott, New Haven Co., Conn.; died in Waterbury, Conn., in March 1842, about age 85. On 23 December 1780, when she was 24, she married **Ichabod MERRILL** in Waterbury, Conn.; born 17 June 1754 in Waterbury; died there, 24 Dec 1829, age 75. They had the following children:

608	i.	Prudence (1782-)
609	ii.	Elijah Frisbie (1788-1852)
610	iii.	Sarah (1791-1813)

222. John FRISBIE was born 8 April 1762 in Waterbury, Conn.; died in Wolcott, New Haven Co., Conn., 1 August 1846, age 84. On 4 January 1787, when he was 24, he married **Rosannah ALCOTT**, daughter of James ALCOTT and Hannah BARNES, in Wolcott, Conn.; born in 1769 in Wolcott; died there, 18 August 1830, about age 61. They had the following children:

611	i.	Amanda
612	ii.	Esther
613	iii.	Ira (-1863)
614	iv.	Levi Collins (1788-1852)
615	v.	James (1799-1862)
616	vi.	Parlia N. (1801-)

223. Susannah GAYLORD was born in 1749 and is said to have died in the same year.

224. Hannah GAYLORD was born on 6 Sep 1749 and died in Cheshire, New Haven Co., Conn., 15 July 1791, age 41. It is possible that Susannah and Hannah are two names for the same person. On 21 April 1774, when she was 24, she married **Reuben BRADLEY** in Cheshire, Conn.; born 30 May 1750 in Wallingford, Conn.; died 7 Jan 1827, age 76.

225. John GAYLORD was born in February 1750 and died in 1750 in Cheshire, Conn.

226. Benjamin GAYLORD[290] was born 25 February 1755 in New Haven, Conn.; died 26 March 1825, age 70. On 4 January 1776, he married **Phebe IVES**, daughter of Jonathan IVES and Thankful COOPER, in Hamden, New Haven, Conn.; born 8 February 1757 in New Haven.; died in 1824, about 66. They had the following children:

617	i.	Merab (1777-1794)
618	ii.	Alling (1778-1794)
619	iii.	Russell (1782-1869)
620	iv.	Loly (1785-1794)
621	v.	Alva (Allen) (1793-1862)
622	vi.	Chester (1796-1852)
623	vii.	Milly (1798-1803)

227. Elizabeth GAYLORD was born in April 1756 and died in same month.

The children of Benjamin and Elizabeth (Pardee) Frisbie are in Jacobus, *Ancient New Haven*[291]

228. Hephzibah FRISBIE was born 19 October 1726 in Wallingford, Conn.

229. James FRISBIE was born on 29 October 1793 in Wallingford, Conn.

230. Jabez FRISBIE was born 30 November 1730 in Wallingford, Conn.

231. Elizabeth FRISBIE was born 2 November 1732 in Wallingford, Conn.

232. Jerusha FRISBIE was born 25 February 1734/5 in Wallingford, Conn.; she was christened in Feb 1734/5 in Cheshire, Conn.

233. Mary FRISBIE was born about 1737 in Cheshire, Conn., and was christened there in April 1737.

234. Benjamin FRISBIE was born on 16 February 1739. He died in the French and Indian War on 30 August 1758, at age 19.

235. Joseph FRISBIE was born on 3 January 1741.

236. Jerusha IVES[292] died in 1805. She married in 1761, as his second wife, **Wise BARNES**, son of Israel BARNES and Mary WISE, who was born in 1720. Wise Barnes married (1) at Branford, Conn., 8 January 1753, Hannah Bartholomew, by whom he had Mary (b. 1750), Wise (b. 1754), Hannah (b. 1756), and Israel (b. 1758). Descendants are known only of Joel 2d, b. 1773, who m. Lucinda Wheeler in 1790 and had a son Sherman Barnes (b. 1793). They had the following children:

624	i.	Elijah
625	ii.	Jerusha
626	iii.	Joel
627	iv.	Joel (1773-)

The children of Benjamin and Jerusha (Frisbie) Gaylord are known only from Ancestry.com[293]

237. Levi GAYLORD was born in 1730.

238. Jersusha GAYLORD was born in 1731.

239. Enos GAYLORD was born 26 January 1733 in Wallingford, New Haven Co., Conn., and died in January 1834 at the age of 100.

The children of Zebulon and Lucy (Lewis) Frisbie are in Jacobus, *Ancient New Haven.*[294]

240. Lucy FRISBIE was born 14 January 1741/2 in Farmington, Hartford Co., Conn.; died in Wolcott, Conn., 11 December 1823, age 82.

241. Mary FRISBIE was born 6 August 1745 in Farmington, Conn.; died there, 22 August 1757, age 12.

242. Elizabeth FRISBIE was born 24 September 1747 in Farmington, Conn.

243. Lola "Lowly" FRISBIE was born 8 November 1749 in Farmington, Conn.

244. Zebulon FRISBIE was born 2 May 1752 in Farmington, Conn.; died in Burlington, Hartford Co., Conn., in 1836, about age 83. He married **Susanna HOTCHKISS**, who was born 20 July 1752. They had one child:

    628   i.   Gad (1778-1854)

245. Levi FRISBIE was born in Jul 1753 and died on 16 Nov 1755, age 2.

246. Abel FRISBIE was born 30 November 1755.

247. Levi [2nd] FRISBIE was born 31 January 1759 in Farmington, Conn.; died in Orwell, Pa., 5 October 1842, age 83. In September 1786, he married **Phebe GAYLORD**; born 19 November 1767 in Bristol, Hartford, Conn.; died in Orwell., 5 Oct 1852, age 84. Two of their five children had descendants. They had the following children:

    629   i.   Chauncey (1787-1864)
    630   ii.   Laura (1790-1879)
    631   iii.   Catherine (1792-1822)
    632   iv.   Levi Randall (1797-1797)
    633   v.   Zebulon (1801-1881)

248. Daniel FRISBIE was born in 1761 in Farmington, Conn.[295]

249. Samuel FRISBIE was born 24 August 1763 in Farmington, Conn.; died in Vernon, N. Y., 19 August 1831, age 67.

The children of Theodore Frisbie[296]

250. Levi FRISBIE, only child of Theodore and Phyllis (___) Frisbie, was born on 6 or 13 Feb 1757 in Wallingford, Conn.

251. Theodore FRISBIE, eldest child of Theodore and Mehitabel (Wheeler) Frisbie, was born 7 August 1759 in Wallingford, Conn.; died in Bristol, Hartford Co., Conn., 9 October 1830, age 71.

252. Luman FRISBIE, second son and second child of Theodore and Mehitabel (Wheeler) Frisbie, was born on 23 Nov 1760 in Wallingford, Conn. He married **Anna PARKER**, daughter of Eldad PARKER and Thankful BELLAMY; born 1 January 1760 in Wallingford, Conn. They had the following children:

    634   i.   Joel
    635   ii.   Levi
    636   iii.   Mehitabel
    637   iv.   Hiram (~1794-)
    638   v.   Eldad (~1794-)
    639   vi.   Luman (~1796-)

253. Mary FRISBIE, daughter and third child of Theodore and Mehitabel (Wheeler) Frisbie, was born 10 October 1763 in Wallingford, Conn.; died there, 21 December 1774, age 11.

Line 2. Great-Grandchildren of Mary Hill[297]

254. Deslah WILCOX was b. 2 March 1739 in Simsbury, Hartford Co., Conn.; d. in Norfolk, Litchfield Co., Conn. She m. **Asaph HUMPHREY**; born 16 May 1732 in Simsbury; died 10 May 1774, age 41. They had one child:

    640   i.   Sarah

255. Elisha WILCOX was born 25 November 1728 in Simsbury, Conn.; died there, 8 October 1812, age 83. In 1748, when he was 19, he married (1) **Abigail CORNISH** in Connecticut; born 5 May 1733 in Simsbury; d. 2 August 1796, age 63.

They had the following children:

641	i.	James
642	ii.	Abigail (1754-1833)
643	iii.	Azariah (1756-1814)
644	iv.	Elisha (1758-1831)
645	v.	Chloe (1760-1835)
646	vi.	Simeon (1764-1825)
647	vii.	Roswell (1764-1831)
648	viii.	George (1768-1842)
649	ix.	Amos (1769-1794)
650	x.	Ozias (1770-1835)

Elisha married (2) **Esther HILL**, whose ancestry is unknown, and who apparently died without progeny.

256. Hannah WILCOX was born 31 July 1732 in Simsbury, Conn.; died 26 August 1802, age 70. In 1750, when she was 17, she is said to have married (1) **Joseph MALLISON** in Connecticut; born in 1728 in Simsbury. In the same year, 1750, when Hannah was 17, she is also said to have married (2) **Elijah CASE** in Simsbury; born in 1726 in Simsbury; died in 1810, age 84. The first marriage may be spurious. Hannah Wilcox and Elijah Case had the following children:

651	i.	Reuben (1755-)
652	ii.	Hannah (1752-1842)
653	iii.	Desiah (1757-1834)
654	iv.	Elijah (1757-)
655	v.	Gabriel (1760-1793)
656	vi.	Asaph (1762-)
657	vii.	Rosette (1766-)
658	viii.	William Palmer (1773-)

257. Mary WILCOX was born 2 September 1734 in Simsbury, Conn.; died in West Simsbury, Hartford Co., Conn., in 1816, age 81. She married **Daniel MOSES**, born 22 June 1729 in Simsbury; died there 8 September 1778, age 49.
They had the following children:

659	i.	Daniel (1758-1805)
660	ii.	Mary (1775-)
661	iii.	Sybil (1763-1854)
662	iv.	Zebina (1764-1815)
663	v.	Lois (1766-1781)
664	vi.	Roger (1767-1828)
665	vii.	Hannah (1769-)
666	viii.	Charlotte (1771-)

258. Lydia WILCOX was born 4 March 1737 in Simsbury, Conn.; died 3 January 1750, age 12.

259. Rachel WILCOX was born 19 March 1743 in West Simsbury, Hartford Co., Conn.; died there in 1817, about 73. On 4 December 1760, at age 17, she m. **Jonathan LATIMER** in West Simsbury; b.13 September 1738 in Wethersfield, Hartford Co., Conn.; d. in West Simsbury in 1826, about 87.
They had the following children:

667	i.	Jonathan (1764-1852)
668	ii.	Lodama (1766-1792)
669	iii.	Rachel (1769-1816)
670	iv.	Sophia (1772-1827)

260. Aaron WILCOX was born 29 March 1745 in Simsbury, Conn. On 17 May 1767, when he was 22, he married **Irana BARNARD** in Simsbury; born 23 October 1747 in Simsbury, Conn.
They had the following children:

671	i.	Borden
672	ii.	Joshua

673	iii.	Philander
674	iv.	William
675	v.	Aaron (1769-1835)
676	vi.	Frederic (1771-1860)
677	vii.	Riverious (1773-)

261. Ziba WILCOX was born 30 June 1749 in Simsbury, Conn.; died in West Simsbury in 1808, about age 58. In 1767, when she was 17, she married **Giles LATIMER** in Connecticut; born in 1745 in Simsbury; died in West Hartford, 22 June 1829, about age 84.
They had one child:

678	i.	Garner

262. Richard Saxton ADAMS was born 16 March 1734 in Simsbury, Conn.; died 23 December 1726 in Hartford, Conn. On 23 December 1762, when he was 28, he married **Lucy MATSON** in Simsbury; born 5 November 1741 in Simsbury; d. in Hartford in 1805, about 63. Four of their children had descendants.
They had the following children:

679	i.	Daniel (1763-1804)
680	ii.	Joseph (1766-)
681	iii.	Richard Saxton (1768-1798)
682	iv.	Lucy (1771-1845)
683	v.	Son (1773-)
684	vi.	Joshua (1780-1863)

263. Lucy ADAMS was born 14 June 1736 in Simsbury, Conn.; died there, 6 January 1801, age 64. In 1756, when she was 19, she married **Martin CASE** in Simsbury; born 2 November 1730 in Simsbury; died there, 18 Apr 1827, he was 96. All of their children married and four had descendants.
They had the following children:

685	i.	Martin (1758-1774)
686	ii.	Roswell (1760-1835)
687	iii.	Mary (1762-1821)
688	iv.	Sybil (1765-1844)
689	v.	Lucy (1766-)
690	vi.	Orpha (1769-)

264. Daniel ADAMS was born 15 November 1738 in Simsbury; died in New Haven, Conn., 20 November 1758, age 20.

265. [Child] ADAMS was born 12 December 1740 in Simsbury; died there, 7 June 1741. Died as an infant, name unknown.

266. Thanks ADAMS was born 16 April 1742 in Simsbury; died in Granby, Hartford Co., Conn., in 1816, age 73. On 5 May 1763, when she was 21, she married **Silas READ** in Simsbury; born 22 June 1737 in Simsbury; died in Granby, 22 Mar 1825, age 87.
They had the following children:

691	i.	Orpha (1764-)
692	ii.	Ruth (1766-1775)
693	iii.	Hannah (1771-)
694	iv.	Alvin (1774-)

267. Elizabeth ADAMS was born 4 February 1745 in Simsbury, Conn.; said to have died in Fairfield, Fairfield Co., Conn., 20 December 1833, age 88. On 2 June 1764, when she was 19, she married **Elisha BARBER** in Simsbury; born 21 August 1742 in Windsor, Hartford Co., Conn.; said to have died in Fairfield, Franklin Co., Vt., 30 November 1806, age 64. The location of death of either Elizabeth or Elisha may have been entered incorrectly.
They had one child:

695	i.	Elisha Westover (1767-)

268. Parmenio (aka Permena, Pernene) ADAMS was born 22 January 1747 in Hartford, Conn.; died in Lysander, N.Y., 18 March 1809, age 62. On 7 May 1772, when he was 25, he married **Chloe NEARING**

in Simsbury, Conn.; born in 1754 in Simsbury, died in Albany, Albany Co., N.Y., 17 May 1787, age 33. They had seven sons, all of whom married; six had descendants.

They had the following children:

696	i.	Charlora (1773-1829)
697	ii.	Alexander (1775-1810)
698	iii.	Parmenio (1776-1832)
699	iv.	John (1778-1857)
700	v.	Dan (1780-1812)
701	vi.	James (1783-1843)
702	vii.	Truman (1785-1832)

269. Oliver ADAMS was born 3 April 1750 in Simsbury, Conn.; died in Bloomfield, Ontario Co., N.Y., 31 March 1804, age 53. He married **Susannah _____**.

270. John ADAMS was born 19 August 1752 in Simsbury; died 4 November 1778, age 26.

271. Mary ENO was born 4 August 1727 in Simsbury, Hartford Co., Conn.; died in Granby, Hartford Co., Conn., 14 October 1804, age 77. She is said to have married twice and had four children by her first husband, of whom three had descendants, and ten children by her second husband, of whom six had descendants. The births of children by her first husband overlap those of her second husband, so it is likely that there is an error in recording of the marriages. In the absence of clear information to confirm one marriage or the other, I will list both as they appear in the published record. In 1747, when she was about 19, she is said to have married (1) **Beriah HILLS** in Goshen, Conn.; born 31 August 1727 in Durham, Middlesex Co., Conn.; died in Winchester, Litchfield Co., Conn., 25 March 1778, age 50.

They had the following children:

703	i.	Mary (1748-)
704	ii.	Lois (1752-)
705	iii.	Chauncey (1754-)
706	iv.	Roger Eno (1755-1833)

On 2 Apr 1752 when she was 24, she is said to have married (2) **Abel PHELPS** in Simsbury, Conn.; born 22 May 1730 in Simsbury; died in Granby, Hartford Co., Conn., 3 January 1805, age 74.

They had the following children:

707	i.	Mary (1754-)
708	ii.	Mehitable (1756-)
709	iii.	Abel (1756-)
710	iv.	Achsah (1758-)
711	v.	Mindwell (1760-1835)
712	vi.	Sarah (1765-1840)
713	vii.	Cynthia (1767-)
714	viii.	Candis (1769-)
715	ix.	James Enos (1771-1822)
716	x.	Benjamin (1773-1848)

272. Major General Roger ENOS Sr.,[298] elder son and second of the five children of David and Mary (Gillett) Eno, was born in 1729 in Simsbury, Hartford Co., Conn.; died at Colchester, Vt., 6 October 1808. He was buried in Greenmount Cemetery, Burlington, Chittenden Co., Vt. He was a lieutenant colonel in the Continental Army and later a major general in the Vermont militia. Enosburg, Vermont, is named for him. He was the father-in-law of Ira Allen.

In 1759 Enos joined the Connecticut militia for the French and Indian War and was commissioned as an Ensign. He was promoted to Lieutenant and became Adjutant of his regiment in 1761. He was promoted to First Lieutenant in 1762 and served in the British expedition against Cuba during the Seven Years War. In 1764 he was promoted to Captain in Israel Putnam's regiment. At the start of the Revolution, Enos was appointed the 22nd Regiment's Lieutenant Colonel for General Benedict Arnold's 1775 Canada expedition.

In September 1775, then-Lt. Col. Roger Enos led the last group of Continental Army troops under the command of Benedict Arnold on an expedition through what is now Maine in an attempt to conquer the British Province of Quebec. The first group departed on 25 September. Arnold's expedition was ultimately a failure. The troops encountered severe weather and heavy flooding, and on 22-25 October several meetings were held as the troops and their leaders tried to decide what to do. Enos voted to proceed but he was pressed by his captains to withdraw. After giving Greene's men some of his supplies, Enos and 450 men turned back. Enos and his detachment arrived back in Cambridge late in November. Enos was court-martialed, charged with "quitting his commanding officer without leave." He was acquitted, but he resigned his commission and saw no more service in the war.

He resigned his Continental Army commission in 1776 and moved to Windsor, Vermont, where he was appointed Colonel in command of a regiment. In the 1780s he was a proprietor of the towns of Waitsfield and Enosburg. In 1781 he was appointed Brigadier General and commander of the Vermont militia. When Vermont reorganized its militia, Enos was appointed commander and Major General of its 1st Division. In 1791 he relocated to Colchester and resigned his commission. Enos was a Member of the Vermont Board of War from 1781 to 1792, served in the Vermont House of Representatives, and was a Trustee of the University of Vermont. He was the father in law of Ira Allen, a founder of Vermont.

On 10 March 1763, when he was 34, he married **Jerusha HAYDEN** in Windsor, Vt.; born 23 November 1739 in Windsor, Conn.; died 20 March 1830, at the home of her daughter, Jerusha Hayden (Enos) Allen, in Irasburg, Vt., at age 90. Her ancestry, according to Orrin Peer Allen, was: Jerusha[5], Daniel[4], Daniel[3], Daniel[2], William[1] Hayden. Roger and Jerusha (Hayden) Enos had four children, Jerusha Hayden (1764-1838), who married General Ira Allen and had descendants; Sibil (1766-1796), who married Roger Bissell and d.s.p.; Roger (1768-1849), who married Emily Paddock and had one child; and Elizabeth (1774-).
They had the following children:

717	i.	Jerusha Hayden (1764-1838)
718	ii.	Sibil (1766-1796)
719	iii.	Roger (1768-1849)
720	iv.	Elizabeth (1774-)

273. Mercy ENO was born in 1734 in Simsbury, Conn.; died in New Britain, Conn. On 12 December 1754, when she was 20, she married **John LANGDON** in New Britain, Conn.; born in 1729 in Simsbury, Hartford Co., Conn.; died in New Britain, Conn., 5 January 1791, age 62.
They had the following children:

721	i.	Sarah (1756-1822)
722	ii.	Hannah (1771-1792)
723	iii.	Abi (1775-1807)

274. Jonathan ENO was born in 1739 in Windsor, Hartford Co., Conn.; died in Simsbury, Conn., 4 December 1813, age 74. On 7 January 1765, when he was 26, he married **Mary HART** in Windsor, Conn.; born 26 December 1744 in Simsbury; died there, 8 October 1834, age 89. They had four children, all of whom had descendants.
They had the following children:

724	i.	Jonathan (1769-1821)
725	ii.	Elizabeth (1773-1868)
726	iii.	Cynthia (1777-1804)
727	iv.	Chauncey (1782-1845)

275. Abigail ENO was born in 1740 in Simsbury, Conn.; died 5 January 1782, about age 42, without progeny. On 2 April 1760, when she was 20, she married **Martin NORTH** in Torrington, Conn.; born 13 December 1734 in Berlin, Hartford Co., Conn.; died in Colebrook, Conn., in 1806, about age 71.

276. Daniel GAINES was b. 5 September 1732 in Simsbury, Hartford Co., Conn. He married **Damaris HOLCOMB**, b. in 1724 in Granby, Hartford Co., Conn.; d. in Southwick, Hampden Co., Mass., 29 April 1797, about age 73. They had eight children, none of whom are known to have had descendants.
They had the following children:

728	i.	Damaris

729	ii.	Daniel
730	iii.	Eunice
731	iv.	Lois
732	v.	Lucretia
733	vi.	Lydia
734	vii.	Lyman
735	viii.	Samuel

Line 3. Great-grandchildren of Eleazer Hill

277. Benjamin HILL was born in 1767. He is not known to have descendants, and this line of descent from Luke and Mary (Hout) Hill thus comes to an end.[299]

Line 4. Great-Grandchildren of Tahan Hill[300]

278. Daniel PARMELEE was born 22 June 1739 in Killingworth, Middlesex Co., Conn.; died 6 May 1800, age 60. He also lived in Claremont, N.H. On 2 January 1763, when he was 23, he married (1) **Mary NETTLETON**.
They had the following children:

736	i.	David (1763-)
737	ii.	Nathan (1766-)
738	iii.	Daniel (1770-)
739	iv.	Bela (1776-)

Daniel married (2) **Damaris PIERSON**, who was born 27 August 1753.

279. Jerusha PARMELEE[301] was born 23 May 1741 and died in 1819, about age 77. On 16 April 1761, when she was 19, she married **Caleb BALDWIN** in Killingworth, Middlesex Co., Conn.; born in 1723 and died in 1823, apparently a centenarian.
They had the following children:

740	i.	Lois (1763-1804)
741	ii.	Eleazer (1764-1835)
742	iii.	Jerusha (1765-1775)
743	iv.	Daniel (1767-1862)
744	v.	Barbara (1769-1770)
745	vi.	Ezra (1771-1772)
746	vii.	Caleb (1776-1836)
747	viii.	Philemon (1778-1857)
748	ix.	Jemima (1780-1781)

280. Samuel PARMELEE was born 6 April 1743 in Killingworth, Conn.; died there, 12 June 1808, age 65. He married **Lois HULL**.
They had one child:

749	i.	Parnel (1769-)

281. Ezra PARMELEE was born 25 August 1745 in Killingworth, Conn.; died in Newport, Sullivan Co., N.H., 18 January 1838, age 92. He married **Sybil HILL**. She was a descendant of John Hill, the emigrant, not Luke Hill Sr.
They had one child:

750	i.	James Hill (1783-1872)

282. Oliver PARMELEE was born 19 March 1748 in Killingworth, Conn.; died in Claremont, Sullivan Co., N.H., 20 April 1821, age 73.

283. Jemima PARMELEE was born 8 August 1750 in Killingworth, Conn.; m. **Peter PARMELEE**.

284. Justin PARMELEE was born in 1750.

285. Elias PARMELEE was born 29 March 1752 in Killingworth, Conn.; died in LeRoy, N.Y., 17 June 1829, age 77. He married **Thankful HILL**, who was born in February 1756 and died 9 October 1799,

age 43. She was a descendant of John Hill, the emigrant, not Luke Hill Sr.
They had the following children:

751	i.	Barbara (1778-)
752	ii.	Hannah (1782-)
753	iii.	Lemuel (1786-)
754	iv.	Elias Harvey (1789-)
755	v.	Thankful (1795-)

286. Hiel PARMELEE was born 23 January 1756 in Killingworth, Conn.; died in Springfield, Otsego Co., N.Y., 23 October 1836, age 80.

Line 5. Great-Grandchildren of Luke Hill Jr. and Hannah Butler

287. Capt. Ambrose HILL,[302] eldest of the seven children of Ensign Ebenezer Hill Jr. and Elizabeth Baldwin, was born at Goshen, Litchfield Co., Conn., 21 March 1743; died in Vermont, or perhaps at Stephentown, N.Y., 10 October 1764. He was a soldier in the Massachusetts militia in the Revolutionary War. He married, at Goshen, Conn., 10 October 1764, **Lucia "Lucy" BEACH** (or Beech), daughter of Edmund and Mary (Deming) Beach; born at Goshen, 27 January 1746; died in Vermont.[303]

It is interesting, but apparently coincidental, that his name is similar that of a famous Confederate officer, Lt. Gen. Ambrose Powell ("A. P.") Hill (1825-1865) [Jr.]. General Hill's ancestry is entirely Virginian, going back to William Russell Hill (1684-1759) and there is apparently no connection in America between Gen. A. P. Hill and Captain Ambrose Hill, a descendant of Luke Hill of Connecticut.
They had the following children:

| 756 | i. | Reuben (1765-1858) |
| 757 | ii. | Electa (1777-1860) |

288. Ebenezer HILL Jr.,[304] second son and second child of Ensign Ebenezer Hill Jr. and Elizabeth Baldwin, was born at Goshen, Conn., 27 August 1746; died there, 3 March 1753, age 6.

289. Samuel HILL,[305] third son and third child of Ensign Ebenezer Hill Jr. and Elizabeth Baldwin, was born at Goshen, Conn., 6 October 1748; died there, 7 October 1766, age 18.

290. Reuben HILL,[306] fourth son and fourth child of Ensign Ebenezer Hill Jr.and Elizabeth Baldwin, was born at Goshen, Conn., 26 March 1751; died there, 24 March 1765, age 13.

291. Chloe (Cloe) HILL,[307] elder daughter and fifth child of Ensign Ebenezer Hill Jr. and Elizabeth Baldwin, was born at Goshen, Conn., 19 February 1754.

292. Ebenezer HILL Jr. [II],[308] fifth son and sixth child of Ensign Ebenezer Hill Jr.and Elizabeth Baldwin, was born at Goshen, Conn., 4 November 1756.

293. Lucina HILL,[309] younger daughter and seventh child of Ensign Ebenezer Hill Jr.and Elizabeth Baldwin, was born at Goshen, Conn., 29 July 1761.

The children of Asa Hill and Elizabeth Richards are from Jacobus, *Ancient New Haven*[310]

294. Jonah HILL,[311] son and eldest child of Asa and Elizabeth (Richards) Hill, was born 15 January 1746 in Goshen, Conn. On 5 May 1768, he married **Lowly BRISTOL**, daughter of Jonathan BRISTOL and Elizabeth HOTCHKISS, in Wallingford, New Haven Co., Conn.; born there, 20 February 1753.
They had the following children:

758	i.	Lucina (1769-)
759	ii.	Mary Ann (1770-)
760	iii.	Samuel (1773-)
761	iv.	Miles (1774-)
762	v.	Lyman (~1777-)
763	vi.	Warren (~1779-)
764	vii.	Clarissa (~1782-)
765	viii.	Roxy (~1784-)
766	ix.	Lowly (~1791-)
767	x.	Eunice (~1793-)

295. David HILL was born 31 Oct 1748 in Harwinton, Litchfield Co., Conn.; died there, 7 April 1749.

296. Elizabeth HILL was born 28 October 1751 in Goshen, Litchfield Co., Conn.; died in Farmington, Trumbull Co., Ohio, 10 July 1825, age 73.

297. Martha HILL was born 16 January 1759 in Goshen, Conn.

298. Sarah HILL was born 6 September 1760 in Goshen.

The children of Asa Hill and Gloriana Wheeler [312]

299. Ithuel HILL.[313] Born in 1769; died in 1821, he was about 52. A stone carver of Sag Harbor, N.Y.; resided at South Hampton, Suffolk Co., N.Y.

300. Uri (Uriah) HILL. Born on 15 May 1771 in Wallingford, Conn.

301. Asa HILL Jr.[314] Born on 31 Jan 1776; died on 13 Mar 1776 in Harwinton, Litchfield Co., Conn.

302. Phineas HILL.[315] Born on 24 Jun 1778 in Harwinton, Litchfield Co., Conn.; died 6 Jan 1844 in Norwalk, Fairfield Co., Conn., age 65. He was a headstone carver. Phineas Hill started working in Danbury; he had advertisements in a Bridgeport newspaper in 1808. By 1818 he was advertising in the Norwalk Gazette as having a shop "a few rods north of the bridge." During this time he was also "commuting" to Huntington Long Island to do work there. He eventually settled permanently on Long Island. With his first wife Mary he was the father of Dr. Asa Hill (1815-1874). Phineas married **Molly "Polly" STONE**. Born in 1779.

They had the following children:

768	i.	Myra (1804-1826)
769	ii.	Horace (1812-1836)
770	iii.	Asa (1815-1874)

The children of Ebenezer and Martha (Hill) Grant [316]

303. Sarah GRANT was born 24 October 1748 in Litchfield, Conn., and died in 1769, about age 20. Ten user-submitted trees agree that she d.s.p.

304. Martha GRANT was born 4 May 1751 in Litchfield, Conn., and died in 1769, about age 17. Ten user-submitted trees agree that she d.s.p.

305. Lydia GRANT was born 18 September 1753 in Litchfield, Conn., and died in 1767, about age 13. Nine user-submitted trees agree that she d.s.p.

306. Elihu GRANT was born 11 October 1756 in Litchfield, Conn. Twelve user-submitted trees provide no more information.

307. Dr. Isaac GRANT,[317] second son and fifth child of Ebenezer and Martha (Hill) Grant, was born at Litchfield, Conn., 3 April 1760; died, probably at Albion, Calhoun Co., Michigan, 9 November 1841, age 81. He is buried in the Riverside Cemetery in Albion, and his gravestone is well marked there. He served as an orderly to General "Mad" Anthony Wayne in the Revolutionary War, when he was but 15 years old. He was a hero at the battle of Stoney Point, and he also served at Valley Forge and Brandywine. He was captured at Ft. Washington in 1776, but he escaped from the Grosvenor ship prison and was one of only four of his company to survive. He later became a physician and was one of the first in the country to employ vaccination for the control of smallpox. He was active in the Methodist Church and was a lay minister for some 30 years. He moved to Albion, Michigan, in 1835, and died there in 1841.

On 26 May 1784, in Sharon Springs, N.Y., he married **Hannah TRACY**, age 19; born at Sharon, Litchfield Co., Conn., 25 February 1765; died at Albion, Michigan, 30 October 1841, age 76, 10 days before he died. Isaac and Hannah (Tracy) Grant had nine children; two of his sons - Isaac and Loring - became Methodist ministers, and there are many descendants of Isaac and Hannah who live in this area.

They had the following children:

771	i.	Isaac (1785-1841)
772	ii.	Elihu (1786-1841)
773	iii.	Loring (1789-1870)
774	iv.	Roswell (1792-1792)
775	v.	Charles (1794-1895)
776	vi.	Marcena (1797-1801)
777	vii.	Maria (1800-1801)

778	viii.	Jesse Chapman (1802-1885)
779	ix.	Juliana Delay (1807-1875)

308. Huldah GRANT was born 19 March 1763 in Litchfield, Conn.

309. Titus (aka Silas) HILL.[318] Born on 1 Apr 1752 in Goshen, Conn. Titus (aka Silas) died in 1820, he was 67. Not known to have married; apparently d.s.p.

310. Arunah HILL I.[319] Born on 16 Apr 1754 in Goshen. Father of 2 by a wife whose name is unknown.

Children:

780	i.	Eli (1782-1838)
781	ii.	Arunah (1793-1856)

311. Nancy HILL. Born in 1757.

312. Elisha HILL. Born in 1759. Elisha died in 1827, he was 68. Patriot Soldier in the Revolutionary War. Elisha married **Hannah GATES**.

They had the following children:

782	i.	Lewis
783	ii.	Daughter of Elisha and Hanna (Gates)

313. Mary HILL. Born in 1763.

314. Lois HILL. Born in 1766. Lois died in 1766.

The children of Zenas Hill and Kezia Hill [320]

315. Frederick (aka Jaldiacek) HILL. Born on 10 Nov 1753 in Goshen, Conn.

316. Ira HILL. Born on 17 Jul 1755 in Goshen, Litchfield Co., Conn.; died in Salem, Washington Co., Ohio on 13 Oct 1841, he was 86. On 2 Feb 1786 when Ira was 30, he married **Esther POST**, daughter of John POST & Abigail LEFFINGWELL, in Conn.; born 22 Jun 1759 in Norwich, New London Co., Conn.; died in Salem, Washington Co., Ohio 15 Aug 1851, she was 92. Two of her children had progeny.

They had the following children:

784	i.	Ira (1787-)
785	ii.	Sally (1792-)
786	iii.	Daniel (1803-)

317. Uri(a) HILL. Born in 1759.[321]

318. Amelia HILL. Born in 1761.

319. Sarah HILL.[322] Born on 20 Mar 1762 in Woodbury, Conn.

320. Zenas HILL.[323] Born on 26 Dec 1764 in Woodbury, Conn.

321. Jesse HILL.[324] Born on 10 Dec 1766 in Woodbury, Conn.

322. Abigail HILL. Born in 1769.

323. Urania HILL. Born 4 Apr 1773 in Richmond, Berkshire Co., Mass.; died 13 Oct 1774, she was 1.

324. Miles HILL.[325] Born in 1766 in Goshen, Litchfield Co., Conn.; died there 10 Mar 1815, he was 49.

The grandchildren of Isaac and Anna (Hill) Cook [326]

325. Chille WHEADON was born 15 April 1751 in Branford, New Haven Co., Conn.

326. Lucene WHEADON was born 15 December 1753 in Branford, Conn.

327. Jonathan WHEATON was born 26 January 1755 in Branford., Conn.; died 23 September 1828 in Millersburg, Holmes Co., Ohio, age 73. On 18 February 1778, when he was 23, he married **Penelope LACY**, daughter of Ebenezer LACEY and Freelove CANFIELD, in New Milford, Litchfield Co., Conn.; born 25 August 1756 in New Milford, Conn.; died in Millersburg, Ohio, 25 July 1826, age 69.

They had the following children:

787	i.	William Anson (1798-)
788	ii.	Anna (1781-)
789	iii.	David (1784-)
790	iv.	Anson Melvin (1786-1857)
791	v.	Jonathan Schuyler (1788-)
792	vi.	Sarah (1792-1864)
793	vii.	Russell (1796-1868)

    794   viii.   Almira (1801-1865)

328. Jane COOK was born 10 April 1751 in Branford, New Haven Co., Conn.

329. Hannah COOK was born 11 March 1753 in Branford, Conn.

330. Jacob COOK was born 15 July 1755 in Branford, Conn.

331. Ebenezer Hubbard COOK was born 6 September 1759 in Branford, Conn.; died in Fitchville, Huron Co., Ohio, 4 September 1847, age 87. He married **Jemima ARCHER** in Benson, Rutland Co., Vt.; born 3 March 1772 in Suffield, Hartford Co., Conn.; died in Huntington, Loraine Co., Ohio, 27 September 1855, age 83. Their only child had descendants.
They had one child:
    795   i.   Rufus Norton (1798-)

332. William COOK was born 9 May 1762 in Branford, Conn.

333. Elizabeth "Betsy" COOK was born 13 March 1764 in Branford, Conn.

334. John COOK was born 14 May 1768 in Guilford or Branford, Conn. He married **Lucy CRUTTENDEN**, born 19 October 1784 in Guilford, Conn. Their only child had descendants.
They had one child:
    796   i.   Amanda (1809-)

335. Hulda COOK was born 14 May 1768 in Branford or Guilford, Conn. Apparently a twin of John.

336. Benjamin COOK was born 6 April 1771 in Branford, Conn.

The children of Uri Hill [327]

337. Uri HILL, son and only child of Uri and Mary (Root) Hill, was born 19 August 1760 in Goshen, Litchfield Co., Conn.

338. Mary Ann HILL, daughter and only child of Uri and Hannah (Beach) Hill, was born 4 February 1766 in Goshen, Conn.

The children of John Jr. and Elizabeth (Holland) Dibble [328]

339. David DIBBLE was born 27 August 1749 in Goshen, Litchfield Co., Conn.

340. Reuben DIBBLE was born 6 March 1755 in Goshen, Litchfield Co., Conn.

341. Harris DIBBLE was born 15 April 1756.

342. _____ DIBBLE married **Shem KENTFIELD**, born in 1750 in Northampton, Hampshire Co., Mass.; died in Albany, Albany Co., N.Y., in June 1782, about age 32. He died during the Revolutionary War, and we wonder if he was a soldier, but the record is silent at this time.
They had the following children:
    797   i.   Palmon (1780-)
    798   ii.   Warren

343. John DIBBLE[329] was born 28 December 1758 in Stamford, Fairfield Co., Conn.; died in Darien, Fairfield Co., Conn., in Apr 1852, age 93. In 1785, when he was 26, he married **Sally**, whose surname may have been **SEELY**. She was born in 1764.
They had the following children:
    799   i.   Maria Seely (1790-1841)
    800   ii.   John (1792-)
    801   iii.   Charles Henry (1794-1850)
    802   iv.   Betsy Ann (1796-)

On 25 Nov 1820 when John was 61, he may have married (2) Fanny **SEELY** in Darien, Fairfield Co., Conn. Born in 1792.

344. Abigail DIBBLE was born 13 March 1762 in Stamford, Fairfield Co., Conn.; died in 1789, about age 26. On 4 December 1780, she married **Isaac NICKERSON** in Stamford, Conn.; born in 1758 in Stamford. His name is spelled Nickason in OWT, but I have used a more traditional spelling.

345. Anna DIBBLE was born 14 March 1765 in Stamford, Conn.; died there, 27 August 1802, age 37. On 5 July 1801, when she was 36, she married **Isaac BELL** in Stamford; born 16 February 1764 in Stamford; died in Darien, Fairfield Co., Conn., 8 September 1840, age 76.

346. Sarah DIBBLE was born 16 January 1771.

347. Alexander DIBBLE was born in 1860 and died 9 September 1819. On 18 January 1787 he married

Betty WATTS in Alsted, N.H.

The children of Elijah and Lydia (Dibble) Birge [330]

348. Rhoda BIRGE was born in 1751.

349. David BIRGE was born 11 December 1753 in Litchfield, Litchfield Co., Conn.; died in Underhill, Chittenden Co., Vt. in 1836, about age 82. On 30 December 1778, when he was 25, he married **Abigail HOWLAND**, daughter of James HOWLAND and Rebecca HALL, in Barnstable, Barnstable Co., Mass.; born 31 December 1754 in Barnstable, Mass.; died in Underhill, Chittenden Co., Vt., in 1830, about age 75. She is a descendant of the Mayflower Pilgrim, John Howland. John and Elizabeth (Tilley) Howland had John, who was born in1627, who had Shubael, who had Jabez, who had James, who was her father. They had the following children:

803	i.	Nancy (1779-1840)
804	ii.	Lydia (1780-1811)
805	iii.	Elijah (1782-1854)
806	iv.	James (1784-1851)
807	v.	Rebecca (1786-1862)
808	vi.	Ansel (1788-1854)
809	vii.	David (1790-)
810	viii.	Abigail (1792-1851)
811	ix.	Warren (1794-1850)
812	x.	Cyrus (1797-1871)

350. Elijah BIRGE was born in 1756 and died in 1829, about age 73.

351. Mabel Leanna HILL,[331] eldest child of Billious and Lydia (Dibble) (Birge) Hill, was born about 1758, probably in Goshen, Litchfield Co., Conn.; died after May 1802, possibly in Canada. She married, in about 1775, probably near Woodbury, Litchfield Co., Conn., **William Belden SKEELS,**[332] son of Samuel SKEELS and Lydia BELDEN; born 15 April 1751 in Southbury, Litchfield Co., Conn.; died in 1821 in Berlin, Delaware Co., Ohio, about age 68.
They had the following children:

813	i.	Molly (~1777-1834)
814	ii.	Joseph (~1777-)
815	iii.	William
816	iv.	Samuel
817	v.	Lydia
818	vi.	Roxana (1799-1883)
819	vii.	Nelson (1802-1859)

352. Chloe HILL,[333] second child and second daughter of Billious and Lydia (Dibble) (Birge) Hill, was born 14 March 1759 in Goshen, Conn.; died in 1814, about age 54. She was the mother of 14 children. On 2 June 1778, when she was 19, she married her brother-in-law **Truman SKEELS**, son of Samuel SKEELS and Lydia BELDEN, in Woodbury, Litchfield Co, Conn.; born 11 February 1753 in Southbury, New Haven Co., Conn.; died in Worthington, Franklin Co., Ohio, in 1814, about 60. William Skeels, older brother of Truman, married Chloe's older sister Mabel Leanna, in about 1775.[334]
They had the following children:

820	i.	Arad (1779-1855)
821	ii.	Belias Hill (1782-1859)
822	iii.	Simeon (1784-1861)
823	iv.	Henry (1786-)
824	v.	Reuben (1788-1864)
825	vi.	Truman (1792->1850)
826	vii.	Harry (1794-~1812)
827	viii.	Almira (1796-1861)
828	ix.	Harvey (1799-1867)
829	x.	Polly (1801-1835)

830	xi.	Susanna (1803->1824)
831	xii.	Chloe (1805-1870)
832	xiii.	daughter of Truman & Chloe (1808-)
833	xiv.	?Sally

353. William HILL, third child and eldest son of Billious and Lydia (Dibble) (Birge) Hill, was born 31 March 1761 in Goshen, Litchfield Co., Conn.; died there, 14 April 1761, at the age of two weeks.

354. Reuben HILL,[335] fourth child and second son of Billious and Lydia (Dibble) (Birge) Hill, was born 13 September 1766 in Woodbury, Conn.; died 2 January 1833, age 66. In October 1794, when he was 28, he married **Jane BRADLEY**, daughter of Miles BRADLEY and Jannetje HOGEBOOM, in New Haven, Addison Co., Vt.; born 15 August 1774 in Salisbury, Conn.; died in 1859, about 84. They had the following children:

| 834 | i. | Bradford (1805-1885) |
| 835 | ii. | perhaps other descendant(s) of Reuben & Jane |

355. Lydia HILL,[336] fifth child and third daughter of Billious and Lydia (Dibble) (Birge) Hill, was born 30 September 1769 in Goshen, Conn. She may have married **Peter BRADLEY**.

The children of Samuel and Mary (Dibble) Benedict [337]

356. Lucy BENEDICT was born 6 January 1772 in Sharon, Vt. On 27 November 1788, when she was 16, she married **David BLODGET**.

357. David BENEDICT was born 27 December 1773 in Sharon, Vt.; died in Aylmer, Quebec, Canada, in Jan 1807, age 33. He married **Jennie McALLISTER**, daughter of William McALLISTER and Peggy _____; born in 1777 in Vermont; died in Aylmer, Quebec, Canada, 23 January 1857, about age 80. They had the following children:

836	i.	John (1800-1859)
837	ii.	Samuel (1805-1848)
838	iii.	David (1807-1849)
839	iv.	Clarissa (1813-1888)

358. Miriam BENEDICT was born 12 December 1775 in Sharon, Vt.; died 11 December 1834, on the day before her 59th birthday. Miriam married (1) **Ebenzer BURNHAM,** and on 7 October 1796, when she was 20, she married (2) **Solomon BLACKMER**, in Massachusetts.

359. Samuel BENEDICT was born 7 January 1778 in Sharon, Vt.; died in Aylmer, Quebec, Canada, in 1869, about age 90. On 28 March 1815, when he was 37, he married **Eleanor SHATFORD**; born 26 December 1793; died in 1872, about age 78. They had the following children:

840	i.	Mary (1816-)
841	ii.	Eunice (1817-)
842	iii.	Lucy (1820-)
843	iv.	Samuel (1822-1906)
844	v.	Moses (1824-)
845	vi.	Joseph (1828-1828)
846	vii.	Margaret (1830-)
847	viii.	Sarah (1834-)

360. Ezra BENEDICT was born 15 January 1780 in Sharon, Vt.; died in Williamtown, Vt., 23 March 1854, age 74. He married **Sarah STOCKWELL**, daughter and one of the fifteen children of Major Moses STOCKWELL and Sarah PIERCE; born in 1779 in Royalston, Mass., or Putney, Vt.; died 24 October 1850, about age 71. They had the following children:

848	i.	Squires (1803-)
849	ii.	Cromwell (1805-)
850	iii.	Daniel (1807-)
851	iv.	Lucy (1809-)
852	v.	Martin Michael (1816-1914)

853 vi. Hannah (1823-)

361. Mary BENEDICT was born 19 November 1785 in Sharon, Vt.; died 16 December 1796, age 11.

362. Rachel BENEDICT was born 26 February 1789 in Sharon, Vt.; died in Aylmer, Hull, Quebec, Canada, 9 October1870, age 81. On 24 November 1805, when she was 16, she married **William GRIMES** in Aylmer, Hull, Quebec, Canada; born 18 January 1779; died there.

They had the following children:

854	i.	William (1806-1897)
855	ii.	Samuel (1809-)
856	iii.	Elizabeth (1811-)
857	iv.	James (1814-1888)
858	v.	Rachel (1822-)
859	vi.	Miriam (1824-)
860	vii.	Mary (1826-)
861	viii.	Triphina (1829-1912)

363. Hannah BENEDICT was born 6 July 1791 in Sharon, Vt.; died in Aylmer, Quebec, 7 September 1812, age 21. On 6 February 1807, when she was 15, she married **Benjamin CHAMBERLAIN** in Aylmer, Quebec; born 13 June 1783 in Northfield, Mass; died 5 December 1845, age 62.

They had the following children:

862	i.	Mehetabel (1806-)
863	ii.	Nathaniel (1808-)

The children of Phineas and Rhoda (Kilborn) Hill [338]

364. Kilbourn (Kilborn) HILL was born 22 August 1786; died after 1849, after age 62, apparently without progeny. He married (1) **Abigail STOKES**, and he married (2) **Deborah SOPER**; died in 1826.

365. Seymour HILL was born 14 February 1788; died 26 October 1796, age 8.

366. Clarissa HILL was born 28 May 1789; died in St. Lawrence, N.Y., 20 May 1821, age 31. She married **Newell FOOTE**.

367. Rose HILL was born 9 March 1792 in Shelburne, Vt.

368. Olive Amanda HILL [339] was born 11 August 1800 in Sunderland, Vt.; died in Arlington, Vt., 24 July 1836, age 35. She married **John Brownson LATHROP**, son of Benjamin LATHROP and Caroline Cornelia BROWNSON; born 29 August 1800 in Sunderland, Vt.; died there, 11 January 1886, age 85. He was buried in Rutland, Vt.

They had the following children:

864	i.	Caroline Clarissa (1828-1828)
865	ii.	Caroline Clarissa [2] (1831-1903)

369. Abraham Enoch HILL [340] eldest son and eldest child of Isaac and Eunice (Mallory) Hill, was born 9 October 1763 in Stratford, Fairfield Co., Conn.; died in 1778, age 14.

370. Major LUKE HILL, [341] second son and second child of Isaac and Eunice (Mallory) Hill, was born about 1764, probably at Woodbury, Litchfield County, Connecticut; died at Chillicothe, Ohio, 28 September 1838. The exact date of his birth is unknown, but he was said to have been 75 when he died, and since his older brother was born in October 1763, we can presume that he was born in about 1764. This is consistent with his appearance in the census of 1790, at which time he was between the ages of 26 and 40, for if he was born in 1764 he would have been 26 in 1790. Born a Connecticut Yankee, he became a soldier, an adventurer, and a Southern planter.

He is said to have served in the Revolutionary War, although the nature of his service is unknown. By 1790, he was living in French Lick Township, Westmoreland County, Pennsylvania, where he appears in the U.S. Census as the head of a household consisting of two free white males between the ages of 26 and 45; and of three white females, one between 26 and 45 and two who were under ten years of age. Presumably one of the males was Luke and the other is unknown; one of the unnamed females was probably his wife and the girls were their two daughters. The other adult male in this household could not have been a younger brother of Luke, because all of them were under age 26, and it probably was not his older brother, Abraham Enoch, because Abraham Enoch is said to have died in 1778.

In the next year, 1791, Luke Hill was in Crawford County, where he participated in the recovery and burial of a man named Darius Mead, who was captured and killed by Indians. Luke Hill was then in the garrison at Franklin, Pennsylvania. Three years later, in August 1794, he was recommended as one of three men who were "competent to act as spies" in pursuit of Indians who had killed a soldier near Franklin. On 14 September 1795, he signed the "Receipt Roll for a Company of Militia at Cossawauga, Allegheny County, for the Defence & Protection of the same, against the insults of the Indians."

By 1800, he had relocated to Meadville Township, Crawford County, Pennsylvania, where he appears as the head of a family of six, five of whom are presumably the same as were in his household in 1790 -- including the unknown male who is about his own age -- and with the addition of a boy, under the age of ten. The records of Woodcock Township show that he purchased 200 acres there on 31 October 1800, and that this land was "repurchased" in 1814, presumably because he had left the area. He is regarded as one of "the early residents of southern Woodcock." In August 1806, he and Frederick Haymaker placed a notice in a Crawford County newspaper offering a reward for the capture of a runaway named Selah Wilcock, aged 21, who had dark complexion and blue eyes and who called himself a "singing-master," who had allegedly run off with clothing owned by Hill and Haymaker.

In December 1806, it was reported that on 24 November, Luke Hill was one of nine or ten men who left Meadville to join the infamous "secret" expedition that was being organized by Aaron Burr. The men from Meadville left in canoes on French Creek to go to a place called Beaver, on the Ohio River, where they were to be met by other adventurers -- some say "more than five thousand men." It was said that they were "all federalists, and cordially unfriendly to the government. They even declared that no democrat, or man friendly to the government should be permitted to participate in the enterprise." Although the purpose of Burr's enterprise was unknown, "Some believe that an attempt is projected to separate the western from the eastern states, and add them to Louisiana."

Within a year, the calendar of James Madison shows that on "15 May 1807, John Wickham wrote, 'As counsel for Aaron Burr, requests that copies be furnished him of three affidavits by Comfort Tyler, Luke Hill, and Frederick Haymaker, filed in the Department of State'." Luke Hill was not charged with disloyalty or treason, as were some members of Burr's expedition, including Burr himself.

In 1810, Luke Hill was back in Meadville as the head of a family that was unchanged, except now ten years older, than it was in 1800. By about 1814, he had left Crawford County, and his lot in Woodcock was sold in that year.

He was in service in the War of 1812, and at the time he died, he was referred to as Major Luke Hill, although the details of his service in that war are unknown. A notice of his death in Chillicothe, Ohio, on 28 September 1838, said that he was then a resident of New Orleans. The census for the Upper Suburbs of New Orleans in 1830 shows that he was the head of a family of three, including two free white females, one of whom was between the ages of 15 and 20, and the other was between 20 and 30. He also had many slaves, the number being difficult to read on the handwritten form, but there were probably at least 33 and perhaps as many as 42. It appears that all but five were young males, all under age 36. Of the five slave women, four were young, and one was over 36. His wife had apparently died by 1830.

Luke Hill married, sometime before 1790 and probably before 1780, a woman whose name is unknown, and by whom he had at least five children, a boy and four girls. Three children -- a boy and two girls -- were in his household in 1790, 1800, and 1810, but the boy and his mother were gone by 1830. Two young women were living in his house in 1830, both of whom were born after 1800. Whether his older daughters had died before 1830, or if they married and left home by then, is unknown.
He married _____, who was born in, say, 1769 and died before 1830.
They had the following children:

866	i.	Son of Luke (~1780-<1830)
867	ii.	Daughter 1 of Luke (~1780-)
868	iii.	Daughter 2 of Luke (~1780-)
869	iv.	Daughter 3 of Luke (~1800-)
870	v.	Daughter 4 of Luke (~1810-)

371. Esther HILL[342] elder daughter and third child of Isaac and Eunice (Mallory) Hill; born about 1765.

372. Isaac HILL Jr. [III],[343] third son and fourth child of Isaac and Eunice (Mallory) Hill, was born at South Britain, Litchfield County, Conn., 6 or 16 November 1772; died at Wakeman Township, Huron County, Ohio, 3 September 1860. He was a blacksmith. He was sometimes called Isaac Hill, Jr., although he was actually the third to be named Isaac Hill in three successive generations in this family. South Britain was then part of Southbury, where his father lived in the latter part of his life, and where he died. Some sources say that Isaac Hill [III] was born in Woodbury, Litchfield County, which is the town immediately to the north of Southbury and South Britain in northwestern Connecticut.

Isaac Hill and four of his brothers moved west by separate paths before, or soon after, the War of 1812. Isaac was married in 1794 and began to raise a family in Woodbury, Connecticut. He moved to Rootstown, Portage Co., Ohio, in 1816, presumably after his youngest child was born in March of that year. He moved on to Wakeman, Ohio, in 1824. Isaac and his family initially lived in a log house in Wakeman which their second son, Leverett, had built for them. In 1828 they moved to a new house across the street, which had also been built for him. This house stood at the northeast corner of what is known as the Westfall Corners in Wakeman. He bought 20 acres in Wakeman in 1825, and in 1830 he obtained 90 acres across the road from his house. His wife, by whom he had thirteen children, died in 1828. Soon thereafter, he began a courtship of Miss Betsy Curtiss, an old acquaintance in South Britain, Conn., and they were married, but she died without issue. After his second wife died, Mr. Hill married a widow, Deborah Woodman, of Oberlin, who survived him.

Isaac Hill was the first blacksmith to settle in Wakeman, and he was said to be a fine man. In a letter written in 1824, the writer said, "We was so plagued for a Blacksmith that I let Isaac Hill have an article of my land off of the west end of my land and took his notes and went to Rootstown and moved him out."

He married (1), at the Oxford Congregational Church, Oxford, New Haven Co., Conn., 17 May 1794, **Elizabeth Ann BUNNELL**, daughter of daughter of Benjamin BUNNELL and Ruth SMITH; born at Danbury, Fairfield Co., Conn., 12 April 1771; died at Wakeman Township, Huron Co., Ohio, 22 August 1828. Isaac and Elizabeth Ann (Bunnell) Hill had thirteen children, born between 1795 and 1816. They had the following children:

871	i.	Maria Ann (1795-1866)
872	ii.	Benjamin (1796-1876)
873	iii.	Leverett (Leveritt) (1798-1851)
874	iv.	Charles W. (1799-1801)
875	v.	Elizabeth Ann (1801-1828)
876	vi.	Sophia (1803-1875)
877	vii.	Ruth Emily (1805-1872)
878	viii.	Charles 2d (1807-1865)
879	ix.	Austin (Justin) (1808-1873)
880	x.	Sylvester (1810-1878)
881	xi.	Esther (1812-1816)
882	xii.	Sarah "Sally" B. (1814-1865)
883	xiii.	Charlotte (1816-)

Isaac Hill married (2) **Betsy CURTIS**, daughter of Dr. Isaac CURTIS and Desire HAWLEY; born 26 February 1785 in Stratford, Litchfield Co., Conn.; died in Wakeman, Huron Co., Ohio, 6 September 1848, age 63; died without issue. He then married (3) **Mrs. Deborah (____) WOODMAN**, born in 1784 in New Hampshire; died after 1850, probably in Huron Co., Ohio; no issue.

373. Benajah HILL,[344] fourth son and fifth child of Isaac and Eunice (Mallory) Hill, was born 3 September 1774 in Stratford, Fairfield Co., Conn.; died in Southbury, New Haven Co., Conn., 29 July 1862, age 87. He was christened 13 September 1774 in Ripton Parish, Stratford, Fairfield Co., Conn. He witnessed his father's pension application on 13 August 1832, and signed his name with a clear hand at age 58. In November 1795, when he was 21, he married (1) **Mary "Molly" JACKSON** in Easton, Fairfield Co., Conn.; b. abt 1776, probably in Fairfield Co., Conn.; d. in Southbury, Conn., before 1850. They had the following children:

884	i.	Isaac (~1804-<1870)

885   ii.   Probably other children

On 9 June 1855, when Benajah was 80, he married (2) **Hannah BRONSON (or BROWN)** in Southbury, New Haven Co., Conn.; born in 1788; died, probably in Southbury, after 1860. Benajah may have married (3) **Huldah _____** in Southbury. She was born about 1780.

374. Seth Slone HILL,[345] fifth son and sixth child of Isaac and Eunice (Mallory) Hill, was born 14 October 1776 in Shelton, Fairfield Co., Conn.; died in Cromwell, Noble Co., Indiana, between 1853 and 18555. He was christened on 1 December 1776 in Ripton Parish, Stratford, Fairfield Co., Conn., and he was buried in Cromwell, Indiana. On 19 June 1796, when he was 19, he married (1) **Mary Ann "Polly" STILSON**, daughter of Thomas STILSON, in Newtown, Fairfield Co., Conn.; born 29 December 1774 in Newtown, Conn.; died after 1810.

They had the following children:

    886   i.   Harvey S. (1799-1852)

    887   ii.   Harriet (1801-1822)

He married (2) **Mary Ann GORMAN**, probably daughter of Michael GORMAN; born 22 November 1797 in Pennsylvania; died in Cromwell, Noble Co., Indiana, after 1860, and was buried there.

They had the following children:

    888   i.   Luke (1826-1923)

    889   ii.   daughter (~1827-)

    890   iii.   Sarah Ann (1828-)

    891   iv.   Charles McNair (1830-1918)

    892   v.   Michael Gorman (1833-1911)

    893   vi.   Joseph (1839-?1860)

375. Ephraim HILL,[346] sixth son and seventh child of Isaac and Eunice (Mallory) Hill, was born at Shelton, Fairfield County, Connecticut, 24 May 1778; died at Painted Post (later Caton), Steuben County, New York, 24 July 1832, age 54. He was baptized at the Shelton-Huntington, Conn., Congregational Church, 12 July 1778. He was a carpenter and a farmer.

Ephraim Hill and two of his brothers, probably Isaac and Seth Sloane, migrated at about the time of the War of 1812 to the "far west," then called the Northwest Territory and now known as the state of Ohio. They had been preceded by their oldest brother, Luke, who moved to Pennsylvania and then turned south. Isaac was in Ohio in 1816 and he stayed there. Seth Slone moved on to Indiana. Ephraim turned back and went north to New York State, where he settled just north of the Pennsylvania border. He lived for a time in Chenango Co., N.Y., and then, ten years later, in 1824, he migrated further west along the border to Steuben County, N.Y., into the wilderness then known as Painted Post Number One.

Ephraim and his wife made their long journey in a covered wagon, with their own team. The wagon carried not only themselves but also their nine children and all of their earthly goods. The area where they chose to live is where the Cohocton and Canisteo Rivers join to form the Chemung River, south of the Finger Lakes. They settled where the village of Caton is now located, nine miles south of Corning, which later became famous for the manufacture of Corning and Steuben glass. Painted Post then included the areas now represented by six townships, including Caton, Corning, Hornby, Campbell, Erwin, and Lindley. Before Steuben County was formed in 1796, the town of Painted Post, Ontario County, included three additional townships to the west, and extended to the western boundary of the present town of Addison.

Ephraim Hill brought the first fruit trees to this part of New York State in 1824, including apple trees and plum trees, which he "brought in an old churn." The land on which he settled east of Caton Center was later known as "the Weale place." The first settler in this area was a man named Ford, who built a log cabin there in 1810. Ford left within two years and abandoned his claim. The land in what is now known as Caton was again unoccupied until new settlers came in 1821-1824, when the Hills arrived.

Ephraim Hill was a Deacon of the Presbyterian Church that was organized in Caton in 1824. In 1832, when he was 54, he fell and died of a broken neck while doing carpentry work on a barn. The barn was still standing in 1921 but it was later torn down, although his house was still in use in the late twentieth century. He was buried in the Gillett Cemetery near the Red School House, two miles east of the village center of Caton. He died intestate. When his estate was administered on 13 August 1832; it was valued at $832.42. Four administrators were named: His sons, William P. Hill and George J. Hill; and John Shoemaker and Samuel Wolcott. There were 12 heirs: seven sons, three daughters, and two sons-in-law. Joseph Gillett, who subsequently married Ephraim's widow, was named as a "special guardian." Two generations later, Gillett's granddaughter married Ephraim's grandson, Charles W. Hill. By coincidence, Ephraim Hill's 92-year old father, Isaac Hill, appeared in court in his home state of Connecticut in the month after Ephraim died, on 13 August 1832, to present his petition for a pension as a Revolutionary War soldier. Isaac Hill died on 1 April 1833 and this document was filed in the Woodbury District Probate Office on 10 January 1834.

Ephraim Hill married, at New Milford, Connecticut, 7 April 1803, **Charlotte PRINCE**,[347] daughter of Edward Howell and Huldah (Oviatt) Prince; born 10 December 1781; died 22 August 1871. Her father was a soldier in the Revolutionary War. Ephraim and Charlotte may not have known it, but they were distant relatives by marriage. They had many cousins in common, through no less than three marriages between members of the Oviatt and Mallory families. Ephraim's great-uncle Moses Mallory was married to Charlotte's great-aunt Frances Oviatt. And there were at least two marriages between the grandchildren of Moses and Frances (Oviatt) Mallory and other members of the two families.

Ephraim and Charlotte (Prince) Hill had 12 children. Two died young, and one died unmarried. The other nine children married members of the Herrick, Riley, Schutt, Gillett, Breese, Howe, Minar, Reed, Tobey, and Holley families. All but one had children of their own, and Ephraim and Charlotte (Prince) Hill had no less than 49 grandchildren. After the death of Ephraim, Charlotte (Prince) Hill married (2), in 1842, Capt. Joseph Gillett, son of Lieut. John and Abigail (Hough) Gillett; born 8 September 1782; died 29 September 1848, age 66. There was no issue from this marriage, although Adelia Riley, Joseph Gillett's granddaughter by his first marriage, later married Charles W. Hill, a grandson of Charlotte (Prince) (Hill) Gillett.[348]

Joseph Gillett left Charlotte "one cow, twenty sheep, one hog, and all my household furniture except the two beds, bedding and the two bedsteads [that he left to his daughters Abigail and Lucy]." He also bequeathed to her youngest son, Isaac E. Hill, a share of various pieces of property, and "two ninths of the right of Dower of the widow Charlotte Hill... which I, the said Joseph Gillet purchased from Ephriam [sic] Hill and Henry Hill, all of which my wife Charlotte shall hold during her lifetime."

In 1850 Charlotte (Prince) (Hill) Gillett was a 67-year old widow, living with her son, Isaac Hill (21), and two of her grandchildren, Emily Hill (16) and Charles Hill (18). Emily and Charles were sons of her oldest child, William; why they were living with Charlotte and not with William is unknown. Her son George (44) and his wife, Esther (44), and their sons Stilson (11) and Joseph (7) lived nearby in one house; and her son Noble (38) and his wife, Jane (36), and their children Cirena (12), Murray (8) and Earle (5) lived nearby in another house. In 1855, at the age of 73, she was living with son Henry and his wife Julia, a short distance from her younger son Ephraim, his wife Mary, and their three children. Henry and Julia Hill were childless. Somewhere nearby at that time lived the recently orphaned children of Charlotte Gillett's step-niece Katherine (Gillett) Riley, including Adelia Catherine, then 14, who later married William's son, Charles W. Hill. At the Hill Family reunion in Caton, New York, in 1920, Charlotte and her second husband, Joseph Gillett, were recalled fondly as "Grandpa and Grandma Gillett" by her grandson, William Edwin Hill (1852-1934).

Ephraim and Charlotte (Prince) Hill had the following children:

894	i.	William Prince [7] (1804-1885)
895	ii.	George J. [8] (1805-1876)
896	iii.	Charlotte J. [9] "Jane" (1807-1892)
897	iv.	Henry [10] (1809-1812)
898	v.	Huldah Jane [11] (1810-1812)
899	vi.	Noble [12] (1812-1903)
900	vii.	Huldah [13] (1815-1885)
901	viii.	Samantha [14] (1817-1878)
902	ix.	Henry [15] (1819-1892)

903	x.	Sylvester J. [16] (1821-1840)
904	xi.	Ephraim Abram [17] (1824-1902)
905	xii.	Isaac Edwin [18] (1829-1904)

376. Sally Betsey HILL,[349] second daughter and eighth child of Isaac and Eunice (Mallory) Hill, was born 10 December 1781, probably in Shelton, Fairfield Co., Conn; died in Wakeman Twp., Huron Co., Ohio, 1 January 1828, age 46. On 16 May 1808, when she was 26, she married **Barzilla Squire HENDRYX** (aka Barzillai HENDRIX, aka HENDRICKS), son of Jedidiah HENDRYX, in Southbury, New Haven Co., Conn.; born about 1776; died in Wakeman Twp., Ohio, 5 February 1830, about age 54. They had one child, who was adopted:

906	i.	Horace (1811-1827)

377. Dolly HILL,[350] third daughter and ninth child of Isaac and Eunice (Mallory) Hill, was born in 1784 in Shelton, Conn., and died on 6 June 1784.

378. VanAger HILL,[351] seventh son and tenth child of Isaac and Eunice (Mallory) Hill, was born about 1785, and died young.

379. Roswell HILL,[352] eighth son and eleventh child of Isaac and Eunice (Mallory) Hill, was born 12 July 1788 in Shelton, Fairfield Co., Conn.; died in Greenfield, Bond Co., Ill., 16 September 1844, age 56. He was a school teacher.

Roswell Hill married in about 1812 and began raising a family that eventually consisted of six sons and two daughters. His youngest daughter, Charlotte Jane, was probably named for his sister-in-law, Ephraim's wife Charlotte (Prince), who also came from New Milford Roswell and his wife and children emigrated from New Milford, Connecticut, to Ross County, Ohio, in the spring of 1832, probably just after his fifth child was born. Three more children were born later, probably all in Ohio. His second child later moved on to Illinois, and Roswell, too, moved to Illinois, where he died at the age of fifty-six. He was buried in Greenfield, Bond County, Illinois. His widow apparently returned to Ohio, probably to stay with her children, and she died there twenty years later.

On 12 December 1808, when he was 20, he married **Frances** (aka Adaline, aka Fanny) **BUCKINHAM**,[353] daughter of John BUCKINHAM and Esther OSBORNE, in Conn.; born 16 April 1791 in Roxbury, Litchfield Co., Conn.; died in West Union, Adams Co., Ohio, 27 January 1864, age 72. They had the following children:

907	i.	Henry
908	ii.	Adeline (aka Adaline) (1815->1870)
909	iii.	Theodore (1817-1896)
910	iv.	George W. (1821-1881)
911	v.	Jane Charlotte (1831-1869)
912	vi.	Addison (?1830->1863)
913	vii.	William Roswell (1832-1900)
914	viii.	James Frederick (1836->1863)

The children of Abraham and Hannah (Ferris) Hill [354]

380. Amy HILL was born 16 May 1769; died 5 July 1818, age 49.

381. Elizabeth HILL was born 24 April 1771.

382. Ferris HILL was born 8 July 1774; died in Lewis Corners, N.Y., 21 November 1863, age 89. He married **Betsy BARSTOW**, born 9 May 1772; died 22 October 1854, age 82. They had the following children:

915	i.	Enos (1793-)
916	ii.	Samuel (1795-1874)
917	iii.	Harsey (1797-1855)
918	iv.	Abraham (1798-1883)
919	v.	Enoch (1800-1867)
920	vi.	Aseph King (1802-1883)

383. Annie HILL, born 10 July 1779 in Carmel, N.Y.; married **Aron BROWN**, b. ca. 1798 in Carmel. They had one child:

| 921 | i. | Norris (1779-) |

384. Samuel HILL was born on 2 October 1781.

He had a child, by a wife whose name is unknown:

| 922 | i. | Eliza |

385. William Sherman BLACKMUN[355] was born 15 December 1816 in Mooers, Clinton Co., N.Y.; died there, 28 Aug 1874, age 57. On 20 February 1838, when he was 21, he married **Philina MANNING** in Mooers, N.Y., or Franklin, Quebec, Canada. She was born in 1818 and died in 1873, about age 55. At least one of their ten children had descendants.

They had the following children:

923	i.	Andrew Perkins (1839-1920)
924	ii.	Cyrus Judson (1841-1910)
925	iii.	William John Manning (1844-1937)
926	iv.	Calvin Luther (1846-1863)
927	v.	Richard Lettin (1849-1937)
928	vi.	Elizabeth Philina (1852-)
929	vii.	Delia J. Sweet (1853-1940)
930	viii.	Sarah Nelly (1856-1857)
931	ix.	Elburt Foster (1857-1868)
932	x.	Emma Jane (1861-)

Line 6. Great-Grandchildren of Abigail Hill and Caleb Parmelee

The children of Cornelius and Abigail (Parmelee) Johnson[356]

386. Cornelius JOHNSON was born in 1744.

387. Lemuel JOHNSON was born in 1745.

388. Caleb JOHNSON was born in 1746 and died in 1771, about age 25.

389. Ruphus JOHNSON was born in 1747.

390. Orphana JOHNSON was born in 1748.

Children of Timothy and Sarah (Parmelee) Allen[357]

391. Parmelee ALLEN,[358] son of Timothy and Sarah (Parmelee) Allen, was born in 1746 in East Haven, New Haven Co., Conn.; died in Granville, Washington Co., N.Y., 2 October 1806, about age 60. There is much confusion in various websites regarding Parmelee Allen and his father, Timothy Allen. This may be because there were two men named Parmelee (spelled variously) Allen, son of Timothy Allen, who lived at about the same time, although this would be an odd and thus an unlikely coincidence.

On 21 July 1768, when he was 22, he married, perhaps as her second husband, **Ann WHEELER** in Woodbury, Litchfield Co., Conn.; born 1743 in Fairfield, Litchfield Co., Conn.; died 1799, about 56. Parmelee and Ann (Wheeler) Allen had one child, who has no known descendants:

| 933 | i. | Prudence (1772-1837) |

He may have married (2), perhaps as her second husband, Deborah **BURROUGHS**, who in some sources is said to have first married a man with the surname of Carl. Deborah Burroughs was born say 1753 in Rumbout (now Fishkill), Dutchess Co, N.Y. In some sources, she is said to have married, as his second wife, Parmelee **ALLEN**, son of Timothy **ALLEN** and Sarah **PARMELEE**, on 18 December 1777 in Pawlet, Rutland Co, Vt. She died on 29 Jan 1843 in Almont Twp., Lapeer Co., Mich, and was buried there in the Sand Hill Cemetery. By this account, Parmelee Allen and Deborah (Burroughs) Carl may have had as many as six children. The names of these children have been given variously but a composite list is as follows (all with the surname Allen): Ethan (1778-1846), William (1782-), Parmelee (1784-), James (1756-), Anna (1791-1866), and Salley Ann (1793-1864).

392. Caleb ALLEN was born in 1759 in Woodbury, Litchfield Co., Conn.; died in Pawlet, Rutland Co., Vt., 24 September 1804, about age 45.

Caleb married **Phebe CURTISS**, born in 1759 in Conn.

They had one child:

934 i. Amy (1782-1856)

Line 7. Great-Grandchildren of Elizabeth Hill
The children of Nathaniel and Elizabeth (Griffin) Griffin[359]

393. Elizabeth GRIFFIN was born 17 February 1728 in Simsbury, Hartford Co., Conn.; died there in Oct 1801, age 73.

394. Chloe GRIFFIN was born in 1731 in Simsbury, Conn.; died in Stephentown, Rensselaer, N.Y., 18 Jul 1805, about age 74.

395. Nathaniel GRIFFIN was born 11 September 1732 in Simsbury, Conn.; died there in 1790, about age 57. In 1757, when he was 24, he married **Abigail FOWLER** in Simsbury, Conn. She was born in 1735 and died in 1828, about age 93.

They had the following children:

  935 i. Nathaniel (1758-)
  936 ii. Wisdom (1760-)
  937 iii. Ezra (1761-1843)
  938 iv. Absolom (1764-1833)
  939 v. Samantha (1767-)
  940 vi. Calvin (1769-)
  941 vii. Chedolaomer (1774-1878)

396. Stephen GRIFFIN was born in 1735 in Simsbury, Hartford Co., Conn.; died in Granby, Hartford Co., Conn. in 1803, about age 68.

397. Micah GRIFFIN was born in 1738 in Simsbury, Conn.; died in East Granby, Hartford Co., Conn., 6 August 1815, about age 77.

398. Elisha GRIFFIN was born in 1740 in Simsbury, Conn.; died there before 1747.

399. Elisha GRIFFIN [2] was perhaps born in 1747 in Simsbury, Conn.

400. Seth GRIFFIN[360] was born in 1747 in Granby, Conn.; died there, 26 March 1817, age 70.

401. Martin GRIFFIN was born in 1754 in Simsbury, Conn.; died in Richfield, Otsego, N.Y., 19 December 1830, about age 76.

Children of Solomon and Sheba (Griffin) Terry[361]

402. Elizabeth TERRY was born in 1749 in Simsbury, Hartford Co., Conn.

403. Stephen TERRY was born 27 September 1751 in Simsbury, Conn.; died in Granby, Hartford Co., Conn., 13 February 1835, age 83. On 5 November 1773, when he was 22, he married **Hannah CHALKERS.** She was born in 1752 and died in 1789, about age 37.

They had one child:

  942 i. Stephen (1784-1857)

404. 4 unnamed children of Solomon and Sheba (Griffin) TERRY.

Line 8. Great-Grandchildren of John Hill
The children of Timothy and Sarah (Strickland) Strong[362]

405. Alexander STRONG was born 23 September 1754 in East Windsor, Hartford Co., Conn.; died 21 January 1755.

406. Eli STRONG was born in 1755 in East Windsor, Conn.; died in Redfield, Oswego, N.Y., in 1825, about age 70. In 1779, when he was 24, he married **Lament SHELDON**, born 13 December 1755 in East Windsor, Conn.; died in Redfield, N.Y. in 1825, about age 69.[363]

They had the following children:

  943 i. Lament Sheldon (1783-1845)
  944 ii. Eli
  945 iii. Sarah (1787-1861)
  946 iv. Sophia (1789-)
  947 v. Julia (Laura) (1791-)

948	vi.	Martha (Mary) (1794-1796)
949	vii.	Anson (1796-1865)
950	viii.	Cynthia (1801-1879)

407. Sarah STRONG[364] was born 6 April 1758 in East Windsor, Conn.; died in Lenox, Berksire, Mass., 8 March 1806, age 47. In 1779, when she was 20, she married **Solomon JONES**. He was born in 1754 and died in 1822, about age 68.

They had the following children:

951	i.	Almira
952	ii.	Anson
953	iii.	Clarissa
954	iv.	Elizabeth "Betsy" Maria
955	v.	Ira
956	vi.	Mary
957	vii.	Nancy
958	viii.	Sarah
959	ix.	Sophia
960	x.	William

408. Samuel STRONG was b. 18 August 1761 in East Windsor, Conn.; d. in Redfield, N.Y., Dec 1821.

409. David STRONG was born 4 June 1764 in East Windsor, Conn., and he died there.

The grandchildren of John Hill Jr.[365]

410. John 4th HILL was born about 1760 in Burlington, Hartford Co., Conn.

411. Mary HILL was born 18 August 1753 in Simsbury, Conn.

412. Elijah HILL was born abt 1754 in Simsbury, Conn. He married **Esther TULER**; born about 1753.

413. Chloe HILL was born about 1755 in Simsbury, Conn. In about 1773, when she was 18, she married **Rufus GARRETT**, who was born about 1755.

414. Keziah HILL was born about 1759 in Simsbury, Conn. She married **Thaddeus TULLER**, who was born about 1772.

415. Anna HILL was born about 1761. She was "of Simsbury" Conn. She married **Nahum BARBER**, who was born about 1761.

416. Jedediah HILL,[366] probably the fifth child of John Hill 3rd and his second wife, Isabel Eggelston, was born 29 March 1761, probably at Simsbury, Conn.; died at Lorraine, N.Y., 28 April 1841, at the age of 80. If the first marriage of John Hill is factual, Jedediah was the seventh of eight children of John Hill 3rd. All the children except John 4th of the first marriage are listed as being born in Simsbury, Conn.

He served two enlistments as a private in the Revolutionary War., during the period 1779-1782. He was 18 and lived in West Simsbury at the time of recruitment into the Connecticut State Troops. On his first enlistment, from October 1779-November 1781, he served in Col. Enos' regiment, which saw action at Horse Neck, Long Island. The regiment was visited by General Washington and General Rufus Putnam on several occasions. On his second enlistment, from November 1781-March 1782, the regiment was commanded by Col. Canfield, and it was in action at Frog Point.

In 1783, at the age of 22, he married **Abigail KILBY**,[367] daughter of Ebenezer and Jerusha (Dix) Kilby; born at Farmington, Conn., 29 July 1760; died at Henderson, Jefferson County, N.Y., 3 November 1859, at the age of 99. She was a descendant of John and Rebecca (Simpkins) Kilby, early settlers in Wethersfield, Conn.

The first census of the United States in 1790 showed Jedediah Hill living in Simsbury, Conn., where his father and grandfather were born. He was then living with his wife and three sons under age 16. He did not appear in the 1800 census in either Simsbury or in Ellisburg, N.Y., but he may have been living in Canton, Conn., where his father was buried. In 1807, he and his family and others moved from Connecticut to Sixtown, Jefferson County, N.Y., on the shore of Lake Ontario. They settled in Ellisburg, which was in the Sixtown area. After a summer of clearing land and building log cabins the men returned home for the winter. The next year they returned to Sixtown with their families, carrying all their tools, furniture, clothing, and some food in ox-drawn wagons. The family tradition has it that Jedediah settled on the bank of Sandy Creek to the east of Sackets Harbor. The 1810 census shows Jed as the head of a family of 11 in Jefferson County, N.Y., where he was buried in 1841.

At the time of the War of 1812 Jedediah and his family were residing near Sackets Harbor on the shores of Lake Ontario. They were farming in that district and during the winter months crossed into Canada to make charcoal for commercial use. The war revived the danger from Indian tribes, who sided with the British. The Hills and other settlers built a log blockhouse at Sackets Harbor for their protection. Later, John, Eben and Ludlow Hill enlisted under Captain George Clark and Capt. Solomon McCumber in a New York militia unit and Jedediah was a private in Carver's 61st Regiment. Their first taste of war soon came, when a British fleet of five ships, headed sailed up to Sackets Harbor and attempted to bombard the fort. The blockhouse stood on a bluff above the lake shore so the Britishers were unable to elevate their cannon for efficient fire on the fort. The Americans also had problems, as the balls for their cannon were too small and would not stick in the barrels when the pieces were depressed. They remedied that somewhat by wrapping the balls in cloth. Later a ball from the British cannon was found to fit the American guns. They scored a direct hit on an attacking vessel and the British withdrew.

The historic battle of Big Sandy Creek took place in the spring of 1814, and the area around the Hill farm remained in the war zone until the end of the war. Jedediah's son, Ladue, was ten or twelve when he went squirrel hunting and heard the cannons at Stony Point. He picked up English musket balls and used them for his squirrel gun.

Jedediah Hill's daughter Abigail Hill died 26 January 1815 and Jed and Abby adopted her daughter, little Abigail, who was then five days old. Little Abigail later married Calvin Leonard and died at the age of 23 years and one month. Her headstone in Woodside Cemetery has the inscription "Erected by her friend, Amasa Hungerford." After the war and the death of his daughter, Abigail, in 1825, Jedediah became the first settler in the hamlet of Rural Hill, in the town of Ellisburg. He constructed a brick house there which is now a national historic site. It is said that he was a Mormon a few years later. According to tradition, his brick house was built for a tavern with six rooms on the first floor, with a fireplace and bake-oven, and upstairs there was a ballroom. Jedediah Hill eventually transferred the mansion, along with the farm on which it stood, to his son, Eben, and after a time Eben conveyed it to his brother, John. In 1836, John and Esther sold the property, amounting to 66 acres, to Amasa Hungerford, one of the best known early residents of Ellisburg. When Amasa Hungerford died in 1848, the mansion and farm went to his son Philo in the resulting distribution of the estate.

Jedediah Hill, age 71, living in Ellisburg, applied for soldier's pension in 1832. The deposition was witnessed by Pitt Morse, clergyman, and Ebben Hill. For unknown reasons, the pension was not granted and the papers were lost. In 1841, Jedediah died at the home of his son, Jedediah Jr., in Loraine; he was buried in the Mixer Cemetery, Ellisburg, N.Y. His widow, Abigail, then lived with her brother, Allen Kilby, and his wife Theda Kilby in Henderson, N.Y. In 1849 she filed for a widow's pension with the aid of a lawyer and a congressman, and her pension was granted. In 1850, at the age of 90, she was living with her daughter Isabel and son-in-law David Boice in Henderson, Jefferson Co., N.Y. In 1855, she applied for a bounty land warrant. She died at the age of 99 years, five months, on 3 November 1859, and was buried in Woodside (Mixer) Cemetery beside her husband, Jedediah.

Jedediah and Abigail (Kilby) Hill had the following children:

961	i.	Jedediah (1784-1858)
962	ii.	John Henry (1786-1869)
963	iii.	Riley (1788-1806)
964	iv.	Ebben (aka Eben) (1791-1876)
965	v.	infant (1793-1793)
966	vi.	Ludlow (1794-1873)
967	vii.	Abigail (1797-1815)
968	viii.	Polly (1800-1806)
969	ix.	Ladue (1803-1886)
970	x.	Isabel (aka Isabella) (1806-1860)

417. Wealthy HILL[368] was born 10 March 1767 in Simsbury, Conn.; died in Sandisfield, Mass., 22

November 1852, age 85. On 30 September 1792, when she was 25, she married **Jabez Oman GLEASON** in West Simsbury, Conn.

418. Jenny HILL was born 4 August 1756 in New Hartford, Conn.

419. Zeruiah HILL was born 6 June 1763 in Simsbury, Conn.

420. Aphia HILL was born in 1764 in Simsbury, Conn.

421. Asenath HILL was born in October 1766 in Simsbury, Conn.

422. Cynthia HILL was born in 1776 in Simsbury, Conn.

423. Eleazer HILL Jr. was born about 1778 in Simsbury, Conn.

424. Lois HILL was born in 1770.

425. Darius HILL was born in 1772.

426. Arden HILL was born in 1775.

427. Sarah HILL was born in 1778.

428. Elias HILL was born in 1780.

429. Rachel HILL was born in 1784.

430. Asa HILL was born in 1787.

431. Mary BUNCE / EDGERTON,[369] was born in 1753 in Hartford Co., Conn.; died in Onondaga County, N.Y., in 1849, she was 96. She married **Joseph BACON**, son of Samuel Bacon; born at West Simsbury [Canton], Hartford Co., Conn., in 1752; died at Onondaga Co., N.Y., in 1833, about 81. They had one child:

| 971 | i. | Phineas (Phinehas) (1783-) |

432. Lydia BARBER[370] was born 26 December 1747 in Simsbury, Hartford Co., Conn.; died in 1783, about age 35. She married **Samuel OLCOTT**.

433. John BARBER[371] was born 29 November 1749 in Simsbury, Conn.; died in Canton, Hartford Co., Conn., 3 November 1825, age 75. In 1773, when he was 23, he married **Elizabeth CASE**, daughter of Capt. Josiah CASE and Hester HIGHLEY, in Canton, Hartford Co., Conn.; born 20 April 1752 in West Simsbury [Canton], Conn.; died in Simsbury, Conn. 26 May 1817, age 65. Of their ten children, 8 married and had descendants.
They had the following children:

972	i.	Infant (1774-1774)
973	ii.	Elizabeth (1775-1817)
974	iii.	Rhoda (1777-)
975	iv.	Cynthia (1779-1840)
976	v.	John (1782-1865)
977	vi.	Abiah "Abi" (1784-1867)
978	vii.	Sylvia (1785-1786)
979	viii.	Sylvia (1787-1861)
980	ix.	Luke (1789-)
981	x.	Austin (1792-)

434. Sarah BARBER[372] was born 1 July 1754 in Simsbury, Conn.; died there, 15 April 1761, age 6.

435. Reuben BARBER[373] was born 7 December 1755 in Simsbury, Conn. He married **Elizabeth CASE**, daughter of Hosea CASE and Mary CASE; born 26 June 1754 in Simsbury, Conn.; died in Canton, Hartford Co., Conn., 2 January 1776, age 21. Of their 8 children, two had descendants.
They had the following children:

982	i.	Mary (1778-1804)
983	ii.	Sadosa (1781-1860)
984	iii.	Elizabeth (1782-1828)
985	iv.	Phoebe (1785-1838)
986	v.	Hosea (1788-1874)
987	vi.	Starling (1790-1801)
988	vii.	Alson (1792-1880)
989	viii.	Sarah (1794-1822)

436. Rhoda BARBER[374] was born 25 April1757 in Simsbury, Conn.; died there, 1 Jun 1761, age 4.

417. Benjamin BARBER,[375] born 3 March 1759/60 in Simsbury, Conn.; died in Otis, Mass., 3 Februrary 1836, age 76. In 1783, when he was 23, he m. **Lydia CASE**, daughter of Hosea CASE and Mary CASE, in Hartford Co., Conn.; b. 25 August 1763 in Simsbury; died in Otis, Mass., 10 November 1843, age 80. They had one child:

990	i.	Ruby

438. Jonathan BARBER was born in 1763 in Simsbury, Hartford Co., Conn.; died in Canton, Hartford Co., Conn., 23 Jan 1817, about age 54. In 1786, when he was 23, he married **Abi MERRELL** in Connecticut; born in Jan 1769 in Canton, Conn.; died there in 1848, about age 78. They had the following children:

991	i.	Seth (1788-1866)
992	ii.	Clarinda (1789-)
993	iii.	Abi (1791-1815)
994	iv.	Henry (1793-)
995	v.	Pluma (1796-1815)
996	vi.	Linda (1799-1879)
997	vii.	Thirza (1801-1887)
998	viii.	Susannah (1803-1888)
999	ix.	Eliza (1806-)
1000	x.	Nancy (1808-)
1001	xi.	Jonathan Sherman (1812-1847)
1002	xii.	Harvey (1814-)

439. Abel BARBER[376] was born in 1765 in Simsbury, Hartford Co., Conn.; died in Canton, Hartford Co., Conn., in 1817, about age 52. In 1789, when Abel was about 24, he married **Chloe CASE**, daughter of Solomon CASE and Anna CASE, in Simsbury, Conn.; born 8 Mar 1769 in Simsbury; died in Canton, 15 Apr 1820, age 51. They had the following children:

1003	i.	Solomon (1791-1820)
1004	ii.	Benjamin (1794-)
1005	iii.	Roena (1802-)
1006	iv.	Abel Lester (1803-)

440. Children of John and Mary (Reade) SEGAR.[377]

441. Jacob READ[378] was born 31 [month omitted] 1767 in Simsbury, Hartford Co., Conn.

442. Elizabeth READ[379] was born 12 December 1769 in Simsbury, Conn.

443. Rhoda READ[380] was born 6 March 1772 in Simsbury, Conn.

Children of Titus and Amy (Case) Reade[381]

444. Titus READE[382] was born 2 November 1765 in Simsbury, Conn.; married **Mary "Polly"** _____. They had the following children:

1007	i.	Titus (1790-)
1008	ii.	Timothy (1796-)
1009	iii.	Hiram (1803-)

445. David READE was born 13 May 1767 in Simsbury, Conn.

446. George READE was born 5 August 1769 in Simsbury, Conn.

447. Amy READE[383] was born 23 February 1772 in Simsbury, Conn.

448. Daniel READE was born 29 May 1774 in Simsbury, Conn.

449. Roswell REED[384] was born 19 August 1776 in Simsbury, Conn.; died in Hartland, Hartford Co., Conn. 5 October 1852, age 76. He resided in 1810 in Granby, Hartford Co., Conn.; in 1820 in Norwalk, Fairfield Co., Conn.; in 1830 in Granby; in 1840 in Fairfield; and in 1850 in Hartland. On 1 December 1799, when he was 23, he married **Eunice CASE**, daughter of Capt. Uriah CASE and Eunice DILL, in Canton, Hartford Co., Conn.; born 19 March 1780 in Simsbury; died in Hartland, 11 Nov 1858, age 78. They had one child:

1010	i.	Roswell P. (1804-1885)

450. Phinehas READE was born 5 January 1781 in Simsbury, Conn.

451. Ruth READE was born 20 September 1782 in Simsbury, Conn.

Children of Silas and Thanks (Adams) Reade[385]

452. Orpha READE was born 17 August 1764 in Simsbury, Conn.

453. Ruth READE was born 17 May 1766 in Simsbury; died there, 15 January 1775, age 8.

454. Hannah READE was born 27 June 1771 in Simsbury, Conn.

455. Alvin READE was born 8 May 1774 in Simsbury, Conn.

Grandchildren of Ephraim and Hannah (Hill) Wilcox[386]

456. Asa WILCOX was born in 1747 in Simsbury, Conn. He married **Ruth TAYLOR**.
They had the following children:

1011	i.	Marcus
1012	ii.	Orra
1013	iii.	Pruna
1014	iv.	Sophronia
1015	v.	Susan
1016	vi.	William "Billy"
1017	vii.	Asa Virgil (1770-)
1018	viii.	Prudence (1772-)
1019	ix.	Edmund (1785-)

457. Chloe WILCOX was born in 1747 in Simsbury, Conn. She married (1) **James OLCOTT**. In 1771, when she was 24, she married (2) **Elijah HUMPHREY** in Simsbury; born 20 September 1747; died in 1788, about age 40.
They had the following children:

1020	i.	Allen (1777-)
1021	ii.	Harry (1780-)
1022	iii.	Chloe (1782-)

458. Jehiel WILCOX was born 17 March 1751 in Simsbury, Conn.; died in Marlboro, Delaware Co., Ohio, 27 September 1848, age 97. In April 1779, when he was 28, he married **Azuba MOORE** in Barkhamsted, Litchfield Co., Conn.; born 6 October 1761 in Simsbury; died in Delaware, Marion Co., Ohio in 1820, about age 58. They had the following children:

1023	i.	Jehiel (1781-)
1024	ii.	Hira (1785-)
1025	iii.	Ezra (1790-)
1026	iv.	Abigail (1797-)

459. Philander WILCOX was born in 1752 in Simsbury, Conn.; died in Barkhamsted, Litchfield Co., Conn., in 1813, about age 61. On 10 December 1776 when he was 24, he married **Mercy MOSES** in Simsbury; born 16 September 1758 in Simsbury; died 12 April 1756 in Barkhamsted, Conn.
They had the following children:

1027	i.	Elizabeth
1028	ii.	? (1790-)

460. Martin WILCOX was born 9 June 1759 in Simsbury, Conn.; died in Cambridge, Washington Co., N.Y., 6 January 1813, age 53. He married **Jerusha DEWEY**. Martin and Jerusha (Dewey) Wilcox apparently had a love for the classics, having named one of their children Lysander and two of the sons, respectively, Romulus and Remus. A search of the Greek and Latin classics would probably reveal the origin of some of the other children's names, too.
They had the following children:

1029	i.	Rodolphus (1788-)
1030	ii.	Clarinda (1791-)
1031	iii.	Romulus Bradford (1793-)
1032	iv.	Zarena (1795-)

1033	v.	Remus (1797-)
1034	vi.	Lysander (1799-)
1035	vii.	Lorenzo (1801-)
1036	viii.	Lorita (1803-)
1037	ix.	Amander N. (1808-)

461. Lyman JACKSON was born 29 February 1756 in Simsbury, Conn.; died in Albion, Erie Co., Penna., 20 March 1835, age 79. On 3 January 1782, when he was 25, he married **Deidama DUNHAM** in Pownal, Vt.; born 25 February 1765 in Pownal; died in Albion, Penna., 2 December 1841, age 76. They had the following children:

1038	i.	Rosanna (1782-)
1039	ii.	Jesse Dunham (1784-)
1040	iii.	Ebenezer (1786-)
1041	iv.	Michael (1788-)
1042	v.	Lyman (1790-)
1043	vi.	John Jay (1792-)
1044	vii.	Obediah (1794-)
1045	viii.	Abner (1795-)
1046	ix.	David (1797-)
1047	x.	Royal (1799-)
1048	xi.	Norman (1801-)
1049	xii.	Susanna (1805-)
1050	xiii.	Lucy Deidamia (1808-)

462. Esther JACKSON,[387] daughter of Michael and Susannah (Wilcox) Jackson, was born at Simsbury, Hartford County, Connecticut, 23 May 1758; died sometime after 1 July 1837. On 1 July 1837, when she was 76, she applied for a Revolutionary War veteran's widow's pension, and the pension was subsequently granted. Nothing is known of her after that date. She married, at New Concord, N.Y, 5 January 1775, when she was 16, **Isaiah J. HENDRYX**, age 19, who may have been the son of William and Eunice (Thorp) Hendryx; born at Redding, Connecticut, 1 December 1756; died at Troy, N.Y., 30 November 1835, age 78. The Hendryx/Hendrix family name appears in the early records of New Amsterdam, and it is likely that Isaiah's ancestors in America were Dutch, but they have not yet been discovered.

Sergeant **ISAIAH J. HENDRYX**[388] was born at Redding, Connecticut, and he lived at New Concord, N.Y., at the time of his enlistment for service in the Revolutionary War. In January 1775, as war with the British was approaching, he was married there at the age of 19; his first child was born the following October.

Isaiah Hendryx was on active duty on three separate occasions during the Revolutionary War, from the time of his enlistment as a Private in 1776 until he was released from service as a Sergeant in 1778. Hendryx served in the Massachusetts line of the Continental Army. He saw duty in New York and Vermont, and he participated in the ill-fated invasion of Quebec. He was at such famous sites as Crown Point, Fort Independence (near Ticonderoga), Bennington, and White Plains. He was away from his young wife for nearly a year, including the period of her second pregnancy. He was proud to have been a "volunteer" who rose to the rank of Sergeant at the age of twenty-one. More than fifty years later, he still recalled vividly many details of his service in the Revolutionary War, and of the officers under whom he served -- including General [Benedict] Arnold, who he called "infamous."

In 1780, after the active fighting was over in the northern colonies, Sergeant Hendryx removed to Bennington, Vermont, with his family, which then consisted of his wife and two girls, one and five years of age. Another daughter had died at the age of one day in 1777. The younger of his two daughters died at the age of thirty, but four sons who were born in Vermont survived to mature years. He signed his petition for a veteran's pension in 1832 with a legible hand at age 75. He died three years later and the pension was eventually granted to his widow.
They had the following children:

1051	i.	Lois (1775-)
1052	ii.	Sally (1777-1777)
1053	iii.	Susannah (1779-1810)
1054	iv.	Beardsley (1782-1829)
1055	v.	David (1784-)
1056	vi.	Isaiah J. (1791-)
1057	vii.	Truman (1800-)

463. Jesse JACKSON was born 26 December 1760; died in 1783, about 22.

464. Abigail JACKSON was born 6 November 1762 in Dover Plains, Dutchess Co., N.Y.; died in 1784.

465. Ebenezer JACKSON was born 6 January 1765 in Nine Partners, Dutchess Co., N.Y.; died in Wellsboro, Tioga, Penna., 25 January 1839, age 74. On 4 November 1786, when he was 21, he married **Abigail KEYS** in Pownal, Bennington, Vt.; born in 1767; died 13 February 1850, about age 83.
They had the following children:

1058	i.	Mary R.
1059	ii.	Esther
1060	iii.	Susanna Samantha (1805-)
1061	iv.	Zilpha Loren (1806-)

466. Keziah JACKSON was born 18 July 1767; died in 1811, about age 43.

467. Mindwell JACKSON was born 17 February 1769 in Dover Plains, Dutchess Co., N.Y.; died in 1800, about age 30.

468. Israel WILCOX was born 15 June 1776 in Alford, Berkshire Co., Mass.; died in 1817, about age 40. On 21 April 1798, when he was 21, he married **Anne FOWLER**.
They had one child:

1062	i.	Elvira (1802-)

469. Asenath WILCOX was born 7 April 1760; died 4 August 1790. She married **Benjamin TOBEY**.

470. Sylvanus WILCOX was born 26 May 1762 in Nine Partners, Dutchess Co., N.Y.; died in Glen, Montgomery Co., N.Y., 10 July 1846, age 84. On 28 April 1785, when he was 22, he married (1) **Sarah JOHNSON**, born 17 March 1765 in Nine Partners, N.Y.; died in Glen, N.Y., 30 July 1830, age 65.
They had the following children:

1063	i.	Amelia (1786-)
1064	ii.	Chestina (1788-)
1065	iii.	Asenath (1790-)
1066	iv.	Elijah (Elisha) (1792-)
1067	v.	Charles (1795-)
1068	vi.	Calvin Pardee (1796-)
1069	vii.	Eliza (1800-)
1070	viii.	Oliver L. (1809-)

On 9 October 1831, when he was 69, he married (2) **Sally HAMILTON**.

471. Rufus WILCOX was born 7 January 1764 in Alford, Berkshire Co., Mass.; died 27 February 1813, age 49. He married **Sarah ADAMS**, born in Lorain, Ohio.
They had the following children:

1071	i.	Chloe
1072	ii.	John
1073	iii.	Julia
1074	iv.	Nancy (1787-)
1075	v.	Ephraim (1791-)
1076	vi.	Chestina (1795-)
1077	vii.	Laura (1797-)
1078	viii.	Caroline (1799-)

472. Reuben WILCOX was born 29 December 1767 in Alford, Berkshire Co., Mass.; died in Huron, Erie, Ohio, 24 Aug 1849, age 81. In 1794, when he was 26, he married (1) **Sophia SPRAGUE**, born 9

July 1774 in Lebanon, Conn.; died 5 November 1804, age 30.
They had the following children:

1079	i.	Charlotte
1080	ii.	Franklin (1798-)
1081	iii.	Erasmus D. (1803-)

He married (2) **Theda MERRILL**.

473. Ralph WILCOX, b. 2 December 1769 in Alford, Berkshire Co., Mass.; married **Minta SPRAGUE**.
They had the following children:

1082	i.	Edward
1083	ii.	Jane
1084	iii.	Marshall
1085	iv.	Ralph (1818-)

474. Oliver WILCOX was born 10 February 1772 in Alford, Berkshire Co., Mass.; died in Buffalo, N.Y., in 1831, about age 58. He married (1) **Betsey SPRAGUE**, born in 1773; died in New York in 1811, about age 38. In 1811, when he was 38, he married (2) **Luna JONES** in Batavia, Genesee, N.Y.; born in 1786 in New Marlboro, Berkshire, Mass.; died in 1862, about age 76.
They had one child:

1086	i.	Hester Malvina (1812-)

475. Chestina WILCOX was born 30 July 1774 in Alford, Mass.; married **William SPOOR**.
They had one child:

1087	i.	Lavina (1799-)

476. Lavina WILCOX was born in 1782 in Alford, Mass. She married **Samuel BARSTOWE**.

477. Pluma WILCOX was born 9 February 1783.

478. William WILCOX was born in 1761 in Amenia, Dutchess Co., N.Y.; died in West Mendon, Monroe, N.Y., in 1828, about age 67. He married **Hannah JOHNSON**, born in 1761 in Massachusetts.
They had the following children:

1088	i.	Eber (1783-)
1089	ii.	Henry (1787-)

479. Abigail WILCOX was born in 1762 in Massachusetts; died in Peoria, Ill., in 1830, about age 68. In 1779, when she was 17, she married **Benjamin STILLMAN** in Stockbridge, Berkshire, Mass.; born in 1760 in Amenia, N.Y.; died in Bloomfield, Hartford Co., Conn., in 1819, about age 59.
They had the following children:

1090	i.	Caroline
1091	ii.	Martha
1092	iii.	Roxanna (1786-)
1093	iv.	Isaiah (1797-)

480. Nathan WILCOX was born on 7 February 1763 in Sheffield, Berkshire, Mass.; died in Salem, Wayne, Mich., 23 April 1844, age 81. In 1787, when he was 23, he married (1) **Sylvia HOPKINS**; born in 1768 in Great Barrington, Mass.; died in East Bloomfield, Ontario Co., N.Y., 13 Feb 1813, age 45.
They had the following children:

1094	i.	John (1796-1839)
1095	ii.	Mark (1800-)
1096	iii.	Newton (1802-)
1097	iv.	Calvin (1804-)

In 1823, when he was 59, he married (2) **Leah HOLLENBECK**, born 3 March 1776 in Egremont, Berkshire, Mass.; died in Salem, Washtenaw, Mich., 19 August 1850, age 74.

481. Enoch WILCOX was born in 1765 in Massachusetts; died in East Bloomfield, Ontario Co., N.Y., 10 July 1835, about age 70. On 7 March 1793, when he was 28, he married **Nancy WOODRUFF** in West Stockbridge, Berkshire, Mass.; born in 1772 in Massachusetts; died in 1850, about age 78.

482. Ezra P. WILCOX was born in 1769 in Massachusetts; died in 1832, about 63. He married **Lavicia (Lovisey) HERRICK**, born in 1784 in Vermont; died in 1832, about 48.

483. Smith WILCOX was born 27 February 1774 in Alford, Berkshire Co., Mass.; died 6 August 1831, age 57. On 12 October 1796, when he was 22, he married **Martha TURNER** in Bloomfield, Ontario, N.Y.; born 1 December 1775 in West Stockbridge, Berkshire, Mass.; died 4 September 1836, age 60. They had the following children:

1098	i.	Angeline (1796-)
1099	ii.	Amanda (1798-)
1100	iii.	Edwin T. (1799-)
1101	iv.	Orrin (1801-)
1102	v.	Elnathan (1804-)
1103	vi.	Peter (1805-)
1104	vii.	Emily (1809-)
1105	viii.	William E. (1811-)
1106	ix.	Electa M. (1813-)
1107	x.	Clarissa (1815-)
1108	xi.	Theodore S. (1818-)

484. Benjamin WILCOX was born in 1776 in New York; died in 1859, about 83.

485. Polly WILCOX was born 9 February 1779 in New York; died in Bristol, N.Y., 18 June 1833, age 54. On 14 September 1792, when she was 13, if this is to be believed, she married **Solomon GOODALE** in Conway, Mass; born 3 August 1767 in Conway, Mass.; died in Bristol, N.Y., 7 November 1862, age 95. Their first child was born in 1797, so it is more likely that she was married in about 1796, at age 17. They had the following children:

1109	i.	Solomon (1797-)
1110	ii.	Harriet (~1797-)
1111	iii.	Charles A. (1798-)
1112	iv.	Osee Montgomery (1800-)
1113	v.	Leonard C. (1803-)
1114	vi.	Lemuel C. (1805-)
1115	vii.	Lucinda (1809-)
1116	viii.	Seymour (1810-)
1117	ix.	Mary (1814-)
1118	x.	Hannah (1817-)

486. Jedediah WILCOX was born in 1770 in Vermont; died in New York in 1823, about age 53. In 1802, when he was about 32, he married **Mary HALLETT**, born in 1785 in Vermont. They had the following children:

1119	i.	Arabelle (1802-1841)
1120	ii.	Ephraim (1803-)
1121	iii.	Dijah (1813-1889)
1122	iv.	Lewis (1819-1891)

487. Jesse WILCOX, born in 1774; died in St. Joseph, Mich., in 1841, about 67; married **Mary _____**.

488. Stephen WILCOX was born in 1776.

489. Jeremiah WILCOX was born in 1780.

490. Joseph WILCOX was born on 4 May 1791; died in Michigan, 12 November 1865, age 74. He married **Jerusha WEBSTER**, born in 1791.

Child of Joseph [Jr.] and Eunice (Coe) Hoskins[389]

491. Theodore HOSKINS was born in April 1766 in Winchester, Litchfield, Conn.; died there 18 December 1839, age 73. He married a woman with the same name as his mother. His wife was the daughter of Thomas Coe, whose ancestry is unknown, but presumably he would be in the same family as his mother. In 1788, when he was 21, he married **Eunice COE**, daughter and seventh of the nine children of Thomas COE and Mary GOODELL, in Connecticut; born 24 July 1766 in Litchfield, Conn.; died in Winchester, Conn., 4 June 1849, age 82. They had one child:

1123   i.   Neri (1796-1865)

Fig. 5-1: Gillett Cemetery, Caton, N.Y. –
Graves of Ephraim Hill (1778-1832) and Charlotte (Prince) (Gillett) Hill (1781-1871)

Fig. 5-2: Other Hill and Gillett graves, Gillett Cemetery, Caton, N.Y.

Photos in Figs. 5-1 and 5-2 by George J. Hill

6

Sixth Generation – The Great-Great-Great-Grandchildren

Line 1 – Descendants of Lydia Hill (continued)[390]
The children of Ebenezer and Hannah (Preston) Babcock[391]

492. Benjamin BABCOCK was born 22 January 1755 in Coventry, Tolland Co., Conn.; died 1796, about age 40. On 13 January 1773, when he was 17, he m. (1) **Julia JUDD**; died bef September 1792. They had the following children:

1124	i.	Saloma (1775-)
1125	ii.	Elias (1778-)
1126	iii.	Lavina (1780-)
1127	iv.	Joseph (1786-)
1128	v.	Anna (1788-)

On 20 September 1792, at age 37, he married (2) **Hannah HAIS**, born in 1759 in Coventry. They had one child:

| 1129 | i. | Susannah (1798-) |

493. Daniel BABCOCK was born 9 October 1756 in Coventry, Conn.; died in 1805, about 48.

494. Joseph BABCOCK was born 7 March 1758 in Coventry; died 11 May 1759, age 1.

495. Redolphus BABCOCK was born 3 March 1761 in Coventry; died in 1762.

496. Hannah BABCOCK was born 3 March 1763 in Coventry; died in Berlin, Delaware Co., Ohio, 9 July 1852, age 89. The coincidence of birth dates of Redolphus and Hannah is suspect.

497. Nathaniel BABCOCK, b. 26 March 1765 in Coventry; d. in Dublin, Delaware Co., Ohio, 4 July 1839, age 74.

498. Mary BABCOCK was born 3 June 1767 in Coventry; died in 1768.

499. Ebenezer BABCOCK was born 3 June 1767 in Coventry; died in 1808, he was 40. If the birth dates of Mary and Ebenezer are correct, they were twins.

500. Tabitha BABCOCK was born 13 March 1770 in Coventry; died in 1786, about age 15.

501. Elisabeth BABCOCK was born in April 1773 in Coventry; died in 1789, about age 15.

502. Lydia BABCOCK was born 27 January 1774 in Coventry; died in Burton City, Geauga Co., Ohio, in 1803, about age 28.

503. Esther BABCOCK was born 23 February 1776 in Coventry; died in Perry, Ohio, in 1827, age 50.

504. Olive BABCOCK was born 17 November 1779 in Murrayfield, Tolland Co., Conn.; died in 1793.

The children of Samuel and Sarah (Babcock) Parker[392]

505. Marah PARKER was born 21 February 1754 in Coventry, Tolland Co., Conn.; died 29 July 1844, age 90. She married **Elias BALLOU**, who was born 24 December 1752 in Cumberland, R.I.; died in Peru, Berkshire Co., Mass., 2 January 1834, age 81. They had the following children:

1130	i.	Amariah (1784-)
1131	ii.	David (1786-)
1132	iii.	Mary (1791-)

506. William PARKER was born 8 June 1755 in Coventry, Conn.; died in Virginia in 1791, about age 35. He married **Elizabeth _____**.

507. Sarah PARKER was born 4 March 1757 in Coventry, Conn.

508. Samuel PARKER was born 14 April 1759 in Coventry; died in Byron, Genesee Co., N.Y., 9 July 1844, age 85. He married (1) **Lucy STEPHENS**, born in 1763 in Killingly, Windham Co., Conn.; died in Partridgefield, Berkshire Co., Mass. in 1788, about age 25.

They had the following children:

1133	i.	Lucy (1784-)
1134	ii.	Samuel (1784-)
1135	iii.	Orra (1788-)

He married (2) **Mary "Polly" RHODES**, b. in 1767; d. in Byron, Genesee Co., N.Y., 4 Apr 1852, abt 85.
They had the following children:

1136	i.	Nelson (1806-)
1137	ii.	Shared (1794-)
1138	iii.	Mary "Polly" (1796-)
1139	iv.	Cynthia (1797-)
1140	v.	Eleazer (1802-)
1141	vi.	Alphonso (1804-)

509. Hannah PARKER was born 21 October 1761 in Coventry, Tolland Co., Conn.

510. Bettie PARKER was born 17 December 1763 in Coventry, Tolland Co., Conn.

511. Elias PARKER was born 13 May 1765 in Coventry, Tolland Co., Conn.; died in Ft. Oswego, N.Y., 5 January 1813, age 47. He probably died in the War of 1812. He married **Elidicy OLDS**, born 18 March 1769 in North Ashford, Conn.; died in Chittenango Falls, Madison Co., N.Y., 14 November 1855.
They had the following children:

1142	i.	Olive
1143	ii.	Orange
1144	iii.	Samuel
1145	iv.	William
1146	v.	Josiah (1812-)

512. Daniel PARKER was born 5 December 1767 in Coventry, Tolland Co., Conn.

513. Triphene PARKER was born 14 December 1769 in Coventry, Conn.; d. in Utica, N.Y., 4 January 1842, age 72. On 22 November 1795, when she was 25, she m. **Elijah SEDGWICK** in Coventry; b. 13 December 1769 in Coventry; d. in Bloomingdale, Du Page Co., Ill., 16 December 1861, age 92.
They had the following children:

1147	i.	Samuel (1803-1847)
1148	ii.	Elijah
1149	iii.	Parker
1150	iv.	Theron
1151	v.	Tryphena
1152	vi.	Amanda
1153	vii.	Betsey

514. Phebe PARKER was born 29 August 1771 in Coventry, Conn.; died 11 February 1830, age 58.
She married **David MANN**, born 22 June 1770 in Chester, Hampden Co., Mass.; died in Byron, Genesee Co., N.Y., 4 August 1850, age 80.
They had the following children:

1154	i.	Betsa (1795-)
1155	ii.	Lydia (1796-)
1156	iii.	Sally (1798-)
1157	iv.	Chester (1800-)
1158	v.	William (1804-)
1159	vi.	Reuben (1810-)

515. Eli PARKER was born 11 July 1774 in Coventry. In 1794, when he was 19, he married **Lydia MANN** in Peru, Berkshire Co., Mass.
They had the following children:

1160	i.	Lydia
1161	ii.	Eli (1798-)

516. Theodore Theodorus BARKER was born about 1780 in New Lebanon, Columbia Co., N.Y.; died in North East, Erie Co., Pa., about 1850-60. Married **Charlotte COLEMAN**, born 1803; died in 1886. They had one child:

    1162   i.   Philo Coleman (1803-1886)

517. Clorinda RICHARDS, born 27 March 1755 in Goshen, Conn.; died there, 17 April 1755.

518. Charity RICHARDS was born 3 June 1757 in Goshen, Conn.

519. Abijah RICHARDS was born 3 November 1759 in Goshen.

520. Ann RICHARDS.

521. Joseph RICHARDS.

522. Lydia RICHARDS.

523. Polly RICHARDS.

524. Sarah RICHARDS.

525. Samuel RICHARDS was born 12 August 1765 in Lenox, Berkshire Co., Mass.; died in Warren, Herkimer Co., N.Y., 2 April 1813, age 47.

526. Chester RICHARDS was born in 1770 in Lenox, Berkshire, Mass.

527. Russell RICHARDS was born 30 March 1773 in Goshen, Litchfield Co., Conn.; died there, 10 January 1853, age 79.

528. Mary RICHARDS was born in 1774 in Goshen, Conn., and died there in the same year.

529. Esther RICHARDS was born in Goshen, Conn.

530. Enos RICHARDS was born in Goshen, Conn., and died there, 22 November 1815.

531. Anna FRISBIE was born 12 April 1761 in Northford, New Haven Co., Conn.; died in Rome, Oneida Co., N.Y., 4 February 1825, age 63. In 1781, at age 19, she married **Abner BARBER**, who was born in 1758 and died in 1815, about age 57.

They had the following children:

    1163   i.   Asa (1785-1813)
    1164   ii.   Anna (1789-1848)

532. John FRISBIE was born 11 August 1762 in Northford, Conn.; died 10 June 1837, age 74.

533. Isaac FRISBIE was born 2 January 1764 in Northford; died in Harwinton, Litchfield Co., Conn., 17 February 1826, age 62.

534. Enos FRISBIE was born 9 March 1766 in Northford; died in Litchfield, Litchfield Co., Conn., 4 April 1829, age 63.

535. Tryphena FRISBIE was b. 13 Jan 1768 in Northford; d. in Harwinton, Conn., 29 Jun 1799, age 31.

536. Adah FRISBIE was born 10 December 1769 in Branford, New Haven Co., Conn.; died 19 April 1730 in Great Barrington, Berkshire Co., Mass., age 60

537. Ezra FRISBIE was born 26 December 1771 in Harwinton; died in Sheffield, Berkshire, Mass., in March 1818, age 46. He married **Deidamia VOSBURGH**, who was born in 1795 and died in 1874, about age 79. One of her children had descendants.

They had the following children:

    1165   i.   Russell B. (1797-1876)
    1166   ii.   Elijah Stanton (1805-1866)
    1167   iii.   Levi S. (1815-)

538. Bede Beda FRISBIE was born 15 March 1774 in Harwinton; died in Winchester, Litchfield Co., Conn., 29 January 1809, age 34.

539. Clarissa FRISBIE was born 27 August 1778 in Harwinton, Conn.; died in Canadice, Ontario Co., N.Y., 28 April 1837, age 58.

540. Relief FRISBIE was born 5 November 1769 in Middletown, Windsor, Vt.; died in Gaines, Orleans Co., N.Y., 30 July 1822, age 52. Two of her children had descendants. She married **Samuel CHUBB**, son of Samuel CHUBB & Prudence FISHER, born 22 April 1751 in Needham, Norfolk Co., Mass.; died in Poultney, Rutland Co., Vt., 3 April 1817, in his 66th year.

They had the following children:

    1168   i.   Lucy (1789-1839)
    1169   ii.   Arba (1791-1875)

1170	iii.	Elizabeth (1794-1843)
1171	iv.	Globe Dugar (1796-1888)
1172	v.	Jonathan Frisbie (1802-1854)
1173	vi.	Rolla Harrison
1174	vii.	Bede (1813-)

541. Anna FRISBIE was born 12 September 1777. In 1796, when she was about 18, she married **Jonathan BUTTS**.

542. Simeon FRISBIE, born 8 November 1781; died in Middletown, Windsor, Vt., in 1807, about 25.

543. Salome FRISBIE was born 21 October 1785; died 3 December 1811, age 26. She married **John ANDERSON**.

544. Elizabeth FRISBIE was born 5 February 1788.

545. William FRISBIE, M.D.,[393] was born 22 May 1769 in Stillwater, Saratoga Co., N.Y.; died in Phelps, N.Y., 30 March 1837, age 67. He married **Elizabeth DAVIDSON**, who was born in 1770 and died in 1850, about age 80. One of her children had descendants.
They had the following children:

1175	i.	Sarah Maria
1176	ii.	Elias Willard (1799-1860)
1177	iii.	Eliza Ann (1801-1880)
1178	iv.	Sarah Maria
1179	v.	Ezra Clark (1805-1867)
1180	vi.	Irene C. (1810-1836)

The children of Jacob and Kezia (Barker) Frisbie[394]

546. Jacob FRISBIE was born in 1767 and died in 1842, about age 75. He married **Polly STREET**.

547. Augustus FRISBIE was born in 1768. He was "of N.Y."

548. Philemon FRISBIE was born in 1772. He was "of N.Y."

549. Bede FRISBIE was born in 1774.

550. Eli FRISBIE was born in 1776. He was "of N.Y."

551. Eunice FRISBIE was born in 1779. She married _____ **HENDRICKS** of Salisbury, N.Y.

552. Dr. Salmon FRISBIE was born in 1782. He was "of N.Y."

553. Sarah FRISBIE was born 22 February 1795.

554. Elizabeth NORTON was born 28 July 1774 in Wolcott, New Haven Co., Conn. In 1794, when she was about 19, she married **Thomas COOK** in Connecticut. He was born in 1776 in Connecticut.

555. Susannah NORTON was born 28 July 1774 in Wolcott, Conn.; died there, 29 June 1806, age 31. If the dates of birth of Elizabeth and Susannah are correct, they were twins. In 1794, when she was about 19, she married **Daniel BYINGTON** in Wolcott, Conn.; born 25 January 1773 in Waterbury, Conn.; died in Camden, Oneida Co., N.Y., 20 August 1843, age 70.
They had the following children:

1181	i.	Hyrum Norton (1800-1887)
1182	ii.	Zina (1795-1885)
1183	iii.	Susia Anna (1797-)

556. Keziah NORTON was born 16 May 1776 in Wolcott, Conn.; died in Plymouth, Litchfield Co., Conn., 3 March 1863, age 86. On 15 June 1798, when she was 22, she married **Daniel LANE** in Connecticut. He was born 25 March 1779 and died in Wolcott, Conn., 4 February 1865, age 85.
They had the following children:

1184	i.	Linus (1799-1880)
1185	ii.	Lucas (1801-1885)
1186	iii.	Lucia (1802-1864)
1187	iv.	Elizabeth (1804-1830)
1188	v.	Leonard (1814-1843)
1189	vi.	Asahel (1817-1885)

557. Jonathan Fowler NORTON was born 31 August 1778 in Wolcott, Conn.; died there, 2 November

1849, age 71. On 23 November 1802, when he was 24, he married **Polly SMITH** in Wolcott; born in 1780 in Connecticut; died in Wolcott, 10 February 1874, about age 94.

538. Moses Frisbie NORTON was born 23 August 1780 in West Wolcott, New Haven Co., Conn., and died in Jones Co., Iowa. On 27 November 1779, when he was 19, he married **Percy BARBER** in Connecticut; born in 1777 in Simsbury, Hartford Co., Conn.; died in Jones Co., Iowa.
They had the following children:

1190	i.	Lauren (1800-1867)
1191	ii.	Harmon (1803-1838)
1192	iii.	Bird (1805-1861)
1193	iv.	Philo (1808-)
1194	v.	Erastus (1809-)
1195	vi.	Theda (1812-1900)
1196	vii.	Esther (1815-)
1197	viii.	Amanda (1817-)
1198	ix.	Perris L. (1821-)

559. Ziba NORTON was born 2 October 1782 in West Wolcott, Conn.; died in Wolcott. He married **Abigail ADKINS**, who was born in 1784 in Connecticut.
They had one child:

1199	i.	Adah (1803-1859)

560. Jedediah Harmon NORTON was born 11 May 1788 in Wolcott, Conn.; died in 1874, about age 85. He married **Hannah ROWE** in Wolcott; born in 1790 in Fair Haven, New Haven, Conn.; died in Wolcott, 9 September 1873, about age 83.
They had the following children:

1200	i.	Ozias Rowe (1806-)
1201	ii.	Rodney Frisbie (1807-1871)
1202	iii.	Stephen Ludington (1810-)
1203	iv.	Matthew Simeon (1812-1874)
1204	v.	Selden S. (1813-)
1205	vi.	Eunice R. (1817-)
1206	vii.	Hannah R. (1819-)
1207	viii.	Jedediah Roswell (1822-)
1208	ix.	Daniel Eli (1826-)

561. Simeon Newton NORTON was born 18 March 1791 in Wolcott, Conn.; died there, 5 Feb 1847, age 55. On 11 November 1812, when he was 21, he married **Rachel Rebecca PACKER** in Connecticut, who was born in 1793 in Connecticut.

562. Russell MUNSON was born 17 August 1784 in Branford, New Haven Co., Conn.

563. Lucretia MUNSON was born 20 April 1786 in Branford, Conn.

564. Sophia MUNSON was born 17 October1789 in Branford.

565. Unetla MUNSON was born in 1789 in Branford.

566. Orpha MUNSON was born in 1792.

567. Aaron MUNSON was born in 1796.

568. Eli MUNSON was born in Oct 1797.

569. Chauncey MUNSON was born 5 March 1806 in Barkhamsted, Conn.

570. Timothy FRISBIE was born 20 April 1769 in Durham, Middlesex Co., Conn.; died in Charlotte, Vt., 10 May 1842, age 73. In 1792, when he was about 22, he married (1) **Percis LOMBARD** in Brimfield, Hampden, Mass.; born 28 June 1770 in Brimfield; died there, 17 March 1801, age 30. They had the following children:

1209	i.	Satira
1210	ii.	Arkemenia (1793-)
1211	iii.	Austin S. (1795-)

On 9 August 1822, when he was 53, he married (2) **Betsey EDWARDS**, born 23 August 1786 in

Gilmartin, N.H.; died in Charlotte, Vt.

They had one child:

    1212   i.   ? (1824-)

571. Thaddeus Granice FRISBIE was born 5 January 1760 in Durham, Conn.

572. Elizabeth FRISBIE was born 23 February 1761 in Durham. In 1792, when she was about 30, she married **Heth CAMP** in New Milford, Litchfield Co., Conn.; born 20 February 1735 in Durham, Conn.; died in Westhaven, Rutland Co., Vt., 15 August 1800, age 65.

They had one child:

    1213   i.   Heth Frisbie (1792-)

573. Rachel FRISBIE. Born on 27 Aug 1763 in Durham, Conn. On 11 February 1780, when she was 16, she married **Noah UPSON** in Bristol, Hartford Co., Conn.; born 26 September 1758 in Waterbury, New Haven Co., Conn.; died in Plymouth, Vt., 21 March 1806, age 47.

They had the following children:

    1214   i.   Sheldon (1785-)

    1215   ii.   Amanda (1799-)

574. Jonah FRISBIE was born 25 August 1765 in Durham, Conn.

575. Dorcas FRISBIE was born 10 June 1767 in Durham; died in Shelburne, Vt., 22 May 1848, age 80. She married **Uzal PIERSON**, born 4 May 1763 in Parsippany, Morris Co., N.J.; died in Shelburne, Vt., 11 January 1836, age 72.

They had the following children:

    1216   i.   John (1790-)

    1217   ii.   Uzal (1791-)

    1218   iii.   Edward (1793-)

    1219   iv.   Betsey (1796-)

    1220   v.   Mary (1798-)

576. James FRISBIE was born 31 July 1771 in Durham, Conn.

557. Asa FRISBIE was born 3 May 1776 in Durham; died in Willsborough, Essex, N.Y., 23 March 1857, age 80. He married **Sarah GREEN**, born in 1783 in Durham, Conn.; died 13 Mar 1860, age 77.

They had the following children:

    1221   i.   Eliza (1804-)

    1222   ii.   Guy Carlton (1805-)

    1223   iii.   Dorcas (1807-)

    1224   iv.   Charlotte (1810-)

    1225   v.   Maria (1812-)

    1226   vi.   Fidelia (1815-)

    1227   vii.   Minerva (1820-)

    1228   viii.   Asa W. (1823-)

578. Archibald FRISBIE was born in 1777 in Durham, Conn.

579. Satira FRISBIE married **Sam CLARK**.

580. Sarah FROST was born 19 October 1789 in Woodbury, Conn.; died in Windsor, Broome Co., N.Y., 19 September 1845, age 55. On 15 March 1810, when she was 20, she married **Joseph Blake GARNSEY** in Windsor, N.Y.; born 8 December 1787 in Watertown, Litchfield Co., Conn.; died in Windsor, N.Y., 2 October 1864, age 76.

They had one child:

    1229   i.   Uri Tracey (1811-1861)

581. Sarah MATTHEWS was born 21 September 1767 in Wallingford, New Haven Co., Conn.

582. William MATTHEWS was born 17 January 1772 in Wallingford, Conn.

583. Reuben MATTHEWS was born 24 January 1774.

584. Ruth Elizabeth MATTHEWS was born 29 May 1776 in Wallingford, Conn.

585. Mary FRISBIE was born 24 March 1780 in Waterbury, Conn.; died in Wolcott, New Haven Co., Conn., 3 February 1852, age 71.

586. David FRISBIE was born 12 January 1782 in Waterbury, Conn.; died in Wolcott, Conn., 25 September 1829, age 47.
587. Hannah FRISBIE was born 10 November 1783 in Waterbury, Conn.; died in Bristol, Dane Co., Wisc., 17 October 1816, age 32.
588. Elizabeth FRISBIE was born 20 August 1769 in Waterbury, Conn.; died 1857, about age 87. Married **Mark WARNER**, born 22 December 1757 in Waterbury; died there, 25 October 1815, age 57. They had one child:
   1230   i.   ? (1808-)
589. Daniel FRISBIE was born 16 January 1771 in Waterbury, Conn.; died in Windsor, Conn., 15 November 1850, age 79. On 29 September 1794, at age 23, he married **Eunice HILL** in Waterbury; her ancestry is unknown; born in 1770 and died in Waterbury, 20 November 1860, about age 90. They had the following children:
   1231   i.   Julia (1795-)
   1232   ii.   Anna (1798-)
   1233   iii.   Lauren Lorrain (1800-)
   1234   iv.   Lucius Daniel (1804-)
   1235   v.   Caroline Eunice (1809-)
   1236   vi.   Mary Chloe (1811-)
590. Ebenezer FRISBIE was born 30 November 1773 in Waterbury, Conn.; died in New Haven, Ohio, 14 May 1835, age 61. On 23 November 1791 when he was 17, he married **Deborah TWITCHELL** in Waterbury, Conn.; born 17 September 1775 in Southington, Conn. They had the following children:
   1237   i.   Richard (1796-)
   1238   ii.   Hannah (1792-)
   1239   iii.   Clara (1794-)
   1240   iv.   Ebenezer Wakelee (1800-)
   1241   v.   Polly (1802-)
   1242   vi.   Reuben (1810-)
   1243   vii.   Emeline (1812-)
591. Abigail FRISBIE was born 9 December 1775 in Waterbury, Conn.
592. Ruth FRISBIE.
593. Sally FRISBIE.
594. Samuel FRISBIE. On 3 February 1813 he married **Isabella BARNES** in Waterbury, Conn. She was born 9 January 1786 and died in Waterbury, 13 December 1816, age 30.
595. Polly FRISBIE was born 21 March 1784 in Waterbury, Conn. In 1806, when she was 21, she married **Daniel Wisdom JACKSON**; born in 1781 in Brookfield, Conn.; died in Naperville, Ill., 2 January 1853, about age 72. They had one child:
   1244   i.   William L. (1808-)
596. Abigail TUTTLE.
597. Benoni TUTTLE.
598. Hannah TUTTLE.
599. Levi TUTTLE.
600. Nancy TUTTLE.
601. Lyman TUTTLE was born 15 November 1769 in Waterbury, Conn.; died in service in 1813 in the War of 1812, about age 43. He married **Anna FROST**, b. in 1773 in Waterbury, Conn. They had one child:
   1245   i.   Ira (1792-1878)
602. Solomon TUTTLE was born 7 September 1773, and he apparently died young.
583. Zophar TUTTLE[395] was born 4 February 1776 in Connecticut. In 1802, when he was 25, he married **Betsy BOWLBY**; born 25 July 1784; died in Morris, Ill., 3 March 1859, age 74.

They had one child:

    1246   i.   Salmon (1815-)

604. Lucinda TUTTLE was born 3 November 1780.

605. Lucy TUTTLE was born 13 April 1796 in Wallingford, Conn.; died in 1847, about age 50.

606. John THRASHER was born 19 March 1779 in Waterbury, Conn.; died in Bloomington, McLean, Ill., 17 June 1856, age 77.

607. Abigail Lucy THRASHER was born 15 December 1781 in Waterbury, Conn.; died in Cattaraugus, Cattaraugus, N.Y. in 1855, about age 73.

608. Prudence MERRILL was born 8 February 1782 in Waterbury, Conn. In 1764 she married **Moses SPERRY**, who was born in 1780 in Oxford, Conn.

609. Elijah Frisbie MERRILL[396] was born 2 April 1788 in Waterbury, Conn.; died there, 2 December 1852, age 64. On 24 April 1811, when he was 23, he married **Anna PERKINS** in Waterbury; born 4 April 1792 in Bethany, New Haven Co., Conn.; died in Waterbury, 1 May 1881, age 89. They had the following children:

    1247   i.   Junius Frisbie (1812-1879)
    1248   ii.   Henry Augustus (1815-1890)
    1249   iii.   Sally Maria (1818-1890)
    1250   iv.   Adeline (1820-1891)
    1251   v.   Nathan F. (1823-1909)
    1252   vi.   Charles Frisbie
    1253   vii.   Huldah
    1254   viii.   Elen Augusta
    1255   ix.   George D.
    1256   x.   Franklin B.
    1257   xi.   John Frederick (1836-)

610. Sarah MERRILL was born 15 July 1791 in Waterbury, Conn.; died there, 13 Sept 1813, age 22.

611. Amanda FRISBIE.

612. Esther FRISBIE.

613. Ira FRISBIE, who died in 1863.

614. Levi Collins FRISBIE was born in 1788 in Wolcott, New Haven Co., Conn.; died in Litchfield, Litchfield Co., Conn., 14 November 1852, about age 64. On 17 October 1811, when he was 23, he married **Abigail DUDLEY**, who was born in 1789. They had the following children:

    1258   i.   Baldwin Augustus (1812-1894)
    1259   ii.   Caroline Collins (1814-1816)
    1260   iii.   Harriet Burnham (1816-)
    1261   iv.   Caroline Collins (1818-)
    1262   v.   Betsey (1820-1877)
    1263   vi.   Freelove (1823-)

615. James FRISBIE was born in 1799 and died in 1862, about age 63.

616. Parlia N. FRISBIE was born in 1801.

617. Merab GAYLORD, born 27 January 1777 in New Haven, Conn.; d 10 October 1794; he was 17.

618. Alling GAYLORD[397] was born 5 November 1778 in New Haven, Conn.; died 1 October 1794.

619. Russell GAYLORD was born 4 November 1782 in Hamden, New Haven Co., Conn.; died 5 September 1869, age 86.

620. Loly GAYLORD was born 26 May 1785 in Hamden, Conn.; died 27 September 1794; she was 9.

621. Alva (Allen) GAYLORD was born 15 June 1793 in Hamden, Conn.; died in 1862, about age 68. On 24 July 1814, when he was 21, he married **Lydia TURNER** in North Haven, Conn. One of their children had descendants.

They had the following children:

    1264   i.   William Lawrence (1815-1884)
    1265   ii.   Adeline (1817-)

1266   iii.   Jennette (1822-1863)

622. Chester GAYLORD was born 4 February 1796 in Hamden, Conn.; died 4 September 1852, age 56.

623. Milly GAYLORD was born 14 July 1798 in Hamden; died 30 January 1803, age 4.

The grandchildren of Elnathan and Abigail (Frisbie) Ives[398]

624. Elijah BARNES.

625. Jerusha BARNES.

626. Joel BARNES.

627. Joel BARNES (2d), born in 1773; married, in 1790, at about age 17, **Lucinda WHEELER.**
They had one child:

1267   i.   Sherman (1793-)

628. Gad FRISBIE was born 14 April 1778 in Farmington, Hartford Co., Conn.; died in Burlington, Hartford Co., Conn., 21 December 1854, age 76. He married **Elizabeth PETTIBONE**, who was born 16 Jun 1803. One of their children had descendants.
They had the following children:

1268   i.   John (1819-1902)
1269   ii.   James (1822-1892)

629. Chauncey FRISBIE was born 16 November 1787 in Bristol, Hartford, Conn.; died in Orwell, Pa., 2 May 1864, age 76. He was married twice but has no known descendants. He married (1) **Chloe HOWARD**, and (2), **Elza HUMPHREY**.

630. Laura FRISBIE was born 1 January 1790 in Bristol, Conn.; died in Orwell, Pa., 15 April 1879, age 89. On 28 August 1814, when she was 24, she married **Ira BRONSON**, born in 1790 in Burlington, Hartford Co., Conn.

631. Catherine FRISBIE was born 1 April 1792 in Bristol, Conn.; died in Orwell, Pa., 27 August 1822, age 30. In October 1815, when she was 23, she married **Abel C. ESTABROOKS**, born 7 April 1788 in Orwell, Pa.; died in Illinois, 14 October 1848, at age 60.
They had the following children:

1270   i.   Aaron Gaylord
1271   ii.   Charles (1816-)
1272   iii.   Laura (1818-)
1273   iv.   Levi (1822-)

632. Levi Randall FRISBIE was born 17 March 1797 in Burlington, Conn.; died there, 20 June 1797.

633. Zebulon FRISBIE was born 4 July 1801 in Orwell, Pa., died there, 29 Aug 1881, age 80. Married **Polly GOODWIN**; born 17 April 1811 in New Hartford, Conn.; died in Orwell, 17 April 1887, age 76.
They had the following children:

1274   i.   Addison Cowles (1829-)
1275   ii.   Warren Rush (1831-)
1276   iii.   William Lawson (1834-)
1277   iv.   Chauncey Montgomery (1837-)
1278   v.   Eliza Maria (1839-)
1279   vi.   Ruby Hannah (1843-)
1280   vii.   Orrin Goodwin (1845-)
1281   viii.   Emily Phoebe (1847-)
1282   ix.   Mary Ellen (1849-)
1283   x.   Olin Gaylord (1852-)

The grandchildren of Theodore and Mehitabel (Wheeler) Frisbie[399]

634. Joel FRISBIE.

635. Levi FRISBIE.

636. Mehitabel FRISBIE.

637. Hiram FRISBIE was christened with Eldad, 8 June 1794 in Hartford, Conn.

638. Eldad FRISBIE was christened with Hiram, 8 June 1794 in Hartford, Conn.

639. Luman FRISBIE was christened 31 July 1796 in Hartford, Conn.

Line 2 – Descendants of Mary Hill (continued) [400]

640. Sarah HUMPHREY.

641. James WILCOX.

642. Abigail WILCOX was born 11 January 1754 in Simsbury, Hartford Co., Conn.; died there in Dec 1833, age 79. She was one of the last of Luke Hill's descendants to live in Simsbury. She married **Moses CASE**, born 8 September 1746 in Simsbury; died there, 18 December 1794, age 48.

They had the following children:

1284	i.	Abigail (1781-)
1285	ii.	Chloe (1785-)
1286	iii.	Violet (1787-)

643. Azariah WILCOXSON was born 18 January 1756 in Simsbury, Conn.; died in 1814, about age 57. He married **Hepzibah HUMPHREYS**.

They had the following children:

1287	i.	Chloe
1288	ii.	Benajah (1780-)
1289	iii.	Hepzibah (1788-)
1290	iv.	Caroline (1790-)
1291	v.	Tammy Lovet (1793-)
1292	vi.	Azariah Jay (1795-)

644. Elisha WILCOXSON was born 5 August 1758 in Simsbury; died there, 6 March 1831, age 72. He married **Elizabeth BABCOCK**.

They had the following children:

1293	i.	Elisha (1790-)
1294	ii.	Harvey (1787-)
1295	iii.	Chester (1801-)

645. Chloe WILCOXSON was born in 1760 in Simsbury, Conn.; died in Granville, Licking Co., O., in February 1835, about age 75. In 1785, when she was 25, she married **Israel WELLS** in Lebanon, New London Co., Conn.; born 3 July 1757 in Lebanon, Conn.; died in Granville, O., 3 April 1831, age 73.

They had the following children:

1296	i.	Ezekial (1787-)
1297	ii.	Israel (1787-)
1298	iii.	Joel (1791-)
1299	iv.	Truman (1797-)
1300	v.	Solomon (1799-)
1301	vi.	Chester (1800-)
1302	vii.	Chloe (1801-)
1303	viii.	Mary (1803-)

646. Simeon WILCOXSON was born in 1764 in Simsbury, Conn.; died in Sharon, Franklin Co., O., 26 April 1825, about age 61. He married **Mary Ann POOLER**.

They had one child:

1304	i.	Harriet

647. Roswell WILCOX was born in 1764 in Simsbury, Conn.; died in Worthington, Franklin Co., O., 27 October 1831, about age 67. In 1789, when he was about 25, he married **Dorcas PINNEY** in Simsbury; born 25 July 1778 in Simsbury; died in Worthington, O., in 1838, about age 59.

They had the following children:

1305	i.	Darius Pinney
1306	ii.	Emily
1307	iii.	George Clinton
1308	iv.	Israel

1309	v.	Leicester
1310	vi.	Lodamia
1311	vii.	Stiles
1312	viii.	Dorcas (1790-)
1313	ix.	Roswell (1792-)

648. George WILCOXSON was born in 1768 in Simsbury, Conn.; died in Sandisfield, Berkshire Co., Mass., 18 November 1842, about age 74. He married **Susannah HUMPHREY**.
They had the following children:

1314	i.	Hiram
1315	ii.	Chauncey (1789-)
1316	iii.	George (1792-)
1317	iv.	Cornish (1796-)
1318	v.	Lavinia (1801-)
1319	vi.	Miriam (1804-)
1320	vii.	Lester (1810-)

649. Amos WILCOXSON was born in 1769 in Simsbury, Conn.; died 27 March 1794, about age 25. He married **Jerusha _____**; born in 1774; died 3 April 1795, about age 21.

650. Ozias WILCOX was born in 1770 in Simsbury, Conn.; died in Sandisfield, Berkshire Co., Mass., 12 September 1835, about age 65.

651. Reuben CASE was born 5 September 1755 in Simsbury, Conn. He married **Lydia PINNEY**, who was born in Jun 1759.
They had the following children:

1321	i.	Arlow
1322	ii.	Calista
1323	iii.	Huldah
1324	iv.	Julia
1325	v.	Lovica
1326	vi.	Parley
1327	vii.	Sarah
1328	viii.	Jonathan (1779-)
1329	ix.	Aminta (1783-)
1330	x.	Lydia (1785-)
1331	xi.	Catherine (1794-)

652. Hannah CASE[401] was born 14 March 1752 in Simsbury, Conn.; died in Barkhamsted, Litchfield Co., Conn., 2 November 1842, age 90. On 2 September 1773, when she was 21, she married **Abner CASE** in Barkhamsted; born 14 August 1752 in Simsbury; died there, 6 October 1807, age 55.
They had the following children:

1332	i.	Lyman
1333	ii.	Hannah (1774-)
1334	iii.	Abner (1776-)
1335	iv.	Candace (1777-)
1336	v.	Imri (1780-)
1337	vi.	Ira (1782-)
1338	vii.	Olive (1785-)
1339	viii.	Eli (1788-)
1340	ix.	Abiel (1792-)

653. Desiah CASE was born 7 February 1757 in Simsbury, Conn.; died in Worthington, Franklin Co., O., 16 April 1834, age 77. In October 1783, when she was 26, she married **Samuel BEACH** in Barkhamsted, Conn.; born 13 August 1763 in Litchfield, Conn.; died in Worthington, O., in 1815, age 51.
They had the following children:

1341	i.	Samuel (1784-)

| 1342 | ii. | Charlotte (1787-) |
| 1343 | iii. | Miles (1791-) |

654. Elijah CASE was born 22 October 1757 in Simsbury, Conn.; died in Boyle, Ontario Co., N.Y. In September 1778, when he was 20, he married **Catherine GANYARD** in Killingworth, Middlesex Co., Conn.; born 3 December 1760 in Killingworth, Conn.; died 26 August 1796, age 35.
They had the following children:

1344	i.	Phebe (1782-)
1345	ii.	Elijah (1784-)
1346	iii.	Esther (1789-)

655. Gabriel CASE was born in 1760 in Simsbury, Conn.; died in Herkimer, N.Y., in 1793, about age 33. On 24 June 1783, when he was 23, he married **Abigail BANNING** in Barkhamsted, Conn.
They had the following children:

1347	i.	Gabriel
1348	ii.	Abigail (1787-)
1349	iii.	Loly (aka Lottie) (1788-)
1350	iv.	Banning (1790-)
1351	v.	Sterling (1806-)

656. Asaph CASE was born in 1762 in Simsbury, Conn. On 7 February 1796, when he was 34, he married **Rhoda HUNGERFORD** in Barkhamsted, Litchfield Co., Conn.

657. Rosette CASE was born in 1766 in Simsbury, Conn. On 21 December 1788, when she was 22, she married **Charles TUTTLE** in Barkhamsted, Conn.; born 30 January 1762 in New Haven, New Haven Co., Conn.; died in Prattsville, N.Y., 5 Apr 1818, age56.
They had the following children:

1352	i.	Charity (1789-)
1353	ii.	Charles (1790-)
1354	iii.	Peniel Case (aka Pernal) (1792-)
1355	iv.	Harvey (1794-)
1356	v.	George Washington (1796-)
1357	vi.	Helpy Rosette (1798-)

658. William Palmer CASE was born in 1773.

659. Daniel MOSES was born in 1758 in Simsbury, Conn.; died in Canton, Conn., 9 September 1805, about age 47. He married **Anna EDGERTON**, who was born in 1775 and died in 1846, about age 71.
They had the following children:

1358	i.	Auria
1359	ii.	Festus
1360	iii.	Daniel (1791-)
1361	iv.	Anna (1792-)
1362	v.	Norman (1797-)

660. Mary MOSES was b. in 1775 in West Simsbury, Hartford Co., Conn.; m. **Hezekiah ANDREWS**.

661. Sybil MOSES was born in 1763 in West Simsbury, Conn.; died in Chautauqua, N.Y., 15 October 1854, about age 91. In 1780, when she was about 17, she married **Martin ROBERTS** in Lincoln, Addison Co., Vt.; born in 1759 in Canton, Conn.; died in Ohio in 1807, about age 48.
They had the following children:

1363	i.	Elisha (1781-)
1364	ii.	Sybil (1782-)
1365	iii.	Martin (1784-)

662. Zebina MOSES was born on 15 April 1764 in West Simsbury, Conn.; died in Simsbury, 23 November 1815, age 51. On 8 January 1786, when he was 21, he married **Theodosia CURTIS** in Simsbury; born in Simsbury; died in Marcellus, Onondaga, N.Y., 29 August 1850.
They had the following children:

| 1366 | i. | Zebina (1786-) |

1367	ii.	Linus (1789-)
1368	iii.	Pliny (1791-)
1369	iv.	Curtis (1792-)
1370	v.	Theodosia (1795-)
1371	vi.	Charlotte (1797-)
1372	vii.	Chester (1800-)
1373	viii.	Horace (1803-)
1374	ix.	Myron (1805-)
1375	x.	Pluma (1807-)
1376	xi.	Elvira (1810-)

663. Lois MOSES was born in 1766 in West Simsbury, Conn.; died in 1781, about age 15.

664. Roger MOSES was born 13 February 1767 in West Simsbury; died in Barkhamsted, Litchfield Co., Conn. in 1828, about age 60. On 9 February 1792, when he was about 24, he married **Prentice Satitha BARBER** in Barkhamsted, where she was born on 17 Mar 1770.
They had the following children:

1377	i.	Mary (1797-)
1378	ii.	Salmon (1792-)
1379	iii.	Almira (1795-)
1380	iv.	Matthew (1799-)
1381	v.	Ruth (1801-)
1382	vi.	Hannah (1805-)
1383	vii.	Lois (1806-)
1384	viii.	Mark (1808-)

665. Hannah MOSES was born in 1769 in West Simsbury, Conn.

666. Charlotte MOSES was born in 1771 in West Simsbury. She married **Job PHELPS**.

667. Jonathan LATIMER was born in 1764 in West Simsbury, Conn.; died in 1852, about age 88. He married **Sarah HUMPHREY**, who was born in 1768 in West Hartford, Conn.

668. Lodama LATIMER was born in 1766 in West Simsbury; died 24 August 1792, about age 26. She married **John EDGERTON**, who was born in 1763 in West Simsbury.

669. Rachel LATIMER was born in 1769 in West Simsbury; died in Simsbury, 28 February 1816, about age 47. On 31 January 1786, when she was about 17, she married **Ariel CASE** in Simsbury; born 23 January 1765 in Simsbury; died there, 17 September 1827, age 62.
They had the following children:

1385	i.	Rachel Lury (1796-)
1386	ii.	Job (1805-)

670. Sophia LATIMER was born in 1772 in West Simsbury; died in Nelson, Portage Co., O., in August 1827, about age 55. On 30 June 1791, when she was about 19, she married **Thomas Delaun MILLS** in Becket, Berkshire Co., Mass.; born 18 December 1770 in Canton, Hartford Co., Conn.; died in Nelson, O., 20 April 1824, age 53.
They had the following children:

1387	i.	Robert (1792-)
1388	ii.	Charlotte (1794-)
1389	iii.	Uriah M. (1799-)
1390	iv.	Harmon (1801-)
1391	v.	William Bainbridge (1805-)
1392	vi.	Homer (1807-)

671. Borden WILCOX.

672. Joshua WILCOX.

673. Philander WILCOX.

674. William WILCOX.

675. Aaron WILCOX was born 26 June 1769 in Simsbury, Conn.; died in Chautauqua, N.Y., in 1835, about age 65. He married **Elizabeth _____**.

676. Frederic WILCOX was born 25 Jan 1771 in Simsbury; died in Cazenovia, Madison Co., N.Y., 29 November 1860, age 89. On 20 August 1792, when he was 21, he married **Eunice _____** in Simsbury. They had the following children:

1393	i.	Frederic (1793-)
1394	ii.	Joseph (1798-)
1395	iii.	Erastus (1801-)

677. Riverious WILCOX was born 15 April 1773 in Simsbury; died in La Salle, Ill. He married **Sopronia _____**.

678. Garner LATIMER was born in West Simsbury, Conn. He married **Ester KIRTLAND**, who was born in West Simsbury.

They had one child:

| 1396 | i. | Harvey (1809-) |

679. Daniel ADAMS was born 20 December 1763 in Simsbury, Conn.; died in Canada in 1804, about age 40. In 1798, when he was about 34, he married **Lois CHAMBERLAIN** in Bastard, Leeds, Quebec, Canada.; born 8 September 1763 in Bastard, Quebec; died in Canada in 1833, about age 69. They had the following children:

1397	i.	Lucy Lovina (1781-)
1398	ii.	Lucinda (1799-)
1399	iii.	Lucy Louisa (1801-)

680. Joseph ADAMS was born 24 May 1766 in Simsbury, Conn.

681. Richard Saxton ADAMS was born 16 September 1768 in Simsbury; died in 1798, about age 29. He married **Nancy STEVENS**; born in 1773 in Pittsford, Rutland Co., Vt.; died in Canada. They had the following children:

1400	i.	Lydia (1790-)
1401	ii.	John (1793-)
1402	iii.	Nancy (1795-)
1403	iv.	Erwin (1801-)

682. Lucy ADAMS was born 6 January 1771 in Upper Canada; died in Montrose, Leeds, Ia., 22 March 1845, age 74. She is perhaps the mother of 12 children. In 1786, when she was about 14, she married **Jonathan STEVENS** in Bastard, Quebec; born in 1766 in Nine Partners, Dutchess Co., N.Y.; died in Fowler Twp., St. Lawrence Co., N.Y. in 1854, about 88. Jonathan and Lucy (Adams) Stevens appear to have been unusually peripatetic, if the record in OneWorldTree can be believed. They had the following children:

1404	i.	Lydia (1786-)
1405	ii.	Jonathan (1794-)
1406	iii.	Warren (1796-)
1407	iv.	Lucy (1798-)
1408	v.	Oliver (1798-)
1409	vi.	Henry (1800-)
1410	vii.	Arnold (1802-)
1411	viii.	Nancy (1804-)
1412	ix.	Lydie (1806-)
1413	x.	Clarissa (1808-)
1414	xi.	Fanny (1809-)
1415	xii.	Henry Adams (1813-)

683. Son [name unknown] ADAMS was born in 1773 in Upper Canada, Canada.

664. Joshua ADAMS was born 5 May 1780 in Rutland, Rutland Co., Vt.; died in Perth, Lanark, Ontario, Canada, 23 April 1863, age 82. On 15 March 1803, when he was 22, he married **Elizabeth CHIPMAN** in Elizabethtown, Lanark, Ontario; born 28 February 1786 in Salisbury, Addison Co., Vt.; died in Adamsville, Lanark, Canada, 29 February 1856, age 70. She was perhaps the mother of 12, the last born when she was nearly 44 years old.

They had the following children:

1416	i.	Arza Matson (1804-)
1417	ii.	Alvah (1805-)
1418	iii.	Richard Saxton (1808-)
1419	iv.	Beulah Everette (1810-)
1420	v.	Barnabas Lothrop (1812-)
1421	vi.	Joshua (1815-)
1422	vii.	Lucy Matson (1817-)
1423	viii.	James (1819-)
1424	ix.	Daniel (1820-)
1425	x.	Franklin Metcalf (1823-)
1426	xi.	Elizabeth Evaline (1827-)
1427	xii.	Lydia Ann (1830-)

685. Martin CASE[402] was born 27 March 1758 in Simsbury, Conn.

686. Roswell CASE was born 20 January 1760 in Simsbury; died there, 24 August 1835, age 75. He was another of the descendants of Luke Hill who lived into the fourth decade of the nineteenth century in Simsbury. In September 1782, when he was 22, he married **Lydia ADAMS** in Simsbury. She died 6 January 1801.

They had the following children:

1428	i.	Truman
1429	ii.	Roswell (1786-)
1430	iii.	Lydia (1788-)
1431	iv.	Grandy (1789-)
1432	v.	Timothy (1791-)
1433	vi.	Riley (1793-)
1434	vii.	Pinney (1796-)
1435	viii.	Lucy (1800-)

687. Mary CASE was born 8 April 1762 in Simsbury; died there, 27 October 1821, age 59. The last of her eight children was born when she was 45 years old. On 19 April 1784, when she was 22, she married **Benajah Philo HOLCOMB** in Simsbury; born there, 5 August 1764; died there, 2 January 1828, age 63.

They had the following children:

1436	i.	Mary (1786-)
1437	ii.	Benajah Philo (1784-)
1438	iii.	Samuel (1786-)
1439	iv.	Hull (1790-)
1440	v.	Linus (1794-)
1441	vi.	Salmon (1797-<1801)
1442	vii.	Salmon (1801-)
1443	viii.	Betsey (1807-)

688. Sybil CASE was born 5 June 1765 in Simsbury; died 29 November 1844, age 79. On 10 April 1783, when she was 17, she married **Seth HILLYER** in Granby, Hartford Co., Conn.

They had the following children:

1444	i.	Sybil (1786-)
1445	ii.	Seth (1788-)
1446	iii.	Chloe (1790-)
1447	iv.	Laura (1792-)
1448	v.	Tracy (1794-)
1449	vi.	Harriet (1797-)
1450	vii.	Alma (1799-)

689. Lucy CASE was born 20 October 1766 in Simsbury. She married **Elisha JUDSON**, born in 1765.

They had the following children:

1451	i.	Alanson
1452	ii.	Gordon
1453	iii.	Lucy
1454	iv.	Sylvanus
1455	v.	Sylvester
1456	vi.	Elisha (1796-)

690. Orpha CASE was born on 16 or 19 October 1769 in Simsbury. She married (1) **Henry CASE**, who was born in 1783 in Connecticut. She married (2) **Elias VINING**, born 16 October 1772 in Simsbury; died 14 April 1852, age 79.

691. Orpha READE was born 17 August 1764 in Simsbury, Hartford Co., Conn.

692. Ruth READ was born 17 May 1766 in Simsbury; died there, 15 Jan 1775, age 8.

693. Hannah READ was born 27 Jun 1771 in Simsbury.

694. Alvin READ was born 8 May 1774 in Simsbury.

695. Elisha Westover BARBER was born 27 May 1767 in Simsbury, Conn. He married **Abigail _____**, who was born in 1787.

They had one child:

1457	i.	Hallett (1798-)

696. Charlora ADAMS was born 22 January 1773 in Hartford, Conn.; died in Lysander, N.Y., 4 March 1829, age 56. In 1792, when he was 18, he married **Phebe ROBINSON** in Lysander, Onondaga Co., N.Y.; born 15 Mar 1772; died in Lysander, 23 March 1832, age 60.

They had the following children:

1458	i.	John (1794-)
1459	ii.	Salina (1796-)
1460	iii.	Mary (1798-)
1461	iv.	William (1800-)
1462	v.	Sarah Ann (1801-)
1463	vi.	Parmelia (1804-)
1464	vii.	Charlora (1812-)

697. Alexander ADAMS was born 15 July 1775 in Simsbury, Conn.; died in Lysander, N.Y., 18 October 1810, at age 35. He married **Sally _____**, who died in 1833 in Canillus, N.Y.

698. Parmenio ADAMS was born 9 September 1776 in Simsbury; died in Alexander, Genesee Co., N.Y., 21 February 1832, age 55. He married **Eleanor WELLS**; born 15 January 1778; died in Attica, Wyoming Co., N.Y., 21 September 1836, age 58.

They had the following children:

1465	i.	James (1796-)
1466	ii.	Sarah (1802-)
1467	iii.	Laura (1807-)

699. John ADAMS was born 3 October 1778 in Simsbury, Conn.; d. in Skaneateles, Onondaga Co., N.Y., 2 August 1857, age 78. He m. **Hannah BAKER** in Onondaga, N.Y.; b. 19 February 1792 in New Marlborough, Berkshire Co., Mass.; d. in Skaneateles, Onondaga Co., N.Y., 15 October 1872, age 80.

They had the following children:

1468	i.	Julia (1802-)
1469	ii.	Almenia (1804-)
1470	iii.	Sally E. (1806-)
1471	iv.	Belinda (1808-)
1472	v.	Chloe (1812-)
1473	vi.	Zilpha (1815-)
1474	vii.	Delia Ann (1819-)

700. Dan ADAMS[403] was b. 28 November 1780 in Simsbury, Conn.; d. at Queenston Heights, Ontario, Canada, 13 October 1812, age 31. He was one of the 100 Americans who were killed in the Battle of

Queenston Heights, the first major battle of the War of 1812. It was a disaster for the United States, which was attempting to invade and conquer Canada, but the Canadians and British also suffered a great loss, when their commander was killed. He m. **Eliza Ann** _____; born in 1785 and died in 1857, about age 72. She was a Widow of the War of 1812. Her youngest was a year old when her husband died. They had the following children:

1475	i.	Ledyard S. (1807-)
1476	ii.	Marcia (1808-)
1477	iii.	Parmenio N. (1810-)
1478	iv.	Elvira (1811-)

701. James ADAMS was born 24 January 1783 in Simsbury, Conn.; died in Springfield, Sangamon Co., Ill., 11 August 1843, age 60. He married **Harriet DENTON**; born 31 January 1787 in Hartford, Conn.; died in Springfield, Ill., 21 August 1844, age 57. They had the following children:

1479	i.	Lovenia Elizabeth (1813-)
1480	ii.	Charlotte Baldwin (1815-)
1481	iii.	Lucian Bonaparte (1816-)
1482	iv.	Vienna Margaret (1818-)

702. Truman ADAMS was born 24 March 1785 in Simsbury, Conn.; died in Elbridge, Onondaga Co., N.Y., 25 March 1832, age 47. He was the father of two children by first wife and one by his second wife. He married (1) **Hannah MUNRO**; born 9 April 1788 in Lanesboro, Mass.; died in Camillus, Onondaga Co., N.Y., 30 March 1822, age 33. She died at about the time of her second child's birth. They had the following children:

| 1483 | i. | Olivia Ann (1811-) |
| 1484 | ii. | Mary (1822-) |

He married (2) **Olive PATCHEN**; born 27 September 1790 in Milton, N.Y.; died in Syracuse, Onondaga Co., N.Y., 3 October 1879, age 89. They had one child:

| 1485 | i. | Hannah Ann (1825-) |

703. Mary HILLS was born 20 March 1748 in Torrington, Litchfield Co., Conn. On 10 January 1766, when she was 17, she married **Elijah BARBER** in Torrington. He was born there in 1742. They had the following children:

1486	i.	Luman (1766-)
1487	ii.	Beriah
1488	iii.	Elijah James
1489	iv.	Olive

704. Lois HILLS was born 2 February 1752 in Torrington, Conn. The last of her seven children was born when she was 44. On 4 June 1773, when she was 21, she married **Hawkins WOODRUFF** in Winchester, Conn.; born 20 October 1750 in Farmington, Conn.; died in Pickering, Ontario, Canada, 1 January 1813, age 62. He died in Ontario during the War of 1812. Was he a soldier? Pickering is 20 miles from York, which was the scene of a great battle in April 1813. They had the following children:

1490	i.	Clarissa (1774-)
1491	ii.	Noadiah (1778-)
1492	iii.	Melinda (1781-)
1493	iv.	Beulah (1783-)
1494	v.	Lauren L. (1788-)
1495	vi.	Elizabeth (1791-)
1496	vii.	Zelotus Harvey (1796-)

705. Chauncey HILLS was born 15 February 1754 in Torrington, Conn. He married **Lois GRANT**, who was born 7 November 1757 in Torrington.

706. Roger Eno HILL was born 16 May 1755 in Torrington, Conn.; died in East Liverpool, O., 11

November 1833, age 78. He was probably named for his uncle Roger Enos – his mother's younger brother – who later became famous as an officer in the Revolutionary War and was a general in the Vermont militia after the war. The family name was spelled variously as Enos and Eno in early generations. Roger Eno Hill married **Elizabeth FARWELL**; born 2 September 1762 in Lowell, Mass.; died in Liverpool Twp., Columbiana Co., O., 8 October 1855, age 93.

They had one child:

    1497   i.   Sanford Clark (1796-)

707. Mary PHELPS was born 6 January 1754 in Simsbury, Conn. She married **A. HULBERT**.

708. Mehitable PHELPS was born 24 March 1756 in Simsbury, a twin of her brother, Abel. She married **A. HAYS**.

709. Abel PHELPS was born on 24 May 1756, a twin of his sister, Mehitable. He married **Cynthia Phelon NELSON**, who was born in 1760.

They had the following children:

    1498   i.   Cynthia (1786-)
    1499   ii.   Abigail (1790-)

710. Achsah PHELPS was born 2 July 1758 in Simsbury. He married **A. LAMPSON**; born in 1758.

711. Mindwell PHELPS was born 21 September 1760 in Simsbury, Conn.; died in Rupert, Vt., 17 September 1835, age 74. She married **Isaac SHELDON**; born 3 July 1752 in Suffield, Conn.; died in Rupert, Vt., 4 January 1810, age 57.

They had the following children:

    1500   i.   Sally (1782-)
    1501   ii.   Isaac (1784-)
    1502   iii.   Abel Phelps (1786-)
    1503   iv.   Phebe (1788-)
    1504   v.   Mary (1791-)
    1505   vi.   Enos (1794-)

712. Sarah PHELPS was born in 1765 in Granby, Connecticut; died in East Rupert, Vt., 15 July 1840, about age 75. She married **William PHELPS**; born 26 October 1762 in Hartford, Conn.; died in East Rupert, Vt., 1 September 1847, age 84. No relationship has been shown between Sarah and William Phelps, although it can be presumed that they are somehow related.

They had the following children:

    1506   i.   Sarah (1786-)
    1507   ii.   William (1794-)
    1508   iii.   John (1795-)
    1509   iv.   Timothy (1796-)
    1510   v.   Willis Abel (1799-)
    1511   vi.   Clarissey (1802-)

713. Cynthia PHELPS was born in 1767 in Granby, Connecticut. On 25 May 1785, when she was 18, she married **Joel HIGLEY** in Simsbury; born 31 July 1764 in Granby, Hartford Co., Conn.; died in Rutland, Meigs Co., O. on 26 Apr 1823, he was 58.

They had the following children:

    1512   i.   Polly (1786-)
    1513   ii.   Elihu (1788-)
    1514   iii.   Lucy (1793-)
    1515   iv.   Sally (1795-)
    1516   v.   Cynthia (1797-)
    1517   vi.   Maria (1799-)
    1518   vii.   Joel Phelps (1802-)

714. Candis PHELPS was born in 1769 in Granby. She married **A. CASE**.

715. James Enos PHELPS was born in 1771 in Granby; died in Meigs, O., 10 September 1822, about age 51. He married **Philinda RICE**, who was born 6 June 1773 in Simsbury, Conn.

They had one child:

| 1519 | i. | James Enos (1793-) |

716. Benjamin PHELPS was born in 1773 in Granby and died on 27 Nov 1848, about age 75. He married **Ester FRISBIE**; born 25 August 1778 in Southampton, Hampshire Co., Conn.; died in Barkhamsted, Litchfield Co., Conn., 8 May 1871, age 92.

They had the following children:

1520	i.	Philo (1804-)
1521	ii.	Lucy (1807-)
1522	iii.	Willis (1810-)
1523	iv.	Mary (1812-)
1524	v.	Lydia (1717-)

717. Jerusha Hayden ENOS[404] was born 6 February 1764 in Colchester, Chittenden Co., Vt.; died 16 May 1838, age 74. She was sometimes referred to as Jerusha Hayden Enos Jr., to distinguish her from her mother. As a wedding present, her husband Ira Allen gave her title to the 24,000 acre township of Irasburg in northern Vermont. That gift was all that Ira's heirs would receive upon his death. Being in his wife's name, it was protected from creditors. Heman Allen, Ira's adopted son and nephew, helped to preserve this property for Jerusha. Of her four children, only one, Col. Ira Hayden Allen (1790-1866),[405] survived and had descendants. He was a Judge of Probate in Irasburg, Vt., in 1822 and president of the Orleans County Bank for many years between 1833 and 1865.

In September 1789, when was 25, she married **Gen. Ira ALLEN**, son of Joseph ALLEN and Mary BAKER, in Hartland, Windsor Co., Vt.; born 21 April 1751 in Cornwall, Conn.; died in Philadelphia, Pa., 15 January 1814, age 62. He was a controversial figure. Some say he was the "Founder of Vermont" and others say he was an opportunistic scoundrel. He was the first Treasurer of the state of Vermont; and a member of the Governor's Council.

IRA ALLEN,[406] was the youngest of the eight children of Joseph and Mary (Baker) Allen. Their eldest child was the famous, or as some would say, notorious, Ethan Allen (1738-1789), head of the Green Mountain Boys. Ethan was thirteen years older than Ira. As a young man, Ira "Stub" Allen was said to have a versatile and penetrating mind, a "Grecian brow," and flashing black eyes. He moved with his older brothers – Ethan, Heman, Heber, Levi, and Zimri – to the area south of Lake Champlain and west of the Green Mountains, then known as the New Hampshire Grants, now Vermont. His oldest brother, Ethan Allen, was the leader of the opposition to control of this area by the large landowners of New York. Ethan became the colonel and commandant of the militia, the "Green Mountain Boys," and was known as the "Hero of Ticonderoga" after he led the capture of that fort from the British in 1775.

Ira Allen also was a patriot. He was a Delegate to the Windsor Convention and aided in drafting the constitution of Vermont in 1777. He served as secretary of the Council of Safety and was a member of the Governor's Council. He was the first treasurer of the state of Vermont and was a representative in negotiations for Vermont's independence. Hoping to force the Continental Congress to recognize Vermont, he joined his brothers in moves to effect a separate peace with Britain, 1780-83. He was also a major general in the state militia and in 1795 he went to Europe to purchase arms for Vermont. He was captured by an English vessel and carried to England, accused of transporting arms for the Irish, who were then in open rebellion. After eight years of litigation, an admiralty court found in his favor, but he died a pauper and was buried in an unmarked grave in Philadelphia. By then the Allens' influence had waned, and his death was not recognized in the public records by the Vermont legislature. He was an interesting and controversial person, who was considered unscrupulous by some, including his brothers. In a poem, his brother Levi allegedly said, "That there's one greater rogue in this world than I... Tis Ira! 'tis Ira! I yield him the prize." However, he adopted Heman, son of his brother Heber, after Heber died in 1782, and he helped Heman to become prominent and successful. He also helped the family of his cousin Remember Baker, after Baker was killed by Indians in 1775.

They had the following children:

| 1525 | i. | Mary F. (1789-) |
| 1526 | ii. | Ira Hayden (1790-1866) |

1527	iii.	Zimri Enos (1792-1813)
1528	iv.	Maria Juliette (1794-1811)

718. Sibil ENOS was born 6 February 1766 in Vermont; died in East Windsor, Conn., 19 June 1796, age 30. On 13 July 1794, when she was 28, she married **Noadiah BISSELL** in Hartford, Vt.; born in 1761.

719. Roger ENOS was born 14 February 1768; died in Irasburg, Orleans Co., Vt., 10 August 1849, age 81. He married **Emily Corning PADDOCK**, who died 1 May 1879.
They had one child:

1529	i.	Ellen Maria

720. Elizabeth ENOS was born 20 May 1774.

721. Sarah LANGDON was born 9 December 1756 in New Britain, Conn.; died in Farmington, Hartford Co., Conn., 14 June 1822, age 65. On 1 January 1778, when she was 21, she married **Elizur HART** in Kensington, Conn.; born 25 December 1752 in Kensington; died in Kingston, Jamaica, in 1794, abt 41.
They had the following children:

1530	i.	Sally (1778-)
1531	ii.	Polly (1781-)
1532	iii.	Sophia (1785-)
1533	iv.	Erastus Langdon (1787-)

722. Hannah LANGDON was born 1 November 1771 in New Britain, Conn.; died 12 November 1792, age 21. In January 1790, when she was 18, she married **Asahel HART** in New Britain; born 24 May 1771 in New Britain; died in Charleston, S.C., 22 July 1804, age 33.
They had one child:

1534	i.	Hannah (1792-)

723. Abi LANGDON was born in 1775 in New Britain, Conn.; died there, 12 Mar 1807, age 32. In 1793, when she was about 18, she married **Ira STANLEY** in New Britain, Conn.; born 12 October 1773 in Farmington, Conn.; died in New Britain, Conn.; 21 December 1854, age 81.
They had the following children:

1535	i.	Ira (1795-)
1536	ii.	Abi Langdon (1807-)

724. Jonathan ENO was born 15 March 1769; died 5 September 1821, age 52. He married **Theodosia CASE**, who was born in 1770.
They had one child:

1537	i.	Jonathan (1793-)

725. Elizabeth ENO was born 8 September 1773 in Simsbury, Conn.; died there, 10 December 1868, age 95. She lived into the seventh decade of the nineteenth century in Luke Hill's hometown of Simsbury. On 12 December 1793, when she was 20, she married **Alexander PHELPS**, son of David PHELPS and Abigail GRISWOLD, in Simsbury; born 26 February 1769 in Simsbury; died there, 25 February 1852, age 82.
They had the following children:

1538	i.	Alexander Cotton (1794-)
1539	ii.	Horace G. (1797-)
1540	iii.	Jaman Hart (1799-)
1541	iv.	Edward (1802-)
1542	v.	Elizabeth (1804-)
1543	vi.	Norman (1806-)
1544	vii.	Mary Ann (1808-)
1545	viii.	John Jay (1810-)
1546	ix.	Sherman David (1814-)

726. Cynthia ENO was born 28 May 1777 in Simsbury, Conn.; died 8 October 1804, age 27. In 1794, when she was about 16, she married **Hezekiah CASE** in Hartford, Conn.; born 11 March 1769 in Simsbury; died in Bloomfield, Hartford Co., Conn., 17 Feb 1859, age 89.
They had the following children:

1547	i.	Hezekiah Hart (1795-)
1548	ii.	Hiram (1799-)

727. Chauncey ENO was born 19 December 1782 in Simsbury; died there, 14 January 1845, age 62. On 4 November 1807, when he was 24, he married **Amaryllis CASE** in Simsbury; born 12 February 1788 in Canton, Conn.; died in Simsbury, 22 August 1860, age 72.
They had the following children:

1549	i.	Elizur Hart (1810-)
1550	ii.	Cordelia (1812-)
1551	iii.	Chauncey E. (1815-)
1552	iv.	Jeanette Amarilla (1818-)
1553	v.	Josiah William (1820-)

728. Damaris GAINES married **Samuel WARNER.**
729. Daniel GAINES.
730. Eunice GAINES.
731. Lois GAINES.
732. Lucretia GAINES.
733. Lydia GAINES.
734. Lyman GAINES.
735. Samuel GAINES.

Line 4 – Descendants of Tahan Hill (continued)[407]
The children of Daniel and Mary (Nettleton) Parmelee[408]

736. David PARMELEE was born 7 December 1763.
737. Nathan PARMELEE was born 24 April 1766.
738. Daniel PARMELEE, born 11 June 1770 and lived in Claremont, N.Y. Married **Abigail STEVENS.**
They had the following children:

1554	i.	David Dudley (1801-1872)
1555	ii.	James Smith (1820-1864)

739. Bela PARMELEE, b 13 July 1776; lived in Killingworth, Conn.; married **Temperence ISBELL.**
They had the following children:

1556	i.	Eliza (-1826)
1557	ii.	Marietta
1558	iii.	Laura P. (1795-1855)
1559	iv.	Almira A. (1811-1855)
1560	v.	Elias

740. Lois BALDWIN was born 1 February 1763 in Killingworth, Middlesex Co., Conn.; died in Clermont, Cheshire Co., N.H., in 1804, about age 40.
741. Eleazer BALDWIN was born 21 October 1764 in Killingworth, Conn.; died in Madisonville, Ohio, 25 November 1835, age 71.
742. Jerusha BALDWIN was born 31 July 1765 in Newtown, Fairfield Co., Conn.; died in 1775, age 9.
743. Daniel BALDWIN was born 23 October 1767 in Killingworth, Middlesex Co., Conn.; died in Clermont, N.H., in 1862, about age 94.
744. Barbara BALDWIN was born 19 October 1769 in Killingworth, Conn.; died in 1770.
745. Ezra BALDWIN was born in 1771 and died in 1772, he was 1.
746. Caleb BALDWIN was born in 1776 and died in 1836, about age 60.
747. Philemon BALDWIN was born on 9 Oct 1778 in Clearmont, Sullivan Co., N.H.; died in Penn Yan, Yates Co., N.Y., in 1857, about age 78. In 1809, when he was about 30, he married **Esther BALDWIN** in Claremont, Sullivan Co., N.H. She was born in 1760 and died in 1815, about age 55. The likely relationship of Philemon and Esther Baldwin has not been determined.[409]
They had the following children:

1561	i.	Amos (1779-1865)
1562	ii.	Mary (1783-1877)
1563	iii.	Philemon H. (1785-1834)
1564	iv.	Rune R. (1789-1834)
1565	v.	Caleb (1791-1849)
1566	vi.	Asa (1795-)
1567	vii.	Elizabeth (1798-1877)
1568	viii.	George (1802-1830)
1569	ix.	Salley Ann (1806-)
1570	x.	Esther (1810-)

748. Jemima BALDWIN was born in 1780; died in 1781, about age 1 .

749. Parnel PARMELEE was born 16 December 1769 in Killingworth, Conn.

750. Rev. James Hill PARMELEE[410] was born 15 May 1783; died 6 April 1872, age 88. He was a graduate of Yale College in 1808. He married (1) **Catherine F. BARKER**; (2) **Priscilla HORN**; and (3) _____ **WILSON**, who was probably the mother of his only child.

He had one child:

1571	i.	Child of Rev. James Hill

The children of Elias and Thankful (Hill) Parmelee[411]

751. Barbara PARMELEE was born 10 December 1778 in Killingworth, Conn.

752. Hannah PARMELEE was born 27 May 1782 in Killingworth, Conn.

753. Lemuel PARMELEE was born 6 October 1786 in Killingworth, Conn.

754. Elias Harvey PARMELEE was born 18 December 1789 in Killingworth, Conn.

755. Thankful PARMELEE was born 12 March 1795 in Killingworth, Conn.

Line 5 – Descendants of Luke Hill Jr. (continued)

756. Patriot Reuben HILL,[412] son and elder child of Ambrose and Lucia (Beach) Hill, was born 19 January 1765 in Goshen, Litchfield Co., Conn.; died in Wauconda, Lake Co., Ill., 31 January 1858, age 93. In 1783, when he was 17, he married **Patience REYNOLDS**; born 3 October 1765 in Rhode Island; died in Wauconda, Lake Co., Ill., 3 August 1856, age 90.

They had one child:

1572	i.	Seth Morris (1799-1896)

757. Electa HILL,[413] daughter and second child of Ambrose and Lucia (Beach) Hill, was born at Goshen, Conn., 1 February 1777; died in New York State, possibly in Alden, Erie Co., 10 December 1860, at age 83. She married, in 1798, **Elisha ROE**, son of Captain Thomas and Mary (Welles) Roe; born at Williamstown, Berkshire Co., Mass., 5 December 1768; died at Medina, Orleans Co., N.Y., 12 January 1830, age 61.

Captain Thomas ROE was born at Suffield, Conn., in November 1736; died in Williamstown, Mass., after 1824; he was a soldier in the French and Indian War. Mary WELLES was the eldest of the seven children of William and Mary (Hunn) Welles. Her father was the son of Capt Thomas Welles, son of Hon. Samuel Welles, who was the son of Governor Thomas Welles. Her mother was the daughter of Samuel Hunn. William was "prob. the Wm. licensed as a 'taverner,' Feb., 1728." Mary Welles m. (1) at Newington, Conn., 17 April 1760, Jonathan Wright, by whom she had two children, Jonathan b. 24 Aug 1762, and Mary bp. 19 Aug 1764. She m. (2), about 1767, Capt. Thomas Roe, by whom she had five children. Her eldest child, Elisha, married Electa Hill, daughter of Captain Ambrose and Lucy (Beech) Hill, and had descendants.

Elisha and Electa (Hill) Roe had the following children:

1573	i.	George Welles (1799-1830)
1574	ii.	Amanda (1800-1870)
1575	iii.	Lydia (1802-)
1576	iv.	William Horace (1803-1886)

1577	v.	James Augustus (1805-1827)
1578	vi.	Lucy (1807-1888)
1579	vii.	Electa (1810-1864)
1580	viii.	Roxana (1812-1900)
1581	ix.	Elisha (1814-1883)
1582	x.	Ambrose Thomas (1817-1879)
1583	xi.	Orvin Sidney (1819-1872)

The children of Jonah and Lowly (Bristol) Hill[414]

758. Lucina HILL was b. 6 Feb 1769 in Wallingford, New Haven Co., Conn.; christened 23 July 1775.

759. Mary Ann HILL was born 30 December 1770 in Wallingford; she was christened 23 July 1775.

760. Samuel HILL was born 22 August 1773 in Wallingford; he was christened 23 July 1775.

761. Miles HILL was born 29 December 1774 in Wallingford, Conn.; he was christened 23 July 1775.

762. Lyman HILL was born about 1777 in Wallingford; he was christened 10 August 1777.

763. Warren HILL was born about 1779 in Wallingford; he was christened 5 December 1779.

764. Clarissa HILL was born about 1782 in Wallingford; she was christened 10 February 1782.

765. Roxy HILL was born about 1784 in Wallingford; she was christened 18 May 1784.

766. Lowly HILL was born about 1791 in Wallingford; she was christened 22 May 1791.

767. Eunice HILL was born about 1793 in Wallingford; she was christened 4 Aug 1793.

The children of Phineas and Molly (Stone) Hill[415]

768. Myra HILL. Born in 1804; died in Norwalk, Conn. on 21 Nov 1826, abt age 22; and buried there.

769. Horace HILL. Born in 1812 in Norwalk, Conn.; died in Norwalk, Conn. on 26 Jan 1836, abt age 24.

770. Asa HILL D.D.S.[416] Born on 20 Nov 1815 in New York; died in Norwalk, Fairfield Co., Conn. on 26 Nov 1874, he was 59. Buried in 1874 in Norwalk, Fairfield Co., Conn., East Norwalk Historical Burying Ground. He was said to be "one of the foremost citizens of Western Connecticut," and he had been the editor of the *American Dental Recorder.* On 11 May 1842 when Asa was 26, he married **Susan ISAACS** in New York City, N.Y. Born in 1819; died in 1886, she was about 67. They had one child:

| **1584** | i. | Rebecca "Betta" Isaacs (1847-1922) |

The children of Isaac and Hannah (Tracy) Grant[417]

771. Isaac GRANT[418] was born 3 February 1785 in Lenox, Mass.; died in Worcester, Mass., 19 October 1841, age 56. On 28 April 1805, when he was 20, he married **Hannah HAMMOND**; born 18 November 1788 in Norwich, N.Y.; died in Worcester, Mass., 27 July 1854, age 65, apparently d.s.p.

772. Elihu GRANT[419] was born 4 November 1786 in Lenox, Mass.; died in Harrisville, Ohio, 26 September 1841, he was 54. On 15 October 1809, when he was 22, he married **Amy MARSH** in Chenango Co., N.Y.; born 7 October 1792 in Vermont; died in Huntington, Ohio, 28 April 1865, age 72. They had the following children:

1585	i.	Elisha (Elizah)
1586	ii.	Lorin Marcina (1810-)
1587	iii.	Hannah (1812-1874)
1588	iv.	Isaac (1814-1833)
1589	v.	John (1816-1887)
1590	vi.	Laura (1817-)
1591	vii.	Sarah (1819-1863)
1592	viii.	Pamelia (1821 1859)
1593	ix.	Lucy Anna (1823-1885)
1594	x.	Jesse C. (1825-1886)
1595	xi.	Nathan Orlando (1828-)

773. Loring GRANT was born 25 February 1789 in Queens, N.Y.; died in Pentwater, Mich., 13 September 1870, age 81. On 4 August 1811, when he was 22, he married **Betsey KEENEY** in Briantrim, Pa.; born 6 April 1796 in Wyalusing, Bradford Co., Pa.; died in Niles, Mich., 10 January 1867, age 70.

They had one child:

    1596   i.   George Roberts (1820-1889)

774. Roswell GRANT was born 9 June 1792 and he died in July 1792.

775. Charles GRANT was born 2 October 1794 in Colerain, Mass.; died in Bengal, Mich., 11 January 1895, age 100. On 26 March 1816, when he was 21, he married (1) **Margaret HINES** in Smithville Flats, Chenango Co., N.Y.; born in Bradford, Pa.; died in Smithville Flats, N.Y., 6 August 1826. They had one child:

    1597   i.   Charles Wesley (1818-)

On 1 February 1831, when he was 36, he married (2) **Matilda CLOSE** in Covington, N.Y.; died 26 Aug 1833 in Perry, N.Y. She d.s.p. On 10 June 1838, when he was 43, he married (3) **Emeline GILLETT**, presumably (but unproved) a descendant of one of the Gillett brothers, Jonathan or Nathan, of Windsor and Simsbury, in Gainesville, N.Y.; born 12 January 1812. She d.s.p.

776. Marcena GRANT was born 21 October 1797 and died in August 1801, age 3.

777. Maria GRANT was born in July 1800 and died in August 1801, age 1.

778. Jesse Chapman GRANT was born 2 September 1802 in Plymouth, N.Y.; died in Minneapolis, Minn., 14 August 1885, age 82. On 25 December 1828, when he was 26, he married **Frances Forbes GERE** in Green, N.Y.; born 22 April 1805 in Norwich, Mass.; died in Minneapolis 3 September 1888. They had one child:

    1598   i.   DeWitt Clinton (1841-)

779. Juliana Delay GRANT, born 2 August 1807 in Smyrna, N.Y.; died in Table Rock, Neb., 25 Feb 1875, age 67. On 15 Jan 1834, when she was 26, she married (1) **Horatio Nelson GERE** in Chenango Co., N.Y.; born 2 April 1802 in Northampton, Mass.; died in Table Rock, Neb., 3 Nov 1862, age 60. They had the following children:

    1599   i.   Charles Henry (1838-)
    1600   ii.   John Nelson (1842-)
    1601   iii.   George Grant (1848-)

In 1867 when she was 59, she married (2) **T. J. McCLURE** in Table Rock, Neb., where he was born.

780. Eli HILL.[420] Born in 1782 in Massachusetts; d. in Berrien, Berrien Co., Mich., 6 Nov 1838, abt 56.

781. Arunah HILL II.[421] Born in 1793 in Massachusetts; died in Clinton, De Kalb Co., Ill., 5 Sep 1856, abt age 63. He was a soldier in the War of 1812, 76th Regt. N.Y. Militia. On 20 Dec 1814 when Arunah was 21, he married **Olivia HALL** in Sackett's Harbor, Jefferson Co., N.Y. Born in 1797 in New York; died in Clinton, De Kalb Co., Ill., after 1880. In 1880, after she was widowed, she lived with her youngest son, George, in Clinton, De Kalb Co., Ill. They had the following children:

    1602   i.   William Smith (1826-1898)
    1603   ii.   Arunah (1828-)
    1604   iii.   Benjamin F. (1830-1905)
    1605   iv.   George W. (1834-)

The children of Elisha Hill and Hannah Gates[422]

782. Lewis HILL. He went to New York State, and then to Illinois. He first married _____. Her name is unknown, and her sons' names are unknown. They had the following children:

    1606   i.   Son #1 of Lewis
    1607   ii.   Son #2 of Lewis

Lewis second married **Rosetta COOK**. They had one child, and perhaps more:

    1608   i.   Herbert

783. Daughter of Elisha and Hanna (Gates) HILL.

The children of Ira and Esther (Post) Hill[423]

784. Ira HILL was born in 1787 in Tinmouth, Rutland Co., Vt. On 4 January 1816, when he was 29, he married **Wealthy** (aka Welthes) **LITTLE** in Lower Newport, Ohio; born 6 May 1793 in Belpre, Ohio;

died in Ohio 2 December 1870, age 77.
They had the following children:

1609	i.	Luther Ira (1816-)
1610	ii.	Harvey Dale (1828-1867)

785. Sally HILL was born 17 April 1792 in Tinmouth, Rutland Co., Vt.

786. Daniel HILL was born 31 January 1803 in Salem, Washington Co., Ohio. On 30 March 1827, when he was 24, he married **Mary MERRIAM** in Washington, Ohio; born 5 December 1805 in New York; died in Washington, Ohio, in April 1843, age 37.
They had the following children:

1611	i.	Unnamed son
1612	ii.	Unnamed son
1613	iii.	Unnamed daughter
1614	iv.	Edwin C. (1828-1829)
1615	v.	Oladine S. (1834-)
1616	vi.	Erwin Dana (1842-1934)

The children of Jonathan and Penelope (Lacy) Wheaton[424]

787. William Anson WHEATON was born 14 March 1798 in Schoharie, N.Y. On 13 January 1820, when he was 21, he married **Sarah HALL** in Coshocton, Ohio.
They had one child:

1617	i.	Anson William (1846-1916)

788. Anna WHEATON was born 4 May 1781 in Washington, Litchfield Co., Conn. Her husband died in the year they were married, and she apparently d.s.p. In 1797, when she was 15, she married _____ **PORTER** in Washington, Conn.; born in 1776 in Washington, Conn.; died there in 1797, age 21.

789. David WHEATON was born 10 September 1784 in Edgermont, Berkshire Co., Mass. He married but apparently d.s.p. On 2 March 1820, when he was 35, he m. **Sarah NOWLES** in Coshocton, Ohio.

790. Anson Melvin WHEATON was born 20 June 1786 in Vershire, Orange Co., Vt.; died in Millersburg, Holmes Co., Ohio, 13 October 1857, he was 71. On 23 March 1820, when he was 33, he married **Rebecca R. COOK** in Holmes, Ohio. She apparently d.s.p.

791. Jonathan Schuyler WHEATON was born on 24 June 1788 in Vershire, Orange Co., Vt.

792. Sarah WHEATON was born 20 October 1792 in Thetford, Orange Co., Vt.; died in Killbuck, Ohio, 6 January 1864, age 71. She had two children, both of whom had descendants. On 26 November 1826, when she was 34, she married **Bartholomew HUSTED** in Holmes, Ohio; born 24 August 1790 in North River, Washington Co., N.Y.; died in Holmes, Ohio, 11 August 1839, age 48.
They had the following children:

1618	i.	Ransom (1827-)
1619	ii.	Huldah (1829-1902)

793. Russell WHEATON was born 20 June 1796 in Schoharie, N.Y.; died in Holmes, Killbuck Co., Ohio, 4 November 1868, age 72. On 11 April 1822, when he was 25, he married **Abigail MARTIN** in Wayne, Ohio; born 30 January 1800 in Pennsylvania; died in Holmes, Ohio, 24 July 1876, age 76. She was the mother of 7, three of whom married and had descendants.
They had the following children:

1620	i.	George (1823-1905)
1621	ii.	John Lacy (1825-)
1622	iii.	James Irvine (1827-)
1623	iv.	Edward Martin (1830-)
1624	v.	Catherine Anne (1834-)
1625	vi.	Nancy Jane (1837-)
1626	vii.	Sarah A. (1840-)

794. Almira WHEATON was born 29 October 1801 in Bridgewater, Luzerne Co., Penn.; died in Fulton Co., Ohio, 5 December 1865, age 64. She married **Reuben S. HALL**; born 27 January 1795 in Pennsylvania; died in Fulton Co., Ohio, 13 August 1875, age 80.

They had the following children:

1627	i.	Sally Ann (1822-1900)
1628	ii.	Eliza Jane (1825-1849)
1629	iii.	Anson W. (1827-1911)
1630	iv.	Washington J. (1829-1909)
1631	v.	Amos W. (1831-1908)
1632	vi.	Mary M. (1833-1913)
1633	vii.	David Schuyler (1836-1926)
1634	viii.	Rebecca (1838-1923)

The grandchildren of Waitstill and Elizabeth (White) Cook[425]

795. Rufus Norton COOK[426] was born 26 March 1798 in Cornwall, Addison Co., Vt. He married **Ester REED**, born 29 July 1797; died in Malden Rock, Pierce Co., Wisc., 13 June 1886, age 88.
They had the following children:

1635	i.	Martha
1636	ii.	Fremont (1821-)
1637	iii.	Nancy Marie (1823-)
1638	iv.	Morton Sonfronian (1825-1907)
1639	v.	Elizabeth (1830-1916)
1640	vi.	Ambrose L. (1835-1911)
1641	vii.	Susan A. (1838-1910)

796. Amanda COOK was born on 15 June 1809 in Guilford, Conn. On 30 July 1827, when she was 18, she married **Benjamin Case LEETE**,[427] son of Edmund LEETE and Fanny GOLDSMITH, in Guilford, Conn.; born 23 September 1804 in Leetes Island, Guilford, Conn.; died in Guilford, 22 October 1883, age 79. He married four times and had descendants by two of his wives.
They had the following children:

1642	i.	John Eugene (1828-1829)
1643	ii.	Daniel Sherwood (1829-1896)
1644	iii.	Benjamin (1831-1833)
1645	iv.	Charity (1832-1854)
1646	v.	Justin Orlando (1834-1863)
1647	vi.	Sarah Page (1837-1902)
1648	vii.	Mary Jane (1838-1899)
1649	viii.	Douglas Merwin (1841-1886)
1650	ix.	Emily Case (1843-1864)
1651	x.	Susan Amanda (1847-1868)

The children of Shem and _____ (Dibble) Kentfield[428]

797. Palmon KENTFIELD was born 17 April 1780 in Charlestown, N.H. On 3 December 1802, when he was 22, he married **Rebecca BAKER** in Remsen, Oneida Co., N.Y.; born 1 October 1780 in Pawtuxet, Providence Co., R.I.; died in Providence, Providence Co., R.I. She was the mother of eight, four of whom married and three had progeny.
They had the following children:

1652	i.	?
1653	ii.	?
1654	iii.	?
1655	iv.	Smith (1804-1804)
1656	v.	Laurana (1805-1864)
1657	vi.	Rebecca (1808-1885)
1658	vii.	Jeremiah B. (1818-1894)
1659	viii.	John (1822-1894)

798. Warren KENTFIELD.

The children of John and Sally Dibble[429]

799. Maria Seely DIBBLE was born in 1790 and died in 1841, about age 51.

800. John DIBBLE was born in 1792. On 25 November 1820, when he was 28, he married **Fanny SEELY** in Darien, Fairfield Co., Conn. She was born in 1792.

801. Charles Henry DIBBLE was born in 1794 and died in 1850, about age 56. On 14 October 1845, when he was 51, he married **Sally Ann WEBB** in Stamford, Fairfield Co., Conn.; born 16 February 1825 in Stamford; died there, 4 October 1851, age 26.

They had one child:

1660	i.	Sarah F. (1846-1850)

802. Betsy Ann DIBBLE was born in 1796.

The grandchildren of Elijah and Lydia (Dibble) Birge[430]

803. Nancy BIRGE was born in 1779 in Lenox, Mass.; died in Bond, Ill. in 1840, about age 61. She was the mother of 11, including a set of twins. All married, and nine of her children had descendants. In 1795, when she was about 16, she married **Joseph BILYEU** in New Jersey; born in 1765 in New Jersey; died in Bond, Ill., in 1845, about age 80.

They had the following children:

1661	i.	Sarah (1799-1850)
1662	ii.	John Birge (1801-1873)
1663	iii.	Isaac Smith (1801-1856)
1664	iv.	Joseph (1804-1868)
1665	v.	Garrett Page (1810-1850)
1666	vi.	Jesse Walker (1811-1860)
1667	vii.	Wesley A. (1812-1867)
1668	viii.	Thomas Coke (1816-1878)
1669	ix.	Mary Magdalene (1820-1853)
1670	x.	Finis (1825-1862)
1671	xi.	William Burge (1826-1851)

804. Lydia BIRGE was born in 1780 in Lenox, Mass.; died on 22 February 1811, about age 31.

805. Elijah BIRGE. Born in 1782 in Lenox, Mass. Elijah died in 1854, about age 72. In 1805, when he was 23, he married **Mary OLDS**; born in 1785 and died in 1869, about age 84.

They had the following children[431]:

1672	i.	Daniel Olds (1806-1846)
1673	ii.	Martin Howland (1806-1906)
1674	iii.	Lucinda (1808-)
1675	iv.	Lydia (1810-1810)
1676	v.	Ebenezer Cross (1810-)
1677	vi.	Ezra (1812-1813)
1678	vii.	Laura (1816-1844)
1679	viii.	J. (1816-1816)
1680	ix.	Cyrus K. (1819-1842)

806. James BIRGE was born in 1784 in Pultney, Vt.; died in Greenville, Bond Co., Ill., in 1851, about age 67. On 5 January 1811, when he was 27, he married **Abilene EATON**, who was born in 1789. One of their six children had descendants.

They had the following children:

1681	i.	Lydia (1811-)
1682	ii.	Lucy (1813-)
1683	iii.	David E. (1815-1860)
1684	iv.	Frances (1823-)
1685	v.	Cyrus (1828-1888)
1686	vi.	Alpheus (1830-)

807. Rebecca BIRGE was born in 1786 in Pulteny, Vt., and died in 1862, about age 76.

808. Ansel BIRGE was born in 1788 in Poultney, Vt., and died 4 October 1854, about age 66. On 10 May 1829, when he was 41, he married **Millicent Clay TWISS**; born in 1808 and died in 1896, about age 88. Four of their seven children had descendants.
They had the following children:

1687	i.	Cyrus (1829-)
1688	ii.	Edwin (1830-1899)
1689	iii.	Julia (1839-1871)
1690	iv.	Emma (1842-1922)
1691	v.	William (1845-1894)
1692	vi.	Laura (1847-1934)
1693	vii.	Alice (1855-1933)

809. David BIRGE was born in 1790. He married **Maria _____**.
They had one child:

1694	i.	Sarah M. (1815-)

810. Abigail BIRGE was born in 1792 in Poultney, Vt., and died in 1851, about age 59.

811. Warren BIRGE was born in 1794 in New Haven, Conn., and died in 1850, about age 56.

812. Cyrus BIRGE was born in 1797 in New Haven; died 21 February 1871, about age 74. On 25 February 1821, when he was 24, he married (1) **Mary HOWELL** in Greenville, Bond Co., Ill.; born in 1805 in New York; died in Greenville, Bond Co., Ill., 23 February 1828, about 23.
They had the following children:

1695	i.	Henry Warren (1823-1909)
1696	ii.	Joseph Howell (1825-)

On 23 September 1828, when he was 31, he married (2) **Adeline FRINK**, who was born in 1808 and died in 1884, about age 76.
They had the following children:

1697	i.	Mary Howell (1830-1912)
1698	ii.	Anna Eliza (1833-1896)

The grandchildren of Billious and Lydia (Dibble) Hill[432]

813. Molly SKEELS was born about 1777 in Glastonbury, Conn.; died in Delaware, Ohio, 28 February 1834, about age 57. She was christened in 1777 in Glastonbury. She married **Ralph CASE**.

814. Joseph SKEELS was christened in 1777.

815. William SKEELS.

816. Samuel SKEELS.

817. Lydia SKEELS married _____ **WHITE**.

818. Roxana SKEELS was born 5 October 1799 in Dunham, Canada East; died in Lee Co., Ill., 7 April 1883, age 83. She married **Russell TOWN**.

819. Nelson SKEELS was born 15 May 1802 in Canada; died 14 November 1859, age 57. He married **Eleanor BENNET**.

820. Arad SKEELS was born on 9 June 1779; died on 21 Jul 1855, age 76. He married (1) **Sarah LAKE** and (2) **Sybilia WOODEN**.

821. Belias Hill SKEELS was born 26 August 1782; died 14 April 1859. He married **Betsy HENDY**.

822. Simeon SKEELS was born 8 September 1784; died 1 March 1861. He married **Roxy DEMING**.

823. Henry SKEELS was born in 1786 and died in N.Y., unmarried.

824. Reuben SKEELS was born on 9 June 1788; died 22 April 1864, age 75. He married **Salley REED**.

825. Truman SKEELS was born in 1792 and died after 1850. He married **Betsey B. BISWELL**.

826. Harry SKEELS was born in 1794 and died about 1812, when he was about 18.

827. Almira SKEELS was born 13 September 1796; died in Adair, Iowa, 12 February 1861, age 64. She married **Azariah ROOT Jr.**

828. Harvey SKEELS was born 12 March 1799 in Essex, N.Y.; died 28 October 1867, age 68. He married (1) **Betsey ANDREWS** and (2) married **Huldah May VINING**.

829. Polly SKEELS was born in 1801 and died 28 February 1835, about age 34. She married (1) **James**

H. WILSON and (2) **Ralph CASE**.

830. Susanna SKEELS was born in 1803 and died after 1824. She married **Silas S. LAMPSON**.

831. Chloe SKEELS was born in 1805; died in Iroquois, Ill., in 1870. She married **John H. KELLY**.

832. Unnamed daughter of Truman and Chloe SKEELS was born in 1808 and died in infancy.

833. ?Sally SKEELS married **Abijah BRADLEY**.

834. Bradford HILL,[433] son of Reuben and Jane (Bradley) Hill, was born at Middlebury or New Haven, Addison Co., Vermont, 8 July 1805; died at Lime Springs, Howard Co., Iowa, 31 August 1885, at age 80. When he was seven, he moved with his parents to Genesee Co., N.Y., where he learned the trade of carpentry, married, and began to raise a family. In 1836, in a "prairie schooner" of his own making, he brought his family to Galena, Illinois. He later removed to Laporte, Indiana, and then in 1842 to Waterloo, Jefferson County, Wisconsin. In 1868, he relocated to Iowa and built a grist mill at Lime Spring(s), Howard County. He died there in 1885 and his wife died there about four years later. He married, in Covington, Genesee Co., N.Y., 22 August 1833, **Catherine CUMMINGS**; born about 1813; died in Lime Springs in about 1889.

They had the following children:

| 1699 | i. | Henry Reuben (1843-) |
| 1700 | ii. | Fred (1844-) |

835. perhaps other descendant(s) of Reuben & Jane HILL.

The grandchildren of Samuel and Mary (Dibble) Benedict[434]

836. John BENEDICT was born 11 May 1800 in Vermont; died in Hull, Quebec, Canada, 13 November 1859, age 59. On 23 March 1836, when he was 35, he married **Mary Ann McALLISTER**, born in 1805 in Hull, Quebec.

They had the following children:

1701	i.	Eleanor (1836-1912)
1702	ii.	Jenny (1839-)
1703	iii.	Solomon (1841-)

837. Samuel BENEDICT was born 27 January 1805 in Lower Canada; died in 1848, about age 42. On 15 July 1847, when he was 42, he married **Eleanor Jane McALLISTER**, who was born in 1810. She may be related to Samuel's sister-in-law, Mary Ann Mcallister, but a relationship is not shown in Ancestry.com.

They had the following children:

1704	i.	Eleanor (1835-)
1705	ii.	Sarah (1837-)
1706	iii.	Charles (1840-)
1707	iv.	Mary Ann (1842-)
1708	v.	Jane "Jenny" (1848-)

838. David BENEDICT was born 17 June 1807 in Lower Canada; died 9 September 1849, age 42. In 1835, when he was about 27, he married **Jane WADSWORTH**, who was born in 1813 and died in 1893, about age 80. At least one of their nine children had descendants.

They had the following children:

1709	i.	David (1835-)
1710	ii.	Matilda (1837-)
1711	iii.	Jerucia (1839-)
1712	iv.	Elizabeth (1841-)
1713	v.	William James (1844-)
1714	vi.	Samuel I. (1845-)
1715	vii.	Samuel John (1846-)
1716	viii.	Dawson Alexander (1848-1941)
1717	ix.	Charles (1850-1851)

839. Clarissa BENEDICT was born 6 September 1813 in Sharon, Windsor Co., Vt.; died in Aylmer, Hull, Quebec, Canada, 4 November 1888, age 75. In 1836, when she was 22, she married **Robert**

STEWART; born in 1811 in Monaghan, Ireland; died in South Hull, Quebec, Canada, 1 Mar 1882, about age 71. Two of their children had descendants.

They had the following children:

1718	i.	Jane (1836-)
1719	ii.	Lucy (1839-1926)
1720	iii.	Maria (1843-)
1721	iv.	David (1844-)
1722	v.	Robert (1845-)
1723	vi.	Samuel (1848-)
1724	vii.	Clarissa (1852-1921)

The children of Samuel and Eleanor (Shatford) Benedict[435]

840. Mary BENEDICT was born 27 January 1816 in Hull, Quebec, Canada. She married **John FARIS**, who was born in 1808 and died in 1897, about age 89.

They had one child:

1725	i.	Jane (1849-1902)

841. Eunice BENEDICT was born 1 July 1817. On 29 January 1850, when she was 32, she married **Henry FARRAR**.

842. Lucy BENEDICT was born 3 February 1820 in Hull, Quebec; died in Hayworth, Quebec, Canada. On 16 March 1848, at age 28, she married **Joseph H. HETHERINGTON**, born 16 August 1821.

They had the following children:

1726	i.	Richard Albert (1849-)
1727	ii.	Eleanor Amelia (1850-)
1728	iii.	Joseph (1852-1925)
1729	iv.	Henry (1855-1885)
1730	v.	Sarah (1856-1885)
1731	vi.	William (1859-1927)
1732	vii.	Thomas H. (1863-)

843. Samuel BENEDICT was born 29 May 1822 and died in 1906, about age 83. On 9 November 1848, when he was 26, he married **Fanny MAXWELL**.

They had the following children:

1733	i.	Harriet Sophia
1734	ii.	Samuel Ezra (1849-)
1735	iii.	Ann Elizabeth (1851-)
1736	iv.	William Henry (1853-)
1737	v.	Amelia Jane (1857-)
1738	vi.	George Frederick (1862-)
1739	vii.	Thomas Walter (1865-)
1740	viii.	Emily Sarah (1869-)

844. Moses BENEDICT was born 22 August 1824. On 30 August 1855, when he was 31, he married **Eleanor BENEDICT** (1701), daughter of John BENEDICT (836) and Mary Ann McALLISTER; born 3 January 1836 and died in 1912, about age 75. Moses Benedict and Eleanor Benedict were first cousins, once removed. Moses was a grandson of Samuel Benedict Sr. and Mary Dibble, and Eleanor was a great-grand daughter of the same couple.

They had the following children:

1741	i.	Eleanor L. (1856-)
1742	ii.	Samuel A. (1858-)
1743	iii.	John Carroll (1860-)
1744	iv.	William (Wilson) Alexander (1864-1865)
1745	v.	Sarah A. (1866-)
1746	vi.	Solomon George (1868-)
1747	vii.	Joseph Franklin (1876-1952)

845. Joseph BENEDICT was born 29 December 1828; died 8 April 1828. On 16 November 1858, when he was 29, he married **Maria HICKS**, who was born in 1839 and died in 1931, about age 92. They had the following children:

1748	i.	Margaret Jane (1860-)
1749	ii.	Thomas Franklin (1862-)
1750	iii.	William Sidney (1864-)

846. Margaret BENEDICT was born 1 December 1830.

847. Sarah BENEDICT was born 7 June 1834. On 29 April 1860, when she was 25, she married **James MAXWELL**, who was born in 1832 and died in 1913, about 81. They had the following children:

1751	i.	Elizabeth (1864-)
1752	ii.	Robert (1865-1931)
1753	iii.	William (1869-1931)
1754	iv.	Sarah (1872-1949)
1755	v.	Jane (1877-)

The children of Ezra and Sarah (Stockwell) Benedict[436]

848. Squires BENEDICT was born 28 July 1803. On 1 December 1825, when he was 22, he married **Adelia Maria ROOD**; born 2 August 1803; died 12 June 1859, age 55. They had the following children:

1756	i.	Armenia Adelia (1826-)
1757	ii.	Sabrina Mable (1828-)
1758	iii.	Ezra Denison (1830-)
1759	iv.	John Rood (1833-)
1760	v.	Charles Rood (1837-)
1761	vi.	Cornelius Nichols (1839-)
1762	vii.	Adna Squires (1841-)
1763	viii.	Mary (Twin) (1843-)
1764	ix.	Martha (Twin) (1843-)

849. Cromwell BENEDICT was born 28 January 1805. On 16 April 1833, when he was 28, he married **Hannah ADAMS**, who was born 11 September 1813. They had the following children:

1765	i.	? [Infant] (1834-)
1766	ii.	Sarah F. (1840-)
1767	iii.	Albert Crumiel (1844-)
1768	iv.	Hannah Amelia (1846-)

850. Daniel BENEDICT was born 13 November 1807. On 14 July 1830, when he was 22, he married **Lucy SMALLEY**, who was born 3 December 1810 and died in 1889, about age 78. They had the following children:

1769	i.	Julius S. (1831-)
1770	ii.	Lydia A. (1833-)
1771	iii.	Carlos N. (1835-)
1772	iv.	Sarah (1837-)
1773	v.	Frederick (1839-)
1774	vi.	Martha S. (1841-)
1775	vii.	Ellen P. (1844-)
1776	viii.	Abby E. (1846-)
1777	ix.	Lunette F. (1849-)
1778	x.	Albert D. (1854-)

851. Lucy BENEDICT was born 7 January 1809.

852. Martin Michael BENEDICT was born 5 August 1816 and died in 1914, about age 97. On 1 January 1844, when he was 27, he married **Althea H. COLEMON**; born 1 September 1820; died in

1912, about age 91.

They had the following children:

    1779   i.   Faber (1845-)

    1780   ii.   Francis Morgan (1847-)

853. Hannah BENEDICT was born 6 July 1823.

The children of William and Rachel (Benedict) Grimes[437]

854. William GRIMES was born in 1806 and died in 1897, about age 91.

855. Samuel GRIMES was born in 1809. He married **Sarah SHATFORD**; born in 1809; died 22 June 1881, about age 72.

856. Elizabeth GRIMES was born 1 May 1811. In 1835, about age 23, she married **Robert KENNY**; born 5 June 1808 in Fernaugh, Ireland; died in Aylmer, Quebec, Canada, 17 March 1896, age 87.

857. James GRIMES was born 23 September 1814 in Quebec, Canada; died in Aylmer, Quebec, Canada, 5 March 1888, age 73. He married **Jane McCONNEL**; born in 1828 in Quebec; died in Aylmer, Quebec, 27 March 1918, about age 90.

They had the following children:

    1781   i.   James Eliot (1851-)

    1782   ii.   Richard Thomas (1854-)

    1783   iii.   Andrew (1865-)

    1784   iv.   Arthur (1872-)

858. Rachel GRIMES was born in 1822.

859. Miriam GRIMES was born in 1824.

860. Mary GRIMES was born in 1826. She married **Gilbert WILCOX**, who died 27 February 1877.

They had one child:

    1785   i.   Franklin (1860-)

861. Triphina GRIMES was born in 1829 and died in 1912, about age 83. She married **Charles PURCELL**, who was born in 1822 and died in 1899, about age 77.

The children of Benjamin and Hannah (Benedict) Chamberlain[438]

862. Mehetabel CHAMBERLAIN was born in 1806. In 1838, she married **Ira MASON**.

863. Nathaniel CHAMBERLAIN was born in 1808. In 1847, he married **Mary Ann SHERMAN**.

The grandchildren of Phineas and Rhoda (Kilbourne) Hill[439]

864. Caroline Clarissa LATHROP was born 20 November 1828; died on 22 November 1828.

865. Caroline Clarissa [2] LATHROP was born 5 August 1831; died 11 January 1903, age 71. On 21 October 1857, when she was 26, she married **Jesse BERDETTE**.

The grandchildren of Isaac and Eunice (Mallory) Hill[440]

866. Son of Luke HILL was born between 1780 and1790; died perhaps before 1830.

867. Daughter 1 of Luke HILL was born between 1780-1790.

868. Daughter 2 of Luke HILL was born between 1780-1790.

869. Daughter 3 of Luke HILL was born between 1800-1810.

870. Daughter 4 of Luke HILL was born between 1810-1815.

The children of Isaac Jr. [III] and Elizabeth Ann (Bunnell) Hill[441]

871. Maria Ann HILL[442] was born 20 March 1795 in Woodbury, Litchfield Co., Conn.; died in Wakeman, Huron Co., Ohio, 20 October 1866, age 71. On 23 April 1817, when she was 22, she married **Bela COE**, son of Israel COE; born 24 April 1795 in Granville, Mass.; died in Wakeman, Huron Co., Ohio, 5 October 1849, age 54.

They had one child:

    1786   i.   Almon Bela (1820-)

872. Benjamin HILL[443] was born 7 November 1796 in Woodbury, Conn.; died in Fairfield Township, Huron Co., Ohio, in 1876, about age 79. He was a blacksmith, who received eight cents per shoe for shoeing horses. He lived in Clarksfield, Ohio, in 1825, and in 1862 he removed to Fairfield Township in Huron County, Ohio. In 1820, when he was about 23, he married (1) **Mary SHANKS** in Portage Co.,

Ohio. She died about 1827. On 18 December 1828, when was about 32, he married (2) **Julia STEPHENS**,[444] daughter of Jonthan STEPHENS and Olive HIETT, in Huron Co., Ohio; died in 1875 in Fairfield Township, Huron Co., Ohio.
They had the following children:

1787	i.	Jonathan
1788	ii.	Hoyt
1789	iii.	Alvin
1790	iv.	Alfred "Fred"

873. Leverett (Leveritt) HILL[445] was born 16 March 1798 in Woodbury, Litchfield Co., Conn.; died in Wakeman, Huron Co., Ohio, 2 October 1851, age 53. He and his wife maintained a station on the Underground Railroad. On 25 April 1829, when he was 31, he married **Esther STRONG**, daughter of Ariel STRONG; born about 1800; died in Wakeman, Ohio, about 1893, about age 93.
They had the following children:

1791	i.	Leverett Benedict (1831-1892)
1792	ii.	Edgar S. (~1834->1896)
1793	iii.	Elizabeth (~1836-1838)
1794	iv.	Edwin Stoddard (1837->1896)
1795	v.	Elizabeth E. (~1839->1896)
1796	vi.	Isaac Curtiss (1843->1896)
1797	vii.	Julius M. (~1847-1902)

874. Charles W. HILL was born 14 August 1799; died 27 September 1801, age 2.

875. Elizabeth Ann HILL was born 31 May 1801; died 22 August 1828, age 27.

876. Sophia HILL[446] was born 25 March 1803; died 10 January 1875, age 71. On 19 November 1847, when she was 44, she married **Asa WHEELER**,[447] son of Asa WHEELER Sr., in Huron Co., Ohio; born about 1793 in Conn.; died 21 January 1875, about 82. He was a farm laborer in Oberlin, Ohio.
They had one child:

| 1798 | i. | Betsy B. (~1844-) |

877. Ruth Emily HILL[448] was born 7 March 1805; died in Oberlin, Ohio in 1872, about age 66. On 17 August 1828, when she was 23, she married, as his second wife, **John HOUGH**,[449] in Huron Co., Ohio; died in 1872 in Oberlin, Ohio. He was a harness and saddle maker, and he was a strong worker for the Underground Railway, having helped 1000 slaves escape.
They had the following children:

1799	i.	Ann (~1830-1854)
1800	ii.	Cordelia
1801	iii.	Ellen (~1838-1855)
1802	iv.	William G. (~1835-1872)
1803	v.	Jonathan T. (~1840-1846)
1804	vi.	Frances M. (~1842-)
1805	vii.	Infant 1
1806	viii.	Infant 2

878. Charles 2d HILL[450] was born 6 March 1807; died in Tabor, Iowa; 7 January 1865, age 57. On 28 July 1830, when he was 23, he married (1) **Elizabeth SPRAGUE** in Huron Co., Ohio. On 24 July 1831, when he was 24, he married (2) **Melinda (Malinda) LYON**, daughter of Charles LYON and Deborah PALMER, in Huron Co., Ohio; born 10 April 1813 in Cayuga Co., N.Y.; died in Tabor, Iowa, 12 August 1892, age 79.
They had the following children:

1807	i.	Charles Willis
1808	ii.	John Watson
1809	iii.	Martha Cornelia

879. Austin (Justin) HILL[451] was born 26 December 1808; died in St. Louis, Michigan, in 1873, about age 64. On 27 September 1830, when he was 21, he married **Cornelia ROWLAND**, daughter of Levi

ROWLAND,[452] in Huron Co., Ohio; born 25 July 1814 in North East, N.Y.; died in Michigan, probably on 13 Jun 1903, age 88.

They had the following children:

1810	i.	Phoebe
1811	ii.	Albert R. (~1838-)
1812	iii.	Jane A. (~1846-)
1813	iv.	Charles E. (~1855-)

880. Sylvester HILL[453] was born 17 December 1810; died in Kansas, 19 November 1878, age 67. On 19 November 1835, when he was 24, he married **Clarissa APPLEBEE (APPLEBY)** in Huron Co., Ohio; born 17 April 1815.

They had the following children:

1814	i.	Isaac H. (1836-1849)
1815	ii.	Truman Olvord "O. B." (1838-)
1816	iii.	Elmore D. (1843-1854)
1817	iv.	Martin L. (1845-1864)
1818	v.	Ellen G. (1848-1853)
1819	vi.	Charles H. (~1851-)
1820	vii.	Homer C. (1852-)
1821	viii.	Benjamin H. (~1854-)
1822	ix.	Horace B. (1855-)

881. Esther HILL was born 20 September 1812; died 30 September 1816, age 4.

882. Sarah "Sally" B. HILL[454] was born 11 March 1814; died 14 October 1865, age 51. In August 1844, when she was 30, she married **Zenus (Zenas) D. BRADISH**,[455] son of Luke BRADISH; born about 1817. He was a wagon maker.

They had the following children:

1823	i.	Elizabeth Ann (~1849-)
1824	ii.	Emily Marie (~1853-)
1825	iii.	Ellen Josephine (~1855-)

883. Charlotte HILL was born 12 March 1816. On 19 November 1835, when she was 19, she married **Rev. William H. NICKERSON, M.D.**; born in 1814 in New York State; died in Jasper Co., Ill., 28 February 1867, age 53. He was a Methodist preacher, a physician, a Mason, and chaplain of 32d Ohio Vol., Union Army, in the Civil War.[456]

They had the following children:

1826	i.	Samuel (~1836-)
1827	ii.	Hoyt H. (1838-1908)
1828	iii.	Elizabeth (~1840->1870)
1829	iv.	Mariah (~1842-)
1830	v.	William V. (~1844-~1865)
1831	vi.	Joseph E. (~1846->1870)
1832	vii.	Charles F. (~1848-<1870)

The children of Benajah and Mary (Jackson) Hill[457]

884. Isaac HILL was born about 1804 in Southbury, Conn.; died before 1870. He was a mechanic. He married Caroline _____, who was born in about 1804-1806.

They had the following children:

1833	i.	Isaac L. (~1831-)
1834	ii.	Henry (~1834-)
1835	iii.	Carlyle (~1840-)
1836	iv.	Mariette (~1842-)
1837	v.	Eunice "Currence" (~1844-)
1838	vi.	Charles L. (~1846-)
1839	vii.	Caroline "Atlanta" (~1849-)

885. Probably other children HILL.

The children of Seth Sloane and Mary Ann "Polly" (Stilson) Hill[458]

886. Harvey S. HILL[459] was born in 1799; died in Derby, Conn., in 1852, about age 53. In 1821, when he was about 22, he married Mehitable BURR; born in 1798; died in 1883, about age 85. They had one child:

| 1840 | i. | William (1831-1891) |

887. Harriet HILL[460] was born in 1801 in Newtown, Conn. On 14 October 1821, when she was about 20, she married **Joseph Middlebrook HUBBELL**, son of Joseph HUBBELL and Eunice HOOKER; born 20 August 1800 in Weston, Conn.; died in Newtown, Conn., 17 Dec 1831, age 31. They had the following children:

1841	i.	Horace (1822-)
1842	ii.	George Albert (1824-)
1843	iii.	Catherine (1826-)
1844	iv.	David Toucey (1827-)
1845	v.	Edward (1830-)

The children of Seth Slone and Mary Ann (Gorman) Hill[461]

888. Luke HILL was born 8 June 1826; died 23 December 1923, age 97. He was a carpenter in Sparta Twp., Noble Co., Ind., in 1870, with a wife and 3 children. He married (1) **Mary Ann MYERS**. They had the following children:

1846	i.	Seth (~1848-)
1847	ii.	Andrew (~1851-)
1848	iii.	Ann (~1854-)

He married (2) married **Lucinda DAVAULT**.
He married (3) **Amanda M. MORRIS**.

889. Daughter HILL was born about 1827.

890. Sarah Ann HILL was born in 1828.

891. Charles McNair HILL,[462] born 19 March 1830 in Titusville, Penn.; died in Yorkville, Kendall Co., Ill., 7 March 1918, age 87. He was buried in the Pavilion Cemetery, Yorkville. He was a mason in Kendall Twp., Ill., in 1860, and in Fox Twp. in 1870. He served in 127th Ill. Vols., Union Army, Civil War, and he was a member of the Pavilion Baptist Church. In 1853, when was about 22, he m. **Sarah Jane JOHNSON** in Pennsylvania; born about 1836 in Indiana; died in Kendall Co., in 1900, about 64. They had the following children:

1849	i.	Myron B. "Myra" (1859-1954)
1850	ii.	Theresa Mary (1861-1951)
1851	iii.	John G. (or U.) (1863-1942)
1852	iv.	Charles A. "Charley" (1868-)
1853	v.	Ernest Oliver "Ernie" (1870-)
1854	vi.	Frank B. (1875-1957)
1855	vii.	Frederick W. (1878-1933)

892. Michael Gorman HILL was born 22 June 1833; died 11 March 1911, age 77. He was a blacksmith in Sparta Twp., Noble Co., Indiana, in 1860, and he did cabinet work in Auglaize Twp., Pauling Co., Ohio, 1870. In about 1859, when he was about 25, he married **Jenette (aka Genette) Catherine KEMP**, who was born in about 1838 in New York State. They had the following children:

1856	i.	John (1860-)
1857	ii.	Nancy (1862-)
1858	iii.	Alice R. (1867-)

893. Joseph HILL was born in 1839 and died in about 1860.

894. William Prince HILL,[463] eldest of the 10 children of Ephraim and Charlotte (Prince) Hill, was born at Litchfield, Connecticut, 28 February 1804; died at Caton Township, Steuben Co., N.Y., 4 August 1885. His parents were the children of Revolutionary War soldiers who lived in southern Connecticut.

His father was born in New Haven County, near Long Island Sound, and his mother was born at New Milford, in the western part of the state. His parents migrated west to what is now Ohio. They traveled by covered wagon with two of William Prince Hill's uncles and at least eight other children at about the time of the War of 1812, when he was eight years old. The brothers separated in Ohio, each going his own way. William's parents went back to New York State, just over the border from Pennsylvania, where they settled in Chenango County. They later went west again, to Steuben County, New York, in 1824. The part of Steuben County where they settled was originally called Painted Post, and later became known as Corning. They were among the founders of a village south of Corning that became known as Caton. As a young man, William worked as a hired laborer on the farm of Ephraim Robbins, who also came to Caton in 1824.

William Hill's father died accidentally in 1832 while doing carpentry work on a barn when William was 28 years old, leaving him to be the head of the large family. His mother remarried ten years later, to a widower with nine children. This family of some seventeen brothers, sisters, step-brothers and step-sisters (two other children had died) was unusually congenial, judging by the names that appeared in their later marriages, and in the will of his step-father, Joseph Gillett. In 1873, the William P. Hill farm was located about one-half mile southeast of Caton Center, NY, immediately south of the farms of J. Gillett, and G. Gillett, who were possibly his step-brothers, and just north of the Gillett cemetery.

William Prince Hill was 44 when his step-father died, leaving his mother, then 67, widowed for a second time. Although she was provided for in the will of her second husband, and by her original dowry, her son William was undoubtedly considered to be responsible for her. She died 23 years later, at the age of 89. William, who together with his wife had raised ten children of his own, lived for another 37 years and died at the age of 81. He was killed in an accident when he was driving a buggy and the horses were startled by a passing train. At least three of his children migrated west to Iowa at about the time of the beginning of the Civil War. William Prince Hill died intestate; his estate was administered on 30 March 1887, in the second year after he died. There were 11 heirs in addition to his wife, Sarah P. Hill: four sons, four daughters, and three grandchildren. He was buried at Caton, N.Y., where his stone is marked "Wm. P. Hill 1804 - 1885 and Family."

He married, probably in New York state, in about 1827-1828, **Sarah P. "Sally" HERRICK**, daughter of Rufus and Jerusha (Palmer) Herrick; born at Guilford, Chenango County, New York, 23 January 1808; died at Corning, Steuben County, N.Y., 27 January 1895. William and Sarah (Herrick) Hill had ten children, born at Steuben County, New York. Eight of the children survived their father, and were still living in 1887 when their father's estate was administered. Charles W. had moved to Iowa, and was the father of George J. Hill, the Iowa Pioneer. Sarah and Harlow also went to Wright County, Iowa, where Harlow soon drowned as a young man; and Diantha went to Michigan. Sarah never married. George Washington, Amanda and Diantha were married, to members of the Breese, Kimball, Richards, and Reed families.

SARAH P. ("Sally") HERRICK,[464] third daughter and probably the youngest of the eight children of Rufus Herrick, was born at Guilford, Chenango County, N.Y., 23 January 1808; died at Corning, Steuben County, N.Y., 27 January 1895, age 87. She was buried 30 January 1895 in Caton, N.Y. She was a daughter of Rufus Herrick by his second wife, Jerusha Palmer. Sarah Herrick moved from Chenango County to Steuben County with her parents in about 1827 when she was nineteen years old. Within a year or two her parents had died. In about 1828 she married William Prince Hill, by whom she had ten children between 1830 and 1847. She survived her husband and was listed as his widow when his estate was administered on 30 March 1887.

They had the following children:

1859	i.	Edgar E. [19] (1829-1901)
1860	ii.	Charles W. [20] (1831-1923)
1861	iii.	Emily [23] "Emma" (1833-1917)
1862	iv.	Sarah [26] (1835-1925)
1863	v.	George Washington [21] (1837-1917)
1864	vi.	Amanda [24] (1838-1887)

1865	vii.	Jerusha [25] "J. M." (~1841-1895)
1866	viii.	Diantha [22] (~1843->1895)
1867	ix.	Mary M. [27] (~1845-)
1868	x.	Harland P. [28] "Harlow" (1847-1869)

895. George J. HILL,[465] second son and second of the twelve children of Ephraim and Charlotte (Prince) Hill, was born at New Milford, Litchfield County, Connecticut, 21 August 1805; died, probably at Caton, New York, 3 November 1876; he was 71. He was buried at Caton.

His parents migrated to the Northwest Territory, now Ohio, in about 1812, with some of his father's siblings, but they did not stay long in that area. They returned east, living for a time in Chenango County, and they then moved again to Steuben County, where they became some of the first settlers in an area south of Painted Post that was known as Caton. Ephraim died eight years after the family arrived in Caton and Charlotte remarried; her second husband was a widower, Joseph Gillette, who -- like Charlotte -- was responsible for a large family.

The Hill and Gillette [aka Gillett, Gillet] families lived in adjacent farms and their descendants intermarried over the next two generations. Other neighboring families were the Herricks (some of who came with the Hills from Chenango County to Steuben County) and the Rileys. The Herricks and Rileys also intermarried with the Hills and Gillettes over the next two generations. George J. Hill's first wife was Esther Jackson Riley, daughter of Josiah and Susannah (Hendryx) Riley. Esther's brother, Simeon, married Katherine Gillett, whose daughter Adelia married Charles W. Hill, a nephew of George J. Hill. Charles and Adelia (Riley) Hill named one of their sons for his uncle; this was George J. Hill (II).

George J. Hill (1805-1876) was the first of three to bear this name. The second was his great-nephew, George J. Hill (1857-1952), the Iowa Pioneer. The third was George James Hill, (b. 1932). None of George Hill's ancestors for several generations were named George, so perhaps he was named for General George Washington (1732-1799). Indeed, his nephew, son of his older brother William, was specifically named for the general: He was George Washington Hill. In 1850, George J. Hill and his wife and two children were living in Caton, New York, near his widowed mother and his brother, Noble, and their families.

George J. Hill married (1), probably in Caton, N.Y., 11 February 1832, **Esther Jackson RILEY,**[466] daughter of Josiah (aka Isaiah) and Susannah (Hendryx) Riley; born at Bennington, Vermont, 1 September 1804; died, probably in Steuben County, N.Y., 16 December 1861; she was 57. George and Esther (Riley) Hill had three children: Mary Amanda (1835-1840); Stilson Edward (1838-1917); and Joseph Gillett (1842-after 1911). Stilson was a Sergeant and Joseph was a Private in the Union Army.[467] After the death of Esther (Riley) Hill, George J. Hill married (2), **Maria C. SCHUTT**; born 24 May 1816; died 31 July 1898, age 82. She was buried in Caton, N.Y. There was no issue from this marriage. George J. Hill and Ester Jackson Riley had the following children:

1869	i.	Mary Amanda [29] (1835-1840)
1870	ii.	Stilson Edward [30] (1838-1917)
1871	iii.	Joseph Gillett [31] (1842->1920)

896. Charlotte J. "Jane" HILL[168] was born 16 August 1807 in Conn.; died 29 September 1892, age 85. She was the mother of 1 as the wife of Aaron Gillett, who became her step-brother following her mother's marriage to his father. In about 1835, when she was about 27, she married **Aaron H. GILLETT**, son of Joseph GILLETT and Catherine HUNT; born in say 1805. He was the Co-executor of his father's estate. In 1835 he was the head of a family of two in Painted Post, with 32 acres of land and 12 meat cattle. They had one child:

| 1872 | i. | Huldah Jane [32] (1836-1886) |

897. Henry HILL was born 6 April 1809; died on 10 Mar 1812, age 2.

898. Huldah Jane HILL was born 10 March 1810; died on 30 Mar 1812, age 2.[469]

899. Noble HILL[470] was born 12 November 1812 in Conn.; died 16 March 1903, age 90, and was buried in Caton, N.Y. He was mentioned in the will of step-father, Joseph Gillett. In 1850 he and his wife and three children were living in Caton, New York, near his widowed mother and his brother, George, and their families. He married **Joanna J. "Jane" BREESE**; born 20 February 1816; died 24 April 1900, age

84, and was buried in Caton, N.Y.

They had the following children:

1873	i.	Syrene C. [35] "Cyrena" (1838-1854)
1874	ii.	Munroe B. [33] "Murray" (1841-1864)
1875	iii.	Earl A. [34] (aka Arthur E.) (1845-1921)
1876	iv.	Nye Robinson [36] "Henry" (1853->1920)

900. Huldah HILL[471] was born 2 April 1815; died 13 March 1885, age 69. She is said to have been the mother of fourteen children, and perhaps more. Her first child was born when she was 16. She married **Lewis GRIDLEY**,[472] perhaps as early as 1830, when she was 14 or 15. He came to Caton in 1822, two years before his father-in-law arrived. In the census of 1830, he appears as the head of the household of 2, with a female 15-20. His residence was adjacent to Ephraim Hill (with a large family), William P. Hill (2 males and 3 females) and Simeon Riley (male, age 20-30; and female, age 15-20).

They had the following children:

1877	i.	Hiram L. [37] (1831-1863)
1878	ii.	Emma A. [38] (1834-<1920)
1879	iii.	Jane C. [39] (1835-1918)
1880	iv.	Emma J. [40] (1836->1920)
1881	v.	Wesley Prince [41] (1838-1904)
1882	vi.	Albert Lavert [42] (1838-1865)
1883	vii.	Elizabeth H. [43] (1842-1863)
1884	viii.	Pliny Fisk [44] (1845-1920)
1885	ix.	Huldah P. [45] (1847-1850)
1886	x.	Elsie P. [46] (1850-1862)
1887	xi.	Manley D. [47] (1852-1856)
1888	xii.	Viola J. [48] (1854-1862)
1889	xiii.	Hettie V. [49] (1855-1862)
1890	xiv.	Alice J. [50] (1857-1862)

901. Samantha HILL[473] was born 13 March 1817; died 29 April 1878, age 61. On 9 July 1835, when she was 18, she married **William P. HOWE**, who died 19 January 1892.

They had the following children:

1891	i.	Gervis P. [51] (1836-1908)
1892	ii.	Augusta E. [52] (1839-1917)
1893	iii.	Francis Sylvester [53] (1842-)
1894	iv.	Charlotte P. [54] (1844-1908)
1895	v.	Mary Jane [55] (1849-)
1896	vi.	Smith J. [56] (1854-1920)
1897	vii.	Lewis [57]

902. Henry HILL[474] was born 7 July 1819; died 2 December 1892, age 73. He was mentioned in the will of his step-father, Joseph Gillett. In 1854-5 his family group (#161 in Caton) included his wife, Julia A. (age 32) and his mother Charlotte Gillett (age 73). He was then 35. Both he and his wife were born in Chenango County; his mother was born in Connecticut. He married **Julia A. MINAR**; born about 1822; died 6 November 1900, about age 78.

903. Sylvester J. HILL[475] was born 8 October 1821; died 2 December 1840, age 19; buried in Gillett cemetery, Caton, N.Y.

904. Ephraim Abram HILL[476] was born 3 March 1824 in New York State; died 16 January 1902, age 77. He was a farmer in Caton, N.Y., in the U.S. Census of 1850, with property worth $1000. He married **Mary M. REED**; born 23 November 1826; died 9 February 1911, age 84.

They had the following children:

1898	i.	Sylvester J. [58] (1846-)
1899	ii.	Julia E. "Juliette" [59] (1849->1920)
1900	iii.	Ezekiel (~1850-)

1901	iv.	Virgil Reed [60] (1853-1895)
1902	v.	Sherman B. [61] (1855->1922)
1903	vi.	Nellie L. [62] (1861-1911)

905. Isaac Edwin HILL[477] was born 14 March 1829 in Caton, N.Y.; died in Ithaca, N.Y., 30 April 1904, age 75. He was an heir of his step-father, Joseph Gillett. On 18 September 1850, when he was 21, he married (1) **Harriet Ruth TOBEY**,[478] daughter of Christopher TOBEY & Fidelia PRESTON; born in 1830 and died in 1870, about age 40. Two of her children died in one week of diphtheria.
They had the following children:

1904	i.	Charles Edwin [63] (1852-1934)
1905	ii.	Noble John Leland [64] (1855-1863)
1906	iii.	Plineas W. C. [65] (1863-1863)
1907	iv.	Elizabeth Merrick [66] (1869-)

On 4 December 1874, when he was 45, he married (2) **Charlotte HOLLEY**.
They had one child:

1908	i.	Clarence Sylvanus [67] (1876-)

906. Horace HENDRYX (HENDRIX)[479] was born in 1811; died in 1827. He was an adopted child.

The children of Roswell and Frances (Buckingham) Hill[480]

907. Henry HILL.

908. Adeline (aka Adaline) HILL was born in 1815 and died after 1870.

909. Theodore HILL, J.P.,[481] was born in 1817; died in West Jefferson, Madison Co., Ohio, 25 November 1896, about age 79. He was a shoemaker and clerk of Marion Township, Ohio. On 26 May 1840, when he was about 23, he married **Ann FILSON**, daughter of George FILSON, in Fayette Co., Ohio.; born about 1815 in Ohio.
They had the following children:

1909	i.	Margaret J. (1844-)
1910	ii.	George R. (1846-)
1911	iii.	William F. (1848-)
1912	iv.	Francis (aka Frances) A. (1850-)
1913	v.	Martha A. (1853-)
1914	vi.	James C. (1857-)

910. George W. HILL[482] was born 6 June 1821 in New Milford, Litchfield Co., Conn.; died in Bond Co., Ill., 13 November 1881, age 60. He was a merchant. On 25 August 1847, when he was 26, he married **Elizabeth Barnes PLANT**, daughter of Williamson PLANT & Martha SUGG; born 28 October 1828 in Pocahontas, Bond Co., Ill.
They had one child:

1915	i.	Lucy I. (~1858-)

911. Jane Charlotte HILL[483] was born 17 April 1831 in New Milford, Litchfield Co., Conn. Jane Charlotte died in Washington Courthouse, Fayette Co., Ohio on 17 Dec 1869, she was 38. On 16 November 1848, when she was 17, she married, as his second wife, **James Mason PAUL** in Lackland, Hamilton Co., Ohio; born 16 August 1821 in Aberdeen, Brown Co., Ohio; died in Washington Courthouse, Fayette Co., Ohio, 4 March 1900, age 78; buried there, 5 March 1900.
They had the following children:

1916	i.	Phonetta A. (1850-)
1917	ii.	Thomas (~1851-~1851)
1918	iii.	Francis "Frank" (1852-1900)
1919	iv.	Roswell Hill (1855-1888)
1920	v.	George W. (1857-)
1921	vi.	Flora C. (1859-)
1922	vii.	Carrie F. (1860-1941)
1923	viii.	Charles B. "Cass" (1862-1941)
1924	ix.	[Baby] (1865-)

912. Addison HILL was born about 1830 and died after 1863. He was buried in Caton, N.Y.
He married **Jemima _____**; born 5 April 1836; died 8 June 1865, age 29. She was buried in Caton, N.Y.
913. William Roswell HILL was born 28 November 1832 in Conn.; died 24 December 1900, age 68. He was a school teacher in Dover Twp., Tuscarawas Co., Ohio, in 1870, when he was 46 years old. He married **Ursula BROWN**, who was born about 1827 in N.Y.
They had the following children:

1925	i.	Lucy (1853-)
1926	ii.	William R. (1855-)
1927	iii.	Henry B. (1857-)
1928	iv.	Mary A. (1858-)
1929	v.	Alice R. (1860-)
1930	vi.	Charles (1863-)
1931	vii.	Edward (1867-)
1932	viii.	Lily (1870-)

914. James Frederick HILL was born in 1836 and died after 1863.

The grandchildren of Abraham and Hannah (Ferris) Hill[484]

915. Enos HILL was born 17 July 1793. He married **Ruth _____**; born about 1790.
They had the following children:

1933	i.	Amanda (-1817)
1934	ii.	Enos
1935	iii.	James (1827-)
1936	iv.	Phoebe (1831-)
1937	v.	Emily (1834-)

916. Samuel HILL was born 20 January 1795; died 24 April 1874, age 79.
890. Harsey HILL[485] was born 11 December 1797 in Patterson, N.Y.; died in Wayne, N.Y., 12 February 1855, age 57. He married **Mary ROGERS**; born 18 February 1805 in Patterson, N.Y.; died in Wayne, N.Y., 10 March 1865, age 60.
They had the following children:

1938	i.	Harmon W. (1821-1901)
1939	ii.	Hansel S. (1822-1893)
1940	iii.	Mary Jane (1824-1892)
1941	iv.	Hannah Eliza (1825-)
1942	v.	Betsey Ann
1943	vi.	Harriet (1827-1853)
1944	vii.	Ferris (1830-)
1945	viii.	Martha (1830-)
1946	ix.	Harsey (1831-1831)
1947	x.	Elizabeth Ann (1832-1921)
1948	xi.	Richard L. [Lord] (1832-1902)
1949	xii.	Amos W.
1950	xiii.	George (1839-1907)

918. Abraham HILL was born 13 October 1798; died 25 December 1883, age 85.
919. Enoch HILL was born 4 August 1800; died 28 July 1867, age 66.
920. Aseph King HILL was born 22 September 1802; died 7 November 1883; married **Maria BRIGS**.
921. Norris BROWN was born 3 December 1779.[486]
922. Eliza HILL. On 25 October 1850 she married **Moses GREGORY** in Merideth, N.Y.[487]

The grandchildren of Luke Sherman and Sally (Foster) Blackmun[488]

923. Andrew Perkins BLACKMUN was born 1 February 1839 in Mooers, Clinton Co., N.Y.; died in St. Paul, Minn., 12 December 1920, age 81. He may have had Civil War service; and citations in Minn. Death Index are mentioned in Ancestry.com.
924. Cyrus Judson BLACKMUN was born 26 January 1841; died 19 April 1910, age 69. He had Civil

War service, according to Ancestry.com.

925. William John Manning BLACKMUN was born 4 January 1844 in Mooers, N.Y.; died in Pelham, N.H., 8 Jul 1937, age 93. He had Civil War service, according to Ancestry.com.

926. Calvin Luther BLACKMUN was born 18 May 1846; died 5 August 1863, age 17. Was he a soldier in the Civil War?

927. Richard Lettin BLACKMUN was b. 15 Jan 1849; d. in Bloomington, Minn., 20 Mar 1937, age 88.

928. Elizabeth Philina BLACKMUN was born in 1852.

929. Delia J. Sweet BLACKMUN,[489] born in 1853 in New York State; died in 1940, about age 87. In 1884, when she was about 31, she m. **Charles Arthur CHASE**; born in 1846; died in 1927, about age 81. They had the following children:

1951	i.	John Wyman "Jay" (1885-1914)
1952	ii.	Annette S. (1888-)
1953	iii.	Nettie (1888-)
1954	iv.	Ethyl (1891-)
1955	v.	Arlia (1893-)

930. Sarah Nelly BLACKMUN was born 18 June 1856; died 28 March 1857.

931. Elburt Foster BLACKMUN, born 1 Sep 1857; died in Mooers, Clinton Co., N.Y., 14 July 1868.

932. Emma Jane BLACKMUN was born in 1861.

Line 6 – Descendants of Abigail Hill (continued)

Child of Parmelee and Ann (Wheeler) Allen[490]

933. Prudence ALLEN was born in 1772 in Whitehall, Mass.; died in Warsaw, Genesee Co., N.Y., 14 April 1837, about age 65. Nothing more is known about her.

934. Amy ALLEN[491] was born in 1782 in Pawlet, Rutland Co., Vt.; died in Oskaloosa, Mahaska Co., Ia., 27 August 1856, about age 74. In 1800 when she was about 18, she married **Willard COBB** in Pawlet, Vt.; born 7 March 1781 in Pawlet, Vt.; died in Oskaloosa, Ia., 23 January 1855, age 73. They had the following children:

1956	i.	Willard Burr (1807-1849)
1957	ii.	Marriett (1808-)
1958	iii.	Reuben Rice (1811-)
1959	iv.	James Hartland (1813-)
1960	v.	Royal Pinckney (1815-)
1961	vi.	Parolina (1817-)

Line 7 – Descendants of Elizabeth Hill (Continued)

The children of Nathaniel and Abigail (Fowler) Griffin[492]

935. Nathaniel GRIFFIN was born in 1758.

936. Wisdom GRIFFIN was born in 1760.

937. Ezra GRIFFIN was born in 1761 and died in 1843, about age 82.

938. Absolom GRIFFIN was born in 1764 and died in 1833, about age 69.

939. Samantha GRIFFIN was born in 1767.

940. Calvin GRIFFIN was born in 1769.

941. Chedolaomer GRIFFIN was born in 1774 and died in 1878. She was about 104.

942. Stephen TERRY[493] was born 19 March 1784 in Granby, Hartford Co., Conn.; died in Plattsburg, N.Y., 10 February 1857, age 72. On 15 October 1815, when he was 31, he married **Catherine CASE** in Granby, Conn. She was born in 1794 and died in 1858, about age 64. They had one child:

| 1962 | i. | Jerome (1821-~1890) |

Line 8 – Descendants of John Hill (Continued)

The grandchildren of Timothy and Sarah (Strickland) Strong[494]

943. Lament Sheldon STRONG[495] was born in 1783 in Granby, Conn.; died in Redfield, Oswego, N.Y. in 1845, about age 62. In 1801, when she was 18, she married **Samuel BROOKS Jr.** in Redfield, Oswego Co., N.Y.; born in 1769; died in 1814, about age 45.

They had the following children:

1963	i.	Frederick (1803-)
1964	ii.	Samuel L. (1805-1897)
1965	iii.	Amos (1807-1850)
1966	iv.	Sheldon (1811-1883)
1967	v.	Sarah (1814-1895)

944. Eli STRONG.

945. Sarah STRONG was b. 28 Feb 1787 in Granby, Hartford Co., Conn.; d.s.p., 20 June 1861, age 74.

946. Sophia STRONG was born in 1789.

947. Julia (? aka Laura) STRONG was born in 1791. The Moore Family Tree says Julia and Laura Strong were both b. in 1791, and d.s.p.

948. Martha (? aka Mary) STRONG was born in 1794 and died in 1796, about age 2. The Moore Family Tree says Martha and Mary were b. 1794, and that Martha d. in 1796.

949. Anson STRONG was born in 1796 and died in 1865, about age 69.

950. Cynthia STRONG was b. in 1801 in Redfield, Oswego, N.Y.; d. in Orwell, N.Y., 13 Aug 1879.

951. Almira JONES.

952. Anson JONES.

953. Clarissa JONES.

954. Elizabeth "Betsy" Maria JONES.

955. Ira JONES.

956. Mary JONES.

957. Nancy JONES.

958. Sarah JONES.

959. Sophia JONES.

960. William JONES.

The grandchildren of John and Isabel (Eggleston) Hill[496]

961. Jedediah HILL Jr.[497] was born on February 1784 in Simsbury, Conn.; died in Lorraine, Jefferson Co., N.Y., 26 May 1858, age 74. He was buried in Lorraine, N.Y. He was a veteran of the War of 1812 who married twice and fathered 11 children, although it is unknown which of his wives was the mother of his children. His brothers John, Eben, and Ludlow Hill were privates in Allen's 55th Regiment, New York Militia, War of 1812. Jedediah, presumably Jedediah Jr., is listed as a private in Carver's 61st Reg., New York Militia, War of 1812. James D. Hill wrote, "Their first taste of war came soon after, when a British fleet of five lake ships, headed by the *Royal George*, sailed up to Sackets Harbor and attempted to bombard the fort. The blockhouse stood on a bluff above the lake shore so the Britishers were unable to elevate their cannon for efficient fire on the fort. The Americans had similar difficulties, as the balls for their cannon were too small and would not stick in the barrels when the pieces were depressed. They remedied that somewhat by wrapping the balls in cloth. Later a ball from the British cannon was found to fit the American guns. They scored a direct hit on an attacking vessel and the British withdrew."

He married (1) **Susannah CASE**, and (2) **Betsy RISLSEY**, widow of George Hitchcok. She may have been the mother of all 11 of the children of Jedediah Hill, Jr.

He had the following children:

1968	i.	Susan (-1806)
1969	ii.	Riley
1970	iii.	Milo
1971	iv.	Polly (1808-1892)
1972	v.	Sophronia
1973	vi.	Julie

1974	vii.	Lorinda
1975	viii.	Clorinda (1823-1905)
1976	ix.	Matilda
1977	x.	Orpha
1978	xi.	Rhoda

962. John Henry HILL, second son and second of the ten children of Jedediah and Abigail (Kilby) Hill, was born at Simsbury, Conn., 29 January 1786; died at Des Moines County, Iowa, 23 February 1869. At the age of 21, he moved to Jefferson County, N.Y., with his father and the rest of his father's family. When he was 22, in February 1809, he married Esther Adams.

During the War of 1812 he served in the Army and saw action at Sacketts Harbor, N.Y., on Lake Ontario, and he was at the Battle of New Orleans on 8 January 1815, under General Andrew Jackson. In an undated letter quoted by James D. Hill, the Quartermaster General of the U.S. Army is said to have written that John Hill enlisted at Sackets Harbor, Jefferson County, New York, and served as private in Capt. G. W. Clark's company of the N.Y. militia from 28 Feb 1813 to 17 Mar 1813 and in Capt. S. McCumber's company of N.Y. militia from July 29, 1814 to August 21, 1814. He was honorably discharged from both enlistments and never requested a pension. On account of this service he was allowed one hundred sixty of bounty land, on his application executed July 9, 1855, at which time he was sixty-seven years old and lived in Des Moines County, Iowa.

In 1820 John Henry Hill was living in Ellisburg, N.Y., with his wife and a boy under the age of ten, who was not his son, but who may have been his younger brother, Ladue. In 1830, a girl under the age of 20 had been added to the family. James D. Hill suggested that she is probably John Henry's niece Abigail Leonard, who had been adopted by his parents, Jedediah and Abigail Hill, after his sister Abigail (Hill) Leonard died soon after giving birth to a daughter, who was also named Abigail. In 1836, John and Esther sold their land and the house in Rural Hill, N.Y., that had been built by John's father Jedediah in 1825. They then moved to bounty land in Iowa. Esther had no children before she died in 1848.

John Henry then sold his prairie farm and moved to Benton Township in Des Moines County, in southeastern Iowa, where he settled near his younger brother Ebben. He married again in 1849, to Sarah Ann Haight, by whom he had three sons and a daughter. Ebben and other members of the family were Baptists, but John was an outsider; his expressed creed was, "Fear God and keep the commandments, and by jiminy, I'll insure the salvation of every one of you." At some time in the 1860s, he went to Missouri and laid two land warrants in Oregon County, planning to leave this land to support his family. He returned ill, and never gave much information to the family about the land. He died at the Des Moines County poor farm near Burlington, Iowa, and was buried in the Kossuth Cemetery, Kossuth, Iowa. His military gravestone is inscribed, "Hill, John, Pvt. N.Y. Militia. War 1812 d. 23 Feb, 1869."

He married (1), in New York State, 22 February 1809, **Esther ADAMS**; born about 1787; died at Kossuth, Des Moines County, Iowa, 20 December 1848. There was no issue from this marriage. He married (2), at Des Moines County, Iowa, 30 October 1849, **Sarah Ann "Sally Ann" HAIGHT**, daughter of Cornelius A. and Abigail (Attwood) Haight; born at Marietta, Ohio, 29 July 1829; died at Sperry, Des Moines County, Iowa, 1 April 1895, age 65. She was buried in Sperry, Iowa, and she was a Presbyterian. John Henry and Sarah Ann (Haight) Hill had four children, John William, James Riley, Cornelius Haight, and Esther Ann.

John Henry and Sarah Ann (Haight) Hill had the following children:

1979	i.	John William (1850-1941)
1980	ii.	James Riley (1852-1906)
1981	iii.	Cornelius Haight (1854-1933)
1982	iv.	Esther Ann (1857-1946)

963. Riley HILL was b. 9 March 1788 in Simsbury, Conn.; d. in Canton, Conn., 18 Sep 1806, age 18.

964. Ebben HILL Sr., also known as Eben, fourth son and fourth of the ten children of Jedediah and Abigail (Kilby) Hill, was born at Simsbury, Conn., 30 March 1791; died at Kossuth, Des Moines County, Iowa, 7 March 1876, age 84, and was buried there. In some records, his surname has been mis-spelled or mis-read as "Hile." Ebben and his brothers John and Ludlow were privates in Allen's 55th Regiment,

New York Militia, in the War of 1812, and his brother Jedediah Jr. was a private in Carver's 61st Regiment.

In 1816 he married (1) a widow, **Mrs. Ruth Ann "Anna" BARNEY**, by whom he had six sons and a daughter between 1816 and 1831 in New York State. She also had two children by her first marriage. Ebben Hill then moved west, and Ruth died in Kossuth, Iowa in 1846, in the year that Iowa achieved statehood. She was buried in Kossuth. In 1850 Ebben was living in the Yellow Springs District of Des Moines County with four children. His older brother John Henry Hill (known as John Hill Sr.) moved to the same part of Iowa soon after Ebben arrived, and the two Hill families appear in census records as neighbors thereafter. Sometime after 1850, Ebben married (2) **Mrs. Malvina Frances "Fannie" TOOLE**, by whom he had two more sons. Ebben Hill was always a farmer, never prosperous, but he was as successful as his neighbors. He died in 1876 and was buried in the Kossuth Cemetery under a military gravestone that is inscribed, "Hill, Eben, Pvt. N.Y. Militia. War 1812 d. 7 Mar, 1876."

Ebben and Ruth Ann (Barney) Hill had the following children:

1983	i.	Eben B. (aka Ebben, aka Ebon) (1821-1868)
1984	ii.	John (1823-)
1985	iii.	Harry "Hervey" (1826-)
1986	iv.	William (1827-)
1987	v.	Lurissa (1829-1855)
1988	vi.	Hiram (1831-)
1989	vii.	Francis (1842-)

Ebben and Malvira Francis (Toole) Hill had the following children:

| 1990 | i. | Judson (1854-) |
| 1991 | ii. | Luther (1856-) |

965. Infant HILL was born 1 June 1793 in Simsbury, Conn.; died 22 June 1793.

966. Ludlow HILL was born 6 August 1794 in Simsbury, Conn.; died in Wonewec, Wisc., 12 July 1873, age 78. The brothers John, Eben, and Ludlow Hill were privates under Capt. George W. Clark in Allen's 55th Regiment, New York Militia, in the War of 1812. Ludlow's service was from 2/8/1813-3/17/1813. James Hill wrote, "Ludlow, having turned eighteen just two months after the war began, in June of 1812, was required to serve in the militia, as were all men from 18 to 45. Only elected officials, slaves, and prisoners were exempt from this duty. Ludlow was stationed at Horse Island and stood guard many a night on the High Rocks from Sackets harbor and along the shore. He also served at the Scotch Settlement and when the British were laying the blockade off of Point Pensholz to ward off the big Galues. He is listed in the index as 'Ludd Hill' and in some of the family records as 'Lud.' John served on the Forseyth Expedition to Frontenac, Canada." Shortly after his daughter Lydia's death in 1838, Ludlow moved his family to Illinois. On 1 Jan 1821 when Ludlow was 26, he married **Lydia PRESLEY** (PRESLY) in N.Y.; b. 24 October 1800 in Hoosic, N.Y.; d. in Wonewec, Wisc., 12 May 1880, age 79.[498] They had the following children:

1992	i.	Ludlow (1821-)
1993	ii.	Orin Rice (1823-1908)
1994	iii.	Lydia Case (1825-1838)
1995	iv.	Ludlow Presly (1829-1915)
1996	v.	Armanda (1831-)
1997	vi.	Abigail Amanda (1832-1869)
1998	vii.	William Riley (1835-)
1999	viii.	Abigail "Abi" (1836-1916)
2000	ix.	Jedediah (1839-)

967. Abigail HILL was born 20 May 1797 in Simsbury, Conn.; died in Ellisburg, Jefferson Co., N.Y., 26 January 1815, age 17, and was buried in Ellisburg. She died 5 days after her daughter was born. She married **Calvin LEONARD**, who died 21 February 1838 in Ellisburg, N.Y., and was buried there. They had one child:

| 2001 | i. | Abigail (1815-1838) |

968. Polly HILL was born 16 August 1800 in Simsbury, Conn.; died there, 21 September 1806, age 6.

969. Ladue HILL, born 4 April 1803 in Simsbury, Conn.; died in Wauconda, Ill., 27 September 1886, age 83. James D. Hill wrote, "The battle of Big Sandy Creek took place in the spring of 1814 and the area around the Hill farm remained in the war zone until the end of the war. Jedediah Jr.'s brother Ladue was ten or twelve when he went squirrel hunting and heard cannon at Stony Point. He picked up English musket balls and used them for his squirrel gun. The War of 1812 was ended by the signing of a treaty in Ghent, Belgium in December of 1814, but news of the treaty didn't reach Sackets Harbor until the spring of 1815." He married **Elizabeth Amelia TAYLOR**, aka Eliza Aurelia Taylor, a school teacher.
They had the following children:

2002	i.	Henry (1827-)
2003	ii.	Emily Welthy (1826-1875)

970. Isabel (aka Isabella) HILL was born 14 March 1806 in Simsbury, Conn.; died in Henderson, Jefferson Co., N.Y., 6 March 1860, age 53. She married (1) **Sylvenas CRITTINDEN**.
They had one child:

2004	i.	Abigail

She married (2) **David BOICE**.
They had the following children:

2005	i.	Fred E. (1841-)
2006	ii.	Helen Cornelia (1843-1864)
2007	iii.	Charlotte Alida (1848-1868)

971. Phineas (Phinehas) BACON[499] was born in say 1783. Phineas Bacon is a well-established name in the Bacon family, going back to the early 1700s. There is also a notable figure in Connecticut history named Phineas Bacon Wilcox, presumably a relative. Phineas Bacon was therefore probably given the name of others who preceded him in the Bacon family, and it was probably a coincidence that his grandfather Bunce's name Phinehas, spelled with an "h," was similar to Phineas. He was biologically a Bunce, and Joseph Edgerton was a step-ancestor. He married **Philura NORTON**, daughter of Bradford NORTON and Abigail "Nabby" BLOOD; born about 1793.
They probably had at least one child:

2008	i.	Perhaps sons and daughters of Phineas and Philura (Norton)

The children of John and Elizabeth (Case) Barber[500]

972. Infant BARBER, whose name is unknown, was born and died in 1774.

973. Elizabeth BARBER was born 27 March 1775 in Simsbury, Hartford Co., Conn.; died in Sheldon, N.Y., 25 January 1817, age 41. In 1795, when she was about 19, she married **Roswell BARBER** in Loundon, Berkshire, Mass.; born in August 1770 in Simsbury, Conn.; died in Sheldon, N.Y., 22 March 1830, age 59. His ancestry is unknown although he is presumably a relative of Elizabeth.
They had the following children:

2009	i.	Laura (1794-)
2010	ii.	Sylvia (1887-)
2011	iii.	Milo R. (1803-)
2012	iv.	Nancy Case (1809-)
2013	v.	Myron Finch (1811-1900)

974. Rhoda BARBER was born in 1777 in Simsbury, Conn. She married **Gordon HURLBUT**, who was born in Wethersfield, Conn.
They had the following children:

2014	i.	Gordon Trumbull (1807-)
2015	ii.	Chauncey Butler
2016	iii.	Rhonda Lucretia
2017	iv.	Talcott Ledyard

975. Cynthia BARBER was born 11 March 1779 in West Simsbury, Hartford Co., Conn.; died in Peru, Ind., 5 January 1840, age 60. She married **Chauncey SADD**, b. 1 June 1779 in Wapping, Conn.
They had the following children:

2018	i.	Maria (1802-)
2019	ii.	William Chauncey (1806-1831)
2020	iii.	Julia Warner (1808-)
2021	iv.	Corinne Gilmore (1801-)
2022	v.	George Franklin (1816-)

976. John BARBOUR[501] was born 18 February 1783 in Canton, Hartford Co., Conn.; died in Sheldon, Wycoming, N.Y., 24 November 1865, age 82. On 13 October 1803, when he was 21, he married (1) **Delight Griswold CASE**, daughter of Elisha CASE and Delight GRISWOLD; born 15 October 1783 in Canton, Hartford Co., Conn.; died there, 13 April 1811, age 27. He is the great-grandfather of Lucius Barnes Barbour, who created the Barbour Collection of Connecticut Vital Records. The spelling of his last name was changed from Barber to Barbour, for unknown reasons, although it appears pretentious. They had the following children:

2023	i.	Lucius (1805-1873)
2024	ii.	Eveline G. (1807-)
2025	iii.	Edwin Case (1810-)

On 15 June 1812, when he was 30, he married (2) **Fanny HUNT**, daughter of George HUNT and Jemima HOLLISTER; born 30 August 1792; died in Sheldon, N.Y. 6 November 1858, age 66. They had the following children:

2026	i.	Selden (1813-1814)
2027	ii.	Fanny Maria (1815-)
2028	iii.	Fidelia Gates (1817-1900)
2029	iv.	Herschell (1819-1819)
2030	v.	Theodore Dwight (1820-1890)
2031	vi.	Silvia (1822-1822)
2032	vii.	Goodrich Hollister (1824-1901)
2033	viii.	John Newton (1828-1874)
2034	ix.	Theron Laselle (1832-1864)
2035	x.	Juliet Louise (1834-)

977. Abiah "Abi" BARBER[502] was born 4 March 1784 in Canton, Hartford Co., Conn.; died in New Hartford, Litchfield Co., Conn., 12 March 1867, age 83. On 7 September 1803, when she was 19, she married (1) **Elisha CASE**, son of Elisha CASE and Delight GRISWOLD, in Canton, Conn.; born 12 August 1781 in Canton; died in New Hartford, Conn., 21 July 1824, age 42. Abi Barber and Elisha Case were twice fourth cousins. They had the following children:

2036	i.	Cynthia Maria (1806-1888)
2037	ii.	Clarissa (1808-1890)
2038	iii.	Erastus (1810-1813)
2039	iv.	Mary Ann (1816-1890)
2040	v.	John Griswold (1818-1879)

She married (2) **John BROWN**. There were no children from this marriage.

978. Sylvia BARBER[503] was born in 1785 and died in 1786.

979. Sylvia BARBER [2d] was b. 9 July 1787 in West Simsbury [Canton], Hartford Co., Conn.; d. there, 24 January 1861, age 73. In 1808, when she was about 20, she married **Dan CASE**, son of Dan CASE and Rachel FOOTE, in Canton, Conn.; b. in 1784 in Canton; d. in 1865, about 81. Dan Case and Sylvia Barber were great-great-greatgrandchildren of John and Sarah (Spencer) Case, so they were 4th cousins. They had the following children:

2041	i.	Austin Barbour
2042	ii.	Calvin
2043	iii.	Child
2044	iv.	George Washington
2045	v.	Harriet Mabel

2046	vi.	Laura Ann
2047	vii.	Sherman Hurlbut

980. Luke BARBER was born 17 December 1789 in Canton, Conn. In 1816, when he was about 26, he married (1) **Clara FOOTE** in Canton, Conn.; born 19 March 1795 in Canton; died 20 Dec 1838, age 43. They had the following children:

2048	i.	Elizabeth (1817-1819)
2049	ii.	Helen M. (1826-)
2050	iii.	Jane (1828-)
2051	iv.	Julia (1832-)

Luke married (2) **Lavinia HOSMER**.

981. Austin BARBER was born in 1792 in West Simsbury [Canton], Conn. On 20 March 1828, when he was 36, he married **Lucy ALLEN** in Becket, Mass.

They had the following children, none of whom are known to have had descendants:

2052	i.	John Austin (1830-)
2053	ii.	Henry Watson (1831-)
2054	iii.	Mary J. (1834-1834)
2055	iv.	James Edwin (1842-)
2056	v.	Benjamin (1845-)

The children of Reuben and Elizabeth (Case) Barber[504]

982. Mary BARBER was born in 1778 in Simsbury, Hartford Co., Conn.; died there in 1804, about age 26. In 1798, when she was about 20, she married **Jonathan NOBLE** in West Simsbury [Canton], b. 22 February 1776 in Simsbury; died in Blendon, Franklin Co., Ohio, 28 March 1832, age 56. They had the following children:

2057	i.	Orin (1800-1844)
2058	ii.	Lester (1802-1850)

983. Sadosa BARBER was born 31 July 1781 in Simsbury, Conn.; died in Canton, Conn., 25 November 1860, age 79. On 4 February 1802, when he was 20, he married **Sarah CLEVELAND**; born 8 August 1784 in Wolcott, New Haven Co., Conn.; died in Canton, Conn. 7 March 1861, age 76.

984. Elizabeth BARBER was born in 1782 in Simsbury, Hartford Co., Conn.; died 24 October 1828, in Canton, St. Lawrence Co., N.Y., age 46. She married (1) **Josiah HARRISON**; born in Canton, Hartford Co., Conn.; died 23 April 1805. On 27 November 1806, when she was about 24, she married (2) **Zimri BARBER [Jr.]**, son of Zimri BARBER; born 21 February 1787 in Simsbury, Conn.; died in Canton, St. Lawrence Co., N.Y. (probably), 16 November 1865, age 78. Zimri Barber and Elizabeth Barber were second cousins, once removed.[505]

They had the following children:

2059	i.	Josiah (1807-)
2060	ii.	Emeline (1809-1813)
2061	iii.	Phoebe (1811-1845)
2062	iv.	Reuben (1814-)
2063	v.	Lorenzo Dow (1817-1887)

985. Phoebe BARBER was born in 1785 in Simsbury, Conn.; died in 1838, about age 53. She married **Uri COOKE**; born 24 December 1779 in Waterbury, Conn.

986. Hosea BARBER was born in 1788 in Simsbury, Conn.; died in Canton, Hartford Co., Conn., 30 July 1874, about age 86. He married **Hannah FULLER**.

987. Starling BARBER was born in 1790 in Simsbury, Conn., and died in 1801, about age 11.

988. Alson BARBER was born 6 May 1792 in Simsbury and d. in Canton, Conn., 4 April 1880, age 87. On 16 November 1814, when he was 22, he m. **Hannah HUMPHREY** in Canton; b. 4 December 1796 in Canton; d. there, 19 April 1877, age 80. She was the mother of 12, four of whom had descendants. They had the following children:

2064	i.	Hannah
2065	ii.	Harriet Elizabeth

2066	iii.	Jeanette
2067	iv.	Luther Humphrey
2068	v.	Martha Jane
2069	vi.	Mary
2070	vii.	Phebe Maria
2071	viii.	Sarah Elvira
2072	ix.	Nelson L. (1819-1885)
2073	x.	Gaylord (1824-1897)
2074	xi.	John (1826-1894)
2075	xii.	Lemuel (1830-1892)

989. Sarah BARBER was born in 1794 in Simsbury, Conn. Sarah died in 1822, about age 28, apparently d.s.p. In November 1821, when she was 27, she married **Harvey PIKE** in Canton, Conn.; born 18 September 1794 in Barkhamsted, Litchfield Co., Conn.

990. Ruby BARBER.

The children of Jonathan and Abi (Merrell) Barber[506]

991. Seth BARBER was born in 1788 in Canton, Hartford Co., Conn.; died in Candor, N.Y., 30 March 1866, about age 78. He married three times; his second and third wives were sisters. He had a son by his first wife and a daughter by his second wife. In 1808, when he was about 20, he married (1) **Tirzah HAYDEN** in Litchfield, Conn.; born 14 April 1789 in Torringford, Conn.; died in Canton, Hartford Co., Conn., 6 December 1819, age 30.

They had one child:

2076	i.	Augustine Hayden (1809-)

On 24 May 1820, when he was about 32, he married (2) **Mehitable CREESY**, daughter of Israel CREESY and Alice WOODRUFF, in Norfolk, Litchfield, Conn.; born 21 July 1785 in Winchester, Litchfield, Conn.; died in Candor, Tioga, N.Y., 8 September 1830, age 45.

They had one child:

2077	i.	Harriet Amelia (1824-1878)

He married (3) **Olive CREESY**, daughter of Israel CREESY and Alice WOODRUFF, and sister of his second wife Mehitable; born 28 January 1795 in Litchfield, Conn.; died in Candor, Tioga, N.Y., 3 February 1865, age 70; d.s.p.

992. Clarinda BARBER was born 11 April 1789 in Canton, Hartford Co., Conn. On 28 November 1807, when she was 18, she married **Miles FOOTE** in Canton, Conn.; born there, 1 April 1788.

They had the following children:

2078	i.	Laura (1809-)
2079	ii.	Henry (1813-)
2080	iii.	Lucius (1817-)
2081	iv.	Eliza M. (1823-)
2082	v.	John M. (1827-)

993. Abi BARBER was born in 1791 in Simsbury, Conn., and died in 1815, about age 24.

994. Henry BARBER was born in 1793 in Simsbury, Conn. He married **Naomi HUMPHREY**; born 28 September 1794 in Bristol, Hartford Co., Conn.; died in Canton, Conn., 7 January 1863, age 68.

995. Pluma BARBER was born in 1796 in Simsbury, Conn., and died in 1815, about age 19.

996. Linda BARBER was born in 1799 in Simsbury, Conn.; died in Canton, Conn., 23 September 1879, about age 80. On 20 March 1822, at about age 23, she married **Uriah HOSFORD**; born 13 November 1796; died in Canton, Conn., 22 October 1866, age 69.

They had one child:

2083	i.	Emerson H. Shaw (1832-1880)

997. Thirza BARBER was b. 1 June 1801 in Simsbury, Conn.; d. in May 1887; m. **Isaac BARNES**.

998. Susannah BARBER was born 29 June 1803 in Simsbury, Conn.; died 9 March 1888, age 84. On 2 March 1825, when she was 21, she married **Imri Lester SPENCER** in Canton, Conn.; born 15 April 1803; died 5 September 1870, age 67.

999. Eliza BARBER was born in 1806 in Simsbury, Conn. She married **Henry A. ADAMS.**

1000. Nancy BARBER was born in 1808 in Simsbury, Conn.

1001. Jonathan Sherman BARBER was born in 1812 in Simsbury, Conn.; died in 1847, about age 35. He married **Satira CHURCH.**

1002. Harvey BARBER was b. in 1814 in Simsbury, Conn. On 20 Nov 1833, age 19, he m. **Lorinda CASE** in Canton, Conn.; born 3 April 1816 in Simsbury; died in Connecticut, 12 October 1859, age 43. They had the following children:

2084	i.	Henrietta (1837-)
2085	ii.	Willard Jonathan (1850-)

The children of Abel and Chloe (Case) Barber[507]

1003. Solomon BARBER was born 19 December 1791 in Otis, Berkshire Co., Mass.; died in Canton, Conn., 15 April 1820, age 28.

1004. Benjamin BARBER was born 11 July 1794 in Otis, Mass.

1005. Roena BARBER was b. 10 Dec 1802 in Otis, Mass. She m. **Jeremiah HUMASON**, b. in 1781. They had one child:

2086	i.	William Lawrence (1821-)

1006. Abel Lester BARBER was born 27 December 1803 in Otis, Mass.

The children of Titus and Amy (Case) Reade[508]

1007. Titus READE was born 4 July 1790 in Simsbury, Conn.

1008. Timothy READE was born 14 July 1796 in Granville, Mass.

1009. Hiram READE was born 10 October 1803 in West Parish, Granville, Mass.

1010. Roswell P. REED[509] was born 22 October 1804 in Granby, Hartford Co., Conn.; died in Higganum, Middlesex Co., Conn., 2 September 1885, age 80. He was a master wool carder. On 16 November 1831, when he was 27, he married **Caroline Mehitable USHER** in Haddam, Conn.; born in 1811 and died in 1885, about age 74.

They had one child:

2087	i.	Albert O. (1844->1910)

The grandchildren of Ephraim and Ruhamah (Pinney) Wilcox[510]

1011. Marcus WILCOX.

1012. Orra WILCOX.

1013. Pruna WILCOX.

1014. Sophronia WILCOX.

1015. Susan WILCOX.

1016. William "Billy" WILCOX.

1017. Asa Virgil WILCOX was born in 1770 in Simsbury, Conn.

1018. Prudence WILCOX was born in 1772 in Simsbury, Conn.

1019. Edmund WILCOX was born 14 March 1785 in Westerly, R.I.

1020. Allen HUMPHREY was born 8 March 1777 in Simsbury, Conn.

1021. Harry HUMPHREY was born 3 December 1780 in New Hartford, Litchfield Co., Conn.

1022. Chloe HUMPHREY was born in 1782 in Canton, Conn.

1023. Jehiel WILCOX was born 16 July 1781 in Barkhamsted, Litchfield Co., Conn.

1024. Hira WILCOX was born 29 April 1785 in Barkhamsted, Conn.

1025. Ezra WILCOX was born in 1790.

1026. Abigail WILCOX was born 3 September 1797 in Barkhamsted, Conn.

1027. Elizabeth WILCOX.

1028. ? WILCOX was born in 1790.

1029. Rodolphus WILCOX was born 22 January 1788.

1030. Clarinda WILCOX was born 15 May 1791.

1031. Romulus Bradford WILCOX was born 15 April 1793.

1032. Zarena WILCOX was probably born in 1795.

1033. Remus WILCOX was born 26 August 1797.
1034. Lysander WILCOX was born 22 August 1799.
1035. Lorenzo WILCOX was born 16 April 1801.
1036. Lorita WILCOX was born 17 November 1803.
1037. Amander N. WILCOX was born 14 December 1808.

The children of Lyman and Deidama (Dunham) Jackson[511]

1038. Rosanna JACKSON was born 9 October 1782 in Pownal, Vt.
1039. Jesse Dunham JACKSON was born 5 May 1784 in Pownal, Vt.
1040. Ebenezer JACKSON was born 15 June 1786 in Pownal, Vt.
1041. Michael JACKSON was born 17 April 1788 in Pownal, Vt.
1042. Lyman JACKSON was born 2 March 1790 in Albany, Otsego, N.Y.
1043. John Jay JACKSON was born 7 February 1792 in Otsego, N.Y.
1044. Obediah JACKSON was born 11 January 1794 in Otsego, N.Y.
1045. Abner JACKSON was born 17 September 1795 in Richfield, Otsego, N.Y.
1046. David JACKSON was born 24 May 1797 in Otsego, N.Y.
1047. Royal JACKSON was born 3 May 1799.
1048. Norman JACKSON was born 2 July 1801 in Pennsylvania.
1049. Susanna JACKSON was born 17 January 1805 in Pennsylvania.
1050. Lucy Deidamia JACKSON was born 6 February 1808 in Pennsylvania.

The children of Sgt. Isaiah J. and Esther (Jackson) Hendryx[512]

1051. Lois HENDRYX was born 29 October 1775 in New Concord, Kings Dist, N.Y.
1052. Sally HENDRYX was born 11 September 1777 in New Concord, N.Y., and died the next day.
1053. Susannah HENDRYX,[513] third daughter and third of the seven children of Sergeant Isaiah and Esther (Jackson) Hendryx, was born at New Concord, Kings District, New York, 5 October 1779; died, probably at Bennington, Vermont, in about 1810. She married at Bennington, Vt., 1 May 1795, when she was 15, **Josiah (Isaiah) RILEY,**[514] son of Simeon RILEY; born 15 October 1773 or 1775; died 22 June 1850 at Coventry, Chenango Co., N.Y. He married (2) Susannah BEARDSLEY, who died 5 December 1810 and was buried in the Old Bennington, Vermont, Cemetery.[515]
Josiah and Susannah (Hendryx) Riley had the following children:

2088	i.	Isaiah Hendryx (1797-1855)
2089	ii.	Simeon (1799-~1848)
2090	iii.	Betsey (1802-1886)
2091	iv.	Esther Jackson (1804-1861)
2092	v.	Josiah B. (1806-)
2093	vi.	Helina (1808-1809)

1054. Beardsley HENDRYX was b. 7 March 1782 or 1788 in Bennington, Vt.; d. 23 May 1829.
1055. David HENDRYX was born 22 June 1784 or 22 June 1786 in Bennington, Vt. On 15 April 1804, he married **Fanny HUNT.**
They had one child:

2094	i.	Fanna (~1820-~1820)

1056. Isaiah J. HENDRYX Jr.[516] was born 26 April 1791 in Bennington, Vt. In 1807, when he was 15, he married **Polly THOMPSON.**
1057. Truman HENDRYX was born 16 January 1800 in Bennington, Vt. He was a tailor in Bennington in 1824, and he appears to have resided at one time at Chestertown, Warren County, N.Y.

The children of Ebenezer and Abigail (Keys) Jackson[517]

1058. Mary R. JACKSON.
1059. Esther JACKSON.
1060. Susanna Samantha JACKSON was born 17 January 1805.
1061. Zilpha Loren JACKSON was born 15 March 1806 in Liberty, Penna.

The grandchildren of Sylvanus and Chestina (Curtis) Wilcox[518]

1062. Elvira WILCOX was born 4 September 1802.

1063. Amelia WILCOX was born 15 August 1786 in Glen, Montgomery Co., N.Y.

1064. Chestina WILCOX was born 17 April 1788 in Glen, N.Y.

1065. Asenath WILCOX was born 17 March 1790 in Glen, N.Y.

1066. Elijah (Elisha) WILCOX was born 10 May 1792 in Glen, N.Y.[519]

1067. Charles WILCOX was born 25 February 1795 in Glen, N.Y.

1068. Calvin Pardee WILCOX was born 4 October 1796.[520]

1069. Eliza WILCOX was born 3 June 1800 in Glen, N.Y.

1070. Oliver L. WILCOX was born 26 June 1809 in Glen, N.Y.

1071. Chloe WILCOX.

1072. John WILCOX.

1073. Julia WILCOX.

1074. Nancy WILCOX.

1075. Ephraim WILCOX was born 20 August 1791.

1076. Chestina WILCOX was born 27 April 1795 in Alford, Berkshire Co., Mass.

1077. Laura WILCOX.

1078. Caroline WILCOX was born in 1799.

1079. Charlotte WILCOX.

1080. Franklin WILCOX was born in 1798 in Huron, Erie, Ohio.

1081. Erasmus D. WILCOX was born 14 January 1803 in Massachusetts.

1082. Edward WILCOX.

1083. Jane WILCOX.

1084. Marshall WILCOX.

1085. Ralph WILCOX was born 9 July 1818 in East Bloomfield, Ontario Co., N.Y.

1086. Hester Malvina WILCOX was born in 1812.

1087. Lavina SPOOR was born 4 November 1799 in Clarence, Erie, N.Y.

The grandchildren of Elnathan and Hannah (Adams) Wilcox[521]

1088. Eber WILCOX was born 13 June 1783 in Massachusetts.

1089. Henry WILCOX was born in 1787 in Gates, Orleans, N.Y.

1090. Caroline STILLMAN was born in New York.

1091. Martha STILLMAN was born in Bloomfield, N.Y.

1092. Roxanna STILLMAN was born 22 March 1786 in Massachusetts.

1093. Isaiah STILLMAN was born in 1797 in Massachusetts.

1094. John WILCOX was born 19 July 1796 in East Bloomfield, Ontario Co., N.Y.; died in Rochester, Mich., 15 January 1839, age 42. On 10 December 1818, when he was 22, he married **Keziah HOPKINS** in East Bloomfield, N.Y.; born 30 September 1795 in East Bloomfield, N.Y.; died in Rochester, Mich., 14 January 1871, age 75.

They had the following children:

2095	i.	John Martin (1819-1907)
2096	ii.	Roxy Ann (1821-)
2097	iii.	Amanda (1826-)
2098	iv.	Horace H. (1831-1832)

1095. Mark WILCOX was born in 1800.

1096. Newton WILCOX was born in 1802.

1097. Calvin WILCOX was born in 1804.

1098. Angeline WILCOX was born 25 March 1796 in Bloomfield, Ontario, N.Y.

1099. Amanda WILCOX was born 22 May 1798 in East Bloomfield, Ontario Co., N.Y.

1100. Edwin T. WILCOX was born 6 December 1799 in Bloomfield, N.Y.

1101. Orrin WILCOX was born 7 April 1801 in Bloomfield, N.Y.

1002. Elnathan WILCOX was born 16 March 1804 in Bloomfield, N.Y.

1003. Peter WILCOX was born 1 October 1805 in Bloomfield, N.Y.

1004. Emily WILCOX was born 26 April 1809 in East Bloomfield, N.Y.

1005. William E. WILCOX was born 16 February 1811 in Bloomfield, N.Y.

1006. Electa M. WILCOX was born 29 June 1813 in Bloomfield, N.Y.

1007. Clarissa WILCOX was born in 1815 in East Bloomfield, N.Y.

1008. Theodore S. WILCOX was born on 26 March 1818 in Bloomfield, N.Y.

1009. Solomon GOODALE was born 5 June 1797 in Brookfield, Mass.

1010. Harriet GOODALE was born about 1797.

1011. Charles A. GOODALE was born in 1798 in Phelps, N.Y.

1012. Osee Montgomery GOODALE was born 27 June 1800 in Phelps, N.Y.

1013. Leonard C. GOODALE was born in 1803 in Phelps, N.Y.

1014. Lemuel C. GOODALE was born in 1805 in Bristol, N.Y.

1015. Lucinda GOODALE was born in 1809 in Bristol, N.Y.

1016. Seymour GOODALE was born in 1810 in Bristol, N.Y.

1017. Mary GOODALE was born in 1814 in Bristol, N.Y.

1018. Hannah GOODALE was born in 1817 in Bristol, N.Y.

The children of Jedediah and Mary (Hallett) Wilcox[522]

1019. Arabelle WILCOX was born in 1802 in Vermont; died in Vermont in 1841, about 39.

1020. Ephraim WILCOX was born in 1803 in New York State. He is said to have resided in Plainfield, Otsego, N.Y., and in Madison, Branch Co., Mich., in 1830, 1840 and 1850.

In 1830, when he was about 27, he married **Miranda STEANS**.

They had the following children:

2099	i.	Eleazer (1831-)
2100	ii.	Lewis (1834-1885)
2101	iii.	Lucie Marie (1836-1914)
2102	iv.	Daniel W. (David) (1839-1913)
2103	v.	Elizabeth (Twin) (1841-1912)
2104	vi.	Robert (Twin) (1841-)
2105	vii.	Mary (1846-1914)

1121. Dijah WILCOX was born in June 1813 in New York State; died in Oakdale, Antelope Co., Neb., 2 March 1889, he was 75. In 1837, when he was about 23, he married **Elvira DOW**, who was born in 1817 and died in 1880, about age 63.

They had one child:

2106	i.	Jedediah Bishop (1851-1944)

1122. Lewis WILCOX was born 8 August 1819 in Conquest, Cayuga, N.Y.; died in Coldwater, Branch Co., Mich. in 1891, about age 71. On 5 March 1839, when he was 19, he married **Elizabeth PITCHER** in Cayuga, Cayuga Co., N.Y.; born in 1819.

They had the following children:

2107	i.	Jedediah (1838-)
2108	ii.	Albert Harley
2109	iii.	Edgar (1864-)

1123. Neri HOSKIN was b. 17 May 1796 in Winsted, Litchfield Co., Conn.; d. in Van Buren, Van Buren Co., Ia., 11 Sep 1865, age 69. On 13 July 1851, when he was 55, he married **Mary Angeline ZUCK**, daughter of Christian ZUCK & Lydia STRATTON, in Des Moines, Van Buren Co. (now Polk Co.), Ia.; born 2 February 1819 in Erie, Erie Co., Penna.; died in Des Moines, Ia., 4 January 1901, age 81.

They had the following children:

2110	i.	Lydia (1852-1853)
2111	ii.	Jasper (1854-1938)
2112	iii.	Inez (1857-1877)
2113	iv.	Neri Brownrigg (1859-1933)

7

Seventh Generation[*]
The Great-Great-Great-Great-Grandchildren

Line 1 – Descendants of Lydia Hill (continued)[523]

1124. Saloma BABCOCK. Born on 18 Jul 1775 in Coventry, Tolland Co., Conn. Saloma died in Indiana. On 19 Oct 1795 when Saloma was 20, she married **Elijah SANDERSON**, in Chester, Hampden Co., Mass. Born on 7 May 1772 in Springfield, Hampden Co., Mass.
They had the following children:
> **2114**   i.   William A.
> **2115**   ii.   Elisha (1803-)

1125. Elias BABCOCK. Born on 5 Jul 1778 in Coventry, Tolland Co., Conn.

1126. Lavina BABCOCK. Born on 23 Jan 1780 in Coventry, Tolland Co., Conn.

1127. Joseph BABCOCK. Born on 9 Apr 1786 in Coventry, Tolland Co., Conn.

1128. Anna BABCOCK. Born on 23 Nov 1788 in Coventry, Tolland Co., Conn.

1129. Susannah BABCOCK. Born on 18 Jul 1798 in Coventry, Tolland Co., Conn.

1130. Amariah BALLOU. Born on 12 Jul 1784.

1131. David BALLOU. Born on 19 Aug 1786.

1132. Mary BALLOU. Born on 2 Aug 1791.

1133. Lucy PARKER. Born on 1 Aug 1784 in Peru, Berkshire Co., Mass.

1134. Samuel PARKER. Born on 14 Dec 1784 in Peru, Berkshire Co., Mass.

1135. Orra PARKER. Born on 12 Dec 1788 in Peru, Berkshire Co., Mass.

1136. Nelson PARKER. Born in 1806.

1137. Shared PARKER. Born on 14 Aug 1794.

1138. Mary "Polly" PARKER. Born on 1 Aug 1796.

1139. Cynthia PARKER. Born on 16 Oct 1797.

1140. Eleazer PARKER. Born on 25 Feb 1802.

1141. Alphonso PARKER. Born on 16 Mar 1804.

1142. Olive PARKER.

1143. Orange PARKER.

1144. Samuel PARKER.

1145. William PARKER.

1146. Josiah PARKER. Born on 12 May 1812.

1147. Samuel SEDGEWICK. Born in 1803 in Herkimer, N.Y. Samuel died in Little Rock, Ill. in 1847, he was 44. On 20 Aug 1826 when Samuel was 23, he married **Ruhana P. KNIGHT**, in Oneida, N.Y. Born on 6 Sep 1809 in Oswego, N.Y. Ruhana P. died in Sandwich, De Kalb Co., Ill. on 8 Aug 1891, she was 81. Occupation: Mother of 9.
They had the following children:
> **2116**   i.   Elijah
> **2117**   ii.   Elizabeth (1830-)
> **2118**   iii.   Parker

---

[*] Beginning with the Seventh Generation, I will allow the formatting automatically produced by my genealogy software, Sierra/Generations, to print the information about each person who is known to me only from Ancestry.com, and about whom I have no additional verifying information. For most entries beginning with the Sixth Generation, I have also reduced the font size from Times New Roman 12 to TNR 11. The age given should be considered as an approximation, unless the dates of birth, marriage, and death are also given. For example, the age at marriage is precise and correct for #1124 (*supra*), but it is only an approximate age for #1147 (*infra*).

2119	iv.	Wrestle W. (1827-1904)
2120	v.	Sarah Ann (1833-1903)
2121	vi.	Louisa Jane (1835-)
2122	vii.	Maria C. (1838-)
2123	viii.	James H. (1840-)
2124	ix.	Joseph White (1846-)

1148. Elijah SEDGWICK.

1149. Parker SEDGEWICK.

1150. Theron SEDGWICK.

1151. Tryphena SEDGWICK.

1152. Amanda SEDGWICK.

1153. Betsey SEDGWICK.

1154. Betsa MANN. Born on 7 Feb 1795.

1155. Lydia MANN. Born on 23 Feb 1796.

1156. Sally MANN. Born on 9 Feb 1798.

1157. Chester MANN. Born on 19 Aug 1800.

1158. William MANN. Born in 1804.

1159. Reuben MANN. Born on 28 Jan 1810.

1160. Lydia PARKER.

1161. Eli PARKER. Born on 2 Mar 1798.

-- [524]

1162. Philo Coleman BARKER. Born on 17 Aug 1803 in Pennsylvania. Philo Coleman died in Brookfield, Linn., Mo. on 1 Dec 1886, he was 83.
Philo Coleman married **Mary G. ADAMS.** Born in 1814. Mary G. died in 1887, she was 73.
They had the following children:

2125	i.	Helen (1842-)
2126	ii.	Wilbur Jay (1843-1918)
2127	iii.	Sarah (~1845-)
2128	iv.	Mary (~1850-1860)

1163. Asa BARBER. Born on 22 Mar 1785 in Harwinton, Litchfield Co., Conn. Asa died in Harwinton, Litchfield Co., Conn. on 7 Nov 1813, he was 28.

1164. Anna BARBER. Born on 12 Aug 1789. Anna died on 13 May 1848, she was 58.

1165. Russell B. FRISBIE. Born in Jun 1797 in Sheffield, Berkshire, Mass. Russell B. died in LaCrosse, Wisc. on 15 Oct 1876, he was 79.
Russell B. married **Mary Taggart PUTMAN.** Born in 1793. Mary Taggart died in 1864, she was 71.
They had the following children:

2129	i.	Asa Putnam (1823-1902)
2130	ii.	Nancy Maria (1826-1904)
2131	iii.	Russell Levi (1830-1906)
2132	iv.	Ann Deidamia (1838-1917)
2133	v.	Mary Josephine (1840-)

1166. Elijah Stanton FRISBIE. Born in 1805 in Sheffield, Berkshire, Mass. Elijah Stanton died in Norfolk, Litchfield Co., Conn. on 15 May 1866, he was 61.

1167. Levi S. FRISBIE. Born in 1815 in Litchfield, Litchfield Co., Conn.

1168. Lucy CHUBB. Born on 17 Oct 1789 in Poultney, Rutland Co., Vt. Lucy died in Gaines, Orleans Co., N.Y. on 2 Jun 1839, she was 49.

1169. Arba CHUBB. Born on 18 Sep 1791 in Poultney, Rutland Co., Vt. Arba died in Ionia Village, Ionia, Mich. on 12 Jan 1875, she was 83.

1170. Elizabeth CHUBB. Born on 7 Mar 1794 in Poultney, Rutland Co., Vt. Elizabeth died in Canton, Wayne Co., Mich. on 9 Feb 1843, she was 48.

1171. Globe Dugar CHUBB.[525] Born on 28 Apr 1796 in Poultney, Rutland Co., Vt. Globe Dugar died in

Nankin, Wayne Co., Mich. on 12 May 1888, he was 92. Globe Dugar married **Pamela PATTISON**. Born on 11 Jun 1808 in New York. Pamela d. in 1884, she was 75. Two of her children had descendants. They had the following children:

2134	i.	Orville Pattison (1830-1894)
2135	ii.	Flora Augusta (1832-1914)
2136	iii.	Alta Delight (1834-1908)
2137	iv.	James Dillon (1837-1920)
2138	v.	Lucius Wolford (1842-1863)
2139	vi.	Hannah Marietta (1845-1849)
2140	vii.	Olive Sophia (1847-1939)

1172. Jonathan Frisbie CHUBB. Born on 29 Nov 1802 in Poultney, Rutland Co., Vt. Jonathan Frisbie died in Grand Rapids, Kent Co., Mich. on 6 Apr 1854, he was 51. He resided in Wyoming, Kent Co., Mich., in the census of 1850. A man of the same name is said to be in the 1860 census in Grand Rapids, Ward 4, and if so, he may have had a son.

1173. Rolla Harrison CHUBB.

1174. Bede CHUBB. Born in 1813.

1175. Sarah Maria FRISBIE.

1176. Elias Willard FRISBIE, M.D. Born on 12 May 1799 in Middletown, Windsor, Vt. Elias Willard died in Phelps, Ontario Co., N.Y. on 31 Jul 1860, he was 61. On 4 May 1825 when Elias Willard was 25, he married **Sophronia BOYNTON**. Born in 1807. Sophronia died in 1883, she was 76.

1177. Eliza Ann FRISBIE. Born on 16 Oct 1801 in Middletown, Windsor, Vt. Eliza Ann died in Walworth, Wayne Co., N.Y. on 16 Apr 1880, she was 78. On 7 Apr 1822 when Eliza Ann was 20, she married **John LEWIS, M.D.** Born in 1793. John died in 1834, he was 41.

1178. Sarah Maria FRISBIE.

1179. Ezra Clark FRISBIE. Born on 21 Mar 1805 in Pitsford, Rutland Co., Vt. Ezra Clark died in Gonzales, Gonzales, Texas on 28 Oct 1867, he was 62. On 16 Aug 1846 when Ezra Clark was 41, he married **Matilda Caroline GIPSON**, in Crittenden, Arkansas. Born in 1824. Matilda Caroline died in 1870, she was 46. Occupation: Mother of 7.

They had the following children:

2141	i.	Francis (-1870)
2142	ii.	Lewis (-1842)
2143	iii.	Clark Lamartine (1848-1930)
2144	iv.	John (1850-)
2145	v.	Julius Caesar (1854-1936)
2146	vi.	Eugenia (Beatrice) (1858-1892)
2147	vii.	Prince William Albert (1865-1915)

1180. Irene C. FRISBIE. Born on 4 Nov 1810 in Middletown, Windsor, Vt. Irene C. died in Phelps, Ontario Co., N.Y. on 20 Aug 1836, she was 25.

1181. Hyrum Norton BYINGTON. Born on 19 Aug 1800 in Wolcott, Conn. Hyrum Norton died in Menan, Jefferson Co., Idaho on 9 Mar 1887, he was 86. On 27 Jan 1828 when Hyrum Norton was 27, he first married **Sarah HOLKINS**, in Camden, Oneida Co., N.Y. Born on 3 May 1808 in Colebrook, Coos Co., N.H. Sarah died in Ogden, Weber Co., Utah on 27 Jan 1870, she was 61. Mother of 4.

They had the following children:

2148	i.	Joseph Henry (1829-1909)
2149	ii.	Hyrum Elliott (1830-1901)
2150	iii.	[Child] of Hyrum and Sarah (Holkins) (1833-1838)
2151	iv.	Susan Augusta (1840-)

On 25 Dec 1849 when Hyrum Norton was 49, he second married **Henrietta NELSON**, in Salt Lake City, Utah. Born on 4 Aug 1812 in Granville, Bradford Co., Penna. Henrietta died in Kanosh, Millard Co., Utah on 2 Dec 1880, she was 68. Hyrum Norton third married **Ann WALTON**. Born in 1802. On 29 Mar 1857 when Hyrum Norton was 56, he fourth married **Julia Phidelia FERRIN**. Born on 2 Nov

1825 in Castle, Genesee Co., N.Y. Julia Phidelia died in Weber, Utah on 12 Sep 1900, she was 74.
His four wives, their birth and death dates, and the dates of their marriages, are as follows:

> Sarah Holkins (1808-1870), married 1828
> Henrietta Nelson (1812-1880), married 1849
> Ann Walton (1802-)
> Julia Phidelia Ferrin (1825-1900), married 1857

He is not said to have divorced any of the wives, so I assume he was polygamous, with at least three and
perhaps four wives living at the same time. His fourth wife, and possibly his third, survived him.

1182. Zina BYINGTON. Born on 20 Jul 1795 in Hartford, Conn. Zina died in Jackson, Mich. on 25 Jan
1885, he was 89. On 14 Feb 1818 when Zina was 22, he married **Huldah WEBSTER**, in Ashtabula,
Ohio. Born on 22 Apr 1797 in Litchfield, Litchfield Co., Conn. Huldah died in Jefferson, Ill. on 5 Aug
1886, she was 89. Occupation: Mother of 4.
They had the following children:

2152	i.	Active Amelia (1819-)
2153	ii.	Hiram Smith (1820-1856)
2154	iii.	Lucius Webster (1828-)
2155	iv.	Augustus (1830-1911)

1183. Susia Anna BYINGTON. Born on 28 Oct 1797 in Wolcott, Conn.

1184. Linus LANE. Born on 21 Feb 1799 in Plymouth, Litchfield Co., Conn. Linus died on 6 Dec 1880,
he was 81. On 25 Mar 1822 when Linus was 23, he married **Jerusha JEWELL**. Born on 2 Mar 1802 in
Litchfield Co., Conn. Jerusha died in Cornwall, Litchfield Co., Conn. on 14 Jan 1856, she was 53.
They had the following children:

2156	i.	Eri Leonard (1824-)
2157	ii.	Lyman Jewell (1827-1863)
2158	iii.	Alfred Henry (1827-)
2159	iv.	Mary Elizabeth (1836-)

1185. Lucas LANE. Born on 19 Jan 1801 in Plymouth, Litchfield Co., Conn. Lucas died in Plymouth,
Litchfield Co., Conn. on 2 Mar 1885, he was 84. On 25 Mar 1823 when Lucas was 22, he married **Mirza
JEWELL**. Born on 10 Apr 1804 in Litchfield Co., Conn. Mirza died on 10 Feb 1887, she was 82.
They had the following children:

2160	i.	Augustus L. (1824-1893)
2161	ii.	Lucia (1829-)
2162	iii.	John D. (1831-1864)
2163	iv.	Charles (1834-1839)
2164	v.	Elizabeth (1843-1846)

1186. Lucia LANE. Born on 12 Nov 1802 in Plymouth, Litchfield Co., Conn. Lucia died in Sullivan,
N.Y. on 7 May 1864, she was 61. Mother of 5, all of whom had descendants.
Lucia married **Erastus TODD**. Born in 1807. Erastus died in Lake Grove, Livingston, N.Y. on 30 Jun
1890, he was 83.
They had the following children:

2165	i.	Dimis Emeline (1832-)
2166	ii.	Olive Ellen (1834-)
2167	iii.	Erastus W. (1839-1890)
2168	iv.	Luther Buckley (1843-)
2169	v.	Elizabeth Eveline (1845-)

1187. Elizabeth LANE. Born on 2 Sep 1804 in Plymouth, Litchfield Co., Conn. Elizabeth died on 18
Dec 1830, she was 26. Elizabeth married **Joel BARNES**.

2170	i.	Elizabeth
2171	ii.	Horace

1188. Leonard LANE. Born on 7 Mar 1814 in Plymouth, Litchfield Co., Conn. Leonard died on 30 Dec
1843, he was 29. In 1833 when Leonard was 18, he married **Lucy JEWELL**. Born on 8 Nov 1813 in

Litchfield, Litchfield Co., Conn. Lucy died on 19 Jul 1884, she was 70.

They had the following children:

2172	i.	Lucinda (1834-1834)
2173	ii.	Robert Orange (1836-1862)
2174	iii.	Ashhel Albert (1838-)
2175	iv.	Horace B. (1842-1862)

1189. Asahel LANE. Born on 10 Apr 1817 in Plymouth, Litchfield Co., Conn. Asahel died in Bristol, Hartford Co., Conn. on 28 Oct 1885, he was 68. On 21 Oct 1841 when Asahel was 24, he married **Harriet MANSFIELD**. Born on 2 Feb 1818. Harriet died on 11 May 1884, she was 66.

They had the following children:

2176	i.	Eugene (1843-)
2177	ii.	Miriam (1844-)
2178	iii.	Frances (1846-)
2179	iv.	Alice (1853-)

1190. Lauren NORTON. Born in 1800 in Connecticut. Lauren died in Lanesboro, Susquehanna, Pa. on 20 Apr 1867, he was 67. Occupation: Father of 3. Lauren married **Lydia BACON**. Born in Connecticut. Lydia died in Lanesboro, Susquehanna, Pa.

They had the following children:

2180	i.	Jennie
2181	ii.	Lydia
2182	iii.	Lauren (1833-)

1191. Harmon NORTON. Born in 1803 in Sappford, Onondaga, N.Y. Harmon died in Kirtland, Lake Co., Ohio in 1838, he was 35. In 1829 when Harmon was 26, he married **Esther Ann PULLMAN**, in Spafford, Onondaga, N.Y. Born on 14 Aug 1813 in Spafford, Onondaga, N.Y. Esther Ann died in Theraples, Mich. in Feb 1883, she was 69.

They had one child:

| 2183 | i. | Emily Caroline (1830-) |

1192. Bird NORTON. B. in 1805 in Spafford, Onondaga, N.Y.; d. in Knoxville, Tenn. in 1861, abt 56.

1193. Philo NORTON. Born in 1808 in Spafford, Onondaga, N.Y.

1194. Erastus NORTON. Born in 1809. Erastus married **Mary ISDELE**.

1195. Theda NORTON. Born in 1812 in Spafford, Onondaga, N.Y. Theda died in 1900, she was 88. She married **Peter PICKETT**. Born in 1800.

They had the following children:

| 2184 | i. | Peres M. (1843-) |
| 2185 | ii. | Lafayette F. (1846-) |

1196. Esther NORTON. Born in 1815 in Spafford, Onondaga, N.Y. Esther married **Royal PULSIFER**.

1197. Amanda NORTON. Born in 1817 in Spafford, Onondaga, N.Y. Amanda married **? WILLIAMS**.

1198. Perris L. NORTON. Born in 1821 in Spafford, Onondaga, N.Y. In Apr 1845 when Perris L. was 24, he married **Sara THAYER**.

1199. Adah NORTON. Born on 23 Jun 1803 in Wolcott, Conn. Adah died on 9 Feb 1859, she was 55. Occupation: Mother of 3. Adah first married **? DOOLITTLE**. On 13 Mar 1827 when Adah was 23, she second married **George William ROYCE**, in Wolcott, Conn. Born in 1789. George William died in Wolcott, Conn. on 11 Oct 1865, he was 76.

They had the following children:

2186	i.	Nancy (1828-1906)
2187	ii.	William Alauson
2188	iii.	Cecilia (1832-)

1200. Ozias Rowe NORTON. Born on 12 Jun 1806. Ozias Rowe married **Fanny ROPER**.

1201. Rodney Frisbie NORTON. Born on 10 Dec 1807 in Plymouth, Litchfield Co., Conn. Rodney Frisbie died in Bristol, Hartford Co., Conn. on 11 Oct 1871, he was 63. Rodney Frisbie married **Lucinda L. BLAKESLEE**. Born in 1817; died in Bristol, Hartford Co., Conn. on 3 Apr 1885, she was 68.

They had the following children:

2189	i.	Lucinda N. (1834-)
2190	ii.	Hellin O. (1843-)

1202. Stephen Ludington NORTON. Born on 23 Jul 1810 in Wolcott, New Haven, Conn. Stephen Ludington married **Lucinda BRADLEY**. Born in Bristol, Hartford Co., Conn. Lucinda died in 1865. Mother of 12, born in 12 successive years according to OneWorldTree.

They had the following children:

2191	i.	Ammon (1841-)
2192	ii.	Lewis (1842-)
2193	iii.	Andrew (1843-)
2194	iv.	Oliver T. (1844-)
2195	v.	Eunice (1845-)
2196	vi.	Sarah M. (1846-)
2197	vii.	Mary (1847-)
2198	viii.	Lydia (1848-)
2199	ix.	Turchus (1849-)
2200	x.	Walter (1850-)
2201	xi.	Addie (1851-)
2202	xii.	Eliott (1852-)

1203. Matthew Simeon NORTON. Born on 19 Aug 1812. Matthew Simeon died in Wolcott, New Haven, Conn. on 22 May 1874, he was 61. On 30 Nov 1831 when Matthew Simeon was 19, he married **Betsey Maria THOMAS**, in Wolcott, New Haven, Conn. Born on 1 Sep 1811 in Wolcott.

1204. Selden S. NORTON. Born on 25 Nov 1813. Selden S. first married **Anna M. DECKER**. Selden S. second married **Aury C. NICHOLS**.

1205. Eunice R. NORTON. Born on 21 Aug 1817.

1206. Hannah R. NORTON. Born on 10 Nov 1819.

1207. Jedediah Roswell NORTON. Born on 28 Jun 1822.

1208. Daniel Eli NORTON. Born on 16 Sep 1826 in Plymouth, Litchfield Co., Conn. On 10 Dec 1867 when Daniel Eli was 41, he married **Mary "Addie" E. RUSSELL**, in New Haven Co., Conn. Born in 1834 in Plymouth, Litchfield Co., Conn.

They had the following children:

2203	i.	Dwight Edward (1868-)
2204	ii.	Jarius Stephen (1871-)
2205	iii.	Nelson B. (1879-)
2206	iv.	Ira R. (1882-)

1209. Satira FRISBIE.

1210. Arkemenia FRISBIE. Born on 12 Sep 1793.

1211. Austin S. FRISBIE. Born on 11 Jun 1795 in Brimfield, Hampden, Mass.

1212. ? FRISBIE. Born on 17 Jun 1824.

1213. Heth Frisbie CAMP. Born in 1792 in Durham, Middlesex Co., Conn. In 1821 when Heth Frisbie was 29, he married **Phoebe BATES**. Born in 1792. Phoebe died in Pennsylvania in 1845, she was 53.

They had the following children:

2207	i.	Elizabeth Mariah (1821-)
2208	ii.	Ebenezer Bates (1825-)
2209	iii.	James (1828-)
2210	iv.	Emily (1831-)
2211	v.	Anna (1837-)

1214. Sheldon UPSON. Born on 24 Mar 1785 in Connecticut.

1215. Amanda UPSON. Born in 1799.

1216. John PIERSON. Born on 17 Feb 1790.

1217. Uzal PIERSON. Born on 7 Nov 1791.

1218. Edward PIERSON. Born on 2 Dec 1793.

1219. Betsey PIERSON. Born on 9 Jan 1796.

1220. Mary PIERSON. Born on 28 Apr 1798 in Shelburne, Chittenden Co., Vt.

1221. Eliza FRISBIE. Born in 1804 in Shelburne, Chittenden Co., Vt.

1222. Guy Carlton FRISBIE. Born on 23 Jul 1805 in Shelburne, Chittenden Co., Vt.

1223. Dorcas FRISBIE. Born on 23 Jul 1807.

1224. Charlotte FRISBIE. Born on 5 Jan 1810 in New York.

1225. Maria FRISBIE. Born on 13 Apr 1812.

1226. Fidelia FRISBIE. Born on 29 Apr 1815 in Willsborough, Essex, N.Y.

1227. Minerva FRISBIE. Born in 1820.

1228. Asa W. FRISBIE. Born in 1823.

1229. Uri Tracey GUERNSEY. Born on 20 Oct 1811 in Windsor, Broome Co., N.Y. Uri Tracey died in Windsor, Broome Co., N.Y. on 11 Sep 1861, he was 49. Uri Tracey married **Lydia Rebina BLETCHLEY**. Born on 19 Jun 1819 in Windsor, Broome Co., N.Y. Lydia Rebina died in Sac City, Sac Co., Ia. on 16 Sep 1910, she was 91. Several of her children and grandchildren went to Iowa, but I cannot find her in a census and I don't see how she got to Sac City.

They had the following children:

2212	i.	Elmer Erastus (1841-1858)
2213	ii.	Ahira Harry Johnson (1842-1919)
2214	iii.	Elliott Birney (1844-1844)
2215	iv.	Flora Ann (1846-1881)
2216	v.	Vesta R. (1849-1850)
2217	vi.	Amy Rosalia (1850-1925)
2218	vii.	Charles Holbrook (1852-1930)
2219	viii.	Mary Arvilla (1854-1920)
2220	ix.	Orpha Jane (1858-1937)

1230. ? WARNER. Born on 30 Aug 1808 in Wolcott, New Haven Co., Conn.

1231. Julia FRISBIE. Born on 2 Nov 1795 in Waterbury, Conn.

1232. Anna FRISBIE. Born on 7 Feb 1798 in Waterbury, Conn.

1233. Lauren Lorrain FRISBIE. Born on 2 Aug 1800 in Waterbury, Conn.

1234. Lucius Daniel FRISBIE. Born on 15 Jun 1804 in Waterbury, Conn.

1235. Caroline Eunice FRISBIE. Born on 1 May 1809 in Waterbury, Conn.

1236. Mary Chloe FRISBIE. Born on 1 Oct 1811 in Waterbury, Conn.

1237. Richard FRISBIE. Born on 26 Jun 1796 in Waterbury, Conn.

1238. Hannah FRISBIE. Born on 2 Jul 1792 in Waterbury, Conn.

1239. Clara FRISBIE. Born on 21 Aug 1794 in Waterbury, Conn.

1240. Ebenezer Wakelee FRISBIE. Born on 7 Apr 1800 in Waterbury, Conn.

1241. Polly FRISBIE. Born on 29 Apr 1802 in Waterbury, Conn.

1242. Reuben FRISBIE. Born on 3 Jul 1810 in Waterbury, Conn.

1243. Emeline FRISBIE. Born on 7 Mar 1812 in Waterbury, Conn.

1244. William L. JACKSON. Born on 20 Aug 1808 in Lanesboro, Mass.

1245. Ira TUTTLE. Born on 11 Feb 1792 in Connecticut. Ira died in Clear Lake, Cerro Gordo Co., Ia. on 18 Oct 1878, he was 86. On 21 Oct 1813 when Ira was 21, he married **Lucy B. BROCKETT**. Born on 8 Dec 1793 in Dolgeville, Bracketts Bridge, N.Y. Lucy B. died in Clear Lake, Cerro Gordo Co., Ia. on 18 Dec 1866, she was 73.

They had the following children:

2221	i.	Eliada (1815-)
2222	ii.	Samantha (1817-)
2223	iii.	Huldah (1820-)
2224	iv.	Elon Augustus (1823-1908)
2225	v.	Alva Brockett (1825-)

2226	vi.	Rhoda (1828-)
2227	vii.	Marcus (1830-)
2228	viii.	Rachel B. (1832-)

1246. Salmon TUTTLE. Born on 12 Aug 1815 in Camden, N.J.

1247. Junius Frisbie MERRILL. Born on 30 Sep 1812 in Waterbury, Conn. Junius Frisbie died in Georgia in 1879, he was 66.

1248. Henry Augustus MERRILL. Born on 1 Jun 1815 in Waterbury, Conn. Henry Augustus died in Brooklyn, Kings Co., N.Y. in 1890, he was 74.

1249. Sally Maria MERRILL. Born on 25 Jun 1818 in Waterbury, Conn. Sally Maria died in Waterbury, Conn. in 1890, she was 71.

1250. Adeline MERRILL. Born on 15 May 1820 in Waterbury, New Haven Co., Conn. Adeline died in Waterbury, New Haven Co., Conn. in 1891, she was 70.

1251. Nathan F. MERRILL. Born on 14 May 1823 in Waterbury, Conn. Nathan F. died in Ansonia, New Haven Co., Conn. on 13 May 1909, he was 85. On 30 Aug 1847 when Nathan F. was 24, he married **Eunice Almira HOADLEY**, in Waterbury, Conn. Born in 1822. Eunice Almira died in 1894, she was 72. Occupation: Mother of 4.
They had the following children:

2229	i.	Mary Elvira (1849->1900)
2230	ii.	Charles (1850-)
2231	iii.	Ellen Taylor (1856-1927)
2232	iv.	Annie (1858-1898)

1252. Charles Frisbie MERRILL.

1253. Huldah MERRILL.

1254. Elen Augusta MERRILL.

1255. George D. MERRILL.

1256. Franklin B. MERRILL.

1257. John Frederick MERRILL. Born in 1836 in Waterbury, Conn. John Frederick married **Susan L. BUCKLEY**. Born in 1838.

1258. Baldwin Augustus FRISBIE. Born on 23 Aug 1812 in Litchfield, Litchfield Co., Conn. Baldwin Augustus died in Granville, Hampden, Mass. on 10 Aug 1894, he was 81. On 1 Jan 1852 when Baldwin Augustus was 39, he married **Elizabeth MOSES**, in Norfolk, Litchfield Co., Conn. Born in 1824. Elizabeth died in 1891, she was 67. Occupation: Mother of 5.
They had the following children:

2233	i.	Nelson Moses (1852-1949)
2234	ii.	Frederick Augustus (1855-1935)
2235	iii.	Theron E. (1858-1926)
2236	iv.	Frank Baldwin (1859-)
2237	v.	Harriet Elizabeth (1868-1930)

1259. Caroline Collins FRISBIE. Born in 1814. Caroline Collins died in 1816, she was 2.

1233. Harriet Burnham FRISBIE. Born in 1816.

1234. Caroline Collins FRISBIE. Born in 1818.

1235. Betsey FRISBIE. Born in 1820. Betsey died in 1877, she was 57.

1236. Freelove FRISBIE. Born in 1823.

1237. William Lawrence GAYLORD. Born on 22 Feb 1815 in Hamden, New Haven, Conn. William Lawrence died in Westfield, Wisc. on 8 Jan 1884, he was 68. On 28 Jun 1837 when William Lawrence was 22, he first married **Harriet YOUNG**. Harriet died on 21 Apr 1838. Occupation: d.s.p. (Did she die in giving birth to a child, a little over 9 months after she was married?) William Lawrence second married **Hannah A. BROWN**. Born on 28 Aug 1821 in Willoughby, Ohio. Hannah A. died in Oxford, Wisc. on 6 Feb 1861, she was 39. She died four months after giving birth to her fifth child.
They had the following children:

2238	i.	William Hepworth (1844-)

2239	ii.	Isaac Brown (1845-1927)
2240	iii.	Frederick Windslow (1848-)
2241	iv.	Fremont (1856-1857)
2242	v.	Minnie (1860-)

On 4 Oct 1862 when William Lawrence was 47, he third married **Catherine CRAWFORD**, in Oxford, Wisc. Born on 12 Aug 1838 in Montreal, East, Canada; died in Oxford, Wisc. on 8 Mar 1876, she was 37. They had one child:

2243	i.	Emma (1863-)

1265. Adeline GAYLORD. Born in 1817.

1266. Jennette GAYLORD. Born in 1822. Jennette died in 1863, she was 41. On 11 Apr 1842 when Jennette was 20, she married **John WOODING**, in Bethany, New Haven Co., Conn.

1267. Sherman BARNES. B. in 1793. In 1813, at abt 20, he m. **Lieuanna SMITH**. Born in 1793. They had one child:

2244	i.	Monroe (1813-)

1268. John FRISBIE. Born on 8 Dec 1819 in Burlington, Hartford Co., Conn. John died in Freeport, Stephenson, Ill. on 6 Dec 1902, he was 82. On 23 Sep 1845 when John was 25, he married **Jane Rosanna LEWIS**, in Burlington, Hartford Co., Conn. Born on 10 Apr 1822 in New York. Jane Rosanna died in Freeport, Stephenson, Ill. on 1 Apr 1863, she was 40. Mother of 6, of whom five had descendants. They had the following children:

2245	i.	Ella Elizabeth (1846-1934)
2246	ii.	Samuel (1850-1930)
2247	iii.	Mary Marilla (1855-1939)
2248	iv.	Horace Cornwall (1858-1859)
2249	v.	Leslie Almon (1861-1921)
2250	vi.	John Case (1863-1915)

1269. James FRISBIE. Born on 11 May 1822 in Burlington, Hartford Co., Conn. James died in Wellsville, Audrain, Mo. on 20 Sep 1892, he was 70. James married **Henrietta PETTIBONE**. Born on 10 Apr 1826 in Burlington, Hartford Co., Conn.; died in Wellsville, Audrain, Mo., 20 Jan 1906, age 79.

1270. Aaron Gaylord ESTABROOKS. Born in Orwell, Bradford, Pa.

1271. Charles ESTABROOKS. Born on 29 Aug 1816 in Orwell, Bradford, Pa.

1272. Laura ESTABROOKS. Born on 15 Aug 1818 in Orwell, Bradford, Pa.

1273. Levi ESTABROOKS. Born on 6 Aug 1822 in Orwell, Bradford, Pa.

1274. Addison Cowles FRISBIE. Born on 20 Oct 1829 in Orwell, Bradford, Pa.

1275. Warren Rush FRISBIE. Born on 31 Aug 1831 in Orwell, Bradford, Pa.

1276. William Lawson FRISBIE. Born on 25 Mar 1834 in Orwell, Bradford, Pa.

1277. Chauncey Montgomery FRISBIE. Born on 12 Nov 1837 in Orwell, Bradford, Pa.

1278. Eliza Maria FRISBIE. Born on 20 Nov 1839 in Orwell, Bradford, Pa.

1279. Ruby Hannah FRISBIE. Born on 15 Jun 1843 in Orwell, Bradford, Pa.

1280. Orrin Goodwin FRISBIE. Born on 8 Jun 1845 in Orwell, Bradford, Pa.

1281. Emily Phoebe FRISBIE. Born on 1 Oct 1847 in Orwell, Bradford, Pa.

1282. Mary Ellen FRISBIE. Born on 6 Oct 1849 in Orwell, Bradford, Pa.

1283. Olin Gaylord FRISBIE. Born on 20 Feb 1852 in Orwell, Bradford, Pa.

Line 2 – Descendants of Mary Hill (continued)[526]

1284. Abigail CASE. Born on 13 Jan 1781.

1285. Chloe CASE. Born in 1785.

1286. Violet CASE. Born in 1787.

1287. Chloe WILCOX.

1288. Benajah WILCOX. Born on 8 Nov 1780.

1289. Hepzibah WILCOX. Born on 20 Jul 1788.

1290. Caroline WILCOX. Born on 6 Nov 1790.
1291. Tammy Lovet WILCOX. Born on 4 Aug 1793.
1292. Azariah Jay WILCOX. Born on 31 Aug 1795.
1293. Elisha WILCOX. Born on 7 Apr 1790 in Hartford, Conn.
1294. Harvey WILCOX. Born in 1787.
1295. Chester WILCOX. Born on 14 Aug 1801.
1296. Ezekial WELLS. Born in 1787 in Simsbury, Hartford Co., Conn.
1297. Israel WELLS. Born in 1787 in Simsbury, Hartford Co., Conn.
1298. Joel WELLS. Born in Oct 1791 in Simsbury, Hartford Co., Conn.
1299. Truman WELLS. Born on 4 Jul 1797 in Simsbury, Hartford Co., Conn.
1300. Solomon WELLS. Born in 1799 in Simsbury, Hartford Co., Conn.
1301. Chester WELLS. Born on 6 Jan 1800 in Simsbury, Hartford Co., Conn.
1302. Chloe WELLS. Born in 1801.
1303. Mary WELLS. Born in 1803 in Simsbury, Hartford Co., Conn.
1304. Harriet WILCOX.
1305. Darius Pinney WILCOX.
1306. Emily WILCOX.
1307. George Clinton WILCOX.
1308. Israel WILCOX.
1309. Leicester WILCOX.
1310. Lodamia WILCOX.
1311. Stiles WILCOX.
1312. Dorcas WILCOX. Born on 17 Jan 1790 in Simsbury, Hartford Co., Conn.
1313. Roswell WILCOX. Born on 23 Jan 1792.
1314. Hiram WILCOX.
1315. Chauncey WILCOX. Born on 20 Aug 1789.
1316. George WILCOX. Born on 6 May 1792.
1317. Cornish WILCOX. Born on 1 Oct 1796.
1318. Lavinia WILCOX. Born on 3 Jun 1801.
1319. Miriam WILCOX. Born on 14 Dec 1804.
1320. Lester WILCOX. Born on 3 May 1810.
1321. Arlow CASE.
1322. Calista CASE.
1323. Huldah CASE.
1324. Julia CASE.
1325. Lovica CASE.
1326. Parley CASE. Born in Granby, Hartford Co., Conn.
1327. Sarah CASE. Born in Granby, Hartford Co., Conn.
1328. Jonathan CASE. Born in 1779 in Granby, Hartford Co., Conn.
1329. Aminta CASE. Born in 1783 in Granby, Hartford Co., Conn.
1330. Lydia CASE. Born in Dec 1785 in Granby, Hartford Co., Conn.
1331. Catherine CASE. Born in Dec 1794 in Granby, Hartford Co., Conn.
1332. Lyman CASE. Born in Barkhamsted, Litchfield Co., Conn.
1333. Hannah CASE. Born on 10 Jul 1774 in Barkhamsted, Litchfield Co., Conn.
1334. Abner CASE. Born on 1 Jan 1776 in Barkhamsted, Litchfield Co., Conn.
1335. Candace CASE. Born on 2 Oct 1777 in Barkhamsted, Litchfield Co., Conn.
1336. Imri CASE. Born on 22 Jan 1780 in Barkhamsted, Litchfield Co., Conn.
1337. Ira CASE. Born on 15 Mar 1782 in Barkhamsted, Litchfield Co., Conn.
1338. Olive CASE. Born on 2 Mar 1785 in Barkhamsted, Litchfield Co., Conn.
1339. Eli CASE. Born on 7 Sep 1788 in Barkhamsted, Litchfield Co., Conn.
1340. Abiel CASE. Born on 10 Aug 1792 in Barkhamsted, Litchfield Co., Conn.

1341. Samuel BEACH. Born on 7 Feb 1784 in Barkhamsted, Litchfield Co., Conn.
1342. Charlotte BEACH. Born on 28 Nov 1787 in Barkhamsted, Litchfield Co., Conn.
1343. Miles BEACH. Born on 30 Sep 1791 in Barkhamsted, Litchfield Co., Conn.
1344. Phebe CASE. Born on 18 Jan 1782 in Barkhamsted, Litchfield Co., Conn.
1345. Elijah CASE. Born on 18 Nov 1784 in Barkhamsted, Litchfield Co., Conn.
1346. Esther CASE. Born on 31 Oct 1789.
1347. Gabriel CASE. Born in Barkhamsted, Litchfield Co., Conn.
1348. Abigail CASE. Born in Feb 1787 in Barkhamsted, Litchfield Co., Conn.
1349. Loly (aka Lottie) CASE. Born on 16 Aug 1788 in Barkhamsted, Litchfield Co., Conn.
1350. Banning CASE. Born on 23 Jun 1790 in Barkhamsted, Litchfield Co., Conn.
1351. Sterling CASE. Born on 12 Feb 1806 in Barkhamsted, Litchfield Co., Conn.
1352. Charity TUTTLE. Born on 8 Mar 1789.
1353. Charles TUTTLE. Born on 16 Sep 1790 in Barkhamsted, Litchfield Co., Conn.
1354. Peniel Case (aka Pernal) TUTTLE. Born on 29 Sep 1792.
1355. Harvey TUTTLE. Born on 21 Apr 1794.
1356. George Washington TUTTLE. Born on 21 Jan 1796.
1357. Helpy Rosette TUTTLE. Born on 6 Mar 1798.
1358. Auria MOSES.
1359. Festus MOSES.
1360. Daniel MOSES. Born on 17 Apr 1791.
1361. Anna MOSES. Born in 1792.
1362. Norman MOSES. Born in 1797.
1363. Elisha ROBERTS. Born in 1781 in Lincoln, Addison Co., Vt.
1364. Sybil ROBERTS. Born in 1782 in West Simsbury, Hartford Co., Conn.
1365. Martin ROBERTS. Born in 1784 in Tyron, N.Y.
1366. Zebina MOSES. Born on 31 Oct 1786.
1367. Linus MOSES. Born on 13 Feb 1789.
1368. Pliny MOSES. Born on 23 Apr 1791 in West Simsbury, Hartford Co., Conn.
1369. Curtis MOSES. Born on 27 Dec 1792.
1370. Theodosia MOSES. Born on 14 Jul 1795.
1371. Charlotte MOSES. Born on 19 Jul 1797.
1372. Chester MOSES. Born on 16 Sep 1800.
1373. Horace MOSES. Born on 3 Jul 1803 in Marcellus, Onondaga, N.Y.
1374. Myron MOSES. Born on 11 May 1805.
1375. Pluma MOSES. Born on 8 Nov 1807.
1376. Elvira MOSES. Born on 18 Oct 1810.
1377. Mary MOSES. Born on 13 Jul 1797 in Barkhamsted, Litchfield Co., Conn.
1378. Salmon MOSES. Born on 10 Aug 1792.
1379. Almira MOSES. Born on 14 Jan 1795.
1380. Matthew MOSES. Born on 17 Jul 1799 in Barkhamsted, Litchfield Co., Conn.
1381. Ruth MOSES. Born on 29 Sep 1801.
1382. Hannah MOSES. Born on 4 Mar 1805.
1383. Lois MOSES. Born on 12 Jun 1806.
1384. Mark MOSES. Born on 18 Jun 1808.
1385. Rachel Lury CASE. Born on 30 Dec 1796 in Simsbury, Hartford Co., Conn.
1386. Job CASE. Born on 28 Jul 1805 in Simsbury, Hartford Co., Conn. He was one of the last of Luke and Mary (Hout) Hill's descendants to be born in their home town of Simsbury.
1387. Robert MILLS. Born on 10 Dec 1792 in Becket, Berkshire Co., Mass.
1388. Charlotte MILLS. Born in 1794 in Becket, Berkshire Co., Mass.
1389. Uriah M. MILLS. Born on 12 Jun 1799 in Nelson, Portage Co., O.
1390. Harmon MILLS. Born in Nov 1801 in Nelson, Portage Co., O.

1391. William Bainbridge MILLS. Born in 1805 in Nelson, Portage Co., O.

1392. Homer MILLS. Born in 1807 in Nelson, Portage Co., O.

1393. Frederic WILCOX. Born on 22 Jul 1793 in Hamilton, Madison Co., N.Y.

1394. Joseph WILCOX. Born on 28 Feb 1798 in Hamilton, Madison Co., N.Y.

1395. Erastus WILCOX. Born on 12 Jun 1801 in Hamilton, Madison Co., N.Y.

1396. Harvey LATIMER. Born in 1809.

1397. Lucy Lovina ADAMS. Born in 1781 in Bastard, Leeds, Quebec, Canada.

1398. Lucinda ADAMS. Born on 13 Dec 1799 in Bastard, Leeds, Quebec, Canada.

1399. Lucy Louisa ADAMS. Born in 1801 in Bastard, Leeds, Quebec, Canada.

1400. Lydia ADAMS. Born in 1790.

1401. John ADAMS. Born in 1793.

1402. Nancy ADAMS. Born in 1795.

1403. Erwin ADAMS. Born in 1801.

1404. Lydia STEVENS. Born on 21 Oct 1786 in Pittsford, Rutland Co., Vt.

1405. Jonathan STEVENS. Born in 1794 in Pittsford, Rutland Co., Vt.

1406. Warren STEVENS. Born in 1796 in Massachusetts.

1407. Lucy STEVENS. Born on 3 Mar 1798 in Barnet, Caledonia Co., Vt.

1408. Oliver STEVENS. Born in 1798 in Bastard, Leeds, Quebec, Canada.

1409. Henry STEVENS. Born in 1800 in Bastard, Leeds, Quebec, Canada.

1410. Arnold STEVENS. Born on 24 Aug 1802 in Bastard, Leeds, Quebec, Canada.

1411. Nancy STEVENS. Born in 1804 in Upper Canada, Canada.

1412. Lydie STEVENS. Born in 1806 in Bastard, Leeds, Quebec, Canada.

1413. Clarissa STEVENS. Born in 1808 in Upper Canada, Canada.

1414. Fanny STEVENS. Born in 1809 in Upper Canada, Canada.

1415. Henry Adams STEVENS. Born on 31 Jul 1813 in Perth, Ontario, Canada.

1416. Matson ADAMS. Born on 22 Jan 1804 in Beverly, Leeds, Ontario, Canada.

1417. Alvah ADAMS. Born on 23 Nov 1805 in Bastard, Leeds, Quebec, Canada.

1418. Richard Saxton ADAMS. Born on 6 Feb 1808 in Bastard, Leeds, Quebec, Canada.

1419. Beulah Everette ADAMS. Born on 26 Jan 1810 in Bastard, Leeds, Quebec, Canada.

1420. Barnabas Lothrop ADAMS. Born on 28 Aug 1812 in Bastard, Leeds, Quebec, Canada.

1421. Joshua ADAMS. Born on 14 May 1815 in Bastard, Leeds, Quebec, Canada.

1422. Lucy Matson ADAMS. Born on 5 Dec 1817 in Perth, Lanark, Ontario, Canada.

1423. James ADAMS. Born on 16 Oct 1819 in Perth, Lanark, Ontario, Canada.

1424. Daniel ADAMS. Born on 14 Oct 1820 in Perth, Lanark, Ontario, Canada.

1425. Franklin Metcalf ADAMS. Born on 27 Jan 1823 in Adamsville, Lanark, Ontario, Canada.

1426. Elizabeth Evaline ADAMS. Born on 3 May 1827 in Adamsville, Lanark, Canada.

1427. Lydia Ann ADAMS. Born on 22 Jan 1830 in Adamsville, Lanark, Ontario, Canada.

1428. Truman CASE. Born in Simsbury, Hartford Co., Conn.

1429. Roswell CASE. Born on 2 Apr 1786 in Simsbury, Hartford Co., Conn.

1430. Lydia CASE. Born on 14 Mar 1788 in Simsbury, Hartford Co., Conn.

1431. Grandy CASE. Born in 1789 in Simsbury, Hartford Co., Conn.

1432. Timothy CASE. Born on 12 Dec 1791 in Simsbury, Hartford Co., Conn.

1433. Riley CASE. Born on 13 Jun 1793 in Simsbury, Hartford Co., Conn.

1434. Pinney CASE. Born on 14 Oct 1796 in Simsbury, Hartford Co., Conn.

1435. Lucy CASE. Born on 25 Sep 1800 in Simsbury, Hartford Co., Conn.

1436. Mary HOLCOMB. Born on 23 Mar 1786 in Simsbury, Hartford Co., Conn.

1437. Benajah Philo HOLCOMB. Born on 18 Jul 1784 in Simsbury, Hartford Co., Conn.

1438. Samuel HOLCOMB. Born on 23 Mar 1786 in Simsbury, Hartford Co., Conn.

1439. Hull HOLCOMB. Born on 4 Feb 1790 in Simsbury, Hartford Co., Conn.

1440. Linus HOLCOMB. Born on 19 Jul 1794 in Simsbury, Hartford Co., Conn.

1441. Salmon HOLCOMB. Born on 4 Jun 1797 in Simsbury, Hartford Co., Conn. Salmon died in

Simsbury, Hartford Co., Conn. (prob.) bef 9 May 1801, he was 3.

1442. Salmon HOLCOMB. Born on 9 May 1801 in Simsbury, Hartford Co., Conn.

1443. Betsey HOLCOMB. Born on 25 Jul 1807 in Simsbury, Hartford Co., Conn. She was one of the last of Luke and Mary (Hout) Hill's descendants to be born in their home town of Simsbury.

1444. Sybil HILLYER. Born on 19 May 1786 in Granby, Hartford Co., Conn.

1445. Seth HILLYER. Born on 17 Jun 1788 in Granby, Hartford Co., Conn.

1446. Chloe HILLYER. Born on 6 May 1790.

1447. Laura HILLYER. Born on 7 Sep 1792 in Granby, Hartford Co., Conn.

1448. Tracy HILLYER. Born on 9 Sep 1794.

1449. Harriet HILLYER. Born on 1 Feb 1797 in Granby, Hartford Co., Conn.

1450. Alma HILLYER. Born on 12 May 1799.

1451. Alanson JUDSON.

1452. Gordon JUDSON.

1453. Lucy JUDSON.

1454. Sylvanus JUDSON.

1455. Sylvester JUDSON.

1456. Elisha JUDSON. Born on 28 Jun 1796 in Kingsboro, Fulton Co., N.Y.

1457. Hallett BARBER. Born in 1798 in New York State.

1458. John ADAMS. Born on 23 Jan 1794 in Albany, Albany Co., N.Y.

1459. Salina ADAMS. Born on 17 Jun 1796.

1460. Mary ADAMS. Born on 3 Apr 1798.

1461. William ADAMS. Born in 1800.

1462. Sarah Ann ADAMS. Born on 22 Jan 1801 in Adams Farm, Lysander, N.Y.

1463. Parmelia ADAMS. Born on 15 Mar 1804.

1464. Charlora ADAMS. Born in Dec 1812.

1465. James ADAMS. Born on 6 Dec 1796 in Hartford, Conn.

1466. Sarah ADAMS. Born on 2 Sep 1802 in Skaneateles, Onondaga Co., N.Y.

1467. Laura ADAMS. Born on 30 Nov 1807 in Attica, Wyoming Co., N.Y.

1468. Julia ADAMS. Born on 14 Dec 1802 in Marcellus, Onondaga, N.Y.

1469. Almenia ADAMS. Born on 16 May 1804 in Marcellus, Onondaga, N.Y.

1470. Sally E. ADAMS. Born on 20 Oct 1806 in Marcellus, Onondaga, N.Y.

1471. Belinda ADAMS. Born on 20 Nov 1808 in Skaneateles, Onondaga Co., N.Y.

1472. Chloe ADAMS. Born in 1812 in Skaneateles, Onondaga Co., N.Y.

1473. Zilpha ADAMS. Born on 8 Jun 1815 in Skaneateles, Onondaga Co., N.Y.

1474. Delia Ann ADAMS. Born on 29 Jun 1819 in Skaneateles, Onondaga Co., N.Y.

1475. Ledyard S. ADAMS. Born in 1807 in Genesee, N.Y.

1476. Marcia ADAMS. Born in 1808 in New York State.

1477. Parmenio N. ADAMS. Born in 1810 in New York State.

1478. Elvira ADAMS. Born in 1811.

1479. Lovenia Elizabeth ADAMS. Born on 3 May 1813 in Oswego, Oswego Co., N.Y.

1480. Charlotte Baldwin ADAMS. Born on 2 May 1815 in Oswego, Oswego Co., N.Y.

1481. Lucian Bonaparte ADAMS. Born on 10 Dec 1816 in Oswego, Oswego Co., N.Y.

1482. Vienna Margaret ADAMS. Born on 10 Jul 1818 in Oswego, Oswego Co., N.Y.

1483. Olivia Ann ADAMS. Born on 31 Jan 1811.

1484. Mary ADAMS. Born in 1822. Her mother died at about the time she was born.

1485. Hannah Ann ADAMS. Born on 15 Jul 1825 in Camillus, Onondaga Co., N.Y.

1486. Luman BARBER. Born on 12 Nov 1766.

1487. Beriah BARBER.

1488. Elijah James BARBER.

1489. Olive BARBER.

1490. Clarissa WOODRUFF. Born on 24 Mar 1774 in Winchester, Litchfield Co., Conn.

1491. Noadiah WOODRUFF. Born on 10 Nov 1778 in Farmington, Conn.

1492. Melinda WOODRUFF. Born in 1781 in Winchester, Litchfield Co., Conn.

1493. Beulah WOODRUFF. Born on 27 May 1783 in Winchester, Litchfield Co., Conn.

1494. Lauren L. WOODRUFF. Born in 1788 in Sheffield, Berkshire Co., Mass.

1495. Elizabeth WOODRUFF. Born in 1791 in Winchester, Litchfield Co., Conn.

1496. Zelotus Harvey WOODRUFF. Born in 1796 in Winchester, Litchfield Co., Conn.

1497. Sanford Clark HILL. Born on 20 Jun 1796 in Pughtown, Hancock Co., Va.

1498. Cynthia PHELPS. Born on 17 May 1786 in Wallingford, New Haven Co., Conn.

1499. Abigail PHELPS. Born on 23 Oct 1790 in Granby, Hartford Co., Conn.

1500. Sally SHELDON. Born in 1782 in Rupert, Vt.

1501. Isaac SHELDON. Born in 1784 in Rupert, Vt.

1502. Abel Phelps SHELDON. Born in 1786 in Rupert, Vt.

1503. Phebe SHELDON. Born in 1788 in Rupert, Vt.

1504. Mary SHELDON. Born in 1791 in Rupert, Vt.

1505. Enos SHELDON. Born in 1794 in Rupert, Vt.

1506. Sarah PHELPS. Born on 15 Jun 1786 in Granby, Connecticut.

1507. William PHELPS. Born in 1794 in Granby, Connecticut.

1508. John PHELPS. Born in 1795 in Granby, Connecticut.

1509. Timothy PHELPS. Born in 1796 in Granby, Connecticut.

1510. Willis Abel PHELPS. Born on 18 Dec 1799 in Granby, Connecticut.

1511. Clarissey PHELPS. Born in 1802 in Granby, Connecticut.

1512. Polly HIGLEY. Born on 26 Nov 1786 in Granby, Hartford Co., Conn.

1513. Elihu HIGLEY. Born on 26 Dec 1788 in Granby, Hartford Co., Conn.

1514. Lucy HIGLEY. Born on 20 Aug 1793 in Granby, Hartford Co., Conn.

1515. Sally HIGLEY. Born on 8 Mar 1795 in North Granby, Conn.

1516. Cynthia HIGLEY. Born on 7 Feb 1797.

1517. Maria HIGLEY. Born on 30 Jul 1799 in Granby, Hartford Co., Conn.

1518. Joel Phelps HIGLEY. Born on 9 Jun 1802 in Granby, Hartford Co., Conn.

1519. James Enos PHELPS. Born in 1793 in Granby, Hartford Co., Conn.

1520. Philo PHELPS. Born on 30 Dec 1804 in Granby, Hartford Co., Conn.

1521. Lucy PHELPS. Born in 1807 in Barkhamsted, Litchfield Co., Conn.

1522. Willis PHELPS. Born on 8 Aug 1810 in Granby, Hartford Co., Conn.

1523. Mary PHELPS. Born on 3 May 1812 in Granby, Hartford Co., Conn.

1524. Lydia PHELPS. Born on 7 Sep 1717 in Granby, Hartford Co., Conn.

1525. Mary F. ALLEN[527] was born in 1789.

1526. Col. Ira Hayden ALLEN,[528] elder son and second of the four children of General Ira and Jerusha Hayden (Enos) Allen, was born at Colchester, Chittenden Co., Vt., 19 July 1790; died at Irasburg, Orleans Co., Vt., 21 April 1866, age 75. He was one of many who competed for a share of his father's estate, and one of the few who were successful. As a young man, he studied at Vermont University, but he withdrew because of poor vision. He later rose in political office was successful in his financial affairs, and he was respected for his many skills and for his integrity. At the age of 26, he was elected Town Clerk of Irasburg, a town that was named for his father and was a wedding gift to his mother. He was a selectman in Irasburg for ten years, and then probate judge. He represented Orleans County on the Vermont Council from 1828 to 1832. He was president of the Orleans County Bank from 1833-49 and from 1863-65, and he was on the board of directors of the bank at the time of his death. His title of Colonel derived from his appointment as aide-de-camp to the governor of Vermont.

He married (1), on 13 January 1842, **Sarah Catherine Tilton PARSONS**; born in 1820; died in Irasburgh, Orleans Co., Vt., 29 February 1844, about age 24. They had two children: Ira Hayden (1842-1863), who died while still a student; and Charles Parsons (1844-1876), who married Lizzzie Pulsifer and had one child, Lizzie Pulsifer (1877-1899). Col. Allen married (2), on 8 July 1848, **Frances Eliza PARSONS**; born 15 August 1828; died at Irasburg, Vt., 1 March 1867. They had three children: Mary

Parsons (1848-1849); Sarah Maria (b. 1850 and was living in Brookline, Mass., in 1907); and Mary Frances (1854-1873), who m. Sydney W. Beanduk (or more likely Beauclerk) and had one surviving child, Mary Frances Beanduk (b. 1873), who m. William O. Wilson (or more likely Stetson) and had a child, Allen Wilson (or Stetson), b. 24 June 1896.

Ira Hayden and Sarah Cathrerine Tilton (Parsons) Allen had the following children:

2251	i.	Ira Hayden (1842-1863)
2252	ii.	Charles Parsons (1844-1877)

Ira Hayden and Frances Eliza (Parsons) Allen had the following children:

2253	i.	Mary Parsons (1848-1849)
2254	ii.	Sarah Maria (1850-)
2255	iii.	Mary Frances (1854-1873)

1527. Zimri Enos ALLEN[529] was born in 1792 in Colchester, Chittenden Co., Vt.; died 22 August 1813, about age 21. He was beginning a career as a lawyer at the time of his death.

1528. Maria Juliette ALLEN[530] was born 22 May 1794 in Colchester, Chittenden Co., Vt.; died in St. Albans, Vt., 18 August 1811, age 17.

_____[531]

1529. Ellen Maria ENO.

1530. Sally HART. Born on 9 Nov 1778 in New Britain, Conn.

1531. Polly HART. Born on 5 Oct 1781 in New Britain, Conn.

1532. Sophia HART. Born on 3 Sep 1785 in New Britain, Conn.

1533. Erastus Langdon HART. Born on 7 May 1787 in New Britain, Conn.

1534. Hannah HART. Born on 7 Oct 1792.

1535. Ira STANLEY. Born on 7 Jul 1795 in New Britain, Hartford Co., Conn.

1536. Abi Langdon STANLEY. Born on 12 Mar 1807 in New Britain, Conn.

1537. Jonathan ENO. Born on 7 Aug 1793 in Simsbury, Hartford Co., Conn. Jonathan married **Orpah Cassett ADAMS.** Born on 17 Feb 1793. Orpah Cassett died on 27 Jun 1867, she was 74.
They had one child:

2256	i.	Eunetia Minerva (1824-1915)

1538. Alexander Cotton PHELPS. Born on 25 Oct 1794 in Simsbury, Hartford Co., Conn.

1539. Horace G. PHELPS. Born on 2 Feb 1797 in Simsbury, Hartford Co., Conn.

1540. Jaman Hart PHELPS. Born on 7 Aug 1799 in Simsbury, Hartford Co., Conn.

1541. Edward PHELPS. Born on 25 Feb 1802 in Simsbury, Hartford Co., Conn.

1542. Elizabeth PHELPS. Born on 30 Jan 1804 in Simsbury, Hartford Co., Conn.

1543. Norman PHELPS. Born on 10 Nov 1806 in Simsbury, Hartford Co., Conn.

1544. Mary Ann PHELPS. Born on 30 Dec 1808 in Simsbury, Hartford Co., Conn.

1545. John Jay PHELPS. Born on 25 Oct 1810 in Simsbury, Hartford Co., Conn.

1546. Sherman David PHELPS. Born in 1814 in Simsbury, Hartford Co., Conn. He was one of the last of Luke and Mary (Hout) Hill's descendants to be born in their home town of Simsbury.

1547. Hezekiah Hart CASE. Born on 7 Jan 1795.

1548. Hiram CASE. Born on 7 Aug 1799 in Simsbury, Hartford Co., Conn.

1549. Elizur Hart ENO. Born in 1810 in Simsbury, Hartford Co., Conn.

1550. Cordelia ENO. Born on 3 Jun 1812.

1551. Chauncey E. ENO. Born on 27 Dec 1815.

1552. Jeanette Amarilla ENO. Born on 8 May 1818.

1553. Josiah William ENO. Born on 23 Feb 1820 in Simsbury, Hartford Co., Conn. He may have been the last of the descendants of Luke and Mary (Hout) Hill to be born in Simsbury.

Line 4 – Descendants of Tahan Hill (continued)[532]

1554. David Dudley PARMELEE.[533] Born on 17 Feb 1801. David Dudley died on 22 May 1872, he was 71. Lived in Middletown, Conn. David Dudley married **Sarah Warne STARR.** Born 23 Feb 1812.

They had the following children:

2257	i.	Adeline Maria (1829-)
2258	ii.	George Stevens (1835-1837)
2259	iii.	Susan Catherine (1837-1869)
2260	iv.	Ermina Starr (1838-1839)
2261	v.	George Stevens (1839-)
2262	vi.	Henry Starr (1842-)
2263	vii.	Ellen Stevens (1846-)
2264	viii.	Charles Henderson (1853-)

1555. James Smith PARMELEE. Born on 22 Sep 1820. James Smith died on 27 May 1864, he was 43. Occupation: Lived in Middletown, Conn., and New York. On 8 Aug 1843 when James Smith was 22, he married **Mary Almira STARR**. Born on 3 Oct 1816.

They had one child:

2265	i.	Emily Starr (1844-)

1556. Eliza PARMELEE. Eliza died on 11 Nov 1826. Unmarried.

1557. Marietta PARMELEE. Marietta married **Alfred NEWTON**.

1558. Laura P. PARMELEE. Born in 1795; died on 13 Dec 1855, abt 60; m. **Abraham BLAKESLEE**.

1559. Almira A. PARMELEE. Born in 1811. Almira A. died on 16 Dec 1855, she was 44. Almira A. married **Richard KIRTLAND**.

1560. Elias PARMELEE. He was of West Meriden, Conn.

------------------------------------534

1561. Amos BALDWIN. Born in 1779. Amos died in 1865, he was 86.

1562. Mary BALDWIN. Born in 1783. Mary died in 1877, she was 94.

1563. Philemon H. BALDWIN. Born in 1785. Philemon H. died in 1834, he was 49.

1564. Rune R. BALDWIN. Born in 1789. Rune R. died in 1834, he was 45.

1565. Caleb BALDWIN. Born in 1791. Caleb died in 1849, he was 58.

1566. Asa BALDWIN. Born in 1795.

1567. Elizabeth BALDWIN. Born in 1798. Elizabeth died in 1877, she was 79.

1568. George BALDWIN. Born in 1802. George died in 1830, he was 28.

1569. Salley Ann BALDWIN. Born in 1806.

1570. Esther BALDWIN. Born in 1810.

1571. Child of Rev. James Hill PARMELEE.

Line 5 – Descendants of Luke Hill Jr. (continued)[535]

1572. Seth Morris HILL,[536] son and only child of Reuben and Patience (Reynolds) Hill, was born at Cambridge, Washington Co., N.Y., 25 August 1799; died at Wauconda, Lake Co., Ill., 15 May 1896, age 96. He married, in New York State, 2 January 1822, **Deborah Ann CLARK**; born 8 September 1803; died 29 July 1874, age 70. They had eight children, of whom the eldest was Morris Seth Hill (1823-1908), a soldier in the Civil War, who had descendants.

They had the following children:

2266	i.	Morris Seth (1823-1908)
2267	ii.	Mary Ann (1825-1855)
2268	iii.	Jerusha (1828-1921)
2269	iv.	Sarah M. (1830-1917)
2270	v.	Eliza Jane (1833-1916)
2271	vi.	Lucy (1836-1909)
2272	vii.	Reuben Clark (1838-1911)
2273	viii.	Frances A. (1845-1853)

1573. George Welles ROE[537] was born 29 May 1799 in Williamstown, Berkshire Co., Mass.; died in Medina, Orleans Co., N.Y., 26 February 1830, age 30. He apparently was unmarried and d.s.p.

1574. Amanda ROE[538] was born 9 June 1800 in Williamstown, Berkshire Co., Mass.; died in Racine, Racine Co., Wisc. in 1870, she was 69. She married **Jasper BARNUM**.

1575. Lydia ROE[539] was b. 22 January 1802 in Williamstown, Berkshire Co., Mass. She was the mother of 5, two of whom had descendants. She m. **Horace WHEELOCK**; b.1802; d. in 1855, abt 53.
They had the following children:

2274	i.	Marian (1831-1913)
2275	ii.	Pamelia (1834-)
2276	iii.	Frances (1836->1880)
2277	iv.	Emily (1838->1860)
2278	v.	Elisha Roe (1842->1860)

1576. William Horace ROE[540] was born 4 November 1803 in Williamstown, Berkshire Co., Mass.; died in Racine, Racine Co., Wisc., 3 September 1886, age 82. On 7 May 1842, when he was 38, he married **Elizabeth Smith PAYNE**, daughter of Harvey PAYNE & Rachel Moss SMITH; born in 1874; died in 1908, about age 34.
They had the following children:

2279	i.	Helen (1844-1882)
2280	ii.	Augustus (1845-1880)
2281	iii.	Lucy (1847-1872)
2282	iv.	Roxanne (1849-1851)
2283	v.	Reuben Smith (1850-1933)
2284	vi.	William H. (1852-1925)
2285	vii.	George (1854-1917)
2286	viii.	Carrie (1857-)
2287	ix.	Harvey P. (1859-1932)
2288	x.	Winnie (1862-1934)
2289	xi.	Nettie (1865-1932)

1577. James Augustus ROE[541] was born 20 November 1805 in Williamstown, Berkshire Co., Mass.; died in Medina, Orleans Co., N.Y., 19 August 1827, age 21.

1578. Lucy ROE[542] was born 22 July 1807 in Williamstown, Berkshire Co., Mass.; died in Chicago, Cook Co., Ill., in Jun 1888, age 80. She resided in Alden, Erie Co., N.Y., in 1860; in Battle Creek, Mich., in 1870; in Geneva, Wisc., in 1880; and she died in Chicago in 1888. In 1831, when she was about 23, she married **Nathan MAYNARD**; born in 1810 in Massachusetts; died in 1877, about age 67.
They had the following children:

2290	i.	Amanda B. (1833-1903)
2291	ii.	Antoinette (1835-1917)
2292	iii.	Eveiline (1836-)
2293	iv.	Henry C. (1846-)

1579. Electa ROE[543] was born 17 March 1810 in Williamstown, Berkshire Co., Mass.; died in Battle Creek, Calhoun Co., Mich., 19 April 1864, age 54. She resided in Johnstown, Barry Co., Mich., in 1850, and in Battle Creek, Mich., in 1860. She married **Orris BARNUM**, who was born in 1805 and died in 1895, about age 90.
They had the following children:

2294	i.	Sophia (1840-)
2295	ii.	James A. (1832-1863)
2296	iii.	Romeo (1847-1863)

1580. Roxana ROE[544] was born 30 January 1812 in Williamstown, Berkshire Co., Mass.; died in Chicago, Cook Co., Ill., in 1900, about age 87. On 16 October 1834, when she was 22, she married **William Henry Harrison PRATT;** born in 1812; died in 1880, about 68.
They had the following children:

| 2297 | i. | George Nathaniel (~1842-1901) |
| 2298 | ii. | Mary F. (~1843-1925) |

2299	iii.	Albert Harrison (1835-1923)
2300	iv.	Ellen (1848-)
2301	v.	Ella A. (1851-1930)

1581. Elisha ROE[545] was born 3 February 1814 in Williamstown, Berkshire Co., Mass.; died in Racine, Racine Co., Wisc. in 1883, about age 68. On 20 March 1836, when he was 22, he married **Eveline KENDALL**; born in 1816; died in 1862, about age 46.
They had the following children:

2302	i.	Marion (1837-)
2303	ii.	Susannah (1839-)
2304	iii.	Electa A. (1842-)
2305	iv.	Mary Frances (1845-)
2306	v.	Josephine (1849-1849)
2307	vi.	Joseph (1849-1849)
2308	vii.	Eveline (1849-)
2309	viii.	Elisha K. (1853-)
2310	ix.	Horace (1854-1870)

1582. Ambrose Thomas ROE[546] was born 2 July 1817 in Williamstown, Berkshire Co., Mass.; died in Charlotte, Mich., 5 January 1879, age 61. He was a vinegar maker. He married **Helen Mar PAINE**; born in 1826; died in 1870, about age 44.
They had the following children:

2311	i.	Birdie (1868-)
2312	ii.	Carrie (1859-)
2313	iii.	Orvin J. (1851-1937)

1583. Orvin Sidney ROE[547] was born 24 November 1819 in Williamstown, Berkshire Co., Mass.; died in New York City, N.Y., 14 September 1872, age 52. He married **Carrie EVANS**.

1584. Rebecca "Betta" Isaacs HILL. Born on 3 Oct 1847 in Norwalk, Conn.; died in Norwalk, Conn. on 26 Apr 1922, she was 74. On 3 Nov 1868 when Rebecca "Betta" Isaacs was 21, she married **Ira COLE** in Norwalk, Conn. Born in 1836. Ira died in 1918, he was 82.
They had the following children:

2314	i.	Edalena "Lena" Hill (1870-1945)
2315	ii.	Anna Louise (1878-1966)
2316	iii.	Alice Isaacs (1881-1957)

1585. Elisha (Elizah) GRANT.

1586. Lorin Marcina GRANT was born 22 July 1810 in Smithville Flats, Chenango Co., N.Y.; died in Harrisville, Medina Co., Ohio. On 4 July 1833, when he was 22, he married **Sarah ROGERS** in Harrisville, Medina Co., Ohio; born on 1 Dec 1811 in Smithville Flats, N.Y.; died 30 June 1892, age 80.
They had one child:

| 2317 | i. | Harriet |

1587. Hannah GRANT. Born on 2 Jan 1812 in Smithville Flats, Chenango Co., N.Y. Hannah died in Woodland, Mich. on 29 Jun 1874, she was 62. Occupation: d.s.p. On 20 Jan 1831 when Hannah was 19, she married **Charles PERKINS**, in Medina, Ohio. Born on 12 Aug 1808 in Otsego, N.Y. Charles died in Hastings, Mich. on 11 Dec 1860, he was 52.

1588. Isaac GRANT. Born in 1814. Isaac died in 1833, he was 19.

1589. John GRANT. Born in 1816 in Smithville Flats, Chenango Co., N.Y. John died in Sunfield, Mich. on 1 Oct 1887, he was 71. Occupation: Married 3 times, had children by 1st two wives. On 19 Feb 1838 when John was 22, he first married **Desire JACKSON**, in Medina, Ohio.
They had one child:

| 2318 | i. | Eliza Desire (1838-1925) |

On 20 Dec 1839 when John was 23, he second married **Lydia M. BIRD**, in Medina, Ohio. Born on 18 Sep 1821 in Massachusetts. Lydia M. died on 20 Dec 1872, she was 51.
They had the following children:

2319	i.	Lydia Maria (1841-1892)
2320	ii.	Samuel Elihu (1843-1934)
2321	iii.	Isaac Jesse (1844-1903)
2322	iv.	John (1847-)
2323	v.	Timothy Burr (1850-)
2324	vi.	Urania (1852-)
2325	vii.	Susanna (1855-1863)
2326	viii.	Julia Eva (Twin) (1858-1867)
2327	ix.	Julius Everett (Twin) (1858-1872)
2328	x.	Alma Virginia (1863-)

John third married **Aseneth A. CLARK**.

1590. Laura GRANT. Born in 1817.

1591. Sarah GRANT. Born on 15 Feb 1819 in Smithville Flats, Chenango Co., N.Y.; died in Medina, Ohio on 8 Jul 1863, she was 44; d.s.p. On 19 Feb 1838 when Sarah was 19, she married **Orrin ROGERS**, in Friendsville, O. Born on 20 Dec 1815 in Smithville Flats, Chenango Co., N.Y.

1592. Pamelia GRANT. Born in 1821. Pamelia died in 1859, she was 38.

1593. Lucy Anna GRANT. Born on 2 Sep 1823 in Norwich, N.Y. Lucy Anna died in Huntington, Ohio on 22 Dec 1885, she was 62; d.s.p. On 6 Jul 1847 when Lucy Anna was 23, she married **Aaron Sewell WARD**, in Harrisville, Medina Co., Ohio. Born on 15 Feb 1818 in Bolton, Quebec, Canada. Aaron Sewell died in Lorain, O. on 23 Aug 1891, he was 73.

1594. Jesse C. GRANT. Born on 4 Nov 1825 in New York; died in Woodland Twp., Barry Co., Mich. on 20 Jun 1886, he was 60. On 5 Jan 1858 when Jesse C. was 32, he married **Elmyra CURTIS**. Born on 1 Aug 1837 in Ontario, Canada; died in Woodland Twp., Barry Co., Mich. on 20 Jun 1886, she was 48.

1595. Nathan Orlando GRANT. Born on 23 Jun 1828 in Smithville Flats, Chenango Co., N.Y. On 30 Aug 1854 when he was 26, he m. **Lydia Ann MELLICK**, in Sharon, O.; b. 4 Feb 1830 in Wadsworth, O.

1596. George Roberts GRANT. Born on 14 Jul 1820 in Reading, Schuyler Co., N.Y.; died in Rocklin, Placer, California, on 22 Jul 1889, he was 69. On 10 Dec 1847 when he was 27, he first married **Maryann Helen VAN ORDEN**, in Winter Quarters, Douglas Co., Neb. Born on 27 Dec 1832 in Moravia, Cayuga, New York. Maryann Helen died in California on 25 Oct 1925, she was 92. They had the following children:

2329	i.	Mary Amelia (1848-)
2330	ii.	Sarah Opehlia (1850-1900)
2331	iii.	George Robert (1852-1895)
2332	iv.	Julia Antoinette (1854-)
2333	v.	Helen Louisa (1856-)
2334	vi.	Henrietta (1858-)
2335	vii.	Gertrude Betsy (1860-1864)
2336	viii.	Henry Loring (1972-1864)
2337	ix.	Charles Lewis (1864-1864)

On 17 Dec 1857 when George Roberts was 37, he second married, as her third husband, **Mary Adelia CARBINE**,[548] daughter of Edmond Zebulon CARBINE & Adelia RIDER, in Kaysville, Davis Co., Utah. Born on 29 Feb 1824 in Cairo, Greene Co., N.Y. She previously married (1) Amos Northrup, by whom she had Eugenia and Llewellyn. Amos was killed and Llewellyn died. She then married (2) Robert C. Petty, by whom she had Adelia and Ella; he died. Her third husband, George Roberts Grant, by whom she had two children, was excommunicated from the Latter Day Saints and moved to California, deserting Mary Adelia, and leaving her to bring up her children in Utah. Francesca was accidentally scalded and died. Mary Adelia then married (4) her brother-in-law, William Warren Taylor, who was married [apparently at the same time] to her sister and had children by both women. Her children by Taylor were Albert, Francis, and James. She died in Delamar, Lincoln, Nevada on 13 Nov 1906, she was 82. It appears that she was married to two men at the same time: George Grant (who deserted her), and William Taylor (who was already married to her sister). George Roberts and Mary Adelia (Carbine) (Northrup)

(Petty) Grant had the following children:

2338	i.	Edmund Carbine (1858-)
2339	ii.	Francesca (1860-)

1597. Charles Wesley GRANT. Born on 15 Mar 1818 in Smithville Flats, Chenango Co., N.Y.

1598. DeWitt Clinton GRANT. Born on 4 Dec 1841 in Cameron, N.Y.

1599. Charles Henry GERE. Born on 18 Feb 1838 in Gainsville, N.Y.

1600. John Nelson GERE. Born on 18 Aug 1842 in Chenango Co., N.Y.

1601. George Grant GERE. Born on 27 Dec 1848 in Greene, Chenango Co., N.Y.

1602. William Smith HILL.[549] Born on 5 Apr 1826 in Brownville, Jefferson Co., N.Y. William Smith died in Clinton, De Kalb Co., Ill. in 1898, abt 71. On 26 May 1851 when William Smith was 25, he first married **Elizabeth FIELD**, daughter of Bennett FIELD & Fanny WAIT, in De Kalb, Ill. Born in 1836. They had the following children:

2340	i.	Sylvester (1855->1930)
2341	ii.	William Smith (1862-1928)

On 22 Sep 1868 at age 42, he second married **Melissa TROUT**, in De Kalb, Ill. She d.s.p.

1603. Arunah HILL III.[550] Born in 1828 in New York, N.Y.

1604. Benjamin F. HILL.[551] Born on 23 May 1830 in Jefferson Co., N.Y.; died in Llewellyn Park, just north of Evanston, Ill. in Oct 1905, he was 75. Occupation: Real estate, at the time of the 1880 census. On 17 Sep 1856 when Benjamin F. was 26, he married **Louisa AUSTIN** in Kane, Ill. Born abt 1837. Mother of eight or more.

They had the following children, and perhaps others:

2342	i.	Gary (~1857-<1870)
2343	ii.	Benjamin F. "Frankie" (~1859-)
2344	iii.	Elizabeth (~1861-)
2345	iv.	Nathaniel (~1865-)
2346	v.	Eugene "Emogene" (~1867-)
2347	vi.	Joab (1869-<1880)
2348	vii.	Albert (~1872-)
2349	viii.	Allison A. (~1874-)

1605. George W. HILL.[552] Born in Aug 1834 in Ohio. He married **Mary E. _____**.

They had the following children:

2350	i.	Elva (Elvira) (~1866-)
2351	ii.	Herbert (~1869-)
2352	iii.	Eugene (~1873-)
2353	iv.	George W. (~1875-)
2354	v.	Reubin (~1879-)

1606. Son #1 of Lewis HILL.

1607. Son #2 of Lewis HILL.

1608. Herbert HILL. Herbert married **Harriet FISHER**.

They had one child:

2355	i.	Theda Albertis (1879-1943)

1609. Luther Ira HILL. Born on 6 Dec 1816 in Newport, Ohio. On 25 Jan 1840 when Luther Ira was 23, he married **Desdamona LACKEY**. Mother of 9, of whom 2 had progeny.

They had the following children:

2356	i.	Dan
2357	ii.	Frances (1841-)
2358	iii.	Henrietta (1843-)
2359	iv.	Wealthia (1845-1888)
2360	v.	Isadora (1846-)
2361	vi.	Ellen (Emily) (1848-1918)
2362	vii.	Wallace (1854-)

2363   viii.   Frank J. (1858-)
2364   ix.   May (1861-)

1610. Harvey Dale HILL. Born in 1828 in Newport, Ohio. Harvey Dale died in 1867, he was 39. In 1855 when Harvey Dale was 27, he married **Angeline Sheets DYE**. Born in 1833 in Center Valley, Wash, Ohio. Angeline Sheets died in Marietta, Ohio in 1910, she was 77. Occupation: Mother of 1. They had one child:

     2365   i.   Willis Edgar (1857-1918)

1611. Unnamed son HILL.

1612. Unnamed son HILL.

1613. Unnamed daughter HILL.

1614. Edwin C. HILL. Born on 1 Apr 1828 in Salem, Washington Co., Ohio. Edwin C. died in Salem, Washington Co., Ohio on 8 Aug 1829, he was 1.

1615. Oladine S. HILL. Born on 26 Feb 1834 in Salem, Washington Co., Ohio. On 21 Oct 1857 when Oladine S. was 23, she married **S. B. HILDRETH**, in Marietta, Ohio. Born on 19 Oct 1831 in Marietta, Washington Co., Ohio. S. B. died on 5 Mar 1916, he was 84. They had one child:

     2366   i.   Zenas Brown (1878-)

1616. Erwin Dana HILL. Born on 21 Jun 1842 in Lower Salem, Washington Co., Ohio. Erwin Dana died in Derby, Oregon on 2 Nov 1934, he was 92. Erwin Dana first married **Hazel TOPPING**. They had one child:

     2367   i.   Hazel (1887-)

Erwin Dana second married Mabel **Elizabeth BABCOCK**. Born on 14 Jul 1851 in Ohio. Mabel Elizabeth died on 13 Sep 1885, she was 34. Mother of 6. They had the following children:

     2368   i.   Carrie Hildreth (1872-)
     2369   ii.   Esther Irene (1874-)
     2370   iii.   Ira Z. (1877-)
     2371   iv.   Della Olaretta (1879-)
     2372   v.   Earl Russell (1881-)
     2373   vi.   Euretta (1883-)

1617. Anson William WHEATON. Born in 1846. Anson William died in 1916, he was 70.

1618. Ransom HUSTED. Born in 1827 in Ohio. Occupation: Married, had children. On 16 Apr 1850 when Ransom was 23, he married **Susan HOWZE**, in Holmes, Ohio. Born in 1825 in Ohio. They had the following children:

     2374   i.   Ella (1853-)
     2375   ii.   Ulysses (1856-)
     2376   iii.   Frank (1858-)

1619. Huldah HUSTED.[553] Born in 1829 in Holmes, Ohio. Huldah died in Holmes, Ohio in 1902, abt 73. On 29 Aug 1847 when Huldah was abt 18, she married **Henry Edwin DAY**, in Killbuck, Holmes Co., Ohio. Born in 1825 in Pennsylvania; died in Holmes, Killbuck Co., Ohio in 1902, he was abt 77. They had the following children:

     2377   i.   Cora Cord (1850-)
     2378   ii.   Anna R. (1860-)
     2379   iii.   Ellen M. (1863-)
     2380   iv.   Shannon (1867-)

1620. George WHEATON.[554] Born on 2 Apr 1823 in Holmes, Killbuck Co., Ohio. George died in Millersburg, Holmes Co., Ohio on 21 Oct 1905, he was 82. On 11 Apr 1844 when George was 21, he married **Delilah WOLGAMOTT**, daughter of Jonathan WOLGAMOTT & Jane BOONE, in Holmes, Killbuck Co., Ohio. Born on 10 Aug 1826 in Hardy, Holmes Co., Ohio. Delilah died in Hardy, Holmes Co., Ohio on 1 Jan 1905, she was 78. Her husband was the brother of Catherine Wheaton (1624), wife of her first cousin, Armstrong Wolgamott.

They had one child:

2381	i.	Laura (1864-1939)

1621. John Lacy WHEATON. Born on 18 Jan 1825 in Holmes, Killbuck Co., Ohio.

1622. James Irvine WHEATON. Born on 3 Feb 1827 in Holmes, Killbuck Co., Ohio.

1623. Edward Martin WHEATON. Born on 4 Jan 1830 in Holmes, Killbuck Co., Ohio.

1624. Catherine Anne WHEATON. Born on 1 Oct 1834 in Ohio. She married **Armstrong WOLGAMOTT**, son of Hiram WOLGAMOTT & Jane MOORE. Born on 1 Apr 1828 in Millersburg, Holmes Co., Ohio; died in Millersburg, Holmes Co., Ohio on 6 Sep 1902, he was 74. He was son of Hiram and grandson of David Wolgamott, and thus was a first cousin of Delilah Wolgamott, who married George Wheaton (1620), his wife's brother.

They had the following children:

2382	i.	Rosella Florence (1858-)
2383	ii.	Joseph Melvin (1859-1903)
2384	iii.	Russell H. (1858-1938)
2385	iv.	John M. (1864-1934)
2386	v.	Nancy Jane (1866-1876)
2387	vi.	Nob (1868-1868)
2388	vii.	Harry L. (Twin) (1869-1946)
2389	viii.	Hattie L. (Twin) (1869-)
2390	ix.	Mary A. (1873-)
2391	x.	Prince A. (1874-1880)
2392	xi.	Charles (1876-)

1625. Nancy Jane WHEATON. Born on 10 Oct 1837 in Holmes, Killbuck Co., Ohio.

1626. Sarah A. WHEATON. Born on 2 May 1840 in Prairie, Holmes Co., Ohio. On 7 Mar 1862 when Sarah A. was 21, she married **Carmi CRAWFORD**, in Holmes, Killbuck Co., Ohio. Born in Dec 1838 in Holmes, Killbuck Co., Ohio. Carmi died in Winfield, Cowley Co., Kansas on 2 Jan 1926, he was 87.

They had the following children:

2393	i.	Genetta Ellen (1864-)
2394	ii.	Franklin Herbert (1866-)
2395	iii.	Anna Nevada (1868-)
2396	iv.	Weldon R. (1871-1953)
2397	v.	Austin (1873-)
2398	vi.	Myron (1879-)

1627. Sally Ann HALL. Born on 19 Jun 1822 in Millersburg, Holmes Co., Ohio. Sally Ann died in Richfield, Lucas Co., Ohio on 16 Jun 1900, age 77, apparently d.s.p. Sally Ann married **Russell TWISS**.

1628. Eliza Jane HALL. Born on 31 Aug 1825 in Millersburg, Holmes Co., Ohio. Eliza Jane died in Sandusky, Ohio on 1 Jun 1849, she was 23, apparently d.s.p. Eliza Jane married **Joseph GEORGE**.

1629. Anson W. HALL. Born on 3 May 1827 in Millersburg, Holmes Co., Ohio. Anson W. died in Fulton, Ohio on 1 Nov 1911, he was 84. Anson W. married **Anna Mariah GILBERT**. Born on 28 May 1835. Anna Mariah died in Fulton, Ohio in 1924, about 88. Mother of 3, of whom one had descendants.

They had the following children:

2399	i.	Ella (-1873)
2400	ii.	Amelia (1859-1867)
2401	iii.	Reuben Anson (1863-)

1630. Washington J. HALL. Born on 3 Feb 1829 in Millersburg, Holmes Co., Ohio. Washington J. died in Fulton, Ohio on 28 Oct 1909, he was 80.

1631. Amos W. HALL. Born on 21 Apr 1831 in Reedtown, Seneca Co., Ohio; died in Fulton, Ohio on 21 Jul 1908, he was 77. Amos W. married **Lucy ?**; d. 21 Nov 1908 in Fulton, Ohio, apparently d.s.p.

1632. Mary M. HALL. Born on 15 Mar 1833 in Reedtown, Seneca Co., Ohio. Mary M. died on 16 May 1913, she was 80, apparently d.s.p. Mary M. married **Hiram ROOT**. Born on 24 Dec 1835.

1633. David Schuyler HALL. Born on 28 Feb 1836 in Reedtown, Seneca Co., Ohio. David Schuyler

died on 17 Jan 1926, he was 89. In 1857 when David Schuyler was 20, he married **Lydia KEENE**, in Seneca, Ohio. Born on 22 Jan 1839 in Seneca, Ohio. Mother of 6, of whom one had progeny.
They had the following children:

2402	i.	Francis Estella (1895-)
2403	ii.	Stephen D. (1860-1933)
2404	iii.	Jesse H. (1863-)
2405	iv.	Mary S. (1866-1871)
2406	v.	Lewis K. (1867-)
2407	vi.	Burton F. (1871-)

1634. Rebecca HALL. Born on 23 Apr 1838 in Reedtown, Seneca Co., Ohio. Rebecca died in Richfield, Lucas Co., Ohio on 5 Feb 1923, she was 84. Mother of 7, of whom 3 had descendants. On 11 Oct 1857 when Rebecca was 19, she married **Horatio Catline SLOAN**, in West Lodi, Seneca Co., Ohio. Born on 5 Feb 1836 in New York. Horatio Catline died in Richfield, Lucas Co., Ohio on 12 Jul 1922, he was 86.
They had the following children:

2408	i.	Melissa Adele (1858-1922)
2409	ii.	Clarinda Jane (1860-1933)
2410	iii.	Almira Ann (1862-1949)
2411	iv.	Russell Franklin (1865-1918)
2412	v.	Phoebe (1867-1867)
2413	vi.	Amos Clinton (1869-1965)
2414	vii.	Arthur Burton (1876-1937)

1635. Martha COOK. Born in Buffalo, Erie Co., N.Y. Martha died in Buffalo, Erie Co., N.Y.

1636. Fremont COOK. Born in 1821 in Vermont.

1637. Nancy Marie COOK. Born in 1823 in Vermont.

1638. Morton Sonfronian COOK.[555] Born on 4 Mar 1825 in Essex, N.Y. Morton Sonfronian died in Tomah, Monroe Co., Wisc. on 5 Jun 1907, he was 82. Morton Sonfronian first married **Mary Elizabeth REMINGTON**, in New York. Born in 1831 in New York. Mary Elizabeth died in Elroy, Juneau Co., Wisc. on 27 Jan 1866, she was 35. Mother of 6.
They had the following children:

2415	i.	Esther L. (1850-1921)
2416	ii.	Levi Hubbard (1852-1896)
2417	iii.	Alice (1856-)
2418	iv.	Charles A. (1858-1896)
2419	v.	Susan Ann (1860-1956)
2420	vi.	Morton Sylvester (1862-1929)

On 27 Apr 1874 when Morton Sonfronian was 49, he second married **Rachel RULON**, in Clayton, Ia. Born in Mar 1832 in Monmouth, N.J.; died in Auburn, Fayette Co., Ia., on 6 Mar 1902, she was 70.
They had the following children:

| 2421 | i. | Len (1873-1885) |
| 2422 | ii. | Anna Rulon (1874-) |

Morton Sonfronian perhaps married (3) **Philande PARDEE**, in Greenfield, Milwaukee Co., Wisc. Born in 1826 in Vermont.

1639. Elizabeth COOK. Born on 21 Jan 1830 in Williston, Chittendon Co., Vt. Elizabeth died in Plymouth, Juneau Co., Wisc. on 11 Oct 1916, she was 86. Mother of 11, including a set of twins; four of her children had descendants. On 12 Oct 1845 when Elizabeth was 15, she married **Lyman BURLINGAME**, in Milwaukee, Wisc. Born on 25 Feb 1820 in Greencastle, Ind. Lyman died in Plymouth, Juneau Co., Wisc. on 14 Nov 1887, he was 67.
They had the following children:

2423	i.	Esther S. (1846-)
2424	ii.	Nancy E. (1848-)
2425	iii.	Spencer Alanson (1850-1931)

2426	iv.	Harriet (Twin) (1852-1928)
2427	v.	Lyman Rufus (Twin) (1852-1941)
2428	vi.	George F. (1856-1935)
2429	vii.	Frederick C. (1858-)
2430	viii.	Betsy A. (1860-)
2431	ix.	John F. (1862-)
2432	x.	Christopher M. (1869-)
2433	xi.	Orley M. (1870-)

1640. Ambrose L. COOK. Born on 12 Jun 1835 in Vermont. Ambrose L. died in Maiden Rock, Pierce Co., Wisc. on 4 Aug 1911, he was 76.

1641. Susan A. COOK. Born on 26 Aug 1838 in Aurora, Erie Co., N.Y. Susan A. died in Elroy, Juneau Co., Wisc. on 21 Apr 1910, she was 71.

1642. John Eugene LEETE. Born on 30 Jun 1828 in Leetes Island, Guilford, Conn. John Eugene died in Leetes Island, Guilford, Conn. on 18 Jul 1829, he was 1.

1643. Daniel Sherwood LEETE. Born on 11 Sep 1829 in Guilford, Conn.; died in 1896, he was 66. On 3 Oct 1851 when Daniel Sherwood was 22, he m. **Cornelia NORTON**. B. on 3 Aug 1831 in Guilford, Conn. Cornelia d. in 1898, she was 66. Mother of 4, of whom 2 married and 1 had descendants.
They had the following children:

2434	i.	Henry Ives (1854-1855)
2435	ii.	Nelson Sherwood (1856-1915)
2436	iii.	Fanny Amanda (1862-1920)
2437	iv.	Eva Rose (1869-1916)

1644. Benjamin LEETE. B. 1 Jan 1831 in Leetes Island, Guilford, Conn.; d. there, 23 Jun 1833, age 2.

1645. Charity LEETE. Born on 15 Sep 1832. Charity died on 2 Aug 1854, she was 21, apparently d.s.p. On 3 Apr 1853 when Charity was 20, she married **William Henry LEE**. Born on 27 Aug 1820 in Guilford, Conn. William Henry died on 12 Jan 1860, he was 39.

1646. Justin Orlando LEETE. Born on 2 Sep 1834. Justin Orlando died on 5 Mar 1863, he was 28. On 25 May 1856 when Justin Orlando was 21, he married **Laura B. JEWELL**. Born in 1836. Laura B. died on 2 Aug 1863, she was 27. Mother of 2, of whom 1 had progeny.
They had the following children:

| 2438 | i. | Henry B. (1857-1918) |
| 2439 | ii. | Jennie Amanda (1859-1906) |

1647. Sarah Page LEETE. Born on 14 Jun 1837 in Leetes Island, Guilford, Conn. Sarah Page died in 1902, she was 64. Occupation: Mother of 6, of whom one had progeny. On 9 Jan 1853 when Sarah Page was 15, she married **Pierre A. GAUCHET**, in Guilford, Conn. Born on 9 Jan 1819 in Paris, France. Pierre A. died in Guilford, Conn. in Feb 1889, he was 70.
They had the following children:

2440	i.	Edward A. (1854-1925)
2441	ii.	Mary (1856-1856)
2442	iii.	Louis "Lewie" Leete (1857-1900)
2443	iv.	James Adolphus (1860-1916)
2444	v.	Daniel Benjamin (1865-1923)
2445	vi.	Frank Henry (1869-)

1648. Mary Jane LEETE. Born on 16 Dec 1838. Mary Jane died in 1899, she was 60. On 1 Jan 1860 when Mary Jane was 21, she married **George L. ROSS**.

1649. Douglas Merwin LEETE. Born on 6 Jan 1841. Douglas Merwin died in 1886, he was 44.

1650. Emily Case LEETE. Born on 31 May 1843. Emily Case died in Clinton, Conn. on 25 Nov 1864, she was 21. On 26 Feb 1862 when Emily Case was 18, she married **Heman PIERSON**. Born in 1828. Heman died in "In the War" on 25 Dec 1863, he was 35.
They had one child:

| 2446 | i. | Orestes Cook (1863-1876) |

1651. Susan Amanda LEETE. Born on 19 Apr 1847. Susan Amanda died on 13 Mar 1868, she was 20.

1652. ? KENTFIELD.

1653. ? KENTFIELD.

1654. ? KENTFIELD.

1655. Smith KENTFIELD. Born in 1804 in Remsen, Oneida Co., N.Y.; d. there in 1804.

1656. Laurana KENTFIELD. Born on 29 Nov 1805 in Remsen, Oneida Co., N.Y. Laurana died in Hadley, Hampshire Co., Mass. on 20 Aug 1864, she was 58, apparently d.s.p. On 24 Nov 1824 when Laurana was 18, she married **Dorus GREEN**, in Amherst, Hampshire Co., Mass. Born on 8 Nov 1801 in Amherst, Hampshire Co., Mass. Dorus died in Hadley, Hampshire Co., Mass. on 26 Oct 1876, he was 74.

1657. Rebecca KENTFIELD. Born on 17 May 1808 in Remsen, Oneida Co., N.Y. Rebecca died in Barrington, Bristol Co., R.I. on 6 Dec 1885, she was 77. None of her children is known to have descendants. On 21 May 1837 when Rebecca was 29, she married **Thomas GREENE**, in Providence, Providence Co., R.I. Born on 25 Mar 1812 in North Kingston, Washington Co., R.I. Thomas died in Providence, Providence Co., R.I. on 23 Jul 1896, he was 84.
They had the following children:

2447	i.	Ardella Robinson (1838-)
2448	ii.	Albert Nathaniel (1840-)
2449	iii.	Charles Thomas (1841-1843)
2450	iv.	Sarah Martha (1846-)
2451	v.	Storrs Douglas (1848-1852)
2452	vi.	Levi Maxley (1851-)

1658. Jeremiah B. KENTFIELD. Born on 15 Jul 1818 in Remsen, Oneida Co., N.Y. Jeremiah B. died in Amherst, Hampshire Co., Mass. on 17 Apr 1894, he was 75. On 10 Apr 1845 when Jeremiah B. was 26, he married **Eleanor Morton GREENE**, in Hampshire, Mass. Born on 26 Apr 1823 in Hadley, Hampshire Co., Mass. Eleanor Morton died in Hampshire, Mass. on 22 May 1905, she was 82.
They had the following children:

2453	i.	Frederick Baker (1845-1927)
2454	ii.	John Greene (1848-)
2455	iii.	Esther Adelia (1858-1923)
2456	iv.	Nellie Rebecca (1860-)
2457	v.	Annie Jane (1862-1939)

1659. John KENTFIELD. Born in 1822 in Remsen, Oneida Co., N.Y. John died in Providence, Providence Co., R.I. on 18 Dec 1894, he was 72. On 11 Jun 1845 when John was 23, he married **Eliza J. SALISBURY**, in Providence, Providence Co., R.I. Born in 1827 in Providence, Providence Co., R.I. Eliza J. died in Providence, Providence Co., R.I. on 8 Mar 1910, she was 83. Occupation: Mother of 4.
They had the following children:

2458	i.	?
2459	ii.	?
2460	iii.	Frank (1858-1901)
2461	iv.	Nellie Lamson (1865-1914)

1660. Sarah F. DIBBLE. Born in 1846 in Stamford, Fairfield Co., Conn.; died in 1850, about 4.

1661. Sarah BILYEU. Born in 1799 in New Jersey. Sarah died in 1850, she was about 51. On 13 Feb 1819 when Sarah was 20, she married **Isaac REED**, in Bond, Ill.

1662. John Birge BILYEU. Born on 11 Dec 1801 in Somerset, N.J. John Birge died in Mulberry Grove, Bond Co., Ill. on 14 Jan 1873, he was 71. On 19 Jul 1825 when John Birge was 23, he married **Martha Houston POWERS**, in Bond, Ill. Born on 5 Aug 1805 in Tennessee. Martha Houston died in Mulberry Grove, Bond Co., Ill. on 14 Mar 1858, she was 52.
They had the following children:

2462	i.	Lewis G. (1827-1893)
2463	ii.	Nancy Birge (1829-1879)
2464	iii.	William Thomas (1831-1903)

2465	iv.	Elizabeth M. (1835-1827)
2466	v.	John F. (1837-1862)
2467	vi.	Peter F. (1839-1909)

1663. Isaac Smith BILYEU. Born on 11 Dec 1801 in Somerset, Mercer Co., N.J. Isaac Smith died in Bond, Ill. on 10 Feb 1856, he was 54. The brothers, Wesley A. and Isaac Smith Bilyeu, married sisters, Kathryn and Sarah File. On 7 Jul 1825 when Isaac Smith was 23, he married **Sarah FILE**, daughter of Henry Oliver FILE & Mary Hasler ANTHONY, in Bond, Ill. Born on 25 Dec 1805 in Cabarrus, N.C. Sarah died in 1888, she was 82. Mother of 9, 3 of whom had descendants.
They had the following children:

2468	i.	Joseph H. (1829-1877)
2469	ii.	John (1834-1915)
2470	iii.	Wesley Asbury (-1899)
2471	iv.	George Harvey (1837-1897)
2472	v.	Sidney M. (1839-1915)
2473	vi.	Andrew (1841-1903)
2474	vii.	Finas (1843-1865)
2475	viii.	Polly Ann (1845-1915)
2476	ix.	Thomas H. (1849-1913)

1664. Joseph BILYEU. Born on 22 Oct 1804 in Tennessee. Joseph died in Bond, Ill. on 10 Nov 1868, he was 64. Occupation: Married 3 times and had 5 children; 1 by 1st wife, 1 by 2nd wife, and 3 by 3rd wife. In 1823 when Joseph was 18, he first married **Malinda H. ?..**
They had one child:

2477	i.	John W. (1827-)

Joseph second married **Mary Ann GILLESPIE**. Born in 1815 in Tennessee. Mother of 1.
They had one child:

2478	i.	William B. (1831-)

Joseph third married **Hannah BILYEU**. Born in 1815 in Tennessee. Mother of 3; she probably was a relative of her husband, or a widow of a man named Bilyeu.
They had the following children:

2479	i.	Jesse Wheeler (1841-1913)
2480	ii.	Simeon Walker (1844-1908)
2481	iii.	Martha Emma (1849-1930)

1665. Garrett Page BILYEU. Born in 1810 in New Jersey. Garrett Page died in Bond, Ill. on 1 Jul 1850, he was 40. Occupation: Married twice; 8 children by second wife. On 19 Aug 1829 when Garrett Page was 19, he first married **Eliza GREGORY**, in Clinton, Ill. Born in 1813. On 18 Feb 1835 when Garrett Page was 25, he second married **Nancy BRYANT**, in Bond, Ill. Born on 5 May 1815 in Richmond, Va. Nancy died in St. Louis, Mo. on 22 Feb 1893, she was 77.
They had the following children:

2482	i.	Mary Jane (1836-)
2483	ii.	Sarah Frances (1840-)
2484	iii.	Lewis Garret (1842-)
2485	iv.	David Allen (1844-)
2486	v.	Emily Caroline (1845-)
2487	vi.	Thomas Newton (1846-)
2488	vii.	Nancy A. (1848-)
2489	viii.	Anna E. (1850-)

1666. Jesse Walker BILYEU. Born in 1811 in Illinois; d. in Bond, Ill., on 26 May 1860, abt 49. On 14 Apr 1832, at abt 21, he m. **Rebecca BURROWS**, in Bond, Ill. B. in 1815 in Tennessee; died in Bond, Ill.
They had the following children:

2490	i.	Mary A. (1835-)
2491	ii.	Irving (1838-)

2492	iii.	Lewis I. (1840-)
2493	iv.	Caroline (1852-)
2494	v.	Emily E. (1849-)
2495	vi.	Francis (1855-)

1667. Wesley A. BILYEU. Born on 25 May 1812 in Kentucky. Wesley A. died on 22 Apr 1867, he was 54. The brothers, Wesley A. and Isaac Smith Bilyeu, married sisters, Kathryn and Sarah File. On 26 May 1836 when Wesley A. was 24, he married **Kathryn FILE**, daughter of Henry Oliver FILE & Mary Hasler ANTHONY, in Bond, Ill. Born in 1818 in Illinois. Kathryn died in Bond, Ill.
They had the following children:

2496	i.	Mary (1836-)
2497	ii.	Martha (1839-)
2498	iii.	John (1844-)
2499	iv.	Emma (1848-)
2500	v.	Sarah (1849-)

1668. Thomas Coke BILYEU. Born on 19 Sep 1816 in Bond, Ill. Thomas Coke died on 28 Mar 1878, he was 61. On 29 Sep 1838 when Thomas Coke was 22, he married **Ann C. BROWN**, in Bond, Ill. Born in 1822 in Indiana. Ann C. died in Bond, Ill.
They had the following children:

2501	i.	Mary (1839-)
2502	ii.	Martha A. (1839-)
2503	iii.	William T. (1842-)

1669. Mary Magdalene BILYEU. Born in 1820 in Bond, Ill.; died there in 1853, she was 33, apparently d.s.p. On 11 Jun 1838 when she was about 18, she married **William MILLS**, in Bond, Ill.

1670. Finis BILYEU. Born on 23 May 1825 in Illinois. Finis died in Bond, Ill. on 26 Jun 1862, he was 37. On 3 Jul 1845 when Finis was 20, he married **Lydia Ann JACKSON**, in Bond, Ill. Born in 2829 in Tennessee. Lydia Ann died in Bond, Ill. Mother of 2.
They had the following children:

2504	i.	Joseph E. (1850-)
2505	ii.	Frank (1857-)

1671. William Burge BILYEU. Born in 1826 in Bond, Ill. William Burge died in Bond, Ill. on 22 Sep 1851, he was 25. On 10 Mar 1847 when William Burge was 21, he married **Martha F. McFERRIN**, in Bond, Ill. Born on 13 Oct 1829 in Tennessee. Martha F. died in Bond, Ill. on 31 Mar 1877, she was 47.
They had one child:

2506	i.	William Burge (1851-)

1672. Daniel Olds BIRGE. Born in 1806 in Underhill, Chittenden Co., Vt. Daniel Olds died in Greenville, Bond Co., Ill. on 28 Jul 1846, he was 40. Daniel Olds married **Laura Eliza PAYNE**. Born on 26 Feb 1821 in Deruyter, N.Y. Laura Eliza died in Dayton, O. on 14 Aug 1881, she was 60.
They had the following children:

2507	i.	Laura C. (1843-1928)
2508	ii.	Edwin D. (1845-1846)

1673. Martin Howland BIRGE. Born in 1806. Martin Howland died in 1906, he was about 100. On 21 Oct 1836 when Martin Howland was about 30, he married **Elizabeth Ann KINGSLEY**, in Sheldon, Vt. Born in 1812. Elizabeth Ann died in 1903, about age 91.
They had the following children:

2509	i.	Julia Elizabeth (1839-1898)
2510	ii.	Mary Olds (1847-)
2511	iii.	George Kingsley (1849-1918)
2512	iv.	Henry Martin (1851-1904)

1674. Lucinda BIRGE. Born in 1808. Lucinda married **Eldred FRINK**.

1675. Lydia BIRGE. Born in 1810. Lydia died in 1810.

1676. Ebenezer Cross BIRGE. Born in 1810. On 26 Dec 1839 when Ebenezer Cross was 29, he

married **Lydia Bacon STEBBINGS**. Born on 1 Jul 1816.
They had the following children:

2513	i.	Laura
2514	ii.	Rose
2515	iii.	Francis
2516	iv.	Mary
2517	v.	Fred
2518	vi.	Ellen
2519	vii.	Blanche

1677. Ezra BIRGE. Born in 1812. Ezra died in 1813, he was 1.

1678. Laura BIRGE. Born in 1816. Laura died in 1844, she was 28.

1679. J. BIRGE. Born in 1816. J. died in 1816.

1680. Cyrus K. BIRGE. Born in 1819. Cyrus K. died in 1842, he was 23. Cyrus K. married **Louisa MARTIN**. Born in 1821. Louisa died in 1843, she was 22.
They had one child:

2520	i.	Olive L.

1681. Lydia BIRGE. Born in 1811.

1682. Lucy BIRGE. Born in 1813.

1683. David E. BIRGE. Born in 1815. David E. died in 1860, he was 45.

1684. Frances BIRGE. Born in 1823.

1685. Cyrus BIRGE. Born in 1828 in Bond, Ill. Cyrus died in Bond, Ill. in 1888, he was 60. On 26 Dec 1850 when Cyrus was 22, he married **Mary Ellen MUNDIS,** in Bond, Ill. Born on 14 Aug 1830 in Madison, Ill. Mary Ellen died in Chetopa, Labette, Ks. on 5 Dec 1893, she was 63. Mother of 3.
They had the following children:

2521	i.	Mamie (1854-)
2522	ii.	Mary M. (1856-)
2523	iii.	Virginia E. (1859-)

1686. Alpheus BIRGE. Born in 1830.

1687. Cyrus BIRGE. Born in 1829. On 26 Dec 1850 when Cyrus was about 21, he married **Mary E. MUNGER**.
They had the following children:

2524	i.	Anna (1853-1893)
2525	ii.	Virginia (1859-)
2526	iii.	Lucy (1864-)
2527	iv.	Charles C. (1893-)

1688. Edwin BIRGE. Born in 1830. Edwin died in 1899, he was 69. On 1 Oct 1857 when Edwin was 27, he married **Martha ETZLER**. Born on 6 Jan 1836. Martha died on 12 Feb 1879, she was 43.

1689. Julia BIRGE. Born in 1839. Julia d. in 1871, when her child was b. She married **Lemuel ADAMS**.
They had one child:

2528	i.	Agatha (1871-1871)

1690. Emma BIRGE. Born in 1842. Emma died in 1922, she was 80.

1691. William BIRGE. Born in 1845. William died in 1894, he was 49. William married **Carry ?.**
They had one child:

2529	i.	Mary (1877-)

1692. Laura BIRGE. Born on 31 Aug 1847 in Greenville, Bond Co., Ill. Laura died in Greenville, Bond Co., Ill. on 28 Feb 1934, she was 86. On 10 Dec 1873 when Laura was 26, she married **Samuel Trotter HENRY**, in Greenville, Bond Co., Ill. Born on 16 Mar 1837 in Greenville, Bond Co., Ill. Samuel Trotter died in Greenville, Bond Co., Ill. on 28 Jun 1921, he was 84.
They had the following children:

2530	i.	Harvey
2531	ii.	John

2532	iii.	Lena
2533	iv.	Mary
2534	v.	Wesley
2535	vi.	William

1693. Alice BIRGE. Born in 1855. Alice died in 1933, she was 78.

1694. Sarah M. BIRGE. Born in 1815.

1695. Henry Warren BIRGE. Born in 1823 in Greenville, Bond Co., Ill. Henry Warren died in Washington in 1909, he was 86. On 18 Sep 1849 when Henry Warren was 26, he married **Anna Chilton PEACHER**, in Covington, Ky. Born on 30 Nov 1830 in Campbell, Ky. Anna Chilton died in Washington in 1920, she was 89. Mother of 8, of whom one had descendants.
They had the following children:

2536	i.	Mary Eliza (1853-1939)
2537	ii.	Ida Virginia (1855-)
2538	iii.	Anna (1860-1934)
2539	iv.	Henry Cyrus (1861-)
2540	v.	Hattie (1862-1932)
2541	vi.	Thomas C. (1864-)
2542	vii.	Henry Cyrus (1864-)
2543	viii.	William E. (1865-)

1696. Joseph Howell BIRGE. Born in 1825 in Greenville, Bond Co., Ill. On 20 Jul 1847 when Joseph Howell was 22, he first married **Harriet W. PERRY**, in Covington, Ky. Born in 1828 in Alabama. Harriet W. died in Greenville, Bond Co., Ill. in 1861, she was 33.
They had the following children:

2544	i.	Eliza Gilbert (1848-1863)
2545	ii.	Lizzie G. (1848-1863)
2546	iii.	Frank Howell (1851-1922)
2547	iv.	Mary A. (1854-1930)
2548	v.	Anna P. (1856-1856)
2549	vi.	Sallie H. (1857-1905)

On 18 Oct 1863 when Joseph Howell was 38, he second married **Sarah L. DUNCAN**, in Bond, Ill. Born in 1842. Sarah L. died in 1929, she was 87.
They had the following children:

2550	i.	Henry Cyrus (1866-1914)
2551	ii.	Eames D. (1864-1886)
2552	iii.	Robert Joseph (1868-1938)
2553	iv.	John Hugh (1871-1950)

1697. Mary Howell BIRGE. Born in 1830. Mary Howell died in 1912, she was 82. On 19 Nov 1854 when Mary Howell was 24, she married **Jeremiah RANKIN**. Born in 1828 in Derry, Ireland. Jeremiah died in 1904, he was 76.
They had the following children:

2554	i.	Eames D. (1856-1890)
2555	ii.	Walter N. (1857-1877)
2556	iii.	Mary F. (1858-1913)
2557	iv.	Andrew R. (1863-1864)
2558	v.	Edith G. (1864-1943)

1698. Anna Eliza BIRGE. Born in 1833. Anna Eliza died in 1896, she was 63.

1699. Henry Reuben HILL.[556] Born on 2 Jan 1843 in Waterloo, Wisconsin. On 12 Dec 1867 when Henry Reuben was 24, he married **Amanda M. LORING**.
They had the following children:

2559	i.	Bradford L. (1868-)
2560	ii.	Daughter of Henry & Amanda Hill

1700. Fred HILL.[557] Born on 18 Jul 1844 in Waterloo, Wisc.; died in Lime Springs, Iowa (prob). Farmer and miller; served in 40th Regt., Wisconsin Volunteers, Civil War. A Presbyterian and a Republican. On 17 Jun 1885 when Fred was 40, he married **Mary Belinda KNIFFEN**, in Darien, Wisc. Born on 22 Apr 1865 in Rutland, Wisc.
They had the following children:

2561	i.	Henry Kniffen (1886-)
2562	ii.	Gertrude Eloise (1887-)
2563	iii.	Helen Winifred (1893-)
2564	iv.	Marion Cecile (1905-)

1701. Eleanor BENEDICT. Born on 3 Jan 1836. Eleanor died in 1912, she was 75. Occupation: Mother of 7. On 30 Aug 1855 when Eleanor was 19, she married **Moses BENEDICT** (817), son of Samuel BENEDICT (339) & Eleanor SHATFORD. Born on 22 Aug 1824. Moses Benedict and Eleanor Bendict were first cousins, once removed. Moses was the grandson of Samuel Benedict Sr. and Mary Dibble, and Eleanor was the great-granddaughter of the same couple.
They had the following children:

1741	i.	Eleanor L. (1856-)
1742	ii.	Samuel A. (1858-)
1743	iii.	John Carroll (1860-)
1744	iv.	William (Wilson) Alexander (1864-1865)
1745	v.	Sarah A. (1866-)
1746	vi.	Solomon George (1868-)
1747	vii.	Joseph Franklin (1876-1952)

1702. Jenny BENEDICT. Born on 3 Nov 1839.

1703. Solomon BENEDICT. Born on 3 Feb 1841. He is said to have m. on 9 Mar 1857 **Mary Ann McALLISTER**, who d. 23 Jan 1858.

1704. Eleanor BENEDICT. Born in 1835.

1705. Sarah BENEDICT. Born in 1837.

1706. Charles BENEDICT. Born in 1840.

1707. Mary Ann BENEDICT. Born in 1842.

1708. Jane "Jenny" BENEDICT. Born on 11 Nov 1848.

1709. David BENEDICT. Born on 24 Dec 1835.

1710. Matilda BENEDICT. Born on 3 Mar 1837.

1711. Jerucia BENEDICT. Born on 20 Oct 1839.

1712. Elizabeth BENEDICT. Born in 1841.

1713. William James BENEDICT. Born on 28 Mar 1844. On 22 Jan 1867 when William James was 22, he married **Emma THOMAS**.

1714. Samuel I. BENEDICT. Born in 1845.

1715. Samuel John BENEDICT. Born on 28 Feb 1846.

1716. Dawson Alexander BENEDICT. Born on 21 Jan 1848; died in 1941, abt age 92. He married **Mary THORP**. Born in 1847; died in 1941, abt 94.
They had the following children:

2565	i.	William James (1872-)
2566	ii.	Mary Elizabeth (1847-)
2567	iii.	Matilda Jane (1875-)
2568	iv.	Ida Florence (1878-)
2569	v.	Ellen Jane (1880-)
2570	vi.	Dawson Alexander (1882-)
2571	vii.	John George (1883-)
2572	viii.	Harriet Maud (1886-)
2573	ix.	Lila Beatrice (1888-)

1717. Charles BENEDICT. Born on 16 Mar 1850. Charles died on 16 Apr 1851, he was 1.

1718. Jane STEWART. Born in 1836. She married **Joseph DOWD**.
They had the following children:

2574	i.	Elizabeth Ann (1855-)
2575	ii.	Hamilton Stewart (1857-)
2576	iii.	Lucy Sophia (1859-)

1719. Lucy STEWART. Born in 1839. Lucy died in 1926, she was 87. Occupation: Mother of 6. Lucy married **Charles WRIGHT**.
They had the following children:

2577	i.	Maria J. (1863-)
2578	ii.	Robert H. (1865-)
2579	iii.	Charles J. (1868-)
2580	iv.	Clarence Peter (1868-)
2581	v.	Lucy (1870-)
2582	vi.	Lillian (1870-)

1720. Maria STEWART. Born in 1843. Maria married **William Blumer McALLISTER**.

1721. David STEWART. Born in 1844. David married **Jane KENNY**. Born in 1840.

1722. Robert STEWART. Born in 1845. Robert married **Elizabeth Ann SMITH**. Born in 1851. Elizabeth Ann died in 1918, she was 67.

1723. Samuel STEWART. Born in 1848. Married twice but d.s.p. Samuel first married **Maria KENNY**. Born in 1852, died in 1922, about 70. Samuel second married **Jennie RADMORE**.

1724. Clarissa STEWART. Born in 1852, died in 1921, abt 69. Clarissa married **Hector McCLEAN**.

1725. Jane FARIS. Born in 1849. Jane died in 1902, she was 53. Mother of 1, who had descendants. In 1866 when Jane was 17, she married **Robert RADMORE**. Born in 1836.
They had one child:

2583	i.	Florence Edith (1883-1954)

1726. Richard Albert HETHERINGTON. Born on 5 Jan 1849. He first married **? MCALESTER**.
They had the following children:

2584	i.	Joseph
2585	ii.	Mary
2586	iii.	Wesley
2587	iv.	Henry (1882-)

Richard Albert second married **Isabella DAVIS**. They had the following children:

2588	i.	Harold
2589	ii.	?
2590	iii.	?
2591	iv.	Lorne Clifford (1890-)
2592	v.	Beatrice (1895-)
2593	vi.	Simpson (1898-)

1727. Eleanor Amelia HETHERINGTON. Born on 21 Jul 1850 in Hayworth, Quebec, Canada. She married **Samuel A. BENEDICT** (1742), son of Moses BENEDICT (844) & Eleanor BENEDICT (1701). Born on 1 Apr 1858. Samuel A. Benedict m. his first cousin, Eleanor Amelia Hetherington. Both are grandchildren of Samuel and Eleanor (Shatford) Benedict.

2594	i.	Ezra
2595	ii.	Thomas

1728. Joseph HETHERINGTON. Born on 13 Jul 1852. Joseph died in Breckenridge, Quebec, Canada on 3 Apr 1925, he was 72. Joseph married **Annie DAVIS**.
They had the following children:

2596	i.	Joseph A.
2597	ii.	William A.
2598	iii.	Lucy (1873-)
2599	iv.	Sarah Elizabeth (1885-)

2600	v.	Mary (1888-)
2601	vi.	Ethyl Emma (1890-)
2602	vii.	Cecil H. (1895-)

1729. Henry HETHERINGTON. Born on 22 Feb 1855. Henry died on 20 Apr 1885, he was 30. He and his sister Sarah died three days apart in Hayworth, Quebec. There must be a sad story here, which we may never know. It is most likely that they were injured in an accident, and one died before the other.

1695. Sarah HETHERINGTON. Born on 8 Dec 1856. Sarah died in Hayworth, Quebec, Canada on 23 Apr 1885, she was 28.

1696. William HETHERINGTON. Born on 19 Jul 1859. William died in Manitou, Manitoba, Canada on 28 Aug 1927, he was 68. William married **Bertha BRECKENRIDGE**. Occupation: Mother of 4. They had the following children:

2603	i.	?
2604	ii.	?
2605	iii.	Robert (1896-)
2606	iv.	Olive J. (1898-)

1732. Thomas H. HETHERINGTON. Born on 27 Mar 1863 in Hayworth, Quebec, Canada. Thomas H. married **Mary MULLIGAN**. Born on 22 Aug 1867. Mary died on 24 Jan 1906, she was 38. They had the following children:

2607	i.	?
2608	ii.	?
2609	iii.	?
2610	iv.	?
2611	v.	Lena May (1899-)
2612	vi.	Percy Robert (1900-)
2613	vii.	Edward John (1902-)
2614	viii.	Margery Rebecca (1905-)

1733. Harriet Sophia BENEDICT.

1734. Samuel Ezra BENEDICT. Born on 10 Aug 1849.

1735. Ann Elizabeth BENEDICT. Born on 3 Feb 1851.

1736. William Henry BENEDICT. Born on 9 Jun 1853.

1737. Amelia Jane BENEDICT. Born on 28 Jul 1857.

1738. George Frederick BENEDICT. Born on 23 Mar 1862.

1739. Thomas Walter BENEDICT. Born on 4 Jul 1865.

1740. Emily Sarah BENEDICT. Born on 3 Feb 1869.

1741. Eleanor L. BENEDICT. Born on 6 Jun 1856.

1742. Samuel A. BENEDICT. Born on 1 Apr 1858. Samuel A. married his first cousin **Eleanor Amelia HETHERINGTON** (1727), daughter of Joseph H. HETHERINGTON & Lucy BENEDICT (842). Born on 21 Jul 1850 in Hayworth, Quebec, Canada. Samuel and Eleanor are grandchildren of Samuel and Eleanor (Shatford) Benedict. They had the following children:

2594	i.	Ezra
2595	ii.	Thomas

1743. John Carroll BENEDICT. Born on 27 Mar 1860.

1744. William (Wilson) Alexander BENEDICT. Born on 3 Nov 1864; died on 29 Apr 1865.

1745. Sarah A. BENEDICT. Born on 18 Feb 1866.

1746. Solomon George BENEDICT. Born on 10 Sep 1868.

1747. Joseph Franklin BENEDICT. Born in 1876. Joseph Franklin died in 1952, he was 76.

1748. Margaret Jane BENEDICT. Born on 20 May 1860

1749. Thomas Franklin BENEDICT. Born on 22 Feb 1862.

1750. William Sidney BENEDICT. Born on 14 Mar 1864.

1751. Elizabeth MAXWELL. Born in 1864. She married **Joseph HILTON**. Born in 1879; died in 1939.

They had one child:

    2615   i.   ?

1752. Robert MAXWELL. Born in 1865. Robert died in 1931, he was 66. In 1905 when Robert was 40, he married **Louisa WRIGHT**. Born in 1869. Louisa died in 1941, she was 72.

1718. William MAXWELL. Born in 1869. William died on 26 Jan 1931, he was 62. William first married **Eleanor ANGUS**. Born in 1872. Eleanor died in 1896, she was about 24.

They had one child:

    2616   i.   Nellie

William second m. **Florence Edith RADMORE**. Born on 5 Dec 1883; died on 28 Jul 1954, she was 70. They had the following children:

    2617   i.   ?
    2618   ii.   Lila (1907-)
    2619   iii.   Doris Elizabeth (1909-)
    2620   iv.   William James (1913-)

1754. Sarah MAXWELL. Born in 1872. Sarah died in 1949, she was 77. In 1903 when Sarah was 31, she married **David Arthur DOWD**. Born in 1866. David Arthur died in 1917, he was 51.

    2621   i.   Velma (1905-)
    2622   ii.   Annie
    2623   iii.   Evelyn
    2624   iv.   Mabel
    2625   v.   ?

1755. Jane MAXWELL. Born in 1877. Jane married **John James MULLIGAN**.

1756. Armenia Adelia BENEDICT. Born on 30 Sep 1826.

1757. Sabrina Mable BENEDICT. Born on 16 Aug 1828.

1758. Ezra Denison BENEDICT. Born on 10 Jun 1830.

1759. John Rood BENEDICT. Born on 13 Jan 1833.

1760. Charles Rood BENEDICT. Born on 12 Mar 1837.

1761. Cornelius Nichols BENEDICT. Born on 11 Feb 1839.

1762. Adna Squires BENEDICT. Born on 19 Mar 1841.

1763. Mary BENEDICT. Born on 10 May 1843.

1764. Martha BENEDICT. Born on 10 May 1843.

1765. ? [Infant] BENEDICT. Born on 23 Feb 1834.

1766. Sarah F. BENEDICT. Born on 20 Jan 1840 in Malone, Franklin Co., N.Y.

1767. Albert Crumiel BENEDICT. Born on 2 Oct 1844.

1768. Hannah Amelia BENEDICT. Born on 20 Dec 1846.

1769. Julius S. BENEDICT. Born on 26 Apr 1831.

1770. Lydia A. BENEDICT. Born on 15 Sep 1833.

1771. Carlos N. BENEDICT. Born on 6 Jan 1835.

1772. Sarah BENEDICT. Born on 22 Jan 1837.

1773. Frederick BENEDICT. Born on 8 Sep 1839.

1774. Martha S. BENEDICT. Born on 13 May 1841.

1775. Ellen P. BENEDICT. Born on 15 Aug 1844.

1776. Abby E. BENEDICT. Born on 7 Oct 1846.

1777. Lunette F. BENEDICT. Born on 26 Oct 1849.

1778. Albert D. BENEDICT. Born on 26 Apr 1854.

1779. Faber BENEDICT. Born on 12 Nov 1845 in Malone, N.Y.

1780. Francis Morgan BENEDICT. Born on 25 Sep 1847 in Malone, N.Y.

1781. James Eliot GRIMES. Born on 9 May 1851 in South Hull, Canada.

1782. Richard Thomas GRIMES. Born on 19 May 1854 in Aylmer, Quebec, Canada. Occupation: OneWorldTree adds: "Communaut Urbaine de Loutanouais Ottawa, Canada".

1783. Andrew GRIMES. Born in 1865.

1784. Arthur GRIMES. Born in 1872.

1785. Franklin WILCOX. Born in 1860 in Rose, Renfrew, Ontario, Canada. On 13 Oct 1896 when Franklin was 36, he married **Jane WRIGHT**, in Ross Township, Renfrew, Ontario, Canada. Born in 1869 in Ross, Renfrew, Ontario, Canada.

-------------------------------------[558]

1786. Almon Bela COE.[559] Born 6 Nov 1820 in Rootstown, Ohio, a cooper; m. **Mary ?**, b. abt 1820. They had the following children:

| 2626 | i. | William (~1845-) |
| 2627 | ii. | Edmund (~1849-) |

1787. Jonathan HILL.

1753. Hoyt HILL.

1754. Alvin HILL. He resided in Fairfield, Huron Co., Ohio.

1755. Alfred "Fred" HILL. He went to sea.

1756. Leverett Benedict HILL.[560] Born on 11 Jun 1831. Leverett Benedict died in Tabor, Iowa on 29 Jan 1892, he was 60. Occupation: farmer. On 30 Mar 1856 when Leverett Benedict was 24, he married **Hannah M. WHITNEY**, in Wakeman, Huron Co., Ohio. Born on 31 Jul 1832 in Newtown, Conn. They had the following children:

| 2628 | i. | Clarence W. (~1857-) |
| 2629 | ii. | Leverett H. (~1859-) |

1792. Judge Edgar S. HILL.[561] Born abt 1834 in Wakeman, Huron Co., Ohio. Edgar S. died in Indianola, Nebraska (prob) aft 1896, he was 62. Occupation: Commissioner of Redwillow County in 1873, 4th California Inf., Union Army, Civil War. County Probate Judge. In 1867 when Edgar S. was 33, he married **Delia JONES**, daughter of Solomon JONES & Mary ESTERBROOK. They had the following children:

2630	i.	George C. (~1868->1896)
2631	ii.	Lena E. (~1869->1896)
2632	iii.	Frank (~1870-)

1793. Elizabeth HILL. Born abt 1836. Elizabeth died in Tabor, Iowa on 20 Jul 1838, she was 2.

1794. Rev. Edwin Stoddard HILL, D.D.[562] Born on 2 Dec 1837 in Wakeman, Huron Co., Ohio. Edwin Stoddard died in National City, Cal. aft 1896, he was 58. Lieut., Union Army, 4th Iowa Vol. Inf.; Pastor of the Congregational Church at Atlantic, Iowa, for forty years. In 1865 when Edwin Stoddard was 27, he first married **Mattie TREAT**. Mattie died abt 1866. They had one child:

| 2633 | i. | Sidney T. (~1866-1895) |

Edwin Stoddard second married **Helen M. JONES**; b. in Vermont, a teacher. Education: Oberlin College.

1795. Elizabeth E. HILL. Born prob abt 1839; died aft 1896. She married **Lemuel E. WEBB**. They had the following children

| 2634 | i. | Herbert (~1858-) |
| 2635 | ii. | Edgar (~1859-) |

1796. Isaac Curtiss HILL. Born on 2 Dec 1843. Isaac Curtiss died in California aft 1896, he was 52. He was a farmer, living with his brother Leverett, in 1860; then Justice of the Peace at Agency, Iowa.

1797. Julius M. HILL. Born abt 1847. Julius M. died in Tabor, Iowa in 1902, he was 55; a teacher.

1798. Betsy B. WHEELER. Born abt 1844 in Ohio. Lived at Pawnee City, Neb.; unmarried.

1799. Ann HOUGH. Born abt 1830; d. in 1854, about 24. Ann married **Philo Oscar STEVENSON**.

1800. Cordelia HOUGH. Cordelia married **William DENMAN**.

1801. Ellen HOUGH. Born abt 1838. Ellen died in 1855, about 17.

1802. William G. HOUGH.[563] Born abt 1835 in Ohio. William G. died in 1872, he was 37. Occupation: farmer. William G. married **Mary E. BARNES**. Born abt 1840 in Ohio.

1803. Jonathan T. HOUGH. Born abt 1840 in Ohio. Jonathan T. died in 1846, he was 6.

1804. Frances M. HOUGH. Born abt 1842 in Ohio. She married **Dr. ? FORDE**. They had one child:

2636   i.   daughter

1805. Infant 1 HOUGH.

1806. Infant 2 HOUGH.

1807. Charles Willis HILL.

1808. John Watson HILL.

1809. Martha Cornelia HILL.

1810. Phoebe HILL.

1811. Albert R. HILL. Born abt 1838 in Ohio.

1812. Jane A. HILL. Born abt 1846 in Ohio.

1813. Charles E. HILL. Born abt 1855 in Ohio.

1814. Isaac H. HILL. Born on 5 Dec 1836. Isaac H. died on 4 Sep 1849, he was 12.

1815. Truman Olvord "O. B." HILL. Born on 13 Jul 1838 in Ohio. Truman Olvord "O. B." married **Susan Alice ANDRE.** Born on 22 Mar 1840 in Van Buren Twp., Hancock Co., Ohio. Susan Alice died in Admire, Lyon Co., Kansas on 8 Aug 1930, she was 90.
They had the following children:

    2637   i.   Alice Clare (1865-1947)
    2638   ii.   Nathan (1865-1900)
    2639   iii.   Sylvester Bruce (1867-1933)

1816. Elmore D. HILL. Born on 5 Aug 1843. Elmore D. died on 25 Sep 1854, he was 11.

1817. Martin L. HILL. Born on 9 Dec 1845. Martin L. died on 7 May 1864, he was 18.

1818. Ellen G. HILL. Born on 5 Sep 1848. Ellen G. died on 10 Sep 1853, she was 5.

1819. Charles H. HILL. Born abt 1851. He appears in the census of 1860 for Waterloo Twp., Breckinridge, KS.

1820. Homer C. HILL. Born on 10 Apr 1852.

1821. Benjamin H. HILL. Born abt 1854. He appears in the census of 1860 for Waterloo Twp., Breckinridge, KS.

1822. Horace B. HILL. Born on 30 Apr 1855.

1823. Elizabeth Ann BRADISH. Born abt 1849.

1824. Emily Marie BRADISH. Born abt 1853 in Ohio.

1825. Ellen Josephine BRADISH. Born abt 1855 in Ohio.

1826. Samuel NICKERSON. Born abt 1836. Samuel died.

1827. Rev. Hoyt H. NICKERSON, M.D.[564] Born on 15 Feb 1838 in Clarksfield, Ohio. Hoyt H. died in Bloomfield, Ind. on 26 Jan 1908, he was 69. Occupation: Blacksmith, and later a minister and physician; 32d Ohio Vol. Inf., Union Army, Civil War, in many battles; an Odd Fellow. On 29 Mar 1864 when Hoyt H. was 26, he married **Mary Margaret CRIDER,** daughter of Tobias CRIDER & Mary KELKEN, in Bloomfield, Ind. Born on 10 Dec 1842 in Massillon, Ohio. Occupation: Mother of 4.
They had the following children:

    2640   i.   Mary Charlotte (~1865-)
    2641   ii.   William T. (~1868->1880)
    2642   iii.   Nellie A.
    2643   iv.   Laura Lenore

1828. Elizabeth NICKERSON. Born abt 1840. Elizabeth died aft 1870, she was 30.

1829. Mariah NICKERSON. Born abt 1842. Mariah died.

1830. William V. NICKERSON.[565] Born abt 1844. William V. died abt 1865, he was 21. Sergeant, 32d Ohio Vol., Civil War; died en route home after the war.

1831. Rev. Joseph E. NICKERSON. Born abt 1846. Joseph E. died aft 1870, he was 24.

1832. Charles F. NICKERSON. Born abt 1848. Charles F. died bef 1870, he was 22.

1833. Isaac L. HILL. Born abt 1831 in prob Southbury, New Haven Co., Conn.

1834. Henry HILL. Born abt 1834 in prob Southbury, New Haven Co., Conn.

1835. Carlyle HILL. Born abt 1840 in prob Southbury, New Haven Co., Conn.

1836. Mariette HILL. Born abt 1842 in prob Southbury, New Haven Co., Conn.

1837. Eunice "Currence" HILL. Born abt 1844 in prob Southbury, New Haven Co., Conn. Was teaching school, living at home, at age 17 in 1860.

1838. Charles L. HILL. Born abt 1846 in prob Southbury, New Haven Co., Conn. Living at home at age 14 in 1860.

1839. Caroline "Atlanta" HILL. Born abt 1849 in prob Southbury, New Haven Co., Conn. Living at home, age 11, in 1860. She was called Atlanta in the 1850 census.

1840. William HILL.[566] Born in 1831. William died in 1891, he was 60. His daughter, Hettie H. Hill, traced her ancestry to her great-great grandfather, the Revolutionary War soldier Isaac Hill (1740-after 1834). In 1857 when William was 26, he married **Eliza J. WOODRUFF**, b. 1836, d. 1898.
They had one child:

    2644   i.   Hettie H.

1841. Horace HUBBELL. Born on 11 Nov 1822.

1842. George Albert HUBBELL. Born on 1 Jun 1824.

1843. Catherine HUBBELL. Born on 20 Feb 1826.

1844. David Toucey HUBBELL. Born on 4 Sep 1827.

1845. Edward HUBBELL. Born on 11 Mar 1830.

1846. Seth HILL.[567] Born abt 1848 in Ohio. Occupation: "Carpenter, living at home in 1870." Seth married **Emma EDWARDS**. Born abt 1852.
They had the following children:

    2645   i.   Charles (~1865-)
    2646   ii.   Myrtle O. "Maybelle" (1878-)
    2647   iii.   Frank (~1871-)

1847. Andrew HILL. Born abt 1851 in Indiana. A farm hand, living at home, in 1870.

1848. Ann HILL. Born abt 1854 in Indiana. Living at home in 1870.

1849. Myron B. "Myra" HILL.[568] Born on 18 Jan 1859 in Yorkville, Ill.; died in Wellington, Kansas on 18 Apr 1954, he was 95. He was also of Winfield, Kansas. On 18 Jan 1889 when he was 30, he married **Ruth Alma WAITE**, daughter of Abraham WAITE & Caroline AUSTIN, in Kendall Co., Ill. Born 11 Dec 1866 in Yorkville, Ill.; died in Winfield, Kansas, 18 Jul 1941, she was 74.
They had the following children:

    2648   i.   Glen W. "Clem" (~1894-)
    2649   ii.   Evelyn R. (~1896-)
    2650   iii.   Lois Erma (~1899-)
    2651   iv.   Orvin J. (~1903-)
    2652   v.   Clarence J. (~1901-)
    2653   vi.   Ruby A. (~1910-)

1850. Theresa Mary HILL. Born on 10 Apr 1861 in Yorkville, Ill. Theresa Mary died in Urbana, Ill. on 1 Sep 1951, she was 90. On 4 Jul 1882 when Theresa Mary was 21, she married **William Jesse SWAIN** in Kendall Co., Ill. Born in 1858. William Jesse died in 1928, he was 70.
They had the following children:

    2654   i.   Fred
    2655   ii.   Frank
    2656   iii.   Florence Rebecca (1888-1961)

1851. John G. (or U.) HILL.[569] Born on 4 Nov 1863 in Fox Township, Ill. John G. (or U.) died in Elgin, Kane Co., Ill. on 25 Nov 1942, he was 79. Occupation: In Kendall Co., Illinois, and later of Minnesota. On 11 Feb 1892 when he was 28, he first married **Hannah Catherine OSTROM** in Kendall Co., Ill. Born in 1864. Hannah Catherine died in 1901, she was 37.
They had one child:

    2657   i.   Ora M. (1892-)

On 24 Dec 1903 when John G. (or U.) was 40, he second married **Cynthia A. DAVIS** in Kendall Co., Ill.

1852. Charles A. "Charley" HILL.[570] Born on 4 Jan 1868 in Illinois. A farmer, of Woodstock, Ill. He married **Harriet M. "Hattie" FAULTZ**. Born abt 1869 in Indiana.

188

They had one child:

    2658   i.   Maurice (~1909-)

1853. Ernest Oliver "Ernie" HILL.[571] Born on 9 Oct 1870 in Fox Station, Ill. He was later of Brookfield, Mo. Ernest Oliver Hill and his wife Myrtle O. Hill are first cousins, once removed; she is one generation younger than he. On 26 Oct 1897 when he was 27, he married **Myrtle O. "Maybelle" HILL** (2646), daughter of Seth HILL (1846) & Emma EDWARDS, in Kendall Co., Ill. B. Apr 1878 in Indiana. They had one child:

    2659   i.   Earnest L. (1899-)

1854. Frank B. HILL.[572] Born on 21 Jun 1875 in Illinois. Frank B. died in Aurora, Ill. on 14 Jan 1957, he was 81. A farm laborer. On 27 Jan 1904 when Frank B. was 28, he married **Jennie A. MORGAN** in Kendall Co., Ill. Born in 1880; died bef 1918.

1855. Frederick W. HILL.[573] Born on 11 Feb 1878 in Illinois. Frederick W. died in Aurora, Ill. on 5 Apr 1933, he was 55. On 3 Feb 1910 when Frederick W. was 31, he married **Lillian WHYNOTT** in Yorkville, Ill. Born in 1889. Lillian died in 1938, she was 49. Occupation: Mother of 3. They had the following children:

    2660   i.   Child of Frederick and Lillian
    2661   ii.   Elizabeth T. (1910-2008)
    2662   iii.   Roy Steven (1912-2004)

1856. John HILL. Born in 1860 in Ohio.

1857. Nancy HILL. Born in 1862 in Indiana.

1858. Alice R. HILL. Born in 1867 in Indiana.

The Ten Children of William P. and Sarah (Herrick) Hill [574]

1859. Edgar E. HILL, [575] eldest of the ten children of William Prince and Sarah P. (Herrick) Hill, was born at Caton, Steuben Co., N.Y., in November 1829; died at Findlay, Hancock Co., Ohio, 18 March 1901. At the age of thirty, he left Caton and went into the lumber business. He initially sold lumber to manufacturers of mowing machines. In 1865, when he was about thirty-six years old, he married and began raising his family in Corning, a few miles north of Caton. He lived at Wall and Third Streets with his wife, two daughters, and two sons at the time of the U.S. census in 1880. He then moved to Cleveland, and then on to Findlay, Hancock County, Ohio, where he built a lumber mill and where he was living with his wife and four children at the time of the census in 1900. He was survived by his wife, about whom nothing more is known. His daughters, too, disappeared from the historical records, and presumably they did not marry. Both of his sons went into the lumber business. His eldest son married and remained in Findlay until sometime after 1930. His younger son married and had a daughter. They were living in Findlay until after 1920. Edgar E. Hill's descendants disappear from the census records after 1930. In 1865 when he was 35, he married **Caroline "Carrie" L. RODGERS,**[576] born in Jul 1842 in New York State; died in 1880, she was 37. They had the following children:

    2663   i.   Kittie A. (1867-)
    2664   ii.   Emma L. (1871-)
    2665   iii.   Fred E. (1872-)
    2666   iv.   Albert G. (1874-)

1860. Charles W. HILL,[577] second son and second child of William and Sarah (Herrick) Hill, was born at Caton, Steuben County, New York, 31 August 1831; died at Rowan, Iowa, 23 September 1923, and was buried in the Graceland Cemetery there. He attended schools in New York State until he was fifteen and assisted his father on the farm. He then left home and worked for monthly wages in the lumbering business, and was also employed on other farms, to send money back to his family. He was married when he was twenty-five and began farming on his own on rental property. He later was able to buy 200 acres of unimproved land in Steuben County. In March 1861, when he was thirty years old and as as the Civil War was about to break out, he moved west with his family and became a pioneer farmer in Wright County, Iowa. Statehood had been granted to Iowa only fifteen years previously, in 1846. Florida, a slave state, was paired with Iowa, a free state, under the terms of the so-called Missouri Compromise.

Much of the state was still unsettled and the land was largely unbroken.

Charles Hill began by renting a farm in Iowa Township, near Clarion, and remained there for 20 years. He started without even a cow, but his hard work and perserverance were rewarded and he was able to buy some land to begin his own farm. On 21 November 1877 he purchased 40 acres of land in Wright County for $200 with a $135 mortgage from Frederick and Sarah Diltz. By 1881 he owned 240 acres, which he purchased at $3 to $5 per acre. With the improvements he had made, it was eventually valued at about $5,000. He moved onto his own farm in 1881 with his wife and two surviving children, whom he protected from prairie fires by plowing around his quarter section of land. In March 1892, when he was serving as President of the Grant Township School Board in the Clarion District, he was appointed by the Board "to represent the Township at a meeting to be called by the County Superintendant to consider the uniform Text Book question." He was a member of the Odd Fellows Lodge at Belmond, Iowa, and was a director of the County Agricultural Society for many years. He was known as a staunch Republican. Charles Hill was "recognized as one of the thriftiest farmers in the county and commands the respect of all who know him."

He married, in New York state, 2 April 1856, **Adelia Catherine RILEY**, daughter of Simeon and Katharine (Gillett) Riley; born at Steuben County, New York, 24 July 1836; died at Rowan, Iowa, 30 July 1887. Simeon Riley is #2089 in this genealogy, a descendant of John Hill, youngest son of Luke Hill Sr. She was buried in Horse Grove, Ia., and her remains were later moved to the Graceland Cemetery in Rowan, Ia. Charles and Adelia (Riley) Hill had three children: George J. (1857-1952); William L. (1860-1869); and Adella L. (1863-1910). William accidentally drowned at age 9, while the other two children reached maturity and had their own families.

Adelia Catharine "Delia" RILEY,[578] daughter and fourth of the five children of Simeon and Katharine (Gillett) Riley, was born at Steuben County, New York, 24 July 1836; died at Rowan, Iowa, 30 July 1887. Her parents died when she was very young; her mother died when she was three years old and her father died when she was about six. In 1848, she and her four brothers were named in the will of her grandfather, Joseph Gillett, to share in the proceeds of sale of two small parcels of land, somewhat more than an acre, which he owned in Caton, Steuben County, NY. Her grandfather Gillett died in 1848 when she was 12, two years after this will was written. Two years later, her grandfather Riley died; she was then 14. At that time she and her two surviving brothers (the youngest, Ransom, is not mentioned at probate) were said to have a General Guardian, one James W. Glover, whose relationship to the family is unknown. Adelia Riley was the step-granddaughter of William Prince Hill's mother, Charlotte (Prince) Hill, through her second marriage, to Joseph Gillett. When she died of "phthisis" or "consumption (tuberculosis)" at the age of 51, her funeral was said to be the largest ever known in Wright County. Some 136 teams of horses were present to bring the mourners to her funeral and to the Horse Grove cemetery, where she was initially buried. Her remains were later moved to the Graceland Cemetery near Rowan, Iowa, where her husband and many of her descendants are buried.

Undoubtedly unknown to them, Charles W. Hill and Adelia Catherine Riley were both descendants of Luke and Mary (Hout) Hill. Charles was a descendant of their son Luke Jr., and Adelia (2928) was a descendant of their son John.

Charles W. Hill and his wife, Adelia (Riley) Hill, had the following children:

2667	i.	George J. [68] (1857-1952)
2668	ii.	William L. [69] (1860-1869)
2669	iii.	Adella L. [70] (1863-1910)

1861. Emily "Emma" HILL,[579] eldest daughter and third child of William P. and Sarah P. (Herrick) Hill, was born in about 1834, probably at Caton, Steuben Co., New York,; died at Corning, Steuben Co., New York, 17 April 1917. She would have been about sixteen years old at the time of the census of 1850, but she was not living at home at that time and her residence is unknown until she appeared in the census of 1880 as the wife of Elias Hungerford in Corning, N.Y. She probably was working as a hired girl in a household somewhere in Steuben County, until she married, sometime between 1870 and 1880, as his second wife, **Elias B. "E. B." HUNGERFORD**; born in Vermont in about 1824; died before 1892, probably at Corning, N.Y. E. B. Hungerford married (1), in say 1848, Betsy Jane (or Jane B.) _____, by whom he had at least seven children: Jerome (b. c. 1849), Alzada J. (b. c. 1851), Cornelia E. (b. c. 1853), Calvin G. (b. c. 1855), Harry (b. c. 1858), Charles (b. c. 1862), and Daniel (b. c. 1865). Elias and Emily (Hill) Hungerford had no children.

Elias Hungerford was living in Painted Post, Steuben Co., N.Y., in 1850 with his wife Jane and a one-year old son, Jerome. In 1860, he was in Corning with his wife Betsy Jane and five children. In 1870 E. B. and Jane Hungerford lived in Corning with six children. In 1880, Elias Hungerford was a wool buyer, living in Corning, N.Y., with his wife Emily, age 44, who was keeping house, and two sons, Daniel (age 15, in school), and Calvin (age 20, an engineer). Emily's step-children disappeared from the census records except for Calvin G. Hungerford, who later married and had descendants. Emily (Hill) Hungerford was living at Corning, New York, on 30 March 1887, when her father's estate was administered. Her mother then moved to her home in Corning and died there eight years later. In 1892, Emily's household included her mother (age 85) and her sisters Sarah Hill (55) and Jerusha Hill (51) and her brother George W. Hill (53).

1862. Sarah HILL,[580] second daughter and fourth child of William Prince and Sarah (Herrick) Hill, was born in New York State, probably at Caton, in March 1835; died at Clarion, Wright Co., Iowa, 4 June 1925, age 90. Sarah Hill never married. She came to Iowa to live with her brother, Charles, following the death in 1917 of her sister Emily, with whom she had been living in Corning, New York. She was affectionately known to her nieces and nephews in Clarion as "Aunt Sarah." She died at Clarion eight years later. Her tombstone is in the oldest part of the Graceland Cemetery, Rowan, Iowa, immediately south of the Hill family obelisk.

1863. George Washington HILL,[581] third son and fifth of the ten children of William Prince and Sarah P. "Sally" (Herrick) Hill, was born in Steuben County (probably in Caton) N.Y., in 1837; died at Corning, Steuben County, N.Y., 17 April 1917. He was 10 years old on 26 July 1850, when the census was taken. He was the Caton Town Collector in 1863. He was still living in Caton, NY in 1887. He married, 6 February 1879, **Stella Comelia BREESE**; born at Caton, N.Y., 7 November 1860; died in 1934, about age 73, and was buried in Caton. George W. and Stella (Breese) Hill had one child, a daughter, Vesta Eloise (b. 1881), who married Harry Lawrence Speer and had five daughters. Three of the daughters were still alive in February 2002.

They had one child:
  2670   i.   Vesta Eloise [71] (1881-1970)

1864. Amanda HILL,[582] third daughter and sixth child of William P. and Sarah (Herrick) Hill, was born in Steuben Co., N.Y., 15 November 1838; died at Caton, N.Y., 13 January 1887, age 48. On 18 April 1859, when she was 20, she married (1) **Chester Lazell KIMBALL**, also known as Luzelle P. Kimball; born in Delmar Township, Tioga Co., Pa., 6 June 1837; died at Wellsboro, Pa., 16 August 1871, age 34. They had the following children:
  2671   i.   Sarah "Sadie" L. [77] (1862->1887)
  2672   ii.   Carrie H. [78] (1866-1894)
  2673   iii.   William E. [79] "Willie" (1868-)
On 29 February 1880, when she was 41, she married (2) **Robert RICHARDS**, in Caton, NY.

1865. Jerusha "J. M." HILL,[583] fourth daughter and seventh child of William P. and Sarah (Herrick) Hill, was born in Steuben County, New York, in about 1841; died at Corning, N.Y., 13 August 1895, age 54. She was named for her maternal grandmother, Jerusha (Palmer) Herrick. She was called Juntia in the census of 1850, when she was nine years old, but she was often referred to as "J. M." when she was an adult. She never married. She was a sales person in New York City for many years, but she returned to Steuben County and was living with her widowed sister Emily "Emma" (Hill) Hungerford in Corning in 1892. Also residing with Emma Hungerford at that time were her unmarried sister Sarah and her brother George, who was apparently a widower at this time, and their widowed mother, then 85. She developed cancer "commencing in the arm pit," which was probably cancer that originated in the breast, and died three years later, seven months after her mother's death.

1866. Diantha HILL,[584] fifth daughter and eighth child of William P. and Sarah (Herrick) Hill, was born in Steuben County, New York, in about 1843; died, probably in Vernon, Michigan, after 1895. On 9 July

1863, when she was about 20, she married **Bertis B. REED**; born 14 November 1834; died at Vernon, Mich., 17 January 1901, age 66.

They had the following children:

2674	i.	Charles C. "Charley" [72] (1865-1926)
2675	ii.	Luella M. [73] (->1920)
2676	iii.	Walter W. [74] (1870-)
2677	iv.	Frank Dubois [75] (1876-)
2678	v.	Deforest H. [76] (1879-)

1867. Mary M. HILL,[585] sixth daughter and ninth child of William P. and Sarah (Herrick) Hill, was born in Steuben County, New York, in about 1845; died at Caton, N.Y., on 21 September, probably 1899, age 44. She managed the family farm in Caton, and never married.

1868. Harland P. "Harley" HILL,[586] fourth son and youngest of the ten children of William P. and Sarah (Herrick) Hill, was born in Steuben Co., N.Y., 23 February 1847; died at Rowan, Wright Co., Iowa, 25 March 1869, age 22. Harland, also known as "Harley" or "Harlow," came to Iowa in 1861 with his brother, Charles and Charles' wife and their two children. His sister Sarah came to Iowa later. Harland drowned eight years after he arrived in Iowa while riding on horseback in the flooded Iowa River near his home. His nine-year-old nephew William drowned with him. Legend has it that he drowned while trying to save his nephews William and George, and although William drowned, George, age 12, survived as a result of Harland's exertions. "Harley" and "Willie" were buried at the top of a small hill about a half mile east of the Iowa River. These were the first graves in what is now known as the Graceland Cemetery in Rowan.

Additional [Numbered] Descendants of Ephraim and Charlotte (Prince) Hill in the Seventh Generation, Who Appear in *Genealogy of the Hill Family in America*

1869. Mary Amanda [29] HILL. Born on 16 May 1835 in Painted Post No. 1, Steuben Co., NY. Mary Amanda [29] died on 4 Jul 1840, she was 5.

1870. Sergeant Stilson Edward [30] HILL.[587] Born on 15 Sep 1838 in Caton, Steuben Co., NY. Stilson Edward [30] died in St. Cloud, FL on 17 Mar 1917, he was 78. He was a Union Army soldier in the Civil War. Stilson Edward [30] married **Amelia L. LOCKWOOD**. Amelia L. died aft Aug 1920. She wrote a letter from her home in St. Cloud, Florida, that was read at the Hill Family Reunion, Corning, N.Y., on 27 August 1920.

1871. Joseph Gillett [31] HILL.[588] Born on 4 Aug 1842. Joseph Gillett [31] died in St. Cloud, Florida (probably) aft Aug 1920, he was 77. He was named for his step-grandfather. He was a Union Army soldier in the Civil War. On 30 Apr 1880 when Joseph Gillett [31] was 37, he first married **Isabelle S. SHANNON**, in Vanango Co., PA. Isabelle S. died on 13 Mar 1908 in Oil City, PA.

1872. Huldah Jane [32] GILLETT. Born on 2 Oct 1836. Huldah Jane [32] died on 6 Oct 1886, she was 50. She and her husband were living with her parents in 1855, at the time of the Caton census. On 1 Jan 1855 when Huldah Jane [32] was 18, she married **Charles WOLCOTT**. Born on 11 Jun 1832 in Chemung Co., N.Y. Charles died on 3 Mar 1915, he was 82. Charles Wolcott owned land abutting Joseph Gillett. His birthplace and age (23) were given in the Caton census of 1855. He was said to be five years older than his wife, Huldah.

They had the following children:

2679	i.	Orson Elvin [80] (1855->1920)
2680	ii.	Charlotte Adelaide [81] (1859->1920)
2681	iii.	Fannie Isabel [82] (1863-1885)
2682	iv.	Pantha Estella [83] (1865-)
2683	v.	Eva Louise [84] (1867-)
2684	vi.	Charles Sidney [85] (1876->1920)

1873. Syrene C. [35] "Cyrena" HILL. Born on 11 Jun 1838. Syrene C. [35] "Cyrena" died on 24 Dec 1854, she was 16. Buried in 1854 in Gillett cemetery, Caton, NY. In 1850 she was living with her father and mother. A grave in the Gillett Cemetery, Caton, NY, is marked with the following inscription, "Syrena C. daughter of Noble & Jane Hill died Dec. 24, 1854."

1874. Munroe B. [33] "Murray" HILL. Born on 26 Aug 1841. Munroe B. [33] "Murray" died on 17 Jul 1864, he was 22. Buried in Caton, N.Y. In 1850 he was living with his father and mother.

1875. Earl A. [34] (aka Arthur E.) HILL.[589] Born in 1845. Earl A. [34] (aka Arthur E.) died on 6 Mar 1921, he was 76. Buried in Caton, N.Y. Religion: Caton, NY, Methodist Church Steward & Trustee. President, Hill Association, at the time of his death in 1921. Earl Hill was a Steward, Trustee, and Class Leader of the Methodist Episcopal Church of Caton, NY, in 1879. Earl A. [34] (aka Arthur E.) married _____ ? (HILL); _____ died aft 1920.

1876. Nye Robinson [36] "Henry" HILL.[590] Born on 7 Jan 1853; died aft 1920, he was 66; he married _____ ? (HILL).
They had one child:
    2685   i.   Louise [86]

1877. Hiram L. [37] GRIDLEY.[591] Born on 28 Sep 1831; died in New Orleans, LA on 27 Nov 1863, he was 32, a Union Army soldier in the Civil War. Hiram L. [37] married _____ ? (GRIDLEY).
They had one child
    2686   i.   _____

1878. Emma A. [38] GRIDLEY.[592] Born on 20 Aug 1834. Emma A. [38] died bef 1920, she was 85. On 6 Oct 1863 when Emma A. [38] was 29, she first married **Charles W. DENNING**. Charles W. died on 4 Apr 1863 in Bell Island Confederate Army Prison. He was a Union Army soldier in the Civil War. They had the following children:
    2687   i.   Daisy Irene [87]
    2688   ii.   Guy Hamilton [88]
On 4 Sep 1871 when Emma A. [38] was 37, she second married **Jacob (Jake) SHAW**. Jacob (Jake) died bef 1920. In 1920, she had her own home in Campbell, Steuben Co., N.Y., and her widowed brother, Albert, was living with her.

1879. Jane C. [39] GRIDLEY.[593] Born on 6 May 1835. Jane C. [39] died on 30 Mar 1918, she was 82. Jane C. [39] first married **Horace GILBERT**. On 21 Jan 1868 when Jane C. [39] was 32, she second married **Eli L. GRIDLEY**. Born in 1848. Eli L. died in 1916, he was 68.
They had the following children:
    2689   i.   Walter E. [89] (1869-)
    2690   ii.   Nettie V. [90] (1871-)
    2691   iii.   Charles L. [91] (1875-<1920)
    2692   iv.   Lena H. [92] (1877-1920)

1880. Emma J. [40] GRIDLEY. Born on 31 Mar 1836. She first married **Sylvester ELDRED**.
They had one child:
    2693   i.   John W. [93]
Emma J. [40] second married **Sanford HOUGH**.
They had the following children:
    2694   i.   Huldah [94]
    2695   ii.   Albert L. [95]
    2696   iii.   Cephas [96]
    2697   iv.   Alice [97]

1881. Wesley Prince [41] GRIDLEY.[594] Born on 10 Apr 1838 at Caton, Steuben Co., N.Y. Wesley Prince [41] died 17 Nov 1904, perhaps with the 1st N.Y. Cavalry; he was 66. He was a Union Army soldier in the Civil War. His father, Lewis Gridley, may have been born 14 December 1801, perhaps the son of Levi Gridley and Mary Gilbert. Wesley Prince Gridley may have married **Sarah BAKER**.
His children were:
    2698   i.   Lavern [98]
    2699   ii.   Cora [99]

1882. Albert Lavert [42] GRIDLEY.[595] Born on 17 Oct 1838, probably at Caton, N.Y. Albert Lavert [42] died on 13 Jun 1865, he was 26. He was living in Michigan in 1877 and 1879, because his daughters were born there in those years. He may have been living in Missiouri in 1893, for his son is said to have been born there in that year. He lived in Ohio in 1900 with his wife and three children, and in 1920 he was widowed and living in the home of his sister, Emma A. Shaw, in Campbell, Steuben Co., N.Y. He was a Union Army soldier in the Civil War. He married, in 1878, **Clara B. _____**; born in New York State in August 1853; died before 1920

They had the following children:

2700	i.	Grace [100] (1877-)
2701	ii.	Rena E. (1879-)
2702	iii.	John S. [101] (1893-)

1883. Elizabeth H. [43] GRIDLEY. Born on 21 Jun 1842. Elizabeth H. [43] died 11 Aug 1863, age 21.

1884. Pliny Fisk [44] GRIDLEY.[596] Born on 10 Jun 1845 at Caton, N.Y. Pliny Fisk [44] died 7 Aug 1920, at Caton, N.Y., he was 75. He was a Union Army soldier in the Civil War. He married, in about 1866, **Maria Ophelia EMERY**; born in 1849 in Hornby, N.Y.; died in Caton, N.Y., in 1924. Pliny and Maria were both buried in the Elmwood Cemetery in Caton.

Their children were:

2703	i.	Frederick Laverne [102] (1867-)
2704	ii.	Earl [103]
2705	iii.	Edwin L. [104]
2706	iv.	Robert M. [105]
2707	v.	Rose M. [106]
2708	vi.	Clara E. [107]
2709	vii.	Bessie [108]
2710	viii.	Jessie [109]
2711	ix.	Edith [110]
2712	x.	Roy H. [111]
2713	xi.	Unknown Child [112]

1885. Huldah P. [45] GRIDLEY. Born on 9 Oct 1847. Huldah P. [45] died on 22 Jan 1850, she was 2.

1886. Elsie P. [46] GRIDLEY. Born on 14 Jan 1850. Elsie P. [46] died on 7 Nov 1862, she was 12.

1887. Manley D. [47] GRIDLEY. Born on 23 Feb 1852. Manley D. [47] died on 24 Sep 1856, he was 4.

1888. Viola J. [48] GRIDLEY. Born on 25 Jan 1854. Viola J. [48] died on 31 Oct 1862, she was 8.

1889. Hettie V. [49] GRIDLEY. Born on 24 Nov 1855. Hettie V. [49] died on 11 Nov 1862, she was 6.

1890. Alice J. [50] GRIDLEY. Born on 25 Mar 1857. Alice J. [50] died on 25 Oct 1862, she was 5.

1891. Gervis P. [51] HOWE. Born on 1 May 1836. Gervis P. [51] died on 12 Oct 1908, he was 72. On 25 Oct 1860 when Gervis P. was 24, he married **Elisabeth C. COLE**. Elisabeth C. died on 31 Dec 1916.

1892. Augusta E. [52] HOWE. Born on 19 Oct 1839. Augusta E. [52] died on 23 Apr 1917, she was 77. On 16 May 1858 when Augusta E. [52] was 18, she married **Carleton PRIEST**.

They had the following children:

| 2714 | i. | William B. [113] (1864-1917) |
| 2715 | ii. | Fred O. [114] (1869-) |

1893. Francis Sylvester [53] HOWE.[597] Born on 28 Aug 1842. He was a Union Army soldier in the Civil War. On 7 Feb 1866 when Francis Sylvester [53] was 23, he married **Mary E. NIVER**.

They had the following children:

| 2716 | i. | Alice B. [115] (1867->1920) |
| 2717 | ii. | Asa L. [116] (1877->1920) |

1894. Charlotte P. [54] HOWE. Born on 12 May 1844. Charlotte P. [54] died on 11 May 1908, she was 63. On 20 Sep 1868 when Charlotte P. [54] was 24, she married **George VAN ARSDALE**.

They had one child:

| 2718 | i. | Jacob A. [117] (1873-) |

1895. Mary Jane [55] HOWE. Born on 18 Aug 1849.

1896. Smith J. [56] HOWE. Born on 5 Aug 1854. Smith J. [56] died on 2 Jun 1920, he was 65. On 26 Nov 1874 when Smith J. [56] was 20, he married **Katherine BECHTEL**. Katherine died aft 1920.

They had one child:

2719   i.   Lora S. [118] (1878->1920)

1897. Lewis [57] HOWE.

1898. Sylvester J. [58] HILL.[598] Born on 3 May 1846. He was a Union Army soldier in the Civil War. On 2 Feb 1872 when Sylvester J. [58] was 25, he first married **Anna A. SOWLES**. Born on 3 Mar 1846. Anna A. died on 10 Sep 1895, she was 49.
They had the following children:

   2720   i.   Alice Mable [119] (1873-)
   2721   ii.   Agnes Lurancy [120] (1875-)
   2722   iii.   Mary Elizabeth [121] (1876-)
   2723   iv.   Edith Laurel [122] (1880-1900)
   2724   v.   Ernest Sylvester [123] (1886->1920)

On 11 Jun 1904 when Sylvester J. [58] was 58, he second married **Jennie BENEDICT**.

1899. Julia E. "Juliette" [59] HILL. Born 19 Jun 1849; died aft 1920. On 25 Oct 1870 when Julia E. "Juliette" [59] was 21, she married **James Abner GILBERT**.[599] James Abner died on 16 Feb 1907.
They had the following children:

   2725   i.   Mary L. [124] (1876-1879)
   2726   ii.   Charles B. [125] (1879-<1920)
   2727   iii.   Roy H. [126] (1889-1889)

1900. Ezekiel HILL.[600] Born abt 1850.

1901. Virgil Reed [60] HILL. Born on 11 Mar 1853. Virgil Reed [60] died on 14 Mar 1895, he was 42. Buried in Caton, N.Y. Virgil Reed [60] married **JoAnna McCARTY**. Born in 1855. JoAnna died in 1929, she was 74. Buried in Caton, N.Y.
They had the following children:

   2728   i.   Frank Sherman [127] (1874-)
   2729   ii.   Frederick E. [128] (1880->1920)

1902. Sherman B. [61] HILL.[601] Born on 20 Dec 1855. Sherman B. [61] died aft 1922, he was 66. Buried in Caton, N.Y. Sherman B. [61] married **Carrie S. ? (HILL)**. Born in 1857. Carrie S. died ? 1902, she was 45. Buried in Caton, N.Y. Her gravestone is referenced for "JoAnne Hill 1855 – 1929" (Identity unknown).

1903. Nellie L. [62] HILL. Born on 25 Dec 1861. Nellie L. [62] died on 22 Feb 1911, she was 49. Buried in Caton, N.Y. Nellie L. [62] married **Lafe F. SMITH**.
They had one child:

   2730   i.   Walter Hill [129] (1889-)

1904. Charles Edwin [63] HILL.[602] Born on 24 Dec 1852 in Caton, Steuben Co., N.Y. Charles Edwin [63] died in Caton, Steuben Co., N.Y. on 13 Sep 1934, he was 81. Buried in Caton, N.Y. Occupation: Farmer at Caton, NY, in 1879. On 28 Sep 1879 when Charles Edwin [63] was 26, he married **Harriett Cynthia BOSTWICK**, in Tioga, Penna. Born on 13 May 1869 in Lawrenceville, Penna. Harriett Cynthia died in Caton, Steuben Co., N.Y. on 26 Aug 1943, age 74. Buried in Caton, N.Y. Mother of 6.
They had the following children:

   2731   i.   Florence Rebecca [130] (1880->1920)
   2732   ii.   William Edwin [131] (1882->1924)
   2733   iii.   Alice Harriet [132] (1885->1920)
   2734   iv.   John Phineas [133] (1891-1996)
   2735   v.   George Noble [134] (1898-1980)
   2736   vi.   Ruth Queenie [135] (1899-2000)

1905. Noble John Leland [64] HILL. Born on 31 Aug 1855. Noble John Leland [64] died on 24 May 1863. Died in his 8th year of diphtheria.

1906. Plineas W. C. [65] HILL. Born on 18 Apr 1863. Plineas W. C. [65] died on 29 May 1863. Died at one month of diphtheria, 5 d. after his brother.

1907. Elizabeth Merrick [66] HILL. Born on 20 Sep 1869. Occupation: Mother of 8. On 20 Aug 1889 when Elizabeth Merrick [66] was 19, she married **William Warner PHILLIPS**.

They had the following children:

2737	i.	Ethel Belle [136] (1890-)
2738	ii.	Harriet Ruth [137] (1893-)
2739	iii.	Mary [138] (1895-)
2740	iv.	Pauline [139]
2741	v.	Henry Clay [140] (1899-)
2742	vi.	Elwin [141] (1901-)
2743	vii.	William [142] (1904-)
2744	viii.	Leslie Lamont [143] (1909-)

1908. Clarence Sylvanus [67] HILL. Born on 12 Jul 1876. On 6 Jul 1898 when Clarence Sylvanus [67] was 21, he married **Lela RUMSEY**.

They had one child:

2745	i.	Sealton [144] (1898-)

-- 603

1909. Margaret J. HILL. Born in 1844 in Ohio.

1910. George R. HILL. Born in 1846 in Ohio.

1911. William F. HILL. Born in 1848 in Ohio.

1912. Francis (aka Frances) A. HILL. Born in 1850 in Ohio. Occupation: domestic servant in 1870, while living at home.

1913. Martha A. HILL. Born in 1853 in Ohio.

1914. James C. HILL. Born in 1857 in Ohio.

1915. Lucy I. HILL. Born abt 1858 in Illinois.

1916. Phonetta A. PAUL. Born on 11 Aug 1850. On 14 Oct 1873 when Phonetta A. was 23, she married **William DICKSON** in Washington Courthouse, Fayette Co., Ohio.

1917. Thomas PAUL. Born abt 1851. Thomas died prob abt 1851.

1918. Francis "Frank" PAUL. Born on 9 Aug 1852; died in Washington Courthouse, Fayette Co., Ohio on 4 Mar 1900, she was 47. Buried on 5 Mar 1900 in Washington Courthouse, Fayette Co., Ohio. She never married, and was known as "Aunt Frank." She lived with her father, and with him brought up the orphaned Charles Ross Paul, son of Roswell Hill Paul and Metha Kearns. She died the day after her father, and they were buried together.

1919. Roswell Hill PAUL. Born on 5 Mar 1855 in Aberdeen, Brown Co., Ohio. Roswell Hill died on 16 May 1888, he was 33. He had one son by first marriage and 3 daughters by second marriage. On 20 Nov 1878 when Roswell Hill was 23, he first married **Metha KEARNS**, in Washington Courthouse, Fayette Co., Ohio. Born abt 1862; died on 26 Jun 1881, she was 19.

They had one child:

2746	i.	Charles Ross "C. R." (1880-1948)

Roswell Hill second married _____ (**PAUL**). Mother of 3 daughters, whose names are unknown.

1920. George W. PAUL. Born on 21 Jul 1857. On 7 Oct 1879 when George W. was 22, he married **Askey A. GREEN** in Washington Courthouse, Fayette Co., Ohio.

1921. Flora C. PAUL. Born on 20 Sep 1859.

1922. Carrie F. PAUL. Born on 16 Oct 1860 in Aberdeen, Brown Co., Ohio. Carrie F. died in Winona, Minn. on 5 Oct 1941, she was 80. On 25 Oct 1883 when Carrie F. was 23, she married **Edward J. POWELL** in Washington Courthouse, Fayette Co., Ohio.

1923. Charles B. "Cass" PAUL. Born on 20 May 1862 in West Union, Adams Co., Ohio; died in Winona, Minn. on 5 Oct 1941, age 79. He m. **Martha "Mattie" SANTEE** in Frankfort, Ross Co., Ohio.

1924. [Baby] PAUL. Born on 22 Mar 1865 in No. Liberty, Adams Co., Ohio.

1925. Lucy HILL. Born in 1853 in Ohio.

1926. William R. HILL. Born in 1855 in Ohio.

1927. Henry B. HILL. Born in 1857 in Ohio.

1928. Mary A. HILL. Born in 1858 in Ohio.

1929. Alice R. HILL. Born in 1860 in Ohio.

1930. Charles HILL. Born in 1863 in Ohio.

1931. Edward HILL. Born in 1867 in Ohio.

1932. Lily HILL. Born in 1870 in Ohio.

------------------------------------ [604]

1933. Amanda HILL. Amanda died on 9 Nov 1817 in Carmel, N.Y.

1934. Enos HILL.

1935. James HILL. Born in 1827. James married **Mary ? (HILL).**

1936. Phoebe HILL. Born in 1831.

1937. Emily HILL. Born in 1834.

1938. Harmon W. HILL. Born on 8 Mar 1821 in Carmel, N.Y.; died in Painted Post, N.Y. on 13 Jul 1901, age 80. He married **Emaline SKINNER**. Born in 1831.
They had the following children:

2747	i.	Emily (1845-)
2748	ii.	Emaline A. (1846-)
2749	iii.	Amy (1858-)

1939. Hansel S. HILL. Born 22 Jul 1822 in Carmel, N.Y.; died on 9 Aug 1893, age 71. Hansel S. married **Margaret _____.**

1940. Mary Jane HILL. Born on 14 May 1824 in Carmel, N.Y. Mary Jane died in Urbana, N.Y. on 12 Dec 1892, she was 68. On 19 Apr 1843 when Mary Jane was 18, she married **John KETCHUM**. Born on 24 Jan 1821; died on 10 Feb 1890, he was 69.
They had the following children:

2750	i.	Wilbur J. (1844-1912)
2751	ii.	Warren B. (1847-1849)
2752	iii.	Charles H. (1850-)
2753	iv.	George W. (1852-1887)
2754	v.	Sarah Emily (1854-1905)
2755	vi.	Ira P. (1857-1942)
2756	vii.	Mary E. (1859-)
2757	viii.	Eliza H. (1863-1941)
2758	ix.	Martha E. (1866-1899)

1941. Hannah Eliza HILL.[605] Born on 9 Nov 1825 in Carmel, N.Y. Hannah Eliza first married **Joseph C. SKINNER**.
They had one child:

2759	i.	George Amos

Hannah Eliza second married **George AXTEL**.
They had the following children:

2760	i.	Mary Elizabeth
2761	ii.	George (~1855-)

1942. Betsey Ann HILL. Betsey Ann married **Anson GOODWIN**.

1943. Harriet HILL. Born 17 Oct 1827; died 31 Dec 1853, she was 26. On 18 Oct 1849 when Harriet was 22, she married **George SHINABARGER** in Hornellsville, N.Y.

1944. Ferris HILL. Born on 29 Jan 1830 in Wayne, N.Y. He married **Unice BIRDSEYE**. Born in 1827.
They had the following children:

2762	i.	George
2763	ii.	Franklin

1945. Martha HILL. Born in 1830 in Wayne, N.Y.

1946. Harsey HILL Jr. Born 1 Apr 1831; died on 23 Dec 1831 in Wayne, N.Y.

1947. Elizabeth Ann HILL. Born on 3 Mar 1832 in Wayne, N.Y. Elizabeth Ann died in Dundee, N.Y. on 7 Apr 1921, she was 89. Elizabeth Ann married **Captain Samuel DUNN**.

1948. Major Richard L. [Lord] HILL I.[606] Born on 25 Dec 1832 in Wayne, N.Y.; died in Corning, N.Y. on 25 Apr 1902, he was 69. Major, 24th Cavalry; wounded at Cold Harbor, Va.; insurance claim adjuster

in Corning and N.Y.C. On 16 Mar 1863 when he was 30, he married **Julia Alice HAVENS** in Corning, N.Y. Born on 26 Jun 1840 in Dresden, N.Y.; died in Corning, N.Y. on 30 Aug 1930, age 90.
They had the following children:

2764	i.	Richard L. (1864-1947)
2765	ii.	Aimee Knox (1889-1918)
2766	iii.	Julia Bovier (1891-1939)
2767	iv.	Alice May
2768	v.	William Ferris
2769	vi.	Joseph Amos
2770	vii.	Amos W. (1873-1887)
2771	viii.	William Amos
2772	ix.	Helen Martha
2773	x.	Lela
2774	xi.	Emma L.

1949. Amos W. HILL.

1950. George HILL. Born on 16 Jun 1839; died on 5 Dec 1907, he was 68.
George first married **Sandie VERNE**.
They had one child:

2775	i.	H. Laverne

George second married **Martha CROSBY**.

1951. John Wyman "Jay" CHASE. Born in 1885; died in 1914, abt age 29.

1952. Annette S. CHASE. Born in 1888.

1953. Nettie CHASE. Born in 1888.

1954. Ethyl CHASE. Born in 1891.

1955. Arlia CHASE. Born in 1893.

Line 6 – Descendants of Abigail Hill (continued)

1956. Willard Burr COBB. Born on 19 Jan 1807 in Pawlet, Rutland Co., Vt.; died in Greensburg, Decatur Co., Ind., 6 Sep 1849, age 42. On 19 Sep 1830 when he was 23, he married **Submitt S. GARLINGHOUSE**, in Tippecanoe, Ind. Born in 1814 in New Jersey; died in 1860, about age 46.
They had the following children:

2776	i.	Sharon J. (1834-)
2777	ii.	Perlina E. (1836-)
2778	iii.	Emma C. (1842-)
2779	iv.	Marietta (1845-)
2780	v.	Alice M. (1849-)

1957. Marriett COBB. Born on 18 Dec 1808. On 22 Aug 1833 when she was 24, she married **William S. DART**. Born in 1805.

1958. Reuben Rice COBB. Born on 2 Jan 1811 in Polleys Landing, Fort Ann, Rutland Co., Vt.; died in Decatur, Ill. On 22 Mar 1842 when he was 31, he married **Amazette H. MORGAN** in Indiana. Born in 1814; died in Decatur, Ill.

1959. James Hartland COBB. Born on 20 Jan 1813.

1960. Royal Pinckney COBB. Born on 24 Jan 1815 in Polleys Landing, Fort Ann, Rutland Co., Vt. On 20 Dec 1842 when he was 27, he married **Ruth A. HOWARD** in Indiana. Born in 1820.

1961. Parolina COBB. Born on 29 Jun 1817 in Polleys Landing, Fort Ann, Rutland Co., Vt. On 25 Jul 1854 when Parolina was 37, she married **William B. STREET** in Mahaska, Iowa. Born on 12 Jul 1819 in Shawneetown, Ill.
They had one child:

2781	i.	Ida Maria

Line 7 – Descendants of Elizabeth Hill (continued)

1962. Jerome TERRY.[607] Born on 31 Dec 1821 in Granby, Hartford Co., Conn. Jerome died in Newport, Herkimer, N.Y. abt 1890, he was 68. In abt 1854 when he was 32, he first married **Lucia Ann WILCOX** in Granby, Hartford Co., Conn. Born in 1825. Lucia Ann died in 1857, she was 32.
They had one child:
   2782   i.   Frederick C. (1855-~1930)
Jerome second married **Caroline A. GRIFFIN**. Born in 1838; died in 1920, she was 82; apparently d.s.p.

Line 8 – Descendants of John Hill (continued)

1963. Frederick BROOKS. Born on 12 Aug 1803 in Redfield, Oswego, N.Y.; died in Oskosh, Wisc.
1964. Samuel L. BROOKS. Born on 9 Jul 1805 in Redfield, Oswego, N.Y. Samuel L. died in Oskosh, Winnebago Co., Wisc. in 1897, he was 91.
1965. Amos BROOKS. Born on 24 Aug 1807 in Redfield, Oswego, N.Y. Amos died in Redfield, Oswego, N.Y. on 1 Nov 1850, he was 43.
1966. Dr. Sheldon BROOKS.[608] Born on 20 May 1811 in Redfield, Oswego, N.Y.; died in Winona, Winona, Minn. on 19 May 1883, he was 71. Physician, State Representative, County Commissioner. On 5 Mar 1844, when he was 32, he married **Jeanette RANNEY** in Smithville, Chenango Co., N.Y. Born in 1811; died in 1894, about age 83.
They had the following children:
   2783   i.   George Sheldon (1845-1861)
   2784   ii.   Lester Ranney (1847-1902)
   2785   iii.   Dwight Frederick (1849-1930)
   2786   iv.   Anson Strong (1852-1937)
1967. Sarah BROOKS. Born in 1814. Sarah died in 1895, she was 81. Her married name is in the Notes for her brother, Dr. Sheldon Brooks. Sarah married _____ **McKINNEY**.
-------------------------------[609]

1968. Susan HILL died in 1806.
1969. Riley HILL.
1970. Milo HILL.
1971. Polly HILL. Born in 1808; died in Ellisburg, Jefferson Co., N.Y., 1 Nov 1892, about 84, and was buried in Mannsville, N.Y. She m. **Hiram WHEELER**.
1972. Sophronia HILL.
1973. Julie HILL.
1974. Lorinda HILL.
1975. Clorinda HILL. Born in 1823. Clorinda died in Mannsville, N.Y. on 6 Sep 1905, about age 82. Buried in 1905 in Mannsville, N.Y.
1976. Matilda HILL.
1977. Orpha HILL.
1978. Rhoda HILL.
1979. John William HILL,[610] eldest child of John Henry and Sarah Ann (Haight) Hill, was born at Kossuth, Des Moines County, Iowa, 27 September 1850; died at Cherryville, Montgomery County, Kansas, 17 June 1941. In 1875, when he was twenty-four years old, he married **Mary Ellen FOX**, a stepdaughter of Sam Wilder, in the home of a Methodist pastor. They had a son, William Henry, and then, before the child was two years old, John William deserted his wife. She returned to the Wilder family and moved to Montana with them; she died in 1946 and is buried in Billings, Montana. She apparently took her son to Montana, for he died in Miles City, Montana, in 1969.

    In the meantime, John William Hill had been operating a saw mill near Oquaqua, Iowa. In 1876, he moved to Medicine Lodge, Kansas, where he homesteaded on government land and hauled freight from the nearest rail point, which was in Wichita. After hunting buffalo and skirmishing with Indians, he returned to Des Moines County, Iowa, in 1879 and worked in a sawmill until 1882, when he married again and began to operate a farm. He is said to have owned and operated the first threshing outfit and did the first plowing in Louisa County, Iowa. He also purchased land on the Mississippi River bank, where he operated a sawmill and floated cut timber to factories in Burlington and Fort Madison. He shipped the sawmill to Oklahoma and he remained there until 1902, when he moved on to Cherryville, Kansas.

For a time, he operated well drilling machinery in Cherryville and Coffeyville, Kansas and in the oil fields of Nowala, Oklahoma. He then purchased a ranch near Holly, Colorado, but in 1921 he disposed of this property and moved again, to a large tract of land near Garden City, Kansas. His second wife, the former Laura Jane Miller, died in 1927 in Tulsa, Oklahoma, having given birth to eight children. Near the end of his life, he returned to Cherryville, where he died in 1941.

John and Mary Ellen (Fox) Hill had one child:

2787	i.	William Henry (1875-1969)

On 18 May 1882 when John William Hill was 31, apparently without divorcing his first wife, he married (2) **Laura Jane MILLER** in Shawnee, Okla.; born 26 Aug 1860 in Mercer Co., Ill.; died in Tulsa, Okla. on 22 Dec 1927, she was 67. They had the following children:

2788	i.	Anna Pearl (1884-1967)
2789	ii.	Emily Christine (1888-1958)
2790	iii.	Frances Esther (1889-1963)
2791	iv.	Ruth Elizabeth (1891-)
2792	v.	John Thomas (1893-)
2793	vi.	Edith Blanch
2794	vii.	Arthur Miller (1898-)
2795	viii.	Josephine (1904-)

1980. James Riley HILL. Born on 12 Aug 1852 in Des Moines Co., Iowa. James Riley died on 24 May 1906, he was 53. Buried in 1906 in Sperry, Des Moines Co., Ia. His spine was injured in a fall from a wagon. James Riley married **Malinda J. CALLOWAY**. Born in 1869. Malinda J. died on 3 Feb 1890, she was 21. Mother of 1; she died at age 21 y, 6 m, 8 d.

2796	i.	Ester M. (1887-)

1981. Cornelius Haight HILL. Born on 9 May 1854 in Des Moines Co., Iowa. Cornelius Haight died on 23 Jun 1933, he was 79. On 14 Jun 1876 when Cornelius Haight was 22, he married **Louise Jane "Luella" "Ella" FOX**, in Cairo, Ill. Born on 15 Aug 1855 in Iowa; died 25 Aug 1933, she was 78. They had the following children:

2797	i.	Mary Jane (1880-1904)
2798	ii.	William John (1877-)
2799	iii.	Nellie (1882-)
2800	iv.	Maude Leoto (1884-)
2801	v.	Marguerite Louise "Maggie" (1885-1959)
2802	vi.	Ada Victoria (1889-)
2803	vii.	Bessie Lyle (1891-)

1982. Esther Ann HILL.[611] Born on 19 Mar 1857 in Des Moines Co., Iowa. Esther Ann died in Independence, Ore. on 12 Mar 1946, she was 88. She was the last living pensioner of the War of 1812 and was an "honor member" of the Daughters of 1812. Esther Ann married **James MORGAN**. Born in 1853 in Alton, Madison Co., Ill. James died in Independence, Ore. in 1945, he was 92. He was a tile factory worker in 1880.

They had the following children

2804	i.	Jesse Riley (1893-)
2805	ii.	?

1983. Eben B. HILL, Jr. (aka Ebben or Ebon), son of Ebben Hill Sr. and his wife, the former Mrs. Ruth Ann Barney, was born at Jefferson County, N.Y., in 1821; died in Oregon, 27 November 1968. He was married in 1845 in Burlington, Iowa. He then moved to Ohio, but he soon went west to Oregon on the Oregon Trail, settling in Hillsboro, Oregon. He and his wife had six children, the youngest of whom was less than two years old when his wife died in 1856. She was buried near Rickreall, Polk County, Oregon.

On 4 Jan 1845 when Eben B. (aka Ebben, aka Ebon) was 24, he married **Elizabeth "Eliza" "Liza" HAIGHT**,[612] daughter of Cornelius A. HAIGHT & Abigail ATTWOOD, in Burlington, Des Moines Co., Ia. Born on 10 Jul 1825 in Ohio; died in Oregon on 27 Nov 1856, she was 31. She was buried in Polk Co., Ore.

They had the following children:

2806	i.	Armilda Abigale
2807	ii.	Annie
2808	iii.	Ester M.
2809	iv.	Larrisa
2810	v.	Lafayette F. (1855-1935)
2811	vi.	Vina

1984. John HILL. Born in 1823 in Jefferson Co., N.Y. On 1 Aug 1846 when John was 23, he married **Armilda HARPER**, in Des Moines [Co.?], Iowa.

1985. Harry "Hervey" HILL. Born in 1826 in Jefferson Co., N.Y.

1986. William HILL. Born in 1827 in New York state. William married _____ **BANTA**, daughter of Abraham BANTA.

1987. Lurissa HILL. Born in Jan 1829 in N.Y. Lurissa died in Kossuth, Iowa on 7 Aug 1855, she was 26. Buried in 1855 in Kossuth, Iowa. Unmarried, a teacher.

1988. Hiram HILL. Born in 1831.

1989. Francis HILL. Born in 1842.

1990. Judson HILL. Born in 1854.

1991. Luther HILL. Born in 1856.

1992. Ludlow HILL Jr. Born in 1821 in Ellisburg, Jefferson Co., N.Y. He is buried in Belleville, N.Y.

1993. Orin Rice HILL. Born on 11 Oct 1823 in Ellisburg, Jefferson Co., N.Y. Orin Rice died in Kenosha, Wisc. on 31 Jan 1908, he was 84. Orin Rice married **Susannah _____**.

1994. Lydia Case HILL. Born in 1825. Lydia Case died in Ellisburg, Jefferson Co., N.Y. on 18 Apr 1838, she was 13. Buried in 1838 in Belleville, N.Y.

1995. Ludlow Presly HILL. Born on 19 Oct 1829 in Ellisburg, Jefferson Co., N.Y. Ludlow Presly died in Kenosha, Wisc. on 10 Oct 1915, he was 85. He married **Cecelia SEAMAN**. Born on 30 Apr 1835; died in Wonewec, Wisc., 14 Jan 1900, she was 64.

They had one child:

2812	i.	William Wallace (1853-1949)

1996. Armanda HILL. Born in 1831 in Ellisburg, Jefferson Co., N.Y. Armanda died in Belleville, N.Y.

1997. Abigail Amanda HILL. Born on 4 Feb 1832 in Ellisburg, Jefferson Co., N.Y. Abigail Amanda died in Wonewec, Wisc. on 12 Nov 1869, she was 37. In about 1850 when Abigail Amanda was about 17, she first married **Robert Ludlow ALCOTT** in Berrington, Ill. Born on 3 May 1828 in England.

They had one child:

2813	i.	Lydia Abi (1851-1922)

Abigail Amanda second married **John L. ROWIN**.

1998. William Riley HILL. Born on 24 Jan 1835 in Ellisburg, Jefferson Co., N.Y.

1999. Abigail "Abi" HILL. Born on 30 Oct 1836 in Jefferson Co., N.Y.; died in Wonewoc, Wisc. on 26 Sep 1916, she was 79. Occupation: One reference says she, not her sister Abigail Amanda, was m. to Robert Alcott. On 1 Jan 1856, when she was 19, she married **John Leroy ROWIN**. Born on 12 Mar 1832 in Ft. Winnebago, Wisc.

They had the following children:

2814	i.	Orilla (1861-)
2815	ii.	Orin (1861-)
2816	iii.	John (1862-)
2817	iv.	Abi (1865-)
2818	v.	Cecelia (1867-)

2819	vi.	Ladue (1869-)
2820	vii.	Lafayette (1872-)
2821	viii.	Bell (Lillian) (1874-)
2822	ix.	Eugennie (1878-)

2000. Jedediah HILL. Born on 11 Nov 1839 in St. Charles, Ill. Jedediah married **Eliza SEAMAN**, aka Eliza Malissa Shaw.

2001. Abigail LEONARD. Born on 21 Jan 1815; died in Ellisburg, Jefferson Co., N.Y. on 21 Feb 1838, she was 23. Buried in 1838 in Ellisburg, Jefferson Co., N.Y. She was adopted by Jedediah and Abigail (Kilby) Hill after her mother died 5 days after she was born.

2002. Henry HILL. Born on 20 Jan 1827 in Ellisburg, Jefferson Co., N.Y.; died in Independence, Ore., and was buried near there. He came by wagon train from St. Joseph, Mo., to Oregon in 1847; was a founder of Independence, Ore.; State Senator; and in Oregon Militia in Civil War. On 14 Jul 1851 when he was 24, he married **Martha Ann VIRGIN**. Born on 18 Dec 1834 in Kentucky.
They had the following children:

2823	i.	Roseltha
2824	ii.	Ladue
2825	iii.	Reason
2826	iv.	Elizabeth (-2010)
2827	v.	Lucy (-2010)
2828	vi.	Nelly
2829	vii.	Homer
2830	viii.	Verd
2831	ix.	Garlin

2003. Emily Welthy HILL. Born in 1826 in Ellisburg, Jefferson Co., N.Y. Emily Welthy died in Coffeyville, Kansas on 21 Apr 1875, she was 49. Emily Welthy married **Asa Wakefield BURBANK**.
They had one child:

2832	i.	Lurissa Rosalia (1845-1924)

2004. Abigail CRITTINDEN.

2005. Fred E. BOICE. Born in 1841.

2006. Helen Cornelia BOICE. Born on 3 Feb 1843. Helen Cornelia died on 30 Apr 1864, she was 21. Buried in 1864 in Henderson, N.Y.

2007. Charlotte Alida BOICE. Born on 23 Jan 1848. Charlotte Alida died on 4 Jun 1868, she was 20. Buried in 1868 in Henderson, Jefferson Co., N.Y.

2008. Perhaps sons and daughters of Phineas and Philura (Norton) BACON.[613]
--------------------------------[614]

2009. Laura BARBER. Born on 16 Jan 1794 in Simsbury, Hartford Co., Conn. Christened on 30 Jan 1883. On 11 Jul 1811 when Laura was 17, she married **Maxon GODFREY**.

2010. Sylvia BARBER. Born on 4 Nov 1887 in Erie, Pa.

2011. Milo R. BARBER. Born on 12 Nov 1803 in Loundon, Berkshire, Mass.
Milo R. married Miranda **Orilla BUTLER**. Born on 10 Apr 1811 in Wyndham, N.Y. Miranda Orilla died in Silver Lake, Ind. on 8 Dec 1886, she was 75. Occupation: Mother of 10.
They had the following children:

2833	i.	Abi Orville (1831-)
2834	ii.	Charles I. (1833-)
2835	iii.	Saphronia (1835-)
2836	iv.	Myron F. (1837-)
2837	v.	Milo R. (1843-)
2838	vi.	Calvin S. (1843-)
2839	vii.	Sylvester (1845-)

2840	viii.	George M. (1849-)
2841	ix.	Edwin Seward (1851-)
2842	x.	Theron L. (1857-)

2012. Nancy Case BARBER. Born on 12 Jun 1809 in Hartford Co., Conn. On 11 Sep 1826 when Nancy Case was 17, she married **Richard ADAMS**, in Sheldon, Genesse, N.Y.

2013. Myron Finch BARBER. Born on 21 Sep 1811 in Sheldon, Genesse, N.Y. Myron Finch died in Fort Wayne, Allen Co., Ind. on 26 Dec 1900, he was 89. Myron Finch first married **Margaret S. McNAUGHTON**. On 14 Mar 1836 when Myron Finch was 24, he second married **Jane SUTTENFIELD**, in Fort Wayne, Allen Co., Ind. Born in 1819 in Fort Wayne, Allen Co., Ind. They had the following children:

2843	i.	Lucius (1842-)
2844	ii.	Sylvia (1844-)
2845	iii.	Myron C. (1845-)
2846	iv.	Elsie A. (1847-)
2847	v.	Eliza J. (1849-)

2014. Gordon Trumbull HURLBUT. Born on 5 Jul 1807.

2015. Chauncey Butler HURLBUT.

2016. Rhonda Lucretia HURLBUT.

2017. Talcott Ledyard HURLBUT.

2018. Maria SADD. Born in 1802. Maria married **Jerot SUTHERLAND**.

2019. William Chauncey SADD. Born in 1806; died in Austerberg, O. in 1831, he was 25.

2020. Julia Warner SADD. Born in 1808 in East Windsor, Hartford Co., Conn. Julia Warner married **Asa JOHNSON**.

2021. Corinne Gilmore SADD. Born in 1801. Corinne Gilmore married **Joseph M. SADD**.

2022. George Franklin SADD. Born in 1816. George Franklin married **Laura ARMSTRONG**.

2023. Deacon Lucius BARBOUR.[615] Born on 26 Jul 1805 in Canton, Hartford Co., Conn. Lucius died in Hartford, Hartford Co., Conn. on 10 Feb 1873, he was 67. On 23 Apr 1840 when Lucius was 34, he married **Harriet Louise DAY**, daughter of Deacon Albert DAY & Louise CHAPIN, in Hartford, Hartford Co., Conn. Born on 2 Feb 1821. Harriet Louise died on 26 Sep 1886, she was 65. They had the following children:

2848	i.	Harriet Louise (1843-1848)
2849	ii.	Lucius Albert (1846-1922)
2850	iii.	Mary Adelia (1851-1851)
2851	iv.	Hattie Day (1860-)

2024. Eveline G. BARBOUR.[616] Born on 22 Jul 1807 in Benton, Ill. In 1824 when Eveline G. was 16, she married **Abel G. BUELL**.

2025. Edwin Case BARBOUR. Born on 26 May 1810. In 1834 when Edwin Case was 23, he first married **Harriet Newell HINMAN**. Born on 17 Jul 1816 in Lee, Mass. Harriet Newell died on 23 Jan 1865, she was 48. They had the following children:

2852	i.	Mary (1834-)
2853	ii.	George (1836-)
2854	iii.	?
2855	iv.	Hattie N. (1844-)
2856	v.	Grovie (1844-)
2857	vi.	Edward (1844-)

In 1867 when Edwin Case was 56, he second married **Widow Ann Maria HINKLEY**.

2026. Selden BARBOUR. Born on 5 Oct 1813. Selden died on 20 Apr 1814.

2027. Fanny Maria BARBOUR. Born on 7 Feb 1815. Fanny Maria married **Lawrence S. PARKER**.

2028. Fidelia Gates BARBOUR. Born on 16 Mar 1817. Fidelia Gates died on 27 Jun 1900, she was 83. Fidelia Gates married **George C. BALDWIN**.

2029. Herschell BARBOUR. Born on 1 Apr 1819. Herschell died on 22 Apr 1819.

2030. Theodore Dwight BARBOUR. Born on 28 Jun 1820 in New York. Theodore Dwight died on 2 Oct 1890, he was 70. On 5 Aug 1850 when Theodore Dwight was 30, he married **Angeline DODGE**. Born on 22 Sep 1819. Angeline died on 20 Jul 1902, she was 82.

They had the following children:

2858	i.	Mary Alice (1852-)
2859	ii.	Clara Agnes (1854-)
2860	iii.	Lucia Ella (1855-)
2861	iv.	Eugene Thomas (1857-)
2862	v.	William Everett (1859-)
2863	vi.	John James (1861-)

2031. Silvia BARBOUR. Born on 28 Jan 1822. Silvia died on 12 Feb 1822.

2032. Goodrich Hollister BARBOUR. Born on 28 Jun 1824. Goodrich Hollister died in Cincinnati, Hamilton Co., Ohio on 19 Dec 1901, he was 77. On 27 Nov 1851 when Goodrich Hollister was 27, he married **Harriet Caroline WARD**, in Leicester, Mass. Born on 6 Nov 1826 in Marietta, Washington Co., O. Harriet Caroline died in Marietta, Washington Co., O. on 21 Mar 1917, she was 90.

2033. John Newton BARBOUR. Born on 22 Jun 1828 in New York; died on 10 Apr 1874, he was 45. John Newton married **Electa HOUGHTON**. Born in 1832 in Michigan; died in 1906, she was 74.

They had the following children:

| 2864 | i. | Hattie |
| 2865 | ii. | Theresa |

2034. Theron Laselle BARBOUR. Born on 20 Feb 1832. Theron Laselle died on 21 Jul 1864; he was 32, and "died unmarried."

2035. Juliet Louise BARBOUR. Born on 28 Sep 1834. Occupation: Married three times; mother of 4 by her first husband. On 22 Aug 1857 when Juliet Louise was 22, she first married **George Gibbs DAVIS**. Born on 26 Oct 1834. George Gibbs died in Varysburg, Wyoming.

They had the following children:

2866	i.	George Monroe (1859-)
2867	ii.	Frederick Charles (1861-)
2868	iii.	Caroline Julia (1862-)
2869	iv.	Theron Dexter (1865-)

Juliet Louise second married **Hiram PECK**.

Juliet Louise third married **Noel MATTISON**.

2036. Cynthia Maria CASE. Born on 6 Jun 1806 in New Hartford, Litchfield Co., Conn. Cynthia Maria died on 12 Dec 1888, she was 82. On 8 Mar 1828 when Cynthia Maria was 21, she married **Israel JONES**. Born on 5 Nov 1801. Israel died in Jul 1846, he was 44.

They had one child:

| 2870 | i. | Lucius Wadsworth (1829-) |

2037. Clarissa CASE. Born on 5 Aug 1808 in New Hartford, Litchfield Co., Conn. Clarissa died in New Hartford, Litchfield Co., Conn. on 8 Aug 1890, she was 82. Married twice; two children by 1st husband, who may have been a relative but the connection is not apparent in Ancestry.com. On 3 May 1830 when Clarissa was 21, she first married **Hiram BARBER**, in New Hartford, Litchfield Co., Conn. Born in 1803 in Harwinton, Conn. Hiram died bef 1852.

They had the following children:

| 2871 | i. | Ellen (1833-) |
| 2872 | ii. | Hiram Lysander (1835-) |

In 1852 when Clarissa was 43, she second married **Judson WADSWORTH**. Born in 1797 in Becket, Mass. Judson died in Winsted, Mass. on 5 Jan 1882, he was 85.

2038. Erastus CASE. Born 25 Sep 1810 in New Hartford, Litchfield Co., Conn.; died 1 Jul 1813, age 2.

2039. Mary Ann CASE. Born on 28 Jan 1816 in New Hartford, Litchfield Co., Conn. Mary Ann died on 19 May 1890, she was 74. On 9 Nov 1837 when Mary Ann was 21, she married **Henry Hubbard**

BARTLETT, in New Hartford, Litchfield Co., Conn. Born on 7 Mar 1813. Henry Hubbard died on 19 Feb 1890, he was 76.
They had the following children:
    2873   i.   Katherine Jane (1847-)
    2874   ii.   Mary Louise (1850-)

2040. John Griswold CASE. Born on 5 Jun 1818 in New Hartford, Litchfield Co., Conn. John Griswold died on 26 Jul 1879, he was 61. John Griswold married **Lucy Ann STODDARD**.

2041. Austin Barbour CASE.

2042. Calvin CASE.

2043. Child CASE.

2044. George Washington CASE.

2045. Harriet Mabel CASE.

2046. Laura Ann CASE.

2047. Sherman Hurlbut CASE.

2048. Elizabeth BARBER. Born on 25 Jan 1817; died on 29 Sep 1819, she was 2.

2049. Helen M. BARBER. Born on 6 Feb 1826. Helen M. married **Henry SPENCER**.

2050. Jane BARBER. Born on 28 Jan 1828. In 1848 when Jane was 19, she married **Edward ROOT**. Born on 31 Dec 1825.

2051. Julia BARBER. Born on 6 Jun 1832. Julia married **Wales TERRELL**. Born in Bethany, Conn.

2052. John Austin BARBER. Born on 11 Jul 1830.

2053. Henry Watson BARBER. Born on 4 Sep 1831.

2054. Mary J. BARBER. Born in 1834. Mary J. died in 1834.

2055. James Edwin BARBER. Born on 1 Jul 1842.

2056. Benjamin BARBER. Born in 1845. Benjamin married **Sabra HAMMOND**.

2057. Orin NOBLE. Born on 14 Dec 1800 in Simsbury, Hartford Co., Conn. Orin died in Franklin, Ohio on 11 Aug 1844, he was 43. On 24 Apr 1825 when Orin was 24, he married **Catherine Elizabeth PRESCOTT** in Litchfield, Woodbury, Conn. Born on 6 Mar 1800 in Litchfield, Woodbury, Conn. Catherine Elizabeth died on 19 Feb 1875, she was 74.
They had the following children:
    2875   i.   Edward Case (1827-)
    2876   ii.   Henry T. (1829-)
    2877   iii.   John Jonathan (1830-)
    2878   iv.   Mary E. (1832-)
    2879   v.   Lucretia A. (1835-)
    2880   vi.   Lester (1837-)
    2881   vii.   Emily E. (1840-)
    2882   viii.   Luther B. (1842-)

2058. Lester NOBLE. Born on 19 Jan 1802 in Simsbury, Hartford Co., Conn. Lester died in Juneau, Dodge Co., Wisc. on 16 Dec 1850, he was 48. On 20 Oct 1828 when Lester was 26, he married **Emily HUMPHREY**. Born on 5 Oct 1806 in Hartford, Hartford Co., Conn.
They had the following children:
    2883   i.   Eliza Jane (1832-)
    2884   ii.   William Jonathan (1833-)
    2885   iii.   Henry Lester (1837-)
    2886   iv.   Susan Delphine (1839-)
    2887   v.   Emily A. (1848-)

2059. Josiah BARBER. Born on 27 Aug 1807 in Canton, St. Lawrence Co., N.Y. On 13 Feb 1831 when Josiah was 23, he married **Nancy Maria PIERCE** in Canton, St. Lawrence Co., N.Y. Born on 18 May 1809 in Canton, St. Lawrence Co., N.Y.
They had the following children:
    2888   i.   Elizabeth M. (1832-)

2889	ii.	Celestia S. (1833-)
2890	iii.	Phebe Jane (1835-)
2891	iv.	Charles B. (1837-)
2892	v.	Julia A. (1839-)
2893	vi.	Harriet P. (1841-)
2894	vii.	Ellen (1843-)
2895	viii.	Gilbert R. (1845-)
2896	ix.	Pliny W. (1849-)

2060. Emeline BARBER. Born on 1 Jan 1809 in Canton, St. Lawrence Co., N.Y. Emeline died on 18 Feb 1813, she was 4.

2061. Phoebe BARBER. Born on 22 Nov 1811 in Canton, St. Lawrence Co., N.Y. Phoebe died in Syracuse, Onondaga Co., N.Y. on 29 Dec 1845, she was 34. Phoebe married **Cornelius R. JONES.**

2062. Reuben BARBER. Born on 18 Feb 1814 in Canton, St. Lawrence Co., N.Y.

2063. Lorenzo Dow BARBER. Born on 11 Oct 1817 in Canton, St. Lawrence Co., N.Y. Lorenzo Dow died in Syracuse, Onondaga Co., N.Y. on 27 Sep 1887, he was 69. Lorenzo Dow married **Mary Ann OSTROM**.

2064. Hannah BARBER.

2065. Harriet Elizabeth BARBER.

2066. Jeanette BARBER.

2067. Luther Humphrey BARBER.

2068. Martha Jane BARBER.

2069. Mary BARBER.

2070. Phebe Maria BARBER.

2071. Sarah Elvira BARBER.

2072. Nelson L. BARBER. Born on 8 Mar 1819 in Canton, Hartford Co., Conn. Nelson L. died on 5 Jan 1885, he was 65. On 12 Sep 1846 when Nelson L. was 27, he married **Zilpah CASE**, daughter of Holcomb CASE & Jane CASE, in Canton, Hartford Co., Conn. Born on 14 Apr 1819 in Simsbury, Hartford Co., Conn. Zilpah died in Canton, Hartford Co., Conn. on 28 Feb 1866, she was 46.

The families of Nelson and Zilpha (Case) Barber are very intertwined: Nelson L. Barber and Zilpah Case are both descendants of Samuel and Sarah (Holcomb) Barber. In addition, her father Holcomb Case is descended from Joshua Holcomb & Mary Hoskins. He is also a great-great grandson of John and Sarah (Spencer) Case. Her mother, Jane Case, is the daughter of Silas Case and Mary Case. Silas Case is the son of Amos Chase and grandson of Bartholomew Chase. Mary Case is the daughter of John Case and Sarah Barber. Her grandparents are John Case & Abigail Humphrey and Samuel Barber & Sarah Holcomb. She is also a descendant of John Case & Sarah Spencer and Joshua and ___ (Sherwood) Holcomb.

They had the following children:

2897	i.	Edda Jane (1847-)
2898	ii.	Adelia (1852-)
2899	iii.	John (1858-)

2073. Gaylord BARBER. Born on 8 May 1824 in Canton, Hartford Co., Conn. Gaylord died in Canton, Hartford Co., Conn. on 21 May 1897, he was 73. On 8 May 1850 when Gaylord was 26, he first married **Catharine HAYDEN** in Barkhamsted, Litchfield Co., Conn. Born on 21 Mar 1826 in Barkhamsted, Litchfield Co., Conn. Catharine died on 12 May 1868, she was 42.

They had the following children:

2900	i.	Adelaide Julia
2901	ii.	Clarence Howard
2902	iii.	Florence Isabella
2903	iv.	Catherine Hayden (1863-)
2904	v.	Alison Hayden (1868-)

On 22 Nov 1868 when Gaylord was 44, he second married **Jerush TAYLOR.**

2074. John BARBER. Born on 6 Oct 1826 in Canton, Hartford Co., Conn. John died in Pacific City, Mills Co., Ia. on 10 Apr 1894, he was 67. John married **Maria MILLS**. Born in Dec 1828 in Canton, Hartford Co., Conn. Maria died in Montana on 22 Sep 1867, she was 38.
They had one child:
   2905   i.   Carrie Ann (1864-1944)

2075. Lemuel BARBER. Born on 16 Aug 1830 in Canton, Hartford Co., Conn. Lemuel died on 13 Feb 1892, he was 61. On 23 Nov 1854 when Lemuel was 24, he married **Susan Eveline CASE**, daughter of Freeman CASE & Sibyl BLISS, in Canton, Hartford Co., Conn. Born on 6 Jul 1834 in Canton, Hartford Co., Conn. Susan Eveline died in Bloomfield, Hartford Co., Conn. on 16 Sep 1913, she was 79. She is twice descended from John and Sarah (Spencer) Case on her father's side.
They had the following children:
   2906   i.   Lucy Amelia (1858-)
   2907   ii.   Cora Lillian (1865-)
   2908   iii.   Infant (1868-)

2076. Augustine Hayden BARBER. Born on 17 Jul 1809 in Connecticut. In 1836 when Augustine Hayden was 26, he married **Frances G. HAYDEN**. Born on 2 Sep 1817 in Windham, Pa. Frances G. died in Fulton, Rock, Wisc. on 9 Mar 1893, she was 75.
They had one child:
   2909   i.   Dorcas (1836-1897)

2077. Harriet Amelia BARBER. Born on 26 May 1824 in Connecticut. Harriet Amelia died in Cheotopa, Cherokee, Kansas, on 14 Apr 1878, she was 53. Ancestry.com says that Samuel Hull and his wife Harriet Barber died on the same day in Cherokee Co., Kansas. If this is true, I suppose it was a tragic accident. On 24 Nov 1842 when Harriet Amelia was 18, she married **Samuel P. HULL** in Candor, Tioga, N.Y. Born on 20 May 1818 in Candor, Tioga, N.Y. Samuel P. died in Chetopa, Cherokee, Kansas on 14 Apr 1878, he was 59.
They had the following children:
   2910   i.   Norman Augustine (1843-)
   2911   ii.   Sabrina (1846-)
   2912   iii.   Harriet Frances (1849-)
   2913   iv.   Wilmot Benjamin (1851-)
   2914   v.   Edwin Alonzo (1853-)
   2915   vi.   Charles Frederick (1859-)
   2916   vii.   Orson LaRue (1863-)

2078. Laura FOOTE. Born on 24 Jun 1809.

2079. Henry FOOTE. Born on 15 Sep 1813.

2080. Lucius FOOTE. Born on 5 Apr 1817.

2081. Eliza M. FOOTE. Born on 7 Mar 1823.

2082. John M. FOOTE. Born on 9 Feb 1827.

2083. Emerson H. Shaw HOSFORD. Born in 1832 in Connecticut. Emerson H. Shaw died in Simsbury, Hartford Co., Conn. in 1880, he was 48. A very late death of a descendant of Luke Hill in Simsbury.

2084. Henrietta BARBER. Born on 10 Jun 1837.

2085. Willard Jonathan BARBER. Born on 21 Nov 1850.

2086. William Lawrence HUMASON. Born on 10 Jan 1821. On 10 Apr 1846 when William Lawrence was 25, he married **Eunetia Minerva ENO** (2256), daughter of Jonathan ENO (1537) & Orpah Cassett ADAMS. Born on 29 Mar 1824 in Simsbury, Hartford Co., Conn. Eunetia Minerva died on 22 Aug 1915, she was 91. She is a descendant of David and Mary (Gillett) Eno. If she died in Simsbury, she must have been the last of the family who lived there.
They had the following children:
   2917   i.   Virgil Pettibone (1847-1905)
   2918   ii.   William Lawrence (1853-)

2087. Albert O. REED. Born in Apr 1844 in Connecticut. Albert O. died in Middletown, Middlesex Co., Conn. aft 1910, he was 65. Albert O. married **Gertrude GLADWIN**. Born in 1844. Gertrude died in 1925, she was 81. Occupation: Mother of 3.

They had the following children:

2919	i.	Edward T. (1879-)
2920	ii.	Albert Gladwin (1880-1952)
2921	iii.	Arthur (1882-)

2088. Isaiah Hendryx RILEY.[617] Born on 1 Mar 1797 in Burlington, N.Y. Isaiah Hendryx died in Caton, Steuben Co., N.Y. on 31 Dec 1855, he was 58. Before 1828 when Isaiah Hendryx was 30, he married **Experience INGRAHAM**. Born in 1801 in Chenango Co., N.Y.; died in Caton, Steuben Co., N.Y.

They had the following children:

2922	i.	Betsey
2923	ii.	3 male children
2924	iii.	3 other female children

2089. Simeon RILEY,[618] second son and second child of Josiah and Susannah (Hendryx) Riley, was born at Bennington, Vermont, 9 December 1799; died between 29 September 1848 (when he was recorded as being alive at the time of his father-in-law's death) and 29 June 1850 (when a deposition following his father's death on 22 June 1850 stated that Simeon was dead and that he was survived by heirs and next of kin his sons William Riley, Horatio Riley, James Riley and a daughter Catherine Adelia Riley, all of whom were under the age of 21). Simeon Riley probably died at Caton, New York, where he had lived with his wife and children. His father was living in Chenano County, N.Y. in the early nineteenth century, and Simeon probably spent his early years there. He was living at Painted Post, New York, in 1830 as the head of a family of two. At that time his neighbors included Ephraim Hill (Sr.) and William P. Hill; and Lewis Gridley, Aaron Gillet, and John Gillet lived nearby. In 1835 he and his wife were living on twenty-five unimproved acres of land near Caton, N.Y., with three young men and one unmarried woman. (The unmarried woman is unidentified. Simeon's only daughter was born the following year, and his youngest son was born about two years later.)

Simeon and his wife Katharine mortgaged 75 acres in Steuben County to John K. Calkins in 1833. In 1836 this property was sold at public auction to Joseph Gillett, Katharine's father, after Simeon and Katharine failed to make the necessary payments to Mr. Calkins. Both of them may already have been ill, for they died within five or six years. Their four young sons and their daughter were left to the care of their relatives, and as wards of Katharine (Gillett) Riley's father, Joseph Gillett.

He married, before 1830, **Katharine "Catherine" GILLETT**, daughter of Joseph and Katherine "Catherine" (Hunt) Gillett; born, probably at Corning, New York, between 1799 and 1810; died after 1839, probably in Painted Post, Steuben Co., N.Y. Simeon and Katharine (Gillett) had five children: William Alanzo (b. about 1830); Horace (about 1832-after 1876); James Gillett (1834-1871); Adelia Catharine (1836-1887); and Ransom (after 1837-1846/1848). Adelia married Charles W. Hill (person #1860 in this genealogy) and was the mother of George J. Hill, the Iowa Pioneer. William Alanzo, Horace, and Ransom were initially named as sons and heirs by Simeon Riley in his will, although William was removed as an heir by a codicil two years later, and Ransom was dead by the time his grandfather Gillett died in 1848. James was also named as an heir, although he was not identified as a son. Horace and James married and had descendants, while William and Ransom died young, without progeny.

Katherine GILLETT,[619] one of the four daughters and five sons of Joseph and Katherine (Hunt) Gillett, was born sometime between 1798/99 and 1815, probably in the area of Painted Post that is now known as Corning, Steuben County, New York; she died sometime after 1839 and prior to 1 August 1846. One of the first three children of Joseph and Katherine Gillett was a daughter, but she was probably not Katherine. It is more likely that Katherine was born between 1810 and 1815, since in the census of 1830 she is said to have been between 15 and 20 years of age. It is certain that her five children were all born after 11 October 1827, since all were under the age of 21 when her father made his will on

11 October 1848. This is confirmed by a deposition on 22 June 1850 which stated that all were still under the age of 21. Indeed, her first child was not born until at least 1830, inasmuch as no children were recorded as living with Katherine and her husband in the census of 1830. Her third child (a son, James) is known to have been born on 8 July 1834 and her fourth child (a daughter Adelia Catherine) was born on 24 July 1836, so her eldest child (William Alonzo) was probably born soon after the census was taken in 1830 and her second child (Horace) was probably born in about 1832. Her fifth child (a son, Ransom) was probably born in about 1838.

Katherine (Gillett) Riley died sometime between about 1838 (when her fifth child was probably born) and 1 July 1846 (when her father made his will, recording that she was deceased). Her husband, Simeon Riley, died sometime between 1 July 1846 (when Katherine Gillett's father named him as a surviving son-in-law) and 22 June 1850 (when a deposition was made to record the names of the children and heirs of his father, who died the previous day; his son, Simeon Riley, was said to be dead, although four of Simeon's children - William, Horace, James, and Catherine Adelia - were said still to be alive and under the age of 21).

They had the following children:

2925	i.	William Alanzo (~1830-)
2926	ii.	Horace (~1832->1876)
2927	iii.	James Gillett (1834-1871)
2928	iv.	Adelia Catharine "Delia" (1836-1887)
2929	v.	Ransom (>1837-1846)

2090. Betsey RILEY, daughter and second child of Josiah and Susannah (Hendryx) Riley, was born in 1802 in Bennington, Bennington Co., Vt.; died at Brookton, N.Y., 1 July 1886, about age 83. She married (1) at Oxford, N.Y., 23 January 1823, **Thomas B. MILLER**; died at Caton, Steuben Co., N.Y., 28 February 1841.

Thomas B. and Betsey (Riley) Miller had one child:

| 2930 | i. | Mary Amanda (1830-1830) |

She married (2) as his second wife, **Rev. Israel WOODWORTH**, Baptist minister of Caton, N.Y. He married (1) Rebecca Pembleton, who was the mother of his children; she died 24 January 1841.

2091. Esther Jackson RILEY.[620] Born on 1 Sep 1804 in Bennington, Vt. Esther Jackson died on 16 Dec 1861, she was 57. On 11 Feb 1832 when Esther Jackson was 27, she married **George J. [8] HILL** (895), son of Ephraim [2] HILL (375) & Charlotte {31} PRINCE. Born on 21 Aug 1805 in New Milford, Litchfield Co., CT. George J. [8] died on 3 Nov 1876, he was 71. Buried in Caton, N.Y.

They had the following children:

1869	i.	Mary Amanda [29] (1835-1840)
1870	ii.	Stilson Edward [30] (1838-1917)
1871	iii.	Joseph Gillett [31] (1842->1920)

2092. Josiah B. RILEY. Born on 7 Aug 1806 in Bennington, Bennington Co., Vt. Josiah and Experience Riley's indenture of 1839 was witnessed by Joseph Gillett. In an indenture of 28 Jan 1856 involving Erastus Riley and wife Fanny Jane Riley, Experience Riley is listed - but not Josiah. Josiah B. married **Experience ? (RILEY).**

2093. Helina RILEY. Born on 27 Feb 1808 in Bennington, Bennington Co., Vt. Helina died on 25 Sep 1809, she was 1.

2094. Fanna HENDRYX.[621] Born abt 1820. Fanna died abt 1820.

---------------------[622]

2095. John Martin WILCOX. Born on 12 Sep 1819 in Bristol, Ontario, N.Y. John Martin died in 1907, he was 87. In 1849 when John Martin was 29, he married **Maria BENNETT**. Born in 1831.

2096. Roxy Ann WILCOX. Born on 16 Aug 1821 in Bristol, Ontario, N.Y. **Roxy Ann WILCOX.** Born on 16 Aug 1821 in Bristol, Ontario, N.Y. On 12 Nov 1846 when she was 25, she married **John William REDMOND**. Born in 1822 in West Bloomfield, Mich.; died in Michigan in 1880.

They had one child:

| 2931 | i. | Josephine (1850-) |

2097. Amanda WILCOX. Born on 10 Dec 1826 in Bristol, Ontario, N.Y. In 1851 when Amanda was 24, she married **Andrew Jackson BENNETT**.

2098. Horace H. WILCOX. Born on 26 Mar 1831 in Bristol, Ontario, N.Y.; died 16 Aug 1832, age 1.

2099. Eleazer WILCOX. Born in 1831.

2100. Lewis WILCOX. Born in 1834. Lewis died in 1885, he was 51.

2101. Lucie Marie WILCOX. Born in 1836; died in 1914, she was about 78.

2102. Daniel W. (David) WILCOX. Born in 1839; died in 1913, about 74.

2103. Elizabeth WILCOX. Born in 1841. Elizabeth died in 1912, about 71.

2104. Robert WILCOX. Born in 1841.

2105. Mary WILCOX. Born in 1846. Mary died in 1914, she was about 68.

2106. Jedediah Bishop WILCOX. Born in 1851; died in 1944, about 93.

2107. Jedediah WILCOX. Born in 1838.

2108. Albert Harley WILCOX.

2109. Edgar WILCOX. Born in 1864.

2110. Lydia HOSKIN. Born on 22 Apr 1852 in Des Moines, Van Buren (now Polk), Ia. Lydia died in Des Moines, Van Buren (now Polk), Ia. on 21 Sep 1853, she was 1.

2111. Jasper HOSKIN. Born on 25 Jan 1854 in Des Moines, Van Buren (now Polk), Ia.; died there in Feb 1938, about 84.

2112. Inez HOSKIN. Born on 5 Mar 1857 in Des Moines, Van Buren (now Polk), Ia.; died there 19 Nov 1877, about 20. She apparently died without marrying.

2113. Neri Brownrigg HOSKIN. Born on 26 Dec 1859 in Des Moines, Van Buren (now Polk), Ia. Neri Brownrigg died in Cantril, Van Buren, Ia. on 13 Oct 1933, he was 73. Neri Brownrigg married **Harriet Cornelia HOLMES**, daughter of John HOLMES & Mary E. CRAIG. Born on 11 Feb 1867 in Jackson, Jackson, Ia. Harriet Cornelia died in Cantril, Van Buren, Ia. on 1 May 1959, she was 92.
They had the following children:

2932	i.	Earl (1885-)
2933	ii.	Carl (1887-)
2934	iii.	Stanley (1889-)
2935	iv.	Stella (1891-)
2936	v.	Affa (1893-1980)
2937	vi.	Neri (1895->1900)
2938	vii.	Garland (1898-)
2939	viii.	Mary (1901->1920)
2940	ix.	Flora (1904->1925)
2941	x.	Lesie V. (1907-1996)

From Ancestry.com

Fig. 7-1: Philo Coleman Barker (1803-1866), great-grandson of Josiah and Mary (Palmer) Richards; and his wife Mary G. (Adams) Barker (1814-1887)

Photos of Graceland Cemetery by George J. Hill

Fig 7-2: Charles W. Hill (1831-1923) and his wife, Adelia Catharine Riley (1836-1887), were fifth cousins, once removed. Charles was a descendant of Luke Hill Jr., and Adelia was a descendant of Luke Jr.'s brother John Hill. They are buried in Graceland Cemetery, Rowan, Iowa. They were the parents of George J. Hill (1857-1952).

Fig. 7-3: Hill Family Graves, Graceland Cemetery, Rowan, Iowa
Three generations of Hills are buried here, including Charles and Adelia (Riley) Hill,
Charles Hill's brother Harland and his sister Sarah, Charles and Adelia's son George J.
and his wife Jessie (Stockwell) Hill, Adelia's brother James Riley, and
George and Jessie's son Gerald and his wife Essie Mae.

Eighth Generation
The 5th-Great-Grandchildren

Line 1 – Descendants of Lydia Hill (continued)[623]

2114. William A. SANDERSON.

2115. Elisha SANDERSON. Born on 4 Jan 1803 in Ontario Co., N.Y. Elisha married **Junia WRIGHT.** Born on 29 Apr 1799 in New York state. Junia died on 7 Mar 1888 in Afton, Ia.
They had the following children:

2942	i.	Mary Ann (1824-1881)
2943	ii.	William Albert (1829-1893)
2944	iii.	Clarinda Jane (1833-1907)
2945	iv.	Adaliza L. (1836-1811)
2946	v.	Julia Dorleska (1839-)

2116. Elijah SEDEGWICK.

2117. Elizabeth SEDGWICK. Born on 3 Apr 1830 in Westmoreland, Oneida Co., N.Y. On 11 Mar 1858 when Elizabeth was 27, she married **Oliver S. HENDEE**, in De Kalb, Ill.

2118. Parker SEDGWICK.

2119. Wrestle W. SEDGEWICK. Born on 7 Jun 1827 in Westmoreland, Oneida Co., N.Y. Wrestle W. died in Sandwich, De Kalb Co., Ill. in Jul 1904, he was 77. In 1848 when Wrestle W. was 20, he married **Sarah Ann TOOMBS**, in Little Rock, Kendall Co., Ill. Born on 22 Nov 1827 in Portage, Wyoming Co., N.Y. Sarah Ann died in Sandwich, De Kalb Co., Ill. on 30 May 1895, she was 67.
They had the following children:

2947	i.	Caroline Gertrude
2948	ii.	Charles T.
2949	iii.	Harvey
2950	iv.	Jennie Mary
2951	v.	Agnes E. (1849-1928)
2952	vi.	S. Parker (1860-1912)
2953	vii.	Charles F. (1865-1915)

2120. Sarah Ann SEDGWICK. Born on 20 Jul 1833 in Westmoreland, Oneida Co., N.Y.; died in Bynumville, Chariton Co., Mo. on 24 Dec 1903, she was 70. On 27 Oct 1858 when she was 25, she married **William Henry BREWER**, in Sandwich, De Kalb Co., Ill. Born on 28 Nov 1831 in Broadalbin, Fulton Co., N.Y.; died in Chariton, Mo. on 3 Jun 1915, he was 83.
They had the following children:

2954	i.	Charles W. (1860-1952)
2955	ii.	Fannie Maria (1868-)
2956	iii.	Elizabeth (1863-)
2957	iv.	Ernest (1873-)

2121. Louisa Jane SEDGWICK. Born on 23 Dec 1835 in Westmoreland, Oneida Co., N.Y.

2122. Maria C. SEDGWICK. Born on 6 Jul 1838 in Licking, Ohio.

2123. James H. SEDGWICK. Born on 4 Aug 1840 in Licking, Ohio.

2124. Joseph White SEDGWICK. Born on 7 May 1846 in Little Rock, Kendall Co., Ill.

2125. Helen BARKER. Born in 1842.

2126. Wilbur Jay BARKER. Born on 13 Aug 1843 in North East, Erie Co., Pa.; died in Montcalm, Manitoba, Canada on 28 May 1918, he was 74. On 10 Jun 1880 when he was 36, he first married **Lovina Gertrude JUDD.** Born in 1850; died in 1887, she was 37.
They had the following children:

2958	i.	Ava Gertrude (1882-1945)
2959	ii.	Edna Belle (1883-1968)
2960	iii.	Elva May (1883-1912)
2961	iv.	Donald Josiah (1887-1950)

On 26 Apr 1893, he m. (2) **Caroline Leonard SMALL**, in Brookfield, Linn., Mo.; b. 1858.
They had the following children:

| 2962 | i. | Zelma Pearl (1894-) |
| 2963 | ii. | Martha Elizabeth (1895-1970) |

2127. Sarah BARKER. Born abt 1845 in Pennsylvania. Sarah married **Loring T. ROSS**. Born in 1847.
They had the following children:

| 2964 | i. | Jessie (1871-) |
| 2965 | ii. | Edith (1878-) |

2128. Mary BARKER. Born abt 1850 in Pennsylvania; d. in North East, Erie Co., Pa. in 1860, abt 10.

2129. Asa Putnam FRISBIE. Born on 28 Jan 1823 in Easton, Washington Co., N.Y. Asa Putnam died in Guthrie, Okla. on 22 Feb 1902, he was 79. He lived in LaFayette, Clinton, Co., Mo., in 1880. Asa Putnam married **Hannah HAZELWOOD**. Born in 1830. Hannah died in 1912, about 82.
They had the following children:

2966	i.	George Elbert (1850-1851)
2967	ii.	Emmarilla Josephine (1852-1946)
2968	iii.	Ida Lizette (1854-1944)
2969	iv.	Mary Isabella (1857-1920)
2970	v.	Minnie Maria (1860-1946)
2971	vi.	Alice Ann (1862-1885)
2972	vii.	Birdie Alvaretta (1865-1938)
2973	viii.	Rosella Putnam (1868-1853)
2974	ix.	Arthur Asa (1871-1926)

2130. Nancy Maria FRISBIE. Born on 27 Nov 1826 in Baldwinsville, Onondaga Co., N.Y. Nancy Maria died in Tecumseh, Johnson Co., Neb. on 27 Dec 1904, she was 78.

2131. Russell Levi FRISBIE. Born on 8 Apr 1830 in Baldwinsville, Onondaga Co., N.Y. Russell Levi died in Burlington, Coffee Co., Kansas on 5 Sep 1906, he was 76.

2132. Ann Deidamia FRISBIE. Born on 17 Nov 1838 in Milwaukee, Wisc. Ann Deidamia died in San Jose, Calif. on 2 Jun 1917, she was 78.

2133. Mary Josephine FRISBIE. Born on 8 Jan 1840 in Summit, Waukesha, Wisc.

2134. Orville Pattison CHUBB. Born on 11 Jun 1830 in Nankin, Wayne Co., Mich. Orville Pattison died in Sioux Falls, Minnehaha Co., So. Dak. on 15 Aug 1894, he was 64.

2135. Flora Augusta CHUBB. Born on 27 Aug 1832 in Nankin, Wayne Co., Mich. Flora Augusta died on 27 Feb 1914, she was 81.

2136. Alta Delight CHUBB. Born on 4 Aug 1834 in Nankin, Wayne Co., Mich. Alta Delight died in Chokio, Stevens Co., Minn. on 10 Jun 1908, she was 73.
Alta Delight married **? CALDWELL**.
They had the following children:

| 2975 | i. | Ida Lenore (1859-1947) |
| 2976 | ii. | Orville Clyde (1861-1935) |

2137. James Dillon CHUBB. Born on 24 Dec 1837 in Knox, Ohio. James Dillon died in Salem, Marion Co., Ore. on 16 Nov 1920, he was 82. James Dillon married **Mary Ann HOWE**. Born in 1839.
They had one child:

| 2977 | i. | Ervin Lyle (a k a Erving) (1863-1942) |

2138. Lucius Wolford CHUBB. Born on 20 Sep 1842 in Nankin, Wayne Co., Mich. Lucius Wolford died in Philadelphia, Pa. on 17 Aug 1863, he was 20. Buried in 1863 in Michigan. Union Army soldier in Civil War, fatally wounded at Gettysburg.

2139. Hannah Marietta CHUBB. B. 24 Mar 1845 in Nankin, Wayne Co., Mich.; d. there, 27 Jun 1849.

2140. Olive Sophia CHUBB. B. on 4 Aug 1847 in Nankin, Wayne Co., Mich.; d. in 1939, abt 91.

2141. Francis FRISBIE. Francis died in 1870.

2142. Lewis FRISBIE. Lewis died in 1842.

2143. Clark Lamartine FRISBIE.[624] Born on 23 Jun 1848 in Sweet Home, Texas. Clark Lamartine died in Sacramento, Sacramento Co., Calif. on 13 Dec 1930, he was 82. Records of three marriages are shown; there may have been more, for he was a mysterious person. On 15 Oct 1867 when Clark Lamartine was 19, he first married **Eliza LOVING (LOVERING)**, in Gonzales Co., Texas. They had one child:

2978	i.	Anna Laura (~1869-1926)

In 1880 when Clark Lamartine was 31, he second married **Elizabeth BARFIELD**. Born in 1852. They had the following children:

2979	i.	Sadie F. (1872-)
2980	ii.	Louis F. (1875-)
2981	iii.	Julius A. (1876-)
2982	iv.	Martha (1877-)
2983	v.	Ezra Clark (1885-)

In 1902 he may have third married **Clara Ellen DOYLE**, in California or Oregon. They had the following children:

2984	i.	? son of Clark Lamartine and Clara (Doyle)
2985	ii.	? son of Clark Lamartine and Clara (Doyle)

2144. John FRISBIE. Born in 1850.

2145. Julius Caesar FRISBIE. Born in 1854. Julius Caesar died in 1936, he was 82.

2146. Eugenia (Beatrice) FRISBIE. Born in 1858. Eugenia (Beatrice) died in 1892, she was 34.

2147. Prince William Albert FRISBIE.[625] Born on 20 Nov 1865 in Hamon, Gonzales Co., Tx. Prince William Albert died in Burnet Co., Tx. on 15 Sep 1915, he was 49. His photo is available on Ancestry.com.

2148. Joseph Henry BYINGTON.[626] Born on 25 Jan 1829 in Sheffield, Ashtabula Co., Ohio. Joseph Henry died in Neely, Power Co., Idaho on 22 Sep 1909, he was 80. He married twice, with overlapping births of 15 children by his two wives. On 25 Dec 1849 when Joseph Henry was 20, he first married **Nancy Mariah AVERY**, in Salt Lake City, Utah. Born on 25 Dec 1830 in Bradford, Mckean, Penna. Nancy Mariah died in Rockland, Power, Idaho on 15 Jan 1914, she was 83. Occupation: Mother of 11. They had the following children:

2986	i.	Nancy Maranda (1850-1876)
2987	ii.	Joseph Hezekiah (1852-1929)
2988	iii.	Oliver Milton (1855-1857)
2989	iv.	Sarah Augusta (1857-1922)
2990	v.	Hyrum Elliot (1859-1939)
2991	vi.	Elizabeth Ann (1862-1942)
2992	vii.	John Henry (1864-1940)
2993	viii.	Jeanette Sophia (1866-1940)
2994	ix.	Noah Samuel (1868-1869)
2995	x.	Ira Zina (1870-1935)
2996	xi.	William Alma (1873-1948)

On 27 Feb 1864 when Joseph Henry was 35, he second married **Hannah MOLLAND** in Salt Lake City, Utah. Born on 21 Jul 1838 in Liverpool, England. Hannah died in Annis, Idaho on 19 Nov 1889, she was 51. Hannah Molland's years of life and the birth years of some of her children overlaps the life of his first wife and the births of some of their children. I suppose that they were Mormons and that following the custom of polygamy, he was married to both women at the same time. They had the following children:

2997	i.	James Henry (1865-1930)
2998	ii.	Hannah Maria (1866-1931)

2999	iii.	Susan Elizabeth (1876-1956)
3000	iv.	John Parley (1880-1964)

2149. Hyrum Elliott BYINGTON. Born on 14 Oct 1830 in on Lake Erie, Ohio. Hyrum Elliott died in Downey, Bannock, Utah on 19 Apr 1901, he was 70. Hyrum Elliott married **Hannah Dyantha HARR**. Born on 3 Aug 1836 in Independence, Jackson, Mo. Hannah Dyantha died in Downey, Bannock, Utah on 7 Jul 1917, she was 80. Occupation: Mother of 8.
They had the following children:

3001	i.	Hyrum Norton (1861-)
3002	ii.	Joseph Henry (1862-)
3003	iii.	Stephen Elliot (1866-)
3004	iv.	Sarah Jane (1867-)
3005	v.	Hannah Elizabeth (1868-)
3006	vi.	Alexander (1873-)
3007	vii.	Rebecca Ann (1874-)
3008	viii.	Nora Isabelle (1876-)

2150. [Child] of Hyrum and Sarah (Holkins) BYINGTON. Born in 1833 in Kirtland, Lake Co., Ohio; died in Bath, Greene Co., Ohio on 8 Aug 1838, about age 5.

2151. Susan Augusta BYINGTON. Born on 25 Sep 1840 in Exeter, Scott Co., Ill. Occupation: Mother of 1. On 20 Aug 1854 when Susan Augusta was 13, she married **Stephen King WILBUR**, in Salt Lake City, Utah. B. 2 Jul 1832 in Providence, R.I.; died in Smoot, Unita, Wyo. on 2 Nov 1905, he was 73.

3009	i.	Susannah (1879-1974)

2152. Active Amelia BYINGTON. Born on 8 Feb 1819. Occupation: Mother of 4.
On 22 Oct 1839 when Active Amelia was 20, she married **Orville OLMSTED**.
They had the following children:

3010	i.	Cyrus
3011	ii.	Frances
3012	iii.	Helen
3013	iv.	Royal

2153. Hiram Smith BYINGTON. Born on 11 Jul 1820. Hiram Smith died on 7 Aug 1856, he was 36.

2154. Lucius Webster BYINGTON. Born on 20 Sep 1828.

2155. Augustus BYINGTON. Born on 27 Apr 1830 in Madison, Ohio. Augustus died in Plymouth, Iowa on 29 Mar 1911, he was 80. On 4 Jul 1854 when Augustus was 24, he married **Ann Eliza MOREY**, in Chicago, Ill. Born in 1830. Ann Eliza died in Plymouth, Iowa on 15 Feb 1901, she was 71.
They had the following children:

3014	i.	Walter Wells (1855-)
3015	ii.	Albert Webster (1856-)
3016	iii.	Edgar Seaburn (1858-)
3017	iv.	Frank Augustus (1861-)
3018	v.	Nelson Smith (Twin) (1862-)
3019	vi.	Nellie Amelia (Twin) (1862-)
3020	vii.	Alice Phoebe (1864-)
3021	viii.	Addie Julia
3022	ix.	Anna Eliza
3023	x.	Martha Luce (1874-)
3024	xi.	Carrie May (1877-)
3025	xii.	Howard Grant (1879-)

2156. Eri Leonard LANE. Born on 12 Jan 1824 in Cornwall, Litchfield Co., Conn. On 11 Jul 1852 when Eri Leonard was 28, he married **Catherine Rebecca SMITH**. Catherine Rebecca died in 1893.
They had the following children:

3026	i.	Florence Selina (1853-)
3027	ii.	Maria Elizabeth (1857-)

3028	iii.	William Edgar (1859-)
3029	iv.	Albert Harry (1861-)

2157. Lyman Jewell LANE. Born on 8 Jan 1827. Lyman Jewell died in Dec 1863, he was 36. In Jan 1850 when Lyman Jewell was 22, he married **Jane LINES.** Born on 21 Dec 1828.
They had the following children:

3030	i.	Harriet Louise (1850-)
3031	ii.	Alfred Henry (1859-)

2158. Alfred Henry LANE. Born in 1827.

2159. Mary Elizabeth LANE. Born in 1836. Occupation: Mother of 2. In 1859 when Mary Elizabeth was 23, she married **Sylvester M. SCOVILLE.** Born in 1815.
They had the following children:

3032	i.	Charles
3033	ii.	George H. (1861-)

2160. Augustus L. LANE.[627] Born on 27 Nov 1824 in Cornwall, Litchfield Co., Conn. Augustus L. died on 9 Jun 1893, he was 68. Resided in Goshen, Litchfield, Conn., in 1850. In 1845 when Augustus L. was 20, he married **Grace MANSFIELD.** Born in 1800. Grace died in 1852, she was 52.
They had the following children:

3034	i.	Bruce B. (1848-)
3035	ii.	Herbert (1849-1893)

2161. Lucia LANE. Born on 2 Jun 1829. Lucia married **Charles PECK.**

2162. John D. LANE. Born on 11 Feb 1831. John D. died in service, in the Civil War on 17 May 1864, he was 33. This was the date of the Battle of Adairsville, in Georgia. It is unknown if he died there, or somewhere else. John D. married **Nancy Ann WILLARD.**

2163. Charles LANE. Born in Sep 1834; died in Cornwall, Conn. 27 Nov 1839, he was 5.

2164. Elizabeth LANE. Born on 16 Jun 1843. Elizabeth died in Feb 1846, she was 2.

2165. Dimis Emeline TODD. Born on 11 Feb 1832. In 1852 when Dimis Emeline was 19, she married **William Wallace L'HOMMEDIEU.**
They had the following children:

3036	i.	Delos Gager (1857-)
3037	ii.	William Albert (1865-)

2166. Olive Ellen TODD. Born on 19 Nov 1834 in Liberty, N.Y. Olive Ellen died in Waterbury, Conn. Occupation: Mother of 3, two of whom had descendants. In 1855 when Olive Ellen was 20, she married **Darius HUMISTON**, in Liberty, N.Y. B. in 1833 in Southington, Conn.; died on 8 Aug 1886, he was 53.
They had the following children:

3038	i.	Warren Todd (1862-1938)
3039	ii.	Glenwood Carlisle (1859-1868)
3040	iii.	Emma Genevieve (1860-1942)

2167. Erastus W. TODD. Born on 5 Sep 1839. Erastus W. died in Trenton, Wayne, Mich. on 1 Jan 1890, he was 50. He married **Ann Jeannette BLAKESLEE.** B. 3 Nov 1841; d. 20 Aug 1891, age 49.
They had the following children:

3041	i.	Eva Adeline (1862-)
3042	ii.	Erwin Wallace (1864-)
3043	iii.	Jennie Laura (1866-)
3044	iv.	Frances Miriam (1871-)
3045	v.	Ethel Winona (1874-)
3046	vi.	Henry Leon (1878-)

2168. Luther Buckley TODD. Born on 8 Aug 1843. On 6 Sep 1870 when Luther Buckley was 27, he married **Caroline Maria PALMER.** Born on 15 Feb 1854.
They had the following children:

3047	i.	Lewis Irving (1872-)
3048	ii.	Florence Emeline (1887-)

2169. Elizabeth Eveline TODD. B. 11 Dec 1845 in Liberty, Sullivan, N.Y. On 1 Jan 1863 when she was 17, she married **Elisha Root NEWELL**, in Southington, Conn. B. 2 Apr 1830 in Southington, Conn.; died in Liberty, N.Y.

They had the following children:

3049	i.	Charles Munde (1863-)
3050	ii.	Eva Lovina (1865-)

2170. Elizabeth BARNES.

2171. Horace BARNES.

2172. Lucinda LANE. Born on 12 Mar 1834. Lucinda died on 12 Dec 1834.

2173. Robert Orange LANE. Born on 1 Dec 1836. Robert Orange died in Cedar Mountain, Conn. on 9 Aug 1862, he was 25.

2174. Ashhel Albert LANE. Born on 27 Mar 1838.

2175. Horace B. LANE. Born on 30 Aug 1842. Horace B. died on 23 Feb 1862, he was 19.

2176. Eugene LANE. Born on 17 Jan 1843 in Wolcott, New Haven, Conn.

2177. Miriam LANE. Born on 11 Dec 1844 in Wolcott, New Haven, Conn. Occupation: Mother of 1. On 18 Jun 1882 when Miriam was 37, she married **Joseph Francis SMITH**, in Bristol, Hartford Co., Conn. Born on 5 Feb 1843.

They had one child:

3051	i.	Donald Joseph (1883-1884)

2178. Frances LANE. Born on 29 Oct 1846 in Wolcott, New Haven, Conn. Occupation: Mother of 4. On 15 Apr 1878 when Frances was 31, she married **Emmett Albert CARLEY**, in Bristol, Hartford Co., Conn. Born on 28 Aug 1846.

They had the following children:

3052	i.	Horatio (1880-)
3053	ii.	Mabel Frances (1881-)
3054	iii.	Julius Munson (1884-)
3055	iv.	Russell Henry (1886-)

2179. Alice LANE. Born on 22 Oct 1853 in Wolcott, New Haven, Conn. Occupation: Mother of 9. Alice married **James Hulbert PRIOR**, in Bristol, Hartford Co., Conn. Born on 6 Jan 1855.

They had the following children:

3056	i.	Ethel Miriam (1878-)
3057	ii.	Orville George (1880-)
3058	iii.	Myrtle Elizabeth (1882-)
3059	iv.	James Murray (1884-)
3060	v.	Leland Jay (1886-)
3061	vi.	Harry (1888-)
3062	vii.	May (1890-)
3063	viii.	Iva Alice (1891-)
3064	ix.	Arline Rose (1893-)

2180. Jennie NORTON.

2181. Lydia NORTON.

2182. Lauren NORTON. Born on 4 Jan 1833 in Spafford, Onondaga, N.Y.

2183. Emily Caroline NORTON. Born on 14 May 1830 in Spafford, Onondaga, N.Y.

2184. Peres M. PICKETT. Born on 30 Jan 1843 in New York.

2185. Lafayette F. PICKETT. Born on 30 Jul 1846 in Michigan.

2186. Nancy ROYCE. Born on 16 Dec 1828 in Middlebury, Conn. Nancy died on 15 Sep 1906, she was 77. On 23 Mar 1845 when Nancy was 16, she married **William Augustus WILLOGHLY**.

2187. William Alauson ROYCE.

2188. Cecilia ROYCE. Born in 1832 in Waterbury, Conn. Cecilia first married **Walter LORD**. Cecilia second married **Lambert WOODING**. Born in 1811 in New Haven, New Haven Co., Conn.

They had the following children:

3065	i.	George
3066	ii.	William

2189. Lucinda N. NORTON. Born on 17 Oct 1834 in Bristol, Hartford Co., Conn.

2190. Hellin O. NORTON. Born on 26 Feb 1843.

2191. Ammon NORTON. Born in 1841.

2192. Lewis NORTON. Born in 1842.

2193. Andrew NORTON. Born in 1843.

2194. Oliver T. NORTON. Born on 4 Mar 1844.

2195. Eunice NORTON. Born in 1845.

2196. Sarah M. NORTON. Born on 6 Jun 1846.

2197. Mary NORTON. Born in 1847.

2198. Lydia NORTON. Born in 1848.

2199. Turchus NORTON. Born in 1849.

2200. Walter NORTON. Born in 1850.

2201. Addie NORTON. Born in 1851.

2202. Eliott NORTON. Born in 1852.

2203. Dwight Edward NORTON. Born on 13 Oct 1868 in Wolcott, New Haven, Conn.

2204. Jarius Stephen NORTON. Born on 21 Nov 1871 in Wolcott, New Haven, Conn.

2205. Nelson B. NORTON. Born on 12 May 1879 in Connecticut.

2206. Ira R. NORTON. Born in May 1882 in Connecticut.

2207. Elizabeth Mariah CAMP. Born on 23 Sep 1821 in Durham, Middlesex Co., Conn.

2208. Ebenezer Bates CAMP. Born on 7 Jun 1825 in Durham, Middlesex Co., Conn.

2209. James CAMP. Born in 1828 in Durham, Middlesex Co., Conn.

2210. Emily CAMP. Born in 1831 in Durham, Middlesex Co., Conn.

2211. Anna CAMP. Born in 1837 in Durham, Middlesex Co., Conn.

2212. Elmer Erastus GUERNSEY. Born on 30 Jan 1841 in Windsor, Broome Co., N.Y. Elmer Erastus died in Windsor, Broome Co., N.Y. on 19 Apr 1858, he was 17.

2213. Ahira Harry Johnson GUERNSEY. Born on 22 Dec 1842 in Windsor, Broome Co., N.Y. Ahira Harry Johnson died in Clebune, Johnson, Texas on 29 Jun 1919, he was 76.

2214. Elliott Birney GUERNSEY. Born on 7 Mar 1844 in Windsor, Broome Co., N.Y. Elliott Birney died on 6 Dec 1844 in Windsor, Broome Co., N.Y.

2215. Flora Ann GUERNSEY. Born on 29 Jun 1846 in Windsor, Broome Co., N.Y. Flora Ann died in Homer, Hamilton Co., Ia. on 14 Mar 1881, she was 34.

2216. Vesta R. GUERNSEY. Born on 17 Nov 1849 in Windsor, Broome Co., N.Y. Vesta R. died on 21 Jan 1850 in Windsor, Broome Co., N.Y.

2217. Amy Rosalia GUERNSEY. Born on 6 Dec 1850 in Windsor, Broome Co., N.Y. Amy Rosalia died in Spokane, Wash. on 24 Jun 1925, she was 74 .

2218. Charles Holbrook GUERNSEY. Born on 13 Jun 1852. Charles Holbrook died in 1930, age 77.

2219. Mary Arvilla GUERNSEY. Born on 9 Aug 1854 in Windsor, Broome Co., N.Y. Mary Arvilla died in Dewey, Okla. on 2 Oct 1920, she was 66. Occupation: Mother of 8. On 25 Feb 1873 when Mary Arvilla was 18, she married **Charles Edwin THOMAS**, in Sheldon, O'Brien Co., Ia. Born in 1852. Charles Edwin died in 1911, he was 59.
They had the following children:

3067	i.	Edna Viola (1874-1879)
3068	ii.	Elmer Elsworth (1878-1965)
3069	iii.	Edgar Louis (1880-1936)
3070	iv.	Charles Ernest (1883-1885)
3071	v.	Earnest L. (1885-)
3072	vi.	Frank Charles (1887-1958)
3073	vii.	Ernest Ray (1889-1955)
3074	viii.	Clarence Irwin (1893-1955)

2220. Orpha Jane GUERNSEY. Born on 10 Jul 1858 in Windsor, Broome Co., N.Y. Orpha Jane died in Denver, Colo. on 18 Jan 1937, she was 78.

2221. Eliada TUTTLE. Born on 2 Jul 1815.

2222. Samantha TUTTLE. Born on 15 Aug 1817.

2223. Huldah TUTTLE. Born on 28 May 1820.

2224. Elon Augustus TUTTLE.[628] B. on 7 Jan 1823 in Salisbury, Herkimer, N.Y.; d. in Clear Lake, Cerro Gordo Co., Ia., 7 Jan 1908, he was 85. On 9 Feb 1843 when he was 20, he first married **Orissa Caroline HUMPHERVILLE**, in New York. B. 20 Jan 1823 in Herkimer, N.Y.; d. in Clear Lake, Ia. on 14 May 1880, she was 57.

They had the following children:

3075	i.	Nellie L. (1844-1929)
3076	ii.	Harriet Eugenia
3077	iii.	Sylvia Jane
3078	iv.	Aldemer M.
3079	v.	Jeanette M.
3080	vi.	Lucien
3081	vii.	Sophia

On 8 Nov 1880 when Elon Augustus was 57, he second married **Anna PARSONS**, in Clear Lake, Cerro Gordo Co., Ia. Born on 8 Nov 1836. Anna died in Clear Lake, Cerro Gordo Co., Ia. on 8 Sep 1907, she was 70. No issue from this marriage.

2225. Alva Brockett TUTTLE. Born on 14 Jan 1825.

2226. Rhoda TUTTLE. Born on 16 Feb 1828.

2227. Marcus TUTTLE. Born on 10 May 1830.

2228. Rachel B. TUTTLE. Born on 28 Feb 1832.

2229. Mary Elvira MERRILL. Born in 1849 in Waterbury, Conn. Mary Elvira died in Ansonia, New Haven Co., Conn. aft 1900. Mary Elvira married **William PARMELEE**. Born in 1849.

2230. Charles MERRILL. Born in 1850 in Waterbury, Conn.

2231. Ellen Taylor MERRILL. Born on 31 Oct 1856 in Waterbury, Conn. Ellen Taylor died in Detroit, Wayne Co., Mich. on 25 Feb 1927, she was 70. Mother of 13, born between 1878 and 1897. On 4 Nov 1876 when Ellen Taylor was 20, she married **William Leroy WHITE**, in New York, N.Y. Born on 27 May 1857 in Hartford, Hartford Co., Conn.; died in Detroit, Wayne Co., Mich., 15 Feb 1927, he was 69.

They had the following children:

3082	i.	Edward Leslie (1878-1960)
3083	ii.	Howard Leroy (1880-1933)
3084	iii.	Percy Lewis (1881-1955)
3085	iv.	Walter Washburn (1883-1885)
3086	v.	Morris Hemingway (1885-1939)
3087	vi.	Merrill Washburn (1887-1951)
3088	vii.	Mary Almira (1889-1940)
3089	viii.	Alma Anna (1890-1985)
3090	ix.	William Wirt (1893-1896)
3091	x.	Twin Son (Twin) (1895-1895)
3092	xi.	Twin Daughter (Twin) (1895-1895)
3093	xii.	Harold (1896-1976)
3094	xiii.	Helen Augusta (1897-1963)

2232. Annie MERRILL. Born on 31 Dec 1858. Annie died in 1898, she was 39.

2233. Nelson Moses FRISBIE. Born in 1852. Nelson Moses died in 1949, he was 97.

2234. Frederick Augustus FRISBIE. Born in 1855. Frederick Augustus died in 1935, he was 80.

2235. Theron E. FRISBIE. Born in 1858. Theron E. died in 1926, he was 68.

2236. Frank Baldwin FRISBIE. Born in 1859.

2237. Harriet Elizabeth FRISBIE. Born in 1868. Harriet Elizabeth died in 1930, she was 62.

2238. William Hepworth GAYLORD. Born on 29 Jan 1844.
2239. Isaac Brown GAYLORD. Born on 25 Aug 1845 in Willoughby, Ohio. Isaac Brown died in Kansas City, Mo. on 7 Feb 1927, he was 81. Isaac Brown married **Lillian Ada BAILEY.** Born on 27 Feb 1848 in Cataragus, N.Y. Lillian Ada died in Kansas City, Mo. on 28 Jun 1933, she was 85. Mother of 12, who were born between 1866 and 1889.
They had the following children:

3095	i.	Fred (1866-)
3096	ii.	Hepworth A. (1868-1928)
3097	iii.	Nellie Ada (1870-)
3098	iv.	William B. (1872-)
3099	v.	Ray B. (1873-)
3100	vi.	Irene B. (1874-)
3101	vii.	Margaret Elsie (1878-)
3102	viii.	Mary D. (1880-)
3103	ix.	Chestley N. (1881-)
3104	x.	Lomar E. (1882-)
3105	xi.	Minnie H. (1885-)
3106	xii.	Laurence I. (1889-)

2240. Frederick Windslow GAYLORD. Born on 5 Jun 1848.
2241. Fremont GAYLORD. Born on 5 Jan 1856; died in Oxford, Wisc. on 26 Aug 1857, he was 1.
2242. Minnie GAYLORD.[629] Born on 11 Oct 1860. On 10 May 1882 when Minnie was 21, she married **Ellis P. MOORE**, in Waupun, Dodge, Wisc. Born in Oct 1858. No known descendants.
2243. Emma GAYLORD. Born on 26 Aug 1863. Emma married **Robert Henry ROBERTS.**
They had the following children:

| 3107 | i. | Catherine |
| 3108 | ii. | Gaylord |

2244. Monroe BARNES. Born in 1813 in Burlington, Hartford Co., Conn. Monroe married **Anne Eliza TOLBERT**. Born in Burlington, Hartford Co., Conn.
They had one child:

| 3109 | i. | Frank Monroe (1859-) |

2245. Ella Elizabeth FRISBIE. Born on 3 Oct 1846 in Burlington, Hartford Co., Conn. Ella Elizabeth died in 1934, she was 87. On 26 Jun 1870 when she was 23, she married **W. M. KEELING**, in Freeport, Stephenson, Ill. Born in Jan 1837 in Manchester, England; d. in Joliet, Ill. on 17 Jun 1895, he was 58.
They had the following children:

| 3110 | i. | Mary Frances (1872-) |
| 3111 | ii. | John Leslie (1883-) |

2246. Samuel FRISBIE. Born on 18 Feb 1850 in Burlington, Hartford Co., Conn. Samuel died in 1930, he was 79. Samuel married **Susan Ellen SMITH**. Born on 12 Jan 1856 in Freeport, Stephenson, Ill..
They had the following children:

3112	i.	Birdie Alice (1876-)
3113	ii.	Henry Case (1878-)
3114	iii.	Lottie May (1881-)
3115	iv.	Jessie Evelyn (1883-)
3116	v.	William (1889-)
3117	vi.	Hazel (1891-)
3118	vii.	John Carlton (1898-)

2247. Mary Marilla FRISBIE. Born on 4 Aug 1855 in Freeport, Stephenson, Ill. Mary Marilla died in 1939, she was 83. She married **Samuel Stern KAUFFMAN**, in Illinois. B. 13 Mar 1855 in Blair, Pa.
They had the following children:

| 3119 | i. | John Earl (1886-) |
| 3120 | ii. | Infant child of Samuel and Mary (Frisbie) |

2248. Horace Cornwall FRISBIE. Born on 16 Apr 1858 in Freeport, Stephenson, Ill. Horace Cornwall died on 15 Jan 1859 in Freeport, Stephenson, Ill.

2249. Leslie Almon FRISBIE. Born on 31 Aug 1861 in Freeport, Stephenson, Ill. Leslie Almon died in Freeport, Stephenson, Ill. on 9 Mar 1921, he was 59. On 20 May 1892 when Leslie Almon was 30, he married **Alice Elizabeth GOCHENOUR,** in Freeport, Stephenson, Ill. Born on 10 Jun 1863 in Freeport, Stephenson, Ill. Alice Elizabeth died in Freeport, Stephenson, Ill. on 3 Feb 1950, she was 86.
They had the following children:

| 3121 | i. | Paul Leslie (1897-) |
| 3122 | ii. | Harold John (1899-) |

2250. John Case FRISBIE. Born on 17 Aug 1863 in Joliet, Ill. John Case died in Silver Creek, Stephenson, Ill. on 15 Feb 1915, he was 51. On 4 Jan 1882 when John Case was 18, he married **Azuba Ann SOPER**, in Freeport, Stephenson, Ill. Born on 7 May 1854 in Freeport, Stephenson, Ill. Azuba Ann died in 1921, she was 66. Occupation: Mother of 1.
They had one child:

| 3123 | i. | Florence (1882-) |

Line 2 – Descendants of Mary Hill (continued)[630]

2251. Ira Hayden ALLEN. Born on 14 Dec 1842. Ira Hayden died on 13 Feb 1863, he was 20. He died while he was a student at a school in Norwich, Vt.

2252. Charles Parsons ALLEN. Born on 16 Feb 1844. Charles Parsons died on 30 May 1877, he was 33. Occupation: Lawyer; a member of the bar. Education: at the Academy in Barton, Vt.; at military school in Norwich; and law in Albany, N.Y. On 1 Feb 1876 when Charles Parsons was 31, he married **Lizzie PULSIFER**. Born in 1854. Lizzie died on 4 Aug 1877, she was 23.
They had one child:

| 3124 | i. | Lizzie Pulsifer (1877-1899) |

2253. Mary Parsons ALLEN. Born on 17 Aug 1848; died 29 Aug 1849, she was 1.

2254. Sarah Maria ALLEN. Born on 18 Oct 1850. Education at Miss Willard's Seminary for Young Ladies. She resided in Brookline, Mass., in 1907.

2255. Mary Frances ALLEN.[631] Born on 31 Jul 1854. Mary Frances died on 17 May 1873, she was 18. Education: at Miss Willard's Seminary. She died seven days after giving birth to her first child. Mary Frances first married **Eben GAYNOR**. Born in 1871.
They had one child:

| 3125 | i. | Charles (~1898-) |

On 2 Jan 1872 when Mary Frances was 17, she second married **Sydney W. (or Thomas Wentworth) BEAUCLERK (or BEANDUK)**.[632] Born on 21 Mar 1847. Sydney W. (or Thomas Wentworth) died in 1938, he was 90.
They had one child:

| 3126 | i. | Mary Frances (1873-1931) |

2256. Eunetia Minerva ENO.[633] Born on 29 Mar 1824 in Simsbury, Hartford Co., Conn. Eunetia Minerva died on 22 Aug 1915, she was 91. Occupation: Mother of 2. She is a descendant of David and Mary (Gillett) Eno. On 10 Apr 1846 when Eunetia Minerva was 22, she married **William Lawrence HUMASON** (2049), son of Jeremiah HUMASON & Roena BARBER (978). Born on 10 Jan 1821.
They had the following children:

| 2917 | i. | Virgil Pettibone (1847-1905) |
| 2918 | ii. | William Lawrence (1853-) |

Line 4 – Descendants of Tahan Hill (continued)[634]

2257. Adeline Maria PARMELEE. Born on 30 Dec 1829. She married **Richard J. LEAYACRAFT.**
2258. George Stevens PARMELEE. Born on 31 Jan 1835; died on 28 Apr 1837, he was 2.
2259. Susan Catherine PARMELEE. Born on 18 Jan 1837; died on 16 Sep 1869, she was 32.

2260. Ermina Starr PARMELEE. Born on 23 Dec 1838. Ermina Starr died on 23 Jan 1839.

2261. George Stevens PARMELEE. Born on 16 Nov 1839.

2262. Henry Starr PARMELEE. Born on 24 Apr 1842.

2263. Ellen Stevens PARMELEE. Born on 10 Jan 1846.

2264. Charles Henderson PARMELEE. Born on 16 Apr 1853.

2265. Emily Starr PARMELEE. Born on 24 Aug 1844. She married **George NICHOLS**.

Line 5 – Descendants of Luke Hill, Jr. (continued)[635]

2266. Morris Seth HILL,[636] only child of Seth Morris and Deborah Ann (Clark) Hill, was born at Steuben Co., N.Y., 24 May 1823; died at Wauconda, Lake Co., Ill., 22 May 1908, two days before his 85th birthday. He was a soldier in the Civil War, whose inscribed sword has been passed down through the generations to his great-great-grandson Richard R. Stanley, Esq. He married, in Lake Co., Ill., 24 May 1849, **Teresa (Terrissa) MILLS**, daughter of Peter and Fanny (Wickham) Mills; born at Catherine, Chemung Co., N.Y., 6 March 1830; died in Lake Co., Ill., 18 December 1911, age 81. They had one child, Clarence Mortimer (1852-1898), who married twice and had descendants.
They had one child:

    3127   i.   Clarence Mortimer (1852-1898)

2267. Mary Ann HILL.[637] Born in 1825. Mary Ann died in Wauconda, Lake Co., Illinois in 1855, she was 30; unmarried; d.s.p.

2268. Jerusha HILL.[638] Born on 11 Jul 1828 in Chemung, Chemung Co., N.Y. Jerusha died in Wauconda, Lake Co., Illinois on 9 Jul 1921, she was 92. Buried in 1921 in Wauconda, Lake Co., Illinois. Jerusha married **Stebbins A. FORD**, son of Zebina FORD & Olive COLEGROVE. Born on 18 Mar 1819 in Massachusetts. Stebbins A. died in Wauconda, Lake Co., Illinois on 12 Feb 1900, he was 80. Buried in 1900 in Wauconda, Lake Co., Illinois.
They had the following children:

    3128   i.   Morris S. (1847-1923)
    3129   ii.   Louis A. (1849-1850)
    3130   iii.   William Henry (1851-)
    3131   iv.   Mary Marie (1855-)
    3132   v.   Nellie F. (1860-)
    3133   vi.   Harry S.
    3134   vii.   Lois Ann

2269. Sarah M. HILL.[639] Born in Jun 1830. Sarah M. died in Wauconda, Lake Co., Illinois in 1917, she was 86; unm.; d.s.p.

2270. Eliza Jane HILL.[640] Born on 24 Mar 1833 in Chemung, Chemung Co., N.Y. Eliza Jane died in Wauconda, Lake Co., Illinois in Jan 1916, she was 82. Occupation: Mother of 3, one of whom had descendants. On 4 Nov 1853 when Eliza Jane was 20, she married **Ambrose Augustus BANGS**, son of Justus BANGS & Louisa OAKS. Born on 18 Nov 1831 in Stamford, Bennington Co., Vt. Ambrose Augustus died in Wauconda, Lake Co., Illinois in Nov 1920, he was 88.
They had the following children:

    3135   i.   Hattie A. (1862-1863)
    3136   ii.   Elva Louise (1863-1907)
    3137   iii.   Fred W. (1866-)

2271. Lucy HILL.[641] Born on 9 Dec 1836 in Elizabethtown, Ontario Co., N.Y. Lucy died in Roseburg, Douglas Co., Ore. on 26 Aug 1909, she was 72. Occupation: No known marriage; probably d.s.p., if she is indeed a child of Seth Morris Hill.

2272. Reuben Clark HILL.[642] Born on 11 Sep 1838 in Chemung, Chemung Co., N.Y. Reuben Clark died in Milwaukee, Wisc. on 2 Oct 1911, he was 73. Occupation: d.s.p.

2273. Frances A. HILL.[643] Born in 1845. Frances A. died in Lake Co., Ill. in 1853, she was 8.

2274. Marian WHEELOCK.[644] Born on 22 Aug 1831 in New York State. Marian died in 1913, she was

81.   Marian married **Truman G. COWLES**.
They had the following children:

3138	i.	Ella J. (1852-)
3139	ii.	Francis (1853-)
3140	iii.	Norman (1858-)
3141	iv.	George (1860-)
3142	v.	Carrie (1862-)
3143	vi.	Mira (1863-)

2275. Pamelia WHEELOCK.[645] Born in 1834 in New York State. Occupation: Mother of 1. Pamelia married **Walter Joseph ROBINSON**.
They had one child:

3144	i.	Winifred Josephine (1867-)

2276. Frances WHEELOCK.[646] Born in 1836. Frances died aft 1880, abt 44.

2277. Emily WHEELOCK.[647] Born in 1838 in Michigan. Emily died aft 1860, she was 22.

2278. Elisha Roe WHEELOCK.[648] Born in 1842 in Michigan. Elisha Roe died aft 1860, he was 18.

2279. Helen ROE.[649] Born in 1844 in New York State. Helen died in Racine, Racine Co., Wisc. on 27 May 1882, she was 38. Her husband was her first cousin; both were grandchildren of Elisha and Electa (Hill) Roe. In 1867 when Helen was 23, she married **Henry C. MAYNARD** (2293), son of Nathan MAYNARD & Lucy ROE (1578), in Racine, Racine Co., Wisc. Born in 1846 in Alden, Erie Co., N.Y.

2280. Augustus ROE. Born in 1845 in New York State, according to census records. Augustus died in Racine, Racine Co., Wisc. on 24 Mar 1880, he was 35.

2281. Lucy ROE. Born in 1847 in Racine, Racine Co., Wisc. Lucy died in Racine, Racine Co., Wisc. on 3 Apr 1872, she was 25, d.s.p.

2282. Roxanne ROE. Born in 1849; died in Racine, Racine Co., Wisc. 18 Sep 1851, abt 2.

2283. Reuben Smith ROE.[650] Born on 26 Oct 1850 in Racine, Racine Co., Wisc. Reuben Smith died in Hudson, St. Croix Co., Wisc. on 14 Oct 1933, he was 82. On 26 Oct 1872 when Reuben Smith was 22, he married **Emma Maria BLODGET**, in Watertown, Walworth Co., Wisc. Born in 1851. Emma Maria died in 1930, she was 79.
They had one child:

3145	i.	Lillian Gertrude "Gertie" (1876-1965)

2284. William H. ROE. Born in 1852. William H. died in 1925, he was 73. Shown in U.S. Census records. Resided in Wisconsin; did not marry; d.s.p.

2285. George ROE. Born in 1854. George died on 23 Jun 1917, he was 63. Resided in Wisconsin; did not m.; d.s.p.

2286. Carrie ROE.[651] Born in 1857 in Racine, Racine Co., Wisc., d.s.p. On 23 Feb 1881 when Carrie was 24, she married **Lafayette PIERCE**, in Racine, Racine Co., Wisc.

2287. Harvey P. ROE.[652] Born in Dec 1859 in Racine, Racine Co., Wisc. Harvey P. died in 1932, he was 72. Harvey P. married **Clarinda STINE**. Born in 1866. Occupation: Mother of 1.
They had one child:

3146	i.	Harvey S.

2288. Winnie ROE.[653] Born in Oct 1862 in Racine, Racine Co., Wisc.; died on 15 Dec 1934, she was 72. On 17 Dec 1889 when Winnie was 27, she married **Ira T. YATES**, in Racine, Racine Co., Wisc.; b.1861.
They had the following children:

3147	i.	Nettie (1891-)
3148	ii.	Bessie (1894-)
3149	iii.	Hellen (1896-)

2289. Nettie ROE.[654] Born on 6 May 1865 in Racine, Racine Co., Wisc. Nettie died in Racine, Racine Co., Wisc. on 15 Apr 1932, she was 66.

2290. Amanda B. MAYNARD.[655] Born in 1833 in New York State. Amanda B. died in 1903, she was 70. Occupation: Mother of 1; she resided in Alden, Erie Co., N.Y., in 1850. On 17 Jun 1858 when

Amanda B. was 25, she married **William Harrison FELLOWS**, in Racine, Racine Co., Wisc. Born in 1836. William Harrison died in 1902, he was 66.

They had one child:

3150   i.   Nettie Louise (1859-1934)

2291. Antoinette MAYNARD.[656] Born in 1835 in New York State. Antoinette died in Battle Creek, Calhoun Co., Mich. in 1917, she was 82. Occupation: Mother of 3. Antoinette married **Ralph N. BUTLER**, son of Samuel M. BUTLER & Julia A. _____. Born in 1832. Ralph N. died in 1878, age 46.

They had the following children:

3151   i.   Samuel Marsh (1854-)
3152   ii.   Jennie (1859-1951)
3153   iii.   Edith B. (1861-)

2292. Eveiline MAYNARD.[657] Born in 1836 in New York State. Occupation: Mother of 2. Eveiline married **Ozias SEYMOUR**.

They had the following children:

3154   i.   Emma M. (1865-)
3155   ii.   Henry O. (1874-)

2293. Henry C. MAYNARD.[658] Born in 1846 in Alden, Erie Co., N.Y. In 1867 when Henry C. was 21, he married **Helen ROE** (2279), daughter of William Horace ROE (1576) & Elizabeth Smith PAYNE, in Racine, Racine Co., Wisc. B. in 1844 in New York State; d. in Racine, Racine Co., Wisc., 27 May 1882, she was 38. Her husband was her first cousin; both were grandchildren of Elisha and Electa (Hill) Roe.

2294. Sophia BARNUM.[659] Born in 1840 in Michigan. Lived in Johnstown, Barry Co., Mich., in 1850.

2295. James A. BARNUM.[660] Born in 1832 in New York State. James A. died in May 1863, about 31. Resided in Johnstown, Barry, Mich., in 1850.

2296. Romeo BARNUM.[661] Born in 1847. Romeo died in 1863, he was 16.

2297. George Nathaniel PRATT.[662] Born abt 1842. George Nathaniel died in 1901, he was 59. George Nathaniel married **Martha Ellen FRACKER**. Born in 1842.

2298. Mary F. PRATT.[663] Born abt 1843 in Vermont. Mary F. died in 1925, she was 82. Mother of 6, none of whom are known to have had descendants. Mary F. married **William Kirby SIDLEY**.

They had the following children:

3156   i.   William Pratt (1868->1880)
3157   ii.   Kyle A. (1870->1880)
3158   iii.   Fred K. (1873->1900)
3159   iv.   Frank C. (1874->1900)
3160   v.   Mollie (1877->1880)
3161   vi.   Ernest S. (1879->1880)
3162   vii.   Thomas H. (1881->1900)

2299. Albert Harrison PRATT.[664] Born in 1835. Albert Harrison died in 1923, he was 88. Albert Harrison married **Mary Adelaide FAY**. Born in 1846. Mary Adelaide died in 1917, she was 71.

2300. Ellen PRATT. Born in 1848.

2301. Ella A. PRATT.[665] Born on 19 May 1851 in Ticonderoga, N.Y. Ella A. died in 1930, she was 78. Mother of 2; one died as an infant, and the other m. and had descendants who are not shown in Roe_Elisha & Electa. Ella A. married **Frederick Morgan STEELE**. Born in 1851. Frederick Morgan died in 1923, he was 72.

They had the following children:

3163   i.   Frederick Pratt (1884-1884)
3164   ii.   Elizabeth Livingston (1886-1959)

2302. Marion ROE.[666] Born in 1837.

2303. Susannah ROE.[667] Born in 1839 in Cattaraugus, N.Y.

2304. Electa A. ROE.[668] Born in Oct 1842 in New York State. On 5 Dec 1866 when Electa A. was 24, she married **Oscar W. NETTLETON**, in Racine, Racine Co., Wisc.

2305. Mary Frances ROE.[669] Born in Feb 1845 in Allegany, N.Y. Occupation: Mother of 1. Mary

Frances married **Charles Atherton CHASE**. Born in 1844.
They had one child:

    3165   i.   Mary (1873-1910)

2306. Josephine ROE.[670] Born on 18 Sep 1849 in Ridgeway, Orleans Co., N.Y. Josephine died on 19 Oct 1849 in Ridgeway, Orleans Co., N.Y.

2307. Joseph ROE.[671] Born on 18 Sep 1849 in Ridgeway, Orleans Co., N.Y. Joseph died on 24 Oct 1849 in Ridgeway, Orleans Co., N.Y.

2308. Eveline ROE.[672] Born on 18 Sep 1849 in Ridgeway, Orleans Co., N.Y.

2309. Elisha K. ROE.[673] Born in 1853 in New York State; d.s.p.

2310. Horace ROE.[674] Born in 1854 in Niagara, N.Y.; died in Racine, Racine Co., Wisc. in 1870, abt 16.

2311. Birdie ROE.[675] Born in 1868 in Michigan.

2312. Carrie ROE.[676] Born in 1859 in New York State.

2313. Orvin J. ROE.[677] Born on 13 Nov 1851 in Shoreham Township, Addison Co., Vt. Orvin J. died in Portland, Ore. on 1 Jul 1937, he was 85. Orvin J. married **Pauline ANSMUS**.
They had one child:

    3166   i.   Ramona (1898-)

--[678]

2314. Edalena "Lena" Hill COLE. Born on 21 Mar 1870 in Norwalk, Conn.; d. in 1945, she was 74. Buried in 1945 in Norwak, Conn. On 25 Jan 1899 when she was 28, she married **David Floyd HUNT** in Norwalk, Conn. Born in 1872. David Floyd died in 1953, he was 81. They were divorced.

2315. Anna Louise COLE. Born on 20 Mar 1878 in Norwalk, Conn. Anna Louise died in Norwalk, Conn. on 14 Jan 1966, she was 87. In abt 1896 when Anna Louise was 17, she first married **Lester HYATT** in Norwalk, Conn. They were divorced. On 12 Dec 1908 when Anna Louise was 30, she second married **Dixon H. McNETTON** in Norwalk, Conn.

2316. Alice Isaacs COLE. Born on 23 Feb 1881 in Norwalk, Conn. Alice Isaacs died in Norwalk, Conn. on 23 Aug 1957, she was 76. Buried in 1957 in Norwalk, Conn. In abt 1912 when Alice Isaacs was 30, she married **Edgar LAUGHTON**. Edgar died in 1920.
They had one child:

    3167   i.   Richard S. (1914-1996)

2317. Harriet GRANT.

2318. Eliza Desire GRANT. Born on 3 Nov 1838 in Levering, Mich. Eliza Desire died in Harbor Springs, Emmet Co., Mich. on 19 Feb 1925, she was 86. On 4 Oct 1857 when Eliza Desire was 18, she married **Hugh KILPATRICK**, in Woodland Twp., Barry Co., Mich. Born on 27 Aug 1832 in Newmilns, Ayrshire, Scotland. Hugh died in Levering, Emmet Co., Mich. on 27 Apr 1921, he was 88.
They had the following children:

    3168   i.   Jesse
    3169   ii.   Fred (1858-)
    3170   iii.   William (1860-)
    3171   iv.   Elmer (1862-)
    3172   v.   Bernard (1865-)
    3173   vi.   Eva (1868-)
    3174   vii.   John (1870-)
    3175   viii.   Nathan (1872-)
    3176   ix.   Lydia May (1875-)
    3177   x.   Hattie (1880-)

2319. Lydia Maria GRANT. Born on 3 Dec 1841. Lydia Maria died in Dec 1892, she was 50; d.s.p. Lydia Maria married **Van NORTWICH**.

2320. Samuel Elihu GRANT. Born on 18 Mar 1843 in Lodi, Ohio. Samuel Elihu died on 12 Apr 1934, he was 91. On 21 Oct 1866 when he was 23, he married **Pamelia J. PERKINS**, in Woodland Twp., Barry Co., Mich. Born on 8 Mar 1850 in Chatham, Medina Co., Ohio; died on 9 Nov 1922, she was 72. They had the following children:

3178	i.	Wirt Ellsworth (1867-)
3179	ii.	Sarah Estella (1869-)
3180	iii.	Elton Durand (1872-)
3181	iv.	Nellie Amy (1874-)
3182	v.	Ola Blanch (1883-)
3183	vi.	Effie Gail (1887-)
3184	vii.	James William (1894-)

2321. Isaac Jesse GRANT. Born on 22 Nov 1844 in Dellwood, Mich. Isaac Jesse died in 1903, he was 58. Isaac Jesse married **Antoinette Nettie HAGAR**. Born in 1854 in Sunfield, Eaton Co., Mich. Antoinette Nettie died in 1932, she was 78.
They had the following children:

3185	i.	John Everett (1879-)
3186	ii.	Mary Ellen (1881-)
3187	iii.	Harman Elihu (1883-)
3188	iv.	Jane (1889-)
3189	v.	Ida Edna (1893-)

2322. John GRANT. Born on 28 Dec 1847 in Woodbury, Mich.

2323. Timothy Burr GRANT. Born on 12 Apr 1850 in Lodi, Ohio. On 16 Nov 1873 when he was 23, he married **Mary Ellen MOORE** in Charleston, Mich. Born 24 Aug 1852 in Cleveland, Ohio. She d.s.p.

2324. Urania GRANT. Born on 21 Oct 1852 in Medina, Ohio. On 20 Oct 1875 when Urania was 22, she married **William MALLORY**, in Woodland Twp., Barry Co., Mich. Born on 20 Jun 1849 in Richland, Ohio. William died in Bliss, Mich. on 26 Jun 1925, he was 76.
They had the following children:

3190	i.	Maud (1876-)
3191	ii.	Claude (1878-)
3192	iii.	Zella (1883-)
3193	iv.	Estella R. (1886-)
3194	v.	John Dow (1888-)
3195	vi.	Gracie (1891-)

2325. Susanna GRANT. Born on 7 Jan 1855; died on 14 Sep 1863, she was 8.

2326. Julia Eva GRANT. Born on 28 Nov 1858 in Sunfield, Eaton Co., Mich.; died in Sunfield, Eaton Co., Mich on 3 Dec 1867, she was 9.

2327. Julius Everett GRANT. Born on 28 Nov 1858 in Sunfield, Eaton Co., Mich. Julius Everett died in Sunfield, Eaton Co., Mich on 20 Nov 1872, he was 13.

2328. Alma Virginia GRANT. Born on 3 Jun 1863 in Sunfield, Eaton Co., Mich. Occupation: Mother of 6. Alma Virginia married **John Lewis SNYDER**. Born on 20 Nov 1853 in Chemung, N.Y. John Lewis died in Muskegon, Mich. on 7 Apr 1920, he was 66.
They had the following children:

3196	i.	Charles Nelson (1883-)
3197	ii.	George Edwin (1886-)
3198	iii.	Earl Dorway (1887-)
3199	iv.	Arthur Leroy (1889-)
3200	v.	Mary (1894-)
3201	vi.	Ella Wilhelmine (1897-)

2329. Mary Amelia GRANT. Born on 22 Dec 1848 in Council Bluffs, Pottawattamie Co., Ia. Married 3 times. May have had 2 children by Gaylord and 5 children by Quirk. On 27 Feb 1867 when Mary Amelia was 18, she first married **Theodore B. GAYLORD**. Born in Aug 1843 in Allen, Ind. Theodore B. died in Porterville, Tulare Co., Calif. in Dec 1878, he was 35. May have been father of 2 by Mary Amelia. On 3 Mar 1874 when Mary Amelia was 25, she second married **James QUIRK**, in San Francisco, Calif. Born in Jul 1837 in Ireland. James died in San Francisco, Calif. on 22 Feb 1892, he was 54. He may have been father of 5. On 3 Jan 1896 when Mary Amelia was 47, she third married **James**

Theophilus PIERCE. Born on 25 Dec 1831 in New Bedford, Mass. James Theophilus died on 26 Oct 1897, he was 65 and d.s.p.

2330. Sarah Opehlia GRANT. Born on 19 Mar 1850 in Council Bluffs, Pottawattamie Co., Ia. Sarah Opehlia died in 1900, she was 49 and mother of 3. Sarah Opehlia married **Robert Smith FRAZEE.** Born in 1848 in Cayuga, N.Y. Robert Smith died in Sacramento, Calif. on 29 Feb 1892, he was 44.

2331. George Robert GRANT. Born on 24 Mar 1852 in Farmington, Davis Co., Utah. George Robert died in Sacramento, Calif. on 10 Sep 1895, he was 43. Occupation: Married and may have had progeny. On 2 Dec 1877 when George Robert was 25, he married **Julia Fidelia SMITH**, in Roseville, Calif. Born on 30 Jun 1858 in Grass Valley, Calif. She may have been the mother of 5.

2332. Julia Antoinette GRANT. Born on 3 Jan 1854 in Farmington, Davis Co., Utah. May have been mother of 4. On 11 Nov 1871 when Julia Antoinette was 17, she married **Leroy Langford CROCKER**, in Roseville, Placer Co., Calif. Born on 8 Aug 1847 in Madison, Wisc. Leroy Langford died in Loomis, Placer Co., Calif. on 30 Oct 1908, he was 61.

2333. Helen Louisa GRANT. Born on 8 Jan 1856 in Farmington, Davis Co., Utah.

2334. Henrietta GRANT. Born on 2 Apr 1858 in Farmington, Davis Co., Utah. No spouses shown in OneWorldTree, but she is said to have had two children by different fathers.

Henrietta first married ____.

They had one child:

    3202   i.   Earle

Henrietta second married ____.

They had one child:

    3203   i.   Longstreth

2335. Gertrude Betsy GRANT. Born on 3 Apr 1860 in Farmington, Davis Co., Utah; died in Sacramento, Calif. in Mar 1864, she was 3.

2336. Henry Loring GRANT. Born 28 April 1862 in Carson City, Nev. Henry Loring died in Jan 1864 in Sacramento, Calif.

2337. Charles Lewis GRANT. Born on 6 Sep 1864 in Sacramento, Calif. Charles Lewis died on 4 Oct 1864 in Sacramento, Calif.

2338. Edmund Carbine GRANT. Born on 11 Sep 1858 in Kaysville, Davis, Utah.

On 4 Feb 1885 when Edmund Carbine was 26, he married **Emily Jane ADAIR**, in Nutrioso, Apache, Ariz. Born on 28 Dec 1865 in Washington, Washington Co., Utah. Emily Jane died in New Harmony, Washington Co., Utah on 3 Oct 1949, she was 83. She may have been mother of 8.

2339. Francesca GRANT. Born in 1860 in Kaysville, Davis Co., Utah. She is not mentioned in the biography of Mary Adelia Carbine, but her b. year and place in OneWorldTree is persuasive enough to list her here.

2340. Sylvester HILL.[679] Born on 7 Jun 1855 in De Kalb, Ill.;died in California (probably) aft 1930. On 12 Oct 1881 when Sylvester was 26, he married **Emma E. McKINZIE.** Born in 1836 in Canada.

They had the following children:

    3204   i.   Berenice (~1874-)
    3205   ii.   Clarence S. (~1887-)

2341. William Smith HILL II.[680] Born on 26 Nov 1862 in Shabbona, De Kalb Co., Ill. William Smith died in Minneapolis, Hennepin Co., Ill. on 31 Jul 1928, he was 65. William Smith married **Harriet Jane "Hattie" EVANS.** Born in 1862 in Minnesota; died in Minneapolis, Hennepin Co., Ill. in 1922, about 60.

They had the following children:

    3206   i.   Raymond Vaughn (1889-1984)
    3207   ii.   William Clayton (1890-1891)
    3208   iii.   David D. (1891-1962)
    3209   iv.   Maurice Gilbert (1893-1952)
    3210   v.   Albert (1894-1895)
    3211   vi.   Mary Abbreata (1894-1895)
    3212   vii.   Ellenore Elizabeth "Florence" (1896-1876)

3213	viii.	Clarice Elva (1898-1977)
3214	ix.	Grace (1898-1898)
3215	x.	Gwendolyn "Babe" (1901-1952)

2342. Gary HILL. Born about 1857 in Illinois; died there before 1870.

2343. Benjamin F. "Frankie" HILL. Born abt 1859.

2344. Elizabeth HILL. Born abt 1861 in Illinois.

2345. Nathaniel HILL. Born abt 1865 in Illinois.

2346. Eugene "Emogene" HILL. Born abt 1867.

2347. Joab HILL. Born in 1869 in Illinois. Joab died bef 1880, he was 11.

2348. Albert HILL. Born abt 1872.

2349. Allison A. HILL. Born abt 1874.

2350. Elva (Elvira) HILL. Born abt 1866 in Illinois.

2351. Herbert HILL. Born abt 1869.

2352. Eugene HILL. Born abt 1873.

2353. George W. HILL. Born abt 1875 in Illinois.

2354. Reubin HILL. Born abt 1879 in Illinois.

2355. Theda Albertis HILL.[681] Born on 21 Aug 1879 in La Clede, Ill. Theda Albertis died in San Francisco, Calif. on 17 Feb 1943, he was 63. Buried in 1943 in Olivet Memorial Park, Colma, Calif. Minister, Free Methodist Church.   Theda Albertis first married **Rushia E. HOLLINGSHEAD**. Born in 1878. Rushia E. died in 1911, she was 33.

They had the following children:

3216	i.	Flora May (1900-)
3217	ii.	Leander Charles (1902-1984)
3218	iii.	Cleo Maxine (1905-1905)
3219	iv.	Glendalia (1909-)

On 17 Apr 1911 when Theda Albertis was 31, he second married **Florence WORKMAN** in Villa Grove, Ill. Born in 1890. Florence died in 1982, she was 92. Buried in 1982 in Colma, California.

They had the following children:

3220	i.	Thelma Louise (1912-2004)
3221	ii.	Herbert Albertis (1914-2005)
3222	iii.	Melvin Leroy (1919-1992)
3223	iv.	Kenneth E. (1923-1990)

2356. Dan HILL.

2357. Frances HILL. Born on 12 Mar 1841 in New Rockford, Ill.

2358. Henrietta HILL. Born on 17 May 1843 in New Rockford, Ill.

2359. Wealthia HILL. Born on 4 Apr 1845 in New Rockford, Ill. Wealthia died in Sanitarium Medical Lake, Washington on 20 Sep 1888, she was 43. Occupation: Mother of 3. On 7 May 1871 when Wealthia was 26, she married **Robert James WILLIAMS**, in Pleasant Prairie, Martin, Minn. Born on 17 May 1844 in New Albion, N.Y. Robert James died in Verona, Fairbault Co., Minn. on 31 Oct 1889, he was 45.

They had the following children:

3224	i.	Infant (1874-)
3225	ii.	Ellen Hope (1876-1879)
3226	iii.	Lydia Faith (1882-1890)

2360. Isadora HILL. Born on 23 Aug 1846 in New Rockford, Ill.

2361. Ellen (Emily) HILL. Born on 10 May 1848 in New Rockford, Ill. Ellen (Emily) died in Minn. on 22 May 1918, she was 70. On 26 Apr 1880 when Ellen (Emily) was 31, she married **Lorenzo WALDREN**, in Fairbault, Minn. Born on 3 Oct 1843 in Peoria, Ill. Lorenzo died in Bass Lake, Fairbault, Minn. on 5 Feb 1918, he was 74.

They had the following children:

3227	i.	Mary Ellen (1882-)

3228	ii.	Martha Maria (1888-)

2362. Wallace HILL. Born on 14 Oct 1854 in Saratoga, Minn.

2363. Frank J. HILL. Born on 8 Jul 1858 in Saratoga, Minn.

2364. May HILL. Born on 21 May 1861 in Saratoga, Minn.

2365. Willis Edgar HILL. Born in 1857. Willis Edgar died in Marietta, Ohio in 1918, he was 61. In 1882 when Willis Edgar was 25, he married **Emma Elizabeth OGLEVEE**. Born in 1859. Emma Elizabeth died in 1888, she was 29.

They had the following children:

3229	i.	David Edgar
3230	ii.	Marion Bradford
3231	iii.	Richard
3232	iv.	Helen C. (1883-)

2366. Zenas Brown HILDRETH. Born on 21 Aug 1878 in Marietta, Ohio.

2367. Hazel HILL. Born in 1887.

2368. Carrie Hildreth HILL. Born on 8 Dec 1872.

2369. Esther Irene HILL. Born on 18 Dec 1874.

2370. Ira Z. HILL. Born on 11 May 1877.

2371. Della Olaretta HILL. Born on 9 May 1879.

2372. Earl Russell HILL. Born on 22 May 1881.

2373. Euretta HILL. Born on 8 Dec 1883.

2374. Ella HUSTED. Born in 1853 in Chester, Morrow Co., Ohio.

2375. Ulysses HUSTED. Born in 1856 in Chester, Morrow Co., Ohio.

2376. Frank HUSTED. Born in 1858 in Chester, Morrow Co., Ohio.

2377. Cora Cord DAY. Born in 1850.

2378. Anna R. DAY. Born in 1860.

2379. Ellen M. DAY. Born in 1863.

2380. Shannon DAY. Born in 1867.

2381. Laura WHEATON. Born on 6 Apr 1864 in Holmesville, Holmes Co., Ohio. Laura died on 9 Aug 1939, she was 75. On 14 Mar 1882 when Laura was 17, she married **James Washington STOCKER** in Holmesville, Holmes Co., Ohio. Born on 30 May 1857 in Newcomerstown, Tuscarawas Co., Ohio. James Washington died on 1 Mar 1946, he was 88.

They had the following children:

3233	i.	Daniel Beers (1882-)
3234	ii.	Elmira (1884-)
3235	iii.	Mittie Leonora (1887-)
3236	iv.	George Washington (1890-)
3237	v.	Ollie (1894-)
3238	vi.	Ellen (1897-)
3239	vii.	Bertha Dell (1900-)
3240	viii.	Ruby (1902-)

2382. Rosella Florence WOLGAMOTT. Born in 1858 in Millersburg, Holmes Co., Ohio, apparently d.s.p. On 22 May 1878 when Rosella Florence was 20, she married **Stanton G. VOORHES** in Holmes, Killbuck Co., Ohio.

2383. Joseph Melvin WOLGAMOTT. Born on 20 May 1859 in Millersburg, Holmes Co., Ohio. Joseph Melvin died in Holmes, Killbuck Co., Ohio on 25 Dec 1903, he was 44. On 1 Jan 1884 when Joseph Melvin was 24, he married **Cora Belle KORNS** in Holmes, Killbuck Co., Ohio. Born on 20 May 1852 in Holmes, Killbuck Co., Ohio. Cora Belle died in Holmes, Killbuck Co., Ohio on 1 Oct 1897, she was 45.

They had the following children:

3241	i.	Milan B. (1884-)
3242	ii.	William Welker (1886-)
3243	iii.	Anna Viola (1888-)

3244   iv.   David Roscoe (1894-)
3245   v.   Burton A. (1897-)

2384. Russell H. WOLGAMOTT. Born in 1858 in Millersburg, Holmes Co., Ohio. Russell H. died in 1938, he was 80. Russell H. married **Ida M. WHEATON**. Born in 1869.

2385. John M. WOLGAMOTT. Born in 1864 in Millersburg, Holmes Co., Ohio. John M. died in 1934, he was 70. John M. married **Etta ALLISON**. Born in 1863. Etta died in 1934, she was 71.

2386. Nancy Jane WOLGAMOTT. Born in 1866 in Millersburg, Holmes Co., Ohio. Nancy Jane died in Holmes, Killbuck Co., Ohio on 7 Sep 1876, about 10.

2387. Nob WOLGAMOTT. Born on 23 Nov 1868 in Holmes, Killbuck Co., Ohio. Nob died on 23 Nov 1868 in Holmes, Killbuck Co., Ohio.

2388. Harry L. WOLGAMOTT. Born on 22 Dec 1869 in Millersburg, Holmes Co., Ohio. Harry L. died in 1946, he was 76. On 27 Oct 1892 when Harry L. was 22, he married **Mary A. PAINTER** in Holmes, Killbuck Co., Ohio. Born in 1873. Mary A. died in 1943, she was 70, apparently d.s.p.

2389. Hattie L. WOLGAMOTT. Born in Dec 1869 in Millersburg, Holmes Co., Ohio. On 20 Jun 1901 when Hattie L. was 31, she married **Franklin Gilbert ANDERSON** in Holmes, Killbuck Co., Ohio. Born in 1856. Franklin Gilbert died in 1938, he was 82.

2390. Mary A. WOLGAMOTT. Born in 1873 in Holmes, Killbuck Co., Ohio.

2391. Prince A. WOLGAMOTT. Born Mar 1874 in Millersburg, Holmes Co., Ohio; died in 1880.

2392. Charles WOLGAMOTT. Born on 14 Mar 1876 in Millersburg, Holmes Co., Ohio. On 24 Aug 1898 when he was 22, he married **Amanda Elzora GRIFFITH**. Born on 12 May 1870 in Holmesville, Holmes Co., Ohio; died in Wooster, Wayne Co., Ohio on 21 Feb 1962, she was 91.
They had the following children:
3246   i.   Miriam Lucille (1901-)
3247   ii.   Russell Griffith (1907-)

2393. Genetta Ellen CRAWFORD. Born in 1864 in Ohio. On 1 Aug 1886 when Genetta Ellen was 22, she married **Lewis YOUNT** in Winfield, Cowley Co., Kansas. Born on 13 Apr 1864 in Martinsville, Morgan Co., Ind. Lewis died in Tonkawa, Kay Co., Okla on 12 May 1923, he was 59.
They had the following children:
3248   i.   Nina Vistula (1888-)
3249   ii.   Inis Beatrice (1892-)
3250   iii.   Roy Oliver (1899-)
3251   iv.   Dean Burdette (1910-)

2394. Franklin Herbert CRAWFORD. Born in 1866 in Ohio. Franklin Herbert died in Holmes, Killbuck Co., Ohio.

2395. Anna Nevada CRAWFORD. Born in 1868 in Holmes, Killbuck Co., Ohio; died in New York.

2396. Weldon R. CRAWFORD. Born on 22 Apr 1871 in Millersburg, Holmes Co., Ohio. Weldon R. died in Tulsa, Tulsa Co., Okla. on 8 Jan 1953, he was 81. Weldon R. married **Mary Alice GILLILAND**. Born in 1872 in Cherokee, Kansas. Mary Alice died in Kay, Okla. in 1942, she was 70. They had the following children:
3252   i.   Margaret Elizabeth
3253   ii.   Mildred (1898-)
3254   iii.   Velma Merle (1899-)
3255   iv.   Hazel Annetta (1901-)
3256   v.   Carmi Russell (1903-)
3257   vi.   Ralph (1906-)
3258   vii.   Lolita Grace (1908-)

2397. Austin CRAWFORD. Born 30 Nov 1873 in Holmes, Killbuck Co., Ohio; died there.

2398. Myron CRAWFORD. Born in 1879 in Ohio. Myron died in Holmes, Ohio.

2399. Ella HALL. Ella died on 23 Jan 1873.

2400. Amelia HALL. Born in 1859. Amelia died on 23 Nov 1867, she was 8.

2401. Reuben Anson HALL. Born on 4 May 1863 in Swanton, Ohio. On 12 Nov 1884 when Reuben

Anson was 21, he married **Dora Bell FAVORITE**. Born on 5 Jan 1865 in Swanton, Ohio. They had the following children:

3259	i.	Floyd Anson (1886-)
3260	ii.	Lola Belle (1888-)
3261	iii.	Clyde Thomas (1890-)
3262	iv.	Pheba Alice (1892-)
3263	v.	Grace Almira (1894-)
3264	vi.	Bertha Jane (1904-)
3265	vii.	Favorite Reuben (1905-)

2402. Francis Estella HALL. Born on 8 Sep 1895 in Fulton, Ohio. Occupation: Married, but apparently d.s.p. Francis Estella married **William G. FLEMING**.

2403. Stephen D. HALL. Born on 3 Apr 1860 in Ohio. Stephen D. died in Fulton, Ohio in 1933, he was 72. In Jun 1890 when Stephen D. was 30, he married **Sarah Jane SMITH**. Born in 1856 in Fulton, Ohio. Sarah Jane died in Fulton, Ohio in 1944, she was 88, apparently d.s.p.

2404. Jesse H. HALL. Born on 16 Mar 1863 in Fulton, Ohio.

2405. Mary S. HALL. Born on 15 Mar 1866 in Ohio. Mary S. died in Mar 1871, she was 4.

2406. Lewis K. HALL. Born on 10 Oct 1867 in Ohio. Lewis K. married **Mabel MAWER**. They had one child:

3266	i.	Price

2407. Burton F. HALL. Born on 22 Feb 1871 in Ohio.

2408. Melissa Adele SLOAN. Born on 11 May 1858 in Seneca, Ohio. Melissa Adele died in Garretsville, Portage Co., Ohio on 17 Nov 1922, she was 64. On 26 Oct 1879 when Melissa Adele was 21, she married **William FARLEY** in Sylvania, Lucas Co., Ohio. Born in 1841 in Ohio. They had one child:

3267	i.	Mary G. (1878-)

2409. Clarinda Jane SLOAN. Born on 22 Jun 1860 in Richfield, Lucas Co., Ohio. Clarinda Jane died in Fulton, Ohio on 3 Jul 1933, she was 73. Married, but apparently d.s.p. On 15 Apr 1879 when she was 18, she married **George Washington TWISS**, in Ohio. Born in 1953 in Amboy, Fulton Co., Ohio.

2410. Almira Ann SLOAN. Born on 18 Apr 1862 in Richfield, Lucas Co., Ohio. Almira Ann died in Toledo, Lucas Co., Ohio on 20 Feb 1949, she was 86. Married but apparently d.s.p. On 18 Jul 1886 when Almira Ann was 24, she married **Elmer J. KLINE** in Ohio.

2411. Russell Franklin SLOAN. Born on 1 Oct 1865 in Cuyahoga, Ohio. Russell Franklin died in Swanton, Fulton Co., Ohio on 20 Nov 1918, he was 53. Married twice and had children by both wives. On 1 Oct 1884 when Russell Franklin was 19, he first married **Mary Ellen BUSKIRK in** Riga, Monroe Co., Mich. Born on 8 Aug 1867 in Hopkins, Allegheny Co., Mich. Mary Ellen died in Richfield, Lucas Co., Ohio on 1 May 1892, she was 24. They had the following children:

3268	i.	William Burton (1885-)
3269	ii.	Daniel Horatio (1887-)
3270	iii.	Daisy Ellen (1889-)

On 24 Aug 1892 when Russell Franklin was 26, he second married **Elizabeth WILL** in Fulton, Ohio. They had the following children:

3271	i.	Carrie Rebecca (1896-)
3272	ii.	Pearl Elizabeth (1905-)

2412. Phoebe SLOAN. Born on 12 Oct 1867 in Richfield Center, Lucas Co., Ohio. Phoebe died on 12 Oct 1867, the day she was born.

2413. Amos Clinton SLOAN. Born on 6 May 1869 in Richfield, Lucas Co., Ohio. Amos Clinton died in Toledo, Lucas Co., Ohio on 9 Nov 1965, he was 96. Married twice; had a daughter by first wife. On 24 Aug 1892 when Amos Clinton was 23, he first married **Francis Siba HALL** in Chester, Dodge Co., Wisc. Born on 24 Feb 1869 in Chester, Dodge Co., Wisc. Francis Siba died in Chester, Dodge Co., Wisc. on 24 Aug 1893, she was 24.

They had one child:

    3273   i.   Siba Zella (1893-)

On 20 Dec 1894 when Amos Clinton was 25, he second married **Jessie Adell HALL**, in Ohio. She apparently d.s.p.

2414. Arthur Burton SLOAN. Born on 24 Jan 1876 in Richfield, Lucas Co., Ohio. Arthur Burton died in Sylvania, Lucas Co., Ohio on 29 Sep 1937, he was 61. On 9 Jun 1909 when Arthur Burton was 33, he married **Florence Louise DECKER** in Ohio. Born in 1878, and apparently d.s.p.

2415. Esther L. COOK. Born on 19 Sep 1850 in Neosho, Dodge Co., Wisc. Esther L. died in Chicago, Cook Co., Ill. on 31 Jan 1921, she was 70. Married but apparently d.s.p. In Nov 1870 when Esther L. was 20, she married **David Jonathan DANFORTH** in Necedah, Juneau Co., Wisc.

2416. Levi Hubbard COOK. Born on 6 Jul 1852 in Neosho, Dodge Co., Wisc. Levi Hubbard died in Gowrie, Webster Co., Ia. on 27 Aug 1896, he was 44. On 29 Jun 1874 when Levi Hubbard was 21, he married **Sarah Maria HUBBARD** in Oakfield, Fond Du Lac Co., Wisc. Born on 13 Aug 1851 in Oakfield, Fond Du Lac Co., Wisc. Sarah Maria died in San Bernardino, Calif. on 5 Jun 1941, she was 89. They had the following children:

    3274   i.   Leon Leslie (1884-)
    3275   ii.   Morton Hubbard (1873-)
    3276   iii.   Fred Lee (1877-)
    3277   iv.   William Warren (1880-)

2417. Alice COOK. Born in 1856 in Fontanelle, Ia. On 23 Nov 1875 when Alice was 19, she married **John Franklin LAGEE** in Milwaukee, Wisc.

2418. Charles A. COOK. Born in 1858 in Iowa. Charles A. died in Denver, Worth Co., Mo. on 18 Apr 1896, he was 38.

2419. Susan Ann COOK. Born in 1860 in Fontanelle, Adair Co., Ia. Susan Ann died in Beloit, Rock Co., Wisc. on 17 Jun 1956, she was 96. Married but apparently d.s.p. On 18 Oct 1882 when Susan Ann was 22, she married **George MILLAR** in Glendale, Monroe Co., Wisc.

2420. Morton Sylvester COOK. Born on 5 Jul 1862 in Horicon, Wisc. Morton Sylvester died in Cedar Rapids, Linn Co., Ia. on 31 Mar 1929, he was 66. Morton Sylvester married **Abigail BOARDMAN**. Born on 28 Oct 1868 in Elkport, Ia.; died in Cedar Rapids, Linn Co., Ia. on 31 Aug 1931, she was 62. They had the following children:

    3278   i.   Elizabeth (1886-)
    3279   ii.   Charles Sylvester (1887-)
    3280   iii.   Alfred (1888-)
    3281   iv.   Clara (1890-)
    3282   v.   Grace (1895-)
    3283   vi.   Frank Leroy (1896-)
    3284   vii.   Fred Emery (1898-)
    3285   viii.   William Ambrose (1901-)
    3286   ix.   Henry "Harry" (1904-)
    3287   x.   Maude Sylvia (1907-)

2421. Len COOK. Born in 1873 in Iowa. Len died in 1885, he was 12.

2422. Anna Rulon COOK. Born in 1874 in Clayton, Ia.

2423. Esther S. BURLINGAME. Born on 2 Nov 1846 in Ashippun, Dodge Co., Wisc.

2424. Nancy E. BURLINGAME. Born on 2 Jun 1848 in Ashippun, Dodge Co., Wisc.

2425. Spencer Alanson BURLINGAME. Born on 5 Aug 1850 in Ashippun, Dodge Co., Wisc. Spencer Alanson died in Elroy, Juneau Co., Wisc. on 7 May 1931, he was 80. On 9 Feb 1875 when Spencer Alanson was 24, he first married **Harriet Rosetta LUKE** in Elroy, Juneau Co., Wisc. Born on 9 Feb 1858; died in Elroy, Juneau Co., Wisc. on 2 Mar 1926, she was 68. They had the following children:

    3288   i.   William Lyman (1876-)
    3289   ii.   Arthur Alanson (1878-)

3290	iii.	Grace Rosetta (1880-)
3291	iv.	Emma Ethyl (1882-)
3292	v.	Clarence Leonard (1885-)

On 6 May 1905 when Spencer Alanson was 54, he second married **Clara KENNEDY** in Elroy, Juneau Co., Wisc. Born in 1861; died in Elroy, Juneau Co., Wisc. in 1924, she was 63; d.s.p.

2426. Harriet BURLINGAME. Born in 1852 in Elroy, Juneau Co., Wisc. Harriet died in Melfort, Saskatchewan, Canada in 1928, she was 76. Harriet married **Hiram Benjamin RUSH.** Born on 2 Jun 1856 in Elroy, Juneau Co., Wisc.; died in Melfort, Saskatchewan, Canada in 1924, he was 67.
They had the following children:

| 3293 | i. | Eben |
| 3294 | ii. | Clarence Benjamin (1893-) |

2427. Lyman Rufus BURLINGAME. Born on 24 Feb 1852 in Ashippun, Dodge Co., Wisc. Lyman Rufus died on 18 Feb 1941, he was 88. On 28 Dec 1882 when Lyman Rufus was 30, he married **Ellen K. PEABODY,**[682] daughter of Horace Emery PEABODY & Catherine DICKINSON, in Elroy, Juneau Co., Wisc. Born on 31 Mar 1862.
They had the following children:

3295	i.	Chester Earl (1883-)
3296	ii.	[Living]
3297	iii.	Gladys Catharine (1890-)
3298	iv.	Marjorie Clare (1898-)

2428. George F. BURLINGAME. Born on 26 Apr 1856 in Ashippun, Dodge Co., Wisc. George F. died in Necedah, Juneau Co., Wisc. on 17 Dec 1935, he was 79. George F. married **Jeanette Mae MOREY.** Born on 14 Nov 1870 in Dane, Wisc.; died in Necedah, Juneau Co., Wisc. on 17 Jun 1960, she was 89.
They had the following children:

3299	i.	Carrie Estell
3300	ii.	Esther Ruhania (1896-)
3301	iii.	Nancy (1899-)
3302	iv.	Sylvia Lavina (1901-)
3303	v.	George Wilfred (1904-)
3304	vi.	Gladys Hazel (1906-)

2429. Frederick C. BURLINGAME. Born on 28 Jun 1858 in Milwaukee, Wisc.

2430. Betsy A. BURLINGAME. Born on 12 May 1860 in Ashippun, Dodge Co., Wisc.

2431. John F. BURLINGAME. Born on 10 Jun 1862 in Ashippun, Dodge Co., Wisc.

2432. Christopher M. BURLINGAME. Born on 15 Feb 1869 in Milwaukee, Wisc.

2433. Orley M. BURLINGAME. Born on 9 Jun 1870 in Ashippun, Dodge Co., Wisc.

2434. Henry Ives LEETE. Born on 16 Jan 1854 in Guilford, Conn.; died on 20 Apr 1855, he was 1.

2435. Nelson Sherwood LEETE. Born on 19 Apr 1856 in Guilford, Conn. Nelson Sherwood died in 1915, he was 58. On 23 Apr 1878 when Nelson Sherwood was 22, he married **Gertrude E. BENEDICT.** Born on 25 Sep 1857 in Woodbridge, Conn. Gertrude E. died in 1917, she was 59.

2436. Fanny Amanda LEETE. Born on 15 May 1862 in Guilford, Conn. Fanny Amanda died in 1920, she was 57. On 23 Apr 1878 when Fanny Amanda was 15, she married **James A. COVILLE.** Born on 25 Sep 1857 in Worcester, Mass. James A. died in 1916, he was 58.
They had the following children:

| 3305 | i. | Minnie Ives (1880-) |
| 3306 | ii. | Alice Belle (1881-) |

2437. Eva Rose LEETE. Born on 18 Jan 1869 in Guilford, Conn. Eva Rose died in 1916, she was 46.

2438. Henry B. LEETE. Born on 4 Nov 1857. Henry B. died in 1918, he was 60. Henry B. married **Louisa QUIST.** Born on 12 Oct 1859 in Gottenberg, Sweden. Louisa died in 1920, she was 60.
They had one child:

| 3307 | i. | William Thomas (1884-) |

2439. Jennie Amanda LEETE. Born on 18 Mar 1859. Jennie Amanda died in 1906, she was 46.

2440. Edward A. GAUCHET. Born on 23 Aug 1854 in Leetes Island, Guilford, Conn. Edward A. died on 16 Jun 1925, he was 70.

2441. Mary GAUCHET. Born on 29 Jun 1856. Mary died on 29 Jun 1856.

2442. Louis "Lewie" Leete GAUCHET. B. 23 Jul 1857 in Guilford, Conn.; died in Feb 1900, age 42.

2443. James Adolphus GAUCHET. Born on 27 Oct 1860 in Leetes Island, Guilford, Conn. James Adolphus died in 1916, he was 55. James Adolphus married **M. A. REDDING**. Born in 1860. M. A. died in 1912, she was 52.

2444. Daniel Benjamin GAUCHET. Born on 27 Jan 1865 in Leetes Island, Guilford, Conn. Daniel Benjamin died on 3 May 1923, he was 58. On 23 Dec 1884 when he was 19, he married **Lottie GREENFIELD**. Born on 5 Oct 1865 in New Haven, Conn.; d. in Lynn, Mass., 18 Feb 1914, she was 48. They had the following children:

3308	i.	Eva Mildred (1886-)
3309	ii.	Daniel Benjamin (1889-)
3310	iii.	Archibald Greenfield (1890-)
3311	iv.	Ezrena Amanda (1894-)

2445. Frank Henry GAUCHET. Born on 20 Sep 1869 in Guilford, Conn. Frank Henry married **Annie HOWARD**. Born in 1878. Annie died in 1960, she was 82.

2446. Orestes Cook PIERSON. Born on 6 Mar 1863 in Clinton, Conn. Orestes Cook died in Clinton, Conn. on 18 Jan 1876, he was 12.

2447. Ardella Robinson GREENE. Born on 5 Jun 1838.

2448. Albert Nathaniel GREENE. Born on 4 Mar 1840.

2449. Charles Thomas GREENE. Born on 5 Sep 1841. Charles Thomas died on 2 Sep 1843, he was 1.

2450. Sarah Martha GREENE. Born on 10 Feb 1846.

2451. Storrs Douglas GREENE. Born on 11 Sep 1848. Storrs Douglas died on 27 Feb 1852, he was 3.

2452. Levi Maxley GREENE. Born on 4 Nov 1851.

2453. Frederick Baker KENTFIELD. Born on 4 Dec 1845 in Hampshire, Mass. Frederick Baker died in Hadley, Hampshire Co., Mass. in 1927, he was 81. After his first wife died of complications of childbirth, and his daughter died at age four, he went to California, where he married for the second time two years after his daughter died. He then returned to Massachusetts and had a family of eight children by his second wife. On 20 Apr 1871 when Frederick Baker was 25, he first married **Mary L. REED** in Hampshire, Mass. Born in 1850 in Amherst, Hampshire Co., Mass. Mary L. died in Hadley, Hampshire Co., Mass. on 4 Feb 1872, she was 22; she d. 6 days after her daughter was b. They had one child:

| 3312 | i. | Mary Lucy (1872-1876) |

On 30 Apr 1878 when Frederick Baker was 32, he second married **Jennie Matilda MANEE** in Stockton, Calif. Born on 4 May 1855 in Westfield, Hampshire Co., Mass. Jennie Matilda died in Hadley, Hampshire Co., Mass. on 7 Dec 1921, she was 66. They had the following children:

3313	i.	?
3314	ii.	Mary Elinor (1880-1926)
3315	iii.	Arthur Baker (1884-1960)
3316	iv.	Nellie Frances (1886-1922)
3317	v.	John Theodore (1891-1950)
3318	vi.	Annie Louise (1892-1950)
3319	vii.	Jennie (1894-1999)
3320	viii.	James Frederick (1895-1971)

2454. John Greene KENTFIELD. Born on 13 May 1848.

2455. Esther Adelia KENTFIELD. Born on 23 Apr 1858 in Hadley, Hampshire Co., Mass. Esther Adelia died in Easthampton, Hampshire Co., Mass. on 3 May 1923, she was 65. Esther Adelia married **William Levi TORREY**. Born on 23 Dec 1856 in Chesterfield, Mass. William Levi died in Easthampton, Hampshire Co., Mass. on 27 May 1936, he was 79.

They had the following children:

3321	i.	Mabel Alice (1881-)
3322	ii.	Orson Winfield (1882-)
3323	iii.	Grace Belle (1884-1949)
3324	iv.	Clara Eleanor (1885-)
3325	v.	Willis Porter (1887-1974)
3326	vi.	Linus Greene (1889-)
3327	vii.	Robert Lorenso (1891-1972)
3328	viii.	Bessie E. (1893-1893)
3329	ix.	Fred Baker (1894-1973)
3330	x.	Ida Marchie (1896-)
3331	xi.	Frank Andrew (1897-1926)
3332	xii.	Edith E. (1899-)
3333	xiii.	Ralph Eugene (1900-1967)
3334	xiv.	Bertha F. (1903-)

2456. Nellie Rebecca KENTFIELD. Born on 9 Sep 1860.

2457. Annie Jane KENTFIELD. Born on 4 Jun 1862. Annie Jane died in Hadley, Hampshire Co., Mass. on 27 Jan 1939, she was 76.

2458. ? KENTFIELD.

2459. ? KENTFIELD married **? HUMES**.

They had the following children, surname Kentfield:

3335	i.	Henry L. (1869-1869)
3336	ii.	Abigail S. (1871-1871)

2460. Frank KENTFIELD. Born in 1858. Frank died on 2 Apr 1901, he was 43.

2461. Nellie Lamson KENTFIELD. Born on 11 Dec 1865 in Providence, Providence Co., R.I. Nellie Lamson died in Providence, Providence Co., R.I. on 16 Mar 1914, she was 48. Occupation: d.s.p. On 9 Apr 1890 when Nellie Lamson was 24, she married **Frank H. BROWN** in Providence, Providence Co., R.I. Born on 16 Feb 1866 in Providence, Providence Co., R.I. Frank H. died in Providence, Providence Co., R.I. on 18 Mar 1934, he was 68.

2462. Lewis G. BILYEU. Born on 27 Aug 1827 in Bond, Ill. Lewis G. died in Mulberry Grove, Bond Co., Ill. on 4 Nov 1893, he was 66. On 6 Feb 1867 when Lewis G. was 39, he first married **Rebecca June Morris** in Fayette, Ill. Born on 1 Mar 1848 in St. Clair, Ill. Rebecca June died in Fayette, Ill. on 5 Dec 1905, she was 57.

They had one child:

3337	i.	Mary Myrtle (1870-)

On 9 Aug 1854 when Lewis G. was 26, he second married **Elizabeth W. BEABOUT** in Bond, Ill. Elizabeth W. died on 7 May 1856 in Illinois.

2463. Nancy Birge BILYEU. Born on 17 Dec 1829 in Bond, Ill. Nancy Birge died in Mulberry Grove, Bond Co., Ill. on 13 Jun 1879, she was 49.

2464. William Thomas BILYEU. Born on 6 Jan 1831 in Mulberry Grove, Bond Co., Ill. William Thomas died in Greenville, Bond Co., Ill. on 15 Sep 1903, he was 72.

2465. Elizabeth M. BILYEU. Born in 1835 in Mulberry Grove, Bond Co., Ill. Elizabeth M. died on 26 Jul 1827 in Bond, Ill.

2466. John F. BILYEU. Born in 1837 in Mulberry Grove, Bond Co., Ill. John F. died in Bond, Ill. on 28 May 1862, he was 25.

2467. Peter F. BILYEU. Born in 1839 in Illinois. Peter F. died in Bond, Ill. on 21 Feb 1909, he was 70.

2468. Joseph H. BILYEU. Born on 7 Feb 1829 in Bond, Ill.; died there, 19 Jun 1877, he was 48.

2469. John BILYEU. Born on 21 Jan 1834 in Bond, Ill. John died in Illinois on 1 Jan 1915, he was 80.

2470. Wesley Asbury BILYEU. Born in Bond, Ill. Wesley Asbury died on 20 Sep 1899 in Bond, Ill. His b.d. of 3 Apr 1834 in OneWorldTree is inconsistent with the entry for his older brother. The brothers, George and Wesley Bilyeu, married sisters, Martha and Elizabeth May. On 15 Dec 1857 Wesley Asbury

married **Elizabeth MAY**, daughter of Morris MAY & Martha OVERSTREET, in Bond, Ill. Born in 1836 in Bond, Ill. Elizabeth died in Sorento, Bond Co., Ill. in 1921, she was 85.
They had one child:

    3338   i.   Sarah (1859-)

2471. George Harvey BILYEU. Born on 22 Feb 1837 in Bond, Ill.; died in Sorento, Bond Co., Ill. on 26 Jul 1897, he was 60. The brothers, George and Wesley Bilyeu, married sisters, Martha and Elizabeth May. George Harvey married **Martha MAY**, daughter of Morris MAY & Martha OVERSTREET. Born in 1837 in Bond, Ill. Martha died in Sorento, Bond Co., Ill. in 1918, she was 81; apparently d.s.p.

2472. Sidney M. BILYEU. Born on 26 Oct 1839 in Bond, Ill.; died there, 25 Jul 1915, he was 75.

2473. Andrew BILYEU. Born in 1841 in Greenville, Bond Co., Ill.; died in Bond, Ill. in 1903, abt 62.

2474. Finas BILYEU. Born in 1843 in Bond, Ill. Finas died in Bond, Ill. in 1865, he was 22.

2475. Polly Ann BILYEU. Born in 1845 in Illinois. Polly Ann died in Litchfield, Montgomery Co., Ill. in 1915, she was 70. On 28 May 1865 when Polly Ann was 20, she married **Francois Eugene MORVILLE**,[683] son of Jean Nicholas MORVILLE & Anne DARDAINE, in Sorento, Bond Co., Ill. Born on 29 Jun 1841 in Salonnes, France; died in Cerro Gordo, Platt Co., Ill. on 19 Apr 1908, he was 66.
They had one child:

    3339   i.   Mary Annette (1867-)

2476. Thomas H. BILYEU. Born on 17 Feb 1849 in Old Ripley, Bond Co., Ill. Thomas H. died in St. Louis, St. Charles Co., Mo. on 10 Feb 1913, he was 63. On 13 Jun 1883 when Thomas H. was 34, he married **Martha A. BILYEU**[684] in Litchfield, Montgomery Co., Ill. Born on 30 Dec 1861 in Litchfield, Montgomery Co., Ill. Martha A. died in Terre Haute, Vigo Co., Ind. on 17 Jan 1940, she was 78.
They had the following children:

    3340   i.   Harry Earle (1886-)
    3341   ii.   Winne Mae (1891-)
    3342   iii.   Roy Sidney (1893-)
    3343   iv.   Olive Marie (1896-)
    3344   v.   Jesse C. (1898-)
    3345   vi.   Charles Clarence (1900-)
    3346   vii.   Vera Bessie (1901-)

2477. John W. BILYEU. Born on 18 Nov 1827 in Illinois. He married **Jane BAKER**. Born in 1830.

    3347   i.   Malinda

2478. William B. BILYEU. Born on 16 Dec 1831 in Illinois. On 11 Aug 1852 when William B. was 20, he married **Sarah McCOLLOM**, in Bond, Ill. Occupation: Mother of 1.
They had one child:

    3348   i.   Henrietta

2479. Jesse Wheeler BILYEU. Born on 20 Sep 1841 in Clinton, Ill. Jesse Wheeler died in Scotia, Greely Co., Neb. on 17 Feb 1913, he was 71. On 22 Mar 1866 when Jesse Wheeler was 24, he married **Emily C. FILE**, in Bond, Ill. Born on 14 Oct 1845.
They had the following children:

    3349   i.   Charles Elmer
    3350   ii.   Fred Ellsworth
    3351   iii.   John Wilson
    3352   iv.   Joseph Nelson
    3353   v.   Lemuel E.

2480. Simeon Walker BILYEU. Born on 17 Aug 1844 in Clinton, Ill. Simeon Walker died in Omaha, Douglas Co., Neb. on 7 Jan 1908, he was 63. On 17 Aug 1865 when Simeon Walker was 21, he first married **Elvira J. HARRIS**, in Pocahontas, Bond Co., Ill. Born on 27 Oct 1847 in Missouri. Elvira J. died in Pocahontas, Bond Co., Ill. on 29 Apr 1875, she was 27.
They had the following children:

    3354   i.   Milo D.
    3355   ii.   Francis Simeon (1869-)

3356	iii.	Nellie E. (1871-)
3357	iv.	Leroy Vernon (1873-)

On 19 Feb 1877 when Simeon Walker was 32, he married (2) **Florinda DONALDSON**, in Merrick, Neb. Simeon Walker third married **Lydia M. HUGHES**. Born in Nov 1864 in Indiana. Lydia M. died in Omaha, Douglas Co., Neb. on 2 Sep 1941, she was 76.

They had the following children:

3358	i.	Willie Ray (1887-)
3359	ii.	Jessie Belle (1889-)
3360	iii.	Lewis (1892-)
3361	iv.	Albert (1897-)

2481. Martha Emma BILYEU. Born in Feb 1849 in Pocahontas, Bond Co., Ill. Martha Emma died in Chadron, Dawes Co., Neb. on 24 Sep 1930, she was 81. Mother of 6. On 26 Feb 1865 when Martha Emma was 16, she married **Andrew Jackson GILLESPIE**, in Pocahontas, Bond Co., Ill. Born on 24 Jan 1839 in Dubuque, Dubuque Co., Ia. Andrew Jackson died on 15 Dec 1911, he was 72.

They had the following children:

3362	i.	Corinore (1863-)
3363	ii.	Sadie (1866-)
3364	iii.	Flora (1868-)
3365	iv.	Mary Temperance (1872-)
3366	v.	Grace A. (1880-)
3367	vi.	Leona (1886-)

2482. Mary Jane BILYEU. Born in 1836 in Illinois. Mary Jane died in Bond, Ill.

2483. Sarah Frances BILYEU. Born in 1840 in Illinois. Sarah Frances died in Bond, Ill.

2484. Lewis Garret BILYEU. Born in 1842 in Illinois. Lewis Garret died in Bond, Ill.

2485. David Allen BILYEU. Born in 1844 in Illinois. David Allen died in Bond, Ill.

2486. Emily Caroline BILYEU. Born in 1845 in Illinois. Emily Caroline died in Bond, Ill.

2487. Thomas Newton BILYEU. Born in 1846 in Illinois. Thomas Newton died in Bond, Ill.

2488. Nancy A. BILYEU. Born in 1848 in Illinois. Nancy A. died in Bond, Ill.

2489. Anna E. BILYEU. Born in 1850.

2490. Mary A. BILYEU. Born in 1835 in Illinois. Mary A. died in Bond, Ill.

2491. Irving BILYEU. Born in 1838 in Illinois. Irving died in Bond, Ill.

2492. Lewis I. BILYEU. Born in 1840 in Illinois. Lewis I. died in Bond, Ill.

2493. Caroline BILYEU. Born in 1852 in Illinois. Caroline died in Bond, Ill.

2494. Emily E. BILYEU. Born in 1849 in Illinois. Emily E. died in Bond, Ill.

2495. Francis BILYEU. Born in 1855 in Illinois. Francis died in Greenville, Bond Co., Ill.

2496. Mary BILYEU. Born in 1836 in Illinois. Mary died in Bond, Ill.

2497. Martha BILYEU. Born in 1839 in Illinois. Martha died in Bond, Ill.

2498. John BILYEU. Born in 1844 in Illinois. John died in Bond, Ill.

2499. Emma BILYEU. Born in 1848 in Illinois. Emma died in Bond, Ill.

2500. Sarah BILYEU. Born in 1849 in Illinois. Sarah died in Bond, Ill.

2501. Mary BILYEU. Born in 1839 in Illinois. Mary died in Bond, Ill.

2502. Martha A. BILYEU. Born in 1839 in Illinois. Martha A. died in Bond, Ill.

2503. William T. BILYEU. Born in 1842 in Illinois. William T. died in Bond, Ill.

2504. Joseph E. BILYEU. Born in 1850 in Illinois. Joseph E. died in Bond, Ill.

2505. Frank BILYEU. Born in 1857 in Illinois. Frank died in Bond, Ill.

2506. William Burge BILYEU. Born in 1851 in Greenville, Bond Co., Ill. On 1 Oct 1871 when William Burge was 20, he married **Martha L. SMITH**, in Bond, Ill. Born on 8 Jan 1855 in Illinois. Martha L. died in Fort Scott, Bourbon Co., Ks. on 8 Dec 1913, she was 58.

They had the following children:

3368	i.	Charles Henry (1874-)
3369	ii.	Maud Ann (1885-)

3370	iii.	Francis Roy (1890-)
3371	iv.	Martha Pearl (1892-)
3372	v.	Harrell H. (1895-)
3373	vi.	Grace Comfort (1899-)

2507. Laura C. BIRGE. Born on 22 Aug 1843 in Seneca Falls, N.Y. Laura C. died in 1928, she was 84.

2508. Edwin D. BIRGE. Born on 15 Apr 1845 in Seneca Falls, N.Y.; died there, 15 Apr 1846, he was 1.

2509. Julia Elizabeth BIRGE. Born in 1839. Julia Elizabeth died in 1898, she was 59.

2510. Mary Olds BIRGE. Born in 1847.

2511. George Kingsley BIRGE.[685] Born in 1849 in Buffalo, N.Y. George Kingsley died in 1918, he was 69. Birge was educated at the Buffalo Academy and Cornell University. He became a partner in the wallpaper establishment in Buffalo that was founded by his father, Martin H. Birge. The company was sold to the National Wall Paper Co. in 1890, but the proprietors bought it back in 1900 and it was continued thereafter as M. H. Birge & Sons Co., which was famous for its 12-color process of wallpaper production. George H. Birge was president of the reorganized company. He was also a director and member of the Executive Committee of the 1901 Pan-American Exposition.

In 1891, Birge and some friends bought into a small manufacturing company that was founded by George N. Pierce in 1880 and that in 1900 was making gas-powered automobiles. The most notable autos produced by the Pierce Company were the fifteen horsepower Arrow and the twenty-four horsepower Great Arrow. The Pierce-Arrow plant in Buffalo eventually employed some 10,000 workers. The founder, Pierce, withdrew from the company in 1908 "in a fit of pique," and Birge was president from 1908-1916, at which time he sold half of his share in the operation for $7 million and retired.

George Kingsley married **Caroline "Carrie" HUMPHREY**, daughter of Hon. James H. HUMPHREY. Born in 1853. Humphrey represented Buffalo in Congress during the Civil War period and later received honors of the bench. Their children were Humphrey, Marion (who married Thomas B. Lockwood), and Allithea (who married a very successful Buffalo architect, George Cary).
George Kingsley and Caroline (Humphrey) Birge had the following children:

3374	i.	Allithea (1860-1918)
3375	ii.	Marion (1871-)
3376	iii.	George Humphrey (1878-1969)

2512. Henry Martin BIRGE. Born in 1851; died in 1904, abt 53. He married **Fannie KING**.

2513. Laura BIRGE.

2514. Rose BIRGE.

2515. Francis BIRGE.

2516. Mary BIRGE.

2517. Fred BIRGE.

2518. Ellen BIRGE.

2519. Blanche BIRGE.

2520. Olive L. BIRGE. On 27 Nov 1861 Olive L. married **Converse E. DAY**.

2521. Mamie BIRGE. Born in 1854 in Bond, Ill.

2522. Mary M. BIRGE. Born in 1856 in Illinois.

2523. Virginia E. BIRGE. Born in 1859 in Bond, Ill.

2524. Anna BIRGE. Born in 1853. Anna died in Pittsford, Crawford Co., Ks. in 1893, she was 40.

2525. Virginia BIRGE. Born in 1859.

2526. Lucy BIRGE. Born in 1864.

2527. Charles C. BIRGE. Born in 1893 in Chetopa, Labette, Ks.

2528. Agatha ADAMS. Born in 1871. Agatha died in 1871.

2529. Mary BIRGE. Born in 1877.

2530. Harvey HENRY.

2531. John HENRY.

2532. Lena HENRY. Lena married **John MULFORD**.

2533. Mary HENRY. Mary married **? CHALMERS**.

2534. Wesley HENRY.

2535. William HENRY.

2536. Mary Eliza BIRGE. Born in 1853 in Washington. Mary Eliza died in 1939, she was 86. Mary Eliza married **C. Owen ABBOTT**.

2537. Ida Virginia BIRGE. Born in 1855.

2538. Anna BIRGE. Born in 1860 in Covington, Ky. Anna died in 1934, she was 74.

2539. Henry Cyrus BIRGE. Born in 1861. Henry Cyrus married **Jeanne Elizabeth RILEY**. Born in 1870. Jeanne Elizabeth died in 1950, she was 80.
They had the following children:

3377	i.	Judith V.
3378	ii.	Warren Riley (1898-)
3379	iii.	Margaret C. (1899-)
3380	iv.	Morgan (1901-)
3381	v.	Henry E. (1907-)

2540. Hattie BIRGE. Born in 1862 in Covington, Ky. Hattie died in 1932, she was 70.

2541. Thomas C. BIRGE. Born in 1864.

2542. Henry Cyrus BIRGE. Born in 1864.

2543. William E. BIRGE. Born in 1865.

2544. Eliza Gilbert BIRGE. Born on 4 Sep 1848. Eliza Gilbert died on 4 Aug 1863, she was 14.

2545. Lizzie G. BIRGE. Born in 1848. Lizzie G. died in 1863, she was 15.

2546. Frank Howell BIRGE. Born in 1851. Frank Howell died in 1922, he was 71. Frank Howell married **Bessie McKINSEY**. Born in 1854. Bessie died in 1925, she was 71.
They had the following children:

3382	i.	Grace (1882-)
3383	ii.	Ethyl (1884-)
3384	iii.	Nellie (1889-)

2547. Mary A. BIRGE. Born in 1854; died 3 Oct 1930, abt 76. Mary A. married **Jim KERNS**.

2548. Anna P. BIRGE. Born in 1856. Anna P. died in 1856.

2549. Sallie H. BIRGE. Born in 1857 in Greenville, Bond Co., Ill. Sallie H. died in Terral, Indian Territory, Okla. on 17 Nov 1905, she was 48. On 9 Feb 1879 when Sallie H. was 22, she married **John F. BARTRUM** in Greenville, Bond Co., Ill. Born on 25 Nov 1853 in Wymondham, Norfolk, England. John F. died in Mobeetie, Wheeler Co., Texas on 30 Aug 1930, he was 76.
They had the following children:

3385	i.	Arthur Henry (1882-)
3386	ii.	James J. (1888-)
3387	iii.	Annie Bell (1894-)
3388	iv.	Maudie Myrtle (1897-)

2550. Henry Cyrus BIRGE. Born in 1866 in Greenville, Bond Co., Ill. Henry Cyrus died in 1914, he was 48. Henry Cyrus first married **Laura HABICH**. Born in 1870. Laura died in 1896, she was 26.
They had one child:

3389	i.	Anna Dell (**1894-**)

Henry Cyrus second married **Alice THOMPSON**.

2551. Eames D. BIRGE. Born in 1864 in Greenville, Bond Co., Ill. Eames D. died in 1886, he was 22.

2552. Robert Joseph BIRGE. Born in 1868. Robert Joseph died in 1938, he was 70. Robert Joseph first married **Effie M. TOPPING**. Robert Joseph second married **Jessie Irene FRY**. Born in 1870 in Iowa. Jessie Irene died in 1947, she was 77.
They had the following children:

3390	i.	Ralph (1895-)
3391	ii.	Ruth (1901-)
3392	iii.	Opal (1905-)

2553. John Hugh BIRGE. Born in 1871 in Illinois. John Hugh died in 1950, he was 79. John Hugh married **Ruth T. ELDRED**. Born in 1892. Mother of 7, only two of whom are named in OneWorldTree. They had the following children:

3393	i.	Jack
3394	ii.	Mary Edna

2554. Eames D. RANKIN. Born in 1856 in Washington. Eames D. died in 1890, he was 34. On 9 Sep 1879 when Eames D. was 23, he married **Martha Jane MILES** in Cook, Ill. Born in 1860 in Illinois. Martha Jane died in Long Beach, Calif. on 20 Jan 1927, she was 67. They had one child:

3395	i.	Edith Miles (1880-)

2555. Walter N. RANKIN. Born in 1857. Walter N. died in 1877, he was 20.

2556. Mary F. RANKIN. Born in 1858. Mary F. died in 1913, she was 55. Mary F. married **Harvey D. GOULDER.**

They had one child:

3396	i.	Harvey D.

2557. Andrew R. RANKIN. Born in 1863. Andrew R. died in 1864, he was 1.

2558. Edith G. RANKIN. Born in 1864. Edith G. died in 1943, she was 79. Edith G. married **William H. WHITE**. Born in 1866. William H. died in 1935, he was 69.

They had the following children:

3397	i.	Mary G. (1901-)
3398	ii.	Evelyn R. (1903-)
3399	iii.	Theodore E. (1904-)

------------------- 686

2559. Bradford L. HILL.[687] Born on 9 Sep 1868 in Lime Springs, Howard County, Iowa. Occupation: Pharmacist. Owned and operated B. L. Hill Drug Co., Olympia, Kansas. Education: Pharmacy Department, University of Kansas. He d.s.p.

2560. Daughter of Henry & Amanda Hill HILL. Teacher, Tacoma Public Schools.

2561. Henry Kniffen HILL. Born on 10 Jun 1886.

2562. Gertrude Eloise HILL. Born on 14 Sep 1887.

2563. Helen Winifred HILL. Born on 4 Nov 1893.

2564. Marion Cecile HILL. Born on 1 May 1905.

------------------- 688

2565. William James BENEDICT. Born in 1872.

2566. Mary Elizabeth BENEDICT. Born in 1847.

2567. Matilda Jane BENEDICT. Born in 1875.

2568. Ida Florence BENEDICT. Born in 1878.

2569. Ellen Jane BENEDICT. Born in 1880.

2570. Dawson Alexander BENEDICT. Born in 1882.

2571. John George BENEDICT. Born in 1883.

2572. Harriet Maud BENEDICT. Born in 1886.

2573. Lila Beatrice BENEDICT. Born in 1888.

2574. Elizabeth Ann DOWD. Born in 1855.

2575. Hamilton Stewart DOWD. Born in 1857.

2576. Lucy Sophia DOWD. Born in 1859.

2577. Maria J. WRIGHT. Born in 1863.

2578. Robert H. WRIGHT. Born in 1865.

2579. Charles J. WRIGHT. Born in 1868.

2580. Clarence Peter WRIGHT. Born in 1868.

2581. Lucy WRIGHT. Born in 1870.

2582. Lillian WRIGHT. Born in 1870.

2583. Florence Edith RADMORE. Born on 5 Dec 1883; died on 28 Jul 1954, she was 70. She married **William MAXWELL**. Born in 1869; died on 26 Jan 1931, abt 62.

They had the following children:

3400	i.	?
3401	ii.	Lila (1907-)
3402	iii.	Doris Elizabeth (1909-)
3403	iv.	William James (1913-)

2584. Joseph HETHERINGTON.

2585. Mary HETHERINGTON.

2586. Wesley HETHERINGTON.

2587. Henry HETHERINGTON. Born on 28 Dec 1882.

2588. Harold HETHERINGTON.

2589. ? HETHERINGTON.

2590. ? HETHERINGTON.

2591. Lorne Clifford HETHERINGTON. Born on 27 Aug 1890 in New Liskeard, Ontario, Canada.

2592. Beatrice HETHERINGTON. Born on 23 Feb 1895.

2593. Simpson HETHERINGTON. Born on 24 Apr 1898 in Teatrenville, Quebec, Canada.

2594. Ezra BENEDICT.

2595. Thomas BENEDICT.

2596. Joseph A. HETHERINGTON.

2597. William A. HETHERINGTON.

2598. Lucy HETHERINGTON. Born on 10 Jun 1873 in Hayworth, Quebec, Canada.

2599. Sarah Elizabeth HETHERINGTON. B. 22 Jul 1885 in Eardley, Quebec, Canada.

2600. Mary HETHERINGTON. Born on 26 Mar 1888.

2601. Ethyl Emma HETHERINGTON. Born on 21 Jan 1890.

2602. Cecil H. HETHERINGTON. Born on 15 Feb 1895.

2603. ? HETHERINGTON.

2604. ? HETHERINGTON.

2605. Robert HETHERINGTON. Born on 2 Jul 1896.

2606. Olive J. HETHERINGTON. Born on 13 May 1898.

2607. ? HETHERINGTON.

2608. ? HETHERINGTON.

2609. ? HETHERINGTON.

2610. ? HETHERINGTON.

2611. Lena May HETHERINGTON. Born on 11 Feb 1899.

2612. Percy Robert HETHERINGTON. Born on 30 Jun 1900.

2613. Edward John HETHERINGTON. Born on 24 Dec 1902.

2614. Margery Rebecca HETHERINGTON. Born on 21 Apr 1905.

2615. ? HILTON.

2616. Nellie MAXWELL.

2617. ? MAXWELL.

2618. Lila MAXWELL. Born on 5 Dec 1907.

2619. Doris Elizabeth MAXWELL. Born on 12 Aug 1909.

2620. William James MAXWELL. Born on 11 Jan 1913.

2621. Velma DOWD. Born in 1905.

2622. Annie DOWD.

2623. Evelyn DOWD.

2624. Mabel DOWD.

2625. ? DOWD.

-------------------- [689]

2626. William COE. Born abt 1845.

2627. Edmund COE.[690] Born abt 1849.

2628. Clarence W. HILL. Born abt 1857.

2629. Leverett H. HILL. Born abt 1859.
2630. George C. HILL. Born abt 1868 in Indianola, Nebraska. George C. died aft 1896. Occupation: Lumber company operator, Cripple Creek, Colo.
2631. Lena E. HILL. B. abt 1869 in Indianola, Neb.; died aft 1896; nurse at St. Luke's Hospital, Denver.
2632. Frank HILL. Born abt 1870 in Indianola, Nebraska. Frank died.
2633. Sidney T. HILL. Born abt 1866. Sidney T. died in Tabor, Iowa on 21 Jul 1895, he was 29.
2634. Herbert WEBB. Born abt 1858 in Iowa.
2635. Edgar WEBB. Born abt 1859 in Iowa.
2636. daughter FORDE.
2637. Alice Clare HILL. Born on 4 Sep 1865. Alice Clare died on 18 Dec 1947, she was 82.
2638. Nathan HILL.[691] Born in 1865 in Kansas City, Jackson Co., Mo. Nathan died in 1900, he was 35.
2639. Sylvester Bruce HILL.[692] Born on 3 Sep 1867 in Admire, Lyon Co., Kansas; died in Zion, Lake Co., Ill. on 4 Sep 1933. On 1 Sep 1896, when he was 28, he married **Janie Sarah COATS**, b 7 Jul 1869. They had the following children:

3404	i.	Elsie (1897-)
3405	ii.	Elva (1900-)
3406	iii.	Louis Sylvester (1905-)
3407	iv.	Raymond Hartley (1907-)

2640. Mary Charlotte NICKERSON. Born abt 1865 in Bloomfield, Ind.
2641. William T. NICKERSON. Born abt 1868 in Bloomfield, Ind. William T. died in perhaps Linton, Ind. aft 1880. He married **Inez HAYWOOD**.
They had the following children:

3408	i.	Hoyt H.
3409	ii.	Alba
3410	iii.	Ruth
3411	iv.	Arthur
3412	v.	Emma Margaret

2642. Nellie A. NICKERSON.
2643. Laura Lenore NICKERSON. Lived in Whitaker, Ind.; mother of 1; married **Pierce JARRELL**. They had one child:

3413	i.	Frank

2644. Hettie H. HILL. Born in Cairo, IL. Occupation: She was DAR member No. 159003.
---------------------------[693]

2645. Charles HILL. Born abt 1865.
2646. Myrtle O. "Maybelle" HILL.[694] Born in Apr 1878 in Indiana. On 26 Oct 1897 when she was 19, she married **Ernest Oliver "Ernie" HILL** (1853), son of Charles McNair HILL (891) & Sarah Jane JOHNSON, in Kendall Co., Ill. Born on 9 Oct 1870 in Fox Station, Ill., and later of Brookfield, Mo. They had one child:

2659	i.	Earnest L. (1899-)

2647. Frank HILL. Born abt 1871.
2648. Glen W. "Clem" HILL.[695] Born abt 1894.
2649. Evelyn R. HILL.[696] Born abt 1896 in Illinois.
2650. Lois Erma HILL.[697] Born abt 1899 in Illinois.
2651. Orvin J. HILL.[698] Born abt 1903 in Illinois.
2652. Clarence J. HILL.[699] Born abt 1901 in Illinois.
2653. Ruby A. HILL.[700] Born abt 1910 in Illinois.
-------------------[701]

2654. Fred SWAIN.
2655. Frank SWAIN.
-------------------------[702]

2656. Florence Rebecca SWAIN. Born on 12 Mar 1888 in Kendall Co., Ill. Florence Rebecca died in

1961, she was 72. On 23 Aug 1910 when Florence Rebecca was 22, she married **Montgomery Frank TILLITSON** in Kendall Co., Ill. Born in 1890. Montgomery Frank died in 1963, he was 73.
They had the following children:

3414	i.	Child of Montgomery and Florence
3415	ii.	Child of Montgomery and Florence
3416	iii.	Swayne George (1912-1982)

2657. Ora M. HILL. Born on 19 Dec 1892 in Kendall Co., Ill.

2658. Maurice HILL.[703] Born abt 1909 in Illinois.

2659. Earnest L. HILL.[704] Born in Jan 1899 in Missouri.

2660. Child of Frederick and Lillian HILL.

2661. Elizabeth T. HILL. Born on 22 Oct 1910 in Illinois. Elizabeth T. died in Aurora, Ill. on 22 Feb 2008, she was 97. On 23 Feb 1928 when Elizabeth T. was 17, she married **Arthur Ervin LEIFHEIT** in Yorkville, Ill. Born in 1905. Arthur Ervin died in 1961, he was 56.
They had the following children:

3417	i.	Child of Arthur and Elizabeth
3418	ii.	Child of Arthur and Elizabeth
3419	iii.	Lorraine Ann (1936-2006)

2662. Roy Steven HILL.[705] Born on 27 Jan 1912 in Yorkville, Ill. Roy Steven died in Aurora, Ill. on 5 Sep 2004, he was 92. On 3 Jul 1937 when Roy Steven was 25, he married **Catherine L. BOWERS.** Born in 1914. Catherine L. died in 2003, she was 89. Occupation: Mother of 2.
They had the following children:

3420	i.	Child of Roy and Catherine
3421	ii.	Melvyn R. (1938-2006)

--- [706]

2663. Kittie A. HILL.[707] Born in Jun 1867 in Corning, Steuben Co., N.Y.

2664. Emma L. HILL.[708] Born in Mar 1871 in Corning, Steuben Co., N.Y.

2665. Fred E. HILL.[709] Born in Dec 1872 in Corning, Steuben Co., N.Y. Timber buyer in 1900; proprietor of lumber yard in 1920; proprietor of lumber factory in 1930.

2666. Albert G. HILL.[710] Albert G. married Mary R. ? (HILL). Born abt 1884 in Michigan.
They had one child:

3422	i.	Caroline L. (~1902-)

--- [711]

2667. George J. [68] HILL,[712] eldest of the three children of Charles W. and Adelia Catharine (Riley) Hill, was born at Caton, Steuben Co., New York, 5 January 1857; died at Clarion, Wright Co., Iowa, 2 June 1952. He was buried in the Graceland Cemetery, Rowan, Wright Co., Iowa.

George J. Hill came to Iowa at the age of four in 1861 with his parents and his brother, who was born in 1860. The family made the trip by train to Dubuque, Iowa, and then by stage coach to Fryeburg, which was later called Rowan, near Clarion, in Wright County, Iowa. His parents purchased land in Grant Township northeast of Clarion for $10 per acre. Part of this original farm was still owned and farmed in 1994 by the descendants of his son, Myron Hill, Sr. George Hill was for many years manager of the Solberg elevator, to which he commuted from his farm home by horse and buggy. He was a charter member of the Harvey Congregational Church in Grant Township, where he was the church janitor and Sunday school teacher. He was Secretary of the Grant Township School Board in 1895-1898, and recorded the minutes of the Board meetings with a bold and legible hand.

George and his wife moved to Clarion in 1913, where he became an active member of the Methodist church. Meanwhile, his family grew and thrived, some in farming, some in business, and others in the field of education. Following the death of his wife, he lived with his daughter, Ruby, in Clarion, until he passed away at the age of 95. In his later years he was one of the town's most visible patriarchs, a quiet dignified gentleman with a full white beard and mustache. Following services at the Methodist church in Clarion, he was buried in the family cemetery at Rowan. This cemetery was near the

Hill family homestead, on the east bank of the Iowa River, close to where his nine year old brother and his 22 year old uncle had drowned in 1869 in an accident that nearly claimed his life, too.

He married,[713] at Fryeburg, Wright Co., Iowa, 7 September 1882, **Jessie Fidelia STOCKWELL**,[714] daughter of Benajah Flavel and Emily Lodiweska (Hyde) Stockwell; born at Peoria, Peoria Co., Illinois, 7 September 1863; died at Clarion, 12 September 1940. George and Jessie (Stockwell) Hill had nine children. Seven of the children lived to maturity, married, and had children. Two young daughters died during a diphtheria epidemic in 1894, and were mourned for the rest of the lives of their parents and their brothers and sisters. When George J. Hill married Jessie Stockwell in 1882, two large families were joined and have since remained close. Many Stockwells looked at George and Jessie as their uncle and aunt, and later generations of Stockwells have been an extended family of first and second cousins of George and Jessie's children. A formal portrait taken in Clarion, Iowa, in 1909 shows 33 members of the Hill and Stockwell family seated on and around a front porch. George and Jessie are there, with his father, Charles Hill, and her father, Benajah Stockwell, and many descendants of each of the two patriarchs.

Jessie Fidelia STOCKWELL was born at Peoria, Illinois, 7 September 1863; died at Clarion, Iowa, 12 September 1940. One of her siblings, a brother, was born in Peoria. The family moved back to Vermont when she was four years old and remained there for three years while her father worked as a school teacher and Methodist preacher. A sister was born there. In the spring of 1870 her parents moved to Iowa with their three children and homesteaded at Fryeburg, near Rowan, in Wright County, on the upper reaches of the Iowa River. Three more children were born to this family in Iowa. Before she was sixteen, her mother died and she became "mother" to her three sisters and two brothers.

She was married on her nineteenth birthday to the son of a neighboring family. She and her husband farmed near Clarion for thirty years, and had nine children. Seven of the children married and had children; two small daughters died during a diphtheria epidemic in 1894. When she lived on the farm she was a member of the Harvey Community Church. She became a member of the Clarion Methodist Church on 18 April 1915 and was a charter member of the Woman's Society of Christian Service. She was also president of the Foreign Missionary Society of the church in Clarion. It was said that as a midwife she attended the birth of countless babies in Wright County, and of all of her grandchildren.

Her nephew, the Rev. F. Olin Stockwell, wrote that she was a thin, spare, and terribly energetic person. Her passion was that her youngest son, Gerald Hill, should not be shunted off to a farm job before he was out of his "teens," but that he should have a chance to get an education. It was this determination that enabled him to get a college education. He believed that "she wanted to make a preacher or a missionary out of him, although he ended up a banker."

Her six living children and many others gathered to celebrate her 77th birthday five days before she died following a short illness. At her funeral, the Rev. H. E. Harvey referred to her as "Sister" Hill, and compared her life to the disciples and heavenly beings arrayed in white, quoting St. John the Divine: "They shall walk with me in white; for they are worthy." (Rev. 3:4)

3423	i.	William Benjamin [145] "Ben" (1883-1924)
3424	ii.	Harland Eugene [146] (1885-1968)
3425	iii.	Leroy George [147] "Lee" (1886-1975)
3426	iv.	Myron Emery [148] (1888-1955)
3427	v.	Nellie Leola [149] (1890-1894)
3428	vi.	Grace Lodawesca [150] (1892-1894)
3429	vii.	Ruby Adella [151] (1896-1995)
3430	viii.	Adelia Emma [152] (1898-1984)
3431	ix.	Gerald Leslie [153] "Gerry" (1905-1979)

2668. William L. [69] HILL.[715] Born in Caton, Steuben Co., N.Y., on 17 Jun 1860. William L. [69] died in Rowan, Wright Co., Iowa (drowned in the Iowa River) on 25 Mar 1869, he was 8. The story that passed to later generations was that he fell off a horse in the flooded river, where it passed through the family farm near Rowan, Ia., while riding with his young uncle Harland "Harley" (Harlow) Hill. He was not quite 9 years old. Since his older brother, George, was 12 at the time, the loss was keenly felt by

George, and the sad story was related in whispered voices ever afterwards. William's only other sibling was his six year old sister, and she, too, must have felt the grief for a long time. The family was then living on land which in 1994 was farmed by Steve and Mark Hill, great-great grandsons of young William's parents. One Otis Tendall was living there in the 1980's.

2669. Adella L. [70] HILL,[716] daughter and third child of Charles W. and Adelia (Riley) Hill, was born in Wright County, Iowa, 14 March 1863; died there, 25 June 1910. She was born shortly after her parents arrived in the then largely unsettled plains of northern Iowa, late in the winter of 1863, only weeks before the outbreak of the Civil War. She was just six years old when her young uncle and one of her brothers drowned in the Iowa River near their farm home. She was said to have been an excellent horseback rider and that she and her older brother secretly watched Indian ceremonies in their county when they were children. When she was older, she was a schoolteacher until she was married at the age of twenty-two. She and her husband had one child, a son, who survived her when she died at the age of forty-seven. Although the cause of her death has not been recorded, we may speculate that she may have died of tuberculosis, which was then the most common cause of death of adults in the United States. Adella's mother died of tuberculosis when she was fourteen; her mother was then fifty-one years old. She married, 26 January 1886, **James W. LINDSAY**; born 30 July 1859 at Waseca County, Minnesota.
They had one child:
   3432   i.   George Edwin "Ed" [154] (1888-1973)

2670. Vesta Eloise [71] HILL.[717] Born on 17 Mar 1881. Vesta Eloise [71] died in 1970, she was 88. The year of her death was provided by Mrs. Ken (Natalie) Rose, who said that she had 15 grandchildren, of whom five were children of Eleanor. On 20 Mar 1900 when Vesta Eloise [71] was 19, she married **Harry Lawrence SPEER**. Born on 5 May 1879 in Halsay Valley, NY.; died in 1943, he was 63.
They had the following children:
   3433   i.   Rosella Amelia [155] (1903-<2002)
   3434   ii.   Harriet Eloise [156] (1912-1912)
   3435   iii.   Arvena Grace [157] (1914-)
   3436   iv.   Bernice Comelia [158] (1920-)
   3437   v.   Eleanor Vesta (->2002)

2671. Sarah "Sadie" L. [77] KIMBALL. Born on 8 Dec 1862; died aft 1887 in Corning, NY, March 1887. She was named as an heir of her grandfather, William Prince Hill, when his estate was administered, 30 Mar 1887. On 3 Sep 1885 when she was 22, she married **Herbert C. AUSTIN** in Caton, NY. Herbert C. died bef 1920.
They had the following children:
   3438   i.   Helen
   3439   ii.   Clarice

2672. Carrie H. [78] KIMBALL. Born on 8 Nov 1866 in Caton, NY. Carrie H. [78] died in Corning, NY on 10 Jan 1894, she was 27.

2673. William E. [79] "Willie" KIMBALL.[718] Born on 18 Jun 1868 in Oatona Steele Co., MN. An heir of the estate of his grandfather, William P. Hill, 30 Mar 1887. On 12 Jan 1892 when he was 23, he first married **Cora Ella CLEVELAND**, in Corning, NY. Cora Ella died on 30 Apr 1906.
They had the following children:
   3440   i.   Everett Cleveland [173] (1900-)
   3441   ii.   Irwing H. [174] (1906-1906)
On 1 Aug 1907 when he was 39, he second married **Bessie C. SMITH**, in Caton, N.Y.

2674. Charles C. "Charley" [72] REED.[719] Born on 28 Apr 1865 in Caton, N.Y.; died 19 April 1926 at Flint, Michigan, age 60. He was a carpenter. He was seriously injured at work in Fenton, Genesee Co., Michigan, where he had lived for nearly twenty years, and he died a week later in the Hurley Hospital, Flint, Michigan. His funeral services were held at the Congregational Church in Vernon, Michigan, where he had previously lived. He was buried in Vernon in the Greenwood Cemetery, beside his wife, who had died in 1917. Two of his sons served in the U.S. Army in France in World War I, and one was

wounded in the eye. He was survived by his five children and also by his brothers Will, of Owosso, Mich; Frank, of Fenton; and D. F., of Vernon; and a sister, Mrs. W. K. Reed, of Vernon. Charles C. Reed married **Frances E. REED**, daughter of George W. and Ellen (Randolph) Reed; born in Michigan, 8 June 1863; died at Fenton, Genesee Co., Mich., 27 January 1917; buried in Greenwood Cemetery, Vernon, Mich. Her parents' ancestors are unknown, and it unknown if Frances was related to her husband.
They had the following children, three sons and two daughters:

3442	i.	Russell Harry (1893-)
3443	ii.	Paul H. (1895-1968)
3444	iii.	Percy G.
3445	iv.	Georgia E. (~1901->1920)
3446	v.	Eleanor D. (~1904->1920)

2675. Luella M. [73] REED. Born on 30 Mar . Luella M. [73] died aft Aug 1920. She and her brother Charles G. Reed attended the Hill Family Reunion at Corning, N.Y., in August 1920. On 1 Mar 1893 Luella M. [73] married **William K. REED**. Born on 18 Apr 1855.

2676. Walter W. [74] REED. Born on 30 Aug 1870. On 17 Nov 1876 when Walter W. [74] was 6, he married **Bertha BRYANT**.
They had the following children:

3447	i.	Gladys [159] (1899-)
3448	ii.	Hazel [160] (1900-)
3449	iii.	Velma L. [161] (1903-)
3450	iv.	Isabell R. [162] (1907-)
3451	v.	Blanche B. [163] (1908-)
3452	vi.	Geraldine [164] (1909-)
3453	vii.	Margaret E. [165] (1911-)
3454	viii.	Vivian B. [166] (1912-)
3455	ix.	Dewey D. [167] (1916-1916)

2677. Frank Dubois [75] REED. Born on 8 Sep 1876. On 27 Jun 1900, he married **Winnie CARLEY**.
They had the following children:

3456	i.	Hobart B. [168] (1901-)
3457	ii.	Leona J. [169] (1905-)
3458	iii.	Zelma L. [170] (1908-)

2678. Deforest H. [76] REED. Born 15 Feb 1879. On 9 Dec 1903, he m. **Ethyl SMEDLEY**.
They had the following children:

3459	i.	Phyllis H. [171] (1904-)
3460	ii.	LaGrand [172] (1906-)

2679. Orson Elvin [80] WOLCOTT. Born on 16 Dec 1855. Orson Elvin [80] died aft 1920, he was 64. On 4 Jul 1876 when Orson Elvin [80] was 20, he married **Melvina RUSSELL**.
They had the following children:

3461	i.	Francis Eugene [175-A] (1877-)
3462	ii.	George Elvin [176-A] (1878-)
3463	iii.	Noble Ernest [177-A] (1882-)
3464	iv.	Flora Melvina [178-A] (1885-)

2680. Charlotte Adelaide [81] WOLCOTT. Born on 24 Feb 1859. Charlotte Adelaide [81] died aft 1920, she was 60. On 1 May 1884 when Charlotte Adelaide [81] was 25, she married **Francis EASTERBROOK**. Born on 6 Jul 1853.
They had the following children:

3465	i.	Harriet Jane [179] (1885-)
3466	ii.	Claude Loraine [180] (1887-)
3467	iii.	Raymond Larne [181] (1890-)
3468	iv.	Lucius Elvin [182] (1892-1915)
3469	v.	Leslie Leone [183] (1896-)

2681. Fannie Isabel [82] WOLCOTT. Born on 23 Sep 1863; died on 4 Feb 1885, she was 21.

2682. Pantha Estella [83] WOLCOTT. Born on 23 Mar 1865; died on 15 Dec ___.

2683. Eva Louise [84] WOLCOTT. Born on 30 Dec 1867. Eva Louise [84] died on 4 Dec ____.

2684. Charles Sidney [85] WOLCOTT. Born on 19 Jun 1876. Charles Sidney [85] died aft 1920. On 28 Oct 1903 when Charles Sidney [85] was 27, he married **Helen W. ROWLEY**. Born on 6 Aug 1879. Helen W. died aft 1920.

They had the following children:

3470	i.	Ezra [230] (1905->1920)
3471	ii.	Frederick John [231] (1906-)
3472	iii.	George Rogers [232] (1909->1920)
3473	iv.	Charlotte Jane [233] (1911-1918)
3474	v.	Clara Louise [234] (1914->1920)

2685. Louise [86] HILL. Louise [86] married **? SOULE**.

They had one child:

3475	i.	Helen [175]

2686. _____ GRIDLEY.

2687. Daisy Irene [87] DENNING.

2688. Guy Hamilton [88] DENNING.

2689. Walter E. [89] GRIDLEY. Born on 4 Mar 1869.

Child:

3476	i.	Clifford H. [176] (1912-)

2690. Nettie V. [90] GRIDLEY. Born on 2 Mar 1871.

2691. Charles L. [91] GRIDLEY. Born on 4 May 1875. Charles L. [91] died bef 1920. On 6 Apr 1898 when Charles L. [91] was 22, he married _____ ? (GRIDLEY).

They had the following children:

3477	i.	Vivian L. [177] (1900->1920)
3478	ii.	Adrian F. [178] (1901-)
3479	iii.	Winifred L. [179] (1910-)

2692. Lena H. [92] GRIDLEY. Born on 20 Jul 1877. Lena H. [92] died on 3 May 1920, she was 42. On 27 Jul 1910 when Lena H. [92] was 33, she married **? HOWARD**.

They had the following children:

3480	i.	Clarence R. [180]
3481	ii.	Violet R. [181] (1915-)
3482	iii.	Virginia L. [182] (1917-)
3483	iv.	Elsie R. [183] (1918-)

2693. John W. [93] ELDRED.

2694. Huldah [94] HOUGH.

2695. Albert L. [95] HOUGH.

2696. Cephas [96] HOUGH.

2697. Alice [97] HOUGH.

2698. Lavern [98] GRIDLEY.

2699. Cora [99] GRIDLEY.

2700. Grace [100] GRIDLEY. Born in Jan 1877 in Michigan.

2701. Rena E. GRIDLEY. Born in Apr 1879 in Michigan.

2702. John S. [101] GRIDLEY. Born in Jul 1893 in Missouri.

2703. Frederick Laverne [102] GRIDLEY. Born on 27 Dec 1867. On 11 Dec 1886 when Frederick Laverne [102] was 18, he married **Ella Mae PALMER**. Born on 22 Mar 1871.

They had the following children:

3484	i.	Earl Fred [184] (1891-)
3485	ii.	Erma Pearl [185] (1900-)
3486	iii.	Clarence LaVerne [185] (1907-)

2704. Earl [103] GRIDLEY.

2705. Edwin L. [104] GRIDLEY.

2706. Robert M. [105] GRIDLEY.

2707. Rose M. [106] GRIDLEY.

2708. Clara E. [107] GRIDLEY.

2709. Bessie [108] GRIDLEY.

2710. Jessie [109] GRIDLEY.

2711. Edith [110] GRIDLEY.

2712. Roy H. [111] GRIDLEY.

2713. Unknown Child [112] GRIDLEY.

2714. William B. [113] PRIEST. Born on 19 Mar 1864. William B. [113] died on 23 Apr 1917, he was 53. On 9 Aug 1899 when William B. [113] was 35, he married **Clara DRAKE**.

2715. Fred O. [114] PRIEST. Born on 22 Nov 1869. On 9 Apr 1902, he married **Nellie MINCH**.

2716. Alice B. [115] HOWE. Born on 8 Sep 1867. Alice B. [115] died aft 1920. On 27 Oct 1886 when Alice B. [115] was 19, she married **Stephen CARMEN**.
They had the following children:

3487	i.	Leta M. [187] (1887-)
3488	ii.	Mabel A. [188] (1889-)
3489	iii.	Florence [189] (1893-)
3490	iv.	Winifred I. [190] (1897-)
3491	v.	William F. [191] (1904-)
3492	vi.	Dorothy [192] (1906-)

2717. Asa L. [116] HOWE. Born on 27 Jun 1877. Asa L. [116] died aft 1920. On 14 Mar 1904 when Asa L. [116] was 26, he married **Nellie CHADWICK**. Nellie died aft 1920.

2718. Jacob A. [117] VAN ARSDALE. B. on 17 Apr 1873. On 12 Jul 1890, he m. **Capitolia RANKIN**.
They had the following children:

3493	i.	Veronica C. [193] (1891-)
3494	ii.	Dorothy [194]
3495	iii.	Archibald J. [195] (1908-)

2719. Lora S. [118] HOWE. Born on 28 Aug 1878. Lora S. [118] died aft 1920. On 17 Sep 1898 when Lora S. [118] was 20, she married **Norman DIMMICK**.
They had the following children:

3496	i.	Edna H. [196] (1899-)
3497	ii.	Mable J. [197] (1904-)
3498	iii.	Uletta C. [198] (1907-)
3499	iv.	Ellen M. [199] (1908-)

2720. Alice Mable [119] HILL. Born on 2 Jul 1873. On 21 Oct 1896 when Alice Mable [119] was 23, she married **Adam Leslie PEART**. Born on 15 Sep 1852.
They had the following children:

3500	i.	Leslie Jay [200] (1897-)
3501	ii.	Ralph Melvin [201] (1903-)
3502	iii.	Edith Reay [202] (1912-)

2721. Agnes Lurancy [120] HILL. Born on 15 Mar 1875.

2722. Mary Elizabeth [121] HILL. Born on 10 Sep 1876. On 25 Oct 1911 when Mary Elizabeth [121] was 35, she married **Elmer Hanson ELWIN**. Born on 30 Oct 1870.
They had the following children:

3503	i.	Elmer Hill [203] (1912-)
3504	ii.	James William [204] (1916-)

2723. Edith Laurel [122] HILL. Born on 2 Aug 1880; died on 12 Sep 1900, she was 20.

2724. Ernest Sylvester [123] HILL.[720] Born on 6 Dec 1886. Ernest Sylvester [123] died aft 1920. Occupation: Civil engineer prior to W.W.I; then co-owner of a storage battery firm in Fargo, N.D.

He wrote a letter that was read at the Hill Family Reunion, Corning, N.Y., in August 1920, in which he said that he gave up his career as a civil engineer because he was blinded in one eye during his service in France. He was co-owner of a storage battery factory in Fargo, N.D., in August 1920; his partner was then ill and was facing the need for surgery. He and his wife had a daughter (unnamed) in June 1920; he did not mention his young son, Gordon (b. 1916). On 25 Oct 1911 when Ernest Sylvester [123] was 24, he married **Florence LUNDIN**, daughter of LUNDIN. Born on 20 Jun 1890; died aft 1920.
They had the following children:

    3505   i.   Gordon Lundin [205] (1916-)
    3506   ii.   _____ (1920->1920)

2725. Mary L. [124] GILBERT. Born on 14 Mar 1876; died on 10 May 1879, she was 3.

2726. Charles B. [125] GILBERT. Born on 5 Oct 1879. Charles B. [125] died bef 1920. On 5 Jun 1900 when Charles B. [125] was 20, he married **Viola TAYLOR**. Viola died bef 1920.
They had the following children:

    3507   i.   Helen Frances [206] (1904-)
    3508   ii.   Leona May [207] (1908->1920)

2727. Roy H. [126] GILBERT. Born on 13 Feb 1889; died on 20 Sep 1889.

2728. Frank Sherman [127] HILL. Born on 25 Aug 1874. He married **Estella OMAN**.
They had the following children:

    3509   i.   Myron [208]
    3510   ii.   Muriel [209]

2729. Frederick E. [128] HILL. Born on 7 Jun 1880; died aft 1920. On 24 Sep 1903 when Frederick E. [128] was 23, he married **Minnie M. PAUL**. Born on 11 Mar 1879. Minnie M. died aft 1920.

2730. Walter Hill [129] SMITH.[721] Born on 26 Oct 1889. On 28 Sep 1919 when Walter Hill [129] was 29, he married **Amy COUCH**.

2731. Florence Rebecca [130] HILL. Born on 3 Oct 1880. Florence Rebecca [130] died aft 1920, she was 39. On 18 Jun 1902 when Florence Rebecca [130] was 21, she married **Jasper J. KINNAN**. Born on 25 May 1875. Jasper J. died "killed by a trolley car" on 13 Oct 1917, he was 42.
They had the following children:

    3511   i.   Wesley Jasper [210] (1903->1920)
    3512   ii.   Ruth Elizabeth [211] (1911->1920)

2732. William Edwin [131] HILL.[722] Born on 17 Sep 1882; died aft 1924. Secretary of the Hill Association, 1921-1924; and author of *Genealogy of the Hill Family in America* (1924). On 5 Jun 1907 when he was 24, he married **Blanche Mae ALLEY**. Born on 16 Aug 1886; died aft 1920.
They had the following children:

    3513   i.   Helen Mae [212] (1919->1920)
    3514   ii.   Marvin Edwin [213] (1920-)

2733. Alice Harriet [132] HILL. Born on 21 Oct 1885. Alice Harriet [132] died aft 1920. On 23 Dec 1913 when Alice Harriet [132] was 28, she married **Roscoe Wellington GREGORY**. Born on 30 Dec 1881; died aft 1920.
They had one child:

    3515   i.   Quincy Wellington [214] (1914->1920)

2734. John Phineas [133] HILL,[723] second son and fourth child of Charles E. and Harriet C. (Bostwick) Hill, was born at Caton, Steuben County, New York, 26 September 1891; died there, 9 March 1996. He served in World War I from November 1917 to August 1919, during which time he was a private first class in the 7th U.S. Infantry regiment, 3rd Division, stationed in France and Germany. He spent his entire life in Steuben County, New York. He was a farmer until World War II, and he was then employed as a mold polisher at Corning, Inc., where he had more than fifty years of active and retired service.

He was a member of the Caton United Methodist Church for over seventy years, and served as the Superintendent of the Church Sunday Schoool and as Treasurer of the Church. He was a member of the Caton Grange for sixty years, a Justice of the Peace, and a member of the Caton Board of Elections. He was also a member of the Mayflower Society and of the Newtown Battlefield Chapter of the Sons of the American Revolution. Tobeytown Road, on which he lived for most of his life, was officially renamed "John Hill Road." When he died at the age of 104, he was survived by his wife of sixty-eight years, two daughters, a son and daughter-in-law, a sister, eight grandchildren, eight great-grandchildren, and one great-great grandson. His memorial service was held at the Caton United Methodist Church, following which he was buried at the Elmwood Cemetery in Caton.

On 14 Sep 1927 when John Phineas [133] was 35, he married **Elizabeth Morse TOBEY**,[724] in Elmira, N.Y. Born on 28 Feb 1907 in Caton, N.Y. Elizabeth Morse died in Caton, N.Y. on 12 Jun 2002, she was 95. Graduated from Corning Free Academy in 1926. Religion: Methodist.
They had the following children:

> 3516   i.   Dean Edwin (1928-)
> 3517   ii.   Iva Louise (1930-)
> 3518   iii.   Constance Elizabeth (1942-)

2735. George Noble [134] HILL. Born on 14 Jan 1898 in Caton, Steuben Co., N.Y. George Noble [134] died on 10 Jun 1980, he was 82. Buried in 1980 in Caton, N.Y. Farmer and factory worker. Protestant.

On 20 Aug 1930 when George Noble [134] was 32, he married **Anna Lois FINCH**, daughter of Elvin FINCH & Emma WELCH, in Clyde, N.Y. Born on 11 Jan 1902 in Clyde (Rose), N.Y. Anna Lois died on 14 Jul 1989, she was 87. Buried in 1989 in Caton, N.Y. Mother of 2 and teacher. Religion: Protestant. She was "A. Lois ___"until publication of the DAR Patriot Index.
They had the following children:

> 3519   i.   Kenneth Elvin (1933-)
> 3520   ii.   Doris Jean (1936-)

2736. Ruth Queenie [135] HILL.[725] Born on 1 Sep 1899. Ruth Queenie [135] died in Elmira, N.Y. on 15 Feb 2000, she was 100. Buried in Feb 2000 in Caton, N.Y. Occupation: a rural schoolteacher and homemaker in the Caton, N.Y., area. She was still living in Caton, N.Y., in March 1996, when her brother, John P. Hill, died there. Her married name appears in her brother's obituary. She later moved into Bethany Manor, Horseheads, N.Y., and lived there until she died at the Arnot Ogden Medical Center, Elmira, N.Y., on 15 February 2000. Arrangements were made by Carpenter's Funeral Home, Corning, N.Y., and graveside services were held at the Elmwood Cemetery, Caton, N.Y. She was predeceased by two sisters and three brothers, and she was survived by several nieces and nephews. She was probably the last survivor of her generation in this branch of the Hill family. On 27 Mar 1937 when Ruth Queenie [135] was 37, she married **Frederick W. KROME**, in Elmira, N.Y. Frederick W. died on 13 Mar 1982.

2737. Ethel Belle [136] PHILLIPS. Born 28 May 1890; married **William OVERBAUGH.**

2738. Harriet Ruth [137] PHILLIPS. Born on 21 May 1893.

2739. Mary [138] PHILLIPS. Born on 5 Sep 1895. Mary [138] married **? GREY.**

2740. Pauline [139] PHILLIPS.

2741. Henry Clay [140] PHILLIPS. Born on 16 Jan 1899.

2742. Elwin [141] PHILLIPS. Born in May 1901.

2743. William [142] PHILLIPS. Born on 17 Aug 1904.

2744. Leslie Lamont [143] PHILLIPS. Born on 13 Mar 1909.

2745. Sealton [144] HILL. Born on 19 Dec 1898.

2746. Charles Ross "C. R." PAUL.[726] Born on 21 Jan 1880 in Washington Courthouse, Fayette Co., Ohio; died in Chillicothe, Ohio on 24 Aug 1948, he was 68. On 26 Jan 1901 when he was 21, he married (1) **Nellie KUNZELMAN** in Chillicothe, Ohio; died 24 Sep 1923 in Columbus, Ohio.
They had the following children:

> 3521   i.   Cora Nellie (1901-1976)
> 3522   ii.   Virginia Helen (1917-1988)
> 3523   iii.   Charles Laurence "Sonny" (1920-)

On 17 Dec 1927 when he was 47, he married (2) **Gertrude Frederica WILHELM**. Born on 5 Nov 1900.
They had the following children:

> 3524   i.   Donald Roswell

3525	ii.	Betty Ann
3526	iii.	Barbara Jean (1933-)

------------------------[727]

2747. Emily HILL. Born in 1845.

2748. Emaline A. HILL. Born in 1846.

2749. Amy HILL. Born in 1858.

2750. Wilbur J. KETCHUM. Born on 17 May 1844; died in Feb 1912, he was 67. On 5 Oct 1870 when Wilbur J. was 26, he married **Sarah GAY** in Urbana, N.Y.

2751. Warren B. KETCHUM. Born in 1847. Warren B. died on 5 Nov 1849, abt 2.

2752. Charles H. KETCHUM. Born on 7 Jul 1850. Did not marry.

2753. George W. KETCHUM. Born on 22 Feb 1852; died 24 Apr 1887, he was 35. On 28 Oct 1874 when George W. was 22, he married **Clara ELLAS**.

2754. Sarah Emily KETCHUM. Born on 16 Jul 1854. Sarah Emily died on 17 Sep 1905, she was 51. On 22 Jun 1880 when Sarah Emily was 25, she married **William E. SEARLES**. Lived in Canisteo, N.Y.

2755. Ira P. KETCHUM. Born on 11 Feb 1857. Ira P. died on 7 Dec 1942, he was 85. Lived in Alpine, Schuyler Co., N.Y. Ira P. married **Lucy HINMAN**.

2756. Mary E. KETCHUM. Born on 8 Apr 1859. Mary E. married **Adelbert WOOD**.

2757. Eliza H. KETCHUM. Born on 1 Jun 1863. Eliza H. died on 23 Mar 1941, she was 77. Lived in Bradford, N.Y. Eliza H. married **Arthur GILMORE**.

2758. Martha E. KETCHUM. Born on 2 Nov 1866. Martha E. died in Urbana, N.Y. on 13 Jul 1899, she was 32. Martha E. married _____ **TOMER**.

2759. George Amos SKINNER. George Amos married **Samantha Arabelle SPITLER**. They had one child:

3527	i.	Francis Hill

2760. Mary Elizabeth AXTEL.

2761. George AXTEL. Born abt 1855.

2762. George HILL.

2763. Franklin HILL.

2764. Richard L. HILL II. Born on 2 Apr 1864 in Corning, N.Y. Richard L. died in Ventura, Calif. on 30 Jun 1947, he was 83. Occupation: Jeweler and watchmaker. Richard L. first married **Emily Knox WHITE**. Born on 3 Jun 1861 in Knoxville, Pa. Emily Knox died in Corning, N.Y. on 6 Jan 1941, she was 79. Richard L. Hill II appears to have left Emily and had a second family in California, although the dates of birth of his second set of children were not provided by Paul F. Hill, and he is now deceased. They had the following children:

3528	i.	Richard L. (1894-1955)
3529	ii.	Dorothy White (1899-1968)

Richard L. second married **Enriquita VALENCIA**. They had the following children:

3530	i.	William George Robert "Bob"
3531	ii.	Harriet Alice
3532	iii.	Hansel Ferris
3533	iv.	Marion Henry

2765. Aimee Knox HILL. Born on 6 Sep 1889. Aimee Knox died in Feb 1918, she was 28. Died in flu epidemic. Aimee Knox married **Howard CLARK**.

2766. Julia Bovier HILL. Born on 16 Sep 1891. Julia Bovier died on 26 Aug 1939, she was 47. Julia Bovier married **Claude GILLIAM**. Born in 1892 in 1961. They had one child:

3534	i.	June (1916-2000)

2767. Alice May HILL. Alice May married **Michael F. MORAN**. They had the following children:

3535	i.	Richard (Harry)

250

3536   ii.   Helen Mary

2768. William Ferris HILL. William Ferris married **Rhemona CRIST**.
They had one child:
    3537   i.   Helen Mildred

2769. Joseph Amos HILL. Joseph Amos married **Hattie Mae WILEY**.
They had one child:
    3538   i.   Richard "Lawrence"

2770. Amos W. HILL. Born on 24 Oct 1873 in Corning, N.Y. Amos W. died on 15 Mar 1887, he was 13. Died of diphtheria.

2771. William Amos HILL. William Amos married **Alice HARTIGAN**.
They had one child:
    3539   i.   Mary Nanno

2772. Helen Martha HILL.

2773. Lela HILL.

2774. Emma L. HILL.

2775. H. Laverne HILL. H. Laverne married **Mertle BALLARD**.

Line 6 – Descendants of Abigail Hill (continued)[728]

2776. Sharon J. COBB. Born in 1834 in Indiana.

2777. Perlina E. COBB. Born in 1836 in Indiana.

2778. Emma C. COBB. Born in 1842 in Indiana.

2779. Marietta COBB. Born on 2 Sep 1845 in Indiana.

2780. Alice M. COBB. Born in 1849 in Indiana.

2781. Ida Maria STREET.

If there are any more descendants of Abigail Hill, they are unknown after this generation.

Line 7 – Descendants of Elizabeth Hill (continued)

2782. Frederick C. TERRY.[729] Born in Dec 1855 in New York state. Frederick C. died in Bristol, Hartford Co., Conn. abt 1930, he was 74. Frederick C. married **Mina N. ? (TERRY)**. Born in 1853. Mina N. died in 1920, she was 67.
They had the following children:
    3540   i.   Lyman Charles (1890-1964)
    3541   ii.   Frederick W. (1892-1913)

Line 8 – Descendants of John Hill (continued)[730]

2783. George Sheldon BROOKS. Born in 1845. George Sheldon died in 1861, he was 16.

2784. Lester Ranney BROOKS. Born in 1847. Lester Ranney died in 1902, he was 55.

2785. Dwight Frederick BROOKS. Born in 1849. Dwight Frederick died in 1930, he was 81.

2786. Anson Strong BROOKS.[731] Born on 6 Sep 1852 in Redfield, Oswego, N.Y. Anson Strong died on 3 August 1937 in Minneapolis, Hennepin County, Minn., he was 84. Telegraph operator as a youth in Winona, Minn. Became Director, National Bank of Commerce, Minneapolis. On 24 Jul 1876 when Anson Strong was 23, he married **Georgia Lillian ANDROS**, in McGregor, Ia.; daughter of Richard Salter Storrs and Maria (Worthing) Andros; born at Garnavillo, Clayton Co., Ia., 28 September 1858; died at Minneapolis, 26 March 1934. They had two children: Paul Andros Brooks (1881-1941) and Stanley Brooks (1886-1907), neither of whom are known to have married and both apparently d.s.p.

2787. William Henry "Will" HILL, son and only child of John William Hill and his first wife, Mary Ellen Fox, was born at Morning Sun, Iowa, 25 December 1875; died at Miles City, Montana, 6 March 1969, age 93. Before he was two years old, his father deserted his mother, who was the step-daughter of Samuel Steven "Sam" Wilder. She returned to the Wilder family and obtained a divorce from John William Hill before 1880. She then married her step-brother, Charles Gifford Wilder, and lived with the

Wilder family as it migrated west, finally settling in Montana. In the meantime, John William Hill also married again, moved west, and had eight children, but he apparently never connected again with his son, William Henry Hill.

Charles Gifford and Mary (Fox) (Hill) Wilder had three children, who grew up with their step-brother William Hill, who was known as "Will." The Wilder family moved to Texas when Will was 10, and they moved into a dugout at the head of Second Creek in Lipscomb County, Texas. They worked on the trail herds that were then being driven from Texas to Miles City, Montana.

In 1901, when he was about 26 years old, Will married Bessie Olive Guenther, one of twelve children, some of whom, like Bessie, were placed with other families when her mother died. Bessie grew up in the Wilder household and was therefore like a step-sister to Will. They were married by an itinerant, tobacco-spitting minister, in Lipscomb County, Texas, and began to raise a family on two-and-a-half sections of land (about 1,500 acres) on Wolf Creek, about four miles from Lipscomb. Their first child, Charlie, was born there. In 1902, Will's step-father, C. G. Wilder, moved to Montana, and the rest of the Wilder clan followed. They shipped their household goods, a herd of 800-900 cattle, and a string of horses from Higgins, Texas, by train to Billings, Montana. They then moved everything to the Clark Tozier ranch, which C. G. Wilder purchased, at the mouth of Sunday Creek from Billings. Will, at age 27, then moved on with his family to the Kinsey valley near Miles City, Montana. His second child, Alma, was born in Miles City. Will then moved to Oregon for a while, and his son Earl was born in Heppner, Oregon. Will worked as a horse merchant and drover in Heppner until he returned to the Yellowstone River valley near Miles City. Another child, Ruth Irene, was born in Miles City in 1911, followed by Edson in 1912. In the 1940s, the members of the family who were still living on the ranch moved into the town of Miles City and built the house in which Bessie died following a stroke in 1962, and in which Will died of heart failure in 1969.

On 17 Feb 1901 when William Henry was 25, he married **Bessie Olive GUENTHER**, daughter of John Franklin GUENTHER & Mary Ellen WEAVER, in Lipscomb Co., Texas. Born on 16 Nov 1881 in Harper, Kansas. Bessie Olive died in Miles City, Mont. on 6 Mar 1962, she was 80. Occupation: Mother of 6; she moved in with the Wilders when her mother died in 1892 and her father had to place some his 12 children with other families.

They had the following children:

3542	i.	Charles Victor (1901-1968)
3543	ii.	Alma Evelyn (1905-)
3544	iii.	Earl Edward (1908-1991)
3545	iv.	Ruth Irene (1911-1982)
3546	v.	Edson Harold (1912->1995)
3547	vi.	Mary Myrtle (1903-1904)

2788. Anna Pearl HILL. Born on 18 May 1884. Anna Pearl died on 11 Nov 1967, she was 83.

2789. Emily Christine HILL. Born on 25 Jan 1888. Emily Christine died on 21 Aug 1958, she was 70.

2790. Frances Esther HILL. Born on 27 Dec 1889. Frances Esther died in Jan 1963, she was 73. Frances Esther married **? PLUMMER**.

2791. Ruth Elizabeth HILL. Born on 10 Sep 1891. Ruth Elizabeth married **? McCULLEY**.

2792. John Thomas HILL. Born on 13 Jan 1893.

2793. Edith Blanch HILL. Edith Blanch married **? TAYLOR**.

2794. Arthur Miller HILL. Born on 20 Jun 1898.

2795. Josephine HILL. Born on 7 Sep 1904.

2796. Ester M. HILL. Born on 10 Sep 1887 in Yellow Springs, Iowa. Her name and year of birth are uncertain; she may have been b. in 1889.

2797. Mary Jane HILL. Born on 2 Jul 1880 in Iowa. Mary Jane died in Mt. Pleasant, Henry Co., Iowa on 30 Sep 1904, she was 24. Buried in 1904 in Mt. Pleasant, Henry Co., Iowa. On 20 Oct 1897 when Mary Jane was 17, she married **Arthur Luther GILLIS**, son of James R. GILLIS & Augusta MOORE, in Wapello, Louisa Co., Iowa. Born abt 1869.

2798. William John HILL Born on 26 May 1877 in Kossuth, Louisa Co., Ia. William John married

Mary K. ? (HILL). Mary K. died in May 1943 in Chicago, Ill. Buried in 1943 in Hannibal, Mo.
2799. Nellie HILL. Born on 21 Sep 1882 in Wapello, Louisa Co., Iowa. On 26 Dec 1905 when Nellie was 23, she married **Frank DeVORE**, in Cass Co., Ill.
They had the following children:

3548	i.	Dale (1901-1996)
3549	ii.	Dayton (1911-1997)
3550	iii.	Donald

2800. Maude Leoto HILL. Born on 1 Oct 1884 in Port Louisa, Louisa Co., Ia. bef 1910 when Maude Leoto was 25, she married **Edward RADEMAKER**.
2801. Marguerite Louise "Maggie" HILL. Born on 26 Feb 1885 in Jefferson Twp., Louisa Co., Ia. Marguerite Louise "Maggie" died in Pomona, Ca. on 5 Feb 1959, she was 73. Buried in 1959 in Dixon Lee Co., Ill. Marguerite Louise "Maggie" married **Charles Oscar JERN**. Born on 17 Jan 1881 in Christianstad, Sweden. Charles Oscar died in Mt. Morris, Ogle Co., Ill. on 19 Feb 1958, he was 77.
They had one child:

3551	i.	Vivian Rosalie (1917-1956)

2802. Ada Victoria HILL. Born on 4 Feb 1889 in Wapello, Louisa Co., Iowa. Ada Victoria first married ? _____
Ada Victoria second married **? KINSEY**.
They had one child:

3552	i.	Forrest

Ada Victoria third married **Charlie WILLIAMS**.
They had one child:

3553	i.	Ruby

2803. Bessie Lyle HILL. Born on 1 Dec 1891 in Wapello, Louisa Co., Iowa.
2804. Jesse Riley MORGAN. Born on 14 Jun 1893. Jesse Riley married **Mildred Rose LAIRD**. Mildred Rose died in Mar 1953.
They had one child:

3554	i.	J. Laird (1932-)

2805. ? MORGAN. Resided in Independence, Oregon, in 1932. ? married **Paul JOHNSON**.
2806. Armilda Abigale HILL. Armilda Abigale married **? ANDERS**.
2807. Annie HILL. Annie married **? HAMMER**.
2808. Ester M. HILL. Ester M. married **? BANTON**.
2809. Larrisa HILL.
2810. Lafayette F. HILL. Born on 28 Jun 1855. Lafayette F. died in Inglewood, Calif. in 1935, he was 79. Lafayette settled in Independence, Oregon. He and his wife later homesteaded in Washtucna, Washington, after Erma was born and they moved to California in 1923, as did several of their children. Lafayette F. married **Emma Melissa LOCKE**. Her parents came to Oregon in 1845 on the Oregon Trail.
They had the following children:

3555	i.	Roy LaFayette (1883-)
3556	ii.	Emma Aurelia (1886-)
3557	iii.	James Lester (1889-)
3558	iv.	Eva Esther (1891-)
3559	v.	Erma Julia (1894-)
3560	vi.	Lolita Fay (1900-)
3561	vii.	Luella Florence (1900-)
3562	viii.	Dale Herschel (1902-)
3563	ix.	Bertram Ladue (1905-)
3564	x.	Herbert H. (1910-)
3565	xi.	Claude Locke (1884-1969)

2811. Vina HILL. Vina married **? KELSO**.
2812. William Wallace HILL. Born on 16 Oct 1853 in Drummond, Mich. William Wallace died in

Kenosha, Wisc. on 25 Aug 1949, he was 95. William Wallace married **Christy McLEOD.** Born on 3 May 1862 in Lochiel, Ont., Canada. Christy died in Kenosha, Wisc. on 25 Mar 1926, she was 63. They had one child:

    3566   i.   Cecelia (1891-)

2813. Lydia Abi ALCOTT. Born on 21 Jul 1851 in St. Charles, Ill.; died in Wonewec, Wisc. on 26 Oct 1922, she was 71. On 19 Oct 1871 when she was 20, she married **Mark Cook BELL.** Born on 19 May 1847 in Independence, Warren Co., N.J.; died in Wonewoc, Wisc. on 4 Jul 1917, he was 70. They had one child:

    3567   i.   Amanda Luella (1873-1931)

2814. Orilla ROWIN. Born in 1861 in Wonewoc, Wisc. She married **Peter MINSTER**, in Wyoming.

2815. Orin ROWIN. Born in 1861 in Wonewoc, Wisc. Orin married **Olive Jane IRR**.

2816. John ROWIN. Born in 1862 in Wonewoc, Wisc.

2817. Abi ROWIN. Born in 1865 in Wonewoc, Wisc.

2818. Cecelia ROWIN. Born in 1867 in Wonewoc, Wisc.

2819. Ladue ROWIN. Born in 1869 in Wonewoc, Wisc.

2820. Lafayette ROWIN. Born in 1872 in Wonewoc, Wisc.

2821. Bell (Lillian) ROWIN. Born in 1874 in Wonewoc, Wisc.

2822. Eugennie ROWIN. Born in 1878 in Wonewoc, Wisc.

2823. Roseltha HILL. Roseltha died in age 9 in Dallas, Ore.

2824. Ladue HILL.

2825. Reason HILL.

2826. Elizabeth HILL. Elizabeth died on as a toddler.

2827. Lucy HILL. Lucy died on as a toddler.

2828. Nelly HILL. First woman to be a law student at Stanford. Nelly married **? DENLINGER**.

2829. Homer HILL.

2830. Verd HILL.

2831. Garlin HILL. Occupation: high school teacher. Education: graduated from Oregon State University when it was Oregon Agricultural College. Garlin married **? COHRS.**

2832. Lurissa Rosalia BURBANK. Born on 21 Jul 1845 in Elgin, Ill. Lurissa Rosalia died in Coffeyville, Kansas on 11 Nov 1924, she was 79. Lurissa Rosalia married **Jacob STAATS Jr**. Born on 25 Dec 1832 in Ripley, W. Va. Jacob died in Coffeyville, Kansas on 17 Dec 1898, he was 65. They had one child:

    3568   i.   Lester Loring (1874-1953)

2833. Abi Orville BARBER. Born in Mar 1831 in Greene, N.Y.

2834. Charles I. BARBER. Born on 13 Apr 1833 in Greene, N.Y.

2835. Saphronia BARBER. Born in 1835 in Greene, N.Y.

2836. Myron F. BARBER. Born on 12 Sep 1837 in Hunter, Greene Co., N.Y.

2837. Milo R. BARBER. Born in Sep 1843 in Seward, Kosciusko, Ind.

2838. Calvin S. BARBER. Born in Sep 1843 in Seward, Kosciusko, Ind.

2839. Sylvester BARBER. Born on 31 Oct 1845 in Seward, Kosciusko, Ind.

2840. George M. BARBER. Born in 1849 in Seward, Kosciusko, Ind.

2841. Edwin Seward BARBER. Born on 9 May 1851 in Silver Lake, Kosciusko, Ind.

2842. Theron L. BARBER. Born on 11 Dec 1857 in Seward, Kosciusko, Ind.

2843. Lucius BARBER. Born in 1842.

2844. Sylvia BARBER. Born in 1844.

2845. Myron C. BARBER. Born in 1845.

2846. Elsie A. BARBER. Born in 1847.

2847. Eliza J. BARBER. Born in 1849.

2848. Harriet Louise BARBOUR. Born on 22 Jun 1843; died 7 Nov 1848, she was 5.

2849. Col. Lucius Albert BARBOUR, Adjutant General of Conn.[732] Born on 26 Jan 1846 in Madison, Indiana; died on 6 Nov 1922, he was 76. He married, February 8, 1877, at Brooklyn, New York, **Harriet**

E. BARNES, born in Brooklyn, N.Y., December 2, 1849, died November 8, 1899, daughter of Alfred Smith and Harriet Elizabeth (Burr) Barnes. Her father was the founder of the publishing house of A. S. Barnes & Company of New York City. His son created the Barbour Collection of Connecticut Records. They had the following children:

    3569   i.   Lucius Barnes (1878-1934)
    3570   ii.   Harriet Burr (1879-)

2850. Mary Adelia BARBOUR. Born on 23 Feb 1851. Mary Adelia died on 6 Mar 1851.

2851. Hattie Day BARBOUR. Born on 18 Jul 1860. Occupation: Mother of 3. On 16 Jun 1880 when Hattie Day was 19, she married **Richard Storrs BARNES**, in Rochester, Monroe Co., N.Y. Born on 21 Nov 1854 in Brooklyn, N.Y. Richard Storrs died on 25 Dec 1913, he was 59.
They had the following children:

    3571   i.   Roderick Barbour (1882-)
    3572   ii.   Hattie Louise (1885-)
    3573   iii.   Goodrich (1887-)

2852. Mary BARBOUR. Born in 1834.

2853. George BARBOUR. Born in 1836.

2854. ? BARBOUR. Christened in 1837.

2855. Hattie N. BARBOUR. Born in 1844 in Indiana.

2856. Grovie BARBOUR. Born in 1844.

2857. Edward BARBOUR. Born in 1844.

2858. Mary Alice BARBOUR. Born on 6 Jul 1852 in Old Barbour Hill Farm, Johnsonburg, N.Y.

2859. Clara Agnes BARBOUR. Born on 24 Apr 1854 in Old Barbour Hill Farm, Johnsonburg, N.Y.

2860. Lucia Ella BARBOUR. Born on 1 Dec 1855 in Old Barbour Hill Farm, Johnsonburg, N.Y.

2861. Eugene Thomas BARBOUR. Born on 30 Dec 1857 in Old Barbour Hill Farm, Johnsonburg, N.Y.

2862. William Everett BARBOUR. Born on 30 Oct 1859 in Old Barbour Hill Farm, Johnsonburg, N.Y.

2863. John James BARBOUR. Born on 21 Aug 1861 in Old Barbour Hill Farm, Johnsonburg, N.Y.

2864. Hattie BARBOUR.

2865. Theresa BARBOUR.

2866. George Monroe DAVIS. Born on 23 Jan 1859.

2867. Frederick Charles DAVIS. Born on 14 Jan 1861.

2868. Caroline Julia DAVIS. Born on 20 Sep 1862.

2869. Theron Dexter DAVIS. Born on 12 Jan 1865.

2870. Lucius Wadsworth JONES. Born on 18 Sep 1829.

2871. Ellen BARBER. Born in 1833.

2872. Hiram Lysander BARBER. Born in 1835 in New Hartford, Litchfield Co., Conn.

2873. Katherine Jane BARTLETT. Born on 27 Apr 1847.

2874. Mary Louise BARTLETT. Born on 2 Mar 1850.

2875. Edward Case NOBLE. Born on 1 Apr 1827 in Litchfield, Woodbury, Conn.

2876. Henry T. NOBLE. Born on 22 Sep 1829 in Franklin, Ohio.

2877. John Jonathan NOBLE. Born on 22 Jun 1830 in Franklin, Ohio.

2878. Mary E. NOBLE. Born on 21 Aug 1832 in Westerville, Ohio.

2879. Lucretia A. NOBLE. Born on 15 Dec 1835 in Franklin, Ohio.

2880. Lester NOBLE. Born on 25 Dec 1837 in Franklin, Ohio.

2881. Emily E. NOBLE. Born on 4 Jan 1840 in Franklin, Ohio.

2882. Luther B. NOBLE. Born on 27 Feb 1842 in Westerville, Ohio.

2883. Eliza Jane NOBLE. Born on 13 Jan 1832 in Tioga, N.Y.

2884. William Jonathan NOBLE. Born on 31 Jul 1833 in Tioga, N.Y.

2885. Henry Lester NOBLE. Born on 5 May 1837 in Tioga, N.Y.

2886. Susan Delphine NOBLE. Born on 5 Jul 1839 in Tioga, N.Y.

2887. Emily A. NOBLE. Born on 26 Dec 1848 in Tioga, N.Y.

2888. Elizabeth M. BARBER. Born on 21 Feb 1832 in Canton, St. Lawrence Co., N.Y.

2889. Celestia S. BARBER. Born on 19 Oct 1833 in Canton, St. Lawrence Co., N.Y.

2890. Phebe Jane BARBER. Born on 26 Jun 1835 in Canton, St. Lawrence Co., N.Y.

2891. Charles B. BARBER. Born on 12 Jun 1837 in Canton, St. Lawrence Co., N.Y.

2892. Julia A. BARBER. Born on 30 Mar 1839 in Canton, St. Lawrence Co., N.Y.

2893. Harriet P. BARBER. Born on 7 Jul 1841 in Canton, St. Lawrence Co., N.Y.

2894. Ellen BARBER. Born on 21 Apr 1843 in Pierrepont, St. Lawrence Co., N.Y.

2895. Gilbert R. BARBER. Born on 21 Oct 1845 in Watertown, Jefferson Co., N.Y.

2896. Pliny W. BARBER. Born on 27 Jun 1849 in Canton, St. Lawrence Co., N.Y.

2897. Edda Jane BARBER. Born on 3 Jul 1847 in Canton, Hartford Co., Conn.

2898. Adelia BARBER. Born on 8 May 1852.

2899. John BARBER. Born on 30 Mar 1858.

2900. Adelaide Julia BARBER.

2901. Clarence Howard BARBER.

2902. Florence Isabella BARBER.

2903. Catherine Hayden BARBER. Born on 1 Jun 1863.

2904. Alison Hayden BARBER. Born on 17 Mar 1868.

2905. Carrie Ann BARBOUR. Born on 24 Apr 1864 in Sheridan, Madison, Montana; died in Ogallala, Keith, Kansas on 8 Mar 1944, age 79. On 14 Sep 1888 when she was 24, she married **Arthur Samuel SMITH**. B. 17 Jan 1864 in Knoxville, Marion, Ia.; d. in Lexington, Dawson, Neb. 23 May 1932, age 68. They had one child:

    3574   i.   Mabel Sarah (1889-)

2906. Lucy Amelia BARBER. Born on 25 Aug 1858 in Canton, Hartford Co., Conn.

2907. Cora Lillian BARBER. Born on 1 Dec 1865 in Canton, Hartford Co., Conn.

2908. Infant BARBER. Born on 6 Jun 1868 in Canton, Hartford Co., Conn.

2909. Dorcas BARBER. Born on 17 Oct 1836 in Chemung, N.Y. Dorcas died in Porter, Rock, Wisc. on 23 Apr 1897, she was 60. Dorcas married **Jason B. MILLER**. Born on 14 Mar 1830 in Vermont. Jason B. died in Porter, Rock, Wisc. on 22 Feb 1894, he was 63.

They had the following children:

    3575   i.   Clifford P.

    3576   ii.   Mildred Gracia (1860-)

    3577   iii.   Flora (1863-)

    3578   iv.   Lois (1865-)

    3579   v.   Fanny (1867-)

    3580   vi.   Frank H. (1869-)

    3581   vii.   Fred S. (1871-)

    3582   viii. Maud E. (1878-)

2910. Norman Augustine HULL. Born on 28 Aug 1843 in Candor, N.Y.

2911. Sabrina HULL. Born on 26 Dec 1846 in Candor, Tioga, N.Y.

2912. Harriet Frances HULL. Born on 4 May 1849 in Candor, Tioga, N.Y.

2913. Wilmot Benjamin HULL. Born on 7 Mar 1851 in Candor, Tioga, N.Y.

2914. Edwin Alonzo HULL. Born on 17 Apr 1853 in Tioga, N.Y.

2915. Charles Frederick HULL. Born on 31 Jul 1859 in Candor, N.Y.

2916. Orson LaRue HULL. Born on 6 Aug 1863 in Tioga, N.Y.

2917. Virgil Pettibone HUMASON. Born on 14 Feb 1847 in Simsbury, Hartford Co., Conn.; died in Yonkers, N.Y. on 6 May 1905, he was 58. Virgil Pettibone first married **Elizabeth Sumner WILSON**. Born on 16 Aug 1846; died in Hartford, Hartford Co., Conn. on 10 Jun 1883, she was 36. They had the following children:

    3583   i.   Elizabeth Catherine (1872-)

    3584   ii.   William Wallace (1873-)

    3585   iii.   John Eno (1876-)

    3586   iv.   Julia Harriet (1883-)

In 1885 when Virgil Pettibone was 37, he second married **Jessie KITTREDGE.** Born on 19 Aug 1845 in Hartford, Hartford Co., Conn. Jessie died on 19 Dec 1929, she was 84. Occupation: d.s.p.

2918. William Lawrence HUMASON. Born on 7 Jun 1853 in Simsbury, Hartford Co., Conn. He is the last known descendant of Luke and Mary (Hout) Hill to be born in Simsbury. On 15 Oct 1884 when William Lawrence was 31, he married **Florence Minerva COLE**, in Kensington, Hartford Co., Conn.; born 3 Jun 1847 in Kensington, Hartford Co., Conn.; died 6 Sep 1903, she was 56.

They had the following children:

3587	i.	Marjorie Florence (1886-)
3588	ii.	Lawrence Cole (1891-)

2919. Edward T. REED. Born in 1879.

2920. Albert Gladwin REED. Born in 1880; died in 1952, abt 72.

2921. Arthur REED. Born in 1882.

2922. Betsey RILEY. She was under 16 in 1835.

2923. 3 male children RILEY.

2924. 3 other female children RILEY. They were under 16 years of age in 1835.

2925. William Alanzo RILEY. William Alanzo RILEY.[733] Born abt 1830. He was probably born after 1830, and he never married.

2926. Horace RILEY.[734] Born abt 1832 in New York state. Horace died in Iowa aft 1876, he was 44. Joseph Gillett's estate records showed that on 11 October 1848 one Ansel I. McCall of Bath, NY, was named special guardian of William Alonzo, Horace, Adelia Catherine and James G. Riley, minors. Horace Riley married, before 1875, Fanny Duffy. They moved to Iowa and had at least one child, Frances M. (1875-1876). It was said that he "came to Iowa and cut logs for a cabin in 1855." His niece, Susan (Riley) Wolfer wrote that he "married Mary Duffy at Rowan Iowa. To them one child was born, Adelia, who married Jap McKinstry at Rowan Iowa." I therefore conclude that Horace and Mary "Fanny" Duffy probably had two children, Frances (who died young), and Adelia (who married). Horace married **Fanny DUFFY.** Fanny died aft 1876 in Iowa.

They had the following children:

3589	i.	Frances M. (1876-1876)
3590	ii.	Adelia

2927. James Gillett RILEY,[735] third son and third child of Simeon and Katharine (Gillett) Riley, was born in New York state, 9 July 1834; died in Wright County, Iowa, 25 September 1871, age 37. He was buried in the Graceland Cemetery, Rowan, Wright County, Iowa. James Riley's father was born in Elmira, Chemung County, New York, and later came to Steuben County, New York, where he met Katharine Gillett, second of the ten children of Joseph and Katherine (Hunt) Gillett. Joseph Gillett, Esq., had been a Lieutenant in the War of 1812 and was wounded in service in Canada. Esquire Gillett married (2) Mrs. Charlotte (Prince) Hill, widow of Ephraim Hill, and thus became the step-father of her 12 children. They lived at Caton, in Steuben County, south of Corning, New York.

James Gillett Riley was skillful with his hands, as shown by descriptions of Corning, New York, that he composed and wrote in the 1840's. In 1849 he joined the gold rush to California, but he returned empty-handed two years later, having formed a "concert company" with his friends to sing their way back home. Mr. Riley came to Wright County, Iowa, in 1856. This was about five years before his sister, Adelia, and her husband, Charles W. Hill, moved to Iowa with their two young children. Charles Hill was a step-first cousin of his wife, Adelia Riley, and her brother James. James Gillett Riley served in the Civil War as a private and Commissary Sergeant in Co. F., Iowa troops. He had tuberculosis, and died at the age of 37. He is buried in the Graceland cemetery, Rowan, Iowa, near the graves of his sister and brother-in-law, Charles and Adelia (Riley) Hill. He married, 2 January 1867, Kate C. "Clara" Archer, by whom he had three children: Isabelle Luella "Totie Belle" (1867-1950); Susan "Sue" Myrtle (d. after 1905); and Stilson James, who died in infancy (b. and d. 1871). On 2 Jan 1867 when James Gillett was 32, he married **Kate C. "Clara" ARCHER.** Born in 1849 in Bedfordshire, ENGLAND; died in 1916, she was 67. Mother of 10: 3 by Riley and 7 by Stout.

Kate C. "Clara" ARCHER,[736] daughter of John Fitzpatrick and Alice Archer, was born at

Bedfordshire, England, in 1849; died at Rowan, Iowa, 1916. Her stepfather was Lawrence McGary of Edinburgh, Scotland. Clara Archer's father, John Fitzpatrick, was a ship builder who came to America before the Civil War and was killed in New Orleans. John and Alice (Archer) Fitzpatrick had three children before he came to America. When he did not return, Alice left her three little children with her mother in Bedfordshire and came to America to see what she could learn of his death. A short time later she married (2), a Mr. Fleming, who had a woolen mill in Cincinnati, Ohio, by whom she had a daughter, Dora Fleming. Mr. Fleming died soon thereafter. Alice Archer apparently married (3), Lawrence McGary, who was described as "dearly loved" by Alice's granddaughter, Susan (Riley) Wolfer. Alice Archer's daughter, Kate "Clara" Archer, apparently took her mother's maiden name for her own, rather than the surname of her mother's husbands.

Clara Archer married twice, and had ten children. She was married first at the age of 18 and was widowed four years later, with three children. Her first husband was a veteran of the Civil War who died of tuberculosis at the age of 37. They lived near where the railroad tracks were being laid through Rowan, Iowa, and she boarded and lodged some of the railroad workers. Her daughter had to sleep on the floor so the railroad workers could have her bed. Clara married again at age 23 and had seven more children before she died at the age of 67. Her second husband was a Methodist preacher who served churches in North Dakota and Iowa. He died 11 years later and was buried at Rowan, Iowa; Clara, too, is presumably buried there.

She married (1), 2 January 1867, James Gillett Riley, son of Simeon and Katharine (Gillett) Riley; born in New York state, 9 July 1834; died in Wright County, Iowa, 25 September 1871. James and Clara (Archer) Riley had three children. She married (2), at Hampton, Iowa, 4 April 1872, James Benward Stout, son of Z. S. and Maryan Stout; born in New Jersey, 7 June 1851; died at Forest City, Iowa (probably), 7 April 1928. James and Clara (Archer) (Riley) Stout had seven children: Three sons, W. Z., Sim and Roy; and four daughters, Jessie, Nellie, Jennie, and Mable (d. before 1928). There were 27 grandchildren and 13 great-grandchildren alive at the time of Mr. Stout's death.

James Gillett and Kate C. (Archer) Riley had the following children:

3591 i. Isabelle "Totie Belle" Luella "Luella" (1867-1950)
3592 ii. Susan Myrtle "Aunt Sue" (->1928)
3593 iii. Stilson James (1871-1871)

2928. Adelia Catharine "Delia" RILEY,[737] daughter and fourth of the five children of Simeon and Katharine (Gillett) Riley, was born at Steuben County, New York, 24 July 1836; died at Rowan, Iowa, 30 July 1887, age 51. Her parents died when she was very young; her mother died when she was three years old and her father died when she was about six. In 1848, she and her four brothers were named in the will of her grandfather, Joseph Gillett, to share in the proceeds of sale of two small parcels of land, somewhat more than an acre, which he owned in Caton, Steuben County, NY. Her grandfather Gillett died in 1848 when she was 12, two years after this will was written. Two years later, her grandfather Riley died; she was then 14. At that time she and her two surviving brothers (the youngest, Ransom, is not mentioned at probate) were said to have a General Guardian, one James W. Glover, whose relationship to the family is unknown.

In 1856 she married a young man from a nearby family which was already connected by marriage to her family; her husband's grandmother Charlotte (Prince) Hill was also her step-grandmother, having married her grandfather Joseph Gillett after his first wife died; and her aunt Esther (Riley) was married to her husband's uncle George Hill. She was 20 and her husband was 25 when they married and began farming on rented land in Steuben County. After about five years, they and their two young sons (a daughter was born later) travelled to Iowa in March 1861 to begin new lives as pioneer farmers in Wright County, initially on rented property. They eventually were able to purchase a quarter section -- 240 acres -- of good farmland near the Iowa River. Their second son died at the age of 9 when he and his 22 year old uncle fell off of a horse and drowned in the flooded river, but the other two children grew to maturity and had children of their own. When she died of "phthisis," also called "consumption" (tuberculosis), at the age of 51, her funeral was the largest ever known in Wright County. Some 136 teams of horses were present to bring the mourners to her funeral and to the Horse Grove cemetery, where she was initially buried. Her remains were later moved to what has become the family cemetery at Rowan, Iowa.

She married, at Caton, Steuben County, New York, 9 April 1856, when she was 19, **Charles W. [20] HILL**, son of William Prince and Sarah (Herrick) Hill; born at Caton, 21 August 1831; died at Rowan, Iowa, 23 September 1923. Adelia Riley was the step-granddaughter of William Prince Hill's mother, Charlotte (Prince) Hill, through her second marriage, to Joseph Gillett. Charles and Adelia (Riley) Hill had three children: George J.; William L.; and Adella L.

They had the following children:

2667	i.	George J. [68] (1857-1952)
2668	ii.	William L. [69] (1860-1869)
2669	iii.	Adella L. [70] (1863-1910)

2929. Ransom RILEY. Born aft 1837. Ransom died in 1846-1848, he was 9. He was listed as a son in the will of his father, Simeon Riley. His grandfather Joseph Gillett listed him as heir, still a minor, in his will, written in 1846, but wrote in a codicil to his will in 1848 that "Ransom Riley the youngest son of my daughter Katharine mentioned in my last will and testament is now dead." The approximate year of his birth is inferred from the years of birth of his older siblings. He was not mentioned as a living heir of his grandfather, Josiah Riley, on 23 August 1850, when Josiah Riley's estate was probated.

2930. Mary Amanda MILLER. Born 9 May 1830 in Coventry, N.Y. Mary Amanda died 8 Aug 1830.

2931. Josephine REDMOND. Born in 1850 in Farmers Creek, Mich.

2932. Earl HOSKINS. Born in 1885.

2933. Carl HOSKINS. Born in Jul 1887 in Iowa. Carl married **Ida Mae SEAVERTON**. Born in 1890. Mother of 3 sons, unnamed in Ancestry.com.

2934. Stanley HOSKINS. Born on 10 Apr 1889 in Iowa. Stanley married Lena **Zenita ? (HOSKIN)**. Born in 1896. Mother of a son and daughter, unnamed in Ancestry.com.

2935. Stella HOSKINS. Born in Mar 1891 in Iowa. In 1910 she was in Chequest, Van Buren, Ia..

2936. Affa HOSKINS. Born on 3 Apr 1893 in Iowa. Affa died in Bloomfield, Davis, Ia. in Jul 1980, she was 87, d.s.p. Affa married **Clarence C. DAY**. Born on 28 Jul 1887 in Bloomfield, Davis, Ia.

2937. Neri HOSKINS. Born in Mar 1895 in Iowa. Neri died aft 1900, he was 4. He disappeared from the record after the census of 1900.

2938. Garland HOSKINS. Born in Apr 1898 in Iowa. He disappeared from the record after the census of 1920, when he was in Des Moines, Ia.

2939. Born in 1901 in Iowa. Mary died aft 1920, she was 19. She resided in Des Moines, Ia., in 1920, and then disappeared from the record.

2940. Flora HOSKIN. Born in 1904 in Iowa. Flora died aft 1925, she was 21. She was in Des Moines, Ia., in 1920 and in Perry, Ia., in 1925, and then disappeared from the record. Flora married **Floyd DOWNING**. Born in 1901. No children are known from this marriage.

2941. Lesie V. HOSKIN. Born on 23 Dec 1907 in Cantril, Van Buren, Ia. Lesie V. died in Marion, Linn Co., Ia. on 22 Oct 1996, he was 88. Lesie V. married **Ruth Alberta Pratt DAVIS**. Born on 10 Oct 1912 in Iowa. Ruth Alberta Pratt died in Marion, Linn Co., Ia. on 11 Feb 1995, she was 82.

They had one child:

3594	i.	Daughter of Lesie and Ruth (Davis)

From Google Images

Fig. 8-1: Birge Mansion, 33 Symphony Circle, Buffalo, N.Y. Home of George Kingsley Birge, designed by his son-in-law, George Cary. 33 Symphony Circle

From Google Images

Fig. 8-2: Birge Memorial, burial place of George Kingsley Birge

Fig. 8-3: Family of George J. and Jessie (Stockwell) Hill, Clarion, Iowa – about 1907
George J. Hill was a great-grandson of Ephraim Hill (d. Caton, N.Y., 1832)

9
Ninth Generation
The 6th-Great-Grandchildren

Line 1 – Descendants of Lydia Hill (continued)[738]

2942. Mary Ann SANDERSON. Born 29 Mar 1824 in Indiana; d. in Monmount, Ore. in 1881, abt 56.

2943. William Albert SANDERSON. Born 25 Sep 1829 in Indiana; d. in Lucas Co., Ia. in 1893, abt 63.

2944. Clarinda Jane SANDERSON. Born on 14 Jul 1833 in Brownstown, Ind. Clarinda Jane died in Chariton, Ia. on 14 Mar 1907, she was 73. Occupation: Mother of 7. On 17 Dec 1850 when Clarinda Jane was 17, she married **John Wesley SHEPPERD,** in Greene Co., Ind. Born on 25 Dec 1826 in Greene Co., Ind. John Wesley died in Des Moines, Polk Co., Ia. on 3 May 1907, he was 80.
They had the following children:

3595	i.	George Washington (1852-1922)
3596	ii.	Bruce Eugene (1854-1943)
3597	iii.	Juniatta L. (1855-1928)
3598	iv.	Clarinda Jane (1859-1893)
3599	v.	Adeliza Bell (1862-1865)
3600	vi.	Mary Melcina (1864-1935)
3601	vii.	John Henry (1869-)

2945. Adaliza L. SANDERSON. Born 18 Apr 1836 in Brownstown, Ind.; d. in Derby, Ia.

2946. Julia Dorleska SANDERSON. Born on 25 Aug 1839 in Brownstown, Ind.; died in Chariton, Ia.

2947. Caroline Gertrude SEDGEWICK. Born in Little Rock, Kendall Co., Ill. On 30 Mar 1876 she married **Webster DYAS** in De Kalb, Ill.

2948. Charles T. SEDGEWICK. Charles T. died in Sandwich, De Kalb Co., Ill.

2949. Harvey SEDGEWICK. Born in Little Rock, Kendall Co., Ill.

2950. Jennie Mary SEDGEWICK. Born in Little Rock, Kendall Co., Ill.; died in Sandwich, Ill.

2951. Agnes E. SEDGEWICK. B. 25 Jul 1849 in Little Rock, Ill.; d. in Sandwich, 27 Jan 1928, age 78.

2952. S. Parker SEDGEWICK. Born on 1 Mar 1860 in Sandwich, Ill.; died there, 17 Jul 1912, age 52.

2953. Charles F. SEDGEWICK. Born 20 Jan 1865 in Little Rock, Ill.; d. in Sandwich, 11 Mar 1915.

2954. Charles W. BREWER. Born on 5 Jun 1860 in Sandwich, De Kalb Co., Ill.; died in Bynumville, Chariton Co., Mo., 10 Mar 1952, he was 91. He married **Grace G. BREWER.** Born on 29 May 1858 in Montezuma, Ia.; died in Bynumville, Chariton Co., Mo., 19 Dec 1932, she was 74.
They had the following children:

3602	i.	LaVerne Sedgwick (1882-1946)
3603	ii.	Ellie L. Corey
3604	iii.	Fannie Z. Miller
3605	iv.	Olive Grace
3606	v.	Leon H.
3607	vi.	Maude C.

2955. Fannie Maria BREWER. Born on 1 Mar 1868.

2956. Elizabeth BREWER. Born in 1863.

2957. Ernest BREWER. Born in 1873.

2958. Ava Gertrude BARKER. Born on 25 Apr 1882 in Brookfield, Linn., Mo. Ava Gertrude died on 24 Sep 1945, she was 63. Occupation: Mother of 4. Ava Gertrude married **Ernest Albert BETT.** Born in 1877. Ernest Albert died in 1931, he was 54.
They had the following children:

3608	i.	Elsie Gertrude (1907-1985)
3609	ii.	Doris Mabel (1908-1994)

| 3610 | iii. | Thomas Barker (1911-1968) |
| 3611 | iv. | Mary Rebecca (1913-1992) |

2959. Edna Belle BARKER. Born in 1883. Edna Belle died in 1968, she was 85.

2960. Elva May BARKER. Born in 1883. Elva May died in 1912, she was 29.

2961. Donald Josiah BARKER. Born on 17 Dec 1887 in Brookfield, Linn., Mo. Donald Josiah died in Brookfield, Linn., Mo. on 15 Dec 1950, he was 62. On 1 Jun 1911 when Donald Josiah was 23, he married **Nellie Hollet MARTIN**. Born in 1888. Nellie Hollet died in 1965, she was 77.
They had the following children:

| 3612 | i. | Wilson Josiah (1912-1994) |
| 3613 | ii. | Donald Junior (1918-1992) |

2962. Zelma Pearl BARKER. Born on 22 Feb 1894 in Brookfield, Linn., Mo.

2963. Martha Elizabeth BARKER. Born on 2 Feb 1895 in Fairplay, Mo. Martha Elizabeth died in Edmonton, Alberta, Canada on 6 Dec 1970, she was 75; d.s.p.

2964. Jessie ROSS. Born in 1871.

2965. Edith ROSS. Born in 1878.

2966. George Elbert FRISBIE. Born in 1850. George Elbert died in 1851, he was 1.

2967. Emmarilla Josephine FRISBIE. Born in 1852. Emmarilla Josephine died in 1946, she was 94.

2968. Ida Lizette FRISBIE. Born in 1854. Ida Lizette died in 1944, she was 90.

2969. Mary Isabella FRISBIE. Born in 1857. Mary Isabella died in 1920, she was 63.

2970. Minnie Maria FRISBIE. Born in 1860. Minnie Maria died in 1946, she was 86.

2971. Alice Ann FRISBIE. Born in 1862. Alice Ann died in 1885, she was 23.

2972. Birdie Alvaretta FRISBIE. Born in 1865. Birdie Alvaretta died in 1938, she was 73.

2973. Rosella Putnam FRISBIE. Born in 1868. Rosella Putnam died in 1853.

2974. Arthur Asa FRISBIE. Born in 1871. Arthur Asa died in 1926, he was 55.

2975. Ida Lenore CALDWELL. Born in 1859. Ida Lenore died in 1947, she was 88.

2976. Orville Clyde CALDWELL. Born in 1861. Orville Clyde died in 1935, he was 74.

2977. Ervin Lyle (a k a Erving) CHUBB. Born in 1863; died in 1942, he was 79.

2978. Anna Laura FRISBIE. Born abt 1869 in Texas. Anna Laura died in Tacoma, Pierce Co., Washington in 1926, she was 57.

2979. Sadie F. FRISBIE. Born in 1872.

2980. Louis F. FRISBIE. Born in 1875.

2981. Julius A. FRISBIE. Born in 1876.

2982. Martha FRISBIE. Born in 1877.

2983. Ezra Clark FRISBIE. Born in 1885.

2984. ? son of Clark Lamartine and Clara (Doyle) FRISBIE.

2985. ? son of Clark Lamartine and Clara (Doyle) FRISBIE.

2986. Nancy Maranda BYINGTON. Born on 4 Dec 1850 in Salt Lake City, Utah. Nancy Maranda died in Ogden, Weber Co., Utah on 10 Nov 1876, she was 25. Occupation: Mother of 1. On 19 Nov 1866 when Nancy Maranda was 15, she married **William STOWE**, in Ogden, Weber Co., Utah. Born on 19 May 1830 in Wayne, Ohio. William died in Ogden, Weber Co., Utah in 1876, he was 45.
They had one child:

| 3614 | i. | Blanch Lillian (1872-1923) |

2987. Joseph Hezekiah BYINGTON. Born on 30 Nov 1852 in Salt Lake City, Utah. Joseph Hezekiah died in Pocatello, Bannock, Idaho on 12 Jun 1929, he was 76. On 26 Sep 1875 when Joseph Hezekiah was 22, he married (1) **Orra "Orry" WAKLEY**, in Utah. Born on 10 Dec 1860 in Willard, Box Elder, Utah; died in Dempsey, Bannock, Idaho on 8 Nov 1893, she was 32.
They had the following children:

3615	i.	Aleanor Elena (1878-)
3616	ii.	Herbert Day (1881-)
3617	iii.	Sylvia Mariah (1883-)
3618	iv.	Leon Nelson (1885-)

3619	v.	Orra Elvira (1887-)
3620	vi.	Joseph Earon (1889-)
3621	vii.	Elmer William (1891-)

On 26 Sep 1895 when Joseph Hezekiah was 42, he married (1) **Mary Ann LASLEY**, in Logan, Cache, Utah. Born 15 Dec 1878 in Calsfort, Box Elder, Utah; died in Jerome, Jerome, Idaho 18 Oct 1964, age 85. They had the following children:

3622	i.	Viola May (1897-)
3623	ii.	Ida May (1898-)
3624	iii.	Ethel Elizabeth (1901-)
3625	iv.	Joseph Lasley (1903-)
3626	v.	John Avery (1909-)
3627	vi.	Heber Thornley (1914-)
3628	vii.	Edna Matilda (1919-)

2988. Oliver Milton BYINGTON. B. 23 Feb 1855 in Tooele, Tooele, Utah; d. 27 Feb 1857, he was 2.

2989. Sarah Augusta BYINGTON. Born on 23 Jun 1857 in Ogden, Weber, Utah. Sarah Augusta died in Montana on 24 Jan 1922, she was 64. May have married twice, but no children are known and no further information about this person is in OneWorldTree.

2990. Hyrum Elliot BYINGTON. Born on 19 Jan 1859 in American Fork, Utah. Hyrum Elliot died in Baker, Baker, Oregon on 23 Nov 1939, he was 80. On 6 Feb 1883 when Hyrum Elliot was 24, he married **Cordelia SIMMONS**, in Utah. Born on 4 Oct 1868 in Sioux City, Mo. (?). Cordelia died in Lava Hot Springs, Bannock, Idaho on 2 Aug 1911, she was 42.
They had one child:

3629	i.	Lottie Faye (1897-1994)

2991. Elizabeth Ann BYINGTON. Born on 27 Jun 1862 in Huntsville, Weber, Utah. Elizabeth Ann died in Blackfoot, Bingham, Utah on 9 Nov 1942, she was 80. She may have married twice and had a child, but this is not clear in OneWorldTree.

2992. John Henry BYINGTON. Born on 20 Sep 1864 in Huntsville, Weber, Utah. John Henry died in Pocatello, Bannock, Idaho on 9 Mar 1940, he was 75. He may have married twice and had a son but this is not clear in OneWorldTree.

2993. Jeanette Sophia BYINGTON. Born on 3 Sep 1866 in Ogden, Weber Co., Utah. Jeanette Sophia died in Pocatello, Bannock, Idaho on 28 Nov 1940, she was 74. She may have married twice and had a daughter, but this is not clear in OneWorldTree.

2994. Noah Samuel BYINGTON. B 28 Sep 1868 in Calls Fort, Box Elder, Utah; d. 27 Nov 1869, age 1.

2995. Ira Zina BYINGTON. Born on 22 Oct 1870 in Calls Fort, Box Elder, Utah; died in Utah 26 Nov 1935, age 65. In Feb 1897 when Ira Zina was 26, he married **Sarah Emma "Sadie Mae" WALKER**.

2996. William Alma BYINGTON. Born on 20 Jul 1873 in Nine Mile, Bannock, Idaho. William Alma died in Boise, Ada, Idaho on 11 Mar 1948, he was 74. William Alma married **Emma HIGGINS**. Born on 5 Jan 1881 in Nephi, Juab, Utah. Emma died in Pocatello, Bannock, Idaho on 21 Jul 1937, she was 56. They had the following children:

3630	i.	Child of William and Emma (Higgins)
3631	ii.	Child of William and Emma (Higgins)
3632	iii.	Emma Elvira (1898-)
3633	iv.	William Leslie (1899-)
3634	v.	Naomia Leona (1908-)
3635	vi.	Harold Ray (1909-)
3636	vii.	Thora (1911-)
3637	viii.	Reba Ilene (1914-)

2997. James Henry BYINGTON. Born on 4 Apr 1865 in Ogden, Weber Co., Utah; died in Lava Hot Springs, Bannock, Idaho on 7 Apr 1930, he was 65. The list of his children in OneWorldTree is inconsistent and will not be reproduced here. On 25 Dec 1890 when he was 25, he married **Sarah Mariah CARR** in Logan, Cache, Utah. Born on 10 Sep 1872 in Promentory Point, Utah; died in Lava

Hot Springs, Bannock, Idaho on 6 Jul 1952, she was 79. Probably had children.

2998. Hannah Maria BYINGTON. Born on 8 Aug 1866 in Ogden, Weber Co., Utah. Hannah Maria died in Logan, Cache, Utah on 22 Mar 1931, she was 64. Probably had children. Hannah Maria married **William BURRUP**. Born on 19 Oct 1861 in Ogden, Weber Co., Utah. William died in Downey, Bannock, Utah on 21 May 1924, he was 62.

2999. Susan Elizabeth BYINGTON. Born on 30 Sep 1876 in Red Rock, Bannock, Utah. Susan Elizabeth died in Rigby, Jefferson, Idaho on 11 Mar 1956, she was 79. Probably had children. Susan Elizabeth married **Isaiah Martin FISHER**. Born on 16 Aug 1873 in Ogden, Weber Co., Utah. Isaiah Martin died in Rigby, Jefferson, Idaho on 12 Dec 1949, he was 76.

3000. John Parley BYINGTON. Born on 23 Mar 1880 in Red Rock, Bannock, Utah. John Parley died in Poplar, Bonneville, Idaho on 20 Feb 1964, he was 83. On 12 Dec 1904 when John Parley was 24, he married **Marguerite Brennetta SMITH**, in Laguna, Utah. Born on 3 Jul 1889 in Nephi, Juab, Utah; died in Idaho Falls, Bonneville, Idaho on 10 Sep 1953, she was 64. Probably had children.

3001. Hyrum Norton BYINGTON. Born on 30 Dec 1861 in Ogden Valley, Weber, Utah.

3002. Joseph Henry BYINGTON. Born on 28 Dec 1862 in Eden, Weber, Utah.

3003. Stephen Elliot BYINGTON. Born on 18 Jan 1866 in Ogden, Weber, Utah.

3004. Sarah Jane BYINGTON. Born on 14 Nov 1867 in Eden, Weber, Utah.

3005. Hannah Elizabeth BYINGTON. Born on 12 Oct 1868 in Ogden Valley, Weber, Utah.

3006. Alexander BYINGTON. Born on 3 Feb 1873 in Bear River City, Box Elder, Utah.

3007. Rebecca Ann BYINGTON. Born on 25 Aug 1874 in Bear River City, Box Elder, Utah.

3008. Nora Isabelle BYINGTON. Born on 3 Feb 1876 in Bear River City, Box Elder, Utah.

3009. Susannah WILBUR. Born on 4 Feb 1879 in Downey, Idaho. Susannah died in Redondo Beach, Calif. on 1 Aug 1974, she was 95. On 25 Oct 1910 when Susannah was 31, she married **Orlando Jackson CARR**, in Annis, Jefferson, Idaho. Born on 22 Feb 1868 in Ogden, Utah. Orlando Jackson died in Annis, Jefferson, Idaho on 19 Jul 1953, he was 85.
They had the following children:

3638	i.	Child of Orlando and Susannah (Wilbur)
3639	ii.	Child of Orlando and Susannah (Wilbur)
3640	iii.	Orlando King (1911-)
3641	iv.	Sylvia Pearl (1912-)
3642	v.	Orville Leui (1918-)
3643	vi.	Clarence (1920-)
3644	vii.	Lavella Ruth (1921-)

3010. Cyrus OLMSTED.

3011. Frances OLMSTED.

3012. Helen OLMSTED.

3013. Royal OLMSTED.

3014. Walter Wells BYINGTON. Born on 2 May 1855 in Jefferson, Ill.

3015. Albert Webster BYINGTON. Born on 10 Dec 1856 in Jefferson, Ill.

3016. Edgar Seaburn BYINGTON. Born on 22 Nov 1858 in Lagrange, Ind.

3017. Frank Augustus BYINGTON. Born on 13 Jan 1861 in Jefferson, Ill.

3018. Nelson Smith BYINGTON. Born on 18 Nov 1862 in Jefferson, Ill.

3019. Nellie Amelia BYINGTON. Born on 18 Nov 1862 in Jefferson, Ill.

3020. Alice Phoebe BYINGTON. Born on 13 Oct 1864 in Jefferson, Ill. OneWorldTree shows Alice, Addie, and Anna are triplets.

3021. Addie Julia BYINGTON. OneWorldTree shows Alice, Addie, and Anna are triplets.

3022. Anna Eliza BYINGTON. OneWorldTree shows Alice, Addie, and Anna are triplets.

3023. Martha Luce BYINGTON. Born on 6 Nov 1874 in Worth, Iowa.

3024. Carrie May BYINGTON. Born on 12 Jul 1877 in Worth, Iowa.

3025. Howard Grant BYINGTON. Born on 17 Oct 1879 in Plymouth, Iowa.

3026. Florence Selina LANE. Born on 9 Jul 1853.

3027. Maria Elizabeth LANE. Born on 28 Oct 1857.

3028. William Edgar LANE. Born on 8 Jan 1859.

3029. Albert Harry LANE. Born on 31 May 1861.

3030. Harriet Louise LANE. Born on 11 Nov 1850.

3031. Alfred Henry LANE. Born on 6 Apr 1859.

3032. Charles SCOVILLE.

3033. George H. SCOVILLE. Born in Jan 1861.

3034. Bruce B. LANE. Born in 1848. In 1874 when Bruce B. was 26, he m. **Allice LANE.** Born in Jun 1856 in New York. Her parents' names are unknown. It is unknown if she is a relative of her husband. They had the following children:

3645	i.	Grace A. (1875->1900)
3646	ii.	Ida M. (~1877->1880)
3647	iii.	Bruce B. (1879->1900)
3648	iv.	Eula (1881->1900)
3649	v.	Allice R. (1883->1900)
3650	vi.	Alice Handsome (~1885->1910)
3651	vii.	Richard J.
3652	viii.	Theodore T. (1889-)
3653	ix.	Harold Charles (1892-)

3035. Herbert LANE. Born in 1849. Herbert died in 1893, he was 44. Information about his marriage and children is from Lane / Ocker Tree (Owner PatLane57). In 1880 when Herbert was 31, he married **Amelia WIEGET.** Born in 1844. Amelia died in 1894, she was 50. Ancestry.com implies that all of her children died as infants, but this is not verified.

They had the following children:

3654	i.	Rufus H. (1884-1885)
3655	ii.	James E. (1886-1887)
3656	iii.	Emily E. (1888-1889)
3657	iv.	Martha (1890-)

3036. Delos Gager L'HOMMEDIEU. Born 20 Sep 1857; m. **Estelle JEFFREY**, b. 29 May 1861.

3658	i.	Perrin
3659	ii.	Ramond D.

3037. William Albert L'HOMMEDIEU. Born 26 May 1865; m. **Susie DURYEA**, b. 9 May 1870. They had the following children:

3660	i.	Albert Whitman (1893-)
3661	ii.	Anella L. (1895-)

3038. Warren Todd HUMISTON. Born on 21 Jun 1862 in Wolcott, New Haven, Conn.; d. in Watertown, Conn., 26 Dec 1938, he was 76. On 25 Dec 1888, when he was 26, he married **Isabel MUNSON.** Born in May 1862 in Nova Scotia, Canada; died in Watertown, Conn.,15 Mar 1933, age 70. They had the following children:

3662	i.	Glenwood Warren (1889-)
3663	ii.	Olive Ellen
3664	iii.	Ralph Carlyle (1890-)
3665	iv.	Clyde Myron (1892-)
3666	v.	Ellsworth Munson (1894-)
3667	vi.	Joseph Harold (1896-)
3668	vii.	Hugh Darius (Twin) (1901-)
3669	viii.	Harry Robert (Twin) (1901-)

3039. Glenwood Carlisle HUMISTON. Born on 30 Mar 1859; died on 4 Jul 1868, he was 9.

3040. Emma Genevieve HUMISTON. Born on 12 Sep 1860 in Wolcott, New Haven, Conn. Emma Genevieve died on 31 Jul 1942, she was 81. Emma Genevieve married **George LEAVENWORTH.** They had one child:

3670   i.   Bertrand Humiston (1884-)

3041. Eva Adeline TODD. Born on 3 Oct 1862 in Meriden, Conn.

3042. Erwin Wallace TODD. Born on 19 Aug 1864 in Meriden, Conn.

3043. Jennie Laura TODD. Born on 18 Dec 1866 in Meriden, Conn.

3044. Frances Miriam TODD. Born on 15 Mar 1871 in Scranton, Lackawanna, Pa.

3045. Ethel Winona TODD. Born on 17 Nov 1874 in Scranton, Lackawanna, Pa.

3046. Henry Leon TODD. Born on 1 Mar 1878 in Scranton, Lackawanna, Pa.

3047. Lewis Irving TODD. Born on 6 Feb 1872.

3048. Florence Emeline TODD. Born on 22 Dec 1887.

3049. Charles Munde NEWELL. Born on 24 Oct 1863 in Southington, Conn.

3050. Eva Lovina NEWELL. Born on 14 Feb 1865 in Southington, Conn.

3051. Donald Joseph SMITH. Born on 19 Aug 1883. Donald Joseph died in 1884.

3052. Horatio CARLEY. Born on 8 Aug 1880.

3053. Mabel Frances CARLEY. Born on 6 Aug 1881.

3054. Julius Munson CARLEY. Born on 17 Apr 1884.

3055. Russell Henry CARLEY. Born on 6 May 1886.

3056. Ethel Miriam PRIOR. Born on 3 Jun 1878 in Bristol, Hartford Co., Conn.

3057. Orville George PRIOR. Born on 29 May 1880.

3058. Myrtle Elizabeth PRIOR. Born on 24 Apr 1882.

3059. James Murray PRIOR. Born on 4 Mar 1884.

3060. Leland Jay PRIOR. Born on 9 Jan 1886.

3061. Harry PRIOR. Born on 14 Mar 1888.

3062. May PRIOR. Born on 16 Feb 1890.

3063. Iva Alice PRIOR. Born on 2 Nov 1891.

3064. Arline Rose PRIOR. Born on 9 May 1893.

3065. George WOODING.

3066. William WOODING.

3067. Edna Viola THOMAS. Born in 1874. Edna Viola died in 1879, she was 5.

3068. Elmer Elsworth THOMAS. Born in 1878. Elmer Elsworth died in 1965, he was 87.

3069. Edgar Louis THOMAS. Born in 1880. Edgar Louis died in 1936, he was 56.

3070. Charles Ernest THOMAS. Born in 1883. Charles Ernest died in 1885, he was 2.

3071. Earnest L. THOMAS. Born in 1885.

3072. Frank Charles THOMAS. Born in 1887. Frank Charles died in 1958, he was 71.

3073. Ernest Ray THOMAS. Born in 1889. Ernest Ray died in 1955, he was 66.

3074. Clarence Irwin THOMAS. Born in 1893. Clarence Irwin died in 1955, he was 62.

3075. Nellie L. TUTTLE. Born on 7 Aug 1844 in Clear Lake, Cerro Gordo Co., Ia. Nellie L. died in Seattle, King Co., Wash. on 7 Mar 1929, she was 84. On 14 Jun 1867 when Nellie L. was 22, she married **Hiram Addison HOUGHTALING**, in Clear Lake, Cerro Gordo Co., Ia. Born on 22 Mar 1843. Hiram Addison died in Algona, Ia. in 1896, abt 52.

They had the following children:

    3671   i.   Myrta May (1868-)

    3672   ii.   Clair Albert (1869-1944)

    3673   iii.   Vera Litta (1882-)

3076. Harriet Eugenia TUTTLE.

3077. Sylvia Jane TUTTLE.

3078. Aldemer M. TUTTLE.

3079. Jeanette M. TUTTLE.

3080. Lucien TUTTLE.

3081. Sophia TUTTLE.

3082. Edward Leslie WHITE. Born in 1878. Edward Leslie died in 1960, he was 82.

3083. Howard Leroy WHITE. Born in 1880. Howard Leroy died in 1933, he was 53.

3084. Percy Lewis WHITE. Born in 1881. Percy Lewis died in 1955, he was 74.

3085. Walter Washburn WHITE. Born in 1883. Walter Washburn died in 1885, he was 2.

3086. Morris Hemingway WHITE. Born in 1885. Morris Hemingway died in 1939, he was 54.

3087. Merrill Washburn WHITE. Born in 1887. Merrill Washburn died in 1951, he was 64.

3088. Mary Almira WHITE. Born in 1889. Mary Almira died in 1940, she was 51.

3089. Alma Anna WHITE. Born in 1890. Alma Anna died in 1985, she was 95.

3090. William Wirt WHITE. Born in 1893. William Wirt died in 1896, he was 3.

3091. Twin Son WHITE. Born in 1895. Twin Son died in 1895.

3092. Twin Daughter WHITE. Born in 1895. Twin Daughter died in 1895.

3093. Harold WHITE. Born in 1896. Harold died in 1976, he was 80.

3094. Helen Augusta WHITE. Born in 1897. Helen Augusta died in 1963, she was 66.

3095. Fred GAYLORD. Born on 6 Aug 1866 in Packwaukee, Marquette, Wisc.

3096. Hepworth A. GAYLORD. Born on 2 Oct 1868 in Grove City, Ia.; died on 9 Feb 1928, he was 59. On 21 Jan 1892 when Hepworth A. was 23, he married **Belle BENNETT**, in Byron, Neb. They had the following children:

3674	i.	Daughter of Hepworth and Belle (Bennett)
3675	ii.	Helen Sabra (1893-)
3676	iii.	Howard (1895-)
3677	iv.	Charles E. (1900-)
3678	v.	Lawrence (1901-)

3097. Nellie Ada GAYLORD. Born on 1 Aug 1870 in Atlantic, Ia.

3098. William B. GAYLORD. Born on 4 Mar 1872 in White Rock, Kansas.

3099. Ray B. GAYLORD. Born in 1873 in Kansas.

3100. Irene B. GAYLORD. Born on 12 Dec 1874 in Gaylords Grove, Kansas.

3101. Margaret Elsie GAYLORD. Born on 27 Feb 1878 in Elma, Kansas.

3102. Mary D. GAYLORD. Born on 17 Feb 1880 in Elma, Kansas.

3103. Chestley N. GAYLORD. Born on 10 Jun 1881 in Harbine, Kansas.

3104. Lomar E. GAYLORD. Born on 18 Dec 1882 in Harbine, Kansas.

3105. Minnie H. GAYLORD. Born on 14 Mar 1885 in Harbine, Kansas.

3106. Laurence I. GAYLORD. Born on 16 Sep 1889 in Byron, Thayer, Neb.

3107. Catherine ROBERTS.

3108. Gaylord ROBERTS.

3109. Frank Monroe BARNES. Born on 27 Jan 1859. Frank Monroe married **Catherine E. WATTS**, daughter of Adam WATTS & Nancy STEWART. Born on 26 May 1859 in Washington, Conn. Catherine E. died on 3 Sep 1930, she was 71. They had one child:

3679	i.	Clarence H. (1885-1952)

3110. Mary Frances KEELING. Born on 14 Apr 1872 in Joliet, Ill.

3111. John Leslie KEELING. Born on 10 Aug 1883 in Joliet, Ill.

3112. Birdie Alice FRISBIE. Born on 4 Jun 1876 in West Union, Fayette, Ia.

3113. Henry Case FRISBIE. Born on 26 Mar 1878 in Lena, Stephenson, Ill.

3114. Lottie May FRISBIE. Born on 21 Mar 1881 in Lena, Stephenson, Ill.

3115. Jessie Evelyn FRISBIE. Born on 10 Apr 1883 in Lena, Stephenson, Ill.

3116. William FRISBIE. Born on 11 Oct 1889 in Lena, Stephenson, Ill.

3117. Hazel FRISBIE. Born on 17 Jul 1891 in Lena, Stephenson, Ill.

3118. John Carlton FRISBIE. Born on 29 Nov 1898 in Lena, Stephenson, Ill.

3119. John Earl KAUFFMAN. Born on 18 Sep 1886 in Freeport, Stephenson, Ill.

3120. Infant child of Samuel and Mary (Frisbie) KAUFFMAN.

3121. Paul Leslie FRISBIE. Born on 29 Jul 1897 in Freeport, Stephenson, Ill.

3122. Harold John FRISBIE. Born on 2 Nov 1899 in Freeport, Stephenson, Ill.

3123. Florence FRISBIE. Born on 22 Nov 1882 in Silver Creek, Stephenson, Ill.

Line 2. Descendants of Mary Hill (continued)[739]

3124. Lizzie Pulsifer ALLEN. Born on 31 Jan 1877; died in Derby, Vt. in Feb 1899, she was 22.

3125. Charles GAYNOR. Born abt 1898.

3126. Mary Frances BEAUCLERK (or BEANDUK). Born on 10 May 1873. Mary Frances died in 1931, she was 57. Her mother died when she was only a week old. Her name in O. P. Allen is Beanduk, and she is in OneWorldTree as Mary Frances Beauclerk. Mary Frances first married **William O. STETSON (or WILSON).** He was of Newport, Vt. He is in OneWorldTree as William O. Stetson. They had the following children:

| 3680 | i. | Allen (1896-) |
| 3681 | ii. | Harold (1898-) |

In 1905 when Mary Frances was 31, she second married **Eben W. GAYNOR.** Born in 1871. Eben W. died in 1919, he was 48. He is in OneWorldTree.
They had the following children:

3682	i.	William Allen (1896-1972)
3683	ii.	Charles Beauclerk
3684	iii.	Harold Wentworth (1899-)

Line 5. Descendants of Luke Hill, Jr. (continued)

------------------------------[740]

3127. Clarence Mortimer HILL,[741] only child of Morris Seth and Teresa (Mills) Hill, was born at Wauconda, Lake Co., Ill., 15 October 1852; died in Lake Co., Ill., 22 March 1898, age 45. He married (1), **Carrie A. BURNHAM**; born in 1852 and died without progeny. He married (2), in Lake Co., Ill., 1 November 1873, **Mary Elizabeth AULT**; born at Natchez, Miss., 23 December 1855; died in Lake Co., Ill., 23 June 1882, at age 26. They had at least three and possibly four children. She died ten days after giving birth to her last child, Sadie W., who survived and had descendants.
Clarence and Mary (Ault) Hill had the following children:

3685	i.	Lulu
3686	ii.	Clarence (1876-)
3687	iii.	Lula A. (1879-)
3688	iv.	Sadie W. (1882-1968)

3128. Morris S. FORD.[742] Born on 21 Feb 1847 in Ela, Lake Co., Ill. Morris S. died in Wauconda, Lake Co., Illinois in 1923, he was 75. On 14 Oct 1868 when Morris S. was 21, he married **Hellen F. TURNER**, in Boone, Boone Co., Ill.
They had the following children:

3689	i.	Harry Lewis (1869-1941)
3690	ii.	Ambrose Elmer (1874-)
3691	iii.	Lida B. (1884-1956)

3129. Louis A. FORD.[743] Born in Oct 1849 in Wauconda, Lake Co., Ill.; died there, 2 Jul 1850.

3130. William Henry FORD. Born on 8 Apr 1851.

3131. Mary Marie FORD. Born in 1855 in Illinois; died in Wauconda, Ill.

3132. Nellie F. FORD. Born in 1860 in Illinois; died in Wauconda, Illinois.

3133. Harry S. FORD.[744] Died in his second year of life.

3134. Lois Ann FORD.[745] Died as an infant.

3135. Hattie A. BANGS.[746] Born on 4 May 1862. Hattie A. died on 4 Mar 1863.

3136. Elva Louise BANGS.[747] Born on 20 Mar 1863 in Wauconda, Lake Co., Illinois. Elva Louise died in Omaha, Douglas Co., Neb. on 7 Jul 1907, she was 44. On 1 Jan 1879 when Elva Louise was 15, she married **Charles H. MYRICK**, in Ida Grove, Ida Co., Ia. Born on 5 Feb 1856 in Unity, Waldo Co., Me. Charles H. died in Excelsior Springs, Clay Co., Mo. on 17 Sep 1908, he was 52.
They had the following children:

3692	i.	Sadie Dell (1879-1960)
3693	ii.	Grace Estelle (1881-)
3694	iii.	Adah Rosina (1883-1919)

3137. Fred W. BANGS.[748] Born in Sep 1866. On 24 Jun 1890 when Fred W. was 23, he married **Jennie E. LONG.** They d.s.p.

3138. Ella J. COWLES. Born in 1852.

3139. Francis COWLES. Born in 1853.

3140. Norman COWLES. Born in 1858.

3141. George COWLES. Born in 1860.

3142. Carrie COWLES. Born in 1862.

3143. Mira COWLES. Born in 1863.

3144. Winifred Josephine ROBINSON.[749] Born in 1867.

3145. Lillian Gertrude "Gertie" ROE.[750] Born on 14 Feb 1876 in Palatine, Ill.; died in Hudson, St. Croix Co., Wisc. on 11 Oct 1965, she was 89. Married twice but d.s.p. On 2 Jun 1902 when she was 26, she first married **Willis James SLAUSON.** Born in 1878; died in 1919, abt 41. In 1915 when she was about 38, she second married **William FISCHER.**

3146. Harvey S. ROE. Apparently d.s.p. Harvey S. married **Josephine PLUCK.** Born in 1890.

3147. Nettie YATES.[751] Born in Jan 1891 in South Dakota. In 1900, she lived in Fairview, Faulk Co., S.Dak., and in 1910 at University Place, Lancaster Co., Neb.

3148. Bessie YATES. Born in Jan 1894 in South Dakota. In 1900, she lived in Fairview, Faulk Co., S.Dak., and in 1910 at University Place, Lancaster Co., Neb.

3149. Hellen YATES. Born in Oct 1896 in South Dakota. In 1900, she lived in Fairview, Faulk Co., S.Dak., and in 1910 at University Place, Lancaster Co., Neb.

3150. Nettie Louise FELLOWS.[752] Born in 1859. Nettie Louise died in 1934, she was 75. Nettie Louise married _____ **OLMSTEAD.**

3151. Samuel Marsh BUTLER. Born in 1854.

3152. Jennie BUTLER. Born in 1859. Jennie died in 1951, she was 92.

3153. Edith B. BUTLER. Born in 1861.

3154. Emma M. SEYMOUR.[753] Born in 1865.

3155. Henry O. SEYMOUR.[754] Born in 1874.

3156. William Pratt SIDLEY.[755] Born in 1868. William Pratt died aft 1880.

3157. Kyle A. SIDLEY.[756] Born in 1870. Kyle A. died aft 1880.

3158. Fred K. SIDLEY.[757] Born in 1873; d. aft 1900. He resided in Chicago in 1880 and 1900.

3159. Frank C. SIDLEY.[758] Born in 1874; died aft 1900. He resided in Chicago in 1880 and 1900.

3160. Mollie SIDLEY.[759] Born in 1877. Mollie died aft 1880. She resided in Chicago in 1880.

3161. Ernest S. SIDLEY.[760] Born in 1879. Ernest S. died aft 1880. He resided in Chicago in 1880.

3162. Thomas H. SIDLEY.[761] Born in 1881; died aft 1900. He resided in Chicago in 1900.

3163. Frederick Pratt STEELE. Born on 6 Aug 1884; died on 17 Sep 1884.

3164. Elizabeth Livingston STEELE,[762] daughter and second child of Frederick Morgan and Ella Amanda (Pratt) Steele, was born in Chicago, Cook Co., Illinois, 27 January 1886; died at Santa Clara, California, 26 June 1959, age 73. She was a descendant of early settlers of New York, including Livingston and Schuyler. She was involved in lineage societies and she was a member of the Chicago Natural History Museum. Two of her three sons married and had descendants.

On 18 Jun 1908 when Elizabeth Livingston was 22, she married **George Washington CHILDS,**[763] son of Robert Andrew CHILDS & Mary Elizabeth COFFEEN. Born on 18 May 1880 in Hinsdale, Lake Co., Ill. George Washington Childs died in Santa Clara, Calif. on 28 Aug 1964, he was 84. Robert Andrew Childs (1845-) was the son of George and Mary C. (Nutter) Childs. George was the son of Jacob, son of Abijah II, son of Abijah and Prisicilla (Morse) Child. All of these ancestors are from New England. George Washington Childs lived at Hinsdale until 1910, when he was in Highland Park, Lake Co., Ill., and in 1920 he was in Deerfield, Lake Co., Ill. In 1930 he was again residing in Highland Park. In 1934 he arrived in New York by ship, and in 1936 he arrived by ship at Los Angeles.

It is curious, but apparently just a coincidence, that this George Washington Childs was a contemporary of a leading citizen of Philadelphia who bore the same name. George Washington Childs (1868-1944) of Philadelphia, who owned the Philadelphia *Public Ledger*, was the son of George Washington Childs (1829-1894), who bought this newspaper in 1864 when it was but a minor publication and built it into Philadelphia's leading newspaper. The elder George W. Childs is said to have been born in Baltimore, 12 May 1829, and came to Philadelphia as a penniless young man, after serving in the Navy. His ancestry is unknown, but he is apparently not related to the George Washington Childs who was born in Illinois in 1880. The Philadelphia man married Emma Bouvier Peterson (b. 1876). His biography is in John St. George Joyce (ed.), *The Story of Philadelphia* (p. 292), available on Google Books. George Washington Childs [Jr.] of Philadelphia was mentioned as a potential candidate for the Presidency of the United States in 1888. He sold the *Ledger* to the *Philadelphia Inquirer*, and the *Ledger* then went out of existence. He had business dealings with the Lippincott and Drexel families and his activities had a nation-wide scope, which leads to some confusion, because George Washington Childs of Illinois also was widely travelled and moved in high level financial and social circles.

George and Elizabeth (Steele) Childs had the following children, two of whom had descendants:

3695	i.	George Frederick (1909-1931)
3696	ii.	Robert Livingston (1912-1992)
3697	iii.	William Coffeen (1916-1997)

3165. Mary CHASE. Born in 1873. Mary died in 1910, she was 37.

3166. Ramona ROE. Born in 1898.

3167. Richard S. LAUGHTON. Born in 1914 in New York City, N.Y. Richard S. died in Norwalk, Conn. on 14 May 1996, he was 82. Richard S. married **? WARREN**, who he later divorced. They had the following children:

3698	i.	Child of Richard S.
3699	ii.	Child of Richard S.
3700	iii.	Child of Richard S.

3168. Jesse KILPATRICK. Born in Levering, Mich.

3169. Fred KILPATRICK. Born in 1858 in Woodlin, Barry Co., Mich.

3170. William KILPATRICK. Born on 8 May 1860 in Woodlin, Barry Co., Mich.

3171. Elmer KILPATRICK. Born on 12 May 1862 in Woodland, Barry Co., Mich.

3172. Bernard KILPATRICK. Born in 1865 in Woodland Twp., Barry Co., Mich.

3173. Eva KILPATRICK. Born in 1868 in Woodland Twp., Barry Co., Mich.

3174. John KILPATRICK. Born in 1870 in Woodland Twp., Barry Co., Mich.

3175. Nathan KILPATRICK. Born on 8 Oct 1872 in Woodland Twp., Mich.

3176. Lydia May KILPATRICK. Born on 7 Apr 1875 in Woodland Twp., Mich.

3177. Hattie KILPATRICK. Born on 15 May 1880 in Levering, Emmet Co., Mich.

3178. Wirt Ellsworth GRANT. Born on 2 Sep 1867 in Woodland Twp., Mich.

3179. Sarah Estella GRANT. Born on 28 Nov 1869 in Woodland Twp., Mich.

3180. Elton Durand GRANT. Born on 9 Jul 1872.

3181. Nellie Amy GRANT. Born on 12 Jan 1874 in Woodland Twp., Mich.

3182. Ola Blanch GRANT. Born on 15 Sep 1883 in Carplake, Mich.

3183. Effie Gail GRANT. Born on 10 Apr 1887 in Carplake, Mich.

3184. James William GRANT. Born on 7 Apr 1894 in Carplake, Mich.

3185. John Everett GRANT. Born on 9 Dec 1879 in Berry, Mich.

3186. Mary Ellen GRANT. Born in 1881.

3187. Harman Elihu GRANT. Born on 20 Jan 1883.

3188. Jane GRANT. Born in 1889.

3189. Ida Edna GRANT. Born on 23 Jul 1893 in Eaton, Mich.

3190. Maud MALLORY. Born on 6 Aug 1876 in Mich.

3191. Claude MALLORY. Born on 22 Oct 1878 in Mich.

3192. Zella MALLORY. Born on 18 Jan 1883.

3193. Estella R. MALLORY. Born on 10 Dec 1886 in Mich.

3194. John Dow MALLORY. Born on 24 Apr 1888 in Eaton, Mich.

3195. Gracie MALLORY. Born on 9 Aug 1891 in Allen, Ky.

3196. Charles Nelson SNYDER. Born on 3 Dec 1883.

3197. George Edwin SNYDER. Born on 16 Jan 1886.

3198. Earl Dorway SNYDER. Born on 7 Nov 1887.

3199. Arthur Leroy SNYDER. Born on 22 Jun 1889.

3200. Mary SNYDER. Born on 6 Dec 1894.

3201. Ella Wilhelmine SNYDER. Born on 29 Jun 1897.

3202. Earle ? (GRANT).

3203. Longstreth ? (GRANT).

3204. Berenice HILL.[764] Born abt 1874 in Illinois.

3205. Clarence S. HILL.[765] Born abt 1887 in Minnesota.

3206. Raymond Vaughn HILL.[766] Born on 3 Jul 1889 in Chicago, Cook Co., Ill. Raymond Vaughn died in Chino, San Bernardino Co., Calif. on 3 Jan 1984, he was 94. On 20 May 1914 when Raymond Vaughn was 24, he married **Edith May WOODFORD** in San Francisco, Calif. Born in 1892.
They had the following children:

3701	i.	Child of Raymond and Edith
3702	ii.	Child of Raymond and Edith
3703	iii.	William (~1915-2005)
3704	iv.	Clyde (1916-1987)
3705	v.	Howard (1918-2004)
3706	vi.	Woodrow (~1919-1986)
3707	vii.	Earl (1920-1988)
3708	viii.	Maxine (1924-1990)

3207. William Clayton HILL.[767] Born on 23 Sep 1890 in Mankato, Blue Earth Co., Minn. William Clayton died on 5 May 1891 in Chicago, Cook Co., Ill. Buried on 7 May 1891 in Chicago, Cook Co., Ill.

3208. David D. HILL.[768] Born on 31 Dec 1891 in Chicago, Cook Co., Ill. David D. died in Hennepin Co., Minn. on 8 Apr 1962, he was 70. In 1929 when David D. was 37, he married **Lillian K. McFARLAND** in Minnesota (probably). Born in 1890. Lillian K. died in 1968, she was 78.

3209. Maurice Gilbert HILL.[769] Born on 1 Apr 1893 in Minnesota. Maurice Gilbert died in Hennepin Co., Minn. on 28 Jul 1952, he was 59. In 1916 when Maurice Gilbert was 22, he married **Blanche Beatrice CHILGREN** in Saint Peter, Nicollet Co., Minn. Born in 1894; died in 1974, about 80.
They had the following children:

3709	i.	Child of Maurice and Blanche
3710	ii.	Child of Maurice and Blanche
3711	iii.	Child of Maurice and Blanche

3210. Albert HILL.[770] B on 9 Jul 1894 in Chicago, Ill.; d. there 6 Feb 1895 and bur 8 Feb.

3211. Mary Abbreata HILL.[771] B. on 9 Jul 1894 in Chicago, Ill.; d there 13 Jan 1895, bur 3 days later.

3212. Ellenore Elizabeth "Florence" HILL.[772] B. on 16 Jul 1896 in Chicago, Cook Co., Ill.; d on 1 Feb 1876 in Minneapolis, Hennepin Co., Ill.; married **Lowell Homer CLARK**. B. in 1894; d in 1972, abt 78.
They had the following children:

3712	i.	Child of Lowell and Ellenore
3713	ii.	Gene Bryant (1922-1980)
3714	iii.	Warren Lowell (1925-1983)
3715	iv.	Kenneth Frederick (~1925-1925)

3213. Clarice Elva HILL. Born on 26 Feb 1898 in Chicago, Cook Co., Ill.; d. in Hennepin Co., Minn., 5 Nov 1977, age 79. She married **? DAHLGREN.** Born in 1890.

3214. Grace HILL.[773] Born on 26 Feb 1898 in Chicago, Ill.; died there 16 Jun 1898; bur there next day.

3215. Gwendolyn "Babe" HILL.[774] Born on 6 Oct 1901 in South Milwaukee, Milwaukee Co., Wisc.; died in Mankato, Minn. in 1952, she was 50; married **Louie SUFFICOOL.** Born in 1900.

3216. Flora May HILL. Born in 1900.

3217. Leander Charles HILL. Born in 1902; died in 1984, about 82.

3218. Cleo Maxine HILL. Born in 1905. Cleo Maxine died in 1905.

3219. Glendalia HILL. Born in 1909.

3220. Thelma Louise HILL. Born in 1912. Christened and died in 2004, about 92.

3221. Herbert Albertis HILL [II]. Born in 1914; died in 2005, about 91.
Child:

3716	i.	Gerald Albert "Jerry"

3222. Melvin Leroy HILL. Born in 1919. Melvin Leroy died in 1992, he was 73.

3223. Kenneth E. HILL.[775] Born on 9 Mar 1923 in Ipava, Fulton Co., Ill. Kenneth E. died in San Joaquin, Calif. on 6 Jan 1990, he was 66. Buried on 17 Jan 1990 in San Francisco, Calif. Kenneth E. first married **Ruth H. WHITNEY**. Born in 1908.
They had the following children:

3717	i.	Gregory
3718	ii.	Mary Ann
3719	iii.	Daughter of Kenneth and Ruth (Whitney)

Kenneth E. second married **? ESCAMOS.**
They had one child:

3720	i.	Daughter of Kenneth and ? (Escamos)

3224. Infant WILLIAMS. Born on 21 May 1874.

3225. Ellen Hope WILLIAMS. Born on 22 Sep 1876 in Verona, Fairbault Co., Minn. Ellen Hope died in Verona, Fairbault Co., Minn. on 28 Jun 1879, she was 2.

3226. Lydia Faith WILLIAMS. Born on 5 Apr 1882 in Verona, Fairbault Co., Minn. Lydia Faith died in Verona, Fairbault Co., Minn. on 11 Sep 1890, she was 8.

3227. Mary Ellen WALDREN. Born on 11 Nov 1882. Mary Ellen married **Earl Deforest REYNOLDS**. Born in 1881 in Minn. Earl Deforest died in Fairbault, Minn. on 7 Sep 1951, he was 70.
They had the following children:

3721	i.	Unnamed son
3722	ii.	Unnamed son

3228. Martha Maria WALDREN. B. 30 May 1888; m. **Bert SOULE**. He died in Winnebago, Minn.
They had the following children:

3723	i.	Glen
3724	ii.	Warren
3725	iii.	Wilbur

3229. David Edgar HILL.

3230. Marion Bradford HILL.

3231. Richard HILL.

3232. Helen C. HILL. Born on 15 Aug 1883 in Lower Newport, Ohio. Occupation: Mother of 1. On 5 Nov 1908 when Helen C. was 25, she married **Clarence R. SLOAN** in Washington, Ohio. Born on 2 Jul 1879 in Williamstown, Wood Co., W.Va.
They had one child:

3726	i.	Unnamed

3233. Daniel Beers STOCKER. Born on 8 Oct 1882 in Holmes, Killbuck Co., Ohio.

3234. Elmira STOCKER. Born on 15 Sep 1884 in Holmes, Killbuck Co., Ohio.

3235. Mittie Leonora STOCKER. Born on 11 Jan 1887 in Wood, Ohio.

3236. George Washington STOCKER. Born on 15 Mar 1890 in Wood, Ohio.

3237. Ollie STOCKER. Born on 29 Aug 1894 in Wood, Ohio.

3238. Ellen STOCKER. Born on 25 Jun 1897 in Wood, Ohio.

3239. Bertha Dell STOCKER. Born on 26 May 1900 in Wood, Ohio.

3240. Ruby STOCKER. Born on 15 Apr 1902 in Wood, Ohio.

3241. Milan B. WOLGAMOTT. Born on 12 Oct 1884.

3242. William Welker WOLGAMOTT. Born on 12 Mar 1886.

3243. Anna Viola WOLGAMOTT. Born on 25 Aug 1888.

3244. David Roscoe WOLGAMOTT. Born on 25 Jul 1894.

3245. Burton A. WOLGAMOTT. Born on 9 Mar 1897.

3246. Miriam Lucille WOLGAMOTT. Born 22 Apr 1901 in Wooster, Wayne Co., Ohio.

3247. Russell Griffith WOLGAMOTT. Born on 8 Oct 1907 in Madisonburg, Ohio.

3248. Nina Vistula YOUNT. Born 22 Feb 1888 in Winfield, Cowley Co., Kansas.

3249. Inis Beatrice YOUNT. Born 4 Nov 1892 in Winfield, Cowley Co., Kansas.

3250. Roy Oliver YOUNT. Born on 2 Nov 1899 in Winfield, Cowley Co., Kansas.

3251. Dean Burdette YOUNT. Born on 31 Jul 1910 in Tonkawa, Kay Co., Okla.

3252. Margaret Elizabeth CRAWFORD.

3253. Mildred CRAWFORD. Born on 2 Dec 1898.

3254. Velma Merle CRAWFORD. Born on 12 Dec 1899.

3255. Hazel Annetta CRAWFORD. Born on 4 Aug 1901.

3256. Carmi Russell CRAWFORD. Born on 30 May 1903.

3257. Ralph CRAWFORD. Born on 27 Aug 1906.

3258. Lolita Grace CRAWFORD. Born on 8 Sep 1908.

3259. Floyd Anson HALL. Born on 22 Feb 1886.

3260. Lola Belle HALL. Born on 25 May 1888.

3261. Clyde Thomas HALL. Born on 4 Oct 1890.

3262. Pheba Alice HALL. Born on 17 Aug 1892.

3263. Grace Almira HALL. Born on 7 Oct 1894.

3264. Bertha Jane HALL. Born on 20 Mar 1904.

3265. Favorite Reuben HALL. Born on 29 Dec 1905.

3266. Price HALL.

3267. Mary G. FARLEY. Born in 1878 in Ohio.

3268. William Burton SLOAN. Born in 1885 in Ohio.

3269. Daniel Horatio SLOAN. Born on 7 Oct 1887 in Richfield, Lucas Co., Ohio.

3270. Daisy Ellen SLOAN. Born in 1889.

3271. Carrie Rebecca SLOAN. Born in 1896 in Ohio.

3272. Pearl Elizabeth SLOAN. Born on 12 Nov 1905 probably in Ohio.

3273. Siba Zella SLOAN. Born on 23 Aug 1893 in Chester, Dodge Co., Wisc.

3274. Leon Leslie COOK. Born on 24 Jul 1884.

3275. Morton Hubbard COOK. Born on 10 Sep 1873.

3276. Fred Lee COOK. Born on 26 Oct 1877.

3277. William Warren COOK. Born on 24 Jan 1880.

3278. Elizabeth COOK. Born on 1 Jan 1886.

3279. Charles Sylvester COOK. Born on 31 Jul 1887.

3280. Alfred COOK. Born on 10 Oct 1888.

3281. Clara COOK. Born on 23 Oct 1890.

3282. Grace COOK. Born on 15 Apr 1895.

3283. Frank Leroy COOK. Born on 27 Dec 1896.

3284. Fred Emery COOK. Born on 11 Dec 1898.

3285. William Ambrose COOK. Born on 29 Apr 1901.

3286. Henry "Harry" COOK. Born on 13 Feb 1904.

3287. Maude Sylvia COOK. Born on 6 Oct 1907.

3288. William Lyman BURLINGAME. Born on 1 Apr 1876.

3289. Arthur Alanson BURLINGAME. Born on 10 Jan 1878.

3290. Grace Rosetta BURLINGAME. Born on 18 Jan 1880.

3291. Emma Ethyl BURLINGAME. Born on 6 Jun 1882.

3292. Clarence Leonard BURLINGAME. Born on 26 Jun 1885.

3293. Eben RUSH. Born in So. Dakota.

3294. Clarence Benjamin RUSH. Born in 1893 in Mellette, S.Dak.

3295. Chester Earl BURLINGAME. Born 28 Dec 1883 in Elroy, Juneau Co., Wisc.

3296. [Living] BURLINGAME.

3297. Gladys Catharine BURLINGAME. Born on 7 May 1890 in So. Dakota.

3298. Marjorie Clare BURLINGAME. Born on 1 Jan 1898 in Hamlin, So. Dak.

3299. Carrie Estell BURLINGAME.

3300. Esther Ruhania BURLINGAME. Born on 11 Sep 1896.

3301. Nancy BURLINGAME. Born on 25 Jun 1899.

3302. Sylvia Lavina BURLINGAME. Born on 25 Oct 1901.

3303. George Wilfred BURLINGAME. Born on 10 Jan 1904.

3304. Gladys Hazel BURLINGAME. Born on 21 Mar 1906.

3305. Minnie Ives COVILLE. Born on 26 Apr 1880.

3306. Alice Belle COVILLE. Born on 27 Dec 1881.

3307. William Thomas LEETE. Born on 9 Feb 1884 in Guilford, Conn.

3308. Eva Mildred GAUCHET. Born on 17 Jun 1886 in Old Lyme, Conn.

3309. Daniel Benjamin GAUCHET. Born on 9 Apr 1889.

3310. Archibald Greenfield GAUCHET. Born on 20 Apr 1890 in Meriden, Conn.

3311. Ezrena Amanda GAUCHET. Born on 12 Sep 1894 in Lynn, Mass.

3312. Mary Lucy KENTFIELD. Born on 29 Jan 1872 in Hadley, Hampshire Co., Mass. Mary Lucy died in Hadley, Hampshire Co., Mass. on 13 Aug 1876, she was 4. Her mother died when she was six days old, and she died at the age of 4.

3313. ? KENTFIELD.

3314. Mary Elinor KENTFIELD. Born on 26 Apr 1880. Mary Elinor died in Apr 1926, she was 45.

3315. Arthur Baker KENTFIELD. Born on 30 Jun 1884. Arthur Baker died in Hadley, Hampshire Co., Mass. in 1960, he was 75.

3316. Nellie Frances KENTFIELD. Born on 15 Feb 1886 in Hadley, Hampshire Co., Mass.; died in Holyoke, Mass. on 29 May 1922, she was 36. On 1 Oct 1907 when she was 21, she married **Clarence M. WOOD** in Plainville, Hadley, Mass. Born on 22 Jul 1882 in N. Amherst, Mass.; died in Manchester, N.H. on 5 Dec 1964, he was 82. He married sisters in sequence, and had children by both wives.
They had the following children:

3727	i.	Estelle Frances
3728	ii.	Ethel Marion
3729	iii.	Harold Kentfield

3317. John Theodore KENTFIELD. Born on 3 Mar 1891. John Theodore died in Mar 1950, he was 58.

3318. Annie Louise KENTFIELD. Born on 31 Jul 1892 in Hadley, Mass.; died in Amherst, Hampshire Co., Mass. 10 May 1950, she was 57. Mother of 2 by her brother-in-law, who she m. as his second wife. She married **Clarence M. WOOD.** Born on 22 Jul 1882 in N. Amherst, Mass.; died in Manchester, N.H. on 5 Dec 1964, he was 82. He married sisters in sequence, and had children by both wives.
They had the following children:

3730	i.	David Frederick
3731	ii.	?

3319. Jennie KENTFIELD. Born on 12 Jun 1894 in Amherst, Hampshire Co., Mass. Jennie died in Amherst, Hampshire Co., Mass. on 10 May 1999, she was 104. Mother of 3, one of whom had 8 children. None are named in OneWorldTree. Jennie married **Winfred Phelps COWLES.** Born on 26 Apr 1890 in Hadley, Hampshire Co., Mass.; died in Amherst, Hampshire Co., Mass. on 9 Sep 1977, he was 87.

3320. James Frederick KENTFIELD. Born on 4 Oct 1895 in Hadley, Hampshire Co., Mass. James Frederick died in Hadley, Hampshire Co., Mass. on 1 Aug 1971, he was 75. On 16 Aug 1922 when he was 26, he married **Helen M. KENTFIELD** in Hadley, Hampshire Co., Mass. Born on 25 Sep 1898 in New London, New London Co., Conn.; died in Greenville, Greene Co., Tenn. on 17 Jun 1999, she was 100. A relationship to her husband may be suspected, but it is unknown. She was the mother of two daughters and one son, who are not named in OneWorldTree.

3321. Mabel Alice TORREY. Born on 21 Feb 1881 in Florence, Mass. On 5 Jun 1907 when Mabel Alice was 26, she married **Charles E. HOLCOMB** in Baltimore, Md. Born on 17 Aug 1882 in Westfield, Hampshire Co., Mass. OneWorldTree says she also m. J. L. Blinn, b. 20 Aug 1836 in Belchertown, Mass. This seems unlikely, for he would have been 45 years senior to her in age.

3322. Orson Winfield TORREY. Born on 16 Apr 1882 in Southampton, Mass.

3323. Grace Belle TORREY. Born on 31 Mar 1884 in Southampton, Mass.; died 16 Jan 1949, she was 64. Mother of 4, none of whom were named in OneWorldTree. On 14 Feb 1906 when she was 21, she married **Levi P. CHASE** in Easthampton, Hampshire Co., Mass.; born 5 Jan 1879 in Bernardston, Mass.

3324. Clara Eleanor TORREY. Born on 22 Sep 1885 in Southampton, Mass. Mother of 3, one of whom was named in OneWorldTree. On 22 Oct 1906 when she was 21, she married **George Peter TRUEHART** in Easthampton, Hampshire Co., Mass. Born on 23 Oct 1884 in Massachusetts. They had the following children:

3732	i.	?
3733	ii.	?
3734	iii.	Hazel M. (1908-)

3325. Willis Porter TORREY. Born on 11 Jul 1887 in Southampton, Mass. Willis Porter died in Tolland, Conn. in Mar 1974, he was 86. On 15 Nov 1916 when he was 29, he married **Hazel R. GRISWOLD** in Thompsonville, Conn. Born on 5 Aug 1897 in Somers, Conn. They had the following children:

3735	i.	?
3736	ii.	?

3326. Linus Greene TORREY. Born on 6 Nov 1889 in Southampton, Mass. On 12 Nov 1912 when he was 23, he married **Marion Jane HARLOW** in Syracuse, N.Y. Born on 12 Nov 1895 in Amherst, N.Y. They had the following children:

3737	i.	?
3738	ii.	?

3327. Robert Lorenso TORREY. Born on 17 Nov 1891 in Southampton, Mass. Robert Lorenso died in Easthampton, Hampshire Co., Mass. in May 1972, he was 80. Robert Lorenso married **Evelyn GRATHER.** Mother of 8, two of whom were named in OneWorldTree. They had the following children:

3739	i.	Chester R. (1922-2001)
3740	ii.	Kenneth (1925-1993)

3328. Bessie E. TORREY. Born on 7 Aug 1893 in Southampton, Mass. Bessie E. died on 29 Aug 1893. She died in the month she was born.

3329. Fred Baker TORREY. Born on 29 Aug 1894 in Southampton, Mass.; died in Springfield, Mass. in Jul 1973, he was 78. On 16 Sep 1916 when Fred Baker was 22, he married **Elinor POMEROY.**

3330. Ida Marchie TORREY. Born on 19 Feb 1896 in Southampton, Mass.

3331. Frank Andrew TORREY. Born 30 May 1897 in Southampton, Mass.; died 9 Aug 1926, age 29.

3332. Edith E. TORREY. Born on 22 Jun 1899 in Southampton, Mass.

3333. Ralph Eugene TORREY. Born on 11 Oct 1900 in Southampton, Mass. Ralph Eugene died in Worcester, Mass. on 17 May 1967, he was 66. In 1921 when he was 20, he married **Olivette BERNIER** in Worcester, Mass. Born on 26 Aug 1900. Olivette died in Worcester, Mass. in Nov 1985, she was 85. They had the following children:

3741	i.	?
3742	ii.	?
3743	iii.	Ralph Bernier (1925-1984)

3334. Bertha F. TORREY. Born on 10 Apr 1903.

3335. Henry L. KENTFIELD. Born on 23 Jul 1869 in Providence, Providence Co., R.I. Henry L. died on 25 Oct 1869 in Providence, Providence Co., R.I. Died at the age of three months.

3336. Abigail S. KENTFIELD. Born on 23 Jun 1871 in Providence, Providence Co., R.I. Abigail S.

died on 14 Aug 1871 in Providence, Providence Co., R.I. Died before she was two months old.

3337. Mary Myrtle BILYEU. Born on 3 Jun 1870 in Mulberry Grove, Bond Co., Ill. On 3 Nov 1891 when Mary Myrtle was 21, she married **Marian M. NEELEY** in Mulberry Grove, Bond Co., Ill. Born in 1862 in Mulberry Grove, Bond Co., Ill.; died there, 6 Oct 1940, about age 78.

They had the following children:

3744	i.	Ralph Bilyeu (1892-)
3745	ii.	Roxie C. (1895-)
3746	iii.	Paul (1897-)
3747	iv.	George L. (1901-)

3338. Sarah BILYEU. Born in 1859 in Illinois.

3339. Mary Annette MORVILLE. Born in 1867 in Sorento, Bond Co., Ill.

3340. Harry Earle BILYEU. Born on 12 Jul 1886 in Sorento, Bond Co., Ill.

3341. Winne Mae BILYEU. Born on 25 Apr 1891 in Bond, Ill.

3342. Roy Sidney BILYEU. Born on 14 Aug 1893 in Vandalia, Audrain Co., Mo.

3343. Olive Marie BILYEU. Born on 14 Aug 1896 in Greenville, Bond Co., Ill.

3344. Jesse C. BILYEU. Born on 17 Aug 1898 in Greenville, Bond Co., Ill.

3345. Charles Clarence BILYEU. Born on 11 Jun 1900 in Greenville, Ill.

3346. Vera Bessie BILYEU. Born on 5 Aug 1901 in Greenville, Bond Co., Ill.

3347. Malinda BILYEU.

3348. Henrietta BILYEU.

3349. Charles Elmer BILYEU.

3350. Fred Ellsworth BILYEU.

3351. John Wilson BILYEU.

3352. Joseph Nelson BILYEU.

3353. Lemuel E. BILYEU.

3354. Milo D. BILYEU.

3355. Francis Simeon BILYEU. Born 13 Mar 1869 in Brainerd, Crow Wing Co., Minn.

3356. Nellie E. BILYEU. Born on 8 Mar 1871.

3357. Leroy Vernon BILYEU. Born on 27 Aug 1873.

3358. Willie Ray BILYEU. Born on 8 Mar 1887 in Nebraska.

3359. Jessie Belle BILYEU. Born on 3 Jan 1889 in Nebraska.

3360. Lewis BILYEU. Born on 4 May 1892 in South Omaha, Douglas Co., Neb.

3361. Albert BILYEU. Born on 6 Feb 1897 in South Omaha, Douglas Co., Neb.

3362. Corinore GILLESPIE. Born in Apr 1863 in Greeley, Neb.

3363. Sadie GILLESPIE. Born in 1866 in Illinois.

3364. Flora GILLESPIE. Born on 7 Nov 1868 in Dubuque, Dubuque Co., Ia.

3365. Mary Temperance GILLESPIE. Born in 1872.

3366. Grace A. GILLESPIE. Born on 24 May 1880 in Chadron, Dawes Co., Neb.

3367. Leona GILLESPIE. Born in Jul 1886 in Nebraska.

3368. Charles Henry BILYEU. Born 22 Mar 1874 in Litchfield, Montgomery Co., Ill.

3369. Maud Ann BILYEU. Born in 1885 in LeRoy, Mo.

3370. Francis Roy BILYEU. Born on 10 Jul 1890 in Missouri.

3371. Martha Pearl BILYEU. Born 13 Feb 1892 in Fort Scott, Bourbon Co., Ks.

3372. Harrell H. BILYEU. Born on 23 Jun 1895 in Fort Scott, Bourbon Co., Ks.

3373. Grace Comfort BILYEU. Born on 22 May 1899 in Arcadia, Ks.

3374. Allithea BIRGE.[776] Born in 1860. Allithea died on 17 Nov 1918, she was 58. In 1908 when Allithea was 48, she married **George CARY,**[777] son of Dr. Walter Cary; born in 1859; died in 1945, about age 86. He was one of seven children in a socially prominent family in Buffalo, New York. He was the grandson of a New York State Senator and a U.S. Congressman. George Cary took his undergraduate work at Harvard and received a Masters of Philosophy degree at Columbia in 1885. He spent a brief apprenticeship with the prestigious New York City architectural firm of McKim, Mead, and White before going to Paris to study. The first Buffalonian to do so, he attended L'Ecole des Beaux-Arts in Paris from 1886 to 1889. This explains the presence of H. H. Richardson (the second American to attend L'Ecole) and Stanford White (who worked for Richardson during some of the construction of the New York State Insane Asylum in Buffalo) as guests at 184 Delaware Ave., since Cary continued to live there as a practicing architect until he married Allithea Birge, the last day of 1908, by which time he was 50.

In 1891 he returned to Buffalo and set up practice. Cary is best known for the Museum and the Pierce-Arrow Motor Car Company Administration Building (1695 Elmwood Avenue at Great Arrow Road), both sites previously occupied by Pan-American Exposition grounds. Cary also designed the Buffalo General Hospital, the Forest Lawn's Delaware Avenue Gate (Neoclassical), and the Forest Lawn Administration Building (Neoclassical). In the mid-1890s, Cary redesigned some rooms in the Ansley Wilcox mansion. He died in 1945, at eighty-six, and was buried in Forest Lawn Cemetery.

3375. Marion BIRGE. Born in 1871. She married **Thomas B. LOCKWOOD.**

3376. George Humphrey BIRGE. Born in 1878 in Buffalo, N.Y. George Humphrey died in Palm Springs, Calif. in 1969, he was 91. In 1906 when he was 28, he married **Ethel RICHARDS** in St. Louis, Mo. Born in 1879 in St. Louis, Mo. Ethel died in Santa Monica, Calif. in 1962, she was 83.
They had the following children:

3748	i.	George Kingsley (1909-1982)
3749	ii.	?
3750	iii.	?

3377. Judith V. BIRGE.

3378. Warren Riley BIRGE. Born in 1898 in District of Columbia.

3379. Margaret C. BIRGE. Born in 1899.

3380. Morgan BIRGE. Born in 1901.

3381. Henry E. BIRGE. Born in 1907.

3382. Grace BIRGE. Born in 1882.

3383. Ethyl BIRGE. Born in 1884.

3384. Nellie BIRGE. Born in 1889.

3385. Arthur Henry Bartrum. Born on 6 Apr 1882 in Montague, Texas.

3386. James J. Bartrum. Born on 30 Aug 1888 in Montague, Texas.

3387. Annie Bell Bartrum. Born on 10 Nov 1894 in Oklahoma.

3388. Maudie Myrtle Bartrum. Born on 13 Jan 1897 in Chickashaw Nation, Indian Territory, Okla.

3389. Anna Dell BIRGE. Born in 1894.

3390. Ralph BIRGE. Born in 1895.

3391. Ruth BIRGE. Born in 1901.

3392. Opal BIRGE. Born on 7 Aug 1905 in Centralia, Clinton Co., Ia.

3393. Jack BIRGE.

3394. Mary Edna BIRGE.

3395. Edith Miles RANKIN. Born on 19 Nov 1880 in Winnetka, Cook, Ill.

3396. Harvey D. GOULDER.

3397. Mary G. WHITE. Born in 1901.

3398. Evelyn R. WHITE. Born in 1903.

3399. Theodore E. WHITE. Born in 1904.

3400. ? MAXWELL.

3401. Lila MAXWELL. Born on 5 Dec 1907.

3402. Doris Elizabeth MAXWELL. Born on 12 Aug 1909.

3403. William James MAXWELL. Born on 11 Jan 1913.

------------------- [778]

3404. Elsie HILL. Born on 21 Jun 1897.

3405. Elva BANGS. Born on 21 Dec 1900.

3406. Louis Sylvester HILL. Born on 31 Aug 1905. On 11 Jun 1925 when he was 19, he married **Vera Ruth BIDDLE.** Vera Ruth died aft 1971. She was of 22 Kemmons Dr., Jackson, TN, in 1971.

They had the following children:

3751	i.	Norma Jean (1927-)
3752	ii.	Gladys Joan (1929-)

3407. Raymond Hartley HILL. Born on 22 May 1907.

3408. Hoyt H. NICKERSON.

3409. Alba NICKERSON.

3410. Ruth NICKERSON.

3411. Arthur NICKERSON.

3412. Emma Margaret NICKERSON.

3413. Frank JARRELL.

3414. Child of Montgomery and Florence TILLITSON.

3415. Child of Montgomery and Florence TILLITSON.

3416. Swayne George TILLITSON. Born on 20 Jan 1912 in Illinois; died in Orange Co., Calif. on 26 May 1982, he was 70. Swayne George married **Vernice Arline TENDALL**, daughter of Randolph Bernhardt TENDALL & Laura Anne WOOD. Born in 1912. Vernice Arline died in 1978, she was 66.

3417. Child of Arthur and Elizabeth LEIFHEIT.

3418. Child of Arthur and Elizabeth LEIFHEIT.

3419. Lorraine Ann LEIFHEIT. Born on 20 Nov 1936 in Aurora, Ill. Lorraine Ann died in Oswego, Ill. on 5 Feb 2006, she was 69. She married **? PATTERSON**.

They had the following children:

3753	i.	Child of Lorraine
3754	ii.	Child of Lorraine
3755	iii.	Child of Lorraine
3756	iv.	Child of Lorraine

3420. Child of Roy and Catherine HILL.

3421. Melvyn R. HILL. Born on 18 Jul 1938 in Aurora, Ill. Melvyn R. died in Aurora, Ill. on 29 Nov 2006, he was 68. Melvyn R. married **? ARCH**.

They had the following children:

3757	i.	Child of Melvyn
3758	ii.	Child of Melvyn
3759	iii.	Child of Melvyn

3422. Caroline L. HILL. Born abt 1902 in Findlay, Hancock Co., Ohio.

------------------------[779]

3423. William Benjamin [145] "Ben" HILL,[780] eldest son of George J. and Jessie Fidelia (Stockwell) Hill, was born at Clarion, Wright County, Iowa, 10 July 1883; died at Cedar Falls, Iowa, 14 September 1924, age 41. His parents were among the earliest settlers of Wright County, in northern Iowa. He grew up on the family farm which was near the upper reaches of the Iowa River. His parents later moved to the county seat of Clarion. At the age of 24 he was married and moved to Cedar Falls, where he taught mathematics at Iowa State Teachers College (now University of Northern Iowa) in 1907-1908. His wife, then 18, did laundry for the students. He later owned a dray line business. He died of a heart attack at age 41 and was buried in the Fairview Cemetery in Cedar Falls.

He married, at Perkins, Payne Co., Oklahoma, 29 May 1907, **Blanche WASHBURN,**[781] daughter of George V. and Barbara Elizabeth (Carson) Washburn; born at Prairie Grove, Washington Co., Arkansas, 16 March 1890; died at Stillwater, Oklahoma, 18 February 1955, age 64. Both William and Blanche were members of the Congregational Church.

When Blanche was married at the age of 18, Oklahoma was still a Territory. She moved with her husband to the town of Cedar Falls, Iowa, in his home state, where he was a mathematics teacher at the "normal school," Iowa State Teachers College. As was the case with many young wives in college towns in those days, she did ironing for the students to earn a bit of money of her own. She and her husband had

278

six children before he died at the age of 41; the children then ranged from three to 15 years of age. She raised them alone as a widow in Cedar Falls for 34 years. Late in life, at the age of 52, she remarried and lived from 1942-1951 in Michigan City, Indiana. She then moved to Missouri, where she died at the age of 65 after a ten year battle with cancer.

William and Blanche (Washburn) Hill had six children, all of whom lived to maturity, married and had children. All were born at Cedar Falls except Paul, who was born at Clarion. Eighteen years after the death of William, Blanche married (2), at Clayton Missouri, 11 August 1942, Albert J. SMITH. William and Blanche (Washburn) Hill had the following children:

3760   i.   Howard Eugene [215] (1909-1983)
3761   ii.   Paul Francis [216] (1911-1997)
3762   iii.   Leola Grace [217] (1913-1983)
3763   iv.   Genevieve Maude [218] (1916-1982)
3764   v.   Ruth Elizabeth [219] (1918-<1997)
3765   vi.   Charles John [220] (1921-1985)

3424. Harland Eugene [146] HILL,[782] second son and second child of George J. and Jessie F. (Stockwell) Hill, was born at Grant Township, near Clarion, Wright County, Iowa, 20 May 1885; died at Clarion, 14 March 1968, age 82. Harland Hill graduated from Clarion High School and then became a farmer in Wright County. For many years he was elected and re-elected as a Wright County Supervisor. He was elected Chairman of the County Board of Supervisors in 1995, and he also was a member of the Solberg Grain Elevator Board. Harland Hill enjoyed working with animals and gave much of his life to community service, working with rural youth programs, with the Farm Bureau, and as member of his church choir. He played the mouth organ and piano for square dances in his community. A tall, quiet and thoughtful man, he was devoted to his wife and vicariously enjoyed her hobby of collecting porcelain objects of art. They were both proud of the achievements of their only son, a teacher and gifted amateur vocalist who became President of the Rochester, Minnesota, Community College. Harland Hill died of pneumonia and was buried at the Evergreen Cemetery in Clarion.

He married, at Clarion, Iowa, 29 December 1909, **Emma Otilda MICKELSON**, daughter of Ole and Lena (Tergeson) Mickelson[783]; born at LaCrosse, Wisconsin, 22 July 1886; died at Belmond, Iowa, 16 September 1977, age 91. Her father was born in Norway in 1856 and came to the United States at age 17. His brother, two years younger, died on the voyage and was buried at sea. Emma Mickelson attended elementary school and became a member of the Methodist Church Sunday School in Clarion on 1 April 1906. She enjoyed music, travel, sewing, and baking. She worked with rural youth and the Farm Bureau in Wright County, Iowa, and sang in the Methodist Church choir. She died of heart failure at the Belmond, Iowa, Nursing Home and was buried at the Evergreen Cemetery in Clarion.

Harland and Emma were married in a triple wedding ceremony at the Methodist Church in Clarion. The other couples were his first cousin, Ed Lindsay and his bride, Mae Huntley; and their friends, Albert and Byrd Thompson.
They had one child,, born at Clarion:

3766   i.   Charles Eugene [221] (1914-)

3425. Leroy George [147] "Lee" HILL,[784] third son and third child of George J. and Jessie F. (Stockwell) Hill, was born at Grant Township, near Clarion, Iowa, 5 August 1886; died at Sumner, Iowa, 1 April 1975, age 88, and was buried at the Wilson Grove Cemetery in Sumner. "Lee" Hill was married in 1908 and began farming in Grant Township, Wright County; his five children were born there. He was originally in partnership with his brothers in the management of the home farm, but in 1911 he purchased one hundred and twenty-four acres in Grant Township and transformed it into a modern farm with entirely new buildings. His barn was forty-eight by sixty-four feet and fifty feet to the peak; it was said to be "one of the largest and most complete barns in the township." The barn was still standing in the summer of 2000. He practiced crop rotation, growing corn, oats, and hay, and raised purebred Duroc-Jersey hogs. The farm was called "Lake View Farm," for its view of Elm Lake, nearby. In 1915 he was a Republican and he served as Assessor of Grant Township, where he and his wife were members of the Harvey Congregational Church.

He and his family moved to a farm near Sumner in 1930, and he lived there until his wife died in 1936. Lee Hill was also a truck driver and a great story teller. With his fine sense of humor, he continued to amuse his nieces and nephews even when he was frail and fading in strength in a nursing home. He died of progressive peripheral vascular insufficiency at the age of 88, survived by 21 grandchildren, 29 great-grandchildren, and one great-great-grandchild, in addition to a brother and two sisters.

He married, in Wright County, Iowa, 7 September 1908, when he was 22, **Luretta Lena SELLERS**,[785] daughter of Chauncey and Mary (Carson) Sellers, when she was 22; born in Louisa County, Iowa, 14 July 1886; died at Sumner, 28 March 1936, age 49. Her father was a native of Louisa County, Iowa, while her mother was born in Ohio and came to Iowa with her parents in 1855 when she was six weeks old. LeRoy and Luretta (Sellers) Hill had five children, four daughters and one son, born at Clarion, all of whom survived her. All five children were married, to members of the Knoedler, Craeger, Gamm, Treloar, and Weston families.

They had the following children:

3767	i.	Velda Mae [222] (1909-1996)
3768	ii.	Max Leroy [223] (1913-1990)
3769	iii.	Marion Carson [224] (1915-)
3770	iv.	La Vonne Ilene [225] "Bonnie" (1919-)
3771	v.	Minnie Marie (1921-2006)

3426. Myron Emery [148] HILL,[786] fourth son and fourth child of George J. and Jessie Fidelia (Stockwell) Hill, was born in Wright County, Iowa, 16 September 1888; died at Clarion, Wright County, Iowa, 16 January 1955, age 66. His farm included a portion of the land that was homesteaded by his grandfather, near the Iowa River in the northern part of the state. As a young man he was a reporter for *The Clipper* newspaper, and as an adult he was one of the most respected men of the county.

He was a calm, quiet man with a sunburned face who stood tall, slender and erect in his old age. He delighted in the productivity of his farm and in the success of his children. Christmas and Thanksgiving dinners at his home brought members of the family together from many miles away. As he grew older, management of the farm was given over to his elder son, Dale. This farm has continued to be productive more than a century after the Hill family first arrived there.

He married, at "The Parsonage," Rowan, Iowa, 20 November 1911, when he was 23, **Julia Lydia WOODIN**,[787] daughter of John Cea and Elizabeth Anna "Lizzie" (Peters) Woodin, age 19; born in Wright County, Iowa, 16 February 1891; died at Clarion, 10 November 1984, age 93. Her parents were pioneer farmers in Wright County, and the Woodin and Hill families were close friends and neighbors. She was educated in the rural school system. Julia Woodin was a short, bright-eyed, sturdy woman, with a quiet voice and an unassuming, calm manner, who was beloved by her family and the entire community. She was widowed after 42 years of marriage and later moved to Clarion. She was buried in the Evergreen Cemetery at Clarion.

His wife's brother, Howard Woodin, was married to Myron's sister, Ruby Hill. The Woodin and Hill families of Wright County are thus joined as "double in-laws" and "double cousins," as well as being friends and neighbors. Myron and Julia (Woodin) Hill had three children. All three children married and had offspring.

They had the following children:

3772	i.	Dale E. [226] (1912-1994)
3773	ii.	Myron Emery (1927-)
3774	iii.	Lela Esther (1930-)

3427. Nellie Leola [149] HILL. Born on 14 Jun 1890. Nellie Leola [149] died in Wright Co., IA on 8 Jan 1894, she was 3. Buried in 1894 in Rowan, Wright Co., IA (Graceland cemetery). Died of diphtheria. The "two little girls," Nellie and Grace, became a sad legend in the family. Nellie was three-and-a-half, and Grace was almost two when they died of diphtheria. Two years later, Ruby was born, and two years after that, Adelia. The last child, little brother Gerald, came as a surprise to everyone, seven years after Adelia. But the parents and the four older brothers never stopped mourning the loss of their little sisters, Nellie and Grace.

3428. Grace Lodawesca [150] HILL. Born on 19 Jan 1892. Grace Lodawesca [150] died in Wright Co., IA on 4 Jan 1894, she was 1. Buried in 1894 in Rowan, Wright Co., IA (Graceland cemetery). Died of diphtheria. Her middle name was taken from the middle name of her maternal grandmother, Emma Lodawisca (Hyde) Stockwell.[788] Little Grace died of diphtheria at age two, a loss keenly remembered forever by her siblings and parents (see notes for her sister Nellie). The cemetery where they are buried in Rowan, Ia., is now known as Graceland cemetery. The graves of the two little girls and their uncles -- who drowned together nearby as young men 23 years earlier -- are among the oldest graves in this cemetery. Could it be that the family named the cemetery for little Grace Hill?

3429. Ruby Adella [151] HILL,[789] third daughter and sixth child of George J. and Jessie F. (Stockwell) Hill, was born in Wright County, Iowa, 27 August 1896; died at Clarion, Iowa, 31 July 1995, age 98, and was buried in the Evergreen Cemetery in Clarion. She attended public school in Wright County and graduated from Clarion High School in 1915. Ruby Hill was the first in her family to go to college. She received a teaching certificate after she attended Morningside College, Sioux City, Iowa, from 1918-1920, and she taught in the Hawarden school in 1919. In 1995 she was probably the oldest living alumna of Morningside College. Ruby lived in Wright County for her entire life, on farms or in Clarion.

On her twenty-third birthday, 27 August 1919, she married her brother-in-law, **Howard Henry WOODIN,**[790] son of John Cea and Elizabeth (Peters) Woodin, age 26; born in Wright County, 22 November 1892; died at Clarion, 14 September 1942, age 49, of cancer of the colon. They were married by the Rev. J. A. LaGrone at the home of her brother, Harland Hill. Howard Woodin completed grammar school in a rural school in Grant Township of Wright County, and he then became a farmer. At the age of 25 he joined the army when the United States entered the Great War that had begun in Europe in August 1914. He served in France with the American Expeditionary Force and he later was a member of the American Legion. After the war he resumed his career as a farmer and became a leader in that profession in Wright County. He was highly regarded by his contemporaries and was for many years a member of the board of trustees of the Methodist Church in Clarion. He was also a member of the Masonic Lodge.

Ruby and Howard Woodin were successful in farming and they had three children, all of whom lived to maturity, and two married. Their youngest child, Mildred, was recognized in infancy to have brain damage of unknown cause -- perhaps from measles or Downs' syndrome. Following Howard's untimely death in 1942, Ruby moved to Clarion. She then devoted her life to the welfare of others in her family and in the community. She cared for her elderly father at her home until he died ten years later at the age of 95, and she provided a loving and supportive home for Mildred until they both moved into an assisted care facility in 1991. After the death of her older brother, Myron, she became the head of the Hill family in Clarion. She was the keeper of the family Bible and the family photograph albums. Many family reunions were held at her home or were organized by her. She quietly provided financial support for many who needed it, through her hard work and oversight of her farm in Wright County. She was an enormously energetic woman with a broad smile and a word of encouragement for everyone. Her kitchen was always a busy place, and as a teacher and practical nurse she provided comfort and healing for countless sick people in Clarion. She was a member of the Order of the Eastern Star, of Navy Mothers, and of the Republican Party. Like her mother, she was active as a lay leader in the Methodist Church in Clarion and she was a member of the Women's Christian Temperance Union. She was still playing hymns for others at her nursing home when she was 95 years old. Ruby lived her entire life according to the precepts set by the women of the Bible.

Howard and Ruby (Hill) Woodin had three children, born in Wright County. John married and had children; Jessie married but had no children; and Mildred, who did not marry, d.s.p. They had the following children:

3775	i.	John Howard "Woody" (1924-)
3776	ii.	Jessie Elizabeth (1927-)
3777	iii.	Mildred Eileen (1932-1997)

3430. Adelia Emma [152] HILL,[791] fourth daughter and eighth child of George J. and Jessie F. (Stockwell) Hill, was born at Clarion, Wright County, Iowa, 16 October 1898; died at Waukesha, Wisconsin, 3 March 1984, age 85. Adelia Hill graduated from Clarion High School. She then attended

Morningside College, Sioux City, Iowa, where she received the B.A. degree in 1921. Her older sister, Ruby, had attended Morningside for two years but had not graduated. Adelia was the first person in her family for countless generations to have graduated from college. She then became an English teacher and taught in a number of communities in Iowa. She was married to a farmer at the age of 27, and they farmed near Goodell, Iowa. Their only child, a son, was born the following year. During her married life she lived and taught at Goodell, Rowan, Maxwell, Corwith, and Lehigh, Iowa. Following retirement from teaching she became a librarian for the Maxwell, Iowa, community. She was awarded the Maxwell, Iowa, Education Association Layman's Award for her contributions to education, "a proven and continuing friend of education since her retirement." After she retired from the Maxwell Library, she and her second husband moved to the I.O.O.F. Home in Mason City. Following her husband's death she moved to Waukesha to be near her son and his family. She was a member of the Rebeccah Lodge for more than 25 years, and was Worthy Matron of the Order of the Eastern Star in 1962. As a devout Methodist churchwoman it was paradoxical that she developed a fatal cancer of the larynx, which is almost always caused by smoking; she was not a smoker.

She was remembered by her family and friends as a shy, gentle and generous person, with a broad smile and an intense interest in the education of her extended family, which included many nieces and nephews. She was also well known as a devoted churchwoman and community volunteer. Her granddaughters were strongly influenced by her work as a Methodist layperson and as a librarian. One became a Methodist minister, and is associate pastor in the denomination in which Adelia's aunt Grace Stockwell entered the mission field; the other granddaughter, who helped Adelia in the library during her summer vacations, now has a Master's degree in library science.

She married, at Clarion, Iowa, 9 June 1926, **Edward Michael HEMENWAY**, son of Frank HEMENWAY & Mary LOGAN; born 2 August 1880 in Aplington, Butler Co., Ia.; died in Corwith, Ia., 26 October 1948, he was 68; buried 30 October 1948 in Clarion. He was a farmer, and he enjoyed music and square dancing. He was raised as a Catholic but became a Methodist when he married. Their son and his wife, Agnes (Beal) Hemenway, had three daughters. One of Adelia's granddaughters became an ordained Methodist minister, thus carrying on a tradition that began with Adelia Hill's grandfather Benajah Stockwell, who was a Methodist lay preacher in Vermont and Iowa.
They had one child:

3778 i. Edward Eugene (1927-1993)

Following the death of Edward Hemenway, Adelia married (2), at Lehigh, Iowa, 26 December 1953, when she was 55, on his 58th birthday, **Harold A. McBETH**[792]; born 26 December 1895; died 3 October 1979, age 83. Adelia and both of her husbands are buried at Clarion, Iowa.

3431. Gerald Leslie [153] "Gerry" HILL,[793] fifth son and youngest of the nine children of George J. and Jessie Fidelia (Stockwell) Hill, was born at Grant Township, near Clarion, Wright Co., Iowa, 18 September 1905; died at Payson, Gila Co., Arizona, 14 June 1979, age 73, from brain damage that was the result of a heart attack about two weeks earlier. He was the first man in his family who had the opportunity to attend college.

He graduated in the Class of 1923 from Clarion High School and then attended Cornell College in Mt. Vernon, Iowa, from which he graduated in 1927 with the B.A. degree. He was employed by Cornell and the Iowa Power and Light Co. as a public relations officer. He also was a part-time sports reporter for the *Cedar Rapids Gazette* and the *Des Moines Register*. He entered the banking profession in 1933, initially in Mt. Vernon and then in the neighboring town of Lisbon, as cashier of the Lisbon Bank and Trust Company. Mr. Hill was the commander of the Lisbon, Iowa, unit of the Civil Air Patrol in the early years of World War II, and he soloed in the Piper "Cub" that was the unit's aircraft. He volunteered for duty with the American Red Cross and was appointed a Red Cross Field Director, a rank equivalent to Army Captain. He served in the European Theatre of Operations in 1945 with the 303rd Infantry Regiment, 97th Division, in General Patton's 3rd Army. His regiment was in combat for the last 30 days of the war. It liberated the infamous concentration camp at Flossenberg and it then drove into Pilsen at the forefront of the Allied liberation of western Czechoslovakia. He was entitled to wear the American Theater Medal, the European Theater Medal, and the World War II Victory Medal.

After the war he resumed his banking career, initially in Perry and later in Sac City, Iowa, and then in Sioux Falls and Aberdeen, South Dakota. In Aberdeen, he was recruited to be the founding Chief Executive Officer (Executive Vice President) of the Farmers and Merchants Bank. This bank became the leading bank of a group known as the Dakotah Bank Holding Corporation. By 1970, the DBHC had become the largest banking organization in South Dakota, and it held the state-wide MasterCard franchise. When Mr. Hill retired from banking at the age of 65, he was President of the Dakotah Bank Holding Corporation (DBHC). This bank system, later known as DakotahBank, recorded $1 billion in deposits by its 40th anniversary in 2004.

Mr. Hill was an avid golfer and bird hunter, and he was active in the Republican Party. He was a member of Delta Phi Rho at Cornell College, and he was active in the Masonic order as a Shriner and as a member of "The Jokers." His other associations included the B.P.O.E. ("Elks") and the Lions Club, which he served as Club Treasurer in many towns. Mr. Hill was raised as a Methodist but was confirmed as an adult in the Protestant Episcopal Church. He was a vestryman of St. Mark's Episcopal Church in Aberdeen, S.D., and of All Saints of the Desert, Sun City, Arizona.

He married, at Mt. Vernon, Iowa, 25 December 1930, when he was 25 and she was 27, **Essie Mae THOMPSON**,[794] daughter of William Henry "Will" and Sarah D. "Sadie" (Rundall) Thompson; born at Spring Grove, Linn County, Iowa, 29 June 1903; died at Sun City, Maricopa Co., Arizona, 15 March 1994, age 90. She was a fellow student and also was his geology teacher at Cornell. She was a member of the Cornell College faculty in geology at the time of their marriage. Gerald and Essie Mae (Thompson) Hill had two sons, born at Cedar Rapids, Iowa. Both of their sons married and had children of their own. Essie Mae Thompson was born in a farmhouse near the Wapsipinicon River, not far from the rural home of the artist Grant Wood, north of Cedar Rapids, Iowa. The white clapboard house where she was born -- with its nine fireplaces -- was still standing in the 1960's. The town of Paris in Spring Grove Township once had shops and stores, but by the 1960s (and continuing into the 1990s) all that remained of the original town of Paris was a cluster of a dozen or so small houses on Paris Road, two miles west of Iowa 13, on the south bank of the Wapsipinicon River.

Essie Mae worked her way through college by teaching in one room country schools near Lisbon after each year at college. She walked the two miles to college and back from her home each day. She majored in geology, with a minor in music, and was both a noted vocalist and a geology teacher at Cornell. She became a full-time mother and a part-time teacher for the next 20 years, until her younger son was enrolled in college. During this time she taught in Cornell College's World War II Naval Flight Preparatory School, and she was certified as an instructor in Navigation by the Civil Aviation Authority. She also was certified as a secondary school teacher in Iowa and South Dakota. She taught vocal music and was a member of various social and professional organizations including Phi Beta Kappa and the American Association of University Women. In 1967 she learned to read and write braille and was a teacher at the South Dakota School for the Blind. She began to compose autobiographical notes and poems, which she published in four books between 1978 and 1988. She was raised in the Methodist faith of her parents, but she was confirmed as an adult in the Protestant Episcopal Church, and she was a member of All Saints of the Desert Episcopal Church in Sun City. She was also a member of the P.E.O. sorority. During her 91st year, she was selected as Resident of the Month at Brighton Gardens by Marriott in Sun City in February 1994, and she quietly passed away two weeks later. Her cremains were interred beside her husband in the Hill family plot, Graceland Cemetery, Rowan, Iowa, on 30 July 1994. They had the following children:

3779   i.   George James (1932-)
3780   ii.   Thomas David "Tom" (1935-2003)

3432. George Edwin "Ed" [154] LINDSAY.[795] Born on 10 Sep 1888 in Clarion, Wright Co., IA.; died in ? Clarion, IA on 14 Dec 1973, he was 85. Buried in 1973 in Clarion, IA (Evergreen Cemetery). Occupation: Farmer. Married in a Triple Wedding ceremony. Religion: Methodist. On 29 Dec 1909 when he was 21, he married **Bertha Mae "Mae" HUNTLEY**, daughter of Albert HUNTLEY & Sarah CANHAM, in Clarion, IA (Methodist Church). Born on 28 Sep 1886 in Cabery, Livingston Co., IL.; died in probably Clarion, IA on 3 Jul 1975, she was 88. Buried in 1975 in Clarion, IA (Evergreen Cemetery).

Religion: Methodist.
They had the following children:

3781	i.	Maxine Bernice [227] (1910-1982)
3782	ii.	James Edwin [228] (1914-1964)
3783	iii.	Adella Helen [229] (1915-)
3784	iv.	Ronald LaVern (1918-1966)

3433. Rosella Amelia [155] SPEER.[796] Born on 12 Nov 1903 in Corning, NY; died bef 2002.

3434. Harriet Eloise [156] SPEER. Born on 15 Jun 1912 in Caton, NY; died on 19 Jun 1912.

3435. Arvena Grace [157] SPEER. Born on 18 Nov 1914 in Caton, NY.

3436. Bernice Comelia [158] SPEER.[797] Born on 24 Mar 1920 in Caton, NY; d. before Feb 2002.
Bernice Comelia [158] married _____ **ROSE**.
They had one child:

3785	i.	Kenneth

3437. Eleanor Vesta SPEER. Eleanor Vesta died aft 2002; she married _____ .
Child:

3786	i.	5 children

3438. Helen AUSTIN.

3439. Clarice AUSTIN.

3440. Everett Cleveland [173] KIMBALL. Born on 3 Jan 1900 in Corning, NY.

3441. Irwing H. [174] KIMBALL. Born on 26 Apr 1906; died on 22 May 1906.

3442. Russell Harry REED. Born on 8 Jan 1893 in Vernon, Genessee Co., Mich. Soldier in World War I. Russell Harry married **Maude M. ?.** Born in 1900. Mother of 2, whose names are unknown.

3443. Paul H. REED. Born on 15 Aug 1895 in Michigan; died in Ann Arbor, Washtennaw Co., Mich. in Aug 1968, he was 72. Soldier in World War I.

3444. Percy G. REED.

3445. Georgia E. REED. Born abt 1901; died aft 1920.

3446. Eleanor D. REED. Born abt 1904; died aft 1920.

3447. Gladys [159] REED. Born on 15 Mar 1899.

3448. Hazel [160] REED. Born on 17 Apr 1900.

3449. Velma L. [161] REED. Born on 9 Sep 1903.

3450. Isabell R. [162] REED. Born on 8 Oct 1907.

3451. Blanche B. [163] REED. Born on 7 May 1908.

3452. Geraldine [164] REED. Born on 11 Aug 1909.

3453. Margaret E. [165] REED. Born on 5 Jun 1911.

3454. Vivian B. [166] REED. Born on 28 Oct 1912.

3455. Dewey D. [167] REED. Born on 8 Aug 1916; died on 29 Nov 1916.

3456. Hobart B. [168] REED. Born on 17 Aug 1901.

3457. Leona J. [169] REED. Born on 26 Sep 1905.

3458. Zelma L. [170] REED. Born on 3 Apr 1908.

3459. Phyllis H. [171] REED. Born on 18 Sep 1904.

3460. LaGrand [172] REED. Born on 18 Jan 1906.

3461. Francis Eugene [175-A] WOLCOTT. Born on 4 Apr 1877. On 11 Oct 1899 when he was 22, he married **Frances DEWOLF**.
They had the following children:

3787	i.	Dorothy [227-A] (1901-)
3788	ii.	Stanley [228-A] (1903-)
3789	iii.	Charles Eugene [229-A] (1920-)

3462. George Elvin [176-A] WOLCOTT. Born on 24 Oct 1878. On 12 Jul 1902 when he was 23, he married **Milly A. CHAPMAN**.
They had the following children:

3790	i.	Hazel Chapman [230] (1903-)

3791	ii.	Edna Mabel [231] (1904-)
3792	iii.	Orson Elvin [232] (1906-)
3793	iv.	Noble Eugene [233] (1910-)
3794	v.	Lanniston [234] (1912-)
3795	vi.	Kenneth [235] (1916-)

3463. Noble Ernest [177-A] WOLCOTT. Born on 25 May 1882. On 15 Jun 1908 when he was 26, he married **Mabel CHAPMAN**.
They had one child:

3796	i.	Mabel Elaine [226-A] (1908-)

3464. Flora Melvina [178-A] WOLCOTT. Born on 28 Dec 1885. On 22 Sep 1908 when she was 22, she married **Walter J. STASCH**; died aft 1920.
They had the following children:

3797	i.	Flora [227-A] (1909-)
3798	ii.	Harold [228-A] (1912-)
3799	iii.	Ruth [229-A] (1917-)
3800	iv.	Donald Lovern [227] (1918-)

3465. Harriet Jane [179] EASTERBROOK. Born on 14 Mar 1885.

3466. Claude Loraine [180] EASTERBROOK. Born on 23 Aug 1887. On 10 Jan 1911 when he was 23, he married **Martha CARPENTER**. Born on 4 Dec 1886.
They had one child:

3801	i.	Thelma Rose [184-A] (1911-)

3467. Raymond Larne [181] EASTERBROOK. Born on 28 Jun 1890.

3468. Lucius Elvin [182] EASTERBROOK. Born on 31 Oct 1892; died on 4 May 1915, he was 22.

3469. Leslie Leone [183] EASTERBROOK. Born on 13 Nov 1896.

3470. Ezra [230] WOLCOTT. Born on 30 May 1905; died aft 1920.

3471. Frederick John [231] WOLCOTT. Born on 9 Dec 1906.

3472. George Rogers [232] WOLCOTT. Born on 1 Jan 1909. George Rogers [232] died aft 1920.

3473. Charlotte Jane [233] WOLCOTT. Born on 8 Sep 1911; died on 19 Mar 1918, she was 6.

3474. Clara Louise [234] WOLCOTT. Born on 27 Feb 1914. Clara Louise [234] died aft 1920.

3475. Helen [175] SOULE.

3476. Clifford H. [176] GRIDLEY. Born on 1 May 1912.

3477. Vivian L. [177] GRIDLEY. Born on 13 Jan 1900. Vivian L. [177] died aft 1920.

3478. Adrian F. [178] GRIDLEY. Born on 23 Nov 1901.

3479. Winifred L. [179] GRIDLEY. Born on 1 Sep 1910.

3480. Clarence R. [180] HOWARD.

3481. Violet R. [181] HOWARD. Born on 10 Sep 1915.

3482. Virginia L. [182] HOWARD. Born on 13 Jun 1917.

3483. Elsie R. [183] HOWARD. Born on 21 Sep 1918.

3484. Earl Fred [184] GRIDLEY. Born on 8 Jun 1891. On 28 Jan 1916 when he was 24, he married **Nellie Hill ALLEN**. Born on 10 Oct 1886.
They had one child:

3802	i.	Vincent Earl [228] (1918-)

3485. Erma Pearl [185] GRIDLEY. Born on 7 Oct 1900.

3486. Clarence LaVerne [185] GRIDLEY. Born on 12 Aug 1907.

3487. Leta M. [187] CARMEN. B. 27 Aug 1887; married, 5 Jul 1907, at 19, **Harry CRANDALL**.
They had the following children:

3803	i.	Clifford [229] (1908-)
3804	ii.	Winifred [230] (1910-)
3805	iii.	Frederick [231] (1912-)
3806	iv.	Alice [232] (1917-)

3488. Mabel A. [188] CARMEN. B. 18 Mar 1889; married, 28 Apr 1909, at 20, **Albert W. ROLFE**.

They had the following children:

   3807   i.   Richard [233] (1913-)
   3808   ii.   Robert [234]

3489. Florence [189] CARMEN. B. 21 Apr 1893; married, 28 Jun 1915, at 22, **George GUISE.**
They had one child:

   3809   i.   Mary Ellen [235] (1918-)

3490. Winifred I. [190] CARMEN. B. on 17 Oct 1897. On 17 May 1918 she m. **William J. MURPHY.**

3491. William F. [191] CARMEN. Born on 21 Sep 1904.

3492. Dorothy [192] CARMEN. Born on 9 Aug 1906.

3493. Veronica C. [193] VAN ARSDALE. Born on 20 Oct 1891.

3494. Dorothy [194] VAN ARSDALE.

3495. Archibald J. [195] VAN ARSDALE. Born on 22 Mar 1908.

3496. Edna H. [196] DIMMICK. B. 24 Sep 1899; m. 1 Jun 1916, at 16, **Wilbert SCHANBACHER.**

3497. Mable J. [197] DIMMICK. Born on 20 Jan 1904.

3498. Uletta C. [198] DIMMICK. Born on 19 Jul 1907.

3499. Ellen M. [199] DIMMICK. Born on 19 Jun 1908.

3500. Leslie Jay [200] PEART. Born on 9 Nov 1897. He married **Sylvia PAJEL.**

3501. Ralph Melvin [201] PEART. Born on 25 Jul 1903.

3502. Edith Reay [202] PEART. Born on 15 Feb 1912.

3503. Elmer Hill [203] ELWIN. Born on 20 Aug 1912.

3504. James William [204] ELWIN. Born on 4 Dec 1916.

3505. Gordon Lundin [205] HILL. Born on 30 Jul 1916.

3506. _____ HILL. Born in Jun 1920 in Fargo, N.D. _____ died aft 1920.

3507. Helen Frances [206] GILBERT. Born on 9 Jan 1904.

3508. Leona May [207] GILBERT. Born on 18 Jan 1908. Leona May [207] died aft 1920.

3509. Myron [208] HILL.

3510. Muriel [209] HILL.

3511. Wesley Jasper [210] KINNAN. B. 25 Nov 1903 in Corning, NY; d. aft 1920.

3512. Ruth Elizabeth [211] KINNAN. B. 10 May 1911 in Canandaigua, NY; d. aft 1920.

3513. Helen Mae [212] HILL. Born on 20 Nov 1919; died aft 1920.

3514. Marvin Edwin [213] HILL. Born on 30 May 1920.

3515. Quincy Wellington [214] GREGORY. Born on 25 Dec 1914 in Caton, NY.; died aft 1920.

---------------------[798]

3516. Rev. Dean Edwin HILL,[799] son of John P. and Elizabeth (Tobey) Hill, was born at Caton, New York, 7 October 1928. He graduated from Mansfield State Teachers College (later Mansfield University), Mansfield, Pennsylvania, in 1951. He graduated from Drew Theological Seminary at Drew University, Madison, New Jersey, in 1954, and was ordained an Elder in the Methodist Church. He was President of the Hill Reunion for several years, and was succeeded in that office by his son John in 2009. The Reunion in August 2009 was held at the Tobeytown School in the southern part of Caton now known as Pine City, N.Y. Dean and Suzanne Hill were then remodeling the school into a home and they have lived there since that time. On 1 Jan 1952 when Dean Edwin was 23, he first married **Ernestine GRIDLEY**, in Caton, N.Y. Born on 3 Mar 1933 in Caton, N.Y. They were divorced in Sep 1980.
They had the following children:

   3810   i.   Paul David (1952-)
   3811   ii.   Mark Dean (1954-)
   3812   iii.   Drew Edwin (1957-)
   3813   iv.   John (1960-)

On 27 Sep 1980 when Dean Edwin was 51, he second married **Suzanne "Susan" DEBRINE**, in Newark, N.J. Born on 23 Dec 1931 in Sodus, N.Y.

3517. Iva Louise HILL.[800] Born on 27 Apr 1930 in Caton, N.Y. Religion: 50 year member of Caton

286

United Methodist Church and the Caton Grange; organist & singer. On 28 Oct 1951 when Iva Louise was 21, she married **Daniel Martin JENKINS** in Caton, N.Y. Born on 23 Jul 1929 in Elmira, N.Y. Occupation: Retiree of Corning, Inc.; veteran of Korean war, where he was a US Marine Corps fighter pilot; woodworker, sawyer, builder. Daniel Martin Jenkins was a graduate of USMC Basic Training "boot camp" at Parris Island in 1946. He then went to Pensacola, Fla., for flight training and graduated as a Naval Aviator. He flew the F4U "gull wing" fighter in the Korean War. He and his wife were the hosts for the 86th Hill Reunion at their home on John Hill Rd. in Pine City, N.Y., in 2010. Caton no longer has a ZIP code and it will probably disappear from maps over the next decade. Their address on John Hill Rd. was formerly a Caton address.

They had the following children:

3814	i.	Timothy Edwin (1953-)
3815	ii.	Scott Douglas (1956-1974)

3518. Constance Elizabeth HILL.[801] Born on 19 Nov 1942 in Caton, N.Y. Occupation: Mother of 3. In March 1996 she was living in Sodus, NY. On 8 May 1971 when Constance Elizabeth was 28, she married **Guy Richard POWELL**, son of Samuel Guy POWELL & Mabel V. SCHULTZ, in Caton, N.Y. Born on 11 Nov 1949 in Corning, N.Y.

They had the following children:

3816	i.	Shannan Elizabeth (1974-)
3817	ii.	Kerry Edward (1975-)
3818	iii.	Joseph Douglass (1977-)

3519. Kenneth Elvin HILL. Born on 31 Dec 1933 in Lyons, Yates(?) Co., N.Y. He married ____.

Children:

3819	i.	Kevin Eugene
3820	ii.	Keith Edwin
3821	iii.	Kerry Edward

3520. Doris Jean HILL.[802] Born on 2 Aug 1936 in Elmira, Chemung Co., N.Y.

3521. Cora Nellie PAUL. Born on 25 Oct 1901 in Logan, Ohio. Cora Nellie died in Athens, Ohio on 15 Feb 1976, she was 74. On 27 Mar 1923 when Cora Nellie was 21, she married **Adolphus Roscoe "Doc" FRAME**, in Chillicothe, Ohio.

3522. Virginia Helen PAUL. Born on 12 Jun 1917 in Chillicothe, Ohio. Virginia Helen died in Chillicothe, Ohio on 28 Nov 1988, she was 71. On 23 Jan 1943 when Virginia Helen was 25, she married **Martin JUDY**, in Chillicothe, Ohio.

3523. Charles Laurence "Sonny" PAUL. Born on 19 Apr 1920 in Chillicothe, Ohio. In Nov 1941 when he was 21, he married **Dorothy PROCTOR**, in Chillicothe, Ohio.

3524. Donald Roswell PAUL.

3525. Betty Ann PAUL. In Jun 1948 she married ____ ?.

3526. Barbara Jean PAUL.[803] Born on 24 Apr 1933 in Chillicothe, Ohio. On 16 Aug 1953 when Barbara Jean was 20, she married **Glenn Ralph LOVENSHEIMER**, in Chillicothe, Ohio.

3527. Francis Hill SKINNER. Francis Hill married **Edith Grace DORMAN**.

They had one child:

3822	i.	Mary Francis

3528. Richard L. HILL III.[804] Born on 19 May 1894. Richard L. died on 11 Nov 1955, he was 61. On 5 Dec 1916 when Richard L. was 22, he married **Ella Mae M. McILWAIN**, in Corning, N.Y. Born on 7 Oct 1899 in Leolyn, Pa.; died in Geneva, N.Y. on 9 Jul 1972, she was 72.

They had the following children:

3823	i.	Nettie "Lorene" (1920-1993)
3824	ii.	Richard L. (1925-)
3825	iii.	Paul Frank (1928-2005)
3826	iv.	Dorothy Claire (1936-)

3529. Dorothy White HILL. Born on 8 Jan 1899; died on 3 Aug 1968, she was 69. On 30 Apr 1917 when she was 18, she m **John Thomas O'CONNELL**, b. 8 Nov 1896; died in May 1968, he was 71.

They had the following children:

3827	i.	John White (1917-1975)
3828	ii.	Aimee (1921-1941)
3829	iii.	James Richard (1923-)

3530. William George Robert "Bob" HILL.

3531. Harriet Alice HILL.

3532. Hansel Ferris HILL.

3533. Marion Henry HILL.

3534. June GILLIAM. Born on 3 Jun 1916. June died on 15 Oct 2000, she was 84. June married **Kenneth MOURHESS.** Born on 15 Oct 1915. Kenneth died on 24 Mar 1967, he was 51.
They had the following children:

3830	i.	Barbara (1937-)
3831	ii.	Byron (1947-)
3832	iii.	Kendra (1949-)

3535. Richard (Harry) MORAN.

3536. Helen Mary MORAN married (1) **Walter MILLER**, and (2) **Frank BLOOMQUIST.**

3537. Helen Mildred HILL married **Lloyd G. WATKINS.**

3538. Richard "Lawrence" HILL married **Margaret LESH.**
They had one child:

3833	i.	Beverly

3539. Mary Nanno HILL.

Line 7. Descendants of Elizabeth Hill (continued)[805]

3540. Lyman Charles TERRY. Born in 1890; died in 1964, about 74.

3541. Frederick W. TERRY. Born in 1892. Frederick W. died in 1913, about 21.

Line 8. Descendants of John Hill (continued)[806]

3542. Charles Victor HILL. Born on 12 Dec 1901 in Lipscomb Co., Texas. Charles Victor died in Colfax, Wash. on 23 Oct 1968, he was 66. Buried in Orofino, Idaho. On 7 Feb 1931 when Charles Victor was 29, he first married **Esther Ruby SMITH**, in Miles City, Custer Co., Mont. Born on 5 Dec 1900 in Mound City, Mo. Esther Ruby died in Miles City, Custer Co., Mont. abt 8 Apr 1995, she was 94.
They had the following children:

3834	i.	Mary Elizabeth (1932-)
3835	ii.	Edwin Kay (1933-)
3836	iii.	Dorothy May (1936-)

Charles Victor second married **Mrs. Catherine DICK.**
They had one child:

3837	i.	Darrell (1948-1978)

3543. Alma Evelyn HILL. Born on 14 Sep 1905 in Miles City, Mont. On 16 Dec 1927 when she was 22, she married **Eric Bradford WILSON**, in Miles City, Custer Co., Mont. Born on 29 Dec 1907 in Walnut Grove, Minn.; died in Polson, Mont. on 25 Jan 1987, he was 79. Agricultural extension agent. Taught at Montana State College, Bozeman, and Washington State College, Pullman, Wash.
They had the following children:

3838	i.	Lenore (1929-1993)
3839	ii.	Marlene Ruth (1932-)

3544. Earl Edward HILL Sr., second son and third of the six children of William Henry and Bessie Olive (Guenther) Hill, was born at Hepner, Oregon, 9 May 1908; died at Helena, Montana, 3 August 1991, age 83. His son, James, wrote that, "at six foot six, he was the largest member of his family, but his father was over six feet tall. He was always soft-spoken and even tempered. . . . After his father died Earl brought Will's agate saw, a diamond studded rotor and lathe arrangement, and the polishing equipment back to Helena and occasionally worked at slicing and polishing agates from the large collection that had been accumulated at the ranch. The best of them were kept in a large trunk and wooden dynamite boxes in the garage." He married, at Miles City, Custer Co., Montana, 30 August 1930, when he was 22 and she was 20, **Elizabeth Campbell "Betty" ANDERSON**; born at McKeesport, Pennsylvania, 21 March 1910. Earl and Betty (Anderson) Hill had three children. All three of the children married, and Earl Jr. and James had descendants. James is the author of the on-line genealogy of the Hill Family, *The Hill Family, From 1651 to 2000: Twelve Generations in America*. Edition 5.0, 2000. His e-book traces the descendants of Luke Hill in the line of their youngest child, John Hill, and his wife Sarah Phelps. James D. Hill, wrote, "Betty and her twin, Bill, were the youngest of their family and were less than two when their father died, so Betty has no memory of him. She remembers her childhood years as being happy, in spite of the family's financial condition. The older brothers and sisters got along well with each other and tended to spoil the 'babies' of the family. There was much humor, especially at the dinner table where all the family convened and talked over the day's events."

They had the following children:

3840	i.	Earl Edward (1931-)
3841	ii.	Raymond Willard (1934-)
3842	iii.	James Dallas (1938-)

3545. Ruth Irene HILL. Born on 3 Nov 1911 in Miles City, Mont. Ruth Irene died on 24 May 1982, she was 70; d.s.p. Ruth Irene married **Carleton MARINER**. Carleton died on 10 Feb 1983.

3546. Edson Harold HILL. Born on 8 Dec 1912 in Miles City, Custer Co., Mont. Edson Harold died aft 1995, he was over 82. Occupation: Dairy employee, Lafayette, Calif. On 5 Mar 1944 when Edson Harold was 31, he married **Arline Hermione WALLER**, daughter of Gilbert Marvin WALLER, in Berkeley, Calif. Arline Hermione died on 7 Oct 1984 in LaFayette, Calif.

They had one child:

| 3843 | i. | Marlynn Ruth "Lynn" (1947-) |

3547. Mary Myrtle HILL. Born on 4 May 1903. Mary Myrtle died on 27 Apr 1904.

3548. Dale DeVORE. Born on 15 May 1901; died in Washington on 28 Mar 1996, age 94.

3549. Dayton DeVORE. B. 15 Mar 1911 in Illinois; d. in Oquawka, Ill. 16 Jan 1997, age 85.

3550. Donald DeVORE.

3551. Vivian Rosalie JERN. Born on 26 Jun 1917 in Mt. Morris, Ogle Co., Ill. Vivian Rosalie died in Mt. Morris, Ogle Co., Ill. on 9 Feb 1956, she was 38. On 12 Dec 1935 when Vivian Rosalie was 18, she married **Franklyn Baird BALLUFF**. Born on 10 Sep 1914 in Malta, De Kalb Co., Ill.

They had one child:

| 3844 | i. | Dennis Michael (1939-) |

3552. Forrest KINSEY.

3553. Ruby WILLIAMS married **Emmett HAWKINS** before 1941.

3554. J. Laird MORGAN. Born on 15 Dec 1932 in Independence, Ore. J. Laird married **Lillian Florence BRUNER**. Born on 31 Oct 1934 in Oakland, Calif.

They had one child:

| 3845 | i. | Loretta Anne (1953-) |

3555. Roy LaFayette HILL. Born in 1883.

3556. Emma Aurelia HILL. Born in 1886.

3557. James Lester HILL. Born in 1889.

3558. Eva Esther HILL. Born in 1891.

3559. Erma Julia HILL. Born in 1894.

3560. Lolita Fay HILL. Born in 1900.

3561. Luella Florence HILL. Born in 1900.

3562. Dale Herschel HILL. Born in 1902.

3563. Bertram Ladue HILL. Born in 1905.

3564. Herbert H. HILL. Born in 1910.

3565. Claude Locke HILL. Born on 21 Jul 1884 in Independence, Ore.; died in 1969, about 84.

Child, by a wife whose name is unknown:

3846   i.   Ruby Alice (1910-)

3566. Cecelia HILL. Born on 21 Jul 1891 in Fish Creek, Wisc. She m. **? BEST**.

3567. Amanda Luella BELL. Born on 5 Jan 1873 in Wonewoc, Wisc. Amanda Luella died in Gary, Ind. on 3 Mar 1931, she was 58. On 18 May 1898 when Amanda Luella was 25, she married **George Wilson TODD**. Born on 8 Sep 1873 in Campbellsford, Canada.

3847   i.   Florence Bell (1908-1995)

3568. Lester Loring STAATS. Born on 28 Jan 1874 in Coffeyville, Kansas. Lester Loring died in Wash. Co., Okla. on 20 Feb 1953, he was 79. Lester Loring married **Eugenia Diana HOLLENBECK**. Born on 11 Apr 1882 in Niobrara, Neb. Eugenia Diana died in Okla. in 1957, she was 74. They had one child:

3848   i.   Lurissa Rosalia Staats (1911-)

_____[807]

3569. Brig. Gen. Lucius Barnes BARBOUR.[808] Born on 1 Feb 1878 in Hartford, Hartford Co., Conn. Lucius Barnes died at Fenwick on 29 Jul 1934, he was 56. He is the eponymous source of the Barbour Collection of Connecticut Vital Records.

He graduated from Hartford Public High School in 1896 and from Yale University in 1900. "Col. Barbour Dies Aged 56 in Fenwick." *Hartford Courant* (30 July 1934), 1: "In 1911, Barbour was appointed the first Examiner of Public Records as assistant to the State Librarian, a position he held until his death. He was captain of Company K in 1916 and trained his company when it was mobilized for service at the Mexican border. He took ill before the troops left for the border and his physicians refused to certify him as fit for active service and he resigned his command. Barbour went to Washington in 1917 to serve on the provost marshal's staff for fifteen months. He was a major of the First Company, Governor's Foot Guard in 1920. He was quartermaster general with the rank of brigadier general on the staff of Governor Lake. Barbour belonged to several organizations including the Acorn Club of Connecticut, the Farmington Country Club, the Fenwick Golf Club, the Hartford Club, Connecticut Society Founders and Patriots of America, Military Order of Foreign Wars, Sphinx Temple, AAONMS, the Society of Colonial Wars, Jeremiah Wadsworth Chapter of the Sons of the American Revolution, the Twentieth Century Club, Yale Alumni Association, Connecticut Historical Society, and the Hartford Oratorio Society." Lucius Barnes married **Charlotte Cordelia HILLIARD**; born on 15 Nov 1876 in Manchester, Hartford Co., Conn.; died 2 Oct 1945. They had the following children:

3849   i.   Lucius Hilliard (1903-)

3850   ii.   Alice Cordelia (1907-)

3570. Harriet Burr BARBOUR. Born on 22 Jul 1879. She married **George Alexander PHELPS**.

3571. Roderick Barbour BARNES. Born on 16 Dec 1882 in Brooklyn, N.Y.

_____[809]

3572. Hattie Louise BARNES. Born on 31 Mar 1885 in Brooklyn, N.Y.

3573. Goodrich BARNES. Born on 30 Jun 1887 in Brooklyn, N.Y.

3574. Mabel Sarah SMITH. Born on 2 Dec 1889 in Omaha, Douglas, Neb.

3575. Clifford P. MILLER.

3576. Mildred Gracia MILLER. Born on 23 Sep 1860 in Fulton, Rock, Wisc.

3577. Flora MILLER. Born on 27 Jul 1863.

3578. Lois MILLER. Born on 12 May 1865.

3579. Fanny MILLER. Born on 31 Dec 1867.

3580. Frank H. MILLER. Born on 20 Nov 1869.

3581. Fred S. MILLER. Born on 4 Mar 1871.

3582. Maud E. MILLER. Born on 10 Oct 1878.

3583. Elizabeth Catherine HUMASON. Born on 16 Jan 1872 in Newark, N.J.

3584. William Wallace HUMASON. Born on 28 Oct 1873.

3585. John Eno HUMASON. Born on 9 Mar 1876.

3586. Julia Harriet HUMASON. Born on 13 Apr 1883 in Yonkers, N.Y.

3587. Marjorie Florence HUMASON. Born on 6 Dec 1886.

3588. Lawrence Cole HUMASON. Born on 16 May 1891 in New Britain, Conn.

—————————————————[810]

3589. Frances M. RILEY.[811] Born on 24 May 1876. Frances M. died on 2 Apr 1876 in Iowa. Buried in Rowan, IA (Graceland cemetery). Her gravestone in Rowan, IA, is inscribed: "RILEY -- Frances M., dau of H. & F. Riley d. Apr 1, 1876 -- aged 10 mo 8 da."

3590. Adelia RILEY. Adelia married **Jap McKINSTRY**, in Rowan, IA.

They had the following children:

3851	i.	Charles
3852	ii.	Albert "Bus"

3591. Isabelle "Totie Belle" Luella "Luella" RILEY,[812] daughter of James Gillett and Kate Clara (Archer) Riley, was born at Fryeburg (now Rowan), Wright County, Iowa, 15 December 1867; died at Mason City, Iowa, 7 March 1950. She was a red-headed girl, who was called "Totie Belle" when she was young, although her Catholic baptismal name was Isabelle Luella. She was known as "Luella" when she was older. She completed grammar school and had some high school education, and then became a school teacher. She took a memorable trip by train from Rowan, Iowa, to Denver, Colorado, when she was twenty-four years old, which she recorded in a diary that she kept from 30 April to 27 September 1891. The diary has been transcribed and copies have been passed down to her descendants. She later returned to Iowa, where she was married and raised a family of four children; her first child was born when she was thirty years old. It was recalled by her daughter, LaVonne, that when she was young, Luella had to sleep on the floor so the railroad workers who were boarding at her home could have her bed. She enjoyed crocheting, quilting, and rug making, and helped anyone in need. In her later years she lived in a nursing home in Mason City, Iowa, and she died there at the age of 82. She was buried three days later at the Oakland Cemetery, Forest City, Iowa, following services led by the Rev. C. Patterson at the Methodist Church in Forest City.

She married **James Peter ANDERSON**[813]; born in Denmark, 19 November 1964; buried in Catskill, N.Y. He was the son of Anders and Mara (Linquist) Anderson. He took pleasure in smoking a pipe and was very skillful in the care of sick animals, as good as a veterinarian would be. They had four children, born in Iowa.

They had the following children:

3853	i.	Ula Myrtle (1897-1981)
3854	ii.	James Adelbert "Delbert" (1900-~1996)
3855	iii.	Haven Riley (1905-1964)
3856	iv.	Mabel LaVonne "LaVonne" (1907-1997)

3592. Susan Myrtle "Aunt Sue" RILEY.[814] Born in Iowa (probably); died aft 1928 in San Diego, CA (probably). She married **James Daniel WOLFER**.

They had the following children:

3857	i.	Susan "Sue"
3858	ii.	Donald Paul (1912-1997)

3593. Stilson James RILEY.[815] Born on 28 Mar 1871 in Wright Co., IA. Stilson James died on 6 Dec 1871 in Wright Co., IA, age 8 months.

———————————————————

3594. Daughter of Leslie and Ruth (Davis) HOSKIN.[816]

10

Tenth Generation
The 7th-Great--Grandchildren
Descendants of 1. Lydia, 2. Mary, 5. Luke Jr., and 8. John

Line 1 – Descendants of Lydia Hill (continued)[817]

3595. George Washington SHEPPERD. Born on 29 Mar 1852 in Chariton, Ia. George Washington died in Caldwell, Ida. on 20 Apr 1922, he was 70. On 21 Jun 1875 when George Washington was 23, he married **Rutha Jane WOODY**, at her home in Iowa. Born on 9 Sep 1848 in Bedford, Ind. Rutha Jane died in Pocatello, Ida. on 19 Mar 1924, she was 75.
They had the following children:

3859	i.	Infant (1877-)
3860	ii.	John Wesley (1878-)
3861	iii.	Bruce Reason (1881-1980)
3862	iv.	Warren Thompson (1883-1971)
3863	v.	Renne Julian (1886-1974)
3864	vi.	Enos Aberdeen (1888-1961)
3865	vii.	Eva Leannah (1890-)

3596. Bruce Eugene SHEPPERD. Born on 25 Apr 1854 in Chariton, Ia.; died in Donna, Tex. in Sep 1943, he was 89. On 13 Jun 1895 when Bruce Eugene was 41, he married **Emma PICKERING**, in Chariton, Ia. Born on 2 Apr 1862 in Richmond, Ind.; died in Donna, Tex. 26 Dec 1934, she was 72.
They had the following children:

3866	i.	William Bruce (1900-)
3867	ii.	Emma Eugenia (1903-)
3868	iii.	Esther Agnes (1905-)

3597. Juniatta L. SHEPPERD. Born on 30 Oct 1855. Juniatta L. died on 10 Mar 1928, she was 72.

3598. Clarinda Jane SHEPPERD. Born on 29 Dec 1859 in Chariton, Ia. Clarinda Jane died in Fargo, N.D. on 12 Mar 1893, she was 33. On 16 Jul 1885 when Clarinda Jane was 25, she married **Willet Martin HAYS**, in Chariton, Ia. Born in Eldora, Ia.; died in West Chester, Pa.
They had the following children:

3869	i.	Martin Willet
3870	ii.	Bessie Shepperd (1887-)

3599. Adeliza Bell SHEPPERD. Born on 7 May 1862. Adeliza Bell died on 16 Nov 1865, she was 3.

3600. Mary Melcina SHEPPERD. Born on 11 Sep 1864 in Chariton, Ia.; died in Cove, Ks. on 8 Feb 1935, she was 70. On 25 Dec 1882 when Mary Melcina was 18, she married **Sanford POWERS**, in Chariton, Ia. Born on 15 Jun 1861 in Chariton, Ia. Sanford died in Cove, Ks. on 20 Feb 1936, age 74.
They had the following children:

3871	i.	Miles Henry (1884-)
3872	ii.	Clara Gertrude (1886-)
3873	iii.	Sumner Leslie (1889-)

3601. John Henry SHEPPERD. Born on 12 Jan 1869.

3602. LaVerne Sedgwick BREWER. Born on 19 Jul 1882 in Bynumville, Chariton Co., Mo.; died in Ottawa, Kan. on 19 Jul 1946, he was 64. LaVerne Sedgwick married **Minnie GIPSON**, in Bynumville, Chariton Co., Mo. Born 11 Apr 1882 in Bynumville, Mo.; died in 1939, about 56.
They had the following children:

3874	i.	Lisle Gipson (1905-1958)

3875	ii.	Ola Verne (1918-)
3876	iii.	Clarene (1918-)
3877	iv.	Margaret G. (1922-)

3603. Ellie L. Corey BREWER.

3604. Fannie Z. Miller BREWER.

3605. Olive Grace BREWER.

3606. Leon H. BREWER.

3607. Maude C. BREWER.

3608. Elsie Gertrude BETT. Born in 1907; died in 1985, about 78.

3609. Doris Mabel BETT. Born in 1908; died in 1994, about 86.

3610. Thomas Barker BETT. Born in 1911; died in 1968, about 57.

3611. Mary Rebecca BETT. Born in 1913; died in 1992, about 79.

3612. Wilson Josiah MARTIN. Born in 1912; died in 1994, about 82. It is not clear why his surname was changed to that of his mother.

3613. Donald Junior BARKER. Born in 1918; died in 1992, about 74. It is not clear why his surname was changed to that of his mother.

3614. Blanch Lillian STOWE. B. 26 Aug 1872 in Ogden, Weber Co., Utah; d. in Idaho Falls, Bonneville, Idaho in 1923. May have married four times. In 1890 when she was 17, she m. **Edward Hunter OLSEN**, in Utah. B. 22 Jan 1865 in Weber, Utah; d. in Salt Lake City, Utah, 7 Jan 1907, age 41. They perhaps had one child:

3878	i.	Stella (1892-)

3615. Aleanor Elena BYINGTON. Born 21 May 1878 in Marshvalley, Bannock, Idaho.

3616. Herbert Day BYINGTON. Born on 5 Feb 1881 in Woodland, Bannock, Idaho.

3617. Sylvia Mariah BYINGTON. Born on 21 Mar 1883 in Dempsey Creek, Marshvalley, Idaho.

3618. Leon Nelson BYINGTON. Born on 25 Mar 1885 in Marshvalley, Idaho.

3619. Orra Elvira BYINGTON. Born on 17 Feb 1887 in Arimo, Bannock, Idaho.

3620. Joseph Earon BYINGTON. Born on 1 Jan 1889 in Dempsey Creek, Idaho.

3621. Elmer William BYINGTON. Born on 4 Apr 1891 in Lava Hot Springs, Bannock, Idaho.

3622. Viola May BYINGTON. Born on 5 Jan 1897 in Rockland, Power, Idaho.

3623. Ida May BYINGTON. Born on 28 Sep 1898 in Rockland, Power, Idaho.

3624. Ethel Elizabeth BYINGTON. Born on 19 Nov 1901 in Rockland, Idaho.

3625. Joseph Lasley BYINGTON. Born on 11 Jun 1903 in Rockland, Power, Idaho.

3626. John Avery BYINGTON. Born on 19 May 1909 in Rockland, Power, Idaho.

3627. Heber Thornley BYINGTON. Born on 21 Dec 1914 in Rockland, Power, Idaho.

3628. Edna Matilda BYINGTON. Born on 27 Jul 1919 in Rockland, Power, Idaho.

3629. Lottie Faye BYINGTON. Born on 10 Oct 1897 in Lava Hot Springs, Bannock, Idaho. Lottie Faye died in Edmonds, Snohomish, Washington on 9 Aug 1994, she was 96. Lottie Faye married **Herman Gilford CORRELL**. Born on 7 Dec 1888 in Stanley, Chippewa, Wisc. Herman Gilford died in Reno, Washoe, Nev. on 17 Apr 1959, he was 70.
They had the following children:

3879	i.	Child of Herman and Lottie (Byington)
3880	ii.	Child of Herman and Lottie (Byington)
3881	iii.	Child of Herman and Lottie (Byington)
3882	iv.	Herman Edward (1917-)
3883	v.	Ray Weldon (1922-)

3630. Child of William and Emma (Higgins) BYINGTON.

3631. Child of William and Emma (Higgins) BYINGTON.

3632. Emma Elvira BYINGTON. Born on 4 Jan 1898 in Dempsey, Bannock, Idaho.

3633. William Leslie BYINGTON. Born on 1 Sep 1899 in Dempsey, Bannock, Idaho.

3634. Naomia Leona BYINGTON. Born on 1 Feb 1908 in Dempsey, Bannock, Idaho.

3635. Harold Ray BYINGTON. Born on 5 Feb 1909 in Idaho.

3636. Thora BYINGTON. Born on 3 Jun 1911 in Rockland, Oneida, Idaho.

3637. Reba Ilene BYINGTON. Born on 1 Nov 1914 in Grace, Idaho.

3638. Child of Orlando and Susannah (Wilbur) CARR.

3639. Child of Orlando and Susannah (Wilbur) CARR.

3640. Orlando King CARR. Born on 30 May 1911 in Annis, Idaho.

3641. Sylvia Pearl CARR. Born on 1 Sep 1912 in Annis, Idaho.

3642. Orville Leui CARR. Born on 14 Apr 1918 in Annis, Idaho.

3643. Clarence CARR. Born on 5 Apr 1920 in Annis, Idaho.

3644. Lavella Ruth CARR. Born on 29 Nov 1921 in Annis, Idaho.

3645. Grace A. LANE. Born in Feb 1875 in Connecticut; died after 1900. In 1880, age 5, she lived in Winchester, Litchfield Co., Conn. In 1900, she was in Bridgeport City, Fairfield Co., Conn.

3646. Ida M. LANE. Born abt 1877. Ida M. died aft 1880.

3647. Bruce B. LANE. Born in Mar 1879 in Connecticut. Bruce B. died aft 1900. Resided in Winchester in 1880, and in Bridgeport in 1900.

3648. Eula LANE. Born in Feb 1881 in Connecticut; d aft 1900. She was in Bridgeport, Conn., in 1900.

3649. Allice R. LANE. Born in Jul 1883 in Connecticut; died aft 1900. She was in Bridgeport in 1900.

3650. Alice Handsome LANE. B. abt 1885 in Connecticut; d aft 1910. She was in Bridgeport in 1910.

3651. Richard J. LANE. In 1900 Richard J. married Katherine **Alghea HAGER**, in Bridgeport City, Fairfield Co., Conn. Born in 1899. Katherine Alghea died in 1995, she was 96.
They had the following children:

3884	i.	Son of Richard and Kathleen (Hager)
3885	ii.	Daughter of Richard and Kathleen (Hager)
3886	iii.	Daughter of Richard and Kathleen (Hager)

3652. Theodore T. LANE. Born in Feb 1889.

3653. Harold Charles LANE. Born on 20 May 1892 in Connecticut. He married **Mabel I. ?**
They had the following children:

3887	i.	Daughter of Harold and Mabel I.
3888	ii.	Daughter of Harold and Mabel I.
3889	iii.	Daughter of Harold and Mabel I.
3890	iv.	Harold Benjamin (1914-1988)

3654. Rufus H. LANE. Born in 1884. Rufus H. died in 1885, about 1.

3655. James E. LANE. Born in 1886. James E. died in 1887, about 1.

3656. Emily E. LANE. Born in 1888. Emily E. died in 1889, about 1.

3657. Martha LANE. Born in 1890.

3658. Perrin L'HOMMEDIEU.

3659. Ramond D. L'HOMMEDIEU.

3660. Albert Whitman L'HOMMEDIEU. Born on 29 Apr 1893.

3661. Anella L. L'HOMMEDIEU. Born on 6 Mar 1895.

3662. Glenwood Warren HUMISTON. Born on 2 Oct 1889 in Waterbury, Conn.

3663. Olive Ellen HUMISTON.

3664. Ralph Carlyle HUMISTON. Born on 12 Jun 1890.

3665. Clyde Myron HUMISTON. Born in Sep 1892.

3666. Ellsworth Munson HUMISTON. Born in Jul 1894.

3667. Joseph Harold HUMISTON. Born in Aug 1896 in Connecticut.

3668. Hugh Darius HUMISTON. Born on 1 Oct 1901 in Connecticut.

3669. Harry Robert HUMISTON. Born on 1 Oct 1901 in Connecticut.

3670. Bertrand Humiston LEAVENWORTH. Born on 24 Feb 1884.

3671. Myrta May HOTELLING. Born on 24 May 1868.

3672. Clair Albert HOTELLING. Born on 22 Jun 1869 in Algona, Kossuth, Ia. Clair Albert died in Los Angeles, Calif. on 5 Jun 1944, he was 74. On 26 Jun 1894 when Clair Albert was 25, he married **Lucy Amelia RAWSON**, in Bancroft, Ia. Born on 1 Jun 1875 in Whittemore, Kossuth, Ia. Lucy Amelia

died in Los Angeles, Calif. on 25 May 1959, she was 83.
They had one child:

3891 i. Four sons and two daughters of Clair and Lucy (Rawson)

3673. Vera Litta HOTELLING. Born on 26 Jun 1882.

3674. Daughter of Hepworth and Belle (Bennett) GAYLORD.

3675. Helen Sabra GAYLORD. Born on 1 Nov 1893.

3676. Howard GAYLORD. Born on 26 May 1895.

3677. Charles E. GAYLORD. Born on 17 Feb 1900.

3678. Lawrence GAYLORD. Born on 9 Dec 1901.

3679. Clarence H. BARNES. Born on 27 Dec 1885 in Litchfield, Litchfield Co., Conn. Clarence H. died on 13 Aug 1952, he was 66. He married **Ida ALLEN**. Born in 1885; died in 1975, about 90.
They had the following children:

3892 i. ?

3893 ii. Dorothy (1916-1994)

Line 2. Descendants of Mary Hill (Continued)[818]

3680. Allen STETSON (or WILSON). Born on 24 Jun 1896.

3681. Harold STETSON (or WILSON). Born in 1898.

3682. William Allen GAYNOR. Born in 1896. William Allen died in 1972, he was 76. In 1922 when William Allen was 26, he married **Leah DIETTE**. Born in 1896. Leah died in 1981, she was 85.
They had the following children:

3894 i. ? [1]
3895 ii. ? [2]
3896 iii. ? [3]
3897 iv. ? [4]
3898 v. ? [5]
3899 vi. ? [6]
3900 vii. Paul (1930-)

3683. Charles Beauclerk GAYNOR.

3684. Harold Wentworth GAYNOR. Born in 1899.

Line 5. Descendants of Luke Hill, Jr. (Continued)
---------------[819]

3685. Lulu HILL.

3686. Clarence HILL.[820] Born in 1876 in Lake Co., Ill.

3687. Lula A. HILL.[821] Born in 1879 in Wauconda, Lake Co., Illinois. Lula A. married _____ **BELT**.

3688. Sadie W. HILL.[822] Born on 13 Jun 1882 in Barrington, Ill. Sadie W. died in Chicago, Cook Co., Ill. in 1968, she was 85. Sadie W. HILL, youngest child of Clarence Mortimer and Mary Elizabeth (Ault) Hill, was born in Barrington, Ill., 13 June 1882; died at Chicago, Cook Co., Ill., in 1968, about age 86. Her mother died 10 days after she was born. She married, 23 September 1910, **Roy A. STANLEY**; born at Princeton, Mo., in 1880; died in Chicago, in July 1941. They had one child, who had descendants. Sadie W. first married _____ **BURDICK**. On 23 Sep 1910 when Sadie W. was 28, she second married **Roy A. STANLEY**. Born in 1880 in Princeton, Mo.; d in Chicago, Cook Co., Ill. in Jul 1941, he was 61.
They had one child:

3901 i. David L. (1920-2006)

3689. Harry Lewis FORD.[823] Born on 17 Aug 1869 in Lake Co., Ill. Harry Lewis died in Delta, Midland Co., Utah on 29 Dec 1941, he was 72. Occupation: d.s.p.

3690. Ambrose Elmer FORD.[824] Born on 15 Jan 1874 in Illinois.

3691. Lida B. FORD.[825] Born on 14 Jan 1884 in Wauconda, Lake Co., Illinois. Lida B. died in Wauconda, Lake Co., Illinois in Apr 1956, she was 72. Mother of 2, one of whom had descendants. On

28 Oct 1902 when Lida B. was 18, she married **Clyde Adair GOLDING**, in Chicago, Cook Co., Ill. Born in 1878. Clyde Adair died in 1955, he was 77.
They had the following children:

3902	i.	Helen Dorothy (1905-1962)
3903	ii.	Alvin Ford (1908-1969)

3692. Sadie Dell MYRICK. Born on 24 Oct 1879 in Ida Grove, Ida Co., Ia. Sadie Dell died in Baytown, Harris Co., Tex. on 27 Jul 1960, she was 80. On 20 May 1903 when Sadie Dell was 23, she married **Ernest Clifford BOND**, in Des Moines, Polk Co., Ia. Born on 26 Apr 1877 in Iowa Falls, Hardin Co., Ia. Ernest Clifford died in Milwaukee, Milwaukee Co., Wisc. on 6 May 1937, he was 60.
They had the following children:

3904	i.	Marge
3905	ii.	Susan
3906	iii.	Clifford M. (1904-)
3907	iv.	Marjorie E. (1906-)

3693. Grace Estelle MYRICK. Born on 23 Aug 1881 in Odeboldt, Sac Co., Ia. Grace Estelle married **Chester W. SOULES**. Born in 1879 in Illinois.
They had one child:

3908	i.	_____

3694. Adah Rosina MYRICK. Born on 11 Dec 1883 in Odeboldt, Sac Co., Ia. Adah Rosina died in Kirksville, Adair Co., Mo. on 8 Feb 1919, she was 35. On 23 Aug 1905 when Adah Rosina was 21, she married **Robert Russell KEITH**, in Des Moines, Polk Co., Ia. Born on 13 Feb 1879 in West Liberty, Muscatine Co., Ia. Robert Russell died in Des Moines, Polk Co., Ia. on 15 Jun 1937, he was 58.
They had the following children:

3909	i.	_____
3910	ii.	_____
3911	iii.	Donald (1906-)
3912	iv.	Dorothy Elliott (1907-)

3695. George Frederick CHILDS.[826] Born on 3 Jul 1909 in Highland Park, Lake Co., Ill. George Frederick died on 10 Jan 1931, he was 21.

3696. Robert Livingston CHILDS.[827] Born on 17 Feb 1912 in Chicago, Cook Co., Ill. Robert Livingston died in Chicago, Cook Co., Ill. on 1 Aug 1992, he was 80. On 20 Sep 1947 when Robert Livingston was 35, he married **Mary Eleanor METCALF**, daughter of John Tucker METCALF. Born in 1924. Mary Eleanor died in 2005, she was 81. Mother of 2, whose names are unknown.
They had the following children:

3913	i.	_____
3914	ii.	_____

3697. William Coffeen CHILDS.[828] Born on 17 Apr 1916 in Chicago, Cook Co., Ill.; died in Wilmette, Ill. on 21 Mar 1997, he was 80. William Coffeen married **Alice GRAFF**. Alice died aft 1997.
They had the following children:

3915	i.	Deborah (->1997)
3916	ii.	Nancy Elizabeth (->1997)

3698. Child of Richard S. LAUGHTON.

3699. Child of Richard S. LAUGHTON.

3700. Child of Richard S. LAUGHTON.

3701. Child of Raymond and Edith HILL.

3702. Child of Raymond and Edith HILL.

3703. William HILL.[829] Born abt 1915 in Aurora, Ill.; died in 2005, about 90.

3704. Clyde HILL.[830] Born on 2 Apr 1916 in Aurora, Ill. Clyde died in South Bend, St. Joseph Co., Indiana in Oct 1987, he was 71.

3705. Howard HILL.[831] Born on 27 Oct 1918 in Aurora, Ill. Howard died in San Andreas, Calaveras Co., Calif. on 22 Aug 2004, he was 85.

3706. Woodrow HILL.[832] Born abt 1919; died in Elgin, Kane Co., Ill. in Mar 1986, about 67.

3707. Earl HILL.[833] Born on 19 Feb 1920 in Aurora, Ill. Earl died in Illinois on 17 May 1988, he was 68.

3708. Maxine HILL.[834] Born on 25 Jul 1924 in Aurora, Ill. Maxine died in Winfield, Winfield Co., Ill. on 27 Mar 1990, he was 65.

3709. Child of Maurice and Blanche HILL.

3710. Child of Maurice and Blanche HILL.

3711. Child of Maurice and Blanche HILL.

3712. Child of Lowell and Ellenore CLARK.

3713. Gene Bryant CLARK. Born on 25 May 1922 in Minneapolis, Hennepin Co., Ill.; died in Minneapolis, Hennepin Co., Ill. on 28 Sep 1980, he was 58.

3714. Warren Lowell CLARK. Born on 13 Aug 1925 in Minneapolis, Hennepin Co., Ill. Warren Lowell died in Alexandria, Minn. on 1 Mar 1983, he was 57.

3715. Kenneth Frederick CLARK.[835] Born abt 1925 in Minna. Kenneth Frederick died on 17 Mar 1925 in Minneapolis, Hennepin Co., Ill.

3716. Hon. Gerald Albert "Jerry" HILL.[836] California State Legislature; Head of the Democratic Party Caucus. Education: University of California at Berkeley. His professional biography states that he was elected to the California State Assembly in November 2008, where he chairs the Majority Caucus in the Assembly and is a member of Speaker Perez' leadership team. He is responsible for negotiating key issues and guiding legislative priorities. Prior to his election to the Assembly, he served 17 years in local government, first as a member of the San Mateo City Council and for 10 years as a San Mateo County Supervisor. As a Supervisor, he led the effort to expand health insurance coverage to every child in San Mateo County without raising taxes. He helped foster a healthy local business climate and he helped deliver a balanced budget for San Mateo County with a fair approach of cuts, belt tightening and fee increases where appropriate.

Jerry Hill has fought to preserve thousands of acres of parks, open space and coastal areas in San Mateo County, while working to set tough limits on air pollution and global warming emissions. He was a member of the California Air Resources Board and he has served on a number of regional boards including the Bay Area Air Quality Management District.

He first married **? ?**

They had one child:

    3917   i.   Taryn

He second married **Karen Loja "Sky" SKAIDRITE.**

3717. Gregory HILL.

3718. Mary Ann HILL.

3719. Daughter of Kenneth and Ruth (Whitney) HILL.

3720. Daughter of Kenneth and ? (Escamos) HILL.

3721. Unnamed son REYNOLDS.

3722. Unnamed son REYNOLDS.

3723. Glen SOULE.

3724. Warren SOULE.

3725. Wilbur SOULE.

3726. Unnamed SLOAN.

3727. Estelle Frances WOOD. Estelle Frances married **William McFALL**. Born on 1 Aug 1904. William died in Thompsonville, Conn. on 15 Nov 1962, he was 58.

3728. Ethel Marion WOOD. Occupation: Mother of 4, of whom nothing is given in OneWorldTree, except that they are "Living." Ethel Marion married **Robert Sinclair SNELL**. Born on 23 Jun 1906 in Sturbridge, Mass. Robert Sinclair died in Southbridge, Mass. on 16 Nov 1980, he was 74.

3729. Harold Kentfield WOOD. Harold Kentfield married **? RICHARDSON.**

3730. David Frederick WOOD.

Child:

    3918   i.   ?

3731. ? WOOD. He has 2 daughters and a son, whose names are not given in OneWorldTree.
? married **?**.

3732. ? TRUEHART.

3733. ? TRUEHART.

3734. Hazel M. TRUEHART. Born on 3 Nov 1908.

3735. ? TORREY.

3736. ? TORREY.

3737. ? TORREY.

3738. ? TORREY.

3739. Chester R. TORREY. Born in 1922. Chester R. died in Easthampton, Hampshire Co., Mass. on 11 Jun 2001, he was 79.

3740. Kenneth TORREY. Born on 16 Jul 1925. Kenneth died in Easthampton, Hampshire Co., Mass. on 29 Mar 1993, he was 67.

3741. ? TORREY. He married **Helen QUINN.** Born on 1 Sep 1926 in Worcester, Mass. Helen died in Worcester, Mass. on 5 Jun 1998, she was 71. Mother of 4, none of whom are named in OneWorldTree.

3742. ? TORREY.

3743. Ralph Bernier TORREY. Born on 2 Apr 1925 in Webster, Mass. Ralph Bernier died in Worcester, Mass. in Dec 1984, he was 59. Ralph Bernier married **Grimala ?.** Mother of 5 children, called "Living" by OneWorldTree.

3744. Ralph Bilyeu Neeley. Born 11 Sep 1892 in Mulberry Grove, Bond Co., Ill.

3745. Roxie C. Neeley. Born on 10 Apr 1895 in Bond, Ill.

3746. Paul Neeley. Born in 1897 in Illinois.

3747. George L. Neeley. Born on 15 Oct 1901 in Mulberry Grove, Bond Co., Ill.

3748. George Kingsley BIRGE. Born on 13 May 1909 in London, England. George Kingsley died in Sunnyvale, Calif. in Aug 1982, he was 73. George Kingsley first married **R. Gretchen NELSON.** In Jul 1937 when George Kingsley was 28, he second married **Mildred ARMSTRONG**, in Reno, Nev. Born on 26 Jul 1909 in Minneapolis, Minn.

They had one child:

   3919   i.   Susan

3749. ? BIRGE.

3750. ? BIRGE.

3751. Norma Jean HILL.[837] Born on 9 Jun 1927.

3752. Gladys Joan HILL. Born on 26 Jun 1929.

3753. Child of Lorraine PATTERSON.

3754. Child of Lorraine PATTERSON.

3755. Child of Lorraine PATTERSON.

3756. Child of Lorraine PATTERSON.

3757. Child of Melvyn HILL.

3758. Child of Melvyn HILL.

3759. Child of Melvyn HILL.

_____[838]

3760. Howard Eugene [215] HILL,[839] son of William Benjamin and Blanche (Washburn) Hill, and first of the twenty-one grandchildren of George J. and Jessie (Fidelia) Stockwell Hill, was born at Cedar Falls, Black Hawk County, Iowa, 1 July 1909; died at Bettendorf, Scott County, Iowa, 23 June 1983. He graduated from the lab high school on the Iowa State Teachers College campus and attended Iowa State University for one year. He was a SeaBee in the U.S. Navy in World War II, stationed in the Philippines and the Fiji Island. After the war, he was employed in the B & H Coal Service and at the B & H Appliance Store, and he was a truck driver for Ruan Transport. He was a 32nd degree Mason and was a member of the American Legion, the V.F.W., the A.A.R.P., and the Diabetic Association.

He married, at Humboldt, Humboldt County, Iowa, 22 March 1941, when he was 31 and she was 34, **Leone Pauline MUNSON**,[840] daughter of Richard Otney and Ada Louise (Rollins) Munson; born at

Humboldt, Iowa, 2 January 1907. Her paternal grandparents were Jonas and Laura (Wetmore) Munson, and her maternal grandparents were Sceva E. and Ella Pauline (Cadett) Rollins. She graduated from Humboldt Public Schools in 1927, and she then attended Iowa State Teachers College, Cedar Falls, from which she received a two year certificate. She also attended additional classes there and at Marycrest and St. Ambrose Colleges in Davenport, Iowa. She was a teacher in country schools in Laurel, Gaza, and Bettendorf, Iowa. She enjoyed reading, watching the Chicago Cubs on television, and work with the church. She was originally a member of the Congregational Church, and became a Presbyterian when she moved to Bettendorf.

They had the following children:

3920	i.	Barbara Jo (1943-)
3921	ii.	Sally Rae (1946-)
3922	iii.	Craig Eugene (1950-)

3761. Paul Francis [216] HILL,[841] second son of William Benjamin and Blanche (Washburn) Hill, was born at Clarion, Iowa, 3 February 1911, and christened in the Congregational Church there on 10 November 1915; died at Littleton, Colorado, 18 April 1997, age 86. His parents lived in Cedar Falls, Iowa, where his father had been a teacher and owned a dray line business. Paul and his five brothers and sisters grew up in Cedar Falls and he attended grade school and high school there. His father died when Paul was 13, so early in life he learned how to save and work for the future. In 1934 he received the B.A. degree from the University of Northern Iowa in Cedar Falls.

For the next five years he taught science and driver education in the public schools of Nora Springs, Tipton, and Des Moines, Iowa. He also took courses in school administration and psychology in the summer at Iowa State College and the University of Iowa. In 1939 the Governor of Iowa appointed him Director of the Iowa State Highway Safety Program, and he served in this position for four years. He was a passionate teacher of safe driving, which he taught by precept ("Keep both hands on the wheel") and by example. In 1943 he was commissioned as a Lieutenant, junior grade, in the U.S. Navy and was called to active duty. He served on the destroyer *USS U. M. Moore* in the Atlantic fleet in 1944, and as educational planning officer and training program director at the U.S. Naval Base, Great Lakes, Ill.

Following his discharge from the Navy, Mr. Hill was appointed Field Representative for the National Safety Council in Chicago. He rose through the ranks during the next 30 years, becoming Manager of all Field Operations by 1955 and Assistant General Manager in 1961. His career culminated with his appointment as Executive Assistant to the President of the National Safety Council from 1974-1976. He retired in 1976, having also served as Consultant to the President's Committee for Traffic Safety, the Council of State Governments, and the American College of Surgeons.

Following retirement from the National Safety Council in 1976, Mr. Hill and his wife moved to Huntington Beach, CA, where he was active in community affairs. In 1983 he and his wife moved to Castle Rock, Colorado, where he continued his activity in community affairs, serving on the Downtown Improvement Committee, the Douglas County Council on Aging, and the city's Parks and Recreation Commission. He was appointed by six successive Mayors to serve as the town representative for the Seniors at the Castle Rock Senior Center. When he died at the age of eighty-six, he was survived by his wife, a sister (Ruth Bowerman), his son and daughter, five grandchildren, three step-grandchildren, and one great-grandson. He was cremated and memorial services were held on 24 April 1994 at the First United Methodist Church, Castle Rock, Colorado.

He married, at Tipton, Iowa, 12 June 1937, when he was 26 and she was 25, **Marie Margaret JOHNSON,**[842] daughter of Fred and Rose (Desmond) Johnson; born at Sioux City, Iowa, 15 January 1912, and christened in the Lutheran Church. She grew up with her grandparents and their daughter, her Aunt Effie, in Alta, Iowa. She graduated from the Alta Consolidated High School in 1931. She then took care of her grandparents for a year, following which she attended Iowa State College. She received the B.S. in Home Economics Education from Iowa State College in June 1935. She taught homemaking to junior high school students in Tipton, Iowa, for the next two years. After Marie was married she became a homemaker herself, and a mother. She was a participant in her children's school activities and Boy Scout and Girl Scout programs. She worked with the United Fund in Wilmette, Illinois, and was active throughout her life in work with the church and the P.E.O. sisterhood. In 1994 she was continuing volunteer work on her church newsletter, her P.E.O. chapter activities, and with Senior Friends. She died in 2000 at the age of eighty-eight. Memorial services were held at the First United Methodist Church in Castle Rock, Colo., on 26 August 2000. She was interred in the Cedar Hill Cemetery in Castle Rock. They had the following children:

3923	i.	Sharon Jean (1939-)
3924	ii.	James William (1940-)

3762. Leola Grace [217] HILL. Born on 8 Aug 1913 in Cedar Falls, Black Hawk Co., IA; died in Cedar Falls, Black Hawk Co., IA on 14 Feb 1983, she was 69. Buried on 17 Feb 1983 in Cedar Falls, Black Hawk Co., IA. She was a ring bearer at the wedding of her aunt Ruby Hill, 27 Aug 1919. On 10 Jun 1933 when Leola Grace [217] was 19, she first married **Robert C. JUHL**, in Cedar Falls, Black Hawk Co., IA. Born on 25 Aug 1912 in Cedar Falls, IA. Robert C. died in Cedar Falls, IA on 3 Nov 1958, he was 46. Buried on 6 Nov 1958 in Cedar Falls, IA. He was the son of Chris and Johanna (Jochumsen) Juhl. They had the following children:

3925	i.	Roberta Marie (1934-1934)
3926	ii.	Grace Leola (1934-1934)
3927	iii.	Richard Harold (1935-)
3928	iv.	Raymond Paul (1938-)
3929	v.	Donald Robert (1939-)
3930	vi.	Ronald Eugene (1941-)

On 17 Jun 1967 when Leola Grace [217] was 53, she second married **Russell H. BISBING**. Occupation: Was a farmer and city employee until he retired in July 1975. He then worked on small yard machines. In April 1996 he was living at Cedar Falls, Iowa.

3763. Genevieve Maude [218] HILL,[843] second daughter and fourth child of William Benjamin and Blanche (Washburn) Hill, was born at Cedar Falls, Iowa, 26 February 1916; died at Cedar Falls, 8 September 1982, age 66. She was born at the family home, and she was eight years old when her father died of a heart attack, leaving her mother with six children to raise. She had attended first grade in Clarion, Iowa, her father's home town, presumably living in the home of her paternal grandparents. She returned to Cedar Falls at age 7 and continued through school there, transferring to College Hill School for the 1923/24 school year. The family moved several times during those years, the first move being the year that she was born, when their home burned down and they moved to another house across the street.

She was married in the famous "Little Brown Church" in the nearby town of Nashua, Iowa, at the age of 22. Thereafter, she and her husband lived in Cedar Falls, where they raised their two daughters. Her husband died at age 43, when they had been married 17 years. In the last three years of his life they owned and operated Gay's Sport Shop. She worked for the F. W. Woolworth Co. at the time of her marriage, and later was a telephone operator at Iowa State Teachers College. She also worked for Enlow's Cash and Carry, a grocery store. On 23 March 1978 she was honored for 25 years of service in executive positions with the Viking Pump Company.

Genevieve Hill became a member of the Daughters of the American Revolution through her descent from Isaac Hill, who was a soldier from Connecticut. She was President of the Business Professional Women's Club of Cedar Falls, and she held many offices in the Order of the Eastern Star and Job's Daughters. She was a Charter Member and Director of the Cedar Falls Historical Society. She loved to play the piano and she and her husband had a small dance band, "The Musikings." She also played accordion and string bass, and she led Christmas carols at home, where she played the organ. She enjoyed knitting and needlework, and made many items of clothing for her daughters and grandchildren, as well as a baby sweater for every expectant mother who worked at Viking Pump for 25 years. She died of a brain tumor at the age of 66 and was buried in the Greenwood Cemetery, Cedar Falls, Iowa.

She married, at Nashua, Iowa, 23 July 1938, when she was 22 and he was 24, **Galen Rose Solomon HUMBERT,**[844] son of George Delos and Eugenia Magdalena (Maier) Humbert; born at Pewaukee, Wisconsin, 15 October 1913, and christened there on 2 November 1913; died at Waterloo, Iowa, 3 November 1956, age 43. He was buried at the Greenwood Cemetery in Cedar Falls, Ia.

He was baptized as Galen Joseph Humbert in the Catholic Church in Pewaukee; he later became a member of the Methodist Church. Mr. Humbert lived all of his life in Cedar Falls, Iowa, with his grandparents, S. B. and Addie Humbert, and his aunt, Erdene Rose. His parents visited him as often as they could, and wrote to him frequently from their home in Pewaukee. He graduated from Cedar Falls High School in 1931 and he then attended Iowa State Teachers College -- now the University of Northern Iowa. He worked as a U. S. Postal Office letter carrier for 15 years until ill health forced his early retirement. In 1954 he purchased Gay's Sport Shop in Cedar Falls and he operated that until he died two years later. He was a member of the Masonic Lodge, Knights of Pythias, the Cedar Falls Municipal Band, Chamber of Commerce, Retired Letter Carriers Association, and the El Kahir Shrine Band of Cedar Rapids, Iowa. He also enjoyed playing cards and cribbage, and he and his wife had a small dance band. They had the following children:

3931	i.	Jeanine Kay (1940-)
3932	ii.	Constance Rose (1945-)

3764. Ruth Elizabeth [219] HILL. Born on 11 Aug 1918 in Cedar Falls, Black Hawk Co., IA. Ruth Elizabeth [219] died bef Mar 1997. On 25 May 1941 when Ruth Elizabeth [219] was 22, she married **Franklin Wesley BOWERMAN**, in Michigan City, La Porte Co., IN. Born on 15 Aug 1913 in South Bend, St. Joseph Co., IN.

They had the following children:

3933	i.	Franklin Peter (1943-)
3934	ii.	Linda Lee (1946-)
3935	iii.	Benjamin (Bennie) Wayne (1949-)

3765. Charles John [220] HILL. Born on 17 May 1921 in Cedar Falls, Black Hawk Co., IA. Charles John [220] died in Michigan City, La Porte Co., IN on 11 Dec 1985, he was 64. Buried on 28 Apr 1986 in Cedar Falls, Black Hawk Co., IA. On 6 Oct 1945 when Charles John [220] was 24, he married **Beverly AUILER**. Born on 28 May 1928. Mother of 1; married (2) Cliff LOFGREN. They were divorced.

They had one child:

3936	i.	Dian Lynn (1946-)

3766. Charles Eugene [221] HILL,[845] only child of Harland and Emma (Mickelson) Hill, was born on a farm in Grant Township near Clarion, Wright Co., Iowa, 11 September 1914. He was christened in the Methodist Church in Clarion, Ia. He grew up on his parents' farm and began school in Clarion while living with his Mickelson grandparents. He then attended a rural one room school for six years, skipping third grade. He entered Clarion High School in 1927 and graduated in 1931. He then attended the University of Northern Iowa, at Cedar Falls, where he received the B.A. degree in 1935. He did graduate work for the next three summers at the University of Michigan, which awarded him the M.A. degree in 1938. He taught English and History at Iowa Falls, IA, from 1935-1937 and was Head of the Social Science Department at William Penn College, Oskaloosa, IA, from 1938-1942. He then was Dean and President of Creston, Iowa, Junior College for eleven years, 1942-1953.

In 1953 Mr. Hill was appointed Dean and President of Rochester, Minn., Junior College. During his 29 years of service there the college grew substantially in enrollment, from 220 to 3,200 students, and in size, from a single building in the city to a college with a large, wooded, campus. When he retired as President Emeritus in August 1982, it had become the Rochester Community College. The newly constructed College Theatre was named for him at its dedication on 18 May 1987.

Charles Hill enjoyed theatre and music as hobbies, and he was a tenor soloist in high school and in college. He continued singing as a soloist with the Rochester Symphony Orchestra until he was 52, in 1966. He also hosted a weekly "big band" program on the college radio station, KRPR-FM. After his retirement he travelled widely, visiting Europe four times and the Caribbean several times. He also travelled to Mexico, Central and South America, Canada, Hawaii, Alsaka, Australia, New Zealand, and the Orient. He played volleyball and golf, and collected coins and stamps. He was a volunteer with the United Way, the Red Cross, the Chamber of Commerce, the YMCA and the Boy Scouts. He was a member of the Senior Citizens Board, and he was an Honorary Member of the 4-H Club. He had a 52 year record of perfect attendance in Kiwanis, which he joined in 1944. In May 1999 he was awarded a plaque and medal to recognize his selection by the Kiwanis International organization as a George F. Hixon Fellow, in recognition of his service, strength of character, and community vision.

He married (1), at Clarion, Iowa, 2 September 1939, when he was 24 and she was 25, **Amy AUSTIN**,[846] daughter of Roland S. and Grace (Barnard) Austin; born at Clarion, 13 February 1914; died at Rochester, 16 September 1974. She attended Clarion Public Schools from kindergarten through the 12th grade and graduated from Clarion High School in 1932. She then attended the University of Northern Iowa, from which she graduated in 1936 with a B.A. in Kindergarten - Nursery School education. She later did advanced study (Reading Specialist) at the University of Minnesota. Amy Austin managed and directed her own dance studio for children each summer for eight years while attending high school and college. She taught kindergarten at Manilla, Iowa, from 1936-1938 and at Hampton, Iowa from 1938-1939, the year in which she was married. After raising her children, she resumed her career as a kindergarten teacher at Rochester, Minnesota, from 1965-1970. She was an Elementary Reading Specialist at Rochester from 1970-1974. She enjoyed reading, sewing, camping, music and ballroom dancing, and she was active as a volunteer with her church and schools, with the YWCA and the Girls Scouts. She travelled with her husband to Hawaii, the Bahamas and Canada. Charles and Amy (Austin) Hill had three children. Her daughters married and had children.

Amy was profoundly affected by the death of her eldest child, Charles ("Chuck"), who was shot and killed by a robber in 1969. She died of heart failure five years later, when she was 60.

Charles and Amy (Austin) Hill had the following children:

3937	i.	Charles Austin "Chuck" (1940-1969)
3938	ii.	Marcella Ann "Sally" (1942-)
3939	iii.	Rebecca Elizabeth "Becky" (1950-)

Following the death of Amy, Charles married (2) **Rose DANZER**, who died of a heart attack in 1987 in the tenth year of their marriage. He then married (3), on 6 November 1987, when he was 73 and she was 72, **Mrs. Helen (JOHNSON) JANES**; born in 1915. There was no issue from the second and third marriages.

3767. Velda Mae [222] HILL,[847] eldest child of Leroy George and Luretta (Sellers) Hill, was born at Clarion, Wright County, Iowa, 9 September 1909; died at Shell Rock, Iowa, 7 May 1996, age 86. She grew up on her parents' farm until she was married at age nineteen. Her parents and her two brothers and two sisters moved eighty miles east, to Sumner, Iowa, in 1930, but Velda and her husband made their home near Clarion until 1937. Her first four children were born at Clarion between 1930 and 1937. Another son died in infancy. Her sixth child was born seventeen years later in Mason City, when she was forty-seven.

In 1937 the family moved to a farm near Britt, Iowa, where they lived until 1952, at which time they moved to the Belmond, Iowa, area. In 1954 they moved to a farm near Sumner. In 1967 they retired from farming and were employed by Travelodge Motels in several locations until they retired again and moved to Shell Rock, southeast of Mason City. Her husband died in 1984. She was active with the Shell Rock Methodist Church and was a 50-Year Member of Zora Rebekah Lodge #189 in Shell Rock. Her last three years were spent as a resident of the Shell Rock Care Center. She was the oldest surviving grandchild of George and Jessie (Stockwell) hill when she died in 1996 at the age of eighty-six.

Velda Mae (Hill) Knoedler was survived by three children, Beth, Lurretta, and Keith, and their spouses; two sisters, Minnie and Lavonne; her brother Marion; eighteen grandchildren; thirty-six great-grandchildren; and one great-greatgrandson. She was preceded in death by her husband and three sons: Elmer, Jr.; John L.; and an infant son. Services were held on 11 May 1996 at the United Methodist Church in Shell Rock, led by Pastor Julie Poore Christensen. The Zora Rebekah Lodge of Shell Rock conducted the Rebekah Service, and burial was at the Evergreen Cemetery, Clarion, Iowa.

She married in the Little Brown Church at Nashua, Iowa, 29 June 1929, when she was 19 and he was about 22, **Elmer Laurel KNOEDLER**,[848] Senior; born at Des Moines, Iowa, about April 1907; died at Waterloo, Iowa, 17 July 1984. He was a farmer and motel manager. Elmer and Velda Mae (Hill) Knoedler had six children, born in Iowa. Five of the children married and had families of their own. They had the following children:

3940	i.	Elmer Laurel (1930-1987)
3941	ii.	John LeRoy (1935-1995)
3942	iii.	Beth Charlene (1936-)
3943	iv.	Keith Maurice (1937-2008)
3944	v.	[Infant son]
3945	vi.	Lurretta (1954-)

3768. Max Leroy [223] HILL,[849] son and second child of Leroy George and Luretta Lena (Sellers) Hill, was born at Clarion, Iowa, 13 January 1913; died at Sumner, Iowa, 30 April 1990, age 77. He attended the Clarion Schools and graduated from Clarion High School in 1930. In the same year he moved with his parents to Sumner and was baptized and confirmed at the Sumner Methodist Church. Initially Mr. Hill worked for the Sumner Municipal Light Plant as a member of the construction crew that paved Highway 93. He then was employed for 33 years by the Butler County Rural Electric Cooperative, from 1943 until he retired in January 1976. He began as a lineman and in later years was in public relations for the REC. During his many years of residence in Sumner, Mr. Hill was a member of the Lions Club and he served on the Sumner City Council. He was also a certified Red Cross instructor. For more than 17 years he was a volunteer and board member of the Hillcrest Home at Sumner, where his father had been a resident for nine years, and his wife's mother, too, had been a resident. He was serving in his thirteenth year as president of the board of Hillcrest Home, and was preparing to host the open house to celebrate its twenty-fifth anniversary, when he suddenly became ill and died shortly thereafter at the Sumner Community Memorial Hospital. He was then 77 years old. The Hillcrest Administrator said of him, "We will all miss Max so much. He was always very concerned about the residents and staff in addition to the operation of the home. His pleasant smile and encouraging comments will never be forgotten."

He married, 2 April 1939, when he was 26 and she was 28, at Sumner, **Mildred CREAGER**, daughter of Warren Oscar Creager; born at Sumner, 10 July 1911. She was a rural school teacher. Max and Mildred (Creager) Hill had two children, born at Sumner, both of whom married and had children. At the time of his death, Max and Mildred had five grandchildren. Mildred returned with her friend Elston Bloom to the Hill Family reunion at Clarion in August 1994. Her middle initial was given on her questionnaire at the Hill reunion in 1997.

Max and Mildred (Creager) Hill had the following children:

3946	i.	Donald Eugene (1939-)
3947	ii.	Steve Clar (1951-)

3769. Marion Carson [224] HILL.[850] Born on 7 Aug 1915 in Clarion, Wright Co., IA. She was of Orlando, Fla., in 1994, when she attended the Hill Reunion. On 3 Sep 1939 when Marion Carson [224] was 24, he married **Geraldine GAMM**, in Sumner, IA. Born on 10 Jun 1920 in Waverly, Ia. Geraldine died in Orlando, Fla. on 30 Mar 1990, she was 69.

They had the following children:

3948	i.	Mary Ann (1941-)
3949	ii.	Carol L. (1943-)
3950	iii.	Janice (1945-)
3951	iv.	Judy (1946-)

3770. La Vonne Ilene [225] "Bonnie" HILL. Born on 13 Jul 1919 in Clarion, Wright Co., IA. Occupation: Mother of 3; of Cornville, AZ, in 1990. Left Sumner, Ia., High School as a junior in 1936. On 25 Nov 1937 when La Vonne Ilene [225] "Bonnie" was 18, she married **Paul Arthur TRELOAR**, in Sumner, IA. Born on 27 Apr 1915 in Sumner, Bremer Co., Ia.

They had the following children:

3952	i.	Michael LeRoy (1938-)
3953	ii.	Nancy Lee (1942-)
3954	iii.	Sharon Jean (1954-)

3771. Minnie Marie HILL.[851] Born on 15 Oct 1921 in Clarion, Wright Co., Iowa. Minnie Marie died in Postville, Iowa on 27 Nov 2006, she was 85. Buried in 2006 in Arlington, Iowa. Occupation: Mother of 7. Earl Blue was her friend for many years. She was living in Arlington, Iowa, in 1990, and she still lived there in 1997. On 30 Sep 1943 when Minnie Marie was 21, she married **Dale WESTON**, in Sumner, IA. Born on 29 Nov 1918. Dale died in Sumner, Bremer Co., Ia. on 13 Feb 1970, he was 51.

They had the following children:

3955	i.	Norma Jean (1945-)
3956	ii.	Ardith Elaine (1947-)
3957	iii.	Janet Marie (1949-)
3958	iv.	Dawn Delight (1951-)
3959	v.	Charlotte Ann (1954-)
3960	vi.	Roger Dale (Twin) (1961-)
3961	vii.	Rose Mary (Twin) (1961-)

3772. Dale E. [226] HILL,[852] eldest child of Myron Emery and Julia Lydia (Woodin) Hill, was born at Clarion, Wright County, Iowa, 10 March 1912; died at Clarion, 11 September 1994, age 82. His great-grandfather Charles W. Hill was a pioneer settler in Wright County. A portion of the original homestead passed down to him and is still farmed by his children. Mr. Hill graduated from Clarion High School in 1929 and then attended Cornell College, Mt. Vernon, Iowa. While at Cornell, he was a member of Delta Phi Rho and the varsity wrestling team. He received the "C" Club award at Cornell for being the varsity athlete with the best overall academic record. He received the B.A. degree from Cornell in 1935.

Mr. Hill returned to Clarion to join his father in farming and raised his family there. He farmed in Grant Township until 1972 when he moved to Clarion. In his middle years he was afflicted by rare neurological illnesses which led to increasing disability, but he maintained the calm demeanor which had characterized him throughout his youth. He was initially diagnosed as having a herniated intervertebral disc of the thoracic spine, and at the age of 44 he was operated on at the Mayo Clinic for spinal stenosis. He subsequently developed Parkinson's disease. After total care at home for more than five years, in May 1991 he entered the Extended Care Ward of the Community Memorial Hospital at Clarion, where he died three years later at the age of 82.

Mr. Hill was active in the Methodist Church, where he held many offices, was a lay leader, and taught an adult Sunday School class for many years. He belonged to the Masonic Lodge and was on the REA Board for many years. Mr. Hill's ownership of the farm that had been in his family for 100 years was recognized by the Iowa Farm Bureau Federation and the Iowa State Secretary of Agriculture in 1977 with the Century Farm Marker and Certificate.

He married, at the First Methodist Church, Des Moines, Iowa, 18 September 1939, when he was 27 and she was 26, **Avis E. BOYINGTON**,[853] daughter of Chester Daniel (aka John) and Harriet (Campbell) Boyington; born at Galt, Wright County, Iowa, 8 September 1913; died at Clarion, Iowa, 31 March 2008, and buried there on 2 April 2008. Avis (Boyington) Hill was raised in Wright County, where her grandparents had been pioneer settlers in the middle years of the previous century. Her parents moved to Clarion in 1918 with Avis, her two brothers and her sister. In 1931 she graduated with honors from Clarion High School. Avis Boyington began working in a law office in 1931. When a member of the law firm was elected State Senator, she went to the legislature to work as a committee clerk and secretary in the Senate for several sessions. She later worked for the State Board of Social Welfare in Des Moines. While so employed she enrolled at the Des Moines College of Law, which later merged with the Drake University Law School. She attended law classes at night school for three years. However, she interrupted her education to be married and raise a family. She then devoted her life to her growing family and to her share of work on the farm that her husband worked with his father and mother.

Avis and her husband farmed the farm of his parents for many years, until his disability from neurological illnesses made it necessary to turn the management of the farm over to the next generation. In 1973 they moved to a house in Clarion. In 1994 Avis sold their home and moved to an apartment in "The Meadows"; her husband had his own room in the adjacent community hospital building.

Avis was an active member of the First Methodist Church of Clarion, in which she held many offices, including serving as President of the U.M.W., Superintendant of the Sunday School, and Sunday School teacher for 11 years. She also served on the Auxiliary of the Clarion Memorial Hospital and was a member of the P.E.O. sisterhood. Throughout her life Avis Boyington Hill carefully kept and catalogued the pictures, letters and other documents about her family and her husband's family. These files and albums were a priceless source for of information about the contemporary members of the Hill family and their in-laws, which she readily shared with all who were interested in family history. She was a member of the Daughters of the American Revolution, and as a member of the Genealogy Society she helped many others to trace their lineage to emigrant ancestors. She was one of the principal organizers of the reunion that brought 108 members of the extended Hill family together in Clarion in July 1994.

After a long illness, she died on 31 March 2008 at the Wright Medical Center, Clarion, Iowa. Funeral services were held at the United Methodist Church in Clarion and she was buried in the Evergreen Cemetery in Clarion.

They had the following children:

3962	i.	Steven Dale (1941-)
3963	ii.	Mark Lynn (1943-)
3964	iii.	Douglas Ray (1947-)

3773. Myron Emery HILL Jr.,[854] second son of Myron and Julia (Woodin) Hill, was born at Clarion, Iowa, 31 August 1927. He was the son, grandson and great-grandson of pioneer farmers in Wright County, Iowa. He continued this tradition by developing his own farm near Clarion, a few miles from where he grew up. His principal crops were corn, soybeans, and hogs. The potential hazards of farm life were vividly illustrated by a barn cat's sudden attack one day on his wife and daughter. The cat had to be killed to disengage it. Laboratory tests later revealed that the cat was rabid and the family was immediately treated with rabies vaccine. Fortunately, none developed rabies.

In 1994 Myron and his wife were living on their farm near Clarion. They had reduced somewhat the acreage that they personally worked, to about 250 acres, and they no longer had any livestock. The trees that they had planted were now tall, and the house that they had built was snug and comfortable. They celebrated their 45th wedding anniversary in October 1994 and enjoyed visits from their children and grandchildren at Thanksgiving. Two of their grandchildren were in college in 1994.

He married, at Spencer, Iowa, 9 October 1949, when he was 22 and she was 20, **Dorla Dean BENSON**, daughter of Louis and Thelma (Brannon) Benson; born at Clarion, 6 October 1929. Myron, Jr., and Dorla (Benson) Hill had five children. Larry was a "blue baby," with a rare type of congenital heart disease. He was helped by palliative surgery at the Mayo Clinic and enjoyed a happy childhood, but he succumbed to his heart disease while in high school. The three daughters married and had children. Kay's second daughter Amber, b. 1981, was married in the spring of 2001 and had twin sons on 22 October 2001; the twins were Myron and Dorla's first great-grandchildren.

They had the following children:

3965	i.	Kay Marie (1951-)
3966	ii.	Willow (b. Cindy Lou) (1954-)
3967	iii.	Michael Dean (1956-1956)
3968	iv.	Julie Lyn (1957-)
3969	v.	Larry Dean (1960-1977)

3774. Lela Esther HILL,[855] daughter and third child of Myron Emery and Julia Lydia (Woodin) Hill, was born at Clarion, Iowa, 27 July 1930. Lela was the granddaughter and great-granddaughter of pioneer Iowa farmers. She grew up on her parents' farm near Clarion and attended the nearby rural school. After graduating from Clarion High School, she attended Iowa State Teachers College in Cedar Falls, now the University of Northern Iowa, from which she received the bachelor's degree in business education. She was a member of the Pi Theta Pi social sorority and the honorary business fraternity, Pi Omega Pi. After graduation she taught business courses at Lohrville and Renwick, Iowa.

Five days after her 23rd birthday she married a young man from a neighboring family. They began to farm near Clarion and to raise a family. All four of their children graduated from college, married and had children. Lela has been active in service to her community and her church. She served on the Clarion School Board for six years and was a member of the Clarion School's Philosophy Committee. She was a member of the Music Boosters board and did volunteer tutoring of students. She also served on the Wright County Extension Council and was a 4-H leader. For many years she was a

Lake Township Election Officer. She has been very active in the Holmes, Iowa, Lutheran Church. She has been a Sunday School teacher, Bible School teacher, Choir Director and pianist, and has held all of the Circle offices at various times. She served as a delegate to the church convention for several years. She has also been a member of the Oakridge Recreation Club, which she served as Secretary and Treasurer of the Women's Board. Lela and her sisters-in-law, Avis Hill and Dorla Hill, were instrumental in bringing 108 members of the extended Hill family together in Clarion for a reunion in July 1994. Four generations of the descendants of George and Jessie Hill and of George Hill's sister, Adella, were represented.

She married, at Clarion, 1 August 1953, when she was 23 and he was 27, **Earl Stenson ("Bud") ODLAND**,[856] son of Earl and Clara (Stenson) Odland; born at Clarion, 23 April 1926. "Bud" Odland grew up on his parents' farm and attended public schools in Wright County. He served in the U.S. Navy in World War II as a WT 3/C (APA) from 1944-1946, and saw both of the American flags raised on Iwo Jima. Earl Odland was a descendant of Lutheran farmers who emigrated to Iowa from Norway. His Odland ancestors have been traced back in the same farming community in Norway for many generations. The Odland and Stenson family homes in Norway are now maintained as museums, and Earl and Lela visited them in 1988. The Odland name is derived from the Norse word for "God," or a principal deity, such as the god of fish, and the word "land"; i.e., "God's land."

The Odlands farmed land in Wright County, Iowa, that was originally only marginally productive. Their fields had been considered risky for planting because there was little natural drainage and pools of water were often standing on them. It was hard and intensive work, but many miles of drainage pipe were placed deep under the topsoil, which were then connected to drainage ditches. The land thus became both productive and valuable. By 1994 the Odlands had for many years specialized in growing corn, soybeans and hogs, with considerable success. Earl Odland has served for more than 30 years on the Holmes, Iowa, Elevator Board, and he has also served on the Wright County Extension Council. He has been active in the Holmes Lutheran Church, as Deacon, Trustee, Secretary, Sunday School teacher, and he was a member of the Building Committee for the new church building. They had the following children:

3970	i.	David Earl "Dave" (1954-)
3971	ii.	Laura Lee (1956-)
3972	iii.	Lisa Ann (1960-)
3973	iv.	Daniel Eugene (1964-)

3775. John Howard "Woody" WOODIN, C.L.U.,[857] only son and eldest child of Howard Henry and Ruby Adella (Hill) Woodin, was born at Belmond, Wright County, Iowa, 21 July 1924, and he was christened in the Methodist Church in Clarion, Iowa. He lived on his parents' farm and went to country school until he entered Clarion High School, from which he graduated in 1942. He matriculated at Cornell College, but left during World War II to accept a commission as an officer in the Supply Corps, U.S. Navy Reserve. He was assigned to the Harvard Business School for two terms, and was eventually discharged with the rank of Lieutenant, SC, USNR. He resumed his studies at Cornell after the war and received the B.A. degree. Following his marriage in 1948, Mr. Woodin moved to Milwaukee and entered the insurance business. He achieved considerable success as an insurance salesman, and was repeatedly recognized with the annual Million Dollar Sales Award. He became a Certified Life Underwriter and was an insurance advisor and investment consultant. He was elected President of the Milwaukee Association of Life Underwriters and was active with the National Association of Life Underwriters. He was also an active member of the Methodist Church, the Harvard Business School Alumni Association and the Acacia Fraternity alumni. Mr. Woodin was a skillful participant in the sport of curling and traveled with his wife on curling trips to many cities in the United States and Europe. He was a member of the International Curling Federation Board in 1990.

He married, at Chicago, 20 March 1948, when he was 23 and she was 20, **Betti Lorraine GRAY**, daughter of John Samuel and Bernice (Foutt) Gray; born at Chicago, 8 November 1927; died in Wisconsin in June 2009, age 81. Betti Woodin developed the Epstein-Barr Virus syndrome in the late 1980s. She learned to live with this disability and continued to serve in the Methodist Church and to enjoy her social activities, bridge and travel with her husband.

John and Betti (Gray) Woodin had two children, born at Milwaukee. Both children remained in Milwaukee, married and had children of their own. Scott joined his father in the insurance business and Wendy developed a professional speakers business.

They had the following children:

3974 i. John Scott "Scott" (1950-)
3975 ii. Wendy Lee (1953-)

3776. Jessie Elizabeth WOODIN, A.S.C.P.,[858] elder daughter and second child of Howard and Ruby (Hill) Woodin, was born in a farm home near Belmond, Wright County, Iowa, 24 June 1927. She began her formal education at a rural school in Grant Township, Wright County, which she attended for eight years, from 1933-1941. She then attended Clarion, Iowa, High School, from which she graduated in 1945. Her father died at the age of 50 in 1942 and her mother moved to Clarion, the county seat of Wright County, to raise her three children. Jessie Woodin attended Cornell College in Mount Vernon, Iowa, and graduated with the B.A. degree in 1950. She studied laboratory technology at St. Lukes Hospital, Cedar Rapids, Iowa, from 1949-1950 and was certified thereafter as A.S.C.P. She later received a B.A. in accounting from the University of Miami, Miami, Florida. She became a laboratory technologist at the Jackson Memorial Hospital and the University of Miami School of Medicine. During her career of 33 years there she rose to the position of chief technologist in the hematology research laboratory and was a Research Assistant Professor of Medicine.

She married, at Clarion, Iowa, 5 October 1952, when she was 24 and he was 25, **Kenneth Ronald KENT,**[859] younger son of Andrew and Grace (Allen) Kent; born at Monmouth, Iowa, 4 May 1927. He was her classmate at Cornell and the University of Miami, and was employed by Eastern Airlines for many years. Ken Kent attended the Grand Mound, Iowa, schools beginning with the first grade in 1932, and he graduated from high school there in 1944. He then spent two years in the U.S. Navy, where he was in the submarine service. After release from the Navy he attended Clinton, IA, Junior College for two years, 1946-1948, and then Cornell College, Mt. Vernon, Iowa, from which he received the B.A. degree in 1950. He later received a B.A. in accounting from the University of Miami, Miami, Florida. Mr. Kent was employed by Eastern Airlines for 25 years in sales and corporate finance, until he retired. He was later employed in the human relations department of Renaissance Cruise Lines, Fort Lauderdale, Florida. He enjoyed golf, gardening and travel.

Jessie and Kenneth Kent lived in a house in Miami, Florida, for forty years, and in 1997 they moved to a townhouse in Pembroke Pines, Florida. They were then spending as much time as possible at their country home in North Carolina. They enjoyed travelling and had a summer home in Beech Mountain, North Carolina. Her activities included herb gardening, gourmet cooking, and golf, and she was a volunteer with the American Heart Association and the American Business Women (ABWA).

3777. Mildred Eileen WOODIN,[860] second daughter and third child of Howard and Ruby (Hill) Woodin, was born at Clarion, Iowa, 1 November 1932; died at Clarion, 30 October 1997, and was buried there on 1 November 1997. As a very young child she was recognized to have severe brain damage, which her older sister, a nationally-recognized medical technologist, believed was probably due to Downs' syndrome or measles in infancy. Mildred lived with her widowed mother, who taught her to read and write simple words, and she enjoyed music and conversation with members of the family, who loved her. She always remained small in stature, and spoke in a shy, quiet voice. In 1991, when she was 59 and her mother was 89, they moved into a nursing home adjacent to the hospital in Clarion. Mildred died there two years after her mother died.

3778. Edward Eugene HEMENWAY,[861] only child of Edward Michael and Adelia Emma (Hill) Hemenway, was born at Hampton, Iowa, 30 May 1927; died at Milwaukee, Wisconsin, 29 March 1993, and was buried on 1 April 1993 at new Berlin, Waukesha Co., Wisc. As a young man, he served with the 3505th U.S. Army Air Force Battalion from May 1944 until May 1946. He earned a Master's degree and had 30 hours of additional credit in graduate school. He was a teacher in Des Moines, Williams, Correctionville, and Perry, Iowa, and at Wauwatosa, Wisconsin. He was also on the staff at the University of Northern Iowa at Cedar Falls for two years. Following retirement he lived in New Berlin, Wisconsin.

In his sixties, he developed progressive intractable heart failure. He died in Milwaukee while awaiting a heart transplant operation, and was buried at New Berlin.

He married, at Primghar, O'Brien Co., Iowa, 9 June 1950, when he was 23 and she was 22, **Agnes Arlene BEAL**, daughter of Arlie A. and Pearl L. (Locke) Beal; born at Bedford, Iowa, 20 November 1927. His wife was a part time teacher. Following Edward's death, Agnes continued to be active in Methodist Church work, and in 1999 she had served for four years as a Chairperson of Missions. She was then also the Chairperson of District United Methodist Women for Social Action. She had been guardian conservator for her aunt Bernita Beal since 1996. Edward and Agnes (Beal) Hemenway had three children:

They had the following children:

3976	i.	Patti Jean (1955-)
3977	ii.	Rhonda Arlene (1958-)
3978	iii.	Michelle Ann (1971-)

3779. George James HILL, M.D., D.Litt.,[862] elder son of Gerald Leslie and Essie Mae (Thompson) Hill, was born at Cedar Rapids, Iowa, 7 October 1932. He was baptized at the Methodist Episcopal Church, Mount Vernon, Iowa, in 1932, and he was accepted into membership in the Methodist Episcopal Church, Lisbon, Iowa, in 1944. He later became an Episcopalian. He attended public schools in Lisbon, Mount Vernon, and Perry, Iowa, and he graduated from Sac City, Ia., High School in 1949. He has earned the degrees of A.B. (Yale), M.D. (Harvard), M.A. (Rutgers), and D.Litt. (Drew). After a career in surgery for forty years, he retired as Professor of Surgery Emeritus, New Jersey Medical School, University of Medicine and Dentistry of New Jersey. He is also a retired Captain, Medical Corps, U.S. Navy Reserve. With the help of many others, he was the compiler of the Hill genealogy and is the author of this book.

He married, as her second husband, at Amagansett, New York, 16 July 1960, when he was 28 and she was 31, **Helene ZIMMERMANN**,[863] daughter of Albert Walter and Barbara (Shoemaker) Zimmermann; she was born at Philadelphia, Pennsylvania, 10 April 1929. Helene Zimmermann's father was a member of the family of carpet manufacturers, John Zimmermann & Sons, and he was later a partner in the firm of Ott and Zimmermann, wool brokers. She attended the Baldwin School, Bryn Mawr, Pa., through the tenth grade, and then the Chatham Hall School, Chatham, Va., from which she graduated in 1946. She studied at Smith College from 1946-50, majoring in premedical studies and French, taking her junior year abroad in Paris. She graduated with the B.A. degree in 1950. She earned the Ph.D. at Brandeis in 1964. She was appointed Professor of Radiology at the UMDNJ-New Jersey Medical School, Newark, NJ, in 1981, and was additionally appointed Professor of Microbiology and Molecular Genetics, and Professor of Biochemistry and Molecular Biology. Her honors include the Smith College Medal and the Lifetime Achievement Award from the Baldwin School.

Helene Zimmermann married (1), at Bryn Mawr, Pennsylvania, 3 May 1952, James Hedgcock GROVER, Esq., son of Charles and Mary (Hedgcock) Grover; born at Boston, Massachusetts, 1917; died in New Hampshire, 1 May 2010. He was a graduate of Harvard College (SB '40) and Boston University Law School; he was an attorney in Boston and later in Sharon, Massachusetts. They were divorced at Montgomery, Alabama, in May 1960 and he married (2) Carol McKinnon; died 1995; they had a daughter, Robin Lee Grover.

George James and Helene (Zimmermann) Hill had two daughters. In 1964 he legally adopted his wife's two sons by her first marriage.

George and Helene (Zimmermann) Hill had the following children:

3979	i.	James Warren "Jim" (1954-)
3980	ii.	David Hedgcock "Dave" (1955-2004)
3981	iii.	Sarah (1962-)
3982	iv.	Helena Rundall "Lana" (1964-)

3780. Thomas David "Tom" HILL Sr., Ph.D.,[864] younger son of Gerald Leslie and Essie Mae (Thompson) Hill, and youngest of the twenty-one grandchildren of George J. and Jessie Fidelia (Stockwell) Hill, was born at Cedar Rapids, Iowa, 3 May 1935; died at Salem, Washington Co., N.Y., 3

July 2003. At the time of his birth, his parents lived at Mt. Vernon, Iowa, where his father was Assistant Cashier of the Mt. Vernon Bank and Trust Company. His family moved when his father accepted positions in banks throughout Iowa and South Dakota, and he attended public schools in Lisbon, Mt. Vernon, Perry, and Sac City, Ia. He graduated from high school at Sioux Falls, S.D., in 1952. He attended the University of Colorado from 1952-56 and received the B.S. in Aeronautical Engineering in 1956. He received the M.S. in Systems Engineering at the Air Force Institute of Technology at Wright-Paterson Air Force Base, Ohio, in 1965, and the Ph.D. in Industrial Engineering from the State University of New York at Buffalo in 1994.

      At his graduation from the University of Colorado he was commissioned as a Second Lieutenant in the U. S. Air Force. After working for a few months at Pratt and Whitney, Hartford, Connecticut, he was called to active duty and spent the next 21 years as an Air Force officer. He earned the Navigator's wings and was assigned to the Strategic Air Command, where he was a prize-winning navigator in the KC-135 jet refueling tanker. He was later assigned as a project engineer to assist in development of the TFX fighter-bomber, later known as the F-111, at Edwards Air Force Base, California. In 1969 he was deployed to Southeast Asia where he was an AC--119 gunship weapons systems operator, principally based at Udorn AFB, Thailand. His final tour of duty was at Andrews Air Force Base, Maryland, and the Pentagon, at which time he lived at Oxon Hill, Maryland. He received numerous decorations, including the Distinguished Flying Cross and the Air Medal with oak leaf clusters. Following retirement from the Air Force in 1977 he was employed as an Operations Researcher at Xerox Corporation, Rochester, New York. His position at Xerox was Manager, Quality Information System; he then lived at Pittsford, NY. After leaving Xerox in 1986, he moved to Buffalo, NY, and took graduate courses in mathematics and engineering, while teaching and conducting personal research. He completed his thesis in Industrial Engineering and received the Ph.D. from SUNY-Buffalo in 1994, at the age of 59. He was believed to be the oldest-ever recipient of the Ph.D. from the School of Engineering at SUNY-Buffalo. Dr. Hill became an Adjunct Professor of Mathematics in the Engineering School at SUNY-Buffalo and was regarded as a popular and skillful teacher. He was an expert on the use of the home computer, and he was a consultant for local law enforcement agencies on the subject of his thesis, "Equity Constrained Preventive Police Patrolling." He retired from teaching in 2002. He enjoyed kite building and flying, and was an avid collector of antique hand tools and other unusual collectibles at flea markets. In 2002, he and his wife, Suzanne Eppley, M.D., moved to a farm in Salem, N.Y. He died there when the tractor that he was driving rolled over.

      He married, (1) at Minot, North Dakota, 25 December 1959, when he was 24 and she was 31, **Keiko NAMBARA**,[865] daughter of Professor Shigeru Nambara and his second wife, Hiroko Nishakawa; born at Tokyo, Japan, 12 November 1928; died at Tokyo, 21 July 1977, of complications of cancer of the maxillary sinus. Her father was President Emeritus of Tokyo University and was the spiritual leader of the non-church indigenous Christian movement in Japan. He was a friend and counselor to many notable world leaders, including Dwight D. Eisenhower -- who was President of Columbia University at that time -- and Emperor Hirohito. Keiko graduated from Joshi Gakuin School in Tokyo and then attended Tokyo Women's Christian College, from which she received the B.A. degree in 1950. She then came to the United States and studied music on a scholarship at St. Olaf College in Northfield, Minnesota, where she received the B.A. in 1955. She did graduate work at the University of Minnesota, and received the M.A. in 1957. She then returned to Japan and began a career as a teacher of industrial relations at St. Paul's Episcopal University in Tokyo, while continuing to study to be a concert pianist.

      By chance in 1959 she met Lieutenant Thomas D. Hill, then a young U.S. Air Force officer who was touring Japan on vacation, and they were married in North Dakota, where he was stationed. As an Air Force officer's wife, she lived in Minot, ND, Wright Paterson Air Force Base, OH, Edwards Air Force Base, CA, and in Oxon Hill, MD, when her husband was working at Andrews Air Force Base and the Pentagon. She continued to study music, to teach, and to paint, and she devoted her many skills to the education of her two children. She was a member of the American Association of Piano Teachers.

      In 1970 she developed cancer of the maxillary sinus, which required extensive surgery to the face and neck, and radiation therapy. Although her cancer was controlled she was left with severe pain and a disfiguring condition from which she never fully recovered. She passed away on a visit home to her family in Japan. Following a funeral service at the Mejiro Episcopal Church and other traditional ceremonies, her ashes were divided; part were interred in a family cemetery near Tokyo, and the remainder were interred in the graveyard of her Episcopal parish church at Oxon Hill, MD. Thomas and Keiko (Nambara) Hill had two children, born at Minot, N.D. Thomas Hill Jr. has a son, Conor Sheehy. Thomas D. and Keiko (Nambara) Hill had the following children:

3983 i. Victoria Grace (1960-)
3984 ii. Thomas David "Tom" (1962-)

Following the death of Keiko, Thomas Hill married (2), at Ridgewood, New Jersey, 29 November 1986, when he was 51 and she was 39, **Suzanne Margaret EPPLEY, M.D.,**[866] daughter of Thomas Joseph and Catherine (Alles) Eppley; born at New Rochelle, New York, 7 October 1947. Dr. Eppley was a graduate of Hunter College of the City University of New York (B.A., 1974) and Tufts University School of Medicine (M.D., 1979). She was Associate Head of the Department of Family Practice of the Health Care Plan of Buffalo, N.Y., until she retired in 2002. While living in Salem, N.Y., she resumed her practice in Washington County, N.Y.

3781. Maxine Bernice [227] LINDSAY.[867] Born on 17 Oct 1910 in Wright Co., IA. Maxine Bernice [227] died on 27 Feb 1982, she was 71. Buried in Vinton, IA (Clark Creek Cemetery [rural]). On 17 Aug 1932 when Maxine Bernice [227] was 21, she married **Clark W. LONG.**

They had the following children:

3985 i. Mildred (1935-)
3986 ii. James (1939-)
3987 iii. Wayne (1942-)
3988 iv. Helen (1947-)

3782. James Edwin [228] LINDSAY.[868] Born on 17 May 1914 in Wright Co., IA. James Edwin [228] died in Hartland, Bath township, Wright Co., IA in Oct 1964, he was 50. Buried in 1964 in Clarion, IA (Evergreen Cemetery). On 4 Jun 1937 when James Edwin [228] was 23, he married **Jeanette LYONS.** Born in 1914.

They had the following children:

3989 i. Louisa Mae (1938-)
3990 ii. Delbert (1941-)
3991 iii. Verlyn (1946-)
3992 iv. Eileen (1948-)

3783. Adella Helen [229] LINDSAY,[869] third child and second daughter of George Edwin and Bertha Mae "Mae" (Huntley) Lindsay, was born at Mora, Minnesota, 11 September 1915. She grew up in Clarion, Iowa. She was a seamstress and a Methodist churchwoman. She and her husband raised a son who married and had two children, one of whom lived to adulthood. During her life she lived in Minnesota, Iowa, Colorado, and then returned to Iowa. In 1996 she was living only a block from where her parents lived when she was born, and from the location of the barn where her father's milk cows were kept. Her recollections of her childhood, and of the stories told to her by her parents and grandparents, provide a vivid image of the family of Charles and Adelia (Riley) Hill who came to Wright County, Iowa, from New York State in the 1860s. She married, 10 March 1939, when she was 23 and he was 21, **Maurice Ray HARSON,** son of L. R. and Zelda (Stuck) Harson; born at Rowan, Wright Co., Iowa, 21 November 1917. Her husband was a carpenter and a member of the Methodist church. Maurice and Adella (Lindsay) Harson had one child, Allen Ray Harson, born at Urbana, Illinois, 18 July 1944. Maurice and Adella (Lindsay) Harson were living in Clarion, Iowa, in 1996.

They had one child:

3993 i. Allen Ray (1944-)

3784. Ronald LaVern LINDSAY,[870] second son and fourth child of George "Ed" and Bertha "Mae" (Huntley) Lindsay, was born 1 January 1918; died June 1966, age 48, and was buried at Clarion in the Evergreen Cemetery. He graduated from Clarion, Iowa, High School in 1937 and was a grain farmer and dairy barn operator in Grant Township, Wright County, for his entire life. He was a member of the

Methodist Church. He died at the age of forty-eight and was buried in the Evergreen Cemetery, Clairon, Iowa. He married, in July 1939, when he was 21 and she was 20, **Grace I. HOYT**, daughter of Everett M. and Jean A. (McCutcheon) Hoyt; born at Goldfield, Iowa, 13 December 1918. She was the mother of three, a homemaker, and a courthouse clerk.

They had the following children:

3994	i.	Donna (1942-)
3995	ii.	Russell Dean (~1947-)
3996	iii.	Edwin Everett "Ed" (1952-1994)

3785. Kenneth ROSE. Kenneth married **Natalie (ROSE).**[871]

They had at least one and probably more children:

3997	i.	"children"

3786. 5 children.

3787. Dorothy [227-A] WOLCOTT. Born on 30 Mar 1901.

3788. Stanley [228-A] WOLCOTT. Born on 12 Sep 1903.

3789. Charles Eugene [229-A] WOLCOTT. Born on 24 Feb 1920.

3790. Hazel Chapman [230] WOLCOTT. Born on 27 May 1903.

3791. Edna Mabel [231] WOLCOTT. Born on 1 Oct 1904.

3792. Orson Elvin [232] WOLCOTT. Born on 6 Jul 1906.

3793. Noble Eugene [233] WOLCOTT. Born on 24 May 1900.

3794. Lanniston [234] WOLCOTT. Born on 21 Jan 1912.

3795. Kenneth [235] WOLCOTT. Born on 18 Jun 1916.

3796. Mabel Elaine [226-A] WOLCOTT. Born on 2 Jan 1908.

3797. Flora [227-A] STASCH. Born on 3 Jul 1909.

3798. Harold [228-A] STASCH. Born on 3 May 1912.

3799. Ruth [229-A] STASCH. Born on 28 Sep 1917.

3800. Donald Lovern [227] STASCH. Born on 1 Jan 1918 in Vinton, Benton Co. A.

3801. Thelma Rose [184-A] EASTERBROOK. Born on 3 Dec 1911.

3802. Vincent Earl [228] GRIDLEY. Born on 19 Dec 1918.

3803. Clifford [229] CRANDALL. Born on 18 Mar 1908.

3804. Winifred [230] CRANDALL. Born on 8 Jul 1910.

3805. Frederick [231] CRANDALL. Born on 18 Mar 1912.

3806. Alice [232] CRANDALL. Born on 24 May 1917.

3807. Richard [233] ROLFE. Born on 14 Mar 1913.

3808. Robert [234] ROLFE.

3809. Mary Ellen [235] GUISE. Born on 13 May 1918.

-------------[872]

3810. Paul David HILL. Born on 22 Nov 1952 in Meshoppen, Pa.

3811. Mark Dean HILL. Born on 8 Sep 1954 in Ithaca, N.Y. Mark Dean married **Deborah YATES**.

They had the following children:

3998	i.	Bryan Mark (1974-)
3999	ii.	Matthew Dean (1976-)
4000	iii.	Michelle (1977-)
4001	iv.	Heather (1982-)

3812. Drew Edwin HILL. Born on 15 Jun 1957 in Cortland, N.Y. On 27 Jul 1984 when Drew Edwin was 27, he married **Elizabeth LAGONEGRO**, in Elmira, N.Y. Born on 6 Sep 1958 in Elmira, N.Y.

They had the following children:

4002	i.	Rebecca Elizabeth
4003	ii.	Kaitlin Margaret Eva (1989-)

3813. John HILL. Born on 18 Dec 1960 in Elmira, N.Y. Re-elected as President of the Hill Reunion in 2010. He manages the website www.Bearprint.net. On 7 Sep 1991 when John was 30, he married **Benita PARKS**. Born on 9 Jul 1980.

3814. Timothy Edwin JENKINS. Born on 7 Apr 1953 in Corning, N.Y. On 5 Jun 1976 when Timothy Edwin was 23, he married **Lois Ann STERLING**, in Caton, N.Y. Born on 3 Jan 1956 in Elimra, N.Y. They had the following children:

  4004 i. Kathleen Ann (1978-)
  4005 ii. John Daniel (1983-)

3815. Scott Douglas JENKINS. B. 21 Apr 1956 in Corning, N.Y.; d. in Caton, N.Y. 16 Aug 1974.

3816. Shannan Elizabeth POWELL.[873] Born on 14 May 1974 in Clifton Springs, Ontario Co., N.Y.

3817. Meredith Louise POWELL. Born on 13 Oct 1975 in Clifton Springs, Ontario Co., N.Y.

3818. Joseph Douglass POWELL. Born on 27 Feb 1977 in Clifton Springs, Ontario Co., N.Y.

3819. Kevin Eugene HILL.

3820. Keith Edwin HILL.

3821. Kerry Edward HILL.

3822. Mary Francis SKINNER.[874] Mary Francis married **George Albert CARLSON**. They had one child:

  4006 i. Thom (~1940-)

3823. Nettie "Lorene" HILL. Born on 24 Nov 1920; died on 20 Nov 1993, she was 72. On 19 Jan 1941 she married **Alvin Raymond TRAVIS**. Born on 1 Jun 1919; died on 18 Jul 1979, he was 60. In 14th Armored Division, WW 2. They had the following children:

  4007 i. Earnest Richard (1942-)
  4008 ii. Alvin Raymond
  4009 iii. Jon Paul (1945-1966)
  4010 iv. Linda Ann (1948-)

3824. Richard L. HILL IV. Born on 23 Jan 1925 in Corning, N.Y. USAAF in WW2. He married **Mary Catherine FLYNN**. Born on 6 Apr 1926; died in Corning, N.Y. on 8 Aug 1992, she was 66. They had the following children:

  4011 i. Michael Richard (1946-)
  4012 ii. Bryan Joseph (1947-)
  4013 iii. Francis Xavier (1951-)
  4014 iv. Paula Marie (1952-)
  4015 v. Patricia Ann (1954-)
  4016 vi. Richard L. (1956-)
  4017 vii. Christopher John (1958-)
  4018 viii. Thomas Flynn (1959-)
  4019 ix. Kathryn Mary (1961-)
  4020 x. Vincent Gerard (1963-)

3825. Paul Frank HILL.[875] Born on 4 May 1928 in Corning, N.Y. Paul Frank died in Sayre, Pa. on 11 Dec 2005, he was 77. Buried on 16 Dec 2005 in Corning, N.Y. Designer, Corning, Inc. Education: Corning High School and Corning Community College (Class of 1970). Religion: Roman Catholic. He was the organizer and genealogist of the descendants of Abraham Hill in Steuben Co., N.Y. He never doubted that proof would be found (as it was), to show that Abraham was the youngest son of Isaac Hill Sr., in spite of apparently conflicting information on Abraham Hill's tombstone in Carmel, N.Y. Paul Frank married **Mary Agnes KEANE**. Born on 11 Sep 1926. Occupation: Credit clerk.

3826. Dorothy Claire HILL. B. 10 Oct 1936. On 29 Jul 1956, at age 19, she m **Dean MICHELSON**. They had the following children:

  4021 i. Douglas (1957-)
  4022 ii. Carey (1960-)
  4023 iii. Tracey

3827. John White O'CONNELL. Born on 10 Dec 1917. John White died on 11 Nov 1975, he was 57. John White married **Eloise ORE**. Born on 13 May 1917. Eloise died on 30 Jul 1987, she was 70. They had the following children:

4024	i.	Dennis Malcolm "Denny" (1947-)
4025	ii.	John White (1948-)
4026	iii.	David Brian (1950-)

3828. Aimee O'CONNELL. Born on 2 Apr 1921; died in Corning, N.Y. on 21 May 1941, she was 20.

3829. James Richard O'CONNELL. Born on 3 Mar 1923. In 2nd Armored Division, WW2; Purple Heart. He married **Edna Mulford COOK**. Born on 15 Apr 1923; died on 24 Nov 2001, she was 78. They had the following children:

4027	i.	Karen Renee (1952-)
4028	ii.	Richard Keith (1952-)
4029	iii.	Kevin Jay (1958-)

3830. Barbara MOURHESS. B. 11 Nov 1937; m. **William DEURLIEN**; b. 13 Jun 1937.

3831. Byron MOURHESS. Born on 6 Jan 1947.

3832. Kendra MOURHESS. Born on 18 Feb 1949.

3833. Beverly HILL. She married (1) **Ronald EAST**.
They had one child:

| 4030 | i. | Penny |

She married (2) **Pete DIAZ**.

Line 8. Descendants of John Hill (Continued)
------------------876

3834. Mary Elizabeth HILL. Born on 25 Feb 1932 in Miles City, Custer Co., Mont. Mary Elizabeth married **John PFAFF**. Ranchers, the Pfaff Homestead, near Miles City, Mont.
They had the following children:

4031	i.	Mark (1954-)
4032	ii.	Lenore (1959-)
4033	iii.	Beverly (1955-)
4034	iv.	Sharon (1961-)

3835. Dr. Edwin Kay HILL. Born on 16 Apr 1933 in Miles City, Custer Co., Mont. Dean of community colleges in Spokane, Wash., and Tucson, Ariz. On 20 Aug 1955 when he was 22, he married (1) **Marie ELLWART**, in Cheney, Wash. They were divorced on 27 Jul 1978 in Waterville, Wash. They had the following children:

4035	i.	Amy Louise (1962-)
4036	ii.	Mary Ellen (1963-)
4037	iii.	Bennet John (1964-)
4038	iv.	James Michael (1968-)

On 19 Aug 1978, he married (2) **Mrs. Jo Anne L. WATSON**, in Chelan, Wash.

3836. Dorothy May HILL. Born on 6 Jun 1936 in Miles City, Custer Co., Mont. On 29 Oct 1960 when Dorothy May was 24, she m **Keith R. WILHELM**, in Bozeman, Mont., a pilot for Alaska Air Lines. They had one child:

| 4039 | i. | Wiley Willy (1966-) |

3837. Darrell HILL. Born in 1948. Darrell died in 1978, about age 30.

3838. Lenore WILSON. Born on 8 May 1929 in Bozeman, Mont. Lenore died in Dillon, Mont. on 7 Apr 1993, she was 63. Buried in Twin Bridge, Mont. Occupation: Teacher and mother. Lenore married **Richard Donald MARSHALL**. Ranch foreman, Newcastle, Wyo.; retired to Twin Bridges, Mont. They had the following children:

| 4040 | i. | Ellen Gail (1953-) |
| 4041 | ii. | James Wilson (1955-) |

3839. Marlene Ruth WILSON. Born on 21 May 1932 in Schnectady, N.Y. She was at the Univ. Montana Business School for 19 years; retired 1993. On 30 Aug 1953 when Marlene Ruth was 21, she married (1) **Dr. Robert Paul YOST**, a sports medicine instructor. They were divorced on 1 Jun 1978.

They had the following children:

4042	i.	Kelly Dawn (1958-)
4043	ii.	Robin Gail (1960-)
4044	iii.	Penney Jeanette (1961-)

On 8 Jun 1980, she married (2) **Richard KOVASH**, in Missoula, Mont.

3840. Earl Edward HILL Jr. Born on 10 Jul 1931 in Miles City, Custer Co., Mont. Occupation: U.S. Naval officer and systems engineer. Education: U.S. Naval Academy, graduated 1953; retired 1998. After graduating from the U.S. Naval Academy in 1953, he served on the *USS Boxer* in Korea and on the *USS Baltimore*. He was Missile Test Officer on the *USS Norton Sound* and he then was assigned to the Lincoln Laboratories at MIT. He was a systems engineer on air defense and NASA satellite tracking and communications systems for the Mitre Corporation until he retired in 1998. On 25 Nov 1955, he married **Ardath Francile CHAMBERLAIN**, daughter of Louis Francis CHAMBERLAIN, in Sioux City, Ia. They had the following children:

4045	i.	Bruce Jon (1956-)
4046	ii.	Molly Regan (1959-)
4047	iii.	Rebecca Leigh (1960-)
4048	iv.	Douglas Campbell (1962-)

3841. Raymond Willard HILL. Born on 13 May 1934 in Miles City, Custer Co., Mont. Occupation: U.S. Naval aviator; retired as Commander, USN; he then was a pilot instructor for the Navy near Pensacola, Fla. Education: U.S. Naval Academy graduate. He married **Barbara HUSSEY**, daughter of Alvin McDowell HUSSEY.

3842. James Dallas HILL. Born on 27 Nov 1938 in Miles City, Custer Co., Mont. Occupation: Communications Dept., *USS Bon Homme Richard* (CVA-31); IBM systems engineer, programmer, analyst, and product assurance and software development quality control; retired 1992; geology, gardening, and genealogy. University of Washington, B.A. in production management; U.S. Naval ROTC. Religion: Congregational Church. In 2000, James D. Hill was Vice President of the North Carolina Society, Sons of the American Revolution. Author of *The Hill Family, From 1651 to 2000: Twelve Generations in America*. <http://files.usgwarchives.net/ct/statewide/history/books/hill51.txt>. This e-book traces the descendants of Luke Hill in the line of his son John Hill and wife Sarah Phelps. It is now in its 5th edition (2000). He married **Susan Elizabeth PECK**. Born on 19 Mar 1938 in Glasgow, Mont. Occupation: University of Washington Nuclear Reactor Laboratory, as a secretary; production coordinator in farm news department for WRAL, Raleigh, N.C.; writes mystery and historical novels. Education: University of Washington. Religion: Congregational. They had the following children:

4049	i.	Tracy Elizabeth (1964-)
4050	ii.	Eric James (1965-)

3843. Marlynn Ruth "Lynn" HILL. Born on 23 Apr 1947 in Oakland, Calif. Occupation: Professional artist. Education: M.A. in fine arts. On 1 Jul 1967 when she was 20, she first married **Ken Victor HAYES Jr**. They were divorced in 1988. They had one child:

4051	i.	Kirk James (1974-)

In Oct 1994 when she was 47, she second m **Eugene H. "Gene" WARREN**, a retired English teacher.

3844. Dennis Michael BALLUFF. Born on 4 May 1939 in Freeport, Stephenson Co., Ill. On 3 Aug 1963 when he was 24, he married **Marsha Rhoda WARK**, in Philadelphia, Pa. They had the following children:

4052	i.	Laura Rosalie (1964-)
4053	ii.	Tammara Margaret (1970-)

3845. Loretta Anne MORGAN. Born 14 Jan 1953 in Jacksonville, Fla.; m **William St. GEORGE**.

3846. Ruby Alice HILL. Born on 13 Mar 1910. Ruby Alice married **? SHERMAN**. They had the following children:

4054	i.	Mary Lou

4055	ii.	Laura Lee
4056	iii.	John Jay
4057	iv.	Paula Jean (1949-)

3847. Florence Bell TODD. Born on 18 May 1908 in Cape Breton Island, Nova Scotia, Canada. Florence Bell died in Tarpon Springs, Fla. on 24 Feb 1995, she was 86. Florence Bell m **James Edward SHAY.** Born on 3 Sep 1907 in Morgantown, W.Va.; died in Holiday, Fla. 27 Jun 1983, he was 75. They had one child:

| 4058 | i. | Linda Lee (1938-) |

3848. Lurissa Rosalia Staats STAATS. Born on 11 Apr 1911 in Wann, Nowata Co., Okla. DAR application #493512 (1963). On 9 Nov 1940 when Lurissa Rosalia Staats was 29, she married **Christoph Henry HANOLD**, in Caney, Kansas. Born on 7 Jul 1908.

-------------------- [877]

3849. Lucius Hilliard BARBOUR. Born on 5 Apr 1903.

3850. Alice Cordelia BARBOUR. Born on 30 Apr 1907.

-------------------- [878]

3851. Charles McKINSTRY. Banker, Waterloo, IA.

3852. Albert "Bus" McKINSTRY. Athletic coach at Fort Dodge, IA.

3853. Ula Myrtle ANDERSON,[879] eldest daughter and eldest child of James Peter and Isabelle Luella (Riley) Anderson, was born at Scarville, Iowa, 10 August 1897; died at Kiester, Minnesota, 20 May 1981, age 83. She attended country schools as a child and continued her education into the second year of high school at Thompson, Iowa. Her parents then were living on a farm about two miles north of Thompson. She was married at the age of 19. She and her husband lived in Iowa until moving to a farm south of Kiester, Minnesota, in 1944. Two years after her husband died she moved into Kiester and she lived there until her death at the age of 83. When she was 75, her daughter wrote, in "My Nice Mother," that "She lived on a farm raising / Livestock and grain, Where irrigation was never heard of cause it always / Would rain." Ula Myrtle was a member of Grace united Methodist Church in Kiester and the Kiester Senior Citizens. Funeral services were held on 23 May 1981 at the Heitner Funeral Home, Wells, Minnesota, and she was buried in the Oakland Cemetery, Forest City, Iowa. She married, at her parents' farm near Thompson, Iowa, 20 June 1917, when she was 19 and he was 28, **Frank Leslie SCHROADER,**[880] son of Herman Ferdinand and Mary Lillian (Olson) Schroader; born in Winnebago County, Iowa, 8 October 1888; died in 1955, age 66. He was the son of Herman Ferdinand and Mary Lillian (Olson) Schroader. They had the following children:

4059	i.	Leona Alice (-<1981)
4060	ii.	Marian Rozella (1920-)
4061	iii.	Leslie Franklin (1927-)

3854. James Adelbert "Delbert" ANDERSON.[881] Born 1 May 1900 in Scarville, IA; died bet 1996-1997, abt 95. Father of 1.

3855. Haven Riley ANDERSON.[882] Born on 24 Jan 1905 in Leland, IA. Haven Riley died in Athens, NY on 7 Nov 1964, he was 59. Buried on 10 Nov 1964 in Catskill Rural Cemetery, from Federated Church, Athens, NY. Occupation: Contractor. Education: High School, Owatonna, IA. He enjoyed flying and volunteer work with the Boy Scouts. On 20 Nov 1931 when Haven Riley was 26, he married **Lillian Maria SORMBERGER**, in Pittsfield, MA. Born on 10 Aug 1908 in Latham, NY. Occupation: Mother of 2; Bookkeeper, Morris Furniture, Catskill, NY. Education: High School, Business College. She is the daughter of Leslie Herman and Hannah (Austin) Sormberger. She enjoys crafts and is a volunteer with RSVP in Catskill, NY. In 1996 she had residences at Athens, NY, and Port Orange, FL. They had the following children:

| 4062 | i. | Lillian Helen (1933-) |
| 4063 | ii. | Haven Leslie (1937-1967) |

3856. Mabel LaVonne "LaVonne" ANDERSON,[883] second daughter and fourth child of James and Isabelle (Riley) Anderson, was born at Leland, Newton Township, Winnebago County, Iowa, 14 January 1907; died in Mason City, Ia., 24 August 1997, age 90. LaVonne Anderson was baptized at the

Sterrenberg School house by the Rev. F. L. Kruwell, 8 February 1914. She attended grammar school near Thompson and three years of high school in Owatonna, Minnesota. She then lived for several years in Catskill, New York, before returning to Forest City, where she worked in a grocery store. She married at the age of thirty-eight and continued working in the grocery store, while also raising two children and doing housework. She also assisted needy families, assisted the school nurse, and did baby sitting. She enjoyed crafts, hand work, reading, and church activities. She was an active member of the United Methodist Church in Forest City for over fifty years, where she taught Sunday School and was active in Circle and UMW. She was a charter member of the Lime Creek Genealogical Society and she enjoyed researching her family's history. She was also a member of the 20th Century Club and Senior Citizens. She entered the Lake Mills Care Center in May 1996 but continued her active correspondence and telephone conversations regarding family history. She had a major stroke in her eighty-ninth year of age and died soon thereafter in a hospice.

Mabel LaVonne Anderson married, at Dows, Iowa, 28 November 1943, when she was 36 and he was 38, **Forest Whitefild OLSON**, son of Olaf and Jane Olson; born at Forest Township, Winnebago County, Iowa, 28 April 1905; died in 1986, age 80. He went to a country grammar school and to Forest City, Iowa, High School. He served in the 133rd Infantry as an antitank gun crewman in World War II. He enjoyed mowing lawns, reading, driving his car, and watching sports.

They had the following children:

| 4064 | i. | Owen James (1945-1988) |
| 4065 | ii. | Jane Luella (1949-) |

3857. Susan "Sue" WOLFER.[884] Occupation: Mother and fundraiser; was living in San Diego in March 1996. Education: San Diego State University. She married _____ **EARNEST**.

They had one child:

| 4066 | i. | Pat |

3858. Donald Paul WOLFER, Ph.D.,[885] son of James Daniel and Susan Myrtle (Riley) Wolfer, was born at San Diego, California, 16 May 1912; died at Sweet Home, Oregon, 12 June 1997, age 85. He received the A.B. from San Diego State University, the M.S. from the University of Southern California, and the Ph.D. from Claremont Graduate School. During World War II he served in the U.S. Navy, rising to the rank of Commander at the time of his retirement. From 1946-1964 Dr. Wolfer was employed as City Manager by Albany, Georgia; by Tuscon, Arizona; and by Fort Lauderdale, Florida. During this period he was also Professor of Public Administration at the University of Chile from 1955-1960. From 1964-1970 he was Budget Director of the San Diego City Schools. He was Professor of Public Administration at San Diego State University from 1964-1977. Following his retirement to Sweet Home, Oregon, Dr. Wolfer continued his interests in gardening and community service projects. In his later years he had a longstanding heart problem which led to his death from heart failure at the age of eighty-five. He married (1) **Lucille KNOWLES**.

Donald Paul and Lucille (Knowles) Wolfer had the following children:

4067	i.	Ann
4068	ii.	Lynn
4069	iii.	Lucia Knowles
4070	iv.	Adele

Following her death, he married (2), at San Diego, on 2 April 1982, **Marcia Loramack HAWKINS**, daughter of Willis Alston and Fredda (Griffin) Hawkins, was born at Tulia, Texas, 27 February 1921. She received the A.B. degree from West Texas State University; the M.S. from San Diego State University; and the Ph.D. from the University of Oregon. During World War II she served with G-2, U.S. Army Intelligence. She was a speech pathologist at San Diego State University and had a private practice in speech pathology until she retired. She enjoyed gardening and community service projects with her husband, who she survived. In 1999 she was living in Sweet Home, Oregon.

11

Eleventh Generation
The 8th-Great--Grandchildren
Descendants of 1. Lydia, 2. Mary, 5. Luke Jr., and 8. John

Line 1 – Descendants of Lydia Hill (continued)

3859. Infant SHEPPERD. Born in Jun 1877.

3860. John Wesley SHEPPERD. Born on 8 Sep 1878. In Sep 1911 when John Wesley was 32, he married **Myrtle WAUGH**, in Kansas City, Mo.

3861. Bruce Reason SHEPPERD. Born on 2 Apr 1881 in Moscow, Ida.; died in Spokane, Wash. 27 May 1980, he was 99. He married **Lucy Christina BURKE**, born 22 Dec 1884 in Pakenham, Ontario, Canada; died in Butte, Mont. on 19 May 1949, she was 64.
They had the following children:

4071	i.	Catherine Patricia (1913-1992)
4072	ii.	Ruth Anne (1915-)
4073	iii.	Bruce Robert (1918-)

3862. Warren Thompson SHEPPERD. Born on 15 Aug 1883 in Troy, Nezperce, Idaho Territory; died in Coeur D'Alene, Ida. on 5 May 1971, he was 87. On 10 Feb 1912 when he was 28, he married **Mildred Blanch DODGE**, in Bellingham, Wash. Born on 29 Feb 1888 in Worcester, Mass.; died in Coeur D'Alene, 20 Nov 1970, she was 82.
They had the following children:

4074	i.	Virgil Earl (1914-1973)
4075	ii.	Hannah Isabel (1916-)
4076	iii.	Winifred Abbey (1917-1988)
4077	iv.	Warren H.
4078	v.	James

3863. Renne Julian SHEPPERD. Born on 3 Feb 1886; died in Los Angeles, Calif. on 27 Jan 1974, he was 87. On 21 Sep 1909 when he was 23, he married **Gertrude WOODY**, in Union, Ore.; b. 2 Feb 1890 in Cedar, Ia.; died in Los Angeles, Calif. 13 Feb 1981, age 91.
They had one child:

| 4079 | i. | Shirley (1911-) |

3864. Enos Aberdeen SHEPPERD. Born on 16 Feb 1888 in Moscow, Ida.; died in San Bernardino, Calif. on 11 Sep 1961, he was 73. On 31 Dec 1913 when he was 25, he m. **Ellen Theresa BURKE**, in Butte, Mont.; born 21 May 1889 in Elmonte, Ontario, Canada; d. in San Bernardino 24 Apr 1976, at 86.
They had the following children:

4080	i.	Kathleen Marie (1916-1987)
4081	ii.	Enid Marguerite (1919-)
4082	iii.	Elizabeth A. (~1921-)
4083	iv.	Bonita L. (~1923-)
4084	v.	George Michael (1925 1999)
4085	vi.	Eva Leannah (1890-1983)

3865. Eva Leannah SHEPPERD. Born on 19 May 1890.

3866 William Bruce SHEPPERD. Born on 27 Sep 1900 in Des Moines, Polk Co., Ia.

3867. Emma Eugenia SHEPPERD. Born on 27 Jan 1903 in Des Moines, Polk Co., Ia.

3868. Esther Agnes SHEPPERD. Born on 25 Apr 1905 in Des Moines, Polk Co., Ia.

3869. Martin Willet HAYS.

3870. Bessie Shepperd HAYS. Born on 12 Apr 1887 in Fargo, N.D.

3871. Miles Henry POWERS. Born on 3 Oct 1884 in Chariton, Ia.

3872. Clara Gertrude POWERS. Born on 26 Sep 1886 in Nebraska.

3873. Sumner Leslie POWERS. Born on 15 Aug 1889 in Nebraska.

3874. Lisle Gipson BREWER. Born 28 Dec 1905 in Bee Branch, Chariton Co., Mo.; d in Elk City, Okla. 8 Oct 1958, he was 52. On 11 Apr 1936 when he was 30, he m **Lavina Margarette BITTICK**, in Amarillo, Tex. Born on 26 Mar 1911 in Leavenworth, Kan.; died in Elk City, 12 Sep 1997, she was 86.

3875. Ola Verne BREWER. Born on 17 Sep 1918 in Brookfield, Mo. She married **Darrell G. BLAKELEY**. Born on 24 Jul 1922 in Ogden, Weber Co., Utah; died in Orange, Calif. on 30 Aug 1990. They had the following children:

4086	i.	Living Child of Darrell and Ola (Brewer)
4087	ii.	Janis Ann (1953-2002)
4088	iii.	Norman (1956-1994)

3876. Clarene BREWER. Born in 1918.

3877. Margaret G. BREWER. Born in 1922. Married twice, survived by second husband and his child.

Margaret G. first married **? HANNAFORD**.

Margaret G. second married **? JOHNSON**.

| 4089 | i. | Living Child of Margaret (Brewer) |

–––––––––––––––––[887]

3878. Stella OLSEN. Born on 22 Oct 1892 in Lorenzo, Idaho.

3879. Child of Herman and Lottie (Byington) CORRELL.

3880. Child of Herman and Lottie (Byington) CORRELL.

3881. Child of Herman and Lottie (Byington) CORRELL.

3882. Herman Edward CORRELL. Born on 17 Mar 1917.

3883. Ray Weldon CORRELL. Born on 27 Apr 1922 in Hagerman, Gooding, Idaho.

3884. Son of Richard and Kathleen (Hager) LANE.

3885. Daughter of Richard and Kathleen (Hager) LANE.

3886. Daughter of Richard and Kathleen (Hager) LANE.

3887. Daughter of Harold and Mabel I. LANE.

3888. Daughter of Harold and Mabel I. LANE.

3889. Daughter of Harold and Mabel I. LANE.

3890. Harold Benjamin LANE. Born on 6 Aug 1914 in Bridgeport City, Fairfield Co., Conn. Harold Benjamin died in Bridgeport City, Fairfield Co., Conn. on 30 Nov 1988, he was 74. Harold Benjamin married **Ruth Etta PELHAM**. Born in 1920. Ruth Etta died in 1989, she was 69. Mother of two sons and one daughter, whose names are not given in Ancestry.com.

3891. Four sons and two daughters of Clair and Lucy (Rawson) HOTELLING.

Line 2 – Descendants of Mary Hill (continued)[888]

3892. ? BARNES.

3893. Dorothy BARNES. Born on 22 Dec 1916 in New Britain, Conn. Dorothy died in Bristol, Hartford Co., Conn. on 29 Oct 1994, she was 77. Mother of 5: 3 daughters and 2 sons. Dorothy married **Leo Harold WRENN**. Born in 1914. Leo Harold died in 1987, he was 73.

3894. ? [1] GAYNOR.

3895. ? [2] GAYNOR.

3896. ? [3] GAYNOR.

3897. ? [4] GAYNOR.

3898. ? [5] GAYNOR.

3899. ? [6] GAYNOR.

3900. Paul GAYNOR. Born in 1939.

Line 5 – Descendants of Luke Hill, Jr. (continued)

3901. David L. STANLEY,[889] only child of Roy A. and Sadie W. (Hill) Stanley, was born at Chicago, Cook Co., Ill., 13 August 1920; died 25 October 2006, age 86. He married, at Evanston, Ill., 24 March 1951, when he was 30 and she was 27, **Alice May ALBRECHTSON**; born at Evanston, 17 July 1923. They had two children. Mary Alice married and had two daughters, both of whom married. They had the following children:

| 4090 | i. | Richard R. (1952-) |
| 4091 | ii. | Mary Alice (1954-) |

-------------------------[890]

3902. Helen Dorothy GOLDING. Born on 4 Jan 1905 in Wauconda, Lake Co., Ill.; died there, Mar 1962, she was 57. She d.s.p. She resided in Chicago, Ward 14, in 1920.

3903. Alvin Ford GOLDING.[891] Born on 3 Mar 1908 in Ill.; died in Wauconda, Lake Co., Illinois in 1969, he was 60. He married **Jessie Lillian BOEHMER.** Born in 1916; died in 1956, she was 40. They had one child:

| 4092 | i. | _____ |

3904. Marge BOND.

3770. Susan BOND.

3771. Clifford M. BOND. Born on 27 Mar 1904 in Des Moines, Polk Co., Ia.

3772. Marjorie E. BOND. Born on 15 Mar 1906 in Waterloo, Black Hawk Co., Ia.

3773. _____ SOULES. _____ married _____ **EBERBACH.**
They had one child, surname Eberbach:

| 4093 | i. | _____ |

3909. _____ KEITH.

3910. _____ KEITH.

3911. Donald KEITH. Born on 30 Aug 1906 in Milwaukee, Milwaukee Co., Wisc.

3912. Dorothy Elliott KEITH. Born on 15 Sep 1907 in Milwaukee, Wisc.

3913. _____ CHILDS-JOHNSON.

3914. _____ CHILDS.

3915. Deborah CHILDS died aft 1997. She resided in Greenwich, Conn., in 1997. She may have been married more than once, for her father had four grandchildren, who are placed with her only because their parents' names are not given in his obituary. They are Elizabeth, William and Charles Schenck and Andrew Buecking.
Deborah married _____ **KESSLER.**
They had the following children:

4094	i.	Elizabeth, surname Kessler
4095	ii.	William, surname Kessler
4096	iii.	Charles, surname Schenck
4097	iv.	Andrew, surname Buecking

3916. Nancy Elizabeth CHILDS. Nancy Elizabeth died aft 1997. She resided in Winnetka, Ill., in 1997.

3917. ? WOOD married (1) **Calvin Dale HALBERSTADT.**
They had the following children:

4098	i.	Angela Lynn
4099	ii.	Bradley Alan
4100	iii.	Douglas James
4101	iv.	Jeffrey Scott
4102	v.	Kenneth Paul

She married (2) **Obie Ray BAKER.**
They had one child:

| 4103 | i. | Brandon Ray |

She married (3) Douglas **Duane ANDERSON.**

3919. Susan BIRGE.

------------------------ [892]

3920. Barbara Jo HILL.[893] Born on 15 Apr 1943 in Davenport, IA. Christened on 21 Nov 1948 in Bettendorf, Iowa. Elementary school teacher. Graduate, Bettendorf [Iowa] High School (1961); B.A. (elementary education) University of Northern Iowa (1965); courses at N.E. Missouri State University, Kirksville, Mo. Religion: Peace United Church of Christ. She was a teacher at Reinbeck, Iowa (1965-1968) and from 1969-1996 was teaching first grade at Elkader, Iowa. She enjoyed reading, sewing, and playing in the community band and she was a volunteer costume mistress for the Opera House Players.

On 26 Nov 1964 when Barbara Jo was 21, she married **Thomas Lee CHANDLER**, in Bettendorf, Scott Co., Ia. Born on 2 Apr 1945 in Des Moines, Iowa. Teacher; band director. Elementary school at LeGrand, Oregon; graduate from Crestwood High School, Cresco, Ia.; B.A., University of Northern Iowa; M.A. North East Missouri State University. He was the son of Arlon Burris and Mary Florence (McLaughlin) Chandler. He enjoyed antique racing cars and sailing; and he was a volunteer with the Opera House Players, the Main Street Program Barber Shoppers; and with the community band. They had the following children:

4104	i.	Randi Rae (1968-)
4105	ii.	Kelly Jo (1974-)
4106	iii.	Katharine Marie (1980-)

3921. Sally Rae HILL. Born on 22 Oct 1946 in Davenport, IA. On 26 Jun 1965 when Sally Rae was 18, she first married **Paul HOCKINGS**, in Bettendorf, IA. They were divorced. They had the following children:

4107	i.	Erika Leigh (1971-)
4108	ii.	Brittany Elissa Anne (1976-)

On 13 Jan 1979 when Sally Rae was 32, she second married **William MATTES**. Born on 25 May 1945. They had the following children:

4109	i.	Graham William (1980-)
4110	ii.	Garrett Rollins (1984-)

3922. Craig Eugene HILL. Born on 21 Feb 1950 in Davenport, IA.

3923. Sharon Jean HILL,[894] daughter and elder child of Paul Francis and Marie Margaret (Johnson) Hill, was born at Des Moines, Iowa, 22 March 1939. She began her education at the Perkins School in Des Moines and continued her education in Denver, Colorado, when her parents moved there. She attended Stedman grade school, Smiley Junior High School, and East High School in Denver. Her parents then moved to Illinois, and she attended New Trier Township High School in Willmette, IL, from which she graduated in 1957. She graduated from Cottey College, Nevada, Missouri, in 1959, and then attended Evanston Business School. She was Secretary to Mr. Hirsch, President of the Turtle Wax Company and later was Executive Secretary to the Vice President of the Kemper Insurance Company. After raising her family and serving as Secretary at her church in Schaumburg, Illinois, she returned to work at the Motorola Corporation. She was living in Schaumburg in April 1997.

She married, at Chicago, Illinois, 25 July 1964, when she was 25, **William Charles SCHNEIDER**, born in Chicago, 1 July 1930, by whom she had three children: Stephen George (b. 1969); Joy Marie (b. 1972); and Matthew Paul (b. 1973). They had the following children:

4111	i.	Stephen George (1969-)
4112	ii.	Joy Marie (1972-)
4113	iii.	Matthew Paul (1973-)

3924. James William HILL,[895] son and younger child of Paul Francis and Marie Margaret (Johnson) Hill, was born at Des Moines, Iowa, 29 November 1940. He began his education at the Perkins School in Des Moines. After his parents moved to Denver, Colorado, he attended Stedman grade school and Smiley Junior High School. His parents then moved to Illinois, and he attended New Trier Township High School in Willmette, IL, from which he graduated in 1959. He then worked for the Boye Needle Co., and the First National Bank and the Methodist Pension Board, in Evanston, Illinois. He enlisted in the U. S. Army, and was stationed at Fort Benning, Georgia; he also served in Vietnam. He moved to Colorado in 1974, where he worked for the Pentax Corporation. In 1995 he was living in Kiowa, Colorado, and in 1997 he was living in Elizabeth, Colorado. He married (1), at Evanston, Illinois, at St. Nicholas Church, when he was 26, **Marilyn Blanche KESSELER**; born at Evanston, 30 July 1939. They had the following children:

4114	i.	(Stillborn) (1972-)
4115	ii.	Randy James (1973-)
4116	iii.	Ryan William (1977-)

After they were divorced, he married (2), 22 March 1980, as her second husband, **Mrs. Mary Lynn (EICHER) LARNER**; born in Illinois, 7 September 1944. She had three children by her first marriage; his stepchildren were Stephen, Scott, and Juli Larner.

3925. Roberta Marie JUHL. Born on 27 Nov 1934; died 27 Nov 1934 in Cedar Falls, IA; bur there.

3926. Grace Leola JUHL. Born on 27 Nov 1934. Grace Leola died on 27 Nov 1934.

3927. Richard Harold JUHL. Born on 26 Nov 1935 in Cedar Falls, IA. On 27 Jul 1958 when Richard Harold was 22, he married **Joann Kay POHL**, in Cedar Falls, IA. Born on 21 Sep 1939. They had the following children:

4117	i.	Connie Rae (1959-)
4118	ii.	Michael Robert (1963-)
4119	iii.	David Stanley (1965-)

3928. Raymond Paul JUHL. Born on 24 Jan 1938 in Cedar Falls, IA. On 28 Aug 1966 when he was 28, he first married **Carol Lee JACKSON**, in Las Vegas, CA. They were divorced in Aug 1978. They had the following children:

| 4120 | i. | Shannon Ca (1968-) |
| 4121 | ii. | Shelly Raye (1970-) |

On 31 Dec 1987 when Raymond Paul was 49, he second married **Anna Paulette ____**.

3929. Donald Robert JUHL. Born on 20 Jun 1939 in Cedar Falls, IA. Donald Robert first married **Norma Kay SHOWERS**. They were divorced. In Jan 1970 when Donald Robert was 30, he second married **Rita Jean GROSVENOR**. They were divorced in May 1987. They had the following children:

| 4122 | i. | Robert Stewart (1971-) |
| 4123 | ii. | Christopher Duane (1973-) |

On 27 Jul 1990 when Donald Robert was 51, he third married **Patricia Kay ADDAMS**.

3930. Ronald Eugene JUHL. Born on 22 Jun 1941 in Cedar Falls, IA. On 2 Jul 1962 when Ronald Eugene was 21, he first married **Kay Leone DAVEY**, in Cedar Falls, IA. Born on 20 Mar 1943. They were divorced in Nov 1969. They had the following children:

4124	i.	Scott Eugene (1963-)
4125	ii.	[male] (1966-1966)
4126	iii.	Tamera Kay (1968-)

On 20 Jul 1970 when Ronald Eugene was 29, he second married **Doris Marcella NISSEN**.

3931. Jeanine Kay HUMBERT,[896] elder child of Galen Rose Solomon and Genevieve Maude (Hill) Humbert, was born at Cedar Falls, Iowa, 2 October 1940. She graduated from Cedar Falls High School and attended the American Institute of Business, from which she graduated in 1959. She has taken continuing education classes every year since then. She has owned and operated Craft Shoppe, Ltd., in Cedar Falls since 1982, and she has been President and Secretary of the Twin Oaks Print / Frame organization. She enjoys needlework and the study of family history and genealogy, and she has been a member of the D.A.R. since 1970. She married, at Cedar Falls, on 30 October 1958, when she was 18, **Garel Lee JOHNSON**, son of Earl Eugene and Ella Inez (Newby) Johnson; born at Dallas Township, Missouri, 9 October 1936; christened in Lost Creek, Santa Rosa Co., Mo. He attended Maysville, Missouri, High School, and has been a repairman for the Viking Pump Company in Cedar Falls, Iowa, since 1959. He has been Vice President and Treasurer of the Craft Shoppe, Ltd., and the Twin Oaks Print

/ Frame organization in Cedar Falls. He enjoys making and shooting antique black powder weapons. They had the following children:

4127	i.	Jeffery Scott (1960-)
4128	ii.	Sheryl Lynn (1963-)

3932. Constance Rose HUMBERT. Born on 30 May 1945 in Cedar Falls, IA, and christened there. On 27 May 1967 at age 21, she married **James Milton CHRISTIANSEN**, son of Milton CHRISTIANSEN & Loretta Crystal GOLLIDAY, in Cedar Falls, IA. Born on 1 Oct 1943 in Waterloo, IA. He is the son of Milton and Loretta Crystal (Golliday) Christiansen.
They had the following children:

4129	i.	Mark Alan (1969-)
4130	ii.	Amy Jo (1971-)

3933. Franklin Peter BOWERMAN. Born on 10 Nov 1943 in Michigan City, La Porte Co., IN. On 16 Aug 1980 when Franklin Peter was 36, he married **Marie Frances WESSEL**. Born on 24 Jul 1946.
They had one child:

4131	i.	Monica Marie (1984-)

3934. Linda Lee BOWERMAN. Born on 5 May 1946 in Michigan City, La Porte Co., IN. On 2 May 1970 when Linda Lee was 23, she first married **Roger JENKINS**, son of Cecil JENKINS. Born on 14 Mar 1947. They were divorced. He was the son of Cecil Jenkins.
They had the following children:

4132	i.	Aundrea Marie (1974-)
4133	ii.	Melissa Lynn (1983-)

On 21 Dec 1991 when Linda Lee was 45, she second married **Roger Le John KERN**. Born in 1937.
3935. Benjamin (Bennie) Wayne BOWERMAN. Born on 18 Sep 1949 in Michigan City, La Porte Co., IN. Benjamin (Bennie) Wayne first married **Linda Sue CHAMBERS**. They were divorced. On 14 Oct 1972 when Benjamin (Bennie) Wayne was 23, he second married **Marilyn JENKINS**, in Michigan City, IN. Born on 13 Aug 1951.
They had the following children:

4134	i.	Douglas Wayne (1975-)
4135	ii.	Kimberly Allison (1978-)

3936. Dian Lynn HILL. Born on 8 Oct 1946. On 15 Jun 1968 when Dian Lynn was 21, she married **James WESNER**. Born on 8 Mar 1944.
They had the following children:

4136	i.	Heather Ann (1972-)
4137	ii.	Scott Alan (1972-)

3937. Charles Austin "Chuck" HILL,[897] eldest child of Charles E. and Amy (Austin) Hill, was born at Oskaloosa, Mahaska Co., Iowa, 5 December 1940; died at St. Louis, Missouri, 14 January 1969. Chuck Hill attended elementary school through the seventh grade at Creston, Iowa. He attended junior high school and high school at Rochester, Minnesota, where he graduated in 1958. As a school boy he was an avid reader and was active with the Boy Scouts. He then entered the U.S. Army for three years. He graduated from Airborne School at Ft. Campbell, Kentucky, and was a paratrooper in the 101st Airborne Division. Specialist Four Charles Hill was honorably discharged in 1961 and returned to Minnesota, where he attended Rochester Community College and received the A.A. degree in 1964. He attended Mankato (MN) State University in 1964-65. He then began work as a tractor-trailer owner-operator, while also enjoying stamp and coin collecting, marksmanship, and camping. On vacations he travelled to the Caribbean, Mexico, and Canada. At the time of his death, Chuck Hill was a Roadmaster and owner-operator of a tractor-trailer with Draymeier Moving and Storage Co., of St. Louis, Missouri, and a contractor with United Van Lines. He was well underway towards success as a tractor-trailer owner-operator, when he was shot and killed by a robber while dining at a restaurant in St. Louis, Missouri. His sudden and completely unexpected death profoundly affected the rest of his family.

3938. Marcella Ann "Sally" HILL,[898] eldest daughter and second child of Charles E. and Amy (Austin) Hill, was born at Creston, Union Co., Iowa, 12 October 1942; christened in the Presbyterian Church at

Creston. She was named for her great-grandfather, Marcelllus Hamilton Austin. Sally Hill attended elementary school at Creston, Iowa, from kindergarten through the fifth grade. She then moved to Rochester, Minnesota, where she attended public schools from the sixth through the twelfth grade. She graduated from the John Marshall High School in Rochester in 1960. She was a student at Rochester Community College for the next two years and received the A.A. degree there in 1962. She completed her baccalaureate work at the University of Minnesota, Minneapolis, with the B.A. degree in Elementary Education in 1964. She took advanced study at St. Thomas University, St. Paul Minnesota, where she received Advanced Reading Specialist and Learning Disabled degrees. In 1994 she was an elementary school teacher in Minneapolis where she worked as a Reading Specialist and Learning Disabled Specialist. She is a poet and composer of music for the piano. She also she enjoys reading, travel, antiques, and listening to music. She is a volunteer in youth activities with her church.

She married at Rochester, Minnesota, 24 August 1969, in the First Presbyterian Church, when she was 26, **C. Robert ELLIOTT**, son of Allen and Elin (Carlson) Elliott; born at Boston, Massachusetts, 7 April 1942, and christened there in a Baptist Church in 1942. He was educated in the public schools of Chicago, where he attended elementary school and high school. He then attended Northwestern College, Minneapolis, Minnesota, where he received the B.A. degree. He later took advanced study courses at the University of Minnesota, St. Thomas University (St. Paul, MN), and at the University of Wisconsin (River Falls, WI). He then became a teacher and in 1994 was a teacher in the Minneapolis Public Schools, specializing in Special Education for the Learning Disabled. He enjoys reading, sports, fishing and camping, and is active in youth work with the Baptist church.

They had the following children:

4138	i.	Amy Elin (1972-)
4139	ii.	John David (1974-)
4140	iii.	Aaron Robert (1976-)

3939. Rebecca Elizabeth "Becky" HILL-SIMPSON,[899] second daughter and third child of Charles E. and Amy (Austin) Hill, was born at Creston, Iowa, 29 July 1950, and christened there in the First Presbyterian Church. She attended public school in Rochester, Minnesota, and graduated from the Mayo High School, Rochester, in 1968. She then attended the Rochester Community College, from which she received the A.A. degree in 1970. She continued her education at Winona State University, Winona, MN, where she graduated with the B.A. in Library Science in 1974. She returned to Rochester Community College for a Medical Secretary degree in 1989. In 1994 she was employed as a medical secretary at the Mayo Clinic, and she was also a pianist and vocalist. She enjoys listening to music, reading, the theatre, and antiques. She also enjoys counted cross stitch sewing, biking and travel, and has visited Australia, Hawaii, and Canada. She has been married twice. Her first marriage ended in divorce and she married (2), at St. Cloud, Minnesota, 19 September 1976, **Lloyd Thomas SIMPSON**; born at Bloomington, Illinois, 25 October 1950. He was a restaurant manager in Minneapolis, who had previously been married and divorced. Tom and Rebecca Hill-Simpson are now divorced.

They had one child:

4141	i.	Matthew David (1981-)

3940. Elmer Laurel KNOEDLER II,[900] eldest child of Elmer L. and Velda M. (Hill) Knoedler, was born at Clarion, IA, 13 January 1930; died at Humboldt, Iowa, 24 June 1987, age 57. His childhood was spent at Britt, Iowa, and he graduated from Britt High School in 1949. He served in the U. S. Navy during the Korean conflict, and he lived in Dike, Ia., and Clarion after his return to civilian life. He moved to Humboldt in 1962. He was a policeman there until 1978 and then managed a hotel and was later employed by Harklau Industries as a machinist until he retired because of health problems. He enjoyed woodworking and fishing and was a member of the Oak Hill Baptist Church and the American Legion. He lived in Humboldt, Iowa, in his later years, and was buried in the Union Cemetery there. He married, at Belmond, Iowa, 13 October 1953, when he was 23, **Louetta May "Lou" FOLLETTE**,[901] daughter of LeRoy and Louise (Wright) Follette; born at Lead, South Dakota, 5 October 1935. She survived her husband and attended the Hill Family Reunion at Clarion, Iowa, in July 1994. E. Laurel and Louetta May (Follette) Knoedler had four children. All four children were married and he had eight grandchildren.

They had the following children:

4142	i.	Roxanne Lee (1954-)
4143	ii.	Deborah Jo (1955-)
4144	iii.	Timothy Laurel "Tim" (1957-)
4145	iv.	Diana Lou (1960-)

3941. John LeRoy KNOEDLER,[902] second son and second child of Elmer Laurel and Velda (Hill) Knoedler, was born at Clarion, Iowa, 27 March 1935; died at Greeley, Colorado, 8 November 1995, age 60. He attended college for two years in Topeka, Kansas. He was a telephone company employee, and was living in Greeley, Colorado, in 1987. Mr. Knoedler was a member of the Free Evangelical Christian Church. He married, on 29 October 1955, **Suzanne Louise STAATS**; born 12 March 1934.

They had the following children:

4146	i.	Cynthia "Cyndee"/ "Cindy" (1959-)
4147	ii.	Vickie Lynn "Vicki" (1960-)
4148	iii.	Lawrence Thomas "Larry" (1964-)
4149	iv.	David John

3942. Beth Charlene KNOEDLER, elder daughter and third child of Elmer Laurel and Velda Mae (Hill) Knoedler), was born at Clarion, Iowa, 24 June 1936. She graduated from Iowa State University and from the secretarial school at the Mayo Clinic, Rochester, Minnesota. She married **Freeman David GATES**; born 6 June 1927; died after July 1997. He was a farmer and warehouse supervisor in Clarion, Iowa, and a member of the Methodist Church. Freeman and Beth (Knoedler) Gates had three children. Bradley married and had children. Freeman and Beth Gates were the organizers and principal hosts for the Hill Family Reunion on 26 July 1997; Freeman died within a year or so after that reunion.

They had the following children:

4150	i.	Brian Freeman (1958-)
4151	ii.	Francine Lea (1961-)
4152	iii.	Bradley Frederick "Brad" (1963-)

3943. Keith Maurice KNOEDLER,[903] third son and fourth child of Elmer and Velda (Hill) Knoedler, was born at Clarion, Iowa, 28 November 1937. He graduated from high school at Maynard, Iowa, and in 1996 was a self-employed building contractor in Shell Rock, Iowa. He is a member of the Lutheran church, and he belongs to the Odd Fellows. In 1996 he had six children and eight grandchildren and he was living in Shell Rock with his wife and youngest child. He married (1), 11 March 1958, **Nancy Elaine LEE**, by whom he had four children. Keith and Nancy (Lee) Knoedler were divorced in 1968.

They had the following children:

4153	i.	Anthony Lee (1959-)
4154	ii.	Andrew Keith (1960-)
4155	iii.	Pamela Lynn (1962-)
4156	iv.	Todd David (1966-)

He married (2), at Stockton, Illinois, 12 June 1969, when he was 31, **Dorothy Anna RODENBECK**, daughter of Herman William and Ann Ann (Dirks) Rodenbeck; born at Waverly, Iowa, 23 June 1942. She graduated from Shell Rock [Iowa] High School and then became a professional underwriter. In 1996 she was the New Business Administrator at Century Companies of America, Waverly, Iowa. She is a volunteer with SHARE Iowa and she belongs to Rebekah's.

They had the following children:

4157	i.	Peggy Ann (1975-)
4158	ii.	Cyndee (Cindy) Kae (1980-)

3944. [Infant son] KNOEDLER.

3945. Lurretta KNOEDLER, second daughter and fifth child of Elmer and Velda (Hill) Knoedler, was born at Mason City, Iowa, 11 February 1954. She graduated from high school at Clinton, Iowa, and then attended Kansas State University for one year. She is a member of the Methodist Church. She married **Roger Fay DAUGHERTY**; born at Quincy, Illinois, 22 August 1953. He was christened in 1965, and is a member of the First Christian Church, Camp Point, Illinois. He attended college for two years in Texas and Illinois, and he has served in the Army National Guard. He is a shop foreman at a Chrysler dealership. The Daughertys were living in Lawrence, Kansas, in 1996.

They had one child:

    4159   i.   Sarah Mae (1982-)

3946. Donald Eugene HILL. Born on 23 Sep 1939 in Sumner, IA. Christened in Sumner, IA (Methodist Church). Occupation: Electronics and computer technician. Education: Sumner, IA, High School; Univ. IA (2 yrs); in USN. Religion: Methodist. Donald Eugene married **Mary Lee MARKSBERRY**. Born abt 23 Jul 1941 in Floyd, IA. Occupation: Secretary, Memorial Hospital, Springfield, IL. Education: Floyd High School graduate; Univ. Iowa graduate. Religion: Methodist.

They had the following children:

    4160   i.   Melissa Ann (1967-)
    4161   ii.   Barbara Lynn (1969-)

3947. Steve Clar HILL. Born on 9 Feb 1951 in Sumner, IA. Occupation: Maintenance worker, Nestle Beverage Corp. Education: Sumner, IA, High School graduate 1969. Religion: Protestant. Steve Clar married **Barbara Kay SCHMIDT**. Born on 26 Jul 1951 in Sumner, IA. Occupation: Secretary, Univ. Northern Iowa, Cedar Falls. Education: Tripoli, IA, High School graduate. Religion: Protestant.

They had the following children:

    4162   i.   Karl LeRoy (1977-)
    4163   ii.   Amanda Kay (1979-)
    4164   iii.   Rhonda Dolores (1981-)

3948. Mary Ann HILL.[904] Born on 27 Aug 1941 in Sumner, Iowa. Occupation: Michelle and Christina Hayner came with her in to the Reunion in Clarion in 1994. Mary Ann married **Bruce HANSEN**.

3949. Carol L. HILL. Born in 1943. Occupation: She lived in Lafayette, Colo. in 2006. She lived for many years in Boulder, Colo., and was living in Broomfield, Colo., in 1997. Attended the Hill Reunion in Clarion in 2006.

3950. Janice HILL. Born in 1945. Of Orlando, FL, in 1994 and 1997, when she attended Hill Reunion.

3951. Judy HILL. Born in 1946. Occupation: of Tampa, FL, in 1994, when attended Hill Reunion in 1997. Judy married **Joe BALES**.

3952. Michael LeRoy TRELOAR. Born in 1938.

3953. Nancy Lee TRELOAR.[905] Born in 1942. Nancy Lee married _____ **MURDOCK**.

They had the following children:

    4165   i.   Donna
    4166   ii.   Cindy
    4167   iii.   Tom
    4168   iv.   Leroy

3954. Sharon Jean TRELOAR. Born in 1954.

3955. Norma Jean WESTON.[906] Born on 31 Dec 1945. Norma Jean married **Kenneth PERRY**.

They had the following children:

    4169   i.   Kenneth D.
    4170   ii.   Kirk
    4171   iii.   Kyle

3956. Ardith Elaine WESTON.[907] Born on 6 Nov 1947. Ardith Elaine married **Richard BARNES**.

They had one child:

    4172   i.   Lana

3957. Janet Marie WESTON.[908] Born on 6 Mar 1949. Janet Marie married _____ **BATTERSON**.

3958. Dawn Delight WESTON.[909] Born on 18 Dec 1951. On 15 January 1972, at Arlington, Iowa, she married **Joel Anthony MENUEY Sr.**, son of Carl and Elba (Larson) Menuey, born at Olwein, Iowa, 25 October 1949.

They had the following children:

    4172a   i.   Michele Leigh (1975-)

4172b	ii.	Douglas Weston (1978-)
4172c	iii.	Joel Anthony (1982-)

3959. Charlotte Ann WESTON.[910] Born on 9 Dec 1954.
Charlotte Ann married **Zeke SEEDORF**.
They had the following children:

4173	i.	Angela
4174	ii.	Michael

3960. Roger Dale WESTON.[911] Born on 31 Aug 1961. Roger Dale married **Judy ? (WESTON)**.
They are believed to have had the following children:

4175	i.	Erin
4176	ii.	Oakley
4177	iii.	Laine

3961. Rose Mary WESTON.[912] Born on 31 Aug 1961.

3962. Steven Dale HILL,[913] eldest child of Dale E. and Avis (Boyington) Hill, was born at Clarion, Iowa, 2 December 1941. He grew up on his parents' farm near Clarion and graduated from Clarion High School in 1960. He attended Iowa State University from 1960-61, and then returned to enter farming with his father. He served in the Iowa National Guard from 1962-1968. The farm which he and his wife operate was previously owned and operated by his father and grandfather. It was designated an Iowa "Century Farm" in 1992.   He married, at Belmond, Iowa, 12 February 1965, **Shirley A. DAVIS**, daughter of Scott and Alva (Berhow) Davis; born at Hampton, Iowa, 22 December 1943. His wife was a graduate of the Thompson School of Cosmetology.
They had the following children:

4178	i.	Kevin Dale (1965-)
4179	ii.	Kristin Sue "Kris" (1968-)

3963. Mark Lynn HILL,[914] second of the three sons of Dale E. and Avis (Boyington) Hill, was born at Clarion, Wright County, Iowa, 25 February 1943; christened in the IOOF Hall in Clarion, 13 June 1943, by the Rev. L. H. Preul. He graduated from Clarion High School and attended Iowa State University for one term in 1963. He then returned to Clarion and began farming, continuing a tradition that began when his great-great grandfather came to Wright County as a pioneer farmer in 1861. He served in the Iowa National Guard during the Vietnam War. Mr. Hill is a member of Ruritan and the Clarion Investment Club. In 1994 he was a member of the Methodist Church Board and the Clarion Park Board. He was formerly a member of the Board of Directors of the Clarion Farmers Cooperative. He enjoys fishing, hunting, and playing card games.

He married, at Clarion, 26 November 1966, when he was 23, **Cynthia Elaine WEBB**, daughter of John and Thelma (Duitscher) Webb of Baltimore, Maryland; they were divorced, without issue, in 1970. He married (2), at Clarion, Iowa, 5 August 1972, **Connie Sue GREIMAN**, daughter of Wayne Warren and Vivian June (Herbert) Greiman; born at Garner, Hancock Co., Iowa, 26 June 1947, a speech therapist. She attended public school at Garner and graduated from Garner-Hayfield High School in 1965. She then attended Makato State University, Mankato, MN, for four years, and received the B.S. in Speech Pathology in 1969. She did graduate work at Colorado State University, Fort Collins, CO, and Mankato State University, from which she received the M.A. in 1976. She achieved the Certificate of Clinical Competence in 1979 and the Iowa License in Speech Pathology in 1980. She is a member of the Iowa Speech Hearing Association, the American Speech Language Hearing Association, and the N.E.A. Her memberships also include A.A.U.W., U.M. Women, Beta Sigma Theta, and P.E.O. In 1994 she was employed as a Speech Language Pathologist by the Northern Trails Area Education Agency, Clear Lake, IA. She was a charter member of the Kids Korner Day Care Center Board, and was a member of the Board of Directors of her local Community Chest. Her hobbies include reading, bridge, crosswords and puzzles, and golf, and she is a Sunday School teacher.

Mark and Connie (Greiman) Hill had two adopted children: Chad Matthew (1979-1988); and Megan Caroline (b. 1985). Chad died as the result of an accident which occurred when he drove his go-cart into the road near his home and was struck by a passing car.

They had the following children:

4180   i.   Chad Matthew (1979-1988)

4181   ii.   Megan Caroline (1985-)

3964. Douglas Ray HILL,[915] youngest of the three sons of Dale and Avis (Boyington) Hill, was born at Clarion, Iowa, 25 August 1947; christened in the Methodist Church in Clarion, 21 March 1948. He attended Grant Township Rural School and then Clarion High School, from which he graduated in 1965. He spent two summers working as a store clerk and waiter at a chateau in Glacier National Park, where his father had worked as a bus driver in the summer of 1934. Doug Hill received the B.B.A. degree from the University of Iowa in 1969 and an M.B.A. from the University of Wisconsin in 1971. He attended banking schools at the University of Wisconsin, the University of Oklahoma, University of Colorado, and Northwestern University. In a career of more than 20 years in banking, he was an officer with the Brenton Bank, Grinnell, Iowa (1973-86), and President of the Brenton Bank, Cedar Rapids (1986-93).

In September 1993 Mr. Hill was elected president of Minowa Bancshares, Decorah, Iowa, and of the Decorah State Bank, one of several banks in Iowa and Minnesota that are owned by Minowa Bancshares. The total consolidated assets of Minowa Bancshares in 1993 were about $230 million. He has served on the Board of Trustees of the Vesterheim Museum in Decorah and of the Colorado School of Banking. He was a volunteer with Decorah Development and is a member of Rotary International. In 1998, he moved to Cedar Rapids, Iowa, as a consultant in the banking industry. His hobbies include swimming, reading, cross country skiing, hiking, and travel. He is a member of the Society of Mayflower Descendants in the line of Matthew Fuller, son of the Pilgrim, Edward Fuller.

He married, at Winfield, Iowa, 23 May 1971, when he was 23, **Linda Kay CARDEN**, daughter of Wade and Ethel (Cook) Carden; born at Burlington, Iowa, 19 November 1946. She was his classmate at the University of Iowa and was later a Personnel Specialist at St. Luke's Hospital, Cedar Rapids. She received the B.B.A. degree from the University of Iowa in 1969 and was an Employment Specialist at St. Luke's Hospital, Cedar Rapids, Iowa, from 1986-1993. Her activities include membership in T.T.T. and St. Luke's Hospital Auxiliary. She is a member of the Methodist Church. Her hobbies include reading, walking and travel.

They had the following children:

4182   i.   Erin Julia (1975-)

4183   ii.   Ryan Douglas (1977-)

3965. Kay Marie HILL. Born on 26 Jan 1951 in Hampton, IA. Occupation: Accounts payable supervisor, Praxair; Mother of 3. Religion: Non-denominational Christian Protestant. Education: Spencer School of Business graduate 1970. On 26 Apr 1975 when Kay Marie was 24, she married **Ken CRUM**, in Des Moines, Iowa. They were divorced in 1992 in Des Moines, Iowa.

They had the following children:

4184   i.   Jessica Dawn (1976-)

4185   ii.   Amber Marie (1981-)

4186   iii.   Hayley Camille (1984-)

3966. Willow (b. Cindy Lou) HILL. Born on 28 Jan 1954 in Clarion, IA. Occupation: Licensed massage therapist, Iowa City, Iowa. Education: Completed one and one-half years at Univ. of Iowa (1972-1974). Religion: She is a member of the Rainbow Family of Living Light. She first married **Bill SOLAWETZ**.

They had one child:

4187   i.   Sienna Glory (1976-)

In 1977 when Willow (b. Cindy Lou) was 22, she second married **Brian (later Osha POV) DAVIDSON**, in Iowa City, Johnson Co., Iowa. They were divorced in 1979 in Iowa City, Johnson Co., Iowa.

They had one child:

4188   i.   Sarah Gray (b. Sarah Rainbow) (1979-)

Willow (b. Cindy Lou) third married **Michael STEPHANS**.

They had one child:

4189   i.   Gwendolyn Ann (1986-)

She fourth common-law married **Jack PHALEN III**, in 1989 in Iowa City, Johnson Co., Iowa.

They had one child:

4190   i.   Govinda Jonas (1992-)

3967. Michael Dean HILL. Born and died at birth, 14 Feb 1956. Buried in Clarion, IA.

3968. Julie Lyn HILL. Born on 5 Mar 1957 in Clarion, IA. Occupation: Medical technologist, Cedar Falls, IA. Religion: Lutheran. On 28 Jul 1979 when Julie Lyn was 22, she married **Paul GLADE**, son of Willard GLADE & Wanda WATNE. Born on 26 Apr 1958 in Clarion, IA. Religion: Lutheran.
They had the following children:

4191   i.   Ryan Jeffrey (1983-)

4192   ii.   Caitlin Marie (1989-)

3969. Larry Dean HILL. Born on 16 Apr 1960 in Clarion, IA; died of congenital heart disease in Rochester, Minn., 9 Sep 1977, age 17. He was a farmer and student at Clarion High School. Methodist.

3970. David Earl "Dave" ODLAND,[916] eldest child of Earl and Lela (Hill) Odland, was born at Clarion, Wright County, Iowa, 28 November 1954. He grew up on his parents' farm in Holmes, Wright County, Iowa, and graduated from Clarion High School as the Salutatorian of the class of 1973. He then attended Iowa State University, from which he received a Bachelor's degree in animal science in 1977. He entered farming with his father, raising corn, beans and pigs. He is involved as a leader in 4-H, and is a member of the Board of the Boone Valley Electric Co-op, the Holmes Co-op Elevator Board, and the Pork Producers Board. He is a lifetime member of the Holmes, Iowa, Lutheran Church, where he is a Sunday School teacher, member of the choir, and in 2000 was President of the church. Dave Odland is a member of Ruritan service club and enjoys sports, being an avid fan of the Iowa State "Cyclones."

He married, at Clarion, 18 August 1984, when he was 29, **Annette Arliene OLSON**, daughter of Larry and Carrie Ann (Richardson) Olson; born at Clarion, 8 March 1963; a nurse.
They had the following children:

4193   i.   Andrew Nels (1985-)

4194   ii.   Cara LeAnn (1990-)

4195   iii.   Colin Earl (1993-)

3971. Laura Lee ODLAND,[917] older daughter and second child of Earl and Lela (Hill) Odland, was born at Clarion, Wright County, Iowa, 28 September 1956. She grew up on her parents' farm in Holmes, Iowa, near Clarion. She graduated from Clarion High School in 1974. She then attended Waldorf College, where she graduated in 1976. She traveled to Norway with the Waldorf Concert Choir. In 1978 she received her bachelor's degree in Elementary Education from Iowa State University. She then became an elementary (fifth grade) teacher in Osage, Iowa. She was married in 1984 and she and her husband began to raise their family. She is involved with many school and community activities and is an active member of the Lutheran Church, teaching and directing children's choirs and singing in the choir.

On 23 Jun 1984 when Laura Lee was 27, she married **Stephen KLAPPERICH**, son of Norbert KLAPPERICH & Mary Ann KOENIG, in Osage, IA. Born on 7 Jul 1957 in Osage, Mitchell Co., IA. Occupation: Machine operator. Religion: Lutheran.
They had the following children:

4196   i.   Allison Lee (1987-)

4197   ii.   Benjamin Stephen "Ben" (1990-)

3972. Lisa Ann ODLAND,[918] second daughter and third child of Earl and Lela (Hill) Odland, was born at Clarion, Iowa, 14 December 1960. She grew up on her parents' farm in Holmes, Iowa, near Clarion. She graduated from Clarion High School in 1979. She then attended Waldorf College, where she graduated in 1981; she travelled to Europe with the Waldorf Concert Choir in the same year. In 1983 she received her bachelor's degree in child development from South Dakota State University. She was married the following year; she and her husband then began to raise their family. She taught at Sioux Falls and Vermillion, South Dakota, and in 1995 was a kindergarten teacher at Akron, Iowa. She is involved in many school and community activities, including the Friendship and Service Club and the Akron Community Theater. She is a member of the Immanuel Lutheran Church of Akron, Iowa, where she is a Sunday School teacher and member of the choir. She enjoys golfing and letter writing.

She married, at Akron, Iowa, 21 July 1984, **Jon Stuart HARRIS**, son of Stuart and Carol (Boe)

Harris; born at Hawarden, Sioux County, Iowa, 3 November 1960; a farmer. He graduated from South Dakota State University with a degree in farm operations and general agriculture, and he is a farmer in Akron, Iowa.

They had the following children:

4198	i.	Nathan Jon (1986-)
4199	ii.	Rachel Ann (1989-)
4200	iii.	Michael Orin (1992-)

3973. Daniel Eugene ODLAND,[919] second son and fourth child of Earl and Lela (Hill) Odland, was born at Clarion, Wright County, Iowa, 25 October 1964. He grew up on his parents' farm near Holmes, Wright County, Iowa, and graduated from Clarion High School in 1983. He attended Waldorf College and travelled to Europe with the Waldorf Concert Choir in 1984. He graduated from Waldorf in 1985. He then attended Iowa State University, from which he graduated in 1987 with a bachelor's degree in agricultural business. He subsequently has been engaged in farming with his father and his older brother, David. He is involved in community affairs as a member of the Wright County 4-H Youth Committee, the Extension Council, and the Farm Bureau Board. Dan Odland is a Lifetime Member of the Holmes Lutheran Church, Holmes, Iowa, where he has been Sunday School Superintendent, Church Secretary, and member of the church choir. He enjoys refinishing furniture, flower gardening, and family history. He builds miniature replicas of houses and other buildings.

He married, at Eagle Grove, Wright County, Iowa, 29 June 1991, **Lynne WILDE**, daughter of Clarence and Betty (Adams) Wilde; born at Fort Dodge, Webster County, Iowa, 21 August 1964; an optometrist's assistant. She received a medical assistant's degree from the Northern Iowa Area Community College.

They had the following children:

4201	i.	Lukas Daniel (1992-)
4202	ii.	Matthew Clarence (1994-)
4203	iii.	Lauren Elizabeth (2001-)

3974. John Scott "Scott" WOODIN. Born on 30 Mar 1950 in Milwaukee, WI. Christened in Jun 1950 in Milwukee, WI (Kingsley Methodist Church). Occupation: Insurance counselor and financial planner. Education: Cornell College BA 1972. Religion: Methodist. In Jun 1972 when he was 22, he first married **Kristine ANDRESEN**, daughter of Richard H. ANDRESEN M.D. & May LONG, in Chicago, IL. Born on 25 Jun 1948 in Chicago, IL. Christened in Daughter of Dr. Richard and May ANDRESEN. Occupation: teacher. Religion: Lutheran. They were divorced in 1983.

They had the following children:

| 4204 | i. | Trevor John (1975-) |
| 4205 | ii. | Erik Richard (1978-) |

In 1987 when he was 36, he second married **Beth RUMMELL**. They were divorced in 1988.

On 25 Aug 1990 when John Scott was 40, he third married **Carol (SCANLAN) CARR-WOODIN**, daughter of Robert SCANLAN, in Milwaukee, WI. Born on 12 Aug 1955 in Arlington Heights, Cook Co., IL. Occupation: Pharmacy Sales Representative. Religion: St. Robert's Church.

They had the following children:

| 4206 | i. | Maggie Carolyn (1992-) |
| 4207 | ii. | Molly Alexandria (1993-) |

3975. Wendy Lee WOODIN.[920] Born on 10 Jan 1953 in Milwaukee, WI. Christened on 15 Mar 1953 in Milwaukee, WI. Occupation: Educator; author; Mother of 1. Religion: St. James Church, Mequon, WI. Author of the book, LEGENDARY TEAM LEADERSHIP, published in 1994. She gave the "Family Reflections" at the memorial service for her aunt Mildred Woodin at Clarion, Iowa, 1 November 1997.

On 5 Nov 1977 when Wendy Lee was 24, she married **Leroy Leonard PECHE**, in Milwaukee, WI. Born on 11 Jul 1950 in Medford, WI. Christened on 30 Jul 1950 in Medford, WI. Occupation: Family Therapist. Religion: St. James Church, Mequon, WI. Son of Leonard and Rosella (HOLBACH) PECHE.

They had one child:

| 4208 | i. | Lauren Gray (1987-) |

3976. Patti Jean HEMENWAY.[921] Born on 11 Aug 1955 in Perry, Dallas Co., IA. Occupation: Director, Kansas' libraries for blind & handicapped. Education: Library Science. Religion: United Methodist. Living in Emporia, Kansas, in December 1999. On 10 Jun 1989 when Patti Jean was 33, she married **Robert Wells LANG**, in West Allis, Milwaukee Co., WI. Born on 10 Oct 1963 in Arlington Heights, IL. Dry cleaner. Religion: United Methodist. He is the son of David and Barbara (Yucker) Lang.
They had one child:

    4209   i.   Ryan Wells (1991-)

3977. Rev. Rhonda Arlene HEMENWAY. Born on 2 Mar 1958 in Des Moines, Polk Co., IA. Occupation: Assoc. Pastor, St. Johns United Methodist Church, Davenport, IA. Religion: United Methodist Church. In 1999 she was in her eighth year as Associate Pastor of St. John's United Methodist Church, Davenport, Iowa. On 1 Nov 1986 when Rhonda Arlene was 28, she married **Craig Charles SCHULTZ D.O.**, son of Charles SCHULTZ Dr. & Florence BOECKEN, in West Allis, Milwaukee Co., WI. Born on 24 Nov 1946 in Madison, Dane Co., WI. Occupation: Physician, Dubuque, IA; was in U.S.A.F. 1972-77. Education: Univ. Iowa BS '69; Coll. Osteop. Des Moines D.O. '73. Religion: United Methodist Church. He is the son of Dr. Charles and Florence (Boecken) Schultz.
They had one child:

    4210   i.   Rachel Elizabeth (1994-)

3978. Michelle Ann HEMENWAY. Born on 4 Dec 1971 in Waukesha, Waukesha Co., WI. Education: U. Of Wisconsin--Madison (Communication Arts) '94. In December 1999 she was employed as an employment counselor at Legal Placement Services in Milwaukee, Wisconsin, and she was living in Wauwatosa, Wisconsin. Michelle Ann married **Ken _____**.
They had the following children:

    4211   i.   Abigail (2005-)
    4212   ii.   Zachary (2008-)
    4213   iii.   Mason Alexander (2010-)

3979. James Warren "Jim" HILL J.D.,[922] eldest child of George James and Helene (Zimmermann) Hill, was born at Boston, Suffolk County, Massachusetts, 23 January 1954; christened at St. Peter's Episcopal Church, Weston, Mass., in 1954. He is the son of Helene Zimmermann by her first marriage to James Hedgcock Grover and was adopted by George Hill in 1964, at which time his surname was changed from Grover to Hill.

He was educated at the Park School in Brookline, Massachusetts, and at public schools in Bethesda, Maryland, and Denver, Colorado. He completed his secondary education at The Gunnery School in Washington, Connecticut. After working in various building trades in Minnesota and West Virginia for ten years he entered Rutgers University in New Brunswick, where he majored in philosophy and graduated with honors in 1985. He continued his education with studies of philosophy and law at Rutgers. He graduated with the J.D. degree in 1993, and became a member of the Bar of New York and New Jersey. He began his career as a public defender in Orange County, N.Y., and he continued this work in Dutchess County, N.Y., where he has resided since 1994. He and his companion **Uma NARAYAN, Ph.D.**, live in Poughkeepsie, N.Y. Dr. Narayan is the Mellon Professor of Philosophy at Vassar College. Mr. Hill enjoys hiking in the Appalachian Mountains and kayaking on rivers and lakes in New York State and New Hampshire. He is also the non-resident manager of his family's nationally-certified forested property, known as Hilltree Farm, in Eaton, New Hampshire. In July 2011, he completed a 45 mile bicycle ride round trip from the east base to the summit of the Kancamangus Pass.

3980. David Hedgcock "Dave" HILL,[923] second child and second son of George J. and Helene (Zimmermann) Hill, was born at Boston, Massachusetts, 29 August 1955; christened in 1955 in St. Peter's Episcopal Church, Weston, Mass.; died at Glen Ridge, N.J., 4 January 2004. He was the son of James Hedgcock Grover, Esq., first husband of Helene Zimmermann; they were divorced in 1960. In 1964 he was adopted by his stepfather and his surname was legally changed to Hill.

Mr. Hill studied at the Dearborn School, Cambridge, Massachusetts, and at private and public schools in Bethesda, Maryland; in Denver, CO; and in the suburbs of St. Louis, Missouri. As a boy he was a Cub Scout and a First Class Boy Scout, and an acolyte in the Episcopal Church. He graduated from

University City, Missouri, High School in 1975. He then attended Fontbonne College in Clayton, Missouri, and later was a student at Glenville, West Virginia, State College. He also attended Union County, N.J., State College. In 1994 he graduated from the Empire Technical School, East Orange, .N.J, as a Certified Medical Secretary. He enjoyed composing music and writing essays and poetry, and some of his works were published during his lifetime and some were edited and published posthumously.

Mr. Hill was employed for several years as a Nursing Assistant at St. Barnabas Medical Center, Livingston, NJ, and in 1994 he was a salesman for Sears, Roebuck, and Co. at Livingston, NJ. He enjoyed walking and long distance bicycle riding, computers, and crossword puzzles and he was a member of the choir and layreader at the Church of the Holy Innocents, West Orange, NJ. He was completely disabled on 20 September 1994 as the result of a severe stroke caused by an occlusion of the right internal carotid artery. It is believed that he probably bruised his carotid artery in a fall at work, but the origin of the occlusion could never be determined. In 2001 he was living near his parents in Essex County, New Jersey, and writing poetry and composing music for the piano and organ. As he became increasingly disabled, he was hospitalized at the Essex County Hospital, Cedar Grove, N.J., and it was there that he had a fatal episode of cerebral ischemia on 25 November 2003, probably due to aspiration of food at breakfast. After resuscitation, he was taken to Mountainside Hospital in Glen Ridge, N.J. It became apparent that he had no hope for recovery; he was taken off of life support on 30 December and he died on 4 January 2004. A memorial service was held at the Church of the Holy Innocents in West Orange on 10 January 2004. His cremains were divided; some were interred in the Bethel Cemetery, Parkersburg, West Virginia, near the grave of his former wife, Sheri (Wilson) (Hill) Graham; some were scattered in the Memorial Garden at the Church of the Holy Innocents, and some were scattered in the Hill plot at the Snowville cemetery, Eaton, New Hampshire.

He married, at Washington Bottom, W.Va., 18 April 1981, when he was 25, **Sheri Lynn WILSON**, daughter of George S. and Regina L. (Marion) Wilson; born at Parkersburg, WV, 4 October 1958; died of an acute asthmatic attack at Parkersburg, 11 February 2003, age 44. She was David Hill's classmate at Glenville State College, and she later became a public school teacher. She received the B.S. from Glenville (WV) State College in 1978, and later the degree of M.Ed. She was employed in the Calhoun County school system for many years and was Principal at Arnoldsburg Elementary School before becoming Assistant Principal at Jackson Junior High School in Parkersburg. She attended Mineral Wells, W.Va., Baptist Church. Services were held on February 15, 2003, at Sunset Memorial Funeral Home, Parkersburg (Minister Robert Summers, officiating), followed by burial in Bethel Cemetery, beside Bethel Baptist Church. They were divorced on 29 July 1983.

David and Sheri (Wilson) Hill had one child:

    4214   i.   Heather Dawn (1982-)

3981. Sarah HILL, M.A., Ph.D.,[924] elder daughter and third child of George J. and Helene (Zimmermann) Hill, was born at Bethesda, Maryland, 5 January 1962. She was baptized later that year at St. Mary Anne's (Episcopal) Church, North East, Maryland, where her father's maternal ancestors had been vestrymen before and during the Revolutionary War. She attended public and private schools in Denver, Colorado; the suburbs of St. Louis, Missouri; and in Huntington, West Virginia. She was a student at Mary Institute, Ladue, Mo., and she graduated in 1980 from Chatham Hall, Chatham, Virginia, where she was a member of the Chatham Athletic Council and the Student Council. She then attended Kenyon College, Gambier, Ohio, where she majored in English and received the B.A., *cum laude*, in 1985. While at Kenyon she played field hockey and lacrosse. She received seven varsity letters and as a senior she was co-captain of the field hockey team which competed in the national NCAA meet.

Ms. Hill spent the summer after her junior year in high school in Nice, France, as a student with the Experiment in International Living. She took a semester off after her third year at Kenyon and worked as a marine biology technician on a Smithsonian Institution research vessel. She spent her last semester in college as an exchange student in Vienna, studying German and teaching English as a foreign language to Viennese high school students. After graduation from college she worked for Lebenthal & Co., N.Y.C; and she was a Development Officer for Very Special Arts in Washington, DC. She then studied Spanish in Antigua, Guatemala, and was a writer for InforPress, Guatemala City. Ms. Hill has also travelled extensively in Europe and Central America. She is fluent in French, German and Spanish. She enjoys photography and is an avid reader, hiker, and runner, and she climbed Mt. Kenya in Africa and several volcanoes in Guatemala.

In 1990 she entered graduate school in the Department of Anthropology at Johns Hopkins University, Baltimore, MD. She completed her course work for the Ph.D. in 1994 and was awarded the M.A. degree; she then began her field work in El Paso, Texas, and Ciudad Juarez, Mexico, on a Fulbright Scholarship. From 1995-98 she lived in El Paso. In 1999 she returned to Baltimore to complete her dissertation; she received her Ph.D. at commencement at Johns Hopkins University in May 2001. She was an Assistant Professor of Anthropology at Temple University in 2001-2, and she then moved to the University of Western Michigan as an Assistant Professor in the Departments of Anthropology and Environmental Studies. She was promoted to Associate Professor with tenure in 2008. She lives with her partner, Megan Reynolds, Esq., and their two daughters in Kalamazoo, Michigan.

Sarah Hill has one child, a daughter, Georgia Clare Hill, born at Kalamazoo, Michigan, 19 September 2004. Her partner, **Megan REYNOLDS, Esq.**, of Wilmington, Delaware, was a midwife and staff member of a large non-profit organization before moving to Michigan. She graduated from Michigan State University Law School in 2008, and in 2009 she was employed in an office providing legal aid for non-citizen farm workers. Megan Reynolds has one child, a daughter, Rosalie Maired Hill, born at Kalamazoo, 14 February 2008. Rosalie and Georgia were both conceived from the same anonymous sperm donor, so they are half-sisters.

Sarah Hill and Megan Reynolds have the following children (surname Hill):

> **4215**   i.   Georgia Clare (2004-)
>
> **4215a**   ii.   Rosalie Maired (2008-)

3982. Helena Rundall "Lana" HILL, younger daughter and fourth child of George J. and Helene (Zimmermann) Hill, was born at Boston, Massachusetts, 1 May 1964, shortly before her mother received her Ph.D. degree; christened about 1964 at St. Paul's Episcopal Church, Brookline, Mass.

She was educated in public and private schools in Denver, Colorado; the suburbs of St. Louis, Missouri; and Huntington, West Virginia. She attended Mary Institute, Ladue, Missouri, and she graduated in 1982 from Chatham Hall, Chatham, Virginia, where she was a member of the Student Council and President of the Chatham Athletic Council. Miss Hill spent a summer in Norway with the Experiment in International Living. She studied environmental engineering for one year at the University of Colorado, where she trained with the Rocky Mountain Rescue organization. In 1985 she received the A.A. degree from Sterling College, Craftsbury Common, Vermont.

Lana Hill has been employed in various outdoor activities, including tree surgeon's assistant, Tamworth, N.H.; and professional ski patroller and ski instructor at Sunday River, Bethel, Maine. From 1987 until 2007 she was principally employed by Outward Bound, beginning at the Hurricane Island, Maine, Outward Bound School, as a rock climbing instructor, trip leader and outdoor educator. From 1992-93 she was Base Site Manager for Outward Bound in Baltimore, Maryland, and she later was Assistant Director for Alumni Relations of the national Outward Bound office.

She has been a certified Wilderness First Responder and a Licensed Maine Guide. Lana Hill is an avid lover of the outdoors, having walked from northern Vermont to the Atlantic Ocean and canoed to Hudson's Bay. She has climbed Mt. Kenya in Africa and volcanoes in Ecuador, and she has climbed many technical "walls" and towers in Utah, West Virginia, and New York State. She was a member of the American Alpine Club. She has rafted the Bio-Bio River in Chile, and she enjoys sea kayaking and "pullboat" sailing off the coast of Maine. She also enjoys handicrafts, working with wood and fabric, and cooking. She has run many marathons, including the Marine Corps, Chicago, San Diego, and New York.

From 2000-2003, she was a member of the faculty and Director of the Hardie Center at the Gilman School in Baltimore, Md. In October 2004, she was appointed Program Director for Outward Bound's Urban Centers in the Mid-Atlantic Region (Philadelphia and Baltimore). From 2007-2010 she was employed by Cradlerock, Inc., a management consulting firm in Stamford, Connecticut, and travelled widely for Cradlerock from her home in Baltimore, Maryland. In 2010 she became a member of the leadership development team of the British Embassy in Washington, D.C., with duties that range over all of the Western Hemisphere.

3983. Victoria Grace HILL,[925] daughter and elder child of Thomas David and Keiko (Nambara) Hill, was born at Minot, N.D., 6 September 1960. She was christened in 1960 at St. Mark's Episcopal Church, Aberdeen, S.D. She received the B.S. degree from Nazareth College and the M.M. (Master of Music in violin performance and chamber music) from the University of Michigan. She has also taken courses toward the M.B.A. On 17 September 1983, when she was 23, she married **Mark David NORFLEET**, son of Ronald J. C. NORFLEET & Carol Irene DICKERSON, in Dexter, Michigan; born in Walled Lake, Mich., 19 September 1956. He is a maker and restorer of violins and other stringed instruments. They live in Ann Arbor, Mich.

3984. Lt. Col. Thomas David "Tom" HILL Jr., USAF (ret),[926] son and younger child of Thomas David and Keiko (Nambara) Hill, and youngest great-grandchild of George J. and Jessie (Fidelia) Stockwell Hill, was born in Minot, N.D., 18 September 1962. He was christened in 1962 at St. Mark's Episcopal Church, Aberdeen, S.D. He graduated in aeronautical engineering from the University of Michigan, where he was a member of the U.S. Air Force ROTC unit. He was commissioned as a second lieutenant in the USAF. He graduated from USAF Navigator School and USAF Pilot School, and was a student at USAF Test Pilot School, Edwards Air Force Base, California, in 1994-95. He holds a Master's degree from the Air Force Institute of Technology, Dayton, Ohio. He was qualified to fly the F-15, F-16, T-38, Sherpa, and C-141 aircraft. In 1999 he was an Exchange Test Pilot at Cold Lake, Alberta, working with the Canadian Air Force. In 2001 he was an instructor in the USAF test pilot school, Edwards AFB, California; his flight nickname was "Sulu." By December 1997, Major Hill had logged over 1,000 flight hours in the F-15 and more than 2,800 hours in thirty-five different aircraft. He was quoted by the magazine *Private Pilot* as saying that "As a military weapon, the F-15 is second to none. . . . The F-15 has recorded 96 victories and zero losses. This is unmatched by any other fighter in history."

Thomas D. Hill, Jr., and **Sheila SHEEHY** had a son, Conor Sheehy, who was born on 29 August 1993; in 1999, Conor was living with his mother in Dutchess County, New York. After Conor was born, she was married, but was divorced and living as a single parent in 2003.

Thomas D. Hill Jr. and Julia Sheehy had one child:

    4216   i.   Conor Patrick Desmond [surname Sheehy] (1993-)

Thomas D. Hill, Jr., when he was 31, married (1), at Austin, Texas, 15 January 1994, **Deana SENN**, daughter of George and Lucie (Patenaude) Senn. She graduated from the Texas A & M University with a degree in biochemistry. They were later divorced.

On 24 Dec 2003 when Thomas David "Tom" was 41, he married (2) **Robin McMACKEN**, in Dayton, Ohio. They have since separated.

There was no issue from either marriage.

––––––––––––––––––––[927]

3985. Mildred LONG. Born on 31 May 1935. Occupation: Mother of 4. She was living in Vinton, Iowa, in 1994. Mildred married **Fred KISLING**. Born on 29 Apr 1934; died on 17 Feb 1988, he was 53. They had the following children:

    4217   i.   Kristi (1955-1979)
    4218   ii.   Lori (1957-)
    4219   iii.   Kenneth (1959-)
    4220   iv.   Beth (1962-)

3986. James LONG. Born on 16 May 1939. He was living in Vinton, Iowa, in 1994. James married **Martha GEATER**. Born on 1 Jul 1939. They had the following children:

    4221   i.   Jimmy (1962-)
    4222   ii.   Ronald (1963-)
    4223   iii.   John (1967-)

3987. Wayne LONG. Born on 18 Feb 1942. Wayne married **Diane CLARK**. Born on 11 Jul 1944. They had the following children:

    4224   i.   Jeff

4225	ii.	Nicole

3988. Helen LONG. Born on 20 Oct 1947. She married **Robert CUMMINGS**.
They had the following children:

4226	i.	Michael (1971-)
4227	ii.	Jennie (1973-)
4228	iii.	Ryan (1974-)

3989. Louisa Mae LINDSAY. Born 20 Aug 1938; married **Loran LUNDAHL**. Born on 17 Sep 1935.
They had the following children:

4229	i.	Tom (1954-)
4230	ii.	Brenda (1957-)
4231	iii.	Rhonda (1960-)
4232	iv.	Paul (1962-)
4233	v.	Mike (1964-)
4234	vi.	Rich (1971-)

3990. Delbert LINDSAY. Born on 3 Jul 1941. She m. **Wanda BRINKMAN**. Born 20 Nov 1944.
They had the following children:

4235	i.	Thresa Jo (1963-)
4236	ii.	James (1966-)

3991. Verlyn LINDSAY. Born on 1 Feb 1946. Verlyn m. **Miate RODRIGUEZ**. Born 21 Nov 1944.
They had the following children:

4237	i.	Mary (1974-)
4238	ii.	James (1970-)

3992. Eileen LINDSAY. Born on 23 Feb 1948; married **John LANGFORD**. Born on 10 Apr 1947.
They had the following children:

4239	i.	Dwight (1970-)
4240	ii.	Kevin (1973-)
4241	iii.	Christine (1976-)

3993. Allen Ray HARSON.[928] Born on 18 Jul 1944 in Urbana, IA. Occupation: Truck driver; was in U.S. Army. Religion: Baptist. He lived in Iowa, Minnesota, and Colorado. Allen and Sue (Smith) Harson were living in Holmes, Wright County, Iowa, in 1996. He was in a serious truck accident in 1995 from which he was still recuperating in February 1996. On 18 Dec 1964 when Allen Ray was 20, he married **Ada Sue SMITH**, daughter of Joel William SMITH II & Brunnie Mae MARTIN, in Phoenix City, AL. Born on 22 Apr 1946 in Jesup, Wayne Co., GA. Occupation: Mother of 2; Clerk of Court. Religion: Baptist. She was the daughter of Joel William Smith II & Brunnie Mae Martin.
They had the following children:

4242	i.	Stacey Carole (1977-)
4243	ii.	Joel Ray (1983-1985)

3994. Donna LINDSAY.[929] Born on 20 Nov 1942 in Clarion, Wright Co., Ia. Occupation: Mother of 2. Education: Graduated, Clarion [Iowa] High School, 1960. Religion: Methodist. She attended grade school in a one room school in Grant Township until she entered eighth grade at Clarion High School, from which she graduated in 1960. During her early married years, she traveled with her husband, who was in the U.S. Air Force. They lived in Nebraska, Oklahoma, Guam, Michigan, Wyoming, and then in Washington state, where she has lived since 1971. She married, 24 September 1961, **Larry McGINNIS**.
They had the following children:

4244	i.	David Lee (1962-)
4245	ii.	Daniel Lee "Dan" (1964-)

3995. Russell Dean LINDSAY. Born abt 9 May 1947 in Clarion, Wright Co., Ia. Occupation: U.S. Air Force active duty, 5 yrs; then telephone company employee. Education: Graduated from Clarion [Iowa] High School. His employment with the telephone company took him from Iowa to Colorado and New Mexico, where he and his family were living in 1996. His USAF duty was performed in Texas, California, and Mildenhall AFB, England. On 1 Mar 1965 when Russell Dean was 17, he married

Connie CEGAN in Clarion, Wright Co., Ia.
They had the following children:

4246	i.	Barbara (1970-)
4247	ii.	Ronald (1977-)
4248	iii.	Lori (1979-)

3996. Edwin Everett "Ed" LINDSAY. Born on 12 Jul 1952 in Clarion, Wright Co., Ia.; died in Oak Park, Ill. on 26 Feb 1994, he was 41. Buried in 1994 in Clarion, Wright Co., Ia. Occupation: Registered Nurse, Oak Park, Ill. Education: Graduated from Clarion [Iowa] High School and Drake University; R.N. training at Oak Park, Ill. Religion: Methodist.
––––––––––––––––––930

3997. "children" ROSE.

3998. Bryan Mark HILL. Born on 23 Jul 1974 in Newark, N.J.

3999. Matthew Dean HILL. Born 28 Jun 1976 in Newark, N.J. He married **Crystal ILLINSWORTH.**
They had one child:

4249	i.	Tyler Dean

4000. Michelle HILL. Born on 5 Jul 1977 in Newark, N.J.

4001. Heather HILL. Born on 7 Dec 1982 in Newark, N.J.

4002. Rebecca Elizabeth HILL.

4003. Kaitlin Margaret Eva HILL. Born on 26 Jan 1989.

4004. Kathleen Ann JENKINS. Born on 26 Oct 1978 in Elmira, N.Y. Information about Kathleen (Jenkins) Smith, her husband Corey, and their children, was given to George J. Hill from her and her parents at the Hill Reunion, 21 August 2010. Kathleen Ann married **Corey SMITH.**
They had the following children:

4250	i.	Damon Mitchell (2000-)
4251	ii.	Dalton Marshal (2002-)

4005. John Daniel JENKINS. Born on 15 Apr 1983 in Elimra, N.Y. He was unmarried as of 21 August 2010, when he attended the Hill Reunion in Caton, N.Y.
––––––––––––––––––

4006. Thom CARLSON Ph.D.[931] Born abt 1940. Philosopher, farmer. Harvard, Ph.D. philosophy, 1990. He is unmarried and lives on his ancestors' farm in Vinton, Ia.
––––––––––––––––––932

4007. Earnest Richard TRAVIS. Born on 5 Mar 1942. He married **Janet STEINBRUNNER.**
They had one child:

4252	i.	Earnest Richard (1943-)

4008. Alvin Raymond TRAVIS Jr. Alvin Raymond married **Sandy MILLER.**
They had the following children:

4253	i.	Todd Thomas
4254	ii.	Jon Paul

4009. Jon Paul TRAVIS. Born 20 May 1945; killed in Viet Nam, 26 Jan 1966, age 20. His name appears on the Viet Nam Wall Message Board: "Sgt Jon Paul Travis, 1st Bn, 7th Cav, KIA 26 Jan 1966."

4010. Linda Ann TRAVIS. Born 3 Nov 1948 in Corning, N.Y., married **Andrew PRYSLOPSKI.**
They had the following children:

4255	i.	Danielle Marie
4256	ii.	Andrew Michael

4011. Michael Richard HILL. Born on 6 Mar 1946.

4012. Bryan Joseph HILL. Born on 26 Feb 1947.

4013. Francis Xavier HILL. Born on 6 Mar 1951.

4014. Paula Marie HILL. Born on 5 Nov 1952.

4015. Patricia Ann HILL. Born on 23 Mar 1954.

4016. Richard L. HILL V. Born on 27 Nov 1956.

4017. Christopher John HILL. Born on 22 Feb 1958.

4018. Thomas Flynn HILL. Born on 27 Apr 1959.

4019. Kathryn Mary HILL. Born on 25 Oct 1961.

4020. Vincent Gerard HILL. Born on 26 Nov 1963.

4021. Douglas MICHELSON. Born on 3 Feb 1957.

4022. Carey MICHELSON. Born on 10 Apr 1960.

4023. Tracey MICHELSON.

4024. Dennis Malcolm "Denny" O'CONNELL. Born on 31 Aug 1947. A member of the Society of Mayflower Descendants in the State of New Jersey.

4025. John White O'CONNELL. Born on 27 Jul 1948.

4026. David Brian O'CONNELL. Born on 16 Jan 1950.

4027. Karen Renee O'CONNELL. Born on 17 Oct 1952. On 26 Oct 1974 when Karen Renee was 22, she married **Harold Lawrence MAHNKE**.
They had one child:
> 4257　　i.　　Adam Richard (1977-)

4028. Richard Keith O'CONNELL. Born on 17 Oct 1952 in Corning, N.Y. On 14 Feb 1976 when Richard Keith was 23, he married **Wendy Jo BANFIELD**. Born on 15 Jul 1956 in Elmira, N.Y.
They had the following children:
> 4258　　i.　　Kenneth Richard (1979-)
> 4259　　ii.　　Gregory Keith (1981-)

4029. Kevin Jay O'CONNELL. Born on 5 Jul 1958. On 12 Jun 1982 when Kevin Jay was 23, he married **Tracey Lynn RANDALL**. Born on 22 Nov 1962 in Dundee, N.Y.
They had one child:
> 4260　　i.　　Joshua Brandon (1987-)

4030. Penny EAST.

Line 8 – Descendants of John Hill (continued)
--------------- 933

4031. Mark PFAFF. Born on 6 Aug 1954 in Miles City, Custer Co., Mont.

4032. Lenore PFAFF. Born on 21 Jun 1959 in Miles City, Custer Co., Mont.

4033. Beverly PFAFF. Born on 14 Dec 1955 in Miles City, Mont. She married **Steve SIMON**.
They had one child:
> 4261　　i.　　Nicole

4034. Sharon PFAFF. Born on 12 Feb 1961 in Miles City, Custer Co., Mont.

4035. Amy Louise HILL. Born on 29 Jan 1962 in Medical Lake, Wash. Occupation: artist.

4036. Mary Ellen HILL. Born on 19 Jun 1963 in Medical Lake, Wash. Occupation: zoologist.

4037. Bennet John HILL. Born on 18 Nov 1964 in Pullman, Wash. Occupation: architect.

4038. James Michael HILL. Born on 9 Mar 1968 in Seattle, Wash. He was adopted; he is a pilot.

4039. Wiley Willy WILHELM. Born on 24 Jul 1966 in Fairbanks, Alaska. Occupation: civil engineer; married twice. Wiley Willy married **Katherine ?(WILHELM).**
They had the following children:
> 4262　　i.　　Charles
> 4263　　ii.　　Katherine
> 4264　　iii.　　Darrel B. (1948-1978)

4040. Ellen Gail MARSHALL. Born on 27 Oct 1953 in Bozeman, Mont. On 4 Aug 1979 when Ellen Gail was 25, she married **Edward Allen BAIRD**, in Dubois, Wyo.
They had one child:
> 4265　　i.　　Mathew (1981-)

4041. James Wilson MARSHALL. Born on 30 Aug 1955 in Bozeman, Mont. Education: Univ. Wyoming, accounting. James Wilson married **Hedi NORGAARD**, in Missoula, Mont.
They had one child:

> **4266**   i.   Elizabeth Ann (1982-)

4042. Kelly Dawn YOST. Born on 18 May 1958 in Missoula, Mont. Education: Graduated Lubbock, Tex. On 8 Jun 1985 when she was 27, she married **Robert Thomas HARPER** in Florida. Golf pro and manager, Pebble Beach, Fla.
They had the following children:

> **4267**   i.   Robert Joshua Taylor (1992-)
> **4268**   ii.   Joseph Michael (1989-)

4043. Robin Gail YOST. Born on 16 Jan 1960 in Spokane, Wash. Occupation: Teaches choir in Great Falls, Mont. Education: Music degree. Religion: Lutheran. On 10 Jun 1979 when Robin Gail was 19, she married **Rev. Mark C. PEDERSON**, in Tacoma, Wash.
They had the following children:

> **4269**   i.   Noel Christine (1987-)
> **4270**   ii.   Paul (1989-)

4044. Penney Jeanette YOST. Born on 5 Jun 1961 in Portland, Ore. Occupation: graphic arts. Education: graduated California Lutheran University. On 12 May 1984 when Penney Jeanette was 22, she married **Michael ADAMS,** in Thousand Oaks, Calif.

4045. Bruce Jon HILL. Born on 26 Oct 1956 in Port Hueneme, Calif. On 8 Sep 1984 when Bruce Jon was 27, he married **Jan REEDY**, in Fairfax County, Va.

4046. Molly Regan HILL. Born on 15 Jan 1959 in Lexington, Mass. Occupation: US Airways flight attendant. abt 1986 when Molly Regan was 26, she married **Bradford PARKER**, in Vienna, Va. Born in 1950s in Berlin, East Germany. They were divorced in 1993.
They had the following children:

> **4271**   i.   Logan Peale (1987-)
> **4272**   ii.   Rebecca Colline (1989-)

4047. Rebecca Leigh HILL. Born on 30 Oct 1960 in Sioux City, Ia. Education: Geology. On 4 Apr 1986 when Rebecca Leigh was 25, she married **Dave DILLER**, in Golden, Colo. Occupation: Software producer for oil exploration enterprises.
They had the following children:

> **4273**   i.   Jedediah Hill (1989-)
> **4274**   ii.   Zachary Travis (1992-)

4048. Douglas Campbell HILL. Born on 28 Dec 1962 in Colorado Springs, Colo. Occupation: flight software production for Titan/Centaur rocket at Lockheed Martin. Education: RPI - computer and systems engineering. On 10 Aug 1990 when he was 27, he married **Linda EUE**, in San Diego, Calif. Born on 18 May 1965 in Redwood Falls, Minn. Occupation: Works in mission analysis, doing Centaur rocket guidance design; mother of 2. Education: Univ. Minnesota, B.S. in mechanical engineering.
They had the following children:

> **4275**   i.   Andrew William (1994-)
> **4276**   ii.   Jason Robert (1996-)

4049. Tracy Elizabeth HILL. Born on 10 Feb 1964 in Cambell, Calif. Occupation: copy editor for newspapers in Durham, N.C.; Pensacola, Fla.; and Raleigh, N.C. Education: North Carolina State University, B.A. in journalism; Florida State University, M.A. in economics.

4050. Eric James HILL. Born on 12 Dec 1965 in Cambell, Calif. Occupation: Wheaton Plastics - Lead mechanic on the injection moulding and blow moulding equipment. On 14 Jun 1987 when Eric James was 21, he married **Karen Denise LEWIS**, in Raleigh, N.C. Born in Georgia. Occupation: operates home businesses for mail-order crafts, constructs custom web pages, and is webmaster for a N.C. publishing house; mother of 3.
They had the following children:

> **4277**   i.   Dustin James (1990-)
> **4278**   ii.   Erica Lemay (1992-)
> **4279**   iii.   Sarah Elizabeth (1992-)

4051. Kirk James HAYES. Born on 4 Oct 1974. Occupation: U.S. Marine Corps until 1997; then works

in computer memory development. Kirk James married **Joni ?(HAYES)**.
They had one child:

    4280   i.   Logan (1995-)

4052. Laura Rosalie BALLUFF. Born on 16 Sep 1964 in St. Louis, Mo.

4053. Tammara Margaret BALLUFF. Born on 30 Jul 1970 in St. Louis, Mo.

4054. Mary Lou SHERMAN.

4055. Laura Lee SHERMAN.

4056. John Jay SHERMAN.

4057. Paula Jean SHERMAN. Born on 28 Jun 1949. Paula Jean married **? BOWDEN**.

4058. Linda Lee SHAY. Born on 22 Mar 1938 in Gary, Ind. On 15 Mar 1957 when Linda Lee was 18, she first married **Emery SHAFFER.**
They had the following children:

    4281   i.   Laurie Kevin (1959-)
    4282   ii.   Shelley Lynn (1963-)

On 30 Jun 1971 when Linda Lee was 33, she second married **Benjamin Herman BABCOCK**. Born on 1 Apr 1923 in Mt. Morris, Mich.
They had one child:

    4283   i.   James Wesley (1972-)
                                      ——————————————————[934]

4059. Leona Alice SCHROADER. Leona Alice died bef 1981. Mother of 1.
Child:

    4284   i.   Sharon

4060. Marian Rozella SCHROADER,[935] second daughter and second child of Frank Leslie and Ula Myrtle (Anderson) Schroader, was born at Thompson, Eden Township, Winnebago County, Iowa, 27 June 1920. She attended grammar school for eight years at Thompson, Iowa, and she graduated from Forest City, Iowa, high school. She later attended Pima Community College in Tucson, Arizona. She was married at the age of 22 and raised eight children. In 1996 she was living in Tucson, Arizona, where she had attended Pima Community College, and she also maintained a home in Minnesota. . She enjoyed gardening and raising A.K.C. registered Pomeranian dogs. She wrote poetry and had published her book of poems, *Thanks for Giving and Other Poems*, in 1990. This book was published in hardbound and softbound editions, and was also the subject of a video recording. She had 12 grandchildren, to whom her book of poetry was dedicated.

       She married, at Des Moines, Iowa, 10 April 1943, when she was 22, **Johnnie Carl BITKER**, son of John Fredrick and Hattie Barbara (Wenig) Bitker; born at Westline Township, Redwood County, Minnesota, 30 April 1914. He completed eight years of grammar school and attended Ventura High School. He later was employed as a farmer and truck driver. He was owner and operator of a freight line and was in the ice cream truck business. He has also been a service station attendant, a city bus driver, a treatment plant operator, and state meat inspector. He has retired as a miner from the Duval Copper Mines. He enjoys reading, working on cars, and dabbling in marketing and sales.
They had the following children, born in Iowa:

    4285   i.   Ula Francis (1943-)
    4286   ii.   Barry Lea (1945-)
    4287   iii.   Lyle Morris "Wylie" (1946-)
    4288   iv.   Leslie Maynard (1946-)
    4289   v.   Joan Carol (1950-)
    4290   vi.   Steven Jay (1954-1979)
    4291   vii.   Marylou Ann (1958-)
    4292   viii.   Tena Marie (1962-)

4061. Leslie Franklin SCHROADER,[936] second son and third child of Frank Leslie and Ula Myrtle (Anderson) Schroader, was born near Thompson, Iowa, 16 May 1927. He was born on his parents' farm, about two miles east of Thompson on Highway 9. He started school at the Varland School, about five miles north of Thompson. After a few months he transferred to another rural school, Madison 3, between Forest City and Crystal Lake, Iowa, where he completed grades 1-6. He attended grades 7-11 at the Hayfield, Iowa, school, and he took his senior year at Forest City, Iowa, High School. After graduation from high school he attended Mankato State College, now Mankato State University, Mankato, Minnesota, where he took a double major in Elementary Education and Art. He received his B.A. degree after four years and took a fifth year as well. He received an NDEA Fellowship to study elementary guidance and counseling at Duluth University. He then was employed as an educational instructor at the Walters School in the Kiester, Minnesota, District School for five years, after which he was a teacher in the Albert Lea, Minnesota, public schools until he retired. He served in the U.S. Army from 1946 to 1948, and he was married five years later.

Mr. Schroader enjoys horses and horticulture. He has been a Judge and Instructor for the National Council of State Garden Clubs, Inc. He completed Teaching Certification for the National Council of State Garden Clubs in 1996. Mr. Schroader has served as a volunteer to drive patients from the airport to the Mayo Clinic. He is also an active compiler of family history and genealogy. In 1996 Mr. and Mrs. Schroader were living in Alden, Minnesota.

He married, at Kiester, Minnesota, 21 June 1953, at the Grace United Methodist Church, when he was 26, **Beata Ida NEUBAUER**, daughter of William and Ida Belle (Rono) Neubauer; born in Bashaw Township, Brown County, Minnesota, 5 February 1929. She received a B.A. degree in Educational Instruction from Mankato, Minnesota, State University (then a state college). She was employed as a teacher at Mountain Lake and St. Peter, Minnesota, and at the Alden-Conger Schools, Alden, Minnesota. She enjoys gardening, quilting, crocheting, and grandmothering.

They had the following children, born at Albert Lea, Minnesota:

4293	i.	Denise Rene (1955-)
4294	ii.	Jacquie Lynne (1957-)
4295	iii.	Scott Leslie (1958-)
4296	iv.	Craig Dean (1960-)
4297	v.	Ramona Gail (1963-)

4062. Lillian Helen ANDERSON.[937] Born on 26 Jun 1933 in Catskill, NY. Occupation: Mother of 3; Clerical worker. Education: High School graduate, and some college courses. On 27 Sep 1953 when Lillian Helen was 20, she married **Dominic Joseph CORNELIUS**, son of Nicholas Ernest and Genevieve Maria (Sasso) Cornelius, in Catskill, NY (St. Patrick's Church); born 26 Jul 1920 in Catskill, NY. Theatre supervisor. High School graduate. He was in the U. S. Army Air Force from 1943-1946. They had the following children:

4298	i.	Barbara Patrice (1958-)
4299	ii.	Diana Leslie (1960-)
4300	iii.	Dominic Joseph (1964-)

4063. Haven Leslie ANDERSON.[938] Born 14 May 1937 in Catskill, NY; died 12 Dec 1967, he was 30.

4064. Owen James OLSON.[939] Born on 24 May 1945 in Forest City, Winnebago Co., IA. Owen James died in Forest City, Winnebago Co., IA on 2 Oct 1988, he was 43. Buried in Forest City, Iowa. Owen James married **Patricia SLATER**. She lived in Rochester, Minn., in August 1997.

4065. Jane Luella OLSON,[940] daughter and second child of Forest and LaVonne (Anderson) Olson, was born at Forest City, Iowa, 31 March 1949. She graduated from Forest City High School in 1967 and then attended Waldorf Junior College in Forest City, where she received the A.A. in 1969. She graduated from Morningside College in Sioux City, Iowa, with a B.A. degree in 1971 and she earned the M.A. from the University of South Dakota, Vermillion, S.D., in 1983. She has obtained sixty additional credit hours of graduate studies in various colleges and universities since then. In 1997 she was a teacher at the Patrick Henry Middle School in Sioux Falls, South Dakota. She enjoyed travel, current events, music, reading, knitting, and outdoor activities. She was a volunteer with her church choir and on various committees, and was a lay delegate to the South Dakota Social Studies Council. She has held various offices in Delta Kappa Gamma and Alpha Delta Pi sororities in North and South Dakota.

She married, at Forest City, Iowa, when she was 40, 29 July 1989, **Robert Hoy LEONHARDT**;

son of Henry and Mildred (Hoy) Leonhardt; born at Winner, South Dakota, 15 March 1940; he is a teacher at the Patrick Henry Middle School in Sioux Falls, South Dakota. He received the B.A. from Black Hills State University and the M.A. from South Dakota State University, and he has obtained thirty-six graduate hours of credit from various colleges and universities. He served in the U.S. Army from 1961-1964, during which he was stationed in Germany as an E-4. He enjoys reading, woodworking, biking, outdoor activities, and current events. He is a volunteer on church committees and he is active with Methodist Men and Habitat for Humanity. He is also a volunteer for Special Olympics.
They had the following children:

    4301   i.   Ross Owen (1991-)
    4302   ii.   Rachel Antoaneta (Adopted) (1992-)

4066. Pat EARNEST. Mother of 2, or possibly more, by a husband whose name is unknown.
Children:

    4303   i.   Kristin
    4304   ii.   Jen

4067. Ann WOLFER. Ann married _____ **PYLE.**
4068. Lynn WOLFER. Lynn married _____ **McDONALD.**
4069. Lucia Knowles WOLFER.
4070. Adele WOLFER. Adele married _____ **JOHNSON.**

12

Twelfth Generation
The 9th-Great--Grandchildren
Descendants of 1. Lydia, 5. Luke Jr., and 8. John

Line 1 – Descendants of Lydia Hill (continued)[941]

4071. Catherine Patricia SHEPPERD. Born on 31 May 1913 in Butte, Mont.; died in Spokane, Wash. on 22 Aug 1992, she was 79. Mother of 3; married twice. She first married **Jerome LEVEQUE.** Born on 19 Mar 1909 in Butte, Mont. Jerome died in Butte, Mont. on 16 Jul 1969, he was 60.
They had the following children:

4305	i.	Living Daughter of Jerome and Catherine (Shepperd)
4306	ii.	Living Son of Jerome and Catherine (Shepperd)
4307	iii.	Ruth Anne (1938-)

On 17 Aug 1974 when Catherine Patricia was 61, she second married **? [Living] LUSSY**, in Butte, Mont.

4072. Ruth Anne SHEPPERD. Born on 14 Jul 1915 in Butte, Mont. Mother of 2. On 31 Oct 1936 when she was 21, she married **Warren Ira TONEY**, in Butte, Mont. Born on 3 Nov 1905 in Coeur D'Alene, Ida. Warren Ira died in Spokane, Wash. on 17 Aug 1976, he was 70.
They had the following children:

4308	i.	Living Son of Warren and Ruth (Shepperd)
4309	ii.	Living Daughter of Warren and Ruth (Shepperd)

4073. Bruce Robert SHEPPERD. Born on 22 Nov 1918 in Spokane, Wash. On 3 Oct 1942 when he was 23, he married **Irene BRITT**, in San Francisco, Calif. Born on 21 Jun 1919 in Flagstaff, Ariz.
They had the following children:

4310	i.	Living Daughter of Bruce and Irene (Britt)
4311	ii.	Living Daughter of Bruce and Irene (Britt)

4074. Virgil Earl SHEPPERD. Born on 5 Nov 1914 in Plummer, Ida. Virgil Earl died in Coeur D'Alene, Ida. on 23 Feb 1973, he was 58. Virgil Earl married **Margaret Alice FREEMAN**. Born on 3 Mar 1915 in Coeur D'Alene, Ida.; died there, 15 Mar 2001, she was 86.
They had the following children:

4312	i.	Living Son of Virgil and Margaret (Freeman)
4313	ii.	Living Son of Virgil and Margaret (Freeman)
4314	iii.	Living Son of Virgil and Margaret (Freeman)
4315	iv.	Living Son of Virgil and Margaret (Freeman)

4075. Hannah Isabel SHEPPERD. Born on 9 Jun 1916 in St. Maries, Ida.; died in Coeur D'Alene, Ida. On 5 Oct 1941 when Hannah Isabel was 25, she married **Gerald E. OLDHAM**, in Coeur D'Alene, Ida. Born on 29 Oct 1919 in Spokane, Wash. Gerald E. died in Coeur D'Alene, 14 Jul 1985, he was 65.
They had the following children:

4316	i.	Living Daughter of Gerald and Hannah (Shepperd)
4317	ii.	Living Daughter of Gerald and Hannah (Shepperd)
4318	iii.	Living Daughter of Gerald and Hannah (Shepperd)
4319	iv.	Living Daughter of Gerald and Hannah (Shepperd)
4320	v.	Living Daughter of Gerald and Hannah (Shepperd)

4076. Winifred Abbey SHEPPERD. Born on 6 Nov 1917 in St. Maries, Ida. Winifred Abbey died in Coeur D'Alene, Ida. on 15 May 1988, she was 70. Winifred Abbey married **? HUNTER**.
They had the following children:

4321	i.	Living Son of Winifred (Shepperd)
4322	ii.	Living Daughter of Winifred (Shepperd)

4323   iii.   Living Daughter of Winifred (Shepperd)

4077. Warren H. SHEPPERD.

4078. James SHEPPERD. James married **? [Living] STODDARD**. Mother of 2.
They had the following children:

    4324   i.   Living Son of James
    4325   ii.   Living Daughter of James

4079. Shirley SHEPPERD. Born in 1911 in La Grande, Ore. Occupation: Mother of 2. In 1933 when Shirley was 22, she married **Manning PHILLIPS**, in Los Angeles, Calif. Born in Los Angeles, Calif.
They had the following children:

    4326   i.   Living Son of Manning and Shirley (Shepperd)
    4327   ii.   Living Daughter of Manning and Shirley (Shepperd)

4080. Kathleen Marie SHEPPERD. Born on 25 Sep 1916 in Spokane, Wash. Kathleen Marie died in San Bernardino, Calif. on 14 Dec 1987, she was 71. On 26 Jan 1941 when Kathleen Marie was 24, she married **Harold Michael RADKE**, in Riverside, Calif.
They had one child:

    4328   i.   Living Son of Harold and Kathleen (Shepperd)

4081. Enid Marguerite SHEPPERD. B. 30 Aug 1919 in Spokane, Wash.; m. **John Alfred AMON**.
They had the following children:

    4329   i.   Living Son of John and Enid (Shepperd)
    4330   ii.   Living Son of John and Enid (Shepperd)
    4331   iii.   Living Daughter of John and Enid (Shepperd)
    4332   iv.   Living Daughter of John and Enid (Shepperd)
    4333   v.   Living Daughter of John and Enid (Shepperd)
    4334   vi.   Living Daughter of John and Enid (Shepperd)
    4335   vii.   Living Daughter of John and Enid (Shepperd)
    4336   viii.   Living Son of John and Enid (Shepperd)
    4337   ix.   Living Daughter of John and Enid (Shepperd)

4082. Elizabeth A. SHEPPERD. Born abt 1921. Elizabeth A. married **Leo Francis BOWLER**.
They had the following children:

    4338   i.   Living Son of Leo and Elizabeth (Shepperd)
    4339   ii.   Living Son of Leo and Elizabeth (Shepperd)
    4340   iii.   Living Son of Leo and Elizabeth (Shepperd)
    4341   iv.   Living Son of Leo and Elizabeth (Shepperd)

4083. Bonita L. SHEPPERD. Born abt 1923. She married **Walter Henry POPPE**. Born on 4 Dec 1916 in Minneapolis, Minn.
They had the following children:

    4342   i.   Living Daughter of Walter and Bonita (Shepperd)
    4343   ii.   Living Son of Walter and Bonita (Shepperd)
    4344   iii.   Living Son of Walter and Bonita (Shepperd)
    4345   iv.   Living Son of Walter and Bonita (Shepperd)

4084. George Michael SHEPPERD. Born on 11 Mar 1925 in Spokane, Wash. George Michael died in San Bernardino, Calif. on 16 Jan 1999, he was 73. George Michael married **? [Living] POTTS**. .
They had the following children:

    4346   i.   Living Son of George
    4347   ii.   Living Son of George
    4348   iii.   Living Daughter of George
    4349   iv.   Living Daughter of George

4085. Eva Leannah SHEPPERD. Born on 19 May 1890 in Moscow, Ida. Eva Leannah died in Spokane, Wash. on 20 Mar 1983, she was 92. Occupation: Mother of 4. On 22 Mar 1911 when Eva Leannah was 20, she married **Maynard Henson McDUFFIE**, in Moscow, Ida. Born on 30 Aug 1890 in Hope, Ida. Maynard Henson died in Spokane, Wash. on 18 May 1977, he was 86.

They had the following children:

4350	i.	Clair (1912-1912)
4351	ii.	Beth Ione (1914-)
4352	iii.	Donald Maynard (Twin) (1916-1986)
4353	iv.	Ronald Clifford (Twin) (1916-1995) *

4086. Living Child of Darrell and Ola (Brewer) BLAKELEY.

4087. Janis Ann BLAKELEY. B. on 1 Mar 1953 in Los Angeles, Calif.; died in Los Angeles, Calif. on 1 Aug 2002, she was 49. Married twice, survived by both spouses and by two children of 1st marriage.

4088. Norman BLAKELEY. Born on 9 Sep 1956 in Los Angeles, Calif. Norman died in Los Angeles, Calif. in 1994, he was 37. On 6 Jun 1931 Norman married **? ? (BLAKELEY)**, in California.

They had one child

4354	i.	Living Child of Norman

4089. Living Child of Margaret (Brewer) JOHNSON.

Line 5 – Descendants of Luke Hill, Jr. (continued)
----------------[942]

4090. Richard R. STANLEY Esq. Born on 23 Jul 1952 in Chicago, Cook Co., Ill. Occupation: Managing Director and Senior Counsel of The Bank of New York Mellon, in November 2010.

4091. Mary Alice STANLEY. Born on 11 May 1954 in Evanston, Ill. In Jun 1978 when Mary Alice was 24, she married **Dan Edward MILLER**. Born on 15 Aug 1954.

They had the following children:

4355	i.	Laura Marie (1980-)
4356	ii.	Jennifer Alice (1984-)

----------------------[943]

4092. _____ GOLDING.

4093. _____ EBERBACH.

4094. Elizabeth KESSLER.

4095. William KESSLER.

4096. Charles SCHENCK.

4097. Andrew BUECKING.

4098. Angela Lynn HALBERSTADT.

4099. Bradley Alan HALBERSTADT.

4100. Douglas James HALBERSTADT.

4101. Jeffrey Scott HALBERSTADT.

4102. Kenneth Paul HALBERSTADT.

4103. Brandon Ray BAKER.

--------------------[944]

4104. Randi Rae CHANDLER. Born on 5 Nov 1968 in Elkader, Clayton Co., IA. Randi Rae married **Peter McNALLY**, in Davenport, Ia.

4105. Kelly Jo CHANDLER. Born on 4 Mar 1974 in Elkader, Clayton Co., IA. Graduated from University of Northern Iowa, 1996.

4106. Katharine Marie CHANDLER. Born on 24 Feb 1980.

4107. Erika Leigh HOCKINGS. Born on 10 Jan 1971 in Davenport, IA.

4108. Brittany Elissa Anne HOCKINGS. Born on 11 Jun 1976 in Davenport, IA.

4109. Graham William MATTES. Born on 3 May 1980.

4110. Garrett Rollins MATTES. Born on 19 Jun 1984.

4111. Stephen George SCHNEIDER. Born on 23 Jan 1969 in Park Ridge, IL. College student at DePaul University, Chicago, IL.

4112. Joy Marie SCHNEIDER.[945] Born on 26 Jan 1972 in Park Ridge, IL. Graduated Rosary Coll., River Forest, IL '94 (*mcl*).

4113. Matthew Paul SCHNEIDER. Born on 10 Nov 1973 in Park Ridge, IL. College student at DePaul University, Chicago, IL.

4114. (Stillborn) HILL. Born in 1972.

4115. Randy James HILL. Born on 8 Jul 1973 in Evanston, IL.

4116. Ryan William HILL. Born on 8 Feb 1977 in Aurora, CO.

4117. Connie Rae JUHL. Born on 21 Mar 1959 in Cedar Falls, IA. On 22 Aug 1981 when she was 22, she married (1) **James WEICKS**. They were divorced. Connie Rae married (2) **Gregory GIUDICI**. They had the following children:

    4357   i.   Danielle Marie (1989-)
    4358   ii.   Derek Alan (1992-)

4118. Michael Robert JUHL. Born on 12 Feb 1963 in Cedar Falls, IA. On 17 Oct 1987 when Michael Robert was 24, he married **Bessie CHAN**, in Cedar Falls, IA.
She was the daughter of Kai Ming Chan.
They had one child:

    4359   i.   Mason Christopher (~1993-)

4119. David Stanley JUHL. Born on 1 Mar 1965 in Cedar Falls, IA. On 2 Sep 1989 when David Stanley was 24, he married **Julie Ann JILOVEC**, in IA.
They had one child:

    4360   i.   Tyler David

4120. Shannon Ca JUHL. Born on 13 Jan 1968 in CA. In Sep 1990 when Shannon Ca was 22, she married **Jeff Scott SHOEMAKE**. They were divorced in Oct 1993.
They had one child:

    4361   i.   Gregory Scott (1991-)

4121. Shelly Raye JUHL. Born on 20 May 1970 in CA. On 15 Apr 2000 when Shelly Raye was 29, she married **Christopher O'BRIEN**.

4122. Robert Stewart JUHL. Born on 14 Oct 1971. On 14 Sep 1996 when Robert Stewart was 24, he married **Margaret Elise McMILLAN**.
They had the following children:

    4362   i.   Donald Tyler (1999-)
    4363   ii.   Joshua Robert (2001-)

4123. Christopher Duane JUHL. Born on 14 Aug 1973.

4124. Scott Eugene TILLEY. Born on 1 Oct 1963 in Cedar Falls, IA. Christened in Cedar Falls, IA. He changed his last name from Juhl to Tilley in 1977. On 29 Jun 1984 when Scott Eugene was 20, he first married **Debra Kay BRANDT**, in Marshalltown, IA. They were divorced in Jan 1991.
They had one child:

    4364   i.   Jared Duane (1987-)

On 5 Oct 1991 when Scott Eugene was 28, he second married **Sherri REESE**.
They had one child:

    4365   i.   Meagan Nichole (1992-)

4125. [male]. Born on 18 Nov 1966 in Waterloo, IA; died on 18 Nov 1966 in Waterloo, IA. Buried in Cedar Falls, IA.

4126. Tamera Kay JUHL. Born on 21 Jul 1968 in IA.
On 22 Sep 1995 when Tamera Kay was 27, she married **Jesse STEELE**.
They had one child:

    4366   i.   Christopher Robert (1996-)

4127. Jeffery Scott JOHNSON.[946] Born on 13 Aug 1960 in Cedar Falls, Black Hawk Co., Ia. Christened on 22 Jan 1961 in Cedar Falls, Ia. (First Methodist Church). Occupation: Works for Pepsi Cola. Education: Cedar Falls High School; U. No. Iowa, BA. Religion: Glad Tidings Assembly of God Church. His hobbies include landscaping, family history, and VW cars. On 26 Apr 1986 when Jeffery Scott was 25, he married **Jillynn Sue AUSTIN**, daughter of Roger Wright AUSTIN & Waival Isabelle CHERRY, in Cedar Falls, IA. Born on 12 Jan 1963 in Waverly, Bremer Co., Ia. Occupation: Teacher;

operates Day Care Center at home. Education: Cedar Falls High School; U. No. Iowa, BA (educat.). Religion: Glad Tidings Assembly of God Church. Her hobbies include needlework and reading.
They had the following children:

- **4367** i. Jeremiah Solomon (1989-)
- **4368** ii. Jacob Austin (1992-)
- **4369** iii. Jonah Scott (1997-)

4128. Sheryl Lynn JOHNSON. Born on 21 Jan 1963 in Cedar Falls, IA. Christened on 7 Apr 1963 in Cedar Falls, IA (First Methodist Church). Occupation: Salesperson, needlework and print / frame shops. Education: Cedar Falls High School; U. Northern IA. Religion: Orchard Hill Reformed Church. She enjoys needlework and designing. On 12 Oct 1991 when Sheryl Lynn was 28, she married **Rodney Lee BRANDHORST**, son of Rodger Lee BRANDHORST & Betty Lou KERN, in Cedar Falls, IA (Orchard Hill Reformed Church). Born on 20 Aug 1967 in Waterloo, IA. Christened in 1972 in Washburn, Black Hawk Co., IA. Occupation: President, Western Auto, Lincoln, Nebraska. Education: High School, Technical school. Religion: Reformed Church.
They had the following children:

- **4370** i. Elizabeth Rose Jane (1992-)
- **4371** ii. Victoria Rose Leigh (1995-)

4129. Mark Alan CHRISTIANSEN. Born 28 Oct 1969 in Waseca, MN; christened there.

4130. Amy Jo CHRISTIANSEN. Born 23 Dec 1971 in Mankato, Blue Earth Co., MN. Christened in Waseca, MN. On 19 Jun 1993 when Amy Jo was 21, she married **Jason METCALF** in Waseca, MN. Born in 1971.

4131. Monica Marie BOWERMAN. Born on 15 Nov 1984 in Green Bay, WI.

4132. Aundrea Marie JENKINS. Born on 5 Jul 1974 in Michigan City, IN.

4133. Melissa Lynn JENKINS. Born on 18 Feb 1983 in Michigan City, IN.

4134. Douglas Wayne BOWERMAN. Born on 20 Jul 1975 in Michigan City, IN.

4135. Kimberly Allison BOWERMAN. Born on 13 Jan 1978 in Michigan City, IN.

4136. Heather Ann WESNER. Born on 26 Jan 1972 in Michigan City, IN.

4137. Scott Alan WESNER. Born on 26 Jan 1972 in Michigan City, IN.

4138. Amy Elin ELLIOTT. Born on 6 Jan 1972 in Edina, Hennepin Co., MN. Occupation: Mother of 1; Pre-school teacher at Children's Beginning, Rochester, Minn. Education: Rochester Community College, A.A.S. Religion: Lutheran. Amy Elin married **Craig KYTONEN**. Born on 13 Aug 1965 in Minnetonka, Minn. Occupation: Auto mechanic.
They had one child:

- **4372** i. Anna (1995-)

4139. John David ELLIOTT. Born on 15 Sep 1974 in St. Louis Park, Hennepin Co., MN.

4140. Aaron Robert ELLIOTT. Born on 3 Sep 1976 in St. Louis Park, Hennepin Co., MN. He was in school in Rochester, MN, in 2010.

4141. Matthew David SIMPSON. Born on 5 Apr 1981 in Bloomington, IL.

4142. Roxanne Lee KNOEDLER.[947] Born on 1 Dec 1954 in Grundy Center, Ia. Occupation: Mother of 3; Manager of Hardee's Restaurant, Humboldt, Ia., in 1995. She married, when she was 18, **Larry A. VESTERBY** on 3 May 1973; they were divorced on 18 July 1990. He was the son of Joy and Gladys M. (Wekling) Vesterby; born at Fort Dodge, Iowa, 11 February 1951. She was working as a Hardee's manager in 1995 and she lived in Humboldt, Iowa.
They had the following children:

- **4373** i. Todd Allen (1973-)
- **4374** ii. Jennifer L. (1976-)
- **4375** iii. Drew Michael (1978-)

4143. Deborah Jo KNOEDLER.[948] Born on 26 Nov 1955 in Grundy Center, Ia. Occupation: Mother of 2; living in St. Paul, Minn., in 1987. She married, when she was 21, at Humboldt, Iowa, 3 April 1977, **Jon L. SPENCE**, son of Lee W. and Joyce A. (Kelly) Spence; born at Cherokee, Iowa, 11 January 1956. She graduated from high school and attended college for two years, studying computers. She was a computer programmer in 1995. She enjoyed golf, fishing, and wood working. Her husband served in the U.S. Air Force and graduated from college with a major in computer science. He was a professional computer engineer and he was a pallbearer at Velda Mae Knoedler's funeral in 1996. In November 1995 the family was living in North St. Paul, Minnesota.

They had the following children:

| 4376 | i. | Jessica Lou (1980-) |
| 4377 | ii. | Nikki Sue (1981-) |

4144. Timothy Laurel "Tim" KNOEDLER,[949] son of E. Laurel and Louett (Follette) Knoedler, was born at Clarion, Iowa, 12 May 1957. He graduated from high school and was the owner-operator of a semi-trailer truck. He married (1) on 17 August 1976, when he was 19, **Jill DAMON**, from whom he was divorced in 1980. Timothy and Jill (Damon) Knoedler had a daughter, Anglea Marie (b. 1977).

They had one child:

| 4378 | i. | Angela Marie (1977-) |

He married (2), at Nashua, Iowa, 13 October 1986, as her second husband, **Mrs. Julie A. (WILLIAMS) BOYD**, daughter of Roger E. and Dora M. (Wilhite) Williams; born at Ft. Dodge, Iowa, 13 May 1958. By her previous marriage, she had two children: Shawna Boyd (b. 1975) and Travis Boyd (b. 1980). Timothy and Julie (Williams) (Boyd) Knoedler had a daughter, Samantha (b. 1988). They lived in Humboldt, Iowa, in 1995.

They had one child:

| 4379 | i. | Samantha J. (1988-) |

4145. Diana Lou KNOEDLER,[950] third daughter and youngest child of E. Laurel and Louetta (Follette) Knoedler, was born at Clarion, Iowa, 9 August 1960. She graduated from high school and in 1995 she and her husband and their daughter were farming at Pomeroy, Iowa. She married at Humboldt, Iowa, 16 March 1988, **John Patrick MURPHY**, son of James and Norma Jean (Boswell) Murphy; born at Ft. Dodge, Iowa, 15 April 1953. She was of Humboldt, Ia., in 1987; and of Pomeroy, Ia., in 1995. He was a high school graduate and was a farmer in Pomeroy, Iowa, in 1995.

They had one child:

| 4380 | i. | Alicia Marie (1988-) |

4146. Cynthia "Cyndee"/ "Cindy" KNOEDLER.[951] Born on 18 Aug 1959; married **Steve NORMAN**.

4147. Vickie Lynn "Vicki" KNOEDLER. Born on 21 Jul 1960.

4148. Lawrence Thomas "Larry" KNOEDLER. Born 11 Nov 1964; married **Jane ? (KNOEDLER)**.

They had the following children:

| 4381 | i. | Matthew Lawrence (1994-) |
| 4382 | ii. | Jonathan Thomas (1996-) |

4149. David John KNOEDLER. On 28 Nov 1992 David John married **Margaret ? (KNOEDLER)**.

They had the following children:

| 4383 | i. | Sarah (1993-) |
| 4384 | ii. | Jacob (1995-) |

4150. Brian Freeman GATES.[952] Born on 13 Jul 1958 in Clarion, IA. Occupation: Computerized fueling of Williams Pipeline trucks. Education: Iowa State Univ. B.S., 1982; Iowa State University, M.S., 1984. He was a pallbearer at the funeral of his grandmother, Velda Mae (Hill) Knoedler. Brian Freeman married **Elizabeth ? (GATES).**

They had the following children:

| 4385 | i. | Elizabeth |
| 4386 | ii. | Chelsea |

4151. Francine Lea GATES.[953] Born on 2 Oct 1961 in Clarion, IA. Occupation: Bookstore at Northern Iowa Community College, Mason City, IA. Education: 2 yrs at Iowa Central Community College. Religion: United Methodist Church. Francine Lea married **Tony PREHM.**

They had the following children:

| 4387 | i. | Coulter |
| 4388 | ii. | Paige |

4152. Bradley Frederick "Brad" GATES. Born on 26 Mar 1963 in Mason City, IA. Occupation: Used tractor parts. Education: 1 yr Iowa Central Community College. Religion: Baptist. He was a pallbearer at the funeral of his grandmother, Velda Mae (Hill) Knoedler. On 9 Mar 1985 when he was 21, he married **Lisa TOURTELOTTE**. Occupation: Mother of 4.
They had the following children:
4389	i.	Leanna
4390	ii.	Benjamin "Ben"
4391	iii.	Katherine "Katie"
4392	iv.	Josiah "Joey"

4153. Anthony Lee KNOEDLER.[954] Born on 1 Jan 1959 in West Union, Ia. In June 1997 he was living in Medford, Oregon. On 25 Dec 1986 when he was 27, he married **Susan RADE**. Born on 15 Aug 1961.
They had the following children:
4393	i.	Destiny Marie (1986-)
4394	ii.	Josiah David (1994-)

4154. Andrew Keith KNOEDLER. Born on 20 Jul 1960.

4155. Pamela Lynn KNOEDLER. Born on 22 Apr 1962 in West Union, Ia. Occupation: Mother of 5. She lived in Spring Grove, Minn., in June 1997. On 1 Oct 1983 when she was 21, she married **Daniel WARD**. Born on 7 Nov 1960.
They had the following children:
4395	i.	Den Anthony (1981-)
4396	ii.	Anthem Lee (1984-)
4397	iii.	Tallen Miles (1986-)
4398	iv.	Ulyssia Autumn (1987-)
4399	v.	Calla Elizabeth (1990-)

4156. Todd David KNOEDLER. Born on 6 Feb 1966 in Waverly, Iowa.

4157. Peggy Ann KNOEDLER. Born on 24 Jul 1975 in Waverly, Iowa. Occupation: Mother of 1. She was a pallbearer at her grandmother Knoedler's funeral in 1996. She was in the U.S. Army in Olympia, Washington, in June 1997.
Peggy Ann first married _____.
They had one child:
4400	i.	Brian Matthew (1994-)

On 22 Dec 1995 when Peggy Ann was 20, she second married **Jerry Jack ANDERSON III**, in Shell Rock, Iowa. Born on 21 May 1971. He and his wife were in the U.S. Army in June 1997.

4158. Cyndee (Cindy) Kae KNOEDLER. Born on 28 Apr 1980 in Waverly, Iowa.
Living with her parents in June 1997. On 9 Aug 2008 when Cyndee (Cindy) Kae was 28, she married **Rubert ZUCK**, in Shell Rock, Iowa.

4159. Sarah Mae DAUGHERTY. Born on 11 Aug 1982 in Decorah, IA.

4160. Melissa Ann HILL. Born on 4 Aug 1967 in San Juan, PR (U.S. Naval Hospital). Physics teacher at Marquette Univ., Milwaukee, WI. Washington Univ. BS; Northwestern Univ. MS. Methodist.

4161. Barbara Lynn HILL. Born on 14 Nov 1969 in San Juan, PR (U.S. Naval Hospital). English teacher at Oshakaga Institute, Japan. Auburn, IL, High School grad.; College graduate. Methodist.

4162. Karl LeRoy HILL. Born on 20 Jul 1977 in Waterloo, IA. Christened in 1977 in Waterloo, IA (Kimball Ave. Methodist Church). Tripoli, IA, High School class of 1995. Religion: Protestant.

4163. Amanda Kay HILL. Born on 4 Nov 1979 in Waterloo, IA. Christened in 1979 in Waterloo, IA (Kimball Ave. Methodist Church). Education: Tripoli schools class of 1998. Religion: Protestant. On 4 Mar 2006 when Amanda Kay was 26, she married **Shawn SHEFFLER**, in Laport City, Iowa.
They had one child:
4401	i.	Olivia Mildred (2008-)

4164. Rhonda Dolores HILL. Born on 20 Oct 1981 in Waterloo, IA. Christened in 1981 in Waterloo, IA (Kimball Ave. Methodist Church). Education: Tripoli schools, class of 2000. Religion: Protestant.

4165. Donna MURDOCK.

4166. Cindy MURDOCK. Cindy married _____ **SPRAGG.**

4167. Tom MURDOCK.

4168. Leroy MURDOCK.

4169. Kenneth D. PERRY.

4170. Kirk PERRY.

4171. Kyle PERRY.

4172. Lana BARNES.[955] Lana married **Jeff OLSON.**
They had the following children:

> **4402** i. Lauri
> **4403** ii. Scott

4172a. Michele Leigh MENUEY,[956] eldest child of Joel and Dawn (Weston) Menuey, was born at West Union, Ia., 16 May 1975. She married, on 6 November 1999, at the Rushford Lutheran Church, Rushford, Minn., **Aaron Anthony EKERN,** son of Roger and Susan Ekern, born 29 November 1969. They are members of the Lutheran Congregations in Mission for Christ and they attend the Rushford Lutheran Church. Michele has a B.S. from Winona State University, Winona, Minn., and a certificate as a Medical secretary/transcriptionist from Rochester Technical College, Rochester, Minn. She is a Receptionist at the Rushford Clinic. Her hobbies are knitting and reading, Girl Scouts, Church youth group, and American Cancer Society Relay for Life.
They had the following child:

> **4403a.** i. Megan Leigh (2003-)

4172b. Douglas Weston MENUEY was b. at Decorah, Ia., 22 August 1978. He m. (1) **Tessa SMITH.**
They had the following child:

> **4403b.** i. Weston Leigh (2005-)

On 26 May 2006, at Janesville, Ia., he married, as her second husband, **Kretta NYHUS,** daughter of Leroy and Marti Nyhus, born 13 January ____. She had previously married (1) Toby Wilkins, by whom she had a son,

> **4403c.** ii. Ethan Leroy (surname Wilkins) (2002-)

Douglas Weston Menuey and Kretta Nyhus had the following son:

> **4403d.** iii. Sidney Henry Ford (2008-)

4172c. Joel Anthony MENUEY was born at Austin, Minn., 15 August 1982. He married, on 30 July 2005, at the Dexter, Minn., United Methodist Church, **Natalie DINGLEY,** born 25 July 1985.
They had the following children:

> **4403e.** i. Hannah Rae (2006-)
> **4403f.** ii. Baby boy (due 8/29/2011)

4173. Angela SEEDORF.

4174. Michael SEEDORF.

4175. Erin WESTON.

4176. Oakley WESTON.

4177. Laine WESTON.

4178. Kevin Dale HILL,[957] son and elder child of Steven D. and Shirley A. (Davis) Hill, was born at Clarion, Iowa, 13 September 1965. He graduated from Clarion High School and then attended Iowa State University, Ames, Iowa, from which he received the B.A. degree in 1989. He worked as a staff writer for the *Daily Gate City* newspaper in Keokuk, Iowa, before returning to graduate school in 1991. He received an M.A. in History in 1994 from Iowa State. His M.A. thesis was a study of the English ancestors of his paternal grandmother, entitled "The Boyntons: A case study of the English gentry, A.D. 1272-1455." He has presented papers on his Ph.D. research at the International Congress on Medieval Studies in Kalamazoo, Michigan, in 1998 and at the American Historical Association Annual Meeting in 2000. In 2000, he was an academic advisor, instructor, and student at Iowa State University, teaching courses on Western civilization, Medieval Europe, and writing his Ph.D. thesis, which is a study of deforestation in twelfth-century England. His other interests include reading, biking, politics, and the movies.

He married, at the First Lutheran Church in Clarion, Iowa, on 1 August 1992, when he was 26, **Lisa Marie WALDON**, adopted daughter of Melvin M. and Dolores M. (Schiek) Waldon; born in Iowa City, Iowa, 18 November 1968. Lisa Waldon graduated from Clarion High School and attended Iowa State University, form which she received a B.A. in 1991. She is on the "Friends" board for the Ames Public Library and is active as a library volunteer and in the library's "Great Books" discussion programs. In the summer of 1999, she was awarded a grant from the National Endowment for the Humanities to study Gothic architecture during an eight-week seminar in Paris, France. In 2000, she was an English teacher in the Colo-Nesco school district, in Colo, Iowa, teaching courses in grammar, literature, creative writing, novel analysis, and college preparation to students in grades 9-12.

4179. Kristin Sue "Kris" HILL,[958] daughter and younger child of Steven Dale and Shirley Ann (Davis) Hill, was born at Clarion, Iowa, 24 September 1968. She attended the Clarion Community School from K-12 and graduated as valedictorian of the class of 1987. She then attended the University of Iowa, from which she received the B.A. in English (1991), having been in the study-abroad program at the University of London in 1990. She did additional coursework in 1991-92 and 1992-93 and received Teaching Certification from the University of Iowa in 1993. In 1994 she was Home Manager for an intermediate care facility for the mentally retarded in Belmond, Iowa. In 2000 she was a Resource Teacher in Special Education and was teaching high school English in Eagle Grove, Ia. She was to receive her M.S. in Special Education from Iowa State University in May 2001. Her hobbies include an interest in sports.

She married, at the First United Methodist Church, Clarion, Iowa, 8 April 1995, when she was 26, **Scott Wayne HARRINGTON**, son of Paul and Sheri (Skrovig) Harrington; born in Wright County, Iowa, 8 September 1968. Scott and Krisin (Hill) Harrington were divorced in 1997. They had one child:

    4404   i.   Elliott (1996-)

4180. Chad Matthew HILL. Born on 4 Aug 1979 in Des Moines, IA. Chad Matthew died in a "go-cart" accident in Clarion, IA on 3 Oct 1988, he was 9. Buried on 6 Oct 1988 in Clarion, IA (Evergreen Cem.). In 3rd grade when he died; was in Cub Scouts & 4-H. First United Methodist Church, Clarion, Ia.

4181. Megan Caroline HILL. Born on 22 Dec 1985.

4182. Erin Julia HILL,[959] elder child of Douglas Ray and Linda Kay (Carden) Hill, was born at Grinnell, Iowa, 10 August 1975. Erin was given her middle name in honor of her great-grandmother. She attended the Grinnell Community School until 1986. Her family later moved to Cedar Rapids, and she remained there for her senior year at Linn-Mar High School when they moved again, to Decorah, Iowa. She was voted "Outstanding Athlete" in track for the '92, '93, and '94 seasons. In 1993 she was elected to the Homecoming Court and she was voted as "Friendliest" in her graduating class. Erin enjoys reading, painting, bike riding, listening to music and being with friends. Her biographical sketch appears in *Who's Who in American High School Students*. She graduated from the University of Iowa in 1998 with a B.B.A. in Business Administration. Erin worked in London, U.K., during the summers of 1997 and 1998. After graduating from college, she completed her internship in the internet industry in Paris, France, before moving to California. In 2000, she was working as a Marketing Associate with "Looksmart.com" and she lived in San Francisco, California.

4183. Ryan Douglas HILL, son of Douglas Ray and Linda Kay (Carden) Hill, was born at Grinnell, Poweshiek County, Iowa, 18 November 1977. He graduated from Decorah, Iowa, high school in 1996, where he was chosen as a member of the Homecoming Court. His hobbies include movies and weight training. In 2000, he was a member of the Kappa Sigma social fraternity at the University of Iowa, where he was expected to graduate in December with a B.B.A. in Business Administration.

4184. Jessica Dawn CRUM. Born on 6 Jul 1976 in Des Moines, IA. Education: Attends Kirkwood Community College, Iowa City (2000). She began college classes at AIB in Des Moines, Iowa, in 1994.

4185. Amber Marie CRUM. Born on 26 Jun 1981 in Des Moines, IA. Occupation: Works at a temporary agency - secretary. Amber Marie married _____ _____.
They had the following children:

    4405   i.   ----- (Twin) (2001-)
    4406   ii.   ----- (Twin) (2001-)

4186. Hayley Camille CRUM. Born on 3 Jan 1984 in Des Moines, IA. Education: In Des Moines Christian School, will enter junior year in 2000.

4187. Sienna Glory HILL. Born on 21 Aug 1976 in Marion, Ill. Occupation: Restaurant manager, Portland, Ore. Education: Graduated Dec. 1998 from Reed College, Portland, Ore. (Anthropology), B.A.

4188. Sarah Gray (b. Sarah Rainbow) DAVIDSON. Born on 6 Jul 1979 in Iowa City, IA. Occupation: Anthropology student, working in Bolivia in summer of 2000. Education: Senior at Cornell University, Ithaca, N.Y. in 2000.

4189. Gwendolyn Ann HILL. Born on 16 Apr 1986 in Leadville, Colo.

4190. Govinda Jonas PHALEN. Born on 4 Dec 1992 in Iowa City, Johnson Co., Iowa. In Iowa City, at Horace Mann Elementary School, 2nd grade, 2000.

4191. Ryan Jeffrey GLADE. Born on 28 Apr 1983 in Cedar Falls, IA.

4192. Caitlin Marie GLADE. Born on 31 Oct 1989 in Cedar Falls, IA.

4193. Andrew Nels ODLAND. Born on 28 Nov 1985 in Clarion, IA.

4194. Cara LeAnn ODLAND. Born on 6 Aug 1990 in Clarion, IA.

4195. Colin Earl ODLAND. Born on 22 Nov 1993 in Clarion, IA.

4196. Allison Lee KLAPPERICH. Born on 17 Feb 1987 in Osage, Mitchell Co., IA.

4197. Benjamin Stephen "Ben" KLAPPERICH. Born on 20 Jan 1990 in Osage, Mitchell Co., IA.

4198. Nathan Jon HARRIS. Born on 19 Apr 1986 in Sioux City, Woodbury Co., IA.

4199. Rachel Ann HARRIS. Born on 22 Feb 1989 in Sioux City, Woodbury Co., IA.

4200. Michael Orin HARRIS. Born on 23 Dec 1992 in Sioux City, Woodbury Co., IA.

4201. Lukas Daniel ODLAND. Born on 20 Oct 1992 in Clarion, IA.

4202. Matthew Clarence ODLAND. Born on 24 Dec 1994.

4203. Lauren Elizabeth ODLAND. Born on 3 Jan 2001.

4204. Trevor John WOODIN. Born on 30 Apr 1975 in Brookfield, Waukesha Co., WI. Occupation: Outstanding student hockey player. Graduated from Brookfield East H.S. 1994. Religion: Lutheran.

4205. Erik Richard WOODIN. Born on 10 Jun 1978 in Brookfield, Waukesha Co., WI. Brookfield East High School, class of 1996. Religion: Lutheran.

4206. Maggie Carolyn WOODIN. Born on 10 Mar 1992 in Milwaukee, WI.

4207. Molly Alexandria WOODIN. Born on 9 Jun 1993 in Milwaukee, WI.

4208. Lauren Gray PECHE. Born on 6 Nov 1987 in Milwaukee, WI. First grade student, 1994-95; soccer player.

4209. Ryan Wells LANG. Born on 14 Aug 1991 in Hoffman Estates, IL. Graduated from Port Charlotte High School (Florida?) in May 2010, lettering in track; Baccalaureate speaker.

4210. Rachel Elizabeth SCHULTZ. Born on 17 Jun 1994 in Dubuque, IA. Education: A high school junior in 2010, a percussionist in the Wind Ensemble, and in Drama Club.

4211. Abigail ? (HEMENWAY). Born in Mar 2005.

4212. Zachary ? (HEMENWAY). Born in Dec 2008.

4213. Mason Alexander ? (HEMENWAY). Born on 24 Sep 2010.

4214. Heather Dawn HILL,[960] only child of David Hedgcock and Sheri Lynn (Wilson) Hill, was born at Spencer, Roane County, West Virginia, 4 October 1982. She attended public schools in West Virginia, and later was a student at Rumsey Hall, Washington, Conn., where she finished eighth grade in 1998. She entered ninth grade at the Greer School in Pennsylvania in the fall of 1998 and studied there for one year. She graduated from high school at South Parkersburg, W. Va., in 2002 and then spent one term in post-graduate study at the Greer School. She has since been a part-time student at the University of West Virginia - Parkersburg, studying business. She enjoys singing and athletics. She is a member of the National Society of the Colonial Dames of America in the State of New Jersey, by right of descent from an ancestor of her grandmother Hill, Toby Leech of Philadelphia.

She married, in Wood County, West Virginia, on 12 September 2002, **Jason Frederick HAUGHT**, son of Frederick John Haught and his second wife Marcina Ann (Plant) Haught. The ceremony was performed by the Rev. Robert A. Waters. He is a computer security technician for U.S. Government, Parkersburg, W.Va.

They had the following children, born at Parkersburg:

    4407   i.   Marcina Lynn (2005-)
    4408   ii.   Landon Jason (2007-)
    4409   iii.   Christian Dean (2009-)

4215. Georgia Clare HILL. Born on 19 Sep 2004 in Kalamazoo, Mich.

4215a. Rosaile Maired HILL. Born on 14 Feb 2008 in Kalamazoo, Mich.

4216. Conor Patrick Desmond SHEEHY. Born 29 Aug 1993 in Tinker Air Force Base, Okla. He is the son of Thomas David Hill Jr., but he retains his mother's maiden name.[961]

4217. Kristi KISLING. Born on 8 Jan 1955. Kristi died on 17 Mar 1979, she was 24.

4218. Lori KISLING. Born on 17 Dec 1957.

4219. Kenneth KISLING. Born on 17 Jul 1959.

4220. Beth KISLING. Born on 2 Jul 1962.

4221. Jimmy LONG. Born on 25 Jul 1962.

4222. Ronald LONG. Born on 7 Nov 1963.

4223. John LONG. Born on 30 Mar 1967.

4224. Jeff LONG.

4225. Nicole LONG.

4226. Michael CUMMINGS. Born on 28 Jan 1971.

4227. Jennie CUMMINGS. Born on 1 Apr 1973.

4228. Ryan CUMMINGS. Born on 27 Dec 1974.

4229. Tom LUNDAHL. Born on 25 Sep 1954.

4230. Brenda LUNDAHL. Born on 20 Apr 1957.

4231. Rhonda LUNDAHL. Born on 15 Feb 1960.

4232. Paul LUNDAHL. Born on 24 Nov 1962.

4233. Mike LUNDAHL. Born on 12 Oct 1964.

4234. Rich LUNDAHL. Born on 18 Apr 1971.

4235. Thresa Jo LINDSAY. Born on 17 Oct 1963.

4236. James LINDSAY. Born on 3 Jul 1966.

4237. Mary LINDSAY. Born on 4 Apr 1974.

4238. James LINDSAY. Born on 22 Aug 1970.

4239. Dwight LANGFORD. Born on 30 Jul 1970.

4240. Kevin LANGFORD. Born on 13 Jun 1973.

4241. Christine LANGFORD. Born on 10 Nov 1976.

4242. Stacey Carole HARSON.[962] Born on 3 Mar 1977 in Aurora, Arapahoe Co., CO. Education: Entered Cottey College, Missouri, as a freshman in 1995.

4243. Joel Ray HARSON. Born on 14 Nov 1983 in Des Moines, Polk Co., IA. Joel Ray died on 19 Dec 1985, he was 2. Buried in 1985 in Clarion, IA (Evergreen Cemetery).

4244. David Lee McGINNIS. Born on 10 Sep 1962 in Clarion, Wright Co., Ia. Occupation: In U.S. Air Force for 8 years; then purchasing agent for construction supply company. Education: High school graduate, Washington state. David Lee married **Sonia ROSAS**.

They had the following children:

    4410   i.   Ryan Daniel (1989-)
    4411   ii.   Lauryn Celia (1992-)

4245. Daniel Lee "Dan" McGINNIS. Born on 2 Dec 1964 in Offut AFB, Nebraska. Occupation: Chef at a hotel. Education: High school graduate, Tacoma, Washington.

4246. Barbara LINDSAY. Born on 11 Feb 1970.

4247. Ronald LINDSAY. Born on 1 Dec 1977.

4248. Lori LINDSAY. Born on 18 Jul 1979.

4249. Tyler Dean HILL.

4250. Damon Mitchell SMITH. Born on 21 Dec 2000 in Elmira, Chemung Co., N.Y. He was at the Hill

Reunion on 21 August 2010.

4251. Dalton Marshal SMITH. Born on 23 Feb 2002 in Elmira, Chemung Co., N.Y. He was at the Hill Reunion on 21 August 2010.

4252. Earnest Richard TRAVIS Jr. Born on 28 Mar 1943.

4253. Todd Thomas TRAVIS.

4254. Jon Paul TRAVIS.

4255. Danielle Marie PRYSLOPSKI.

4256. Andrew Michael PRYSLOPSKI.

4257. Adam Richard MAHNKE. Born on 1 Mar 1977 in Elmira, N.Y. On 22 Jul 2000 when Adam Richard was 23, he married **Christina BURRIS**. Born on 27 Sep 1978 in California.

4258. Kenneth Richard O'CONNELL. Born on 20 Feb 1979 in Elmira, N.Y.

4259. Gregory Keith O'CONNELL. Born on 1 Jul 1981 in Elmira, N.Y.

4260. Joshua Brandon O'CONNELL. Born on 26 Jun 1987 in Elmira, N.Y.

Line 8 – Descendants of John Hill (continued)
-------------963

4261. Nicole SIMON. Nicole married **Simon (PFAFF)**. Born on 25 Jul 1990.

4262. Charles WILHELM.

4263. Katherine WILHELM.

4264. Darrel B. WILHELM. Born on 16 Nov 1948. Darrel B. died in 1978, he was 29.

4265. Mathew BAIRD. Born on 22 Oct 1981 in Riverton, Wyo.

4266. Elizabeth Ann MARSHALL. Born on 30 Dec 1982. A daughter by Hedi's previous marriage.

4267. Robert Joshua Taylor HARPER. Born on 18 Feb 1992 in Pebble Beach, Calif.

4268. Joseph Michael HARPER. Born on 2 Jan 1989 in Pebble Beach, Calif.

4269. Noel Christine PEDERSON. Born on 21 Jul 1987 in Berkeley, Calif.

4270. Paul PEDERSON. Born on 25 Mar 1989 in Berkeley, Calif.

4271. Logan Peale PARKER. Born on 24 Mar 1987 in Fairfax County, Va.

4272. Rebecca Colline PARKER. Born on 27 Jan 1989 in Fairfax County, Va. She married **? BECCA**.

4273. Jedediah Hill DILLER. Born on 7 Apr 1989 in Littleton, Colo.

4274. Zachary Travis DILLER. Born on 8 Jan 1992 in Littleton, Colo.

4275. Andrew William HILL. Born on 13 Oct 1994 in San Diego, Calif.

4276. Jason Robert HILL. Born on 12 Sep 1996 in Englewood, Colo.

4277. Dustin James HILL. Born on 28 Apr 1990 in Raleigh, N.C.

4278. Erica Lemay HILL. Born on 30 Mar 1992 in Raleigh, N.C.

4279. Sarah Elizabeth HILL. Born on 30 Mar 1992 in Raleigh, N.C.

4280. Logan HAYES. Born in Jan 1995.

4281. Laurie Kevin SHAFFER. Born on 26 Oct 1959. On 30 Jun 1984, she married **Barry WILBUR**. They had the following children:

4412	i.	Danielle (1985-)
4413	ii.	Mathew Robert
4414	iii.	Ashley Lindsey (1989-)

4282. Shelley Lynn SHAFFER. Born on 24 Jul 1963.

4283. James Wesley BABCOCK. Born on 7 Aug 1972 in Dunedin, Fla. On 14 Nov 1998 when James Wesley was 26, he married **Judith Marie SUPPERER**. Born on 2 Oct 1975 in Philadelphia, Pa. They had the following children:

4415	i.	Shelley Marie (1993-)
4416	ii.	Jamie Lee (1995-)

-------------------964

4284. Sharon NESHEIM. Occupation: Mother of 2. In March 1996 she was living in Midland, SD.

4285. Ula Francis BITKER. Born on 1 Feb 1943 in Forest City, IA.

4286. Barry Lea BITKER. Born on 3 Aug 1945 in Mason City, IA.

4287. Lyle Morris "Wylie" BITKER. Born on 4 Aug 1946 in Mason City, IA. His mother said he was like her uncle Roy, a "prince of a guy." (From *Thanks for Giving*, page 10).

4288. Leslie Maynard BITKER. Born on 4 Aug 1946 in Mason City, IA.

4289. Joan Carol BITKER. Born on 24 Aug 1950 in Greene, IA.

4290. Steven Jay BITKER. Born on 9 Aug 1954 in Tucson, AZ. Steven Jay died in San Francisco, CA on 28 Mar 1979, he was 24. Buried in Mar 1979 in Services at So. Lawn, Tucson (AZ) Memorial Park.

4291. Marylou Ann BITKER. Born on 5 Sep 1958 in Forest City, IA.

4292. Tena Marie BITKER, fourth daughter and eighth child of Johnnie Carl and Marian Rozella (Schroader) Bitker, was born at Forest City, Iowa, 13 September 1962. Her parents moved to Tucson, Arizona, and she attended grammar school there for eight years. She then attended Sunnyside High School, Tucson, and graduated in three years. In April 1996 she was living at home and was a student at Pima Community College in Tucson. She enjoyed line dancing, gardening, interior design, and landscaping. She was engaged to marry, in April 1997, **Richard Wayne STARK**, son of Richard Lee and Linda Rae (Good) Stark; born at Paris, Illinois, 12 July 1965. Her fiancé had attended grammar school for eight years in Benson, Arizona, and graduated from Sunnyside High School, Tucson, after three years. He was service manager of a family business, Trailer Refrigeration, Inc., in Tucson. He enjoyed fishing, hunting, carpentry, and landscaping.

4293. Denise Rene SCHROADER. Born on 6 Jan 1955 in Albert Lea, Freeborn Co., MN (Naeve Hosp.). In 1996 she lived in Tabor, Iowa. She was married to _____ **ABU RAMEH OLSEN**.

4294. Jacquie Lynne SCHROADER. Born on 20 Aug 1957 in Albert Lea, Freeborn Co., MN (Naeve Hosp.). In 1996 she was living in Helena, Montana. Jacquie Lynne married _____ **GILHAM**.

4295. Scott Leslie SCHROADER, elder son and third child of Leslie Franklin and Beata Ida (Neubauer) Schroader, was born at the Naeve Hospital, Albert Lea, Minnesota, 18 December 1958. He attended kindergarten through third grade at Alden, Minnesota, and fourth grade at the Indian School, Duluth, Minnesota. He was again at Alden for 5th and 6th grades and then attended Alden High School, from which he graduated in 1977. In 1978-79 he attended Austin VoTech School, from which he received a Degree of Proficiency in Carpentry. In 1996 he was living at Albert Lea, Minnesota, where he was employed as a Set-up Technician at Streater. He enjoys hunting, fishing, and bowling. He married, at the Church of Christ, Albert Lea, 20 August 1994, as her second husband, **Janice Elaine VanRYSWYK GULBERTSON**, daughter of Lester Lyle and Dolores June (Giles) VanRyswyk; born at Albert Lea, 6 June 1950. She attended first grade at Myrtle, Minnesota, and was at the Manchester School for the next three years. She attended 5th through the 8th grades in Albert Lea and 9th through 12th grades at the Freeborn, Minnesota, High School. She is a Residential Development Worker at the Crest Group Home in Albert Lea and is also a baby sitter. She enjoys doing embroidery work, walking, and crafts. She is active in the Christian Church in Albert Lea as Chairman of the Women's Circle and Coordinator of the Junior Church, and she helps teach the Toddler Sunday School. She married (1) _____ Gunderson, by whom she had three children, born at Albert Lea: Chad (b. 1971); Tara (b. 1977); and Jenilee (b. 1982).

4296. Craig Dean SCHROADER. Born on 27 Sep 1960 in Albert Lea, Freeborn Co., MN (Naeve Hosp.). In 1996 he was living in Mapleton, MN.

4297. Ramona Gail SCHROADER. Born on 5 Sep 1963 in Albert Lea, Freeborn Co., MN (Naeve Hosp.). In 1996 she was living in Albert Lea, MN. Ramona Gail married _____ **ANDERSON**.

4298. Barbara Patrice CORNELIUS. Born 23 Jul 1958 in Catskill, NY; married _____ **PREMO**.

4299. Diana Leslie CORNELIUS. Born on 19 May 1960 in Catskill, NY; married _____ **SMITH**.

4300. Dominic Joseph CORNELIUS III. Born on 25 Dec 1964 in Catskill, NY.

4301. Ross Owen LEONHART. Born on 13 Sep 1991 in Sioux Falls, S.D.

4302. Rachel Antoaneta LEONHARDT. Born on 16 May 1992 in Lagovgrad, BULGARIA. Her birth name in Bulgaria was Antoneta Simeonova Terzyiska. She was adopted by Robert and Jane Leonhardt in February 1999. She was then in an orphanage in Tetrovo, in southern Bulgaria.

4303. Kristin.

4304. Jen. She has a B.A. degree, and is a skier.

13

Thirteenth Generation
The 10th-Great--Grandchildren
Descendants of 1. Lydia, 5. Luke Jr., and 8. John

Line 1 – Descendants of Lydia Hill (continued)[965]

4305. Living Daughter of Jerome and Catherine (Shepperd) LEVEQUE.

4306. Living Son of Jerome and Catherine (Shepperd) LEVEQUE.

4307. Ruth Anne LEVEQUE. Born on 20 Jun 1938 in Butte, Mont. She m. **? [Living] PALMER.** They had the following children:

| 4417 | i. | Living Daughter of Ruth (Leveque) |
| 4418 | ii. | Living Daughter of Ruth (Leveque) |

4308. Living Son of Warren and Ruth (Shepperd) TONEY.

4309. Living Daughter of Warren and Ruth (Shepperd) TONEY.

4310. Living Daughter of Bruce and Irene (Britt) SHEPPERD.

4311. Living Daughter of Bruce and Irene (Britt) SHEPPERD.

4312. Living Son of Virgil and Margaret (Freeman) SHEPPERD.

4313. Living Son of Virgil and Margaret (Freeman) SHEPPERD.

4314. Living Son of Virgil and Margaret (Freeman) SHEPPERD.

4315. Living Son of Virgil and Margaret (Freeman) SHEPPERD.

4316. Living Daughter of Gerald and Hannah (Shepperd) OLDHAM.

4317. Living Daughter of Gerald and Hannah (Shepperd) OLDHAM.

4318. Living Daughter of Gerald and Hannah (Shepperd) OLDHAM.

4319. Living Daughter of Gerald and Hannah (Shepperd) OLDHAM.

4320. Living Daughter of Gerald and Hannah (Shepperd) OLDHAM.

4321. Living Son of Winifred (Shepperd) HUNTER.

4322. Living Daughter of Winifred (Shepperd) HUNTER.

4323. Living Daughter of Winifred (Shepperd) HUNTER.

4324. Living Son of James SHEPPERD.

4325. Living Daughter of James SHEPPERD.

4326. Living Son of Manning and Shirley (Shepperd) PHILLIPS.

4327. Living Daughter of Manning and Shirley (Shepperd) PHILLIPS.

4328. Living Son of Harold and Kathleen (Shepperd) RADKE.

4329. Living Son of John and Enid (Shepperd) AMON.

4330. Living Son of John and Enid (Shepperd) AMON.

4331. Living Daughter of John and Enid (Shepperd) AMON.

4332. Living Daughter of John and Enid (Shepperd) AMON.

4333. Living Daughter of John and Enid (Shepperd) AMON.

4334. Living Daughter of John and Enid (Shepperd) AMON.

4335. Living Daughter of John and Enid (Shepperd) AMON.

4336. Living Son of John and Enid (Shepperd) AMON.

4337. Living Daughter of John and Enid (Shepperd) AMON.

4338. Living Son of Leo and Elizabeth (Shepperd) BOWLER.

4339. Living Son of Leo and Elizabeth (Shepperd) BOWLER.

4340. Living Son of Leo and Elizabeth (Shepperd) BOWLER.

4341. Living Son of Leo and Elizabeth (Shepperd) BOWLER.

4342. Living Daughter of Walter and Bonita (Shepperd) POPPE.

4343. Living Son of Walter and Bonita (Shepperd) POPPE.
4344. Living Son of Walter and Bonita (Shepperd) POPPE.
4345. Living Son of Walter and Bonita (Shepperd) POPPE.
4346. Living Son of George SHEPPERD.
4347. Living Son of George SHEPPERD.
4348. Living Daughter of George SHEPPERD.
4349. Living Daughter of George SHEPPERD.
4350. Clair McDUFFIE. Born on 15 Jan 1912. Clair died in Dec 1912.
4351. Beth Ione McDUFFIE. Born on 17 Mar 1914. On 6 Jun 1942 when Beth Ione was 28, she married **Gerald GILBERT** in Camp Roberts, Calif.
They had the following children:
> **4419** i. Living Son of Gerald and Beth (McDuffie)
> **4420** ii. Living Son of Gerald and Beth (McDuffie)

4352. Donald Maynard McDUFFIE. Born on 13 Feb 1916 in Sand Point, Ida. Donald Maynard died in Albany, Ore. on 9 Jan 1986, he was 69. On 15 Apr 1945 when Donald Maynard was 29, he married **Kathryn RHOADS** in Spokane, Wash.
They had one child:
> **4421** i. Living Daughter of Donald and Kathryn (Rhoads)

4353. Ronald Clifford McDUFFIE. Born on 13 Feb 1916 in Sand Point, Ida. Ronald Clifford died in Coos Bay, Ore on 25 Jul 1995, he was 79. On 28 May 1942 when Ronald Clifford was 26, he married **Betty WARD** in Fort Lewis, Wash. Betty died in 1991 in Coos Bay, Ore.
They had the following children:
> **4422** i. Living Daughter of Ronald and Betty (Ward)
> **4423** ii. Living Son of Ronald and Betty (Ward)

4354. Living Child of Norman BLAKELEY.

Line 5 – Descendants of Luke Hill, Jr. (continued)

4355. Laura Marie MILLER.[966] Born on 6 Jul 1980. In Jun 2006, she married **Timmon FAVARO**.
4356. Jennifer Alice MILLER. Born on 24 Sep 1984. On 25 Sep 2009, she married **James HEIMAN**.

--------------------[967]

4357. Danielle Marie GIUDICI. Born on 21 Mar 1989 in MI.
4358. Derek Alan GIUDICI. Born on 17 Feb 1992 in MI.
4359. Mason Christopher JUHL. Born abt 10 Aug 1993 in TX.
4360. Tyler David JUHL.
4361. Gregory Scott SHOEMAKE. Born on 20 Jun 1991.
4362. Donald Tyler JUHL. Born on 1 Apr 1999.
4363. Joshua Robert JUHL. Born on 6 Feb 2001.
4364. Jared Duane TILLEY. Born on 26 Oct 1987 in TX.
4365. Meagan Nichole TILLEY. Born on 12 Mar 1992.
4366. Christopher Robert STEELE. Born on 16 Aug 1996.
4367. Jeremiah Solomon JOHNSON. Born on 18 Jun 1989 in Waterloo, IA. Christened on 22 Jul 1989 in Cedar Falls, IA.
4368. Jacob Austin JOHNSON. B. 8 Apr 1992 in Waterloo, IA. Christened in 1992 in Cedar Falls, IA.
4369. Jonah Scott JOHNSON. Born on 25 Feb 1997 in Waterloo, Black Hawk Co., Ia.
4370. Elizabeth Rose Jane BRANDHORST. Born on 15 Aug 1992 in Waterloo, IA. Christened on 22 Nov 1992 in Cedar Falls, IA.
4371. Victoria Rose Leigh BRANDHORST. Born on 19 May 1995 in Clinton, IA. Her parents moved to Lincoln, Nebraska, soon after she was born.
4372. Anna KYTONEN.[968] Born on 5 Jul 1995 in Rochester, Minn.

----------------969

4373. Todd Allen VESTERBY. Born on 7 Dec 1973.

4374. Jennifer L. VESTERBY. Born on 19 May 1976 in Humboldt, Ia.

On 10 Aug 1996 when Jennifer L. was 20, she married Michael JANSSEN.

4375. Drew Michael VESTERBY. Born on 30 Dec 1978 in Humboldt, Ia.

4376. Jessica Lou SPENCE. Born on 16 Jan 1980.

4377. Nikki Sue SPENCE. Born on 10 Jun 1981.

4378. Angela Marie KNOEDLER. Born 14 Jun 1977; lived in Ames, Iowa, in 1995.

4379. Samantha J. KNOEDLER. Born on 13 Dec 1988.

4380. Alicia Marie MURPHY. Born on 31 Oct 1988 in Ft. Dodge, Iowa.

4381. Matthew Lawrence KNOEDLER. Born on 9 Nov 1994.

4382. Jonathan Thomas KNOEDLER. Born on 19 Jun 1996.

4383. Sarah KNOEDLER. Born on 6 Apr 1993. Her date of birth is from a questionnaire completed 7 Aug 1997 by her father for the Hill family reunion.

4384. Jacob KNOEDLER. Born on 13 Jul 1995.

His date of birth is from a questionnaire completed 7 Aug 1997 by his father for the Hill family reunion.

4385. Elizabeth GATES.

4386. Chelsea GATES.

4387. Coulter PREHM.

4388. Paige PREHM.

4389. Leanna GATES.

4390. Benjamin "Ben" GATES.

4391. Katherine "Katie" GATES.

4392. Josiah "Joey" GATES.

4393. Destiny Marie KNOEDLER. Born on 25 Nov 1986.

4394. Josiah David KNOEDLER. Born on 2 Jan 1994.

4395. Den Anthony WARD. Born on 23 Oct 1981.

4396. Anthem Lee WARD. Born on 7 Apr 1984.

4397. Tallen Miles WARD. Born on 1 Jan 1986.

4398. Ulyssia Autumn WARD. Born on 21 Dec 1987.

4399. Calla Elizabeth WARD. Born on 12 Aug 1990.

4400. Brian Matthew KNOEDLER. Born on 26 Sep 1994.

4401. Olivia Mildred SHEFFLER. Born 5 Nov 2008 in Waterloo, Black Hawk Co., Iowa.

4402. Lauri OLSON.

4403. Scott OLSON.

4403a. Megan Leigh EKERN.[970] Born at Rochester, Minn. 15 April 2003.

4403b. Weston Leigh EKERN. Born at Austin, Minn., 24 June 2005.

4403c. Ethan Leroy WILKINS. Born 18 December 2002.

4403d. Sidney Henry Ford EKERN. Born at Austin, Minn., 8 Feb 2008.

4404e. Hannah Rae EKERN. Born at Austin, Minn., 21 Jan 2006.

4404f. Baby boy EKERN. Birth expected, 29 August 2011

4404. Elliott HARRINGTON. Born on 24 Jun 1996 in Mason City, Iowa. Information from family reunion, 8 July 2000.

4405. ----- ____. Born on 22 Oct 2001.

4406. ----- ____. Born on 22 Oct 2001.

4407. Marcina Lynn HAUGHT.[971] Born on 27 Dec 2005 in Parkersburg, W. Va.

4408. Landon Jason HAUGHT. Born on 26 Aug 2007 in Parkersburg, West Virginia.

4409. Christian Dean HAUGHT. Born on 5 Jan 2009 in Parkersburg, W.Va.

Born at 10:27 p.m., 7 lbs 4 oz., 21 in.

4410. Ryan Daniel McGINNIS. Born on 11 May 1989.

4411. Lauryn Celia McGINNIS. Born on 30 Sep 1992.

Line 8 – Descendants of John Hill (continued)[972]

4412. Danielle WILBUR. Born on 7 Feb 1985.

4413. Mathew Robert WILBUR.

4414. Ashley Lindsey WILBUR. Born on 19 Jan 1989.

4415. Shelley Marie BABCOCK. Born on 12 Aug 1993.

4416. Jamie Lee BABCOCK. Born on 20 Nov 1995.

14

Fourteenth Generation
The 11th-Great—Grandchildren

Line 1. Descendants of Lydia Hill (continued)[973]

4417. Living Daughter of Ruth (Leveque) PALMER.
4418. Living Daughter of Ruth (Leveque) PALMER.
4419. Living Son of Gerald and Beth (McDuffie) GILBERT.
4420. Living Son of Gerald and Beth (McDuffie) GILBERT.
4421. Living Daughter of Donald and Kathryn (Rhoads) McDUFFIE.
4422. Living Daughter of Ronald and Betty (Ward) McDUFFIE.
4423. Living Son of Ronald and Betty (Ward) McDUFFIE.

Bibliography

Abbreviations and Short Titles of Sources

ACB, *Windsor* = A. C. B. [Albert Carlos Bates] (ed.), *Some Early Records and Documents of and Relating to the Town of Windsor, Connecticut, 1639-1703*. Hartford, Conn.: Connecticut Historical Society, 1930.

AGBI = *American Genealogical-Biographical Index*.

AGRI, *Hill* = American Genealogical Research Institute. *The Hill Family*. Washington, D.C.: Heritage Press, Inc., 1975.

Ancestry.com = Ancestry.com, and related links to www.familysearch.org, OneWorldTree, and specific family trees, some with sources, documents, and photographs, and some without references, details below.
   Family trees include: "Andre," "Baldwin," "Brooks," "Frisbie/Criger," "Golding," "Hill" by Norris, "Pratt," "PrestonSmith," "Roe," "Tompkins," "Winters," and "Wiswedel"

Anderson, *Great Migration Begins* = Anderson, Robert Charles, *The Great Migration Begins: Immigrants to New England, 1620-1633*. Vols 1-3.

Avis Hill = Hill, Avis (Boyington) [Mrs. Dale E.], letters to George James Hill, M.D., 1970ff. [hereafter, Avis Hill]

Bassett = Bassette, Buell Burdett. *One Bassett Family in America: With All Connections in America and Many in Great Britain and France*. Springfield, Mass.: F. A. Bassette Co., 1926.

Barber FH = Morris, Andrew J., "Family History of Thomas Barber (ca 1614-1662)" in "Connecticut Genealogy: Frequent posts of genealogical and family history information, record extracts and indices, and similar useful information for anyone interested in the people of Connecticut's past." < http://connecticut-genealogy.blogspot.com/2010/07/family-history-of-thomas-barber-ca-1614.html>, accessed 8/8/2010.

Barbour Collection = Barbour, Lucius Barnes. *Connecticut Town Birth Records, pre-1870* (from various sources).

Barbour, *Early Hartford* = Barbour, Lucius Barnes, *Families of Early Hartford, CT: 1600s-1800s*, Baltimore, Md.: Genealogical Publishing Co., (1977), 1982. *CD #515 (2002): CD-ROM of Family Tree Maker, Local and Family Histories: Connecticut, 1600s-1800s*.

Bates, *Simsbury* = Bates, Albert C. *Simsbury, Connecticut, Births, Marriages and Deaths, Transcribed from the Town Records, and Published by Albert C. Bates.* Hartford, Conn.: The Case, Lockwood & Brainard Co., 1898.

Brodnax = Brodnax, Christine. "Ancestors of Thomas Byron Brodnax," re Pierre LaDou and Jeanne Anneraud, parents of Jeanne Ladue, first wife of John Hill Jr.

Carlson, "Hill" = Carlson, Thom, Ph.D. "Some Descendants of Isaac Hill Sr. & Eunice Mallory."

Hill: The Ferry Keeper and His Family for 14 Generations

Compiled by Thom Carlson, and sent to George J. Hill, M.D., 3 December 2008ff.

Colket = Colket, Meredith B., Jr. *Founders of Early American Families: Emigrants from Europe 1607-1657.* Revised Edition (Cleveland, Ohio: General Court of the Order of Founders and Patriots of America, 1985).

Connecticut Public Records or *Connecticut Probate Records* = *The Public Records of the Colony of Connecticut*, Vol. 4. Accessed 4/15/2010 from Ancestry.com. And *A Digest of the Early Connecticut Probate Records, 1723-1729*, 121-4 (Will of Eleazer Hill, Windsor), accessed from Ancestry.com, 6/14/2010. Also includes *Early Connecticut Probate Records*, v. 2, p. 473 (accessed from NEHGS, 25 June 2010). Record of 31 March 1736 re Ebenezer Hill, Jr., Luke Hill, and Isaac Hill, near the town lines of Litchfield and Torrington, Conn.

Cutter, *New England Families* = Cutter, William Richard. *New England Families: Genealogical and Memorial: A Record of the Achievements of Her People in the Making of Commonwealths and the Founding of a Nation*, 1913.

Edwin Hill, "John Hill" = Hill, Edwin A. "Notes on the Family of John Hill of Guilford, Conn." In *Genealogies of Connecticut Families*. CD#179. Vol. 2, 164-6, "Luke Hill of Windsor, Conn., and John Hill of Guilford, Conn."

GHFA 1e = [Hill, William Edwin]. *Genealogy of the Hill Family in America* [Hill Family Association], 1921. Typed, mimeographed, and stapled.

GHFA 2e = Hill, George James. *Genealogy of the Hill Family in America: Seven Generations of the Family of Isaac Hill (1740-1833) of Guilford and Southbury, Connecticut*. 2nd Edition. West Orange, N.J., 2000. Privately printed, with cardstock covers.

GJH = George J. Hill, M.D., aka George James Hill (b. 1932)

"Early Guilford" = "Families of Early Guilford, Connecticut," *Local and Family Histories: CT, 1600s-1800s,* Family Tree Maker, CD515, 2000.

Harson = Harson, Adella Helen [228] (Lindsay). Recollections and handwritten notes [untitled] to George J. Hill, 1994-96.

Hibbard, *Goshen* = Hibbard, A. G. *History of the Town of Goshen, Connecticut*. Hartford, Conn.: Press of the Case, Lockwood & Brainard Co., 1897.

High, *Manly* = High, Grace Mildred Ridings. *The Manly Family: A Record of the Descendants of William Manly and Rachel Jackson Manly, His Wife, of Cecil County, Maryland.* Claflin, Kansas: Claflin Clarion, for Grace High, 1962.

Hill, *Melanchton Hill* = Hill, Francis C. *Biographical Sketch and Genealogical Record of the Descendants of Melanchthon Hill, of Connecticut: 1610 to 1895*. New York City, N.Y.: T. A. Wright, 1895.

Hill, "Twelve Generations" = Hill, James D. "The Hill Family, from 1651 to 2000: Twelve Generations in America" Edition 5.0.

Hinman, *Connecticut Settlers* = Hinman, R. R. *Catalogue of the Names of the Puritan Settlers of the Colony of Connecticut: With the Time of Their Arrival in the Colony, and Their Standing in Society, Together with Their Place of Residence, As Far As Can be Discovered by the Records. Collected from the State and Town Records.* Vol. 1. Hartford, Conn.: Printed by E. Gleason, 1946.

IGI = International Genealogical Index (from The Church of Jesus Christ of Latter-day Saints).

Jacobus, *Ancient New Haven* = Jacobus, Donald Lines (compiler). *Families of Ancient New Haven.* 9 vols. in 3. Baltimore, Md.: Genealogical Publishing Co., 1981. Accessed on Family Tree Maker, CD#179 Family History: Connecticut Genealogies #1.

Johnson = Johnson, Jeanine Humbert; correspondence with George James Hill.

Kennedy, *Stockwell* = Kennedy, Mabel Stockwell. *The Stockwell Genealogy.* Lebanon, N.H.: Stockwell Family Assoc., 1983.

NEHGS = New England Historic Genealogical Society

NEHGR = *New England Historic Genealogical Register*, aka "The Register"

OFPA, *Lineages* = The Order of the Founders and Patriots of America. *Register of Lineages of Associates, 1993-2000.* Vol. 5. *Corrections, Additions, & Supplements; and Nos. 4968 Thru 5383. Index.* Williamsburg, Va.: The General Court of the Order, 2002.

Olson = Olson, Mabel LaVonne (Anderson). Information from LaVonne (Anderson) Olson by telephone, and in a Biographical Information Form prepared for her late sister, Ula (Anderson) Schroader, 4 Mar 1996.

OWT = OneWorldTree, a computerized synthesis of family trees, available on Ancestry.com. Information on OWT is considered as "possible," but is not verified, unless supported with additional information.

Parsons, "Windsor" = Parsons, Samuel H. "Record of Marriages and Births, in Windsor, Ct." *NEHGR* 5 (April 1851): 225-8ff.

Paul Hill = Correspondence of Paul F. Hill, Corning, N.Y., with George James Hill, 2004ff, including "Descendants of Abraham Hill" and related matters.

Phelps, "Family History" = Phelps, Brian. "Phelps Family History in America: Family of Joseph and Hannah (Newton) Phelps of Simsbury, Conn. (Sources are given at the website: http://www.phelpsfamilyhistory.com/ (2008ff; last updated and accessed 10 August 2010). [hereafter, Phelps "Family History]

Phelps, *Simsbury* = Phelps, Noah A. *History of Simsbury, Granby and Canton, from 1642 to 1845* Hartford, Conn.: Case, Tiffany and Burnham, 1845.

Pitman, "Nathan Gillett" = Pitman, Leon S. "Some Descendants of Nathan Gillett of Windsor and Simsbury, Connecticut," Modesto, California, [1999] 2002, 5 pp., with references. Downloaded from Ancestry.com, where it appeared in a search for Gillett, Nathan, on 23 August 2009.

Priest, "Gillett" = Priest, Alice Lucinda. "The Brothers Jonathan and Nathan Gillett and Some of Their

Descendants" *New England Historical Genealogical Register,* October 1946: 272-277.

Ptak = Ptak, Diane Snyder, C.A.L.S., 12 Tice Road, Albany, NY 12203-9721 (518) 456-3370. Research conducted on Hill families in New York state and Connecticut, 1994 ff., for George J. Hill, M.D.

Roberts, *Connecticut Genealogies* = Roberts, Gary Boyd. *Family History: Connecticut Genealogies. Genealogies of Connecticut Families from the* New England Historic and Genealogical Register. 3 vols. Baltimore: Genealogical Publishing Co., 1983.

Rose = Rose, Mrs. Ken (Natalie), E-mail to George J. Hill, 2002 ff.

Savage, *Genealogical Dictionary* = Savage, James. *A Genealogical Dictionary of the First Settlers of New England, Showing Three Generations of Those Who Came Before May, 1692.* Boston, 1861. 4 vols.

Schroader = Correspondence with George James Hill, M.D., including documents related to Riley, Olson, and Hill families.

Smith and Steiner, "Luke Hill" = Smith, Hon. Ralph D. and Dr. Bernard C. Steiner. "Luke Hill of Windsor, Conn., and John Hill of Guilford, Conn., and Their Descendants." *NEHGR* 57 (Jan. 1903): 87-93.

Smith and Steiner, "Parmelee" = Smith, Hon. R. D., and Bernard C. Steiner. "The Descendants of John Parmelee." In *Genealogies of Connecticut Families*. CD#179. Vol. 3, 24-30.

Stanley, "Hill" = Stanley, Richard R. E-mail to George J. Hill from Richard R. Stanley, 29 January 2005. Re: His line of descent from Luke Hill Jr.'s son Ebenezer, and Ebenezer Jr.'s son Ambrose. rrstanley@bankofny.com and leyric@comcast.net

Stiles, *Ancient Windsor* (1859) = Stiles, Henry R., M.D. *The History of Ancient Windsor, Connecticut* . . . New York: Charles B. Norton, 1859.

Stiles, *Ancient Windsor* (1892) = Stiles, Henry R. *Families of Ancient Windsor, Connecticut*, Vol. 2, *Genealogies*. 1892. On CD#515, "Family Tree Maker's Family Archives: Local and Family Histories: Connecticut, 1600s-1800s" © 2000.

Stiles, *Wethersfield* = Stiles, Henry R., A.M., M.D. *The History of Ancient Wethersfield, Connecticut:* . . . . 2 vols. New York City, N.Y.: The Grafton Press, 1904.

Stockwell, GSF = Stockwell, Foster Paul. "Genealogy of the Stockwell Family and Other Related Families." Typed MS, ca. 1970, with computer-printed addendum, 10 December 1988.

TAG = The American Genealogist

Torrey, *New England Marriages* = Torrey, Clarence Almon. *New England Marriages Prior to 1700.* 6th printing. Genealogical Publishing Co., (1984) 2004.

Yale and Jacobus, "Isaac Hill" = Connecticut Historical Society, letter of Allen R. Yale to Mrs. Jeanine Humbert Johnson, 17 July 1992, and part of a letter of Donald Lines Jacobus to Mrs. H. A. Thomas (1952) regarding Isaac Hill and his ancestors.

Books and Book Chapters

Abbott, Susan Woodruff, and Jacquelyn L. Ricker. *Families of Early Milford, Connecticut,* Baltimore: Genealogical Publishing Co. (on CD-ROM, 2000), 1979. Selected pages copied, from D. S. Ptak to George J. Hill, 9 Feb 1994.

Allen, Orrin Peer. *The Allen Memorial: Descendants of Samuel Allen of Windsor, Connecticut, 1640-1907* (Palmer, Mass.: C. B. Fiske & Co., 1907 [paperback reprint by Kessinger Publishing Co., Breingsville, Pa., 2010].

American Genealogical-Biographical Index [hereafter *AGBI*]: "Mary Hout / Birth Date: 1630 / Birthplace: Connecticut" / Volume: 84 / Page Number 340 / Reference: Gen. Column of the *Boston Transcript* 1906-1941 ... (14 Jan 1920), 8127. Accessed and printed from Amazon.com, in a search for "Mary Hout" (4/5/2010).
    "Eleazer Hill was b. 1657 in Connecticut." From *AGBI* 79, p.347 (accessed on Ancestry.com, 6/14/2010), referencing James Savage, *A Genealogical Dictionary of the First Settlers of New England, Showing Three Generations of Those Who Came Before May, 1692,* (Boston, 1861), 4 vols., v.2:418.

American Genealogical Research Institute. *The Hill Family.* Washington, D.C.: Heritage Press, Inc., 1975. [hereafter AGRI, *Hill*]. Also, *American Genealogical-Biographical Index[AGBI]*, other pages accessed and printed from Amazon.com, 5 April 2010ff.

Anderson, Robert Charles. *The Great Migration Begins: Immigrants to New England, 1620-1633.* Vols 1-3. On-line from NEHGS, 2002, New England Historic Genealogical Society, 1995. [hereafter, Anderson, *Great Migration Begins*]

Anon. *History of Chittenden County, Vermont.* Syracuse, NY: D. Mason & Co., 1886.
Avery, Kent C. L., Donna Siemiatkoski, and Robert T. Silliman. *The Settlement of Windsor, Connecticut.* 4th ed., by Richard C. Roberts. Windsor, Conn.: The Descendants of the Founders of Ancient Windsor, Inc., 2008. Pamphlet, 32 pp.

Barber, Gertrude A. *Index of Wills of Chenango County, New York.* 1 (1797-1850), 2 (1851-1875), Salem, Mass.: Higginson Book Co. [reprint, 1999]. Vol. 1, 1935; 2, 1951.

Barr, John L. *The Genealogy of Ethan Allen and His Brothers and Sisters.* Burlington, Vt.: Ethan Allen Trust, 1991.

[Bates] A. C. B. [Albert Carlos Bates] (ed.), *Some Early Records and Documents of and Relating to the Town of Windsor, Connecticut, 1639-1703.* Hartford, Conn.: Connecticut Historical Society, 1930; facsimile reproduction by Higginson Book Co., Salem, Mass., 1995. [hereafter ACB, *Windsor*]

Bates, Albert C. *Simsbury, Connecticut, births, marriages and deaths, transcribed from the town records, and published by Albert C. Bates.* Hartford, Conn.: The Case, Lockwood & Brainard Co., 1898. Accessed as Simsbury, Connecticut, Vital Records, 1665-1886 (Online Database: NewEnglandAncestors.org, New England Historic Genealogical Society, 2008.) [hereafter, Bates, *Simsbury*]

Bates, Samuel P. *History of Crawford County, Pennsylvania.* Chicago: Warner, Beers & Co, 1885. [quoted by Carlson, op. cit.]

Barbour, Lucius Barnes, *Families of Early Hartford, CT: 1600s-1800s*, Baltimore, Md.: Genealogical

Publishing Co., (1977), 1982. *CD #515 (2002): CD-ROM of Family Tree Maker, Local and Family Histories: Connecticut, 1600s-1800s.* [hereafter, Barbour, *Early Hartford*]

_____. *Connecticut Town Birth Records, pre-1870 (Barbour Collection).* See internet sources (below) utilized for access to these documents.

Bassette, Buell Burdett, *One Bassett Family in America: With All Connections in America and Many in Great Britain and France* (Springfield, Mass.: F. A. Bassette Co., 1926; reprinted by Higginson Book Co., Salem, Mass., 28 August 1997). "The John Hill Family" is pp. 425-29, and "The Luke Hill Family" is pp. 430-34. "The Gillett Family" is pp. 321-33. [hereafter, Bassette]

Beach and Hibbard, *History of the Town of Goshen, Connecticut* [quoted by Carlson]

Biographical Memoirs of Greene County, Indiana. Indianoplis: B. F. Bowen & Co. [quoted by Thom Carlson].

Birdsall, B. P. (ed.). *History of Wright County Iowa: Its People, Industries and Institutions.* Indianapolis: B. F. Bowen & Co., 1915.

Bitker, Marian Rozella (Schroader). *Thanks For Giving And Other Poems.* Privately printed, 1990

Brown, Abiel. *Early Settlers of West Simsbury* [Canton], 1856. [quoted by Carlson]

Brownson, Ernest Ray. *Genealogy of One Branch of the Richard Brownson Family*, 1631-1951. Mayville, N.D.: n.s., 1951.

Burkhardt, Frederick, et al. (eds.). *Concise Dictionary of American Biography*. New York City, N.Y.: Scribners, 1961.

Buys, Barbara Smith (B.A. Vassar, 1946; M.A., C.A.L.S.), *Old Gravestones of Putnam County, New York: Together with Information from Ten Adjacent Dutchess County Burying Grounds,* Baltimore, Md.: Gateway Press, Inc., 1975 [from Tuttle Antiquarian Books, 2004].

Chapman, Frederick William. *Descendants of Thomas Buckingham, One of the First Settlers of Milford, Conn.* Case, Lockwood & Brainard, 1872. [quoted by Carlson]

Child, Hamilton. *Gazetteer and Business Directory of Addison County, Vt., for 1881-82.* Syracuse, NY: H. Child, 1882. [quoted by Carlson]

Clayton, W. W. *History of Steuben County, New York, with Illustrations and Biographical Sketches of Some of Its Prominent Men and Pioneers.* Vol. 1, Philadelphia: J. B. Lippincott/Lewis, Peck & Co., 1879 [Reprint from Higginson Books, Salem, Mass., 2000].

Colket, Meredith B., Jr. *Founders of Early American Families: Emigrants from Europe 1607-1657.* Revised Edition (Cleveland, Ohio: General Court of the Order of Founders and Patriots of America, 1985). [hereafter, Colket]

Compendium of History Reminiscence and Biography of Western Nebraska. Chicago: Alden Publishing Co, 1912. [quoted by Carlson]

Connecticut State Library, *Shelton, Connecticut Huntington Congregational Church and Ecclesiastical Society Records, 1717-1917* [5 vols.]

Cook, Lorraine, ed. *The Barbour Collection of Connecticut Town Vital Records.* Vol. 1-55. Baltimore, Md.: Genealogical Publishing Co., 1994-2002.

Cooke, Edward S., Jr., *The Social Economy of the Preindustrial Joiner in Western Connecticut, 1750-1800* [quoted by Carlson, op. cit.]

Cothren, William. *History of Ancient Woodbury, Connecticut: From the First Indian Dead in 1659. . .* [quoted by Carlson, op. cit.]

Curley, Juanita Bradish, Patrick Joseph Curley, Robert L. Mittino, *Genealogy & History of Robert Bradish in America* (2000) [quoted by Carlson, op. cit.]

Cutter, William Richard (ed.) and William Frederick Adams (assistant), *Genealogical and Personal Memoirs Relating to the Families of the State of Massachusetts.* Lewis Historical Publishing Co., 1910. [quoted by Carlson]

Cutter, William Richard. *Genealogical and Family History of the State of Connecticut: A Record of the Achievements of Her People in the Making of a Commonwealth and the Founding of a Nation.* New York, N.Y.: Lewis Publishing Company, 1911. [quoted by Thom Carlson]

_____. *New England Families: Genealogical and Memorial: A Record of the Achievements of Her People in the Making of Commonwealths and the Founding of a Nation* (1913. Reprinted for Clearfield Company, Inc., by Genealogical Publishing Co., Inc., Baltimore Md., 1994, 1995. 3 vols. On Family Tree Maker, CD515 Local and Family Histories: CT, 1600s-1800s, Disk 1, New England Families, vol. 1. The Buckland Line is on p. 1305. [hereafter, Cutter, *New England Families*]

Davis, Betsey Warren. *The Warren, Jackson, and Allied Families.* Philadelphia: J. B. Lippincott, 1903.

Dimitroff, Thomas P., and Lois S. Janes. *History of the Corning-Painted Post Area: 200 Years in Painted Post Country.* Corning, N.Y.: Corning Area Bicentennial Committee, (n.d., ?ca. 1976).

Depuy, Henry W. *Ethan Allen and the Green-Mountain Heroes of '76 with a Sketch of the Early History of Vermont.* New York: Phinney, Blakeman & Mason, 1861. Facsimile Reprint by Heritage Books, Bowie, Md., 1994.

"Families of Early Guilford, Connecticut," *Local and Family Histories: CT, 1600s-1800s,* Family Tree Maker, CD515, 2000. [hereafter, "Early Guilford"]

Fernald, Natalie R. *The Genealogical Exchange.* 1904. [quoted by Thom Carlson]

Foote, Abram W. *Foote Family: Comprising the Genealogy and History of Nathaniel Foote, of Wethersfield, Conn.* Rutland, VT: Tuttle Co., 1907. [quoted by Carlson]

Garnett, R. S. *History of Bond and Montgomery Counties, Illinois.* Chicago: O.L. Baskin & Co., 1882. [quoted by Carlson]

Goodwin, Joseph O. *East Hartford: Its History and Traditions.* Hartford, Conn.: Press of the Case, Lockwood & Brainard Co., 1879 (accessed via Google, 7/24/10).

Harrison, Bruce H. *Descendants of Pieter Tjercks (Schuyler)*. Kamuela, Hawaii: Millisecond Publishing Co., n.d.

Hakes, Harlow (Editor). *Landmarks of Steuben County, New York*. Syracuse, N.Y.: D. Mason & Co., Publishers, 1896 [Reprinted by Higginson Books, Salem, Mass., 2000].

Herringshaw, Mae Felts. *Chicagoans of 1916: Ten Thousand Biographies. Herringshaws City Blue Book of Biography*. Chicago: Clark J. Herringshaw, 1916.

Hibbard, A. G. *History of the Town of Goshen, Connecticut*. Hartford, Conn.: Press of the Case, Lockwood & Brainard Co., 1897 [selected pages from Thom Carlson] [hereafter, Hibbard, *Goshen*].

High, Grace Mildred Ridings. *The Manly Family: A Record of the Descendants of William Manly and Rachel Jackson Manly, His Wife, of Cecil County, Maryland*. Claflin, Kansas: Claflin Clarion, for Grace High, 1962. [hereafter, High, *Manly*]

Hill, David Hedgcock. "The Statue and the Strands," in Deborah Case and Sharon Derderian (Editors), *Passages: An Anthology of Contemporary Literature*. Troy, Mich.: Iliad Press/Cader Publishing Co., 1992. [ISBN 0-8187-0164-1], p. 80;

_____. (edited by George J. Hill, M.D.) *A Lesson in Reality: Poems and Essays, 1991-2000*. West Orange, N.J.: Hilltree Farm Press, 2007, 67 pp.

Hill, Edwin A. "Notes on the Family of John Hill of Guilford, Conn." In *Genealogies of Connecticut Families*. CD#179. Vol. 2, 164-6, "Luke Hill of Windsor, Conn., and John Hill of Guilford, Conn." [hereafter, Edwin Hill, "John Hill"]

Hill, Essie Mae Thompson. *Prairie Daughter*. Phoenix, Ariz.: O'Sullivan, Woodside, 1973.

Hill, Francis C. *Biographical Sketch and Genealogical Record of the Descendants of Melanchthon Hill, of Connecticut: 1610 to 1895*. New York City, N.Y.: T. A. Wright, 1895. Reprint from Higginson Book Co., Salem, Mass., July 1998. [hereafter, Hill, *Melanchthon Hill*]

Hill, George James. *Genealogy of the Hill Family in America: Seven Generations of the Family of Isaac Hill (1740-1833) of Guilford and Southbury, Connecticut*. 2nd Edition. West Orange, N.J., 2000. Includes reproduction of GHFA 1e, reduced to 80 percent of original size. Privately printed, with cardstock covers. [hereafter *GHFA* 2e]

Hill, George J[ames]. *John Saxe, Loyalist (1732-1808) and His Descendants for Five Generations*. Westminster, Md.: Heritage Books, 2010.

[Hill, William Edwin]. "Genealogy of the Hill Family in America." [Hill Family Association], 1921. 14 page typescript, 14 in. by 8 1/2 in., printed single-sided, mimeographed, and stapled. [hereafter GHFA 1e]

Hinman, R. R. *Catalogue of the Names of the Puritan Settlers of the Colony of Connecticut: With the Time of Their Arrival in the Colony, and Their Standing in Society, Together with Their Place of Residence, As Far As Can be Discovered by the Records. Collected from the State and Town Records*. Vol. 1. Hartford, Conn.: Printed by E. Gleason, 1946. Available on-line from Ancestry.com, accessed 4/15/2010. [hereafter, Hinman, *Connecticut Settlers*]

Historical Collections of Ohio. Henry Howe & Son, 1891. [quoted by Thom Carlson]

Hollister, Hiel. *Pawlet, Vermont: One Hundred Years.* Albany, N.Y.: J. Munsell, 1867. "Biography of Allen Surname of Pawlet, Vermont" [quoted by Thom Carlson]

Hosley, Eva Loesa Hill (compiler). *Descendants of William Hill of Fairfield, Conn., Who came from Exeter, England, June 5, 1632, in Ship* William and Frances: *With Genealogical Notes and Biographical Sketches of His Descendants as Far as Can be Obtained Including Notes on Collateral Branches.* Meriden, Conn.: Horton Press, 1909. 8vo., boards, 55 pp.

Hoyt, David Webster. *A Genealogical History of the Hoyt, Haight, and Hight Families.* Providence, 1871. [available as pdf file on Google books]

Hoyt, Edwin P. *The Damndest Yankees: Ethan Allen & His Clan.* Brattleboro, Vt.: The Stephen Greene Press, 1976.

Huidekoper, Alfred. "Incidents in the Early History of Crawford County, Pennsylvania" in *Memoirs of the Historical Society of Pennsylvania.* Vol. 2, Part 2. Philadelphia: Henry C. Baird, 1850.

Jacobus, Donald Lines. *Families of Ancient New Haven.* 9 vols. in 3. Baltimore, Md.: Genealogical Publishing Co., 1981. Orig. in *New Haven Genealogical Magazine,* 1922-1932; and Rome, N.Y.: Clarence D. Smith, 1923ff. In Family Tree Maker's Family Archives: "Connecticut Family Histories #1, 1600s-1800s," CD#179, from Genealogy.com, © 2000. [hereafter, Jacobus, *Ancient New Haven*]

Jacobus, Donald Lines (compiler). "Hill Family, Family 5. Luke, s. of Luke & Mary (Hart)," in Family Tree Maker, CD#179 Family History: Connecticut Genealogies #1, Families of Ancient New Haven, Vol. 3, "Family Statistics," 743. [hereafter, Jacobus, "Hill Family"]

Jackson, Francis. *A History of the Early Settlement of Newton, County of Middlesex, Massachusetts, from 1639 to 1800, with a Genealogical Register of its Inhabitants Prior to 1800.* Boston: Stacy and Richardson, Facsimile Reprint ed. by Heritage Books, Bowie, Md., (1854) 1987. Includes unpaginated additional index and plat map of Newton, 1700.

Jackson, Mary S., and Edward F. Jackson. *Marriage Notices from Steuben County, New York, Newspapers: 1797-1884.* Bowie, Md.: Heritage Books, 1998.

Jackson, Mary S., and Edward F. Jackson. *Death Notices from Steuben County, New York Newspapers: 1797-1884.* Bowie, Md.: Heritage Books, 1998.

Johnson, Jeanine Humbert, and Cynthia Huffman Sweet. *Since I Started for the War: The Letters and Diary of Solomon B. Humbert, Co. B, 31st Iowa Volunteer Infantry.* Cedar Falls, Ia.: Sweet Press, 2007.

Kennedy, Mabel Stockwell. *The Stockwell Genealogy.* Lebanon, N.H.: Stockwell Family Assoc., 1983. [hereafter, Kennedy, *Stockwell*]

Kilbourne, Payne K. *History and Genealogy of the Kilbourn Family in the United States.* Hartford, CT: Brown & Parsons, 1845. [quoted by Thom Carlson]

Knapp, Chauncey L. *Rolls of the Soldiers in the Revolutionary War, 1775 to 1783 in Vermont.* [quoted by Thom Carlson]

Latzman, Valerie. *The City of Wayne*. Philadelphia, Pa.: Tempus Publishing/Arcadia Press, 2003.

Lu, Helen M. and Gwen B. Neumann, *Revolutionary War Period: Bible, Family & Marriage Records Gleaned from Pension Applications*, 1998. [quoted by Carlson]

Lyon Memorial. 3 vols. Lyons, A. B., M.D., and G. W. A. Lyon, M.D. (Editors); and Eugene F. McPike (Associate Editor), *Lyon Memorial: Massachusetts Families Including Descendants of the Immigrants William Lyon, of Roxbury, Peter Lyon, of Dorchester, [and] George Lyon, of Dorchester, with Introduction Treating of the English Ancestry of the American Families*. Detroit, Michigan: William Graham Printing Co., 1905; reprint edition by Higginson Press, Salem, Mass., 2002. Miller, Robert B. (Editor) and A. B. Lyons, M.D. (Associate Editor). *Lyon Memorial: New York Families Descended from the Immigrant Thomas Lyon, of Rye, with Introductory Chapter by Dr. G. W. A. Lyon on the English Lyon Families*. 1907; reprint by Higginson Books, Salem, Mass., 2002. Lyon, Sidney Elizabeth (Editor), and Louise Lyon Johnson and A. B. Lyons, M.D. (Associate Editors), *Lyon Memorial: Families of Connecticut and New Jersey Including Records of the Descendants of the Immigrants Richard Lyon, of Fairfield [and] Henry Lyon, of Fairfield*. Detroit, Michigan: William Granham Printing Co., 1907; reprint by Higginson Books, Salem, Mass., 2002.

Lytle, James R. *20th Century History of Delaware County, Ohio*. Chicago: Biographical Pub. Co, 1908. [quoted by Thom Carlson]

Manwaring, Charles W. *A Digest of the Early Connecticut Probate Records*. R. S. Peck & Co. Printers, Hartford, CT, 1904. In "A Digest of the Early Connecticut Probate Records" Online database: NewEnglandAncestors.org, New England Historic Genealogical Society, 2006. *Early Connecticut Probate Records*, v. 2, p. 473 (accessed from NEHGS, 25 June 2010). Vol. 12, p. 42, Record of 31 March 1736 re Ebenezer Hill, Jr., Luke Hill, and Isaac Hill, near the town lines of Litchfield and Torrington, Conn.

Marquis, Albert Nelson. *The Book of Minnesotans: A Biographical Dictionary of Leading Living Men of the State of Minnesota*. Albert Nelson Marquis & Co., 1907. [quoted by Thom Carlson]

Memorial and Biographical Record of Iowa. Chicago: Lewis Publishing Co, 1896. [quoted by Thom Carlson]

Morgan, Ted. *A Shovel of Stars: The Making of the American West, 1800 to the Present*. New York: Simon and Schuster, 1995.

Orcutt, Samuel. *History of the Towns of New Milford and Bridgewater, Connecticut, 1703-1882*. Hartford, Conn.: Case, Lockwood and Brainard, 1882.

Peeke, Hewson L. *A Standard History of Erie County, Ohio*. Chicago: Lewis Pub. Co., 1916. [quoted by Thom Carlson]

Phelps, Noah A. *History of Simsbury, Granby and Canton, from 1642 to 1845*. Hartford, Conn.: Case, Tiffany and Burnham, 1845. [hereafter, Phelps, *Simsbury*] Mark Norris found this book at: http://www.archive.org/details/historyofsimsbur00p hel. It can also be downloaded as a pdf file from Google books.

Phoenix, S. Whitney, *The Whitney family of Connecticut*. New York: Priv. print., 1878.

Pope, Charles Henry, *The Pioneers of Massachusetts: A Descriptive List, Drawn from Records of the Colonies, Towns and Churches, and other Contemporaneous Documents,* n.p. [Facsimile Reprint by Heritage Books, Bowie, Md., (n.d.) 1991]

Powell, Esther Weygandt. *Ohio Records and Pioneer Families.* 2001.[quoted by Carlson]

Prince, Helen Wright. *Descendants of Captain John Prince of Southold, New York and Their Place in Local History.* Blacksburg, Va.: Kopy Korner (c/o Weathervane Shop, Suffolk Co. Historical Society, 300 West Main St., Riverhead, NY 11901), n.d. Selected pages from Diane Snyder Ptak to G. J. Hill, 26 February 1994.

Prosser, William F. *History of the Puget Sound Country.* The Lewis Publishing Company, 1903. [quoted by Thom Carlson]

Putnam, Rufus. *Pioneer Record and Reminiscences of the Early Settlers and Settlement of Fayette County, Ohio.* Cincinnati: Applegate, Pounsford & Co. Print, 1872. [quoted by Thom Carlson]

Reynolds, John Earle. *In French Creek Valley.* Meadville, PA.: Crawford County Historical Society, 1938. [quoted by Thom Carlson]

Roberts, Gary Boyd. *Family History: Connecticut Genealogies. Genealogies of Connecticut Families from the* New England Historic and Genealogical Register. 3 vols. Vol. 1. *Adams-Gates.* Vol. 2. *Geer-Owen.* Vol. 3. *Painter-Wylls.* Baltimore: Genealogical Publishing Co., 1983. In Family Tree Maker's Family Archives: "Connecticut Family Histories #1, 1600s-1800s," CD#179, from Genealogy.com, © 2000. [hereafter, Roberts, *Connecticut Genealogies*]

_____, *The Royal Descent of 600 Immigrants to the American Colonies or the United States.* Genealogical Publishing Co., 2004.

Roberts, Millard F. (Compiler and Editor), *Historical Gazetteer of Steuben County, New York, with Memoirs and Illustrations,* Part 1, Syracuse, N.Y.: Millard F. Roberts, Publisher, 1891.

Robinson, Rowland Evans. *Vermont: A Study of Independence.* Boston, Mass.: Houghton, Mifflin and Co., 1892 [paperback reprint by BiblioBazaar, Charleston, S.C., 2010.]

Savage, James. *A Genealogical Dictionary of the First Settlers of New England, Showing Three Generations of Those Who Came Before May, 1692.* Boston, 1861. 4 vols. [hereafter, Savage, *Genealogical Dictionary*]

Shoemaker, Benjamin H. *Genealogy of the Shoemaker Family of Cheltenham, Pennsylvania.* Philadelphia, Pa.: J. B. Lippincott, 1903.

Smith (aka Smyth), Ralph D. *Luke and John Hill of Connecticut* (1903). A reprint by Higginson Books of Hon. Ralph D. Smith and Dr. Bernard C. Steiner. "Luke Hill of Windsor, Conn., and John Hill of Guilford, Conn., and Their Descendants." *NEHGR* 57 (Jan. 1903): 87-93. For corrections, see H. A. Thomas, *NEHGR* 107 (Jan. 1953): 71). [hereafter, Smith and Steiner, "Luke Hill"]

Smith, Stephen R., Frederick E. Camp, Lucius A. Barbour, and George M. White. *Record of Service of Connecticut Men in the War of the Revolution.* Hartford: Authority of the General Assembly, 1889. [quoted by Thom Carlson]

Stiles, Henry R., M.D. *The History of Ancient Windsor, Connecticut, Including East Windsor, South Windsor, and Ellington, Prior to 1768, the Date of Their Separation from the Old Town: and Windsor, Bloomfield and Windsor Locks, to the Present Time. Also the Genealogies and Genealogical Notes of Those Families Which Settled Within the Limits of Ancient Windsor, Connecticut, Prior to 1800.* New York: Charles B. Norton, 1859 [copy from Google, digitized]. Also available as a Facsimile Reprint from Heritage Books, Bowie, Md., 1997. 2 vols., bound as Part One [History] (pp. xiv, 1-511) and Part Two, "Genealogies and Genealogical Notes of Those Families Which Settled Within the Limits of Ancient Windsor, Conn., Prior to 1800" (pp. 512-922). [hereafter, Stiles, *Ancient Windsor* (1859)].

_____. *Families of Ancient Windsor, Connecticut: Consisting of Volume II of The History and Genealogies of Ancient Windsor, Connecticut; Including East Windsor, South Windsor, Bloomfield, Windsor Locks, and Ellington, 1635-1891.* Hartford, Conn., 1892. Reprinted for Clearfield Company, Inc., by Genealogical Publishing Co., Inc., Baltimore, Md., 1999. ISBN: 0-8063-4922-0. On CD#515, "Family Tree Maker's Family Archives: Local and Family Histories: Connecticut, 1600s-1800s" © 2000. ISBN 1-57944-241-2. [hereafter, Stiles, *Ancient Windsor* (1892)].

_____. *The History of Ancient Wethersfield, Connecticut: Comprising the Present Towns of Wethersfield, Rocky Hill, and Newington; and of Glastonbury Prior to Its Incorporation in 1693, from Date of Earliest Settlement Until the Present Time, With Extensive Genealogies and Genealogical Notes on Their Early Families.* 2 vols. Vol. 1. History (pp. 1-995). Vol. 2. Genealogies and Biographies (pp. 1-946). New York City, N.Y.: The Grafton Press, 1904; reprint by Higginson Book Company, Salem, Mass., 1995. Also in *Local and Family Histories: Connecticut, 1600s-1800s.* CD #515. (Family Tree Maker, 2000). On this CD, see Henry R. Stiles, *The History of Ancient Wethersfield.* Vol. 2. (1904; Wethersfield Historical Society, 1975). [hereafter, Stiles, *Wethersfield*].

Stockwell, Mabel Kennedy. *The Stockwell Genealogy.* Lebanon, N.H.: Stockwell Family Assoc., 1983.

The Order of the Founders and Patriots of America. *Register of Lineages of Associates, 1993-2000.* Vol. 5. *Corrections, Additions, & Supplements; and Nos. 4968 Thru 5383. Index.* Williamsburg, Va.: The General Court of the Order, 2002. [hereafter, OFPA, *Lineages*]. George James Hill, General no. 5298. Society: NJ 384 (pp. 4253-4).

The Public Records of the Colony of Connecticut, Vol. 4. Accessed 4/15/2010 from Ancestry.com. And *A Digest of the Early Connecticut Probate Records, 1723-1729*, 121-4 (Will of Eleazer Hill, Windsor), accessed from Ancestry.com, 6/14/2010. Includes *Early Connecticut Probate Records*, v. 2, p. 473 (accessed from NEHGS, 25 June 2010). Record of 31 March 1736 re Ebenezer Hill, Jr., Luke Hill, and Isaac Hill, near the town lines of Litchfield and Torrington, Conn. And, *A Digest of the Early Connecticut Probate Records.* 1723 to 1729. Hartford, Connecticut Probate Records, 1700-29. [all hereafter as *Connecticut Public Records* or *Connecticut Probate Records*]

Torrey, Clarence A. *New England Marriages Prior to 1700.* 6th printing. Genealogical Publishing Co., [1984] 2004), 371: "… HILL, Luke (-1690, Simsbury) & Mary HOUT/HOYT/HART; 6 May 1651; Windsor, CT" (Accessed and printed via Ancestry.com, 4 April 2010). Originally published as: *New England Marriages Prior to 1700.* CD-ROM. Boston, Mass.: New England Historic Genealogical Society, 2001 [hereafter, Torrey, *New England Marriages*].

Tuttle, Charles. *A Partial Record of One Branch of the Hyde Family.* Rutland, Vt.: Tuttle., 1931.

Ward, Andrew Henshaw. *Ward Family: Descendants of William Ward, Who Settled in Sudbury, Mass., in 1639. With an Appendix, Alphabetically Arranged, of the Names of the Families That Have Intermarried with Them.* Boston: Samuel G. Drake, 1851. Extracted in *New England Historical and Genealogical*

Register 5 (No. 3, July 1851): 271-274, with a portrait of Gen. Ward (Reprinted by Heritage Books, Inc., Bowie, Md., 1994).

Virgil D. White, Abstractor, *Genealogical Abstracts of Revolutionary War Pension Files,* vol. 2 [F-M] (Waynesboro, Tenn.: National Historical Publishing Co., 1991).

Weis, Frederick Lewis. *The Magna Charta Sureties, 1215: The Barons Named in the Magna Charta, 1215 and Some of their Descendants Who Settled in America During the Early Colonial Years,* 5th Edition, Baltimore, Md.: Genealogical Publishing Co., Inc., [1955] 1999.

Collections

Family Tree Maker's Family Archives: CD#515, "Local and Family Histories: Connecticut, 1600s-1800s." Genealogy.com, 2000.

Family Tree Maker's Family Archives: CD#179, "Connecticut Family Histories #1, 1600s-1800s." Genealogy.com, 2000.

"SAR Patriot Index," Progeny Publishing, PP-9905, 1999.

Journal and Magazine Citations

Adams, Nelson D. "Adams" *NEHGR* (1879): 107.

Atwood, Mrs. George H. "George Adams" *NEHGR* 65 (1911): 302.

Hill, George J. "From Salem to Kalamazoo – A 14-Generation Family Odyssey" *About Towne: Quarterly Newsletter of the Towne Family Association* 26 (No. 3, July-September) 2006: 50-56; and (No. 4, October-December) 2006: 74-78.

_____. "Signatures of Two 17th Century Emigrants Once Believed to be the Same Henry Herrick" *The Mayflower Quarterly* (March 2007), 46-49.

_____. "Was James Prescott of Hampton, New Hampshire (in 1665), the Son of Sir William and Margaret (Babington) Prescott (bp. 1637/8), for Whom an Arrest Warrant Was Issued in 1659/60?" *The Mayflower Quarterly* (September 2008), 245-268.

Hill, George J., and Sarah Hill. "Lead Poisoning due to Hai Ge Fen." Letter to the Editor of the *Journal of the American Medical Association*, 1994.

Hill, Mrs. Louis, *The Holy Bible containing the Old and New Testaments ...,* New York: American Bible Society, 1858. Transcribed in *Mid-West Tennessee Genealogical Society. Family Findings* 3 (No. 1, January 1971).

Jackson, Robert F., "Texas Compatriot Bush Elected U.S. President," *SAR Magazine,* 95 (No. 3, Winter), 2001. This article shows the lineage of Presidents George H. W. Bush and George W. Bush from their Revolutionary War ancestor, Col. Samuel Herrick of the Vermont Militia.

Jackson, Mary S. and Edward F. Jackson *Death Notices from Steuben County, New York Newspapers: 1797-1884.* Bowie, Md.: Heritage Books, 1998.

Jacobus, Donald Lines. "The Josiah Adkins Family of Connecticut," *TAG* 33 (1957), 242-5.

_____. "Edgerton Family of Simsbury," *TAG* 41 (1965): 227-30.

McCracken, George E. "Dr. Philip Reade and His Earlier Descendants" *NEHGR* 112 (April 1958): 119-132. [hereafter, McCracken, "Dr. Philip Reade"]

_____. "John Griffin of Windsor and Simsbury, Connecticut" *The American Genealogist* [*TAG*] 38 (1962): 100-111.

_____. *TAG* 56 (1980):130.

Parsons, Gerald James. "The Early Parsons Families of the Connecticut River Valley," *NEHGR* 148 (1994): 354 (re constable Eleazer Hill of Hartford Co., Conn.,1692/3).

Parsons, Samuel H. "Record of Marriages and Births, in Windsor, Ct." *NEHGR* 5 (April 1851): 225-8ff (continued from p. 66 of this volume). [hereafter, Parsons, "Windsor"]

Priest, Alice Lucinda. "The Brothers Jonathan and Nathan Gillett and Some of Their Descendants" *New England Historical Genealogical Register,* October 1946: 272-277. [hereafter, Priest, "Gillett]

Smith, Hon. Ralph D. and Dr. Bernard C. Steiner. "Luke Hill of Windsor, Conn., and John Hill of Guilford, Conn., and Their Descendants." *NEHGR* 57 (Jan. 1903): 87-93. Also appears separately as Ralph D. Smith (aka Smyth), *Luke and John Hill of Connecticut* (1903), reprinted by Higginson Books. For corrections, see H. A. Thomas, *NEHGR* 107 (Jan. 1953): 71). [hereafter, Smith and Steiner, "Luke Hill"]

_____. "The Descendants of John Parmelee." In *Genealogies of Connecticut Families*. CD#179. Vol. 3, 24-30. [hereafter, Smith and Steiner, "Parmelee"]. "John Parmelee,"
Thomas, H. A. "Notes: Luke Hill of Windsor, Conn., and John Hill of Guilford, Conn., and Their Descendants: Additions and Corrections" *NEHGR* 107 (Jan. 1953): 71. "These additions and corrections are to the article [by Smith and Steiner] which appeared in *The Register*, vol. 57, p. 87 et seq., and are taken from the notes of Donald Lines Jacobus. "Luke[1] Hill married 6 May 1651 Mary Hout (Windsor Records, *The Register* 5:228). Her name is shown as Hoyt in Stile's "History of Windsor", 2:292, and in Savage's "Genealogical Dictionary," 2:418. The spelling Hart, appearing in *The Register*, 57:87, may be a mis-reading of the original text."

Ullmann, Helen Schatvet. "Hartford District Probate Records from 1750, As Abstracted by Lucius Barnes Barbour from Volume 19 (1761-1764)," *The Connecticut Nutmegger,* 2006, March: 581ff.

Wolcott, Samuel. "List of Freemen of Windsor, Ct." *NEHGR* 5 (April 1851), 246-7.

Newsletters and Newspaper Articles

[Barbour, Lucius] "Col. Barbour Dies Aged 56 in Fenwick." *Hartford Courant* (30 Jul 1934), 1.

Norfolk Gazette and Publick Ledger (29 December 1806).

Spear, Burton W. (ed.), *Mary and John Clearinghouse Newsletter.* 5602 - 305th St., Toledo, OH 43611 (multiple dates in 20th century). Volumes 1, 2, 3, 5, 13, 14, 18, 24, and 25.

Wonewoc Reporter [Wisc.] (July 17, 1919) [quoted by Hill, "Twelve Generations"]

Maps, Documents, and Unpublished Manuscripts

[Barbour] RG 074:036, Lucius B. Barbour Genealogical Collection Inventory. Finding aid prepared by Connecticut State Library staff. Includes biography of Lucius Barnes Barbour. Copyright © 2009 by the Connecticut State Library.

FamilyTreeDNA Certificate – Y-DNA … Dr. George J. Hill, 2010; and "Certificate of Y-chromosome DNA testing of George James Hill," 2 December 2005;

Francis, Helen Ingraham. "Herrick Family: Some of the Herrick Genealogy" (Reserve, N.M., 16 February 1961). This 22 page manuscript was provided to George J. Hill, M.D., by Alton Herrick of Lindley, N.Y., on 10 March 2000.

Hernstadt, Gertrude Elizabeth (Gillett). Application for Membership to the National Society of the Daughters of the American Revolution, Washington, D.C., 30 June 1969. National Number 543167, by right of lineal descent from John Gillett, born in Litchfield, Connecticut, 9 February 1733/4; died, probably in N.Y. or Vt., after October 1799.

Hill, Stockwell, and Riley gravestones in Graceland Cemetery, Rowan, Iowa, photographed and transcribed by George James Hill, M.D., 1973-2007. Inscriptions of the Hill and Stockwell obelisks and stones for 20 individuals.

Hill, Isaac [Sr.] New Haven Probate Files: File 4963. Estate of Isaac Hill of Wallingford. Bond of Esther Hill, Executrix (signed by mark, 29 Jan 1741/2), copy from Connecticut Historical Society to Jeanine Humbert Johnson, 17 July 1992, forwarded to George J. Hill.

Hill, Isaac [Jr.]. Deposition for pension application as a Revolutionary War Soldier (application approved) at Woodbury District Probate Court, State of Connecticut, 13 August 1832.

Hill, William Edwin. *Brief Account of the Hill Reunion Held at Dennison Park [Corning, N.Y.], August 27, 1920.* Genesee, N.Y.: William Edwin Hill, 1920. 6 pp., mimeographed typescript. Photocopy provided on 10 April 2002 to George J. Hill by Mrs. Kenneth (Natalie) Rose, 610 Martz Road, Sykesville, MD 21784. An 11 page annotated transcription of the 6 pp. typescript was prepared by George J. Hill on 14 April 2002.

Pitman, Leon S. "Some Descendants of Nathan Gillett of Windsor and Simsbury, Connecticut," Modesto, California, [1999] 2002, 5 pp., with references. Downloaded from Ancestry.com, where it appeared in a search for Gillett, Nathan, on 23 August 2009. [hereafter, Pitman, "Nathan Gillett"]

Riley, Josiah. Last Will and Testament (21 June 1850); and depositions regarding his death (22 June 1850) and the disposition of his estate (23 August 1850) in Chenango Co., N.Y. Copies enclosed with letter from D.S. Ptak to George J. Hill, 2 December 1996.

Stockwell, Foster Paul. "Genealogy of the Stockwell Family and Other Related Families." Typed MS, ca. 1970, with computer-printed addendum, 10 December 1988.

Toelke, Ronald. *Connecticut* [Map]. 1975. Shows founding of Windsor 1633, Wethersfield 1634, Hartford 1635, Saybrook 1635, New Haven 1638, Milford 1639, Guilford 1639, Stratford 1639, Fairfield 1639, Farmington 1640, Greenwich 1640, Stamford 1641, Branford 1644, Simsbury 1664.

Weeks, F. E. *Pioneer History of Clarksfield* (MS, Huron Co, OH, 1938). [quoted by Thom Carlson]
Internet Sources

Ancestry.com.: Includes links to U.S. Federal Census and original records such as passport applications, passenger ship manifests, biographies, photographs, cemetery records. Also includes citations from FamilySearch.org, at www.familysearch.org," 6 June 2000, and thereafter, Family Search Internet Genealogy Service, Church of Jesus Christ of Latter-Day Saints, copyright 1999, Intellectual Reserve, Inc.; citations from OneWorldTree (a computerized synthesis of information submitted in family trees [hereafter OWT]; and specific family trees, viz.:

"Andre Family Tree," owned by KWAndre51, for "Hill, Sylvester Bruce," accessed 22 January 2010 [hereafter, Ancestry.com, "Andre"]

"Baldwin Family Tree," accessed 15 June 2010 [Ancestry.com, "Baldwin"]

"Brooks, Truchon, Wimer, Barlow, Dumais Families," owned by dotruchon1957, accessed 4/15/2010 [hereafter, Ancestry.com, "Brooks"]

"Frisbie/Criger Family Tree," owned by ercriger, accessed 8/23/2010 [hereafter, Ancestry.com, "Frisbie/Criger"]

"Golding Family Tree," owned by katesgolding [Ancestry.com, "Golding"]

"Hill Family Tree," owned by marknorris59, accessed 1/10/2011ff [hereafter, Ancestry.com, "Hill" by Norris]

"Pratt and Webster Family Tree," owned by PriscillaR, accessed 11/4/2010 [hereafter, Ancestry.com, "Pratt"]

"PrestonSmith," accessed 4/20/2010, owned by Wendy Proudfoot [hereafter, Ancestry.com, "PrestonSmith"]

"Roe_Elisha & Electa Family Tree" [hereafter, Ancesty.com, "Roe"]

"Tompkins Family Tree," owned by FranklinTompkins18, accessed 8/23/2010 [hereafter, Ancestry.com, "Tompkins]

.   "Winters Family," owned by mythtown1958, accessed 4/15/2010 [hereafter, Ancestry.com, "Winters"]

"Wiswedel Family Tree," owned by gwiswedel, accessed 8/23/2010 [hereafter, Ancestry.com "Wiswedel"]

Ancestry.com. "OneWorldTree takes family trees submitted by Ancestry members and "stitches" them together with family trees and historical records from other sources. OneWorldTree identifies probable name."

[Barber] Morris, Andrew J. "Family History of Thomas Barber (ca 1614-1662)" in "Connecticut Genealogy." < http://connecticut-genealogy.blogspot.com/2010/07/family-history-of-thomas-barber-ca-1614.html>, accessed 8/8/2010. [hereafter, Barber FH]

Barbour, Lucius Barnes. *Connecticut Town Birth Records, pre-1870* (from various sources) [hereafter all sources combined, as *Barbour Collection*]. Includes:
"Wallingford, New Haven Co., Ct., Vital Records from Barbour, 1670-1850," transcribed by Coralynn Brown, accessed on Ancestry.com, 8/21/2009. Other pages from Connecticut Historical Society to Jeanine Johnson, 17 July 1992, forwarded to George J. Hill.
"Goshen, Litchfield Co. Ct., Vital Records from Barbour, 1739-1854, transcribed by Coralynn Brown, from New Horizons Genealogical Services [NHGS], http://www.newhorizonsgenealogicalservices.com/barbour-collection.htm, accessed 6/26/2010ff.
"Farmington Vital Records 1645-1850," From Ancestry.com [database on-line]. Original data: White, Lorraine Cook, ed., *The Barbour Collection of Connecticut Town Vital Records*. Vol. 1-55.

Baltimore, Md.: Genealogical Publishing Co., 1994-2002.

"Branford Vital Records," accessed on Ancestry.com, 8/19/2010.

Also, copies of selected pages in the following v.r. from Connecticut Historical Society   to Jeanine Johnson, 17 July 1992 (copy to George J. Hill):

"Stratford Vital Records," Vol. LR5, p. 72; "Wallingford Vital Records"; "Guilford Vital Records"; and "Stratford Vital Records"

Brodnax, Christine. "Ancestors of Thomas Byron Brodnax" (with many references). http://www.familyorigins.com/users/b/r/o/Christine-E-Brodnax-1/FAMO1-0001/d949.htm (accessed 9/13/2010). Re: Pierre LaDou and Martha Anneraud, whose fifth child, Jeanne Ladue, was the first wife of John Hill Jr. and mother of John III, Ebenezer, Martha, and Mary. By Christine Brodnax / 9839 Walnut St. T-109 / Dallas, TX 75243. [hereafter, Brodnax]

Early Connecticut Probate Records (4 September 1697) and 1723-1729. Accessed via New England Historic Genealogical Society (NEHGS) @ AmericanAncestors.org., and Ancestry.com

Frisbie-Frisbee Family Association of America, Inc (FFFAA) www.fffaa.org/

Hartford County, Conn. Index to Hartford County, Connecticut, County Court Minutes, Volumes 3 and 4, 1663-1687, 1697. (Online database: AmericanAncestors.org., New England Historic Genealogical Society, 2007).

Hill, James D. "The Hill Family, From 1651 to 2000: Twelve Generations in America. Edition 5.0, 2000," Accessed 1/31/2010, 151 pp. on monitor, 51 pp. printed with 10-point. http://files.usgwarchives.net/ct/statewide/history/books/hill51.txt. [hereafter, Hill, "Twelve Generations"]

Hill Family of Connecticut Vital Records to 1800 accessed 8/20/2010ff at http://freepages.genealogy.rootsweb.ancestry.com/

International Genealogical Index (The Church of Jesus Christ of Latter-day Saints) [IGI].

Lu, Helen M., and Gwen B. Neumann, *Revolutionary War Period: Bible, Family & Marriage Records Gleaned from Pension Applications*, 1998. v. 19 [quoted by Carlson]

"[LDS] www.familysearch.org," 6 June 2000, and thereafter, Family Search Internet Genealogy Service, Church of Jesus Christ of Latter-Day Saints; copyright 1999, Intellectual Reserve, Inc. (See Ancestry.com)

Money, current value. http://www.measuringworth.com/glossary/

Painter, George. "The Sensibilities of Our Forefathers: The History of Sodomy Laws in the United States (1991-2001)," a copyrighted web page accessed 7/22/2010.

Phelps, Brian. "Phelps Family History in America: Family of Joseph and Hannah (Newton) Phelps of Simsbury, Conn. (Sources are given at the website: http://www.phelpsfamilyhistory.com/ (2008ff; last updated and accessed 10 August 2010). [hereafter, Phelps "Family History]

"Simsbury Connecticut, Vital Records, 1665-1886," from New England Ancestors.org. / NEHGS (now AmericanAncestors.org).

The Public Records of the Colony of Connecticut, Vol. 4. Arthur Henbury's estate, accessed 4/15/2010

from Ancestry.com.

Wikipedia. For "Ira Allen," "Roger Enos," "Enosburg," and Irasburg," and Benedict Arnold" (accessed 12 May 2010).

Correspondence and e-Correspondence

Carlson, Thom, Ph.D. "Some Descendants of Isaac Hill Sr. & Eunice Mallory." Compiled by Thom Carlson, and sent to George J. Hill, M.D., 3 December 2008. Address: 2667 61st St. Lane, Vinton, IA 52349. tywaz@intergate.com. (E-mails to GJH 2 Feb 2004 and 3 December 2008). Includes "Descendants of Hannah Eliza Hill & Joseph C. Skinner" [hereafter, Carlson, "Hill"]

Connecticut Historical Society, letter of Allen R. Yale to Mrs. Jeanine Humbert Johnson, 17 July 1992, re Isaac Hill (b. c. 1740); 10 pp., including 3 pp. of copies of Connecticut vital records of Hill Family, and part of a letter of Donald Lines Jacobus to Mrs. H. A. Thomas (1952) regarding Isaac Hill and his ancestors. [hereafter Yale and Jacobus, "Isaac Hill"]

Harson, Adella Helen [228] (Lindsay). Recollections and handwritten notes [untitled] to George J. Hill, 1994-96. [hereafter, Harson] 8 May 1994 (AL); 30 July 1994 (AL, 4 pages); 20 February 1996 (ALS and markup of 5 generation Descendant Chart of James and Adella (Hill) Lindsay, and markup of draft of Lindsay family history); 13 March 1996 (additional markup of Lindsay Family Register Report); 15 March 1996 (AN).

Hill, Avis (Boyington) [Mrs. Dale E.], letters to George James Hill, M.D.," 1970ff. [hereafter, Avis Hill] Includes French and Indian War and Revolutionary War service records of Isaac Hill [Jr.], and copies of the District of Woodbury, New Haven County, Connecticut, documents of 13 August 1832 in which Isaac Hill applied for and was granted a pension, with copy of cover letter of 10 April 1924 from the Acting Commissioner of military records to Camp Stanley, M.D., Washington, D.C.

Also, application by Doris Jean Hill for membership in the Daughters of the American Revolution shows Isaac Hill's death on 3/31/1833 at Southbury, CT. Miss Hill was the great-great-great granddaughter of Isaac Hill. The application was filed 16 Sep 1966 and was approved 1 Feb 1967. Her membership number is 521680.

Hill, Donald. "Leroy Hill Family." Letters to George James Hill, 23 December 2008 and 3 January 2009.

Hill, Paul F., 35 Pershing St., Corning, NY 14830-2032 (609) 936-6069; letters and enclosures to George J. Hill, April 1996 ff. [hereafter, Paul Hill].

Enclosures include Hill Family History Worksheet from Isaac Hill (b. ca 1740) to Dean Hill, Iva (Hill) Jenkins and Constance (Hill) Powell, the three children of John P. and Elizabeth (Tobey) Hill; obituary for John P. Hill (9/26/1891-3/9/1996); and letter from Dean Hill. Letter of 25 April 2002 updated the information about descendants of Ephraim Hill in Caton/Corning area, and included his ancestral charts going back to Abraham Hill (b. c. ?1747 "Lived in Bullet Hole?" d 5-11-1817 Carmel, N.Y.) and his wife Hannah Ferris (b. c 1748; d. 6-5-1818, Carmel, N.Y.). Also, typed genealogy of Abraham Hill's descendants from Dennis O'Connell (*q.v.*).

Hurtuk, Marjorie K. (compiler). Connecticut Historical Society to George J. Hill, M.D., 8 November 1999 and 24 January 2000, re: Hendrix and Riley families.

Johnson, Jeanine K. Humbert. Personal communications with George J. Hill, 1994-2010.

Norris, Mark. Telephone and e-mail communications with George J. Hill, 8 January 2011ff, from mark-norris@sbcglobal.net. He is marknorris59, author/owner of "The Hill Family Tree" on Ancestry.com.

O'Connell, Dennis. "Directory of Ancestors and Descendants of Abraham Hill & Hannah Ferris" 18 pp., some printed double sided, n.d. [2004]. Copy from Paul F. Hill, Corning, N.Y., to George J. Hill (*q.v.*)

Olson, Mabel LaVonne (Anderson). Information from LaVonne (Anderson) Olson by telephone, and in a Biographical Information Form prepared for her late sister, Ula (Anderson) Schroader, 4 Mar 1996. [hereafter, Olson]

Ptak, Diane Snyder, C.A.L.S., 12 Tice Road, Albany, NY 12203-9721 (518) 456-3370. Research conducted on Hill families in New York state and Connecticut, 1994 ff., for George J. Hill, M.D. (Correspondence in his files). [hereafter, Ptak]

Rose, Mrs. Ken (Natalie), E-mail to George J. E-mail from Mrs. Ken (Natalie) Rose to George J. Hill, 2002 ff., from kenrose@hotmail.com. [hereafter, Rose]

Schroader, Leslie. Correspondence with George James Hill, M.D., including documents related to Riley, Olson, and Hill families. [hereafter, Schroader]

Stanley, Richard R. E-mail to George J. Hill from Richard R. Stanley, 29 January 2005. Re: His line of descent from Luke Hill Jr.'s son Ebenezer, and Ebenezer Jr.'s son Ambrose. rrstanley@bankofny.com and leyric@comcast.net [hereafter, Stanley, "Hill"]

Index

Franklin Metcalf (1823 -)	1425
Hannah (1813 -)	spouse of 849
Hannah (1742 - 1825)	spouse of 171
Hannah Ann (1825 -)	1485
Henry A.	spouse of 999
James (1819 -)	1423
James (1783 - 1843)	701
James (1796 -)	1465
John (1752 - 1778)	270
John (1793 -)	1401
John (1778 - 1857)	699
John (1794 -)	1458
Joseph (1766 -)	680
Joshua (1780 - 1863)	684
Joshua (1815 -)	1421
Julia (1802 -)	1468
Laura (1807 -)	1467
Ledyard S. (1807 -)	1475
Lemuel	spouse of 1689
Lovenia Elizabeth (1813 -)	1479
Lucian Bonaparte (1816 -)	1481
Lucinda (1799 -)	1398
Lucy (1736 - 1801)	263
Lucy (1771 - 1845)	682
Lucy Louisa (1801 -)	1399
Lucy Lovina (1781 -)	1397
Lucy Matson (1817 -)	1422
Lydia (1790 -)	1400
Lydia (- 1801)	spouse of 686
Lydia Ann (1830 -)	1427
Marcia (1808 -)	1476
Mary (1798 -)	1460
Mary (1822 -)	1484
Mary G. (1814 - 1887)	spouse of 1162
Michael	spouse of 4044
Nancy (1795 -)	1402
Oliver (1750 - 1804)	269
Olivia Ann (1811 -)	1483
Orpah Cassett (1793 - 1867)	spouse of 1537
Parmelia (1804 -)	1463
Parmenio (1776 - 1832)	698
Parmenio (aka Permena, Pernene) (1747 - 1809)	268
Parmenio N. (1810 -)	1477
Richard	spouse of 2012
Richard Saxton (1734 - 1726)	262
Richard Saxton (1768 - 1798)	681
Richard Saxton (1808 -)	1418
Salina (1796 -)	1459
Sally (?) (- 1833)	spouse of 697
Sally E. (1806 -)	1470
Samuel (1689 -)	39
Samuel (~1664 - >1701)	spouse of 8
Sarah (1802 -)	1466
Sarah	spouse of 471

Sarah Ann (1801 -)	1462
Son (1773 -)	683
Susannah (?)	spouse of 269
Thanks (1742 - 1816)	266
Thanks	spouse of 164
Truman (1785 - 1832)	702
Vienna Margaret (1818 -)	1482
William (1800 -)	1461
Zilpha (1815 -)	1473

ADDAMS

Patricia Kay	spouse of 3929

ADKINS

Abigail (1784 -)	spouse of 559

ALBRECHTSON

Alice May (1923 -)	spouse of 3901

ALCOTT

Lydia Abi (1851 - 1922)	2813
Robert Ludlow (1828 -)	spouse of 1997
Rosannah (1769 - 1830)	spouse of 222

ALFORD

Isabell (1733 -)	spouse of 147

ALLEN

Amy (1782 - 1856)	934
Caleb (1759 - 1804)	392
Charles Parsons (1844 - 1877)	2252
Ida (1885 - 1975)	spouse of 3679
Gen. Ira [E.8] {51} (1751 - 1814)	spouse of 717
Col. Ira Hayden (1790 - 1866)	1526
Ira Hayden (1842 - 1863)	2251
Lizzie Pulsifer (1877 - 1899)	3124
Lucy	spouse of 981
Maria Juliette (1794 - 1811)	1528
Mary F. (1789 -)	1525
Mary Frances (1854 - 1873)	2255
Mary Parsons (1848 - 1849)	2253
Nellie Hill (1886 -)	spouse of 3484
Parmelee [aka Parmlee, Parmalee] (1746 - 1806)	391
Prudence (1772 - 1837)	933
Sarah Maria (1850 -)	2254
Timothy (1715 - 1806)	spouse of 132
Zimri Enos (1792 - 1813)	1527

ALLEY

Blanche Mae (1886 - >1920)	spouse of 2732

ALLISON

Etta (1863 - 1934)	spouse of 2385

ALVORD

Jerusha (1743 - 1793)	spouse of 186

AMON

John Alfred	spouse of 4081
Living Daughter of John and Enid (Shepperd)	4331
Living Daughter of John and Enid (Shepperd)	4332
Living Daughter of John and Enid (Shepperd)	4333
Living Daughter of John and Enid (Shepperd)	4334
Living Daughter of John and Enid (Shepperd)	4335

Living Daughter of John and Enid (Shepperd)   4337
Living Son of John and Enid (Shepperd)   4329
Living Son of John and Enid (Shepperd)   4330
Living Son of John and Enid (Shepperd)   4336
ANDERS
  ?   spouse of 2806
ANDERSON
  ———   spouse of 4297
  Douglas Duane   spouse of 3918
  Elizabeth Campbell (1910 -)   spouse of 3544
  Franklin Gilbert (1856 - 1938)   spouse of 2389
  Haven Leslie (1937 - 1967)   4063
  Haven Riley (1905 - 1964)   3855
  James Adelbert "Delbert" (1900 - ~1996)   3854
  James Peter (1864 -)   spouse of 3591
  Jerry Jack III (1971 -)   spouse of 4157
  John   spouse of 543
  Lillian Helen (1933 -)   4062
  Mabel LaVonne "LaVonne" (1907 - 1997)   3856
  Ula Myrtle (1897 - 1981)   3853
ANDRE
  Susan Alice (1840 - 1930)   spouse of 1815
ANDRESEN
  Kristine (1948 -)   spouse of 3974
ANDREWS
  Betsey   spouse of 828
  Hezekiah   spouse of 660
Andros
  Georgia L.   spouse of 2786
ANGUS
  Eleanor (1872 - 1896)   spouse of 1753
ANSMUS
  Pauline   spouse of 2313
APPLEBEE APPLEBY
  Clarissa (1815 -)   spouse of 880
ARCH
  ?   spouse of 3421
ARCHER
  Jemima (1772 - 1855)   spouse of 331
  Kate C. "Clara" (1849 - 1916)   spouse of 2927
ARMSTRONG
  Laura   spouse of 2022
  Mildred (1909 -)   spouse of 3748
ARSDALE
  Archibald J. [195] (VAN) (1908 -)   3495
  Dorothy [194] (VAN)   3494
  George (VAN)   spouse of 1894
  Jacob A. [117] (VAN) (1873 -)   2718
  Veronica C. [193] (VAN) (1891 -)   3493
AUILER
  Beverly (1928 -)   spouse of 3765
AULT
  Mary Elizabeth (1855 - 1882)   spouse of 3127
AUSTIN

Amy Ruth (1914 - 1974)   spouse of 3766
Clarice   3439
Helen   3438
Herbert C. (- <1920)   spouse of 2671
Jillynn Sue (1963 -)   spouse of 4127
Louisa (~1837 -)   spouse of 1604

AVERY
Nancy Mariah (1830 - 1914)   spouse of 2148

AXTEL
George   spouse of 1941
George (~1855 -)   2761
Mary Elizabeth   2760

BABCOCK
Anna (1788 -)   1128
Benjamin (1697 - 1751)   spouse of 50
Benjamin (1757 -)   182
Benjamin (1755 - 1796)   492
Benjamin Herman (1923 -)   spouse of 4058
Daniel (1756 - 1805)   493
Ebenezer (1730 -)   177
Ebenezer (1767 - 1808)   499
Elias (1778 -)   1125
Elisabeth (1773 - 1789)   501
Elizabeth   spouse of 644
Esther (1776 - 1827)   503
Hannah (1736 -)   180
Hannah (1763 - 1852)   496
James Wesley (1972 -)   4283
Jamie Lee (1995 -)   4416
Joseph (1758 - 1759)   494
Joseph (1786 -)   1127
Lavina (1780 -)   1126
Lydia (1774 - 1803)   502
Mabel Elizabeth (1851 - 1885)   spouse of 1616
Mary (1737 -)   181
Mary (1767 - 1768)   498
Nathaniel (1765 - 1839)   497
Olive (1779 - 1793)   504
Redolphus (1761 - 1762)   495
Saloma (1775 -)   1124
Sarah (1734 -)   179
Shelley Marie (1993 -)   4415
Susannah (1798 -)   1129
Tabitha (1770 - 1786)   500
William (1732 -)   178

BACON
Joseph (1752 - 1833)   spouse of 431
Lydia (- 0187)   spouse of 1190
Perhaps sons and daughters of Phineas and Philura (Norton)   2008
Phineas (Phinehas) (1783 -)   971

BAILEY
Lillian Ada (1848 - 1933)   spouse of 2239

BAIRD
Edward Allen   spouse of 4040

Mathew (1981 -)   4265

BAKER

Brandon Ray   4103
Hannah (1792 - 1872)   spouse of 699
Jane (1830 -)   spouse of 2477
Obie Ray   spouse of 3918
Rebecca (1780 -)   spouse of 797
Sarah   spouse of 1881

BALDWIN

Amos (1779 - 1865)   1561
Asa (1795 -)   1566
Barbara (1769 - 1770)   744
Caleb (1723 - 1823)   spouse of 279
Caleb (1776 - 1836)   746
Caleb (1791 - 1849)   1565
Daniel (1767 - 1862)   743
Eleazer (1764 - 1835)   741
Elizabeth (1798 - 1877)   1567
Elizabeth (1722 -)   spouse of 94
Esther (1760 - 1815)   spouse of 747
Esther (1810 -)   1570
Ezra (1771 - 1772)   745
George (1802 - 1830)   1568
George C.   spouse of 2028
Hannah (1746 - 1829)   spouse of 216
Jemima (1780 - 1781)   748
Jerusha (1765 - 1775)   742
Lois (1763 - 1804)   740
Mary (1783 - 1877)   1562
Philemon (1778 - 1857)   747
Philemon H. (1785 - 1834)   1563
Rune R. (1789 - 1834)   1564
Salley Ann (1806 -)   1569

BALES

Joe   spouse of 3951

BALLARD

Mertle   spouse of 2775

BALLOU

Amariah (1784 -)   1130
David (1786 -)   1131
Elias (1752 - 1834)   spouse of 505
Mary (1791 -)   1132

BALLUFF

Dennis Michael (1939 -)   3844
Franklyn Baird (1914 -)   spouse of 3551
Laura Rosalie (1964 -)   4052
Tammara Margaret (1970 -)   4053

BANFIELD

Wendy Jo (1956 -)   spouse of 4028

BANGS

Ambrose Augustus (1831 - 1920)   spouse of 2270
Elva (1900 -)   3405
Elva Louise (1863 - 1907)   3136
Fred W. (1866 -)   3137

Hattie A. (1862 - 1863)	3135
BANNING	
Abigail	spouse of 655
BANTA	
?	spouse of 1986
BANTON	
?	spouse of 2808
BARBER	
Abel (1765 - 1817)	439
Abel Lester (1803 -)	1006
Abi (1791 - 1815)	993
Abi Orville (1831 -)	2833
Abiah "Abi" (1784 - 1867)	977
Abigail (?) (1787 -)	spouse of 695
Abner (1758 - 1815)	spouse of 531
Adelaide Julia	2900
Adelia (1852 -)	2898
Alison Hayden (1868 -)	2904
Alson (1792 - 1880)	988
Anna (1789 - 1848)	1164
Asa (1785 - 1813)	1163
Augustine Hayden (1809 -)	2076
Austin (1792 -)	981
Benjamin (1759 - 1836)	437
Benjamin (1845 -)	2056
Benjamin (1794 -)	1004
Beriah	1487
Calvin S. (1843 -)	2838
Catherine Hayden (1863 -)	2903
Celestia S. (1833 -)	2889
Charles B. (1837 -)	2891
Charles I. (1833 -)	2834
Clarence Howard	2901
Clarinda (1789 -)	992
Cora Lillian (1865 -)	2907
Cynthia (1779 - 1840)	975
Dorcas (1836 - 1897)	2909
Edda Jane (1847 -)	2897
Edwin Seward (1851 -)	2841
Elijah (1742 -)	spouse of 703
Elijah James	1488
Elisha (1742 - 1806)	spouse of 267
Elisha Westover (1767 -)	695
Eliza (1806 -)	999
Eliza J. (1849 -)	2847
Elizabeth (1775 - 1817)	973
Elizabeth (1817 - 1819)	2048
Elizabeth (1782 - 1828)	984
Elizabeth M. (1832 -)	2888
Ellen (1833 -)	2871
Ellen (1843 -)	2894
Elsie A. (1847 -)	2846
Emeline (1809 - 1813)	2060
Florence Isabella	2902

Gaylord (1824 - 1897)	2073
George M. (1849 -)	2840
Gilbert R. (1845 -)	2895
Hallett (1798 -)	1457
Hannah	2064
Harriet Amelia (1824 - 1878)	2077
Harriet Elizabeth	2065
Harriet P. (1841 -)	2893
Harvey (1814 -)	1002
Helen M. (1826 -)	2049
Henrietta (1837 -)	2084
Henry (1793 -)	994
Henry Watson (1831 -)	2053
Hiram (1803 - <1852)	spouse of 2037
Hiram Lysander (1835 -)	2872
Hosea (1788 - 1874)	986
Infant (1774 - 1774)	972
Infant (1868 -)	2908
James Edwin (1842 -)	2055
Jane (1828 -)	2050
Jeanette	2066
John (1719 - 1797)	spouse of 158
John (1749 - 1825)	433
John (1826 - 1894)	2074
John (1858 -)	2899
John Austin (1830 -)	2052
Jonathan (1763 - 1817)	438
Jonathan Sherman (1812 - 1847)	1001
Josiah (1807 -)	2059
Julia (1832 -)	2051
Julia A. (1839 -)	2892
Laura (1794 -)	2009
Lemuel (1830 - 1892)	2075
Linda (1799 - 1879)	996
Lorenzo Dow (1817 - 1887)	2063
Lucius (1842 -)	2843
Lucy Amelia (1858 -)	2906
Luke (1789 -)	980
Luman (1766 -)	1486
Luther Humphrey	2067
Lydia (1747 - 1783)	432
Martha Jane	2068
Mary (1778 - 1804)	982
Mary	2069
Mary J. (1834 - 1834)	2054
Milo R. (1803 -)	2011
Milo R. (1843 -)	2837
Myron C. (1845 -)	2845
Myron F. (1837 -)	2836
Myron Finch (1811 - 1900)	2013
Nahum (~1761 -)	spouse of 415
Nancy (1808 -)	1000
Nancy Case (1809 -)	2012
Nelson L. (1819 - 1885)	2072

Olive	1489
Percy (1777 -)	spouse of 558
Phebe Jane (1835 -)	2890
Phebe Maria	2070
Phoebe (1785 - 1838)	985
Phoebe (1811 - 1845)	2061
Pliny W. (1849 -)	2896
Pluma (1796 - 1815)	995
Prentice Satitha (1770 -)	spouse of 664
Reuben (1755 -)	435
Reuben (1814 -)	2062
Rhoda (1757 - 1761)	436
Rhoda (1777 -)	974
Roena (1802 -)	1005
Roswell (1770 - 1830)	spouse of 973
Ruby	990
Sadosa (1781 - 1860)	983
Saphronia (1835 -)	2835
Sarah (1754 - 1761)	434
Sarah (1794 - 1822)	989
Sarah Elvira	2071
Seth (1788 - 1866)	991
Solomon (1791 - 1820)	1003
Starling (1790 - 1801)	987
Susannah (1803 - 1888)	998
Sylvester (1845 -)	2839
Sylvia (1787 - 1861)	979
Sylvia (1887 -)	2010
Sylvia (1844 -)	2844
Sylvia (1785 - 1786)	978
Theron L. (1857 -)	2842
Thirza (1801 - 1887)	997
Willard Jonathan (1850 -)	2085
Zimri (1787 - 1865)	spouse of 984
BARBOUR	
?	2854
Alice Cordelia (1907 -)	3850
Carrie Ann (1864 - 1944)	2905
Clara Agnes (1854 -)	2859
Edward (1844 -)	2857
Edwin Case (1810 -)	2025
Eugene Thomas (1857 -)	2861
Eveline G. (1807 -)	2024
Fanny Maria (1815 -)	2027
Fidelia Gates (1817 - 1900)	2028
George (1836 -)	2853
Goodrich Hollister (1824 - 1901)	2032
Grovie (1844 -)	2856
Harriet Burr (1879 -)	3570
Harriet Louise (1843 - 1848)	2848
Hattie	2864
Hattie Day (1860 -)	2851
Hattie N. (1844 -)	2855
Herschell (1819 - 1819)	2029

John (1782 - 1865)	976	
John James (1861 -)	2863	
John Newton (1828 - 1874)	2033	
Juliet Louise (1834 -)	2035	
Lucia Ella (1855 -)	2860	
Deacon Lucius (1805 - 1873)	2023	
Col. Lucius Albert Adjutant General, Conn. (1846 - 1922)		2849
Brig. Gen. Lucius Barnes (1878 - 1934)	3569	
Lucius Hilliard (1903 -)	3849	
Mary (1834 -)	2852	
Mary Adelia (1851 - 1851)	2850	
Mary Alice (1852 -)	2858	
Selden (1813 - 1814)	2026	
Silvia (1822 - 1822)	2031	
Theodore Dwight (1820 - 1890)	2030	
Theresa	2865	
Theron Laselle (1832 - 1864)	2034	
William Everett (1859 -)	2862	

BARFIELD

Elizabeth (1852 -)	spouse of 2143

BARKER

Anna (1706 - 1762)	spouse of 60
Ava Gertrude (1882 - 1945)	2958
Catharine F.	spouse of 750
Donald Josiah (1887 - 1950)	2961
Donald Junior (1918 - 1992)	3613
Edna Belle (1883 - 1968)	2959
Elva May (1883 - 1912)	2960
Helen (1842 -)	2125
Kezia (~1743 - 1788)	spouse of 196
Martha Elizabeth (1895 - 1970)	2963
Mary (~1850 - 1860)	2128
Philo Coleman (1803 - 1886)	1162
Sarah (~1845 -)	2127
Solomon Damon (~1737 -)	spouse of 185
Theodore Theodorus (~1780 - ~1850)	516
Wilbur Jay (1843 - 1918)	2126
Zelma Pearl (1894 -)	2962

BARNARD

Irana (1747 -)	spouse of 260

BARNES

?	3892
Clarence H. (1885 - 1952)	3679
Dorothy (1916 - 1994)	3893
Elijah	624
Elizabeth	2170
Frank Monroe (1859 -)	3109
Goodrich (1887 -)	3573
Harriet Elizabeth (1849 - 1899)	spouse of 2849
Hattie Louise (1885 -)	3572
Horace	2171
Isaac	spouse of 997
Isabella (1786 - 1816)	spouse of 594
Jerusha	625

Joel	626
Joel (1773 -)	627
Joel	spouse of 1187
Lana	4172
Mary E. (~1840 -)	spouse of 1802
Monroe (1813 -)	2244
Richard	spouse of 3956
Richard Storrs (1854 - 1913)	spouse of 2851
Roderick Barbour (1882 -)	3571
Samuel (~1714 -)	spouse of 131
Sherman (1793 -)	1267
Wise (1720 -)	spouse of 236

BARNEY

Mrs. Ruth Ann "Anna" (1789 - 1846)	spouse of 964

BARNUM

James A. (1832 - 1863)	2295
Jasper	spouse of 1574
Orris (1805 - 1895)	spouse of 1579
Romeo (1847 - 1863)	2296
Sophia (1840 -)	2294

BARSTOW

Betsy (1772 - 1854)	spouse of 382

BARSTOWE

Samuel	spouse of 476

BARTLETT

Henry Hubbard (1813 - 1890)	spouse of 2039
Katherine Jane (1847 -)	2873
Mary Louise (1850 -)	2874

Bartrum

Annie Bell (1894 -)	3387
Arthur Henry (1882 -)	3385
James J. (1888 -)	3386
John F. (1853 - 1930)	spouse of 2549
Maudie Myrtle (1897 -)	3388

BATES

Phoebe (1792 - 1845)	spouse of 1213

BATTERSON

_____	spouse of 3957

BEABOUT

Elizabeth W. (- 1856)	spouse of 2462

BEACH

Charlotte (1787 -)	1342
Miles (1791 -)	1343
Samuel (1763 - 1815)	spouse of 653
Samuel (1784 -)	1341

BEACH aka BEECH

Lucia "Lucy" (1746 -)	spouse of 287

BEACH BEECH

Hannah (1745 - 1826)	spouse of 112

BEAL

Agnes Arlene (1927 -)	spouse of 3778

BEAUCLERK or BEANDUK

Mary Frances (1873 - 1931)	3126
Sydney W. (or Thomas Wentworth) (1847 - 1938)	spouse of 2255

BECCA

?	spouse of 4272

BECHTEL

Katherine (- >1920)	spouse of 1896

BELL

Amanda Luella (1873 - 1931)	3567
Isaac (1764 - 1840)	spouse of 345
Mark Cook (1847 - 1917)	spouse of 2813

BELT

_____	spouse of 3687

BENEDICT

? [Infant] (1834 -)	1765
Abby E. (1846 -)	1776
Adna Squires (1841 -)	1762
Albert Crumiel (1844 -)	1767
Albert D. (1854 -)	1778
Amelia Jane (1857 -)	1737
Ann Elizabeth (1851 -)	1735
Armenia Adelia (1826 -)	1756
Carlos N. (1835 -)	1771
Charles (1840 -)	1706
Charles (1850 - 1851)	1717
Charles Rood (1837 -)	1760
Clarissa (1813 - 1888)	839
Cornelius Nichols (1839 -)	1761
Cromwell (1805 -)	849
Daniel (1807 -)	850
David (1773 - 1807)	357
David (1807 - 1849)	838
David (1835 -)	1709
Dawson Alexander (1848 - 1941)	1716
Dawson Alexander (1882 -)	2570
Eleanor (1836 - 1912)	spouse of 844
Eleanor (1836 - 1912)	1701
Eleanor (1835 -)	1704
Eleanor L. (1856 -)	1741
Elizabeth (1841 -)	1712
Ellen Jane (1880 -)	2569
Ellen P. (1844 -)	1775
Emily Sarah (1869 -)	1740
Eunice (1817 -)	841
Ezra (1780 - 1854)	360
Ezra	2594
Ezra Denison (1830 -)	1758
Faber (1845 -)	1779
Francis Morgan (1847 -)	1780
Frederick (1839 -)	1773
George Frederick (1862 -)	1738
Gertrude E. (1857 - 1917)	spouse of 2435
Hannah (1791 - 1812)	363
Hannah (1823 -)	853
Hannah Amelia (1846 -)	1768
Harriet Maud (1886 -)	2572
Harriet Sophia	1733

Ida Florence (1878 -)	2568
Jane "Jenny" (1848 -)	1708
Jennie	spouse of 1898
Jenny (1839 -)	1702
Jerucia (1839 -)	1711
John (1800 - 1859)	836
John Carroll (1860 -)	1743
John George (1883 -)	2571
John Rood (1833 -)	1759
Joseph (1828 - 1828)	845
Joseph Franklin (1876 - 1952)	1747
Julius S. (1831 -)	1769
Lila Beatrice (1888 -)	2573
Lucy (1772 -)	356
Lucy (1820 -)	842
Lucy (1809 -)	851
Lunette F. (1849 -)	1777
Lydia A. (1833 -)	1770
Margaret (1830 -)	846
Margaret Jane (1860 -)	1748
Martha (1843 -)	1764
Martha S. (1841 -)	1774
Martin Michael (1816 - 1914)	852
Mary (1785 - 1796)	361
Mary (1816 -)	840
Mary (1843 -)	1763
Mary Ann (1842 -)	1707
Mary Elizabeth (1847 -)	2566
Matilda (1837 -)	1710
Matilda Jane (1875 -)	2567
Miriam (1775 - 1834)	358
Moses (1824 -)	844
Moses (1824 -)	spouse of 1701
Rachel (1789 - 1870)	362
Sabrina Mable (1828 -)	1757
Samuel (1744 - 1820)	spouse of 123
Samuel (1778 - 1869)	359
Samuel (1805 - 1848)	837
Samuel (1822 - 1906)	843
Samuel A. (1858 -)	spouse of 1727
Samuel A. (1858 -)	1742
Samuel Ezra (1849 -)	1734
Samuel I. (1845 -)	1714
Samuel John (1846 -)	1715
Sarah (1834 -)	847
Sarah (1837 -)	1705
Sarah (1837 -)	1772
Sarah A. (1866 -)	1745
Sarah F. (1840 -)	1766
Solomon (1841 -)	1703
Solomon George (1868 -)	1746
Squires (1803 -)	848
Thomas	2595
Thomas Franklin (1862 -)	1749

Thomas Walter (1865 -)	1739
William Henry (1853 -)	1736
William James (1844 -)	1713
William James (1872 -)	2565
William Sidney (1864 -)	1750
William (Wilson) Alexander (1864 - 1865)	1744

BENNET

Eleanor	spouse of 819

BENNETT

Andrew Jackson	spouse of 2097
Belle	spouse of 3096
Maria (1831 -)	spouse of 2095

BENSON

Dorla Dean (1929 -)	spouse of 3773

BERDETTE

Jesse	spouse of 865

BERNIER

Olivette (1900 - 1985)	spouse of 3333

BEST

?	spouse of 3566

BETT

Doris Mabel (1908 - 1994)	3609
Elsie Gertrude (1907 - 1985)	3608
Ernest Albert (1877 - 1931)	spouse of 2958
Mary Rebecca (1913 - 1992)	3611
Thomas Barker (1911 - 1968)	3610

BIDDLE

Vera Ruth (- >1971)	spouse of 3406

BILYEU

Albert (1897 -)	3361
Andrew (1841 - 1903)	2473
Anna E. (1850 -)	2489
Caroline (1852 -)	2493
Charles Clarence (1900 -)	3345
Charles Elmer	3349
Charles Henry (1874 -)	3368
David Allen (1844 -)	2485
Elizabeth M. (1835 - 1827)	2465
Emily Caroline (1845 -)	2486
Emily E. (1849 -)	2494
Emma (1848 -)	2499
Finas (1843 - 1865)	2474
Finis (1825 - 1862)	1670
Francis (1855 -)	2495
Francis Roy (1890 -)	3370
Francis Simeon (1869 -)	3355
Frank (1857 -)	2505
Fred Ellsworth	3350
Garrett Page (1810 - 1850)	1665
George Harvey (1837 - 1897)	2471
Grace Comfort (1899 -)	3373
Hannah (1815 -)	spouse of 1664
Harrell H. (1895 -)	3372
Harry Earle (1886 -)	3340

Henrietta	3348
Irving (1838 -)	2491
Isaac Smith (1801 - 1856)	1663
Jesse C. (1898 -)	3344
Jesse Walker (1811 - 1860)	1666
Jesse Wheeler (1841 - 1913)	2479
Jessie Belle (1889 -)	3359
John (1834 - 1915)	2469
John (1844 -)	2498
John Birge (1801 - 1873)	1662
John F. (1837 - 1862)	2466
John W. (1827 -)	2477
John Wilson	3351
Joseph (1765 - 1845)	spouse of 803
Joseph (1804 - 1868)	1664
Joseph E. (1850 -)	2504
Joseph H. (1829 - 1877)	2468
Joseph Nelson	3352
Lemuel E.	3353
Leroy Vernon (1873 -)	3357
Lewis (1892 -)	3360
Lewis G. (1827 - 1893)	2462
Lewis Garret (1842 -)	2484
Lewis I. (1840 -)	2492
Malinda	3347
Malinda H. (?)	spouse of 1664
Martha (1839 -)	2497
Martha A. (1861 - 1940)	spouse of 2476
Martha A. (1839 -)	2502
Martha Emma (1849 - 1930)	2481
Martha Pearl (1892 -)	3371
Mary (1836 -)	2496
Mary (1839 -)	2501
Mary A. (1835 -)	2490
Mary Jane (1836 -)	2482
Mary Magdalene (1820 - 1853)	1669
Mary Myrtle (1870 -)	3337
Maud Ann (1885 -)	3369
Milo D.	3354
Nancy A. (1848 -)	2488
Nancy Birge (1829 - 1879)	2463
Nellie E. (1871 -)	3356
Olive Marie (1896 -)	3343
Peter F. (1839 - 1909)	2467
Polly Ann (1845 - 1915)	2475
Roy Sidney (1893 -)	3342
Sarah (1799 - 1850)	1661
Sarah (1859 -)	3338
Sarah (1849 -)	2500
Sarah Frances (1840 -)	2483
Sidney M. (1839 - 1915)	2472
Simeon Walker (1844 - 1908)	2480
Thomas Coke (1816 - 1878)	1668
Thomas H. (1849 - 1913)	2476

Thomas Newton (1846 -)	2487
Vera Bessie (1901 -)	3346
Wesley A. (1812 - 1867)	1667
Wesley Asbury (- 1899)	2470
William B. (1831 -)	2478
William Burge (1826 - 1851)	1671
William Burge (1851 -)	2506
William T. (1842 -)	2503
William Thomas (1831 - 1903)	2464
Willie Ray (1887 -)	3358
Winne Mae (1891 -)	3341

BIRD

Lydia M. (1821 - 1872)	spouse of 1589

BIRDSEYE

Unice (1827 -)	spouse of 1944

BIRGE

?	3749
?	3750
Abigail (1792 - 1851)	810
Alice (1855 - 1933)	1693
Allithea (1860 - 1918)	3374
Alpheus (1830 -)	1686
Anna (1853 - 1893)	2524
Anna (1860 - 1934)	2538
Anna Dell (1894 -)	3389
Anna Eliza (1833 - 1896)	1698
Anna P. (1856 - 1856)	2548
Ansel (1788 - 1854)	808
Blanche	2519
Carry (?)	spouse of 1691
Charles C. (1893 -)	2527
Cyrus (1797 - 1871)	812
Cyrus (1828 - 1888)	1685
Cyrus (1829 -)	1687
Cyrus K. (1819 - 1842)	1680
Daniel Olds (1806 - 1846)	1672
David (1753 - 1836)	349
David (1790 -)	809
David E. (1815 - 1860)	1683
Eames D. (1864 - 1886)	2551
Ebenezer Cross (1810 -)	1676
Edwin (1830 - 1899)	1688
Edwin D. (1845 - 1846)	2508
Elijah (1731 - 1756)	spouse of 119
Elijah (1756 - 1829)	350
Elijah (1782 - 1854)	805
Eliza Gilbert (1848 - 1863)	2544
Ellen	2518
Emma (1842 - 1922)	1690
Ethyl (1884 -)	3383
Ezra (1812 - 1813)	1677
Frances (1823 -)	1684
Francis	2515
Frank Howell (1851 - 1922)	2546

Fred	2517
George Humphrey (1878 - 1969)	3376
George Kingsley (1849 - 1918)	2511
George Kingsley (1909 - 1982)	3748
Grace (1882 -)	3382
Hattie (1862 - 1932)	2540
Henry Cyrus (1861 -)	2539
Henry Cyrus (1864 -)	2542
Henry Cyrus (1866 - 1914)	2550
Henry E. (1907 -)	3381
Henry Martin (1851 - 1904)	2512
Henry Warren (1823 - 1909)	1695
Ida Virginia (1855 -)	2537
J. (1816 - 1816)	1679
Jack	3393
James (1784 - 1851)	806
John Hugh (1871 - 1950)	2553
Joseph Howell (1825 -)	1696
Judith V.	3377
Julia (1839 - 1871)	1689
Julia Elizabeth (1839 - 1898)	2509
Laura (1816 - 1844)	1678
Laura	2513
Laura (1847 - 1934)	1692
Laura C. (1843 - 1928)	2507
Lizzie G. (1848 - 1863)	2545
Lucinda (1808 -)	1674
Lucy (1813 -)	1682
Lucy (1864 -)	2526
Lydia (1780 - 1811)	804
Lydia (1810 - 1810)	1675
Lydia (1811 -)	1681
Mamie (1854 -)	2521
Margaret C. (1899 -)	3379
Maria (?)	spouse of 809
Marion (1871 -)	3375
Martin Howland (1806 - 1906)	1673
Mary	2516
Mary (1877 -)	2529
Mary A. (1854 - 1930)	2547
Mary Edna	3394
Mary Eliza (1853 - 1939)	2536
Mary Howell (1830 - 1912)	1697
Mary M. (1856 -)	2522
Mary Olds (1847 -)	2510
Morgan (1901 -)	3380
Nancy (1779 - 1840)	803
Nellie (1889 -)	3384
Olive L.	2520
Opal (1905 -)	3392
Ralph (1895 -)	3390
Rebecca (1786 - 1862)	807
Rhoda (1751 -)	348
Robert Joseph (1868 - 1938)	2552

Rose	2514
Ruth (1901 -)	3391
Sallie H. (1857 - 1905)	2549
Sarah M. (1815 -)	1694
Susan	3919
Thomas C. (1864 -)	2541
Virginia (1859 -)	2525
Virginia E. (1859 -)	2523
Warren (1794 - 1850)	811
Warren Riley (1898 -)	3378
William (1845 - 1894)	1691
William E. (1865 -)	2543

BISBING

Russell H.	spouse of 3762

BISSELL

Noadiah (1761 -)	spouse of 718

BISWELL

Betsey B.	spouse of 825

BITKER

Barry Lea (1945 -)	4286
Joan Carol (1950 -)	4289
Johnnie Carl (1914 -)	spouse of 4060
Leslie Maynard (1946 -)	4288
Lyle Morris "Wylie" (1946 -)	4287
Marylou Ann (1958 -)	4291
Steven Jay (1954 - 1979)	4290
Tena Marie (1962 -)	4292
Ula Francis (1943 -)	4285

BITTICK

Lavina Margarette (1911 - 1997)	spouse of 3874

BLACKMAN

Andrew (1740 - 1821)	spouse of 31

BLACKMER

Solomon	spouse of 358

BLACKMUN

Andrew Perkins (1839 - 1920)	923
Calvin Luther (1846 - 1863)	926
Cyrus Judson (1841 - 1910)	924
Delia J. Sweet (1853 - 1940)	929
Elburt Foster (1857 - 1868)	931
Elizabeth Philina (1852 -)	928
Emma Jane (1861 -)	932
Luke Sherman (1775 - 1855)	129
Richard Lettin (1849 - 1937)	927
Sarah Nelly (1856 - 1857)	930
William John Manning (1844 - 1937)	925
William Sherman (1816 - 1874)	385

BLAKELEY

? (?)	spouse of 4088
Darrell G. (1922 - 1990)	spouse of 3875
Janis Ann (1953 - 2002)	4087
Living Child of Darrell and Ola (Brewer)	4086
Living Child of Norman	4354
Norman (1956 - 1994)	4088

BLAKESLEE
    Abraham   spouse of 1558
    Ann Jeannette (1841 - 1891)   spouse of 2167
    Lucinda L. (1817 - 1885)   spouse of 1201
BLETCHLEY
    Lydia Rebina (1819 - 1910)   spouse of 1229
BLODGET
    David   spouse of 356
    Emma Maria (1851 - 1930)   spouse of 2283
BLOOMQUIST
    Frank   spouse of 3536
BOARDMAN
    Abigail (1868 - 1931)   spouse of 2420
BOEHMER
    Jessie Lillian (1916 - 1956)   spouse of 3903
BOICE
    Charlotte Alida (1848 - 1868)   2007
    David   spouse of 970
    Fred E. (1841 -)   2005
    Helen Cornelia (1843 - 1864)   2006
BOND
    Clifford M. (1904 -)   3906
    Ernest Clifford (1877 - 1937)   spouse of 3692
    Marge   3904
    Marjorie E. (1906 -)   3907
    Susan   3905
BOSTWICK
    Harriett Cynthia (1869 - 1943)   spouse of 1904
BOWDEN
    ?   spouse of 4057
BOWERMAN
    Benjamin (Bennie) Wayne (1949 -)   3935
    Douglas Wayne (1975 -)   4134
    Franklin Peter (1943 -)   3933
    Franklin Wesley (1913 -)   spouse of 3764
    Kimberly Allison (1978 -)   4135
    Linda Lee (1946 -)   3934
    Monica Marie (1984 -)   4131
BOWERS
    Catherine L. (1914 - 2003)   spouse of 2662
BOWLBY
    Betsy (1784 - 1859)   spouse of 603
BOWLER
    Leo Francis   spouse of 4082
    Living Son of Leo and Elizabeth (Shepperd)   4338
    Living Son of Leo and Elizabeth (Shepperd)   4339
    Living Son of Leo and Elizabeth (Shepperd)   4340
    Living Son of Leo and Elizabeth (Shepperd)   4341
BOYINGTON
    Avis E. (1913 - 2008)   spouse of 3772
BOYNTON
    Sophronia (1807 - 1883)   spouse of 1176
BRADISH
    Elizabeth Ann (~1849 -)   1823

Ellen Josephine (~1855 -)   1825
Emily Marie (~1853 -)   1824
Zenus (Zenas) D. (~1817 -)   spouse of 882

BRADLEY
??Peter   spouse of 355
Abijah   spouse of 833
Jane (1774 - 1859)   spouse of 354
Lucinda (- 1865)   spouse of 1202
Reuben (1750 - 1827)   spouse of 224

BRANDHORST
Elizabeth Rose Jane (1992 -)   4370
Rodney Lee (1967 -)   spouse of 4128
Victoria Rose Leigh (1995 -)   4371

BRANDT
Debra Kay   spouse of 4124

BRECKENRIDGE
Bertha   spouse of 1731

BREESE
Joanna J. "Jane" (1816 - 1900)   spouse of 899
Stella Comelia (1860 - 1934)   spouse of 1863

BREWER
Charles W. (1860 - 1952)   2954
Clarene (1918 -)   3876
Elizabeth (1863 -)   2956
Ellie L. Corey   3603
Ernest (1873 -)   2957
Fannie Maria (1868 -)   2955
Fannie Z. Miller   3604
Grace G. (1858 - 1932)   spouse of 2954
LaVerne Sedgwick (1882 - 1946)   3602
Leon H.   3606
Lisle Gipson (1905 - 1958)   3874
Margaret G. (1922 -)   3877
Maude C.   3607
Ola Verne (1918 -)   3875
Olive Grace   3605
William Henry (1831 - 1915)   spouse of 2120

BRIGS
Maria   spouse of 920

BRINKMAN
Wanda (1944 -)   spouse of 3990

BRISTOL
Lowly (1753 -)   spouse of 294

BRITT
Irene (1919 -)   spouse of 4073

BROCKETT
Lucy B. (1793 - 1866)   spouse of 1245

BRONSON
Ira (1790 -)   spouse of 630

BRONSON or BROWN
Hannah (1788 - >1860)   spouse of 373

BROOKS
Amos (1807 - 1850)   1965
Anson Strong (1852 - 1937)   2786

Dwight Frederick (1849 - 1930)	2785
Frederick (1803 -)	1963
George Sheldon (1845 - 1861)	2783
Lester Ranney (1847 - 1902)	2784
Samuel Jr. (1769 - 1814)	spouse of 943
Samuel L. (1805 - 1897)	1964
Sarah (1814 - 1895)	1967
Dr. Sheldon (1811 - 1883)	1966

BROWN

Ann C. (1822 -)	spouse of 1668
Aron (~1798 -)	spouse of 383
Frank H. (1866 - 1934)	spouse of 2461
Hannah A. (1821 - 1861)	spouse of 1264
John	spouse of 977
Mary (1732 -)	spouse of 188
Norris (1779 -)	921
Ursula (~1827 -)	spouse of 913

BRUNER

Lillian Florence (1934 -)	spouse of 3554

BRYANT

Bertha	spouse of 2676
Nancy (1815 - 1893)	spouse of 1665

BUCKINHAM

Frances (aka Adaline, aka Fanny) (1791 - 1864)	spouse of 379

BUCKLAND

Jane	spouse of 56

BUCKLEY

Susan L. (1838 -)	spouse of 1257

BUECKING

Andrew	4097

BUELL

Abel G.	spouse of 2024
Hannah (1684 - 1725)	spouse of 16

BUNCE

Phinehas (~1727 - <1763)	spouse of 157

BUNCE EDGERTON

Mary (1753 - 1849)	431

BUNNELL

Elizabeth Ann (1771 - 1828)	spouse of 372

BURBANK

Asa Wakefield	spouse of 2003
Lurissa Rosalia (1845 - 1924)	2832

BURDICK

_____	spouse of 3688

BURKE

Ellen Theresa (1889 - 1976)	spouse of 3864
Lucy Christina (1884 - 1949)	spouse of 3861

BURLINGAME

Arthur Alanson (1878 -)	3289
Betsy A. (1860 -)	2430
Carrie Estell	3299
Chester Earl (1883 -)	3295
Christopher M. (1869 -)	2432
Clarence Leonard (1885 -)	3292

Addie Julia	3021	
Albert Webster (1856 -)	3015	
Aleanor Elena (1878 -)	3615	
Alexander (1873 -)	3006	
Alice Phoebe (1864 -)	3020	
Anna Eliza	3022	
Augustus (1830 - 1911)	2155	
Carrie May (1877 -)	3024	
[Child] of Hyrum and Sarah (Holkins) (1833 - 1838)		2150
Child of William and Emma (Higgins)	3630	
Child of William and Emma (Higgins)	3631	
Daniel (1773 - 1843)	spouse of 555	
Edgar Seaburn (1858 -)	3016	
Edna Matilda (1919 -)	3628	
Elizabeth Ann (1862 - 1942)	2991	
Elmer William (1891 -)	3621	
Emma Elvira (1898 -)	3632	
Ethel Elizabeth (1901 -)	3624	
Frank Augustus (1861 -)	3017	
Hannah Elizabeth (1868 -)	3005	
Hannah Maria (1866 - 1931)	2998	
Harold Ray (1909 -)	3635	
Heber Thornley (1914 -)	3627	
Herbert Day (1881 -)	3616	
Hiram Smith (1820 - 1856)	2153	
Howard Grant (1879 -)	3025	
Hyrum Elliot (1859 - 1939)	2990	
Hyrum Elliott (1830 - 1901)	2149	
Hyrum Norton (1800 - 1887)	1181	
Hyrum Norton (1861 -)	3001	
Ida May (1898 -)	3623	
Ira Zina (1870 - 1935)	2995	
James Henry (1865 - 1930)	2997	
Jeanette Sophia (1866 - 1940)	2993	
John Avery (1909 -)	3626	
John Henry (1864 - 1940)	2992	
John Parley (1880 - 1964)	3000	
Joseph Earon (1889 -)	3620	
Joseph Henry (1829 - 1909)	2148	
Joseph Henry (1862 -)	3002	
Joseph Hezekiah (1852 - 1929)	2987	
Joseph Lasley (1903 -)	3625	
Leon Nelson (1885 -)	3618	
Lottie Faye (1897 - 1994)	3629	
Lucius Webster (1828 -)	2154	
Martha Luce (1874 -)	3023	
Nancy Maranda (1850 - 1876)	2986	
Naomia Leona (1908 -)	3634	
Nellie Amelia (1862 -)	3019	
Nelson Smith (1862 -)	3018	
Noah Samuel (1868 - 1869)	2994	
Nora Isabelle (1876 -)	3008	
Oliver Milton (1855 - 1857)	2988	
Orra Elvira (1887 -)	3619	

Reba Ilene (1914 -)	3637
Rebecca Ann (1874 -)	3007
Sarah Augusta (1857 - 1922)	2989
Sarah Jane (1867 -)	3004
Stephen Elliot (1866 -)	3003
Susan Augusta (1840 -)	2151
Susan Elizabeth (1876 - 1956)	2999
Susia Anna (1797 -)	1183
Sylvia Mariah (1883 -)	3617
Thora (1911 -)	3636
Viola May (1897 -)	3622
Walter Wells (1855 -)	3014
William Alma (1873 - 1948)	2996
William Leslie (1899 -)	3633
Zina (1795 - 1885)	1182

CALDWELL

?	spouse of 2136
Ida Lenore (1859 - 1947)	2975
Orville Clyde (1861 - 1935)	2976

CALLOWAY

Malinda J. (1869 - 1890)	spouse of 1980

CAMP

Anna (1837 -)	2211
Ebenezer Bates (1825 -)	2208
Elizabeth Mariah (1821 -)	2207
Emily (1831 -)	2210
Heth (1735 - 1800)	spouse of 572
Heth Frisbie (1792 -)	1213
James (1828 -)	2209

CAMPBELL

Sarah (1745 - 1772)	spouse of 195

CARBINE

Mary Adelia (1824 - 1906)	spouse of 1596

CARDEN

Linda Kay (1946 -)	spouse of 3964

CARLEY

Emmett Albert (1846 -)	spouse of 2178
Horatio (1880 -)	3052
Julius Munson (1884 -)	3054
Mabel Frances (1881 -)	3053
Russell Henry (1886 -)	3055
Winnie	spouse of 2677

CARLSON

George Albert	spouse of 3822
Thom Ph.D. (~1940 -)	4006

CARMEN

Dorothy [192] (1906 -)	3492
Florence [189] (1893 -)	3489
Leta M. [187] (1887 -)	3487
Mabel A. [188] (1889 -)	3488
Stephen	spouse of 2716
William F. [191] (1904 -)	3491
Winifred I. [190] (1897 -)	3490

CARPENTER

Martha (1886 -)	spouse of 3466
CARR	
Child of Orlando and Susannah (Wilbur)	3638
Child of Orlando and Susannah (Wilbur)	3639
Clarence (1920 -)	3643
Lavella Ruth (1921 -)	3644
Orlando Jackson (1868 - 1953)	spouse of 3009
Orlando King (1911 -)	3640
Orville Leui (1918 -)	3642
Sarah Mariah (1872 - 1952)	spouse of 2997
Sylvia Pearl (1912 -)	3641
CARY	
George (1859 - 1945)	spouse of 3374
CASE	
A.	spouse of 714
Abiel (1792 -)	1340
Abigail (1787 -)	1348
Abigail (1781 -)	1284
Abner (1752 - 1807)	spouse of 652
Abner (1776 -)	1334
Amaryllis (1788 - 1860)	spouse of 727
Aminta (1783 -)	1329
Amy (1744 - 1782)	spouse of 163
Ariel (1765 - 1827)	spouse of 669
Arlow	1321
Asaph (1762 -)	656
Austin Barbour	2041
Banning (1790 -)	1350
Calista	1322
Calvin	2042
Candace (1777 -)	1335
Catherine (1794 -)	1331
Catherine (1794 - 1858)	spouse of 942
Child	2043
Chloe (1785 -)	1285
Chloe (1769 - 1820)	spouse of 439
Clarissa (1808 - 1890)	2037
Cynthia Maria (1806 - 1888)	2036
Dan (1784 - 1865)	spouse of 979
Delight Griswold (1783 - 1811)	spouse of 976
Desiah (1757 - 1834)	653
Eli (1788 -)	1339
Elijah (1726 - 1810)	spouse of 256
Elijah (1757 -)	654
Elijah (1784 -)	1345
Elisha (1781 - 1824)	spouse of 977
Elizabeth (1752 - 1817)	spouse of 433
Elizabeth (1754 - 1776)	spouse of 435
Erastus (1810 - 1813)	2038
Esther (1789 -)	1346
Eunice (1780 - 1858)	spouse of 449
Gabriel (1760 - 1793)	655
Gabriel	1347
George Washington	2044

Grandy (1789 -)	1431
Hannah (1752 - 1842)	652
Hannah (1774 -)	1333
Harriet Mabel	2045
Henry (1783 -)	spouse of 690
Hezekiah (1769 - 1859)	spouse of 726
Hezekiah Hart (1795 -)	1547
Hiram (1799 -)	1548
Huldah	1323
Imri (1780 -)	1336
Ira (1782 -)	1337
Job (1805 -)	1386
John Griswold (1818 - 1879)	2040
Jonathan (1779 -)	1328
Joseph (1722 - 1801)	spouse of 165
Julia	1324
Laura Ann	2046
Loly (aka Lottie) (1788 -)	1349
Lorinda (1816 - 1859)	spouse of 1002
Lovica	1325
Lucy (1766 -)	689
Lucy (1800 -)	1435
Lydia (1785 -)	1330
Lydia (1788 -)	1430
Lydia (1763 - 1843)	spouse of 437
Lyman	1332
Martin (1730 - 1827)	spouse of 263
Martin (1758 - 1774)	685
Mary (1762 - 1821)	687
Mary Ann (1816 - 1890)	2039
Moses (1746 - 1794)	spouse of 642
Olive (1785 -)	1338
Orpha (1769 -)	690
Ozias	spouse of 156
Parley	1326
Phebe (1782 -)	1344
Pinney (1796 -)	1434
Rachel Lury (1796 -)	1385
Ralph	spouse of 813
Ralph	spouse of 829
Reuben (1755 -)	651
Riley (1793 -)	1433
Rosette (1766 -)	657
Roswell (1760 - 1835)	686
Roswell (1786 -)	1429
Sarah	1327
Sherman Hurlbut	2047
Sterling (1806 -)	1351
Susan Eveline (1834 - 1913)	spouse of 2075
Susannah	spouse of 961
Sybil (1765 - 1844)	688
Theodosia (1770 -)	spouse of 724
Timothy (1791 -)	1432
Truman	1428

Elizabeth (1786 - 1856)	spouse of 684

CHRISTIANSEN

Amy Jo (1971 -)	4130
James Milton (1943 -)	spouse of 3932
Mark Alan (1969 -)	4129

CHUBB

Alta Delight (1834 - 1908)	2136
Arba (1791 - 1875)	1169
Bede (1813 -)	1174
Elizabeth (1794 - 1843)	1170
Ervin Lyle (a k a Erving) (1863 - 1942)	2977
Flora Augusta (1832 - 1914)	2135
Globe Dugar (1796 - 1888)	1171
Hannah Marietta (1845 - 1849)	2139
James Dillon (1837 - 1920)	2137
Jonathan Frisbie (1802 - 1854)	1172
Lucius Wolford (1842 - 1863)	2138
Lucy (1789 - 1839)	1168
Olive Sophia (1847 - 1939)	2140
Orville Pattison (1830 - 1894)	2134
Rolla Harrison	1173
Samuel (1751 - 1817)	spouse of 540

CHURCH

Satira	spouse of 1001

CLARK

Aseneth A.	spouse of 1589
Child of Lowell and Ellenore	3712
Deborah Ann (1803 - 1874)	spouse of 1572
Diane (1944 -)	spouse of 3987
Gene Bryant (1922 - 1980)	3713
Howard	spouse of 2765
Kenneth Frederick (~1925 - 1925)	3715
Lowell Homer (1894 - 1972)	spouse of 3212
Sam	spouse of 579
Warren Lowell (1925 - 1983)	3714

CLEVELAND

Cora Ella (- 1906)	spouse of 2673
Sarah (1784 - 1861)	spouse of 983

CLOSE

Matilda (- 1833)	spouse of 775

COATS

Janie Sarah (1869 -)	spouse of 2639

COBB

Alice M. (1849 -)	2780
Emma C. (1842 -)	2778
James Hartland (1813 -)	1959
Marietta (1845 -)	2779
Marriett (1808 -)	1957
Parolina (1817 -)	1961
Perlina E. (1836 -)	2777
Reuben Rice (1811 -)	1958
Royal Pinckney (1815 -)	1960
Sharon J. (1834 -)	2776
Willard (1781 - 1855)	spouse of 934

Willard Burr (1807 - 1849)   1956
COE
 Almon Bela (1820 -)   1786
 Bela (1795 - 1849)   spouse of 871
 Edmund (~1849 -)   2627
 Eunice (1742 - 1810)   spouse of 176
 Eunice (1766 - 1849)   spouse of 491
 Mary (?) (~1820 -)   spouse of 1786
 William (~1845 -)   2626
COHRS
 ?   spouse of 2831
COLE
 Alice Isaacs (1881 - 1957)   2316
 Anna Louise (1878 - 1966)   2315
 Edalena "Lena" Hill (1870 - 1945)   2314
 Eisabeth C. (- 1916)   spouse of 1891
 Florence Minerva (1847 - 1903)   spouse of 2918
 Ira (1836 - 1918)   spouse of 1584
COLEMAN
 Charlotte (1803 - 1886)   spouse of 516
COLEMON
 Althea H. (1820 - 1912)   spouse of 852
COOK
 Alfred (1888 -)   3280
 Alice (1856 -)   2417
 Amanda (1809 -)   796
 Ambrose L. (1835 - 1911)   1640
 Anna (1724 - 1759)   106
 Anna Rulon (1874 -)   2422
 Benjamin (1771 -)   336
 Charles A. (1858 - 1896)   2418
 Charles Sylvester (1887 -)   3279
 Clara (1890 -)   3281
 Demetrius (1718 -)   104
 Desire (1729 -)   108
 Ebenezer Hubbard (1759 - 1847)   331
 Edna Mulford (1923 - 2001)   spouse of 3829
 Elizabeth (1830 - 1916)   1639
 Elizabeth (1886 -)   3278
 Elizabeth "Betsy" (1764 -)   333
 Esther L. (1850 - 1921)   2415
 Frank Leroy (1896 -)   3283
 Fred Emery (1898 -)   3284
 Fred Lee (1877 -)   3276
 Fremont (1821 -)   1636
 Grace (1895 -)   3282
 Hannah (1753 -)   329
 Henry "Harry" (1904 -)   3286
 Hulda (1768 -)   335
 Isaac (1692 - 1762)   spouse of 26
 Isaac (1716 - 1760)   103
 Jacob (1755 -)   330
 Jane (1751 -)   328
 Jerusha (1736 -)   110

CRAEGER
    Mildred L. (1911 - 2008)   spouse of 3768
CRAMPTON
    Demetrius   spouse of 130
CRANDALL
    Alice [232] (1917 -)   3806
    Clifford [229] (1908 -)   3803
    Frederick [231] (1912 -)   3805
    Harry   spouse of 3487
    Winifred [230] (1910 -)   3804
CRAWFORD
    Anna Nevada (1868 -)   2395
    Austin (1873 -)   2397
    Carmi (1838 - 1926)   spouse of 1626
    Carmi Russell (1903 -)   3256
    Catherine (1838 - 1876)   spouse of 1264
    Franklin Herbert (1866 -)   2394
    Genetta Ellen (1864 -)   2393
    Hazel Annetta (1901 -)   3255
    Lolita Grace (1908 -)   3258
    Margaret Elizabeth   3252
    Mildred (1898 -)   3253
    Myron (1879 -)   2398
    Ralph (1906 -)   3257
    Velma Merle (1899 -)   3254
    Weldon R. (1871 - 1953)   2396
CREESY
    Mehitable (1785 - 1830)   spouse of 991
    Olive (1795 - 1865)   spouse of 991
CRIDER
    Mary Margaret (1842 -)   spouse of 1827
CRIST
    Rhemona   spouse of 2768
CRITTINDEN
    Abigail   2004
    Sylvenas   spouse of 970
CROCKER
    Leroy Langford (1847 - 1908)   spouse of 2332
CROSBY
    Martha   spouse of 1950
CRUM
    Amber Marie (1981 -)   4185
    Hayley Camille (1984 -)   4186
    Jessica Dawn (1976 -)   4184
    Ken   spouse of 3965
CRUTTENDEN
    Lucy (1784 -)   spouse of 334
CULVER
    Abigail (1718 - 1771)   spouse of 67
CUMMINGS
    Catherine (~1813 - ~1889)   spouse of 834
    Jennie (1973 -)   4227
    Michael (1971 -)   4226
    Robert   spouse of 3988

Ryan (1974 -)	4228
CURTIS	
Betsy (1785 - 1848)	spouse of 372
Chestina (Justina) (1742 - 1816)	spouse of 170
Comfort (1744 - 1825)	spouse of 190
Elmyra (1837 - 1886)	spouse of 1594
Theodosia (1787 - 1850)	spouse of 662
CURTISS	
Phebe (1759 -)	spouse of 392
DAHLGREN	
? (1890 -)	spouse of 3213
DAILEY	
? (~1737 -)	spouse of 153
DAMON	
Jill	spouse of 4144
DANFORTH	
David Jonathan	spouse of 2415
DANZER	
Rose (1924 - 1987)	spouse of 3766
DART	
William S. (1805 -)	spouse of 1957
DAUGHERTY	
Roger Fay (1953 -)	spouse of 3945
Sarah Mae (1982 -)	4159
DAVAULT	
Lucinda	spouse of 888
DAVEY	
Kay Leone (1943 -)	spouse of 3930
DAVIDSON	
Brian (later Osha POV)	spouse of 3966
Elizabeth (1770 - 1850)	spouse of 545
Sarah Gray (b. Sarah Rainbow) (1979 -)	4188
DAVIS	
Annie	spouse of 1728
Caroline Julia (1862 -)	2868
Cynthia A.	spouse of 1851
Frederick Charles (1861 -)	2867
George Gibbs (1834 -)	spouse of 2035
George Monroe (1859 -)	2866
Isabella	spouse of 1726
Ruth Alberta Pratt (1912 - 1995)	spouse of 2941
Shirley Ann (1943 -)	spouse of 3962
Theron Dexter (1865 -)	2869
DAY	
Anna R. (1860 -)	2378
Clarence C. (1887 -)	spouse of 2936
Converse E.	spouse of 2520
Cora Cord (1850 -)	2377
Ellen M. (1863 -)	2379
Harriet Louise (1821 - 1886)	spouse of 2023
Henry Edwin (1825 - 1902)	spouse of 1619
Shannon (1867 -)	2380
DEBRINE	
Suzanne "Susan" (1931 -)	spouse of 3516

DECKER
Anna M.	spouse of 1204
Florence Louise (1878 -)	spouse of 2414

DEMING
Roxy	spouse of 822

DENLINGER
?	spouse of 2828

DENMAN
William	spouse of 1800

DENNING
Charles W. (- 1863)	spouse of 1878
Daisy Irene [87]	2687
Guy Hamilton [88]	2688

DENTON
Harriet (1787 - 1844)	spouse of 701

DEURLIEN
William (1937 -)	spouse of 3830

DeVORE
Dale (1901 - 1996)	3548
Dayton (1911 - 1997)	3549
Donald	3550
Frank	spouse of 2799

DEWEY
Jerusha	spouse of 460

DEWOLF
Frances	spouse of 3461

DIAZ
Pete	spouse of 3833

DIBBLE
?	342
Abigail (1762 - 1789)	344
Alexander (1860 - 1819)	347
Anna (1765 - 1802)	345
Betsy Ann (1796 -)	802
Charles Henry (1794 - 1850)	801
David (1749 -)	339
Hannah (?)	spouse of 118
Harris (1756 -)	341
Israel (1729 -)	118
John (1702 - 1756)	spouse of 29
John Jr. (1725 - 1790)	116
John (1758 - 1852)	343
John (1792 -)	800
Josiah (1737 -)	121
Lydia (1731 - 1805)	119
Lydia (1731 - 1805)	spouse of 125
Maria Seely (1790 - 1841)	799
Mary (1747 - 1825)	123
Rachel (1740 -)	122
Reuben (1727 - 1779)	117
Reuben (1755 -)	340
Sarah (1771 -)	346
Sarah F. (1846 - 1850)	1660
Susannah (1735 -)	120

DIBBLE aka DIBIL
Martha Wealthy (1697 - 1758)   spouse of 25
DICK
Mrs. Catherine   spouse of 3542
DICKSON
William   spouse of 1916
DIETTE
Leah (1896 - 1981)   spouse of 3682
DILLER
Dave   spouse of 4047
Jedediah Hill (1989 -)   4273
Zachary Travis (1992 -)   4274
DIMMICK
Edna H. [196] (1899 -)   3496
Ellen M. [199] (1908 -)   3499
Mable J. [197] (1904 -)   3497
Norman   spouse of 2719
Uletta C. [198] (1907 -)   3498
DINGELY
Natalie   spouse of 4172c
DODGE
Angeline (1819 - 1902)   spouse of 2030
Mildred Blanch (1888 - 1970)   spouse of 3862
DONALDSON
Florinda   spouse of 2480
DOOLITTLE
?   spouse of 1199
DORMAN
Edith Grace   spouse of 3527
DOW
Elvira (1817 - 1880)   spouse of 1121
DOWD
?   2625
Annie   2622
David Arthur (1866 - 1917)   spouse of 1754
Elizabeth Ann (1855 -)   2574
Evelyn   2623
Hamilton Stewart (1857 -)   2575
Joseph   spouse of 1718
Lucy Sophia (1859 -)   2576
Mabel   2624
Velma (1905 -)   2621
DOWNING
Floyd (1901 -)   spouse of 2940
DOYLE
Clara Ellen   spouse of 2143
DRAKE
Clara   spouse of 2714
DUDLEY
Abigail (1789 -)   spouse of 614
DUFFY
Fanny (- >1876)   spouse of 2926
DUNCAN
Sarah L. (1842 - 1929)   spouse of 1696

DUNHAM
    Deidama (1765 - 1841)   spouse of 461
DUNN
    Captain Samuel   spouse of 1947
DURHAM
    Mary (- 1770)   spouse of 33
DURYEA
    Susie (1870 -)   spouse of 3037
DYAS
    Webster   spouse of 2947
DYE
    Angeline Sheets (1833 - 1910)   spouse of 1610
EARNEST
    UNNAMED   spouse of 3857
    Pat   4066
EAST
    Penny   4030
    Ronald   spouse of 3833
EASTERBROOK
    Claude Loraine [180] (1887 -)   3466
    Francis (1853 -)   spouse of 2680
    Harriet Jane [179] (1885 -)   3465
    Leslie Leone [183] (1896 -)   3469
    Lucius Elvin [182] (1892 - 1915)   3468
    Raymond Larne [181] (1890 -)   3467
    Thelma Rose [184-A] (1911 -)   3801
EATON
    Abilene (1789 -)   spouse of 806
EBERBACH
    _____   spouse of 3908
    _____   4093
EDGERTON
    Anna (1775 - 1846)   spouse of 659
    John (1763 -)   spouse of 668
    Jonathan   spouse of 157
EDWARDS
    Betsey (1786 -)   spouse of 570
    Emma (~1852 -)   spouse of 1846
    Thankful (1742 -)   spouse of 211
EGGLESTON
    Isabel (1732 - 1818)   spouse of 147
EICHER
    Mary Lynn (1944 -)   spouse of 3924
EKERN
    Aaron Anthony (1969-)   spouse of 4172a
    Megan Leigh (2003-)   4403a
ELDRED
    John W. [93]   2693
    Ruth T. (1892 -)   spouse of 2553
    Sylvester   spouse of 1880
ELLAS
    Clara   spouse of 2753
ELLIOTT
    Aaron Robert (1976 -)   4140

Amy Elin (1972 -)	4138
Carl Robert "Bob" (1942 -)	spouse of 3938
John David (1974 -)	4139
ELLWART	
Marie	spouse of 3835
ELWIN	
Elmer Hanson (1870 -)	spouse of 2722
Elmer Hill [203] (1912 -)	3503
James William [204] (1916 -)	3504
EMERY	
Maria Ophelia (1849 - 1924)	spouse of 1884
ENO	
Abigail (1740 - 1782)	275
Chauncey (1782 - 1845)	727
Chauncey E. (1815 -)	1551
Cordelia (1812 -)	1550
Cynthia (1777 - 1804)	726
David (1702 - 1745)	spouse of 83
Elizabeth (1773 - 1868)	725
Elizur Hart (1810 -)	1549
Ellen Maria	1529
Eunetia Minerva (1824 - 1915)	spouse of 2086
Eunetia Minerva (1824 - 1915)	2256
Jeanette Amarilla (1818 -)	1552
Jonathan (1739 - 1813)	274
Jonathan (1769 - 1821)	724
Jonathan (1793 -)	1537
Josiah William (1820 -)	1553
Mary (1727 - 1804)	271
Mercy (1734 - 1860)	273
ENOS	
Elizabeth (1774 -)	720
Jerusha Hayden Jr. (1764 - 1838)	717
Major General Roger Sr. (1729 - 1808)	272
Roger (1768 - 1849)	719
Sibil (1766 - 1796)	718
ENSIGN	
Anna (1706 - 1786)	spouse of 55
EPPLEY	
Suzanne Margaret "Suzie" , M.D. (1947 -)	spouse of 3780
ESCAMOS	
?	spouse of 3223
ESTABROOKS	
Aaron Gaylord	1270
Abel C. (1788 - 1848)	spouse of 631
Charles (1816 -)	1271
Laura (1818 -)	1272
Levi (1822 -)	1273
ETZLER	
Martha (1836 - 1879)	spouse of 1688
EUE	
Linda (1965 -)	spouse of 4048
EVANS	
Carrie	spouse of 1583

Harriet Jane "Hattie" (1862 - 1922)	spouse of 2341
FARIS	
Jane (1849 - 1902)	1725
John (1808 - 1897)	spouse of 840
FARLEY	
Mary G. (1878 -)	3267
William (1841 -)	spouse of 2408
FARRAR	
Henry	spouse of 841
FARWELL	
Elizabeth (1762 - 1855)	spouse of 706
FAULTZ	
Harriet M. "Hattie" (~1869 -)	spouse of 1852
FAVARO	
Timmon	spouse of 4355
FAVORITE	
Dora Bell (1865 -)	spouse of 2401
FAY	
Mary Adelaide (1846 - 1917)	spouse of 2299
FELLOWS	
Nettie Louise (1859 - 1934)	3150
William Harrison (1836 - 1902)	spouse of 2290
FERRIN	
Julia Phidelia (1825 - 1900)	spouse of 1181
FERRIS	
Hannah (~1748 - 1818)	spouse of 128
FIELD	
Elizabeth (1836 -)	spouse of 1602
FILE	
Emily C. (1845 -)	spouse of 2479
Kathryn (1818 -)	spouse of 1667
Sarah (1805 - 1888)	spouse of 1663
FILSON	
Ann (~1815 -)	spouse of 909
FINCH	
Anna Lois (1902 - 1989)	spouse of 2735
FISCHER	
William	spouse of 3145
FISHER	
Harriet	spouse of 1608
Isaiah Martin (1873 - 1949)	spouse of 2999
FLEMING	
William G.	spouse of 2402
FLYNN	
Mary Catherine (1926 - 1992)	spouse of 3824
FOLLETTE	
Louetta May "Lou" (1935 -)	spouse of 3940
FOOTE	
Clara (1795 - 1838)	spouse of 980
Eliza M. (1823 -)	2081
Elizabeth (1697 - 1725)	spouse of 33
Henry (1813 -)	2079
John M. (1827 -)	2082
Joseph	spouse of 12

Laura (1809 -)	2078
Lucius (1817 -)	2080
Miles (1788 -)	spouse of 992
Newell	spouse of 366
FORD	
Ambrose Elmer (1874 -)	3690
Harry Lewis (1869 - 1941)	3689
Harry S.	3133
Lida B. (1884 - 1956)	3691
Lois Ann	3134
Louis A. (1849 - 1850)	3129
Mary Marie (1855 -)	3131
Morris S. (1847 - 1923)	3128
Nellie F. (1860 -)	3132
Stebbins A. (1819 - 1900)	spouse of 2268
William Henry (1851 -)	3130
FORDE	
Dr. ?	spouse of 1804
daughter	2636
FOSTER	
Sally (1780 - 1827)	spouse of 129
FOWLER	
Abigail (1735 - 1828)	spouse of 395
Anne	spouse of 468
FOX	
Louise Jane "Luella" "Ella" (1855 - 1933)	spouse of 1981
Mary Ellen (1858 - 1946)	spouse of 1979
FRACKER	
Martha Ellen (1842 -)	spouse of 2297
FRAME	
Adolphus Roscoe "Doc"	spouse of 3521
FRAZEE	
Robert Smith (1848 - 1892)	spouse of 2330
FREDERICK	
Sarah (1704 -)	spouse of 28
FREEMAN	
Margaret Alice (1915 - 2001)	spouse of 4074
FRINK	
Adeline (1808 - 1884)	spouse of 812
Eldred	spouse of 1674
FRISBIE	
? (1824 -)	1212
? son of Clark Lamartine and Clara (Doyle)	2984
? son of Clark Lamartine and Clara (Doyle)	2985
Abel (1755 -)	246
Abigail (1709 - 1778)	71
Abigail (1746 -)	218
Abigail (1775 -)	591
Adah (1769 - 1730)	536
Addison Cowles (1829 -)	1274
Alice Ann (1862 - 1885)	2971
Amanda	611
Ann Deidamia (1838 - 1917)	2132
Anna (1761 - 1825)	531

Anna (1777 -)	541
Anna (1798 -)	1232
Anna Laura (~1869 - 1926)	2978
Archibald (1777 -)	578
Arkemenia (1793 -)	1210
Arthur Asa (1871 - 1926)	2974
Asa (1776 - 1857)	577
Asa Putnam (1823 - 1902)	2129
Asa W. (1823 -)	1228
Augustus (1768 -)	547
Austin S. (1795 -)	1211
Baldwin Augustus (1812 - 1894)	1258
Bede (1774 -)	549
Bede Beda (1774 - 1809)	538
Benjamin (1679 - 1724)	spouse of 13
Benjamin (1705 - ?1758)	70
Benjamin (1739 - ?1758)	234
Betsey (1820 - 1877)	1262
Birdie Alice (1876 -)	3112
Birdie Alvaretta (1865 - 1938)	2972
Caroline Collins (1814 - 1816)	1259
Caroline Collins (1818 -)	1261
Caroline Eunice (1809 -)	1235
Catherine (1792 - 1822)	631
Charles (1752 -)	219
Charlotte (1810 -)	1224
Chauncey (1787 - 1864)	629
Chauncey Montgomery (1837 -)	1277
Chloe (1737 - 1749)	207
Chloe (1750 -)	209
Clara (1794 -)	1239
Clarissa (1778 - 1837)	539
Clark Lamartine (1848 - 1930)	2143
Daniel (1771 - 1850)	589
Daniel (1761 -)	248
David (1782 - 1829)	586
Dorcas (1767 - 1848)	575
Dorcas (1807 -)	1223
Ebenezer (1773 - 1835)	590
Ebenezer Wakelee (1800 -)	1240
Eldad (~1794 -)	638
Eli (1776 -)	550
Elias Willard M.D. (1799 - 1860)	1176
Elijah (1717 - 1800)	67
Elijah Stanton (1805 - 1866)	1166
Eliza (1804 -)	1221
Eliza Ann (1801 - 1880)	1177
Eliza Maria (1839 -)	1278
Elizabeth (1744 -)	197
Elizabeth (1732 -)	231
Elizabeth (1747 -)	242
Elizabeth (1757 - 1827)	204
Elizabeth (1788 -)	544
Elizabeth (1761 -)	572

Elizabeth (1769 - 1857)   588
Ella Elizabeth (1846 - 1934)   2245
Emeline (1812 -)   1243
Emily Phoebe (1847 -)   1281
Emmarilla Josephine (1852 - 1946)   2967
Enos (1766 - 1829)   534
Ester (1778 - 1871)   spouse of 716
Esther (1743 - 1795)   215
Esther   612
Eugenia (Beatrice) (1858 - 1892)   2146
Eunice (1779 -)   551
Ezra (1771 - 1818)   537
Ezra Clark (1805 - 1867)   1179
Ezra Clark (1885 -)   2983
Fidelia (1815 -)   1226
Florence (1882 -)   3123
Francis (- 1870)   2141
Frank Baldwin (1859 -)   2236
Frederick Augustus (1855 - 1935)   2234
Freelove (1823 -)   1263
Gad (1778 - 1854)   628
George Elbert (1850 - 1851)   2966
Guy Carlton (1805 -)   1222
Hannah (1720 - 1803)   68
Hannah (1792 -)   1238
Hannah (1783 - 1816)   587
Hannah Amelia (1738 - 1810)   220
Harold John (1899 -)   3122
Harriet Burnham (1816 -)   1260
Harriet Elizabeth (1868 - 1930)   2237
Hazel (1891 -)   3117
Henry Case (1878 -)   3113
Hephzibah (1726 -)   228
Hiram (~1794 -)   637
Horace Cornwall (1858 - 1859)   2248
Huldah (1715 - 1797)   66
Ida Lizette (1854 - 1944)   2968
Ira (- 1863)   613
Irene C. (1810 - 1836)   1180
Isaac (1764 - 1826)   533
Israel (1709 - 1787)   63
Israel (1754 -)   210
Jabez (1730 -)   230
Jacob (1740 - 1823)   196
Jacob (1767 - 1842)   546
James (1793 -)   229
James (1732 -)   205
James (1771 -)   576
James (1799 - 1862)   615
James (1822 - 1892)   1269
Jedediah (1705 - 1736)   61
Jerusha (1712 -)   72
Jerusha (1735 -)   232
Jessie Evelyn (1883 -)   3115

Joel (1747 -)	198
Joel	634
John (1676 - 1736)	spouse of 12
John (1703 - 1786)	60
John (1731 - 1817)	193
John (1762 - 1846)	222
John (1762 - 1837)	532
John (1850 -)	2144
John (1819 - 1902)	1268
John Carlton (1898 -)	3118
John Case (1863 - 1915)	2250
Jonah (1724 -)	69
Jonah (1734 -)	206
Jonah (1765 -)	574
Jonathan (1734 - 1818)	194
Joseph (1741 -)	235
Judah (1744 - 1817)	216
Julia (1795 -)	1231
Julius A. (1876 -)	2981
Julius Caesar (1854 - 1936)	2145
Keziah (1748 - 1821)	201
Laura (1790 - 1879)	630
Lauren Lorrain (1800 -)	1233
Leslie Almon (1861 - 1921)	2249
Levi (1719 -)	75
Levi (1753 - 1755)	245
Levi (1759 - 1842)	247
Levi (1757 -)	250
Levi	635
Levi Collins (1788 - 1852)	614
Levi Randall (1797 - 1797)	632
Levi S. (1815 -)	1167
Lewis (- 1842)	2142
Lola "Lowly" (1749 -)	243
Lottie May (1881 -)	3114
Louis F. (1875 -)	2980
Lucius Daniel (1804 -)	1234
Lucy (1741 - 1823)	240
Luman (1760 -)	252
Luman (~1796 -)	639
Maria (1812 -)	1225
Martha (1877 -)	2982
Mary (1714 -)	73
Mary (~1737 -)	233
Mary (1745 - 1757)	241
Mary (1763 - 1774)	253
Mary (1780 - 1852)	585
Mary Chloe (1811 -)	1236
Mary Ellen (1849 -)	1282
Mary Isabella (1857 - 1920)	2969
Mary Josephine (1840 -)	2133
Mary Marilla (1855 - 1939)	2247
Mehitabel	636
Minerva (1820 -)	1227

Minnie Maria (1860 - 1946)	2970
Miriam (1746 - 1824)	200
Moses (1754 -)	203
Nancy Maria (1826 - 1904)	2130
Nathaniel (1711 - 1711)	64
Nelson Moses (1852 - 1949)	2233
Olin Gaylord (1852 -)	1283
Orrin Goodwin (1845 -)	1280
Parlia N. (1801 -)	616
Paul Leslie (1897 -)	3121
Philemon (1772 -)	548
Phillis (?) (- 1757)	spouse of 76
Polly (1784 -)	595
Polly (1802 -)	1241
Prince William Albert (1865 - 1915)	2147
Rachel (1763 -)	573
Relief (1769 - 1822)	540
Reuben (1746 - 1824)	217
Reuben (1810 -)	1242
Richard (1796 -)	1237
Rosella Putnam (1868 - 1853)	2973
Ruby Hannah (1843 -)	1279
Russell B. (1797 - 1876)	1165
Russell Levi (1830 - 1906)	2131
Ruth	592
Sadie F. (1872 -)	2979
Sally	593
Dr. Salmon (1782 -)	552
Salome (1785 - 1811)	543
Samuel (~1707 - 1708)	62
Samuel	594
Samuel (1763 - 1831)	249
Samuel (1850 - 1930)	2246
Sarah (1756 - 1842)	221
Sarah (1795 -)	553
Sarah Maria	1175
Sarah Maria	1178
Satira	579
Satira	1209
Simeon (1781 - 1807)	542
Simon (1743 - 1777)	199
Susannah (1713 -)	65
Susannah (1750 -)	202
Tamer (1739 -)	208
Thaddeus Granice (1760 -)	571
Theodore (1723 - 1764)	76
Theodore (1759 - 1830)	251
Theron E. (1858 - 1926)	2235
Timothy (1769 - 1842)	570
Tryphena (1768 - 1799)	535
Warren Rush (1831 -)	1275
William (1737 - 1813)	195
William M.D. (1769 - 1837)	545
William (1889 -)	3116

William Lawson (1834 -)	1276
Zebulon (1717 - 1800)	74
Zebulon (1752 - 1836)	244
Zebulon (1801 - 1881)	633

FROST

Anna (1773 -)	spouse of 601
Joseph (1711 -)	spouse of 65
Sarah (1789 - 1845)	580
Solomon (1742 - 1838)	211

FRY

Jessie Irene (1870 - 1947)	spouse of 2552

FULLER

Hannah	spouse of 986

GAINES

Damaris	728
Daniel (1732 -)	276
Daniel	729
Daniel (aka David) (1700 -)	spouse of 85
Eunice	730
Lois	731
Lucretia	732
Lydia	733
Lyman	734
Samuel	735

GAMM

Geraldine (1920 - 1990)	spouse of 3769

GANYARD

Catherine (1760 - 1796)	spouse of 654

GARLINGHOUSE

Submitt S. (1814 - 1860)	spouse of 1956

GARNSEY

Joseph Blake (1787 - 1864)	spouse of 580

GARRETT

Rufus (~1755 -)	spouse of 413

GATES

Benjamin "Ben"	4390
Bradley Frederick "Brad" (1963 -)	4152
Brian Freeman (1958 -)	4150
Chelsea	4386
Elizabeth (?)	spouse of 4150
Elizabcth	4385
Francine Lea (1961 -)	4151
Freeman David (1927 - >1997)	spouse of 3942
Hannah	spouse of 312
Josiah "Joey"	4392
Katherine "Katie"	4391
Leanna	4389

GAUCHET

Archibald Greenfield (1890 -)	3310
Daniel Benjamin (1865 - 1923)	2444
Daniel Benjamin (1889 -)	3309
Edward A. (1854 - 1925)	2440
Eva Mildred (1886 -)	3308
Ezrena Amanda (1894 -)	3311

Frank Henry (1869 -)	2445
James Adolphus (1860 - 1916)	2443
Louis "Lewie" Leete (1857 - 1900)	2442
Mary (1856 - 1856)	2441
Pierre A. (1819 - 1889)	spouse of 1647

GAY

Sarah	spouse of 2750

GAYLORD

Adeline (1817 -)	1265
Alling (1778 - 1794)	618
Alva (Allen) (1793 - 1862)	621
Benjamin (1722 - 1801)	spouse of 68
Benjamin	spouse of 72
Benjamin (1755 - 1825)	226
Charles E. (1900 -)	3677
Chester (1796 - 1852)	622
Chestley N. (1881 -)	3103
Daughter of Hepworth and Belle (Bennett)	3674
Elizabeth (1756 - 1756)	227
Emma (1863 -)	2243
Enos (1733 - 1834)	239
Fred (1866 -)	3095
Frederick Windslow (1848 -)	2240
Fremont (1856 - 1857)	2241
Hannah (1749 - 1791)	224
Helen Sabra (1893 -)	3675
Hepworth A. (1868 - 1928)	3096
Howard (1895 -)	3676
Irene B. (1874 -)	3100
Isaac Brown (1845 - 1927)	2239
Jennette (1822 - 1863)	1266
Jersusha (1731 -)	238
John (1750 - 1750)	225
Laurence I. (1889 -)	3106
Lawrence (1901 -)	3678
Levi (1730 -)	237
Loly (1785 - 1794)	620
Lomar E. (1882 -)	3104
Margaret Elsie (1878 -)	3101
Mary D. (1880 -)	3102
Merab (1777 - 1794)	617
Milly (1798 - 1803)	623
Minnie (1860 -)	2242
Minnie H. (1885 -)	3105
Nellie Ada (1870 -)	3097
Phebe (1767 - 1852)	spouse of 247
Ray B. (1873 -)	3099
Russell (1782 - 1869)	619
Susannah (1749 - 1749)	223
Theodore B. (1843 - 1878)	spouse of 2329
William B. (1872 -)	3098
William Hepworth (1844 -)	2238
William Lawrence (1815 - 1884)	1264

GAYNOR

? [1]	3894
? [2]	3895
? [3]	3896
? [4]	3897
? [5]	3898
? [6]	3899
Charles (~1898 -)	3125
Charles Beauclerk	3683
Eben (1871 -)	spouse of 2255
Eben W. (1871 - 1919)	spouse of 3126
Harold Wentworth (1899 -)	3684
Paul (1930 -)	3900
William Allen (1896 - 1972)	3682

GEATER

Martha (1939 -)	spouse of 3986

GEORGE

Joseph	spouse of 1628
William? (St.)	spouse of 3845

GERE

Charles Henry (1838 -)	1599
Frances Forbes (1805 - 1888)	spouse of 778
George Grant (1848 -)	1601
Horatio Nelson (1802 - 1862)	spouse of 779
John Nelson (1842 -)	1600

GILBERT

Anna Mariah (1835 - 1924)	spouse of 1629
Charles B. [125] (1879 - <1920)	2726
Gerald	spouse of 4351
Helen Frances [206] (1904 -)	3507
Horace	spouse of 1879
James Abner (- 1907)	spouse of 1899
Leona May [207] (1908 - >1920)	3508
Living Son of Gerald and Beth (McDuffie)	4419
Living Son of Gerald and Beth (McDuffie)	4420
Mary L. [124] (1876 - 1879)	2725
Roy H. [126] (1889 - 1889)	2727

GILHAM

————	spouse of 4294

GILLESPIE

Andrew Jackson (1839 - 1911)	spouse of 2481
Corinore (1863 -)	3362
Flora (1868 -)	3364
Grace A. (1880 -)	3366
Leona (1886 -)	3367
Mary Ann (1815 -)	spouse of 1664
Mary Temperance (1872 -)	3365
Sadie (1866 -)	3363

GILLET

Elizabeth	spouse of 22

GILLETT

Aaron H. (1805 -)	spouse of 896
Emeline (1812 -)	spouse of 775
Eunice (1707 - 1740)	85
Huldah Jane [32] (1836 - 1886)	1872

Jonathan (1701 - 1719)	82
Katharine "Catherine" (~1810 - ~1840)	spouse of 2089
Mary (1703 - 1760)	83
Richard (1705 - 1719)	84
Sarah (1651 - 1737)	spouse of 4
William (1673 - 1718)	spouse of 17
William (1700 - 1736)	81
GILLIAM	
Claude (1892 -)	spouse of 2766
June (1916 - 2000)	3534
GILLILAND	
Mary Alice (1872 - 1942)	spouse of 2396
GILLIS	
Arthur Luther (~1869 -)	spouse of 2797
GILMORE	
Arthur	spouse of 2757
GIPSON	
Matilda Caroline (1824 - 1870)	spouse of 1179
Minnie (1882 - 1939)	spouse of 3602
GIUDICI	
Danielle Marie (1989 -)	4357
Derek Alan (1992 -)	4358
Gregory	spouse of 4117
GLADE	
Caitlin Marie (1989 -)	4192
Paul (1958 -)	spouse of 3968
Ryan Jeffrey (1983 -)	4191
GLADWIN	
Gertrude (1844 - 1925)	spouse of 2087
GLEASON	
Jabez Oman	spouse of 417
GOCHENOUR	
Alice Elizabeth (1863 - 1950)	spouse of 2249
GODFREY	
Maxon	spouse of 2009
GOLDING	
_____	4092
Alvin Ford (1908 - 1969)	3903
Clyde Adair (1878 - 1955)	spouse of 3691
Helen Dorothy (1905 - 1962)	3902
GOODALE	
Charles A. (1798 -)	1111
Hannah (1817 -)	1118
Harriet (~1797 -)	1110
Lemuel C. (1805 -)	1114
Leonard C. (1803 -)	1113
Lucinda (1809 -)	1115
Mary (1814 -)	1117
Osee Montgomery (1800 -)	1112
Seymour (1810 -)	1116
Solomon (1767 - 1862)	spouse of 485
Solomon (1797 -)	1109
GOODWIN	
Anson	spouse of 1942

Polly (1811 - 1887)	spouse of 633
GORMAN	
Mary Ann (1797 - >1860)	spouse of 374
GOULDER	
Harvey D.	spouse of 2556
Harvey D.	3396
GRAFF	
Alice (- >1997)	spouse of 3697
GRANNIS	
Elizabeth (1708 - 1760)	spouse of 63
GRANT	
Alma Virginia (1863 -)	2328
Charles (1794 - 1895)	775
Charles Lewis (1864 - 1864)	2337
Charles Wesley (1818 -)	1597
DeWitt Clinton (1841 -)	1598
Earle (?)	3202
Ebenezer (1723 - 1765)	spouse of 96
Edmund Carbine (1858 -)	2338
Effie Gail (1887 -)	3183
Elihu (1786 - 1841)	772
Elihu (1756 -)	306
Elisha (Elizah)	1585
Eliza Desire (1838 - 1925)	2318
Elton Durand (1872 -)	3180
Francesca (1860 -)	2339
George Robert (1852 - 1895)	2331
George Roberts (1820 - 1889)	1596
Gertrude Betsy (1860 - 1864)	2335
Hannah (1812 - 1874)	1587
Harman Elihu (1883 -)	3187
Harriet	2317
Helen Louisa (1856 -)	2333
Henrietta (1858 -)	2334
Henry Loring (1972 - 1864)	2336
Huldah (1763 - 1764)	308
Ida Edna (1893 -)	3189
Isaac (1785 - 1841)	771
Isaac (1814 - 1833)	1588
Dr. Isaac (1760 - 1841)	307
Isaac Jesse (1844 - 1903)	2321
James William (1894 -)	3184
Jane (1889 -)	3188
Jesse C. (1825 - 1886)	1594
Jesse Chapman (1802 - 1885)	778
John (1816 - 1887)	1589
John (1847 -)	2322
John Everett (1879 -)	3185
Julia Antoinette (1854 -)	2332
Julia Eva (1858 - 1867)	2326
Juliana Delay (1807 - 1875)	779
Julius Everett (1858 - 1872)	2327
Laura (1817 -)	1590
Lois (1757 -)	spouse of 705

Longstreth (?)	3203
Lorin Marcina (1810 -)	1586
Loring (1789 - 1870)	773
Lucy Anna (1823 - 1885)	1593
Lydia (1753 - 1767)	305
Lydia Maria (1841 - 1892)	2319
Marcena (1797 - 1801)	776
Maria (1800 - 1801)	777
Martha (1751 - 1769)	304
Mary Amelia (1848 -)	2329
Mary Ellen (1881 -)	3186
Nathan Orlando (1828 -)	1595
Nellie Amy (1874 -)	3181
Ola Blanch (1883 -)	3182
Pamelia (1821 - 1859)	1592
Roswell (1792 - 1792)	774
Samuel Elihu (1843 - 1934)	2320
Sarah (1819 - 1863)	1591
Sarah (1748 - 1769)	303
Sarah Estella (1869 -)	3179
Sarah Opehlia (1850 - 1900)	2330
Susanna (1855 - 1863)	2325
Timothy Burr (1850 -)	2323
Urania (1852 -)	2324
Wirt Ellsworth (1867 -)	3178

GRATHER

Evelyn	spouse of 3327

GRAY

Betti Lorraine (1927 - 2009)	spouse of 3775

GREEN

Askey A.	spouse of 1920
Dorus (1801 - 1876)	spouse of 1656
Sarah (1783 - 1860)	spouse of 577

GREENE

Albert Nathaniel (1840 -)	2448
Ardella Robinson (1838 -)	2447
Charles Thomas (1841 - 1843)	2449
Eleanor Morton (1823 - 1905)	spouse of 1658
Levi Maxley (1851 -)	2452
Sarah Martha (1846 -)	2450
Storrs Douglas (1848 - 1852)	2451
Thomas (1812 - 1896)	spouse of 1657

GREENFIELD

Lottie (1865 - 1914)	spouse of 2444

GREGORY

Eliza (1813 -)	spouse of 1665
Moses	spouse of 922
Quincy Wellington [214] (1914 - >1920)	3515
Roscoe Wellington (1881 - >1920)	spouse of 2733

GREIMAN

Connie Sue (1947 -)	spouse of 3963

GREY

?	spouse of 2739

GRIDLEY

_____ (?)	spouse of 2691
_____ (?)	spouse of 1877
_____	2686
Adrian F. [178] (1901 -)	3478
Albert Lavert [42] (1838 - 1865)	1882
Alice J. [50] (1857 - 1862)	1890
Bessie [108]	2709
Charles L. [91] (1875 - <1920)	2691
Clara B. (?) (1853 - <1920)	spouse of 1882
Clara E. [107]	2708
Clarence LaVerne [185] (1907 -)	3486
Clifford H. [176] (1912 -)	3476
Cora [99]	2699
Earl [103]	2704
Earl Fred [184] (1891 -)	3484
Edith [110]	2711
Edwin L. [104]	2705
Eli L. (1848 - 1916)	spouse of 1879
Elizabeth H. [43] (1842 - 1863)	1883
Elsie P. [46] (1850 - 1862)	1886
Emma A. [38] (1834 - <1920)	1878
Emma J. [40] (1836 - >1920)	1880
Erma Pearl [185] (1900 -)	3485
Ernestine (1933 -)	spouse of 3516
Frederick Laverne [102] (1867 -)	2703
Grace [100] (1877 -)	2700
Hettie V. [49] (1855 - 1862)	1889
Hiram L. [37] (1831 - 1863)	1877
Huldah P. [45] (1847 - 1850)	1885
Jane C. [39] (1835 - 1918)	1879
Jessie [109]	2710
John S. [101] (1893 -)	2702
Lavern [98]	2698
Lena H. [92] (1877 - 1920)	2692
Lewis (0180 - 1878)	spouse of 900
Manley D. [47] (1852 - 1856)	1887
Nettie V. [90] (1871 -)	2690
Pliny Fisk [44] (1845 - 1920)	1884
Rena E. (1879 -)	2701
Robert M. [105]	2706
Rose M. [106]	2707
Roy H. [111]	2712
Unknown Child [112]	2713
Vincent Earl [228] (1918 -)	3802
Viola J. [48] (1854 - 1862)	1888
Vivian L. [177] (1900 - >1920)	3477
Walter E. [89] (1869 -)	2689
Wesley Prince [41] (1838 - 1904)	1881
Winifred L. [179] (1910 -)	3479

GRIFFIN

Absolom (1764 - 1833)	938
Anna (Hannah) (1713 -)	137
Calvin (1769 -)	940
Caroline A. (1838 - 1920)	spouse of 1962

Chedolaomer (1774 - 1878)	941
Chloe (1731 - 1805)	394
Elisha (1740 - <1747)	398
Elisha (1747 -)	399
Elizabeth (~1709 - 1800)	136
Elizabeth (1728 - 1801)	393
Ephraim (1668 - 1725)	spouse of 38
Ephraim (~1718 -)	139
Ezra (1761 - 1843)	937
Martin (1754 - 1830)	401
Micah (1738 - 1815)	397
Nathaniel (1706 - 1786)	spouse of 136
Nathaniel (1732 - 1790)	395
Nathaniel (1758 -)	935
Samantha (1767 -)	939
Seth (1747 - 1817)	400
Sheba (Phoebe, Pheba) (~1722 -)	140
Silence (~1716 - >1726)	138
Stephen (1735 - 1803)	396
Wisdom (1760 -)	936

GRIFFITH

Amanda Elzora (1870 - 1962)	spouse of 2392

GRIMES

Andrew (1865 -)	1783
Arthur (1872 -)	1784
Elizabeth (1811 -)	856
James (1814 - 1888)	857
James Eliot (1851 -)	1781
Mary (1826 -)	860
Miriam (1824 -)	859
Rachel (1822 -)	858
Richard Thomas (1854 -)	1782
Samuel (1809 -)	855
Triphina (1829 - 1912)	861
William (1779 - 1805)	spouse of 362
William (1806 - 1897)	854

GRISWOLD

Hazel R. (1897 -)	spouse of 3325

GROSVENOR

Rita Jean	spouse of 3929

GROVER

Matthew	spouse of 47

GUENTHER

Bessie Olive (1881 - 1962)	spouse of 2787

GUERNSEY

Ahira Harry Johnson (1842 - 1919)	2213
Amy Rosalia (1850 - 1925)	2217
Charles Holbrook (1852 - 1930)	2218
Elliott Birney (1844 - 1844)	2214
Elmer Erastus (1841 - 1858)	2212
Flora Ann (1846 - 1881)	2215
Mary Arvilla (1854 - 1920)	2219
Orpha Jane (1858 - 1937)	2220
Uri Tracey (1811 - 1861)	1229

Vesta R. (1849 - 1850)	2216
GUISE	
George	spouse of 3489
Mary Ellen [235] (1918 -)	3809
HABICH	
Laura (1870 - 1896)	spouse of 2550
HAGAR	
Antoinette Nettie (1854 - 1932)	spouse of 2321
HAGER	
Katherine Alghea (1899 - 1995)	spouse of 3651
HAIGHT	
Elizabeth "Eliza" "Liza" (1825 - 1856)	spouse of 1983
Sarah Ann "Sally Ann" (1829 - 1895)	spouse of 962
HAIS	
Hannah (1759 -)	spouse of 492
HALBERSTADT	
Angela Lynn	4098
Bradley Alan	4099
Calvin Dale	spouse of 3918
Douglas James	4100
Jeffrey Scott	4101
Kenneth Paul	4102
HALL	
Amelia (1859 - 1867)	2400
Amos W. (1831 - 1908)	1631
Anson W. (1827 - 1911)	1629
Bertha Jane (1904 -)	3264
Burton F. (1871 -)	2407
Clyde Thomas (1890 -)	3261
David Schuyler (1836 - 1926)	1633
Eliza Jane (1825 - 1849)	1628
Ella (- 1873)	2399
Favorite Reuben (1905 -)	3265
Floyd Anson (1886 -)	3259
Francis Estella (1895 -)	2402
Francis Siba (1869 - 1893)	spouse of 2413
Grace Almira (1894 -)	3263
Isaac	spouse of 209
Jesse H. (1863 -)	2404
Jessie Adell	spouse of 2413
Lewis K. (1867 -)	2406
Lola Belle (1888 -)	3260
Lucy (?) (- 1908)	spouse of 1631
Mary M. (1833 - 1913)	1632
Mary S. (1866 - 1871)	2405
Mindwell (1730 -)	spouse of 97
Olivia (1797 - 1880)	spouse of 781
Pheba Alice (1892 -)	3262
Price	3266
Rebecca (1838 - 1923)	1634
Reuben Anson (1863 -)	2401
Reuben S. (1795 - 1875)	spouse of 794
Sally Ann (1822 - 1900)	1627
Sarah	spouse of 787

Stephen D. (1860 - 1933)	2403
Washington J. (1829 - 1909)	1630
HALLETT	
Mary (1785 -)	spouse of 486
HAMILTON	
Sally	spouse of 470
HAMMER	
?	spouse of 2807
HAMMOND	
Hannah (1788 - 1854)	spouse of 771
Sabra	spouse of 2056
HANNAFORD	
?	spouse of 3877
HANOLD	
Christoph Henry (1908 -)	spouse of 3848
HANSEN	
Bruce	spouse of 3948
HARLOW	
Marion Jane (1895 -)	spouse of 3326
HARPER	
Armilda	spouse of 1984
Joseph Michael (1989 -)	4268
Robert Joshua Taylor (1992 -)	4267
Robert Thomas	spouse of 4042
HARR	
Hannah Dyantha (1836 - 1917)	spouse of 2149
HARRINGDEN	
Hezekiah (~1744 -)	spouse of 154
HARRINGTON	
Elliott (1996 -)	4404
Scott Wayne (1968 -)	spouse of 4179
HARRIS	
Elvira J. (1847 - 1875)	spouse of 2480
Jon Stuart (1960 -)	spouse of 3972
Michael Orin (1992 -)	4200
Nathan Jon (1986 -)	4198
Rachel Ann (1989 -)	4199
HARRISON	
Jemima (1692 - 1766)	spouse of 33
Josiah (- 1805)	spouse of 984
HARSON	
Allen Ray (1944 -)	3993
Joel Ray (1983 - 1985)	4243
Maurice Ray (1914 -)	spouse of 3783
Stacey Carole (1977 -)	4242
HART	
Asahel (1771 - 1804)	spouse of 722
Elizur (1752 - 1794)	spouse of 721
Erastus Langdon (1787 -)	1533
Hannah (1792 -)	1534
Mary (1744 - 1834)	spouse of 274
Polly (1781 -)	1531
Sally (1778 -)	1530
Sophia (1785 -)	1532

HARTIGAN
  Alice   spouse of 2771
HAUGHT
  Christian Dean (2009 -)   4409
  Jason Frederick (1971 -)   spouse of 4214
  Landon Jason (2007 -)   4408
  Marcina Lynn (2005 -)   4407
HAVENS
  Julia Alice (1840 - 1930)   spouse of 1948
HAWKINS
  Emmett   spouse of 3553
  Marcia Loramack (1921 -)   spouse of 3858
HAYDEN
  Catharine (1826 - 1868)   spouse of 2073
  Frances G. (1817 - 1893)   spouse of 2076
  Jerusha (1739 - 1830)   spouse of 272
  Tirzah (1789 - 1819)   spouse of 991
HAYES
  Ken Victor Jr.   spouse of 3843
  Kirk James (1974 -)   4051
  Logan (1995 -)   4280
HAYS
  A.   spouse of 708
  Bessie Shepperd (1887 -)   3870
  Martin Willet   3869
  Silence (1737 -)   spouse of 174
  Willet Martin (1895 -)   spouse of 3598
HAYWOOD
  Inez   spouse of 2641
HAZELWOOD
  Hannah (1830 - 1912)   spouse of 2129
HEIMAN
  James   spouse of 4356
HEMENWAY
  Abigail (?) (2005 -)   4211
  Edward Eugene (1927 - 1993)   3778
  Edward Michael (1880 - 1948)   spouse of 3430
  Ken (?)   spouse of 3978
  Mason Alexander (?) (2010 -)   4213
  Michelle Ann (1971 -)   3978
  Patti Jean (1955 -)   3976
  Rev. Rhonda Arlene (1958 -)   3977
  Zachary (?) (2008 -)   4212
HENBURY
  Arthur (~1646 - 1697)   spouse of 2
  Elizabeth (~1684 -)   13
  Hannah (1674 - 1759)   11
  Lydia (<1687 - 1689)   15
  Mary (1672 - 1759)   10
  Samuel (1686 - <1687)   14
  Susanna (1682 - 1767)   12
HENDEE
  Oliver S.   spouse of 2117
HENDRICKS

?	spouse of 551
HENDRYX	
Beardsley (1782 - 1829)	1054
David (1784 -)	1055
Fanna (~1820 - ~1820)	2094
Isaiah J. Jr. (1791 -)	1056
Sergeant Isaiah J. (1756 - 1835)	spouse of 462
Lois (1775 -)	1051
Sally (1777 - 1777)	1052
Susannah (1779 - 1810)	1053
Truman (1800 -)	1057
HENDRYX aka HENDRIX, aka HENDRICKS	
Brazilla (aka Barzillai) Squire (~1776 - 1830)	spouse of 376
HENDRYX HENDRIX	
Horace (1811 - 1827)	906
HENDY	
Betsy	spouse of 821
HENRY	
Harvey	2530
John	2531
Lena	2532
Mary	2533
Samuel Trotter (1837 - 1921)	spouse of 1692
Wesley	2534
William	2535
HERRICK	
Lavicia (Lovisey) (1784 - 1832)	spouse of 482
Sarah P. "Sally" (1808 - 1895)	spouse of 894
HETHERINGTON	
?	2589
?	2590
?	2603
?	2604
?	2607
?	2608
?	2609
?	2610
Beatrice (1895 -)	2592
Cecil H. (1895 -)	2602
Edward John (1902 -)	2613
Eleanor Amelia (1850 -)	1727
Eleanor Amelia (1850 -)	spouse of 1742
Ethyl Emma (1890 -)	2601
Harold	2588
Henry (1855 - 1885)	1729
Henry (1882 -)	2587
Joseph (1852 - 1925)	1728
Joseph	2584
Joseph A.	2596
Joseph H. (1821 -)	spouse of 842
Lena May (1899 -)	2611
Lorne Clifford (1890 -)	2591
Lucy (1873 -)	2598
Margery Rebecca (1905 -)	2614

Mary	2585
Mary (1888 -)	2600
Olive J. (1898 -)	2606
Percy Robert (1900 -)	2612
Richard Albert (1849 -)	1726
Robert (1896 -)	2605
Sarah (1856 - 1885)	1730
Sarah Elizabeth (1885 -)	2599
Simpson (1898 -)	2593
Thomas H. (1863 -)	1732
Wesley	2586
William (1859 - 1927)	1731
William A.	2597

HICKOK

Elizabeth (1738 -)	spouse of 206

HICKS

Maria (1839 - 1931)	spouse of 845

HIGGINS

Emma (1881 - 1937)	spouse of 2996

HIGLEY

Cynthia (1797 -)	1516
Elihu (1788 -)	1513
Joel (1764 - 1823)	spouse of 713
Joel Phelps (1802 -)	1518
Lucy (1793 -)	1514
Maria (1799 -)	1517
Polly (1786 -)	1512
Sally (1795 -)	1515

HILDRETH

S. B. (1831 - 1916)	spouse of 1615
Zenas Brown (1878 -)	2366

HILL

? (?)	spouse of 2802
?	spouse of 782
? (?)	spouse of 3716
_____ (1920 - >1920)	3506
_____ (?) (- >1920)	spouse of 1875
_____ (?)	spouse of 1876
Abigail (1664 - 1737)	7
Abigail (1797 - 1815)	967
Abigail (1741 -)	115
Abigail (1769 -)	322
Abigail "Abi" (1836 - 1916)	1999
Abigail Amanda (1832 - 1869)	1997
Abraham (~1740 - 1817)	128
Abraham (1798 - 1883)	918
Abraham Enoch (1763 - 1778)	369
Ada Victoria (1889 -)	2802
Addison (?1830 - >1863)	912
Adelia Emma [152] (1898 - 1984)	3430
Adeline (aka Adaline) (1815 - >1870)	908
Adella L. [70] (1863 - 1910)	2669
Agnes Lurancy [120] (1875 -)	2721
Aimee Knox (1889 - 1918)	2765

Albert (1894 - 1895)	3210
Albert (~1872 -)	2348
Albert G. (1874 -)	2666
Albert R. (~1838 -)	1811
Alfred "Fred"	1790
Alice Clare (1865 - 1947)	2637
Alice Harriet [132] (1885 - >1920)	2733
Alice Mable [119] (1873 -)	2720
Alice May	2767
Alice R. (1867 -)	1858
Alice R. (1860 -)	1929
Allison A. (~1874 -)	2349
Alma Evelyn (1905 -)	3543
Alvin	1789
Amanda (- 1817)	1933
Amanda [24] (1838 - 1887)	1864
Amanda Kay (1979 -)	4163
Capt. Ambrose (1743 - 1816)	287
Amelia (1761 -)	318
Amos W.	1949
Amos W. (1873 - 1887)	2770
Amy (1769 - 1818)	380
Amy (1858 -)	2749
Amy Louise (1962 -)	4035
Andrew (~1851 -)	1847
Andrew William (1994 -)	4275
Ann (~1854 -)	1848
Anna (~1761 -)	415
Anna (1692 -)	26
Anna Pearl (1884 - 1967)	2788
Annie (1779 -)	383
Annie	2807
Aphia (?) (~1731 -)	spouse of 148
Aphia (1764 -)	420
Arden (1775 -)	426
Armanda (1831 -)	1996
Armilda Abigale	2806
Arthur Miller (1898 -)	2794
Arunah I (1754 -)	310
Arunah II (1793 - 1856)	781
Arunah III (1828 -)	1603
Asa (1787 -)	430
Asa Jr. (1776 - 1776)	301
Asa (1719 - 1809)	95
Asa D.D.S. (1815 - 1874)	770
Asenath (1766 -)	421
Aseph King (1802 - 1883)	920
Austin (Justin) (1808 - 1873)	879
Barbara Jo (1943 -)	3920
Barbara Lynn (1969 -)	4161
Benajah (1774 - 1862)	373
Benjamin (1796 - 1876)	872
Benjamin (1735 -)	87
Benjamin (1767 -)	277

Benjamin F. (1830 - 1905)	1604
Benjamin F. "Frankie" (~1859 -)	2343
Benjamin H. (~1854 -)	1821
Bennet John (1964 -)	4037
Benoni (1736 - 1737)	152
Berenice (~1874 -)	3204
Bertram Ladue (1905 -)	3563
Bessie Lyle (1891 -)	2803
Betsey Ann	1942
Beverly	3833
Billious (aka Billie, aka Bellas) (1738 - 1807)	spouse of 119
Billious (aka Billie, aka Bellas) (1738 - 1807)	125
Bradford (1805 - 1885)	834
Bradford L. (1868 -)	2559
Bruce Jon (1956 -)	4045
Bryan Joseph (1947 -)	4012
Bryan Mark (1974 -)	3998
Carlyle (~1840 -)	1835
Carol L. (1943 -)	3949
Caroline (?) (1804 -)	spouse of 884
Caroline "Atlanta" (~1849 -)	1839
Caroline L. (~1902 -)	3422
Carrie Hildreth (1872 -)	2368
Carrie S. (?) (1857 - ?1902)	spouse of 1902
Cecelia (1891 -)	3566
Chad Matthew (1979 - 1988)	4180
Charles (1863 -)	1930
Charles (~1865 -)	2645
Charles 2d (1807 - 1865)	878
Charles A. "Charley" (1868 -)	1852
Charles Austin "Chuck" (1940 - 1969)	3937
Charles E. (~1855 -)	1813
Charles Edwin [63] (1852 - 1934)	1904
Charles Eugene [221] (1914 -)	3766
Charles H. (~1851 -)	1819
Charles John [220] (1921 - 1985)	3765
Charles L. (~1846 -)	1838
Charles McNair (1830 - 1918)	891
Charles Victor (1901 - 1968)	3542
Charles W. (1799 - 1801)	874
Charles W. [20] (1831 - 1923)	1860
Charles W. [20] (1831 - 1923)	spouse of 2928
Charles Willis	1807
Charlotte (1816 -)	883
Charlotte J. [9] "Jane" (1807 - 1892)	896
Child of Frederick and Lillian	2660
Child of Maurice and Blanche	3709
Child of Maurice and Blanche	3710
Child of Maurice and Blanche	3711
Child of Melvyn	3757
Child of Melvyn	3758
Child of Melvyn	3759
Child of Raymond and Edith	3701
Child of Raymond and Edith	3702

Child of Roy and Catherine	3420
Chloe (1759 - 1814)	352
Chloe (~1755 -)	413
Chloe (Cloe) (1754 -)	291
Christopher John (1958 -)	4017
Clarence (1876 -)	3686
Clarence J. (~1901 -)	2652
Clarence Mortimer (1852 - 1898)	3127
Clarence S. (~1887 -)	3205
Clarence Sylvanus [67] (1876 -)	1908
Clarence W. (~1857 -)	2628
Clarice Elva (1898 - 1977)	3213
Clarissa (1789 - 1821)	366
Clarissa (~1782 -)	764
Claude Locke (1884 - 1969)	3565
Cleo Maxine (1905 - 1905)	3218
Cloe (1733 - 1749)	124
Clorinda (1823 - 1905)	1975
Clyde (1916 - 1987)	3704
Constance Elizabeth (1942 -)	3518
Cornelius Haight (1854 - 1933)	1981
Craig Eugene (1950 -)	3922
Cynthia (1776 -)	422
Dale E. [226] (1912 - 1994)	3772
Dale Herschel (1902 -)	3562
Dan	2356
Daniel (1803 -)	786
Daniel (1734 - >1810)	100
Darius (1749 -)	155
Darius (1772 -)	425
Darrell (1948 - 1978)	3837
daughter (~1827 -)	889
Daughter 1 of Luke (~1780 -)	867
Daughter 2 of Luke (~1780 -)	868
Daughter 3 of Luke (~1800 -)	869
Daughter 4 of Luke (~1810 -)	870
Daughter of Elisha and Hanna (Gates)	783
Daughter of Henry & Amanda Hill	2560
Daughter of Kenneth and ? (Escamos)	3720
Daughter of Kenneth and Ruth (Whitney)	3719
David (1748 - 1749)	295
David D. (1891 - 1962)	3208
David Edgar	3229
David Hedgcock "Dave" (1955 - 2004)	3980
dead child (1700 - 1700)	42
Rev. Dean Edwin (1928 -)	3516
Deliverance (1738 -)	31
Della Olaretta (1879 -)	2371
Dian Lynn (1946 -)	3936
Diantha [22] (~1843 - >1895)	1866
Dolly (1784 - 1784)	377
Donald Eugene (1939 -)	3946
Doris Jean (1936 -)	3520
Dorothy Claire (1936 -)	3826

Dorothy May (1936 -)	3836
Dorothy White (1899 - 1968)	3529
Douglas Campbell (1962 -)	4048
Douglas Ray (1947 -)	3964
Drew Edwin (1957 -)	3812
Dustin James (1990 -)	4277
Earl (1920 - 1988)	3707
Earl A. [34] (aka Arthur E.) (1845 - 1921)	1875
Earl Edward Sr. (1908 - 1991)	3544
Earl Edward Jr. (1931 -)	3840
Earl Russell (1881 -)	2372
Earnest L. (1899 -)	2659
Ebben (aka Eben) Sr. (1791 - 1876)	964
Eben B. (aka Ebben, aka Ebon) Jr. (1821 - 1868)	1983
Ebenezer (1687 - 1758)	25
Ebenezer (1756 -)	292
Ens. Ebenezer Jr. (1717 - ~1765)	94
Ebenezer (1746 - 1753)	288
Edgar E. [19] (1829 - 1901)	1859
Judge Edgar S. (~1834 - >1896)	1792
Edith Blanch	2793
Edith Laurel [122] (1880 - 1900)	2723
Edson Harold (1912 - >1995)	3546
Edward (1867 -)	1931
Edwin C. (1828 - 1829)	1614
Dr. Edwin Kay (1933 -)	3835
Rev. Edwin Stoddard D.D. (1837 - >1896)	1794
Eleazer (1694 - 1741)	22
Eleazer Jr. (~1778 -)	423
Eleazer (1732 -)	86
Eleazer (? aka Ebenezer) (~1656 - 1724)	4
Eleazer B. (1727 - >1790)	148
Electa (1777 - 1860)	757
Eli (1782 - 1838)	780
Elias (1780 -)	428
Elijah (~1754 -)	412
Elisha (1759 - 1827)	312
Eliza	922
Eliza Jane (1833 - 1916)	2270
Elizabeth (1710 - >1740)	46
Elizabcth (1681 -)	19
Elizabeth (1771 -)	381
Elizabeth (~1836 - 1838)	1793
Elizabeth (?) (~1700 - 1738)	spouse of 43
Elizabeth (- 2010)	2826
Elizabeth (1666 - >1689)	8
Elizabeth (1751 - 1825)	296
Elizabeth (~1861 -)	2344
Elizabeth Ann (1832 - 1921)	1947
Elizabeth Ann (1801 - 1828)	875
Elizabeth E. (~1839 - >1896)	1795
Elizabeth Merrick [66] (1869 -)	1907
Elizabeth T. (1910 - 2008)	2661
Ellen (Emily) (1848 - 1918)	2361

Ellen G. (1848 - 1853)	1818
Ellenore Elizabeth "Florence" (1896 - 1876)	3212
Elmore D. (1843 - 1854)	1816
Elsie (1897 -)	3404
Elva (Elvira) (~1866 -)	2350
Emaline A. (1846 -)	2748
Emily (1834 -)	1937
Emily (1845 -)	2747
Emily [23] "Emma" (1833 - 1917)	1861
Emily Christine (1888 - 1958)	2789
Emily Welthy (1826 - 1875)	2003
Emma Aurelia (1886 -)	3556
Emma L.	2774
Emma L. (1871 -)	2664
Enoch (1800 - 1867)	919
Enos (1793 -)	915
Enos	1934
Ephraim [2] (1778 - 1832)	375
Ephraim Abram [17] (1824 - 1902)	904
Eric James (1965 -)	4050
Erica Lemay (1992 -)	4278
Erin Julia (1975 -)	4182
Erma Julia (1894 -)	3559
Ernest Oliver "Ernie" (1870 -)	1853
Ernest Oliver "Ernie" (1870 -)	spouse of 2646
Ernest Sylvester [123] (1886 - >1920)	2724
Erwin Dana (1842 - 1934)	1616
Ester M. (1887 -)	2796
Ester M.	2808
Esther (~1765 -)	371
Esther (1812 - 1816)	881
Esther	spouse of 255
Esther Ann (1857 - 1946)	1982
Esther Irene (1874 -)	2369
Eugene (~1873 -)	2352
Eugene "Emogene" (~1867 -)	2346
Eunice (~1793 -)	767
Eunice (1770 - 1860)	spouse of 589
Eunice "Currence" (~1844 -)	1837
Euretta (1883 -)	2373
Eva Esther (1891 -)	3558
Evelyn R. (~1896 -)	2649
Ezekiel (~1850 -)	1900
Father of Georgia and Rosalie	father of 4215 and 4215a
Ferris (1774 - 1863)	382
Ferris (1830 -)	1944
Flora May (1900 -)	3216
Florence Rebecca [130] (1880 - >1920)	2731
Frances (1841 -)	2357
Frances A. (1845 - 1853)	2273
Frances Esther (1889 - 1963)	2790
Francis (1842 -)	1989
Francis (aka Frances) A. (1850 -)	1912
Francis Xavier (1951 -)	4013

Frank (~1870 -)	2632
Frank (~1871 -)	2647
Frank B. (1875 - 1957)	1854
Frank J. (1858 -)	2363
Frank Sherman [127] (1874 -)	2728
Franklin	2763
Fred (1844 -)	1700
Fred E. (1872 -)	2665
Frederick (aka Jaldiacek) (1753 -)	315
Frederick E. [128] (1880 - >1920)	2729
Frederick W. (1878 - 1933)	1855
Garlin	2831
Gary (~1857 - <1870)	2342
Genevieve Maude [218] (1916 - 1982)	3763
George (1839 - 1907)	1950
George	2762
George C. (~1868 - >1896)	2630
George J. [68] (1857 - 1952)	2667
George J. [8] (1805 - 1876)	895
George J. [8] (1805 - 1876)	spouse of 2091
George James M.D., D.Litt. (1932 -)	3779
George Noble [134] (1898 - 1980)	2735
George R. (1846 -)	1910
George W. (1821 - 1881)	910
George W. (1834 -)	1605
George W. (~1875 -)	2353
George Washington [21] (1837 - 1917)	1863
Georgia Clare (2004 -)	4215
Hon. Gerald Albert "Jerry"	3716
Gerald Leslie [153] "Gerry" (1905 - 1979)	3431
Gertrude Eloise (1887 -)	2562
Gladys Joan (1929 -)	3752
Glen W. "Clem" (~1894 -)	2648
Glendalia (1909 -)	3219
Gordon Lundin [205] (1916 -)	3505
Grace (1898 - 1898)	3214
Grace Lodawesca [150] (1892 - 1894)	3428
Gregory	3717
Gwendolyn Ann (1986 -)	4189
Gwendolyn "Babe" (1901 - 1952)	3215
H. Laverne	2775
Hannah (~1706 - 1766)	45
Hannah (1689 - 1775)	23
Hannah Eliza (1825 -)	1941
Hansel Ferris	3532
Hansel S. (1822 - 1893)	1939
Harland Eugene [146] (1885 - 1968)	3424
Harland P. [28] "Harlow" (1847 - 1869)	1868
Harmon W. (1821 - 1901)	1938
Harriet (1827 - 1853)	1943
Harriet (1801 - 1822)	887
Harriet Alice	3531
Harry "Hervey" (1826 -)	1985
Harsey (1797 - 1855)	917

Harsey Jr. (1831 - 1831)	1946
Harvey Dale (1828 - 1867)	1610
Harvey S. (1799 - 1852)	886
Hazel (1887 -)	2367
Heather (1982 -)	4001
Heather Dawn (1982 -)	4214
Helen C. (1883 -)	3232
Helen Mae [212] (1919 - >1920)	3513
Helen Martha	2772
Helen Mildred	3537
Helen Winifred (1893 -)	2563
Helena Rundall "Lana" (1964 -)	3982
Henrietta (1843 -)	2358
Henry	907
Henry (~1834 -)	1834
Henry (1827 -)	2002
Henry [10] (1809 - 1812)	897
Henry [15] (1819 - 1892)	902
Henry B. (1857 -)	1927
Henry Kniffen (1886 -)	2561
Henry Reuben (1843 -)	1699
Herbert	1608
Herbert (~1869 -)	2351
Herbert Albertis [II] (1914 - 2005)	3221
Herbert H. (1910 -)	3564
Hettie H.	2644
Hiram (1831 -)	1988
Homer	2829
Homer C. (1852 -)	1820
Horace (1812 - 1836)	769
Horace B. (1855 -)	1822
Howard (1918 - 2004)	3705
Howard Eugene [215] (1909 - 1983)	3760
Hoyt	1788
Hulda (1742 -)	102
Huldah (?) (~1780 -)	spouse of 373
Huldah (1736 - 1737)	101
Huldah [13] (1815 - 1885)	900
Huldah Jane [11] (1810 - 1812)	898
infant (1793 - 1793)	965
Infant (~1700 - 1702)	41
Ira (1755 - 1841)	316
Ira (1787 -)	784
Ira Z. (1877 -)	2370
Isaac (~1804 - <1870)	884
Isaac Sr. (1703 - 1741)	30
Isaac [1] [Jr.] (1740 - 1833)	127
Isaac [5] Jr. [III] (1772 - 1860)	372
Isaac Curtiss (1843 - >1896)	1796
Isaac Edwin [18] (1829 - 1904)	905
Isaac H. (1836 - 1849)	1814
Isaac L. (~1831 -)	1833
Isabel (aka Isabella) (1806 - 1860)	970
Isadora (1846 -)	2360

Keith Edwin	3820
Kenneth E. (1923 - 1990)	3223
Kenneth Elvin (1933 -)	3519
Kerry Edward	3821
Kerry Edward (1975 -)	3817
Kevin Dale (1965 -)	4178
Kevin Eugene	3819
Kezia (1724 - 1726)	111
Kezia (1733 - 1801)	spouse of 98
Kezia (1733 - 1801)	113
Keziah (~1759 -)	414
Keziah (1695 -)	27
Kilbourn (Kilborn) (1786 - >1849)	364
Kittie A. (1867 -)	2663
Kristin Sue "Kris" (1968 -)	4179
La Vonne Ilene [225] "Bonnie" (1919 -)	3770
Ladue (1803 - 1886)	969
Ladue	2824
Lafayette F. (1855 - 1935)	2810
Larrisa	2809
Larry Dean (1960 - 1977)	3969
Leander Charles (1902 - 1984)	3217
Lela	2773
Lela Esther (1930 -)	3774
Lena E. (~1869 - >1896)	2631
Leola Grace [217] (1913 - 1983)	3762
Leroy George [147] "Lee" (1886 - 1975)	3425
Leverett Benedict (1831 - 1892)	1791
Leverett H. (~1859 -)	2629
Leverett (Leveritt) (1798 - 1851)	873
Lewis	782
Lily (1870 -)	1932
Lois (1770 -)	424
Lois (1766 - 1766)	314
Lois Erma (~1899 -)	2650
Lolita Fay (1900 -)	3560
Lorinda	1974
Louis Sylvester (1905 -)	3406
Louise [86]	2685
Lowly (~1791 -)	766
Lucina (1769 -)	758
Lucina (1761 -)	293
Lucy (1853 -)	1925
Lucy (- 2010)	2827
Lucy (1836 - 1909)	2271
Lucy I. (~1858 -)	1915
Ludlow (1794 - 1873)	966
Ludlow Jr. (1821 -)	1992
Ludlow Presly (1829 - 1915)	1995
Luella Florence (1900 -)	3561
Luke (1826 - 1923)	888
Luke [III] (1698 - 1772)	28
Luke Jr. (1661 - 1740)	6
Luke Sr. (~1613 - ~1695)	1

Mary Jane (1824 - 1892)	1940
Mary Jane (1880 - 1904)	2797
Mary K. (?) (- 1943)	spouse of 2798
Mary M. [27] (~1845 -)	1867
Mary Myrtle (1903 - 1904)	3547
Mary Nanno	3539
Mary R. (?) (~1884 -)	spouse of 2666
Matilda	1976
Matthew Dean (1976 -)	3999
Maude Leoto (1884 -)	2800
Maurice (~1909 -)	2658
Maurice Gilbert (1893 - 1952)	3209
Max Leroy [223] (1913 - 1990)	3768
Maxine (1924 - 1990)	3708
May (1861 -)	2364
Megan Caroline (1985 -)	4181
Melissa Ann (1967 -)	4160
Melvin Leroy (1919 - 1992)	3222
Melvyn R. (1938 - 2006)	3421
Michael Dean (1956 - 1956)	3967
Michael Gorman (1833 - 1911)	892
Michael Richard (1946 -)	4011
Michelle (1977 -)	4000
Miles (1774 -)	761
Miles (1766 - 1815)	324
Milo	1970
Minnie Marie (1921 - 2006)	3771
Molly Regan (1959 -)	4046
Morris Seth (1823 - 1908)	2266
Mrs. Luke (1769 - <1830)	spouse of 370
Munroe B. [33] "Murray" (1841 - 1864)	1874
Muriel [209]	3510
Myra (1804 - 1826)	768
Myron [208]	3509
Myron B. "Myra" (1859 - 1954)	1849
Myron Emery Jr. (1927 -)	3773
Myron Emery [148] (1888 - 1955)	3426
Myrtle O. "Maybelle" (1878 -)	spouse of 1853
Myrtle O. "Maybelle" (1878 -)	2646
Nancy (1862 -)	1857
Nancy (1757 -)	311
Nathan (1865 - 1900)	2638
Nathaniel (~1865 -)	2345
Nellie (1882 -)	2799
Nellie L. [62] (1861 - 1911)	1903
Nellie Leola [149] (1890 - 1894)	3427
Nelly	2828
Nettie "Lorene" (1920 - 1993)	3823
Noble [12] (1812 - 1903)	899
Noble John Leland [64] (1855 - 1863)	1905
Norma Jean (1927 -)	3751
Nye Robinson [36] "Henry" (1853 - >1920)	1876
Oladine S. (1834 -)	1615
Olive Amanda (1800 - 1836)	368

Ruby Alice (1910 -)	3846
Ruth (?) (~1790 -)	spouse of 915
Ruth Elizabeth (1891 -)	2791
Ruth Elizabeth [219] (1918 - <1997)	3764
Ruth Emily (1805 - 1872)	877
Ruth Irene (1911 - 1982)	3545
Ruth Queenie [135] (1899 - 2000)	2736
Ryan Douglas (1977 -)	4183
Ryan William (1977 -)	4116
Sadie W. (1882 - 1968)	3688
Sally (1792 -)	785
Sally Betsey (1781 - 1828)	376
Sally Rae (1946 -)	3921
Samantha [14] (1817 - 1878)	901
Samuel (1781 -)	384
Samuel (1795 - 1874)	916
Samuel (1773 -)	760
Samuel (1748 - 1766)	289
Sanford Clark (1796 -)	1497
Sarah (1697 - 1736)	40
Sarah (~1687 -)	21
Sarah (1740 -)	153
Sarah (1778 -)	427
Sarah (1737 -)	114
Sarah (1762 -)	319
Sarah M.A., Ph.D. (1962 -)	3981
Sarah (1760 -)	298
Sarah [26] (1835 - 1925)	1862
Sarah Ann (1828 -)	890
Sarah Elizabeth (1992 -)	4279
Sarah M. (1830 - 1917)	2269
Sarah "Sally" B. (1814 - 1865)	882
Sealton [144] (1898 -)	2745
Seth (1734 - 1736)	151
Seth (~1848 -)	1846
Seth [6] Slone (1776 - 1853)	374
Seth Morris (1799 - 1896)	1572
Seymour (1788 - 1796)	365
Sharon Jean (1939 -)	3923
Sherman B. [61] (1855 - >1922)	1902
Sidney T. (~1866 - 1895)	2633
Sienna Glory (1976 -)	4187
Son #1 of Lewis	1606
Son #2 of Lewis	1607
Son of Luke (~1780 - <1830)	866
Sophia (1803 - 1875)	876
Sophronia	1972
Stephen (1737 -)	88
Steve Clar (1951 -)	3947
Steven Dale (1941 -)	3962
(Stillborn) (1972 -)	4114
Stilson Edward [30] Sergeant (1838 - 1917)	1870
Susan (- 1806)	1968
Susannah (?)	spouse of 1993

Sybil	spouse of 281	
Sylvester (1810 - 1878)	880	
Sylvester (1855 - >1930)	2340	
Sylvester Bruce (1867 - 1933)	2639	
Sylvester J. [16] (1821 - 1840)	903	
Sylvester J. [58] (1846 -)	1898	
Syrene C. [35] "Cyrena" (1838 - 1854)	1873	
Tahan (1691 -)	24	
Tahan "Tahay" (1659 - 1692)	5	
Taryn	3917	
Thankful (1756 - 1799)	spouse of 285	
Theda Albertis (1879 - 1943)	2355	
Thelma Louise (1912 - 2004)	3220	
Theodore J.P. (1817 - 1896)	909	
Theresa Mary (1861 - 1951)	1850	
Thomas David "Tom" Sr., Ph.D. (1935 - 2003)	3780	
Lt. Col. Thomas David "Tom" Jr., USAF (ret) (1962 -)		3984
Thomas Flynn (1959 -)	4018	
Titus (aka Silas) (1752 - 1820)	309	
Titus (Linas) (1725 - >1790)	97	
Tracy Elizabeth (1964 -)	4049	
Truman Olvord "O. B." (1838 -)	1815	
Tyler Dean	4249	
Unnamed daughter	1613	
Unnamed son	1611	
Unnamed son	1612	
Urania (1773 - 1774)	323	
Uri (1760 -)	337	
Uri (1759 -)	317	
Uri (1729 - <1769)	112	
Uri (Uriah) (1771 -)	300	
VanAger [4] (~1785 -)	378	
Velda Mae [222] (1909 - 1996)	3767	
Verd	2830	
Vesta Eloise [71] (1881 - 1970)	2670	
Victoria Grace (1960 -)	3983	
Vina	2811	
Vincent Gerard (1963 -)	4020	
Virgil Reed [60] (1853 - 1895)	1901	
Wallace (1854 -)	2362	
Warren (~1779 -)	763	
Wealthia (1845 - 1888)	2359	
Wealthy (1767 - 1852)	417	
William (1831 - 1891)	1840	
William (1761 - 1761)	353	
William (1827 -)	1986	
William (~1915 - 2005)	3703	
William Amos	2771	
William Benjamin [145] "Ben" (1883 - 1924)	3423	
William Clayton (1890 - 1891)	3207	
William Edwin [131] (1882 - >1924)	2732	
William F. (1848 -)	1911	
William Ferris	2768	
William George Robert "Bob"	3530	

William Henry (1875 - 1969)	2787
William John (1877 -)	2798
William L. [69] (1860 - 1869)	2668
William Prince [7] (1804 - 1885)	894
William R. (1855 -)	1926
William Riley (1835 -)	1998
William Roswell (1832 - 1900)	913
William Smith (1826 - 1898)	1602
William Smith II (1862 - 1928)	2341
William Wallace (1853 - 1949)	2812
Willis Edgar (1857 - 1918)	2365
Willow (b. Cindy Lou) (1954 -)	3966
Woodrow (~1919 - 1986)	3706
Zenas (1764 -)	320
Zenas (1730 -)	98
Zenas (1730 -)	spouse of 113
Zeruiah (1763 -)	419
Zervia B. (?) (~1731 -)	spouse of 148

HILLIARD

Charlotte Cordelia (1876 -)	spouse of 3569

HILLS

Beriah (1727 - 1778)	spouse of 271
Chauncey (1754 -)	705
Lois (1752 -)	704
Mary (1748 -)	703

HILL-SIMPSON

Rebecca Elizabeth "Becky" (1950 -)	3939

HILLYER

Alma (1799 -)	1450
Chloe (1790 -)	1446
Harriet (1797 -)	1449
Laura (1792 -)	1447
Seth	spouse of 688
Seth (1788 -)	1445
Sybil (1786 -)	1444
Tracy (1794 -)	1448

HILTON

?	2615
Joseph (1879 - 1939)	spouse of 1751

HINES

Margaret (1700 - 1826)	spouse of 775

HINKLEY

Widow Ann Maria	spouse of 2025

HINMAN

Harriet Newell (1816 - 1865)	spouse of 2025
Lucy	spouse of 2755

HOADLEY

Eunice Almira (1822 - 1894)	spouse of 1251

HOCKINGS

Brittany Elissa Anne (1976 -)	4108
Erika Leigh (1971 -)	4107
Paul	spouse of 3921

HOLCOMB

Benajah Philo (1764 - 1828)	spouse of 687

Benajah Philo (1784 -)	1437
Betsey (1807 -)	1443
Caleb (1695 - 1758)	spouse of 38
Charles E. (1882 -)	spouse of 3321
Damaris (1724 - 1797)	spouse of 276
Hull (1790 -)	1439
Jonathan	spouse of 17
Linus (1794 -)	1440
Mary (1786 -)	1436
Salmon (1797 - <1801)	1441
Salmon (1801 -)	1442
Samuel (1786 -)	1438

HOLKINS

Sarah (1808 - 1870)	spouse of 1181

HOLLAND

Elizabeth (1729 -)	spouse of 116

HOLLENBECK

Eugenia Diana (1882 - 1957)	spouse of 3568
Leah (1776 - 1850)	spouse of 480

HOLLEY

Charlotte	spouse of 905

HOLLINGSHEAD

Rushia E. (1878 - 1911)	spouse of 2355

HOLMES

Harriet Cornelia (1867 - 1959)	spouse of 2113

HOPKINS

Keziah (1795 - 1871)	spouse of 1094
Sylvia (1768 - 1813)	spouse of 480

HORN

Priscilla	spouse of 750

HOSFORD

Emerson H. Shaw (1832 - 1880)	2083
Uriah (1796 - 1866)	spouse of 996

HOSKIN

Daughter of Lesie and Ruth (Davis)	3594
Flora (1904 - >1925)	2940
Inez (1857 - 1877)	2112
Jasper (1854 - 1938)	2111
Lena Zenita (?) (1896 -)	spouse of 2934
Lesie V. (1907 - 1996)	2941
Lydia (1852 - 1853)	2110
Mary (1901 - >1920)	2939
Neri (1796 - 1865)	1123
Neri Brownrigg (1859 - 1933)	2113

HOSKINS

Affa (1893 - 1980)	2936
Carl (1887 -)	2933
Earl (1885 -)	2932
Garland (1898 -)	2938
Joseph (1698 - 1782)	spouse of 46
Joseph (1731 - 1818)	176
Neri (1895 - >1900)	2937
Stanley (1889 -)	2934
Stella (1891 -)	2935

Theodore (1766 - 1839)	491
HOSMER	
Lavinia	spouse of 980
HOTCHKISS	
Susanna (1752 -)	spouse of 244
HOTELLING	
Clair Albert (1869 - 1944)	3672
Four sons and two daughters of Clair and Lucy (Rawson)	3891
Myrta May (1868 -)	3671
Vera Litta (1882 -)	3673
HOUGH	
Albert L. [95]	2695
Alice [97]	2697
Ann (~1830 - 1854)	1799
Cephas [96]	2696
Cordelia	1800
Ellen (~1838 - 1855)	1801
Frances M. (~1842 -)	1804
Huldah [94]	2694
Infant 1	1805
Infant 2	1806
John (- 1872)	spouse of 877
Jonathan T. (~1840 - 1846)	1803
Sanford (- <1920)	spouse of 1880
William G. (~1835 - 1872)	1802
HOUGHTALING	
Hiram Addison (1843 - 1896)	spouse of 3075
HOUGHTON	
Electa (1832 - 1906)	spouse of 2033
HOUT aka HOYT, HART	
Mary (<1636 - >1697)	spouse of 1
HOWARD	
?	spouse of 2692
Annie (1878 - 1960)	spouse of 2445
Chloe	spouse of 629
Clarence R. [180]	3480
Elsie R. [183] (1918 -)	3483
Ruth A. (1820 -)	spouse of 1960
Violet R. [181] (1915 -)	3481
Virginia L. [182] (1917 -)	3482
HOWE	
Alice B. [115] (1867 - >1920)	2716
Asa L. [116] (1877 - >1920)	2717
Augusta E. [52] (1839 - 1917)	1892
Charlotte P. [54] (1844 - 1908)	1894
Francis Sylvester [53] (1842 -)	1893
Gervis P. [51] (1836 - 1908)	1891
Lewis [57]	1897
Lora S. [118] (1878 - >1920)	2719
Mary Ann (1839 -)	spouse of 2137
Mary Jane [55] (1849 -)	1895
Smith J. [56] (1854 - 1920)	1896
William P. (- 1892)	spouse of 901
HOWELL	

Mary (1805 - 1828)   spouse of 812

HOWLAND

Abigail (1754 - 1830)   spouse of 349

HOWZE

Susan (1825 -)   spouse of 1618

HOYT

Grace I. (1918 -)   spouse of 3784

HUBBARD

Sarah Maria (1851 - 1941)   spouse of 2416

HUBBELL

Catherine (1826 -)   1843

David Toucey (1827 -)   1844

Edward (1830 -)   1845

George Albert (1824 -)   1842

Horace (1822 -)   1841

Joseph Middlebrook (1800 - 1831)   spouse of 887

HUGHES

Lydia M. (1864 - 1941)   spouse of 2480

HULBERT

A.   spouse of 707

HULL

Charles Frederick (1859 -)   2915

Edwin Alonzo (1853 -)   2914

Harriet Frances (1849 -)   2912

Lois   spouse of 280

Norman Augustine (1843 -)   2910

Orson LaRue (1863 -)   2916

Sabrina (1846 -)   2911

Samuel P. (1818 - 1878)   spouse of 2077

Wilmot Benjamin (1851 -)   2913

HUMASON

Elizabeth Catherine (1872 -)   3583

Jeremiah (1781 -)   spouse of 1005

John Eno (1876 -)   3585

Julia Harriet (1883 -)   3586

Lawrence Cole (1891 -)   3588

Marjorie Florence (1886 -)   3587

Virgil Pettibone (1847 - 1905)   2917

William Lawrence (1821 -)   2086

William Lawrence (1821 -)   spouse of 2256

William Lawrence (1853 -)   2918

William Wallace (1873 -)   3584

HUMBERT

Constance Rose (1945 -)   3932

Galen Rose Solomon (1913 - 1956)   spouse of 3763

Jeanine Kay (1940 -)   3931

HUMES

?   spouse of 2459

HUMISTON

Clyde Myron (1892 -)   3665

Darius (1833 - 1886)   spouse of 2166

Ellsworth Munson (1894 -)   3666

Emma Genevieve (1860 - 1942)   3040

Glenwood Carlisle (1859 - 1868)   3039

Glenwood Warren (1889 -)	3662
Harry Robert (1901 -)	3669
Hugh Darius (1901 -)	3668
Joseph Harold (1896 -)	3667
Olive Ellen	3663
Ralph Carlyle (1890 -)	3664
Warren Todd (1862 - 1938)	3038
HUMPHERVILLE	
Orissa Caroline (1823 - 1880)	spouse of 2224
HUMPHREY	
Allen (1777 -)	1020
Asaph (1732 - 1774)	spouse of 254
Caroline "Carrie" (1853 -)	spouse of 2511
Chloe (1782 -)	1022
Elijah (1747 - 1788)	spouse of 457
Elza	spouse of 629
Emily (1806 -)	spouse of 2058
Hannah (1796 - 1877)	spouse of 988
Harry (1780 -)	1021
Naomi (1794 - 1863)	spouse of 994
Sarah	640
Sarah (1768 -)	spouse of 667
Susannah	spouse of 648
HUMPHREYS	
Hepzibah	spouse of 643
HUNGERFORD	
E. B. (- <1892)	spouse of 1861
Rhoda	spouse of 656
HUNT	
David Floyd (1872 - 1953)	spouse of 2314
Fanny	spouse of 1055
Fanny (1792 - 1858)	spouse of 976
HUNTER	
?	spouse of 4076
Living Daughter of Winifred (Shepperd)	4322
Living Daughter of Winifred (Shepperd)	4323
Living Son of Winifred (Shepperd)	4321
HUNTLEY	
Bertha Mae "Mae" (1886 - 1975)	spouse of 3432
HURLBUT	
Chauncey Butler	2015
Gordon	spouse of 974
Gordon Trumbull (1807 -)	2014
Rhonda Lucretia	2016
Talcott Ledyard	2017
HUSSEY	
Barbara	spouse of 3841
HUSTED	
Bartholomew (1790 - 1839)	spouse of 792
Ella (1853 -)	2374
Frank (1858 -)	2376
Huldah (1829 - 1902)	1619
Ransom (1827 -)	1618
Ulysses (1856 -)	2375

Frank	3413
Pierce	spouse of 2643
JEFFREY	
Estelle (1861 -)	spouse of 3036
JENKINS	
Aundrea Marie (1974 -)	4132
Daniel Martin (1929 -)	spouse of 3517
John Daniel (1983 -)	4005
Kathleen Ann (1978 -)	4004
Marilyn (1951 -)	spouse of 3935
Melissa Lynn (1983 -)	4133
Roger (1947 -)	spouse of 3934
Scott Douglas (1956 – 1974)	3815
Timothy Edwin (1953 -)	3814
JERN	
Charles Oscar (1881 - 1958)	spouse of 2801
Vivian Rosalie (1917 - 1956)	3551
JEWELL	
Jerusha (1802 - 1856)	spouse of 1184
Laura B. (1836 - 1863)	spouse of 1646
Lucy (1813 - 1884)	spouse of 1188
Mirza (1804 - 1887)	spouse of 1185
JILOVEC	
Julie Ann	spouse of 4119
JOHNSON	
?	spouse of 3877
_____	spouse of 4070
Asa	spouse of 2020
Caleb (1746 - 1771)	388
Cornelius (1705 - 1768)	spouse of 130
Cornelius (1744 -)	386
Garel Lee (1936 -)	spouse of 3931
Hannah (1761 -)	spouse of 478
Jacob Austin (1992 -)	4368
Jeffery Scott (1960 -)	4127
Jeremiah Solomon (1989 -)	4367
Jonah Scott (1997 -)	4369
Lemuel (1745 -)	387
Living Child of Margaret (Brewer)	4089
Marie Margaret (1912 - 2000)	spouse of 3761
Orphana (1748 -)	390
Paul	spouse of 2805
Ruphus (1747 -)	389
Sarah (1765 - 1830)	spouse of 470
Sarah Jane (1835 - 1899)	spouse of 891
Sheryl Lynn (1963 -)	4128
JOHNSON JANES	
Helen V. Mrs. (1915 -)	spouse of 3766
JONES	
Almira	951
Anson	952
Clarissa	953
Cornelius R.	spouse of 2061
Delia	spouse of 1792

Elizabeth "Betsy" Maria	954
Helen M.	spouse of 1794
Ira	955
Israel (1801 - 1846)	spouse of 2036
Lucius Wadsworth (1829 -)	2870
Luna (1786 - 1862)	spouse of 474
Mary	956
Nancy	957
Sarah	958
Solomon (1754 - 1822)	spouse of 407
Sophia	959
William	960

JUDD

Ebenezer (1703 - 1734)	spouse of 52
Hannah (1731 - 1736)	184
Julia (- <1792)	spouse of 492
Lovina Gertrude (1850 - 1887)	spouse of 2126
Ruth (1733 - 1736)	183

JUDSON

Alanson	1451
Elisha (1765 -)	spouse of 689
Elisha (1796 -)	1456
Gordon	1452
Lucy	1453
Sylvanus	1454
Sylvester	1455

JUDY

Martin	spouse of 3522

JUHL

Anna Paulette (?)	spouse of 3928
Christopher Duane (1973 -)	4123
Connie Rae (1959 -)	4117
David Stanley (1965 -)	4119
Donald Robert (1939 -)	3929
Donald Tyler (1999 -)	4362
Grace Leola (1934 - 1934)	3926
Joshua Robert (2001 -)	4363
[male] (1966 - 1966)	4125
Mason Christopher (~1993 -)	4359
Michael Robert (1963 -)	4118
Raymond Paul (1938 -)	3928
Richard Harold (1935 -)	3927
Robert C. (1912 - 1958)	spouse of 3762
Robert Stewart (1971 -)	4122
Roberta Marie (1934 - 1934)	3925
Ronald Eugene (1941 -)	3930
Shannon Ca (1968 -)	4120
Shelly Raye (1970 -)	4121
Tamera Kay (1968 -)	4126
Tyler David	4360

KAUFFMAN

Infant child of Samuel and Mary (Frisbie)	3120
John Earl (1886 -)	3119
Samuel Stern (1855 -)	spouse of 2247

KEANE
Mary Agnes (1926 -)   spouse of 3825
KEARNS
Metha (~1862 - 1881)   spouse of 1919
KEELING
John Leslie (1883 -)   3111
Mary Frances (1872 -)   3110
W. M. (1837 - 1895)   spouse of 2245
KEENE
Lydia (1839 -)   spouse of 1633
KEENEY
Betsey (1796 - 1867)   spouse of 773
KEITH
_____   3909
_____   3910
Donald (1906 -)   3911
Dorothy Elliott (1907 -)   3912
Robert Russell (1879 - 1937)   spouse of 3694
KELLY
John H.   spouse of 831
KELSO
?   spouse of 2811
KEMP
Jenette (aka Genette) Catherine (~1838 -)   spouse of 892
KENDALL
Eveline (1816 - 1862)   spouse of 1581
KENNEDY
Clara (1861 - 1924)   spouse of 2425
KENNY
Jane (1840 -)   spouse of 1721
Maria (1852 - 1922)   spouse of 1723
Robert (1808 - 1896)   spouse of 856
KENT
Kenneth Ronald (1927 -)   spouse of 3776
KENTFIELD
?   1652
?   1653
?   1654
?   2458
?   2459
?   3313
Abigail S. (1871 - 1871)   3336
Annie Jane (1862 - 1939)   2457
Annie Louise (1892 - 1950)   3318
Arthur Baker (1884 - 1960)   3315
Esther Adelia (1858 - 1923)   2455
Frank (1858 - 1901)   2460
Frederick Baker (1845 - 1927)   2453
Helen M. (1898 - 1999)   spouse of 3320
Henry L. (1869 - 1869)   3335
James Frederick (1895 - 1971)   3320
Jennie (1894 - 1999)   3319
Jeremiah B. (1818 - 1894)   1658
John (1822 - 1894)   1659

John Greene (1848 -)	2454
John Theodore (1891 - 1950)	3317
Laurana (1805 - 1864)	1656
Mary Elinor (1880 - 1926)	3314
Mary Lucy (1872 - 1876)	3312
Nellie Frances (1886 - 1922)	3316
Nellie Lamson (1865 - 1914)	2461
Nellie Rebecca (1860 -)	2456
Palmon (1780 -)	797
Rebecca (1808 - 1885)	1657
Shem (1750 - 1782)	spouse of 342
Smith (1804 - 1804)	1655
Warren	798

KERN

Roger Le John (1937 -)	spouse of 3934

KERNS

Jim	spouse of 2547

KESSELER

Marilyn Blanche (1939 -)	spouse of 3924

KESSLER

Elizabeth	4094
William	4095
_____	spouse of 3915

KETCHUM

Charles H. (1850 -)	2752
Eliza H. (1863 - 1941)	2757
George W. (1852 - 1887)	2753
Ira P. (1857 - 1942)	2755
John (1821 - 1890)	spouse of 1940
Martha E. (1866 - 1899)	2758
Mary E. (1859 -)	2756
Sarah Emily (1854 - 1905)	2754
Warren B. (1847 - 1849)	2751
Wilbur J. (1844 - 1912)	2750

KEYS

Abigail (1767 - 1850)	spouse of 465

KILBOURN

Sybil (1732 - 1789)	spouse of 116

KILBOURNE AKA KILBORN

Rhoda (1759 - >1849)	spouse of 126

KILBY

Abigail (1760 - 1859)	spouse of 416

KILPATRICK

Bernard (1865 -)	3172
Elmer (1862 -)	3171
Eva (1868 -)	3173
Fred (1858 -)	3169
Hattie (1880 -)	3177
Hugh (1832 - 1921)	spouse of 2318
Jesse	3168
John (1870 -)	3174
Lydia May (1875 -)	3176
Nathan (1872 -)	3175
William (1860 -)	3170

KIMBALL

Carrie H. [78] (1866 - 1894)	2672
Chester Lazell (or Luzelle P.) (1837 - 1871)	spouse of 1864
Everett Cleveland [173] (1900 -)	3440
Irwing H. [174] (1906 - 1906)	3441
Sarah "Sadie" L. [77] (1862 - >1887)	2671
William E. [79] "Willie" (1868 -)	2673

KING

Fannie	spouse of 2512

KINGSLEY

Elizabeth Ann (1812 - 1903)	spouse of 1673

KINNAN

Jasper J. (1875 - 1917)	spouse of 2731
Ruth Elizabeth [211] (1911 - >1920)	3512
Wesley Jasper [210] (1903 - >1920)	3511

KINSEY

?	spouse of 2802
Forrest	3552

KIRTLAND

Ester	spouse of 678
Richard	spouse of 1559

KISLING

Beth (1962 -)	4220
Fred (1934 - 1988)	spouse of 3985
Kenneth (1959 -)	4219
Kristi (1955 - 1979)	4217
Lori (1957 -)	4218

KITTREDGE

Jessie (1845 - 1929)	spouse of 2917

KLAPPERICH

Allison Lee (1987 -)	4196
Benjamin Stephen "Ben" (1990 -)	4197
Stephen (1957 -)	spouse of 3971

KLINE

Elmer J.	spouse of 2410

KNIFFEN

Mary Belinda (1865 -)	spouse of 1700

KNIGHT

Ruhana P. (1809 - 1891)	spouse of 1147

KNOEDLER

Andrew Keith (1960 -)	4154
Angela Marie (1977 -)	4378
Anthony Lee (1959 -)	4153
Beth Charlene (1936 -)	3942
Brian Matthew (1994 -)	4400
Cyndee (Cindy) Kae (1980 -)	4158
Cynthia "Cyndee"/ "Cindy" (1959 -)	4146
David John	4149
Deborah Jo (1955 -)	4143
Destiny Marie (1986 -)	4393
Diana Lou (1960 -)	4145
Elmer Laurel Sr. (~1907 - 1984)	spouse of 3767
Elmer Laurel II (1930 - 1987)	3940
[Infant son]	3944

Jacob (1995 -)	4384
Jane (?)	spouse of 4148
John LeRoy (1935 - 1995)	3941
Jonathan Thomas (1996 -)	4382
Josiah David (1994 -)	4394
Keith Maurice (1937 - 2008)	3943
Lawrence Thomas "Larry" (1964 -)	4148
Lurretta (1954 -)	3945
Margaret (?)	spouse of 4149
Matthew Lawrence (1994 -)	4381
Pamela Lynn (1962 -)	4155
Peggy Ann (1975 -)	4157
Roxanne Lee (1954 -)	4142
Samantha J. (1988 -)	4379
Sarah (1993 -)	4383
Timothy Laurel "Tim" (1957 -)	4144
Todd David (1966 -)	4156
Vickie Lynn "Vicki" (1960 -)	4147

KNOWLES

Lucille	spouse of 3858

KORNS

Cora Belle (1852 - 1897)	spouse of 2383

KOVASH

Richard	spouse of 3839

KROME

Frederick W. (- 1982)	spouse of 2736

KUNZELMAN

Nellie (- 1923)	spouse of 2746

KYTONEN

Anna (1995 -)	4372
Craig (1965 -)	spouse of 4138

LACKEY

Desdamona	spouse of 1609

LACY

Penelope (1756 - 1826)	spouse of 327

LADIEU

Jane (~1708 - 1732)	spouse of 43

LAGEE

John Franklin	spouse of 2417

LAGONEGRO

Elizabeth (1958 -)	spouse of 3812

LAIRD

Mildred Rose (- 1953)	spouse of 2804

LAKE

Sarah	spouse of 820

LAMPSON

A. (1758 -)	spouse of 710
Silas S.	spouse of 830

LANE

Albert Harry (1861 -)	3029
Alfred Henry (1827 -)	2158
Alfred Henry (1859 -)	3031
Alice (1853 -)	2179
Alice Handsome (~1885 - >1910)	3650

Allice (1856 -)	spouse of 3034
Allice R. (1883 - >1900)	3649
Asahel (1817 - 1885)	1189
Ashhel Albert (1838 -)	2174
Augustus L. (1824 - 1893)	2160
Bruce B. (1848 -)	3034
Bruce B. (1879 - >1900)	3647
Charles (1834 - 1839)	2163
Daniel (1779 - 1865)	spouse of 556
Daughter of Harold and Mabel I.	3887
Daughter of Harold and Mabel I.	3888
Daughter of Harold and Mabel I.	3889
Daughter of Richard and Kathleen (Hager)	3885
Daughter of Richard and Kathleen (Hager)	3886
Elizabeth (1804 - 1830)	1187
Elizabeth (1843 - 1846)	2164
Emily E. (1888 - 1889)	3656
Eri Leonard (1824 -)	2156
Eugene (1843 -)	2176
Eula (1881 - >1900)	3648
Florence Selina (1853 -)	3026
Frances (1846 -)	2178
Grace A. (1875 - >1900)	3645
Harold Benjamin (1914 - 1988)	3890
Harold Charles (1892 -)	3653
Harriet Louise (1850 -)	3030
Herbert (1849 - 1893)	3035
Horace B. (1842 - 1862)	2175
Ida M. (~1877 - >1880)	3646
James E. (1886 - 1887)	3655
John D. (1831 - 1864)	2162
Leonard (1814 - 1843)	1188
Linus (1799 - 1880)	1184
Lucas (1801 - 1885)	1185
Lucia (1802 - 1864)	1186
Lucia (1829 -)	2161
Lucinda (1834 - 1834)	2172
Lyman Jewell (1827 - 1863)	2157
Mabel I. (?)	spouse of 3653
Maria Elizabeth (1857 -)	3027
Martha (1890 -)	3657
Mary Elizabeth (1836 -)	2159
Miriam (1844 -)	2177
Richard J.	3651
Robert Orange (1836 - 1862)	2173
Rufus H. (1884 - 1885)	3654
Son of Richard and Kathleen (Hager)	3884
Theodore T. (1889 -)	3652
William Edgar (1859 -)	3028

LANG

Robert Wells (1963 -)	spouse of 3976
Ryan Wells (1991 -)	4209

LANGDON

Abi (1775 - 1807)	723

Susan Amanda (1847 - 1868)	1651
William Thomas (1884 -)	3307

LEIFHEIT
Arthur Ervin (1905 - 1961)	spouse of 2661
Child of Arthur and Elizabeth	3417
Child of Arthur and Elizabeth	3418
Lorraine Ann (1936 - 2006)	3419

LEONARD
Abigail (1815 - 1838)	2001
Calvin (- 1838)	spouse of 967

LEONHARDT
Rachel Antoaneta (1992 -)	4302
Robert Hoy (1949 -)	spouse of 4065

LEONHART
Ross Owen (1991 -)	4301

LESH
Margaret	spouse of 3538

LEVEQUE
Jerome (1909 - 1969)	spouse of 4071	
Living Daughter of Jerome and Catherine (Shepperd)		4305
Living Son of Jerome and Catherine (Shepperd)	4306	
Ruth Anne (1938 -)	4307	

LEWIS
Jane Rosanna (1822 - 1863)	spouse of 1268
John M.D. (1793 - 1834)	spouse of 1177
Karen Denise	spouse of 4050
Lucy (1724 - 1789)	spouse of 74

LHOMMEDIEU
Albert Whitman (1893 -)	3660
Anella L. (1895 -)	3661
Delos Gager (1857 -)	3036
Perrin	3658
Ramond D.	3659
William Albert (1865 -)	3037
William Wallace	spouse of 2165

LINDSAY
Adella Helen [229] (1915 -)	3783
Barbara (1970 -)	4246
Delbert (1941 -)	3990
Donna (1942 -)	3994
Edwin Everett "Ed" (1952 - 1994)	3996
Eileen (1948 -)	3992
George Edwin "Ed" [154] (1888 - 1973)	3432
James (1966 -)	4236
James (1970 -)	4238
James Edwin [228] (1914 - 1964)	3782
James W. (1859 -)	spouse of 2669
Lori (1979 -)	4248
Louisa Mae (1938 -)	3989
Mary (1974 -)	4237
Maxine Bernice [227] (1910 - 1982)	3781
Ronald (1977 -)	4247
Ronald LaVern (1918 - 1966)	3784
Russell Dean (~1947 -)	3995

Thresa Jo (1963 -)	4235
Verlyn (1946 -)	3991
LINES	
Jane (1828 -)	spouse of 2157
LITTLE	
Wealthy (Welthes) (1793 - 1870)	spouse of 784
LOCKE	
Emma Melissa	spouse of 2810
LOCKWOOD	
Amelia L. (- >1920)	spouse of 1870
Thomas B.	spouse of 3375
LOMBARD	
Percis (1770 - 1801)	spouse of 570
LONG	
Clark W.	spouse of 3781
Ebenezer (1707 -)	51
Helen (1947 -)	3988
James (1939 -)	3986
Jeff	4224
Jennie E.	spouse of 3137
Jimmy (1962 -)	4221
John (1967 -)	4223
Lydia (1697 -)	47
Mary (1703 -)	50
Mildred (1935 -)	3985
Nicole	4225
Ronald (1963 -)	4222
Sarah (1701 -)	49
Wayne (1942 -)	3987
William (1689 - 1740)	spouse of 10
William (1699 -)	48
LOOMIS	
Ebenezer	spouse of 137
LORD	
Walter	spouse of 2188
LORING	
Amanda M.	spouse of 1699
LOVENSHEIMER	
Glenn Ralph	spouse of 3526
LOVING LOVERING	
Eliza	spouse of 2143
LUKE	
Harriet Rosetta (1858 - 1926)	spouse of 2425
LUNDAHL	
Brenda (1957 -)	4230
Loran (1935 -)	spouse of 3989
Mike (1964 -)	4233
Paul (1962 -)	4232
Rhonda (1960 -)	4231
Rich (1971 -)	4234
Tom (1954 -)	4229
LUNDIN	
Florence (1890 - >1920)	spouse of 2724
LUSSY	

? [Living]   spouse of 4071
LYON
    Melinda (Malinda) (1813 - 1892)   spouse of 878
LYONS
    Jeanette (1914 -)   spouse of 3782
MAHNKE
    Adam Richard (1977 -)   4257
    Harold Lawrence   spouse of 4027
MALLISON
    Joseph (1728 -)   spouse of 256
MALLORY
    Claude (1878 -)   3191
    Estella R. (1886 -)   3193
    Gracie (1891 -)   3195
    John Dow (1888 -)   3194
    Maud (1876 -)   3190
    William (1849 - 1925)   spouse of 2324
    Zella (1883 -)   3192
MALLORY MALLARY MALLERY
    Eunice (1747 - 1805)   spouse of 127
MALTBY
    Hannah (1746 - 1778)   spouse of 199
MANEE
    Jennie Matilda (1855 - 1921)   spouse of 2453
MANN
    Betsa (1795 -)   1154
    Chester (1800 -)   1157
    David (1770 - 1850)   spouse of 514
    Lydia (1796 -)   1155
    Lydia   spouse of 515
    Reuben (1810 -)   1159
    Sally (1798 -)   1156
    William (1804 -)   1158
MANNING
    Philina (1818 - 1873)   spouse of 385
MANSFIELD
    Grace (1800 - 1852)   spouse of 2160
    Harriet (1818 - 1884)   spouse of 1189
MARINER
    Carleton (- 1983)   spouse of 3545
MARKSBERRY
    Mary Lee (~1941 -)   spouse of 3946
MARSH
    Amy (1792 - 1865)   spouse of 772
MARSHALL
    Elizabeth Ann (1982 -)   4266
    Ellen Gail (1953 -)   4040
    James Wilson (1955 -)   4041
    Richard Donald   spouse of 3838
MARTIN
    Abigail (1800 - 1876)   spouse of 793
    Louisa (1821 - 1843)   spouse of 1680
    Nellie Hollet (1888 - 1965)   spouse of 2961
    Wilson Josiah (1912 - 1994)   3612

MASON
  Ira   spouse of 862
MATSON
  Lucy (1741 - 1805)   spouse of 262
MATTES
  Garrett Rollins (1984 -)   4110
  Graham William (1980 -)   4109
  William (1945 -)   spouse of 3921
MATTHEWS
  Aaron (1721 - 1806)   spouse of 66
  Aaron (1744 - 1802)   213
  Caleb   spouse of 13
  Hannah   spouse of 100
  Reuben (1743 - 1777)   212
  Reuben (1774 -)   583
  Ruth Elizabeth (1776 -)   584
  Samuel (1761 - 1812)   214
  Sarah (1767 -)   581
  William (1772 -)   582
MATTISON
  Noel   spouse of 2035
MAWER
  Mabel   spouse of 2406
MAXWELL
  ?   3400
  ?   2617
  Doris Elizabeth (1909 -)   3402
  Doris Elizabeth (1909 -)   2619
  Elizabeth (1864 -)   1751
  Fanny   spouse of 843
  James (1832 - 1913)   spouse of 847
  Jane (1877 -)   1755
  Lila (1907 -)   3401
  Lila (1907 -)   2618
  Nellie   2616
  Robert (1865 - 1931)   1752
  Sarah (1872 - 1949)   1754
  William (1869 - 1931)   spouse of 2583
  William (1869 - 1931)   1753
  William James (1913 -)   3403
  William James (1913 -)   2620
MAY
  Elizabeth (1836 - 1921)   spouse of 2470
  Martha (1837 - 1918)   spouse of 2471
MAYNARD
  Amanda B. (1833 - 1903)   2290
  Antoinette (1835 - 1917)   2291
  Eveiline (1836 -)   2292
  Henry C. (1846 -)   spouse of 2279
  Henry C. (1846 -)   2293
  Nathan (1810 - 1877)   spouse of 1578
MCALESTER
  ?   spouse of 1726
McALLISTER

Eleanor Jane (1810 -)	spouse of 837
Jennie (1777 - 1857)	spouse of 357
Mary Ann (1805 -)	spouse of 836
William Blumer	spouse of 1720

McBETH

Harold (1895 - 1979)	spouse of 3430

McCARTY

JoAnna (1855 - 1929)	spouse of 1901

McCLEAN

Hector	spouse of 1724

McCLURE

T. J.	spouse of 779

McCOLLOM

Sarah	spouse of 2478

McCONNEL

Jane (1828 - 1918)	spouse of 857

McCULLEY

?	spouse of 2791

McDONALD

____	spouse of 4068

McDUFFIE

Beth Ione (1914 -)	4351	
Clair (1912 - 1912)	4350	
Donald Maynard (1916 - 1986)	4352	
Living Daughter of Donald and Kathryn (Rhoads)		4421
Living Daughter of Ronald and Betty (Ward)	4422	
Living Son of Ronald and Betty (Ward)	4423	
Maynard Henson (1890 - 1977)	spouse of 4085	
Ronald Clifford (1916 - 1995)	4353	

McFALL

William (1904 - 1962)	spouse of 3727

McFARLAND

Lillian K. (1890 - 1968)	spouse of 3208

McFERRIN

Martha F. (1829 - 1877)	spouse of 1671

McGINNIS

Daniel Lee "Dan" (1964 -)	4245
David Lee (1962 -)	4244
Larry	spouse of 3994
Lauryn Celia (1992 -)	4411
Ryan Daniel (1989 -)	4410

McILWAIN

Ella Mae M. (1899 - 1972)	spouse of 3528

McKEAN

Elizabeth	spouse of 212

McKINNEY

?	spouse of 1967

McKINSEY

Bessie (1854 - 1925)	spouse of 2546

McKINSTRY

Albert "Bus"	3852
Charles	3851
Jap	spouse of 3590

McKINZIE

Emma E. (1836 -)	spouse of 2340
McLEOD	
Christy (1862 - 1926)	spouse of 2812
McMACKEN	
Robin	spouse of 3984
McMILLAN	
Margaret Elise	spouse of 4122
McNALLY	
Peter	spouse of 4104
McNAUGHTON	
Margaret S.	spouse of 2013
McNETTON	
Dixon H.	spouse of 2315
MELLICK	
Lydia Ann (1830 -)	spouse of 1595
MENUEY	
Baby boy (2011-)	4404f
Douglas Weston (1978-)	4172b
Hannah Rae (2006-)	4404e
Joel Anthony Jr. (1982-)	4172c
Joel Anthony Sr. (1949-)	spouse of 3958
Michele (1975-)	4172a
Sidney Henry Ford (2008-)	4403d
Weston Leigh (2005-)	4403b
MERRELL	
Abi (1769 - 1848)	spouse of 438
MERRIAM	
Mary (1805 - 1843)	spouse of 786
MERRILL	
Aaron	spouse of 57
Adeline (1820 - 1891)	1250
Annie (1858 - 1898)	2232
Charles (1850 -)	2230
Charles Frisbie	1252
Elen Augusta	1254
Elijah Frisbie (1788 - 1852)	609
Ellen Taylor (1856 - 1927)	2231
Franklin B.	1256
George D.	1255
Henry Augustus (1815 - 1890)	1248
Huldah	1253
Ichabod (1754 - 1829)	spouse of 221
John Frederick (1836 -)	1257
Junius Frisbie (1812 - 1879)	1247
Mary Elvira (1849 - >1900)	2229
Nathan F. (1823 - 1909)	1251
Prudence (1782 -)	608
Sally Maria (1818 - 1890)	1249
Sarah (1791 - 1813)	610
Theda	spouse of 472
METCALF	
Jason (1971 -)	spouse of 4130
Mary Eleanor (1924 - 2005)	spouse of 3696
MICHELSON	

Carey (1960 -)	4022
Dean	spouse of 3826
Douglas (1957 -)	4021
Tracey	4023

MICKELSON

Emma Otilda (1886 - 1977)	spouse of 3424

MILES

Martha Jane (1860 - 1927)	spouse of 2554

MILLAR

George	spouse of 2419

MILLER

Clifford P.	3575
Dan Edward (1954 -)	spouse of 4091
Fanny (1867 -)	3579
Flora (1863 -)	3577
Frank H. (1869 -)	3580
Fred S. (1871 -)	3581
Jason B. (1830 - 1894)	spouse of 2909
Jennifer Alice (1984 -)	4356
Laura Jane (1860 - 1927)	spouse of 1979
Laura Marie (1980 -)	4355
Lois (1865 -)	3578
Mary Amanda (1830 - 1830)	2930
Maud E. (1878 -)	3582
Mildred Gracia (1860 -)	3576
Sandy	spouse of 4008
Thomas B. (- 1841)	spouse of 2090
Walter	spouse of 3536

MILLS

Charlotte (1794 -)	1388
Harmon (1801 -)	1390
Homer (1807 -)	1392
Maria (1828 - 1867)	spouse of 2074
Robert (1792 -)	1387
Teresa (Terrissa) (1830 - 1911)	spouse of 2266
Thomas Delaun (1770 - 1824)	spouse of 670
Uriah M. (1799 -)	1389
William	spouse of 1669
William Bainbridge (1805 -)	1391

MINAR

Julia A. (~1822 - 1900)	spouse of 902

MINCH

Nellie	spouse of 2715

MINSTER

Peter	spouse of 2814

MOLLAND

Hannah (1838 - 1889)	spouse of 2148

MOORE

Azuba (1761 - 1820)	spouse of 458
Ellis P. (1858 -)	spouse of 2242
Mary Ellen (1852 -)	spouse of 2323
Rachel (1780 - 1855)	spouse of 685

MORAN

Helen Mary	3536

Michael F.	spouse of 2767
Richard (Harry)	3535
MOREY	
Ann Eliza (1830 - 1901)	spouse of 2155
Jeanette Mae (1870 - 1960)	spouse of 2428
MORGAN	
?	2805
Amazette H. (1814 -)	spouse of 1958
J. Laird (1932 -)	3554
James (1853 - 1945)	spouse of 1982
Jennie A. (1880 - <1918)	spouse of 1854
Jesse Riley (1893 -)	2804
Loretta Anne (1953 -)	3845
MORRIS	
Amanda M.	spouse of 888
Rebecca June (1848 - 1905)	spouse of 2462
MORVILLE	
Francois Eugene (1841 - 1908)	spouse of 2475
Mary Annette (1867 -)	3339
MOSES	
Almira (1795 -)	1379
Anna (1792 -)	1361
Auria	1358
Charlotte (1771 -)	666
Charlotte (1797 -)	1371
Chester (1800 -)	1372
Curtis (1792 -)	1369
Daniel (1729 - 1778)	spouse of 257
Daniel (1758 - 1805)	659
Daniel (1791 -)	1360
Elizabeth (1824 - 1891)	spouse of 1258
Elvira (1810 -)	1376
Festus	1359
Hannah (1769 -)	665
Hannah (1805 -)	1382
Horace (1803 -)	1373
Linus (1789 -)	1367
Lois (1749 -)	spouse of 155
Lois (1766 - 1781)	663
Lois (1806 -)	1383
Mark (1808 -)	1384
Mary (1775 -)	660
Mary (1797 -)	1377
Matthew (1799 -)	1380
Mercy (1758 - 1756)	spouse of 459
Myron (1805 -)	1374
Norman (1797 -)	1362
Pliny (1791 -)	1368
Pluma (1807 -)	1375
Roger (1767 - 1828)	664
Ruth (1801 -)	1381
Salmon (1792 -)	1378
Sybil (1763 - 1854)	661
Theodosia (1795 -)	1370

Zebina (1764 - 1815)	662
Zebina (1786 -)	1366
MOSS	
Anna (1750 -)	spouse of 194
MOURHESS	
Barbara (1937 -)	3830
Byron (1947 -)	3831
Kendra (1949 -)	3832
Kenneth (1915 - 1967)	spouse of 3534
MULFORD	
John	spouse of 2532
MULLIGAN	
John James	spouse of 1755
Mary (1867 - 1906)	spouse of 1732
MUNDIS	
Mary Ellen (1830 - 1893)	spouse of 1685
MUNGER	
Mary E.	spouse of 1687
MUNRO	
Hannah (1788 - 1822)	spouse of 702
MUNSON	
Aaron (1796 -)	567
Chauncey (1806 -)	569
Eli (1797 -)	568
Elizabeth (1717 - 1777)	spouse of 61
Isabel (1862 - 1933)	spouse of 3038
Leone Pauline (1907 -)	spouse of 3760
Lucretia (1786 -)	563
Orpha (1792 -)	566
Russell (1784 -)	562
Samuel (1741 - 1791)	spouse of 201
Sophia (1789 -)	564
Unetia (1789 -)	565
Waitstill (1755 -)	spouse of 204
MURDOCK	
——	spouse of 3953
Cindy	4166
Donna	4165
Leroy	4168
Tom	4167
MURPHY	
Alicia Marie (1988 -)	4380
John Patrick (1953 -)	spouse of 4145
William J.	spouse of 3490
MYERS	
Mary Ann	spouse of 888
MYRICK	
Adah Rosina (1883 - 1919)	3694
Charles H. (1856 - 1908)	spouse of 3136
Grace Estelle (1881 -)	3693
Sadie Dell (1879 - 1960)	3692
NAMBARA	
Keiko (1928 - 1977)	spouse of 3780
NEARING	

Mary (1847 -)	2197
Matthew Simeon (1812 - 1874)	1203
Moses Frisbie (1780 -)	558
Nelson B. (1879 -)	2205
Oliver T. (1844 -)	2194
Ozias (1753 - 1840)	spouse of 200
Ozias Rowe (1806 -)	1200
Perris L. (1821 -)	1198
Philo (1808 -)	1193
Philura (~1793 -)	spouse of 971
Rodney Frisbie (1807 - 1871)	1201
Sarah M. (1846 -)	2196
Selden S. (1813 -)	1204
Simeon Newton (1791 - 1847)	561
Stephen Ludington (1810 -)	1202
Susannah (1774 - 1806)	555
Theda (1812 - 1900)	1195
Turchus (1849 -)	2199
Walter (1850 -)	2200
Ziba (1782 -)	559

NORTWICH
Van	spouse of 2319

NOWLES
Sarah	spouse of 789

NYHUS
Kretta	spouse of 4172b

OBRIEN
Christopher	spouse of 4121

OCONNELL
Aimee (1921 - 1941)	3828
David Brian (1950 -)	4026
Dennis Malcolm "Denny" (1947 -)	4024
Gregory Keith (1981 -)	4259
James Richard (1923 -)	3829
John Thomas (1896 - 1968)	spouse of 3529
John White (1917 - 1975)	3827
John White (1948 -)	4025
Joshua Brandon (1987 -)	4260
Karen Renee (1952 -)	4027
Kenneth Richard (1979 -)	4258
Kevin Jay (1958 -)	4029
Richard Keith (1952 -)	4028

ODLAND
Andrew Nels (1985 -)	4193
Cara LeAnn (1990 -)	4194
Colin Earl (1993 -)	4195
Daniel Eugene (1964 -)	3973
David Earl "Dave" (1954 -)	3970
Earl Stenson "Bud" (1926 -)	spouse of 3774
Laura Lee (1956 -)	3971
Lauren Elizabeth (2001 -)	4203
Lisa Ann (1960 -)	3972
Lukas Daniel (1992 -)	4201
Matthew Clarence (1994 -)	4202

OGLEVEE
    Emma Elizabeth (1859 - 1888)   spouse of 2365
OLCOTT
    James   spouse of 457
    Samuel   spouse of 432
OLDHAM
    Gerald E. (1919 - 1985)   spouse of 4075
    Living Daughter of Gerald and Hannah (Shepperd)   4316
    Living Daughter of Gerald and Hannah (Shepperd)   4317
    Living Daughter of Gerald and Hannah (Shepperd)   4318
    Living Daughter of Gerald and Hannah (Shepperd)   4319
    Living Daughter of Gerald and Hannah (Shepperd)   4320
OLDS
    Elidicy (1769 - 1855)   spouse of 511
    Mary (1785 - 1869)   spouse of 805
OLMSTEAD
    _____   spouse of 3150
OLMSTED
    Cyrus   3010
    Frances   3011
    Helen   3012
    Orville   spouse of 2152
    Royal   3013
OLSEN
    Edward Hunter (1865 - 1907)   spouse of 3614
    Stella (1892 -)   3878
OLSON
    Annette Arliene (1963 -)   spouse of 3970
    Forest Whitefield (1905 - 1986)   spouse of 3856
    Jane Luella (1949 -)   4065
    Jeff   spouse of 4172
    Lauri   4402
    Owen James (1945 - 1988)   4064
    Scott   4403
OMAN
    Estella   spouse of 2728
ORDEN
    Maryann Helen (VAN) (1832 - 1925)   spouse of 1596
ORE
    Eloise (1917 - 1987)   spouse of 3827
OSTROM
    Hannah Catherine (1864 - 1901)   spouse of 1851
    Mary Ann   spouse of 2063
OVERBAUGH
    William   spouse of 2737
PACKER
    Rachel Rebecca (1793 -)   spouse of 561
PADDOCK
    Emily Corning (- 1879)   spouse of 719
PAINE
    Helen Mar (1826 - 1870)   spouse of 1582
PAINTER
    Mary A. (1873 - 1943)   spouse of 2388
PAJEL

Sylvia   spouse of 3500

PALMER

? [Living]   spouse of 4307
Caroline Maria (1854 -)   spouse of 2168
Ella Mae (1871 -)   spouse of 2703
Living Daughter of Ruth (Leveque)   4417
Living Daughter of Ruth (Leveque)   4418
Mary (1708 -)   spouse of 53

PARDEE

Elizabeth   spouse of 70
Philande (1826 -)   spouse of 1638

PARKER

Alphonso (1804 -)   1141
Anna (1760 -)   spouse of 252
Bettie (1763 -)   510
Bradford (1950 -)   spouse of 4046
Cynthia (1797 -)   1139
Daniel (1767 -)   512
Eleazer (1802 -)   1140
Eli (1774 -)   515
Eli (1798 -)   1161
Elias (1765 - 1813)   511
Elizabeth (?)   spouse of 506
Hannah (1761 -)   509
JOsiah (1812 -)   1146
Lawrence S.   spouse of 2027
Logan Peale (1987 -)   4271
Lucy (1784 -)   1133
Lydia   1160
Marah (1754 - 1844)   505
Mary "Polly" (1796 -)   1138
Nelson (1806 -)   1136
Olive   1142
Orange   1143
Orra (1788 -)   1135
Phebe (1771 - 1830)   514
Rebecca Colline (1989 -)   4272
Samuel (~1730 - 1814)   spouse of 179
Samuel (1759 - 1844)   508
Samuel (1784 -)   1134
Samuel   1144
Sarah (1757 -)   507
Shared (1794 -)   1137
Triphene (1769 - 1842)   513
William (1755 - 1791)   506
William   1145

PARKS

Benita (1980 -)   spouse of 3813

PARMELEE

Abigail (1703 - 1733)   36
Abigail (1721 -)   130
Adeline Maria (1829 -)   2257
Almira A. (1811 - 1855)   1559
Barbara (1778 -)   751

Bela (1776 -)	739
Benjamin (1705 -)	37
Caleb (1663 - 1714)	spouse of 7
Caleb Jr. (1696 - 1750)	33
Charles Henderson (1853 -)	2264
Child of Rev. James Hill	1571
Chloe (1739 -)	134
Daniel (1739 - 1800)	278
Daniel (1770 -)	738
David (1763 -)	736
David Dudley (1801 - 1872)	1554
Elias (1752 - 1829)	285
Elias	1560
Elias Harvey (1789 -)	754
Eliza (- 1826)	1556
Ellen Stevens (1846 -)	2263
Emily Starr (1844 -)	2265
Ermina Starr (1838 - 1839)	2260
Ezra (1745 - 1838)	281
Ezra (aka Ezrah) (1714 - 1800)	spouse of 90
George Stevens (1835 - 1837)	2258
George Stevens (1839 -)	2261
Hannah (1667 - >1693)	spouse of 5
Hannah (1694 - 1761)	32
Hannah (1782 -)	752
Henry Starr (1842 -)	2262
Hiel (1756 - 1836)	286
Rev. James Hill (1783 - 1872)	750
James Smith (1820 - 1864)	1555
Jemima (1750 -)	283
Jerusha (1741 - 1819)	279
Jerusha (1729 -)	133
Josiah (1701 - 1720)	35
Justin (1750 -)	284
Laura P. (1795 - 1855)	1558
Lemuel (1786 -)	753
Lydia (1699 - 1726)	34
Marietta	1557
Mary (1722 -)	131
Nathan (1766 -)	737
Oliver (1748 - 1821)	282
Parnel (1769 -)	749
Peter	spouse of 283
Rebecca (1741 -)	135
Samuel (1743 - 1808)	280
Sarah (1724 - 1767)	132
Susan Catherine (1837 - 1869)	2259
Thankful (1795 -)	755
William (1849 -)	spouse of 2229

PARRISH

John (1671 - 1748)	spouse of 32

PARSONS

Anna (1836 - 1907)	spouse of 2224
Frances Eliza (1828 - 1867)	spouse of 1526

Sarah Catherine Tilton (1820 - 1844)	spouse of 1526
PATCHEN	
Olive (1790 - 1879)	spouse of 702
PATTERSON	
?	spouse of 3419
Child of Lorraine	3753
Child of Lorraine	3754
Child of Lorraine	3755
Child of Lorraine	3756
PATTISON	
Pamela (1808 - 1884)	spouse of 1171
PAUL	
_____	spouse of 1919
_____ (?)	spouse of 3525
[Baby] (1865 -)	1924
Barbara Jean (1933 -)	3526
Betty Ann	3525
Carrie F. (1860 - 1941)	1922
Charles B. "Cass" (1862 - 1941)	1923
Charles Laurence "Sonny" (1920 -)	3523
Charles Ross "C. R." (1880 - 1948)	2746
Cora Nellie (1901 - 1976)	3521
Donald Roswell	3524
Flora C. (1859 -)	1921
Francis "Frank" (1852 - 1900)	1918
George W. (1857 -)	1920
James Mason (1821 - 1900)	spouse of 911
Minnie M. (1879 - >1920)	spouse of 2729
Phonetta A. (1850 -)	1916
Roswell Hill (1855 - 1888)	1919
Thomas (~1851 - ~1851)	1917
Virginia Helen (1917 - 1988)	3522
PAYNE	
Elizabeth Smith (1874 - 1908)	spouse of 1576
Laura Eliza (1821 - 1881)	spouse of 1672
PEABODY	
Ellen K. (1862 -)	spouse of 2427
PEACHER	
Anna Chilton (1830 - 1920)	spouse of 1695
PEART	
Adam Leslie (1852 -)	spouse of 2720
Edith Reay [202] (1912 -)	3502
Leslie Jay [200] (1897 -)	3500
Ralph Melvin [201] (1903 -)	3501
PECHE	
Lauren Gray (1987 -)	4208
Leroy Leonard (1950 -)	spouse of 3975
PECK	
Charles	spouse of 2161
Hiram	spouse of 2035
Susan Elizabeth (1938 -)	spouse of 3842
PEDERSON	
Rev. Mark C.	spouse of 4043
Noel Christine (1987 -)	4269

Paul (1989 -)	4270
PELHAM	
Ruth Etta (1920 - 1989)	spouse of 3890
PERKINS	
Anna (1792 - 1881)	spouse of 609
Charles (1808 - 1860)	spouse of 1587
Pamelia J. (1850 - 1922)	spouse of 2320
PERRY	
Harriet W. (1828 - 1861)	spouse of 1696
Kenneth	spouse of 3955
Kenneth D.	4169
Kirk	4170
Kyle	4171
PETTIBONE	
Elizabeth (1803 -)	spouse of 628
Henrietta (1826 - 1906)	spouse of 1269
PFAFF	
Beverly (1955 -)	4033
John	spouse of 3834
Lenore (1959 -)	4032
Mark (1954 -)	4031
Sharon (1961 -)	4034
Simon (1990 -)	spouse of 4261
PHALEN	
Govinda Jonas (1992 -)	4190
Jack III	spouse of 3966
PHELPS	
Abel (1730 - 1805)	spouse of 271
Abel (1756 -)	709
Abigail (1790 -)	1499
Achsah (1758 -)	710
Alexander (1769 - 1852)	spouse of 725
Alexander Cotton (1794 -)	1538
Benjamin (1773 - 1848)	716
Candis (1769 -)	714
Clarissey (1802 -)	1511
Cynthia (1767 -)	713
Cynthia (1786 -)	1498
Edward (1802 -)	1541
Elizabeth (1804 -)	1542
George Alexander	spouse of 3570
Horace G. (1797 -)	1539
Jaman Hart (1799 -)	1540
James Enos (1771 - 1822)	715
James Enos (1793 -)	1519
Job	spouse of 666
John (1795 -)	1508
John Jay (1810 -)	1545
Lucy (1807 -)	1521
Lydia (1717 -)	1524
Mary (1754 -)	707
Mary (1812 -)	1523
Mary Ann (1808 -)	1544
Mehitable (1756 -)	708

Mindwell (1760 - 1835)	711
Norman (1806 -)	1543
Philo (1804 -)	1520
Sarah (1672 - ~1707)	spouse of 9
Sarah (1765 - 1840)	712
Sarah (1786 -)	1506
Sherman David (1814 -)	1546
Timothy (1796 -)	1509
William (1762 - 1847)	spouse of 712
William (1794 -)	1507
Willis (1810 -)	1522
Willis Abel (1799 -)	1510

PHILLIPS

Elwin [141] (1901 -)	2742
Ethel Belle [136] (1890 -)	2737
Harriet Ruth [137] (1893 -)	2738
Henry Clay [140] (1899 -)	2741
Leslie Lamont [143] (1909 -)	2744
Living Daughter of Manning and Shirley (Shepperd)	4327
Living Son of Manning and Shirley (Shepperd)	4326
Manning	spouse of 4079
Mary [138] (1895 -)	2739
Pauline [139]	2740
William [142] (1904 -)	2743
William Warner	spouse of 1907

PICKERING

Emma (1862 - 1934)	spouse of 3596

PICKETT

Lafayette F. (1846 -)	2185
Peres M. (1843 -)	2184
Peter (1800 -)	spouse of 1195

PIERCE

James Theophilus (1831 - 1897)	spouse of 2329
Lafayette	spouse of 2286
Nancy Maria (1809 -)	spouse of 2059

PIERSON

Betsey (1796 -)	1219
Damaris (1753 -)	spouse of 278
Edward (1793 -)	1218
Heman (1828 - 1863)	spouse of 1650
John (1790 -)	1216
Mary (1798 -)	1220
Orestes Cook (1863 - 1876)	2446
Uzal (1763 - 1836)	spouse of 575
Uzal (1791 -)	1217

PIKE

Harvey (1794 -)	spouse of 989

PINNEY

Dorcas (1778 - 1838)	spouse of 647
Lydia (1759 -)	spouse of 651
Ruhamah (- 1776)	spouse of 168

PITCHER

Elizabeth (1819 -)	spouse of 1122

PLANT

Abraham	spouse of 208
Elizabeth Barnes (1828 -)	spouse of 910
PLUCK	
Josephine (1890 -)	spouse of 3146
PLUMB	
Sibble	spouse of 121
PLUMMER	
?	spouse of 2790
POHL	
Joann Kay (1939 -)	spouse of 3927
POMEROY	
Elinor	spouse of 3329
POOLER	
Mary Ann	spouse of 646
POPPE	
Living Daughter of Walter and Bonita (Shepperd)	4342
Living Son of Walter and Bonita (Shepperd)	4343
Living Son of Walter and Bonita (Shepperd)	4344
Living Son of Walter and Bonita (Shepperd)	4345
Walter Henry (1916 -)	spouse of 4083
PORTER	
? (1776 - 1797)	spouse of 788
Post	
Esther (1759 - 1851)	spouse of 316
POTTS	
? [Living]	spouse of 4084
POWELL	
Edward J.	spouse of 1922
Guy Richard (1949 -)	spouse of 3518
Joseph Douglass (1977 -)	3818
Meredith Louise (1975 -)	3817
Shannan Elizabeth (1974 -)	3816
POWERS	
Clara Gertrude (1886 -)	3872
Martha Houston (1805 - 1858)	spouse of 1662
Miles Henry (1884 -)	3871
Sanford (1861 - 1936)	spouse of 3600
Sumner Leslie (1889 -)	3873
PRATT	
Albert Harrison (1835 - 1923)	2299
Ella A. (1851 - 1930)	2301
Ellen (1848 -)	2300
George Nathaniel (~1842 - 1901)	2297
Mary F. (~1843 - 1925)	2298
William Henry Harrison (1812 - 1880)	spouse of 1580
PREHM	
Coulter	4387
Paige	4388
Tony	spouse of 4151
PREMO	
_____	spouse of 4298
PRESCOTT	
Catherine Elizabeth (1800 - 1875)	spouse of 2057
PRESLEY PRESLY	

Lydia (1800 - 1880)	spouse of 966
PRESTON	
Hannah (1734 -)	spouse of 177
PRIEST	
Carleton	spouse of 1892
Fred O. [114] (1869 -)	2715
William B. [113] (1864 - 1917)	2714
PRINCE	
Charlotte {31} (1781 - 1871)	spouse of 375
PRIOR	
Arline Rose (1893 -)	3064
Ethel Miriam (1878 -)	3056
Harry (1888 -)	3061
Iva Alice (1891 -)	3063
James Hulbert (1855 -)	spouse of 2179
James Murray (1884 -)	3059
Leland Jay (1886 -)	3060
May (1890 -)	3062
Myrtle Elizabeth (1882 -)	3058
Orville George (1880 -)	3057
PROCTOR	
Dorothy	spouse of 3523
PRYSLOPSKI	
Andrew	spouse of 4010
Andrew Michael	4256
Danielle Marie	4255
PULLMAN	
Esther Ann (1813 - 1883)	spouse of 1191
PULSIFER	
Lizzie (1854 - 1877)	spouse of 2252
Royal	spouse of 1196
PURCELL	
Charles (1822 - 1899)	spouse of 861
PUTMAN	
Mary Taggart (1793 - 1864)	spouse of 1165
PYLE	
_____	spouse of 4067
QUINN	
Helen (1926 - 1998)	spouse of 3741
QUIRK	
James (1837 - 1892)	spouse of 2329
QUIST	
Louisa (1859 - 1920)	spouse of 2438
RADE	
Susan (1961 -)	spouse of 4153
RADEMAKER	
Edward	spouse of 2800
RADKE	
Harold Michael	spouse of 4080
Living Son of Harold and Kathleen (Shepperd)	4328
RADMORE	
Florence Edith (1883 - 1954)	2583
Florence Edith (1883 - 1954)	spouse of 1753
Jennie	spouse of 1723

Robert (1836 -)	spouse of 1725
RAMEH OLSEN	
____ (ABU)	spouse of 4293
RANDALL	
Tracey Lynn (1962 -)	spouse of 4029
RANKIN	
Andrew R. (1863 - 1864)	2557
Capitolia	spouse of 2718
Eames D. (1856 - 1890)	2554
Edith G. (1864 - 1943)	2558
Edith Miles (1880 -)	3395
Jeremiah (1828 - 1904)	spouse of 1697
Mary F. (1858 - 1913)	2556
Walter N. (1857 - 1877)	2555
RANNEY	
Jeanette (1811 - 1894)	spouse of 1966
RAWSON	
Lucy Amelia (1875 - 1959)	spouse of 3672
READ	
Alvin (1774 -)	694
Elizabeth (1769 -)	442
Hannah (1771 -)	693
Jacob (1767 -)	441
John	spouse of 36
John (1728 - <1775)	159
Mary (Polly) (?)	spouse of 444
Rhoda (1772 -)	443
Ruth (1766 - 1775)	692
Silas (1737 - 1825)	spouse of 266
READE	
Abijah (1743 - >1775)	166
Alvin (1774 -)	455
Amy (1772 -)	447
Daniel (1774 -)	448
David (1767 -)	445
George (1769 -)	446
Hannah (1771 -)	454
Hiram (1803 -)	1009
Orpha (1764 -)	691
Orpha (1764 -)	452
Phinehas (1781 -)	450
Ruth (1782 -)	451
Ruth (1766 - 1775)	453
Sarah (1733 - 1736)	162
Sarah (1740 -)	165
Silas (1738 -)	164
Timothy (1796 -)	1008
Titus (1735 - 1788)	163
Titus (1765 -)	444
Titus (1790 -)	1007
READE aka READ	
Jacob Jr. (1731 -)	161
REDDING	
M. A. (1860 - 1912)	spouse of 2443

REDFIELD
    Lydia   spouse of 67
REDMOND
    John William (1822 - 1880)   spouse of 2096
    Josephine (1850 -)   2931
REED
    Albert Gladwin (1880 - 1952)   2920
    Albert O. (1844 - >1910)   2087
    Arthur (1882 -)   2921
    Bertis B. (1834 - 1901)   spouse of 1866
    Blanche B. [163] (1908 -)   3451
    Charles C. "Charley"[72] (1865 - 1926)   2674
    Deforest H. [76] (1879 -)   2678
    Dewey D. [167] (1916 - 1916)   3455
    Edward T. (1879 -)   2919
    Eleanor D. (~1904 - >1920)   3446
    Ester (1797 - 1886)   spouse of 795
    Frances E. (1863 - 1917)   spouse of 2674
    Frank Dubois [75] (1876 -)   2677
    Georgia E. (~1901 - >1920)   3445
    Geraldine [164] (1909 -)   3452
    Gladys [159] (1899 -)   3447
    Hazel [160] (1900 -)   3448
    Hobart B. [168] (1901 -)   3456
    Isaac   spouse of 1661
    Isabell R. [162] (1907 -)   3450
    LaGrand [172] (1906 -)   3460
    Leona J. [169] (1905 -)   3457
    Luella M. [73] (- >1920)   2675
    Margaret E. [165] (1911 -)   3453
    Mary L. (1850 - 1872)   spouse of 2453
    Mary M. (1826 - 1911)   spouse of 904
    Maude M. (?) (1900 -)   spouse of 3442
    Paul H. (1895 - 1968)   3443
    Percy G.   3444
    Phyllis H. [171] (1904 -)   3459
    Roswell (1776 - 1852)   449
    Roswell P. (1804 - 1885)   1010
    Russell Harry (1893 -)   3442
    Salley   spouse of 824
    Velma L. [161] (1903 -)   3449
    Vivian B. [166] (1912 -)   3454
    Walter W. [74] (1870 -)   2676
    William K. (1855 -)   spouse of 2675
    Zelma L. [170] (1908 -)   3458
REED AKA READ, READE
    Amy (- >1775)   167
    Elizabeth (1729 - <1775)   160
    Dr. Jacob (1700 - 1775)   spouse of 44
    Lydia (1726 - 1806)   158
    Mary (1724 -)   157
REEDY
    Jan   spouse of 4045
REESE

?	spouse of 3729	
RILEY		
3 male children	2923	
3 other female children	2924	
Adelia	3590	
Adelia Catharine "Delia" (1836 - 1887)	spouse of 1860	
Adelia Catharine "Delia" (1836 - 1887)	2928	
Betsey (1802 - 1886)	2090	
Betsey	2922	
Esther Jackson (1804 - 1861)	spouse of 895	
Esther Jackson (1804 - 1861)	2091	
Experience (?)	spouse of 2092	
Frances M. (1876 - 1876)	3589	
Helina (1808 - 1809)	2093	
Horace (~1832 - >1876)	2926	
Isabelle "Totie Belle" Luella "Luella" (1867 - 1950)		3591
Isaiah Hendryx (1797 - 1855)	2088	
James Gillett (1834 - 1871)	2927	
Jeanne Elizabeth (1870 - 1950)	spouse of 2539	
Josiah B. (1806 -)	2092	
Josiah (Isaiah) (1773 - 1850)	spouse of 1053	
Ransom (>1837 - 1846)	2929	
Simeon (1799 - ~1848)	2089	
Stilson James (1871 - 1871)	3593	
Susan Myrtle "Aunt Sue" (- >1928)	3592	
William Alanzo (~1830 -)	2925	
RISLEY		
Betsy	spouse of 961	
ROBERTS		
Catherine	3107	
Elisha (1781 -)	1363	
Gaylord	3108	
Martin (1759 - 1807)	spouse of 661	
Martin (1784 -)	1365	
Robert Henry	spouse of 2243	
Sybil (1782 -)	1364	
ROBINSON		
Phebe (1772 - 1832)	spouse of 696	
Walter Joseph	spouse of 2275	
Winifred Josephine (1867 -)	3144	
RODENBECK		
Dorothy Anna (1942 -)	spouse of 3943	
RODGERS		
Caroline "Carrie" L. (1842 - 1880)	spouse of 1859	
RODRIGUEZ		
Miate (1944 -)	spouse of 3991	
ROE		
Amanda (1800 - 1870)	1574	
Ambrose Thomas (1817 - 1879)	1582	
Augustus (1845 - 1880)	2280	
Birdie (1868 -)	2311	
Carrie (1857 -)	2286	
Carrie (1859 -)	2312	
Electa (1810 - 1864)	1579	

Electa A. (1842 -)	2304
Elisha (1768 - 1830)	spouse of 757
Elisha (1814 - 1883)	1581
Elisha K. (1853 -)	2309
Eveline (1849 -)	2308
George (1854 - 1917)	2285
George Welles (1799 - 1830)	1573
Harvey P. (1859 - 1932)	2287
Harvey S.	3146
Helen (1844 - 1882)	2279
Helen (1844 - 1882)	spouse of 2293
Horace (1854 - 1870)	2310
James Augustus (1805 - 1827)	1577
Joseph (1849 - 1849)	2307
Josephine (1849 - 1849)	2306
Lillian Gertrude "Gertie" (1876 - 1965)	3145
Lucy (1807 - 1888)	1578
Lucy (1847 - 1872)	2281
Lydia (1802 -)	1575
Marion (1837 -)	2302
Mary Frances (1845 -)	2305
Nettie (1865 - 1932)	2289
Orvin J. (1851 - 1937)	2313
Orvin Sidney (1819 - 1872)	1583
Ramona (1898 -)	3166
Reuben Smith (1850 - 1933)	2283
Roxana (1812 - 1900)	1580
Roxanne (1849 - 1851)	2282
Susannah (1839 -)	2303
William H. (1852 - 1925)	2284
William Horace (1803 - 1886)	1576
Winnie (1862 - 1934)	2288

ROGERS

Elizabeth (1720 - 1807)	spouse of 104
Freelove (1737 - 1806)	spouse of 193
Mary (1805 - 1865)	spouse of 917
Orrin (1815 -)	spouse of 1591
Sarah (1811 - 1892)	spouse of 1586

ROLFE

Albert W.	spouse of 3488
Richard [233] (1913 -)	3807
Robert [234]	3808

ROOD

Adelia Maria (1803 - 1859)	spouse of 848

ROOT

?	spouse of 197
Azariah Jr.	spouse of 827
Edward (1825 -)	spouse of 2050
Hiram (1835 -)	spouse of 1632
Mary	spouse of 112

ROPER

Fanny	spouse of 1200

ROSAS

Sonia	spouse of 4244

ROSE

————	spouse of 3436
"children"	3997
Kenneth	3785
Natalie	spouse of 3785

ROSS

Edith (1878 -)	2965
George L.	spouse of 1648
Jessie (1871 -)	2964
Loring T. (1847 -)	spouse of 2127

ROWE

Hannah (1790 - 1873)	spouse of 560

ROWIN

Abi (1865 -)	2817
Bell (Lillian) (1874 -)	2821
Cecelia (1867 -)	2818
Eugennie (1878 -)	2822
John (1862 -)	2816
John L.	spouse of 1997
John Leroy (1832 -)	spouse of 1999
Ladue (1869 -)	2819
Lafayette (1872 -)	2820
Orilla (1861 -)	2814
Orin (1861 -)	2815

ROWLAND

Cornelia (1814 - 1903)	spouse of 879

ROWLEY

Helen W. (1879 - >1920)	spouse of 2684

ROYCE

Cecilia (1832 -)	2188
George William (1789 - 1865)	spouse of 1199
Nancy (1828 - 1906)	2186
William Alauson	2187

RULON

Rachel (1832 - 1902)	spouse of 1638

RUMMELL

Beth	spouse of 3974

RUMSEY

Lela	spouse of 1908

RUSH

Clarence Benjamin (1893 -)	3294
Eben	3293
Hiram Benjamin (1856 - 1924)	spouse of 2426

RUSSELL

Mary "Addie" E. (1834 -)	spouse of 1208
Melvina	spouse of 2679

SADD

Chauncey (1779 -)	spouse of 975
Corinne Gilmore (1801 -)	2021
George Franklin (1816 -)	2022
Joseph M.	spouse of 2021
Julia Warner (1808 -)	2020
Maria (1802 -)	2018
William Chauncey (1806 - 1831)	2019

SALISBURY

Eliza J. (1827 - 1910)	spouse of 1659

SANDERSON

Adaliza L. (1836 - 1811)	2945
Clarinda Jane (1833 - 1907)	2944
Elijah (1772 -)	spouse of 1124
Elisha (1803 -)	2115
Julia Dorleska (1839 -)	2946
Mary Ann (1824 - 1881)	2942
William A.	2114
William Albert (1829 - 1893)	2943

SANTEE

Martha "Mattie"	spouse of 1923

SAXTON

Adam (1710 - 1774)	79
Hannah (1707 - 1725)	77
John (~1682 - 1766)	18
Lucy (1712 - 1784)	80
Mary (1709 - 1776)	78
Richard (1673 - 1714)	16

SAXTON aka SEXTON

John (1649 - 1718)	spouse of 3

SAXTON SEXTON

Mary (1678 - >1721)	17

SCANLAN CARR-WOODIN

Carol (1955 -)	spouse of 3974

SCHANBACHER

Wilbert	spouse of 3496

SCHENCK

Charles	4096

SCHMIDT

Barbara Kay (1951 -)	spouse of 3947

SCHNEIDER

Joy Marie (1972 -)	4112
Matthew Paul (1973 -)	4113
Stephen George (1969 -)	4111
William Charles (1930 -)	spouse of 3923

SCHROADER

Craig Dean (1960 -)	4296
Denise Rene (1955 -)	4293
Frank Leslie (1888 - 1955)	spouse of 3853
Jacquie Lynne (1957 -)	4294
Leona Alice (- <1981)	4059
Leslie Franklin (1927 -)	4061
Marian Rozella (1920 -)	4060
Ramona Gail (1963 -)	4297
Scott Leslie (1958 -)	4295

SCHULTZ

Craig Charles "David" D.O. (1946 -)	spouse of 3977
Rachel Elizabeth (1994 -)	4210

SCHUTT

Maria C. (1816 - 1898)	spouse of 895

SCOVILLE

Charles	3032

George H. (1861 -)	3033
Sylvester M. (1815 -)	spouse of 2159
SEAMAN	
Cecelia (1835 - 1900)	spouse of 1995
Eliza	spouse of 2000
SEARLES	
William E.	spouse of 2754
SEAVERTON	
Ida Mae (1890 -)	spouse of 2933
SEDEGWICK	
Elijah	2116
SEDGEWICK	
Agnes E. (1849 - 1928)	2951
Caroline Gertrude	2947
Charles F. (1865 - 1915)	2953
Charles T.	2948
Harvey	2949
Jennie Mary	2950
Parker	1149
S. Parker (1860 - 1912)	2952
Samuel (1803 - 1847)	1147
Wrestle W. (1827 - 1904)	2119
SEDGWICK	
Amanda	1152
Betsey	1153
Elijah (1769 - 1861)	spouse of 513
Elijah	1148
Elizabeth (1830 -)	2117
James H. (1840 -)	2123
Joseph White (1846 -)	2124
Louisa Jane (1835 -)	2121
Maria C. (1838 -)	2122
Parker	2118
Sarah Ann (1833 - 1903)	2120
Theron	1150
Tryphena	1151
SEEDORF	
Angela	4173
Michael	4174
Zeke	spouse of 3959
SEELY	
Fanny (1792 -)	spouse of 343
Fanny (1792 -)	spouse of 800
Sally (?) (1764 -)	spouse of 343
SEGAR	
Children of John and Mary (Reade)	440
John	spouse of 160
SELLERS	
Luretta Lena (1886 - 1936)	spouse of 3425
SENN	
Deana Katherine (1966 -)	spouse of 3984
SEWARD	
Ruth (1755 - 1833)	spouse of 217
SEYMOUR	

Emma M. (1865 -)	3154
Henry O. (1874 -)	3155
Ozias	spouse of 2292
SHAFFER	
Emery	spouse of 4058
Laurie Kevin (1959 -)	4281
Shelley Lynn (1963 -)	4282
SHANKS	
Mary (- ~1827)	spouse of 872
SHANNON	
Isabelle S. (- 1908)	spouse of 1871
SHATFORD	
Eleanor (1793 - 1872)	spouse of 359
Sarah (1809 - 1881)	spouse of 855
SHAW	
Jacob (Jake) (- <1920)	spouse of 1878
SHAY	
James Edward (1907 - 1983)	spouse of 3847
Linda Lee (1938 -)	4058
SHEEHY	
Conor Patrick Desmond (1993 -)	4216
Julia "Sheila"	spouse of 3984
SHEFFLER	
Olivia Mildred (2008 -)	4401
Shawn	spouse of 4163
SHELDON	
Abel Phelps (1786 -)	1502
Enos (1794 -)	1505
Isaac (1752 - 1810)	spouse of 711
Isaac (1784 -)	1501
Lament (1755 - 1825)	spouse of 406
Mary (1791 -)	1504
Phebe (1788 -)	1503
Sally (1782 -)	1500
SHEPPERD	
Adeliza Bell (1862 - 1865)	3599
Bonita L. (~1923 -)	4083
Bruce Eugene (1854 - 1943)	3596
Bruce Reason (1881 - 1980)	3861
Bruce Robert (1918 -)	4073
Catherine Patricia (1913 - 1992)	4071
Clarinda Jane (1859 - 1893)	3598
Elizabeth A. (~1921 -)	4082
Emma Eugenia (1903 -)	3867
Enid Marguerite (1919 -)	4081
Enos Aberdeen (1888 - 1961)	3864
Esther Agnes (1905 -)	3868
Eva Leannah (1890 -)	3865
Eva Leannah (1890 - 1983)	4085
George Michael (1925 - 1999)	4084
George Washington (1852 - 1922)	3595
Hannah Isabel (1916 -)	4075
Infant (1877 -)	3859
James	4078

John Henry (1869 -)	3601
John Wesley (1826 - 1907)	spouse of 2944
John Wesley (1878 -)	3860
Juniatta L. (1855 - 1928)	3597
Kathleen Marie (1916 - 1987)	4080
Living Daughter of Bruce and Irene (Britt)	4310
Living Daughter of Bruce and Irene (Britt)	4311
Living Daughter of George	4348
Living Daughter of George	4349
Living Daughter of James	4325
Living Son of George	4346
Living Son of George	4347
Living Son of James	4324
Living Son of Virgil and Margaret (Freeman)	4312
Living Son of Virgil and Margaret (Freeman)	4313
Living Son of Virgil and Margaret (Freeman)	4314
Living Son of Virgil and Margaret (Freeman)	4315
Mary Melcina (1864 - 1935)	3600
Renne Julian (1886 - 1974)	3863
Ruth Anne (1915 -)	4072
Shirley (1911 -)	4079
Virgil Earl (1914 - 1973)	4074
Warren H.	4077
Warren Thompson (1883 - 1971)	3862
William Bruce (1900 -)	3866
Winifred Abbey (1917 - 1988)	4076

SHERMAN

?	spouse of 3846
John Jay	4056
Laura Lee	4055
Mary Ann	spouse of 863
Mary Lou	4054
Paula Jean (1949 -)	4057

SHERWOOD

Ann (1731 - 1829)	spouse of 117

SHINABARGER

George	spouse of 1943

SHOEMAKE

Gregory Scott (1991 -)	4361
Jeff Scott	spouse of 4120

SHOWERS

Norma Kay	spouse of 3929

SIDLEY

Ernest S. (1879 - >1880)	3161
Frank C. (1874 - >1900)	3159
Fred K. (1873 - >1900)	3158
Kyle A. (1870 - >1880)	3157
Mollie (1877 - >1880)	3160
Thomas H. (1881 - >1900)	3162
William Kirby	spouse of 2298
William Pratt (1868 - >1880)	3156

SIMMONS

Cordelia (1868 - 1911)	spouse of 2990

SIMON

Nicole	4261
Steve	spouse of 4033
SIMPSON	
Lloyd Thomas "Tom" (1950 -)	spouse of 3939
Matthew David (1981 -)	4141
SKAIDRITE	
Karen Loja "Sky"	spouse of 3716
SKEELS	
?Sally	833
Almira (1796 - 1861)	827
Arad (1779 - 1855)	820
Belias Hill (1782 - 1859)	821
Chloe (1805 - 1870)	831
daughter of Truman & Chloe (1808 -)	832
Harry (1794 - ~1812)	826
Harvey (1799 - 1867)	828
Henry (1786 -)	823
Joseph (~1777 -)	814
Lydia	817
Molly (~1777 - 1834)	813
Nelson (1802 - 1859)	819
Polly (1801 - 1835)	829
Reuben (1788 - 1864)	824
Roxana (1799 - 1883)	818
Samuel	816
Simeon (1784 - 1861)	822
Susanna (1803 - >1824)	830
Truman (1753 - 1814)	spouse of 352
Truman (1792 - >1850)	825
William	815
William Belden (1751 - 1821)	spouse of 351
SKINNER	
Emaline (1831 -)	spouse of 1938
Francis Hill	3527
George Amos	2759
Joseph C.	spouse of 1941
Mary Francis	3822
SLATER	
Patricia	spouse of 4064
SLAUSON	
Willis James (1878 - 1919)	spouse of 3145
SLOAN	
Almira Ann (1862 - 1949)	2410
Amos Clinton (1869 - 1965)	2413
Arthur Burton (1876 - 1937)	2414
Carrie Rebecca (1896 -)	3271
Clarence R. (1879 -)	spouse of 3232
Clarinda Jane (1860 - 1933)	2409
Daisy Ellen (1889 -)	3270
Daniel Horatio (1887 -)	3269
Horatio Catline (1836 - 1922)	spouse of 1634
Melissa Adele (1858 - 1922)	2408
Pearl Elizabeth (1905 -)	3272
Phoebe (1867 - 1867)	2412

?	spouse of 2685
Bert	spouse of 3228
Glen	3723
Helen [175]	3475
Warren	3724
Wilbur	3725
SOULES	
———	3908
Chester W. (1879 -)	spouse of 3693
SOWLES	
Anna A. (1846 - 1895)	spouse of 1898
SPEER	
Arvena Grace [157] (1914 -)	3435
Bernice Comelia [158] (1920 -)	3436
Eleanor Vesta (- >2002)	3437
Harriet Eloise [156] (1912 - 1912)	3434
Harry Lawrence (1879 - 1943)	spouse of 2670
Rosella Amelia [155] (1903 - <2002)	3433
SPENCE	
Jessica Lou (1980 -)	4376
Jon L. (1956 -)	spouse of 4143
Nikki Sue (1981 -)	4377
SPENCER	
Henry	spouse of 2049
Imri Lester (1803 - 1870)	spouse of 998
SPERRY	
Moses (1780 -)	spouse of 608
SPITLER	
Samantha Arabelle	spouse of 2759
SPOOR	
Lavina (1799 -)	1087
William	spouse of 475
SPRAGG	
———	spouse of 4166
SPRAGUE	
Betsey (1773 - 1811)	spouse of 474
Elizabeth	spouse of 878
Minta	spouse of 473
Sophia (1774 - 1804)	spouse of 472
STAATS	
Jacob Jr. (1832 - 1898)	spouse of 2832
Lester Loring (1874 - 1953)	3568
Lurissa Rosalia Staats (1911 -)	3848
Suzanne Louise (1934 -)	spouse of 3941
STANLEY	
Abi Langdon (1807 -)	1536
David L. (1920 - 2006)	3901
Ira (1773 - 1854)	spouse of 723
Ira (1795 -)	1535
Mary Alice (1954 -)	4091
Richard R. Esq. (1952 -)	4090
Roy A. (1880 - 1941)	spouse of 3688
STARR	
Mary Almira (1816 -)	spouse of 1555

Sarah Warne (1812 -)   spouse of 1554

STASCH

Donald Lovern [227] (1918 -)   3800
Flora [227-A] (1909 -)   3797
Harold [228-A] (1912 -)   3798
Ruth [229-A] (1917 -)   3799
Walter J. (- >1920)   spouse of 3464

STEANS

Miranda   spouse of 1120

STEBBINGS

Lydia Bacon (1816 -)   spouse of 1676

STEELE

Christopher Robert (1996 -)   4366
Elizabeth Livingston (1886 - 1959)   3164
Frederick Morgan (1851 - 1923)   spouse of 2301
Frederick Pratt (1884 - 1884)   3163
Jesse   spouse of 4126

STEINBRUNNER

Janet   spouse of 4007

STEPHANS

Michael   spouse of 3966

STEPHENS

Julia (- 1875)   spouse of 872
Lucy (1763 - 1788)   spouse of 508

STERLING

Lois Ann (1956 -)   spouse of 3814

STETSON or WILSON

Allen (1896 -)   3680
Harold (1898 -)   3681
William O.   spouse of 3126

STEVENS

Abigail   spouse of 738
Arnold (1802 -)   1410
Clarissa (1808 -)   1413
Fanny (1809 -)   1414
Henry (1800 -)   1409
Henry Adams (1813 -)   1415
Jonathan (1766 - 1854)   spouse of 682
Jonathan (1794 -)   1405
Lucy (1798 -)   1407
Lydia (1786 -)   1404
Lydie (1806 -)   1412
Nancy (1773 -)   spouse of 681
Nancy (1804 -)   1411
Oliver (1798 -)   1408
Warren (1796 -)   1406

STEVENSON

Philo Oscar   spouse of 1799

STEWART

Clarissa (1852 - 1921)   1724
David (1844 -)   1721
Jane (1836 -)   1718
Lucy (1839 - 1926)   1719
Maria (1843 -)   1720

Robert (1811 - 1882)	spouse of 839
Robert (1845 -)	1722
Samuel (1848 -)	1723
STILLMAN	
Benjamin (1760 - 1819)	spouse of 479
Caroline	1090
Isaiah (1797 -)	1093
Martha	1091
Roxanna (1786 -)	1092
STILSON	
Mary Ann "Polly" (1774 - >1810)	spouse of 374
STINE	
Clarinda (1866 -)	spouse of 2287
STOCKER	
Bertha Dell (1900 -)	3239
Daniel Beers (1882 -)	3233
Ellen (1897 -)	3238
Elmira (1884 -)	3234
George Washington (1890 -)	3236
James Washington (1857 - 1946)	spouse of 2381
Mittie Leonora (1887 -)	3235
Ollie (1894 -)	3237
Ruby (1902 -)	3240
STOCKWELL	
Jessie Fidelia [1741371] (1863 - 1940)	spouse of 2667
Sarah (1779 - 1850)	spouse of 360
STODDARD	
? [Living]	spouse of 4078
Lucy Ann	spouse of 2040
STOKES	
Abigail	spouse of 364
STONE	
Esther (Ester, Hester) (1711 - 1797)	spouse of 30
Molly "Polly" (1779 -)	spouse of 302
STOWE	
Blanch Lillian (1872 - 1923)	3614
William (1830 - 1876)	spouse of 2986
STREET	
Ida Maria	2781
Polly	spouse of 546
William B. (1819 -)	spouse of 1961
STRICKLAND	
Elizabeth (1731 -)	145
Hannah (1729 -)	144
Joseph (1721 -)	141
Mary (1722 -)	142
Orpha (1733 -)	146
Samuel (1697 -)	spouse of 40
Sarah (1724 - 1769)	143
STRONG	
Alexander (1754 - 1755)	405
Anson (1796 - 1865)	949
Cynthia (1801 - 1879)	950
David (1764 -)	409

Eli (1755 - 1825)	406
Eli	944
Esther (~1800 - ~1893)	spouse of 873
Julia (Laura) (1791 -)	947
Lament Sheldon (1783 - 1845)	943
Martha (Mary) (1794 - 1796)	948
Samuel (1761 - 1821)	408
Sarah (1758 - 1806)	407
Sarah (1787 - 1861)	945
Sophia (1789 -)	946
Timothy (1719 - 1803)	spouse of 143

SUFFICOOL
Louie (1900 -)	spouse of 3215

SUPPERER
Judith Marie (1975 -)	spouse of 4283

SUTHERLAND
Jerot	spouse of 2018

SUTTENFIELD
Jane (1819 -)	spouse of 2013

SWAIN
Florence Rebecca (1888 - 1961)	2656
Frank	2655
Fred	2654
William Jesse (1858 - 1928)	spouse of 1850

TAYLOR
?	spouse of 2793
Elizabeth Amelia	spouse of 969
Jerush	spouse of 2073
Ruth	spouse of 456
Viola (- <1920)	spouse of 2726

TENDALL
Vernice Arline (1912 - 1978)	spouse of 3416

TERRELL
Wales	spouse of 2051

TERRY
4 unnamed children of Solomon and Sheba (Griffin)	404
Elizabeth (1724 -)	spouse of 139
Elizabeth (1749 -)	402
Frederick C. (1855 - ~1930)	2782
Frederick W. (1892 - 1913)	3541
Jcrome (1821 - ~1890)	1962
Lyman Charles (1890 - 1964)	3540
Mina N. (?) (1853 - 1920)	spouse of 2782
Sarah (1668 - ~1740)	spouse of 9
Solomon (1720 -)	spouse of 140
Stephen (1751 - 1835)	403
Stephen (1784 - 1857)	942

THAYER
Sara	spouse of 1198

THOMAS
Betsey Maria (1811 -)	spouse of 1203
Charles Edwin (1852 - 1911)	spouse of 2219
Charles Ernest (1883 - 1885)	3070
Clarence Irwin (1893 - 1955)	3074

Earnest L. (1885 -)	3071
Edgar Louis (1880 - 1936)	3069
Edna Viola (1874 - 1879)	3067
Elmer Elsworth (1878 - 1965)	3068
Emma	spouse of 1713
Ernest Ray (1889 - 1955)	3073
Frank Charles (1887 - 1958)	3072

THOMPSON

Alice	spouse of 2550
Essie Mae (1903 - 1994)	spouse of 3431
Polly	spouse of 1056

THORP

Mary (1847 - 1941)	spouse of 1716

THRASHER

Abigail Lucy (1781 - 1855)	607
Elnathan (1750 - 1810)	spouse of 220
John (1779 - 1856)	606

TILLEY

Jared Duane (1987 -)	4364
Meagan Nichole (1992 -)	4365
Scott Eugene (1963 -)	4124

TILLITSON

Child of Montgomery and Florence	3414
Child of Montgomery and Florence	3415
Montgomery Frank (1890 - 1963)	spouse of 2656
Swayne George (1912 - 1982)	3416

TOBEY

Benjamin	spouse of 469
Elizabeth Morse (1907 - 2002)	spouse of 2734
Harriet Ruth (1830 - 1870)	spouse of 905

TODD

Dimis Emeline (1832 -)	2165
Elizabeth Eveline (1845 -)	2169
Erastus (1807 - 1890)	spouse of 1186
Erastus W. (1839 - 1890)	2167
Erwin Wallace (1864 -)	3042
Ethel Winona (1874 -)	3045
Eva Adeline (1862 -)	3041
Florence Bell (1908 - 1995)	3847
Florence Emeline (1887 -)	3048
Frances Miriam (1871 -)	3044
George Wilson (1873 -)	spouse of 3567
Henry Leon (1878 -)	3046
Jennie Laura (1866 -)	3043
Lewis Irving (1872 -)	3047
Luther Buckley (1843 -)	2168
Olive Ellen (1834 -)	2166

TOLBERT

Anne Eliza	spouse of 2244

TOMER

_____	spouse of 2758

TONEY

Living Daughter of Warren and Ruth (Shepperd)	4309
Living Son of Warren and Ruth (Shepperd)	4308

Warren Ira (1905 - 1976)   spouse of 4072
TOOLE
Mrs. Malvira Francis "Fannie"   spouse of 964
TOOMBS
Sarah Ann (1827 - 1895)   spouse of 2119
TOPPING
Effie M.   spouse of 2552
Hazel   spouse of 1616
TORREY
?   3735
?   3736
?   3737
?   3738
?   3741
?   3742
Bertha F. (1903 -)   3334
Bessie E. (1893 - 1893)   3328
Chester R. (1922 - 2001)   3739
Clara Eleanor (1885 -)   3324
Edith E. (1899 -)   3332
Frank Andrew (1897 - 1926)   3331
Fred Baker (1894 - 1973)   3329
Grace Belle (1884 - 1949)   3323
Grimala (?)   spouse of 3743
Ida Marchie (1896 -)   3330
Kenneth (1925 - 1993)   3740
Linus Greene (1889 -)   3326
Mabel Alice (1881 -)   3321
Orson Winfield (1882 -)   3322
Ralph Bernier (1925 - 1984)   3743
Ralph Eugene (1900 - 1967)   3333
Robert Lorenso (1891 - 1972)   3327
William Levi (1856 - 1936)   spouse of 2455
Willis Porter (1887 - 1974)   3325
TOURTELOTTE
Lisa   spouse of 4152
TOWN
Russell   spouse of 818
TRACY
Hannah (1765 - 1841)   spouse of 307
TRAVIS
Alvin Raymond (1919 - 1979)   spouse of 3823
Alvin Raymond Jr.   4008
Earnest Richard (1942 -)   4007
Earnest Richard Jr. (1943 -)   4252
Jon Paul   4254
Jon Paul (1945 - 1966)   4009
Linda Ann (1948 -)   4010
Todd Thomas   4253
TREAT
Mattie (- ~1866)   spouse of 1794
TRELOAR
Michael LeRoy (1938 -)   3952
Nancy Lee (1942 -)   3953

Paul Arthur (1915 -)	spouse of 3770
Sharon Jean (1954 -)	3954
TROUT	
Melissa	spouse of 1602
TRUEHART	
?	3732
?	3733
George Peter (1884 -)	spouse of 3324
Hazel M. (1908 -)	3734
TULER	
Esther (~1753 -)	spouse of 412
TULLER	
Thaddeus (~1772 -)	spouse of 414
TURNER	
Hellen F.	spouse of 3128
Lydia	spouse of 621
Martha (1775 - 1836)	spouse of 483
TUTTLE	
Abigail	596
Aldemer M.	3078
Alva Brockett (1825 -)	2225
Benoni	597
Charity (1789 -)	1352
Charles (1762 - 1818)	spouse of 657
Charles (1790 -)	1353
Dan (1746 - 1816)	spouse of 218
Eliada (1815 -)	2221
Elon Augustus (1823 - 1908)	2224
George Washington (1796 -)	1356
Hannah (1747 - 1813)	spouse of 213
Hannah	598
Harriet Eugenia	3076
Harvey (1794 -)	1355
Helpy Rosette (1798 -)	1357
Huldah (1820 -)	2223
Ira (1792 - 1878)	1245
Jeanette M.	3079
Levi	599
Lucien	3080
Lucinda (1780 -)	604
Lucy (1796 - 1847)	605
Lyman (1769 - 1813)	601
Marcus (1830 -)	2227
Nancy	600
Nellie L. (1844 - 1929)	3075
Peniel Case (aka Pernal) (1792 -)	1354
Rachel B. (1832 -)	2228
Rhoda (1828 -)	2226
Salmon (1815 -)	1246
Samantha (1817 -)	2222
Solomon (1773 -)	602
Sophia	3081
Sylvia Jane	3077
Zophar (1776 -)	603

TWISS
George Washington (1953 -)   spouse of 2409
Millicent Clay (1808 - 1896)   spouse of 808
Russell   spouse of 1627

TWITCHELL
Deborah (1775 -)   spouse of 590

UPSON
Amanda (1799 -)   1215
Noah (1758 - 1806)   spouse of 573
Sheldon (1785 -)   1214

USHER
Caroline Mehitable (1811 - 1885)   spouse of 1010

VALENCIA
Enriquita   spouse of 2764

VanRYSWYK
Janice Elaine (1950 -)   spouse of 4295

VERNE
Sandie   spouse of 1950

VESTERBY
Drew Michael (1978 -)   4375
Jennifer L. (1976 -)   4374
Larry A.   spouse of 4142
Todd Allen (1973 -)   4373

VINING
Elias (1772 - 1852)   spouse of 690
Huldah May   spouse of 828

VIRGIN
Martha Ann (1834 -)   spouse of 2002

VOORHES
Stanton G.   spouse of 2382

VOSBURGH
Deidamia (1795 - 1874)   spouse of 537

WADSWORTH
Jane (1813 - 1893)   spouse of 838
Judson (1797 - 1882)   spouse of 2037

WAITE
Ruth Alma (1866 - 1941)   spouse of 1849

WAKELEE
Hannah (1751 - 1778)   spouse of 217

WAKLEY
Orra "Orry" (1860 - 1893)   spouse of 2987

WALDON
Lisa Marie (1968 -)   spouse of 4178

WALDREN
Lorenzo (1843 - 1918)   spouse of 2361
Martha Maria (1888 -)   3228
Mary Ellen (1882 -)   3227

WALKER
Sarah Emma "Sadie Mae"   spouse of 2995

WALLER
Arline Hermione (- 1984)   spouse of 3546

WALTON
Ann (1802 -)   spouse of 1181

WARD

Aaron Sewell (1818 - 1891)	spouse of 1593
Anthem Lee (1984 -)	4396
Betty (- 1991)	spouse of 4353
Calla Elizabeth (1990 -)	4399
Daniel (1960 -)	spouse of 4155
Den Anthony (1981 -)	4395
Harriet Caroline (1826 - 1917)	spouse of 2032
Tallen Miles (1986 -)	4397
Ulyssia Autumn (1987 -)	4398

WARK

Marsha Rhoda	spouse of 3844

WARNER

? (1808 -)	1230
Mark (1757 - 1815)	spouse of 588
Samuel	spouse of 728

WARREN

?	spouse of 3167
Eugene H. "Gene"	spouse of 3843

WASHBURN

Blanche (1890 - 1955)	spouse of 3423

WATKINS

Lloyd G.	spouse of 3537

WATSON

Mrs. Jo Anne L.	spouse of 3835

WATTS

Betty	spouse of 347
Catherine E. (1859 - 1930)	spouse of 3109

WAUGH

Myrtle	spouse of 3860

WEBB

Cynthia Elaine	spouse of 3963
Edgar (~1859 -)	2635
Herbert (~1858 -)	2634
Lemuel E.	spouse of 1795
Sally Ann (1825 - 1851)	spouse of 801

WEBSTER

Huldah (1797 - 1886)	spouse of 1182
Jerusha (1791 -)	spouse of 490

WEICKS

James	spouse of 4117

WELLS

Chester (1800 -)	1301
Chloe (1801 -)	1302
Eleanor (1778 - 1836)	spouse of 698
Ezekial (1787 -)	1296
Israel (1757 - 1831)	spouse of 645
Israel (1787 -)	1297
Joel (1791 -)	1298
Mary (1803 -)	1303
Solomon (1799 -)	1300
Truman (1797 -)	1299

WESNER

Heather Ann (1972 -)	4136
James (1944 -)	spouse of 3936

Marian (1831 - 1913)	2274
Pamelia (1834 -)	2275

WHITE

_____	spouse of 817
Alma Anna (1890 - 1985)	3089
Edward Leslie (1878 - 1960)	3082
Elizabeth (1727 - 1812)	spouse of 107
Emily Knox (1861 - 1941)	spouse of 2764
Evelyn R. (1903 -)	3398
Harold (1896 - 1976)	3093
Helen Augusta (1897 - 1963)	3094
Howard Leroy (1880 - 1933)	3083
Mary Almira (1889 - 1940)	3088
Mary G. (1901 -)	3397
Merrill Washburn (1887 - 1951)	3087
Morris Hemingway (1885 - 1939)	3086
Percy Lewis (1881 - 1955)	3084
Theodore E. (1904 -)	3399
Twin Daughter (1895 - 1895)	3092
Twin Son (1895 - 1895)	3091
Walter Washburn (1883 - 1885)	3085
William H. (1866 - 1935)	spouse of 2558
William Leroy (1857 - 1927)	spouse of 2231
William Wirt (1893 - 1896)	3090

WHITNEY

Hannah M. (1832 -)	spouse of 1791
Ruth H. (1908 -)	spouse of 3223

WHYNOTT

Lillian (1889 - 1938)	spouse of 1855

WIEGET

Amelia (1844 - 1894)	spouse of 3035

WILBUR

Ashley Lindsey (1989 -)	4414
Barry	spouse of 4281
Danielle (1985 -)	4412
Mathew Robert	4413
Stephen King (1832 - 1905)	spouse of 2151
Susannah (1879 - 1974)	3009

WILCOX

? (1790 -)	1028
Aaron (1745 - 1750)	260
Aaron (1769 - 1835)	675
Abigail (1754 - 1833)	642
Abigail (1797 -)	1026
Abigail (1762 - 1830)	479
Albert Harley	2108
Amanda (1798 -)	1099
Amanda (1826 -)	2097
Amander N. (1808 -)	1037
Amelia (1786 -)	1063
Angeline (1796 -)	1098
Arabelle (1802 - 1841)	1119
Asa (1747 -)	456
Asa Virgil (1770 -)	1017

Asenath (1760 - 1790)	469
Asenath (1790 -)	1065
Azariah (1706 - 1776)	spouse of 78
Azariah Jay (1795 -)	1292
Benajah (1780 -)	1288
Benjamin (1776 - 1859)	484
Borden	671
Calvin (1804 -)	1097
Calvin Pardee (1796 -)	1068
Caroline (1790 -)	1290
Caroline (1799 -)	1078
Charles (1795 -)	1067
Charlotte	1079
Chauncey (1789 -)	1315
Chester (1801 -)	1295
Chestina (1774 -)	475
Chestina (1788 -)	1064
Chestina (1795 -)	1076
Chloe	1287
Chloe (1747 -)	457
Chloe	1071
Clarinda (1791 -)	1030
Clarissa (1815 -)	1107
Cornish (1796 -)	1317
Daniel W. (David) (1839 - 1913)	2102
Darius Pinney	1305
Desiah (1739 - 1750)	254
Dijah (1739 - 1805)	174
Dijah (1813 - 1889)	1121
Dorcas (1790 -)	1312
Eber (1783 -)	1088
Edgar (1864 -)	2109
Edmund (1785 -)	1019
Edward	1082
Edwin T. (1799 -)	1100
Eleazer (1831 -)	2099
Electa M. (1813 -)	1106
Elijah (Elisha) (1792 -)	1066
Elisha (1728 - 1812)	255
Elisha (1790 -)	1293
Eliza (1800 -)	1069
Elizabeth (?)	spouse of 675
Elizabeth (1841 - 1912)	2103
Elizabeth	1027
Elnathan (1734 - 1826)	171
Elnathan (1804 -)	1102
Elvira (1802 -)	1062
Emily	1306
Emily (1809 -)	1104
Enoch (1765 - 1835)	481
Ephraim (1727 -)	168
Ephraim (1803 -)	1120
Ephraim (1791 -)	1075
Erasmus D. (1803 -)	1081

Erastus (1801 -)	1395
Eunice (?)	spouse of 676
Ezra (1790 -)	1025
Ezra P. (1769 - 1832)	482
Franklin (1860 -)	1785
Franklin (1798 -)	1080
Frederic (1771 - 1860)	676
Frederic (1793 -)	1393
George (1792 -)	1316
George Clinton	1307
Gilbert (- 1877)	spouse of 860
Hannah (1732 - 1802)	256
Harriet	1304
Harvey (1787 -)	1294
Henry (1787 -)	1089
Hepzibah (1788 -)	1289
Hester Malvina (1812 -)	1086
Hira (1785 -)	1024
Hiram	1314
Horace H. (1831 - 1832)	2098
Israel	1308
Israel (1776 - 1817)	468
James	641
Jane	1083
Jedediah (1770 - 1823)	486
Jedediah (1838 -)	2107
Jedediah Bishop (1851 - 1944)	2106
Jehiel (1751 - 1848)	458
Jehiel (1781 -)	1023
Jeremiah (1780 -)	489
Jerusha (?) (1774 - 1795)	spouse of 649
Jesse (1774 - 1841)	487
John	1072
John (1796 - 1839)	1094
John Martin (1819 - 1907)	2095
Joseph (1798 -)	1394
Joseph (1791 - 1865)	490
Joshua	672
Julia	1073
Laura (1797 -)	1077
Lavina (1782 -)	476
Lavinia (1801 -)	1318
Leicester	1309
Lester (1810 -)	1320
Lewis (1834 - 1885)	2100
Lewis (1819 - 1891)	1122
Lodamia	1310
Lorenzo (1801 -)	1035
Lorita (1803 -)	1036
Lucia Ann (1825 - 1857)	spouse of 1962
Lucie Marie (1836 - 1914)	2101
Lydia (1737 - 1750)	258
Lysander (1799 -)	1034
Marcus	1011

Mark (1800 -)	1095
Marshall	1084
Martin (1759 - 1813)	460
Mary (1734 - 1816)	257
Mary (1846 - 1914)	2105
Mary (?)	spouse of 487
Miriam (1804 -)	1319
Nancy (1787 -)	1074
Nathan (1763 - 1844)	480
Newton (1802 -)	1096
Oliver (1772 - 1831)	474
Oliver L. (1809 -)	1070
Orra	1012
Orrin (1801 -)	1101
Ozias (1770 - 1835)	650
Peter (1805 -)	1103
Philander	673
Philander (1752 - 1813)	459
Pluma (1783 -)	477
Polly (1779 - 1833)	485
Prudence (1772 -)	1018
Pruna	1013
Rachel (1743 - 1817)	259
Ralph (1769 -)	473
Ralph (1818 -)	1085
Remus (1797 -)	1033
Reuben (1767 - 1849)	472
Riverious (1773 -)	677
Robert (1841 -)	2104
Rodolphus (1788 -)	1029
Romulus Bradford (1793 -)	1031
Rosannah (1741 -)	175
Roswell (1764 - 1831)	647
Roswell (1792 -)	1313
Roxy Ann (1821 -)	2096
Rufus (1764 - 1813)	471
Smith (1774 - 1831)	483
Sophronia	1014
Sopronia (?)	spouse of 677
Stephen (1776 -)	488
Stiles	1311
Susan	1015
Susannah (1731 - 1803)	169
Sylvanus (1733 - 1821)	170
Sylvanus (1762 - 1846)	470
Tammy Lovet (1793 -)	1291
Theodore S. (1818 -)	1108
Willard (1737 - 1825)	173
William	674
William (1761 - 1828)	478
William "Billy"	1016
William E. (1811 -)	1105
Zachariah (1735 - 1821)	172
Zarena (1795 -)	1032

Adelbert	spouse of 2756
Clarence M. (1882 - 1964)	spouse of 3316
Clarence M. (1882 - 1964)	spouse of 3318
David Frederick	3730
Estelle Frances	3727
Ethel Marion	3728
Harold Kentfield	3729
Rebecca	spouse of 161

WOODEN
Sybila	spouse of 820

WOODFORD
Edith May (1892 -)	spouse of 3206

WOODIN
Erik Richard (1978 -)	4205
Howard Henry (1892 - 1942)	spouse of 3429
Jessie Elizabeth A.S.C.P. (1927 -)	3776
John Howard "Woody" C.L.U. (1924 -)	3775
John Scott "Scott" (1950 -)	3974
Julia Lydia (1891 - 1984)	spouse of 3426
Maggie Carolyn (1992 -)	4206
Mildred Eileen (1932 - 1997)	3777
Molly Alexandria (1993 -)	4207
Trevor John (1975 -)	4204
Wendy Lee (1953 -)	3975

WOODING
George	3065
John	spouse of 1266
Lambert (1811 -)	spouse of 2188
William	3066

WOODMAN HILL
Mrs. Deborah (?) (1784 - >1850)	spouse of 372

WOODRUFF
Beulah (1783 -)	1493
Clarissa (1774 -)	1490
Eliza J. (1836 - 1898)	spouse of 1840
Elizabeth (1791 -)	1495
Hawkins (1750 - 1813)	spouse of 704
Lauren L. (1788 -)	1494
Melinda (1781 -)	1492
Nancy (1772 - 1850)	spouse of 481
Noadiah (1778 -)	1491
Zelotus Harvey (1796 -)	1496

WOODWORTH
Rev. Israel	spouse of 2090

WOODY
Gertrude (1890 - 1981)	spouse of 3863
Rutha Jane (1848 - 1924)	spouse of 3595

WORKMAN
Florence (1890 - 1982)	spouse of 2355

WRENN
Leo Harold (1914 - 1987)	spouse of 3893

WRIGHT
Charles	spouse of 1719
Charles J. (1868 -)	2579

Clarence Peter (1868 -)	2580
Jane (1869 -)	spouse of 1785
Junia (1799 - 1688)	spouse of 2115
Lillian (1870 -)	2582
Louisa (1869 - 1941)	spouse of 1752
Lucy (1870 -)	2581
Maria J. (1863 -)	2577
Robert H. (1865 -)	2578

YATES

Bessie (1894 -)	3148
Deborah	spouse of 3811
Hellen (1896 -)	3149
Ira T. (1861 -)	spouse of 2288
Nettie (1891 -)	3147

YOST

Kelly Dawn (1958 -)	4042
Penney Jeanette (1961 -)	4044
Dr. Robert Paul	spouse of 3839
Robin Gail (1960 -)	4043

YOUNG

Harriet (- 1838)	spouse of 1264
John	spouse of 34

YOUNT

Dean Burdette (1910 -)	3251
Inis Beatrice (1892 -)	3249
Lewis (1864 - 1923)	spouse of 2393
Nina Vistula (1888 -)	3248
Roy Oliver (1899 -)	3250

ZIMMERMANN

Helene "Lanie" Ph.D. (1929 -)	spouse of 3779

ZUCK

Mary Angeline (1819 - 1901)	spouse of 1123
Rubert	spouse of 4158

Notes
Chapter 1 – Luke Hill and Mary Hout

[1] The first document in which this Luke Hill is mentioned is in his marriage record, on 6 May 1651: [Bates] A. C. B. [Albert Carlos Bates] (ed.), *Some Early Records and Documents of and Relating to the Town of Windsor, Connecticut, 1639-1703* (Hartford, Conn.: Connecticut Historical Society, 1930), 47.

[2] Samuel H. Parsons, "Record of Marriages and Births, in Windsor, Ct." *New England Historic Genealogical Register* [hereafter *NEHGR*] 5 (April 1851): 225-8ff. On p. 228: "LUKE HILL, m. Mary Hout, 6 May, 1651. This appears to be the earliest published record of the marriage of Luke Hill, and here his wife's name is spelled Hout.

Henry R. Stiles, M.D., *The History of Ancient Windsor, Connecticut, Including East Windsor, South Windsor, and Ellington, Prior to 1768, the Date of Their Separation from the Old Town: and Windsor, Bloomfield and Windsor Locks, to the Present Time. Also the Genealogies and Genealogical Notes of Those Families Which Settled Within the Limits of Ancient Windsor, Connecticut, Prior to 1800* (New York: Charles B. Norton, 1859), 664: Luke Hill m. Mary Hout. Also, Henry R. Stiles, *Families of Ancient Windsor, Connecticut: Consisting of Volume II of The History and Genealogies of Ancient Windsor, Connecticut; Including East Windsor, South Windsor, Bloomfield, Windsor Locks, and Ellington, 1635-1891* (Hartford, Conn., 1892), 392. In this edition, Luke Hill m. Mary "Hoyt."

Hon. Ralph D. Smith and Dr. Bernard C. Steiner, "Luke Hill of Windsor, Conn., and John Hill of Guilford, Conn., and Their Descendants" *NEHGR* 57 (Jan. 1903): 87-93. This paper is also available as Ralph D. Smith (aka Smyth), *Luke and John Hill of Connecticut* (1903; reprinted by Higginson Book Co., Salem, Mass., 1995); and with addenda, in Gary Boyd Roberts and Elizabeth Petty Bentley, *Genealogies of Connecticut Families from the* New England Historical and Genealogical Register. Vol. 2: Geer – Owen (Baltimore, Md.: Genealogical Publishing Co., 1983), 156-165.

Buell Burdett Bassette, *One Bassett Family in America: With All Connections in America and Many in Great Britain and France* (Springfield, Mass.: F. A. Bassette Co., 1926), Luke Hill family.

[3] American Genealogical Research Institute [hereafter AGRI], *The Hill Family* (Washington, D.C.: Heritage Press, Inc., 1975), 3; and Luke Hill on pp. 32, 44-5, 91.

[4] Bassette, *Bassett Family*, 430-34.

[5] FamilyTreeDNA Certificate – Y-DNA: Dr. George J. Hill, 2010 (study of 37 alleles); and "Certificate of Y-chromosome DNA testing of George James Hill," 2 December 2005 (study of 12 alleles).

[6] AGRI (op. cit.) shows many other unrelated Hill immigrants, adding: "By the time of the 1790 census in America, Hill was the 16th most common surname in the country, numbering around 7,162." For example, Abraham Hill arrived in Boston, and he is not related to Luke. Nor are three other men named Hill who immigrated to this part of Connecticut related to Luke. They are William Hill, who came to Windsor and left before Luke arrived; John Hill, who founded a larger and "more important family" in Guilford than Luke's family in Windsor and Simsbury; and a mysterious man named Melanchthon Hill, of whom nothing is known. See: Stiles, *Ancient Windsor* (1859 and 1892) for William and Luke Hill; AGRI, 28 (for Abraham Hill), and 35 (for William Hill). Eva Loesa Hill Hosley (compiler), *Descendants of William Hill of Fairfield, Conn., Who came from Exeter, England, June 5, 1632, in Ship* William and Frances: *With Genealogical Notes and Biographical Sketches of His Descendants as Far as Can be Obtained Including Notes on Collateral Branches* (Meriden, Conn.: Horton Press, 1909); Bassette, *Bassett Family*, 425-9 (John Hill family); and Francis C. Hill, *Biographical Sketch and Genealogical Record of the Descendants of Melanchthon Hill, of Connecticut: 1610 to 1895* (New York City, N.Y.: T. A. Wright, 1895).

The Order of the Founders and Patriots of America has accepted the m record of Luke Hill and Mary Hout as evidence for his arrival in America before 1657. See Meredith B. Colket, Jr., *Founders of Early American Families: Emigrants from Europe 1607-1657.* Revised Edition (Cleveland, Ohio: General Court of the Order of Founders and Patriots of America, 1985), 155; and The Order of the Founders and Patriots of America, *Register of Lineages of Associates, 1993-2000.* Vol. 5. *Corrections, Additions, & Supplements; and Nos. 4968 Thru 5383. Index.* (Williamsburg, Va.: The General Court of the Order, 2002), 4253-4. Lineage of George James Hill . . . Descended from Generation 9 (Founder) Luke Hill Sr.; m. Mary Hoyt (Hart or Hout)."

[7] See David Webster Hoyt, *A Genealogical History of the Hoyt, Haight, and Hight Families* (Providence, 1871), 633-4.

[8] Torrey, Clarence A. *New England Marriages Prior to 1700.* 6th printing. Genealogical Publishing Co., [1984] 2004), 371: "... HILL, Luke (-1690, Simsbury) & Mary HOUT/HOYT/HART; 6 May 1651; Windsor, CT" (Accessed and printed via Ancestry.com, 4 April 2010).

     American Genealogical-Biographical Index (*AGBI*): "Mary Hout / Birth Date: 1630 / Birthplace: Connecticut / Volume: 84 / Page Number 340 / Reference: Gen. Column of the *Boston Transcript* 1906-1941 ... (14 Jan 1920), 8127. Accessed and printed from Amazon.com, in a search for "Mary Hout" on 5 April 2010.

     H. A. Thomas, "Notes: Luke Hill of Windsor, Conn., and John Hill of Guilford, Conn., and Their Descendants: Additions and Corrections" *NEHGR* 107 (Jan. 1953): 71. "These additions and corrections are to the article which appeared in *The Register*, vol. 57, p. 87 et seq., and are taken from the notes of Donald Lines Jacobus. Luke[1] Hill married 6 May 1651 Mary Hout (Windsor Records, *The Register* 5:228). Her name is shown as Hoyt in Stile's 'History of Windsor,' 2:292, and in Savage's 'Genealogical Dictionary,' 2:418. The spelling Hart, appearing in *The Register*, 57:87, may be a mis-reading of the original text. The possibility exists that Mary may have been an unrecorded daughter of Reverend Ephraim Huit or of Simon Hoyt, both among the earliest settlers of Windsor. Note that the eldest daughters of both Rev. Ephraim and Luke were named Lydia." G. J. Hill comments: Notwithstanding the tempting speculation of H. A. Thomas, I am skeptical of his suggestion. It is hard for me to imagine that the birth or baptism of a prominent clergyman's daughter would not have been recorded in the church records (*O.C.R.*), and that a clergyman's daughter would have married a yeoman, Luke Hill, without any further reference to her origin or to her siblings in the historical record over the next forty years.

[9] Ronald Toelke, *Connecticut* [Map] (1975), purchased at Windsor Historical Society, shows the earliest towns in Connecticut as Windsor (1633), Wethersfield (1634), Hartford (1635), and Saybrook (1635). The Dutch settlement near Hartford ("Fort Good Hope") was in existence from 1633-54. Kent C. L. Avery, et al, *The Settlement of Windsor, Connecticut* (Windsor, Conn.: Descendants of the Founders of Ancient Windsor, 2008), 4: "Windsor was settled in 1633 by 'Pilgrims' and in 1635 by two groups of Puritans."

[10] Bassette, *Bassett Family*, 430, citing Vol. 1:152 LR. The lot of "W. Gaylord" and the "Hi Way" are adjacent to the "Burying place" on the *Plan of the Ancient Palisado Plot in Windsor* in Stiles, *History of Ancient Windsor* (1859), 121, but a man named John brook (or Brook) is not on the map or in the Index. John Brooke is, however, later seen in the Simsbury record of 1681/2 (*infra*).

[11] Most writers agree that Luke and Mary Hill's third child was born in Farmington in March 1656/7 and that he was named Ebenezer at birth. In later years, he was known as Eleazer (also spelled Elezer and Eliazer) when he resided with the rest of the Hill family in Simsbury. The birth of Ebenezer in Farmington appears in *Connecticut Town Birth Records, pre-1870 (Barbour Collection)*, 244: "HILLS, HILL ... Ebenezer, s. Luck, b. Mar. about 20, 1656/7." Ref: Vol. LR2, p. 328, citing Farmington Vital Records 1645-1850).

[12] Bassette, *Basset Family*, 430: "The birth of son Eliazer this month at Farmington, Ct., as here reported, would indicate the family was living there. If so it could not be for long for in the following record we see him purchasing another dwelling in Windsor. Stiles says that was in Backer Row and that he sold it in a few months and moved to Middletown. The fact, however, is certain that he returned in a year or two to Windsor, since Mr. Grant shows that seven of the eight children were born at Windsor. In this connection we have searched both the land and the town meeting records in both Farmington and Middletown; but we could not find any reference to the Hills whatever."

[13] The land acquisitions in 1658 and 1660 are in Bassette, 430, citing Vol. 1:165, LR.

[14] Bassette, 430-1, for Capt. Aran Cooke's suit against Luke Hill, citing Vol. 3: 9 C C, 3 Dec 1663.

[15] Bassette, 431; and Stiles, *Ancient Windsor* (1859), 151 (canoe) and 157 (1 April and 27 April, 1667); and 160 (19 July 1671, Corporal Marshall's boat is back).

[16] Bassette, 431, citing Stiles; Stiles (1859), 160.

[17] Bassette, 431, showing that Luke Hill had been a freeman in Windsor and was now a freeman in Massaco, citing 13 May 1669 and 11 Oct 1669, Vol. 2:274 G C; and 12 May 1670, Vol. 3:1, G C.

[18] James D. Hill, "The Hill Family, From 1651 to 2000: Twelve Generations in America. Edition 5.0, 2000," Accessed 1/31/2010, 151 pp. on monitor, 51 pp. printed with 10-point font; includes many references. http://files.usgwarchives.net/ct/statewide/history/books/hill51.txt.

[19] Bassette, 431, citing 2 March 1681/2, Vol. 3:49 C C. The weekly payment to Hill was to be 3*s*, 6*d*.

[20] Bassette, 431, citing "History of 200dth anni of Simsbury Church," and James D. Hill, "The Hill Family," op. cit. Also, Luke Hill appears as one of the 32 legal voters of Simsbury in 1638 in Noah A. Phelps, *History of Simsbury, Granby and Canton, from 1642 to 1845* (Hartford, Conn.: Case, Tiffany and Burnham, 1845), 47. Eleazer Hill, presumably his son, is on this list, and his son-in-law, Arthur Henbury.

[21] Bassette, 431, the will of Arthur Henbery, citing vol. 6:18 C C, 25 June 1687; and Lucius Barnes Barbour, *Families of Early Hartford, CT: 1600s-1800s* (Baltimore, Md.: Genealogical Publishing Co., [1977], 1982). *CD #515 (2002): CD-ROM of Family Tree Maker, Local and Family Histories: Connecticut, 1600s-1800s.* Henbury and his family are on pp. 300-1. Sad to say, although Arthur Henbery recovered, his daughter Lydia – who was provided for in this will – and his wife Lydia both died in 1689.

[22] Bassette, 432, citing Vol. 4:204 P C, 21 May 1688 ("Stony Brook"); Vol. 1:64 T V, Simsbury, 26 March 1688/9, ("highway"); op. cit., 87, 27 Feb. 1692/3 ("East Corner"), 88 ("Goodman Hills"); 4:199 P C, 8 Sep 1693 ("aged 80"); Simsbury taxes, Vol. 2 ½ , 2 T V, 1693: Luke Hill, Jr. (06*s*-03*d*), Sr. (13*s*-06*d*).

[23] Bassette, 432-3, quotes the will of Luke Hill, 13 February 1693/4, in Vol. 1:167 T Acts. Luke Hill (presumably Luke Sr.) was freed from the tax lists on 9 May 1695 (citing Vol. 3:259 G C, 9 May 1695). Luke Hill (presumably Luke Jr.) was taxed in 1696 (ref. Vol. 2½ , p. 3 T V).

[24] Bassette, 433.

[25] *New Netherland Register* 1 (January 1911), a Severyen Ten Hout witnessed a document.

[26] Robert B. Miller (Editor) and A. B. Lyons, M.D. (Associate Editor), *Lyon Memorial: New York Families Descended from the Immigrant Thomas Lyon, of Rye, with Introductory Chapter by Dr. G. W. A. Lyon on the English Lyon Families* (1907), 25. This volume is about Thomas Lyon of "of Rye," of Fairfield Co., Conn., and his descendants. On p.28: he was b. abt 1621, d. 1690. He m. (1) Martha Joanna Winthrop; and (2) Mary Hoyt, dau. of Simon (p. 47, 279-80).

[27] See references *supra* for the marriage of Mary Hout, her complaint in April 1667, her place in Luke Hill's will, and the record of her observation in 1697, viz.: *Early Connecticut Probate Records* (4 September 1697), re Arthur Henbury: "afforsd. Arthur henbury to declare before me and the Wif of Luke Hill senr" (accessed via NEHGS, 25 June 2010).

[28] The list of Founders of Windsor appears in Avery, *Settlement of Windsor*, 29.

Chapter 2 – The Children

[29] Lydia Hill's birth is recorded in ACB, *Windsor*, 47; Stiles, *Ancient Windsor* (1859), 2:664; Ibid. (1892), 392; Smith and Steiner, "Luke Hill" (1903), for b. of Lydia; Bassette, *Bassett*, 430-4; and Parsons, "Windsor." Also see OneWorldTree for descendants of Lydia Hill and Arthur Henbury.

[30] Barbour, *Early Hartford*, 300-1, 369-70, 477-8 (for Arthur Henbury and his descendants). Bassette, *Bassett* (Hill Family), 431 (for will of Arthur Henbery [sic] on 25 June 1687, when he believed he was dying); and 433 (for b., m., and d. of Lydia; d. and estate of Henbery; and his second m to Widow Martha Bement in 1688). Hill, "Twelve Generations," gives Arthur Henbury's b as: "1648, Hartford, Conn."

Phelps, *Simsbury*, 45-47. [p. 45, the residents of Simsbury in 1683 are] . . . [p. 46] "Arthur Henbury." 47fn: "This list of names, containing thirty-two persons, comprised, it is believed, all the legal voters of the town in 1683. Of these, Arthur Henbury removed to Hartford about 1691, where he died without male issue."

R. R. Hinman, *Catalogue of the Names of the First Puritan Settlers of the Colony of Connecticut: With the Time of Their Arrival in the Colony, and Their Standing in Society, Together with Their Place of Residence, as Far as Can be Discovered by the Records* (Hartford: E. Gleason, 1840), 34: "Henbury, Arthur, land record, Windsor, 1669." Page 163: "*First Settlers of Windsor. . . .* The following list of names are found in the land record of Windsor . . . Arthur Henbury."

The Public Records of the Colony of Connecticut, Vol. 4. Accessed 4/15/2010 from Ancestry.com. 1699, p. 293: "Liberty and full power is by this Assembly granted to William Long of Hartford, administrat^r to the estate of Arthur Henbury deceased, to sell so much of the lands belonging to [330] the estate of the said Arthur as shall be necessary / for the paym^t of such just debts as are due from the said estate."

[31] Arthur and Lydia (Hill) Henbury had six children, all b Simsbury: **Mary** (Barbour, *Early Hartford*, 301, 369, 370); **Hannah** (op. cit., 301, 344, 394-5, 476-9); **Elizabeth** (op. cit., 301, and Ancestry.com, "Brooks, Truchon, Wimer, Barlow, Dumais Families," by dotruchon1957, accessed 4/15/2010) [hereafter, Ancestry.com, "Brooks"]; **Susannah** (Barbour, *Early Hartford*, 301; and Ancestry.com, "Brooks");

Samuel (Barbour, *Early Hartford*, 301; and Bassette, "Luke Hill Family," 431); and **Lydia** (Barbour, *Early Hartford*, 301; and Bassette, "Luke Hill," 431).

[32] Mary Hill's b is recorded in ACB, *Windsor*, 47; Stiles, *Ancient Windsor* (1859), 2:664; Ibid. (1892), 392; Smith and Steiner, "Luke Hill" (1903); AGRI, *Hill*, 32, which also records her marriage on p. 45; Bassette, *Bassett*, 430-4; and Parsons, "Windsor," 228. Descendants of Mary Hill and John Saxton from OneWorldTree [OWT] and other sources cited *infra.*

[33] For the b, ancestry, m, life, and descendants of John Sexton/Saxton, see "The Sexton Family" in Bassette, *Bassett*, 652-60. The m of John Saxton and Mary Hill is in Smith and Steiner, "Luke Hill," 87. Richard Saxton is on the list of names "found in the land record of Windsor" in 1652, in Hinman, *Connecticut Settlers*, 163. Stiles, *Ancient Windsor*, Vol. 2. *Genealogies*, "The Sexton Family," 677-8: origin of the Sexton family in Yorkshire, England, and the supposed connection to the first earl of Limerick; arrival of Richard and George Sexton in America; 6 ch of Richard Sexton; the family of his s John Sexton, who m Mary Hill (dau. of Luke) on 30 July 1677; and their dau Mary, b. 4 May 1678. Much of this information is also in OWT, without sources.

[34] For the m and family of Mary Sexton and William Gillett, and of his ancestors in America, see Bassette, *Bassett*, "The Gillett Family," 321-33; and the family of Roger Eno, his dau Jerusha, and her h Ira Allen, in "The Eno Family," 246-61.

[35] I cannot find a primary source that unequivocally shows that Eleazer Hill of Simsbury, Conn., was the s of Luke Hill and Mary Hout of Windsor, Conn., and that he was the same person as the Ebenezer, s of Luck (a k a Luik) Hill, who was b in March 1656/7 in Farmington, Mass. This information does, however, appear in countless websites in which Luke and Mary Hill are shown as having a third ch whose name is either Ebenezer or Eleazer. It is not unusual to have a name change such as this, and the weight of evidence suggests that it probably did happen in this instance. Primary and secondary sources in which Ebenezer and Eleazer Hill are mentioned as the third ch of Luke Hill and his wife Mary include the following:

"Ebenezer Hill, s. Luck, b. Mar. abt. 20, 1656" appears in the *Barbour Collection*, Farmington, 12:244; referencing Vol. LR2, p. 328. Ancestry.com and many other secondary sources presume that "Luck" Hill in this transcribed b.r. is actually Luke Hill, so Ebenezer Hill, b. about 20 March 1656/7 (N.S.), would be the first s and third ch of Luke and Mary Hill. Their other seven ch were born at intervals of 2-3 years, and the b of Ebenezer thus fits nicely into the five year gap between their dau Mary (b. 1654) and their s Tahan (b. 1659). We do not know why Luke's w Mary would have been in Farmington when her third ch was born, but it is clear from the historical record that Ebenezer/Eleazer was not born in Windsor. This s does not appear in the Old Church Records [O.C.R.] of Windsor (transcribed in ACB, *Windsor* [1930] and Parsons, "Windsor" [1851]).

James Savage wrote in 1861 that Eleazer Hill was b. 1657 in Connecticut. From *AGBI* 79:347, referencing Savage, *A Genealogical Dictionary of the First Settlers of New England, Showing Three Generations of Those Who Came Before May, 1692* (Boston, 1861), 2:418.

Eleazer Hill is shown as the s of Luke and Mary Hill in Stiles, *Ancient Windsor* (1892), where he appears as the third ch of Luke Hill and Mary Hoyt (sic), viz.: "3. *[Eleazer, b. 1657; not rec. *O.C.R.*]." The assertion that Eleazer is the s of Luke Hill does not, however, appear in the first edition of Stiles, *Ancient Windsor* (1859). In this edition, only seven ch of Luke and Mary Hill are shown, and Eleazer is not one of them. Instead, in the 1859 edition, the name of Eleazer Hill appears immediately after the entry for Luke and Mary and their ch. Unfortunately, the f and s, Eleazer Hill Sr. and Jr., are inadvertently conflated by Stiles in 1859.

In 1895, Francis Hill wrote a short monograph in which he asserted that the name of the f of Ebenezer Hill in the Farmington records was actually spelled "Lank," and that he believed this was an abbreviation for the name Melanchthon Hill. See: Francis C. Hill, *Biographical Sketch and Genealogical Record of the Descendants of Melanchthon Hill, of Connecticut: 1610 to 1895* (New York City, N.Y.: T. A. Wright, 1895). Francis Hill believed that this Ebenezer Hill had two sons, Joseph and George, who went respectively to Goshen and Norwalk, Conn. Francis Hill's narrative is rambling and confusing, his genealogy is deeply flawed, and there is little reason to believe his assertion that the father of Ebenezer Hill was an otherwise unknown man named Melanchthon Hill, who disappeared from the historical record after fathering Ebenezer Hill.

Smith and Steiner, "Luke Hill," show Ebenezer, not Eleazer, as the third ch of Luke Hill and Mary Hart (sic). Bassette asserted that Eleazer Hill was the third ch of Luke and Mary Hoyt (sic) Hill. AGRI, *Hill*: The third ch of Luke Hill and Mary Hoyt was Eleazur (p. 32); Elezer Hill m. Sarah Gillett (p. 45).

Hill, "Twelve Generations," says that Eleazer Hill was b. 7 Mar 1657, citing three sources, one of which is "New England Marriages Prior to 1700." I cannot confirm this statement. Eleazer Hill's b or m may be in this book, although it is not in the Index of the copy that I reviewed, nor do I see his b in this book. Leon S. Pitman also says that Eleazer Hill was b on 7 March 1657 in Farmington, Conn., citing references. From Pitman, "Some Descendants of Nathan Gillett of Windsor and Simsbury, Connecticut," Modesto, California, [1999] 2002, from Ancestry.com, 23 August 2009.

On the basis of the many primary and secondary sources quoted above, I conclude that Ebenezer Hill (who was b in Farmington in March 1656/7 but was not mentioned in later records of that town) is probably the same person as Eleazer Hill (who appeared in Simsbury in 1679 as an adult). This presumes that Ebenezer Hill (b. Farmington, 1656/7) was known as Eleazer Hill when he m Sarah Gillet/Gillett in 1679 and that he continued to be known as Eleazer Hill for the rest of his life.

[36] Alice Lucinda Priest, "The Brothers Jonathan and Nathan Gillett and Some of Their Descendants" *NEHGR* (October 1946): 272-277. Robert Charles Anderson, *The Great Migration Begins: Immigrants to New England, 1620-1633*. Vols 1-3. Some secondary sources give the date of his birth as 7 March 1656/7, but the date in the Farmington records transcribed in the *Barbour Collection* is "b. Mar. abt. 20, 1656," which we would now write as "abt. 20 March 1656/7." The brothers Jonathan and Nathan Gillett, who came to America on the *Mary and John* in the Winthrop Fleet in 1630, are believed to be sons of the Rev. William Gylett, Rector of Chaffcombe, Somersetshire, England. He is said to have come from Bergerac, Guyenne, France, and his descendants are eligible for membership in the Huguenot Society of America.

[37] Pitman, Ibid.

[38] Anderson, *Great Migration Begins*, "Nathan Gillett" (dau Sarah): vi. SARAH, b. 13 July 1651; m. Simsbury 29 December 1679 Eleazer Hill [Referencing Simsbury Vital Records, *Barbour Collection*, 61. Also in Torrey, *New England Marriages*: "Hill, Eleazer - Eleazer [-1725?] & Sarah GILLET; 29 Dec 1679; Simsbury, CT [Simsbury CT VR 12; Hartford Prob. 2:525]."

[39] U.S. and International Marriage Records, 1560-1900 (Ancestry.com, Source Citation: Source number: 2512.000, 6/14/2010): "Eleazer Hill, male, b. CT, 1656; Spouse Sarah Gillett, b. CT, 1651; m. 1679, CT."

[40] Phelps, *Simsbury*, 46 (Eleazer Hill, resolution signed 1683), 55 (1697, church covenant), 152 (taxes 1694, 1696). "On 31 January 1692/3, several acres of [Ebenezer Parson's] land . . . were seized by the constable, Eleazer Hill, and delivered to Peter Mills to satisfy the judgment" (Gerald James Parsons, "The Early Parsons Families of the Connecticut River Valley," *NEHGR* 148 [1994]: 354).

[41] *Early Connecticut Probate Records*, accessed 6/15/10 from NEHGS. The Alverd family (Record 1, 2:6ff); Rowley inventory (Record 2, 2:7-8); Clark estate (Record 4, 2:370); Goring inventory (Record 5, 2:390); Will and probate of Eleazer Hill (Record 6, 2:525).

[42] *A Digest of the Early Connecticut Probate Records, 1723-1729*, 121-4 (Eleazer Hill, Windsor), accessed from Ancestry.com, 6/14/2010. I have not found a source for the Eleazer's d.d; 3 March 1724/5 is in Burdette, *Burdette*.

[43] She is probably the "HILL ...Wid. SARAH, d. Sept. 30, 1737" in Stiles, *Windsor* (1859), 664. For the ancestry and descendants of Sarah (Gillett) Hill, w of Eleazer Hill, see: Pitman, "Nathan Gillett," "4: vi. SARAH, b. 13 July 1651, m. 29 Dec. 1679 in Simsbury 29 Dec. 1659 to ELEAZER HILL, who was b. 7 March 1656/7 in Farmington, Conn.[28] He d. at Windsor 3 Mar. 1724/5. In April 1688 Eleazer Hill, as a son-in-law of Nathan Gillett, was granted land in the Nathan Gillett Weatogue Meadow tract in Simsbury.[29] His lot abutted that of brother-in-law Nicholas Gozzard. Children born in Simsbury, surname **Hill**, include: (1) *Elizabeth*, b. 29 July 1681; (2) *Mary*, b. 6 Dec. 1685, d. 5 Dec. 1697 in Simsbury; (3) *Eleazer*, b. 20 Jul. 1694, (4) *Sarah*. [30]." References to this paragraph in Pitman: George E. McCracken, *The American Genealogist [TAG]* 56 [1980]:130. John W. Harms and Pearl Goddard Harms, *The Goddard Book*, 2 vols. (Baltimore, 1984) [hereinafter Harms & Harms] 1:36, 37. Includes the data on their children; 22. Simsbury Vital Records in Albert C. Bates, *Simsbury, Connecticut, Births, Marriages and Deaths* (Hartford, 1898) [hereinafter Simsbury VRs in Bates], 11, 40. John Slater's will is printed in Charles William Manwaring, *A Digest of The Early Connecticut Probate Records* 1904-06, 3 vols. (reprinted, Baltimore, 1995). [hereafter Manwaring], 2:296; 28. In Bates, *Simsbury VRs*, [note 22] 12, Sarah who m. Eleazer Hill, is identified as the dau of Nathan Gillett. Also included are the b.d's. for

Elizabeth, Mary, and Eleazer and the d.d. for Mary; 29. Simsbury Deeds 1-1/2:72, 73, 125.

[44] The order of b of Eleazer Hill's four ch is given differently in Pitman, *Nathan Gillett* (2002), *supra.*, and in Hill, "Twelve Generations," who says there were but three: Elizabeth 29 Jul 1681, Mary 1685-97, Eliezer Jr. 20 Jul 1694. I cannot find a primary source for the b year of Sarah, who was mentioned in her father's will in 1717, but it is reasonable to assume that she was born in the interval between Mary (1685) and Eleazer Jr. (1694). The order of b and dates of b and d of the four ch has thus been chosen arbitrarily from the various primary and secondary sources.

[45] ACB, *Windsor*, 47: "his fonn Tahan Hill was Borne . noumbr . 23 . 1659." Stiles, *Ancient Windsor* (1859) "Tahan, b. Nov. 23, 1659"; also, Stiles, *Ancient Windsor* (1892), v.2: Children of Luke and Mary (Hoyt –sic) Hill include "3. *[Eleazer, b. 1657; not rec. *O.C.R.*]; 4. Tahan, b. 23 Nov., 1659." And "Families of Early Guilford, Connecticut," *Local and Family Histories: CT, 1600s-1800s,* Family Tree Maker, CD515, 2000, "Parmelee Family, 943-982; 943: John Parmelee, the Immigrant, and his wife Hannah ___ had a child, John, who married three times. He m. (3), in 1659, Hannah ____, and had at Guilford a child Hanna (b. 5 Nov 1667), who mar. Tahan Hill. Page 1262, "Hannah mar/2 Thomas Merrill." There are many women named Hannah Parmelee and Hannah Hill (including at least three citations for wid. Hannah Hill) and Hannah Merrill in this volume, and it is not clear from these records that it is the widow Hannah (Parmelee) Hill who "mar/2 Thomas Merrill." Parsons, "Windsor," 228: "LUKE HILL, m. Mary Hout, 6 May, 1651; chil. Liddya, b. 18 Feb. 1651; Mary, b. 20 Sept. 1654; Tahan, b. 23 Nov. 1659." Smith and Steiner, "Luke Hill": b. of Tahan, 16 or 18 Dec 1692; m. 29 Nov 1688, Hannah Parmelee; was of Guilford in 1690; ch. Hannah, b. 17 Nov 1689, m. 31 Mar 1710 Samuel Bushnell, and Tahan [Jr.] b. 1691. This information is repeated verbatim without a source in Bassette, *Bassett*, "Luke Hill Family," 433. The information above is repeated in James D. Hill, "Hill Family"; and in Ancestry.com, OWT. His nickname, "Tahay," appears in Hill, "Twelve Generations," without a source.

[46] His m is in *TAG*, 13 (1936), 184: "Hill, Tahane / Parmely, Hannah / both of Gilford / married By Mr Andrew Leete Justis Later end Nov. 1688."

[47] Parmelee family in "Early Guilford, 943-82. On 943: John Parmelee (who was one of the twenty-five signers of the Guilford Plantation Covenant on June 1, 1689) and his wife Hannah ___ had a son John Jr., who m. (3) in 1659, Hannah ____ and had, at Guilford, a daughter Hannah, b. 5 Nov 1667, who m. Tahan Hill. Nothing more is stated here about this m or of any progeny of Tahan and Hannah (Parmelee) Hill. On p. 1262 it is said that "Hannah mar/2 Thomas Merrill." It is not stated on either p. 943 or 1262 that it was Hannah (Parmelee) Hill who m. Thomas Merrill. However, OWT (accessed 6/18/10) says that Thomas Merrill (b. 1646, Hartford) m. 25 May 1693 at Saybrook, Hannah (Parmelee) Hill, and he died 7 Nov 1711. The same information about John Parmelee Sr., John Parmelee Jr., his daughter Hannah, and her m to Tahan Hill is also in Smith and Steiner, "The Descendants of John Parmelee," 24-29. Smith and Steiner, "Luke Hill": Tahan Hill, son of Luke Hill and Mary Hart (sic) m. 29 Nov 1688, Hannah Parmelee; he d. 16 or 18 Dec 1692 and she m. (2) "Thomas Merrill of Saybrook."

[48] Zoeth D. Eldridge in *NEHGR* 54 (1900), 353: "MERRILLS - Book 1, page 3, Hartford records, has the following 'Thomas Merrills, son of Thomas Merrills, was baptized Nov. 1, 1646.' Can any one tell me the fate of this child? I have long sought for the record of Thomas Merrills of Saybrook, who was married in that place May 25, 1693, to Hannah, daughter of John Parmelee of Guilford, and widow of Tahan Hill."

[49] An alternate second m for Hannah (Parmelee) (Hill) is given in Smith and Steiner, "Descendants of John Parmelee," 25: "The children of John and Hannah Parmelee were: . . . vi. Hannah, b. Nov. 5, 1667; m. 1st, Tahan Hill, son of Luke of Windsor, November, 1688; he d. Dec. 16, 1692; 2d, Josiah Stevens of Killingworth. . . ."

[50] This account of the life and family of Luke Hill Jr., is based on many sources, some of which are more reliable than others. Some of these allege to be transcriptions or quotations from primary sources, while others are secondary sources that are derived from previous transcriptions. Some are simply assertions made in public websites. The principal collections of references are the catalog of the New England Historic Genealogical Society (NEHGS), in which the name Luke Hill appears 40 times; two CDs of Family Tree Maker's Family Archives (CD#515, "Local and Family Histories: Connecticut, 1600s-1800s; and CD#179, "Connecticut Family Histories #1, 1600s-1800s), which were searched for numerous references to Luke Hill; and the *Barbour Collection of Connecticut Vital Records*, which was searched for the names of Luke Hill and his children.

The 40 citations to Luke Hill (which include references to Luke Sr., Jr., and III) in the NEHGS database were all examined and those that are relevant are incorporated into the present work. On CD#179 (*supra*), the Index shows 9 pages on which references to Luke Hill appear and one on which Luke Jr. appears. All of these pages were examined and relevant information was incorporated into this work. However, the most important information about Luke Hill, Jr. in CD#179 is inexplicably absent from the Index. I discovered it by chance when searching for Luke Jr.'s son-in-law, John Dibble. It is in "Families of Ancient New Haven," vol. 3, "Family Statistics," 743: "Hill family 5: Luke, s. of Luke & Mary (Hart) [sic]." This page shows the m of Luke Jr. to Hannah Butler, their 6 ch, ch of two of their sons (Ebenezer and Luke [III]); and a second m to Deliverance _____, by whom Luke Jr. had a seventh ch, Deliverance. On CD#515 (*supra*), the Index shows 4 pages on which references to Luke Hill appear. All of these pages were examined and relevant information was incorporated into the present work.

The *Barbour Collection* was accessed in two ways: (1) through Ancestry.com, which provided copies of specific pages of *Connecticut Town Birth Records, pre-1870 (Barbour Collection)*; from Ancestry.com [database on-line]. Original data: Lorraine Cook, ed. *The Barbour Collection of Connecticut Town Vital Records.* Vol. 1-55. Baltimore, Md.: Genealogical Publishing Co., 1994-2002; and (2) through New Horizons Genealogical Services [NHGS] "Barbour Collection of Vital Records," trans. Coralynn Brown, at www.newhorizonsgenealogicalservices.com/barbour-collection.htm (accessed 6/26/2010ff).

Also, the names of Luke Hill, his w, and his descendants were sought for on Ancestry.com, beginning with OWT. The OWT synthesis for Luke Hill and his w Hannah Butler was said to be derived from 90 User-submitted trees. OWT (accessed 6/25/2010) was correct in some respects, but it included some obvious errors. For example, the d.d and d.p. for Hannah (Butler) Hill is probably for another woman named Hannah Hill; and Luke Hill Jr. is given a seventh ch (Uri), who is actually a ch of Luke [III] and his w Sarah, not Luke Jr. and his w Hannah. OWT must therefore be regarded warily in regard to the information it provides about Luke Hill and his w and ch.

[51] ACB, *Windsor*, 47: "[53] Luke Hill married mary Hout . may . 6 . 1651. . . . his fonn Luke Hill was Borne . march . 6 . 1661"; Stiles, *Ancient Windsor* (1859), 664: "LUKE, m. Mary Hout, May 6, 1651. *Children* – . . . Luke, b. March 6, 1661"; Stiles, *Ancient Windsor* (1892), 392: "HILL ... "Luke (no evid. of relationship to Mr. William); m. Mary Hoyt [sic], 6 May, 1651 (*O.C.R.*); . . . *Ch.*: . . . 5. Luke, b. 6 Mch., 1661"; Smith and Steiner, "Luke Hill": "LUKE[1] HILL, of Windsor . . . married Mary Hart [sic] . . . Their children were: . . . 3. v. LUKE[2], b. March 6, 1661. . . . 3. LUKE Hill, JR. (*Luke*[1]), born March 6, 1661, married Hanna _____, or Anna _____, and lived for a time at Guilford. He seems to have been of roving disposition."

Donald Lines Jacobus, *Families of Ancient New Haven.* 9 vols. in 3 (Baltimore, Md.: Genealogical Publishing Co., 1981): "Butler Family": FAM. 1. JOHN, of Bd, d. 1679; m (1) ---------; m (2) Bendicta ----------. . . . (By 2): 6 JOHATHAN; m Lydia -----; 10 children. 7 JONAH, d. s. p. 28 Feb 1710 *BdV* [1710/1]; 8 HANNAH; m Luke Hill." "BdV" refers to Branford, Conn., Vital Records. Hill, "Twelve Generations": "LUKE HILL . . . Children: . . . 2. Luke Hill (2nd) B. 06 Mar 1661/2, Windsor, CT. D. 20 May 1740, Wallingford, CT. M: Hannah Butler B. [1687] Simsbury, CT."; [Hill] AGRI, *The Hill Family* (1975), 32: "*Luke Hill* . . . married to Mary Hoyt [sic]; children were Lydia, Mary, Eleazur, Tahan, Luke . . ."; Parsons, "Windsor": 228: "LUKE HILL, m. Mary Hout, 6 May, 1651; chil. . . Luke, b. 6 March, 1661. NHGS, *Barbour Collection*, Wallingford VR [Transcribed by Coralynn Brown]: Hill, Isaac, d. Oct 25, 1741." Bassette, *Bassett Family*, 430-3: The ch of Luke Hill and Mary Hoyt (sic) were eight, including "5. LUKE b. Mch. 6, 1661; m. Hanna _____ 6 ch. After m they lived up to about 1693 at Guilford; then to about 1696 at Wethersfield; then Simsbury to about 1703; then Branford. He had namesake whose will was filed Apl. 7, 1772 at Litchfield, Ct." And, p. 433: "1696. Vol. 2 ½, p 3 T V: Here is spread against 68 citizens of Simsbury 'Mr. Dudley Woodbridges rate made and published for 1696'. Luk Hill pays L00-11-03. There is but one Luke Hill in the list, and we take this as referring to son Luke since Luke Sen'r is freed from taxes anyway, as per the preceding item. From this point in the records and running into the next century there are various references to Luke Hill, but we can find nothing further re Luke Hill Sen'r."

[52] Phelps, *Simsbury*: Luke Hill Sr. and Jr. were both listed in Town Rates in 1694 (p. 152); Luke Hill (presumably Jr.) was in Minister's Rates in 1696 (p. 152), and in Minister's Rates in 1701 (p. 153).

[53] The m of Luke Hill Jr. to Deliverance _____ and the b of their dau Deliverance Hill is in Jacobus, *Ancient New Haven*, v. 3, "Family Statistics," Hill. Fam. 5. Luke, s. of Luke & Mary (Hart), 743. The m of Deliverance Hill to Andrew Blackman is in the *Barbour Collection*, Woodbury VR, 11 January 1764.

Ancestry.com, without sources, says that Luke Hill Jr. m. Deliverance Cooke Falconer, and their daughter Deliverance m. Andrew Blackmun. There are many descendants of Andrew and Deliverance (Hill) Blackmun in various family trees in Ancestry.com, and this appears to be legitimate, although it is unreferenced in the initial generations.

For Deliverance (Cooke) Falconer, said in Ancestry.com to be Deliverance ____, second w of Luke Hill Jr.: Her b is in the *Barbour Collection*: "Deliverance Cook [Cooke] / female / b.d. 12 Jan 1695 / Guilford / Parent Thomas / Parent Sarah." Her ancestry, b, and first m is in *Genealogies of Connecticut Families* and *Families of Ancient New Haven*. I cannot find a record of her second m to Luke Hill Jr., and neither Gary Boyd Roberts (for Cooke) nor Jacobus (for Falconer) says anything about a second m of Deliverance (Cooke) Falconer.

Smith and Steiner, "Thomas Cooke of Guilford, Conn. and His Descendants," in Roberts, *Genealogies of Connecticut Families* 1:477-ff: She was the tenth and youngest ch of Thomas Cooke Jr. and Sarah Mason; he was the s of Thomas and Elizabeth Cooke. Thomas Cooke Sr. was an original signer of the plantation covenant of Guilford and was the last survivor of the original signers. He was a member of the General Assembly and a "Juror" of Guilford. Thomas Cooke Jr. was a carpenter of Guilford. He m, 15 April 1677, Sarah Mason, who died 6 July 1701. They had ten ch, of whom the sixth was (Rev.) Samuel (A.B., Yale), and the youngest was Deliverance.

The Rev. Samuel Cooke (1687-1747), older brother of Deliverance, was of Stratfield or Bridgeport, Conn. He graduated A.B. from Yale College in 1705. He m four times: m (1) 30 Nov 1706, Anna, dau of John Trowbridge of New Haven; d. 11 Aug 1721; m (2) Esther, dau of Nathaniel Burr and wid of John Sloss of Fairfield; d. 1723; m (3) Elizabeth, dau. of Joseph Platt of Norwalk; b. 2 Dec 1701; d. 16 May 1732; m (4) 16 Aug 1733 Abigail, dau. of Rev. Samuel Russel of Branford and wid of Rev. Joseph Moss. He had 8 ch, three of whom graduated from Yale. The first seven were ch of Anna Trowbridge, and the eighth, including one of the Yale graduates, was by Elizabeth Platt.

Jacobus, *Ancient New Haven*, v. 3 "Family Statistics, Ewen, Faircild, Falconer, Fanning, Farnes, Farrand, Farren," 597: "FALCONER. Varian FAULKNER. PATRICK, b.c. 1660, d 27 June 1692 ae. 33 Newark, N.J.; m. 2 Oct 1689 NHV -- Hannah da. William & Hanna (Eaton) Jones, b.c. 1660, d 29 May 1717 StV; she m (2) James Clark . . . 1 HANNAH, b c.1640; m 7 Aug 1710 GV -- Seth Morse. 2 PATRICK, b 12 Aug 1692 (posthumous) NHV, bp 14 Aug 1692 NHC1, d 1735; res. G; m Deliverance Cooke, who d 1781; children: Hannah (1723-1765) m Charles Miller; Sarah (1727-1797); Mary (1729-) m Simeon Norton; Charles (1731-1803) m (1) Hannah Morse & (2) Mary Bly; Rebecca (1734-1816)."

Ancestry.com says (7/20/10) without a source, that her name is Deliverance Cooke Falconer, and that her daughter Deliverance Hill, b. 20 July 1738, m. Andrew Blackmun (b. 3 Jan 1740), and d. Clinton, Mooers, N.Y., 2 Oct 1821). This b.d. for Deliverance Hill is consistent with the known years of Luke Hill Jr. (d. 26 May 1740).

[54] From Thom Carlson to GJH, 3 December 2008. Carlson quotes Beach, *History of Cheshire*; and Hibbard, *History of the Town of Goshen*, Chapter 3, 42-4.

[55] *Early Connecticut Probate Records*, 2:473: Record of 31 March 1736 re Ebenezer Hill, Jr., Luke Hill, and Isaac Hill, near the town lines of Litchfield and Torrington, Conn. "Page 42 (Vol. XII) 31 March, 1736: It appears to this Court that there was 300 acres of land granted by the General Assembly of the Colony of Connecticut to James Wadsworth, John Hall and Hezekiah Brainard, Esq., bounded south by the Litchfield line and every way else by common land, lying neare the west line of the place called Torrington. Sd. Wadsworth hath sold his third part as undivided to Ebenezer Hill, Jr., Luke Hill and Isaac Hill, and sd. Hall's part now belongs to his eldest son John Hall of Wallingford, and in the dist. of sd. Brainard's estate according to his last will his third part of sd. land fell to his son Israel Brainard, who is yet under age, who, together with the other owners of sd. land viz., John Hall and the sd. Ebenezer, Luke and Isaac Hill, moves this Court that James Wadsworth, Esq., and James Wadsworth, Jr., of Durham, might assist Hezekiah Brainard, guardian to sd. minor, to divide the sd. 300 acres of land by meets and bounds, that each owner may know their part thereof."

[Comment by GJH: It appears that these three men named Hill are contemporaries, but it is not clear who they were. Ebenezer, Luke, and Isaac Hill were the names of sons of Luke Hill Jr. and his wife Hannah Butler. This Ebenezer had a son, who would have been known as Ebenezer Jr. while his father was still alive, and the other two men were probably brothers of Ebenezer (Sr.). This Luke Hill was therefore Luke (III), a grandson of Luke and Mary (Hout) Hill, and Isaac was later known as Isaac Hill, Sr., who married Esther Stone.]

[56] Smith and Steiner, "Luke Hill":

3. LUKE Hill, JR. (*Luke[1]*), born March 6, 1661, married Hanna _____, or Anna _____, . . . His children were:

     i.   EBENEZER,[3] b. Nov. 23, 1687, at Guilford.
     ii.   ANNA, b. Dec 3, 1692.
     iii.   KEZIAH, b. Feb. 24, 1695, at Wethersfield.
     iv.   LUKE, b. at Simsbury, Sept. 16, 1698.
     v.   LYDIA, b. at Simsbury, Feb. 25, 1700.
     vi.   ISAAC, b. at Branford, May 27, 1703.

[57] *Barbour Collection*, Goshen, Litchfield Co., Ct., VR: Hill, Ebenezer, m Martha DIBAL, Jan 3, 1716/17 . . . Hill, Ebenezer, son Ebenezer & Martha, b Oct 24, 1717. OWT states without a source that Ebenezer Hill d. in 1758, and that his wife Martha Dibble was b. in Saybrook, Conn, 14 Nov 1697; d. 1758.

[58] Jacobus, *Ancient New Haven.* 2:435-6: "Cook Family" COOK. FAM. 1. HENRY of Salem, Mass., d 25 Dec 1661; m June 1639 *SalemV* – Judith Birdsall. . . . [They had 10 children] 1 ISAAC. . . 2 SAMUEL . . . 8 HENRY, b 30 Dec 1652 *SalemV*, d 1705; m 30 Sep 1678 *SalemV* – Mary da. John & Jane (Woolen) Hall, b c. 1654, d 31 July 1718 *WV*. [They had 11 children, of whom the 6th was Isaac]

       vi Isaac, b c. 1692; rem. to Bd; m Anna da. Luke & Hannah (Butler) Hill, b 30 Dec 1692 (at Simsbury) *BdV*. Children, recorded *WV*: 1 Isaac, b July 1716; 2 Demetrius, b 2 Apr 1718; 3 Uzziel, b 9 May 1722; 4 Anna, b 24 June 1724; 5 Waitstill, b 8 Jan 1727; 6 Desire, b 21 July 1729; 7 Lydia, b 4 Feb 1732."

OWT, citing "29 User-submitted trees," states that Anna was b. at Guilford.

[59] Jacobus, *Ancient New Haven.* 3:623-4: "Frederick Family": "FREDERICK. WILLIAM, res. W & Wy; m (1) Mary da. Jonathan & Rebecca (Bell) Tuttle, b 17 Feb 1666 *NHV*; m (2) Abigail da. Abraham & Abigail (Moss) Doolittle, b 26 Feb 1668 *WyV*, d 26 Aug 1760 ae. 55 *NHT1*; m 18 Dec 1718 *NHV* – Josiah Todd. [They had 8 children] . . . 8 SARAH, b 18 Oct 1704 *WV*; m 19 Dec 1723 *WV* – Luke Hill."

    Barbour Collection, Wallingford, New Haven Co., Ct. VR, 1670-1850 [Transcribed by Coralynn Brown]: Hill, Luke, m. Sarah FRED[E]RICK, Dec. 19, 1723, by Capt John Hall.

    OWT states without a source that Luke Hill d. Mar 1772 at Goshen, Litchfield Co., Conn.

[60] Jacobus, *Ancient New Haven.* 3:535-6: "Dibble Family": "DIBBLE. FAM. 1. JOHN, res. W, rem. To L before 1753; m 14 Apr 1725*WV* – Lydia da. Luke & Hannah (Butler) Hill, b 26 Feb 1700 (at Simsbury) *BdV*.

    1 JOHN, b 26 July 1725 *WV*.
    2 REUBEN, b 6 Mar 1727 *WV*.
    3 LYDIA, b 29 May 1731 *WV*.
    4 SUSANNA, b 30 Mar 1735*WV*.
    5 JOSIAH, b 3 Mar 1737*WV*.

OWT, without a source, says Lydia (Hill) Dibble d. at Goshen, Conn., in 1756.

[61] *Barbour Collection*, Wallingford: Hill, Isaac, m. Esther STONE, Jan. 16, 1733 / Hill, Isaac, d. Oct 25, 1741

[62] Deliverance Hill, daughter of Luke Jr. and his wife Deliverance, from Jacobus, *Ancient New Haven*, 3:743, "Family Statistics," Hill. Fam. 5. Luke, s. of Luke & Mary (Hart).

[63] Abigail Hill's birth is recorded in ACB, *Windsor*, 47; Stiles, *Ancient Windsor* (1859), Part 2, 664; Ibid. (1892), 392; Smith and Steiner, "Luke Hill"; and Bassette, *Bassett*, 430-4. Also see OWT for descendants of Abigail Hill and Caleb Parmelee.

    Parmelee family in "Families of Early Guilford, Connecticut," 943-82: John Parmelee (who was one of the twenty-five signers of the Guilford Plantation Covenant on June 1, 1689) and his wife Hannah ___ had a son John Jr., who m. (3) in 1659, Hannah _____ and had, at Guilford, a daughter Hannah, b. 5 Nov 1667, who m. Tahan Hill.

[64] Smith and Steiner, "Descendants of John Parmelee," 24-29: CALEB[3] PARMELEE (*John[2]*, *John[1]*) of Branford, husbandman, married first, Abigail Johnson, daughter of John of Guilford, April 11, 1690, who

died May 8, 1692; second, Abigail Hill, April 23, 1693. She died at Branford, Oct. 6, 1737.

The child of Caleb and Abigail (Johnson) Parmelee was:

i. Samuel[4], b. April 26, 1691; d. Dec. 18, 1692.

The children of Caleb and Abigail (Hill) Parmelee were:

ii. Hannah, b. March 28, 1694; joined the Branford church, Nov. 5, 1714.

iii. Caleb, b. Aug. 28, 1696; d. July 14, 1750; m. 1st, Elizabeth Foote, 1720; she d. 1725,
        ae. 28; 2d, Jemima Harrison, March 25, 1728; she d. 1730; 3d, Mary Durham, Jan. 11, 1737; she
        d. October 1770. By his first wife he had: 4. *Abigail*[5], b. April 16, 1721; m. Cornelius Johnson of
        Branford. 2. *Mary*, b. Dec. 25, 1722; m. Samuel Barnes of East Haven, Aug. 2, 1739. 3. *Sarah*, b.
        Oct. 16, 1724; joined Branford church Aug. 30, 1741; m. Timothy Allen, Nov. 23, 1744. By his
        second wife he had: 4. *Jerusha*, b. Feb. 16, 1729; m. Stephen Smith, September, 1747. By his
        third wife he had: 5. *Chloe*, b. April 2, 1739. 6. *Rebecca*, b. April 12, 1741.

iv. Lydia, b. Mar 8, 1699; d. Oct. 8, 1726; m. John Young, Feb 3, 1725-6; joined Branford ch Sept. 2, 1716.

v. Josiah, b. Dec. 28, 1701; joined Branford church Sept. 2, 1716.

vi. Abigail, b. March 12, 1703; m. John Read of Branford, May 3, 1727.

vii. Benjamin, b. June 26, 1705.

[65] *Barbour Collection*, Guilford V.R., 243: "PARMELEE, PARMELE, PARMELY, PARMELIN, PARMILIE, PARMERLY … Calib, m. Abigail JOHNSON, b. of G[u]ilford, Apr 21, 1690, by Mr. Andrew Leete" (cites A:80).

[66] William Plaine was was executed in Guilford in 1646 under a sodomy law. He had been found guilty of masturbating a number of young men. The execution may not have been legal, given the definition of sodomy at that time. See George Painter, "The Sensibilities of Our Forefathers: The History of Sodomy Laws in the United States (1991-2001)," a copyrighted web page accessed 7/22/2010. Painter cites James Savage (ed.), John Winthrop, *The History of New England from 1630 to 1649* (Boston: Little, Brown, 1853), 2:324.

[67] *TAG* 16 (1939), 182 (accessed via NEHGS), shows m of Caleb and Abigail (Hill) Permelee and the b of four of their ch, citing Guilford, Conn., VR:

[p. 20] Permele, Calib of gilford   married   By Mr highly Justis
      hill, abygell of Semsbury   23 Apr. 1793 [*sic*] [error noted by editor of *TAG*]

[p. 21] Births / Permele, Hanah da. Calib & Abigell   b. 28 Mar. 1694
         Calib s. Calib & Abigell   b. 23 Aug. 1696
         Lidiah da. Calib & Abigell   b. 8 Mar. 1699
         Josiah s. Calib & Abigell   b. 28 Dec. 1701
         Abigell da. Calib & Abigell   b. 12 Mar 1702/3

[68] Bassette, *Bassett*, 433: "Abigail Parmerly receives £14 in settlement deed of 1693/4." The will of Luke Hill Sr., written on 13 February 1693/4 states: "my sd Son John Hill is to pay and fully discharge all my debts, as also to pay his sister Abigall Parmerly her portion which is Fourteen pounds as also to do it as soon as he can conveniently, and whereas sd Abigall had given her the grat Iron Pot she shall not have it till after her parants death; but that beed with the filling therein and one bolster and pillow sd abigall is to have after our death. Freely it is given her; but the pot above mentioned is to goe to her for part of her portion." Abigail and John are the only ch that Luke mentioned in his will. He mentioned that "Fourteen pounds" is "her portion," so it may be that the other ch were given equal portions, i.e. £14, in the distribution of the estate, but the record of the distribution has not been found.

[69] Jemima (Harrison) Parmelee was the dau of Thomas Harrison, who served in King Philip's War, was ensign in 1697, was a lieutenant in 1709 in Queen Anne's War, and was also in the expedition to Canada. He was the father of 9 ch by Margaret Stent, dau of his step-mother. Their second ch, Jemima, m as his second w, Caleb Parmelee Jr., who m. (1) Elizabeth Foote and (3) Mary Durham. The record of her d in 1730 in *Families of Early Guilford* must be erroneous or a misinterpretation by me, because Findagrave.com shows (on 7/23/2010) the following grave with a photo of a gravestone, viz.: Birth: 1692 / Death: Jun. 9, 1766 / Note: wife of Caleb, age 74 years / Burial: Branford Center Cemetery, Branford, New Haven County, Connecticut, USA (Created by: Judith / Record added: Aug 06, 2005 / Find A Grave Memorial #11486279).

[70] ACB, *Windsor*, citing Matthew Grant 'Old Church Record' of Windsor, 47: "[53] Luke Hill married mary Hout . may . 6 . 1651. . . .his Daughter elifabeth was Born . octobr . 8 . 1666. Parsons, "Windsor,"

228: "LUKE HILL, m. Mary Hout, 6 May, 1651; chil. . . . Elisabeth, b. 8 Oct. 1666." Smith and Steiner, "Luke Hill . . . children were: . . . vii. Elizabeth, b. Oct. 18 [sic], 1666." Stiles, *Ancient Windsor* (1859), 664: LUKE, m. Mary Hout, May 6, 1651. *Children* – . . . Elizabeth, Oct. 8, 1666. Stiles, *Ibid.* (1892), 392: "HILL . . . Luke . . . m. Mary Hoyt [sic], 6 May, 1651. . . . *Ch.* . . . 7. Elizabeth, b. 8 Oct., 1666; m. Wm. Buckland. Bassette, *Bassett*, 433: "The Luke Hill Family . . . Children . . . born at Windsor . . . 7. ELIZABETH b. Oct. 8 or 18, 1666; m. William Buckland; she d. ____ he d. Dec. 12, 1724. 6 ch." The b, m, or d of Elizabeth Hill is not in the *Barbour Collection*.

[71] AGBI: Elizabeth Hill / b.d. 1666 / birth place Connecticut / vol. 79 / page 352 (cites Savage, *Genealogical Dictionary* 2:418 (printed from Ancestry.com, 7/26/2010).

[72] Stiles, *Ancient Windsor* (1892), 2:392; and Bassette, *supra.*

[73] Jacobus, "The Josiah Adkins Family of Connecticut," *TAG* 33 (1957), 242-5. Barbour, *Families of Early Hartford, Conn.* (1977): "William Buckland (Buckline) d. 12 Dec 1724 mar. Elizabeth Hills dau of John Hills & Margaret Dix" (p. 95). Also see "John Hills" and his children in this work.

[74] *Barbour Collection* (p. 96, town and vol. not specified, from Ancestry.com/imageservice, citing 2:34).

[75] George E. McCracken, "John Griffin of Windsor and Simsbury, Connecticut," *TAG* 38 (1962), 100-111 (page 110 is quoted). Also, U.S. and International Marriage Records, 1560-1900: Elizabeth Hill / female / b. place CT / b. year 1666 / Spouse Name: Samuel Adams (Yates Publishing, database on-line, Provo, UT, 2004), printed from Ancestry.com, 7/26/2010).

[76] "Simsbury Connecticut, Vital Records, 1665-1886," from New England Ancestors.org. / NEHGS. Three citations for Adams family: 1689 - Samuel Addams Son to Samuel Addams Senior Which his Wife Elizebeth bore to him Was borne the Twenty Sixth of October Annoq Christi 1689 / 1754 - Mary Adams Daughter of Samuel Adams the 3rd and mary his wife was Born January 15th 1754. / 1764 - Elizabeth Adams the wife of Samuel Adams the Elder Departed this Life the 17th : of May A : D : 1764. Aged 74:

[77] The marriages of the Pinneys and Adamses are in Nelson D. Adams, "Adams," *NEHGR* (1879): 107. Reprinted Roberts (ed.), *Genealogies of Connecticut Families*, 1:2 "Adams." For George Adams (d. at Watertown, Mass., 10 Oct 1696) and his family see Mrs. George H. Atwood, *NEHGR* 65 (1911): 302.

For George Adams of Watertown, Mass., and his children, also see: William Richard Cutter (ed.) and William Frederick Adams (assistant), *Genealogical and Personal Memoirs Relating to the Families of the State of Massachusetts* (Lewis Historical Publishing Co., 1910), v. 3, 1867-8: "George Adams [had] wife Frances. [On] November 4, 1664 [he] removed to Cambridge Farms (now Lexington), Massachusetts, [where he was] killed by a fall of rock, October 10, 1696. [He had] Children: John, George, Daniel, Joseph and Mary." The information was amplified in Cutter, *New England Families: Genealogical and Memorial. A Record of the Achievements of Her People in the Making of Commonwealths and the Founding of a Nation.* Third Series, 3:1584-5: "George Adams, the immigrant ancestor, was b in England. He settled in Watertown, Massachusetts, as early as 1645. . . . Children: John, b October 16, 1645; Daniel, mentioned below ['was born about 1650']; Joseph, March 6, 1657; George; Mary; and perhaps others."

[78] For the b of John Hill in Windsor, his residence as a ch in Massaco/Simsbury, his first m, a ch by that m, and his residence in Saybrook , see: ACB, *Windsor*, 47: "[53] Luke Hill married mary Hout . may . 6 . 1651. . . . his fonn John Hill was borne . noumber . 28 . 1668; Stiles, *Ancient Windsor* (1859), 664: "HILL . . . LUKE, m. Mary Hout, May 6, 1651. *Children* – . . . John, b. Nov. 28, 1668"; Ibid. (1892), 392: "HILL . . . "Luke (no evid. of relationship to Mr. William); m. Mary Hoyt, 6 May, 1651 (*O.C.R.*) . . . adm. freeman at Massaco, 1669. *Ch.*: . . . 8. John, b. 28 Nov., 1668"; Smith and Steiner. "Luke Hill" *NEHGR* 57 (Jan. 1903): 87-93: "LUKE[1] HILL, of Windsor, later removed to Simsbury, where he was living in 1694. Married Mary Hart [sic], May 6, 1651. Their ch were: . . . 4. viii. JOHN, b. Nov. 28, 1668. . . . 4. JOHN[2] HILL, (*Luke*[1]), of Saybrook, born Nov. 28, 1668, married April 14, 1670 Jane Bushnell. Their ch was: i. SAMUEL[3], b. May 29, 1671." GJH comments: I believe Smith and Steiner erred; this John Hill (son of Luke) probably did not live in Saybrook, and he did not m. Jane Bushnell; and the ch Samuel (b. 1671) was not his (see text).

[79] U.S. and International Marriage Records, 1560-1900, accessed from Ancestry.com 8/2/2010: "John Hill, male, b. CT, 1668, m. Sarah Phelps, b. CT 1672." "John Hill, male, b. CT, 1668, m. 1708 CT Sarah Terry, b. CT 1668." Also, Phelps, *Simsbury*, 172-3: "William Phelps m in England. He d July 14, 1672, and his widow, Nov, 27, 1675, both at an advanced age. He had [six ch, of whom the fourth was] Joseph Phelps, m Hannah Newton, Sept. 20, 1660 — he d at Simsbury in 1684. [They had four ch , of whom the third,] Sarah, m John Hill, of Simsbury." John Hill's youngest child was by his second wife, Sarah Terry: "Elizabeth Hill, b. 14 Dec 1710, Simsbury, daughter of John Hill and Sarah Terry," is in "HILL Family of

Connecticut VITAL RECORDS TO 1800," http://freepages.genealogy.rootsweb.ancestry.com/ (accessed 8/2/2010), citing *Barbour Collection*. Hill, "Twelve Generations," says that Sarah Terry was the daughter of Lieut. John Terry, Bates, Albert C.: "Simsbury, Connecticut, Births, Marriages, and Deaths" transcribed from the town records, 1898 (LDS microfilm 0896756).

[80] Phelps, *Simsbury*, 11, 14, 16, and 17: "In 1674, the town ordered a ferry place to be established at the mouth of Hop brook. This, however, meant only that the inhabitants might enjoy the privilege of passing the river at this place. It was many years after this time before any thing like a ferry, furnished with a boat large enough to transport even a horse across the river, was established. At the same time, a road leading from Hop meadow to East Weatauge was laid out, crossing the river at this place." The Connecticut Society of Genealogists (http://www.csginc.org/), accessed 8/2/2010: "People from Windsor settled this land on the Tunxis River by 1663. In 1666 lots were laid out from Nod Meadow (Avon) to Hop Meadow. By 1670, areas of Windsor called Weatoque, Hop Meadow, Terry's Plain and The Falls, petitioned for town privileges. The area was known as Massaco Plantation. In May 1670, the Court ordered that Massaco Plantation be named Simsbury, but locally it continued to be known as Massaco until 1742. Town vital records begin 1670. Barbour Collection records cover 1670-1855. People from Windsor settled this land on the Tunxis River by 1663."

[81] Bassette, *Bassett*, 432-3: Luke Hill, Sr., 26 February 1693/4, from Simsbury Town Acts, 1:167: "That this my sonne [John Hill] to whom I bare good will and affection too being now present with me, being in the 25 year of his agge, & Further desiring him my sd sonne to be with me and to take yee care of me and his aged mother during the full time of our life providing good cloaths, Phisicks & all such necessaries as is nedfull for us Durring life," Luke granted his son John and "his heyrs executors Administrators and assigns for ever all and singular" his "Measuag or Tenements and those parcells of land" and a long list of household and farm items. John was instructed "to pay and fully discharge all my debts" and to pay his sister Abigail Parmerly "her portion which is Fourteen pounds" and also the "grat Iron Pot . . . after her parants death . . . the beed with the filling therein and one bolster and pillow." Luke gave John "all the sd Parcells of land Mesuage and appurtinances" without reservation. In return, John, "upon consideration of sd premises . . . do convenant to & with my father & mother Mary Hill to Continue with them . . . for food, cloathing, phisick, & other necessities."

[82] Bassette, *Bassett*, 433: "JOHN b. Nov. 28, 1668; m. Apl. 22, 1708, Sarah Terrey / He was chosen Hayward in Simsbury on Mch. 14, 1693/4. They resided later in Saybrook, Conn." Phelps, *Simsbury*, 152 (Minister's Rate, 1696), 173 (m to Sarah Phelps, dau. of Joseph), 153 (freeman, 1701).

[83] Phelps, *Simsbury*, 34 (military service, 1724). John is also said by Bassette (*supra*) to have lived for some time at Saybrook, Conn., but when he left for Saybrook, and when he returned to Simsbury is not stated. GJH says: I doubt that he ever lived in Saybrook, for he was a citizen of substance in Simsbury, and his record there is otherwise unbroken.

[84] "Probate Records of Hartford Co., CT, 13:284: Distribution of John Hill's property after his death. A transcript of the original record can be seen on the NEHGS website. Page 253-325 (in the original records). "Hill, John, Simsbury. Died 1st November, 1740. Invt. £1339-09-07. Taken 25 November, 1740, by Joseph Case, Joseph Case Jr., and Michael Humphrey. Court Record, Page 78 - 3 December, 1740: The widow, Sarah Hill, having been notified that Adms. would be granted, and not appearing, letters of Adms. were granted to John Hill and Ephraim Wilcockson of Simsbury. Recog., £600 with Jacob Reed." Page 86-7 April 1741: "Sarah Hill, the widow, asked this Court to set out her dower. And this Court appoint John Humphery, James Case and David Holcomb to set out 1-3 part of the lands and buildings of sd. deceased." 14:8, 6 July 1742: "John Hill and Ephraim Wilcock, Adms., exhibit an account of their Adms. Accepted. Order to distribute as follows (in pounds, shilling, pence): To Sarah Hill, the widow, her thirds 71-06-02 / To John Hill, eldest son, his double part 47-10-08. To the heirs of Sarah Strickland, 23-15-05 / to Mary Read, to Hannah Wilcock, and to Elizabeth Hoskins, to each of them the sum of, 23-15-05. And appoint James Case, Jonathan Case and Andrew Robe distributors."

[Comment by GJH: The estate of John Hill was substantial, amounting to over £1339!! The distributions listed above total about £810, and presumably the widow's dower would have been the rest (about £429), although this is not specified in these documents. As the daughter of one of the town's leading citizens, she probably had a large dowry, which she was entitled to receive after her husband's death, and to dispose of as she wished. £1339 in English pounds in 1740 would be worth about £160,000 in 2008, using the retail price index, and £1,980,000 using average earnings. From http://www.measuringworth.com/glossary/ (accessed 8/3/2010)]

[85] Phelps, *Simsbury*, 48 (meeting house, 1671); 90 (bridge, 1734); 91 (legal ferry with rates, 1756)

[86] James D. Hill, "The Hill Family" (Hill, "Twelve Generations") John Hill's descendant James D. Hill first gave his d date as 1 Nov 1668, Windsor, Conn., and later that it was 1 Nov 1740. The former statement is clearly a misprint, inasmuch as John Hill m for the second time in 1708 (according to Bassette, *supra*), and his last ch was born in about 1714. James D. Hill gives his first m. as "ca. 1696 at Simsbury" and that his first ch, Sarah, was b. 1697. A precise date of 22 April 1708 is in Ancestry.com, unsourced, but this was the year of his second m; and given the b. year of Sarah, I will accept the m. of her parents as "ca. 1696."

Jeanine K. (Humbert) Johnson concluded that this John Hill probably m three times, including the two marriages shown above. She cites *Phelps Family of America* (Minnesota Historical Society); and Hartford Co. Probate, estate of John Hill. Smith and Steiner, "Luke Hill," says that John Hill, eighth ch of Luke Hill of Windsor, was b. 28 Nov 1668 and m. 14 April 1670 Jane Bushnell; their son, Samuel, was b. 29 May 1671. The m. of John Hill and Jane Bushnell on 14 April 1670 is also given on "HILL Family of Connecticut VITAL RECORDS TO 1800," at: http://freepages.genealogy.rootsweb.ancestry.com/ (accessed 8/2/2010). GJH comments: These dates are clearly impossible for John Hill (b. 1668), s of Luke Hill, so I conclude that this John Hill was not the husband of Jane Bushnell. If he m someone between the time that Sarah (Phelps) d and he m Sarah (Terry), and indeed I see no reason to posit a third m.

Chapter 3 – The Grandchildren

[87] Barbour, *Early Hartford*, 300-1, 369-70, 477-8. Arthur Henbury and his family are on pp. 300-1 (301: "Children: Mary b Aug 31, 1672 (Simsby Rec [Simsbury Vital Records]) m William Long."). Arthur Henbury's son-in-law, William Long, and his family are on pp. 369-70, and Arthur Henbury's son-in-law, Samuel Richards, and his family are on pp. 477-8.

"Brooks, Truchon, Wimer, Barlow, Dumais Families," by dotruchon1957, Ancestry.com., accessed 4/15/2010, says Arthur Henbury was b 1643 England, d 1 Sep 1687 Hartford, Conn.; Lydia Hill d. bef Jul 1687; gives ch: Hannah, Lydia, Mary, Elizabeth (b abt 1680 Hartford), Susanna (b 1682 Hartford, d 17 May 1767, North Branford, Ct.). Elizabeth m Benjamin Frisbie, had dau Abigail who m Elusthan Ives, traces this family for 8 generations. Susannah m John Frisbie & gives b.d. & place of 10 ch. No references cited but overall, most of the information appears reasonable.

OWT - Descendants of Arthur Henbury and Lydia Hill, on Ancestry.com, accessed 4/18/2010ff: William Long m. Mary Henbury; ch Lydia, William, Sarah, Mary+, Ebenezer; Mary Long m. Benjamin Babcock; ch Ebenzer+, William, Sarah+, Hannah, Mary, Benjamin; Ebenezer Babcock m. Hannah Preston; ch Benjamin, Daniel, Joseph, Redolphus, Hannah, Nathaniel, Mary, Ebenezer, Tabitha, Elisabeth, Lydia, Esther, Olive; Sarah Babcock m. Samuel Parker; ch Marah, William, Sarah, Samuel, Hannah, Bettie, Elias, Daniel, Triphene, Phebe, Eli.

[88] Barbour, *Early Hartford,* 301, 369-70. 301: "Arthur Henbury born ca 1646 died Aug 1, 1697 mar / 1 May 5, 1670 (Simsby Rec) Lydia Hill dau of Luke Hill. . . . Ch. . . . Hannah m Samuel Richards (Simsby Rec) . . . Hannah Henbury m Samuel Richards June 14, 1697 (HTR [Hartford Vital Records]). 477-8: "SAMUEL RICHARDS / "Samuel Richards s of John & Lydia (Stocking) died 1733 mar / 1 Mary Graves dau of George Graves. Mar / 2 June 14, 1697 (HTR) Hannah Henbury dau of Arthur Henbury and Lydia Hill. Samuel Richards owned cov 1 Ch [1st Church, Hartford] Feb 23, 1695-6, ad full com June 6, 1697. Mary wife of Samuel Richards ad full com 1 Ch June 6, 1697. Children:

Lydia b Mch 14, 1696 (HTR) bp Mch 15, 1695-6 (1 Ch Rec) m John Merrill

Hannah b June 17, 1700 (HTR) bp June 23, 1700 (1 Ch Rec) m Ebenezer Judd

Josiah b Feb 15, 1702 (HTR) bp Jonah Feb 7, 1702-3 (2 Ch Rec [2nd Church Hartford Records]) m
   Mary Palmer July 27, 1726 (Branford)

James b Feb 2, 1705-6 (HTR) bp Feb 3, 1705-6 (1 Ch Rec) m Anna Ensign

Daniel b Dec 25, 1708 (HTR) bp Dec 26, 1708 (1 Ch Rec) m Jane Buckland Dec 26, 1734 (HTR)

Esther b June 18, 1713 (HTR) bp June 21, 1713 (1 Ch Rec) m Aaron Merrill? Apl 9, 1740

Samuel?

Jane Buckland was probably dau of Charles & Hannah (Shepard) Buckland"

Additional unverified information about the children of Samuel and Hannah (Henbury) Hill is derived from various Family Trees on Ancestry.com., including two ch (Mary and Hezekiah) who are not in *Families of Early Hartford*. Some of the information in Ancestry.com is inconsistent and some is implausible. I have omitted a second Josiah Richards, who could not have been a ch of Hannah Henbury. I have selected what I think is reasonable for presentation here. Images are from the family tree known as Hattersley2006.

[89] Barbour, *Early Hartford*: The children of Hannah and Samuel (Richards) Henbury were Hannah, born 17 Jun 1700, baptized 23 Jun 1700 (1 Ch Rec), married Ebenezer Judd; Josiah, born 15 Feb 1702, baptized Jonah 7 Feb 1702/3 (2 Ch Rec), married Mary Palmer 27 July 1726 (Branford); perhaps Mary, born 1 July 1705; James, born 2 Feb 1705/6, baptized 3 Feb 1705/6 (1 Ch Rec), married Anna Ensign; Daniel born 25 Dec 1708, baptized 26 Dec 1708 (1 Ch Rec), married Jane Buckland 26 Dec 1734, probably daughter of Charles and Hannah (Shepard) Buckland; Esther born 18 June 1713, baptized 21 June 1713 (1 Ch Rec); married Aaron Merrill(?) 9 April 1740; probably also Samuel; and perhaps also Hezekiah, born about 1715.

[90] Jacobus, *Ancient New Haven*, shows 9 ch of John and Ruth (Bowers) Frisbie. One additional ch, Jonah, their last ch, appears in *Barbour Collection* for Branford.

Barbour, *Early Hartford*, 300-1: "Arthur Henbury born ca 1646 died Aug 1, 1697 mar / 1 May 5, 1670 (Simsby Rec) Lydia Hill dau of Luke Hill. . . . [301] "Children: . . . Elizabeth bp Mch 26, 1693 (1 Ch Rec) m () Frisbie; Susannah bp Mch 26, 1693 m () Frisbie . . . John Frisbie of Branford, Benjamin Frisbie of Branford . . . married daughters of Arthur Henbury."

OWT shows ten ch of John [Jr.] and Susannah (Henbury) Frisbie, b in Branford, New Haven Co., Conn. between 1704 and 1724, and also adds a s Jonah (b. 1724) to the nine in Jacobus. Other family trees in Ancestry.com show varying numbers and names. OWT also shows a second m of Susannah (Henbury) Frisbie to Joseph Foote when she was 58 years old, and this is confirmed by Jacobus.

[91] John Frisbie's name appears in *Families of Early Hartford* as one of the two Frisbie men who married daughters of Arthur Henbury. In the *Barbour Collection* of Hartford V.R., the entries for FRISBEE, John show three generations of men named John Frisbee: "John, s. Edward, b. July 17, [1650]; m. Ruth BOWERS, Dec. 2, [16]74; John, s. John, b. May 23, 1676; m. Susanna HENBERRY, Apr. 7, 1703, by Mr. Russell; John, s. John & Susanna, b. Mar. 11, 1703/4; John Jr., of Branford, m. Freelove ROGERS, of New Haven, July 31, 1760, by Josiah Rogers, J.P.; John, s. John, Jr. & Freelove, b. Aug. 11, 1762." In Jacobus, *Ancient New Haven*, 3:626-30, the family of Edward and Hannah (?Culpepper) Frisbie is seen. Two of their 11 ch are relevant to our story: Edward's first ch John (b. 1650) m. Ruth Bowers and had nine ch, of whom the eldest, John [Jr.] m. Susannah Henbury. They had 9 ch, whose marriages and ch are listed. Edward's fourth ch Benoni (d. 1700) m. Hannah Rose. They had two ch, of whom the eldest, Benjamin, m. Elizabeth Henbury. They had 7 ch, whose marriages and ch are listed.

Additional details are from various Ancestry.com family trees, some of which conflicts with the information in *Families of Ancient New Haven*. In these instances, I will accept *Families of Ancient New Haven* as being definitive. The information in later generations of the Frisbie family is mainly from the Maney Family Tree (owner Fred Seiber), and OneWorldTree, both of which were accessed on 8/18/2010.

Also see www.fffaa.org/ Web page of the Frisbie-Frisbee Family Association of America, Inc (FFFAA): "Edward Frisbie first appears in 1646 as a young man in the village of Branford, in what is now Connecticut. . . . Edward had eight sons and three daughters, all born in Branford between 1650 and 1672. Three sons died without issue."

[92] Jacobus, *New Haven*, "Frisbie Family," 3:626-30: "John, b 23 May 1676, d 14 Jan 1736; m 7 Apr 1703 – Susanna da. Arthur & ___ (Hill) Henbury who d 17 May 1767; she m (2) 8 Sep 1741 Joseph Foote."

[93] Barbour, *Families of Early Hartford,* 301-2. [300] "ARTHUR HENBURY / "Arthur Henbury . . . mar / 1 May 5, 1670 (Simsby Rec) Lydia Hill dau of Luke Hill. . . . [301] "Children: . . . Elizabeth bp Mch 26, 1693 (1 Ch Rec) m () Frisbie; Susannah bp Mch 26, 1693 " m () Frisbie Hfd 1691; had been of Simsbury; John Frisbie of Branford, Benjamin Frisbie of Branford . . . married daughters of Arthur Henbury."

Benjamin Frisbie's name and his m. date and place to Elizabeth Henbury is in *Families of Early Hartford*. His b.d., b.p., and information about his parents are in "Brooks" (Ancestry.com / dotruchon1957). The ancestry of Benjamin Frisbie and his brother John, whose s John m Benjamin's sister-in-law Susannah Henbury, is also in "Maney Family" (Ancestry.com / FredSeiber), 8/18/2010.

[94] Benjamin Frisbie's ancestry, marriage, and children is taken from Jacobus, *Families of Ancient New*

Haven, 3:626-30: "Frisbie Family" [626]: Fam. 1. Edward of Bd, d 10 May 1690; m Hannah [?Culpepper]

1 JOHN, b 17 July 1650, d Mar 1697; Sgt; m 2 Dec 1674 Ruth da. John & Rebecca (Gregson) Bowers, bp 20 Dec 1657, d 26 apr 1736; she m (2) William Hoadley.

i. John, b 23 May 1676, d 14 Jan 1736; m 7 Apr 1703 – Susanna da. Arthur & ___ (Hill) Henbury who d 17 May 1767; she m (2) 8 Sep 1741 Joseph Foote. FAM 2.

[eight other ch of John and Ruth (Bowers) Frisbie are then listed with spouses and some of their ch]

[Edward and Hannah (?Culpepper) Frisbie had eleven children, of whom #1, John, married Ruth Bowers; #4 was Benoni, who m. Elizabeth Henbury]

FAM. 4. BENJAMIN & ELIZABETH (HENBURY) FRISBIE:

1 BENJAMIN, b 16 July 1705; res. Goshen & L; m Elizabeth da. George & Mercy (Denison) Pardee. . .

2 ABIGAIL, b 23 June 1709, d 1778 ae. 69; m 7 May 1730 Elnathan Ives.

3 JERUSHA, b 10 Mar 1712; m 8 Jan 1729 Benjamin Gaylord.

4 MARY, b 10 Oct 1714

5 ZEBULON, b 10 May 1717, d 12 Aug 1800 ae. 84; m 2 Apr 1740 Lucy da. Barnabas & Elizabeth Lewis, b 23 Mar 1724, d 18 Sep 1789 ae. 66. Children: . . .

6 LEVI, b 3 Dec 1719, d young.

7 THEODORE, b 27 Mar 1723, d 31 Jan 1764; m (1) Phyllis ____, "wife of Theodore" d June 1757; m (2) 11 June 1758 Mehitabel da. William & Jemima (Plumb) Wheeler. . .

Jacobus also says that Elizabeth (Henbury) Frisbie m. (2) Caleb Matthews, but there are no descendants shown from this marriage. Benjamin Frisbie's name and his m. date and place to Elizabeth Henbury are also in Barbour, *Families of Early Hartford*. Also, *Barbour Collection*: "Branford Vital Records" – "Frisbie, Benjamin, s. Benoni, b. Jan. 24, 1679; Benjamin, m. Elisabeth HENBRY, Dec. 8, 1703, by Rev. Sam[ue]ll Russell; Benj[ami]n, s. Benj[ami]n & Elsabeth, b. July 16, 1705; Benj[ami]n, d. Sept. 10, 1724; Benjamin, s. Ebenzer, Jr. & Silence, b. Apr. 28, 1736; Benjamin, s. Joseph, 2d, & Sarah, b. Dec. 17, 1752." His b.d., b.p., and information about his parents are in "Brooks" (Ancestry.com / dotruchon1957). Both of these sources show only one ch, Abigail.

Also see www.fffaa.org/ Web page of the Frisbie-Frisbee Family Association of America, Inc.

[95] His early death can be presumed because he was not mentioned in his father's will. Barbour, *Families of Early Hartford*, 301; and Bassette, *Basseett* (Hill Family), 431.

[96] Barbour, *Families of Early Hartford*, 301, lists her name after Samuel, which probably indicates that she was b after Samuel, and gives her date of d in 1689. We know she was alive on 25 June 1687, because she was mentioned in her father's will, quoted in Bassette (*supra*). Arthur Henbury's will, written 25 June 1687, shows that Lydia had died, because he said that what remained of his wife's "portion" be given Lydia's father and mother to care for his youngest dau, just a baby, with a "wekly body." This ch, Lydia, is not mentioned again in historical records, and must have died soon thereafter.

[97] That Richard Saxton was the s of John and Mary (Hill) Saxton was shown above, and is summarized as follows: Although Richard's b.r. has not been found, "John Sexton Snr of Symsbury" made his will on 9 March 1716/7. He gave most of his land and goods to his s John Jr., except for specific grants to his "daughter" Hannah, who was the widow of his late s Richard, on condition that she keep her ch with her, including her three daughters, who were referred to as "orphans." He also gave six acres of land in Bissell's Marsh to his son-in-law William Gillett. His remaining outlands were to be divided into three equal parts and given to his "son" William Gillett, Richard's three daughters, and his "Loving son John." Also, in Simsbury V.R., accessed 26 August 2010 from NEHGS: "Richard Saxtone of Simfbery Departed this life march the twenty 7th 1714." Richard Saxton's death and the disposition of his estate is in Connecticut Probate Records, viz.: A DIGEST OF THE EARLY CONNECTICUT PROBATE RECORDS, 1710 to 1715, and 1715 to 1723 (From Ancestry.com, 15 May 2010). Name. Richard Saxton Location. Simsbury / Inventory on File. Invt. £65-15-08. Taken 27 March, 1714, by John Case, Sen., John Roberts, Sen., and Jonathan Westover. The children: Hannah, Mary and Lucy. . .[the estate continues for a full page]"

[98] Hannah Buell is in Simsbury V.R. as the dau of Peter Buell and the w of Richard Saxton, but not the b. year and b.d. that are given in Ancestry.com. Simsbury V.R.: "Richard Saxton of Simsbury the Son of John Saxton was Married to Hanah Buell the daughter of Peter Buell of Simsbury June 20th Anno. 1706-."

[99] Priest, "Gillett": Jonathan Gillett Jr., p. 276, had by his first wife Anna Kelsey the following children, born in Windsor, Conn.: iv. WILLIAM, of Windsor and Simsbury, b. 4 Dec., 1673; d. in Simsbury 27 Jan.

1718-19; m. in Simsbury, 14 Sept. 1699, MARY SAXTON (SEXTON) of Simsbury, b. in Simsbury 4 May 1673. She m. (2) in Simsbury, 22 June 1721, Jonathan Holcomb of Simsbury:

      1. *William*,[4] b. 1 Sept. 1700; d. 16 July 1736 or 1737 (Simsbury record).

      2. *Jonathan*, b. 1 Oct. 1701; d. in Simsbury 7 Jan. 1719.

      3. *Mary*, b. 29 Feb. 1702-3; d. in Simsbury 23 Nov. 1760, aged 58; m. in
          Simsbury, 20 Oct. 1726, David Eno, b. in 1702, d. in 1745, son of James Eno.

      4. *Richard*, b. in 1705; d. in Simsbury 3 Jan. 1719.

      5. *Eunice*, d. in Simsbury 24 May 1740; m. there, 3 Dec 1728, David Gaines. 7 children.

[100] Simsbury V.R. (accessed 8-26-2010 from NEHGS) says the m. was in 1690, not 1699 as appears in the other sources: "William Gillet the Son of Jonathan Gillet of windfor was married to mary the daughter of John Saxton ye 14th of feptember 1690." She was only 12 in 1690 and their first ch was born in 1700, so the transcription by NEHGS must be incorrect. The b. of William Gillett, s of Jonathan Jr. and Anna (Kelsey) Gillett is in *History of Ancient Windsor*, 2:289 (b. 4 Dec 1673). His m. and d. are not shown there.

[101] Marriage of Mary (Saxton) Gillett to Jonathan Holcomb in Priest, "Gillett," *NEHGR* (*supra*).

[102] "John Sexton Snr of Symsbury" made his will on 9 March 1716/7. He gave most of his land and goods to his s John Jr.. His remaining outlands were to be divided into three equal parts and given to his "son" [actually, son-in-law] William Gillett, Richard's three daughters, and his "Loving son John," who was named as his sole executor. The death d. of John Sexton/Saxton Jr. is Simsbury V.R., accessed from NEHGS: "John Saxton Departed this Life the 13th : day of October A : D : 1766."

[103] Pitman cites the following sources:

1. Anderson, *Great Migration Begins*, 2:769; and Stiles, *Ancient Windsor, Connecticut* (1892), 2:289.

13. Stiles [*supra*, note 1], 1:478.

16. All of Nathan's children and their birthdates are listed in the "Records of Windsor," *NEHGR* 5 (1851): 226. Rebecca, Elias, Sarah, Benjamin, and Nathan; their birthdates are in Windsor VRs 1:14. Stiles [note 1], 2:297. Anderson [note 1], 2:771,772.

17. McCracken, *TAG*, 56 (1980): 130. John W. Harms and Pearl Goddard Harms, *The Goddard Book*, 2 vols. (Baltimore, 1984) 1:36, 37. Includes the data on their ch.

22. ACB, *Windsor*, 11, 40. John Slater's will is printed in Charles William Manwaring, *A Digest of The Early Connecticut Probate Records 1904-06*, 3 vols, (reprinted, Baltimore, 1995), 2:296.

28. In Bates, Simsbury VRs, [*supra*, note 22]12, Sarah who m. Eleazer Hill, is the dau of Nathan. Gillett. Also included are the birthdates for Elizabeth, Mary, and Eleazer and the death date for Mary.

30. Daughter Sarah is mentioned in Eleazer Hill's will, 1717, in Manwaring [*supra*, note 22], 2:525; b.d. undetermined. McCracken [*supra*, note 17], 132,133.

Hill, "Twelve Generations," named the three ch who are shown in Bates, but he did not identify Sarah, who was named by Pitman. James D. Hill wrote of Eleazer, his wife and Sarah Gillett, and their ch: Eleazer and Sarah (Gillett) Hill: Eleazer Hill B. 07 Mar 1657, Windsor <27> D. 1725. M: on 29 Dec 1679 at Simsbury to <4,31,39> Sarah Gillett B. 13 Jul 1651 / Children: Elizabeth 29 Jul 1681, Mary 1685-97, Eliezer Jr. 20 Jul 1694 <39>. James D. Hill's sources were given in brackets and are shown in his "References and Acknowledgments," viz.: <4> American Genealogical Institute, "The Hill Family" (Wash. D.C., 1975). <27> Savage, James: *A Genealogical Dictionary Of The First Settlers Of New England, Showing Three Generations Of Those Who Came Before 1692, On The Basis Of Farmer's Register* (four vols., 1986); (References to Luke Hill, and the Eggleston, Phelps, and Hoyt families). <31> "New England Marriages Prior To 1700" <39> "Bates, Albert C., *Simsbury, Connecticut, Births, Marriages, and Deaths transcribed from the town records*, 1898 (LDS microfilm 0896756).

The NEHGS index of the Simsbury V.R. shows only Mary Hill, and not the other three ch. The NEHGS citation confirms that Mary was the "second daughter" of Eleazer Hill. None of the four ch of Eleazer and Sarah (Gillett) Hill are in Ancestry.com's index of the *Barbour Collection*, and none are in the on-line Hartford V.R. from Barbour, transcribed by Coralynn Brown for NHGS. The information in Ancestry.com conflates the information about Elizabeth Hill, the youngest daughter of Luke Hill Sr. (who Ancestry.com and others erroneously states married William Buckland), with Elizabeth Hill, daughter of Eleazer and Sarah (Gillett) Hill. The b.d. of 29 July 1681 for Eleazer's daughter Elizabeth is correct, as we see above, and the death date given in Ancestry.com (5 April 1725) for Eleazer's daughter Elizabeth is therefore incorrect. This error is perpetuated in Ancestry.com, which also shows the same death date, 5 April 1725, for Eleazer's daughter Sarah Hill.

[104] Her b.d. and b.p. are shown in the previous note. I have not found a record of her death, but will accept the date given in Ancestry.com as possible.

[105] From Simsbury V.R., accessed on the NEHGS website: "Mary Hill the fecond daughter to Eliezr Hi[ ] was borne Defember the fixth 1685. Mary Hill the fecond daughter to Eliezr Hi[ ] dyed December the 5th day Annoq 1697 buried Decemb 26. mary Hill daughter of Elezr Hill eliezr hill his daughter mary dyed the fifth day of december 1697."

[106] She is known only because she was mentioned in the will of her father, written in 1717. Her d. date is given by Ancestry.com, and because it is the same as the date given in Ancestry.com for her sister Elizabeth, I believe either one or the other or both of these dates are probably incorrect.

[107] Stiles, *Ancient Windsor* (1859), 664: "HILL . . . Sgt. ELEAZER, m. Elizabeth Gillet, July 8, 1731; he d. March 3, 1724-5. *Children* – Eleazer, b. May 15, 1732; Benjamin, b. July 17, 1735; Stephen, b. Oct. 2, 1737." Stiles, Ibid., (1892), 392: "Eleazer (Sgt.) m. Elizabeth Gillet, 8 July 1731; he d. 3 Mch., 1725/5. *Ch.:* 1. Eleazer, b. 15 May, 1732. 2. Benjamin, b. 17 July, 1735. 3. Stephen, b. 2, bp. 9 Oct., 1737.

[108] This Elizabeth Gillett does not appear in any of the usual sources for information about the Gillett family, including Pitman's "Nathan Gillett" and Priest's "Jonathan and Nathan Gillett." The latter, in spite of its title, is entirely about the descendants of Jonathan Gillett and not at all about his brother Nathan. Pitman's work is more recent than Priest's and it is apparently more thoroughly documented, so I doubt if he missed this Elizabeth. She is, therefore, more likely to be an unrecorded descendant of Jonathan Gillett.

[109] Bassette, "Luke Hill Family,"433, says that Tahan Hill and Hannah Parmelee had 2 children, but does not name them. Smith and Steiner, "Luke Hill," 87: "Tahan Hill . . . married Nov. 29, 1688, Hannah Parmelee. . . . Their children were: i. Hannah, b. Nov. 17, 1680; m. March 31, 1710, Samuel Bushnell. ii. Tahan, b. 1691." Hannah's death date is from Ancestry.com, Baldwin Family Tree, and is is considered possible but unconfirmed. Her m. is shown in Smith, but not her children.

[110] The parents and b. of Samuel Bushnell Jr. are in the Barbour Collection for Saybrook, Conn., either via Ancestry.com, or at http://dunhamwilcox.net/barbour/saybrook_barbour_e-j.htm (Coralynn's transcription), accessed 8/28/2010. The m. of Samuel Bushnell Jr. and Hannah Parmelee is in Coralynn's transcription, and also the births of three of their ch: Jeremiah, Jemimah, and Hannah. The other two ch (Samuel and Patience) are known only from Ancestry.com (Baldwin Family Tree), which lists all five ch, and until their existence is confirmed, they can be considered only as "possible." No further information is seen on Barbour about the five ch, and we are dependent on Ancestry.com's unsourced list for the m. and descendants of Jemima.

[111] His b. year is in Smith and Steiner, "Luke Hill."

[112] Smith and Steiner, "Luke Hill," 87: "3. LUKE HILL, JR. (*Luke*[1]), b March 6, 1661, m Hannah ___, or Anna ___, and lived for a time at Guilford. . . . His ch were: i. EBENEZER, b. Nov. 23, 1687, at Guilford. ii. ANNA, b. Dec. 3, 1692. iii. KEZIAH, b. Feb. 24, 1695, at Wethersfield. iv. LUKE, b. at Simsbury, Sept. 16, 1698. v. LYDIA, b. at Simsbury, Feb. 25, 1700. vi. ISAAC, b. at Branford, May 27, 1703."

[113] Smith and Steiner, "Luke Hill." Stiles, *Families of Ancient Wethersfield*, 777: "Elisha (Roe), b. 4 Dec., 1768; m. 1798, Electa (dau. *Capt. Ambrose,*[5] *Ens. Ebenezer,*[4] *Ebenzer,*[3] *Luke,*[2] *Luke*[1]) Hill, b. 1 Feb., 1777; rem. to Medina, N.Y., she d. 10 Dec., 1860, ae. 84." Information about Ebenezer Hill and his brothers in Litchfield County is from Carlson to GJH (e-mails, 2008). Carlson quotes from Beach and Hibbard, *History of the town of Goshen, Connecticut*, Chapter 3, 42-4. Additional details are from OWT and various family trees in Ancestry.com., and are considered as "possible."

[114] *Barbour Collection*, Saybrook V.R. for her b., Goshen V.R. for her m.; and also unverified details from OWT and family trees in Ancestry.com., some of which are conflicting. (OWT says she was b. and m. in Saybrook.) I have decided to accept eight possible ch, although some lists show seven and at least one list shows nine. Her d. year is unverified and must be considered doubtful. However, this is the same year that her neighbor Benjamin Frisbie, an in-law, died in the French and Indian War, and it could have been a common disaster. Her death d. and place is from Norris, "Hill Family Tree," without a source that I can see. Norris says her middle name was Wealthy.

[115] Smith and Steiner, "Luke Hill," 87; Jacobus, *Ancient New Haven.*: "Cook Family," 2:435-6: "COOK. FAM. 1. HENRY of Salem, Mass., d 25 Dec 1661; m June 1639 SalemV - Judith Birdsall. . . . [They had 10 ch] 1 ISAAC. . . 2 SAMUEL . . . 8 HENRY, b 30 Dec 1652 SalemV, d 1705; m 30 Sep 1678 SalemV - Mary da. John & Jane (Woolen) Hall, b c. 1654, d 31 July 1718 WV. [They had 11 ch, of whom the 6th

was Isaac] . . . vi Isaac, b c. 1692; rem. to Bd; m Anna da. Luke & Hannah (Butler) Hill, b 30 Dec 1692 (at Simsbury) BdV. Children, recorded WV [Wallingford V.R.]: 1 Isaac, b July 1716; 2 Demetrius, b 2 Apr 1718; 3 Uzziel, b 9 May 1722; 4 Anna, b 24 June 1724; 5 Waitstill, b 8 Jan 1727; 6 Desire, b 21 July 1729; 7 Lydia, b 4 Feb 1732."

    In OWT, Isaac Cook is said to be a s of Henry and Mary (Hall) Cook, s of Henry and Judith (Birdsall) Cook, s of Edmund and E. (Nicholls) Cook, s of Henry and Anne (Goodere) Cook. Judith Birdsall is the dau of Henry and Judith (Kempe) Birdsall; Henry is the s of Henry and A. (de Doncaster) Birdsall. The family of Isaac Cook and Anna Hill in OWT is based on 29 User-submitted trees.

[116] Smith, op. cit., and Jacobus, op. cit. Nothing more about her in Ancestry.com and OWT.

[117] Smith, op. cit., and Jacobus, op. cit. Bassette, "Hill Family" (op.cit.). His b. and m. are in *Barbour Collection* for Wallingford: "Hill, Luke, m. Sarah FRED[E]RICK, Dec. 19, 1723, by Capt John Hall." Bassette (p. 433) says that Luke Hill Jr. "had namesake whose will was filed Apl. 7, 1772 at Litchfield, Ct." so we can accept a death year of about 1772.

[118] The m of Luke [III] and Sarah Frederick is in *Ancient New Haven*: "Frederick Family," 3:623-4: "FREDERICK. WILLIAM, res. W & Wy; m (1) Mary da. Jonathan & Rebecca (Bell) Tuttle, b 17 Feb 1666 NHV; m (2) Abigail da. Abraham & Abigail (Moss) Doolittle, b 26 Feb 1668 WyV, d 26 Aug 1760 ae. 55 NHT1; m 18 Dec 1718 NHV - Josiah Todd. [They had 8 ch]. . . . 8 SARAH, b 18 Oct 1704 WV; m 19 Dec 1723 WV - Luke Hill." The five ch of Luke [III] and Sarah (Frederick) Hill are 3:743: "4 LUKE, b 16 Sep 1698 (at Simsbury) *BdV*; m 19 Dec 1723 *WV* – Sarah da. William & Abigail (Doolittle) Frederick, b 18 Oct 1704 *WV*. i. Kezia, b 28 Sep 1724 *WV*, d 14 Oct 1726 *WV*. ii. Uri, b 19 June 1729 *WV*. iii. Kezia, b 1 Dec 1788 *WV*. iv. Sarah, b 2 Oct 1737 *WV*. v. Abigail, b 12 June 1741 *WV*."

    OWT erroneously puts this Uri as a s of Luke Jr., and says Luke [III] and Sarah Frederick had four ch: Abigail, Sarah, Uri and Keziah, giving a b. year only for Kezia (1733, Goshen). OWT says Luke [III] d. at Goshen in Mar 1772, but this is not in Jacobus, *Ancient New Haven*, or in the *Barbour Collection*.

[119] Jacobus, op. cit.; *Barbour Collection* for towns cited; and OWT/Ancestry.com, unproved but "possible."

[120] Records of the births of ch of John and Lydia (Hill) Dibble are found in Jacobus, *Ancient New Haven*; in the *Barbour Collection*; and in OWT. None of these sources show all eight ch, but their names appear as follows, with abbreviations of Jacobus [J], Barbour [B], and OWT [O]:

1. John (1725) J,B,O
2. Reuben (1727) J,B,O [OWT says b. Stamford, but this is unlikely]
3. Israel (1729) O
4. Lydia (1731) J,B,O
5. Susannah (1735) J,B,O
6. Josiah (1737) J,B,O
7. Rachel (1740) B
8. Mary (1746) B,O

Jacobus, op. cit. Page 535: "DIBBLE. FAM. 1. JOHN, res. W, rem. To L before 1753; m 14 Apr 1725WV - Lydia da. Luke & Hannah (Butler) Hill, b 26 Feb 1700 (at Simsbury) BdV.

  1 JOHN, b 26 July 1725 WV.

  2 REUBEN, b 6 Mar 1727 WV.

  3 LYDIA, b 29 May 1731 WV.

  4 SUSANNA, b 30 Mar 1735WV.

  5 JOSIAH, b 3 Mar 1737WV."

[121] *Barbour Collection*, Wallingford VR, trans. Brown: DIBBLE, DIBBELL, DIBBELLS, DIBBLL, DIBLE [The names that may be related to this John Dibble, his wife, and his children, are as follows]: John, m. Lidea HILL, Apr. 14, 1725, by Capt. Yall / John, son John & Lidea, b. July 26, 1725 / Josiah, son John & Lidea, b. Mar. 3, 1737 / Lidea, dau. John & Lidea, b. May 19, 1731 / Reuben, son John & Lidea, b. Mar. 6, 1727 / Susannah, dau. John & Lidea, b. Mar. 30, 1735.

Barbour Collection, Goshen VR, trans. Brown: DIBBLE, DIBELL, DIBAL: David, son John, b Aug 27, 1749 / Harris, son Jno., b Apr 15, 1756 / John Jr, m Elizabeth HOLLAND, Oct 6, 1746. / John, m Sibel KILLBORN, June 20, 1751 / John, died Apr 7, 1756 / Josiah, m Sibble PLUMB, Mar 18, 1756

Martha, m Ebenezer HILL, Jan 3, 1716/17 [but this was before Goshen was settled!!] / Mary*, m John WILLOUGHBY, Oct 2, 1728 (*Arnold Copy has "Mary TIBELL") Mary, dau John, b May 30, 1747 / Rachel, dau John, b Jan 30, 1740 / Reuben, son John Jr, b Mar 6, 1755

[122] Branford, CT, VR, 2:346: "ISAAC HILL (son of Luke, son of Luke), born 27 May 1703 in Branford, Conn., married 16 Jan. 1733, Esther Stone, daughter of Benajah and Hannah of Guilford" (Wallingford V.R., 5:509). He died 25 Oct. 1741 (Wallingford V.R., 5:549). Esther married secondly, 9 May 1745, Ebenezer Shelly of Guilford (Guilford V.R., 2:59).

Children of Isaac and Esther Hill: Chloe, born 20 Nov. 1733 (Wallingford V.R.., 5:506). Bille, Phineas, Isaac, Abraham [all four from] New Haven Probate File No. 4963, 6 Nov 1741. Child of Ebenezer and Esther (Hill) Shelley: Ebenezer, born 18 April 1746 (Guilford V.R. 2:79). Isaac and his brothers, Ebenezer and Luke, were first settlers of Goshen, Conn., from Roberts, "Genealogies of Connecticut Families," 2:165. Smith and Steiner, "Luke Hill," 87: "Luke Hill, Jr. [and] Hannah ___ [had] vi. Isaac, b. at Branford, May 17, 1703."

[123] The life of Isaac Hill Sr. is pieced together from many sources. A concise summary, weighing all of the evidence, is in a letter from Donald Lines Jacobus, in the files of the Connecticut Historical Society. Jacobus summarized his research as follows: "The Isaac Hill who married Esther Stone and lived and died in Wallingford was undoubtedly of the Luke Hill family which was very migratory; at that period, several members of this family lived in Wallingford; they had an interest in Goshen and some members of this family settled there. I have no doubt that search of land records of Branford, Wallingford, Goshen and Stratford would add to the evidence and provide further details but while it might be of interest, it seems genealogically unnecessary. This is not the Isaac Hill family which settled in the Bethlehem section of Woodbury, coming there from Guilford. To make this absolutely sure, I looked up a few records of this family group . . .

"Isaac himself, although of Wallingford at death, owned a right in Goshen, as reported above from his inventory . . . It looks as if Isaac moved there, which explains why only his first child was recorded in Wallingford, but returned to Wallingford before his death. There are some omissions of birth records anyway, so the youngest children may have been born in Wallingford and simply not recorded. But it is possible that Isaac (1740) was born in Goshen just before the family returned to Wallingford."

Jacobus' letter was provided to me on 17 July 1992 by Jeanine Humbert Johnson, who obtained a copy from the Connecticut Historical Society, located in the Society's file on Isaac Hill (b. c. 1740), and sent with a cover letter from Allen R. Yale to Mrs. Jeanine Humbert Johnson. This letter encloses 10 pp., including 3 pp. of copies of Connecticut vital records of Hill Family, and a portion of a letter of Jacobus to Mrs. H. A. Thomas (1952) regarding Isaac Hill and his ancestors.

Jacobus continues (p.2), "I worked out the fourth and last marriage of Hannah (DeWolf) Stone and then located her will, which proves the second marriage of her daughter Esther (Stone) Hill; and it is this second marriage of Esther which brought her son Isaac to Guilford and later to Stratford. Proof was also found that Isaac and Esther of Wallingford had a son Isaac." In a 4 page enclosure to this letter, entitled "Isaac Hill," Jacobus provided citations and quotations from documents that he had reviewed. These citations included the following:

Wallingford Vital Records: Isaac Hill m. 16 Jan 1733 Esther [Stone]. LRS:50; Cloe dau. of Isaac & Esther Hill

New Haven Probate Files: File 4963. Estate of Isaac Hill of Wallingford. Bond of Esther Hill, Executrix (signed by mark, 29 Jan 1741/2) "57 acres with house and barn; pieces of 38 and 50 acres . . . and 1/2 an undivided right in Goshen. File 4949. Guardianship bond of Esther Hill of Wallingford, 26 Oct1743 as guardian to Cloe, Billie, Phineas, Isaac, & Abraham Hill, five minor children of Isaac Hill late of Wallingford, Dec'd. [From this record, Jacobus estimates the year of Isaac's birth as c.1739-40; he refers to him as Isaac, Jr.; he believes Abraham may have been born posthumously; he believes that Isaac was probably born in Wallingford, although he grew up in Guilford with his mother and stepfather, Ebenezer Shelley; and that Isaac may therefore have thought he was born in Guilford, which is what he said in his deposition at age 92, in 1832]

Guilford Vital Records: Ebenezer Shelley m. (1) 5 Aug 1730, Comfort Everest (who d. 26 Sep 1743); m. (2) 8 May 1745 Esther Hill, widow, late of Wallingford, now of Guilford. 2:59. Ebenezer son of Ebenezer and Esther Shelley, b.18 Apr 1746. 2:79

Ebenezer Shelley of Stratford m.20 May 1766 Sarah Peirson of Guilford 2:229. [Jacobus believes this was a 3rd marriage, after the death of Esther (Stone) (Hill), his 2nd wife]

Stratford Vital Records: Isaac Hill m. 29 Sep 1762 Eunice Mallery. A child, Abraham Enoch, b. 9 Oct 1763 LR5:72. Benajah Mallory m. 20 Jan 1742/3 Elizabeth Crane. Children: Enoch b. 8 Jul 1744, d. 10 Feb 1746; Eunice b. 7 Jan 1747; and Sarah b. Feb 1748.

Some descendants of Abraham Hill, the last child of Isaac and Esther (Stone) Hill, believe Isaac Hill, Sr., died later, in 1747 or 1751. This erroneous belief is based on a misinterpretation of Abraham Hill's gravestone in Carmel, N.Y., which states that he d. at age ~70 on 11 May 1817. Dennis O'Connell, however, suggested what I believe is the correct interpretation of this stone. His descendants who ordered the stone to be carved did not know his exact age or date of birth, so they used the symbol ~ to show an approximate age at the time of death. The New Haven Probate Files clearly confirm that Isaac Hill Sr. was dead by 29 January 1741/2 and that Abraham was last in the list of his five minor children. Isaac Jr. was b. on 16 April 1740, and Esther could have had another son by, say March 1740/41. If the record of death of Isaac Sr. on 25 October 1741 is correct, Abraham could have been born while his father was still alive; otherwise, he would have been born posthumously, as Jacobus opines.

[124] From Carlson to GJH, 3 December 2008, quoting *History of Litchfield County, Connecticut*, 25:251-2.

[125] Carlson to Hill, quoting Smith and Steiner, "Luke Hill," 332: "ROBERT SHELLEY." Carlson: "It is not clear if Sarah (Pierson) Shelley died within the first month of her marriage, or whether there were two Ebenezer Shelleys living in Stratford. The children of Ebenezer & Abigail are recorded at Stratford." And Christ Episcopal Church, Stratford, CT, m. records: Ebenezer Shelley md. Abigail Bundy 13 Jul 1766.

[126] From Carlson to Hill: 1790 Federal Census; there are no Shelley families in Stratford in 1800 census.

[127] From Carlson to Hill, quoting Hibbard, *History of the Town of Goshen, Connecticut.*

[128] Her b. and m. and her husband's b. and m. and the b. of their child are a composite of information in Jacobus, *Ancient New Haven* and Lorraine Cook, *Barbour Collection* v. 14, Goshen 1739-1854, Granby 1886-1850, Greenwich 1640-1848 (Baltimore: Genealogical Publishing Co., 1994). This information is also in various family trees of Ancestry.com and is linked with these family trees in later generations that are beyond Jacobus and the Barbour Collection in this branch of the family. The later generations must be considered only as "possible."

[129] Stiles, *Ancient Windsor* (1892); and *Families of Early Guilford.*

[130] Little information is available about her supposed husband John Parish/Parrish. However, there are two sources that may be helpful: Roswell Parish Jr., "John Parish of Groton, Mass., and Some of His Descendants," in *Genealogies of Connecticut Families*, 3:15: John Parish of Groton, Mass., "probably the first of the line in New England. . . . married first, 30 June 1664, Hannah Jewell, born 12 Dec. 1648," by whom he had a daughter Hannah, b. in Braintree, 3 July 1665; died a spinster in Concord, 17 June 1753. He then had a son Samuel, a son Benjamin (both of whom had descendants who were traced), and a fourth child, John, "b. prob. in Mendon, Mass. One of this name bought land in Branford, Conn., in 1717." Also, the *Barbour Collection* reports the death of John Parish on 23 March 1748 in Branford, Conn.

[131] The names of seven ch of John and Hannah (Parmelee) Parish/Parrish are given by websites on Ancestry.com: DeGe's Family, Noyes Family Tree, and Curtis Family Tree, except that Noyes does not list the 7th child, Joel.

[132] Stiles, *Ancient Windsor* (1892); and *Families of Early Guilford.* Additional information on family trees of Ancestry.com that appears to be consistent and reasonable is added to this branch of the family as "possible"; or as "probable," if supported by additional information such as census records.

[133] *Families of Early Guilford.*

[134] The record of Jemima's death in 1730 in *Families of Early Guilford* must be erroneous or a misinterpretation by me, because Findagrave.com shows (on 7/23/2010) the following grave with a photo of a gravestone "Created by Judith," viz.: "Parmelee, Jemima b. 1692 d. Jun. 9, 1766" in Branford Center Cemetery, New Haven Co., Conn.: Birth: 1692 / Death: Jun. 9, 1766 / Note: wife of Caleb, age 74 year / Burial: Branford Center Cemetery / Branford / New Haven County / Connecticut, USA / Record added: Aug 06, 2005 / Find A Grave Memorial# 11486279.

[135] *Families of Early Guilford.*

[136] Ibid., and Roberts, *Genealogies of Connecticut Families.* No more information on Ancestry.com.

[137] Ibid.

---

[138] Ibid.

[139] Ibid.

[140] McCracken, "Griffin": 100-111: John Griffin of Windsor and Simsbury (d. there Aug 1681) was once said to be the son of John Griffin of Wales by his wife Ann Langford, and was b. in 1609. McCracken says, however, that "the first evidence of our John Griffin really consists of his marriage at Windsor on 13 May 1647 to Ann Bancroft who may have been the daughter of John Bancroft. They had 10 children who were named in his estate inventory, including Ephraim, then age 12. John Griffin became commander of the Simsbury train band, as sergeant, in July 1675 and was Deputy to the colonial legislature 1670-74. His 9th child Ephraim (b 1 Mar 1668/9; d 26 Sep 1725) m. Simsbury 9 Dec 1707 Elizabeth Adams b Simsbury 21 Feb 1686/7, dau of 'Samuel and Elizabeth (Hill) Adams.' She m (2) Sept 1725, Joshua Holcomb. Children by Griffin: i. Elizabeth b c1707, may have m. her 1st cousin Nathaniel Griffin. ii. Anna or Hannah, b Simsbury 26 Jul 1713, m Simsbury 17 May 1736 Ebenezer Loomis. iii. Silence, b c1716, age 10 in 1726. iv. Ephraim, b c1718, age 14 in 1731/2, m Elizabeth Terry b 3 Feb 1724/5 dau of John and Mary (Robe) Terry. v. Sheba b c1722; age 4 in 1726 said to m Solomon Terry b Simsbury 5 Mar 1720 son of John and Mary (Robe) Terry; had 6 children at Simsbury 1749-59, the eldest a dau Phebe."

There are many unsourced family trees of Elizabeth Adams on Ancestry.com. The most compelling is "My Comprehensive Family Tree," accessed 7/29/2010. It states that Elizabeth Adams (1687-1726) had by Ephraim Griffin (1662-1725) the following children: Elizabeth (1709-1800), Ephraim (1712-), Hannah/Anna (1713-1745), Silence (1716-1726), and Phoebe (1722-); and that she m. (2) Caleb Holcomb (1695-1758). This website shows children of the daughter Elizabeth, but only one child of Phoebe, who m. Solomon Terry, whose name is given as Stephen Terry. McCracken said that Phebe 1722 m. Solomon Terry and had six children, one of whom was Elizabeth. I will therefore utilize both McCracken and Ancestry.com in preparing the list of descendants of Solomon and Phebe (Griffin) Terry. Another Ancestry.com family tree (Cathy Starnes-Bancroft Family Tree) shows previous child named Ephraim (b. 1712), which of course is possible, but without supporting information I am not convinced that he is a child of Ephraim and Elizabeth (Adams) Griffin.

[141] Unsourced websites in Ancestry.com say that Mary Adams 1754 was the daughter of Samuel 1698 (son of Daniel 1652 and Mary [Phelps] Adams) and Mary Reade. I find this to be a likely scenario. Samuel Adams 3rd was therefore the son of Samuel "the Elder," and grandson of Daniel Adams. Samuel 3rd may have been called "3rd" because he was the third oldest of the men then living in Simsbury who were named Samuel Adams.

"Simsbury Connecticut, Vital Records, 1665-1886" / NEHGS

Three citations for Adams family: 1689 - Samuel Addams Son to Samuel Addams Senior Which his Wife Elizebeth bore to him Was borne the Tweenty Sixth of October Annoq Christi 1689 / 1754 - Mary Adams Daughter of Samuel Adams the 3rd and mary his wife was Born January 15th 1754. / 1764 - Elizabeth Adams the wife of Samuel Adams the Elder Departed this Life the 17th : of May A : D : 1764. Aged 74:

[142] Her birth is in the *Barbour Collection* for Simsbury, viz.: B Sarah HILL / F /28 Jul 1697 / Simsbury / Hartford CT / John. Her birth is also in Bates, *Simsbury, Connecticut, Vital Records*, 30 (seen on NEHGS website): "Sarah Hill the firft Daug of John Hill was Born ye 28th day of Jully : 1697 . and Baptifed the Twenty 21 eight day of Nouember 1697." "Birth: 1697 - Sarah Hill the firft Daugh of John Hill was Borne ye 28th day of Jully: 1697." "Baptism: 1697 - Sarah Hill the firft Daugh of John Hill was Baptifed the Twenty 21 eight day of Nouember 1697."

Her marriage is in Bates, *Simsbury, Connecticut, Vital Records*: Marriage: 1720 - Samuell Strickland and Sarah hill both of the Town of Simfbery : were married July : the : 28th: 1720." Her heirs were listed as recipients of a portion of the estate of her father, John Hill: "To the heirs of Sarah Strickland, 23-15-05."

[143] Samuel Srickland's m is in Bates, *Simsbury, Connecticut, Vital Records*. A search there for the Strickland family reveals the b. of Samuel, m. to Sarah Hill, d. of Sarah (Hill) Strickland, and the b. of their children Joseph, Mary, and Orpha: Strickland Family / Samuel Strickland: Birth: 1697 - Samuel Stricktland the Son of Jofeph ftricktland was borne the 11th of Nouember 1697 . and Baptifed ye 14th of Nouember 1697. Death: 1736 - Sarah Strickland the wife of Samuel Strickland Departed this Life Decembr : 25th 1736 : [Birth: 1735 - Samuel the firft Sone of Edward Strickland was born april the : 24th A : D : 1735/6 - N.b., not a child of Samuel]. Birth: 1733 - Orpha Strickland the Daughter of Samuel

Strickland was born January the : 4th : 1733/4 : M: 1720 - Samuell Strickland and Sarah hill both of the Town of Simfbery : were married July : the : 28th: 1720. Birth: 1722 - Mary Strickland the daughter of Samuel Strickland was Borne ye 23 day of October 1722. Birth: 1721 - Jofeph Stricland : the Son of Samuel ftrickland was borne may 10th 1721

He is not in the *NEHGR*. His estate was not shown in the probate records of early Connecticut, although he was involved in the estate of his brother Joseph, June 1714 (accessed via NEHGS website).

Ancestry.com / OWT shows three other ch of Samuel and Sarah (Hill) Strickland, who will be listed here, although with no particular enthusiasm: Sarah, said to have m. Timothy Strong; Hannah; Elizabeth. OWT also shows a d. of both Sarah and Samuel on 25 Dec 1736. Sarah's d is in Simsbury V.R. Unless they d in an accident, it appears unlikely that Samel d then, too, so I will disregard this information. It appears more likely that he would have remarried and had a step-mother for his ch. Another wife appears on Ancestry.com and I will accept this as possible. She is Tamar Younglove, b. 4 Jan 1705, m. in Suffield, Hartford Co., Conn., 6 October 1737.

[144] From Simsbury V.R.: Death: 1702 – "an Infant of John Hils dyed April 2d 1702."

[145] "John Hills wife was deliuered of a dead child janry 29th 1700 / 1701"

[146] Hill, "Twelve Generations." I find no reason to believe that John Jr. was born on the day the infant died in 1702, it is reasonable to estimate his b. year as about 1702. Stiles, *Ancient Windsor*, v. 2. Bates, *Simsbury, Connecticut, Vital Records, 1665-1886.*

[147] Her b and m is in Hill, "Twelve Generations," with references; her d is in Simsbury V.R.: "Death: 1732 - Jane Hill ye wife of John hill Junr departed this life nouember ye 2d – 1732."

[148] Hill, "Twelve Generations": Jane (LaDieu) Hill two ch, but by the known date of her d and the years of b of the next two ch in this account, she must also have been their mother. I therefore have moved them to that position. Jane d about eight months after the b of her fourth ch.

[149] Simsbury V.R.: "Death: 1738 - Elizabeth Hill the wife of John Hill Jur Departed this Life September : 21 : A : D : 1738 :" Her approximate b. year and the names and dates of her ch are from Hill, ibid.

[150] The Wilcox/Wilcoxson family (with various spellings) appears many times in the genealogy of Luke Hill's descendants. I cannot, however, find where John Jr.'s w Abigail fits into the Wilcox/Wilcoxson genealogy. In Simsbury V.R., accessed via NEHGS, the Wilcox family (soundex) includes Wilcocks, Wilcockson, Wilcockson, and perhaps others. From several hundred names, on 14 pages, these four are related to the family of Luke Hill Sr., although there may be more:
Birth: 1727 - Ephraim wilcockson ye fon of Ephraim wilcockfon was Borne may ye 24- 1727
Birth: 1731 - fufannah wilcockfon ye daughter of Ephraim wilcockfon was born Aprill 17th - 1731
Marriage: 1726 - Ephraim willcockfon and hannah Hill ware married Aprill ye fifth - 1726
Marriage: 1738/9 - John Hill Jur : & Abigail Willcockfun were Married february 21st 1738/9 :

[151] U.S. and International Marriage Records, 1560-1900 (accessed from Ancestry.com, 8/4/2010): "Mary Hill married Jacob Reed in CT, 1724." "Probate Records of Hartford Co., CT," vol. 13, page 284: Distribution of John Hill's property after his death. Page 8 (Vol. 14) 6 July, 1742: John Hill and Ephraim Wilcock, Adms., . . . distribute as follows (in pounds, shilling, pence): To Sarah Hill, the widow, her thirds 71-06-02 / To John Hill, eldest son, his double part 47-10-08. To the heirs of Sarah Strickland, 23-15-05 / to Mary Read, to Hannah Wilcock, and to Elizabeth Hoskins, to each of them the sum of, 23-15-05."

[152] Phelps, *History of Simsbury*, has two citations for Jacob Reed: 153 - Minister's Rates, 1701; 175 - Taxed in 1701. Also, Death: 1736 - Sarah Reade Daughter of Jacob Reade Departed this Life

----

Reade/Reed Family (from NEHGS, Simsbury V.R.):
Jacob Reed (18 records, and they all relate to the Jacob Reed who m. Mary Hill, daughter of John and granddaughter of Luke Sr.):
1700 - Jacob Reade the Son of Jacob reade was born the fifteenth of may one Thoufand feuen Hundred
1736 - Sarah Reade Daughter of Jacob Reade Departed this Life December the : 11th A : D : 1736 :
1728 - John Read the Sone of Doctr : Jacob Read was Born June the : 20th : Anno Dom : 1728 :
1731 - Jocob Reade ye fon of Jacob Read was born Auguft 20th -1731 :

Birth: 1735/6 - Titus- the fone of Jacob Reade was Born January the : 9th A : D : 1735/6
Birth: 1738 - Silas Son of Jacob Reade was Born June 22nd 1738 :
Birth: 1740 - Sarah Daughter of Jacob Reade was Born July : 8th 1740 :
Birth: 1743 - Abijah Reade Son of Jacob Reade was Born July : 13th 1743 :
Birth: 1724/5 - Mary Reed the daughter of Jacob Reed was borne January ye 10th - 1724/5
Birth: 1726 - Lidia Read ye daughter of Jacob Read was born nouember 18th-1726
Birth: 1729 - Elizabeth Read the daughter of Jacob Read was born Aprill 27(?) - 1729
Marriage: 1724 - Jacob Reed and Mary Hill ware Maried Aprill ye 9th- 1724
Death: 1773 - Mary Read the wife of Jacob Read Departed this Life the Day of May A. D. 1773.
Death: 1775 - Jacob Read Departed this Life the 8th : Day of January Anno Do : 1775 .
Jacob Read Junr: of Simfbury and Rebecca Wood of New Haven were Joined in Marriage December 7th : A.D . 1766.
Jacob Read the Son of Jacob Read Junr: by Rebecca his wife was Born in Simfbury the 31st : A . D. 1767 .
Elifabeth Read the Daughter of Jacob Read Junr: by Rebecca his wife was Born in Simfbury December the 12th : A D . 1769.
Rhoda Read the Daughter of Jacob Read by Rebecca his wife was Born in Simfbury March 6th : A . D . 1772 .

[153] The ancestry of this Jacob Reed/Read/Reade is in the *NEHGR* . McCracken is quoted: "Dr. Philip Reade, shows that he is the son of Dr. Jacob Reade and grandson of Dr. Philip Reade: 6. DR. JACOB3 READ, son of Dr. Jacob2 Reade (Philip1) by his wife Elizabeth Law, was born in Simsbury, Conn., 15 May 1700, baptized there on 19 May 1700, and died there 8 Jan. 1775. He married there, 9 April 1724, MARY HILL, died in May 1773, daughter of John. Jacob Read's will is dated 14 Dec. 1774 (Simsbury Records, 1:175). It lists the children as below; in the distribution made by the daughter Mary on 3 June 1774 (ibid., 1:211), the children appear as Mary, Lydia, Elizabeth, Jacob, Titus, Sarah, Silas, Abijah, and Amy. William Moses, stepfather to this Jacob Read, conveyed to him on 24 July 1735 (ibid., vol. 6)."

McCracken then lists Mary, Lydia, John, Elizabeth, Jacob, Titus, Sarah, Silas, Sarah, and Amy. He says Amy's b was not recorded and she was not mentioned in the will but appears in the distribution. He says Abijah was listed in the distribution just before Amy, but he forgot to add Abijah to the list; this would make 11. He shows the first Sarah, who d. in 1736, as b. between Titus and Silas, although there is no particular reason given for this. I have listed her as first, not knowing when she was b. The information about the ten ch named by McCracken is entered in their Notes. Abijah's information is from the V.R.

[154] Bates, Simsbury V.R. In Simsbury V.R., accessed via NEHGS -- Wilcox family (soundex), includes Wilcocks, Wilcockson, Wilcockson, and perhaps others. From several hundred names, on 14 pages, these 4 are related to the family of Luke Hill Sr., although there may be more:
Birth: 1727 - Ephraim wilcockson ye fon of Ephraim wilcockfon was Borne may ye 24- 1727
Birth: 1731 - fufannah wilcockfon ye daughter of Ephraim wilcockfon was born Aprill 17th - 1731
Marriage: 1726 - Ephraim willcockfon and hannah Hill ware married Aprill ye fifth - 1726
Marriage: 1738/9 - John Hill Jur : & Abigail Willcockfun were Married february 21st 1738/9 :
[155] (aka WILCOXSON, WILCOCKSON, WILLCOCKSON, WILCOCK, WILLCOX) .
[156] From Phelps, *History of Simsbury*: 174 - Sergeant Samuel Willcoxson, (Willcox) was an early settler. He resided at Meadow plain, and died March 12, 1713. He removed from Hartford. He left, it is supposed, three sons, Samuel, William and Joseph. Samuel had Joseph, born Aug. 1701, and Ephraim, Feb. 4 1707, and perhaps other children. William married Elizabeth Willson, by whom he had John, William, Amos, and Azariah, born July 27, 1706. William was a deacon in the church, and was living in 1770. Amos married Joanna Hillyer, Nov. 6, 1725. His widow married a Mr. Bishop, and died at about one hundred years of age. Their children were, Amos, born May 15, 1729. Elijah, born Sept. 25, 1743. Ruth, born Jan. 10, 1733. Lucy,-married Ariel Lawrence. Ezekiel, born June 10, 1735. Esther. Joanna, born May 26, 1740. James, born Feb. 10, 1751. Joseph, had Joseph, born Feb. 9, 1705, and perhaps other children. He settled at Westover's plain. Some of his descendants, it is supposed, settled at Salmon brook. Joseph and Ephraim Willcox were taxed there in 1734.
[157] None of the supposed ch of Ephraim and Hannah (Hill) Wilcox appear in Simsbury V.R., even when a Soundex search is used in the search. None of the b dates of these ch can be considered as proved, and I therefore consider them only as "possible," although presumably someone had a reason for assigning

specific b dates to Susannah, Ephraim, and Sylvanus.

[158] In Simsbury V.R. (and *Barbour Collection*): "Birth: 1710 - Elizabeth Hill the daughter of John Hill, wch his wif Sarah bare whof maiden nam was Sarah Terrey was born december fourtenth 1710." She received a distribution from her father's estate: "To Mary Read, to Hannah Wilcock, and to Elizabeth Hoskins, to each of them the sum of 23-15-05."

She is not in OWT. The information about her life, m, and descendants is unsourced, compiled from several family trees, principally "Martin Franks Sedlacek Simanek [MFSS] Family Tree" of Ancestry.com. She must have been alive in 1740 at the time her father's estate was distributed, so her death date of 5 April 1725 in MFSS Family Tree will be disregarded.

[159] If Ancestry.com is to be believed, Eunice Coe was the daughter of Ebenezer and Jane (Elmer) Coe. Ebenezer was the son of Robert and Barbara (Parmelee) Coe. Barbara Parmelee was the daughter of John Parmelee of Guilford, Conn. The Parmelee family of Guilford also appears in the marriage of Tahan and Abigail Hill, son and daughter of Luke Hill Sr., who married, respectively, Hannah and Caleb Parmelee. They were children of John Parmelee Jr., one of the three children of John Parmelee, a founder of Guilford, Conn. This John Parmelee (Sr.) had only three children: John, Hannah, and Mary. Barbara (Parmelee) Hoskins must therefore have been the child of a John Parmelee in a later generation -- or the genealogy is mixed up in some way.

Three of the descendants of John Parmelee Jr. married three descendants of Luke Hill Sr. John Parmelee's son Caleb and his daughter Hannah married, respectively, Luke Hill's daughter Abigail and his son Tahan. The Hill and Parmelee families were joined again several generations later, when John Parmelee Jr.'s great-granddaughter Eunice Coe married Joseph Hoskins Jr. He was a great-grandson of Luke Hill Sr., in the line of Luke's son John, whose daughter Elizabeth Hill married Joseph Hoskins Sr.

Chapter 4 – The Great-grandchildren

[160] *Families of Early Hartford*, 370; OWT, "Descendants of Arthur Henbury and Lydia Hill," Ancestry.com, accessed 4/18/2010ff; and "Winters Family," mythtown1958, Ancestry.com., 4/15/2010.

[161] Nothing more about this person in Ancestry.com.

[162] *Families of Early Hartford*, 477-8; and OWT, "Arthur Henbury and Lydia Hill," op. cit.

[163] Her b.d. and the name of her dau is from Ancestry.com.

[164] Her d. date and place is from Ancestry.com. Her m is from *Families of Early Hartford*.

[165] See www.fffaa.org/ Web page of the Frisbie-Frisbee Family Association of America, Inc (FFFAA).

[166] *Barbour Collection*, Branford V.R., entries for FRISBEE, John; *Families of Ancient New Haven*, 628.

[167] OWT gives 8 Feb 1731 as the date of her b and m. I will accept the m date.

[168] *Barbour Collection*, Branford V.R., for FRISBIE, Jedediah; *Families of Ancient New Haven*; and OWT.

[169] He is not in the *Barbour Collection* for Hartford V.R.; he is in *Families of Ancient New Haven*.

[170] *Barbour Collection*, Hartford V.R., for FRISBIE, Israel. The names of his ch are from OWT.

[171] *Barbour Collection*, Branford V.R., for FRISBIE, Nathaniel.

[172] *Barbour Collection*, Branford V.R., for FRISBIE, Susannah; Jacobus, *Early New Haven*; and OWT.

[173] *Barbour Collection*, Branford V.R., for FRISBIE, Huldah; Jacobus, *Early New Haven*; and OWT.

[174] *Barbour Collection*, Branford V.R. for FRISBIE, Elijah; Jacobus, *Ancient New Haven*; and OWT.

[175] There are 15 entries for Hannah Frisbie in *Barbour Collection*, Branford V.R., but only one is relevant: "Hannah, d. John & Susanna, b. June 24, 1720." Also, Jacobus, *Ancient New Haven*; OWT; and Wiswedel Family Tree (Owner gwiswedel), accessed on Ancestry.com (8/23/2010).

[176] *Barbour Collection*, Branford V.R., for Frisbie, Jonah; and OWT.

[177] Jacobus, *Ancient New Haven*: FAM. 4. BENJAMIN & ELIZABETH (HENBURY) FRISBIE.

[178] *Barbour Collection*, for Branford Vital Records. Elnathan is given by Jacobus, *Ancient New Haven*.

[179] Jacobus, op. cit.; and Frisbie/Criger Family Tree, Owner ercriger, accessed 8/23/2010.

[180] Jacobus, op. cit.

[181] Jacobus, op. cit.; OWT, and Farmington Vital Records.

[182] Jacobus, op. cit.. There is nothing more about him in Ancestry.com.

[183] Jacobus, op. cit.

[184] Hannah, Mary, Adam, and Lucy Saxton are in NEHGS, "Simsbury Connecticut, V.R., 1665-1886."

[185] Stiles, *Ancient Windsor* (1892), v.2; and Priest, "Gillett." There is nothing more about him in OWT.

[186] Stiles, op cit.; and Priest, "Gillett."

[187] Stiles, op cit.; and Priest, "Gillett."; and "The Siege of Louisbourg," Wikipedia, accessed 5 May 2010.

[188] "Descendants of John Saxton and Mary Hill," Ancestry.com, accessed 4/23/2010ff.

[189] "Descendants of John Saxton and Mary Hill," op. cit.

[190] Stiles, *Ancient Windsor* (1859 and 1892); OWT; and Pitman, "Nathan Gillett," with sources.

[191] Stiles, *Ancient Windsor* (1859 and 1892).

[192] Stiles, *Ancient Windsor* (1859 and 1892).

[193] Coralynn's transcription of Saybrook *Barbour Collection*: BUSHNELL Jeremiah.

[194] Jemima (Bushnell) Parmelee was the mother of 8 or 9, four of whom were followed for additional generations in "Families of Early Guilford." One of these was followed in Baldwin Family Tree, Ancestry.com (accessed 6/15/2010). Also, "Families of Early Guilford," (Parmelee Family), 953; and Roberts, "Genealogies of Connecticut Families," v. 1.

[195] *Barbour Collection* of Saybrook V.R.: "Hannah, dau Samuell Jr & Hannah, b Dec 8, 1719."

[196] Known only from Ancestry.com, and no other information there.

[197] Ibid.

[198] *Ancient New Haven*, 3:743: Hill Family #5; Smith and Steiner, "Luke Hill"; and *History of Wethersfield*, v.2. The name of the wife of Ebenezer Jr. is from Ancestry.com. Also, e-mail to GJH from Richard R. Stanley, 29 January 2005ff; and Mark Norris, "Some descendants of Ebenezer Hill, son of Luke Hill Jr.," Telephone conversations with Mark Norris, 650-349-6380, 7 January 2011ff, and e-mail exchanges, mark-norris@sbcglobal.net; Mark Norris (owner), The Hill Family (on Ancestry.com); Hill Family of Connecticut Vital Records to 1800 at http://freepages.genealogy.rootsweb.ancestry.com/ and Rootsweb, based on Barbour Collection; Church Records.

[199] Jacobus, *Ancient New Haven*, 3:743; and OWT; Mark Norris, Ibid. His b. 22 Nov 1719 is in Rootsweb's Hill Family of Connecticut VR. His m. to Elizabeth Richards, 13 Mar 1745, Ibid. His 2nd m. to Gloriana _____ is from Ibid.; her b. is est at 1749 and their m. est at 1769, in Wallingford. Jacobus says she had a dau. Martha b. 16 Jan 1759, but if the v.r. is correct for Gloriana's est. b., Martha must have been a child of Elizabeth, and I will place her there. Mark Norris: Asa and his sons were professional gravestone carvers. http://www.norwalkhistoricalsociety.org/BuryingGround5.html.

[200] Rootsweb, Hill Family of Connecticut VR shows Barbour Collection: Marriage Asa Hill her birth est 1725 marriage 13 Mar 1745 Goshen Litchfield CT Elizabeth Richards. Mark Norris said she had six ch, but names only 5: Jonah, David, Elizabeth, Martha, and Sarah. I will therefore show only five.

[201] Jacobus gives only her first name. Her surname is from Ancestry.com (accessed 2/13/2011).

[202] Jacobus, *Ancient New Haven*; and OWT, citing 42 user-submitted trees.

[203] *Barbour Collection* for Wallingford: "Hill, Titus, son Ebenezer, b. Mar. 22, 1726." OWT says she d.s.p., but Mark Norris (op. cit., *supra*) names six children and descendants of one of them.

[204] References cited by Mark Norris: Connecticut Soldiers, French and Indian War, 1755-62; Connecticut Town Birth Records, pre-1870 (Barbour Collection), and Connecticut Town Marriage Records, pre-1870 (Barbour Collection). Norris says she had a son, Elisha, who had descendants.

[205] Ancestry.com; Barbour Collection; and Mark Norris: "Military service, Massachusetts, 17 July 1777," citing *Massachusetts Soldiers and Sailors of the Revolutionary War*.

[206] *Barbour Collection*: "Hill, Zenas"; Jacobus, *Ancient New Haven* ("Zenas, b 4 Jan 1730"); and OWT.

[207] Ancestry.com gives a b.d. of 4 Jan 1734, which is unlikely, given the birth of the next child in June of the same year. The b.d. of 2 Apr 1732 is from Jacobus. OWT concludes that he d. 26 May 1740.

[208] 8 user-submitted trees are referred to for Daniel Hill (b. 1734). Norris cites U.S. Federal Census records for 1790, 1800, 1810, AGBI, and Connecticut v.r. (Barbour Collection and Town of Goshen v.r.) and says the child of this marriage was Miles Hill (b. 1766). It is confusing, but there is another Daniel Hill who is contemporaneous in Connecticut, a descendant of James Hill (1646-1715) and his wife Sarah Griswold.

[209] Mark Norris located her b. and d. record in the Barbour Collection for Goshen, Conn., page 28, viz.: "Huldah, d. [Ebenezer], b. Nov. 15, 1736; d. Sept. 6, 1737" citing in the original record 1:253.

[210] Jacobus, *Ancient New Haven*: "COOK . . . HENRY."

[211] His b. is in Jacobus, op. cit. Married, but d.s.p. according to OWT.

[212] His b. is in Ibid. No additional information about him in OWT.

[213] Her b. is in Ibid. Her m. and children are from OWT.

[214] His b. is in Ibid. His m. and children are from OWT.

[215] Her b. is in Ibid. No additional information about her in OWT.

[216] Her b. is in Ibid. No additional information about her in OWT.

[217] OWT. She apparently d.s.p.

[218] Jacobus, op cit.

[219] *Barbour Collection*, Wallingford: "Uri, son Luke, & Sarah, b. June 19, 1729"; and OWT.

[220] Kezia Hill is in Jacobus, op. cit. For her m. and ch, see Zenas Hill (*supra*). Norris: "Military service, Massachusetts, 17 July 1777," *Massachusetts Soldiers and Sailors of the Revolutionary War.*

[221] His b. in Wallingford is in Barbour Collection: Hill, Zenas, son Ebenezer & Martha, b. Jan. 4, 1730. OWT, based on 4 user-submitted references, shows the same children and adds Sarah, Zenas, and Jesse.

[222] Jacobus, *Ancient New Haven.*

[223] Jacobus, op. cit.

[224] Jacobus, op. cit.; *Barbour Collection*; and OWT.

[225] Reuben Dibble is in the *Barbour Collection* and Jacobus, op. cit. Also see OWT.

[226] Known only from OWT. He does not appear in Jacobus, op. cit., or the *Barbour Collection.*

[227] Lydia Dibble is in Jacobus, op. cit., and the *Barbour Collection*; and Hibbard, *Goshen, Connecticut.*

[228] Susannah Dibble is in Jacobus, op. cit., and the *Barbour Collection* but not in OWT.

[229] OWT gives Josiah Dibble's b.d. as 30 March 1737, but it is 3 March in Jacobus and *Barbour.*

[230] Rachel Dibble's b. is in the *Barbour Collection*, but nothing more is known about her.

[231] Mary Dibble's b. is in the *Barbour Collection*. Also see OWT.

[232] Roberts, *Genealogies of Connecticut Families*, 165; and Carlson to GJH, 3 December 2008.

[233] Carlson to GJH: Hibbard, *Goshen*, 42-4; Edward S. Cooke Jr., *The Social Economy of the Preindustrial Joiner in Western Connecticut, 1750- 1800*; Sale 7443 – American Furniture. Christie's Auction House, New York, NY, 22 June 1993; and *Massachusetts Soldiers and Sailors in the War of the Revolution.*

[234] Carlson to GJH, quoting New Haven Colony probate file #4963 6 Nov 1741 names Bille, Phineas, Isaac, & Abraham; also quotes Payne K. Kilbourne, *History and Genealogy of the Kilbourn Family in the United States* (Hartford, CT: Brown & Parsons, 1845), 89; and *History of Chittenden County, Vermont* (Syracuse, NY: D. Mason & Co., 1886), 674; and quotes from Abram W. Foote, *Foote Family: Comprising the Genealogy and History of Nathaniel Foote, of Wethersfield, Conn.* (Rutland, VT: Tuttle Co., 1907). 264. Relevant U.S. Federal censuses include 1790, 1800, 1810, and 1820 (Chittenden Co., VT).

[235] [Hill, William Edwin]. "Genealogy of the Hill Family in America."[GHFA] [Hill Family Association], 1921. The numbers in brackets, eg. [2], [3], refer to the listing in GHFA: "1. Isaac Hill was born about 1740." Isaac Hill gave a deposition at Woodbury District, Conn., probate court on 13 August 1832. The DAR application of Doris Hill (1966) shows 31 March 1833 as his date of d at Southbury. However, GJH found a record of his d on 1 April 1833 in the Town Office at Southbury, Conn., in a volume entitled *Vital Statistics of the Town of Southbury, Conn., Taken from Early Church Records*: "Hill Isaac SBC 1 Apr 1833." SBC refers to the South Britain Congregational Church, which is located in the northern part of Southbury. His burial site is unknown. The m of Isaac Hill and Eunice Mallary (sic) at Stratford, CT, appears on LR5 page 72 of the "Record of marriages in the Town of Stratford, Connecticut." Isaac Hill is in *Record of Service of Connecticut Men in the War of the Revolution*, 655. Hettie H. Hill (b. Cairo, IL), D.A.R. No. 159003, was a great-great granddaughter of this Isaac Hill, in *Lineage Book: National Society of the D.A.R.*, v. 160, 1920; Washington, DC, 1938, p. 2. Roberts, *Genealogies of Connecticut Families*, 156; VR Branford, CT, 2:346 (for his b); VR Wallingford, CT, 5:509 (for his m to Ester Hester Stone, b. 1711 in Guilford, Ct., on 16 Jan 1733 in Wallingford); and VR Wallingford, Ct., 5:549 (for his d in 1751).

[236] Her birth is recorded on LR5, page 50, of the Vital Statistics "Record of births in the Town of Stratford , 1868 (sic)-1914." Carlson, quoting Stratford, CT, in *Barbour Collection.* Eunice Mallory was a descendant of Thomas Trowbridge, who emigrated to New Haven and then returned to d in Taunton, England. His ancestry has been traced back to Charlemagne. See Gary Boyd Roberts, *The Royal Descents of 600 Immigrants to the American Colonies or the United States* (Genealogical Publishing Co., 2004).

[237] A photograph of Abraham Hill's tombstone in Carmel, N.Y., was sent to GJH by Dennis O'Connell on 2-2-2004. It shows that he died on "11 May 1817, age ~70." The record in Barbara Smith Buys, *Old Gravestones of Putnam County, New York: Together with Information from Ten Adjacent Dutchess County Burying Grounds* (Baltimore: Gateway Press, 1975), 207: "Hill, Abraham, d. May 11, 1817, 70y.; and Hill,

Hannah, w. Abraham, d. July 5, 1818, 70y." Buys' transcription missed the symbol ~, which is clearly visible on the stone, and which shows his age at death was approximately 70.

[238] Hannah's gravestone (*supra*); lineage of descendants of Abraham Hill, from Paul F. Hill, Corning, N.Y.

[239] All that is known about Luke Blackmun, his wife, and ch, is from OWT.

[240] *Families of Early Guilford, Connecticut*; Ancestry.com and OWT.

[241] Roberts, *Genealogies of Connecticut Families*; OWT.

[242] *Families of Early Guilford.*

[243] Her m is in "Barnes Family," *Families of Early Guilford.*

[244] *Families of Early Guilford* for Sarah Parmelee; Roberts, *Connecticut Families* for Timothy Allen; OWT; Kingsley Family Tree (owner: USAF_Kingsley); Hiel Hollister, *Biography of Allen Surname of Pawlet, VT*: *Pawlet (VT) One Hundred Years* (Albany, N.Y.: J. Munsell, 1867): ALLEN, TIMOTHY. It is odd but perhaps true that there were two men who were named Timothy Allen, each of whom had a son Pamelee (various spellings), and who lived at about the same time. One of them was said to be a "cousin" of Ethan Allen. His son Parmelee was a Captain in the Vermont Militia in the Revolutionary War. Orrin Allen Peer's genealogy shows that the Timothy Allen who was a cousin of Ethan was actually a 3d cousin, once removed. The ancestry of the other Timothy Allen is unknown; he m Sarah Parmelee and had a son Parmelee, who m Ann Wheeler and had a dau Prudence.

[245] Roberts, *Connecticut Families*. There is nothing more about them in Ancestry.com.

[246] Roberts, op. cit. and *Families of Early Guilford.*

[247] Ibid.

[248] McCracken, "Griffin"; and Ancestry.com "My Comprehensive Family Tree" (accessed 7/29/2010).

[249] Anna Griffin and Ebenezer Loomis in McCracken, op. cit.

[250] McCracken, op. cit. Nothing more about this person in Ancestry.com.

[251] McCracken, op. cit. Nothing more about them in Ancestry.com.

[252] McCracken, op. cit., and Ancestry.com.

[253] Bates, Simsbury V.R.; and Ancestry.com.

[254] Bates, Simsbury V.R. No further information about her in OWT.

[255] "Moore Family Tree" (accessed from Ancestry.com, 8/5/2010); *Barbour Collection*; Wayne Hollister, "BROOKS FAMILY OF OSWEGO COUNTY NEW YORK AND WINNEBAGO COUNTY WISCONSIN" <http://www.rootsweb.ancestry.com/~nyoswego/biographies/ brooks.html> (accessed 8/6/2010); and OWT.

[256] Bates, Simsbury V.R. No further information about her in OWT.

[257] Bates, Simsbury V.R. No further information about her in OWT.

[258] Bates, Simsbury V.R. No further information about her in OWT.

[259] Simsbury V.R.: "Birth: 1725 - John Hill ye fon of John Hill Jur was born february the third-1725/6." Also, *Barbour Collection*; and Hill, "Twelve Generations," including sources; and from "HILL Family of Connecticut" http://freepages.genealogy.rootsweb.ancestry.com/ (accessed 8/20/2010ff).

[260] James D. Hill, "Twelve Generations," with sources provided.

[261] *Barbour Collection*: "B Martha HILL F 21 Jun 1730 Simsbury Hartford CT John."

[262] *Barbour Collection*: B Mary HILL F 28 Sep 1732 12 Nov 1733 Simsbury Hartford CT John; Simsbury V.R.: "Death: 1733 - Marey Hill The Daughter of John Hill Jur : departed This Life November : 12th : 1733."

[263] *Barbour Collection*

[264] S VR: "Death: 1737 - Bennoni Hill the Son of John Hill Jur: Departed this Life November : 21 : 1737."

[265] Ibid. "Birth: 1739/40 - Sarah Daughter of John Hill Jur : was Born January : 6th 1739/40":

[266] *Barbour Collection*: "B Phebe HILL F 17 Jul 1746 Simsbury Hartford CT John."; and James D. Hill.

[267] James D. Hill, "Twelve Generations," with sources provided.

[268] James D. Hill, Ibid..

[269] Bates, Simsbury V.R.: "Mary Reed . . . Phinehas Bunce and Mary Reade"; McCracken, "Dr. Philip Reade and His Earlier Descendants," *NEHGR* 112 (April 1958): 119-132; Jacobus, "XII. Edgerton Family of Simsbury," *TAG [TAG]*, 41: 227-30, 1965; Helen Schatvet Ullmann, "Hartford District Probate Records from 1750, As Abstracted by Lucius Barnes Barbour from Volume 19 (1761-1764)," *The Connecticut Nutmegger,* 2006, March: 581ff.

[270] Bates, Simsbury V.R.: "Lidia Read"; Stiles, *Ancient Windsor* (1859); and McCracken, Ibid.

[271] Andrew J. Morris, "Family History of Thomas Barber (ca 1614-1662)" in "Connecticut Genealogy" < http://connecticut-genealogy.blogspot.com/2010/07/family-history-of-thomas-barber-ca-1614.html>, accessed 8/8/2010. Cites William Richard Cutter,*Genealogical and Family History of the State of Connecticut: A Record of the Achievements of Her People in the Making of a Commonwealth and the Founding of a Nation* (New York, NY, USA: Lewis Publishing Company, 1911); John Barber in Simsbury V.R.: Barber Family.

[272] Simsbury V.R.: "John Read"; and McCracken: "John, b. 20 June 1728; d. *vita patris*, not in the will."

[273] Simsbury V.R..: "Elizabeth Read"; and McCracken, Ibid.

[274] Simsbury V.R.: "Jocob Reade"; and McCracken, Ibid.

[275] Simsbury V.R.: "Sarah Reade."

[276] Simsbury V.R.: "TituS- the fone of Jacob Reade"; McCracken, Ibid; and U.S. and International Marriage Records, 1560-1900 (accessed on Ancestry.com, 8/4/2010): Titus Reade.

[277] Simsbury V.R.: "Silas Son of Jacob Reade"; McCracken, Ibid., "Silas Read."

[278] Simsbury V.R. "Sarah Daughter of Jacob Reade"; McCracken, Ibid., "b. 8 July 1740."

[279] Simsbury V.R.: "Abijah Reade"; McCracken says he was named in the distribution of his f's estate.

[280] McCracken: "x. Amy, birth not recorded, not mentioned in the will, but appears in the distribution."

[281] In Simsbury V.R.: Wilcox family (soundex), includes Wilcocks, Wilcockson, Wilcockson, and perhaps others. From several hundred names, on 14 pages, at least four, and perhaps more, are related to the family of Luke Hill Sr.

[282] "I Michael Jackson of Richfield was Baptized the 29th Day of October 1796 . . . My wife Susanna" [annex to the war record of his son-in-law, Sergeant Isaiah Hendryx, W21305]. Also see OWT; and Edwards/Biddlecome Family Tree on Ancestry.com (accessed 10 August 2010).

[283] The six youngest ch of Ephraim and Hannah (Hill) Wilcox are from Ancestry.com, and is unsourced.

[284] Information about Joseph Hoskins and Eunice Coe is from Ancestry.com.

Chapter 5 – Fifth Generation

[285] The information about Ebenezer and his family and the other ch of Benjamin and Mary (Long) Babcock is from OWT and Ancestry.com. "PrestonSmith," owned by Wendy Proudfoot (4/20/2010).

[286] Ruth & Hannah Judd are in "Families of Early Hartford." We note, sadly, that they died one day apart.

[287] The 8 children of Josiah and Mary (Palmer) Richards are known from Ancestry.com.

[288] The grandchildren of John and Susannah (Henbury) Frisbie are from Ancestry.com. and OWT; also, "Brooks," and "Harper Family Tree," owned by Laurin50; "Steele Family Tree," owned by Steelesvineyard; "Humphries Family Tree," owned by zredhd; and www.fffaa.org/.

[289] Jacobus, *Ancient New Haven*; OWT; Ancestry.com, "Tompkins Family Tree," owned by FranklinTompkins18; and "Bill & Judy VanNewkirk's Family Tree," Judy VanNewkirk, Ancestry.com.

[290] OWT; and Ancestry.com, "Wiswedel Family Tree."

[291] The children of Benjamin and Elizabeth (Pardee) Frisbie were named in Jacobus, *Ancient New Haven*.

[292] Information about Jerusha Ives and Wise Barnes and his first m and their ch are from Ancestry.com.

[293] The ch of Benjamin and Jerusha (Frisbie) Gaylord are known only from Ancestry.com.

[294] All of the ch except the two youngest are in Jacobus, Ibid. These are in Ancestry.com and OWT.

[295] Daniel and Samuel Frisbie are known only from Ancestry.com.

[296] Children of Theodore Frisbie by his two wives are from Jacobus, *Ancient New Haven*.

[297] "Descendants of John Saxton and Mary Hill," Ancestry.com, accessed 4/23/2010ff; and *A Digest of the Early Connecticut Probate Records, 1715 to 1723*: Name: Richard Saxton Location: Simsbury

[298] Orrin Peer Allen, *The Allen Memorial: Descendants of Samuel Allen of Windsor, Connecticut, 1640-1907* (Palmer, Mass.: C. B. Fiske & Co., 1907), 54-6; Roger Enos is on p. 54. Also see: Edwin P. Hoyt, *The Damndest Yankees: Ethan Allen & His Clan* (Brattleboro, Vt.: The Stephen Greene Press, 1976), many citations of Ira Allen; Roger Enos is on p. 220; Rowland Evans Robinson, *Vermont: A Study of Independence* (Boston, Mass.: Houghton, Mifflin and Co., 1892), 216. Gravestone on "findagrave."

[299] OWT, Ancestry.com, accessed 6/15/2010.

[300] *Families of Early Guilford*, 953, 962, Ancestry.com family trees and OWT; "Baldwin Family Tree."

[301] "Baldwin," Ibid.; and *Early Guilford*.

[302] Richard R. Stanley, e-mail to GJH, 29 January 2005; "History of Wethersfield," v.2; Connecticut Town Birth Records, pre-1870 (*Barbour Collection*); OWT; and "Hill Family Association/Hill Family Club" <reocities.com/Heartland/hills/9493/hillrevw.html> (accessed 11-2-2010); and "Golding Family Tree"

[303] Lucy Beach/Beech is in "Golding"; also see "Roe_Elisha & Electa Family Tree," *Barbour Collection*; and "Pratt and Webster Family Tree," owned by PriscillaR, accessed 11/4/2010.

[304] Six younger ch of Ebenezer Hill Jr. from Norris, who cited Hill Family of Connecticut Vital Records.

[305] B Samuel HILL M 6 Oct 1748 7 Oct 1766 Goshen Litchfield CT Ebenezer Jr.

[306] Hill Family (Ibid.): B Reuben HILL M 26 Mar 1751 Goshen Litchfield CT Ebenezer

[307] Hill Family (Ibid.): B Chloe HILL (Cloe) F 19 FEb 1754 Goshen Litchfield CT Ebenezer Jr.

[308] Hill Family (Ibid.): B Ebenezer HILL M 4 Nov 1756 Goshen Litchfield CT Ebenezer Jr.

[309] Hill Family (Ibid.): B Lucina HILL F 29 Jul 1761 Goshen Litchfield CT Ebenezer

[310] The wives and ch of Asa Hill are from Jacobus, *Ancient New Haven*, 3:743; OWT; and Mark Norris.

[311] His wife and ch are Hill Family 6, on Jacobus, Ibid., 743ff.

[312] Information about the children of Asa Hill and Gloriana Wheeler is largely from Mark Norris (op. cit.).

[313] Norris says Ithuel Hill was a headstone carver: http://www.brecknock.org/construction.htm.

[314] Hill Family (Ibid.): Asa HILL M b 31 Jan 1776 d 13 Mar 1776 Harwinton Litchfield Par Asa Gloriana.

[315] From Mark Norris: http://www.flickr.com/photos/cemeteryrodeo/sets/72157612214746022/ "Phineas Hill (1778-1844) is the son of a headstone carver Asa Hill …" And "wtcole67": Three children by wife Mary "Polly" Stone: Myra (d.s.p.), Horace (d.s.p.), and Asa (1815-1874), who had descendants.

[316] Ebnezer and Martha (Hill) Grant's ch are from 30 user-submitted family trees on Ancestry.com.

[317] A biography of Dr. Isaac Grant by Frank Passic, Albion Historian; and an article in the *Morning Star* (21 January 2001) are in the Hill Family website of Ancestry.com that is owned by marknorris59.

[318] Mark Norris cites Barbour Collection for b. of Silas, s of Titus and Mindwell (Hall) Hill, 1 Apr 1752. In "thehills45" on Ancestry.com, he is "Titus Jr.," b 1 Apr 1752, d. date unk, lived at Richmond, Mass.

[319] The website for "thehills45" on Ancestry.com shows that Titus Hill was b. in Goshen, Litchfield Co., Conn., on 22 Mar 1726, son of Ebenezer and Martha (Dibble) Hill, and by wife Mindwell Hall (dates and ancestry unknown), he had children Titus Jr. and Arunah Hill.

[320] Hill Family of Connecticut VR (Ibid.).

[321] OneWorldTree says his name is Uria and does not give a gender. Nothing more about him/her is given.

[322] Woodbury V.R. in Barbour Collection (p. 161): "Sarah, d. Zenas & Kezia, b. Mar. 20, 1762."

[323] Woodbury V.R. in Barbour Collection (p. 161), "Zenas, s. Zenas & Kezia, b. Dec. 26, 1764."

[324] Woodbury V.R. in Barbour Collection (p. 161): "Jesse, s. Zenas & Kezia, b. Dec. 10, 1766."

[325] Jacobus and Norris (op. cit.)

[326] Information about Isaac and Anna (Hill) Cook is from OWT and various family trees in Ancestry.com.

[327] Uri Hill and his marriages are in the *Barbour Collection*. His children are from Ancestry.com

[328] Jacobus, *Ancient New Haven*; OWT, and various family trees in Ancestry.com, unverified.

[329] Some of the information about John Dibble in OWT is probably incorrect; it shows him marrying twice.

[330] The children of Elijah and Lydia (Dibble) Birge are from OWT. This information has not been verified.

[331] Carlson, "Some Descendants of Isaac Hill Sr. & Eunice Mallory," to GJH, 3 December 2008, sourced.

[332] Carlson quotes Hamilton Child, *Gazetteer and Business Directory of Addison County, Vt., for 1881-82* (Syracuse, NY: H. Child, 1882), 219; and James R. Lytle, *20th Century History of Delaware County, Ohio* (Chicago: Biographical Pub. Co, 1908), 474.

[333] Carlson quotes 1790 Federal Census, Addison Co, VT / Town of New Haven (Bilious and Reuben Hill).

[334] Carlson names the ch of Truman and Chloe (Hill) Skeels.

[335] Carlson cites 1790 and 1800 Federal Census for Addison Co, VT; and he quotes William F. Prosser, *History of the Puget Sound Country* (The Lewis Publishing Company, 1903), v. 2.

[336] Carlson, op. cit.

[337] All that is known about this family is from OWT, except that Maj. Moses Stockwell, father-in-law of Ezra Benedict, is in Mabel Kennedy Stockwell, *The Stockwell Genealogy* (Lebanon, N.H.: Stockwell Family Assoc., 1983). Moses Stockwell is person #1252; b about 1746 at Sutton, Mass., he was at Valley Forge and was present at the surrender of Cornwallis in 1781. Sarah Stockwell was one of the 15 ch of Moses and Sarah (Pierce) Stockwell.

[338] The ch of Phineas Hill are from Carlson, op. cit. Additional unverified details are from OWT.

[339] Carlson quotes Ernest Ray Brownson, *Genealogy of One Branch of the Richard Brownson Family*, 1631-1951 (Mayville, N.D.?: unknown, 1951), 237.

[340] Carlson, op. cit.

[341] Carlson, op. cit., quotes Alfred Huidekoper, "Incidents in the Early History of Crawford County, Pennsylvania" in *Memoirs of the Historical Society of Pennsylvania*. Vol. 2, Part 2. (Philadelphia: Henry C. Baird, 1850), 125, 149. Also, Genealogical Data contained in the Statutes at Large, Commonwealth of PA: LAWS PASSED SESSION 1816/17 / HARRISBURG, PA. / SIMON SNYDER, Governor, 116; Samuel P. Bates, *History of Crawford County, Pennsylvania* (Chicago: Warner, Beers & Co, 1885), 697-8; *Norfolk Gazette and Publick Ledger* (29 December 1806); John Earle Reynolds, *In French Creek Valley* (Meadville, PA.: Crawford County Historical Society, 1938), 129-30 [*Crawford Weekly Messenger*, November 27, 1805.]; Natalie R. Fernald, *The Genealogical Exchange* (1904), 23. Luke Hill is in 1790 Federal Census, Westmoreland Co., PA; 1800 Federal Census, Crawford Co, PA; 1810 Federal Census, Crawford Co, PA; and 1830 Upper Suburbs of New Orleans, LA.

[342] Carlson, op. cit.

[343] Carlson provides sources for: Isaac b. 16 Nov 1772 d. 3 Sep 1860 Huron OH m 1) Elizabeth Ann BUNNELL / 2) Betsey CURTIS / 3) Deborah WOODMAN; and ch by Elizabeth Ann Bunnell are named. Carlson also quotes Hewson L. Peeke, *A Standard History of Erie County, Ohio* (Chicago: Lewis Pub. Co., 1916), 460-1; and he quotes "Family Findings" 3 (No. 1, January 1971), *Mid-West Tennessee Genealogical Society*, 11-2: Transcription of HILL FAMILY BIBLE RECORDS, contributed by Mrs. Louis Hill, owner of the Bible from which these records were taken. TITLE PAGE: *The Holy Bible containing the Old and New Testaments, Translated out of The Original Tongues; and with The Former Translations Diligently Compared and Revised*. New York: American Bible Society, Instituted in the Year MDCCCXVL. 1858 / FAMILY RECORD (Hill Family): Marriages Isaac Hill Junior to Elizabeth Ann Bunnell May 17th 1794 [and 11 others]; Births [and 17 others] Isaac Hill Junior, November 6th 1772 /Elizabeth Ann Bunnell, April 12th 1771; Children Maria Hill, March 20th 1795 [and 12 others]; Deaths [and 13 others] Charles W. Hill, September 27th 1801/ Isaac Hill junior, September 3d 1860.

[344] Carlson, op. cit., cites U.S. Federal Censuses for 1820, 1830, and 1850; and Helen M. Lu and Gwen B. Neumann, *Revolutionary War Period: Bible, Family & Marriage Records Gleaned from Pension Applications*, 1998. 19:20: CT/CT ISAAC HILL in 1832, aged 92, res New Haven, CT, b 16 Apr 1740, Guilford, Middlesex Co., CT. Son BENAJAH HILL aged 7 in 1781; dau SALLY b 10 Dec 1781. S-31747.

[345] Carlson cites LDS Pedigree Resource File for Ephraim Hill, Benajah Hill and Seth Stone Hill (Ripton Parish, Stratford, Fairfield, Connecticut); also, quotes Julia H. Brush Genealogical Collection, Cyrenius H. Booth Library, Newtown, CT, manuscripts; and 1810 U.S. Federal Census, Newton, Fairfield Co., CT (Thos Stillson and Seth Hill).

[346] William Edwin Hill (1st ed.); GJH (2nd ed. editor), *Genealogy of the Hill Family in America* (William E. Hill, Genesee, N.Y. (1921); GJH, West Orange, N.J. (2000). Ephraim Hill is person #2 in William E. Hill's edition; Thomas P. Dimitroff and Lois S. Janes, *History of the Corning-Painted Post Area: 200 Years in Painted Post Country* (Corning, N.Y.: Corning Area Bicentennial Committee, n.d. ?1976); W. W. Clayton, *History of Steuben County, New York, with Illustrations and Biographical Sketches of Some of Its Prominent Men and Pioneers* (Philadelphia: J. B. Lippincott/Lewis, Peck & Co., 1879; Samuel Orcutt, *History of the Towns of New Milford and Bridgewater, Connecticut, 1703-1882* (Hartford, Conn.: Case, Lockwood and Brainard, 1882); Harlow Hakes (ed.), *Landmarks of Steuben County, New York* (Syracuse, N.Y.: D. Mason & Co., Publishers, 1896; Torrey, *New England Marriages*; Millard F. Roberts (Compiler and Editor), *Historical Gazetteer of Steuben County, New York, with Memoirs and Illustrations* (Syracuse, N.Y.: Millard F. Roberts, Publisher, 1891); Mary S. Jackson and Edward F. Jackson, *Death Notices from Steuben County, New York Newspapers: 1797-1884* (Bowie, Md.: Heritage Books, 1998).

Baptismal record of "Ephraim, son of Isaac Hill" at Shelton / Huntington Congregational Church, 12 July 1778 (Baptism #102 for 1778), linking him to Isaac Hill, from Connecticut State Library's volumes entitled *Shelton, Connecticut Huntington Congregational Church And Ecclesiastical Society Records, 1717-1917*, Vol. 1; Orcutt, *New Milford and Bridgewater, Connecticut*, 711; tombstone inscription in Gillett Cemetery in yard in East school house, Caton, Dist. 4., D.A.R.

[347] Charlotte Prince, in *GHFA*, page 1; b appears in records of New Milford, CT. She is #31 in the Helen Prince, *Descendants of Captain John Prince of Southold, New York and Their Place in Local History*

(Blacksburg, Va.: Kopy Korner), n.d.; Orcutt, 711;and will of Joseph Gillet [sic], 4 pp, MS, 1 July 1846. She is a descendant of Elder John Prince of Hull, Mass., of Edward Howell of the Hamptons, Long Island, of Edward Fuller the Mayflower Pilgrim, and of George Morton, presumed author of *Mourt's Relation*.

[348] Joseph Gillett was wounded as an officer in the War of 1812. He was the son of John Gillett, a Revolutionary War soldier, whose descendants qualify for membership in the D.A.R. and S.A.R. His ancestry traces back to Jonathan Gillett of Windsor and Simsbury, Conn., who appears earlier in this book..

[349] Carlson, op. cit., for m of Sally Betsey Hill to Barzillai Squire Hendryx; 1820 U.S. Federal Census for Wakeman Twp, Huron Co., OH; and quotes F. E. Weeks, "History of Wakeman," MS, 1938: re HENDRYX, Barzilla S.; also quotes Lu and Neumann, *Revolutionary War Period*, 20.

[350] Carlson says: Dolly b. 1784   d. 6 Jun 1784.

[351] VanAger Hill is person #4 in *GHFA*. Carlson says only that he was b. about 1785 and d. young.

[352] The Roswell Hill family line is from information to GJH from Jeanine Johnson, that she had received by letter and Family Group Records in 1991 from Roswell Hill's descendant, Barbara Paul Lovensheimer; also from Carlson, op. cit., for Roswell Hill m Frances Buckingham; Rufus Putnam, *Pioneer Record and Reminiscences of the Early Settlers and Settlement of Fayette County, Ohio* (Cincinnati: Applegate, Pounsford & Co. Print, 1872), 108; Frederick William Chapman, *Descendants of Thomas Buckingham, One of the First Settlers of Milford, Conn.* (Case, Lockwood & Brainard, 1872), p. 66: 453; and from GoogleBooks: Esther Weygandt Powell, *Ohio Records and Pioneer Families* (2001), 131. Carlson also cites U.S. Federal Census 1820, Newton, Fairfield Co., OH; and quotes *Historical Collections of Ohio* (Henry Howe & Son, 1891), 3:185; R. S. Garnett, *History of Bond and Montgomery Counties, Illinois* (Chicago: O.L. Baskin & Co., 1882), part 2:19.

[353] Another name, "Fanny," appears from an unknown source; Carlson says she was Frances Buckingham.

[354] The children of Abraham and Hannah (Ferris) Hill are from Paul F. Hill letter to GJH, 25 April 2002, with ancestral charts going back to an Abraham Hill (b. c 1747 "Lived in Bullet Hole?" d 5-11-1817 Carmel, N.Y.) and his wife Hannah Ferris (b. c 1748; d. 6-5-1818, Carmel, N.Y.).

[355] The information about William Sherman Blackmun is unverified, from Ancestry.com and OWT.

[356] The ch of Cornelius and Abigail (Parmelee) Johnson are unverified, from Ancestry.com and OWT.

[357] The ch of Timothy and Sarah (Parmelee) Allen are unverified, from Ancestry.com and OWT (*supra*): It is likely that there were two men named Parmelee Allen who lived at about the same time.

[358] OWT; Ancestry.com: Kingsley Family Tree; William Cothren, *History of Ancient Woodbury, Connecticut : From the First Indian Dead in 1659. . .* 3:41 "Parmelee Allen and Ann Wheeler"; *Pawlet, Vermont in the Revolutionary War: Originally Part of New Hampshire Colony*; Steven J. Warling, http://members.cox.net/swarling/burroughs/newtown000t.htm#toc0 (accessed accessed 11/18/10): "Descendants of John Burroughs"; Chauncey L. Knapp, *Rolls of the Soldiers in the Revolutionary War, 1775 to 1783 in Vermont* (from Google search), shows many entries for Capt. Parmelee Allen and Company; and Orrin Allen Peer (compiler), *The Allen Memorial: Descendants of Samuel Allen of Windsor, Connecticut, 1640-1907* (Palmer, Mass.: C. B. Fiske and Co., 1907).

[359] The ch of Nathaniel and Elizabeth (Griffin) Griffin are unverified, from Ancestry.com and OWT.

[360] Ancestry.com., AGBI; U.S. censuses of 1790 - 1810; and "Connecticut Men in the Revolutionary War."

[361] McCracken, "Griffin."

[362] The ch of Timothy and Sarah (Strickland) Strong are unverified, from Ancestry.com and OWT.

[363] OWT says Eli Strong m. Lament Sheldon and d.s.p., but the Moore Family Tree shows 9 ch.

[364] OWT lists 10 different ch for Sarah Strong, plus duplicates; Moore Family Tree says she d.s.p.

[365] James D. Hill, "Twelve Generations"; and Hill Family of Connecticut VR.

[366] James D. Hill, op. cit.

[367] Jedediah Hill's Marriage to Abigail Kilby, from James D. Hill, op. cit.

[368] *Barbour Collection*: O Wealthy HILL F 10 Mar 1767 Simsbury Hartford CT John Isabel .

[369] Jacobus, XII. "Edgerton Family of Simsbury" *TAG* 41 (1965): 227-30; Abiel Brown, *Early Settlers of West Simsbury*, 1856; and 1810, 1820,1830 U.S. Census / Joseph Bacon / Onondaga / State: New York

[370] Bates, Simsbury V.R.; and Andrew J. Morris, "Family History of Thomas Barber (ca 1614-1662)" in "Connecticut Genealogy" < http://connecticut-genealogy.blogspot.com/2010/07/family-history-of-thomas-barber-ca-1614.html>, accessed 8/8/2010.

[371] Simsbury V.R; "Family History of Thomas Barber."

[372] Simsbury V.R.: Sarah Barber Daughter of John Barber was born the firft Day of July 1754. Sarah Barber the Daughter of John Barber Departed this Life the 15th : of April 1761.

[373] Simsbury V.R.: Birth: 1755 - Reuben Barber Son of John Barber was Born December 7th 1755. Ancestry.com (OWT) says he was b. 7 Dec 1751 but I accept the date in Simsbury V.R. The parents of Elizabeth Case were second cousins. Both were great-grandchildren of John and Sarah (Spencer) Case.

[374] Simsbury V.R.: Rhoda Barber the Daughter of John Barber was Born in Simfbury the 25th day of April 1757. Rhoda Barber the Daghter of John Barber Departed this Life June firft day A: D : 1761. From "Family History of Thomas Barber": (IV) John, . . . Rhoda, born April 25, 1756, died June 1, 1761.

[375] Simsbury V.R.: "Benjamin Barber the Son of John Barber was born the 3rd : Day of March A : D : 1760." Lydia Case's parents were both great-grandchildren of John and Sarah (Spencer) Case.

[376] Both of Chloe Case's parents were great-grandchildren of John and Sarah (Spencer) Case; they were second cousins. Her maternal grandmother was Abigail Barber, but she is not a descendant of Samuel Barber. Abigail's Barbers go back through three generations named Thomas Barber, not in Ancestry.com.

[377] McCracken, "Dr. Philip Reade and His Earlier Descendants" *NEHGR* 112 (April 1958): 119-132.

[378] McCracken, "Reade": "Jacob Read."

[379] McCracken, "Reade": "Elifabeth Read."

[380] McCracken, "Reade"; and Simsbury V.R.: "Rhoda Read."

[381] The children of Titus and Amy (Case) Reade are from McCracken (op. cit.).

[382] McCracken, "Reade": "Titus."

[383] She could have been the Amy Reade who was in the distribution of the estate of Dr. Jacob Reade.

[384] Information in McCracken is supplemented with unverified information from Ancestry.com.

[385] The ch of Silas and Thanks (Adams) Reade are from McCracken (op. cit.).

[386] The grandchildren of Ephraim and Hannah (Hill) Wilcox are from Ancestry.com.

[387] Her husband d 30 November 1835; she was granted a Rev War soldier's widow's pension (W21305).

[388] Isaiah Hendryx was the Grantee of ten pieces of property in Bennington, Vt., between 1785 and 1825. The Grantors included Josiah Riley (9 Aug 1806), p. 233. He is mentioned in the Revolutionary War veteran petition of his son, Isaiah J. Hendryx, of 5 June 1833.

[389] Known only from Ancestry.com, and not verified.

Chapter 6 – Sixth Generation

[390] Ancestry.com and OWT, "Descendants of Arthur Henbury and Lydia Hill," accessed 4/18/2010ff.

[391] From "PrestonSmith" by Wendy Proudfoot, Ancestry.com. (accessed 4/20/2010), and OWT, "Descendants of Arthur Henbury and Lydia Hill" (unverified).

[392] OWT, "Descendants of Arthur Henbury and Lydia Hill."

[393] William Frisbie and his descendants from Humphries Family Tree (zredhd, Ancestry.com), 8/22/2010.

[394] Jacobus, *Ancient New Haven.*

[395] The information in OWT is difficult to reconcile. It says Zophar Tuttle was b. in Connecticut (which is all right), that Betsy Bowlby died in Morris, Ill., but that their son Salmon was born in Camden, N.J. OWT says Zophar's father Dan Tuttle died in Camden, N.Y., so perhaps we need to change N.J. to N.Y.

[396] Bill & Judy VanNewkirk's Family Tree, Owner Judy VanNewkirk, Ancestry.com (8/23/2010).

[397] 1826 is given as a d year by the Wiswedel Family Tree.

[398] The grandchildren of Elnathan and Abigail (Frisbie) Ives are known only from Ancestry.com.

[399] The grandchildren of Theodore and Mehitabel (Wheeler) Frisbie are from Jacobus, *Ancient New Haven.*

[400] Except where otherwise noted, the descendants of Mary Hill (Line 2 in this genealogy) are from "Descendants of John Saxton and Mary Hill," on Ancestry.com, accessed 4/23/2010ff.

[401] Ancestry.com says she m. (1) Peter Rogers and had 1 child by him.

[402] OWT says this Martin Case died in Simsbury, Conn., 2 June 1774, age 16, and also that he married Rachel MOORE, who was born in 1780 in Simsbury and died in Delaware Co., O. in 1855, about age 75. This information is inconsistent, and some of it must be wrong.

[403] Wikipedia (5 May 2010): "The Battle of Queenston Heights was the first major battle in the War of 1812 and resulted in a British victory. It took place on 13 October 1812."

[404] Henry W. Depuy, *Ethan Allen and the Green-Mountain Heroes of '76 with a Sketch of the Early History of Vermont* (New York: Phinney, Blakeman & Mason, 1861), 129; Frederick Burkhardt, et al. (eds.),

Concise Dictionary of American Biography (New York City, N.Y.: Scribners, 1961); John L. Barr, *The Genealogy of Ethan Allen and His Brothers and Sisters* (Burlington, Vt.: Ethan Allen Trust, 1991); Orrin Peer Allen, *The Allen Memorial: Descendants of Samuel Allen of Windsor, Conn., 1640-1907*, 2d series (Palmer, Mass.: Allen, 1907).

[405] The descendants of Ira Hayden Allen, son of Ira and Jerusha (Enos) Allen, have been followed for five more generations, to children born in the 1960's, in Ancestry.com.

[406] For Ira Allen, see Allen, *The Allen Memorial*, 54-6; Roger Enos is on p. 54. Also see: Edwin P. Hoyt, *The Damndest Yankees: Ethan Allen & His Clan* (Brattleboro, Vt.: The Stephen Greene Press, 1976), many citations of Ira Allen; Roger Enos is on p. 220. And Rowland Evans Robinson, *Vermont: A Study of Independence* (Boston, Mass.: Houghton, Mifflin and Co., 1892, for Ira Allen; Roger Enos is on p. 216.

[407] The descendants of Tahan Hill in Generation 6 are from Ancestry.com.

[408] The ch of Daniel and Mary (Nettleton) Parmelee are from "Families of Early Guilford, Connecticut."

[409] The Baldwin Family tree on Ancestry.com says Philemon has 13 ch, but three are duplicates. I am dubious about the 10 alleged ch, said to be descendants of Philemon and Esther (Baldwin) Baldwin.

[410] The Rev. James Hill Parmelee, his wives, and his son, are in "Families of Early Guilford."

[411] The ch of Elias and Thankful (Hill) Parmelee are in "Families of Early Guilford."

[412] Reuben Hill in Golding Family Tree (owned by katesgolding), accessed 11/1/2010; also see *Barbour Collection* for Goshen, Conn.; and e-mails from Richard Stanley, Esq. (*supra*).

[413] The *History of Ancient Wethersfield* shows Electa as a ch of Ambrose Hill and as the w of Elisha Roe, son of Capt. Thomas and Mary (Welles) Roe (p. 777); also, Ancestry.com " Roe_Elisha & Electa."

[414] The wife and ch of Jonah Hill are from Hill Family 6, in Jacobus, *Ancient New Haven*.

[415] The ch of Phineas Hill are from Mark Norris (op. cit.) amplified on various sites in Ancestry.com.

[416] Google search for "Dr. Asa Hill" -- From *Pennsylvania Journal of Dental Science*, 1:514."

[417] The ch of Isaac and Hannah (Tracy) Grant are from Ancestry.com, and are unverified. 30 user-submitted trees were synthesized to provide a record of Isaac Grant's b., m., and 9 children.

[418] Isaac Grant (Jr.)'s vital information and marriage are in OWT, with 10 user-trees cited.

[419] Fourteen user-submitted trees for Elihu Grant are cited by OWT.

[420] The Ancestry.com website owned by "thehills45" shows his b. in Massachusetts in 1782, and it shows his residences in Livonia, Ontario, N.Y., in 1810; in Wyoming Co., N.Y., in 1820; and his death in Berrien, Mich., in 1838, at age 56. He apparently did not marry and died without progeny; James H. Smith and Hume H. Cale, *History of Livingston County, New York: with illustrations and biographical sketches of some of its prominent men and pioneers*, 1687-1881 (Syracuse: D. Mason & Co., 1881), 390; *History of Berrien and Van Buren Counties, Michigan : with illustrations and biographical sketches of its prominent men and pioneers* (Philadelphia: D. W. Ensign & Co., press of J. B. Lippincott, 1880), 280.

[421] The Ancestry.com website owned by "thehills45" shows his m. to Olivia Hall on 20 Dec 1814 at Sacketts Harbor, Jefferson Co., N.Y.; their residence in Le Ray, Jefferson, N.Y. in 1820; in Brownville, Jefferson, N.Y., in 1830; in Cook Co., Ill., in 1836 and 1840; in Clinton Twp., Ill., in 1846 and 1850 and 1855; and his d. there on 5 Sep 1846, at age 63. The Service Pension record image that is attached to this website shows that Olivia Hill, widow of Arunah Hill, was m. 20 Dec 1814.

[422] The ch of Elisha and Hannah (Gates) Hill are from Mark Norris (op. cit.).

[423] The ch of Ira and Esther (Post) Hill are from Ancestry.com, and are unverified.

[424] The ch of Jonathan and Penelope (Lacy) Wheaton are from Ancestry.com, and are unverified.

[425] The grandchildren of Waitstill and Elizabeth (White) Cooke are from Ancestry.com.

[426] Ancestry.com says that Rufus Norton Cooke was b. in in "Vt Ma, Canada," which is unintelligible.

[427] From Wikipedia and various sources on a Google search: Benjamin Case Leete was a great-great grandson of Pelatiah Leete I (*Benjamin*[5] *Case, Edmund*[4], *Daniel*[2-3], *Pelatalia I*[1]) . He was a 1C2R of Pelatiah III, who built the Pelatiah Leete III House in about 1765. The Leetes have owned Leetes Island since 1640, when the town granted the island to William Leete, one of the founders of Guilford.

[428] Shem Kentfield and his descendants are from Ancestry.com and are unverified.

[429] The ch of John and Sally Dibble are from Ancestry.com and are unverified.

[430] The grandchildren of Elijah and Lydia (Dibble) Birge are from Ancestry.com and are unverified.

[431] Three pairs of these ch are shown in Ancestry.com to have been born in the same years. It is possible but unlikely that there are three sets of twins in this family.

[432] The grandchildren of Billious and Lydia (Dibble) Hill are from Carlson to GJH, 3 December 2008.

[433] Carlson to GJH, quoting Cyrus H. Brown, *Genealogical record of Nathaniel Babcock, Simeon Main, Issac Miner, Ezekiel Main* (Boston: Everett Press, 1909), 110-1.

[434] The grandchildren of Samuel and Mary (Dibble) Benedict are from various family trees on Ancestry.com, and a synthesis of these trees on OWT. I have edited this information for consistency.

[435] The ch of Samuel and Eleanor (Shatford) Benedict are from Ancestry.com, and are unverified.

[436] The ch of Ezra and Sarah (Stockwell) Benedict are from Ancestry.com, and are unverified.

[437] The ch of William and Rachel (Benedict) Grimes are from Ancestry.com, and are unverified.

[438] The ch of Benjamin and Hannah (Benedict) Chamberlain are from Ancestry.com, and are unverified.

[439] The Grandchildren of Phineas and Rhoda (Kilbourne) Hill are from Carlson (*supra*).

[440] For the grandchildren of Isaac and Eunice Hill, Carlson to GJH, 5 December 2008 (e-mail).

[441] Mrs. Louis Hill, *The Holy Bible containing the Old and New Testaments* ... (New York: American Bible Society, 1858), from Mid-West Tennessee Genealogical Society (*supra*); and Carlson (op. cit.)

[442] Carlson to GJH quotes Joseph Gardner Bartlett, *Robert Coe, Puritan*, 290; and Gertrude Van Wickham (ed.), *Memorial to the Pioneer Women of the Western Reserve* (Woman's Department of the Cleveland Centennial Commission, 1896), 559-563.

[443] Carlson quotes F. E. Weeks, *Pioneer History of Clarksfield.* [MS, Huron Co, OH, 1938].

[444] Elvira Stevens Barney, *The Stevens Genealogy* (Salt Lake City, UT: Skelton Publishing, 1907), 141-2.

[445] Carlson quotes W. W. Williams, *History of Huron and Erie Counties, Ohio* (1879); and *Memorial and Biographical Record of Iowa* (Chicago: Lewis Publishing Co, 1896).

[446] Carlson, Ibid.; and 1850 and 1860 U.S. Federal Censuses for Wakeman Twp, OH.

[447] Carlson quotes F. E. Weeks, *Pioneer History of Clarksfield* (op. cit.).

[448] Ibid.; and 1860 U.S. Federal Census: John Hough and w Ruth E. Hough, dau Francis M., son John.

[449] Carlson, Ibid.

[450] Carlson to GJH, 5 Dec 2008.

[451] Carlson, Ibid.

[452] Carlson quotes F. E. Weeks, *Pioneer History of Clarksfield* (MS, Huron Co, OH, 1938).

[453] Carlson to GJH, 5 Dec 2008.

[454] Carlson quotes Mrs. Louis Hill, *The Holy Bible containing the Old and New Testaments* ... (New York: American Bible Society, 1858), from Mid-West Tennessee Genealogical Society (*supra*).

[455] Carlson quotes Juanita Bradish Curley, Patrick Joseph Curley, Robert L. Mittino, *Genealogy & History of Robert Bradish in America* (2000), 204.

[456] Carlson quotes Huron Co, OH marriage records, and *Biographical Memoirs of Greene County, Indiana* (Indianoplis: B. F. Bowen & Co.), 2:548-51; and Bethel/Fox: Cemetery Fox Twp, Jasper County, IL.

[457] The children of Benajah and Mary (Jackson) Hill are from Thom Carlson, e-mail, with references.

[458] The ch of Seth Sloane and Mary Ann "Polly" (Stilson) Hill are from Carlson, Ibid., and Ptak, op. cit.

[459] Harvey Hill m. Mehitable Burr. He was son of Seth Hill (b. 1776), (son of Isaac Hill), who m. Polly Stinson [sic] (b. 1779). Miss Hettie H. Hill, D.A.R. No. 159003, was a descendant of this Isaac Hill.

[460] Edward Hooker says she died in Huntington, Conn., 5 February 1822, age 21, but this d.d. is impossible, if she was indeed the mother of five children, b between 1822 and 1830. Carlson quotes Edward Hooker, *Descendants of Rev. Thomas Hooker, Hartford, Connecticut, 1586-1908* (Edward Hooker, 1909), 29.

[461] The children of Seth Slone and Mary Ann (Gorman) Hill are from Carlson, Ibid.

[462] Carlson quotes [Kendall Co, IL] *Kendall County Record* (13 Mar 1918) for Charles McNair Hill.

[463] William Edwin Hill, (1st ed.) and GJH (2nd ed. editor), *Genealogy of the HillFamily in America* (William E. Hill, Genesee, N.Y. [1921]; GJH, West Orange, N.J. [2000]); Dimitroff and Janes, *History of the Corning-Painted Post*; Clayton, *History of Steuben County*; Orcott, *New Milford and Bridgewater, Connecticut*; and Roberts, *Steuben County, New York*, 219; William P. Hill is person 7 in GHFA; "William Prince Hill, Son of Ephraim Hill & Charlotte his wife was born the 28th day of February 1804"; Orcutt, 711; D. C. Beers, W. C., Kewen, and W. Upton, *Atlas of Steuben County New York* (Phila.: D. C. Beers & Co., 1873); Marion Springer, Steuben County Clerk, Bath, NY, June 1995, to Ptak, transmitted to GJH, 14 June 1995: "William Prince Hill d. 4 Aug 1885 Caton age 81 buried CT 1 - pg 23 Father - Ephraim Hill Mother - Charlotte Prince"; William P. Hill appears as the subject of two Abstracts of Wills and

Administrations in Caton Township, New York: "Case No. 5477, Bk. 3-A, Pg. 56, Ephraim Hill, Painted Post Township, Date of Adm. Aug. 13, 1832"; and "Case No. 5487, Bk. 8-A, Pg. 721, William P. Hill."

[464] Sarah P. Herrick's father Rufus was actually Rufus Herrick III. His descent from Henry Heyrick, who was admitted as a freeman of Salem on 19 October 1630. Her middle initial appears in the 1855 census and in the Abstract of Administration of her husband's estate, 30 March 1887, which showed the widow's name as Sarah P. Hill, 30 March 1887. Her death registration shows Sarah P. Hill, age 87 years and 4 days; retired; born at Guilford, N.Y., daughter of Rufus Herrick (born in N.Y.) and Jerusha Palmer (birthplace not given); of cardiac failure, 4 days duration; attended by J. L. Miller; buried at Caton, N.Y. Her obituary is in the *[Corning, N.Y.] Daily Democrat* for 28 January [1895]. The children of William and Sarah Herrick are identified by brackets [ ] which show their numbers in GHFA. Henry Herrick is the subject of George J. Hill, "Signatures of Two 17th Century Emigrants Once Believed to be the Same Henry Herrick" *The Mayflower Quarterly* (March 2007), 46-49.

[465] He is person #8 in GHFA; also Clayton, *Steuben County*; Ptak, correspondence; and Helen Wright Prince, *Descendants of Captain John Prince of Southold, New York* (Blacksburg, Va.: Kopy Korner (n.d.).

[466] Connecticut Historical Society (Marjorie K. Hurtuk) to George J. Hill, M.D., letters of 8 November 1999 and 24 January 2000.

[467] William Hill, "Brief Account of the Hill Reunion Held at Dennison Park, Aug 27, 1920."

[468] Person #9 in *GHFA*; and Orcott, *History of the Towns of New Milford and Bridgewater*, 710-11, 748-52.

[469] Henry was person #10 and Huldah Jane was person #11 in *GHFA*.

[470] Person #12 in *Genealogy of the Hill Family in America*. The months and years of his birth and death were confirmed in June 1995 by the Steuben Co., NY, Clerk; to Ptak and thence to G. J. Hill, 14 Jun 1995.

[471] Person #13 in *GHFA*. In addition to the fourteen children listed in this *Genealogy*, four other children are mentioned in this family group in the Caton census of 1855. Also, Millard F. Roberts, *Historical Gazetteer of Steuben County, New York, with Memoirs and Illustrations*. Part 1. (Syracuse, N.Y.: Millard F. Roberts, Publisher, 1891), 225: "Huldah, daughter of Ephraim Hill, married Lewis Gridley, who settled in Caton in 1822."

[472] If OWT (accessed 11/29/2010) is credible, Lewis Gridley was born 14 December 1801, son of Levi Gridley and Mary Gilbert, and died at Caton, N.Y., 3 December 1878.

[473] She is person #14 in *Genealogy of the Hill Family in America*.

[474] He was person #15 in *GHFA*. Charlotte Gillett, then 73, was living with Henry and Julia A. Hill.

[475] He is person #16 in *Genealogy of the Hill Family in America*. A grave in the Gillett cemetery, Caton, NY: "Sylvester, son of Ephriam and Charlotte Hill died July 2, 1840, aged 18 yrs 9 mo. & 5 das."

[476] Person #17 in *GHFA*.. "E. A. Hill" was a town officer (assessor) of Caton, NY, in 1895.

[477] Person #18 in *GHFA*. The years of her birth and death were given in the SAR Patriot Index (1999).

[478] S.AR. Patriot Index (1999), PP-9905.

[479] Thom Carlson to George J. Hill, "Children of Isaac and Eunice Hill."

[480] Carlson, "Some Descendants of Isaac Hill Sr. & Eunice Mallory," sent to GJH, 3 December 2008.

[481] From Carlson, p. 26: Rufus Putnam, *Pioneer record and reminiscences of the early settlers and settlement of Fayette County, Ohio* (Cincinnati: Applegate, Pounsford & Co. Print, 1872), 108: "Isaac Hill, grandfather of T. Hill, was in the revolutionary war. He had the measles while he was out of the service, and lost one of his eyes. He died in New Britain, Connecticut, aged 98."

[482] R. S. Garnett, *History of Bond and Montgomery Counties, Illinois*, Part 2 (Chicago: O.L. Baskin & Co., 1882), 19 [quoted by Carlson] "G. W. HILL, retired, P.O. Greenville."

[483] Carlson to Hill, 5 December 2008.

[484] Paul F. Hill, 35 Pershing St., Corning, NY 14830-2032; letters and enclosures to George J. Hill.

[485] According to information developed by Paul F. Hill and his other relatives, the descendants of this Abraham Hill (Generation 1), who lived in Bullet Hole?, N.Y. before moving to Carmel, N.Y., included Ferris Hill (Generation 2) (b. 8 July 1774; d. 21 September 1863, Lewis Corners, N.Y.) m. Betsy Barstow (b. 9 May 1772; d. 22 Oct 1854). One of their children was Harsey Hill (Generation 3), who m. Mary Rogers. Of their children, Richard L. [Lord] Hill I (Generation 4), was the father of Richard L. Hill II (Generation 5), father of Richard L. Hill III (Generation 6), father of Paul F. [Frank] Hill (b. 4 May 1928, Corning N.Y., a designer for Corning, Inc.), who m. Mary Agnes Keane (b. 11 September 1926, a credit clerk at Corning, N.Y.).

[486] Paul F. Hill, 35 Pershing St., Corning, NY 14830-2032; letters and enclosures to George J. Hill.

[487] Paul F. Hill, 35 Pershing St., Corning, NY 14830-2032; letters and enclosures to George J. Hill.

[488] The grandch of Luke Sherman and Sally (Foster) Blackmun are from Ancestry.com, and are unsourced.

[489] According to Ancestry.com, she lived in Walden, Pope Co., Minn., in 1900.

[490] See the entry for Timothy and Sarah (Parmelee) Allen for the uncertainty regarding Parmelee Allen.

[491] Amy Allen, her husband, and her children, are known only from Ancestry.com.

[492] The ch of Nathaniel and Abigail (Fowler) Griffin are known only from Ancestry.com and are unverified.

[493] Stephen Terry, his wife, and his child are known only from Ancestry.com and are unverified.

[494] Grandch of Timothy and Sarah (Strickland) Strong are known from Ancestry.com and are unverified.

[495] Lament Sheldon Strong is given no children in OWT; Moore Family Tree is not sourced.

[496] Grandch of John and Isabel (Eggleston) Hill are from Hill, "Twelve Generations," referenced.

[497] Census Data, Jedediah Hill Family (From James D. Hill, op. cit.), 1790-1850.

[498] The following is taken from the *Wonewoc Reporter [Wisc.]* (July 17, 1919): "Something more than three quarters of a century ago, Ludlow Hill and his wife, Lydia Presley Hill, left Sackets Harbor . . ."

[499] Phineas or Phinehas Bacon is mentioned by Jacobus as a s of Joseph Bacon and Mary Edgerton. Jacobus, XII. "Edgerton Family of Simsbury" *TAG* 41 (1965): 227-30. Also, GenForum, presented by Genealogy.com (8/8/2010): Re: Phineas Bacon, b. 1783, Posted on 6 Apr 2004 by: mary mahon (mmahon@tampabay.rr.com).

[500] Information about the children of John and Elizabeth (Reed) Barber is from Bates, *Simsbury*; and Andrew J. Morris, "Family History of Thomas Barber (ca 1614-1662)" in "Connecticut Genealogy" <http://connecticut-genealogy.blogspot.com/2010/07/family-history-of-thomas-barber-ca-1614.html>, Morris cites Cutter, *Connecticut*; Also, Ancestry.com.

[501] Morris, "Family History of Thomas Barber"

[502] Elisha Case & Abi Barber had in common their gr-gr-gr-grandparents John Case & Sarah Spencer.

[503] "Family History of Thomas Barber'" says she was b. 1785, d. 1786.

[504] The ch of Reuben and Elizabeth (Case) Barber are known only from Ancestry.com and are unverified.

[505] Elizabeth, who is younger than Zimri, is from a generation earlier than he is.

[506] The ch of Jonathan and Abi (Merrell) Barber are known only from Ancestry.com and are unverified.

[507] The children of Abel and Chloe (Case) Barber are known only from Ancestry.com and are unverified.

[508] The ch of Titus and Amy (Case) Reade are from McCracken, "Dr. Philip Reade."

[509] Roswell Reed in several U.S. Federal Censuses. Ancestry.com says he was a master wool carder.

[510] The grandch of Ephraim and Ruhamah (Pinney) Wilcox are from Ancestry.com and are unverified.

[511] The ch of Lyman and Deidama (Dunham) Jackson are known only from Ancestry.com.

[512] The children of Isaiah J. and Esther (Jackson) Hendryx are from Virgil D. White, Abstractor, *Genealogical Abstracts of Revolutionary War Pension Files,* vol. 2 [F-M] (Waynesboro, Tenn.: National Historical Publishing Co., 1991), p. 1604: "Hendryx, Isaiah, Esther, W21305, MA Line, sol appl 14 Aug 1832 at Bennington VT . . ."; and Connecticut Historical Society (Marjorie K. Hurtuk) to GJH.

[513] Josiah (Isaiah) Riley's putative gr-gr grandfather John Riley (also spelled Ryly and Reilly), "the Settler," came to Wethersfield, Conn. in ca 1643-1645, and d there in May or June 1674. There are 58 entries for Riley in Stiles' *History of Ancient Wethersfield, Connecticut* (1904). Stiles says that almost all Rileys in the northeast section of our country came from the "Old Weathersfield stock of Rileys."

[514] Josiah (Isaiah) Riley was usually known as Josiah, but his name has also been given as Isaiah Riley. He was very peripatetic. He apparently lived for a time in Caton, Steuben Co., N.Y., and he resided in Coventry, N.Y. from at least 1830 until his death there 20 years later.

[515] Schroader states that she d 5 December 1810 and was buried in the Old Bennington, Vt., cemetery. The widow of Josiah Riley was referred to as Susannah Riley in his will dated 21 June 1850; this was his second wife, Susannah [Beardsley] Riley. An article in the *Boston Transcript* (7 February 1923) says that Susannah Hendryx was "born in New Concord in Kings Street, State of New York, Oct. 5, 1779, married Isaiah [sic] Riley at Bennington, Vt., May 7, 1795, and died, Nov. 4, 1810, in Bennington."

[516] His father's middle initial can be deduced from the fact that his son, Isaiah Hendryx, Jr., used the middle initial "J" at least after 1804-1805, when he was thirteen or fourteen years old.

[517] The ch of Ebenezer and Abigail (Keys) Jackson are known only from Ancestry.com and are unverified.

[518] The grandch of of Sylvanus and Chestina (Curtis) Wilcox are known only from Ancestry.com.

[519] OWT says that two sons were born on the same day, Elijah and Elisha Wilcox.

[520] Ancestry.com says Calvin Pardee Wilcox was born 4 October 1796 in Lagrange, Lorain Co., Ohio. The the birth place in Ohio is very odd, and must be considered suspicious or spurious until proved.

[521] The grandch of Elnathan and Hannah (Adams) Wilcox are known only from Ancestry.com.

[522] The ch of Jedediah and Mary (Hallett) Wilcox are known only from Ancestry.com and are unverified.

Chapter 7 – Seventh Generation

[523] #1124-1161 are from OWT, "Descendants of Arthur Henbury and Lydia Hill" (Ancestry.com, accessed 4/18/2010ff). There is much detail there, but it is not independently verified. #1162-1283 are known only from Ancestry.com and are unverified, except when additional information is inserted in the text or notes.

[524] #1162-1283 are known only from Ancestry.com and are unverified, except when additional information is inserted in the text or notes.

[525] Valerie Latzman, *The City of Wayne* (Philadelphia, Pa.: Tempus Publishing/Arcadia Press, 2003), 58 (accessed from Google Books): "Globe Dugar Chubb was born on April 26, 1796 . . . Pamela Pattison Chubb was born on June 11, 1808." Their photographs accompany this story.

[526] #1284-1524 are from "Descendants of John Saxton and Mary Hill," some of whom are supplemented from other sources, as noted below.

[527] She is not in Orrin Peer Allen's genealogy of the Allen Family, so her existence is not verified.

[528] Allen, *Allen Memorial*; Hoyt, *Damndest Yankees*; "Descendants of John Saxton and Mary Hill."

[529] O. P. Allen (p. 56): "He pursued a course of study at the Vermont University for a while...."

[530] Her b.d. and b.p. are from "Descendants of John Saxton and Mary Hill; d.d and d.p. from O. P. Allen.

[531] #1529-1533 are from "Descendants of John Saxton and Mary Hill."

[532] #1554-1560 are from "Families of Early Guilford, Connecticut ," Local and Family Histories, CD 515.

[533] He is on pp. 972 and 979 of "Families of Early Guilford."

[534] #1561-1571 are from Ancestry.com and are unverified.

[535] #1572-1785 are from Ancestry.com. Many are unverified, but others are supported by notes (*infra*).

[536] Ancestry.com; and Richard Stanley to George Hill. His name is in Golding Family Tree (owned by katesgolding), accessed 11/1/2010, which says he d. in 1896; and OWT.

[537] From Roe_Elisha & Electa, citing American Genealogical-Biographical Index.

[538] From Roe_Elisha & Electa, citing U.S. Federal Census of 1850; AGBI; and Headstone, Mound Cemetery, Racine, Wisc.: She resided in Shorham, Addison Co., Vt., in 1850, and d.s.p. in Racine, Wisc.

[539] From Roe_Elisha & Electa, citing U.S. Federal Censuses of 1850, 1860, 1870, and 1880.

[540] From Ancestry.com: Roe_Elisha & Electa (accessed 11/2/2010).

[541] Ibid.

[542] Ibid., citing U.S. Federal Censuses of 1850, 1860, and 1880.

[543] Ibid., cites U.S. Federal Censuses of 1850 and 1860; AGBI; Oak Hill Cemetery records, Battle Creek, Mich.; and "Transcript - Genealogy Column."

[544] Roe_Elisha & Electa cites U.S. Federal Censuses for Ticonderoga, N.Y., for 1850; and for Chicago.

[545] Roe_Elisha & Electa, citing U.S. Federal Census of 1850; D.A.R. Record of Electa Roe Nettleton; and Revolutionary War Pension of John & Betsey Bostwick.

[546] Roe_Elisha & Electa (accessed 11/2/2010), citing U.S. Federal Censuses for 1860 and 1870; and AGBI.

[547] Roe_Elisha & Electa (accessed 11/2/2010), citing AGBI.

[548] Sheldon B Grant with Kay Daun Pace Edwards, "Mary Adelia Carbine" in "The Harmony Valley - and New Harmony, Utah - History and Memories"; Shari H. Franke, "Family History of the Joseph Taylor, Jr. & Sarah Best Family"in www.taylorassociation.org/biographies/taylor/taylor_william_w_1828-1892.htm (accessed 6/30/2010) for more on the complex history of this Mormon family.

[549] The Ancestry.com website owned by "thehills45" shows an image of a plat map on which his name "W. S. Smith" appears. His second wife does not appear in the census records, so it is not clear what her relationship was to the family. Was this a polygamous Mormon family? And where did she live after she married William Smith Hill?

[550] He is known only from the Ancestry.com website owned by "thehills45."

[551] He is known from the Ancestry.com website owned by "thehills45."

[552] "thehills45," in which his b. is shown, and U.S. Federal Censuses of 1870, 1880, and 1900 are cited.

[553] Three children are shown in OWT, at least one of whom must be of another family named Day.

[554] Ancestry.com says Wolgamott is the Americanized spelling of German Wohlgemuth.

[555] The entries in Ancestry.com for Morton Sonfronian Cook are inconsistent and cannot be reconciled.

[556] From Carlson, pp. 17-18, citing Prosser, *History of the Puget Sound Country* for Bradford L. Hill.

[557] From Thom Carlson, "Some Descendants of Isaac Hill Sr. & Eunice Mallory," 16-18, for Fred Hill.

[558] #1786-1858 from Thom Carlson, "Some Descendants of Isaac Hill Sr. & Eunice Mallory."

[559] 1850 census: Belah Coe 55 m farmer MA / Maria Coe 55 f CT . . .

[560] Carlson: S. Whitney Phoenix, *The Whitney family of Connecticut* (New York: Priv. print., 1878), 743

[561] Carlson, citing "Judge Edgar S. Hill" in *Compendium of History Reminiscence and Biography of Western Nebraska* (Chicago: Alden Publishing Co, 1912), pp. 944-5.

[562] Carlson, citing "Rev. Edwin Stoddard Hill" in *Biographical Record of Iowa*.

[563] From Carlson, 5 Dec 2008, p.12

[564] Carlson cites *Greene County, Indiana*, Vol. 2, 548-51. "Hoyt H. Nickerson."

[565] Carlson, 5 Dec 2008, p. 20: Bethel/Fox: Cemetery Nickerson, W.H. - d. 1866 Civil War.

[566] Miss Hettie H. Hill (b. Cairo, IL), D.A.R. No. 159003, was a descendant of Isaac Hill by William Hill.

[567] A Seth Hill (b. abt 1848), is shown in the Ancestry.com website owned by "SuePopulorum."

[568] No children are shown in Ancestry.com, but U.S. Federal Census records show ch in 1900, 1910, 1920.

[569] U.S. Federal Censuses of 1900 with a dau, Ora M., and in the 1910 census with his w (2), Cynthia.

[570] Charles A. Hill is probably seen in U.S. Federal Census records of 1900, 1910, and 1920.

[571] Myrtle O. appears as "Maybelle Hill," age 22, wife of "Ernie" Hill, in Marion, Hannibal Co., Mo.

[572] He may be the "Frank Hill" age 36, b. Illinois, who was married to "Jennie M. Hill" age 36 (or 30).

[573] Frederick W. Hill was unknown to me until 24 April 2011, when I discovered him in the My FTDNA project / Hill Family / Group 47. Of the 55 Groups in the Hill Family project, one (and only one) has descendants of Luke Hill Sr. There are two in this group (#47). The grandson of Charles McNair Hill and I have a "match" at 25 marker/genetic distance 1. The line from Luke Hill Sr. to Isaac Hill Jr. is identical for both of us. I am, however, a descendant of Isaac Jr.'s son Ephraim, whereas Charles McNair is a son of Seth Stone Hill. Several other children of Charles McNair Hill were already in my database, but Frederick W. is now added, along with his son, Roy Steven Hill (1912-2004). Additional information about Frederick W. Hill is from the Ancestry.com website owned by "Supopulorum," without sources; and from U.S. Census records. The other "match" in group 47, with the same FTDNA 25 marker, distance 1, is to Roy Hill, whose line is similar. Roy and I are, I believe, 3rd cousins, twice removed.
Direct paternal lineage of DNA participant 20044:
Luke HILL (1613 ENG - 1696 CT)
Luke HILL (1661/2 CT - 1740 CT)
Isaac HILL (1703 CT - 1741 CT)
Isaac HILL (1740 CT - 1833 CT)
Seth Stone HILL (1776 S CT - 1853/5 IN)
Charles McNair HILL (1830 PA - 1918 IL)
Frederick W. HILL (1878 IL - 1933 IL)
Roy Steven HILL (1912 IL - 2004 IL)

[574] William Hill and George Hill, *GHFA* (1921, 2000); Dimitroff and Janes, *History of the Corning-Painted Post Area*; Clayton, *History of Steuben County, New York*; Roberts, *Steuben County, New York*.

[575] He is person #19 in *Genealogy of the Hill Family in America* (1e). He was of Findley, Ohio, in 1895, when his mother died (see her obituary). His obituary was sent from Natalie Rose, 20 April 2002.

[576] Carrie L. Hill, b July 1842, U.S. census of 1900, Findlay Ward 6, Ohio, with her husband Edgar E. Hill..

[577] He is person #20 in *GHFA* (1e). Also, Birdsall, *History of Wright County Iowa: Its People, Industries and Institutions*, 481.

[578] The record of her d was provided by the Wright County Registrar of Vital Records on 9 December 2002.

[579] Emily Hill is person #23 in *Genealogy of the Hill Family in America*.

[580] She is person #26 in *Genealogy of the Hill Family in America*.

[581] Person #21 in *GHFA*. Information about his descendants is from Kenneth Rose, his great-grandson.

[582] She is person #24 in *Genealogy of the Hill Family in America*.

[583] "Jerusha M. / J. M." Hill was listed as a son [sic] and heir of William P. Hill.

[584] She was person #22 in *Genealogy of the Hill Family in America.*

[585] She was person #27 in *Genealogy of the Hill Family in America.* She was living in Caton, NY, in 1887; obituary was sent by e-mail to GJH from Mrs. Natalie Rose.

[586] He is person #28 in *Genealogy of the Hill Family in America.*

[587] From *GHFA*: "Stilson Edward Hill enlisted Sept. 2, 1861, for three years in the 50th Engineers."

[588] *GHFA*: "He enlisted as a private in the 141st Inf. Co. F. Sept. 14, 1864 and was discharged June 26, 1865." (person 31). He recalled that "Grandmother Gillett" was "head of the family in those days."

[589] The "Brief Account of the Hill Reunion Held at Dennison Park, Corning, N.Y., August 27, 1921" by William E. Hill, Secretary, states that "During the year our president, Mr. Earl A. Hill had died."

[590] "Nye R. Hill ch/ Noble Hill & Joanna (Jane) Breese 1853-1925 Cg City."

[591] *GHFA*: "He enlisted in the 161st. Aug. 10, 1862, and died in a hospital," person 37.

[592] *GHFA*: "He enlisted Sept. 1862, was taken prisoner Dec. 29. 1863, and died," 1st h of person 38.

[593] *GHFA*: "She m (first) Horace Gilbert . . . She married (second) Eli Gridley Jan. 21, 1868," person 39.

[594] From *GHFA*: "Wesley P. Gridley enlisted Sept. 14, 1864, for one year," person 41.

[595] *GHFA*: "Albert Levert Gridley enlisted as a private Aug. 26, 1861, for three years," person 42.

[596] *GHFA*: "Pliny Fisk Gridley enlisted Aug. 15, 1864, in the 50th Eng. Co.F," person 44..

[597] *GHFA*: "Francis Sylvester Howe enlisted Aug. 22, 1862, for 3 years," person 53.

[598] *GHFA*: "He enlisted as a private in the 141st. Inft. Co. F. Sept.14, 1864," person 58.

[599] *GHFA*: "James Abner Gilbert enlisted for 2 years as a private July 16, 1862," husband of person 59.

[600] Ezekiel was mentioned in a handwritten note from Marion Springer, on 16 Feb 2000.

[601] From "The Hill Reunion" announcement for Saturday, August 26, 1922.

[602] Clayton, (p. 454) reports, "Hill, Charles E., Farmer, b. New York, s. 1852, p. o. add. Caton."

[603] Entries for Margaret J. Hill #1909 (b. 1844) to Lily Hill #1932 (b. 1870) from Thom Carlson.

[604] #1933 (Amanda Hill, d. 1817) - #1950 (George Hill, b. 1839) from Paul F. Hill, 1996ff.

[605] One of her descendants in 2004 is Thom Carlson, Ph.D. (Harvard), e-mail to GJH 2/2/04.

[606] Information developed by Paul F. Hill on the descendants of Abraham Hill.

[607] Federal Census resided in Hartland, Hartford Co., Conn., in 1860, 1870, and 1880.

[608] Moore Family Tree (Ancestry.com): Brooks served as a county commissioner, Univ. Minn. Archives.

[609] #1968 (Susan Hill, d. 1806) - #2007 (Charlotte Alida Boice, b. 1848) from Hill, "Twelve Generations."

[610] His biography appeared in a 1946 newspaper article in either *Miles City Star* or *The Billings Gazette.*

[611] The Pension File of John H. Hill; " Mrs. Morgan . . . draws a federal pension of $20."

[612] She was in generation 6 in descendants of Cornelius Haight.

[613] Jacobus, XII. "Edgerton Family of Simsbury" *TAG* 41 (1965): 227-30.

[614] #2009 (Laura Barber, b. 1794) - #2087 (Albert O. Reed, b. 1844) from Ancestry.com.

[615] From "Family History of Thomas Barber (ca 1614-1662)" in "Connecticut Genealogy...": (VII) Lucius (3), son of John and Delight Griswold (Case) Barbour, was born July 26, 1805, in Canton, Connecticut, died February 10, 1873. He was a trustee of the Hartford Theological Seminary, a director of the American Asylum for the Deaf and Dumb, and of the Charter Oak Bank.

[616] Nothing more about this person in Ancestry.com, or "Family History of Thomas Barber."

[617] The purchase of land by Isaiah Riley and his wife, Experience, in 1828 was witnessed by John Gillett.

[618] Simeon Riley's b in AGBI: "Simeon, born in Bennington, Vt., Dec. 9, 1799," desc of Hendryx family.

[619] Census of 1830, Painted Post, Steuben Co., NY.: Simeon Riley was the head of a family of two. Joseph Gillett, father of Catherine, was a descendant of Johnathan Gillett, a founder of Windsor and Simsbury. Jonathan and his brother Nathan came to America in 1630 on the *Mary and John.* They appear in the Second Generation of this genealogy. Joseph was the son of John, a soldier in the Revolution, whose descendants qualify for the D.A.R. Joseph was an officer in the War of 1812, and his descendants qualify for membership in the Society of the War of 1812. The Gillett Cemetery on his farm in Caton is the location of burial of many members of the Hill and Gillett families.

[620] Census 1890, Caton, N.Y.: George Hill 44 M Farmer $2500 real estate Birth Conn. Esther Hill 44 F.

[621] A marginal note on the Family Group Record of Isaiah and Esther (Jackson) Hendryx.

[622] #2095-2113 are from Ancestry.com and are unverified.

Chapter 8 – Eighth Generation

[623] The descendants of Lydia Hill in Gen 8 are from Ancestry.com, except those with additional Notes.

[624] Ancestry.com Humphries Family Tree: "Lamartine Frisbie was arrested for murder and later acquitted."

[625] zredhdadded accessed on Ancestry.com: "Malinda's grandfather was Carmon Ross who fought in the Texas Revolution and died in service of the U.S. Army in 1847 at (we believe) the Battle of Cerro Gordo."

[626] Joseph Henry Byington's two m and his many ch and their descendants appear on OWT.

[627] Information about his marriage and children is from Lane / Ocker Tree (Owner PatLane57).

[628] Nellie's husband died in Iowa in 1896 and she died in Seattle, Washington, in 1929.

[629] OWT says she d. 28 Feb 1861, but shows her m. to Ellis P. Moore in 1882. This is impossible.

[630] The descendants of Mary Hill in the eighth generation are named by Allen, *The Allen Memorial.*

[631] Mary Frances Allen is in OWT and Ancestry.com, in Allen-Taylor -30052009 Family Tree.

[632] He is in OWT as Thomas Wentworth Beauclerk. O. P. Allen says his name was Sydney W. Beanduk.

[633] She is known only from "Descendants of John Saxton and Mary Hill," on Ancestry.com

[634] #2257-2265 are from "Families of Early Guilford, Connecticut" on CD 515.

[635] The descendants of Luke Hill Jr. in the eighth gen are from Ancestry.com and are largely unverified..

[636] E-Correspondence from Richard R. Stanley to George Hill, and Pratt and Webster Family Tree.

[637] From Golding Family Tree (Owner: katesgolding), Ancestry.com. No sources cited.

[638] From Golding Family Tree, citing U.S. Federal Censuses for 1850, 1860, 1870, 1880, 1900, and 1920.

[639] From Golding Family Tree (Owner: katesgolding), Ancestry.com. No sources cited.

[640] Her name was not given by Richard Stanley, but in OWT it is shown as Eliza Jane Hill.

[641] Golding Family Tree. The b and d places of this ch of Seth Morris Hill are strange.

[642] Golding Family Tree. No sources cited.

[643] Golding Family Tree. No sources cited.

[644] From Roe_Elisha & Electa, citing U.S. Federal Censuses of 1850, 1870, 1880, 1900, and 1910.

[645] From Roe_Elisha & Electa, citing U.S. Federal Censuses of 1850, 1860, and 1880.

[646] From Roe_Elisha & Electa, citing census records: She resided in Michigan.

[647] From Roe_Elisha & Electa, citing census records: She resided in Michigan.

[648] From Roe_Elisha & Electa, citing census records: She resided in Michigan.

[649] Roe_Elisha & Electa, 1850 U.S. census; Wisconsin Marriage Index and Wisconsin Deaths, 1820-1907.

[650] Roe_Elisha & Electa, citing U.S. Federal Censuses for 1880, 1900, 1910, and 1930.

[651] Roe_Elisha & Electa, citing 1880 Federal Census and Wisconsin Marriages prior to 1907.

[652] Roe_Elisha & Electa, citing U.S. Federal Census of 1880.

[653] Roe_Elisha & Electa, citing U.S. Federal Censuses of 1880, 1900, and 1910.

[654] Roe_Elisha & Electa Family Tree, citing 1870, 1880, 1900, 1910, and 1920 U.S. Federal Censuses.

[655] From Ancestry.com: Roe_Elisha & Electa (accessed 11/2/2010), citing U.S. Federal Census of 1850; D.A.R. Record of Nettie Fellows Olmstead; and Wisconsin Marriage Index.

[656] Roe_Elisha & Electa, citing Federal Censuses of 1850-1910; and Oak Hill Cemetery records.

[657] Roe_Elisha & Electa (accessed 11/2/2010), citing U.S. Federal Censuses of 1850 and 1880.

[658] Roe_Elisha & Electa, (accessed 11/2/2010), citing 1850 census, and other documents.

[659] Roe_Elisha & Electa (accessed 11/2/2010), citing U.S. Census of 1850.

[660] Roe_Elisha & Electa, citing U.S. Censuses and Oak Hill Cemetery records, Battle Creek, Mich.

[661] From Ancestry.com: Roe_Elisha & Electa (accessed 11/2/2010).

[662] Roe_Elisha & Electa, citing U.S. Federal Census for Ticonderoga, Essex Co., N.Y., 1850.

[663] Roe_Elisha & Electa, citing U.S. Federal Censuses of 1850, 1880, and 1900.

[664] Roe_Elisha & Electa, citing U.S. Federal Census of 1850.

[665] Roe_Elisha & Electa, citing U.S. Federal Census of 1900.

[666] Roe_Elisha & Electa, citing U.S. Federal Census for 1850.

[667] Roe_Elisha & Electa, citing U.S. Federal Census for 1850.

[668] Roe_Elisha & Electa, citing Federal Censuses for 1850-920; and Wisconsin Marriage Index.

[669] Roe_Elisha & Electa, citing U.S. Federal Census for 1880, 1900, and 1910.

[670] Roe_Elisha & Electa (accessed 11/2/2010), citing Orleans Co. Vital Statistics.

[671] Roe_Elisha & Electa (accessed 11/2/2010), citing Orleans Co. Vital Statistics.

[672] Roe_Elisha & Electa, although a "possible error" is mentioned on Ancestry.com.

[673] Roe_Elisha & Electa, citing U.S. Federal Census for 1910 and 1920.

[674] Roe_Elisha & Electa, citing Federal Census for 1870 and headstone in Mound Cemetery, Racine, Wisc.

[675] From Ancestry.com: Roe_Elisha & Electa (accessed 11/2/2010), citing U.S. Federal Census for 1870.

[676] Roe_Elisha & Electa, citing U.S. Federal Censuses for 1860 and 1870.

[677] Roe_Elisha & Electa, citing Federal Censuses for 1880-1930; and Oregon Death Index.

[678] #2314-2502 (Edalena Cole to Edith G. Rankin) are from various family trees and OWT on Ancestry.com and are unverified, except when supplemented with additional notes, *infra*.

[679] The Ancestry.com website owned by "thehills45" cites six U.S. Federal Census records.

[680] His wife and 10 children are named in the Ancestry.com website owned by "thehills45."

[681] Documents cited by Mark Norris show that he resided in La Clede, Fayette Co., Ill., in 1880, with his parents, Herbert A. and Harriet (Fisher) Hill. The Hill Family Tree entry for Theda Hill shows a photo of him and a photo of his tombstone, with two hearts - one for Theda and one for Florence.

[682] OneWorldTree says she is a descendant of Francis Peabody (1694-1769) of Topsfield, Mass.

[683] He does not appear to be a figure in history but Hugh de Morville was one of the four conspirators who assassinated Thomas a Becket at the instigation of Henry II of England.

[684] I suppose she is a blood relative of her husband or his in-law (i.e., a widow of a Bilyeu).

[685] From Google, 7/13/10: "Birge was president of the auto company from 1908-1916."

[686] #2559-2564 are from Thom Carlson, Ph.D., "Some Descendants of Isaac Hill Sr. & Eunice Mallory."

[687] From Carlson, Prosser, *History of the Puget Sound Country*, "Bradford L. Hill."

[688] #2565-2625 are from Ancestry.com, and are unverified.

[689] #2626 (William Coe) – 2644 (Hettie Hill) are from Thom Carlson, Ph.D.

[690] 1850 census: Belah Coe 55 m farmer MA / Maria Coe 55 f CT / Almond B. . . ."

[691] Carlson to George Hill, op. cit., and Sylvester Bruce Hill in Ancestry.com, Andre Family Tree.

[692] Sylvester Bruce Hill from Carlson, and Ancestry.com (Ibid.)

[693] #2645 (Charles Hill) – 2653 (Ruby A. Hill) from Ancestry.com.

[694] "Maybelle Hill," age 22, wife of Ernes O. "Ernie" Hill are first cousins, once removed.

[695] He is in the U.S. Federal Census of 1900 and 1910, accessed via Ancestry.com.

[696] She is in the U.S. Federal Censuses of 1900 and 1910, accessed via Ancestry.com.

[697] She is in the U.S. Federal Censuses of 1900, 1910, and 1920, accessed via Ancestry.com.

[698] He is in the U.S. Federal Censuses of 1910 and 1920, accessed via Ancestry.com.

[699] He is in the U.S. Federal Census of 1910 and 1920, accessed via Ancestry.com.

[700] She is in the U.S. Federal Censuses of 1910 and 1920, accessed via Ancestry.com.

[701] Fred amd Frank Swain from Carlson, op. cit.

[702] #2656 (Florence Swain) – 2661 (Elizabeth T. Hill) are from Ancestry.com, in U.S. Census records.

[703] He is known only from the U.S. Federal Census of 1920, where he is the only child, age 11.

[704] He is known only from one U.S. Federal Census record (1900), accessed via Ancestry.com.

[705] Roy Steven Hill is in the "My FTDNA" project/Hill Family/Group 47. We have a "match" at 25 markers, genetic distance 1. See his father, Frederick W. Hill (*supra*).

[706] #2663-2666 are from Ancestry.com, supplemented as shown in text.

[707] Kittie A. (#2663) and Emma L. (#2664) are mentioned in the obituary of their father in 1901.

[708] Emma L. appears in the census records of the family of Edward Hill of Corning, N.Y., in 1880.

[709] Fred E. Hill, son of Edgar E. Hill, is white; and Fred E. Hill, son of Thomas H. Hill, is black.

[710] Albert G. Hill appears in the census records of the family of Edward Hill of Corning, N.Y., in 1880.

[711] #2667 - #2745, numbered [ ], from William Edwin Hill, *Genealogy of the Hill Family in America* (1e).

[712] George J. Hill is person #68 in *GHFA*..

[713] Memory book of "Jessie F. Stockwell, Fryburgh, May 19, 1878." (copy from Mrs. Dale Hill's records).

[714] She is in Mabel Kennedy Stockwell, *The Stockwell Genealogy* (Lebanon, N.H.: Stockwell Family Association, 1983). On her father's side, she is descended from John Saxe, who was expelled to Canada from Dutchess County, N.Y., after the Revolution; see George J. Hill, *John Saxe, Loyalist (1732-1808) and His Descendants for Five Generations* (Westminster, Md.: Heritage Books, 2010); and Richard Singletary of Haverhill, Mass., who is also an ancestor of Barack Obama's mother. On her mother's side, she is a descendant of Sergeant Jonathan Hyde, an early settler of Newton, Mass.; William Ward, a founder of Marlboro, Mass., and an ancestor of General Artemus Ward; Robert Long, an early member of the Ancient

and Honorable Artillery Company; Samuel Allen, an early settler of Windsor, Mass., whose descendants also include Ethan Allen; Captain Roger Clapp, who came on the *Mary and John*; and of several of the early settlers of Rhode Island: Jonathan Holmes, Richard Borden, Pardon Tillinghast, Robert Potter, and John Irish; and John Alcock, a founder of Maine.

[715] He is in *GHFA*, p. 8, sheet #7, person 69. Research by Mrs. Dale (Avis Boyington) Hill, Clarion, IA.

[716] Her granddaughter, Adella Lindsay Harson, reviewed the Lindsay Family Register Report.

[717] William E. Hill, "Brief Account of the Hill Reunion Held at Dennison Park [Corning, N.Y.], August 27, 1920"; and e-mail from Mrs. Ken (Natalie) Rose to George J. Hill, 2002ff.

[718] William E. Kimball was "in charge of the music" and the "song fest" at the Hill Family Reunion.

[719] He is person #72 in *GHFA*.

[720] From *GHFA*: "He saw service in France and was wounded in one eye."

[721] From *GHFA*: "He served 2 years in France as First Sergeant in Training Camp."

[722] Records of the Hill Reunions held at Dennison Park, Corning, N.Y., in August 1921, 1922, 1923, and 1924 were prepared by William E. Hill, Secretary of Hill Association. He was also Treasurer in 1921. The announcement of the 1923 meeting states that he was then living in Genessee, N.Y.; he asked for records of the family that were "not contained in the present genealogy" to be sent to him there.

[723] *GHFA* "He was drafted Nov. 23, 1917, and discharged Aug. 27, 1919." John Phineas Hill was a member of the Society of Mayflower Descendants in the State of Massachusetts by right of his mother's descent from the Pilgrim Myles Standish.

[724] Her maiden name is from a Hill Family History Worksheet prepared by Paul F. Hill to George J. Hill, 2 April 1996, where she was called Elizabeth M. Tobey. In the DAR Patriot Index (CD-ROM), 1999, she is clled Elizabeth Morse.

[725] Her obiturary from Horseheads [N.Y.] was forwarded on 25 April 2002 to George Hill by Paul F. Hill.

[726] Charles Ross Paul from Thom Carlson, op. cit.

[727] #2747 (Emily Hill) to #2775 (H. LaVerne Hill) from Paul F. Hill, Corning, N.Y. (op. cit.)

[728] From Ancestry.com, unverified by primary sources.

[729] Ancestry.com cites U.S. Census records of 1860, 1870, 1880, 1900, 1920, and 1930, and the AGBI.

[730] Line 8, Descendants of John Hill, is from James D. Hill, "Twelve Generations" supplemented as noted.

[731] Albert Nelson Marquis, *The Book of Minnesotans: A Biographical Dictionary of Leading Living Men of the State of Minnesota* (Albert Nelson Marquis & Co., 1907).

[732] "Family History of Thomas Barber (ca 1614-1662)" in "Connecticut Genealogy": (VIII) Lucius Albert Barbour, son of Lucius and Harriet Louise (Day) Barbour, was born January 26, 1846, at Madison, Indiana, and came when young with his parents to Hartford, Connecticut. . . . Colonel Barbour was one of the most popular officers connected with the National Guard and his selection later as adjutant-general of the state met with popular approval throughout the state.

[733] He was named as an heir in the will written in 1846 by his grandfather, Joseph Gillett.

[734] He appears as the oldest child on a Family Group record of Joseph [Simeon] Riley and Katherine Gillett.

[735] A handwritten chart that accompanied a letter from Leslie Schroader to GJH, 28 Mar 1996, gave the name of the wife of James Gillett Riley, and the mother of his children Isabell, Susan, and Stilson James, as Alice Fitzpatrick, not Kate Archer. (w/o attribution). His photograph in the uniform of a U.S. Army enlisted soldier was enclosed with the Biographical Information form of 20 March 1997 submitted by his great-granddaughter, Jane Luella (Olson) Leonhardt, to GJH.

[736] Information by letter from Leslie Schroader to GJH, 20 Mar 1996.

[737] The record of her death was provided by the Wright County Registrar of Vital Records on 9 Dec 2002.

[738] #2942 (Mary Ann Sanderson)-#3124 (Lizzie Pulsifer Allen) are from OWT and specific notes.

Chapter 9 – Ninth Generation

[739] #3125-3126 are from Ancestry.com and are unverified.

[740] #3127 (Clarence Mortimer Hill)-#3403 (William James Maxwell) are from Ancestry.com and are unverified, except when additional notes are provided by Richard Stanley, et al.; and #3216 (Flora May Hill)-#3223 (Kenneth E. Hill) are from Mark Norris, op. cit.

[741] From Richard Stanley, op. cit.; and Pratt and Webster Family Tree (Owner: PriscillaR).

[742] Golding Family Tree, citing U.S. Census records of 1850, 1860, 1870, 1880, and 1900.

[743] His name and date of death at 5 months is on his parents' tombstone in Wauconda Cemetery.

[744] His name and date of death at 1 year 9 months is on his parents' tombstone in Wauconda Cemetery.

[745] Her date of death as "Baby" is on her parents' tombstone.

[746] From Golding Family Tree (Owner: katesgolding), Ancestry.com. No sources cited.

[747] From Carlson to George Hill, op. cit.; and Golding Family Tree (Owner: katesgolding), Ancestry.com.

[748] Fred W. Bangs is from Golding Family Tree. Jennie E. Long is known only from OWT.

[749] From Roe_Elisha & Electa, citing U.S. Federal Censuses of 1860 and 1880.

[750] From Roe_Elisha & Electa, citing 1880, 1900, and 1910 U.S. Federal Censuses.

[751] Sources cited by Roe_Elisha & Electa: U.S. Federal Censuses of 1900 and 1910.

[752] Roe_Elisha & Electa (11/2/2010), cites D.A.R. Record of Nettie Fellows Olmstead.

[753] From Ancestry.com: Roe_Elisha & Electa (11/2/2010), citing U.S. Federal Censuses of 1850 and 1880.

[754] From Ancestry.com: Roe_Elisha & Electa (11/2/2010), citing U.S. Federal Censuses of 1850 and 1880.

[755] Roe_Elisha & Electa (11/2/2010), citing U.S. Federal Census of 1880: He resided in Chicago in 1880.

[756] Roe_Elisha & Electa (accessed 11/2/2010), citing U.S. Federal Census of 1880.

[757] From Ancestry.com: Roe_Elisha & Electa (11/2/2010), citing U.S. Federal Censuses of 1880 and 1900.

[758] From Ancestry.com: Roe_Elisha & Electa (11/2/2010), citing U.S. Federal Censuses of 1880 and 1900.

[759] From Ancestry.com: Roe_Elisha & Electa (11/2/2010), citing U.S. Federal Census of 1880.

[760] From Ancestry.com: Roe_Elisha & Electa (11/2/2010), citing U.S. Federal Census of 1880.

[761] From Ancestry.com: Roe_Elisha & Electa (accessed 11/2/2010), citing U.S. Federal Census of 1900.

[762] Roe_Elisha & Electa, citing U.S. Federal Censuses of 1910 and 1930, and California Death Index; Bruce H. Harrison, *Descendants of Pieter Tjercks (Schuyler)* (Kamuela, HI: Millisecond Publishing Co., n.d).; http://www.FamilyForest.com) (accessed via Google, 11/5/2010), 164-5: Children of Elizabeth Livingston Steele and George Washington[11] Childs were as follows:

886   i   George Frederick[12] Childs, born 3 Jul 1909 in Highland Park, IL; died 10 Jan 1931.

887   ii   Robert Livingston Childs, born 17 February 1912 in Chicago, IL.

888   iii   William Coffeen Childs, born 17 April 1916 in Chicago, IL.

[763] For George Washington Childs, the Roe_Elisha&Electa family tree of Ancestry.com cites U.S. Federal Censuses for 1880, 1910, 1920, and 1930; California Death Index, 1940-1997; SSDI; Passenger and Crew Lists from California (1893-1957) and New York (1820-1957); and Draft Registration Cards for World War I (1917-1918) and World War II (1942). Also, from Mae Felts Herringshaw, *Chicagoans of 1916: Ten Thousand Biographies. Herringshaws City Blue Book of Biography* (Chicago: Clark J. Herringshaw, 1916; accessed via Google, 11/5/2010).

[764] The Ancestry.com website owned by "thehills45" cites the Census of 1910.

[765] The Ancestry.com website owned by "thehills45" cites the Census of 1910.

[766] The Ancestry.com website owned by "thehills45" shows m to Edith May Woodford and their eight children (of whom six are named); his residences after marriage in Kane, Ill., in 1920 and 1930; his WWI and WWII Draft Registration Cards; and his death in California.

[767] The Ancestry.com website owned by "thehills45" shows his b., d., and burial at just over 7 months old.

[768] The Ancestry.com website owned by "thehills45" shows b, residences, military service, m, and death.

[769] "thehills45" shows his b, m, draft registration in Nicollet Co., Minn., on 5 Jun 1917; d and bur in Minnesota at age 59. Three unnamed children are shown on the website.

[770] He is shown without sources in the Ancestry.com website owned by "thehills45."

[771] "thehills45": She died as an infant, about 3 weeks before her twin brother.

[772] "thehills45": Her m. and four children, of whom three are named; censuses; Minnesota Death Index.

[773] She is shown in the website owned by "thehills45," dying at a little over 3 months of age.

[774] "thehills45," census records of 1920 and 1930.

[775] Information from Mark Norris, on Hill Family Tree: He was born in Ipava, Fulton Co., Ill., and died at 66; buried 11 days later at the Presidio National Cemetery in San Francisco; two of his ch were named

[776] "Allithea Birge Cary" by Patrick Kavanagh, History of Women in Forest Lawn Lawn Cemetery. Allithea m George Cary on 12/13/1908. George's marriage to Allithea secured his place in Buffalo society.

[777] Pan-American Expo: At the age of 40, Cary became one of the three local architects on the Board of Architects of the 1901 Pan-American Exposition.

[778] #3404 (Elsie Hill)-#3422 (Caroline Hill) are from Thom Carlson to George J. Hill, op. cit., except that Tillitsons and Leifheits are expanded from information in Ancestry.com.

[779] #3423 (William Benjamin Hill)-#3515 (Quincy Wellington Gregory) are from *GHFA* and William E. Hill, "Brief Account of the Hill Reunion Held at Dennison Park [Corning, N.Y.], August 27, 1920," supplemented with additional notes, *infra*.

[780] He person #145 in *GHFA*. Research by Jeanine Kay (Humbert) Johnson, his granddaughter: Obituary: Waterloo, IA, *Daily Courier* (September 1924). Burial at Fairview Cemetery, Cedar Falls, IA; Brown Funeral Home.

[781] Research by Jeanine Kay (Humbert) Johnson, her granddaughter. Obituary: *Sedalia (Missouri) Capital Newspaper* and *Stillwater (Oklahoma) News* (Feb 20, 21, 1955). Burial at Crown Hill Cemetery, Sedalia, Mo., and monument stone in Cedar Falls, Ia.

[782] *Wright County Monitor*: The wedding was described, 12/29/09. The triple wedding ceremony was the only one ever performed by the Rev. William H. Spence, then the minister at the Methodist Episcopal Church in Clarion. He was the subject of a biography, *One Foot in Heaven*, written by his son, Hartzell Spence, which became a best seller and was a Warner Brothers movie starring Frederick March (*Monitor*, Dec 1941). Notes reviewed and corrected by Charles E. [221] Hill to George J. Hill, M.D., 30 July and 7 Sep 1994. Family Group Record prepared by Charles E. Hill, August 1994.

[783] Ole Mickelson was b. in Norway, 25 Aug 1856. He and his brother came to the U.S. in about 1873. Lena Tergeson was b. at LaCrosse, WI, 22 Aug 1863. Ole and Lena (Tergeson) Mickelson were married at LaCrosse, WI, 4 Oct 1882. He d. 1941 and she d. 1948, both at Clarion, IA, and both were buried at the Evergreen Cemetery in Clarion.

[784] Recollections of his niece by marriage, Essie Mae (Thompson) Hill, to her son, George, about 1953; and by his nephew, Myron Hill, Jr., to George Hill. His barn was described by Birdsall (1915), 921-2. The farm was later owned by his sister, Ruby (Hill) Woodin and later by descendants of his brother Myron.

[785] In 1997 her name was spelled Loretta by her daughter, Minnie.

[786] He is person #148 in *GHFA*. "Harvey People Wed," a newspaper clipping of six paragraphs provided by his daughter-in-law, Mrs. Dale (Avis Boyington) Hill. Myron and Julia Hill took the train to Chicago for a honeymoon in Illinois. Family Group record prepared by Avis (Boyington) Hill, 30 July 1994.

[787] She appears on Sheet #11 of GHFA, the wife of person #148. Family Group record for Myron and Julia Hill was completed by Avis (Boyington) Hill, September 1994.

[788] Her grandmother's maiden name was Emma (or Emily) Lodiweska (spelled variously). The origin of her middle name was a puzzle until it was clarified in a search on "Google." "Lodoiska" became famous as the result of the success of the heroic comedy by that name by Luigi Cherubini (1760-1842).

[789] Biographical Information form and Family Group Record prepared July 1994 by her daughter, Jessie (Woodin) Kent. Obit from the *Wright County Monitor*, "Ruby A. Woodin died . . . July 30, 1995."

[790] Biographical Information form prepared by his daughter, Jessie (Woodin) Kent, July 1994. Obituary of Howard Henry Woodin, *Wright County Monitor*.

[791] Person #152 in *GHFA*. A copy of her obituary was provided on 7 Sep 1995 by her nephew, Charles E. Hill, without a source. Burial was in the Evergreen Cemetery, Clarion.

[792] Funeral services were held at the Eyler-Williams Funeral Home, Clarion, Iowa, 6 October 1979.

[793] He is person #153 in *GHFA*; Grace Miller Ridings High, *The Manly Family* (1962); and Essie Mae Thompson Hill, *Prairie Daughter* (1973).

[794] Essie Mae (Thompson) Hill wrote four books, all of which were published privately in Sun City, Az.: *Prairie Daughter*, 1978 (123 pp.); *Let Thy Handmaidens Speak*, 1983 (46 pp.); *Essie Mae's Cookbook*, 1987 (186 pp.); and *Flapper Fun: Other Poems and Stories*, 1988 (87 pp.). She appears in Grace Miller Ridings High, *The Manly Genealogy*,45. She is a descendant of Rebecca (Towne) Nurse, who was hanged at Salem in 1692, in the genealogy described by George J. Hill, "From Salem to Kalamazoo – A 14-Generation Family Odyssey" *About Towne: Quarterly Newsletter of the Towne Family Association* 26 (No. 3, July-September) 2006: 50-56; and (No. 4, October-December) 2006: 74-78. In this line, she is also a Putnam, and General Israel Putnam is a collateral ancestor. She is also a descendant of James Prescott of Hampton, N.H., who was the subject of George J. Hill, "Was James Prescott of Hampton, New Hampshire (in 1665), the Son of Sir William and Margaret (Babington) Prescott (bp. 1637/8), for Whom an Arrest Warrant Was Issued in 1659/60?" *The Mayflower Quarterly* (September 2008), 245-268. She is a

descendant of William Rundle, a founder of Greenwich, Conn., and his wife Amy Hobby, who is a descendant of James Feake, Sr., goldsmith of London, an "adventurer of purse" in the Jamestowne Society. She is also a descendant of John Manley, a founder of Maryland, and of John Sharpless, who came on the William Penn fleet and was a founder of Chester, Penn.

[795] Person #154 in GHFA, known as Edward Lindsay. Adella Lindsay Harson reviewed the Linsay Family Register Report of 13 March 1996 and returned it with corrections to George J. Hill, M.D., 15 March 1996.

[796] Her demise before Feb 2002 was given to George Hill by e-mail from Mrs. Ken (Natalie) Rose on 3 February 2002 <kennrose@hotmail.com>.

[797] Her demise before Feb 2002 was given to George Hill by e-mail from Mrs. Ken (Natalie) Rose on 3 February 2002 <kennrose@hotmail.com>.

[798] #3516 (Dean Edwin Hill)-#3539 (Mary Nanno Hill) are from Paul F. Hill, op. cit., supplemented with additional notes, *infra*.

[799] Dean Edwin Hill was of Oxbow, N.Y., in 1996 and 2003. (From Hill Family History Worksheet prepared by Paul F. Hill, 35 Pershing St., Corning, NY 14830-2032, to George J. Hill, 2 April 1996; and the obituary of his mother in 2002). His middle name is from DAR Patriot Index (1999). Also, from letter of 16 September 2003 from Dean E. Hill to George J. Hill.

[800] In March 1996 she was living in Caton, NY. From Hill Family History Worksheet prepared by Paul F. Hill, 35 Pershing St., Corning, NY 14830-2032, to George J. Hill, 2 April 1996.

[801] Constance Elizabeth Hill and Guy Richard Powell are from the worksheet prepared by Paul F. Hill.

[802] At the Hill Reunion in 2010, she submitted a Family Group Record for her parents' family group.

[803] Barbara Lovensheimer's ltr to Jeanine Humbert Johnson and Family Group Records that she compiled.

[804] According to information developed by Paul F. Hill and his other relatives, Richard L. [Lord] Hill I (Generation 4), was the father of Richard L. Hill II (Generation 5), father of Richard L. Hill III (Generation 6), father of Paul F. [Frank] Hill (b. 4 May 1928, Corning N.Y., a designer for Corning, Inc.), who m. Mary Agnes Keane (b. 11 September 1926, a credit clerk at Corning, N.Y.).

[805] These two descendants of Elizabeth Hill in the 9th generation are known only from Ancestry.com, and this line apparently becomes extinct with this generation.

[806] The descendants of John Hill in the 9th generation from #3542 (Charles Victor Hill) - #3568 (Lester Loring Staats) are from Hill, "Twelve Generations" with references.

[807] #3569-3571 are from Andrew J. Morris, "Thomas Barber" in "Connecticut Genealogy"

[808] Ancestry.com.; and RG 074:036, "Lucius B. Barbour Genealogical Collection Inventory: Finding aid prepared by Connecticut State Library staff," Connecticut State Library, 2009.

[809] #3572 (Hattie Barnes) – #3588 (Lawrence Humason) are from Ancestry.com

[810] #3589 (Frances M. Riley) - #3593 (Stilson James Riley) are from Leslie Schroader, letters to GJH re Anderson; Olson; Riley; Hendryx; Allen. Letters of 23 and 28 March 1996, enclosing Family Group Records for Josiah and Susanna (Hendryx) Riley; and of her parents, Isaiah and Esther (Jackson) Hendryx.

[811] From Mrs. Dale E. (Avis Boyington) Hill to George J. Hill, 21 Aug 1995.

[812] Information from her granddaughter, LaVonne (Anderson) Olson, and her grandson, Leslie Schroader, to GJH March 1996; and from Biographical Information Form of Luella (Riley) Anderson prepared 14 Mar 1996 by La Vonne (Anderson) Olson.

[813] From Biographical Information Form of Luella (Riley) Anderson prepared 14 Mar 1996 by La Vonne (Anderson) Olson, mailed to George J. Hill, M.D.

[814] Sue (Riley) Wolfer described her ancestors and her immediate family in a typewritten page (attributed to her by La Vonne Olson), a copy of which was sent by Mrs. Olson to GJH, 28 Mar 1996.

[815] Letter from Leslie Schroader to GJH, 19 Mar 1996, who wrote, "I believe this information came from LaVonne's records." He is buried beside his father in Graceland Cemetery, Rowan, Iowa.

[816] #3594 is from Ancestry.com and is unverified.

Chapter 10 – Tenth Generation

[817] #3595 (George Washington Shepperd) - #3679 (Clarence H. Barnes) are from Ancestry.com. #3595-#3607 (Maude C. Brewer) are supplemented with information from OWT - Descendants of Arthur Henbury and Lydia Hill, Ancestry.com, accessed 4/18/2010ff.

[818] The descendants of Mary Hill, #3680-3684, are from Ancestry.com, OWT, and are unconfirmed.

---

[819] #3685 (Lulu Hill) - #3622 (?Birge), are from various Family Trees on Ancestry.com, and OWT, supplemented with additional notes, *infra*. #3685 - #3688 (Sadie W. Hill) are from From Pratt and Webster Family Tree, Ancestry.com, accessed 11/9/2010.

[820] The Pratt and Webster Family Tree cites U.S. Federal censuses, U.S. Passport Applications and World War I Draft Registration Cards, 1917-1918.

[821] The Pratt and Webster Family Tree cites 1880 and 1900 U.S. Federal Censuses.

[822] Pratt and Webster Family Tree cites 1900 U.S. Federal Census; information from Richard Stanley (q.v.).

[823] From Golding Family Tree, Ancestry.com, accessed 11/1/2010.

[824] From Golding Family Tree, Ancestry.com, accessed 11/1/2010.

[825] From Ancestry.com, Golding Family Tree and from Pratt and Webster Family Tree.

[826] He appears as George F. Childs, b. 1910, in the Johnson Family Tree (owner: johnsoem1).

[827] He appears in the Johnson Family Tree (owner: johnsoem1) of Ancestry.com (accessed 11/5/2010). His photo as a young rugby player is included in this page. He is in New York Passenger Lists, 1820-1957, arriving in New York on 17 September 1934, and he resided in Wayne, Ill., in 1987, at age 75.

[828] See Notes for his mother: "888 iii William Coffeen12 Childs, born 17 April 1916 in Chicago, IL."

[829] "thehills45" shows his b and c and cites 1920 and 1930 U.S. Federal Census records.

[830] "thehills45" shows his b and d and cites 1920 and 1930 U.S. Federal Census records.

[831] "thehills45" shows his b and d and cites 1920 and 1930 U.S. Federal Census records.

[832] "thehills45" shows his b and d and cites 1920 and 1930 U.S. Federal Census records.

[833] "thehills45" shows his birth and death and cites the 1930 U.S. Federal Census record.

[834] "thehills45" shows his birth and death and cites 1930 census; WWII Army enlistment; and SSDI.

[835] He died in the year of his birth, according to the website owned by "thehills45."

[836] From http://democrats.assembly.ca.gov/members/a19/Biography/default.aspx and Project Vote Smart http://www.votesmart.org/bio.php?can_id=81552, and *San Mateo Daily Journal* Editorial (15 Dec 2010). His name was given to me by Mark Norris, who directed me to this website.

[837] #3751-2 are from Thom Carlson to George J. Hill, op. cit.

[838] #3760 (Howard Eugene Hill) - #4005 (John Daniel Jenkins) are from *GHFA* (1st and 2nd eds), supplemented with additional notes. Numbers in brackets, such as [215], are from 1st edi.

[839] The Family Group Record prepared on 2 July 1996 by his daughter, Barbara Jo (Hill) Chandler, gives his place of marriage as Forest City, Iowa, by a Justice of the Peace, and his place of d as Davenport, Iowa.

[840] Information from her niece, Jeanine (Humbert) Johnson

[841] Person #216 in *GHFA*. Paul F. Hill: Biography, on file with University of Northern Iowa Alumni Association. A copy of *The Denver Post* obit came from Mrs. Virginia W. Thompson of Littleton, Colo.

[842] 1994 Christmas letter of Paul and Marie Hill, and note from Marie (Johnson) Hill to George J. Hill, 6 June 1995. The card for her memorial service was sent by her children to George Hill on 28 Aug 2000.

[843] Research done by her daughter, Jeanine Kay (Humbert) Johnson: A delayed birth certificate was filed 6 March 1957. Her obituary appeared in the *Waterloo Courier* (9 and 10 September 1982).

[844] George Delos Humbert (b. 1867, nr. Cedar Falls, IA; d. 1944, Milwaukee, WI; m. 1911 at San Antonio, TX, Eugenia Magdelina Maier) was the son of Solomon Barrick Humbert (b. 1842, Potter, NY; d. 1938, Cedar Falls, IA; m. 1866 at Shoptierre, WI, Adaline Rose, who was b. 1841, Cambria Twp., NY, and d. 1924, Cedar Falls, IA). His m to Genevieve Hill at the Little Brown Church in Nashua, IA, was recorded e Chickasaw Co. Court House, Book 26:95, and published in the *Cedar Falls Daily Record* (23 July 1938).

[845] He is person #221, sheet #11, in *GHFA*. Shortly before his fifth birthday he and his cousin [Leola] Grace Hill were ring bearers at the wedding of their aunt Ruby Adella Hill.

[846] The b and d of her parents were provided on an Ancestral Chart, completed August 1994 by Charles E. Hill. Services by Towey Funeral Home at Rochester, MN; burial at Evergreen Cemetery, Clarion, IA.

[847] #222 in *GFFA*. Obituary of her s, E. Laurel Knoedler, II, says that she was of Shell Rock, IA, in 1987.

[848] Knoedler Family Register Report (5 Jan 1997) by GJH was corrected by Dorothy Knoedler on 4 June 1997 and is the basis for these Notes.

[849] Person #223 in *GHFA*. "Max Hill... 18 years of dedicated service," *Sumner Gazette* (3 May 1990), 3.

[850] person #224 in *GHFA*. He was of Orlando, Fla., in 1994, when he attended Hill Reunion. Family history given directly to George J. Hill at Hill Family Reunion, 30 July 1994.

[851] Avis Hill to George Hill, 8 Aug 1994.

[852] Person #226 in *GHFA*. Services at First United Methodist Church, Clarion; burial at Evergreen Cemetery, Clarion, 13 Sep 1994.

[853] Biographical information was provided by Avis (Boyington) Hill regarding the Dale and Avis Hill family, and about her Boyington and Campbell ancestors. Her 1931 Essay was quoted in the brochure, "Iowa High School Seniors Win Valuable Prizes." Obit in *Globe Gazette* on 4/1/2008.

[854] Christmas letter, 1994. Myron Hill Jr. received the Hill Family Bible from his aunt Ruby (Hill) Woodin after she died, and it was in his possession in the first decade of the twenty-first century.

[855] Conversation with Lela (Hill) and Earl Odland, 31 July 1994, and letter from Lela (Hill) Odland to George J. Hill, 18 Oct 1995. Updated 1 August 2000 by letter from Avis Hill to George Hill.

[856] Family Group record completed by Lela (Hill) Odland; conversation with Earl S. Odland, 30 July 1994. He had sisters Segnora (d. 1994) and Norine. Updated 1 August 2000 by letter from Avis Hill to GJH.

[857] Family Group record prepared by John Howard Woodin. Addittional comments to George J. Hill, 29 July 1994, and in the Christmas newsletter, 1994; other notes from Christmas messages of 1987 and 1990.

[858] Biographical Information and Family Record forms for Jessie Woodin and Kenneth Kent were completed in November 1994 by Jessie (Woodin) Kent.

[859] In November 1994, the Family Record of Kenneth Ronald Kent was prepared by his wife, Jessie (Woodin) Kent, and sent to George J. Hill, M.D.

[860] Family Group Record and other information from Jessie (Woodin) Kent, July 1994.

[861] Correspondence from Agnes (Beal) Hemenway to George J. Hill, M.D., most recently on 29 December 1999. Arlie A. Beal (27 Dec 1897-21 Feb 1975) was the son of Elmer and Cassie (Ashcroft) Beal. Pearl L. Locke (21 Nov 1903-27 July 1929) was the dau. of Frank R. and Rulenna (Slemp) Locke; he was the son of Edward F. and Juliana (Janvrin) Locke.

[862] His biography appears in *Who's Who in the United States*, and on his website, www.georgejhill.com.

[863] Her biography appears in *Who's Who in America*. Her most frequently cited paper is Hill, HZ: "The function of melanin or six blind people examine an elephant" *BioEssays* 14:49-56, 1992. She is descended from John Thorndike and Thomas Trowbridge, gateway ancestors in Roberts, *The Royal Descents of 600 Immigrants*. She is a member of the National Society, Colonial Dames of America by right of descent from Toby Leech; and the Welcome Society, as a descendant of George and Sarah Shoemaker.

[864] His teaching at the University of Buffalo was praised by his students. Lee Koslowski, "Department Fills Demand to Retain Popular Professor" *The Spectrum*, SUNY at Buffalo 49 (No. 39, 8 Dec 1999): "We just told him [the department chairman] that Dr. Hill was one of our best professors."

[865] Hill, G.L.: "A Tribute to Keiko Nambara Hill," in E. M. T. Hill, *Prairie Daughter*, 116-7.

[866] Dr. Eppley was certified by the American Board of Family Practice in 1982 and was recertified by examination in 1989. She is a member of the American Academy of Family Practice, Physicians for Social Responsibility, and The Hunger Project.

[867] Adella Lindsay Harson reviewed the Lindsay Family Register Report of 13 March 1996 and returned it with corrections to GJH, 15 March 1996.

[868] From his obituary (copy from Mrs. Lavonne [Anderson] Olson to Mrs. Avis [Boyington] Hill, and thence to George J. Hill, 21 Aug 1995).

[869] She is person #229 in *GHFA*. Family Group record of Maurice and Adella (LINDSAY) HARSON family completed by Maurice R. Harson, 8 May 1994.

[870] Adella Harson reviewed the Linsay Family Register Report and gave handwritten comments.

[871] Natalie Rose wrote to George Hill on 3 February 2002 asking for information regarding the descendants of William P. and Sarah (Herrick) Hill. In response to this information, she said "Vesta and Harry had five daughters. The youngest is Eleanor Vesta. As she is still living I will stop."

[872] #3810 (Paul David Hill) - #3833 (Beverly Hill) are from Paul F. Hill, letters and enclosures to George J. Hill, April 1996 ff, some of whom are supplemented with additional notes.

[873] #3816-8 are on Family Group Record prepared by Constance Elizabeth Hill, 3 Sep 2010.

[874] From Thom Carlson to George J. Hill, op. cit.

[875] From George J. Hill, M.D. / August 12, 2003: "Dear Paul, Thank you ever so much for your letter and the enclosures of August 12. You and your cousins have done a marvelous job in tracing your branch of the Hill family back to Abraham, the son of Isaac Hill Sr, our common great x5 grandfather."

[876] #3834 (Mary Elizabeth Hill) - #3848 (Lurissa Rosalia Staats) from Hill, "Twelve Generations," op. cit.

[877] #3849-50 from Andrew J. Morris, "Family History of Thomas Barber," op. cit.

[878] #3851 (Charles McKinstry) - #3858 (Donald Peck Wolfer) from Leslie Schroader to George Hill, "Riley Family," 23 and 28 March 1996, supplemented with information from LaVonne Olson to George Hill, 28 March 1996, enclosing Susan Wolfer, "Riley Family History."

[879] Biographical Information Form completed by Leslie Schroader, 4 Mar 1996, for GJH. "My Nice Mother," by Marian Rozella (Schroader) Bitker, in her book, *Thanks For Giving And Other Poems*, 1990.

[880] From a Biographical Information form regarding Ula Myrtle (Anderson) Schroader, completed 4 Mar 1996 by Leslie Schroader, and mailed to George J. Hill, M.D.

[881] His b was obtained from Biographical Information Form of Luella (Riley) Anderson prepared 14 Mar 1996 by La Vonne (Anderson) Olson, mailed to GJH. He was living in Des Moines, Iowa, in 1997, but his sister LaVonne's memorial card says that he had died by the time of her death in August 1997.

[882] Biographical Information Form completed Mar 1996 by Lillian (Sormberger) Anderson, and mailed to GJH. He also appeared on the Biographical Information Form of Luella (Riley) Anderson prepared 14 Mar 1996 by La Vonne (Anderson) Olson.

[883] Biographical Information Form prepared for her late sister, Ula (Anderson) Schroader, 4 Mar 1996, and form completed by La Vonne (Anderson) Olson, March 1996, and additional information from form completed by her daughter, Jane Luella (Olson) Leonhardt, 20 March 1997.

[884] Her husband's family name was in a letter from her first cousin, La Vonne (Anderson) Olson, to GJH, 28 Mar 1996. Mrs. Olson enclosed a letter from Susan (Wolfer) Earnest of 9 Jan 1995.

[885] Marcia (Hawkins) Wolfer discovered a Biographical Information Form in her late husband's effects and forwarded it to GJH on 17 April 1999.

Chapter 11 – Eleventh Generation

[886] #3859-3877 are from "Descendants of Arthur Henbury and Lydia Hill," op. cit.

[887] #3878-91 are from Ancestry.com and are unverified.

[888] #3892-3900 are from Ancestry.com and are unverified.

[889] Richard R. Stanley, e-mail to George J. Hill, 29 January 2005ff.

[890] #3902-19 are from Ancestry.com and are unverified except for information provided *infra.*.

[891] Golding Family Tree cites U.S. Federal Censuses for 1910, 1920, and 1930, and SSDI.

[892] The great-grandchildren of George J. and Jessie (Fidelia) Stockwell Hill, #3920 (Barbara Jo Hill) - #3984 (Thomas David Hill Jr.), are from Family Group Records submitted by their parents and grandparents to George J. Hill, M.D., plus sources shown in Notes, *infra.*

[893] She completed the Biographical Information form for her immediate family on 11 July 1996.

[894] She was born at the Methodist Hospital, Des Moines, Iowa. (Letter from her m to GJH, 22 Sep 1995)

[895] He was born at the Methodist Hospital, Des Moines, IA. (Letter from his m to GJH, 22 Sep 1995)

[896] Biographical Information Form prepared by Jeanine (Humbert) Johnson for GJH, July 1995. Her Mayflower Society numbers are: National 67129 and Iowa 1145.

[897] His picture appeared in the Rochester, MN, *Post Bulletin* (28 Apr 1955), in Scout uniform. The man who shot Chuck Hill in the back of the head, and who also killed a waitress at the same restaurant, confessed to two other killings in the St. Louis area. This man, one Ronald Hoelzer, received two 99 year sentences (from *Overdrive Magazine*, 1 August 1969, 39). His sister Sally wrote poems to him, posthumously, "Touch me not / My heart is sore. / I cannot love him / Anymore. . ."

[898] Information from her father, Charles E. Hill, 7 Sep 1994 on Biographical Information and Family Group Record forms. At age 8, she wrote, "Happy, Happy Mothers Day / Gentle Wishes Are On Their Way."

[899] Notes written by her father, Charles E. Hill, 30 July and 7 Sep 1994. At age 15, she wrote "A Poem" on Mother's Day, "I got up very early, / just to pick you some flowers. / It's funny what you'll find."

[900] Family Group record and obituary provided by Avis Hill, 4 Sep 1994. Additional information in Biographical Information sheets completed for GJH by his widow, Louetta Knoedler, 25 Nov 1995.

[901] Biographical Information sheets completed for GJH by Louetta (Follette) Knoedler, 25 Nov 1995.

[902] Obituary of E. Laurel Knoedler, II. Her d of b is from by her son, David for the 1997 Hill reunion.

[903] Biographical Information form provided by Keith and Dorothy (Rodenbeck) Knoedler, 27 August 1996.

[904] Her birth date and place from her sister, Carol, to George Hill, 8 July 2000.

[905] Her married name comes from two questionnaires completed for the Hill family reunion in Clarion, Iowa, in 1997. She is presumed to have four children, two sons and two daughters.

[906] Her date of b and married name from her m at Hill Family reunion at Clarion, Iowa, on 26 July 1997.

[907] Her date of b and married name from her m at Hill Family reunion at Clarion, Iowa, on 26 July 1997. The questionnaire also mentions four whose names are otherwise unknown (perhaps a daughter, son-in-law, and grandchildren?): Lauri Olson (Montgomery St., Decorah), Jeff and Lana Olson (101 R. St., West Union, Ia.), and Scott Olson (Oelwein, Ia.)

[908] Her date of b and married name from her m at Hill Family reunion at Clarion, Iowa, on 26 July 1997.

[909] Her date of b and married name from her m at Hill Family reunion at Clarion, Iowa, on 26 July 1997. Also, from Michele Menuey Ekern, 7/14/11ff, by e-mail: ekern_michele@hotmail.com.

[910] Her date of b and married name from her m at Hill Family reunion at Clarion, Iowa, on 26 July 1997. The names of Zeke, Angela, and Michael appear on another questionnaire; their relationships are presumed.

[911] His d of birth from his m at Hill Family reunion at Clarion, Iowa, on 26 July 1997. His w's name and those of her children are presumed from their appearance on a questionnaire.

[912] Her d of b is from a questionnaire completed by her mother on 26 July 1997.

[913] Iowa Century Farm certificate, and story with photograph of Steven and Shirley (Davis) Hill. Biographical Information form completed by Steven Dale Hill, 30 July 1994.

[914] Obituary of Chad Matthew Hill provided by Avis (Boyington) Hill. Biographical Information from Connie Sue (Greiman) Hill, 25 Aug 1994.

[915] "Hill elected president of Minowa Bancshares board," *Decorah (Iowa) Journal* (Thurs., 30 Sep 1993), page A-4. Biographical Information provided by Linda Kay (Carden) Hill, 30 Jul 2000.

[916] Conversation with Lela (Hill) and Earl Odland, 31 July 1994; ltr from Lela Odland to GJH, 18 Oct 1995.

[917] Conversation with Lela (Hill) Odland, 31 Jul 1994, and letter from Lela Odland to George J. Hill, 18 Oct 1995, updated by Lela in July 2000 (by letter from Avis Hill to George Hill, 1 August 2000).

[918] Conversation with Lela (Hill) and Earl Odland, 31 July 1994; ltr from Lela Odland to GJH, 18 Oct 1995.

[919] Conversation with Lela (Hill) and Earl Odland, 31 July 1994; ltr from Lela Odland to GJH, 18 Oct 1995.

[920] Research: Family Group record completed by Wendy (Woodin) Peche, July 1994.

[921] Patti Jean (Hemenway) Lang marked up on 12 July 1997 the draft of the Hemenway Family Register Report of 28 June 1997. The revised information was entered on 15 June 2000.

[922] *New York* magazine, regarding his client, Gary McGivern, 6 Mar 1995, p. 14.

[923] David Hill, "The Statue and the Strands," in Deborah Case and Sharon Derderian (Editors), *Passages: An Anthology of Contemporary Literature* (Troy, Mich.: Iliad Press/Cader Publishing Co., 1992) [ISBN 0-8187-0164-1], p. 80; and David Hedgcock Hill (edited by George J. Hill, M.D.), *A Lesson in Reality: Poems and Essays, 1991-2000* (West Orange, N.J.: Hilltree Farm Press, 2007, 67 pp.).

[924] Her b is in *The Manly Genealogy*, 45. Sarah Hill, Untitled. Her black and white photograph of a children's swing was published facing the back cover in the Kenyon College literary magazine, *Hika*, v. 44, no. 2, 1984. G. J. Hill and S. Hill, "Lead Poisoning due to Hai Ge Fen," Letter to the Editor of the *Journal of the American Medical Association*, 1994.

[925] e-mail from Victoria Hill Norfleet to George Hill, 10 May 1999.

[926] His photograph and an interview with him appear in Robert D. Mulcahy, Jr., "The F-15 Eagle Celebrates 25 Years of Service" in *Private Pilot* (December 1997), 80-81.

[927] #3985 (Mildred Long) - #3996 (Edwin Lindsay) are from Adella Lindsay Harson, Lindsay Family Register Report of 13 March 1996, to George J. Hill, M.D., 15 March 1996.

[928] Family Group record for Allen Ray and Ada Sue (Smith) Harson family completed by Sue Harson, 8 May 1994. Additional information by letter from Adella (Lindsay) Harson, 20 Feb 1996.

[929] Adella Lindsay Harson reviewed the Linsay Family Register Report of 13 March 1996 and returned it with corrections to George J. Hill, M.D., 15 March 1996. This Note is based on her handwritten additions.

[930] #3997-4005 are from Hill Family Reunion, Caton, N.Y., August 2010.

[931] Thom Carlson, Ph.D., to George J. Hill, M.D., op. cit.

[932] #4007 (Ernest Travis) - #4030 (Penny East) are from Paul F. Hill to George J. Hill, M.D., op cit.

[933] #4031 (Mark Pfaff) - #4058 (Linda Lee Shay) are from James D. Hill, "Twelve Generations," op. cit.

[934] #4059 (Leona Alice Schroader) – 4070 (Adele Wolfer) are from letter from Leslie Schroader to GJH, 19 Mar 1996; and Biographical Information Form completed by Marian (Schroader) Bitker, 15 Apr 1996.

[935] Leslie Schroader to GJH, 19 Mar 1996. Biographical Information Form completed by Marian (Schroader) Bitker and *Thanks for Giving and Other Poems* (Kiester, Minn.: Marian Bitker, 1990).

[936] Information sent to GJH by letters on 4, 5, 18, 19, and 20 Mar 1996, and a large packet of information was sent on 28 Mar 1996. He completed the Biographical Information Form for his mother on 4 Mar 1996.

[937] Biographical Information Form Mar 1996 by Lillian Helen (Anderson) Cornelius, and mailed to GJH.

[938] Biographical Information Form Mar 1996 by Lillian (Sormberger) Anderson for GJH.

[939] His name and that of his wife were in a letter from his mother to GJH., 28 Mar 1996. He died at home in Forest City, Winnebago County, Iowa, of a malignant brain tumor.

[940] Biographical Information Form completed by LaVonne (Anderson) Olson, March 1996. Jane (Olson) Leonhardt lived in Sioux Falls, S.D., in August 1997.

Chapter 12 – Twelfth Generation

[941] The descendants of Lydia Hill in the 12th generation are from OWT - Descendants of Arthur Henbury and Lydia Hill, Ancestry.com, accessed 4/18/2010ff.

[942] #4090-1 are from Richard R. Stanley, Esq., to GJH, "Ambrose Hill Family," 13 November 2010.

[943] #4092-4103 are from Ancestry.com and are unverified.

[944] #4104-4216 are descendants of George J. and Jessie (Stockwell) Hill. The information about them is derived from interviews, letters, and Family Group Records given to George J. Hill, M.D., by their parents and grandparents, in Notes, *supra*.

[945] Christmas note from her grandparents, 1994, and ltr from Marie (Johnson) Hill to GJH, 22 Sep 1994.

[946] #4127-8, Biographical Information Form prepared by Jeanine (Humbert) Johnson for GJH, July 1995.

[947] Biographical Information sheets completed for George J. Hill, M.D., by Louetta Knoedler, 25 Nov 1995.

[948] Biographical Information sheets completed for GJH by Louetta Knoedler, 25 Nov 1995. Deborah (Knoedler) Spence completed the questionnaire about her family on 15 May 1997.

[949] Biographical Information sheets completed for George J. Hill, M.D., by Louetta Knoedler, 25 Nov 1995.

[950] Biographical Information sheets completed for George J. Hill, M.D., by Louetta Knoedler, 25 Nov 1995.

[951] #4146-9 are from form on 7 Aug 1997 by their brother, David (#4149) for the Hill family reunion.

[952] The names of his wife and daughters are presumed from the questionnaire that was turned in at the Hill family reunion in 1997: "Velda's grandson: Brian, Betsy, Elizabeth, & Chelsea Gates."

[953] Her married name, her husband's name, and her children's names come from a questionnaire completed for the Hill Family reunion at Clarion, Iowa, on 26 July 1997.

[954] #4153-8 are from Biographical Information form provided by Keith and Dorothy (Rodenbeck) Knoedler, 27 August 1996; and update on Family Register Report 2 June 1997 by Dorothy Knoedler.

[955] Her name comes from a questionnaire completed for the Hill Family reunion at Clarion, Iowa, on 26 July 1997; the relationship of this family group is presumed, but not established.

[956] Information re the children of Dawn Delight (Weston) Menuey (4172a, b, c) is from Michele Menuey Ekern, 7/14/11ff, by e-mail: ekern_michele@hotmail.com.

[957] Hill, Kevin D.: "Closing Iowa courthouse isn't civilized," Iowa View op/ed column, *Des Moines Register*, Wed., 17 Feb 1993. Biographical Information form completed by Kevin D. Hill, 29 July 1994 and updated on 30 July 2000 (forwarded to George Hill by Avis Hill, 1 August 2000),

[958] Biographical Information form completed by Kristin Sue Hill, 30 July 1994. Update sent by Avis Hill to George Hill, 1 August 2000. Marriage program of Kristin Sue Hill and Scott Wayne Harrington, 8 Apr 1995, provided by her grandmother, Avis (Boyington) Hill.

[959] Biographical Information form completed by Linda (Carden) Hill, 30 Jul 1994. Family History edited by Avis (Boyington) Hill, 4 Sep 1994.

[960] The m was recorded in Wood County, W.Va., Marriage Record No. 120, page 160, on 12 Sept 2002.

[961] #4217 (Kristi Kisling) - #4260 (Joshua Brandon O'Connell) are from Paul F. Hill to George J. Hill, op. cit., and information obtained by George J. Hill at Hill Reunions, Caton, N.Y., 1997-2010.

[962] #4242-3 from Adella (Lindsay) Harson, 20 Feb 1996.

[963] #4261 (Nicole Simon) - #4283 (James Wesley Babcock) are from Hill, "Twelve Generations," op. cit.

[964] #4284 (Sharon Nesheim) - #4304 (Jen) from Biographical Information Form completed by Scott Leslie and Janice Elaine Schroader, 15 March 1996; telephone from Jane (Olson) Leonhardt to GJH, 10 September 2000; and Biographical Information Form by Tena Bitker and sent to GJH, 15 Apr 1996.

Chapter 13 – Thirteenth Generation

[965] #4305 (Living Daughter) - #4354 (Living Child of Norman Blakeley) are from from OWT - Descendants of Arthur Henbury and Lydia Hill, Ancestry.com, accessed 4/18/2010ff.

[966] #4355-6 are from Richard R. Stanley, Esq., to George J. Hill, M.D., op. cit.

[967] #4357 (Danielle Giudicci) - #4371 (Victoria Brandhorst) are from Jeanine Humbert Johnson to GJH; Johnson and Cynthia Huffman Sweet *Since I Started for the War: The Letters and Diary of Solomon B. Humbert, Co. B, 31st Iowa Volunteer Infantry* (Cedar Falls, Ia.: Sweet Press, 2007).

[968] From Charles Hill to George J. Hill, M.D.

[969] #4373-4411 from Hill Family Reunion, Clarion, Ia., August 1997, with narrative information and questionnaires, or entered directly into the computer of George J. Hill, M.D.

[970] #4403a-f are from Michele Menuey Ekern, op cit.

[971] #4407-9 from Heather Haught Hill; great-grandchildren of GJH, author of this work, and Helene Z. Hill.

[972] The known descendants of John Hill end with this generation; from Hill, "Twelve Generations."

Chapter 14 – Fourteenth Generation

[973] The descendants of Arthur Henbury and Lydia Hill in the 14th generation are from Ancestry.com, and are unsourced.

ABOUT THE AUTHOR

GEORGE J. HILL, M.D., M.A., D.Litt., is Professor of Surgery Emeritus at the New Jersey Medical School, University of Medicine and Dentistry of New Jersey. He has been a Fellow in Molecular Biology at Princeton University and he was an Adjunct Professor of History at Kean University, Union, New Jersey.

A native of Iowa, Dr. Hill received his B.A. degree with honors from Yale University and the M.D. from Harvard. After retiring from the practice of surgery, he earned an M.A. in history at Rutgers-Newark and the D.Litt. in history from Drew University. Dr. Hill has written more than a dozen books on a wide range of topics, including prize-winning books on surgery,

©*JanPressPhotomedia*

oncology, and leprosy. His master's thesis became a book on the environmental impact of Thomas Edison, and his doctoral thesis on a secret project of Church and State in the U.S. and Liberia was also published as a book. His most recent book is the story of his ancestor, John Saxe, who was a Loyalist in the American Revolution, and the Saxe family for five generations.

Dr. Hill was a non-commissioned officer in the U.S. Marine Corps Reserve during the Korean War, and he was on active duty with the U.S. Public Health Service during the Cuban Missile Crisis. As a U.S. Navy Medical Officer, he served in Vietnam and he was recalled for duty as a surgeon during the First Gulf War. He was awarded the U.S. Meritorious Service Medal when he retired as a Captain in 1992. Dr. Hill is also an alpinist and an explorer, having hiked and climbed on all seven continents.

As a student of genealogy, Dr. Hill has proved his descent from many early Americans. He is a member of forty-two lineage societies and he is a past or current national officer in seven of these societies. His ancestors include James Feake, Sr., a goldsmith of London in 1615; Edward Fuller, who came on the *Mayflower* in 1620, and his son, Doctor Matthew Fuller; Luke Hill and Mary Hoyt, who were married in Windsor, Connecticut, in 1651; Jonathan Gillett, who died there in 1677; Henry Herrick, who became a freeman of Salem, Massachusetts, in 1630; Rebecca (Towne) Nurse, who was hanged there in 1692; Lord of the Manor Edward Howell, who became a freeman of Boston in 1638 and was a founder of the Hamptons on Long Island; Thomas Trowbridge, who was in New Haven, Connecticut, in 1638; Robert Long, who was a member of the Ancient and Honorable Artillery Company in 1639; the Rev. Obadiah Holmes, who was a founder of Rhode Island; James Prescott, of Hampton, New Hampshire, in 1665; William Rundle, a freeholder of Greenwich, Connecticut, in 1667; John Sharples, who came to Pennsylvania in 1682; John Manley, of Cecil County, Maryland, in 1712; and John Archibald, who died in Derry, New Hampshire, in 1651, and whose descendants were pioneer settlers of Truro, Nova Scotia.

www.ingramcontent.com/pod-product-compliance
Lightning Source LLC
Chambersburg PA
CBHW052128020426
42334CB00023B/2645

* 9 7 8 0 7 8 8 4 5 3 6 7 0 *